Encyclopedia of the
MODERN WORLD
1900 TO THE PRESENT

Encyclopedia of the
MODERN WORLD

1900 TO THE PRESENT

VOLUME I

A–F

William R. Keylor

GENERAL EDITOR

Michael McGuire

ASSOCIATE EDITOR

Facts On File

An imprint of Infobase Publishing

Encyclopedia of the Modern World: 1900 to the Present

Copyright © 2007 by William R. Keylor

Facts On File, Inc.
An imprint of Infobase Publishing
132 West 31st Street
New York NY 10001

Library of Congress Cataloging-in-Publication Data

The encyclopedia of the modern world: 1900 to the present / William R. Keylor, general editor ;
Michael McGuire, associate editor. p. cm.
ISBN 0-8160-4872-X (HC. : alk. paper)
1. History, Modern—20th century—Encyclopedias. 2. World politics—20th century—Encyclopedias.
3. Twentieth century—Encyclopedias. I. Keylor, William R., 1944– II. McGuire Michael (Michael E.), 1976–
D419.E53 2005
909.82′03—dc22   2004061975

Facts On File books are available at special discounts when purchased in bulk quantities for businesses, associations, institutions, or sales promotions.
Please call our Special Sales Department in New York at
(212) 967-8800 or (800) 322-8755.

You can find Facts On File on the
World Wide Web at http://www.factsonfile.com

Text design by Dorothy M. Preston
Cover design by Nora Wertz
Illustrations by Dale Williams

Printed in the United States of America

VB Hermitage 10 9 8 7 6 5 4 3 2 1

This book is printed on acid-free paper.

To James Arthur Keylor
with brotherly love

Contents

Introduction

When asked to edit the *Encyclopedia of the Modern World*, I immediately began to ponder the challenge of such an assignment in light of the extraordinary transformation that the world has undergone since the appearance of its predecessor, *The Facts On File Encyclopedia of the 20th Century*, in 1991. The Union of Soviet Socialist Republics, the United States's old adversary in the cold war, disappeared and disintegrated into 15 sovereign states. Then Yugoslavia also broke apart and became the scene of the first serious outbreak of violence and ethnic strife in Europe since the end of the Second World War. The long-standing conflict between Israel and the Palestinians finally seemed headed toward a peaceful settlement during the 1990s, only to resume with all of its familiar ferocity and destructiveness as the 21st century dawned. After so many false starts and wrong turns since the 1950s, the movement toward European economic and political integration gathered steam; the newly renamed European Union recorded astonishing progress with the admission of new states to the east, the creation of a common European currency, and the adoption of the goal of a common foreign and security policy for the united continent. The People's Republic of China was transformed from a backward, impoverished country to a major industrial power in the world. The United States, after a decade of basking in the afterglow of the collapse of communism and relishing its enviable position as the world's sole remaining superpower, discovered its vulnerability to a new global threat with the terrorist attacks in New York City and Washington, D.C., on September 11, 2001. A new war on terrorism replaced the cold war as the defining theme of our time.

Amid these revolutionary changes in the political and economic landscape, the social and cultural world also underwent a fundamental transformation as a result of spectacular changes in the field of information technology. Innovations in fiberoptics and microchip technologies spawned the creation of a worldwide communications network that brought people across the globe in much closer contact with one another than ever before. The Internet, facsimile transmission, satellite television and other technological breakthroughs in communications have made the world of the 21st century radically different from the world that was referenced in the previous work. I have attempted in this encyclopedia to take account this radically changed world and the people who played a prominent role in shaping it.

I would like to acknowledge two people for their critical contributions to this volume: Owen Lancer at Facts On File conceived of the project for the second edition and shepherded this book throughout the various editorial stages with great skill, tact and forbearance. Michael McGuire, the associate editor, devoted prodigious effort to identifying sources of information and collecting data from an extraordinarily wide variety of fields. I also was able to rely on the advice of Professors Standish Hartman and Robert Hausman for assistance with entries in the natural sciences, of Robert Grenoble for assistance with entries in the field of music, and of Dr. Rheta G. Keylor for assistance with entries in the field of mental health. Any errors of fact that have crept into this book are entirely my own responsibility.

William R. Keylor
Boston, Massachusetts
February 15, 2006

Entries A to F

A

Aalto, Alvar *(1898–1976)* Finnish architect and designer. Aalto is one of the most renowned of 20th-century architects. He began his career in the 1920s and soon became a leading member of the International Modern school of architecture, with projects such as the library in Viipuri, Finland (1927–35). Aalto drew heavily upon native Finnish lumbers in his projects of this period. He also designed wooden furniture and, in 1932, invented the basic process for bent plywood furniture. After WORLD WAR II, Aalto designed what most critics feel to be his finest architectural projects, most of which showed his independent creative spirit and featured curved walls and single-pitched roofs. These include the Hall of Residence at the Massachusetts Institute of Technology (1947–49) and the Hall of Culture in Helsinki, Finland (1958).

Aarnio, Eero *(1932–)* Finnish interior and industrial designer trained in Helsinki at the Institute of Industrial Arts. Aarnio's best known designs are for chairs using plastics as the primary material. His Ball, or Globe, chair of 1960 is a sphere, open on one side to permit the occupant to move into its upholstered interior. The Gyro chair of 1968 is a round, hollowed-out form of FIBERGLASS in which seating space is a simple hollow in what appears to be a solid, flattened spherical mass.

Aaron, Henry Louis "Hank" *(1934–)* American baseball player and executive. Aaron is Major League Baseball's all-time home run leader, with a career total of 755. He broke the record of 714, previously held by Babe RUTH, in April 1974, after a year of building pressure and anticipation. He began his career in the NEGRO LEAGUES, playing two seasons for the Indianapolis Clowns. He spent most of his major league career (1954–74) with the Braves organization, playing his final year with the Milwaukee Brewers, and was named an All-Star every one of those years. Averaging 33 home runs per season, he batted in over 100 runs 15 times. In addition to his batting prowess, he was a skilled fielder, winning four Gold Gloves for his right field play. He was inducted into the Baseball Hall of Fame in 1982. Upon his retirement from baseball in 1976, Aaron began a new career as a member of the Braves' front office staff as a vice president and director of player development. In December 1989 Aaron was promoted to senior vice president and assistant to the president of the Atlanta Braves. He has also served on the board of directors for the national cable station Turner Broadcasting Station (TBS).

Abacha, Sani *(1943–1998)* Military ruler of NIGERIA (1993–98). Educated at a variety of Nigerian and British military and policy schools, Abacha ascended the ranks in the Nigerian army, from second lieutenant in 1963 to chief of staff of the army in 1985, to chairman of the joint chiefs of staff in 1989. During that time, he also held an appointment as minister of defense in the 1985 BABANGIDA government, whose cause he supported when it annulled the election victory of an opposition candidate. In 1990 he obtained a position in the Nigerian ministry of defense, which he again headed in 1993 under the government of President Ernest Shonekan. In 1993 he toppled Shonekan in a bloodless coup and assumed the Nigerian presidency. In his capacities as military and political leader, Abacha developed a history of repressing various elements of Nigeria. In 1985 the Nigerian army killed more than 200 civilians demonstrating against the elections that had been annulled earlier that year. Throughout the 1990s he repeatedly thwarted and repressed the separatist desires of the Ogoni people in the oil-rich Nigerian delta. Finally, in 1994, he ordered the arrest of Mashood ABIOLA, a Nigerian chief who declared himself the victor of recent elections and head of a government of national unity. Such actions bred constant friction and discontent between Abacha and large segments of the Nigerian population and resulted in Nigeria's suspension from the British Commonwealth. After his death, the presidency was assumed by General Abdusalami Abubakar.

Abadan Crisis Crisis of 1951–54, developing from the expulsion by the Iranian government of Western companies from Abadan oil refineries, and the nationalization of the Anglo-Iranian

Oil Company. Rather than alleviating poverty, the resulting fall in production and exports undermined the position of Premier Mohammed MOSSADEQ, who was ousted. In August 1954 the oil company was placed under the control of an international consortium.

Abaiang Atoll Coral atoll (formerly known as Charlotte Island) in Kiribati chain (formerly the Gilbert Islands) in the west-central Pacific Ocean. During WORLD WAR II, it was occupied by the Japanese from 1941 to 1943. After its conquest by American forces, it served as a base of operations for the subsequent capture of the Marshall Islands.

Abbado, Claudio *(1933–)* Italian conductor. Born in Milan of a musical family, Abbado graduated from the Verdi Conservatory (1955) and also studied conducting with Hans Swarowsky at the Vienna Academy. He made his conducting debut in Trieste in 1958 and debuted in the U.S. conducting the New York Philharmonic in 1963. He made his Metropolitan Opera debut in 1968, became the permanent conductor of Milan's La Scala in 1969 and was appointed its artistic director in 1977. There he instituted a number of innovations, including lengthening the season and broadening the repertoire to include such contemporary composers as Luigi DALLAPICCOLA and Luigi NONO. After the death of Herbert von KARAJAN in 1989, Abbado was appointed music director of the Berlin Philharmonic. In 1992 Abbado received the German government's highest civilian honor, the Bundesverdienstkreuz. In 1994 Abbado received the Ernst-von-Siemens music prize, the most prestigious musical award presented in Germany. That year Abbado also established the Salzburg Easter Festival, an annual competition among international composers located in Vienna, Austria. His tenure as music director of the Berlin Philharmonic ended with retirement in 2002.

Abbas, Ferhat *(1899–1985)* Algerian political leader. Abbas's *Manifesto of the Algerian People,* published in 1943, was vital to ALGERIA's fight for independence from FRANCE. In 1958, during Algeria's war for independence, he was named president of the first provisional government declared by the National Liberation Front, a post he held until 1961. In 1962 he was elected president of the National Assembly. He resigned from that position in 1963, when he became dissatisfied with the policies of Algeria's first president, Ahmed BEN BELLA. Ben Bella had him placed under house arrest in 1964. Abbas was not officially rehabilitated until 1984.

Abbas, Mahmoud *(1935–)* Palestinian political leader. Popularly known as Abu Mazen ("father of Mazen," his eldest son), Abbas became a refugee in Syria from the newly created state of ISRAEL in 1948. After teaching in an elementary school, he earned his undergraduate degree in law from Damascus University and his Ph.D. in history from the Oriental College in Moscow. A founding member of the Fatah movement, he joined the Palestinian National Council in 1968. Abbas was elected to the Executive Committee of the PALESTINE LIBERATION ORGANIZATION (PLO) in 1980 and rose to the position of PLO secretary general in 1996, a position that made him in effect Yasir ARAFAT's second-in-command. Throughout his career Abbas maintained close relations with Israeli critics of the hardline policies of the LIKUD Party concerning the issue of Palestinian statehood, at a time when most Palestinian officials refused any contact with Israeli groups. He was actively involved in the negotiations between Israeli and Palestinian representatives at the Madrid Conference of 1991 and then headed the Palestinian delegation to the Oslo negotiations that produced a breakthrough agreement in 1993. On behalf of the PLO, he signed the peace agreement that was reached at the Oslo conference and then the interim agreement of 1995 that was designed to pave the way for the eventual establishment of a Palestinian state.

On his return to the occupied territories after 48 years in exile, Abbas was elected to the Palestinian Legislative Council in 1996. He was designated as the first prime minister of the PALESTINIAN AUTHORITY (PA) in 2003, but Arafat's insistence on maintaining personal control over the PA budget and the security forces that it controlled led to Abbas's resignation after only six months in office. After Arafat's death in late 2004, of an undisclosed ailment, Abbas was elected president of the PA on January 9, 2005, with a 62% majority. Abbas has been severely criticized by hard-line Palestinian opponents for his willingness to make concessions to Israel at the expense of his people's interests; he has been praised in Israel and the United States for abandoning Arafat's uncompromising posture and representing a pragmatic interlocutor with whom Israel can negotiate an end to the bloody conflict that has taken so many Palestinian and Israeli lives since 1948.

Abbey Theatre Dublin theater, founded in 1904 by Annie HORNIMAN to provide a venue for Irish drama. Opened with a presentation of work by W. B. YEATS and Lady Augusta GREGORY, the theater became home to the Irish National Dramatic Society and a focus for the IRISH LITERARY REVIVAL. In 1907 the production of J. M. SYNGE's *Playboy of the Western World* caused riots. However, despite frequent public controversy, the theater continued to produce new works by Synge, AE, G. B. SHAW, and later Sean O'CASEY. Following World War I, the Abbey began to suffer financially, but in 1925 it received a grant from the new government of Eire, becoming the first state-subsidized theater in the English-speaking world. The theater burned down in 1951 but was rebuilt in 1966. The main Abbey Theatre continued to present largely Irish drama, while experimental works were produced in the Peacock Theatre, opened in 1925 and reopened in 1967.

Abbott, Berenice *(1898–1991)* American photographer known for a design-oriented, documentary approach. Abbott went to Paris in 1921 as an art student and, while there, became an assistant to the avant-garde photographer Man RAY. In 1925 she set up practice as a professional portrait photographer. Also during that year, she met French photographer Eugène ATGET, then an elderly and little-known commercial photographer who had, over a lifetime, documented Paris with a huge collection of photos. Abbott acquired his negatives, eventually arranging to have them sold to the MUSEUM OF MODERN ART in New York. After returning to New York in 1929, Abbott turned to documentary photography, taking on the 1935 WPA photo project known as "Changing New York." Later she worked in scientific photography and on a documentary project, "U.S. Route 1." The direct and unsentimental character of her images gave them a design-oriented quality of a kind that came to typify "modern photography." She taught at the New School in New York beginning in 1934 and continued until 1958. She was the author of several technical photography books.

Abbott, Grace *(1878–1939)* American social reformer. After finishing graduate work at the University of Nebraska in Lincoln, Abbott joined Jane ADDAMS at Hull-House in Chicago (1908). That same year she was made director of the Immigrants' Protective League. In the period 1909–10 her series of articles for the *Chicago Evening Post* exposed the exploitation of immigrants. She joined the faculty of the Chicago School of Civics and Philanthropy in 1910. In 1917 she became director of the child-labor division of the Children's Bureau in Washington, D.C., and administered the first child-labor law. Her subsequent moves took her to various federal and state government posts and finally to the University of Chicago, where she was a professor of public welfare until her death. At Chicago she also edited the *Social Service Review* (1934–39). Her best-known work is considered to be *The Child and the State,* in two volumes (1938).

Abbott and Costello The comedy team of **Bud Abbott** (William Abbott, 1895–1974) and **Lou Costello** (Louis Francis Cristillo, 1906–59) enjoyed huge popularity in the 1940s and early 1950s. Abbott and Costello were unsuccessful veterans of the vaudeville circuit when they met in 1931. They worked the vaudeville and burlesque theaters in the 1930s, then won national fame after appearing on the Kate SMITH radio show in 1938. Throughout the 1940s they were one of Hollywood's top box-office draws, appearing in farcical slapstick comedies. These include their phenomenally successful *Buck Privates* (1941), *Hold That Ghost* (1942), *The Naughty Nineties* (1945) (featuring the duo's famous "Who's on First?" stand-up routine) and *Abbott &*

Costello Meet Frankenstein (1948). Abbott typically played the "straight man" (although he was often a con man at the same time), while Costello was his bumbling sidekick. Their comedy routines relied heavily on mistaken identity and verbal misunderstandings, usually carried to a ridiculous extreme. Abbott and Costello appeared frequently on the live-television variety shows of the early 1950s and also had a successful TV series of their own, *The Abbott and Costello Show.*

ABC (American Broadcasting Company) The third of the three major television broadcasting networks in the U.S., ABC was formed in 1943 when Edward J. Noble, head of Life Savers candy, purchased the so-called Blue network of six radio stations from NBC. ABC merged with United Paramount Theaters in 1952. While its larger rivals NBC and CBS prospered throughout the 1950s and 1960s, ABC subsisted on a diet of westerns and popular melodramas but consistently remained in third place, drawing fewer viewers and losing money. The network finally came into its own in the mid-1970s, and during the 1975–76 season it beat CBS and NBC in the ratings for the first time. This success was largely due to ABC's innovative sports programs, produced by Roone ARLEDGE. Situation comedies and made-for-TV movies also featured in the network's programming. The network's news coverage increased and improved during the 1980s (again under Arledge, who had become president of ABC news). ABC and its affiliate local stations led the way in popularizing news broadcasts with light human-interest features and newsroom chat. ABC was acquired by Capital Cities Communications, Inc., in 1986; the new company was known as Capital Cities/ABC, Inc. In addition to its television and radio broadcasting interests, the company is also involved in publishing, recording and other facets of the entertainment industry. In 1996 ABC was purchased by the Walt Disney Corporation.

Abd el-Krim *(1882–1963)* Nationalist leader of the Rif tribes in Morocco. A public official and newspaper editor in Spanish Morocco, he was infuriated by Spain's corrupt colonial practices. He led a small rebel force in victorious

sorties against the Spanish army in 1921. During the next four years Abd el-Krim led his troops against the Spanish in a number of successful engagements, culminating in his advance into French Morocco in 1925. There he was defeated by a massive Franco-Spanish army led by Marshal PÉTAIN. Exiled to Réunion, he was detained there for over 20 years. In 1947 he escaped to Egypt, where he continued to encourage Arab resistance to imperialism.

abdication crisis Crisis provoked in the United Kingdom in 1936 by the abdication of King EDWARD VIII so that he could marry the American divorcée Wallis SIMPSON. The marriage was opposed by the government of Prime Minister Stanley BALDWIN. Edward insisted on the right to marry the woman he loved; Baldwin and the British cabinet felt the marriage was constitutionally and doctrinally unsound. After efforts to create a morganatic marriage failed, Edward decided to abdicate, a decision announced in a moving radio address to the realm on December 11, 1936. Created duke of WINDSOR, he went into voluntary exile in France, marrying Mrs. Simpson there in 1937. Edward, the first British monarch to abdicate voluntarily, was succeeded by GEORGE VI.

Abdul Hamid II (Abdulhamid II) *(1842–1918)* Sultan of TURKEY (1876–1909). The son of Sultan Abdul Majid, he succeeded his insane brother, Murad V. During 1876–77, after the Berlin Treaty, which reduced Turkey's European territory, he ruled constitutionally, but after May 1877 he ruled as an absolute monarch. Despite some local administrative reforms in the Asiatic provinces, the sultan's ministers adamantly opposed reform, and in 1895–96 his inability to restrain irregular troops during the Armenian massacres made him notorious throughout Europe. Turkey's main European ally was now GERMANY. In 1908 the YOUNG TURKS forced Abdul Hamid to summon a parliament. An attempted counterrevolution resulted in his overthrow and exile from the capital in April 1909. (See also OTTOMAN EMPIRE.)

Abdul-Jabbar, Kareem (Ferdinand Lewis [Lew] Alcindor Jr.) *(1947–   )* American basketball player. Beginning with his years as a high school star center at Power Memorial Academy in New York City, Abdul-Jabbar dominated every court he played on. First known as Lew Alcindor, he later joined the BLACK MUSLIMS and took the name Kareem Abdul-Jabbar. During his years at UCLA (1965–68), the team won three National Collegiate Athletic Association (NCAA) championships. He turned pro with the NBA Milwaukee Bucks in 1969 and was named that season's rookie of the year. While with the Bucks, he twice led the league in scoring and game point average and led the team to a championship. In 1975 he was traded to the Los Angeles Lakers, where he would be a part of championship teams. He announced his retirement before the 1988–89 season, and was honored in every city in the league. Abdul-Jabbar finished his career with 38,387 points, eclipsing Wilt CHAMBERLAIN's record of 31,419. He has written two autobiographical books, *Giant Steps* (1985) and *Kareem* (1990). In May 1995 Abdul-Jabbar was enshrined in the National Basketball Hall of Fame.

Abdullah, King of Jordan (1962–)

Assuming the throne of the Hashemite Kingdom of JORDAN on February 7, 1999, upon the death of his father, King HUSSEIN, under the title of King Abdullah II, he is head of that nation's constitutional monarchy. Abdullah received his primary and secondary education in Jordan, the United Kingdom, and the United States. Additionally, he studied international and Middle Eastern affairs both at Oxford and later Georgetown (where he obtained a master's degree) and obtained his extensive military training in British and American military academies. During his service in the Jordanian armed forces, he held diverse positions in the armored, airborne, and special operations divisions, reformed the Jordanian armored and special operations forces and rose to the rank of major general. In affairs of state, he functioned as the regent on numerous occasions when King Hussein's duties took him out of the country and repeatedly participated in diplomatic missions on behalf of the royal government. As king, Abdullah launched a variety of initiatives to improve the condition of his country, most notably in the economic sphere. He oversaw Jordan's admission to the WORLD TRADE ORGANIZATION and has repeatedly advocated greater privatization and development of information technology and foreign investment within Jordan's economy.

Abdullah, King of Saudi Arabia (1924–)

One of 37 sons of IBN SAUD, the ruler of the Nejd who unified the Arabian Peninsula under Saudi control by 1926 and established the independent Kingdom of Saudi Arabia in 1932, Abdullah emerged as the effective head of Saudi Arabia after the 1995 stroke of his elder half brother, King FAHD. Abdullah's appointment in 1975 as second deputy prime minister in 1975 and his rise to power as deputy prime minister in 1982 gave him great exposure to and involvement in Saudi Arabia's relations with foreign powers, especially the UNITED STATES. He was crowned king in 2005, after the death of Fahd.

Opinion remains divided over Abdullah's stance toward the U.S. in the aftermath of the SEPTEMBER 11, 2001, terrorist attacks. Critics have pointed to Abdullah's stern disapproval of America's support for ISRAEL, nonrecognition of the PALESTINIAN AUTHORITY and relations with the TALIBAN regime in AFGHANISTAN, his rapprochement with Iran and his affinity for Arab and Islamic causes as distinct signs of anti-Americanism. Other analysts, however, have noted his acceptance of increasing military and economic links between Saudi Arabia and the U.S., and his 2002 Middle East peace plan, which called for Israeli withdrawal from Palestinian territories and return to its pre–SIX-DAY WAR borders in exchange for acceptance of formal and peaceful relations between Israel and the Arab states.

Domestically, Abdullah repeatedly labored to improve and modernize the Saudi national guard (which he has headed since 1962), to balance the Saudi budget, to introduce an element of frugality into the 20,000-member royal family and to improve the library establishments of both his country and MOROCCO. Additionally, Abdullah tolerated a certain amount of domestic criticism of the royal government in the Saudi press and has hinted that restrictions on women in the workplace should be liberalized. In all these matters, Abdullah is said to consult regularly with key Saudi Muslim clerics.

Abdullah ibn Hussein (1882–1951)

King of JORDAN. Second son of Emir Hussein and brother of King FAISAL I, he was also the king of Hejaz (1916–24). During WORLD WAR I, Abdullah was associated with T. E. LAWRENCE and was a leader of the Arab revolt against the Ottoman Turks. His guerrilla raids isolated Turkish troops

King Abdullah of Jordan (right) meets with Israeli prime minister Ehud Barak in July 1999. (REUTERS/CORBIS)

in MEDINA, in western Arabia. In 1921 Britain recognized Abdullah as emir of Transjordania—the eastern portion of the PALESTINE mandate taken from Turkey after 1918. Abdullah remained on good terms with the British, becoming king of Transjordan (renamed Jordan in 1949) when the mandate expired in 1946. After the failure of an attempt to unite Palestine under his rule in 1949, Abdullah accepted the throne of the Hashemite Kingdom of the Jordan—the eastern part of the former Palestine mandate. He was assassinated on June 20, 1951, in Jerusalem.

Abe Kobo (Abe Kimifusa) *(1924–1993)* Japanese novelist, short story writer, dramatist, essayist. Abe received an M.D. from Tokyo University in 1948, but his first short story collection, *The Wall*, established his reputation in Japan in 1951. The most avant-garde and metaphysical author of modern Japan, Abe was influenced by DADA and SURREALISM, but he brought a scientist's point of view to his fiction. He is often compared to KAFKA and BECKETT. His greatest success both at home and abroad was the existentialist novel *Woman in the Dunes* (1962; tr. 1964), which he adapted for film. Abe also wrote for radio and television. Other novels in translation include *Inter Ice Age Four* (1959; tr. 1970), *The Face of Another* (1964; tr. 1966), *The Ruined Map* (1967; tr. 1969), *The Box Man* (1973; tr. 1975) and *Secret Rendezvous* (1977; tr. 1979); his first English-language collection of stories was *Beyond the Curve* (1991). On January 22, 1993, shortly after releasing his work *Three Plays*, Abe died.

Abel, Iorwith Wilbur *(1908–1987)* U.S. labor leader. Abel helped found the United Steelworkers of America and served as the union's third president from 1965 to 1977. During that period union membership rose dramatically, and a strike fund of more than $85 million was amassed. Abel was instrumental in the historic 1973 no-strike agreement to end production and stockpiling swings.

Abel, John Jacob *(1857–1938)* American biochemist. Abel was educated at the University of Michigan, Johns Hopkins University, and at universities in Leipzig, Heidelberg, Wurzburg, Vienna, Bern and Strasbourg, where he received an M.D. in 1888. He worked briefly at the University of Michigan before being appointed in 1893 to the first chair of pharmacology at Johns Hopkins, a post he retained until his retirement in 1932. Abel had first-rate training in chemistry and was convinced that the study of molecules and atoms was as important as the observation of multicellular tissues under the microscope. He thus began by working on the chemical composition of various bodily tissues and fluids and, in 1897, succeeded in isolating a physiologically active substance from the adrenal glands, which he named epinephrine, also known as **adrenaline.**

As early as 1912 Abel formulated the idea of an artificial kidney and in 1914 isolated for the first time amino acids from the blood. He was less successful with his search (1917–24) for the pituitary hormone, as he was unaware that several hormones were involved. His 1926 announcement that he had crystallized INSULIN met with considerable skepticism, especially regarding its protein nature. This work was not generally accepted until the mid-1930s.

After his retirement Abel devoted himself to a study of the tetanus toxin.

Abell, George *(1927–1983)* American astronomer and cosmologist. He was known for his discovery of the **Abell Galaxy,** which was for many years considered the largest known object in the universe. His *Abell Catalogue of Clusters* (1958) was long the standard catalog of clusters of galaxies visible from the Northern Hemisphere; it was used by astronomers throughout the world. Abell helped popularize astronomy with his books, lectures and television appearances. He was also a public critic of popular claims of supernatural phenomena. He taught at the University of California for 17 years.

Abell, Kjeld *(1901–1961)* Danish playwright and artist. He studied economics and later worked as a commercial artist in Paris and London, resettling in Denmark in 1930 to work as a stage designer. His early works, including *Melodien der blevvock (The Melody That Got Lost,* 1931), wittily as-sailed bourgeois values and pettiness. Most notable is *Anna Sophie Hedvig* (1939), which expresses his dismay at the failure of the middle classes to rise up against FASCISM. Other works include *Dan bla pekineser (The Blue Pekingese,* 1954) and *Skiget (The Scream,* 1961). Abell's plays reject naturalism in favor of experimentalism.

Abelson, Philip Hauge *(1913–2004)* American physical chemist. Abelson was educated at Washington State College and at the University of California at Berkeley, where he obtained his Ph.D. in 1939. Apart from the war years at the Naval Research Laboratory in Washington, D.C., he spent his entire career at the Carnegie Institution, also in Washington. He served as the director of the geophysics laboratory from 1953 and became president of the institute in 1971. In 1940 he assisted Edwin McMILLAN in creating the first transuranic element, neptunium, by bombarding uranium with neutrons in the Berkeley cyclotron.

Abelson next worked on separating the isotopes of uranium by thermal diffusion. Collecting sufficient uranium 235 involved Abelson in massive research and engineering projects possible only in wartime. In the Philadelphia Navy Yard, he constructed 100 or so 48-foot precision-engineered pipes through which steam was pumped. From this Abelson was able to obtain uranium enriched to 14 U-235 atoms per 1,000.

Although this was still too weak a mixture for a bomb, it was sufficiently enriched to use in other separation processes. A bigger plant was constructed at Oak Ridge, Tennessee, and provided enriched material for the separation process from which came the fuel for the first atomic bomb (see ATOMIC BOMB DEVELOPMENT). After the war Abelson extended the important work of Stanley MILLER on the origin of vital biological molecules. He found that amino acids could be produced from a variety of gases if carbon, nitrogen, hydrogen and oxygen were present. He was also able to show the great stability of amino acids by identifying them in 300-million-year-old fossils. In 1985 the American Association for the Advancement of Sciences (AAAS) established the Philip Hauge Abelson Award in honor of Abelson's contributions to science. The Abelson Award is given annually in recognition of the recipient's contributions to advancing scientific knowledge and community service. Since the award's creation until his death, Abelson served as a scientific adviser for the AAAS.

Abemana Atoll Coral atoll (formerly known as Roger Simpson Island) in Kiribati (formerly the Gilbert Islands chain) in the west-central Pacific Ocean; site of the formal British annexation of the Gilbert Islands in 1892. Held by Japanese forces during WORLD WAR II, from 1942 to 1943, when it was captured by the American military.

Abercrombie, Lascalles (1881–1938) British poet and critic. Born in Cheshire, Abercrombie was educated at Malvern College and Manchester University. He began his career as a journalist and reviewer, publishing his first collection of verse, *Interludes in Poems,* in 1908. He became lecturer in poetry at the University of Liverpool and, eventually, Goldsmith's Reader of English at Oxford. A contributor to *Georgian Poetry,* he was admired by fellow contributor Rupert BROOKE. Abercrombie's work reflects his marvel at the rapid changes of the early 20th century. Highly regarded during his lifetime, Abercrombie has been overshadowed by the modernist poets who followed him (see MODERNISM). Other works include *The Sale of St. Thomas* (1931), a play; *Thomas Hardy* (1912) and *Principles of Literary Criticism* (1932).

Aberfan disaster Slide of 2 million tons of coal waste, mud and rocks that occurred in the Welsh village of Aberfan on the morning of October 21, 1966. Engulfing a schoolhouse, farm and 16 cottages in debris that reached a height of 45 feet, the avalanche of slag from a mountain of mine waste caused 192 deaths, 113 of them children.

Abernathy, Ralph David (1926–1990) American leader of the CIVIL RIGHTS movement. Abernathy was a top aide to the Rev. Martin Luther KING Jr. in the 1950s and 1960s. The two organized the MONTGOMERY BUS BOYCOTT (1955) after a black woman, Rosa PARKS, was arrested for refusing to give up her seat to a white person. Aber-

nathy was also a leading figure in the 1963 MARCH ON WASHINGTON. Following King's assassination in 1968, Abernathy became head of the SOUTHERN CHRISTIAN LEADERSHIP CONFERENCE, a position he held for nine years. His 1989 autobiography, *And the Walls Came Tumbling Down,* caused a storm of controversy. In the book, Abernathy alleged that King had had an adulterous affair on the night before he was killed.

Abiola, Mashood (1937–1998) A principal figure in the prodemocracy movement within NIGERIA, Abiola ran for president in that country's 1993 national elections. When voting returns indicated he was the victor of that campaign, a coup led by General Sani ABACHA overthrew the government and annulled the elections. Soon after this, Abiola declared himself president and began forming a coalition government, prompting Abacha to charge Abiola with treason, order his arrest in 1993 and keep him in prison until Abiola's death in 1998. Although the Nigerian government insisted that Abiola's death, which quickly followed the passing of Abacha, was due to a heart attack, his family repeatedly insisted his passing was the result of foul play.

ABM Treaty The Anti-Ballistic Missile Treaty, signed by the U.S. and the Soviet Union on May 26, 1972, sought to maintain the nuclear balance of power by limiting both nations' ability to deploy anti-nuclear weapons systems. In 1967, President Lyndon JOHNSON had first suggested an ABM treaty; negotiations began at the SALT I talks in 1969, and the treaty was signed with the rest of the SALT I agreement three years later. The ABM Treaty later figured prominently in debate of the STRATEGIC DEFENSE INITIATIVE, because critics of that system contended that it was in violation of the earlier agreement. On December 13, 2001, U.S. president George W. BUSH informed Russian president Vladimir PUTIN that the U.S. would unilaterally withdraw from the ABM Treaty the following year. Bush announced that the reason for his decision was to allow the U.S. to develop his National Missile Defense (NMD) program.

abortion Abortion has been perhaps the most controversial moral, legal and

political issue in the U.S. since the late 20th century. In technical terms, abortion is a method of preventing the birth of an unwanted child by inducing a miscarriage. Although the procedure itself is relatively simple when practiced by a qualified medical person, the issue of whether abortion is an appropriate means of ending a pregnancy is one fraught with emotional and philosophical repercussions.

Advocates of legalized abortion, who regard themselves as "pro-choice," claim that a fetus is not a person and that a woman should have the right to make her own reproductive decisions; government regulation of abortion is seen as an unconstitutional intrusion of government into a private matter. Abortion rights advocates also cite the high incidence of serious injury or death from illegal abortions performed under unsanitary conditions by unskilled abortionists. In the U.S. and Western Europe, the demand for the legalization of abortion was led by the WOMEN'S MOVEMENT in the 1960s and 1970s. In asserting the right to abortion in ROE V. WADE (1973), the U.S. Supreme Court invoked the right to privacy implicit in the Constitution and affirmed earlier in *GRISWOLD V. CONNECTICUT.*

Opponents of abortion, mainly Roman Catholics and Protestant fundamentalists who regard themselves as "pro-life," rely largely on moral and religious arguments. Many abortion opponents believe that human life begins at the moment of conception, or at least that a fetus is more than a mere collection of tissues; in this view, abortion is therefore murder. Some opponents of abortion claim that if abortion can be justified, any means can be used to justify any end. For them, the fact that a baby is unwanted is not sufficient cause to justify abortion. Antiabortion activists have sought to protect the rights of the unborn, but most U.S. courts ruling on the issue have ruled in favor of the woman's rights over those of the fetus. The Supreme Court decision in *WEBSTER V. REPRODUCTIVE HEALTH SERVICES* (1989) neither upheld nor overturned the ruling in *Roe v. Wade* but gave states the right to regulate abortion. Subsequently, abortion again became a major issue in state and local elections.

Public opinion polls in the U.S. in the late 1980s and early 1990s showed that the American population was almost evenly divided over the issue. Despite the polarized views on abortion, most Americans believed that abortions should not be undertaken lightly or encouraged as a routine method of birth control; on the other hand, few believed that prohibitions on abortion should be absolute, but rather that exceptions may be made in cases in which the fetus is deformed, the mother's health is at risk, or of rape. Abortion laws were liberalized in the UNITED KINGDOM in 1967, and abortion is currently legal, to various degrees, in all the nations of western Europe.

Abortion remained a contentious political issue throughout the 1990s and into the 21st century. Repeated controversy followed congressional Republican efforts to ban partial-birth abortions during the presidential administrations of Bill CLINTON and George W. BUSH. President Bush also supported a May 2004 ruling by the Food and Drug Administration (FDA) to ban over-the-counter sales of Plan B, a morning-after contraception.

Abrahams, Peter Henry (1919–) South African novelist and journalist. Born in Vrededorp near Johannesburg to an Ethiopian father and a mother of mixed race, Abrahams did not learn to read until he was nine but was later educated at St. Peter's College and Teacher's Training College. He held many menial jobs and tried unsuccessfully to start a school for poor Africans. After publication of his first volume of poetry, *A Black Man Speaks of Freedom* (1940), he enlisted on a British ship and moved to England, where he worked as a journalist. He was commissioned by the British government to write *Jamaica* (1957); while researching the book he was seduced by the charm of the island and moved there. Abrahams's writing explores the problems and history of Africa, at times angrily denouncing the racism and repression of his birthplace. His other works include *Mine Boy* (1946), *This Island Now* (1966), *The View from Coyaba* (1985), all novels, and two volumes of autobiography, *Return to Goli* (1953) and *Tell Freedom* (1954). Abrahams has continued to write, producing such tomes as *Tongues of*

Fire (1982) and the quasi-autobiographical *The Black Experience in the 20th Century* (2000). (See also APARTHEID, SOUTH AFRICA.)

Abrams, Creighton Williams, Jr. (1914–1974) U.S. Army general; commander of U.S. forces in VIETNAM. A graduate of West Point in 1936, Abrams served as deputy to General William WESTMORELAND, then succeeded him as commander of U.S. forces in Vietnam in July 1968, when Westmoreland was named army chief of staff. In his new position, Abrams was faced with the difficult tasks of reducing U.S. troop levels and "Vietnamizing" the war; he also planned the 1970 invasion of CAMBODIA. In 1972, Abrams was named army chief of staff.

ABSCAM Bribery scandal that resulted in the conviction of several congressmen and a U.S. senator in 1980–81. Representative John W. Jenrette Jr. (Ohio) and Senator Harrison Williams (New Jersey), among other officials, were lured into a "sting" operation conducted by FBI agents posing as wealthy Arabs wishing to pay cash bribes in return for legislative favors. During the scandal the nightly news included film of several congressmen receiving and stuffing cash into their pockets. A congressional investigation was followed by federal prosecution. Despite pleas that they were "entrapped" by overzealous government agents, most of the participants were ultimately convicted. All of the wrongdoers either resigned or were defeated for reelection to Congress.

abstract art Term applied to a dominant movement in 20th-century art that abandoned the traditional Western aesthetic view that art should imitate the forms of nature. Instead, abstract art validates the analytical and imaginative creation by artists of new pictorial and sculptural realities that either drastically simplify natural forms or resort to altogether nonrepresentational geometric or random forms. The Russian painter Wassily KANDINSKY is commonly regarded as the first purely abstract painter by virtue of his 1910 geometric canvases, while the Romanian sculptor Constantin BRANCUSI pioneered the use of abstract forms in sculpture in the subsequent decade.

Another early, influential abstract painter was the Dutch artist Piet MONDRIAN, who was a member of the abstract-influenced de STIJL group formed in 1917. By the 1930s, abstract art had become a widely accepted form of artistic expression.

abstract expressionism Emerged in New York in the late 1940s and flourished in the 1950s; in essence an intensification of ABSTRACT ART aesthetics. The term *abstract expressionism* was first applied to the work of the Russian painter Wassily KANDINSKY, but in general usage it refers to the works of a group of Manhattan-based painters of the postwar period, most notably Arshile Gorky, Franz KLINE, Willem DE KOONING, Jackson POLLOCK and Mark ROTHKO. Abstract expressionism was the first American artistic movement to have a dominant influence on European painting. Its primary tenets were an emphasis on intuitive, emotional expression over prescribed technique, a denial of the classical ideal of a "finished" work of art that concealed the creative process and a celebration of self-determined aesthetic standards. A famous form of abstract expressionism was the "action" paintings of Pollock, who spattered his canvases with paint to allow for free-form energy patterns in his work.

Abu Dhabi One of the emirate states located on the west coast of the Persian Gulf. Abu Dhabi became a British protectorate in 1892. After it was granted independence in 1971, it joined six other emirates to become the UNITED ARAB EMIRATES, with the city of Abu Dhabi as capital. Abu Dhabi is the largest and most economically powerful of the emirates.

Abu Nidal (nom de guerre of Sabry al-Banna) (1937–2002) Palestinian terrorist. Born in Jaffa (now part of ISRAEL), he was educated at a private Palestinian school in Jerusalem. Committing himself to the cause of Palestinian liberation, he received military training in North Korea (1970). He joined the Al-Fatah party of Yasir ARAFAT but broke with it in 1973 over policy disputes and founded the radical FATAH REVOLUTIONARY COUNCIL in 1974. Abu Nidal directed numerous terrorist attacks on Israelis, on Western targets, on moderate Arabs and on rival terrorist leaders. He vowed to kill Arafat after Arafat and the PLO publicly renounced terrorism in 1988. In 1989 he was arrested in Libya, probably at the insistence of Arab governments and the PLO, who could no longer tolerate his violent hard line. In August 2002 Abu Nidal was found dead in an Iraqi hotel room shortly after he allegedly told a meeting of the Al-Fatah Revolutionary Council that he had masterminded the midair destruction of PAN AM 103 on December 21, 1998, that killed all 259 passengers and crew members as well as 11 people on the ground at Lockerbie, Scotland.

Abu Simbel Archaeological dig site on the Nile River, in Egypt's Aswân province. Abu Simbel, once a center of the ancient Nubian civilization, is the site of two sandstone temples constructed c. 1250 B.C. These temples were rediscovered in 1812 but were subsequently threatened by the waters banked up by the ASWÂN DAM. In the 1960s, UNESCO completed a rescue effort in the course of which the temples were cut out of their surrounding cliffs and reassembled on higher ground 200 feet up.

Abwehr German intelligence agency during WORLD WAR II. Formed after the Nazis came to power in 1933, in contravention of the terms of the VERSAILLES TREATY, it became extremely powerful under the direction of Admiral Wilhelm CANARIS, who took command in 1935. The agency was active in information-gathering and counterespionage work but was rendered less efficient by the meddling of Reinhard HEYDRICH, head of the army's intelligence services. Gradually, after 1938, the Abwehr became a center of conspiracy against HITLER's regime, while still being involved in intelligence work. Heinrich HIMMLER, who also distrusted the Abwehr and its leader, was instrumental in having Canaris dismissed in 1944, and the Abwehr was absorbed into a combined intelligence service called the Militarische Amt.

Abzug, Bella *(1920–1998)* U.S. political leader. Bella Abzug was born in the Bronx, New York, and practiced law in New York City beginning in

1944. In the 1960s she was a founder of Women's Strike for Peace, and in 1970 she was elected to Congress as a Democrat from Manhattan. In the House, she was an outspoken advocate of welfare reform, women's rights and other liberal causes and an outspoken critic of the war in Vietnam. She resigned her congressional seat in 1976 to run for the U.S. Senate but lost to Daniel Patrick Moynihan in the primary. After leaving office, Abzug remained active in politics and was an active supporter of the EQUAL RIGHTS AMENDMENT.

Academy Awards Annual U.S. awards, popularly known as the Oscars, bestowed by the Academy of Motion Picture Arts and Sciences upon films and film artists and technicians. The first awards ceremony, on May 16, 1929—presided over by academy president Douglas FAIRBANKS Sr.—was a small, informal banquet where a handful of members voted several merit awards for 1927–28, including a best picture award to the aviation epic *Wings*. Voting was soon extended to the entire membership. In 1941 the policy of using sealed envelopes was begun. Four years later national radio covered the event; and in 1953 network television broadcast it nationwide. Today the nominations are made from each of 13 art and craft branches—actors selecting actors, editors selecting editors, etc.—and the entire membership, which has held steady at 4,000, then votes by secret ballot on the final winners in all categories. Legend holds that the "Oscar" nickname comes from Bette DAVIS, who declared the figurine resembled her first husband, Harmon Oscar Nelson Jr. Each statuette—the original design is by MGM art director Cedric Gibbons—is valued at $100, but the box-office benefits to a film can be enormous. For example, when *Platoon* (1986) won several Oscars (including best picture), its box-office income exceeded $138 million in a matter of weeks. All-time winners in the Oscar sweepstakes include *Ben Hur* (1959) with 11 Oscars, John FORD with four best director Oscars and Katharine HEPBURN with three best actress Oscars. Some celebrities have refused their awards (George C. Scott in 1970 for *Patton* and Marlon BRANDO in 1972 for THE GODFATHER) and others

have never won at all (GARBO, HITCHCOCK, MONROE, BARRYMORE and Cary GRANT, to name but a few). Although the academy insists that its awards honor the work and not the particular person, many critics and artists insist that it is a popularity contest. In 1998 James Cameron's *Titanic* (1997) tied the record set by *Ben Hur.*

Academy of Sciences of the USSR Founded in St. Petersburg in 1724 by Peter the Great as the Russian Academy of Sciences. From the Russian Revolution (1917) until 1925 it was known as the Academy of Sciences of Russia. It was the chief coordinating body for scientific research within the USSR, directing the work of over 260 scientific institutions. With the disintegration of the Soviet Union in December 1991, the Academy of Sciences dissolved into the affiliates associated with each of the 15 former Soviet Socialist Republics.

Aceh A northwest region of the Indonesian island of Sumatra that repeatedly resisted Dutch and, later, Indonesian rule. From 1873 the Achinese waged a conventional and, later, unconventional war against Dutch forces that lasted until the Japanese invasion of the Dutch East Indies in 1942. In 1959, as a result of Islamic separatist efforts on the island of JAVA, the young Indonesian government declared Aceh a "special territory" of INDONESIA, granting it considerable autonomy in religious, educational and cultural affairs. In 1976 dissatisfaction with autonomy led to the formation of the dissident Aceh Merdeka, or "Free Aceh," an armed resistance group headed by Tengku Hasan di Tiro, which again sought to use guerrilla tactics to obtain independence. Though repeated arrests and repression by the Indonesian government effectively thwarted the movement for 13 years, a new group calling itself the Aceh-Sumatra National Liberation Front (ASNLF) emerged in 1989 and began attacks on police and military installations throughout the region, prompting the government to place it under military control from 1991 to 1999. Unlike EAST TIMOR, where the independence movement reflected religious and ethnic differences between that region and the island on which it was located, the independence movement in Aceh stemmed largely from resentment against the disproportionately low employment of Aceh's inhabitants within the region's industries and the subsequent migration of Java residents to the region in search of work. Aceh was hard hit by the tsunami that swept through the Indian Ocean in late December 2004.

Achebe, Chinua *(1930–)* Nigerian novelist. Born in Nigeria, he was among the first students to pursue a degree at the University College of Ibadan. He later worked for the Nigerian Broadcasting Company. He is perhaps best known for his first four novels, *Things Fall Apart* (1958), *No Longer at Ease* (1960), *Arrow of God* (1964) and *A Man of the People* (1966), which examined the clash between tradition and modern civilization. A prolific writer, his other works include *Ant Hills of the Savannah* (1988) and *Hopes and Impediments* (1989). Achebe's often angry, deft satire and his keen ear for spoken language have made him one of the most highly esteemed African writers in English. In 1990 Achebe was involved in an automobile accident that left him paralyzed from the waist down. Since the accident, Achebe has lived in the United States, teaching at Bard College. In 2000 he published a book of essays, *Home and Exile.*

Acheson, Dean Gooderham *(1893–1971)* American statesman and secretary of state (1949–53); a key figure in planning U.S. foreign policy in the immediate post–World War II period. Born in Middletown, Connecticut, Acheson attended Yale University and graduated from Harvard Law School in 1918. He was private secretary to Supreme Court associate justice Louis D. BRANDEIS from 1919 to 1921, afterward joining a Washington, D.C., law firm. Acheson entered government service in 1933 as undersecretary of the treasury under President Franklin D. ROOSEVELT. He joined the State Department in 1941, serving as assistant secretary of state until 1945, as undersecretary of state from 1945 to 1947 and as secretary of state from 1949 to 1953. Acheson was instrumental in planning and carrying out America's activist role in the postwar world and in instituting the economic

and military containment of communist expansion that was to be the cornerstone of U.S. COLD WAR policy for over four decades. Consistent with this stance, he was also important in establishing the NORTH ATLANTIC TREATY ORGANIZATION (NATO). His attempts to disengage the U.S. from its commitment to the Nationalist Chinese regime drew a great deal of criticism, as did his support of American involvement and failure to achieve peace in the KOREAN WAR. In spite of his unswerving anticommunist stand, Acheson became the target of the reigning red-baiters of the 1950s, in particular, of their leader, Senator Joseph R. MCCARTHY. He left government service in 1953 but retained an unofficial role by advising Presidents John F. KENNEDY and Lyndon B. JOHNSON.

Achille Lauro **hijacking** On October 7, 1985, Palestinian terrorists hijacked an Italian cruise liner, the *Achille Lauro,* in the Mediterranean and murdered an invalid American passenger. The hijackers surrendered in Egypt on October 9 in return for safe passage to Tunis. American jets intercepted the aircraft taking the hijackers to Tunis on October 10 and forced it to land in Sicily, where the Italian authorities arrested them.

Achinese Rebellion of 1953–1959 In 1953 Muslim Achinese rebels in northern Sumatra protested against the annexation of the state of Achin (ACEH) to the republic of INDONESIA, formed in 1950. On September 20, Tengku Daud Beureuh, military governor of Achin before its annexation, led an open armed rebellion against the government of President SUKARNO. Achinese attacked police and army posts, attempting to obtain more arms for a full-scale rebellion. Scattered guerrilla fighting continued until a cease-fire was arranged in March 1957, when Achin was declared a separate province. Native revolts broke out on other Indonesian islands that sought more autonomy. The Achinese rebels resumed fighting, which resulted in Sukarno's declaring Achin a special district with autonomy in matters of religion and local law.

Achinese War of 1873–1907 After the British recognized Dutch influence

in Achin (ACEH), a Muslim state in northern Sumatra, the Dutch sent two expeditions to conquer the Achinese in 1873. The Achinese palace in the capital, Kutaraja, was seized. In 1903 the sultan of Achin, Muhammed Daud, concluded a treaty with the Dutch, recognizing Dutch sovereignty and relinquishing his throne. Many Achinese refused to accept Dutch rule and continued to wage war. Slowly, using a "castle strategy" (establishing fortresses for Dutch troops throughout the area), the Dutch were able to pacify the Achinese by the end of 1907.

acid rain Precipitation (rain, snow, sleet and hail) containing acid pollutants, usually sulfuric or nitric acid. This rain has a pH of 2.4–4.5 as opposed to the 5.0 pH of unpolluted precipitation. The rain is basically an industrial phenomenon, resulting from the chemical reaction of airborne water vapor with the sulfur dioxide and nitrogen oxides contained in such pollutants as the exhaust from automobiles and the high-sulfur materials expelled from factory smokestacks. Acid rain has been a particularly disturbing environmental problem since the 1950s, polluting lakes, rivers and streams and destroying aquatic life; killing trees and plants; contaminating drinking water with acid-laced soil leachates and eroding such human-made objects as buildings, bridges and outdoor sculptures. The problem has yet to be solved, although it has been treated by devices that reduce sulfur and nitrogen compounds in car and factory emissions, by the addition of alkaline lime to certain bodies of water and by other measures.

ACLU See AMERICAN CIVIL LIBERTIES UNION.

Acmeists Group of Russian poets formed in 1912 in ST. PETERSBURG in reaction to the SYMBOLISTS. The leading members were Anna AKHMATOVA, her husband Nikolai Stepanovich GUMILEV and Osip MANDELSTAM; other members included Mikhail Kuzmin and Sergei Gorodetsky. Their work was published in the journal *Apollon*, edited by Sergei Makovsky. Acmeist poetry was highly individualistic and was marked by a strong emphasis on aesthetics and form, concise imagery and direct expression. In contrast to the FUTURISTS, the Acmeists had great respect for tradition. Mandelstam described Acmeism as "a longing for world culture." The group disbanded in 1917, and its members went their separate ways.

Action Française Rightist political movement in France (1899–1944). It was founded by poet and journalist Charles Maurras (1868–1952) and championed by essayist and journalist Léon DAUDET. Through its eponymous newspaper and through student groups such as the Camelots du Roi, it attacked the democratic institutions of the Third Republic, supported royalism and nationalism and espoused ANTI-SEMITISM. Pope PIUS XI condemned the movement in 1926, and it was banned by the French government 10 years later. Action Française continued as an underground movement, surfacing to support the VICHY government during World War II. It was disbanded in 1944 when France was liberated, and Maurras was sentenced to life imprisonment for collaboration.

Adamawa Former African tribal kingdom, located near the Benue River basin. After its conquest by the British in 1901, Adamawa was divided between Britain's NIGERIA colony and the German colony of Kamerun. The German portion was conquered by Allied forces during WORLD WAR I and was placed under joint British and French mandate in 1922. (See also CAMEROON.)

Adams, Ansel Easton (1902–1984) American photographer. One of the most widely exhibited photographers in the U.S., Adams was best known for his majestic black-and-white landscapes of the American West. He began taking photographs at the age of 14. Adams was credited with pioneering innovations in photographic technology and helping to gain recognition for photography as a legitimate art form. In a career spanning more than 50 years, he had photographs published in more than 35 books and portfolios. He cofounded the department of photography at the MUSEUM OF MODERN ART in New York City. An avid environmentalist, Adams became the official photographer of the

Ansel Adams in Yosemite National Park, photographed by Imogen Cunningham, 1953 (LIBRARY OF CONGRESS, PRINTS AND PHOTOGRAPHS DIVISION)

Sierra Club in 1928 and served as a director of the club for 37 years.

Adams, Gerry (1948–) Leader of SINN FÉIN (1983–), the political wing of the IRISH REPUBLICAN ARMY (IRA), and member of the British Parliament (1983–92, 1997–). Born in Belfast, Northern Ireland, Adams became involved with the IRA as a young man and worked toward the paramilitary group's goal of liberating Northern Ireland from British rule. In 1971 Adams was arrested on suspicion of serving as the IRA leader in the West Belfast area, but he was released in 1972 to serve as an intermediary in secret discussions between the IRA and the British secretary of state for Northern Ireland, William Whitelaw. Adams's continued association with the IRA again landed him in prison in 1973. During this second imprisonment Adams began to write political tracts for the *Republican News*, a pro-IRA newspaper, advocating the establishment of a political platform to complement the IRA's paramilitary effort. A year after his release in 1977, he was elected vice president of the Irish nationalist political party Sinn Féin, a position he held until becoming the party's president in 1983. In the same year he won election to the British Parliament as an Abstentionist candidate, and used his authority to advance Sinn Féin's agenda. Adams also overcame the objections of traditional IRA members and announced that Sinn Féin would sponsor candidates for the Dáil, the national parliament of Ireland. Adams's rise was not without setbacks, as he survived an assassination attempt in 1984 and lost his Parliament seat in April 1992.

In August 1994 Adams played a pivotal role in producing a cease-fire agreement between the IRA and the British government. However, the IRA refused the British government's demand to disband and subsequently broke the cease-fire in February 1996. The talks later served as the model for the May 1998 Good Friday Agreement that produced a joint Catholic-Protestant coalition government for Northern Ireland. Although Adams supported the Good Friday Agreement, he refused a position in the coalition. He instead focused on winning reelection to Parliament in 1997 and on improving Sinn Féin's representation in the Dáil and in the Northern Ireland parliament.

Adams, John Bertram *(1920–1984)* British nuclear physicist. Adams was considered the architect of the giant atom smasher built in the early 1970s for the European Center for Nuclear Research (CERN). He directed the center from 1976 to 1981. Under his leadership, the laboratory discovered the W and Z particles, subatomic particles considered to be keys to the understanding of matter.

Adams, John Michael Geoffrey "Tom" *(1931–1985)* Barbadan politician. Adams became prime minister of BARBADOS in 1976 when his Barbados Labour Party won an election after 15 years in opposition. A staunch anticommunist and a firm ally of the U.S. in the Caribbean, he gave strong support to the U.S.-led invasion of GRENADA in October 1983. He served as prime minister until his death.

Adams, Maude (Maude Adams Kiskadden) *(1872–1953)* American stage actress. Daughter of the leading lady of a Salt Lake City stock company, Adams played most of the standard child roles of the day, including Little Eva in *Uncle Tom's Cabin,* before she was 15. Her big break came when legendary Broadway producer Charles Frohman introduced her to writer James M. BARRIE. The three collaborated on a string of sensational successes, with Adams appearing in Frohman's American productions of the popular Scottish writer work's: as Lady Babbie in *The Little Minister* (1897); Miss Phoebe in *Quality Street* (1902); Maggie Wylie in *What Every Woman Knows* (1908); and the title role in *Peter Pan.* From opening night, November 6, 1905, to her farewell as "Pan" in 1915, Adams played the flying boy more than 1,500 times in New York and on tour. Onstage, she seemed a boy-girl, or a woman-child—a curious hybrid of earthy experience and elfin charm. Offstage, she had a passion for privacy, despite a string of unsuccessful suitors. At the peak of her success she was the top moneymaking star in America, averaging $20,000 a week. She retired in 1918. Perhaps her greatest tribute came from Barrie himself: "I believe you have become Peter

Pan in such a magical way that my only fear is your flying clear away out of the theatre some night."

Adams, Michael *(1930–1967)* U.S. test pilot; killed while making the 191st flight of the U.S.'s most famous experimental plane—the X-15. He was the only X-15 test flight fatality, with just eight more flights to go before completion of the tests. Adams, who had flown 49 combat missions in Korea, had joined the Air Force Test Pilot School at Edwards Air Force Base in California in 1962. Originally chosen to participate in the Air Force Manned Orbiting Laboratory programs, Adams chose in 1966 to fly the X-15 instead. During his final flight, Adams pushed the X-15 rocket plane to an altitude of 50.4 miles, qualifying him for U.S. Air Force astronaut wings.

Adams, Roger *(1889–1971)* American organic chemist. Adams studied chemistry at Harvard, where he obtained his Ph.D. in 1912, and at the University of Berlin. After working briefly at Harvard, he joined the staff of the University of Illinois in 1916 and later served as professor of organic chemistry from 1919 until his retirement in 1957. Adams was one of the most important chemists in the U.S. in the interwar period, and under him the University of Illinois became one of the leading centers of American chemistry.

Adams, Samuel A. *(1934–1988)* Central Intelligence Agency analyst; a codefendant in General William WESTMORELAND's libel suit against CBS, Inc. A Southeast Asia expert, Adams was a consultant and major contributor to the CBS documentary "The Uncounted Enemy: A Vietnam Deception," which accused Westmoreland of conspiring to underestimate enemy troop strength in 1967. Before resigning from the CIA's VIETNAM desk in 1968, Adams expressed his belief that the army was minimizing North Vietnamese and VIET CONG troop strength for political reasons. He first expressed his views publicly as a witness for the defense in the PENTAGON PAPERS espionage trial of Daniel Ellsberg and Anthony J. Russo, telling the court that the "facts" revealed by Ellsberg were false and therefore not state secrets.

Adams, (Llewellyn) Sherman *(1899–1986)* American politician. In 1952, during his second term as governor of New Hampshire, Adams played a key role in securing victory for Dwight D. EISENHOWER in that state's early presidential primary. He then served as special adviser to President Eisenhower from 1953 to 1958. In that post he wielded so much power that he came to be known as "assistant president." He resigned under fire in 1958 after a scandal in which he admitted accepting gifts, including a vicuna coat, from Bernard Goldfine, a Boston industrialist. In later years Adams operated a ski resort in his home state.

Adams, Walter Sydney *(1876–1956)* American astronomer. Adams was the son of missionaries working in Syria, then part of the Ottoman Empire, who returned to the U.S. in 1885. He graduated from Dartmouth College in 1898 and obtained his A.M. from the University of Chicago in 1900. After a year in Munich he began his career in astronomy as assistant to George Hale in 1901 at the Yerkes Observatory. In 1904 he moved with Hale to the newly established Mount Wilson Observatory, where he served as assistant director from 1913 to 1923 and then as director from 1923 until his retirement in 1946. At Mount Wilson Adams was able to use first the 60-inch and, from 1917, the 100-inch reflecting telescopes in whose design and construction he had been closely associated. His early work was mainly concerned with solar spectroscopy, studying sunspots and solar rotation, but he gradually turned to stellar spectroscopy.

In 1914 he showed how it was possible to distinguish between a dwarf and a giant star merely from their spectra. He also demonstrated that it was possible to determine the luminosity—intrinsic brightness—of a star from its spectrum. This led to Adams's introducing the method of spectroscopic parallax whereby a star's distance from the Earth could be estimated using the luminosity deduced from the star's spectrum. This method has been used to calculate the distance of many thousands of stars. He is better known for his work on the orbiting companion of Sirius, named Sirius B. Adams succeeded in obtaining the spectrum of

Sirius B in 1915 and found it to be considerably hotter than the Sun. He realized that such a hot body, just eight light-years distant, could remain invisible to the naked eye only if it was very much smaller than the Sun, no bigger in fact than the Earth. Adams had thus discovered the first known "white dwarf"—a star that has collapsed into a highly compressed object after its nuclear fuel is exhausted. If such an interpretation was correct, then Sirius B should possess a very strong gravitational field. According to EINSTEIN's general theory of RELATIVITY, this strong field should shift the wavelength of light waves emitted by it toward the red end of the spectrum. In 1924 Adams made the difficult spectroscopic observations and detected the predicted red shift, which confirmed his own account of Sirius B and provided strong evidence for general relativity.

Addams, Charles *(1912–1988)* American cartoonist. Born in Westfield, New Jersey, and educated at Colgate University, the University of Pennsylvania and Grand Central School of Art, he was noted for the ghoulish, gallows-humor cartoons that appeared primarily in THE NEW YORKER from 1935 onward. His work inspired a 1960s television series, *The Addams Family.* Twelve collections of his morbid cartoons were published, the last of them, *Creature Comforts,* in 1982. His work was also displayed at the Metropolitan Museum of Art, the Fogg Art Museum and the Museum of the City of New York.

Addams, Jane *(1860–1935)* American settlement worker who won the NOBEL PRIZE for peace in 1931. After graduating from Rockford College, Addams attended Woman's Medical College in Philadelphia until failing health caused her to leave in 1882. While visiting Europe in 1887–88, she became interested in the British settlement houses. Inspired by the movement to help the urban poor, she returned and founded Hull-House in Chicago in 1889. There the working poor could leave their children for care and instruction, and adults could come together for study and socialization. Addams's dedication soon earned the respect and help of many Chicagoans. By 1905 she was acknowledged to

have created by far the finest facilities and program for working-class education and recreation in the U.S. and the most famous settlement house in the world. Her many books, such as *Twenty Years at Hull-House* (1910), helped to bring her work to public attention. She later branched out to aid the woman suffrage movement and cause for world peace. Addams was accepted as one of the greatest women of her time.

Adderley, Julian "Cannonball" *(1928–1975)* American jazz musician. Adderley played alto, tenor and soprano saxophone as well as the flute. He led his own quintet and also worked with Miles DAVIS and John COLTRANE. Adderley won a Grammy Award in 1968 for his album *Mercy, Mercy.*

Addis Ababa Capital of ETHIOPIA. Addis Ababa was founded in 1887 by King Menelik II and became the capital in 1896. The city was conquered by the Fascist Italian forces of Benito MUSSOLINI in 1936 but was retaken by British forces in 1943, during WORLD WAR II. In 1963, it was named the headquarters of the ORGANIZATION OF AFRICAN UNITY.

Ade, George *(1866–1944)* U.S. playwright and humorist. Ade joined the staff of the *Chicago Record* in 1890. Eleven volumes written by Ade pointed out the follies and foibles of his peers. Many have considered his work to be a master portrait of the common man. He was especially praised for his use of the vernacular. As a playwright Ade once had three plays in New York running simultaneously. He also wrote a number of motion picture scripts. In 1936 Ade wrote the popular book *The Old Time Saloon.*

Aden See YEMEN, REPUBLIC OF.

Adenauer, Konrad *(1876–1967)* German statesman, first chancellor of the Federal Republic of GERMANY (1949–63). Born in Cologne, Adenauer studied law at the universities of Freiburg, Munich and Bonn and became a lawyer in his native city. Elected Cologne's mayor and a member of the provincial diet from 1917 to 1933, he was a staunch opponent of HITLER and

in 1933 was banned from the city, forced to flee and finally arrested by the GESTAPO. After escaping to Switzerland, he returned to Germany at the outbreak of WORLD WAR II and led a relatively uneventful life until he was rearrested by the Nazis in 1944. After the Allied victory, Adenauer was returned (1945) to the mayor's office in Cologne but was dismissed after the city was transferred to British military control. He founded the CHRISTIAN DEMOCRATIC UNION (CDU) in the mid-1940s, was elected president of the constituent assembly in 1948 and helped to write the new constitution for the Bonn republic. When the CDU gained a majority in the 1949 elections, Adenauer was appointed chancellor; he also served as foreign minister from 1951 to 1955. During his long tenure as chancellor he attempted to achieve reconciliation with France, relaxation of occupation laws and an end to the dismantling of German industry.

Adenauer developed a thriving economy and a successful political democracy out of the wartime ruins and is widely regarded as the architect of West Germany's remarkable postwar recovery. A strong opponent of communist East Germany, he also worked to reinstate West Germany as a member of the EUROPEAN COMMUNITY. A CDU defeat in 1961 and a cabinet scandal the following year forced him to resign in 1963. Nonetheless, "Der Alte" (the old one) continued to be an influential and popular figure in West Germany until his death.

Adivar, Halide Ebib *(1883–1964)* Turkish novelist. Adivar was educated in the U.S. and served for a time in the Anatolian nationalist army, an experience that inspired *The Daughter of Smyrna* (1922). This and Adivar's other early fiction examines the role of women in Turkish society. After living abroad for several years, Adivar wrote *The Clown and His Daughter* (1935) in English; she translated it into Turkish in 1936. Considered her most important work, the novel assesses the effects of westernization on Turkish society.

Adler, Alfred *(1870–1937)* Austrian psychologist. Adler achieved renown, along with Carl Gustav JUNG, as one of the rare disciples of Sigmund

FREUD to emerge from Freud's shadow with a distinctive psychological theory of his own. Adler graduated from the University of Vienna Medical School in 1895. Freud invited Adler to join his psychoanalytic discussion group on the basis of an insightful review Adler had written in 1902 of a book by Freud on dream interpretation. But Adler always maintained an intellectually independent status and left the group with nine followers in 1911, establishing his own "Individualpsychologie." In *The Neurotic Constitution* (1912), Adler stressed a teleologic (goal-oriented) basis for neurotic behavior as opposed to Freud's focus on infantile sexuality. In 1925 Adler coined the term *inferiority complex* to apply to those who adapted badly to physical or other disabilities. Adler's *Understanding Human Nature* (1927) is based on a series of his lectures that drew wide audiences in both Europe and America.

Adler, Mortimer Jerome *(1902–2001)* American educator and writer. Adler, one of the most influential intellectuals of mid-20th-century America, wrote a wide range of books and articles but is best remembered for his cofounder role (along with Robert HUTCHINS) in establishing the GREAT BOOKS PROGRAM—a 54–volume collection (1952) of the great writings of Western civilization designed for broad educational use. Adler earned a doctorate at Columbia University in 1928, having already established himself as an opponent of the pragmatism of Columbia philosopher John Dewey. Dewey held that truth was whatever is useful to a society in a given stage of its evolution. Adler countered that certain moral and spiritual values were absolute truths and that the progressive education system fostered by pragmatism was producing a half-educated public trained for money-making but not for living the inspired Greek ideal of the "good life." In the 1940s, while teaching at the University of Chicago, Adler guided a team of scholars in the production of the Syntopicon, a synthesis of the great ideas of Western civilization that was published along with the Great Books collection. In addition to his philosophical works, Adler also addressed other topics, as indicated by *The Common Sense of Politics* (1971) and *The Paideia Program: An Educational Syllabus* (1984). Adler also developed an increasing interest in Christianity, converting to the Episcopalian faith in 1984 and then to the Roman Catholic faith in 1999. Adler died at his home on June 28, 2001, of natural causes.

Adler, Peter Herman *(1899–1990)* U.S. conductor. As music and artistic director of the NBC Opera between 1949 and 1959, he pioneered the broadcasting of opera on U.S. television. Among the works he commissioned was Gian Carlo MENOTTI's *Amahl and the Night Visitors*. He served as music director of the Baltimore Symphony from 1959 until 1968.

Adler, Renata *(1938–)* American author and journalist. Born in Italy, she was educated at Bryn Mawr, the Sorbonne and Harvard, later earning a law degree from Yale. From 1962 she worked intermittently for THE NEW YORKER as a film critic and writer-reporter. She is the author of two unconventional novels, *Speedboat* (1976), an amalgamation of short, overlapping stories, and *Pitch Dark* (1983), variously described as minimalist and an "antinovel." She brought her legal training to bear in *Reckless Disregard: Westmoreland v. CBS et al.; Sharon v. Time* (1986), an examination of media ethics in two important libel cases of the 1980s. Much of the work first appeared in *The New Yorker*, which was itself embroiled in a lawsuit by CBS as a result. Adler has contributed articles and short stories to various publications under the pseudonym Brett Daniels and has also published collections of film criticism and reportage. In 2000 Adler released her latest book, *Gone: The Last Days of The New Yorker*, which chronicled what she regarded as the decline of *The New Yorker* magazine.

Adler, Samuel *(1898–1979)* American abstract painter, sculptor and educator. Adler was best known for his paintings and collages, which were once described as "ghostly presences and dreamlike memories." His artwork was exhibited in more than 150 national and international shows and was included in the collections of 25 public museums.

Admiralty Islands (Admiralties) Group of islands in the Bismarck Archipelago, north of the New Guinea. The admiralty Islands were annexed by Germany to its New Guinea colony in 1884. During WORLD WAR I, the islands were seized by Australian forces and placed under Australian mandate in 1921. They were held by Japanese forces from 1942 to 1944, during WORLD WAR II, and are now a part of the independent Papua–New Guinea.

Adorno, Theodor (Theodor Weisengrund) *(1903–1969)* German philosopher, sociologist, literary and music critic. Adorno was one of the most influential German cultural critics of his generation, along with Walter Benjamin and Georg LUKACS, with whom Adorno was often linked due to his Marxist-influenced approach to the interpretation of societal patterns and literary works. Adorno joined the renowned philosophical faculty of Frankfurt University in 1930 but emigrated from Germany to Oxford in 1933 to escape the Nazi regime. In 1938 Adorno came to America, where he formed a friendship with fellow German émigré Thomas MANN. In 1950 he returned to Frankfurt, where he headed the Institute of Social Relations from 1958 to 1959. Adorno's most famous works are *The Dialectic of Enlightenment* (1947), which argues that reason has become an instrument of totalitarian control, and *the Authoritarian Personality* (1950), a study of FASCISM. His posthumous *Collected Writings* appeared in 16 volumes (1970–80).

Adoula, Cyrille *(1921–1978)* Premier of the Republic of the Congo (now Democratic Republic of CONGO) (1961–64). Adoula later served as ambassador to Belgium (1964–66), ambassador to the U.S. (1966–69), and foreign minister (1969–70).

adrenaline See John Jacob ABEL; Thomas Renton ELLIOTT.

Adrian, Edgar Douglas (Baron Adrian of Cambridge) *(1889–1977)* British neurophysiologist. Adrian, a lawyer's son, studied at Cambridge University and St. Bartholomew's Hospital, London, where he obtained his M.D. in 1915. He returned to Cambridge in 1919, was appointed professor of physiology in 1937 and became the master of Trinity College in 1951, an office he retained until his retirement in 1965. He was made a peer in 1955.

Adrian's greatest contribution to neurophysiology was his work on nerve impulses. When he started his work, it was known that nerves transmit nerve impulses as signals, but little was known of the frequency and control of such impulses. The first insight into this process came from Adrian's colleague Keith Lucas, who demonstrated in 1905 that the impulse obeyed the "all-or-none" law. This asserted that below a certain threshold of stimulation a nerve does not respond. But once the threshold is reached, the nerve continues to respond by a fixed amount, however much the stimulation increases. Thus increased stimulation, although it stimulates more fibers, does not affect the magnitude of the signal itself.

It was not until 1925 that Adrian advanced beyond this position. By painstaking surgical techniques he succeeded in separating individual nerve fibers and amplifying and recording the small action potentials in them. He demonstrated how the nerve, even though it transmits an impulse of fixed strength, can still convey a complex message. He discovered that as the extension increased, so did the frequency of the nerve impulse, rising from 10 to 50 impulses per second. Thus he concluded that the message is conveyed by changes in the frequency of the discharge. For this work Adrian shared the 1932 NOBEL PRIZE for physiology or medicine with Charles Sherrington.

Adwa (Adowa) See ETHIOPIA.

Ady, Endre *(1877–1919)* Hungarian poet, critic and journalist. Ady is generally recognized as the finest Hungarian poet of the 20th century. He created a sensation in his native land with the appearance of his very first volume of verse, *New Poems* (1906). Ady's lyrics defied the social and poetical conventions of the era by including highly charged erotic imagery as well as scenes of intense violence. Ady was an expressionistic poet who wrote fervently of his own spiritual torment as one unable to find faith or certainty in any creed or personal relationship.

The combined horror and release of death was a frequent theme in his work. English translations of Ady's verse have been issued as *Poems* (1969) and *The Explosive Country* (1977).

AE (pen name of George William Russell) *(1867–1935)* Irish poet, playwright and nationalist. AE (an abbreviation of *AEon*) studied art in Dublin and published his first collection of poetry, *Homeward* (1894), with the encouragement of W. B. YEATS, with whom, along with Lady GREGORY, AE later helped form the ABBEY THEATRE. AE's first play, *Deirdre,* a poetic drama, was performed at the Irish National Theatre, an early incarnation of the Abbey, in 1902. From 1905 to 1923 AE edited *The Irish Homestead,* a publication encouraging Irish culture, and from 1923 to 1930 he served as editor of *The Irish Statesman,* which advocated Irish independence. He is perhaps best known for *The Avatars* (1933), a poetic, futuristic fantasy. Other poetic works include *Midsummer Eve* (1928), *The House of the Titans* (1934) and *Selected Poems* (1935). AE also contributed political articles to various journals and was a mentor to many young Irish writers, among them Padraic COLUM and James STEPHENS.

AEG (Allgemeine Elektrizitäts-Gesellschaft) Giant German manufacturer of electrical products, founded in 1883 by Emil Rathenau. It became a significant force in the design world through its patronage of the designer and architect Peter BEHRENS in the early 20th century. Behrens designed the AEG trademark, such products as electric fans and lighting fixtures and many brochures and other graphic materials. The AEG turbine factory he designed in Berlin is an important pioneering work of modern architecture. In 1985 the German automotive firm Daimler-Benz purchased AEG. Daimler-Benz closed the electronics firm 11 years later as part of its corporate restructuring.

Aehrenthal, Count Alois Lexa von *(1854–1912)* Diplomat and politician of the Austro-Hungarian Empire. He was ambassador to St. Petersburg (1898–1906) and foreign minister (1906–12). While he was foreign minister, Austria-Hungary, with German approval, annexed BOSNIA AND HERZE-GOVINA (1908); this action raised the threat that Russia would make war and was one of the incidents leading to WORLD WAR I.

aerodynamic styling Design using forms derived from the science of aerodynamics, which developed in connection with aviation and is concerned with the study of the movement of solid bodies through the air. In the 1920s and 1930s it became known that certain shapes, such as the bullet-shaped front and tapering rear typical of large dirigibles, were maximally efficient for aircraft. Such forms came to be called streamlined and were associated with concepts of MODERNISM, speed and progress. Aerodynamic forms were adopted by industrial designers for locomotives, automobiles and eventually for such illogical applications as pencil sharpeners and toasters. In recent years, a more serious interest in aerodynamics has developed in automotive design in an effort to improve fuel efficiency. Minimizing air resistance has led to many recent designs characterized by flowing shapes and smooth surfaces.

Aerosmith American rock and roll band. Formed in 1969, Aerosmith united Steven Tallarico (Tyler) of the group Chain Mail with Joe Perry, Joey Kramer and Ray Tabano. They debuted as Aerosmith in 1970 by entertaining a large crowd in the student union building at Boston University. In 1972 Aerosmith signed with Columbia Records, recorded its self-titled album, and released it in 1973. The band's appeal expanded to areas outside Boston the following year after the appearance of its second album, *Get Your Wings.*

Personnel changes, in addition to Tyler's efforts to recover from a motorcycle accident in 1981, resulted in a four-year void in which the band did not release an album. In April 1984 the original members reunited for a *Back in the Saddle* tour across the U.S.

After a brief break in the mid-1990s, the band again returned to the studio and recorded *Nine Lives,* which debuted at number one on the *Billboard* chart its first week and reached double platinum three weeks later. Since 1999 Aerosmith has slowed the pace of its production and promotion, releasing only two albums in four

Aerosmith. photographed by Ron Pownall (PHOTOFEST)

years. However, despite a quantitative slowdown, the band's songs did well as singles, resulting in Aerosmith's induction into the Rock and Roll Hall of Fame.

affirmative action programs Programs implemented in the U.S. after the 1970s to encourage racial and sexual equality in schools and workplaces in order to redress past inequities. Although the CIVIL RIGHTS ACT OF 1964 and its amendments outlawed discriminatory hiring by most private employers and most discriminatory school and college admission policies, the results of historical discrimination remained. Affirmative action programs—some voluntary and some imposed by court order—were designed to encourage diversity by giving preference to minority groups and women in hiring and in college admissions. The programs were extremely controversial, and white men objected that the result was "reverse discrimination" because they were passed over despite having better qualifications than successful minority group members. The Supreme Court in a number of decisions upheld the use of affirmative action programs so long as they did not impose rigid racial or sexual quotas. In 2003, the U.S. Supreme Court ruled that colleges and universities could consider an applicant's race as a factor in the admissions process but declared

that assigning a quantitative value to race was unconstitutional.

Affirmed *(1975–2001)* American thoroughbred racehorse. In 1978 Affirmed became the second half of racing's first back-to-back Triple Crown sweep, after SEATTLE SLEW took the honors in 1977. Affirmed, the top-rated two year-old of 1977, spent much of his racing life fighting off ALYDAR, who handed the horse his only defeats in his first season. The following season, the two colts finished one-two in all three Triple Crown races. Affirmed was ridden by Steve CAUTHEN, who became the second youngest rider ever to take the Kentucky Derby. Their Belmont Stakes battle is particularly remembered as a racing classic, as the two horses were stride for stride through two-thirds of the race and finished with the third fastest time in the history of the race. In 2001, following months of problems with the use of his legs, Affirmed died.

Afghan Civil War of 1928–1929
Opponents to internal reforms caused a large-scale revolt in November 1928 as AMANULLAH KHAN, emir of AFGHANISTAN, attempted to modernize his country. In mid-January 1929 Amanullah abdicated in favor of his weak older brother, but an outlaw leader led a strong band to capture the Afghan capital of Kabul and proclaimed himself

emir as Habibullah Ghazi. At Kandahar, Amanullah assembled an army and began a march on Kabul to retake the throne in the spring of 1929; he was defeated and fled the country. Other early claimants to the throne were also unsuccessful. Then General Muhammad NADIR KHAN, an Afghan officer and Amanullah's cousin, organized an army after returning from Europe and marched against Habibullah, defeating him and taking Kabul in October 1929. Habibullah was captured and executed, and Khan took the throne, renaming himself Nadir Shah. With British assistance he instituted reforms, restored order and placated Amanullah's loyal followers. In 1932 he established a constitutional government.

Afghan Civil War of 1979–2001
The Soviet invasion of AFGHANISTAN in late December 1979 dramatized a momentous failure in Soviet foreign policy. When Afghanistan became a republic in 1973, the USSR increased its efforts to make the country a buffer state against Pakistan by supporting radical political parties like the Khalq (People's Democratic) Party. In 1978 Khalq militants assassinated Afghanistan's first president; a Khalq leader became president but was ousted by his prime minister (September 1979), who himself was overthrown (December 27, 1979) by another leftist, Babrak Karmal, who had Soviet backing. When Karmal's attempt to impose Russianization met with armed resistance, he asked for Soviet aid to crush the opposition. Despite having modern equipment, more than 100,000 Soviet troops found it difficult to defeat the Afghan rebels, whose guerrilla tactics and sabotage confused the invaders. Ancient tribal antagonisms and linguistic differences prevented the rebels from developing a unified strategy to defeat the Soviets and the official Afghanistan army, the latter so riddled by defections that in 1984 the Kabul government was drafting 14-year-olds. The civil war, labeled by some as the Soviets' "Vietnam," embarrassed the USSR internationally. The Soviets signed a UN-sponsored withdrawal agreement on April 14, 1988. They began to withdraw on May 15 and completed their withdrawal by early 1989.

The withdrawal of Soviet troops did not immediately mean the end of the

Afghan communist government. Led by Dr. Mohammed NAJIBULLAH, the government continued to fight against the various bands of mujahideen, or Islamic freedom fighters, from 1986 until 1992, when Najibullah was forced from power, executed and replaced by the Islamic Council of Mujahideen (ICM). Led by Burhanuddin Rabbani, the ICM ruled most of Afghanistan. However, in the mid-1990s the ICM faced an insurgency by the TALIBAN, a group of Islamic clerics espousing an extreme form of Islamism. Led by Mullah Mohammed OMAR, the Taliban acquired the support of mujahideen bands that desired the strict application of sharia, or Islamic law, to Afghanistan. In 1996 the Taliban took over Kabul and forced the retreat of the ICM, which later renamed itself the Northern Alliance. Although the Taliban increased its control over Afghanistan to approximately 90% of the state's territory by 2001, it was driven from power in an October 2001 offensive by U.S. military forces, because of the Taliban's support for the terrorist group al-QAEDA, and its leader, Osama BIN LADEN, who had orchestrated the terrorist attacks of SEPTEMBER 11, 2001. Since then, the country has been under the rule of Hamid KARZAI, an Afghanistan official from the same clan as King Zahir Shah. In 2002 Karzai was elected president of Afghanistan by the Loya Jirga, a national council convened traditionally by the Afghanistan head of state; he was subsequently reelected in the country's first nationwide popular vote.

Afghanistan Country in southwestern Asia; bounded by TURKMENISTAN, UZBEKISTAN, TAJIKISTAN and CHINA to its north, PAKISTAN to its south and east, and IRAN to its west. With a long history of fierce resistance to outside pressures, Afghanistan remained neutral during WORLD WAR I and was recognized as an independent nation by Britain, Persia (Iran), Russia and TURKEY. AMANULLAH KHAN, a progressive monarch, took office in 1919 and oversaw the adoption of a written constitution in 1923. But Khan was overthrown in 1929, due to opposition to his efforts to westernize Afghanistan (see AFGHAN CIVIL WAR OF 1928–1929). Mohammed NADIR SHAH, his successor, was killed in 1933. Mohammed Zahir Shah, NADIR SHAH's son, continued westernization efforts. He also helped to found, in 1937, the Oriental Entente, consisting of Afghanistan, Iran, IRAQ and Turkey. Afghanistan again was neutral during WORLD WAR II. In the 1950s and 1960s, westernization

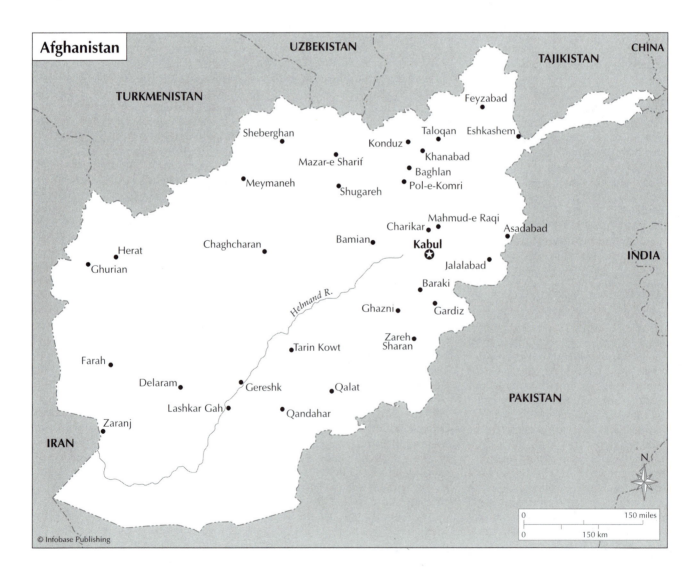

© Infobase Publishing

AFGHANISTAN	
1919	Independence confirmed by British.
1921	Treaty of Friendship signed with Soviet Union.
1929	British intervene to establish General Nadir Shah on throne after brigands seize Kabul.
1961	U.S. president John F. Kennedy offers to mediate border dispute with Pakistan.
1965	First Marxist party formed, People's Democratic Party of Afghanistan (PDPA).
1978	Military dictator Mohammed Daoud Khan killed in Marxist coup.
1979	Soviet troops invade to fight Muslim rebels threatening communist government; identified as major supplier of heroin to Western Europe.
1989	Last of Soviet troops are withdrawn in accordance with UN-sponsored agreement; civil strife continues.
1992	Communist regime overthrown by Islamic groups.
1996	Taliban gains control of country.
2001	U.S. military forces overthrow the Taliban.
2004	Hamid Karzai reelected president.
2005	National Assembly elections held.

efforts continued in an attempt to modernize the Afghan economy. In 1973, the monarchy was overthrown and a republican form of rule established. A pro-USSR communist government emerged, and in 1979 Soviet troops occupied Afghanistan to strengthen that government, which had been in danger of toppling. After a decade of armed resistance to its pacification efforts, Soviet forces withdrew in 1989. But fighting continued between the communist Afghan government and anticommunist rebel forces. In 1992 the communist government of Afghanistan was overthrown by the bands of mujahideen, or Islamic freedom fighters, that had conducted a guerrilla war against the government, and the Soviet occupation force that had remained until 1989. After the president of the communist government, Mohammed NAJIBULLAH, was driven from power in 1992, his government was replaced by the Islamic Council of Mujahideen (ICM).

Headed by Burhanuddin Rabbani, the ICM ruled most of Afghanistan and laid claim to the country's seat in the UN. But the ICM's authority was later challenged by the TALIBAN, a group of Islamic clerics espousing an extreme form of Islamism. Led by Mullah Mohammed OMAR, the Taliban acquired the support of mujahideen bands that desired the strict application of sharia, or Islamic law. The conflict between the ICM and the Taliban continued until 1996, when Taliban forces took control of Kabul and forced the ICM into the northern regions of Afghanistan, where it regrouped and renamed itself the Northern Alliance. The Taliban remained in power until October 2001, when U.S. military forces invaded Afghanistan and deposed it, on account of the Taliban's refusal to hand over Osama BIN LADEN, the al-QAEDA terrorist leader responsible for the attacks of September 11, 2001. The Taliban was replaced by Hamid KARZAI, an Afghanistan official from the regime of Zahir

Shah, who was later elected president of Afghanistan in 2002 by the constituted *loya jirga,* or grand council. Karzai was reelected in 2004 in the first nationwide democratic election in Afghanistan's history. In September 2005 parliamentary elections were held for the first time in 30 years, and in December the new parliament held its first session. (See also AFGHAN CIVIL WAR OF 1979–2001).

Afinogenov, Alexander Niko-layevich *(1904–1941)* Russian playwright, one of the few important dramatists to emerge immediately after the Russian Revolution. *The Strange Fellow* (1928) and *Fear* (1931) were his best-known plays and dealt with the difficulties of change in a new social order. Subsequent plays—*The Distant, Greetings Spain, Mashenka* and *On the Eve*—were more acceptable politically to the regime. He was killed in a German air raid during World War II.

Aflaq, Michel *(1910–1989)* Syrian political leader. Together with Salah Baytar, he founded the BAATH movement in SYRIA in 1940. The Baathists, who advocated Arab nationalism and socialism, came to power in Syria in 1963 and Iraq in 1968, but a split between factions forced Aflaq to move to Iraq in 1968. He was said to have been out of the mainstream of Arab politics since that time.

AFL-CIO See AMERICAN FEDERATION OF LABOR AND CONGRESS OF INDUSTRIAL ORGANIZATIONS.

African National Congress (ANC) Organization formed in 1912 to promote the rights of the black people of SOUTH AFRICA. Growing out of the Native Education Association (established in Cape Colony in 1882), the ANC joined forces with representatives of the South African Indian community in 1927. Thereafter, it sought a unified, multiracial and democratic country offering full citizenship to all South Africans. The ANC adopted a strategy of passive resistance, particularly under the leadership (1952–67) of Albert LUTHULI, but was nonetheless banned by South African authorities in 1960. From then on, the organization operated underground or in exile. Maintaining its goal of total abolition of APARTHEID, the ANC was later split between those who continued to support nonviolence and militants who supported armed insurrection. After the legalization of the ANC by South African president F. W. DE KLERK and the release of its long-imprisoned leader Nelson MANDELA in 1990, the organization abandoned the threat of guerrilla warfare while orchestrating a campaign of strikes, marches, boycotts and other protests. During the 1990s, the ANC moved toward a new identity as a viable political party. In 1997, Mandela was succeeded as ANC president by Thabo MBEKI, an ANC member and activist since 1956. Mbeki was the party's candidate in the 1999 presidential elections and succeeded Mandela as president of South Africa. Mbeki has been responsible for transforming the ANC into a political organization capable of establishing its own national agenda, at times independent of its political rivals, the Inkatha Freedom Party and the National Party.

Aga Khan The hereditary title for the spiritual leader (imam) of the Ismaili sect of Shiite Muslims, whose greatest population concentration is in Africa and parts of Asia. It was first used by the imam Hassan Ali Shah in the 1800s and represents the belief that the Aga Khan is a direct descendant of Mohammad's daughter, Fatima, through the Fatimid caliphs of Egypt. **Aga Khan III** (1877–1957) worked to improve Muslim education and representation in Hindu-dominated INDIA. He helped to establish the Muslim League, which gave the impetus for the creation of the independent country of PAKISTAN. He also represented India at the LEAGUE OF NATIONS (1932; 1934–37). His grandson, Karim Al Hussaini Shah, succeeded him as **Aga Khan IV** in 1957 and continues to work for the welfare of his followers.

Agee, James (1909–1955) American author. Agee was born in Tennessee and educated at Exeter and Harvard. His first poetry collection, *Permit Me Voyage,* appeared in the 1934 Yale Series of Younger Poets. In 1936 Agee and photographer Walker EVANS were commissioned to depict the lives of rural Alabama sharecroppers. The product of their observations, *Let Us Now Praise Famous Men*

(1939), is a poignant, lyrical description of the American South during the GREAT DEPRESSION. Agee is perhaps best known for the loosely autobiographical novel *A Death in the Family* (1957), which examines the effect on a family of the father's death in an automobile accident, but he was a poet, film critic and screenwriter as well.

Agent Orange One of the terrible legacies of the VIETNAM WAR is what many veterans believe to be their contamination with the herbicide Agent Orange. The major herbicides sprayed in Vietnam were assigned code names corresponding to the color of identification bands painted on their storage drums. Agent Orange was sprayed by the U.S. Air Force in a defoliation operation called Ranch Hand from 1962 to 1970. The chemical contained minute amounts of a poisonous type of dioxin, which has been claimed to result in various health problems.

During the initial stages of light herbicide use in Vietnam, from 1962 through 1964, the most commonly used herbicides were Purple and Pink. During this period of Operation Ranch Hand, approximately 145,000 gallons of Purple and 123,000 gallons of Pink were sprayed in South Vietnam. After 1964 the most widely used herbicides were Orange, White and Blue, which rapidly replaced Purple and Pink. Heavily sprayed areas included inland forests near the DMZ; inland forests at the junction of the borders of Cambodia, Laos and South Vietnam; inland forests north and northwest of Saigon; mangrove forests on the southernmost peninsula of Vietnam; and mangrove forests along major inland shipping channels southeast of Saigon. Crop destruction missions were concentrated in northern and eastern central areas of South Vietnam. The primary use of herbicide was to kill vegetation and thereby deny cover to enemy forces. By making ambushes more difficult, Agent Orange undoubtedly saved American lives. Often confused with pesticides that were sprayed directly over U.S. installations to control malaria-carrying mosquitoes, Agent Orange was not normally sprayed directly on troops. But soldiers did come in contact with it as they moved through jungle areas that had been defoliated.

Beginning in the late 1970s, Vietnam veterans began citing dioxin as the cause of health problems ranging from skin rashes to cancer to birth defects in their children. Although dioxin has proven extremely poisonous in laboratory animals, considerable controversy still exists over its effect on humans. While not admitting any liability, chemical companies that manufactured the herbicide have agreed to establish a $180 million fund to be distributed to eligible veterans by a "special master" appointed by the U.S. District Court in Brooklyn, New York. The agreement was made in response to a class action suit by veterans. According to the terms of the settlement, a claimant "who dies or becomes totally disabled from an illness (not caused by trauma such as auto accident or gunshot wound) anytime during the period from the Vietnam war to December 31, 1994" and who meets the exposure standards will be eligible. Since the late 1970s the Veterans Administration has provided free medical tests to veterans citing health problems that they believe may be related to Agent Orange.

Agnew, Spiro Theodore (1918–1996) Vice president of the UNITED STATES (1969–73). Perhaps the most controversial U.S. vice president in the 20th century, Agnew was the son of Greek immigrants. A native of Baltimore, Maryland, he attended Johns Hopkins University and Baltimore Law School. After army service in World War II, he received his law degree (1947). He became active in Maryland state politics in the 1950s. Elected governor in 1966, he was the surprise choice as Richard M. NIXON's vice presidential running mate in the 1968 national elections. During the campaign Agnew established himself as a champion of law and order and a leading spokesman for the U.S. right wing. He gained particular attention for his colorful and uncompromising rhetoric as he castigated antiwar demonstrators and liberals in the news media as an "effete corps of impudent snobs." Throughout Nixon's first term and during the 1972 reelection campaign, Agnew continued his defense of the administration's VIETNAM WAR policy and his condemnation of administration opponents. Nixon and Agnew were reelected in 1972.

Former U.S. vice president Spiro T. Agnew (LIBRARY OF CONGRESS, PRINTS AND PHOTOGRAPHS DIVISION)

Agnew was not implicated in the developing WATERGATE scandal, but he soon faced his own legal troubles. In mid-1973 he was charged with having committed numerous criminal acts, including extortion and bribery while governor of Maryland and earlier. Though protesting his innocence, he was ultimately forced to resign the vice presidency (October 10, 1973). He pleaded no contest and was fined $10,000 and sentenced to three years unsupervised probation. Disbarred and disgraced, Agnew disappeared from the political scene. Nixon chose Gerald FORD as Agnew's replacement; Ford in turn succeeded to the presidency after Nixon's resignation the following year. Agnew became a business consultant and in 1980 published his autobiography, *Go Quietly or Else.* Agnew died in Berlin, Maryland, on September 17, 1996.

Agnon, Shmuel Yosef (pen name of Halevi Czaczkes) *(1880–1970)* Israeli poet and novelist. Born in Galicia (then a region of Austria-Hungary, now part of Poland), he received a traditional Talmudic education and studied Jewish and Hebrew literature. He published his first poems in his teens, when he also became an active Zionist (see ZIONISM). In 1908 he moved to Jerusalem, where he published his first novel, *Agunot* (1909), from which he

derived his pen name. In 1912 he moved to Berlin, where he helped found the journal *Der Jude* (The Jew), and where he met businessman Salman Schocken, who became his lifelong friend, patron and publisher. He later settled in Palestine. Agnon's work, written in Hebrew, is rich in folklore and fantasy. *The Bridal Suite* (1931) is the story of a poor Hasidic Jew searching for husbands and dowries for his daughters. Other works include *A Guest for the Night* (1937) and *A Simple Story* (1935). Critic Edmund WILSON was an admirer of Agnon's work and was instrumental in his nomination for the NOBEL PRIZE in literature, which Agnon received in 1966 along with Nelly SACHS. Agnon received numerous honors during his lifetime and is considered to be among the finest writers of Hebrew fiction.

Agricultural Adjustment Administration (AAA) U.S. government agency, established as part of President Franklin D. ROOSEVELT'S NEW DEAL during the GREAT DEPRESSION. The AAA was created in May 1933, during the Roosevelt administration's first HUNDRED DAYS. It attempted to raise farm prices by lowering production of certain agricultural goods. The AAA's policy of paying farmers to grow less food was highly controversial. In 1936 the U.S. Supreme Court declared that the AAA was unconstitutional.

Ahidjo, Ahmadou *(1924–1989)* First president of CAMEROON (1960–82). Ahidjo was elected shortly after independence and reelected four times (1965, 1970, 1975, 1980). His rule was authoritarian, but the country became self-sufficient in food. Ahidjo put down several rebellions and survived a coup attempt in 1970. A year after his resignation in 1982, he was charged with plotting against his successor, Paul Biya. He went into exile and was sentenced to death in absentia. Although the sentence was later commuted to indefinite detention, he never returned to Cameroon.

Ahren, Uno *(1897–1977)* Swedish architect and designer who was a pioneer in introducing the concepts of MODERNISM into Sweden in the 1920s. Ahren collaborated with Sven Markelius and E. Gunnar ASPLUND in buildings for

the Stockholm exhibition of 1930 and was the designer of a Ford factory of 1929 and a 1930 cinema in Stockholm that were among the first major modernist works in Sweden. Ahren exerted a significant influence on the development of the style known as Swedish Modern.

Aideed, Mohammed Farah *(1934–1996)* Somali warlord. Originally an ambassador to India during the administration of strongman Mohammad Siad Barre of SOMALIA, Aideed was solicited by the leadership of his family clan, Habr Gadir, to head a rebellion against Siad. Though the insurrection toppled Siad's regime in January 1991, a struggle for power emerged among the northern Somali National Movement, the southern-based Somali Patriotic Movement, and the United Somali Congress (USC), for which Aideed served as its supreme military commander. Complicating matters further was the struggle within the USC between General Aideed and his associate, Ali Mahdi Mohammad, leader of both the USC and the Abgadir subclan. In December 1992 this escalating civil conflict precipitated U.S. president George H. W. BUSH to launch Operation Restore Hope and deploy 20,000 troops to Somalia in an effort to bolster the UN forces already there. After repeated attacks on UN personnel, one of which resulted in the deaths of 24 Pakistani soldiers, the Clinton administration expanded the scope of Restore Hope to include the removal of Aideed, whom by mid-1993 the U.S. and UN had identified as the principal individual disrupting the multinational force's task. Aideed, however, repeatedly thwarted efforts to capture him, such as the disastrous October 3–4, 1993, U.S. raid in Mogadishu that led to the deaths of 18 U.S. Army Rangers. Though some argued that the assault, in which the Rangers established a 10-to-1 kill ratio and which captured many USC personnel, was a military success, the televised dragging of the dead Americans through the streets of Mogadishu while their corpses were repeatedly beaten by Somalis generated an enormous public outcry in the U.S. that resulted in the withdrawal of American forces from the UN operation in 1994. Without the substantial American presence, the UN left the following year, followed soon by the remaining international relief agencies. In an effort to solidify his position within Somalia, Aideed repeatedly cultivated support within Somalia's Muslim-dominated northern region by both providing support to Islamic militant groups based in that area, such as al-Islam and Jihad al-Islam, and encouraging impoverished Somalis to conduct a raid into ETHIOPIA. Aideed died in 1996 of a heart attack related to a gunshot wound. He was succeeded by his son, Hussein, who later participated in the formation of the UN-recognized Transitional National Government.

AIDS (acquired immunodeficiency syndrome) A serious disorder that became one of the health scourges of the late 20th century. First identified in 1981 in the U.S., AIDS affects the ability of the body's immune system to fight disease. It is caused by a retrovirus—isolated in France in 1983 and in the U.S. in 1984—that has come to be known as **HIV** (human immunodeficiency virus). Researchers have speculated that AIDS may have arisen on the African continent (where it is now a leading cause of death in many countries) as a virus of monkeys or primates that has since undergone mutation. However, the nature of the genesis of AIDS, like so much about the disorder, has yet to be definitely established.

Two separate HIV viruses have been discovered that share about 40% of their genetic makeup; HIV-1 was identified in 1984 and HIV-2 the following year. Within each of these viruses there are a multiplicity of different strains. The virus has been shown to have an unusually long incubation period and, after initial introduction into the body, can lie dormant for up to 10 years in a symptom-free individual before manifesting itself. It strikes mainly the body's disease-fighting white blood cells, particularly the T-helper cells, leaving the infected person vulnerable to a number of opportunistic infections.

The earliest sign of infection is the production of HIV antibodies, a state in which an individual is commonly known as HIV-positive. Normally, the first signs of HIV infection are several of a cluster of symptoms called ARC

(AIDS-related complex). These include tiredness, fevers, night sweats, enlarged lymph glands, diarrhea and severe weight loss. In full-blown AIDS a number of previously rare diseases tend to manifest themselves in the infected individual. These include Kaposi's sarcoma, a skin cancer characterized by bruise-like patches that spread throughout the body, and *Pneumocystis carinii* pneumonia, a parasitic lung infection. Among other infections often accompanying AIDS are cytomegalovirus, which often produces blindness, and diseases of the central nervous system that sometimes lead to an AIDS-related dementia.

AIDS has been shown to spread from one individual to another by contact with bodily fluids such as blood and semen. Never found to be spread by casual contact, it is passed through sexual contact, by blood-to-blood transmission or from an infected mother to her unborn fetus, resulting in an AIDS-infected newborn. The AIDS virus was first detected in the U.S. and most Western countries in homosexual or bisexual men. Since the early 1980s it has spread through a large percentage of the homosexual population, especially affecting large urban areas. In the late 1980s and early 1990s, the disorder became extremely prevalent among minority communities in large cities, spread mostly by intravenous drug use with infected needles and by sexual transmission from drug users to their partners.

After tests for the HIV virus became available in 1985, the nation's blood supply was tested and, to a very great degree, made safe. However, before testing was available, some of the blood supply was tainted and many hemophiliacs, who must use large quantities of blood products, and some recipients of blood transfusions, were infected with AIDS.

No cure for the virus had been found and, while more persons with AIDS (PWAs) are surviving for longer periods of time, the diseases brought on by the virus have invariably proved to be fatal. Promising research on a number of vaccines is in progress, but no effective vaccine has yet been discovered, although a number of medications have been found to slow the course of the disorder by treating the underlying disease and the opportunistic infections that characterize it.

The former treatments include **AZT** (zidovudine, earlier called azidothymidine) and DDI; the latter group includes aerosolized pentamidine, an inhalant used to prevent symptoms of *Pneumocystis carinii,* several interferons and fluconizole. But with no cure for the disease found and since all treatments discovered to date merely slow its course, the best defense against AIDS has been education into its causes and avoidance of such high-risk behaviors as unprotected intercourse or needle-sharing.

New and deadly, AIDS has strained society's resources in dealing with the pandemic and raised difficult moral and social questions. Many activists advocate early education to help prevent the spread of AIDS, but school programs involving the discussion of sexual behavior and the distribution of condoms to students have generated much controversy. Movements to provide drug addicts with sterile needles have met with a similar disapproval from citizens who feel that such distribution will only condone and encourage drug use. AIDS patients have sometimes been socially stigmatized, denied care and housing and often pauperized by their disease; issues of confidentiality regarding HIV status have become extremely important.

The health care system has also been strained, and new types of treatment, such as increased outpatient care for the sick and hospice care for the dying, have increasingly been implemented. Dissatisfied with the slow pace of public and government reaction to the AIDS crisis, many advocacy and activist groups have been formed to educate the public and lobby for action. Research into the treatment and prevention of AIDS is likely to remain among the greatest medical challenges of the 21st century.

Aiken, Conrad (*1889–1973*) American poet, novelist and critic. Born into a prosperous southern family, Aiken used an independent income to support his writing career. His early work was influenced by his Harvard classmate T.S. ELIOT, by the IMAGISM of John Gould Fletcher and by the French Symbolists (see SYMBOLISM). After graduating, he spent several years in London, where he edited the *Dial* (1916–19). He was also American correspondent of

THE NEW YORKER (1933–36). A prolific writer, he produced over two dozen volumes of poetry and 10 volumes of fiction between 1914 and 1952. His *Selected Poems* won a PULITZER PRIZE in 1929; in 1950–51 he was poetry consultant at the Library of Congress; and in 1953 his *Collected Poems* won the National Book Award. His autobiography, *Ushant,* appeared in 1952.

Ailey, Alvin *(1931–1989)* American dancer, choreographer and ballet director. Born in Texas, Ailey discovered dance as a Los Angeles high school student. While at UCLA, he studied modern dance with Lester Horton, who became his mentor and was a prime influence, along with Katherine DUNHAM and Martha GRAHAM, on his choreographic style. After Horton's death in 1953, Ailey left for New York City to dance in the Broadway musical *House of Flowers* with Carmen de Lavallade. He founded his own company in 1958; its first concert included *Blues Suite,* which, with his company's signature piece *Revelations* (1960) and *Cry* (1971), made his name as a choreographer who eloquently dramatized the black experience. His choreography blended elements of classical ballet, JAZZ, Afro-Caribbean dance and modern dance. In 1971 he established the Alvin Ailey American Dance Center. His company, interracial since 1963, has performed worldwide. Ailey also choreographed for Broadway musicals, opera and other dance companies. In 1988 he received one of the Kennedy Center Honors in recognition for his lifetime of achievement in modern dance. Ailey arguably did more than anyone else to open up opportunities for black dancers.

air-conditioning A technological means of controlling the temperature within a room or building, cooling and dehumidifying the air in order to make it comfortable for human habitation. Air-conditioning is a phenomenon of life in the late 20th century, particularly in the U.S. and in affluent warm-weather countries such as Australia and Saudi Arabia; it is less common in Europe and the developing world. Willis H. Carrier, who presented a paper on the subject to the American Society of Mechanical Engineers in 1911, is commonly considered the inventor of the air conditioner; credit is sometimes given to Stuart W. Cramer, who rigged a primitive air conditioner in 1906. Air-conditioning was introduced in public buildings in the U.S. in the 1920s; by the 1960s, it had become a common feature in American homes. Although most commonly thought of strictly in terms of cooling, air-conditioning is also intended to filter out impurities. However, air-conditioning systems can be breeding grounds for harmful microorganisms, as with Legionnaire's disease, first identified in the 1970s. Some people feel that air-conditioning is one more artificial barrier between human life and nature; the American writer Henry MILLER titled one of his books *The Air-Conditioned Nightmare* (referring to U.S.). Nonetheless, on hot, humid summer days in city offices and apartment buildings, few would scorn this 20th-century invention.

Airflow Chrysler Chrysler and DeSoto 1934 automobile developed by Carl Breer with curving, streamlined forms derived from aerodynamics. Its appearance was so startlingly unlike that of other, more boxlike automotive products that public acceptance was very poor. The Airflow Chrysler has come to be considered a classic case of a consumer design ahead of its time, although later admired for being inventive and advanced.

Airstream Brand name of the travel trailers manufactured by the firm of the same name founded by Wally Byam, an advertising executive and publisher. Byam built a trailer for his own use as a hobby in 1934. He used ALUMINUM for a streamlined unit based on aircraft technology. Its light weight and lowered air resistance were highly functional, but its striking shape and gleaming exterior finish made the Airstream trailer handsome in contrast with most competitors. Over the years since its mid-1930s introduction, various improvements and varied designs have been introduced by Airstream, but all Airstreams retain an elegantly streamlined, functional form and aluminum exterior finish.

Aisne River River that flows northwestward from France's Argonne Forest to join with the Oise River. The Aisne served as a key battlefield line during WORLD WAR I, with major battles along its shores in 1914, 1917 and 1918. In the latter engagement, Germany launched its last major offensive from the Aisne River, only to see it decisively halted at the MARNE River.

Aitken, Sir (John William) Maxwell *(1910–1985)* British newspaper publisher. Born in Canada, Aitken was raised and educated in England. He joined the Royal Air Force just before the outbreak of WORLD WAR II and was a hero of the BATTLE OF BRITAIN. After the war he was a Conservative member of Parliament until 1950. Upon his father's death in 1964, he became chairman of Beaverbrook Newspapers, which included the *Daily Express,* the *Sunday Express* and London's *Evening Standard.* He held that post until 1977, when the group was sold to Trafalgar House. After the sale, Aitken stayed on as life president.

Aitken, Robert Grant *(1864–1951)* American astronomer. Aitken obtained his A.B. in 1887 and his A.M. in 1892 from Williams College, Massachusetts. He began his career at the University of the Pacific, then in San Jose, as professor of mathematics from 1891 until 1895, when he joined the staff of Lick Observatory, Mount Hamilton, California. He remained at Lick for his entire career, serving as its director from 1930 until his retirement in 1935. Aitken did much to advance knowledge of binary stars, pairs of stars orbiting about the same point under their mutual gravitational attraction. He described over 3,000 binary systems and published in 1932 the comprehensive work *New General Catalogue of Double Stars Within 120° of the North Pole.* He also produced the standard work *The Binary Stars* (1918).

Akers, Sir Wallace Allen *(1888–1954)* British industrial chemist. Akers, the son of an accountant, was educated at Oxford University. He first worked for the chemical company Brunner Mond from 1911 to 1924. After four years in Borneo with an oil company, in 1928 he returned to Brunner Mond, which had become part of ICI. From 1931 he was in charge of the Billingham Research Laboratory and from 1944 was the company director responsible for all ICI research. In WORLD WAR II Akers worked under Sir John Anderson, the government minister responsible for work on the atom bomb (see ATOMIC BOMB DEVELOPMENT). He was put in charge of Tube Alloys, the Ministry of Supply's front for secret nuclear work. Akers led the mission of British scientists in 1943 to the U.S. to work out details of collaboration, although he proved unacceptable to the Americans and was replaced by James CHADWICK. Akers returned to head Tube Alloys in the United Kingdom. After the war one of his main tasks was setting up the Central Research Laboratory for ICI at Welwyn near London, later named the Akers Research Laboratory. He was knighted in 1946.

Akhmadulina, Bella *(1937–)* Russian poet. Influenced by the ACMEISTS, and by Anna AKHMATOVA and Marina TSVETAEVA in particular, Akhmadulina's work has been noted for its "surprising imagery" and sense of humor as well as its ability to find significance in the most seemingly trivial things and events. Though published infrequently, she is probably best known for her collections *String* (1962) and *Music Lesson*. Akhmadulina's first marriage was to fellow poet Yevgeny YEVTUSHENKO in 1955.

Akhmatova, Anna *(1889–1966)* Russian poet. Considered Russia's greatest woman poet, Akhmatova belonged to the group of poets called the ACMEISTS before 1918. Her first two collections of poetry, *Evening* (1912) and *Rosary* (1914), established her reputation. She was married to fellow poet Nikolai GUMILEV (1910–18), and his execution in 1921 by the BOLSHEVIKS stigmatized her. From 1923 to 1940 she had practically no publications, suffered from hardships, isolation and official censorship, and supported herself by doing translations. Her great work, *Poem Without a Hero* (1943), exemplifies her characteristic way of merging personal emotions and memories with important events. Other poetry collections include *In 1940* and the famous *Requiem* (1935–40). Her complete poems were issued in 1990 in a definitive bilingual (Russian and English) edition.

Akihito *(1933–)* Emperor of Japan (1989–); eldest son of Emperor HIROHITO and Empress Nagako. Crown Prince Akihito studied marine biology at Jakushuin University. He has traveled widely, knows English and is well versed in Western culture. He assumed imperial duties in September 1988 when his father became ill. On January 7, 1989, upon Hirohito's death, Akihito rose to the Chrysanthemum Throne and became Japan's emperor. He and his wife, Empress Michiko, were married in 1959.

Akins, Zoe *(1886–1958)* American author, poet, dramatist and screenwriter. Akins won a PULITZER PRIZE in 1935 for her play *The Old Maid*. This work, along with several of her nondramatic works, was adapted for audiences. She also wrote a screenplay based on Edna FERBER's *Showboat*. Her major poetic works are *Interpretations* (1911) and *The Hills Grow Smaller* (1937).

Aksyonov, Vassily Pavlovich *(1932–)* Russian author. Aksyonov was born in Kazan, USSR; his parents were political prisoners exiled in Siberia for 18 years. He spent his youth in an orphanage for Children of Enemies of the State, was educated at the first Leningrad Medical Institute and practiced as a physician at Leningrad Hospital from 1956 to 1960. His first novel, *Zvezdnyi Bilit* (1961; translated both as *A Starry Ticket,* 1962, and as *A Ticket to the Stars,* 1963), drew comparisons to the work of J.D. SALINGER because of its exploration of the yearnings of youth, a theme he carried through in successive fiction. In 1980 Aksyonov left the Soviet Union because of increasing government harassment and his frustration at his inability to get his work published there. He went to the U.S., serving as writer-in-residence at the University of Southern California in 1981, George Washington University in 1982, and Goucher College in 1984, and settled in Washington, D.C. Other works include *The Island of Crimea* (1983), *The Burn* (1984) and *Searching for Melancholy Baby* (1987). Aksyonov has also written short stories and a play. He published *The New Sweet Style* in 1999 and currently teaches at George Mason University.

Akutagawa Ryunosuke *(1892–1927)* Japanese short story writer and novelist. Akutagawa was influenced by his teachers Soseki Natsume and Ogai Mori, the two greatest figures of the late-19th-century Meiji period. At Tokyo Imperial University he specialized in English literature and published his first short stories in student magazines. These included "Rashomon," the source for Akira KUROSAWA's 1951 film masterpiece. Akutagawa's stories drew heavily on Chinese and Japanese history and ancient story books. A profound individualist with a precise and elegant style, he has been compared to both Aubrey Beardsley and Jonathan Swift. Sensitive, morose and frail in health, he committed suicide in 1927, leaving a legacy of about 150 short stories, a novel (*Kappa*) and some poems and essays.

Alamein, El Town on the Mediterranean Sea, 62 miles west-southwest of Alexandria, Egypt. During WORLD WAR II it was the most advanced point reached by the Axis forces under General Erwin ROMMEL in their attack against Egypt. The Axis advance stalled there on June 30, 1942. Field Marshal MONTGOMERY's Eighth Army counterattacked on October 23; in a battle that lasted until November 3, the Allies won one of their most decisive victories of the war and went on to a total defeat of Axis forces in Africa.

Alamogordo City in the U.S. state of New Mexico, west of the Sacramento Mountains. The first test detonation of an atomic bomb took place on June 16, 1945, at the nearby White Sands Missile Range. (See ATOMIC BOMB DEVELOPMENT.)

Alaska Highway Highway extending some 1,523 miles, from Dawson Creek in British Columbia, northwest to Fairbanks, Alaska; formerly known as the Alcan Highway. Built by the United States in 1942 during WORLD WAR II, it served as a strategic supply road for American forces stationed in Alaska to defend against Japanese invasion.

Alaska pipeline Pipeline, about 800 miles long, that carries crude oil from Prudhoe Bay on the Arctic north coast of Alaska to the port of Valdez on the state's south coast. Massive petroleum deposits were discovered at Prudhoe Bay in 1968. Because Prudhoe Bay is locked in by ice for much of the year, the oil companies required a pipeline to transport the oil across Alaska to the south coast for shipment to refineries. The pipeline became a major political issue. Environmental groups opposed it, fearing that an accidental leak could contaminate Alaska's pristine environment. However, many state residents felt that the pipeline would bring new jobs and an influx of money. The pipeline was built between 1974 and 1977. (See also *EXXON VALDEZ*.)

Alba Iulia (Alba Julia) Town in Romania's Transylvania; a center of Romanian nationalism in the first two decades of the 20th century, in a region otherwise dominated by Hungarian sympathies. It was the site of the December 1, 1918, proclamation of Transylvanian and Romanian union and of the 1922 coronation of King Ferdinand I and Queen Marie.

Albania (People's Republic of Albania) European nation located in the Balkans and on the east shore of the Adriatic Sea; bordered to its north by Serbia and Montenegro, to its east by Macedonia and to its south by Greece. Scholars trace the ancestry of the Albanian populace to the ancient Illyrian and Thracian peoples. The nation is naturally isolated by mountains, forests and swampland. For centuries a part of the OTTOMAN EMPIRE, Albania asserted its independence during the First BALKAN WAR in 1912. The Serbian invasion of 1913 and the intensive fighting of WORLD WAR I interrupted, and independence was not fully reestablished until the 1920s. The conservative leader Ahmed Zogu became King Zog in 1928. In 1939, at the outset of WORLD WAR II, Italy seized Albania. During the war, partisan forces led by communist leader Enver HOXHA were aided exclusively by Britain and France, leading to the postwar establishment of a European communist state free of Soviet economic or military dependence. Albania broke diplomatic relations with the USSR in 1961 to ally itself with the more doctrinally pure communist Chinese regime. Albania remained isolated and

subject to a repressive regime that frequently employed purges. However, in 1990 the communist regime announced that opposition parties would be allowed. Many Albanians began fleeing to Greece and Yugoslavia, and in early 1991 there were anticommunist demonstrations. Albania experienced a peaceful transfer of power from the Communist Party to the Democratic Party in 1992. In 1999 Albania became the temporary exile of thousands of Kosovars who fled the ethnic cleansing of Serbian leader Slobodan MILOŠEVIĆ in the Serbian province of KOSOVO. Preliminary talks leading to possible future EU admittance were launched in 2003, but mittance were launched in 2003, but

Albania was advised in 2004 that further economic and social reforms were necessary.

Albanian Uprising of 1910 A rebellion of about 8,000 Albanians in the northern part of the country beginning in March 1910. The Albanians had aided the YOUNG TURKS of the OTTOMAN EMPIRE after being promised autonomy and relief from oppressive Turkish taxation. However, once in power the Young Turks reneged and levied new taxes. The uprising spread to southeastern Albania and western Macedonia. Albanian leaders in Montenegro issued a memorandum demanding Albanian self-government.

ALBANIA

1912   Ottoman Empire breaks up; patriots led by Ismail Quemal Bey proclaim independence for Albania.

1915   Secret Treaty of London; Allied powers prepare to divide Albania among Greece, Italy and Serbia.

1920   Partisans drive out Italians and reestablish independence.

1923   Albanian Muslims (69% of its population) declare their autonomy from outside authority.

1924   Ahmet Zogu declares himself president, begins modernization.

1928   Zogu crowns himself Zog I.

1939   Italians annex Albania; Zog flees.

1944   Communist-dominated government takes power following internal struggle.

1946   People's Republic of Albania proclaimed; Enver Hoxha consolidates dictatorial power.

1961   Hoxha breaks relations with USSR, forms alliance with China.

1969   Last Catholic church closes; all organized religious activity ended.

1982   China severs relations; Albania becomes one of the world's most isolated countries.

1985   Hoxha dies; replaced by Ramiz Alia.

1987   Tentative moves to make contact with Greece and other neighbors.

1990   Thousands protesting communist government jam foreign embassies; many are allowed to emigrate.

1991   In the face of a general strike and violent protests, communist regime overthrown.

1992   Presidential election is won by Sali Berisha of the Democratic Party; Alia and other Communist Party officials are charged with corruption and abuse of power; Totalitarian and Communist Parties are banned.

1993   Conflict erupts between Albanians and ethnic Greeks following purge of Greeks from senior positions in civil service and army; Alia is sentenced to eight years' imprisonment.

1995   Alia is released from prison but is banned, along with fellow Communists, from local and national elections until 2002.

1997   Antigovernment riots break out following collapse of bogus investment schemes, southern Albania falls under rebel control; national election is won by former Communist Party; Rexhep Meidani is elected president and Fatos Nano prime minister.

1998   Prime Minister Nano resigns and former student activist Pandeli Majko becomes new prime minister.

1999   NATO conducts air strikes against Yugoslav military targets; hundreds of thousands flee from Kosovo into Albania; Prime Minister Majko resigns after losing a Socialist Party leadership vote; Iler Meta, 30, becomes Europe's youngest prime minister.

2001   Albania and former Yugoslavia reestablish diplomatic ties broken off during the Kosovo crisis in 1999.

2002   Nano becomes prime minister.

2003   Albania and EU begin talks seen as possible first step in future EU membership.

2004   Opposition demands Nano's resignation and protests against government failure to improve the standard of living.

2005   Former president Sali Berisha wins in the July general election.

The Turkish government rejected it, and a large Turkish army crushed the uprising in June 1910.

Albanian Uprisings of 1932, 1935 and 1937 ALBANIA's King Zog I (1895–1961) faced insurrections in 1932, 1935 and 1937 from groups of liberal reformers and Marxist-oriented Muslim radicals. A dictator who ruled autocratically to preserve Albania's feudal society, Zog easily put down these relatively small and poorly planned uprisings. His punishment was lenient: Only a few ringleaders were executed; minor social and administrative reforms were undertaken. Zog's rule ended on April 7, 1939, when ITALY, Albania's sole foreign support, declared Albania a protectorate and invaded, forcing Zog to flee into exile.

Albee, Edward *(1928–)* American playwright. Albee is perhaps the best-known American playwright of his generation, primarily due to the great critical and popular success of *WHO'S AFRAID OF VIRGINIA WOOLF?* (1962). Albee first earned recognition through his one-act play *The Zoo Story* (1959), which explores the illusions people cherish in the face of a harsher reality. Albee won Pulitzer Prizes for two subsequent dramas, *A Delicate Balance* (1966) and *Seascape* (1975). His other plays include *Tiny Alice* (1964), *Counting the Ways* (1976) and *The Man Who Had Three Arms* (1983). In 1981 he adapted the Vladimir NABOKOV novel *Lolita* for the Broadway stage. In 1994 Albee premiered *Three Tall Women,* a play in which three apparently different female characters portrayed in the first act are later revealed to be representations of the same woman at different points in her life. *Three Tall Women* proved to be a critically acclaimed work, and won Albee his third PULITZER PRIZE in 1994.

Albéniz, Isaac *(1860–1909)* Spanish composer and pianist. Born in Camprodon, Catalonia, the piano virtuoso made his debut at the age of four. A young adventurer, he left his home at 13, traveling to Central America, South America and the U.S., supporting himself by playing the piano. Settling in Paris in 1893, he was strongly influenced by DEBUSSY and D'INDY, and his

teacher, Felipe Pedrell, interested Albéniz in the music of his native Spain. The best known of his compositions are those he wrote for the piano, with strong Spanish dance rhythms and pervasive musical references to Spanish folk themes. The most important of these is *Iberia* (1906–09), a group of 12 piano pieces. Albéniz also wrote several operas, such as *Pepita Jiménez* (1896), and a number of other vocal works.

Albers, Anni *(1899–1994)* German designer whose special interests were weaving and textile design, fields in which she was a leader in the development of a modern, fully abstract approach. Born in Berlin, in 1922 Albers became a student at the BAUHAUS, where she met and married Josef ALBERS. She taught with her husband at Black Mountain College in North Carolina until 1949 when she moved to New Haven, Connecticut. Her work as a weaver was widely respected, and she taught and lectured in many universities in the U.S., Europe, and Japan. Her books, *On Designing* (1959) and *On Weaving* (1965), are definitive works in their area.

Albers, Josef *(1888–1976)* German-American painter, printmaker, designer and art theorist. Born in Bottrop, Germany, he studied in Berlin (1913–15), Essen (1916–19), Munich (1919–j20) and finally at the BAUHAUS in Weimar (1920–23), where he became an instructor (in Weimar, Dessau and Berlin) from 1923 to 1930. In this period he began his experiments with optics, color and light. In 1933 he and his wife, the weaver Anni ALBERS, immigrated to the U.S., and he became a citizen in 1939. A popular and influential teacher, he headed the art department at Black Mountain College until 1940 and was director of the Department of Design at Yale University from 1950 to 1958. Albers's many books on color theory include the massive *Interaction of Color* (1963). His best-known works, *Homage to the Square,* are a series of geometrical paintings and graphics begun in 1949 and continued until his death.

Albert I (King of the Belgians) *(1875–1934)* Succeeding his uncle, Leopold II (1835–1909), he reigned

from 1909 to 1934. He was married (1900) to the Bavarian princess Elizabeth. A courageous and popular monarch, he strongly resisted the German invasion of Belgium (1914) during WORLD WAR I. Albert spent the duration of the war commanding the nation's army, and in 1918 he headed the final Allied offensive. After the war he supported economic reconstruction, worked to improve social conditions at home and in the BELGIAN CONGO and promoted currency reform (1926). He was killed in a mountain-climbing accident in 1934 and was succeeded by his son, LEOPOLD III.

Alberti, Rafael *(1902–1999)* Spanish poet and playwright. A member of the GENERATION OF 1927 in Spain, Alberti began his career as a painter but turned to poetry in 1923. His first book, *Marinero en tierra* (1925, Sailor on land), won the Premio Nacional de Literatura. His finest work, *Sobre los ángeles* (1929, About the angels), was abstract and difficult and showed the influence of SURREALISM. After 1931 Alberti professed Marxism. A Loyalist in the SPANISH CIVIL WAR, he went into exile in Argentina after the triumph of FRANCO, only returning to Spain in 1977. His later poetry was lyrical and spiritual. His work shows the influence of Juan Ramón JIMÉNEZ and the classical Spanish poets, especially Góngora. Shortly after his return to Spain, Alberti helped develop the catalog and design the posters for a retrospective exhibit of Pablo PICASSO, marking the first exhibit of Picasso in Spain since the 1920s.

Albery, Sir Donald *(1914–1988)* British theater manager. Albery was the chairman and manager of Wyndham Theatres Ltd. of London and supported playwrights such as Samuel BECKETT, John OSBORNE and Edward ALBEE. Besides now-standard modern works such as *WAITING FOR GODOT, A Taste of Honey, WHO'S AFRAID OF VIRGINIA WOOLF?* and Graham GREENE's *The Living Room,* he staged box office smashes such as *Oliver!* Born into a four-generation theater family, he was the first to recognize the importance of American tourists to the economic health of the West End theater.

Albright, Ivan de Lorraine *(1897–1983)* American painter associated with the 1930s style called MAGIC REALISM. Labeled by critics "the painter of horrors" and "the specialist in the repulsive," he was best known for his painting *The Window* and for the portraits used in a film version of Oscar Wilde's *The Picture of Dorian Gray.*

Albright, Madeleine *(1937–)* U.S. secretary of state (1997–2001). Born in Prague, Albright fled Czechoslovakia with her family in 1939 when Adolf HITLER moved to incorporate the Czech portion of the country into Germany. Eventually settling in the U.S., Madeleine Korbel (her maiden name) attended and graduated from Wellesley College, where she studied Eastern European affairs and political science. The year of her graduation, she married Joseph Albright, with whom she had three daughters; they divorced in 1981. Albright returned to academia in the 1960s, obtaining an M.A. (1968) and a Ph.D. (1976) in international affairs from Columbia University. While at Columbia, she impressed one of her professors, Zbigniew BREZINSKI, who later became President Jimmy CARTER's national security advisor. In 1978 Brezinski asked Albright to serve on the National Security Council as a legislative liaison. Upon leaving the White House in 1981, Albright received a fellowship from the Woodrow Wilson Center for Scholars and for two years worked on a book that analyzed the importance of the indigenous press in producing political change within POLAND.

In 1982 she joined the faculty of Georgetown University, where for seven years she taught courses on international studies, foreign policy and Eastern European politics. By 1989 she had left Georgetown to head the Center for National Policy, an eight-year-old think tank formed by the DEMOCRATIC PARTY. Throughout the 1980s Albright worked repeatedly to advise Democratic presidential candidates, and she became a senior foreign policy adviser to Bill CLINTON during the 1992 presidential campaign. Appointed in 1993 by President Clinton as ambassador to the UN, Albright gained positive national press exposure as a staunch defender of America's international goals while serving as an influential member of Clinton's National Security Council. When Clinton's first secretary of state, Warren CHRISTOPHER, resigned following Clinton's reelection, the president nominated Albright to fill the position, and she was confirmed by a unanimous Senate vote in January 1997.

As secretary of state, Albright helped redefine the U.S.'s international aims in the post–cold war world. She proved instrumental in forcing SERBIA to accept a NATO-led Kosovo peacekeeping force (KFOR) in 1999 and in promoting the expansion of NATO to include eastern European states such as Poland and the Czech Republic. Moreover, she helped develop the early U.S. response to increasing terrorist attacks on U.S. embassies and forces abroad by fundamentalist Islamic groups such as al-QAEDA, which included cruise missile strikes on al-Qaeda training camps in TALIBAN-controlled AFGHANISTAN. In Middle Eastern affairs, Albright participated in the abortive efforts of the Clinton administration to broker a peace settlement between ISRAEL and the PALESTINIAN AUTHORITY and SYRIA over the WEST BANK and the GOLAN HEIGHTS, respectively. Albright repeatedly worked to build an international consensus in support of these and other U.S. policies. After leaving office in 2001 with the end of the Clinton administration, Albright became a strong critic of the administration of George W. BUSH (2001–) for what she perceived as its relative lack of interest in building a strong international coalition to conduct the war on terrorism.

Alcatraz U.S. island in California's San Francisco Bay. From 1859 to 1934 it was the site of an American military prison. Thereafter, it became a maximum security, civilian facility for prisoners deemed to be hard cases. After closing in 1963, the island and its prison became a popular tourist site. Alcatraz was briefly seized by American Indian activists demanding civil rights for their people.

Alcock and Brown British aviator John William Alcock (1892–1919) and his navigator, Arthur Whitten Brown (1886–1948), made the first nonstop flight over the Atlantic Ocean, in a Vickers-Vimy biplane, on June 14, 1919. Flying from St. John's, Newfoundland, to Clifden, Ireland, the men made the historic 1,960-mile trip in 16 hours, 27 minutes. Both were knighted by King George V; one week later, Alcock was killed in an airplane crash in France.

Alcoholics Anonymous (AA) Alcoholics Anonymous is an international, nonprofit self-help organization for alcoholics, dedicated to helping members maintain sobriety. AA was founded in 1935 by Bill Wilson, an alcoholic Wall Street worker, who built on the concepts and techniques of the nondenominational OXFORD GROUP. Wilson's book *Alcoholics Anonymous*

Secretary of State Madeleine Albright addresses the UN. 2000. (PHOTOGRAPHED BY ESKINDER DEBEBE, UN/DPI)

was published in 1939, and in 1946 "the Twelve Traditions" were promulgated to formalize the organization's goals and practices. Today there are estimated to be more than 2 million AA members worldwide.

Aldanov, Mark (Mark Aleksandrovich Landau) *(1886–1957)* Russian writer. Aldanov left Russia for France in 1919 and wrote a series of books on the French revolutionary period. His essay on LENIN (1912) compared the French and RUSSIAN REVOLUTIONS. In *The Fifth Seal* (1939) he depicted the decline in revolutionary idealism that followed the Russian Revolution. Among his later works are *A Night at the Airport* (1949) and *The Escape* (1950). After 1941 he lived in the U.S.

Alden, John G. *(1884–1962)* American designer of yachts and other craft, particularly known for his schooners based on traditional New England fishing boats. Alden was a largely self-taught naval architect, although he worked for eight years for the firm of B.B. Crowninshield, a Boston specialist in Gloucester fishing schooners. After World War I he established himself as a designer of yachts as well as a dealer and marine insurance broker. By the time of his retirement in 1955, Alden had designed some 900 yachts, many of them ocean-racing schooners, ketches or yawls.

Alder, Kurt *(1902–1958)* German organic chemist. Alder studied chemistry in Berlin and Kiel, receiving his doctorate in 1926 under Otto DIELS. In 1928 the two discovered the chemical reaction that bears their names. Alder was professor of chemistry at Kiel (1934), chemist with I.G. Farben at Leverkusen (1936) and director of the Chemical Institute at the University of Cologne (1940). In 1950 Diels and Alder jointly received the NOBEL PRIZE in chemistry for their discovery.

Aldington, Richard *(1892–1962)* British author. Aldington was born in Hampshire and educated at University College in London, though he did not complete a degree there. As a young imagist poet, Aldington became acquainted with Ezra POUND, Ford Maddox FORD and Hilda DOOLITTLE (HD),

whom he married in 1913, while he was assistant editor of *The Egoist*. His first volume of poetry, *Images 1910–1915,* was published in 1915. WORLD WAR I left Aldington psychologically scarred and bitter. His first novel, *Death of a Hero* (1929), depicts a frivolous young civilian, George Winterbourne, his transformation into a soldier and, finally, his death. The book's anger and graphic descriptions of the atrocities of war made an impact unmatched by his following novels, such as *The Colonel's Daughter* (1931) and *All Men are Enemies* (1933). During WORLD WAR II, Aldington moved to the U.S. where he wrote the biographies *Wellington* (1946); *Portrait of a Genius, But . . .* (1950) about D. H. LAWRENCE; and *Lawrence of Arabia: A Biographic Enquiry* (1955), which raised hackles for its negative portrayal of T. E. LAWRENCE. He also wrote an autobiography, *Life for Life's Sake* (1941). (See also IMAGISM.)

Aldiss, Brian *(1925–)* British science fiction writer. Aldiss holds a secure position in the front rank of contemporary science fiction writers by virtue of his prolific output of stories, novels, critical essays and anthologies. Aldiss published his first stories in the mid-1950s; they were distinguished by their literary style and their deemphasis of strict scientific plausibility in favor of imaginative plot development. In 1962 he won a Hugo Award (the highest honor in the genre) for the Hothouse Series of novelettes depicting a future humanity living in the branches of a continent-wide tree. Aldiss has also won a Nebula Award and a British Science Fiction Award. Notable novels by Aldiss include *Greybeard* (1964), *Cryptozoic!* (1967), *The Malacia Tapestry* (1976) and *Helliconia Spring* (1982) and its two sequels. He has also written a compendious history of science fiction, *The Billion-Year Spree* (1973, revised 1989).

Aldrin, Edwin Eugene "Buzz," Jr. *(1930–)* U.S. astronaut. "We both landed at the same time," Aldrin would usually reply when introduced as the "second man to land on the moon." As lunar module pilot of the most famous flight in space history, Aldrin was the second human to set foot on the Moon, following APOLLO 11 commander Neil ARMSTRONG down the ladder of the

lunar lander to the Moon's dusty surface only 15 minutes after Armstrong's famous "small step." "Magnificent desolation" was how Aldrin described the Moon's surface—without the ring of Armstrong's words. Being the second man to walk the surface of the Moon was a hard act to follow, and that historic mission of July 16–24, 1969, was the restless Aldrin's last spaceflight.

Born in Montclair, New Jersey, he was a West Point graduate and served as a combat pilot in the KOREAN WAR, flying over 60 combat missions before returning to the U.S. to become an aide to the dean of faculty at the U.S. Air Force Academy. After three years he moved to Germany and spent the next three years as an F-100 pilot with the 36th Fighter Day Wing at Bitburg. Joining NASA in October 1963, he served as capcom (capsule communicator) for *Gemini 5* and *Gemini 10*, making his first spaceflight on *Gemini 12* (November 11–15, 1966), the last Gemini mission. Spending four days in space, Aldrin put in over five hours of EVA (extravehicular activity) in one of the most successful space walks of the Gemini program.

Gemini 12 and *Apollo 11* were Aldrin's only spaceflights. Resigning from NASA in July 1971, he was appointed commander of the Test Pilot School at Edwards Air Force Base in California. While there he upset some conservative NASA officials by participating in a march after the death of civil rights activist Dr. Martin Luther KING, Jr. His return to the air force was cut short in 1972 when he suffered a nervous breakdown and retired from the service. *The Eagle Has Landed* was the name of a popular NASA motion picture detailing the historic flight of *Apollo 11*. He authored a 1973 autobiography, *Return to Earth,* and a 1989 book about the Apollo program, *Men from Earth.*

Aleichem, Sholom (Sholem Rabinowitz) *(1859–1916)* Yiddish author. Sholom Aleichem (literally, "peace be unto you") was born in the Poltava province of the USSR, where he attended a government school. He worked intermittently at the Kiev bourse (stock exchange) but in 1903 dedicated himself solely to writing. Around this time he also coedited a Russian anthology of Yiddish writing with Maxim GORKY. Aleichem fled the POGROMS of 1905, living in Italy from 1908 to 1914, when the advent of WORLD WAR I drove him to the U.S. He is best known for his humorous, tender short stories depicting Russian Jewish peasants. English-language editions of his works include *The Old Country* (1946), *Some Laughter Some Tears* (1968) and a novel, *The Adventures of Manahem-Mendle* (1969). The short story collection *Tevye's Daughters* (1949) was adapted as the Broadway musical *Fiddler on the Roof* (1964) and a film (1971).

Aleixandre, Vicente *(1898–1984)*

Spanish poet. Aleixandre earned his degrees in law and business management from the University of Madrid but wrote poetry in secret. A member of the GENERATION OF 1927, he published his first book, *Ambito*, in 1928. The influence of Sigmund FREUD is evident in *Espadas como labios* (1932) and *Pasión de la tierra* (1935). His intensely erotic *La destrucción o el amor* won the National Prize for literature in 1934. Because of illness, Aleixandre remained in Spain during the SPANISH CIVIL WAR, but his work was banned. *Sombra del paraíso* (1944) and *Historia del corazón* (1954) concerned man's place in the universe. Later works include *En un vasto dominio* (1962), *Poemas de la consumación* (1968) and *Diálogos del conocimiento* (1974). He was a major influence in Spanish poetry in the 20th century and won the NOBEL PRIZE in literature in 1976.

Alekhine, Alexander Alexandrovich *(1892–1946)*

A Russian who became a French citizen, Alekhine was world chess champion (1927–33) when he defeated Capablanca, and again from 1937 until his death.

Alekseyev, Michael Vasilyevich *(1857–1918)*

Russian general. Alekseyev was commander in chief on the Western Front (1915) and chief of staff to Czar NICHOLAS II (1915–17) during WORLD WAR I. For a brief period after the overthrow of the czar he was chief of staff to KERENSKY. In 1918 he took the initiative to organize the White (anti-BOLSHEVIK) forces in the RUSSIAN CIVIL WAR. He died soon afterward of pneumonia.

Aleutian Islands

Archipelago extending from the Alaska Peninsula of the U.S. to the Kamchatka Peninsula of the USSR. The Bering Sea is to the north of the Aleutians, while the Pacific Ocean is to the south. Certain of the Aleutians—Attu, Agattu, Dutch Harbor (or Unalaska) Island and Kiska—were briefly occupied or attacked by Japanese forces during WORLD WAR II. At present, the U.S. military utilizes the Aleutians for military and radar installations.

Alexander *(1888–1934)*

King of Yugoslavia (1921–34) and son and successor of the Serbian king Peter I (1844–1921), he was a member of the Karadjordjević family. Alexander commanded the Serbian army during World War I and, upon his father's death in 1921, became king of the newly created Kingdom of Serbs, Croats and Slovenes, which he later renamed Yugoslavia to promote unity. Nonetheless, strife among nationalities, notably between Serbs and Croats, caused him to abolish the constitution in 1929 and assume absolute rule. While an end to his dictatorship was announced in 1931, Alexander continued to hold the reins of power, antagonizing separatist minorities. On October 9, 1934, during a state visit to France, Alexander was assassinated by a Croatian terrorist. He was succeeded by his 11-year-old son PETER II, with Prince Paul (1893–1976) acting as chief regent until 1941.

Alexander, Harold Rupert Leofric George (Viscount [1946] and first earl of Tunis [1952]) *(1891–1969)*

British general in WORLD WAR II. Educated at Harrow and Sandhurst, he was commissioned in the Irish Guard and was a decorated batallion commander in France during World War I. Between the wars (1934–38), he served as an officer in India. One of Britain's most celebrated commanders, he led the retreats at Dunkirk (1940) and Burma (1942), going on the offensive as he directed the great Allied advance across North Africa to Tunis and led the invasion of Sicily and Italy (both 1943). In 1944 he was appointed field marshal, acting as supreme Allied commander in the Mediterranean from 1944 to 1945. Alexander served as governor-general of Canada (1946–52) and as minister of defense (1952–54) in the cabinet of Sir Winston CHURCHILL.

Alexander, Samuel *(1859–1938)*

British philosopher and essayist. Alexander was one of the few British philosophers of the 20th century to devote his primary efforts to metaphysical questions. Alexander's magnum opus, *Space, Time and Deity* (1920), remains a basic text for philosophers interested in explaining the human perception of a space-time continuum within reality. In that work, Alexander argued that metaphysical questions—such as the existence of God or the nature of time—were nonempirical in that they were not subject to direct verification by experiment. But Alexander also insisted that the observation of human metaphysical beliefs was an empirical activity that could be aided by the experimental findings of physiological psychology, a newly emerging field that Alexander championed in British academic circles. Alexander, who was educated at Oxford and was the first Jew to win a fellowship there, taught for most of his academic career at the University of Manchester.

Alexanderson, Ernst *(1878–1975)*

Swedish-born engineer. Alexanderson is credited as the inventor of the first home television (1927). A pioneer in the development of radio broadcasting, he was responsible for the device that first made voice communication possible (1906). Altogether he held 322 patents.

Alexandra, queen of England *(1844–1925)*

Queen of EDWARD VII of England. A princess of Denmark, Alexandra married Edward in 1863, when he was still Prince of Wales. On Victoria's death in 1901, Edward ascended to the throne, and Alexandra became queen. A popular figure, she was known for her charitable work, and she helped to establish a military nursing service. Tolerant of her husband's many marital infidelities, Alexandra outlived the king by 13 years and was buried beside him at Windsor.

Alexandra Fedorovna *(1872–1918)*

Empress of All the Russians. Born a princess of Hesse-Darmstadt and a granddaughter of Queen Victoria, she married (1894) NICHOLAS II of Russia. Her belief in the powers of the monk RASPUTIN to cure the young czarevich of HEMOPHILIA brought her under Rasputin's disastrous domination and encouraged her to exert an unfortunate political influence, much resented by the czar's ministers and the population at large. After the 1917 RUSSIAN REVOLUTION she was murdered along with her husband and children.

Alexandretta City and province on the Mediterranean Sea's Gulf of Iskenderun. Due to its strategic location, Alexandretta was the source of international controversy in the decades between the two world wars. The French ceded it to Syria under the Treaty of Sevres in 1920. It briefly became the independent Republic of Hatay in 1938 before being reconsolidated into TURKEY in 1939.

Alexandria Quartet, The Four related novels by Lawrence DURRELL—*Justine* (1957), *Balthazar* (1958), *Mountolive* (1950) and *Clea* (1960)—set in Alexandria, Egypt, just before World War II. The first three books describe the same events and time period; only in *Clea* is there a regular chronological narrative. The main characters are Darley, a novelist and narrator of the first two books; Melissa, his mistress; Justine and her husband Nessim; Mountolive, the British ambassador; Pursewarden, a British intelligence agent; and Clea, an artist. All are involved with one another, often sexually. Durrell examines the shifting nature of truth by presenting the same events through different character's eyes, always with a strong dose of ambiguity. The writing is sensual and explores a common theme in Durrell's writing: the nature of love and sexuality. Alexandria is presented as decadent and corrupt, a cauldron of urbanity, ancient tradition and exotic ethnicity. The Alexandria Quartet shows Durrell's departure from realism and the influence of James JOYCE and Henry MILLER. While critics have argued about the work's significance, The Alexandria Quartet has achieved cult status among readers.

Alexis (Sergei Vladimirovich Simanskyl) (*1873–1970*) Patriarch of Moscow and All Russia (1945–70). He was

ordained bishop in 1913 and was archbishop (1929), metropolitan of Novgorod (1932) and metropolitan of Leningrad (1933). From about 1925 he cooperated with the Soviet authorities and secured considerable expansion of church activity as a result.

Alfonsín, Raúl (*1927– *) President of Argentina. After earning a law degree in 1950, Alfonsín joined the Radical Civic Union political party. Over the next two decades he held seats in provincial and national legislatures, but his failed attempt to assume party control from Ricardo Balbín in 1972 appeared to put his political career at an end. In 1983, however, when the military stepped down from power, after Argentina's defeat in the FALKLAND ISLANDS WAR, Alfonsín won his party's nomination and was elected president of the country. Despite assassination attempts and threatened coups, he brought many members of the preceding military governments, including three former presidents, to trial for human rights violations. In the middle to late 1980s, Alfonsín imposed economic austerity measures in an attempt to reduce Argentina's crushing foreign debt. He resigned the presidency in 1989, five months before the end of his six-year term, citing the nation's loss of confidence in his ability to lead the country out of its worst economic crisis. Succeeded in the presidency by Carlos Saúl MENEM, Alfonsín remained leader of the RCU. Although Alfonsín did not seek other political offices upon his departure from the presidency, he remained involved in Argentinian affairs. In December 1997 he openly criticized two former U.S. ambassadors for their efforts as paid lobbyists for groups seeking to purchase recently privatized Argentinian companies.

Alfonso XIII (*1886–1941*) King of Spain (1902–31), the posthumous son and successor of Alfonso XII; his mother, Queen Maria Christina of Hapsburg (1858–1929), was regent during his minority. In 1906 he married Princess Victoria Eugenia of Battenberg (1887–1969), a granddaughter of Britain's Queen Victoria. His early reign was beset by problems: political instability and corruption, labor disputes, Catalan separatism and the rise of socialism and ANARCHISM. Alfonso

kept Spain neutral in World War I but suffered the decline of his prestige in the 1920s, largely due to the 1922 defeat of the Spanish army in Morocco by ABD EL-KRIM. The king supported the 1923 coup d'état of General Miguel PRIMO DE RIVERA and the military dictatorship that ensued. After Primo de Rivera was deposed in 1930 and Republicans won landslides in municipal elections, Alfonso was almost completely discredited. He left Spain in 1931, going into self-imposed exile in Italy, where he died 10 years later. There was no reigning king in Spain until the accession of Alfonso's grandson, JUAN CARLOS, in 1975.

Alfvén, Hannes Olof Gösta (*1908–1995*) Swedish physicist. Alfvén was educated at the University of Uppsala, where he received his Ph.D. in 1934. He served as professor of electronics at the Royal Institute of Technology, Stockholm, from 1945 until 1963 when a special chair of plasma physics was created for him. He became a professor at the University of California at San Diego in 1967. Alfvén is noted for his pioneering theoretical research in the field of magnetohydrodynamics—the study of conducting fluids and their interaction with magnetic fields. This work, for which he shared the 1970 NOBEL PRIZE in physics with Louis Neel, is mainly concerned with plasmas—ionized gases containing positive and negative particles. He investigated the interactions of electrical and magnetic fields and showed theoretically that the magnetic field, under certain circumstances, can move with the plasma. In 1942 he postulated the existence of waves in plasmas; these **Alfven waves** were later observed in both liquid metals and ionized plasmas. Alfvén applied his theories to the motion of particles in the Earth's magnetic field and to the properties of plasmas in stars. In 1942 and later in the 1950s he developed a theory of the origin of the solar system. This he assumed to have formed from a magnetic plasma, which condensed into small particles that clustered together into larger bodies. His work is also applicable to the properties of plasmas in experimental nuclear fusion reactors.

Algeciras Port city in the region of Andalusia. It is Spain's southernmost Mediterranean port and was the site in

1906 of the **Algeciras Conference** that established a privileged hegemony for France and Spain in Morocco.

Algeria (Democratic and Popular Republic of Algeria) Country in North Africa bound on the north by the Mediterranean Sea, on the east by Tunisia and Libya, on the south by Mali and Niger and on the west by Mauritania and Morocco. A French colony at the start of the century, Algeria was ruled by a French governor-general. Prior to WORLD WAR II, over 1 million French settlers had colonized Algeria, but after the war an anticolonial Arab nationalist movement gained strength and ultimately started a violent civil war (see ALGERIAN WAR OF 1954–1962). Estimates as of 1960 placed the number of dead at 10,000 each for the French and Arab sides. The EVIAN Accords of 1962 established an independent Algeria. The government was led initially by the moderate Ben Khedda; he was soon replaced by the nationalist leader Ahmed BEN BELLA. In the following year, most of the French residents of Algeria returned to their native land (a "native land" that many of them had never seen), thereby severely disrupting the Algerian economy. In 1965 Ben Bella was deposed by his defense minister, Houari BOUMEDIENNE. Income from Algerian oil fields in the Sahara helped stabilize the country; the fields were nationalized in 1971. In 1976 a new national charter (approved by 99% of the voters) declared Algeria a socialist and Islamic state; one-party rule was also ratified. Economic problems led to riots in the late 1980s. Political parties were legalized in 1989. One of the newly legalized parties was the Islamic Salvation Front (FIS), a political-religious organization espousing a form of Islamism for Algeria, which desired the application of sharia, or Islamic law, throughout the country. In local elections held in 1990 the FIS won 55% of the popular vote. The following year the Algerian government announced it would organize free multiparty national elections for June 1991. However, these elections were postponed until December on account of FIS protests over government regulations prohibiting campaigning in mosques. When the December elections occurred, the FIS emerged as the dominant party and ap-

peared to be on the verge of obtaining an absolute parliamentary majority. In an effort to avert the creation of an Algerian theocracy, the military leadership deposed the government on January 4, 1992, and declared the elections void. In response, street riots erupted between FIS supporters and government forces, beginning a seven-year guerrilla war pitting the FIS's Islamic Salvation Army and the Armed Islamic Group against the government. In 1999 Algerian president Liamine Zeroual announced that he had secretly negotiated a truce with the FIS and released several imprisoned members of the Islamic Salvation Army. However, extremist Islamist activists continue to stage terrorist attacks on government buildings, which along with the violent clashes between government police forces and Berbers has served to destabilize the nation regularly. By 2000, violence had claimed the lives of more than 100,000 Algerians. Former prime minister Aldelaziz Bouteflika, elected in 1999, agreed in 2001 to some demands of the Berbers,

including official recognition of their language. Bouteflika was reelected in April 2004, promising to devote himself to national reconciliation.

Algerian-Moroccan War of 1963–1964 In October 1963 Algerian and Moroccan forces began a border war after ALGERIA separated from FRANCE (see ALGERIAN WAR OF 1954–1962). The French had established the shared boundary between Algeria and MOROCCO (to which France had relinquished its rights in 1956) without consulting either former possession. Demands for adjustment by Algerian president BEN BELLA were ignored. Many lives were lost before the ORGANIZATION OF AFRICAN UNITY (OAU), led by Ethiopian emperor HAILE SELASSIE and Mali's president Modibo Keita, intervened and arranged a cease-fire (February 20, 1964). Relations between Algeria and Morocco remained strained and border clashes resumed in 1967. In 1976 when the Spanish Sahara (renamed Western Sahara) became independent, Algeria and Morocco began a

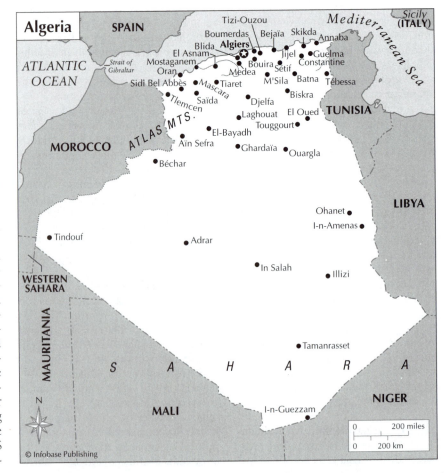

ALGERIA

1900	Algeria gains autonomy from France.
1942	Becomes North African base for Allied armies.
1945	Nationalists kill 88 Europeans; French kill several thousand Muslims in reprisal, dampening hopes for independence.
1955	Front de Liberation National massacres dozens of settler families.
1959	After fierce fighting between French and Muslims, de Gaulle concedes that Algerian self-rule should be put to a vote.
1961–62	OAS opposes Algerian independence, launches unsuccessful coup to overthrow de Gaulle.
1962	France recognizes new state of Algeria.
1965	Coup led by defense minister Houari Boumedienne deposes President Ben Bella.
1971	French oil and gas companies nationalized, become mainstay of economy.
1985	Referendum providing for some private enterprise approved.
1989	Referendum legalizes multiple political parties.
1990	Led by four recently formed opposition parties, tens of thousands of Algerians march through capital to support democracy and oppose Islamic fundamentalism.
1992	Military deposes government and declares elections of 1991, which were won by Islamic Salvation Front (FIS), null and void.
1999	President Liamine Zeroual negotiates truce with FIS; former foreign minister Abdelaziz Bouteflika is elected president; opposition candidates had withdrawn from the race, fearing reprisals. Voters approve civil accord pardoning FIS and other armed groups.
2000	Violence is estimated to have claimed the lives of more than 100,000 Algerians since 1992, despite truce.
2001	The mainly Berber Rally for Culture and Democracy party withdraws from the government in protest against the authorities' handling of Berber militants; government agrees to grant Berber language official status, as part of a series of concessions.
2002	Prime Minister Ali Benflis's National Liberation Front (FLN) wins general elections amid violence and a low turnout.
2003	An earthquake kills more than 2,000 people and injures thousands.
2004	President Bouteflika is reelected to a second term in a landslide victory.
2005	Voters approve government plans to offer amnesty to those involved in post-1992 killings; opposition parties retain their majority in local elections.

low-key military dispute over ownership of that region.

Algerian National Movement See BEN BELLA, MOHAMMED AHMED.

Algerian War of 1954–1962 Algerian Muslims of the Front de Liberation National (FLN, or National Liberation Front) began open warfare against French rule in 1954. They raided French army installations and European holdings. In 1957 the French government refused to grant Algeria independence, and thousands of French troops were sent to crush the Algerian rebels. After taking office as president of France (1958), Charles DE GAULLE offered a plan of self-determination for Algeria and later sought a cease-fire with Algerian rebel leaders in 1960. Raoul SALAN, a French general opposed to the plan, led an unsuccessful insurrection in Algiers in April 1961, trying to thwart Algerian independence from France. French and Algerian rebel leaders signed a cease-fire in March 1962, but Salan led the illegal Algerian Secret Army Organization (OAS) in revolt against it. Loyal French forces seized Salan, but the French-OAS war continued. On July 1, 1962, Algerians, voting in a national referendum, approved independence, and two days later France recognized Algeria's sovereignty.

Algiers Port city and capital of Algeria, located on the Bay of Algiers; the city was conquered by the French in 1830. During WORLD WAR II, Algiers became the provisional capital in exile of the FREE FRENCH forces led by Charles DE GAULLE. After the war, it became a center of anticolonial resistance to French rule and was the site of the unsuccessful, procolonial putsch of General SALAN in 1958, which helped to overturn the French Fourth Republic and return de Gaulle to power, who would eventually grant independence to the Arabs). (See also ALGERIAN WAR OF 1954–1962.)

Algren, Nelson (*1909–1981*) American novelist. Born in Detroit, Michigan, Algren was raised in Chicago and educated at the University of Illinois School of Journalism. During the GREAT DEPRESSION he worked as a salesman, migrant laborer and writer on the WPA Writers Project and for the Chicago Board of Health in venereal disease control. He sought out the underclass of depression-era Chicago, and his realistic writing depicts the desolation and brutality of that life. His first novel was *Somebody in Boots* (1935). He is best known for the ground-breaking *Man with the Golden Arm* (1949; filmed 1955), a novel about drug addiction that won the NATIONAL BOOK AWARD in 1950. Other work includes *Chicago: City on the Make* (1951), a prose poem; *Walk on the Wild Side* (1956; filmed 1962); and *The Last Carousel* (1973), a collection of short stories. Following WORLD WAR II, Algren traveled occasionally with Simone de BEAUVOIR and became acquainted with Jean-Paul SARTRE. His work was much admired by Ernest HEMINGWAY.

Ali, Muhammad (**Cassius Clay**) (*1942–*) U.S. boxer; burst on the boxing world in 1960, winning the amateur light heavyweight championship, the Golden Gloves heavyweight title and an Olympic gold medal. He then turned professional, taking the national heavyweight championship from Sonny Liston in 1964; he defeated Liston in a rematch the following year.

A handsome and glib man, given to reciting his own poetry, he brought a sense of style to boxing. In 1967 Clay converted to the Muslim religion and took the name Muhammad Ali. Later that year, when he refused to enter U.S. military service, he was stripped of his title. He began a comeback in 1970, which led to a series of historic fights throughout the 1970s against such opponents as Joe FRAZIER and George FOREMAN, winning, losing and regaining his championship title. Ali retained the heavyweight title until he lost it to Leon Spinks in February 1978, only to regain it seven months later in a rematch. In June 1979 Ali announced his first retirement from professional boxing. A year later he returned to the ring to challenge heavyweight champion Larry Holmes. The fight was disastrous for Ali, when Holmes knocked him out in the 11th round. In December 1981 Ali retired permanently.

Despite exhibiting increasingly visible symptoms of Parkinson's disease since the late 1980s, Ali has remained involved in a variety of activities. In November 1990 he made a personal visit to Iraqi dictator Saddam HUSSEIN in an effort to arrange a peaceful settlement to the standoff between Iraq and the U.S. over the Iraqi invasion of Kuwait. Six years later Ali carried the Olympic torch into the main stadium in Atlanta, Georgia, and lit the Olympic flame for the 1996 games. Not long after his Olympic appearance Ali volunteered his time to help the refugee camps that had sprung up in East Africa to cope with the displacement of millions of Hutus and Tutsis (see TUTSI AND HUTU MASSACRES).

Aliger, Margarita Iosifovna (*1915–1979*) Soviet poet who was first published in 1933 but who gained fame during World War II with her patriotic poems, including "Zoya" (1942). Her poem "The Most Important Thing" (1948) caused her to be criticized by the authorities.

Allegret, Yves (*1907–1987*) French film director. He was a leading light of post–World War II French cinema. He made a series of starkly realistic dramas of social criticism, some of which starred Simone SIGNORET, to whom Allegret was married from 1944 to 1949. Perhaps his most notable film was *Les orgueilleux* (*The Proud and the Beautiful,* 1953).

Allen, Edgar (*1892–1943*) American endocrinologist. Allen, the son of

Muhammad Ali, 1965 (LIBRARY OF CONGRESS, PRINTS AND PHOTOGRAPHS DIVISION)

a physician, was educated at Brown University. After war service he worked at Washington University before being appointed (1923) to the chair of anatomy at the University of Missouri. In 1933 he moved to a similar post at Yale and remained there until his death.

In 1923 Allen, working with Edward Doisy, began the modern study of the sex hormones. It was widely thought that the female reproductive cycle was under the control of some substance found in the corpus luteum, the body formed in the ovary after ovulation. But Allen thought that the active ingredient was probably in the follicles surrounding the ovum. To test this he made an extract of the follicular fluid. On injection, he found it induced the physiological changes normally found only in the estrous cycle. Allen had in fact discovered estrogen, although it was only identified some six years later by Adolf BUTENANDT.

Allen, Fred (John Florence Sullivan) (1894–1956) American humorist.

Allen began performing in vaudeville as "Freddy James, the World's Worst Juggler." Moving to Broadway in the early 1920s, he appeared in revues such as *The Passing Show of 1922* and *Greenwich Follies of 1924*. But it was in the 1930s on radio that Allen developed his famous laid-back, detached comic style. His show featured a hilarious segment known as "Allen's Alley," in which he played straight man to the fictional Mrs. Nussbaum, Ajax Cassidy, Senator Claghorn and Titus Moody. In the 1950s Allen was fortunate enough to capitalize on the nationwide craze for game shows and appeared regularly on the quiz program *What's My Line.* The stress of the live weekly show eventually caused heart problems, and Allen collapsed on St. Patrick's Day.

Allen, Steve (1921–2000) American television personality, composer, pianist, comedian and social satirist,

arguably the most versatile showman in the history of radio and television. Allen is best known for the creation in 1954 of the original TONIGHT SHOW, the model for various broadcast incarnations ever since. He was born in New York City to vaudeville parents, and his early years were spent mostly on the road, in and out of 18 schools. He

began his broadcasting career in 1942 in Phoenix, Arizona, and continued in Los Angeles after 1945 on several network radio programs. *Smile Time* and *The Steve Allen Show* helped him to develop and refine the "ad lib" comedy that is his trademark. These verbal pyrotechnics, facility at the piano and utter fearlessness in front of an audience won him a national following on the NBC television airwaves. He hosted or appeared in 20 network and/or syndicated shows, including the Peabody Award–winning *Meeting of the Minds* (1977–81). He also recorded music albums, authored books of poetry, fiction and social commentary, wrote Broadway shows (*Sophie*) and appeared in movies (*The Benny Goodman Story,* 1956). On October 30, 2000, Allen died of heart failure.

Allen, Woody (Allen Stewart Konigsberg) (1935–   ) American film director,

actor, screenplay writer and comedian; the most critically acclaimed American film director of his generation. Born in Brooklyn, New York, Allen briefly attended New York University but flunked out. He quickly moved on to comedy writing for Sid Caesar's 1950s television program *Your Show of Shows.* In the early 1960s Allen became a highly popular stand-up comedian with his persona of neurotic but articulate everyman. Turning his attention to films, Allen wrote, directed and starred in two highly successful comedies—*Take the Money and Run* (1969) and *Bananas* (1971)—that earned him financial and creative freedom. His numerous films since then have ranged from farces to intense dramas, but the best of them have successfully blended comedy and drama. These include *Annie Hall* (1977), which won that year's ACADEMY AWARD for best picture (as well as best director and best screenplay Oscars for Allen), *Manhattan* (1979), *Zelig* (1983), *The Purple Rose of Cairo* (1985), *Hannah and Her Sisters* (1986), *Crimes and Misdemeanors* (1989) and *Alice* (1990). Like the Swedish director Ingmar BERGMAN, whose films have influenced him, Allen draws upon a core group of actors who work with him from one film to the next. His collaborations (both as actor and director) with Diane Keaton and Mia Farrow have been particularly noteworthy. Allen continued producing a variety of offbeat movies throughout the

Woody Allen. in a poster for his film Annie Hall. *1977* (LIBRARY OF CONGRESS. PRINTS AND PHOTOGRAPHS DIVISION)

1990s and into the 2000s, such as *Shadows and Fog* (1992), *Husbands and Wives* (1992), *Bullets Over Broadway* (1994), *Mighty Aphrodite* (1995), *Deconstructing Harry* (1997), *Celebrity* (1998), *Sweet and Lowdown* (1999), *Small Time Crooks* (2000), and *Melinda and Melinda* (2005), as well as the musical *Everybody Says I Love You* (1997).

In 1992 Allen began a romantic relationship with one of the children adopted by Farrow, Soon Yi Previn, who at the time was 21. The love affair between Allen and Previn led to the abrupt end of Allen and Farrow's 12-year relationship and resulted in a civil trial for the custody of Farrow's then seven-year-old daughter, Dylan, in which it was alleged that Allen molested her. No charges were ever filed.

Allenby, Edmund Henry Hynman (first viscount Allenby) (1861–1936)

British general. Educated at Sandhurst, he was a cavalry officer in South Africa (1899–1902). After the outbreak of WORLD WAR I, he was stationed in France with the British Expeditionary Force (BEF), first commanding a cavalry division. As general of the Third Army (1915–17), he commanded British forces at the battle of ARRAS (1917). Posted to EGYPT in 1917, he conducted a successful cavalry campaign against the Turks, invading PALESTINE and capturing JERUSALEM in

December of that year. A skilled tactician, he was victorious at the **battle of Megiddo** (September 18–21, 1918), pushing the Turks back through Syria. Allenby served as high commissioner for Egypt from 1919 to 1925.

Allende Gossens, Salvador *(1908–1973)* President of Chile (1970–73). A Marxist democrat who served as a Chilean Socialist Party deputy from 1937 to 1945 and senator from 1945 to 1970, after three unsuccessful attempts he won the 1970 presidential election. His efforts to bring social reform by democratic means encountered increasing opposition and unrest, supported in part by the CIA. In 1973 he was overthrown in a military coup led by General PINOCHET and died during fighting at the presidential palace. His niece **Isabel Allende** is a noted novelist.

Alliance Political party in NORTHERN IRELAND, founded in 1970 by Oliver John Napier (1935–). Its members are moderate, mostly middle-class people—both Protestants and Catholics—opposed to sectarian violence in the region. The party enjoyed some initial success; members were elected to provincial and local offices but never to the British Parliament. Alliance hoped to play a conciliatory role and provide an alternative to the more established and extremist Northern Irish parties. However, by 1985 it seemed destined to remain a minority party. In 1994, following establishment of a cease-fire by the IRISH REPUBLICAN ARMY (IRA), Alliance leader Lord Alderdice helped persuade the political wing of the IRA, SINN FÉIN, to enter into negotiations with the British. In 1998 the Alliance Party lent its support to the Good Friday Agreement, which established a government for Northern Ireland in which power was shared by Protestant and Catholic political leaders like David TRIMBLE and John HUME. Alliance announced its hopes that the accord would lead to a high degree of autonomy for Northern Ireland on the same model as the Scottish Parliament proposed by British prime minister Tony BLAIR.

Alliance for Progress Program to promote the economic and social development of Latin America; proposed by President John F. KENNEDY and established at a conference at Punta del Este, Uruguay, in August 1961. Embodied in a treaty signed by the U.S. and the 19 nations of Latin America (excluding Cuba), the alliance pledged members to coordinate their economies, to institute tax and land reform and to resist communist expansion within their borders. The initial aim of the alliance was a 2.5% annual increase in per capita income in Latin American countries, a goal that was never reached. In all, the U.S. government spent about $100 billion on Alliance for Progress programs, which included health and education programs, housing projects and general economic development. Faced by mounting criticism during the Johnson and Nixon administrations, the alliance ceased operation in 1974 when U.S. financial support was withdrawn.

Alliluyeva, Svetlana Iosifovna *(1927–)* The daughter of Josef STALIN by his second wife, Nadezhda Alliluyeva, Svetlana Alliluyeva defected to the U.S. in March 1967, at the U.S. embassy in New Delhi, India. She arrived in New York in April, saying she had come to "seek the self-expression that has been denied me for so long in Russia." Stalin's only daughter and last surviving child, she was stripped of her Soviet citizenship in December 1969. In 1973 Alliluyeva divorced her American husband, William Peters, and in November 1984, after living in Great Britain for two years, she returned, with her daughter, Olga Peters, to the Soviet Union, where she attacked Western "pseudodemocracy." Her Soviet citizenship was restored, but in April 1986 she fled to the U.S. again, returning her daughter to boarding school in Great Britain. In the early 1990s Alliluyeva again departed the U.S., this time settling in Britain.

All in the Family Long-running comedy series that changed the course of American television entertainment. From the first telecast on CBS (January 12, 1971) to the last (September 21, 1983) the address of the Archie Bunker residence in New York's Queens—704 Houser Street—was the place to be each week for millions of viewers. Producers Norman LEAR and Bud Yorkin and cast members Jean Stapleton (Edith), Carroll O'Connor (Archie), Sally Struthers (Gloria) and Rob Reiner (the "Meathead," Mike) took an obscure British TV series called *Till Death Us Do Part* and transplanted its Cockney sensibilities to Queens. The program challenged conventional values, using comedy to skewer the hypocrisies of racism and sexism as well as air out issues like abortion and homosexuality. There were two spinoffs: *Maude,* based on a relative of Edith's played by Beatrice Arthur, debuted in 1972; *The Jeffersons,* based on characters who lived next door, debuted three years later. In 1979, after Stapleton, Struthers and Reiner had left the program, Archie bought Kelsey's Bar, and the series continued under the title, *Archie Bunker's Place.* In the words of the *All in the Family* theme song, "Those were the days." *Archie Bunker's Place* remained on the air until April 1983, when CBS announced it was canceling the show.

Allison, Fran *(?–1989)* U.S. singer and entertainer. She was best known as the human star of the children's television program *Kukla, Fran, and Ollie* in the late 1940s and 1950s. The pioneering show, which was created by puppeteer Burr TILLSTROM in 1947, soon became one of the most popular television programs in the U.S. Allison, a former teacher, played the warm-hearted human companion to two eccentric puppets—Kukla, an earnest clown, and Ollie, a roguish dragon. The show ended in 1957 but was revived briefly on public television (1969–71) and in syndication (1975–76).

Allon, Yigal *(1918–1980)* Israeli military and political leader, a hero of the Jewish struggle for independence in PALESTINE. Allon held a series of cabinet posts, including deputy prime minister and foreign minister in the Labor government of Golda MEIR. He was known for his controversial peace plan put forward after the SIX-DAY WAR (1967). He proposed returning most of the WEST BANK territory to JORDAN in exchange for a narrow security strip along the Jordan River. The plan was not carried out.

All Quiet on the Western Front Novel by German author Erich Maria

REMARQUE, filmed in 1930. First serialized in a German magazine in 1928, it tells the story of a young German soldier in WORLD WAR I who enlists in a burst of patriotic fervor but who soon awakens to the horrors of trench warfare. The book was later banned by the NAZIS because of its pacifism and was also forbidden in MUSSOLINI's Italy and in the USSR for several years following WORLD WAR II. The intensely moving novel is considered a classic of war fiction and is studied in schools and universities. A sequel, *The Road Back,* was published in 1931.

All-Russian Directory A Russian counterrevolutionary organization consisting of five members. It was established in Omsk in September 1918. (See also RUSSIAN REVOLUTION.)

All the King's Men Novel by Robert Penn WARREN, published in 1946. Awarded the PULITZER PRIZE in 1947, the novel portrays Willie Stark, a profligate, influence-wielding southern governor who is loosely based on former Louisiana governor Huey LONG. The story is told from the perspective of Jack Burden, an aide to Stark, and his discovery of the identity of his father, a seemingly incorruptible judge known to him since childhood, is an important subplot. The writing vacillates between a gripping realism and poetic intensity. The film made from the book won the ACADEMY AWARD for best picture in 1949.

Alonso, Alicia (Alicia Martínez) (1921–) Cuban ballerina and ballet director. Educated in Havana and at the School of American Ballet in New York City, she was first married to fellow dancer Fernando Alonso; now she is married to Pedro Simón. She earned an international reputation in ballet after beginning as a dancer in musical theater. Alonso joined Lincoln KIRSTEIN's touring company, Ballet Caravan, in 1939, then performed regularly with AMERICAN BALLET THEATRE (1941–60) and the Ballet Russes de Monte Carlo (1955–57), as well as in concert with Andre Eglevsky, Royes Fernández and Igor Youskevitch with whom she formed a legendary partnership. Among the roles created for her were those of the ballerina in *Theme and Variations* (1947) by George BALANCHINE and the Accused in *Fall River Legend* (1948) by Agnes DE MILLE. She was also considered one of the outstanding "Giselles" of her generation. In 1947 Alonso received Cuba's Decoration of Carlos Manuel de Cespedes, and in 1959 a Dance Magazine Award. In 1948 she established her own dance company in Cuba; with the rise of Fidel CASTRO it became known as the National Ballet of Cuba. She has also choreographed several ballets and staged ballets for other companies. In 1999 Alonso was awarded the Pablo Picasso Medal by the UNITED NATIONS EDUCATIONAL, SCIENTIFIC AND CULTURAL ORGANIZATION (UNESCO) in recognition of her contribution to ballet and dance.

Alonso, Dámaso (1898–1990) Spanish poet, literary critic and scholar. Alonso was a member of the so-called GENERATION OF 1927, a literary group that also included Federico GARCÍA LORCA and Rafael ALBERTI. Alonso's best-known work appeared in the books *Pure Poems, Poems of the City* (1921), *The Sons of Anger* (1944) and *Man and God* (1955). He was also a director of the Royal Academy of the Spanish Language. In 1978 he was awarded Spain's Miguel de Cervantes Prize, considered the highest literary prize for Spanish writers.

Alpher, Ralph Asher (1921–) American physicist. Alpher studied at George Washington University, Washington, D.C., where he obtained his B.S. in 1943 and his Ph.D. in 1948. He spent the war as a physicist with the U.S. Navy's Naval Ordnance Laboratory in Washington, followed by a period (1944–55) with the applied physics laboratory of Johns Hopkins University, Baltimore. In 1955 Alpher joined the staff of the General Electric Research and Development Center, in Schenectady, New York.

At George Washington, Alpher came under the influence of the physicist George GAMOW with whom he collaborated on a number of papers. With Hans BETHE they produced a major paper on the origin of the chemical elements, sometimes called the Alpher-Bethe-Gamow theory, which was incorporated into Gamow's modern form of the BIG-BANG THEORY of the origin of the universe, published in 1948. In the same year Alpher and Herman published a remarkable paper in which they predicted that the big bang should have produced intense radiation that gradually lost energy as the universe expanded and by now would be characteristic of a temperature of about minus 268°C. Unlike its later independent formulation by Robert Dicke in 1964, the 1948 paper had surprisingly little impact. Alpher did approach a number of radar experts but was informed that it was then impossible to detect such radiation. When this radiation was discovered by Arno Penzias and Robert Wilson in 1964–65, a major revolution in cosmology and astrophysics began. Alpher repeatedly protested the fact that the credit for the detection of the radiation was given to Penzias and Wilson and intensified his efforts to receive his due honors when both men won the 1978 NOBEL PRIZE in physics. Alpher later ceased his protestations shortly after recovering from a heart attack.

Alsace-Lorraine Ancient region of eastern France bordering on Germany, Luxembourg and Switzerland. Created as a territory in 1871, it was carved from French lands by a victorious Germany in the Treaty of Frankfurt, to recognize German victories in the Franco-Prussian War. After WORLD WAR I control of the region returned to France, but it was seized again by the Germans during WORLD WAR II. Since 1945 it has remained under French control, its area distributed among several modern French departments.

Althusser, Louis (1918–1990) French Marxist philosopher. A longtime member of the French Communist Party, he became an outspoken critic of Soviet and French communism in the 1970s. He taught at the École Normale Superieure in Paris for more than three decades. A victim of manic-depression, his career virtually ended in 1980 after he strangled his wife. He was judged mentally incompetent to stand trial and was institutionalized until 1984.

Altman, Robert (1925–) American film director, best known for his irreverent views of America in the 1970s. A pilot in World War II, Altman returned to his native Kansas City, Missouri, to make industrial films. After working on the television series *Whirlybirds* and *Bonanza,* he scored his first big movie success with M*A*S*H in 1970, a savage antiwar comedy about army medics in Korea. For the next five years he averaged two films a year, presenting an unbroken string of commercially successful and critically praised hits. He satirized the western (*McCabe and Mrs. Miller,* 1971), the psychological drama (*Images,* 1972), the gangster thriller (*The Long Goodbye,* 1973) and the caper film (*California Split,* 1974). Films far more difficult to categorize during this time included an allegory about a flying boy (*Brewster McCloud,* 1970), Altman's personal favorite; a poignant story about a trio of young robbers (*Thieves Like Us,* 1974); and the masterful, densely textured *Nashville* (1975). Subsequently he has directed a number of stage plays and a string of quirky, occasionally bewildering films, including the science fiction allegory *Quintet* (1979) and *Come Back to the Five and Dime, Jimmy Dean* (1982). Altman received critical acclaim for *The Player* (1992), a film that portrayed the more scandalous elements of the Hollywood industry, and *Gosford Park* (2001), an Academy Award–winning dark comedy that narrates familial intrigue in 1930s Britain. Altman has said he is preoccupied in his pictures with the "flexible boundary between sanity and insanity."

aluminum Lightweight, silvery metal refined from bauxite ore, a naturally occurring mineral. Because aluminum is lighter than steel but of comparable strength, it came to be used in the construction of aircraft. It is also nonrusting (although it develops a surface oxide) and so is widely used for kitchen cookwear, household utensils, and decorative objects. Because of its recent availability and its association with aviation, it came to be associated with MODERNISM in the 1920s and 1930s.

Alvarez, Alfred *(1929–)* British critic and author. Born in London, he was educated at Corpus Christi College, Oxford, where he later served as a senior research scholar and tutor in English. He established himself as literary critic with his first book, *Stewards of Excellence* (1958). In *The Savage God* (1971) he coined the term *extremists,* referring to poets such as Sylvia PLATH and Robert LOWELL, whose work explores their personal obsessions. While he helped to popularize these CONFESSIONAL POETS, he was also criticized for promoting the view that madness is necessary for creating great literature. His first novel, *Hers,* was published in 1975; a volume of poetry, *Autumn to Autumn: Selected Poems 1953–1976,* in 1976. Alvarez's eclectic nonfiction includes *Life After Marriage: People in Divorce* (1982), *The Biggest Game in Town* (1983) and *Offshore: A North Sea Journey* (1986). Other works of fiction include *Day of Atonement* (1991). In 1999 Alvarez published his memoir, *Where Did It All Go Right?* He has contributed to THE NEW YORKER.

Alvarez, Luis *(1911–1988)* American scientist, winner of the 1968 NOBEL PRIZE in physics for his use of bubble chambers to detect new subatomic particles. A member of the team at Los Alamos that developed the atomic bomb (see ATOMIC BOMB DEVELOPMENT), Alvarez witnessed its first use at Hiroshima in WORLD WAR II. He also supported the development of the HYDROGEN BOMB. Alvarez joined his son Walter in supporting a controversial theory holding that one or more asteroid impacts were responsible for the extinction of the dinosaurs and thousands of other species 65 million years ago.

Alwyn, William *(1905–1985)* British composer. Alwyn was for many years a professor of composition at London's Royal Academy of Music. In addition to writing much concert music, including five symphonies, he wrote many film scores, including those for *Odd Man Out* and *Fallen Idol.*

Alydar *(1975–1990)* American thoroughbred racehorse who faced off against AFFIRMED in one of the most celebrated rivalries in racing history. Alydar finished second to Affirmed in all three 1978 Triple Crown races, with the total distance between them amounting to less than two lengths. While Alydar beat Affirmed only three times in his career, he captured the public imagination with his courage and his unfaltering will to win. His post-racing career at stud assured his place in the annals of thoroughbred history, as he sired such major stakes winners as Alysheba, Easy Goer and Strike the Gold. At the time of his death from complications following a broken leg, Alydar's offspring were approaching the $35 million mark in winnings.

Amado, Jorge *(1912–2001)* Brazilian novelist. Amado enjoyed the relatively rare status of a novelist both lionized by critics and read avidly by a worldwide general public. Born on a plantation in northeast Brazil, Amado studied law and began his writing career as a popular proletarian novelist. *The Violent Land* (1943) is the major work of this early phase. From 1946 to 1948, Amado was elected as a Communist to the Brazilian parliament; his political career ended when his Communist Party was outlawed. Amado nonetheless continued to express populist themes in his fiction while transforming his style to utilize picaresque narratives full of bawdy humor and folk wisdom. His novels include *Gabriela, Cinnamon and Clove* (1958), *Dona Flor and Her Two Husbands* (1966), *Home Is the Sailor* (1968) and *Tent of Miracles* (1969).

Amahl and the Night Visitors The first full-length opera to be presented on network television December 24, 1951. Composer Gian Carlo MENOTTI was commissioned by the NBC network in the fall of 1950 to compose an original opera. He prepared his own text, the story of an encounter between a crippled beggar boy and the Magi on the way to Bethlehem. Mr. Joyce C. HALL, founder of Hallmark Cards, Inc., of Kansas City, sponsored the project as a "thank you" to customers. Hosted by the composer and actress Sarah Churchill (daughter of Winston), the "live" telecast made television history and launched what would become known as THE HALLMARK HALL OF FAME anthology series. The program was rebroadcast on April 13, 1952. Again Churchill and Menotti hosted, and the cast was repeated. (Chet Allen and Rosemary Kuhlman portrayed, respectively,

Amahl and his mother; Thomas Schippers conducted.) Hallmark sponsored four other television versions including a color telecast on NBC on December 20, 1953 (the first color telecast in television history) and a remounting on December 12, 1965, with an entirely new cast—Kurt Haghjian as Amahl and Martha King as his mother. With the premiere telecast in 1951, wrote critic Olin Downes, "television, operatically speaking, has come of age."

Amaldi, Edoardo *(1908–1989)* Italian physicist. Amaldi graduated from the University of Rome in 1929, where he had studied under Enrico FERMI. Together with Fermi and others he discovered that fast-moving neutrons are slowed down (moderated) by substances containing hydrogen and can thus be brought to energies at which they more easily interact with nuclei. He also contributed to the study of taumesons, hyperons and antiprotons. In 1937 he was made professor of general physics at the University of Rome, and from 1952 until 1954 he was secretary-general of the European Organization for Nuclear Research. He also served as president of the International Union of Pure and Applied Physics (1957–60) and president of the Istituto Nazionale di Fisica Nucleare (1960–65). Amaldi was a constant advocate for the greater pooling of scientific research and technical information and was one of the primary sponsors of what became the European Space Agency (ESA). On December 8, 1989, Amaldi died during his tenure as the president of the Accademia dei Lincei.

Amal militia Shiite Muslim militia in LEBANON and one of the most important political and military groups in the country. Founded in 1974, it is the military arm of the large Shiite faction originally headed by Imam Musa Sadr, who disappeared during a visit to Libya in 1978. Led by Nabih Berri and closely aligned with Syria, it existed alongside the PALESTINE LIBERATION ORGANIZATION until the Israeli invasion of Lebanon (1982), after which it became the sole militia in southern Lebanon. It was temporarily aligned with the Druze forces of Walid Jumblat. The Islamic Amal, a more militant offshoot and now a

rival of the Amal with headquarters in the Bekaa Valley, was involved in a variety of terrorist attacks, including the raid on the U.S. embassy and the U.S. Marines barracks. Two other Shiite extremist groups also oppose the Amal, the HEZBOLLAH (Party of God) and the Islamic Jihad (Islamic Holy War). Since 1982 the Amal militia has continued to fight Hezbollah through guerrilla means, such as the July 2000 attack that killed two Hezbollah soldiers. It has also continued its fight against ISRAEL. In August 1999 the Amal movement announced that it had orchestrated a successful attack on 10 Israeli and Israeli-allied outposts in southern Lebanon. In response, Israel ordered air strikes on alleged Amal staging grounds in the region.

Amalrik, Andrei Alekseyevich *(1938–1980)* Soviet writer, historian, dissident and human rights activist. During the 1960s and 1970s Amalrik was a leader in the movement for intellectual and political freedom in the USSR. He was the first dissident to seek out American news correspondents in Moscow in the mid-1960s, thereby establishing a link between Soviet political dissidents and the West. Because of his beliefs he was expelled from his university (1965), harassed by the KGB and eventually exiled to Siberia (1965). In 1976 he was pressured to

leave the USSR. He gained worldwide attention for his unrelenting criticism of repression and backwardness in Soviet society. His books include *Revolutionary Journey to Siberia* (1970) and *Will the Soviet Union Survive Until 1984?* (1970).

Amanpour, Christiane *(1958–)* U.S. television news personality. Born to Patricia and Mohammed Amanpour in London, she belonged to a wealthy family that had fled Iran in 1979 because of its close association with the deposed shah's regime. Settling in the U.S., she obtained a degree in journalism from the University of Rhode Island and then worked as a journalist within the greater Providence area. In 1983 she joined the young Cable News Network (CNN) as a news assistant and over the next seven years advanced up the ranks to become a news producer and foreign correspondent. From that position she covered stories throughout Europe and the Middle East on topics ranging from the end of the COLD WAR, the Iraqi invasion of Kuwait, the PERSIAN GULF WAR, the Kurdish refugee crisis, the conflict in the former Yugoslavia, and the U.S.-led war on terrorism. As one of CNN's senior foreign correspondents and also an occasional correspondent for CBS's *60 Minutes*, Amanpour has received numerous

CNN reporter Christiane Amanpour (right) with Gouli Imami in Tehran. 2000 (PHOTOFEST)

awards for her journalism, including a news and documentary Emmy. She was named a fellow of the Society of Professional Journalists in 1997.

Amanullah Khan (*1892–1960*) King of AFGHANISTAN (1919–29). He ended British control of Afghanistan, but revolts forced him to abdicate when he tried to end the slavery of women and to introduce monogamy. (See also AFGHAN CIVIL WAR OF 1928–1929.)

Ambartsumian, Viktor Amazaspovich (*1908–1996*) Soviet astrophysicist. Ambartsumian, the son of a distinguished Armenian philologist, graduated from the University of Leningrad in 1928 and did graduate work at nearby Pulkovo Observatory from 1928 to 1931. He was professor of astrophysics from 1934 to 1946 at Leningrad and held the same post from 1947 at the State University of Yerevan in Armenia. In 1946 he organized the construction, near Yerevan, of the Byurakan Astronomical Observatory, having been appointed its director in 1944. Ambartsumian's work was mainly concerned with the evolution of stellar systems, both galaxies and smaller clusters of stars, and the processes taking place during the evolution of stars. In 1947 Ambartsumian introduced into astronomy the idea of a stellar "association." These associations are loose clusters of hot stars that lie in or near the disk-shaped plane of our galaxy. They must be young, no more than a few million years old, as the galaxy's gravitational field will tend to disperse them. Thus star formation is still going on in the galaxy. He also argued in 1955 that the idea of colliding galaxies proposed by Rudolph Minkowski and Walter BAADE to explain such radio sources as Cygnus A would not produce the required energy. Instead he proposed that the source of energy was gigantic explosions occurring in the dense central regions of galaxies.

Ambassadors, The Novel by Henry JAMES, published in 1903. The work examines the reactions of several Americans to European mores and morals in the early 20th century. The story revolves around a young American, Chad Newsome, who is living a reputedly dissolute life in Paris, and the "ambassador" of the story, Lambert

Strether, who has been sent by Chad's mother to fetch her son back. The middle-aged Strether is initially caught up in the happy atmosphere of Paris and takes Chad's side; ultimately, his loyalty to Mrs. Newsome prevails. James captured American and European "types" of the period with wit and deftness of perception. Many critics consider *The Ambassadors* to be his finest novel.

Amchitka One of the ALEUTIAN ISLANDS, in the U.S. state of Alaska. It was the site of a U.S. Army Air Force base during WORLD WAR II. Designated for underground nuclear weaponry testing in 1967, the first test was conducted in 1971.

Amendola, Giorgio (*1907–1980*) Italian Communist Party leader. Amendola began his political career as a staunch opponent of Benito MUSSOLINI. He was arrested in 1932 and later exiled. During the German occupation of ITALY toward the end of WORLD WAR II, he led guerrillas against the NAZIS in northern Italy. He served in all postwar Italian parliaments up to his death. He was among party leaders who denounced the SOVIET INVASION OF CZECHOSLOVAKIA in 1956.

America First Isolationist movement that attempted to maintain American neutrality as WORLD WAR II raged in Europe and Japanese expansionism swept Asia. It was spearheaded by the America First Committee, an organization that was formed in 1940 and reached a membership of some 800,000. The group argued that the U.S. should maintain a strong defense and avoid foreign entanglements. It was abruptly disbanded after the Japanese attack on PEARL HARBOR (December 7, 1941) catapulted the U.S. into war.

American Ballet Theatre (ABT) Ballet company founded by Richard Pleasant in New York City in 1939 with a core group of dancers and a repertory primarily from the Russian dance companies. Pleasant managed the company with dancer and heiress Lucia CHASE until resigning in 1941, whereupon his place was taken by designer Oliver Smith. Smith and Chase were succeeded by Mikhail BARYSHNIKOV

(1980–89). Jane Herman took over the management in 1989. From the start, ABT was envisioned as an eclectic repository for the best dances of the Russian, English, Spanish, American and popular heritages and as a venue for star dancers (Natalia MAKAROVA, Fernando Bujones) from all corners of the world. Though not marked by one choreographer's imprimatur, the company's general tenor and broad-based appeal were established by choreographers Antony TUDOR (*Pillar of Fire*) and Jerome ROBBINS (*Fancy Free*) during the 1940s. Today the company performs works from the classical and romantic ballet tradition by such choreographers as Agnes DE MILLE, Kenneth MACMILLAN and George BALANCHINE, as well as dances in the modern and postmodern vein by Twyla THARP, Paul TAYLOR, Mark Morris and others.

American Broadcasting Company
See ABC.

American Civil Liberties Union (ACLU) A U.S. public interest group founded to protect individual liberties as guaranteed by the U.S. Constitution's Bill of Rights. Although the group's espoused aims seem uncontroversial, the group has been involved in constant controversy since its founding in 1920, because of its support for polemical and often unpopular causes.

The ACLU was founded by a number of prominent Americans, including Jane ADDAMS, Roger Baldwin, Felix FRANKFURTER, Helen KELLER and Norman THOMAS. The organization has brought numerous court challenges against statutes violative of the Bill of Rights, including the famous Scopes monkey trial, which involved a law banning the teaching of the theory of evolution in Tennessee public schools. The ACLU has defended Jews and Nazis alike whenever individual rights are imperiled. Critics maintain that its rigid adherence to principle sometimes conflicts with common sense, but despite the criticism the organization continues as a vigorous champion of American individual rights.

American Dance Festival (ADF) An annual event since 1948, the ADF presents dance companies, choreographers, dance critics and others from the U.S. and abroad in a series of public performances, workshops and seminars. The festival's original focus was modern dance, featuring the works of Martha GRAHAM, Doris Humphrey, José LIMÓN, Alwin Nikolais, Merce CUNNINGHAM and Paul TAYLOR. Notable festival premieres included Graham's *Diversion of Angels* (1948) and Limón's *The Moor's Pavane* (1949). Not until the 1960s did the artistic agenda grow to include ethnic dance, such as that from Korea, Spain and Jamaica, as well as other dance forms. Under the direction of Charles Reinhart since 1969, the festival has grown steadily more eclectic. Though housed for many years at Connecticut College, the ADF has been based at Duke University in Durham, North Carolina, since 1978.

American Federation of Labor and Congress of Industrial Organizations (AFL-CIO)
Federation of over 100 autonomous labor unions. Primarily an American body with a membership of about 13 million, it also has international members in U.S. territories, Puerto Rico, Canada and Panama. The federation was created in 1955 with the merger of the AFL, a group consisting mainly of craft unions, and the CIO, an organization of industrial unions. The history of the AFL stretches back to 1881, when a number of trade unions meeting in Pittsburgh established the Federation of Organized Trades and Labor Unions of the U.S. and Canada. The group reorganized in 1886 and changed its name to the American Federation of Labor. From its inception, the AFL was a trade union, organizing workers by their individual skills. Led by Samuel GOMPERS until his death in 1924, it acted as a lobbying group to secure labor-rights legislation, helped to organize workers and was successful in securing such benefits as a shorter work day, higher wages, worker's compensation and laws prohibiting child labor. Led later by William GREEN and George MEANY, it became America's largest and most important labor federation.

The CIO, originally called the Committee for Industrial Organization, was formed within the AFL in 1935 to organize factory workers on an industry-wide basis. Expelled from the AFL in 1938 in a dispute over whether mass-production workers should be organized on an industrial or craft basis, it

changed its name to the Congress of Industrial Organizations and elected John L. LEWIS as its head. Lewis, who served until 1940, was succeeded by Phillip MURRAY, who headed the federation until his death in 1952. The group was extremely successful in organizing large industries such as steel and automobiles.

As an antiunion climate began to prevail in the 1950s and the distinctions between craft and industrial unions were perceived as less important, the groups reunited in 1955 and elected George Meany as president. Under a 1957 antirackets provision, the AFL-CIO expelled the Teamsters Union (readmitted in 1987). Led by Walter REUTHER, the United Automobile Workers left the federation in 1968, only to reaffiliate in 1981. The AFL-CIO acts as the collective representative of labor, seeking to influence prolabor legislation on the federal and state levels. It is active politically and has traditionally supported Democratic candidates. It assists its member unions in organizing activities and maintains a staff to handle research, information, publicity, legal affairs and various special issues such as civil rights and veterans' interests. It is also active in general social welfare and community-building areas. The AFL-CIO is governed by a convention that meets biennially. It is headed by a president, a secretary-treasurer and 33 vice presidents, who form an executive council that governs between conventions and carries out convention decisions. In 2003 the AFL-CIO's leadership announced that the union would openly oppose the invasion of Iraq proposed by U.S. president George W. BUSH. In the early stages of the 2004 Democratic primary season, the AFL-CIO chose not to endorse a candidate, although the Teamsters, one of its subsidiary unions, did endorse Missouri congressman Richard Gephardt.

American Friends Service Committee (AFSC)
A social service organization founded by Quakers in Philadelphia in 1917, it grew from opposition to WORLD WAR I. The organization proposed various methods of noncombatant service for Quakers and other conscientious objectors. The group's first chairman, philosophy professor Rufus M. Jones, established voluntary civilian work in France, much

of it in hospitals, as an alternative to military service. After the war the AFSC distributed food and clothing in Germany, and in the early 1920s it worked to ameliorate famine in the USSR. Between the world wars the committee worked in four basic areas: foreign, interracial, peace and home service. In the years preceding World War II, the AFSC provided relief in the SPANISH CIVIL WAR and aided Jews persecuted by the Nazi regime. During WORLD WAR II, it administered public service camps, assisted interned Japanese Americans and undertook relief efforts in China, France, England and other areas. In the postwar era the organization distributed food, clothing, medical supplies and other relief to refugees worldwide. The AFSC was particularly active in humanitarian programs during the KOREAN WAR and the VIETNAM WAR. In 1947 the AFSC shared the NOBEL PRIZE for peace with the British FRIENDS SERVICE COUNCIL. The AFSC also sent volunteer workers and humanitarian aid to Third World areas beset by violence, such as Algeria (1962), North and South Vietnam (1966), Laos (1972), Zimbabwe (1980–81), Cambodia (1981), Honduras (1985) and Somalia (1993).

American Popular Revolutionary Alliance (APRA)
Marxist political movement in PERU. (See also Víctor Raúl HAYA DE LA TORRE.)

American Samoa
Chain of islands that form the eastern portion of the Samoa chain in the southwest Pacific Ocean. The U.S. won control of them pursuant to a 1899 treaty with Germany and Great Britain. Until 1951 they were administered by the U.S. Navy, which also established a now defunct base at Pago Pago, the capital. Also known as Eastern Samoa, the islands presently form an unincorporated territory administered by the U.S. Department of the Interior.

American Tragedy, An
Novel by Theodore DREISER. Considered to be his masterpiece, it is a pioneering psychological study of a murderer. Unlike literary precedents in Poe, Dostoyevsky and CONRAD, the crime is not motivated by passion, alienation or madness so much as by simple expedience. Clyde Griffiths murders Roberta

Alden, a mill worker he has seduced, because her unexpected pregnancy threatens his courtship of a socially prominent debutante. The novel grew out of several of Dreiser's preoccupations—an absorbing interest in real-life crime stories (the murder by Chester Gillette of Grace Brown in Moose Lake, New York, in 1906), his growing frustration with his own loveless marriage and his readings in Sigmund FREUD and Jacques Loeb of the biological, subconscious and mechanistic forces that work upon our lives. The book, published in 1925, became Dreiser's most successful novel, selling 25,000 copies in the first six months. Critic Joseph Wood Krutch called it the greatest book of its generation; criminal lawyer Clarence DARROW praised its "fanatical devotion to truth"; and, more recently, critic Ellen Moers in her classic study, *The Two Dreisers,* appraised it as a modern version of the Aladdin myth. Unimpressed, the city of Boston banned it. Two watered-down movie versions have appeared—a 1931 version by Josef von STERNBERG and one in 1951 by George STEVENS.

American Volunteer Group See FLYING TIGERS.

Ames, Aldrich (*1941–   *) American CENTRAL INTELLIGENCE AGENCY (CIA) official and double agent for the Soviet Union. Ames began his tenure at the CIA in 1962. In 1974 the CIA assigned him to manage a newly acquired double agent, Alexander Dmitrievich Ogorodnik, a diplomat in the Soviet Foreign Ministry. Ogorodnik continued to provide Ames and the CIA with top-secret transmissions until Ogorodnik committed suicide in 1977 upon learning that the Soviets had got wind of his activities. Ames continued to manage other Soviet double agents, such as Sergeii Fedorenko, a Soviet nuclear official with the UN, and Arkadii Shevchenko, a high-ranking Soviet diplomat at the UN.

Ames was transferred to Mexico City in 1981 with instructions to recruit Mexican bureaucrats and foreign diplomats as CIA operatives. Two years later he returned to the U.S. to serve as the counterintelligence chief of Soviet operations in the agency's New York City branch. Ames's triumphal return later produced complications for his

personal and professional life. During his two years in Mexico, Ames began an affair with an official at the Colombian embassy, María del Rosario Casas Dupuy. Shortly before his return to America, Ames informed Rosario that he was married and would soon return with his wife. However, the relationship resumed several months after Ames's transfer, when Rosario moved to Virginia and convinced Ames to divorce his wife. The ensuing legal fees complicated Ames's finances, as did Rosario's spendthrift ways. His financial difficulties drove Ames into collusion with the Soviet intelligence agency, the KGB, in late 1984. Soviet operatives desired Ames's assistance in identifying Soviet officials who were working for the CIA. Ames soon provided the KGB with information on every Soviet double agent and U.S. intelligence operation in the Soviet Union that he could identify. This led to the arrest of many U.S. agents and a drastic decline in the CIA's intelligence from the USSR, which prompted a full-scale investigation to determine if the Soviets had acquired a mole within the CIA. To deflect from himself, Ames obtained a transfer to the CIA's Rome branch, where he and Rosario adopted an even more opulent lifestyle. In 1987 Ames's spendthrift habits caught the attention of Dan Payne, a CIA official and former accountant charged with finding the mole. The financial evidence against Ames steadily accumulated after his return to the U.S. in 1989, leading the FBI to place numerous bugs in Ames's home, office and car. The FBI's big break came in October 1993, when it retrieved computer ribbon from Ames's trash cans that contained copies of several letters to the KGB. By February 1994 the FBI had obtained enough information to arrest Ames and Rosario (who, it was discovered, knew all about Ames's espionage activities). Both were tried and convicted later that year, with Ames sentenced to life imprisonment, and Rosario to five years, after which she was deported to Colombia.

Amethyst Incident Attack on the British frigate HMS *Amethyst* by Chinese Communist troops on April 20, 1949. The ship was fired on while sailing up the Yangtze River with supplies for the British community in Nanjing.

Occurring during the final phase of the Chinese revolution, the attack was assumed to be an assertion of Chinese sovereignty over the waterway. Seventeen of the *Amethyst's* crew were killed, 30 were wounded, and the ship was detained in China. After attempts to rescue the vessel failed, the ship successfully sailed downriver, reaching the sea on July 31, 1949, an escape that was greeted with great joy in Great Britain.

Amfiteatrov, Alexander Valentinovich (*1862–1938*) Russian journalist. He was exiled by the czarist government for his satirical piece "The Obmanovs" (1902). In 1905 he went abroad and published *Krasni Flag,* a revolutionary magazine. On his return to Russia he became editor of the newspaper *Russkaya Svoboda* (Russian freedom). He left Russia again after the Russian Revolution and wrote articles against the BOLSHEVIKS. His books include *Maria Luseva* (1904), *Those of the Eighties* (1907–08) and *Those of the Nineties* (1910).

Amichai, Yehuda (*1924–2000*) Israeli poet. Born in Germany, Amichai immigrated to Palestine in 1936. He served in the Israeli army during the ARAB-ISRAELI WAR OF 1948. His novel *Not of This Time, Not of That Place* (translated from the Hebrew in 1968), concerns the author's ambivalence about his citizenship and the situation of the Jewish writer. His lyrical, highly metaphoric and psalm-like poetry focuses on the themes of love, war and loss. His collections include *Songs of Jerusalem and Myself* (translated 1973) and *Amen* (translated 1977). In 1982 Amichai was awarded the Israel Prize, the highest literary honor awarded in ISRAEL, in recognition of his distinctive use of the Hebrew language in poetry. Amichai is generally considered to have been Israel's foremost poet.

Amin, Idi (*ca. 1925–2003*) President of Uganda (1971–79). A Muslim and a member of the Kakwa tribe, he served as a sergeant in the British colonial army and later rose in the Ugandan military to become commander in chief in 1966. That year he aided Prime Minister Milton OBOTE in the overthrow of President Kabaka Mutesa II. In 1971, while Obote was out of the country, Amin seized control and proclaimed himself president. Brutal and unpredictable, he was regarded as a buffoon by some and a monster by others. He established a dictatorship, expelled most resident Asians, feuded with neighboring African republics and was responsible for the slaughter of hundreds of thousands of Ugandans. As the Ugandan economy worsened and his abuses of power became widely known, Amin's prestige in the international community rapidly waned; he was condemned after giving haven to the Palestinian hijackers of an Israeli airliner in 1976 (see ENTEBBE, RAID ON). In 1979 Tanzanian troops invaded Uganda and forced Amin into exile; he reportedly settled in Libya and then Saudi Arabia. Amin remained in Saudi Arabia until his death in 2003.

Amis, Kingsley *(1922–1995)* British author. Born in London, Amis was educated at St. John's College, Oxford, where he met Philip LARKIN. His first novel, *Lucky Jim* (1954), was a popular and critical success and earned him a reputation as one of the ANGRY YOUNG MEN. Though best known for his comic satires, such as *Take a Girl Like You* (1960), *Jake's Thing* (1978) and *The Old Devils* (1987; Booker Prize), Amis also tried his hand at other literary genres, including detective stories (published under the pseudonym Robert Markham) that reveal his enthusiasm for author Ian FLEMING. He was an accomplished poet as well; his early verse appeared in the MOVEMENT anthology *New Lines* (1956). Like many of the Angry Young Men, Amis later embraced conservative values. His son Martin AMIS is also an author.

Amis, Martin *(1949–)* British author. Born in Oxford and educated there at Exeter College, Amis is the son of author Kingsley AMIS. Martin Amis's first novel, *The Rachel Papers* (1973), which explores adolescent sexuality, established him as a satirist of contemporary British middle-class life. His steady output of dark, comedic fiction upholds this reputation. His works include *Money* (1984), *Success* (1987) and *London Fields* (1990). Amis also served as editorial assistant of the *Times Literary Supplement* (1972–75), assistant literary editor of *The New* *Statesman* and writer for the *Observer*. His literary journalism has appeared in periodicals in Britain and the U.S. In 1995 Amis concluded the trilogy of novels that began with *Money* and continued with *London Fields*, when he published *The Information*. In 2000 his autobiography, *Experience*, won the James Tait Black Memorial Prize.

Ammann, Othmar H. *(1875–1965)* Distinguished Swiss-born American structural engineer and designer of many major bridges. Ammann received his training in engineering at the Swiss Federal Polytechnical Institute before moving to the U.S. in 1904. Ammann designed the steel arch Bayonne Bridge over the Kill van Kull, connecting New Jersey and Staten Island with a span of 1,675 feet, with partner Allston Dana in 1927. As chief engineer for the Port of New York Authority, Ammann was in charge of the design of the George Washington Bridge (1931), the Goethals Bridge and Outerbridge Crossing (1928), the Triborough Bridge (1936) and the Bronx-Whitestone Bridge (1939). He was a consultant for the design of the Golden Gate Bridge in San Francisco (1937). As a partner in the firm of Ammann and Whitney, he was responsible for the design of the Throgs Neck (1961) and Verrazano-Narrows (1964) suspension bridges as well as many other structures, including several very wide-span airplane hangars.

Ammons, Archie Randolph *(1926–2001)* American poet. Born on a farm near Whiteville, North Carolina, Ammons worked in a shipyard after high school. After World War II he graduated from Wake Forest College on the GI Bill and attended Berkeley. For eight years he was vice president of a glassware manufacturing firm in New York State. In 1953 his first poems appeared in *The Hudson Review*. In 1965 he attracted attention with *Corsons Inlet* and *Tape for the Turn of the Year*, a witty poem-diary written on adding machine tape. *Collected Poems 1951–1971* won a National Book Award in 1973, and he received the BOLLINGEN PRIZE in 1974–75. Other works include *Sphere: The Form of a Motion* (1974), *Diversifications* (1975) and *The Snow Poems* (1977). He taught at Cornell University. Ammons was a meditative writer in the transcendentalist tradition of Emerson, Dickinson and Whitman. He wrote in open, expansive forms. While working at Cornell, Ammons continued to publish such volumes of poetry as *A Coast of Trees* (1981), *Garbage* (1993), and *Glare* (1997). *Garbage* in particular acquired a great deal of critical acclaim and won a National Book Award in 1994. In 1998 Ammons received the American Academy of American Poets' Tanning Prize.

Amnesty International (AI) International civil liberties organization. Founded in 1961 as an outgrowth of British barrister Peter Benenson's (1921–2005) year-long campaign "Appeal for Amnesty," which called for the release of all "prisoners of conscience" worldwide, AI has grown into a global organization dedicated to ensuring that all nations adhere to the UN's 1948 Universal Declaration on Human Rights. A nongovernmental organization (NGO), AI seeks to raise world awareness and condemnation of unjust trials, capital and brutal corporal punishment and the disappearance, murder and abuse of dissidents by governments and terrorist organizations.

In its first seven years, AI accomplished its goals by organizing a global letter-writing campaign to various governmental officials and media outlets on behalf of prisoners of conscience throughout the world. Though originally winning popular acclaim by bringing about the release of prisoners in Ireland, Romania, and Egypt, AI suffered a decline in membership and revenues when reports surfaced linking AI donations to the U.S. CENTRAL INTELLIGENCE AGENCY and suggesting that Sean MACBRIDE, a former officer in the IRISH REPUBLICAN ARMY and one of AI's founders, had thwarted AI's efforts to investigate his former organization. In 1968 this led to a series of institutional reforms inaugurated by AI's then secretary general, Martin Ennals, to prevent investigations of countries by nationals from that country. Ennals also expanded AI's focus beyond the realm of political prisoners to include campaigns against rape, torture and executions committed for nonpolitical reasons. Its evolving foci have generated criticism from both conservative and liberal quarters: conservative intellectual William F. BUCKLEY, Jr., left the organization when it began to condemn the practice of capital punishment, while supporters of Nelson MANDELA protested AI's refusal to classify him as a prisoner of conscience following his 1964 life sentence because Mandela had encouraged violent actions against the South African government. However, AI has generally received praise throughout the world for its campaigns against alleged human rights abuses in Indonesia, Somalia, Kenya, Saudi Arabia, Israel, and even the U.S. government's treatment of alleged al-QAEDA operatives held in Guantanamo Bay, Cuba. Its highest honor came in 1977, when AI received the Nobel Peace Prize, adding to the NOBEL PRIZE won by MacBride in 1974.

Amoco Cadiz Supertanker that broke up and sank off Portsall, on France's Brittany coast, in March 1978, resulting in the spill of 68 million gallons of oil. A total of $665 million in claims were filed against Standard Oil Co. as a result of the spill, which was one of the worst on record.

Amos and Andy An immensely popular radio program that changed the hours and the routine of millions of American families and may have had as great an influence on the development of radio as Milton BERLE's *TEXACO STAR THEATER* had on early television. The show swiftly became an American institution after it hit the airwaves in 1929; from then until 1951, when it moved to television, *Amos and Andy* suffered little controversy over its depiction of black stereotypes. The main radio characters—Andy Brown and Amos Jones—were created by white vaudevillians Charles Correll and Freeman Gosden, who performed on stage in "blackface." But for television, black comedians were selected for all the roles, with Alvin Childress as Amos, Spencer Williams as Andy and Tim Moore as "Kingfish," the show's key figure. That made the television show funnier and more real—and just a bit embarrassing to a newly enlightened American public. The show lasted for two seasons and, after the late 1950s, disappeared from syndication. In spite of continuing controversy over the show's dialogue humor and simple characters—actually, little different from *The Jeffersons* of the 1980s—*Amos and Andy* has contin-

ued to influence comedians and find a cult audience.

Amritsar Massacre On April 12, 1919, in the city of Amritsar in the Punjab, INDIA, five British subjects were killed during a riot by Indian nationalists protesting antisedition measures (the Rowlatt Acts). About 10,000 unarmed Indians assembled the next day to continue the protest. Refusing to disperse, the Indians were fired upon by Gurkha troops under the command of British brigadier general Reginald Dyer (1864–1927); 379 Indians were killed and about 1,200 wounded. Dyer then imposed martial law and ordered floggings. His actions were denounced in the British House of Commons but upheld by the House of Lords. An army council later called the massacre "an error in judgment."

Amundsen, Roald (Engelbregt Gravning) *(1872–1928)* Norwegian explorer who led the first expedition to reach the SOUTH POLE. Born near Oslo, Amundsen attended university and medical school but left in 1897 to join a two-year Belgian expedition to the Antarctic. From then on the polar regions of the Earth were to haunt him, and he was to return to the frozen wastes time and time again. From 1903 to 1906 he commanded the ship *Gjoa* in the Arctic Ocean, negotiating the Northwest Passage. After long preparation to conquer the North Pole, he learned (1909) that Robert E. PEARY had reached this destination, and so Amundsen turned his attention to the South Pole. With this goal in mind, he sailed from Norway in 1910 in a ship borrowed from NANSEN, the *Fram*, racing a British expedition under Robert Falcon SCOTT. Well prepared for this venture, Amundsen used dogsleds and took a shorter overland route across Antarctica. He and four compatriots reached the South Pole on December 14, 1911. Scott reached the Pole 35 days later, but he and his men died on their return trip. After a shipboard journey along the northern coast of Europe and Asia in 1918–19, Amundsen turned to exploring by air. He and Lincoln ELLSWORTH tried unsuccessfully to fly across the North Pole in 1925. The following year the two explorers and Italian airman General Umberto NOBILE were able to fly over

Norwegian explorer Roald Amundsen. 1906 (LIBRARY OF CONGRESS, PRINTS AND PHOTOGRAPHS DIVISION)

the Pole and to explore the northern Arctic Ocean. Two years later Nobile crashed in another dirigible, the *Italia*, and Amundsen disappeared while trying to rescue his colleague. His autobiography, *My Life as an Explorer*, was published in 1927, and he was the author and coauthor of several volumes describing his explorations.

Anami, Korechika *(1887–1945)* Japanese general. A career officer and graduate of the Army War College, Anami held a number of posts before WORLD WAR II. From 1938 to 1943 he commanded various Japanese armies in China, and in 1943 he directed operations in western New Guinea. The following year he was appointed inspector general of army aviation. As the tide of war turned against Japan in 1945, Anami became the nation's last war minister, serving in the cabinet of Kantaro Suzuki. He advocated improving his nation's bargaining posture by attacking the expected Allied invasion forces and, after the atomic bomb attack on HIROSHIMA, continued to strive for conditional rather than unconditional surrender. Certain of defeat, he committed suicide in August 1945.

anarchism A political philosophy holding that government is evil and that it should be abolished in favor of free agreements between individuals. First formulated by ancient Greek Stoics, its modern manifestations were outlined by such philosophers as William Godwin (1756–1836) and Pierre-Joseph Proudhon (1807–65). In Russia the theory was espoused by Mikhail Bakunin (1814–76), who provided much of the violent and revolutionary tone that persisted into the 20th century. Anarchism was suppressed by the BOLSHEVIKS after the RUSSIAN REVOLUTION. In the late 19th and early 20th centuries the movement became closely associated with a series of assassinations, including those of French president Sadi-Carnot (1894), Austrian empress Elizabeth (1898), Italian king Umberto I (1900) and U.S. president William MCKINLEY (1901). Anarchists were forbidden entry into the U.S. early in the 20th century, and some adherents of the movement, such as Emma GOLDMAN, were deported (1919). In Europe anarchism was linked with syndicalism and gained considerable public support. The movement had much less currency as the 20th century progressed, after Spain's anarchists and communists clashed during the SPANISH CIVIL WAR and Soviet power grew in the 1940s. While anarchist thought was somewhat revived during the 1960s and anarchist terror resurfaced in the contemporary world in actions by such groups as West Germany's BAADER-MEINHOF, today anarchism is more important as a theoretical construct than as a political movement.

Anastasia Nikolayevna *(1901– 1918)* Youngest daughter of Czar NICHOLAS II of Russia, murdered along with the rest of the Russian royal family at Yekaterinburg in 1918. In 1929 a German citizen named Anna ANDERSON claimed to be Anastasia. The dispute was definitively settled during the period of GLASNOST, or political openness, enacted in the Soviet Union by Mikhail GORBACHEV. Gorbachev authorized the releasing of documents that indicated

where the bodies of the entire czarist family were buried. A criminal forensics team later confirmed this information using the skeletal remains of Czar Nicholas II and the rest of his family.

Andean Community Regional economic organization. Established in 1969 by the nations of Bolivia, Chile, Colombia, Ecuador, and Peru, the Andean Community is dedicated to establishing a free trade area and an eventual a full common market among its members, and to coordinating its participants' tariff policies to produce a common external tariff. Its membership has changed slightly over the years: In 1973 Venezuela joined the community, while three years later Chile left its ranks; Peru also left in 1991 but rejoined the community in 1995 in order to improve its own economy without foreign interference. The Andean Community has regularly entered into negotiations with other similar multinational economic entities, such as ASEAN and the EUROPEAN UNION (EU), in an effort to benefit its participants through collective action. On account of its successful encouragement of trade among its members, it has endeavored since 1996 to expand the scope of the community from a common economic policy among the five states to include a court of justice and parliament, and the development of a common foreign policy, in emulation of the EU.

Anders, William *(1933–)* U.S. astronaut. Aboard *Apollo 8* (December 21–27, 1968) Bill Anders was one of the first three men to orbit the Moon. Anders, Frank BORMAN and James LOVELL began their historic orbit on Christmas Eve 1968 after escaping from Earth orbit via NASA's Apollo workhorse, the powerful Saturn 5 rocket. Circling the Moon 10 times, the crew of *Apollo 8* were the first humans ever to see its far side with their own eyes. After his historic flight, Anders became executive secretary for the National Aeronautics and Space Council in 1969 and remained with the council until 1973, when he was appointed to the Atomic Energy Commission. Later serving as first chairman of the Nuclear Regulatory Commission in 1975, he left in 1976 to become U.S. ambassador to Norway. Anders left government ser-

vice in 1977 to enter private industry. *Apollo 8* was his only spaceflight. By 1989 Anders had become the chairman and chief executive officer–designate of General Dynamics. Five years later he retired from General Dynamics.

Anderson, Anna *(1901–1984)* Woman who claimed to be Grand Duchess Anastasia, the youngest daughter of Czar NICHOLAS II of Russia; allegedly the only member of the Russian imperial family to survive execution by the BOLSHEVIKS in 1918. The fate of the real Anastasia (and the identity of Anna Anderson) remains one of the great nonmysteries of the 20th century. Anderson spent some 60 years trying to prove her claim. In 1967 a German court rejected her claim after she had sued the duchess of Mecklenburg for part of the imperial Russian fortune; however, the court said that its decision did not settle the identity of Anderson. The duchess contended that "Anastasia" was really one Franziska Schanzkowski, the daughter of a Polish worker. Her life was the basis of the movie *Anastasia* (1957). Anderson's claims were later invalidated by documents released under Soviet leader Mikhail GORBACHEV's policy of GLASNOST, or openness. The documents revealed that Anastasia was killed and buried along with the rest of her family, which was later confirmed by a team of criminal forensic technicians.

Anderson, Carl David *(1905–1991)* American physicist. Anderson, the son of Swedish immigrants, was educated at the California Institute of Technology where he obtained his Ph.D. in 1930 and where he remained for his entire career, serving as professor of physics from 1939 until his retirement in 1978. Anderson was deeply involved in the discovery of two new elementary particles. In 1930 he began to study cosmic rays by photographing their tracks in a cloud chamber. He was able to determine the existence of the positron, or positive electron, in September 1932. In the following year his results were confirmed by Patrick Blackett and Giuseppe Occhialini. Anderson won the 1936 NOBEL PRIZE in physics. In the same year Anderson noted some further unusual cosmic-ray tracks, which appeared to be made by a particle more massive than an electron but lighter than a proton. The particle was initially named the mesotron or yukon. From 1938 the particle became known as the meson. The confusion was partly dispelled in 1947 when Cecil Powell discovered another and more active meson, which became known as the pi-meson or pion, to distinguish it from Anderson's mu-meson or muon.

Anderson, Jack (Jackson Northman Anderson) *(1922–2005)* American newspaper columnist. Born in Long Beach, California, Anderson was raised in Salt Lake City and began his career in journalism in the 1930s as a reporter for the *Deseret News* and later for the *Salt Lake Tribune*. Much of the moral fervor that marked his reporting was shaped by his Mormon upbringing and his years (1941–44) as a missionary in the South. After service as a war correspondent in 1945, he became (1947) an assistant to the muckraking columnist Drew PEARSON, inheriting the column after Pearson's death in 1969. Anderson is particularly noted for his exposé of the pro-Pakistan U.S. policy during the INDO-PAKISTAN WAR OF 1971 (which won him a 1972 PULITZER PRIZE), of CIA plots to assassinate various foreign leaders, including Fidel CASTRO, of FBI wiretappings and of the WATERGATE affair. His syndicated column remained influential into the 1990s. He retired from journalism in July 2004.

Anderson, John *(1922–   )* U.S. congressman. Born in Rockford, Illinois, Anderson graduated from the University of Illinois in 1943 and obtained his law degree there in 1946. He was an adviser to the U.S. High Commission for Germany (1952–55) before returning home to become state's attorney (1956–60). A Republican, he entered the House of Representatives in 1961, serving there for 20 years. Gradually moderating his once conservative views, he often opposed party policy but was nevertheless elected chairman of the House Republican Conference, serving from 1968 to 1979. In 1979 he campaigned for the Republican nomination for president but was defeated by Ronald REAGAN. In the 1980 campaign, Anderson ran as an independent and garnered some 7% of the popular vote. He retired from the House in 1981. Upon retirement from

Congress, Anderson entered academia, where he served as a visiting professor at Bryn Mawr, Brandeis, Stanford, Oregon State, the University of Illinois, and Nova Southeastern Law Center.

Anderson, Lindsay *(1923–1994)* British film director and critic. A controversial figure in British cinema, Anderson was best known for combining cinematic experimentation with a strident social consciousness. Born in India, the son of a Scottish general, Anderson moved to London as a young man and in the 1950s became a leading film critic who called for British cinema to tackle the issues of a troubled postwar society. In 1954 his short documentary film, *Thursday's Children,* won an Oscar, and Anderson became a key figure in the emerging British Free Cinema movement that also included Tony Richardson and Karel Reisz. Anderson made his full-length directorial debut in 1963 with the highly acclaimed *This Sporting Life,* starring Richard Harris. Other Anderson films include *If . . .* (1968), *O Lucky Man!* (1973) and *The Whales of August* (1987). He also had a small acting role in *Chariots of Fire* (1981). On August 30, 1994, Anderson died of a heart attack.

Anderson, Marian *(1902–1993)* American concert and opera singer. Born in Philadelphia, Anderson began singing in church choirs and studied voice privately. Possessed of an extraordinarily rich contralto voice, she began her concert career after graduation from high school, winning a New York Philharmonic Orchestra guest appearance in 1925. Her first CARNEGIE HALL recital was held in 1929, and she soon made extremely popular tours of Europe. Primarily a concert singer, she excelled at spirituals as well as at the classical repertoire, but as a black artist she encountered prejudice in her native country. In 1939 she was denied access to Constitution Hall in Washington, D.C., by the Daughters of the American Revolution and instead gave a triumphal concert to some 75,000 on the steps of the Lincoln Memorial. In 1955 she became the first black permanent member of the Metropolitan Opera Company. Named a delegate to the UN in 1958, she retired from her performing career in 1965. One of the most popular clas-

Opera singer Marian Anderson (LIBRARY OF CONGRESS. PRINTS AND PHOTOGRAPHS DIVISION)

sical artists of her day, she is known for a variety of outstanding recordings. Anderson was named to the National Arts Hall of Fame in 1972 and was one of the Kennedy Center's first honorees in 1978. Her autobiography, *My Lord, What a Morning,* was published in 1956.

Anderson, Maxwell *(1888–1959)* American playwright known for historical dramas that embody satire and social commentary. Originally a journalist, Anderson gained success with the production of his first play, *What Price Glory?* an antiwar drama. *Winterset* (1935), written in verse, examines the SACCO AND VANZETTI CASE. *Key Largo* (1939) and *Anne of the Thousand Days* (1948) were later adapted as movies. Anderson collaborated with composer Kurt WEILL on the musicals *Knickerbocker Holiday* (1938) and *Lost in the Stars* (1940) and won a PULITZER

PRIZE for *Both Your Houses* (1933), a satire on the U.S. Congress.

Anderson, Philip Warren *(1923–)*

American physicist. Anderson obtained his B.S. (1943), M.S. (1947) and Ph.D. (1949) at Harvard University, doing his doctoral thesis under John Van Vleck. He spent 1943 to 1945 at the Naval Research Laboratory working on antenna engineering. Upon receiving his doctorate, Anderson joined the Bell Telephone Laboratories at Murray Hill, New Jersey. Anderson's main research has been in the physics of the solid state, incorporating such topics as superconductors and nuclear theory. In 1959 he developed a theory to explain "superexchange"—the coupling of spins of two magnetic atoms in a crystal through their interaction with a nonmagnetic atom located between them. He went on to develop the theoretical treatments of antiferromagnetics ferroelectrics, and superconductors. In 1961 Anderson conceived a theoretical model to describe what happens when an impurity atom is present in a metal—now widely known and used as the **Anderson model.** Also named for him is the phenomenon of **Anderson localization,** describing the migration of impurities within a crystal. In the 1960s Anderson concentrated particularly on superconductivity and superfluidity. Along with Van Vleck and the British physicist Nevill MOTT, Anderson shared the 1977 NOBEL PRIZE in physics "for their fundamental theoretical investigation of the electronic structure of magnetic and disordered systems." In 1984 Anderson retired from Bell Laboratories and began devoting part of his time to teaching courses as a visiting professor at Cambridge University and at Princeton.

Anderson, Sherwood *(1876–1941)*

U.S. author. After a childhood of poverty in Camden, Ohio, he moved to Chicago where he joined the National Guard. He served in Cuba during the Spanish-American War (1898–99). After preparatory studies in Chicago, he became an advertising executive. He went back to Elyria, Ohio, where he opened a paint factory. After five years in the business, he came back to Chicago and associated himself with the Chicago Circle of writers. His first novel was *Windy McPherson's Son* (1916), followed by *Marching Men* (1917). His most famous book was a collection of short stories and sketches with interrelated themes, entitled *Winesburg, Ohio* (1919); it was followed by *Poor White* (1920) and *The Triumph of the Egg* (1921). He dealt with the conflict of the individual against organized industrial society. Many critics contend that his short stories contain the best expression of his talent.

Andorra (Principality of Andorra)

Andorra is a small, neutral European coprincipality (formed by a treaty in 1278) situated in the eastern Pyrenees roughly midway between Barcelona, Spain, and Toulouse, France. Historically protective of the right to Andorran citizenship, Andorrans reacted to a modest extension of the franchise in 1933 by staging a mild revolution, which was eventually ended by a force of French gendarmes. In the postwar era, as tourism rapidly developed into the main industry, the non-Andorran (mainly Spanish) population increased. Previously confined to male citizens of the third generation, the franchise was progressively extended to all citizens in the 1970s, although with a higher age qualification for first-generation Andorrans. Under a 1981 constitutional agreement providing for a separation of legislative and executive functions, Andorra's first executive council (government) was formed in January 1982 under the leadership of a prime minister. This office was initially held by Oscar Ribas Reig and after May 1984 by Josep Pintat Solens. The December 1985 elections to the General Council of the Valleys produced, in the absence of formal parties, a mainly conservative new legislature, which confirmed Pintat in his post. In a general election in December 1989, however, Ribas Reig was returned to office. In 1990 Andorra entered the customs union of what would later become the EUROPEAN UNION (EU). Three years later Andorra joined the UN and enacted constitutional reforms that reduced the powers of its two princes and established executive, legislative and judicial branches of the government.

Andrea Doria

Shortly before midnight on July 25, 1956, the 29,083-ton Italian luxury liner *Andrea Doria,* en route from Genoa to New York, was rammed by the 12,644-ton Swedish liner *Stockholm,* en route from New York to Europe. The *Andrea Doria* began taking on water and sank at 10:15 A.M. on July 26. More than 500 survivors were picked up off Nantucket Island by the *Stockholm,* which remained afloat, and returned to New York. The liner *Ile de France* also helped in the rescue, arriving three hours after the collision and taking aboard 753 of the *Doria's* 1,709 passengers and crew. More than 50 passengers died. Both liners in the collision were equipped with RADAR. An investigation later determined that crew members on both ships had made errors that resulted in the collision.

Andreotti, Giulio *(1919–)*

Italian politician. After studying law Andreotti became president of the Catholic Action student movement and a reporter for an underground Christian Democrat newspaper during World War II. Winning election to the Chamber of Deputies in Italy's first postwar election in 1946, he became a protégé of the country's powerful Christian Democratic prime minister, Alcide DE GASPERI. He retained his seat in the chamber from 1946 to 1991, when he was named senator for life. Andreotti held several high posts in Christian Democrat governments. He was prime minister seven times between 1972 and 1992 and foreign minister six times. During his last term as prime minister (1989–92), accusations of corruption and connections to the Mafia led to his political downfall and the erosion of Christian Democratic power. In 1993 he was formally accused of corruption and ties to the Mafia. He was eventually acquitted of all charges and resumed his political career. In 2006 Andreotti was barely defeated for the presidency of the Senate. During his long career he was a staunch supporter of NATO and a devout Catholic.

Andretti, Mario *(1940–)*

Italian-born race car driver. Born in Trieste, Italy, Andretti began driving in the Formula, Jr. class at the age of 13 in Italy. In 1955 his family immigrated to the U.S. In 1965 he captured his first national championship with 3,110 points. In 1966 he repeated as national champion, posting eight wins. In 1969 he won the Indy 500 with a record speed of 156.867 mph and was again national champion. He competed in every Indy 500 from 1965 to 1990 except one and has the record for number of laps driven—7,236. He is second to A. J. FOYT in career victories, with 67. In 1992 Andretti won a pole (one of the stages) at the Michigan International Speedway. A year later he won his last Indy car victory at Phoenix.

Andrew, Bishop Agnellus (*1908–1987*) Pioneer of religious broadcasting on radio and television for the BRITISH BROADCASTING CORPORATION (BBC). He was the first Roman Catholic priest to appear on British television and the first in Europe to become a television producer.

Andrews, Julie (Julia Elizabeth Welles) (*1935–   *) English singer and actress of stage, screen and television, Andrews was born in Walton-on-Thames, a small town west of London. Boasting a full-grown larynx as a child, Andrews quickly became a professional singer and performer. She made her stage debut at 12 in a musical review, and at 19 she became a star in the U.S. in the British musical *The Boy Friend.* Her next stage appearance, in 1956 as Eliza Doolittle in *My Fair Lady,* received glowing reviews in England and the U.S. Andrews triumphed in Lerner and Loewe's *Camelot* and become a popular figure on American TV variety shows. She made her movie debut in the Walt Disney adaptation of the P. L. Travers fantasy, *Mary Poppins* (1964), and won a best actress ACADEMY AWARD. This was followed by a straight role in the antiwar comedy *The Americanization of Emily* (1964). Her most successful film was undeniably *The Sound of Music* (1965), which earned her a second Oscar nomination and brought her "Star of the Year" awards in 1966 and 1967 (voted by the Theater Owners of America). In the late 1960s film projects like *Star* and *Darling Lili* were expensive failures, but her marriage to director Blake Edwards in 1969 led to several pleasing collaborative efforts: *The Tamarind Seed* (1974), *10* (1979), *S.O.B.* (1981) and *Victor/Victoria* (1982), which earned her another Oscar nomination. Andrews continued to appear in films and on television specials and wrote several children's books (as "Julie Andrews Edwards"). In 1995 she returned to Broadway, where she starred in the musical version of *Victor/Victoria.* For her contributions to theater, music and film, Andrews was made a Dame Commander of the British Empire by Queen Elizabeth II in May 2000.

Andrews, Roy Chapman (*1884–1960*) U.S. explorer and scientist. A graduate of Beloit College in Wisconsin (1906), he joined the staff of the American Museum of Natural History in New York, where he specialized in the study of whales and became recognized as the world's top cetologist. In 1914 he became head of the museum's division of Asian exploration, and from 1914 to 1932 Andrews led scientific expeditions to Alaska, northern Korea, Tibet, southwestern China, Burma, northern China and Outer Mongolia. On his 1919 expedition to Central Asia, he was the discoverer of the first known dinosaur eggs, perfectly preserved. He was the first to find evidence of the baluchitherium, the largest known land animal, and made other important discoveries of prehistoric life, including some of the world's largest fossil fields. Andrews was the director of the American Museum of Natural History from 1935 to 1942.

Andreyev, Leonid Nikolayevich (*1871–1919*) Russian author and playwright. He began his career as a lawyer and then turned to journalism. He was a friend of Maxim GORKY, whose influence is evident in his early short stories; his later works show the influence of Dostoyevsky and Tolstoy. In his prime he was regarded as highly as Gorky, but his popularity did not endure. His best-known works include the short stories *The Red Laugh* (1904) and *The Seven Who Were Hanged* (1908) and the plays *To The Stars* (1906) and *Anathema* (1909). While he supported the moderates in the early phases of the RUSSIAN REVOLUTION, he became fiercely anti-BOLSHEVIK and in 1917 fled to Finland, where he died in poverty two years later.

Andrić, Ivo (*1892–1975*) Yugoslavian author and diplomat. Born in the village of Dolac in Bosnia, he joined the revolutionary organization Young Bosnia (Mlada Bosna) while a student in Zagreb. When Gavrilo Princip, another member of the organization, assassinated Archduke Franz Ferdinand in 1914, precipitating WORLD WAR I, Andrić was among those arrested. He spent three years in jail, where he immersed himself in the works of Dostoyevsky and Kierkegaard, which greatly influenced his outlook. After the war he studied languages, history and philosophy at the universities of Zagreb, Vienna, Kraków and Graz. Shortly thereafter he joined the diplomatic corps, serving in various European capitals during the 1920s and 1930s. On the eve of World War II he was in Berlin as Yugoslavia's minister to Germany. He spent the war in Belgrade under German house arrest, and during this time (1941–45) wrote the three novels (known as the Bosnian Trilogy) that made his reputation: *Na Drini ćuprija* (*The Bridge on the Drina,* 1945), *Travnička chrónika* (*Bosnian Chronicle,* 1945), and *Gospodjica* (*The Woman from Sarajevo,* 1945). These works draw on the complex history, cultural diversity and ethnic folklore of his native Bosnia and reflect his fundamentally pessimistic outlook. After the war Andrić, a supporter of Yugoslav premier TITO and was president of the Union of Yugoslav Writers; in the late 1950s he was elected to Yugoslavia's federal assembly. Andrić received the NOBEL PRIZE in literature in 1961. His other works include *Prokleta avlija* (*The Devil's Yard,* 1954) and *Nove pripovetke* (*New Stories,* 1948).

Andropov, Yuri (*1914–1984*) Soviet official and general secretary of the Communist Party (1982–84). Andropov served as ambassador to Hungary (1954–57), where he played a major role in suppressing the HUNGARIAN UPRISING OF 1956. Secretary to the Central Committee of the Communist Party (1957–67), he was subsequently chairman of the KGB (1967–82). In this latter post he became identified with the 1968 invasion of CZECHOSLOVAKIA, the 1979 invasion of AFGHANISTAN and the 1980 military crackdown in POLAND. He became general secretary on BREZHNEV's death in 1982. Although ill health dimmed his brief tenure as party head (and, thus, as top political leader in the USSR), he did initiate a drive for economic reform. His proposal for arms reduction was greeted with skepticism in the West. Andropov's protégé, Mikhail GORBACHEV, would later implement several of his proposed reforms.

Andrzjewski, Jerzy *(1909–1983)* Polish author and political dissident. His best-known novel is *Ashes and Diamonds,* which depicts political struggles in POLAND after World War II; in 1961 the book was made into a widely acclaimed film by Andrzej Wajda. Andrzjewski helped found the Workers' Defense Committee (KOR) in 1976 to aid families of striking workers who were jailed or dismissed from their jobs.

Andy Griffith Show, The Popular American television series noted for its gentle, homespun comedy. Monday nights on CBS, from October 3, 1960, to September 16, 1968, millions of viewers were willingly whisked away to bucolic Mayberry, tucked away in the North Carolina hills. A spinoff of *The Danny Thomas Show,* it portrayed Andy at first as loutish country sheriff (Andy Taylor). With the growing popularity of his bumbling sidekick Barney, Andy mellowed and yielded the floor to a growing cast of outrageous but likable characters: A new series, *Mayberry, R.F.D.,* retained the setting and some of the characters. During the 1980s, former child star Ron Howard, who played Andy Taylor's son Opie, emerged as a successful HOLLYWOOD director.

Anfinsen, Christian Boehmer *(1916–1995)* American biochemist. Anfinsen was educated at Swarthmore College, the University of Pennsylvania and Harvard University, where he obtained his Ph.D. in 1943. He taught at Harvard Medical School from 1943 to 1950, when he moved to the National Heart Institute at Bethesda, Maryland, where from 1952 to 1962 he served as head of the laboratory of cellular physiology. In 1963 Anfinsen joined the National Institute of Arthritis and Metabolic Diseases at Bethesda, where he was appointed head of the laboratory of chemical biology. Anfinsen was concerned with the shape and structure of the enzyme ribonuclease and the forces that permit it always to adopt the same unique configuration. He found that the minimum of chemical intervention—merely putting the enzyme into a favorable environment—was sufficient to induce the ribonuclease to adopt the one configuration that restores enzymatic activity. From this

observation Anfinsen drew the important conclusion that the protein's sequence of amino acids—its primary structure—must contain all the information for the assembly of the three-dimensional protein. He went on to show similar behavior in other proteins. For this work Anfinsen shared the 1972 NOBEL PRIZE in physiology or medicine with Moore and Stein.

Ángeles, Victoria de los *(1923–2005)* Spanish soprano. Born in Barcelona, de los Ángeles studied at the Instituto Balmes and the Conservatorio del Liceo. She made her concert debut at the Barcelona Conservatory in 1946 and her operatic debut at the Teatro Lirico, Barcelona, as the Countess in *The Marriage of Figaro.* After successful European and South American tours, she made her American debut at CARNEGIE HALL in 1950. She performed with the Metropolitan Opera from 1950 to 1961. De los Ángeles performed at Bayreuth, Covent Garden and other leading theaters and festivals throughout the world. She is noted for her exquisitely lyrical voice, her superb musicianship and her extensive command of the operatic repertoire.

Angel Island Island in California's San Francisco Bay. During WORLD WAR II, it was the site of both a U.S. military base and an immigration intake station, as well as a camp for PRISONERS OF WAR.

Angell, Sir Norman (Ralph Norman Angell Lane) *(1873–1967)* British writer and peace activist. Born in Lincolnshire, Angell was educated in England, France and Switzerland. In 1891 he traveled to the U.S., where he took odd jobs and worked as a journalist in various cities. Settling in Paris in 1898, he became the editor of the Paris edition of London's *Daily Mail* and wrote *The Grand Illusion* (1910, rev. ed. 1933), a widely celebrated book that pointed out, in economic terms, the interdependence of nations and the stupidity of war. In 1913 the periodical *War and Peace* was established to disseminate his views. Angell's concepts of an international association were instrumental in the formation of the LEAGUE OF NATIONS. In 1934 he was awarded the NOBEL PRIZE for peace. Angell was opposed to the

British policies of APPEASEMENT toward Nazi Germany, Japan and Italy, views he articulated in *Peace with the Dictators?* (1938). During World War II he worked in the U.S. to seek support for the British war effort, remaining in New York City until 1951. Returning to England, he continued to write and to work for the cause of international peace.

Angelou, Maya (Marguerite Ann Johnson) *(1928–)* American memoirist and poet. Born in St. Louis, Angelou is best known for four volumes of autobiography: *I Know Why the Caged Bird Sings* (1970), *Gather Together in My Name* (1974), *Singin' and Swingin' and Gettin' Merry Like Christmas* (1976) and *The Heart of a Woman* (1981). Her memoirs describe the small, rural black community of her childhood, her struggles to support herself as a young unwed mother in San Francisco, her burgeoning theatrical career and her experiences with the black liberation movement in the 1960s and as a writer and administrator in Africa. Her poetry, which has been less successful than her powerful and engaging prose, ranges from love lyrics to harsh public condemnation of racism in America. She has also produced and acted in a number of plays. On January 20, 1993, Angelou read her poem "On the Pulse of Morning" at the inauguration of President Bill CLINTON. In 2000 she received the National Medal of Arts.

Anghelis, Odysseus *(1912–1987)* Greek military leader. He was a leading member of the military junta that ruled GREECE from 1967 to 1974 (see GREEK COLONELS). After the junta was overthrown, he was sentenced to 20 years in Korydallos Prison, where he later committed suicide.

Angleton, James Jesus *(1917–1987)* U.S. intelligence officer. He joined the CENTRAL INTELLIGENCE AGENCY (CIA) at its inception in 1947 and served for more than 20 years as the head of its counterintelligence office, whose purpose was to protect the agency from infiltration by foreign agents. Over the years his efforts to unmask Soviet agents came to be regarded as overzealous, and at the end of 1974 he was forced to resign his post. With his departure from the CIA, the agency cut its counterintelligence staff from

300 to 80 and moved away from some of the techniques he had introduced.

Anglo-Egyptian Sudan Former British colony, now the country of SUDAN in northeastern Africa. Jointly ruled by Egypt and Great Britain from 1899, in practice real control was exercised by the British. Sudanese resistance persisted, even after Britain established North and South Sudan as separate colonial entities. In 1952 an agreement in principle was reached to establish Sudan's independence, which was accomplished in 1956.

Anglo-French Entente See ENTENTE CORDIALE.

Anglo-Irish Civil War of 1916–1923 Irish nationalism generated by the Anglo-Irish Union of 1800 led to the British granting home rule in 1914 but postponing it until 1920 because of WORLD WAR I. Frustrated, the Irish began the final phase of their struggle against the British in the unsuccessful 1916 EASTER RISING. After executing the rebel leaders, the British tried to achieve an all-Ireland consensus through an Irish National Convention (1917). However, announcement of Irish conscription (1918)—a never-fulfilled plan—resulted in Irish terrorism and political resistance. SINN FÉIN, an Irish political society, won 73 parliamentary seats assigned to the Irish; they refused to go to London and instead set up the DÁIL Eireann (Irish Assembly). The British promptly arrested 36 members of the society, but the remaining 37 ratified the Irish republic proclaimed during the Easter Rising. A provisional Irish government was established, and the IRISH REPUBLICAN ARMY (IRA) and the Irish Volunteers engaged in two and a half years of guerrilla warfare (called "the Troubles" by the Irish) against the Royal Irish Constabulary (Black and Tans). The republicans were supported by the public, Irish Americans and isolated heroic acts like the Lord Mayor of Cork's successful 1920 hunger strike. The British government was slowly conciliated; after granting a separate Irish parliament in 1920, Sinn Féin took almost all seats. A truce led to an Anglo-Irish Treaty, opposed by both Ulster (NORTHERN IRELAND) and

Dublin (EIRE) because it split the country. Fighting broke out between protruce and antitruce factions within the IRA. Granted both free state and dominion status (1921), Dublin finally accepted the partition and became the capital of the IRISH FREE STATE in 1922. However, fighting continued into the following year.

Anglo-Russian Entente An agreement signed in St. Petersburg on August 31, 1907, that laid down English and Russian spheres of interest in Persia, England taking the Persian Gulf and Russia the north of Persia. The aim was to keep a check on German expansion in the Near East. The entente formed a link in the ENTENTE CORDIALE among England, France and Russia and was a basis for the Allied coalition in WORLD WAR I.

Angola (People's Republic of Angola) Angola is situated on the west coast of Africa, south of the equator, and has an area of 481,226 square

miles. The frontiers of Angola were fixed by the conventions of 1891, following the 1884–85 Congress of Berlin, which had divided the map of Africa among the colonial powers. PORTUGAL, which had established a lucrative slave-trading presence on the coast in the 16th century, was granted rights of occupation over Angola, but Portuguese rule did not effectively begin until 1910–20. Following the overthrow of the Portuguese Republic in 1926 and the establishment of Dr. Antonio SALAZAR's Estado Novo four years later, the decentralization policy of the early colonial period ended and was replaced by a system whereby the interests of the colonies were more directly subjugated to the immediate interest of Portugal, eventually leading to a rebellion in Luanda in February 1961. Severe repression followed, but armed resistance to Portuguese rule in Angola was under way. In the 13 years until April 1974, when a military coup in Lisbon led directly to the ending of the Portuguese colonial wars, the na-

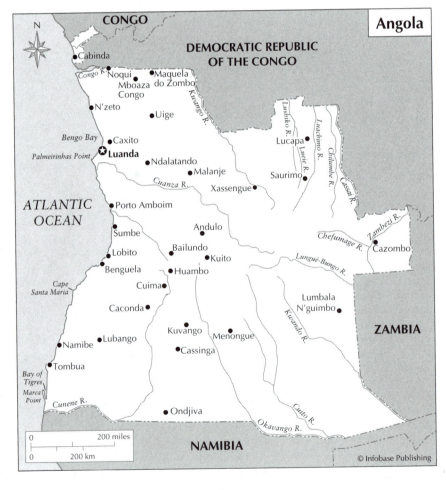

ANGOLA

1954–74	Rival rebel groups MPLA, FNLA and UNITA fight Portuguese rule.
1975	Portugal grants Angolan independence; MPLA takes power, forms Marxist-Leninist government and establishes ties to SWAPO movement in Namibia.
1976	UNITA calls on U.S. blacks to come and fight for "liberty"; one American and three British mercenaries executed despite U.S. and UK appeals for clemency.
1988	Namibian independence linked to Cuban troop withdrawal in Brazzaville Accord.
1990	Angolan government and UNITA rebels agree to cease-fire; ruling party adopts "democratic socialism."
1991	Rivals sign peace agreement in Portugal (Bicesse Accords).
1994	New peace accords signed (Lusaka Accords).
2002	UNITA leader Jonas Savimbi killed; UNITA and government agree to another cease-fire.
2003	Fernando da Piedade Días dos Santos (Nando) appointed prime minister, ending a three-year vacancy of the post.

tionalist guerrilla armies were able to establish military and political control over large parts of eastern Angola and to press westward toward the country's central and western districts.

Three nationalist movements were involved in the struggle for independence. The Popular Movement for the Liberation of Angola (Movimento Popular de Libertação de Angola—MPLA) was formed in December 1956 with the aim of ending colonial rule and building a new and unified society. It was led by Agostinho NETO. The National Front of Angolan Liberation (Frente Nacional de Libertação de Angola—FNLA), essentially a tribalist movement, was formed in 1962, operating in the north of the country and led by Holden Roberto. The National Union for the Total Independence of Angola (Uniao Nacional para a Independencia Total de Angola—UNITA) was formed in 1966 under Dr. Jonas SAVIMBI, operating mainly in eastern Angola.

Following the military coup in Portugal a tripartite transitional government was formed by the three nationalist movements, but armed conflict soon broke out between the MPLA and the others (see ANGOLAN CIVIL WAR). A socialist regime was established; in December 1977 the MPLA was restructured as a Marxist-Leninist party, with the state becoming an instrument of the party. President Neto died on September 10, 1979, and was succeeded by MPLA veteran José Eduardo DOS SANTOS. Elections to the assembly were held in 1980 and 1986, but political power remained firmly in the control of the 90-member central committee and the 15-member political bureau of the MPLA.

South African incursions into Angola continued sporadically until August 1988, despite a formal withdrawal in April 1985 following the signing of the Lusaka Accord in February 1984. South Africa also continued to provide logistical backing to UNITA as the latter waged a guerrilla campaign against the Angolan government. The U.S. Congress in June 1985 voted to repeal the Clark Amendment (enacted in 1976), which prohibited U.S. military and financial support for UNITA.

As part of the peace process designed to bring independence to Namibia, South African forces were finally withdrawn from Angola on August 30, 1988, and under a U.S.-mediated agreement signed in New York on December 22, 1988, Cuba and Angola agreed on a gradual and total withdrawal of the estimated 50,000 Cuban troops from Angola, while South Africa agreed to withdraw from Namibia to allow free elections to be held there prior to independence. In December 1988 the Angolan government offered a one-year amnesty to UNITA supporters, but this was rejected by the UNITA leadership. President dos Santos had declared in mid-1987 that the war against UNITA and its South African backers had cost Angola $12 billion in terms of economic sabotage, 60,000 citizens killed and 600,000 displaced.

In 1991 the Angolan Civil War ended as a result of the Bicesse Accords, in which both the MPLA and UNITA agreed to a cease-fire, the creation of a national Angolan army integrating both MPLA and UNITA officers, and scheduling elections for 1992. However, the UNITA presidential candidate, Savimbi, alleged that the voting was fraudulent, and the civil war resumed. The 1994 Lusaka Accords, produced by UNITA and MPLA leaders, again brought peace to Angola by calling for Savimbi and MPLA leader dos Santos to form a government of national unity. However, hostilities continued between the government and UNITA members, and a renewed civil war began in 1998. In February 2002 Savimbi was killed by government forces. Two months later, the government and UNITA signed a third cease-fire.

Angolan Civil War (1975–2002) When the Popular Movement for the Liberation of Angola (MPLA) gained control of the government of Angola in 1976 (see ANGOLAN WAR OF INDEPENDENCE), UNITA and the FNLA refused to recognize the new Marxist-oriented government. In 1977 the MPLA captured UNITA's major stronghold and drove its leaders into ZAIRE and ZAMBIA. UNITA regrouped and revived its guerrilla activities. It was aided by South African and Portuguese white mercenaries and by covert American arms. In the early 1980s UNITA had extended its control over central and southeastern Angola. UNITA also won support from Great Britain, France, the U.S., Saudi Arabia and several African nations. The MPLA was backed by the USSR and Cuba. Continual warfare disrupted the Angolan economy and displaced one-sixth of its people, many of whom became refugees in Zaire, Zambia and the Congo. In 1988 Cuba, Angola and South Africa signed accords that promised the departure of all Cuban troops by July 1991. Cuban withdrawal began in 1989. After the 1991 signing of the Bicesse Accords, the Angolan Civil War continued sporadically. Although Bicesse and the later Lusaka Accords established periods of peace in Angola from 1991 to 1992 and from 1994 to 1998, they failed to develop a permanent peace between the MPLA government and the UNITA rebels, as fighting occurred between 1992 and 1994, and 1998 and 2002. In April 2002 the government and UNITA agreed to a third cease-fire arrangement, after UNITA leader Jonas SAVIMBI was killed by government troops.

Angolan War of Independence

(1961–1976) The Marxist Popular Movement for the Liberation of Angola (MPLA) revolted against Portuguese rule in the capital of Portuguese West Africa in February 1961. About a month later the moderate Union of Peoples of Angola (UPA) joined the rebellion in the north. The rebels were suppressed, and an estimated 20,000 black Africans were killed in the fighting. The MPLA shifted its activities to the country's eastern section, where it waged guerrilla campaigns from bases in neighboring ZAMBIA. In 1966 the UPA split into two prowestern groups, the socialist Front for the Liberation of Angola (FNLA) and the National Union for the Total Independence of Angola (UNITA), which moved its guerrilla operations into the south-central region. The antigovernment forces confined their actions to ambushes and hit-and-run attacks, but they tied down a sizable Portuguese force. By the late 1960s half of PORTUGAL's national budget was being spent on its armed forces in Africa (see GUINEA-BISSAUAN WAR OF INDEPENDENCE; MOZAMBIQUE). Many

young Portuguese officers came to resent the unrelieved bush fighting and the inefficiency of the bureaucracy running the war in Lisbon. In April 1974 they toppled the national government and installed a leftist regime that was willing to relinquish Portuguese West Africa once an orderly succession could be ensured. Twice the three main liberation movements formed a coalition government, and twice the coalitions collapsed. When the Portuguese finally withdrew in November 1975, they left a country divided by civil war, with UNITA and the FNLA pitted against the MPLA. The MPLA held the capital and received Soviet aid and Cuban soldiers, which turned the tide in its favor. Although South African forces and American supplies came to the aid of FNLA and UNITA, the MPLA seized control of the government (February 1976) and was recognized by the ORGANIZATION OF AFRICAN UNITY (OAU) as the legitimate authority in newly independent ANGOLA. Portuguese colonialism in Africa had ended. (See also ANGOLAN CIVIL WAR.)

Angry Young Men

A term coined in the mid-1950s to describe several young British writers including Kingsley AMIS, John BRAINE and John OSBORNE, among others, whose works are characterized by their protagonists' anarchistic, antiestablishment views, lower middle-class origins, restlessness and sense of social ostracism. Among the most notable and representative works fitting this description are Amis's LUCKY JIM, Braine's Room at the Top, Osborne's Look Back in Anger and John WAIN's Hurry on Down. Ironically, most of the Angry Young Men resisted the label, and several of them later became figures of the establishment. The name is believed to have been taken from the book Angry Young Men (1951) by Irish writer Leslie Paul.

Anheuser, Eberhard

(1880–1963) U.S. businessman. He formed a partnership with Adolphus Busch in 1896 and purchased a bankrupt St. Louis brewery. Together they developed a method of brewing beer without pasteurization and pioneered in bottling beer. Anheuser began serving as chairman of the board in 1950.

Animal Farm

An allegorical satire of the aftermath of the RUSSIAN REVOLUTION, the novel by George ORWELL describes the revolt of the animals on a farm and their overthrow of their human keepers. The clever pigs seize power and are soon corrupted by it; their slogan is "All animals are equal, but some animals are more equal than others." The calculating, tyrannical pig Napoleon, who represents Josef STALIN, ousts the more idealistic Snowball, who represents Leon TROTSKY. The kind-hearted horse Boxer symbolizes the strength, goodness and innocence of the common man, and is eventually crushed by the despotic government imposed by the pigs.

animal rights movement

The modern animal rights movement dates from the publication of Animal Liberation (1975) by Peter Singer, a philosophy lecturer at University College, Oxford. Singer documented inhumane conditions under which animals were used as subjects for medical experiments and in which they were kept on so-called factory farms. According to Singer, research animals were subjected to extreme pain and distress in the course of cruel "experiments," while farm animals were confined for their entire lives in small, crowded pens. Subsequent investigations, reported in newspapers and magazines and on television, have periodically uncovered similar stories. The animal rights movement seeks to stop these practices and to ensure that all animals can live natural, healthy lives. However, animal rights activists have sometimes crossed the line into activity that the law may deem criminal. This often involves releasing animals from cages where they are confined; it has occasionally extended to bombing or otherwise damaging facilities where animals are allegedly mistreated. Most medical researchers defend experiments on animals, claiming that important medical advances that save human lives would not be possible without such experiments, and charging that animal rights activists are naive in their assumptions about the use of animals for such testing. While the animal rights movement has not developed the sort of political influence that other contemporary rights movements (for African Americans, women, homosexuals, the disabled and other minorities, for example) have come to enjoy, it has received public attention and has helped to change many people's attitudes toward the treatment of animals, particularly in the U.S., Britain and western Europe. For example, many people now find the purchase and wearing of fur coats unacceptable; many boycott specific products, such as brands of shampoo or cologne, whose development involved animal testing; still others have become vegetarians.

animated film Animated film creates the illusion of life in static drawings and inanimate objects by adapting graphic arts techniques to the film process. Animation is produced by a progressive build-up of images, frame by frame, using one of several methods, such as "cel animation" or "silhouette animation," to make each frame and link them together. The introduction of a computerized animation process by Bell Telephone Company in the mid-1960s revolutionized animation. Walt Disney Studio has produced the best-known animated films, from short cartoons featuring such characters as MICKEY MOUSE to the full-length *Snow White and the Seven Dwarfs*. The memorable animated images of Disney's *FANTASIA* (1941) reflect the mood of particular works of classical music. Animated films are also used in television commercials, industrial presentations and in education. In more recent years several Eastern European countries took animation in another direction by using fable and myth to deal with serious subjects. Although computer-animated graphics began to be used in the 1980s, it was not until the 1990s that this new technology began to appear in animated films, such as Disney's *Beauty and the Beast* (1991) and *Aladdin* (1992). In 1995 Disney and Pixar Studios, a firm that specialized in computer-generated imagery (CGI), released *Toy Story*, the first feature film completely composed of CGI. The popularity of CGI films led to the 2001 creation of the Academy Award for best animated feature.

Ankara (Angora) Capital of TURKEY, at the juncture of the Ankara and Cubuk Rivers. In 1920 it was established as the nationalist capital by Kemal ATATÜRK, and in 1923 it became the official capital of the Republic of Turkey.

Annan, Kofi *(1938–)* UNITED NATIONS secretary-general (1996–). Born in Kumasi, Ghana, to an aristocratic family, Annan attended Kumasi's University of Science and Technology and Manchester College in the U.S., where he graduated with a degree in economics in 1961. He spent the next two years at the Institut universitaire des hautes études internationales in Geneva, where he took graduate courses in economics. Leaving his studies in 1963, Annan began work for the UN as a budget officer for the Geneva offices of the WORLD HEALTH ORGANIZATION. In addition to serving other divisions of the UN, such as its Economic Commission for Africa, and its Emergency Force in Ismalia, Egypt, Annan attended the Massachusetts Institute of Technology where in 1972, as a Sloan Fellow, he received his M.S. in management. Annan's management skills aided him greatly in his duties as UN High Commissioner for Refugees, assistant secretary general for human resources management and security coordinator, and assistant secretary general for program planning, budget and finance control. His experience in the field of preserving refugees served him well in 1990 when then secretary general Javier PÉREZ DE CUÉLLAR asked him to supervise the repatriation of more than 900 foreign nationals from Iraq. After the defeat of Iraq in 1991, he established a program in which proceeds from Iraqi oil would provide humanitarian aid for Iraqi citizens. Annan also served under then secretary general Boutros BOUTROS-GALI as assistant secretary general for peacekeeping operations in 1992–93 and as undersecretary general in 1993–96. In the latter post he increased the size and scope of UN peacekeeping operations and participated in the creation of the 1995 DAYTON AGREEMENT. In 1996, following the U.S. veto of a second term for Boutros-Galli, Annan was elected secretary general. He was reelected by the General Assembly and Security Council in 2001. As secretary general, Annan has championed a variety of issues, such as an increased international commitment to improving the economic situation in Africa, the independence of East Timor, the Israeli withdrawal from Lebanon, and a renewed international effort to contain and reduce the AIDS epidemic. His reputation was tarnished after the U.S.-led invasion of Iraq in 2003, when evidence surfaced about his son Kojo's relationship with a Swiss firm that won a lucrative contract to oversee relief efforts in Iraq. Though an investigation found no proof that the secretary-general had influenced the procurement process in favor of the company, critics of his leadership called for his resignation.

Anouilh, Jean-Marie-Lucien-Pierre *(1910–1987)* French playwright. Anouilh first achieved international popularity with theater audiences through the success of his modern adaptation of *Antigone* (1944), from the classic Greek tragedy by Sophocles. Born in the Bordeaux region, Anouilh began his career as a playwright in the 1930s and continued to produce plays at a prolific rate for over five decades. Anouilh cannot easily be linked with any particular school or trend in the modern theater. Rather, he maintained an intellectual independence that showed itself in the sheer diversity of his works, which ranged in tone from high drama to absurdist farce. His plays frequently dealt with the themes of loss of idealistic innocence and the societal pressures that dictate compromise of one's most cherished values. Other major plays by Anouilh include *The Traveller Without Baggage* (1937), *Point of Departure* (1942), *Ring Round the Moon* (1947), *The Rehearsal* (1950), *The Waltz of the Toreadors* (1952), *Medea* (1953) and *Becket, or the Honour of God* (1959).

Anschluss German term for the 1938 union of Austria with Germany. Favored by German-speaking subjects of the failed Hapsburg monarchy, by German nationalists and by Austrians who wished to expand their country's status after World War I, it was forbidden by the terms of the Treaties of VERSAILLES and St. Germain (both 1919). Demands for *Anschluss* became insistent with the ascendancy of Adolf HITLER as German chancellor in 1933. It was accomplished in March 1938, when Hitler occupied Austria and incorporated it into Germany as a province. The *Anschluss* was annulled by the Allied powers in 1943 when they also agreed on the establishment of an independent Austria after WORLD WAR II; Austria was formally recognized in 1946.

Ansermet, Ernest *(1883–1969)* Swiss conductor and founder of the L'Orchestre de la Suisse Romande, renowned for his interpretations of Russian and French ballet music. Ansermet was born into a musical family in Vevey in the French-speaking region of Switzerland. After several years spent teaching mathematics in Geneva and Lausanne, he turned to music and from 1919 to 1923 conducted the BALLETS RUSSES of Serge DIAGHILEV. He led world premieres of many important works, including Maurice RAVEL's *La Valse* and Manuel de FALLA's *The Three-Cornered Hat*. In 1922 he gave the first performance in Germany of Igor STRAVINSKY's *Le Sacre du printemps*. In 1918 he founded the L'Orchestre de la Suisse Romande with which he would be linked for the next 50 years. His extensive recording career began in 1929. His most notable records were made with Decca, beginning in 1946. Never wholly comfortable with the German repertoire, Ansermet specialized in the ballet music of Stravinsky, Ravel, BARTOK, PROKOFIEV and DEBUSSY. His cool temperament and precise, elegant sensitivity to textures made him the ideal interpreter of these scores. He regarded the atonal ambitions of Arnold SCHOENBERG with hostility and expressed his distrust of these contemporary directions in his book, *The Foundations of Music in the Human Consciousness* (1916). His lifelong conviction was that the spirit of the composer, not the temperament of the conductor, should be observed.

Antarctica Southernmost continent, encompassing the South Pole and composed of two major landmasses joined and overlayed by an ice cap thousands of feet thick. Within the Antarctic Circle, it has the coldest climate on Earth. The first permanent base was established by Norwegian naturalist Carsten E. Borchgrevink in 1899. A major expedition from 1907 to 1909, led by British explorer Sir Ernest SHACKLETON, resulted in the discovery of the magnetic South Pole and the first ascent of Mount Erebus, one of the tallest volcanoes on Earth. On December 14, 1911, Norwegian explorer Roald AMUNDSEN became the first person to reach the South Pole. He was followed, a month later, by British naval officer Robert F. SCOTT. Airplanes were first used for exploration in the 1920s. Sir Hubert Wilkins of Britain became the first person to fly over the continent in 1928, while Americans Richard E. BYRD and Bernt Balchen became the first to fly over the South Pole itself in 1929, and American Lincoln ELLSWORTH the first pilot to traverse the entire continent in 1936. In 1958–59, Sir Vivian FUCHS of Britain made the first complete overland crossing. In 1989–90, an international team led by Will Steger made the first crossing by dogsled. Since the 1930s numerous claims have been made by various nations as to control of Antarctic territory. The U.S. has refrained from such claims and recognizes none made by other countries. Antarctica has become the site of several major scientific research stations. The Antarctic Treaty of 1959 was signed by 12 nations that participated in the 1957–58 INTERNATIONAL GEOPHYSICAL YEAR. In the late 1980s Antarctica again became a subject of international debate between those who wished to exploit its natural resources and those who favored leaving the continent in its natural state.

Antheil, George *(1900–1959)* American composer, pianist and writer whose music in the 1920s was an important force in the avant-garde. He was born in Trenton, New Jersey, of German-Polish ancestry. His early musical studies were with Ernest BLOCH and at the Settlement School in Philadelphia (renamed the Curtis Institute). He toured London, Berlin and Paris in the early 1920s as a pianist-composer. He earned the nickname "the Bad Boy of Music" because of his iconoclastic music, feisty manner and the loaded .32 automatic revolver he reputedly kept in his coat pocket to master unruly audiences. His *Mechanisms* (later renamed *Ballet Mecanique*) caused a riot in 1923. This "Message to Mars," as he called it, utilized 10 pianos, bells, sirens and an airplane propeller to create a cold, hard, precise sound—a prophecy and a warning about the impending mechanization of society. He injected jazz idioms into his opera, *Transatlantic* (1930), and contemporary "pop" music into his six symphonies. After 1933 Antheil spent much of his time in HOLLYWOOD, writing a column on music and the movies and scoring many motion pictures, including *The Plainsman* (1937), *In a Lonely Place* (1952) and *The Pride and the Passion* (1955). A man of diverse interests, he also wrote mystery stories under the pen name Stacey Bishop and studied electronics and criminology. His importance as a composer stems largely from the pre-Hollywood period. He was an innovator in the use of sounds produced by nonmusical instruments. "I have only used these sounds because they are part of the musical sound of our modern life," he wrote, ". . . as steel and aluminum are now part of the material of modern buildings." Before his death he wrote an opera and a ballet for the new medium of television—*Volpone* and *Capital of the World* (both 1953).

Anti-Comintern Pact A five-year agreement for mutual defense against communist subversive activities; signed by Germany and Japan on November 24, 1936, and later joined by Italy (1937). The Western democracies held that the pact was designed to dominate Europe rather than to combat COMMUNISM. From 1939 to 1941 other countries, including Bulgaria, Finland, Hungary, Romania, Slovakia and Spain, signed the pact.

Antigua and Barbuda The nation of Antigua and Barbuda consists of three islands in the eastern Caribbean, along the outer rim of the West Indies' Leeward Islands chain. Antigua, formerly a British colony, saw universal adult suffrage introduced in 1951, when the Antigua Labour Party (ALP), the political arm of the Antigua Trade and Labour Union, led by Vere Bird, won all eight elective seats on the Legislative Council. A system of ministerial government was introduced in 1956, and in 1960 Bird became chief minister. The territory became an "associate state" in 1967, with full internal government. The ALP lost the 1971 general election to the opposition Progressive Labour Movement, and George Walter became premier. The ALP regained power at

ANTIGUA AND BARBUDA

1958	The Leeward Islands Federation becomes the West Indies Federation.
1967	Antigua and Barbuda becomes an associated state within the Commonwealth.
1971	Progressive Labor Movement wins elections with George Walter as prime minister.
1976	ALP regains power and remains in power for the rest of the century.
1981	Antigua and Barbuda becomes a sovereign state.
1993	Lester Bird succeeds his father as prime minister.
1995	Hurricane Luis damages or destroys at least 75% of homes in Antigua and Barbuda, causing an estimated $300 million worth of damage.
1996	To improve its tarnished antinarcotics image, Antigua establishes an office to control illicit drugs.
1997	Antigua and Barbuda takes steps to eliminate money laundering and organized crime within its borders, closing 11 offshore banks and initiating legislation to close loopholes used by international criminal organizations.
1999	Lester Bird of the Antigua Labour Party is reelected for a sixth term.
2004	Baldwin Spencer of the United Progressive Party is elected prime minister.

elections in 1976 and, after elections in 1980, opened negotiations with Britain for full independence. Opposition to independence came from the island of Barbuda, which wanted greater autonomy for itself. The territory became an independent state within the COMMONWEALTH on November 1, 1981. Bird became the first prime minister. In the early 1990s the Bird family experienced two setbacks to its control of Antigua and Barbuda. In 1991 Vere Bird, Jr., was removed from his position in the national government on charges of gun smuggling. Two years later, his father resigned as prime minister amid allegations of corruption and was succeeded by another son, Lester. Lester Bird remained prime minister from 1993 to 2004, when he lost to Baldwin Spencer of the United Progressive Party.

Anti-Party Group Crisis The Anti-Party was the name given by Soviet premier Nikita KHRUSHCHEV to large and inefficient central ministries that, he felt, were usurping the COMMUNIST PARTY's role in industry. Members of the group included MALENKOV, MOLOTOV and KAGANOVICH. In meetings of the central committee and the Supreme Soviet, seven members of the Presidium had remained silent, forming a majority against Khrushchev and calling on him to resign as first secretary. Khrushchev refused and rallied his supporters. On June 22, 1957, the vast majority of central committee members supported Khrushchev, the Anti-Party group was defeated and a new Presidium of the USSR elected.

anti-Semitism Prejudice against JEWS. Anti-Semitism had a religious basis until the 19th century. The liberalization of western Europe in the 18th century, brought on by the Enlightenment and the French Revolution, resulted in the emancipation of Europe's Jews and the granting of legal and religious freedoms. Subsequent 19th-century prejudices were based on theories that saw Jews as a distinct and inferior race and nationalist concerns, especially where Jews formed a large minority. In czarist RUSSIA, ROMANIA, POLAND and HUNGARY, attacks on Jews, known as POGROMS, were organized and deadly. Pseudoscientific theories of ARYAN racial superiority and Jewish inferiority, espoused by the French ethnologist J. A. Gobineau (1816–82) and the Anglo-German Houston Stewart CHAMBERLAIN, were important in the formation of racist policies.

In GERMANY, Adolf HITLER and his NAZI Party advocated the idea of an Aryan "master race" and targeted Jews as scapegoats for Germany's misfortunes after World War I. German anti-Semitism was codified in the Nuremberg Laws of 1935, and Jewish property was confiscated in 1938. Ultimately, Germany's official FINAL SOLUTION resulted in the extermination of some 6 million Jews in the HOLOCAUST. After WORLD WAR II anti-Semitism was particularly prevalent in USSR, where continued persecution in the 1950s, 1960s and 1970s led to large-scale immigration of Jews to ISRAEL and the U.S. Anti-Semitism remains a factor in the Middle East, where it is related to the ongoing Arab-Israeli conflict. With the waning of the Soviet empire in Russia and Eastern Europe in the late 1980s and early 1990s and the concurrent rise of religious orthodoxy and political nationalism, anti-Semitism again became a serious problem in Europe. As Germany moved toward unification in 1990 and the Soviet Union disintegrated in 1991, some observers worried that a renewal of nationalism within a united Germany and the independent republics of the former Soviet Union would lead to a revival of anti-Semitism. While these fears were not borne out, sympathy for the plight of the Palestinians and antagonism toward Israel led to several anti-Semitic acts in countries with large Muslim populations, such as France.

antiwar movement Term generally used for the movement that developed in the U.S. in opposition to American involvement in the VIETNAM WAR. The earliest dissent originated with foreign

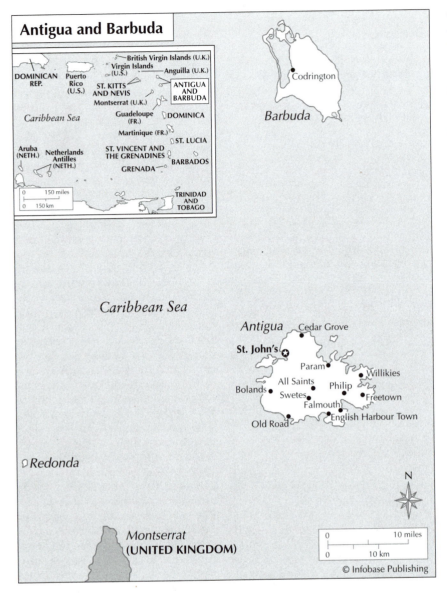

Antigua and Barbuda

British Virgin Islands (U.K.)
Virgin Islands (U.S.)
DOMINICAN REP.
Puerto Rico (U.S.)
Anguilla (U.K.)
ST. KITTS AND NEVIS
ANTIGUA AND BARBUDA
Montserrat (U.K.)
Caribbean Sea
Guadeloupe (FR.)
DOMINICA
Martinique (FR.)
ST. LUCIA
Aruba (NETH.)
Netherlands Antilles (NETH.)
ST. VINCENT AND THE GRENADINES
BARBADOS
GRENADA
TRINIDAD AND TOBAGO

0   150 miles
0   150 km

Codrington
Barbuda

Caribbean Sea

Antigua
Cedar Grove
St. John's
Param
Willikies
All Saints
Philip
Bolands
Swetes
Freetown
Falmouth
Old Road
English Harbour Town

Redonda

Montserrat
(UNITED KINGDOM)

N

0   10 miles
0   10 km

© Infobase Publishing

policy experts who saw little of vital interest for the U.S. in Southeast Asia. Opposition among private citizens was first manifested by pacifists and social activists. Many of these early opponents spoke at college campuses, where a core of student activists against the war was formed. Gaining momentum after President JOHNSON's escalation of the war in 1965, the movement came to encompass a large and vocal segment of the American population. The first college "teach-in" was held at the University of Michigan, Ann Arbor, in March 1965, with such events occurring regularly at colleges and universities thereafter. That same year a number of organizations and peace coalitions were formed to try to put an end to the war: the Women's Strike for Peace, Committee for a Sane Nuclear Policy (SANE) and the Vietnam Day Committee. Their tactics varied from peaceful marches to draft-card burnings.

By 1967 a radical and confrontational segment had formed, helping to create the mass march on the Pentagon in October 1967, student takeovers of university buildings at various campuses and the bloody riots outside the Democratic Convention in Chicago in August 1968. As war casualties rose and the cost increased, a credibility gap arose between the Johnson administration and the American public. The TET OFFENSIVE of 1968 lent momentum to the antiwar movement, and vocal el-

ements within the public, Congress and the media all pressed for an end to the war. Within the DEMOCRATIC PARTY, Senators Eugene MCCARTHY and Robert KENNEDY entered the 1968 presidential primaries as antiwar candidates. This opposition forced Johnson from the White House and helped to defeat his heir, Hubert HUMPHREY, and to elect Richard NIXON, who claimed to have a secret plan to finish the war.

In January 1969 the first Moratorium Against the War was held in a number of U.S. cities, and public opposition grew after the KENT STATE killings in 1970. The Nixon administration felt besieged as the antiwar movement grew, and pressure increased with the publication of the PENTAGON PAPERS in 1971. Two mass bombings of Hanoi in 1972 brought further criticism from press and public alike. Vice President Spiro AGNEW vociferously denounced the antiwar protesters as left-wing radicals, and Nixon himself appealed to what he called the "silent majority," those who did not protest but who patriotically supported the government. The movement quieted as Nixon deescalated the war, and it was finally silenced when South Vietnam fell in 1975.

Arguments continue as to the antiwar movement's effectiveness and its motives; some critics of the movement have charged that it undermined the U.S. war effort, giving aid and comfort to the Vietnamese communists and thus contributing directly to the perceived U.S. defeat and the eventual communist takeover of all of Vietnam.

Antonescu, Ion (1882–1946) Romanian dictator during WORLD WAR II. A military officer, he served in World War I and was briefly chief of the general staff (1937). Pro-NAZI and supported by the fascist Iron Guard and the German government, he was appointed premier by King CAROL II in 1940. He quickly forced the king's abdication, and Antonescu ruled Romania in the name of Carol's young son King Michael. During his four years in power, Antonescu allied Romania with the AXIS powers, giving HITLER virtual control over the country. On August 23, 1944, with Soviet troops at Romania's borders, King Michael seized control of the government and arrested Antonescu. Tried for war crimes, he was condemned and executed on June 1, 1946.

Antoniadi, Eugene Michael *(1870–1944)* Greek-French astronomer. Antoniadi established quite early a reputation as a brilliant observer and in 1893 was invited by Camille Flammarion to work at his observatory at Juvisy near Paris. From 1909 Antoniadi worked mainly with the 33-inch refracting telescope at the observatory at Meudon. He became a French citizen in 1928. In his two works *La Planète Mars* (1930) and *La Planète Mercure* (1934) Antoniadi published the results of many years' observations and presented the best maps of Mars and Mercury to appear until the space probes of recent times. He took a strong line regarding Mars: "Nobody has ever seen a genuine canal on Mars," attributing the "completely illusory canals" "seen" by astronomers such as Percival Lowell and Flammarion to irregular natural features of the Martian surface. Antoniadi also observed the great Martian storms of 1909, 1911 and 1924, noting after the last one that the planet had become covered with yellow clouds and had a color similar to Jupiter. On Mercury his observations made between 1914 and 1929 seemed to confirm Giovanni Schiaparelli's rotation period of 88 days, identical with the planet's period of revolution around the Sun. The effect of this would be for Mercury always to turn the same face to the Sun, in the same way as the Moon always turns the same face to the Earth. Antoniadi cited nearly 300 observations of identifiable features always in the same position, as required by the 88-day rotation period. However, radar studies of Mercury in 1965 revealed the planet has a 59-day rotation period. When the planet returns to the same favorable viewing position in the sky, at intervals of 116 days, it does present the same face to observers.

Antonioni, Michelangelo *(1912–)* Italian film director. A graduate of the University of Bologna, Antonioni won worldwide praise for his film *L'Avventura* in 1959. In this film and in his other works, including *La Notte* (1961), *The Eclipse* (1962), *Red Desert* (1964), *Blow-Up* (1966), *Zabriskie Point* (1970) and *The Passenger* (1975), Antonioni explores the alienation of modern life. Although Antonioni suffered a stroke in 1985 that left him partially paralyzed, he remained involved in the filmmaking industry, and in 1995 collaborated with Wim Wenders to direct *Par-delà les nuages* and was presented an Academy Award for lifetime achievement.

Antonov-Ovseyenko, Vladimir Aleksandrovich *(1884–1939?)* Russian revolutionary with MENSHEVIK leanings who joined the Social-Democratic Labor Party in 1903. He was an organizer of the OCTOBER REVOLUTION and conducted the capture of the Winter Palace. He commanded various army groups during the Russian civil war, but as a supporter of TROTSKY he was dismissed from the army in 1925. He then held diplomatic posts abroad and disappeared in the GREAT PURGE of 1936–38.

Antonov Uprising *(1919–1921)* An uprising in the Tambov province of Russia, led by A. S. Antonov, a socialist revolutionary. It was anticommunist, and as many as 50,000 peasants and deserters from the Red Army took part. Soviet troops defeated the movement on several occasions, but it collapsed only with the onset of the NEW ECONOMIC POLICY.

Anzac Acronym for the Australian and New Zealand Army Corps. Anzacs became famous for their eight-month stand against the Turks during the disastrous GALLIPOLI campaign of 1915. They later fought at Arras and Messines, served under General ALLENBY in Palestine (1917) and resisted German advances on the Western Front (1918).

Aparicio, Luis *(1934–)* Venezuelan-born baseball player. Considered by many to be the finest shortstop ever, Aparicio won the Gold Glove for that position nine times. He was named Rookie of the Year in 1956, and while with the Chicago White Sox (1956–63), he and Nellie Fox formed one of the most efficient infield combinations in baseball history. Traded to the Orioles in 1963, he returned to Chicago five years later and finished his career in Boston in 1973. Aparicio led American League shortstops in fielding eight consecutive years and was a 10-time All-Star. A workmanlike hitter, he reached the .300 mark only once, in 1970. His basepath speed gave him seventh position on the all-time stolen bases roster, with 506. Aparicio was named to the Hall of Fame in 1984.

apartheid An Afrikaner term (literally, "apartness") referring to the South African policy of racial segregation and economic and political discrimination against nonwhites. Practiced unofficially since colonial times, the policy became politically entrenched with the 1948 victory of the white supremacist Afrikaner National Party. As part of apartheid the Bantu Self-Government Act (1959) provided for the establishment of seven native African areas to be run by nonwhite chief ministers. International opposition to the policy began in 1952 and intensified during the 1970s and 1980s, resulting in an economic boycott of SOUTH AFRICA by many countries. The controversy led to South Africa's leaving the British COMMONWEALTH and becoming an independent republic in 1961. Major anti-apartheid riots occurred at Sharpeville (1960; see SHARPEVILLE MASSACRE) and SOWETO (1976). Black leader Steve BIKO died in detention in 1977, causing increased anger over the policy. Beginning in 1989 the government of South Africa under F. W. DE KLERK slowly moved toward discussions on ending apartheid and released AFRICAN NATIONAL CONGRESS leader Nelson MANDELA from prison. In 1992 de Klerk organized a national referendum on apartheid. Two-thirds of South African voters participated in the vote, which sanctioned de Klerk's ultimate goal of removing apartheid as a practice in South Africa. The result was a 1994 constitution that answered the ANC's call for "one man, one vote," and created a multiparty executive in 1994. In elections held later that year, the ANC became the country's ruling party, and the last vestiges of apartheid disappeared.

Apollinaire, Guillaume (**Wilhelm-Apollinaris de Kostrowitski**) *(1880–1918)* French poet and art critic. Apollinaire is perhaps the most widely read and influential French poet of the 20th century. Born of a Polish mother and an Italian-Swiss father, young Apollinaire adopted the French language when he was sent to school in Monaco. His first lyric poems, written in his early 20s in Paris, showed the marked influence of 19th-century French symbolist poets, such as Baudelaire, Rimbaud and Verlaine. But in 1905 Apollinaire established friendships with a group of young painters, including Pablo PICASSO, who were creating the new aesthetics of CUBISM. Apollinaire championed their work and was also the first critic to praise the visionary canvases of Henri Rousseau. In his poems, Apollinaire combined cubist experimentation with his own natural lyrical bent. *Alcools* (1913) and *Calligrammes* (1918) are his two major volumes of poems. He served in the French army during WORLD WAR I and died on November 9, 1918, two days before the Armistice, of complications from a head wound.

Apollo 11 Manned spaceflight launched on July 16, 1969, as a part of the APOLLO PROJECT; on July 20 it landed the first men on the Moon. The mission's crew consisted of its commander, Neil ARMSTRONG, Edwin "Buzz" ALDRIN and Michael Collins. With Collins orbiting the Moon in the command module *Columbia,* Armstrong and Aldrin piloted the lunar module *Eagle* to a landing on the Moon's Sea of Tranquility. Upon landing, they broadcast to Earth: "Houston, Tranquility Base here. The *Eagle* has landed." Armstrong was the first man to stand upon the lunar surface. Stepping onto Earth's satellite at 10:56 P.M., EST, he made the now-famous statement: "That's one small step for [a] man, one giant leap for mankind." Aldrin then joined Armstrong, and the two spacesuit-clad men set up a battery of scientific instruments, including a seismometer, an aluminum foil apparatus to catch solar wind particles and a laser beam reflector. They also erected an American flag. The two astronauts photographed the Moon's surface and collected more than 50 pounds of lunar rock and soil. Altogether, the two men spent two hours and 13 minutes on the Moon. Returning to *Columbia* in the ascent stage of the lunar module, Armstrong and Aldrin rejoined the command module, jettisoned *Eagle* into lunar orbit and returned to a splashdown in the Pacific Ocean on July 24, 1969.

Astronaut Buzz Aldrin descending from the lunar module during the Apollo 11 *spaceflight. 1969* (LIBRARY OF CONGRESS, PRINTS AND PHOTOGRAPHS DIVISION)

Apollo project American space program initiated in 1961 by President John F. KENNEDY, who pledged the nation to land men on the Moon and return them safely to Earth by 1970. The undertaking that realized that goal became the biggest technological program to date, encompassing 17 missions, and the most expensive, costing some $25 billion. Overseen by the NATIONAL AERONAUTICS AND SPACE ADMINISTRATION (NASA), the Apollo spacecraft was developed from research conducted in the earlier MERCURY and GEMINI programs. The Apollo spacecraft were launched from the Kennedy Space Center in Florida by a three-stage Saturn V rocket, 363 feet in length, weighing over 3,000 tons and developing a liftoff thrust of 7.5 million pounds. The spacecraft itself consisted of a three-man command module, a service module and a lunar excursion module (LEM). When in Moon orbit, the LEM, with a crew of two, detached from the command and service modules and landed on the Moon. After exploration, one part of the LEM remained on the lunar surface, while the other rejoined the spacecraft and was discarded after the astronauts reentered the command module. On returning to Earth, the service module was jettisoned, and only the command module and its crew splashed down to complete the journey.

The first six Apollo flights were unmanned tests. The only fatalities of the project occurred during this testing phase when three astronauts were killed in a launchpad fire early in

1967. The first manned flight, *Apollo 7,* took place in October 1968 and demonstrated the spaceworthiness of the craft. *Apollo 8,* in December 1968, was successful in orbiting both the Earth and the Moon. *Apollo 9* (March 1969) tested a lunar module in Earth orbit, and *Apollo 10* (May 1969) saw the piloting of the LEM within 50,000 feet of the Moon. The goal of the Apollo program was finally reached with APOLLO 11, which successfully landed men on the Moon. Scientific exploration began in earnest in November 1969 with *Apollo 12,* which employed the first Apollo Lunar Scientific Package (ALSEP) and brought back almost 75 pounds of lunar material. *Apollo 13* (April 1970) was aborted after an explosion in the service module but returned safely to Earth. *Apollo 14* (January–February 1971) did additional scientific exploration, and *Apollo 15* (July–August 1971) was the first mission to use an exploration vehicle, the Lunar Rover, on the surface of the Moon. The last two Apollo missions, *Apollo 16* (April 1972) and *Apollo 17* (December 1972), explored the lunar highlands with the aid of the Lunar Rover and collected a total of over 450 pounds of lunar rocks.

Altogether, Apollo astronauts collected and brought back to Earth for investigation some 900 pounds of lunar material the Apollo Project also involved a Soviet-American cooperative effort in space. Initiated in an agreement of 1972, a link-up of Soviet and U.S. spacecraft was achieved on July 17, 1975, when *Apollo 18* docked in space with the Soviet *Soyuz*

19 spacecraft. The two ships were linked for almost two days. Mounting costs finally terminated the Apollo project, and work on manned space exploration was continued with the SKYLAB program.

Apollo-Soyuz Test Project (ASTP)

Historic cooperative program between the U.S. and the USSR resulting in a joint space mission in July 1975. Two Soviets and three Americans met in space when the orbiting SOYUZ and APOLLO spacecraft linked up. The term *test project* was used because only one mission was planned.

Apostles, the

A secret society at Cambridge University whose members idealized the Soviet Union. During the 1930s, Cambridge don Anthony BLUNT worked with undergraduate Guy Burgess to turn the Apostles into a Marxist cell and to recruit potential spies from among its ranks. In addition to Blunt and Burgess, the group's most notable members included Donald Maclean and Kim PHILBY, all of whom actively worked as double agents for the Soviet Union during WORLD WAR II and in the early stages of the COLD WAR. (See also BURGESS-MACLEAN SPY CASE.)

appeasement

Foreign policy that causes a nation or nations to concede certain matters to an aggressor country rather than risk war. In the 20th century the term is usually applied to attempts by Great Britain and France to appease Adolf HITLER by making agreements with Germany and Italy in the years from 1936 to 1939. It is particularly associated with the efforts of British prime minister Neville CHAMBERLAIN. Appeasement permitted German reoccupation of the RHINELAND, the ANSCHLUSS with Austria and Czechoslovakia's surrender of the Sudetenland in the MUNICH PACT. The policy came to an end as a result of Germany's occupation of the rest of Czechoslovakia in 1939.

Appiah, Joseph Emmanuel "Joe"

(1918–1990) Ghanaian political leader and diplomat. Appiah was a close associate of Ghanaian leader Kwame NKRUMAH before GHANA achieved independence from Britain in 1957. However, he eventually split with Nkrumah over Nkrumah's increasingly authoritarian policies and became a prominent opposition leader. Appiah served as Ghana's representative to the UN (1977–78). Appiah attracted widespread publicity in 1953 when he married an Englishwoman, Peggy Cripps, the daughter of former chancellor of the Exchequer Sir Stafford CRIPPS.

Apple Computer

Computer manufacturing firm based in Cupertino, California, founded by Steven Jobs, a computer expert who successfully challenged such major manufacturers as IBM with a product line not compatible with other manufacturers' systems. Apple computers have been of distinguished design, developed by the German-American industrial design firm Frogdesign. The very successful Apple IIC, the Macintosh, and Apple IIGS units are examples of the compactness and neat detailing typical of Apple products. Apple introduced a new line of Macintosh computers in 1990. In 1998 Apple introduced a new brand of computers, the iMac, a Macintosh-like design that featured a single-piece computer and monitor, with the monitor covered in a variety of colored transparent plastic shells. Another distinguishing feature was that the iMac did not have an internal 3.5-inch floppy disk drive, although one could be attached to the computer through a cable connection. Shortly after the success of the iMac, Apple released the iBook, the laptop version of the iMac with an 3.5-inch disk drive, and the iPod, an MP3 player that allowed one to download several digital copies of various songs into a device roughly the size of a pager.

Appleton, Sir Edward Victor

(1892–1965) British physicist. Appleton studied physics at Cambridge University from 1910 to 1913. During World War I, while he was serving in the Royal Engineers, he developed his interest in radio that was to influence his later research. After the war he returned to Cambridge and worked in the Cavendish Laboratory from 1920. In 1924 he was appointed Wheatstone Professor of Experimental Physics at King's College, London. There, in his first year, he used a BBC transmitter to conduct a famous experiment that established beyond doubt the presence of a layer of ionized gas in the upper atmosphere capable of reflecting radio waves. The existence of such a layer had been postulated by Oliver Heaviside and Arthur Kennelly to explain MARCONI's transatlantic radio transmissions. Furthermore, the experiment measured the height of the layer, which Appleton estimated at 60 miles. He proceeded to do theoretical work on the reflection or transmission of radio waves by the ionized layer and found, using further measurements, a second layer above the Heaviside-Kennelly layer. The **Appleton layer** undergoes daily fluctuations in ionization, and he established a link between these variations and the occurrence of sunspots. In 1936 he became the Jacksonian Professor of Natural Philosophy at Cambridge, and during the war years until 1949 he was secretary of the department of scientific and industrial research, while he led research into RADAR and the atomic bomb (see ATOMIC BOMB DEVELOPMENT). For his great achievements in ionospheric physics he was knighted in 1941 and in 1947 won the NOBEL PRIZE in physics.

April Theses

(April 1917) On his return to Petrograd, April 16, 1917, LENIN published the so-called April Theses, a policy statement that defined his own position and was intended to direct the BOLSHEVIKS toward the seizure of power. The theses contributed to the OCTOBER REVOLUTION because in effect they were asking the Bolsheviks to withdraw support from the provisional government. In the theses Lenin opposed continuation of WORLD WAR I; proposed that power be handed over to the Soviets, including control of banks, production and distribution of goods; advocated abolition of the existing police force, army and bureaucracy and the confiscation of all private land; and suggested that the Social-Democratic Party be called the COMMUNIST PARTY and the Socialist International be reconstructed.

The theses met with considerable opposition even from within the Bolshevik Party; and the Petrograd and Moscow Bolshevik committees voted against them, but within a few weeks they were adopted by the Bolsheviks.

Aquino, (Maria) Corazon (Cori Aquino)

(1933–) President of the Philippines (1986–92). From 1980 to

1983 Aquino lived in exile with her husband, **Benigno Aquino,** who led the opposition to President Ferdinand Marcos. Following Benigno Aquino's assassination on his return to Manila in 1983, she became increasingly active politically and was chosen as a compromise candidate to contest the presidential election against Marcos in 1986. Although Marcos claimed victory, international pressure in the face of widespread corruption led to his resignation and Aquino's accession to the presidency. As president, Aquino pledged economic and political reforms but faced opposition from both the right and the left, including several attempted coups. Aquino left the presidency in 1992 and assured the peaceful and lawful transition of her successor, Fidel V. Ramos. She subsequently served on the Benigno S. Aquino Jr. Foundation, an organization in the Philippines that awards education scholarships to promising students.

Arab-Israeli War of 1948–1949

Arab forces from Egypt, Syria, Transjordan (Jordan), Lebanon and Iraq invaded Israel on May 14, 1948, the day the state of Israel was proclaimed. The Arabs pushed into southern and eastern Palestine and Jerusalem's Old City before the Israelis halted them. In June the United Nations succeeded in a securing a four-week truce. After fighting resumed in July, the Israeli forces gained territory until another truce went into effect for about three months. The Israelis then pushed the Arab forces back on all fronts, gaining the Negev desert region (except for the Gaza Strip). Between February and July 1949 Israel signed armistice agreements with the Arab states (except Iraq, which refused to sign but did withdraw its troops). At the end of the war Israel occupied most of the disputed areas of Palestine, increasing its territory by one-half. It also developed a formidable standing army. About 400,000 Palestinian Arabs fled, settling in refugee camps in neighboring Arab countries. (See also Arab-Israeli War of 1956.)

Arab-Israeli War of 1956

Brief war, from October 29 to November 6, between Israel and Egypt, prompted by the Egyptian nationalization of the Suez Canal. The Israeli attack on Egypt (October 29) was secretly instigated by Britain and France, which sought to topple Egyptian president Nasser and protect their own interests in the canal zone. Actively supported by Britain and France, Israel achieved its military goals in less than a week. However, the French and British role in the affair resulted in severe domestic and international political crises for these nations. (See also Suez Crisis.)

Arab-Israeli War of 1973 (Yom Kippur War)

Fighting continued off and on between the Arabs and Israelis after the Six-Day War of 1967. Frustrated over Israeli refusal to negotiate a return of the Occupied Territories, Arab states launched a surprise attack on Israel on October 6, 1973, the Jewish holy day of Yom Kippur. Egyptian forces attacked from the east across the Suez Canal, while Syrian troops moved from the north into Israel. The Egyptian and Syrian armies, joined by Iraqi, Jordanian and Libyan units, inflicted heavy losses on the Israelis, who were caught off guard. The Israeli armies eventually counterattacked and drove into Syria to within 20 miles of Damascus. They also encircled the Egyptian army by crossing the Suez and establishing troops on the canal's west bank. Israel agreed to a cease-fire called for by the U.S. and the USSR, but fighting continued until a UN peacekeeping force was moved into the war zone and a cease-fire agreement was signed on November 11, 1973. By a 1974 agreement Israel withdrew into Sinai west of the Mitla and Gidi Passes, and Egypt reduced forces on the Suez's east bank. A UN buffer zone was established between Israel and Syria.

Arab League (League of Arab States)

Organization formed in 1945 by Egypt, Iraq, Lebanon, Saudi Arabia, Syria, Transjordan (now Jordan) and Yemen (later North Yemen, or the Yemen Arab Republic). Its purpose was to provide a political voice for the Arab states, to strengthen ties among Arab nations and to preserve the sovereignty of member states. The league has remained a loose confederation without a strong central authority. At first involved in anti-Israeli activities and in efforts to curb French influence, its militancy was tempered by the founding of the Palestine Libera-tion Organization (PLO). In the early 1990s the league had a membership of 22 (including the PLO) and acted largely as a mouthpiece for moderate Arab thought and as a coordinator of Arab economic affairs. In 1993 the league included 22 members, the newest addition being the small African island country of Comoros.

The Arab League has sought to use its power to influence international relations in the Middle East. It voted unanimously to condemn such actions as the 1990 invasion of Kuwait by Iraq and the U.S. cruise missile attacks on Afghanistan and Sudan in 1998. However, its members have disagreed on issues such as the U.S.-led Operation Iraqi Freedom in March 2003 that deposed Saddam Hussein, with Syria criticizing the operation, and states such as Kuwait, Qatar and Bahrain assisting U.S. operations. In September 2003 the league permitted the U.S.-appointed Iraqi Governing Council to assume the Iraqi seat in league meetings.

Arafat, Yasir (Yasser Arafat) (1929–2004)

Palestinian leader, chairman of the Palestine Liberation Organization (PLO) from 1968 until his death. Active in the League of Palestinian Students in the 1940s and 1950s, he formed the al-Fatah movement in 1956. Although the PLO was associated with many terrorist incidents, Arafat was regarded by some as a moderate Palestinian leader and, as such, was recognized by much of the international community as someone with whom negotiations should take place. In 1988 Arafat informed the UN that the PLO would seek diplomatic conversations with Israel and would consider recognizing Israeli sovereignty. Although U.S.-sponsored meetings in Madrid in 1991 between Palestinian leaders not affiliated with the PLO and members of the Israeli government failed, secret meetings between Israeli prime minister Yitzak Rabin and Arafat in Oslo, Norway, led to the signing of the Oslo Peace Accords in 1993. The accords established a rough framework for the creation of an autonomous Palestinian Authority (PA), which would assume increasing control of domestic affairs in the Gaza Strip and the West Bank. In 1994 Arafat, Rabin, and Israeli foreign min-

Palestinian leader Yasir Arafat (right) at the Arab Summit Conference in 1969 (Bettman/Corbis)

ister Shimon PERES shared the Nobel Peace Prize for their work. In 1998 Arafat also proved willing to sign the Wye River Memorandum, an agreement that further defined the Israel-PA relationship. However, Arafat proved unwilling to finalize this relationship in a 2000 meeting with U.S. president Bill CLINTON and Israeli prime minister Ehud BARAK, in which Barak offered Arafat full statehood for Gaza and most of the West Bank in exchange for an end to all terrorist attacks on Israel. Arafat's refusal was shortly followed by an outbreak of renewed Palestinian terrorist attacks on Israelis (see INTIFADA II). Barak's successor, Ariel SHARON, responded by laying siege to Arafat inside his home in the West Bank city of Ramallah and issuing repeated calls for his removal as PA president. Arafat's health deteriorated in 2004; flown to Paris for medical treatment, he died there on November 11, 2004, from an undisclosed illness.

Aragon, Louis *(1897–1982)* French poet, novelist, essayist and journalist. Aragon first came to prominence as a surrealist poet in the 1920s, most notably in his book *Perpetual Movement* (1926). That same year he published a novel, *Le Paysan de Paris,* which evokes the everyday life of Paris in a fantastical style. Aragon joined the Communist Party in 1927 and visited the Soviet Union in 1930. In the 1930s and after,

he abandoned his surrealistic style in favor of a committed political realism. During World War II, Aragon became a hero of the French RESISTANCE both by publishing clandestine newspapers and by expressing the yearning for liberty in his traditional lyric poems of the war years. Aragon continued to write novels in the postwar years, such as the six-volume series *The Communists* (1949–51), as well as volumes of love poems, such as *Elsa* (1959).

Arbenz Guzmán, Jacobo *(1913–1971)* Guatemalan political leader. Arbenz served as Guatemala's defense minister (1945–50) before being elected president in 1950. An independent radical with the support of both the army and left-wing political groups, Arbenz in 1952 launched a controversial land reform program that resulted in the confiscation of holdings of the United Fruit Company, an American firm. As a result, the U.S. government denounced the Arbenz government as communist, and in 1954 a U.S.-backed coup replaced Arbenz with the right-wing colonel Carlos Castillo Armas.

Arber, Werner *(1929–)* Swiss microbiologist. Arber graduated from the Swiss Federal Institute of Technology in 1953 and gained his Ph.D. from the University of Geneva in 1958. He spent a year at the University of South-

ern California before returning to Geneva where he became professor of molecular genetics in 1965. In 1970 Arber moved to Basel to take the chair of molecular biology. In the early 1950s Giuseppe Bertani reported a phenomenon he described as "host-controlled variation" in which phage (the viruses that infect bacteria) successfully growing on one host found it difficult to establish themselves on a different bacterium. In 1962 Arber proposed that bacteria possess highly specific enzymes capable of destroying invading phage by cutting up their DNA. The existence of such "restriction enzymes," as they came to be called, was later established by Hamilton Smith. As restriction enzymes were found to leave DNA strands "sticky" and ready to combine with certain other "sticky" strands, it was soon apparent to molecular biologists that genetic engineering was at last a practical proposition. For his work on restriction enzymes Arber shared the 1978 NOBEL PRIZE in physiology or medicine with Smith and Daniel Nathans.

Arbuckle, Roscoe "Fatty" *(1887–1933)* American comedy film actor. Originally a member of the silent screen's bumbling Keystone Kops, the chubby clown became a star in his own right at the Mack SENNETT studio from 1912 to 1915. In 1920 he began to make his own feature-length comedies. His career ended after a 1921 scandal involving the death of a young actress. Although cleared of rape and manslaughter charges, a discredited Arbuckle was unable to work in the film industry again, although he had a brief stint as a writer and director under the pseudonym William B. Goodrich from 1931 to 1932.

Arbus, Diane (Diane Nemerov) *(1923–1971)* American photographer. The sister of American poet Howard Nemerov, she married fellow fashion photographer Allan Arbus in 1941, and the two operated a successful commercial studio until 1958. In 1959 she studied with the photographer Lisette Model. She is best known for her unblinkingly direct studies of unconventional, strange or freakish people. Among her best-known photographs are images of twins (1966), a photograph of a Jewish "giant" (1970) and studies of prostitutes, transvestites and dwarfs. Not all of her subjects were unusual, but she brought a jarringly powerful vision and a pervasive sense of unease to portrayals of even the most ordinary people. Arbus committed suicide in 1971.

Arbuzov, Alexei Nikolayevich (*1908–1986*) Russian playwright. Arbuzov was one of the best known of Soviet dramatists, both at home and abroad. His plays were first published in 1930. *Tanya* is generally considered to be one of the foremost plays of the 1930s. In later years, music hall and vaudeville features colored his work.

Arcaro, Eddie (**George Edward Arcaro**) (*1916–1997*) American jockey. Over a 30-year career, Arcaro rode in 24,092 races. A stable boy at the age of 13, he rode the first of his 4,779 winners at a Mexican track in 1932. A four-time Kentucky Derby winner, he was the only jockey ever to ride two Triple Crown winners, WHIRLAWAY in 1941 and CITATION in 1948. He was known early in his career as a down-and-dirty rider and was suspended during the 1942–43 racing season for his tactics. He later reformed and became known for his skill and tactical ability. Arcaro led all jockeys in winnings in 1949, 1950, 1952 and 1955. In 1951 he won the Preakness, followed in 1952 by a victory in the Kentucky Derby and the Belmont, and in the Preakness again in 1955. Among his best-known mounts were NATIVE DANCER, NASHUA and the incomparable KELSO.

Archipenko, Alexander (*1887–1965*) Russian sculptor. His development paralleled that of the cubist painters (see CUBISM). A gradual simplification of human contours brought him to the point of expressing the nude figure entirely in geometrical shapes.

Arcos Raid Diplomatic incident of May 1927 in the UNITED KINGDOM. Under orders from Stanley BALDWIN's government, which suspected that the USSR was meddling in British affairs, Scotland Yard agents raided and searched the London offices of the Soviet trading company known as Arcos. Although no evidence was found, the British nevertheless maintained that the Soviets were plotting against British imperial interests. Diplomatic relations were subsequently broken off but were resumed in 1929 when anti-Soviet sentiments had somewhat subsided.

Arden, Eve (**Eunice Quedens**) (*1908–1990*) U.S. film and television actress. She appeared in such films as *Stage Door* (1937), *Mildred Pierce* (1945), for which she was nominated for an ACADEMY AWARD, and *Anatomy of a Murder* (1959). She was best known for her role as the sharp-tongued but lovable schoolteacher in the long-running television series *Our Miss Brooks* (1948–57). She went on to star in *The Eve Arden Show* and costarred with Kaye Ballard in the series *The Mothers-in-Law.*

Arendt, Hannah (*1906–1975*) German-born American philosopher and social critic. Arendt was one of the most influential political writers in the U.S. in the decade following World War II. She earned her Ph.D. in philosophy in 1928 at the University of Heidelberg, where she studied under the renowned philosopher Karl JASPERS. Due to her Jewish ancestry, Arendt was forced to flee the German Nazi regime in 1933, moving first to Páris and then, in 1941, to the U.S., where she was actively involved in Jewish refugee relief efforts. Her first major work, *The Origins of Totalitarianism* (1951), argued that totalitarian regimes were growing in strength throughout the Western world due to an increasing sense of political and personal alienation among the ruled populaces. Considerable controversy developed over *Eichmann in Jerusalem* (1963), in which Arendt stated that the trial of Nazi death camp officer Adolf EICHMANN illustrated the "banality of evil." Her other major works include *The Human Condition* (1958) and *On Violence* (1970).

Arens, Egmont (*1888–1966*) American industrial and packaging designer whose work of the 1930s followed the streamlined direction typical of the most advanced work of the time. His 1932 book, *Consumer Engineering* (written with Roy Sheldon), was influential during the depression in promoting the idea that improved design could be a tool to increase product sales. Many of his package designs, such as the coffee bags for A&P food stores, were once universally familiar. His Kitchen Aid mixer (c. 1946) is a typical example of his approach to product design.

Arévalo, Juan José (*1904–1990*) President of Guatemala (1945–51). Arévalo began his career in Guatemala's Education Ministry but soon exiled himself in political protest to Argentina, where he was a professor of literature and ethics and wrote textbooks. After a 1944 coup ended 14 years of military dictatorship in Guatemala, Arévalo returned and was elected president, his tenure beginning in 1945. He overturned repressive laws banning free press and labor unions and encouraged the formation of political parties. He also initiated social security and public health reforms and attempted to bring Guatemala's Indian population into government. Arévalo described himself as a socialist, but many accused him of being a communist. As a more radical left gained increasing control of his party, he faced many attempts to oust him by the right. He was succeeded in 1951 by Jacobo ARBENZ GUZMÁN, who was overthrown in 1954 by a military coup backed by the U.S. CENTRAL INTELLIGENCE AGENCY. A military dictatorship was reestablished that eliminated many of Arévalo's reforms and maintained a brutal repression almost continuously until 1985. Arévalo went into exile and did not return permanently to Guatemala until the mid-1970s. He authored *The Shark and the Sardines* (1961) in which he criticized U.S. involvement in Latin America.

Argentina Argentina occupies almost the whole of the southern part of the South American continent and extends from Bolivia to Cape Horn, a distance of nearly 2,149 miles. From 1880 to the 1920s, the attraction of foreign investment and labor became the primary concern of governments. Argentina's population was boosted by European immigration. The honest administration of the 1912 Electoral Law, which insisted on universal and compulsory male suffrage, secret ballots and permanent voter registration, brought the radicals to power in 1916 under Hipólito Yrigoyen. The radicals held the presidency for the next 14 years but never seriously threatened the power base of the ruling class. In September 1930, amid economic crisis, government corruption and popular disillusionment, a coup brought Argentina's first military government to power. Far from providing stability, the coup brought harsh repression and corruption, the period from 1930 to 1943 being known as the "Era of Patriotic Fraud," when the Conservatives, together with civilian and military political opportunists, rigged successive elections. Such abuses in turn antagonized the growing industrial middle class and an increasingly militant working class. The heightened tension developing between these two forces persuaded the military to take the helm again in 1943.

The 1943 coup brought Colonel Juan Domingo PERÓN on to the political stage. As the military's minister of labor, Perón believed that the state could play the key role in industrializing and diversifying the economy and that it could be assisted by the urban working class. Perón sanctioned progressive labor legislation, encouraged trade union growth and organization and substantially raised wages. In the presidential elections of 1946 Perón, now the candidate of the Argentine Labor Party, defeated the single candidate of the traditional parties. He, along with his second wife, Eva ("Evita," a legend for her social welfare programs), mobilized the labor movement into a single General Labor Confederation (CGT) fiercely loyal to him. Such loyalty persisted even when Perón (reelected in 1951 as the automatic candidate of the new Peronist Party) became increasingly authoritarian as economic growth slowed. Strikes were repressed, wages driven down and opposition leaders were harassed or exiled. By 1955 Peronism had strained its appeal among the rank-and-file of the labor movement, and the Catholic Church had withdrawn its support. In September the military overthrew Peron and forced him into an 18-year exile.

The succeeding 20 years were characterized by accelerating inflation, strikes, high unemployment and political instability. The military, which had closed the Congress and dissolved all

political parties in 1966, was unable to deal with the high level of political violence, which their own repression had stoked up. General Alejandro Lanusse allowed the Peronists to contest the elections of March 1973, and

ARGENTINA

1902	Long dispute with Chile over Patagonian border settled.
1910	International exhibition in Buenos Aires marks centennial of first independence struggle; peak of economic and population boom based on export of beef to Europe.
1916	After electoral reforms, Radical Party takes over government; fails to challenge entrenched agricultural and business interests.
1919	Argentina joins League of Nations; withdraws following year to protest Allied treatment of defeated Germany.
1930	First military coup ends period of reform.
1943	Labor unrest leads to second coup, by army colonels including Juan Perón.
1944	Publication of *Ficciones* by Jorge Luis Borges.
1946	Perón elected president; attempts to pacify labor movement and industrialize the country.
1952	Death of Perón's wife Eva, whose advocacy of social programs made her a hero to many Argentines.
1966	Military suspends Congress and dissolves political parties.
1973	Elections resume and Perón returns from exile; he is reelected.
1976	Inflation cripples economy; Perón forced out in coup.
1977	"Dirty War"; army kills thousands of perceived subversives.
1982	Military discredited after defeat by Britain in war over Falkland (Malvinas) Islands; junta leaves power and elections are scheduled.
1986	Argentina wins the World Cup in soccer.
1989	Peronists return to power with election of Carlos Saúl Menem; hyperinflation again batters the economy.
1990	Menem authorizes the military to suppress civil unrest for the first time since 1983; in December a bloody uprising by several hundred Argentine army troops is quashed by forces loyal to Menem; Menem grants pardons to eight military men, including former junta members responsible for the "Dirty War."
1991	Argentine workers stage wildcat strikes to protest economic austerity measures.
1993	The country's 11-year debt crisis comes to an end.
1997	Violent protests erupt in several major cities over growing unemployment (20% in some areas); the governing Peronist Party suffers heavy losses in midterm legislative elections; the economy pulls out of recession, posting 8% GDP.
1998	Trials of military officers accused of waging the "Dirty War" begin.
2001	Newly installed president Fernando de la Rúa forms a government of national unity incorporating several parties from across Argentina's political spectrum; protests greet planned austerity measures; Argentina nears default on IMF payments; on December 20, de la Rúa resigns after widespread street protests and rioting leave at least 25 people dead.
2002	Congress elects Peronist senator Eduardo Duhalde president; banking and foreign exchange activities are suspended; protests occur; Argentina defaults on World Bank payments.
2003	Nestor Kirchner becomes president and renegotiates IMF payments to cover only interest.

their successful candidate, Héctor Campora, then resigned within 50 days, forcing fresh elections to clinch the presidency for Perón, who had returned from exile. Both Perón and his third wife, "Isabel" (who succeeded him as president after his death), failed to deliver any significant social and economic changes, with record inflation in 1975 and 1976. In 1975 there was the threat of the first general strike against a Peronist government. The radical youth wing of the Peronist movement initiated a campaign of urban guerrilla warfare to destabilize the government. The military returned to power in a coup on March 24, 1976, arresting Isabel Perón and proceeding to torture, murder and abduct thousands of perceived opponents in a campaign later known as the ARGENTINE "DIRTY WAR."

At the end of 1981 military hardliners installed a junta led by the commander in chief of the army, General Leopoldo GALTIERI. By 1982 the military had so discredited itself that it gambled on invasion of the Falkland (Malvinas) Islands on April 2 to restore its national credibility (see FALKLAND ISLANDS WAR). Defeat by British forces made the resignation of Galtieri's military junta inevitable. In the presidential elections of October 1983 Raúl ALFONSÍN was the surprise victor. The Alfonsín administration promised peace, freedom and progress but faced military unrest and a multitude of economic problems that deepened throughout its term, notably the spiraling inflation and foreign debt that topped $60 billion at the close of 1988. Groups of army officers led a series of rebellions in 1987 and 1988, protesting against government efforts to bring to trial the military personnel responsible for human rights violations. The Peronists returned to power with the victory of Carlos Saúl MENEM over the UCR candidate Eduardo Angeloz in May 1989. They also won control of the Congress. In 1990 Argentina and Britain restored full diplomatic relations, although Argentina continued to claim the Falklands. Two years later, in an effort to stabilize the country's economy, President Menem introduced the peso as the new currency and pegged it to the U.S. dollar. Later that year Menem ordered a government investigation into the bombing of the Is-

raeli embassy in Buenos Aires, in which 29 people died, as well as a similar attack on a Jewish community center in 1994. Menem also supported the 1998 efforts of the Argentine judicial system to bring to trial officers and soldiers associated with atrocities in the "Dirty War." The Argentine economy collapsed in 2001 under President Fernando de la Rúa, and violent protests erupted. The economy stabilized under President Nestor Kirchner.

Argentine "Dirty War" (1976–1983)

On March 24, 1976, the Argentine armed forces overthrew the government of President Isabel Perón (see Juan PERÓN). A three-man junta led by General Jorge Videla began a ruthless campaign against leftists, liberals and terrorists. An estimated 6,000 to 15,000 Argentines disappeared between 1976 and 1981. The flagrant violations of human rights caused the U.S. government under President CARTER to stop sending Argentina military aid. Several prominent prisoners were freed and allowed to leave the country, and gradually the security forces reduced their "Dirty War" activities in response to worldwide public opinion. Argentina's return to civilian rule under President Raúl ALFONSÍN (December 10, 1983) resulted in the prosecution of former military presidents Videla, General Roberto Viola and General Leopoldo GALTIERI and six other members of the former junta.

Argentine Revolt of 1951

Argentina became a virtual dictatorship under President Juan Domingo PERÓN, who was assisted by his wife Eva (Evita) PERÓN. In 1951 the country's economy was in bad shape, with decreasing exports, climbing inflation and several strikes. Declaring martial law, Perón broke the strikes with force and claimed they were instigated by "foreign agitators." Riots erupted when he suspended the newspaper La Prensa, Argentina's largest independent newspaper, which had criticized the government. Perón attempted to have his wife nominated for vice president, but the prospect of a woman succeeding to the presidency and as commander of armed forces outraged some generals, who led an unsuccessful revolt in September 1951. Eva withdrew

her bid for the vice presidency. In the national election on November 11, 1951, Perón was reelected by a two-to-one majority.

Argentine Revolt of 1955

Juan Domingo PERÓN, president and dictator of ARGENTINA, began to lose power after the death of his wife Eva (Evita) PERÓN (1952), who had a strong political following among women, labor and the poor. Many Argentines were also upset by the deteriorating economy and increasing totalitarianism. Fearing a growing Christian socialist movement, Perón turned against the Catholic Church, a former ally. He arrested priests, fired clerical teachers and stopped all financial support of church educational facilities. Opposition to these measures increased, and many government officials resigned in protest. Perón introduced bills to end religious instruction in the schools and to tax church property. Catholics held religious processions that turned into antigovernment demonstrations, which the police suppressed. After a Corpus Christi celebration in June 1955, two high-ranking bishops were deported. The Vatican retaliated by excommunicating Perón (June 16, 1955). That same day part of the navy and air force staged an unsuccessful revolt in Buenos Aires. Perón later offered to resign (August 31, 1955), but the workers, who still supported him, called a general strike until he promised to remain in office. On September 16, 1955, army revolts broke out against Perón. The navy and air force soon joined and threatened to bomb Buenos Aires unless Perón resigned. Perón fled to Paraguay and went on to exile in Spain. Five days after Perón was ousted, General Eduardo Lonardi became provisional president (September 23, 1955).

Argentine Revolts of 1962–1963

Peronist candidates were permitted to run for the first time since President Juan Domingo PERÓN's ouster (1955). The Peronists won a slight majority in the Chamber of Deputies and nine of 14 governorships. The anti-Peronist military leadership refused to allow the Peronists to take office, deposed President Arturo Frondizi and seized control of the government. Fighting erupted within the military over whether to allow elections or to establish a dictatorship. In the elections of 1963 Peronists were forbidden to run candidates, and so cast blank ballots in protest as they had in 1957, when they tried to disrupt the voting. Intrigue, secret alliances, street fighting, intimidation by the military, hardening hatreds and an economy in shambles characterized Argentina when Umberto ILLIA was elected president in 1963.

Arghezi, Tudor *(1880–1967)* Romanian poet. A controversial figure, Arghezi began publishing his work in 1896 while eking out a modest existence in Bucharest. He entered a monastery in 1899 and stayed for four years before returning to Bucharest to write and edit a literary journal of his own devising, *The Straight Line* (it was the first in a succession of such magazines). Frequently in trouble for his tendency to issue alienating, radically inconsistent political tirades, he was imprisoned after World War I for contributing to a pro-German newspaper. His first book of poems was not published until 1927. Five novels appeared in the 1930s, as well as further collections of poetry. Called a "Faustian" by some, Arghezi was nonetheless seen as a poet of the first rank, writing with ferocity of the world's evils and compensatory pleasures.

Ariane Three-stage rocket developed by the European Space Agency (ESA). The Ariane project, designed to create an independent European capability in launching a variety of satellites, ran into a number of difficulties in its early days, at the beginning of the 1980s. Declared operational in January 1982, Ariane 1 failed in its first launch in September 1982. Subsequent launches met with some successes and some failures, including rockets that had to be destroyed after launching in September 1985 and May 1986. Ariane 4 was developed during 1987–88 and successfully launched for the first time, in June 1988. Ariane 5, scheduled for development in the 1990s, was planned to bring Europe into satellite-launching parity with the U.S. and the USSR and to place the ESA's planned Hermes space shuttle in orbit. Launched from Kourou, French Guiana, Ariane is 155.45 feet tall, has a lift-off weight of 463,643 pounds and can carry a payload of up to 4.6 tons. In December 1999, after two years of unsuccessful tests, the Ariane 5 was successfully used to deploy an X-ray observation satellite. However, the program was briefly suspended after a July 2001 failure to place two satellites in their desired orbit. In an effort to rectify this error, the ESA deployed the ESC-A, a variant on the Ariane 5 design, in December 2002.

Arias, Roberto Emilio *(1918–1989)* Panamanian lawyer, journalist and diplomat. In 1955 he married the British ballerina Dame Margot FONTEYN, whom he had known for many years. In 1959 he and Fonteyn were charged with attempting to smuggle guns into PANAMA aboard their yacht as part of a plot to overthrow President Ernesto de la Guardia Jr. Fonteyn was deported and Arias took refuge in the Brazilian embassy until the charges were dropped. In 1964 Arias was shot and partially paralyzed by a former political associate in a dispute over his election to the national assembly.

Arias Madrid, Arnulfo *(1901–1988)* Panamanian politician; three times elected president of Panama, he was three times overthrown by the Panamanian military or police. An old-style nationalist, Arias Madrid first popularized the slogan "Panama for the Panamanians" in an unsuccessful attempt to gain the PANAMA CANAL Zone from the U.S. His fascist sympathies and his refusal to allow the U.S. to arm Panamanian ships bringing Lend-Lease weapons to Great Britain led to his first U.S.-backed removal in a bloodless coup in 1940.

Arias Sánchez, Oscar *(1940-)* Costa Rica politician and Nobel laureate. After receiving an undergraduate degree in law and economics, Arias obtained a doctorate in political science from the University of Essex, in England. In 1970 he entered politics as an assistant to former president José Figueres during the latter's successful campaign for the presidency. In 1972 Arias was named minister of national planning and political economy. His National Liberation Party chose him as its general secretary in 1979. After serving in the Costa Rican parliament for several years, Arias was elected president in 1980. A year later he persuaded the presidents of Guatemala, El Salvador, Honduras and Nicaragua to endorse his plan for the restoration of peace in Nicaragua, which was engulfed in a bloody civil war between the left-wing Sandinista government and a rebel group known as the contras that was backed by the United States. As a result of the Arias Peace Plan, he was awarded the Nobel Peace Prize in 1987. After retiring from the presidency in 1990, Arias became active in several international organizations dedicated to world peace.

Aristide, Jean-Bertrand *(1953-)* President of Haiti (1991, 1994, 2001–04). Born in Port-Salut, Aristide attended a Catholic school and seminary with the intention of joining the priesthood. However, his superiors grew concerned that Aristide's fascination with LIBERATION THEOLOGY would bring him into conflict with the repressive government of Haitian strongman Jean-Claude Duvalier, and so they sent him to study abroad in Israel, Britain, and Canada. In 1982 Aristide returned to Haiti, where he was ordained in the Salesian order. Three years later he was assigned as pastor to a small parish in Port-au-Prince, where he regularly participated in protests against Duvalier. When Duvalier fled Haiti in 1986 and a civilian and military cabal assumed control, Aristide continued to lead protests and organizations against the Haitian oligarchy. These activities resulted in the Salesian order's expulsion of Aristide on grounds that he had incited people to violence. Because of his popularity among Haitians for his democratic stance, Aristide won the presidency in the December 1990 elections and entered office the following February. Seven months later a junta led by General Raoul CÉDRAS removed Aristide, and he began a three-year exile in the U.S. Eventually, under threat of an impending American invasion, Cédras agreed to a proposal offered by former American president Jimmy CARTER and former chairman of the Joint Chiefs of Staff Colin POWELL, and Aristide resumed his presidency in October 1994. He immediately began tackling the governmental corruption and social and economic problems besetting his

Jean-Bertrand Aristide (EMBASSY OF HAITI)

country. Although Aristide originally enjoyed amicable relations with the U.S., American diplomats grew concerned that he would convince himself that Haiti's continued economic hardships required his continued rule of the island state beyond the expiration of his term in 1996. Although the American-Haitian relationship frayed over these differences and concerns, as well as the canceling of $4.5 million in aid from the U.S. and the establishment of diplomatic relations between Haiti and Cuba, Aristide did step aside and permit René Préval to assume the presidency in 1996 after his election the previous year. Upon the expiration of Préval's term in 2001, Aristide ran for and was reelected to the presidency. However, his return to power was marred by controversy, as opponents of Aristide boycotted the election, claiming that he was becoming a political strongman in the mold of Duvalier. In 2004 Aristide resigned and fled the country amid political chaos and mounting criticism of his authoritarian, corrupt policies.

Arkan (Zeljko Raznatović) (*1952–2000*) Alleged Serbian war criminal. Born in Slovenia, Arkan originally gained notice for petty crimes such as stealing purses in Belgrade, despite the efforts of his father and Yugoslav state security to reform him. Arrested and convicted in Belgium for bank robbery, he escaped from jail in 1977. In 1979 Dutch police arrested him for his crimes in Belgium, but he escaped again in 1981 and fled through Germany to Yugoslavia, where a court ac-

quitted him of the charges levied against him in Belgium. During this time he allegedly functioned as a hit man for the Yugoslav government, assassinating high-profile Yugoslav émigrés who caused trouble for the regime at home. After he returned to Yugoslavia, Arkan opened a pastry shop and began to lead the Red Star Belgrade supporters' club; this was a fan club dedicated to the Yugoslav soccer team of the same name that later served as the recruiting base for the Serbian Volunteer Guard, or "the Tigers," formed and led by Arkan in 1990. When YUGOSLAVIA began to disintegrate in the early 1990s, Arkan expanded his repertoire to include gun running, for which the Croatian police arrested him in 1990. Between 1991 and 1995, his paramilitary unit participated in looting, smuggling and ETHNIC CLEANSING in eastern Slovenia and Bosnia; its most infamous operation was the Vukovar hospital massacre, in which over 200 Croats and other non-Serbs were killed. For his actions, the HAGUE WAR CRIMES TRIBUNAL indicted him as a war criminal in 1997. On January 15, 2000, he was assassinated in the Intercontinental Hotel in Belgrade.

Arledge, Roone Pinckney, Jr. (*1931–2002*) American TELEVISION producer. As president of ABC Sports (1968–77), Arledge transformed the very "look" and pacing of live and taped sports television. He insisted on using the latest technical advances in his programs, and his innovations were copied by other networks and quickly became standard practice in television sports broadcasting. Most notably, Arledge introduced the instant replay and its variations: stop-action replay, slow-motion replay and replays shot from different cameras and camera angles. He also pioneered the use of computer-generated graphics on the screen. The two showcases for Arledge's style were *Monday Night Football* and *Wide World of Sports;* he also brought a new level of coverage to the OLYMPIC GAMES in 1968 and subsequent years. In 1977 Arledge became head of ABC News and responsible for introducing America to anchors such as Peter Jennings and Diane Sawyer.

Arlen, Harold (Hyman Arluck) (*1905–1986*) U.S. composer. During

his Broadway and HOLLYWOOD career, Arlen created some of the most enduring and popular tunes in the history of American popular music. He started out hoping to succeed as a singer but switched full time to composition in the late 1920s. His first hit was "Get Happy," written in collaboration with lyricist Ted Koehler. Among their other hits were "I Love a Parade" and "Stormy Weather." During the Great Depression, Arlen left Broadway for Hollywood, where he collaborated with E. Y. Harburg on the songs for *The Wizard of Oz*. Arlen won an Oscar in 1939 for that film's "Over the Rainbow." He was nominated for five other songs, including "Blues in the Night" and "That Old Black Magic."

Armani, Giorgio (*1935– *) Italian fashion designer, known for work that is characterized by a quality of casual elegance, a quality that has even been described as "over-serious." Armani's educational background included two years of medical school followed by military service. In the 1950s he took a job designing windows for La Rinascente, moving into buying and then to fashion design. He was associated with La Rinascente until he established his own design studio in 1970, producing designs for various manufacturers. In 1975 he founded his own label. He now operates a chain of shops, designs leatherware for Mario Valentino and has even designed uniforms for the Italian air force. His style depends heavily on the traditional detailing of men's clothing, adapting that vocabulary to jackets and skirts for women with a reserved, tailored dignity. He was the winner of a 1979 Neiman Marcus Award. Armani has remained a popular designer, in part because of his willingness to design outfits for media celebrities such as Robert DE NIRO and Michelle Pfeiffer.

Armenia Russian and Ottoman territory (1820–1918), independent nation (1918–20), Soviet territory (1920–91) and independent republic (1991–). Armenia's history in the 20th century was largely one of unfulfilled nationalism. Before WORLD WAR I (1914–18), several political organizations in Armenia, particularly the Armenian Revolutionary Federation (ARF) and the socialist Hunchak party, attempted to gain autonomy for Armenian subjects in Russia and the Ottoman Empire. Instead, Russian troops and government officials repressed Armenians by closing their schools and divesting their churches of property, as these two structures were seen as sources of nationalism. The Ottomans were more severe in their plunder and murder of Armenians within their borders. During World War I, the Ottoman state deported 90% of the Armenians within its borders. The Ottoman sultan justified this act by claiming that the Armenians represented a "fifth column" within his state that would operate at the behest of the Russians, with whom the sultan was at war. In this exodus an estimated 800,000 Armenians died as they marched into present-day Syria (then an Ottoman possession).

In 1916 this persecution briefly ended when Russian forces occupied all Ottoman lands inhabited by Armenians. When the BOLSHEVIKS took power in November 1917, the Russian Empire collapsed in civil war, allowing Armenians briefly to form their own independent state under the ARF in May 1918. Armenia immediately waged war against the newly independent states of Georgia and Azerbaijan, both of which ruled over ethnic Armenians. Though failing to acquire these regions, such as the Azerbaijani-controlled Nagorno-Karabakh district, Armenia gained Ottoman recognition in August 1920 at the Treaty of SÈVRES. The peace created at Sèvres only lasted a month. In September 1920 the nationalist Mustafa Kemal (later Kemal ATATÜRK) established a new government that renounced the treaty and invaded Armenia. At this time the Bolsheviks also invaded Armenia after winning their civil war and another conflict with Poland (1920), and the Bolshevik and Turkish states each acquired portions of Armenia. The Bolshevik forces that entered Armenia signed a December accord with the ARF that created the Armenian Socialist Soviet Republic out of the Armenian territories now in Bolshevik possession, including the ethnically Armenian regions of Naxçivan and Nagorno-Karabakh. By 1922 the ARF was forced out of all government posts by the Bolsheviks, and Armenia was united with Georgia and Azerbaijan in

the Transcaucasian Soviet Federated Socialist Republic, one of the four states that founded the Union of Soviet Socialist Republics (USSR). The new Soviet leadership soon returned Naxçivan and Nagorno-Karabakh to Azerbaijan, outlawed all noncommunist parties, attempted to eradicate the Armenian church and persecuted thousands of Armenian nationalists. During STALIN's reign, the only improvement in the condition of Armenia and Armenians came in 1936, when the Transcaucasian republic dissolved and Armenia was allowed to reemerge as a Soviet Socialist Republic within the USSR.

While persecution of Armenians lessened after Stalin's death in 1953, their subjugation remained unchanged until Mikhail GORBACHEV came to power in 1985 and soon introduced his political philosophy of GLASNOST, or "openness." Glasnost allowed Soviets civil liberties, particularly the ability to criticize government policies. By February 1988, many Armenians used these liberties to rally for the reannexation of Nagorno-Karabakh from Azerbaijan. By 1991 escalating tensions

between these Soviet Socialist Republics led to a war between them when Armenia seceded from the USSR in late 1991. Initially the Armenians fared poorly due to an Azerbaijani blockade and the collapse of order in neighboring Georgia, which interrupted Armenian imports. However, Armenian victories in 1993 and multilateral mediation procured a cease-fire in May 1994. Two months after the truce, the ARF protested against the ruling Pan-Armenian National Movement's (PNM) willingness to place Nagorno-Karabakh under joint rule with Azerbaijan, to give the Armenian president greater powers and to introduce capitalism gradually into the Armenian economy. The PNM responded by declaring the ARF illegal on account of its alleged ties to recent terrorist incidents. The ARF's suppression helped the PNM retain power in the 1995 national elections, although several opposition parties claimed the elections were fraudulent. Similar complaints were made in the 1996 reelection of PNM presidential candidate Levon Ter-Petrossian, who had served as presi-

ARMENIA

1915	Suspected of pro-Russian sympathies, two-thirds of Armenia's population of 2 million are deported to Syria and Palestine. Around 600,000 to 1 million die en route; the survivors contribute towards an Armenian diaspora in Europe and North America.
1916	Armenia is conquered by tsarist Russia and becomes part of a brief "Transcaucasian Alliance" with Georgia and Azerbaijan.
1918	Armenia becomes an independent republic.
1920	The Allies recognize Armenia as a sovereign nation; the Turks, who refuse to recognize the independence of Armenia, seize the regions of Kars and Alexandropol and continue the forced repatriation of ethnic Armenians, a process begun in 1915 and in which 1.5 million perish; the government of Armenia, a coalition of communists and Dashnaks, pronounces Armenia a Soviet republic.
1921	Communists force the Dashnaks out of government, who stage a revolt but fail to regain power.
1922	Armenia, Georgia, and Azerbaijan form the Transcaucasian Soviet Federated Socialist Republic, then join the Soviet Union.
1923	The Soviet Union assigns control of Nagorno-Karabakh, a region disputed by Armenia and Azerbaijan, to Azerbaijan.
1926	Joseph Stalin comes to power in Moscow and initiates both the industrialization of Armenia and the systematic suppression and murder of the country's political and intellectual elite, a campaign known as the Great Terror.
1936	The Soviet Union makes Armenia Georgia, and Azerbaijan distinct republics within the union.
1953	Stalin dies; Nikita Khrushchev becomes the leader of the Soviet Union.
1974	Moscow appointee Karen Demirchian assumes control of the Communist Party of Armenia (CSA), further entrenching its notorious corruption.
1985	Mikhail Gorbachev becomes leader of the Soviet Union.
1988	A massive earthquake kills 55,000 in Armenia.
1989	Soviet authorities arrest members of the Karabakh Committee, a political group dedicated to regaining the Nagorno-Karabakh region from Azerbaijan; the dispute with Azerbaijan over the Nagorno-Karabakh enclave escalates into war.
1991	Armenia declares its independence following the collapse of the Soviet Union; Levon Ter-Petrosian is elected president; Armenia joins 10 other former Soviet countries as a member of the Commonwealth of Independent States.
1992	The Armenian army carves a supply route, the Lachin corridor, through Azerbaijan and occupies Nagorno-Karabakh.
1994	Russia brokers a cease-fire between Armenia and Azerbaijan in which Armenia retains control over most of the Nagorno-Karabakh enclave.
1998	President Ter-Petrosian resigns unexpectedly; the government legalizes the Dashnak party, which Ter-Petrosian had outlawed; Prime Minister Robert Kocharian is elected president.
1999	Five terrorists enter the National Assembly and open fire, killing the prime minister, speaker, and six other members of parliament.
2001	Armenia becomes a full member of the Council of Europe.
2003	Kocharian wins presidential election; international observers find parliamentary elections flawed; six are sentenced for their roles in 1999 shooting.
2004	Thousands protest against president.
2006	Gas supply is nearly curtailed owing to explosions in Russia that damage pipeline; price of Russian gas doubles.

dent since his election in 1991. While protesters of the election were suppressed, Ter-Petrossian resigned as president in February 1998 after continued unpopularity over the joint administration of Nagorno-Karabakh. Robert Kocharian was elected president in 1998 and reelected in 2003.

Armenian Massacres of 1909 In April 1909 thousands of Armenians were killed by Turks in Cilicia, present-day southern Turkey, on the order of Sultan ABDUL HAMID II. The massacres were reprisals for Armenian revolutionary activity. The U.S. and other major powers intervened to stop the slaughter. (See also YOUNG TURKS.)

Armenian Massacres of 1915–1923 Armenian revolutionaries, hoping to achieve independence, captured the Ottoman fortress of Van, in the east of the empire, on April 20, 1915. Aided by the Russians, they held the fortress until August, when Turks regained control. The YOUNG TURK government declared the Armenian people dangerous, accused them of helping Russian invaders in WORLD WAR I and ordered them killed or deported. About 1 million Armenians fled or were killed, and 600,000 died of starvation, disease and exhaustion during forced marches through swamps and deserts of Syria and Mesopotamia. Many were massacred when they could go no farther.

Armory Show (International Exposition of Modern Art) Popularly known as the Armory Show, the International Exposition of Modern Art was held February 15 to March 15, 1913, in the 69th Regiment Armory in New York City. It introduced modern art in America. Organized by the Association of American Painters and Sculptors (founded in 1911), the show provided an outlet for artists ignored by the academically dominated shows usually presented and introduced Americans to the European art movements of FAUVISM and CUBISM. Approximately 1,000 American artists, including John SLOAN and Maurice PRENDERGAST, and 500 Europeans, such as Pablo PICASSO and Paul Cézanne, were represented. Although the public and the press ridiculed and condemned many of the paintings and sculptures, the show became a watershed in the development American art.

Armstrong, Edwin *(1890–1954)* American inventor, radio pioneer. Armstrong received his bachelor of electrical engineering from Columbia University, New York City, in 1913 and taught there from 1934 to 1954. He is best known for developing the regenerative or feedback circuit (1912) and superheterodyne circuit (1918) that formed the basic design for AM radios. In 1933 Armstrong invented the frequency modulation (FM) technique, which reduced static and improved radio reception. Patent disputes over his inventions marred his later years, and in 1954 he committed suicide.

Armstrong, Henry (Henry Jackson) *(1912–1988)* American boxer, the only man to have held three world titles simultaneously. In 1938 Armstrong reigned as the featherweight, lightweight and welterweight champion. He was inducted into boxing's Hall of Fame in 1954. He suffered a series of illnesses in his later years, some of which doctors suspected were caused by the many punches he had taken.

Armstrong, Lance (Lance Edward Gunderson) *(1971-)* American cyclist. The dominant athelete of the cycling world through the late 1990s until his retirement from cycling in 2005, Armstrong holds the record for most Tour de France wins. Armstrong began his career in the mid-1990s, showing promise with several wins at some major races but sidelined in 1996 when he was diagnosed with cancer and given less than even odds by the doctors that he would survive. With treatment and a strict regime of diet and training, not only did Armstrong survive, but he stunned the cycling world when he went on to win the Tour de France seven consecutive times from 1999 to 2005. Since his retirement he has been active in charity work for cancer research and has written a book about his life, *It's Not About the Bike: My Journey Back to Life* (2000).

Armstrong, (Daniel) Louis *(1900–1970)* American jazz musician. Born in New Orleans, Armstrong began playing the cornet at the age of 13 in the Waifs' Home band in his native city. He subsequently (1918–21) became a soloist with various New Orleans and Mississippi riverboat bands. He moved to Chicago in 1922 and gained recognition as a trum-

pet player with King OLIVER, later soloing with Fletcher HENDERSON in New York. Armstrong returned to Chicago in 1925 and organized his own band, the Hot Five. He made the first of many successful European tours in 1932 and gained the nickname of "Satchmo," a London critic's misspelling of the earlier appellation "Satchelmouth." Armstrong made a number of memorable recordings and became a familiar figure at jazz festivals and on television. An enormously popular musician, he was known for his brilliant improvisational style with the cornet and trumpet and for his gravelly-voiced "scat" singing. His autobiography, *Satchmo,* was published in 1954.

Armstrong, Neil Alden *(1930–)* U.S. astronaut and the first man on the Moon. He received his pilot's license at the age of 16. A naval air cadet at Purdue University, he was called to active duty in the KOREAN WAR. He received the Air Medal three times for his 78 combat missions. He returned to Purdue where he graduated in 1955. In 1962 he was accepted as a NASA pilot. On his first spaceflight in 1966, he commanded *Gemini 8* and performed the first manual docking maneuver in space. He commanded the *APOLLO 11* flight, and on July 10, 1969, he landed the lunar landing module on the Moon's surface. As the first man to set foot on a nonterrestrial surface, he made one of the notable comments of all time when he declared: "That's one small step for (a) man, one giant leap for mankind." With his companion Edwin E. ALDRIN, he set up experiments on the Moon and gathered a quantity of Moon material. In 1970 Armstrong resigned from the astronaut program and became a NASA administrator. In 1971 he joined the faculty of the University of Cincinnati. Armstrong left Cincinnati in 1979 and has since served in a variety of positions, such as on the National Commission of Space (1985–86) and as chairman of Computing Technologies for Aviation, Inc. (1982–92).

Army-McCarthy Hearings Soon after the end of World War II, the U.S. found itself in the grip of an anticommunist hysteria that became known as MCCARTHYISM, in tribute to the senator from Wisconsin. Like the PALMER RAIDS that followed World War I, many individuals were unfairly labeled as communists or FELLOW TRAVELERS and careers and lives were ruined as a result. Although Joseph R. MCCARTHY's tactics were brutal, he initially enjoyed broad popular support because of his seemingly patriotic opposition to COMMUNISM. McCarthy met his own downfall in 1953 at televised hearings in which the senator attempted to implicate the U.S. Army as harboring subversives. McCarthy was aided by his chief counsel, attorney Roy COHN, who held a personal grudge against the army because of its perceived abuse of his friend G. David Schine. McCarthy and Cohn, relishing the spotlight, turned the proceeding into a televised witchhunt. But McCarthy's antics and bullying of witnesses soured the public who came to admire army counsel Joseph Welch. The most memorable moment occurred when McCarthy accused Welch himself of employing subversives, and Welch shot back asking McCarthy "Have you no sense of decency at long last?" After the hearings McCarthy's power and prestige waned, and in late 1954 he was censured by the full Senate.

Arnaz, Desi (Desiderio Alberto Arnaz y de Acha III) *(1917–1986)* Cuban-born entertainer and producer. He and his first wife, Lucille BALL, designed, starred in and produced the pioneering TELEVISION comedy series *I LOVE LUCY*. The show dominated the U.S. airwaves from 1951 to 1957 and continues to entertain in syndication throughout the world. In the show Arnaz played Ricky Ricardo, a bandleader bedeviled by his wife's attempts to break into show business. The couple, married for 20 years, built a show business empire called Desilu Productions. They were divorced in 1960. After selling his interest in Desilu to Ball, Arnaz devoted himself to raising thoroughbred horses.

Arness, James *(1923–)* American television and movie actor. Arness (originally spelled Aurness) began his movie career after working in advertising. He played minor roles in such movies as *The Thing* in 1951 before creating the role of Marshal Matt Dillon on television's long-running dramatic series *Gunsmoke* (1955–75). Arness, six feet seven inches in height, was suggested for the role by John WAYNE. From February 12, 1978, to April 23, 1979, Arness played the role of Zeb

Macahan in the television series *How the West Was Won*.

Arnhem Netherlands port on the lower Rhine River. In September 1944, during WORLD WAR II, it was the target of a major Allied airborne and armored offensive, led by British general Bernard MONTGOMERY, that was designed to capture the Rhine River bridges and drastically shorten the war—a tragically bungled operation. Arnhem was not taken by the Allies until April 1945.

Arno, Peter *(1904–1968)* American cartoonist. Born Curtis Arnoux Peters in Rye, New York, he attended Yale University. He became famous for his cartoons, principally published in *THE NEW YORKER*. Heavily outlined with spikey expressive lines, the charcoal and watercolor drawings cleverly portray New York society, from high to low life, from the flapper-era 1920s to the hippie-filled 1960s. Recurrent in his delightful cast of characters were pompous businessmen, endearing drunks, overstuffed socialites and bosomy young things. Among his cartoon collections are *Peter Arno's Parade* (1929), *Man in the Shower* (1944), *Sizzling Platter* (1949) and *Lady in the Shower* (1967).

Arnold, Henry Harley "Hap" *(1886–1950)* U.S. Army and Air Force general. Born in Gladwyn, Pennsylvania, Arnold attended West Point, graduating in 1907. He took flying lessons from Orville Wright (see WRIGHT BROTHERS), and for the next three decades he advanced in the U.S. Army Air Corps, finally becoming chief of the corps in 1938. Arnold was long a believer in the strategic importance of air power, and in the years preceding WORLD WAR II he aggressively maximized the air corps' combat readiness despite a sharply limited budget. At his urging, American airplane manufacturers increased their production capacity six-fold during this period, and the air corps' pilot-training program greatly expanded its capacity through Arnold's scheme of sending pilots to civilian training programs. In World War II, Arnold was commander of the U.S. Army Air Force and played an instrumental role in planning the Allied war effort. In 1944 he was promoted to general of the army. In 1947, due largely to Arnold's lobbying, the air

force was made an independent branch of the armed forces, and in 1949, Arnold was named the first general of the U.S. Air Force.

Arnoldson, Klas Pontus *(1844–1916)* Swedish journalist and peace activist. Born in Göteborg, he was a railway stationmaster who was self-taught in many disciplines. During the 1870s he began to write articles that stressed individual conscience and freedom of thought. In 1881 he decided to devote all his time to journalism and the promotion of world peace. The following year he was elected to parliament, where he advocated neutrality and served until 1887. He edited a number of progressive journals and wrote several novels and many widely read books on peace and religion. One of the most influential figures in the European peace movement, he was important in preventing war with Norway after the Norwegian parliament voted for independence in 1905. In 1908 Arnoldson shared the NOBEL PRIZE for peace with the Danish pacifist Fredrik BAJER.

Aron, Jean-Paul *(1925–1988)* French writer and philosopher. Aron was the nephew of philosopher Raymond ARON and member of a distinguished Alsace family. Aron taught philosophy at the universities of Tourcoing and Lille and wrote books on the social manners and mores of 19th-century France. He also wrote novels and plays and contributed to the newspapers *Le Matin* and *Le Monde*. One of the first public figures in France to admit that he was suffering from AIDS, he said on French television that he would never have admitted he was homosexual had he not suffered from AIDS.

Aron, Raymond Claude *(1905–1983)* French political theorist, sociologist, historical philosopher, writer and teacher. During WORLD WAR II, after the Germans occupied FRANCE, he escaped to England and became editor of *La France Libre*, the official newspaper of Charles de GAULLE's FREE FRENCH government-in-exile. After the war he was a political columnist for *Le Figaro* for 30 years (1947–77), then served on the editorial board of the weekly *L'Express* (1977–83), for which he also wrote a regular column. Politically right of center, Aron championed individual freedom above all else and vigorously opposed COMMUNISM and TOTALITARIANISM. He carried on a well-known, long-standing antagonistic relationship with the French philosopher and writer Jean-Paul SARTRE. He wrote more than 30 books including *Main Currents in Sociological Thought* (1965).

Arp, Jean Hans *(1887–1966)* French painter, sculptor and poet. A student at the Weimar Academy (1905–07) and the Académie Julien, Paris (1908), he was associated with the BLAUE REITER group in Germany, exhibiting with them in 1913. In 1916 he was a cofounder of the DADA movement, contributing art and poetry to dada publications. From 1919 to 1920, he worked on dadaist projects with Max ERNST, and in 1925 he collaborated with El LISSITZKY on *The Isms of Art,* a survey of contemporary art. The following year he moved to Meudon near Paris and became a member of the surrealist group (1926–30). Arp is known for his inventive abstract work in many media—painted reliefs, collages, cut-outs, bas-reliefs and sculptures in the round. He is best remembered for the sculptures he began about 1930, works called "Concretions" that are richly organic in form. Represented in many museum collections, he is also noted for large commissioned works such as the wood relief executed for Harvard University in 1950 and the bronze created for the University of Caracas in 1953.

Arpino, Gerald *(1928–   )* American dancer and choreographer. Born in New York City, Arpino studied with Mary Ann Wells and May O'Donnell. He was one of six dancers who, with Robert JOFFREY, formed the Joffrey Ballet in 1956. Now best known as a choreographer and, after Joffrey's death in 1989, as artistic director of the company, Arpino has set a distinctly contemporary stamp on ballet with such works as his rock ballet *Trinity* (1970), *Viva Vivaldi!* (1965) and *Italian Suite* (1983). He has also danced in and choreographed Broadway musicals and operas and worked for television. In 1974 he received a Dance Magazine Award. Arpino is noted for his use of avant-garde music and the contemporary themes of his works.

Arrhenius, Svante August *(1859–1929)* Swedish physical chemist. Arrhenius originally went to Uppsala University to study chemistry, changing later to physics. He transferred to Stockholm in 1881 to do research under the physicist Erik Edlund, working initially on electrical polarization and then on the conductivity of solutions (electrolytes). This work won Arrhenius a high international reputation but only limited acclaim in Sweden. Despite this he returned to Stockholm in 1891 as lecturer at the Technical Institute and in 1895 became professor there. In 1903 he was awarded the NOBEL PRIZE in chemistry, and in 1905 he became the director of the Nobel Institute, a post he held until shortly before his death.

Arrhenius was a man of wide-ranging intellect. Besides developing his work on solutions, in later life he worked on cosmogony and serum therapy, being especially interested in the relation between toxins and antitoxins. He also investigated the GREENHOUSE EFFECT by which carbon dioxide regulates atmospheric temperature and calculated the changes that would have been necessary to have produced the Ice Ages.

Arroyo, Gloria Macapagal *(1947–   )* President of the Philippines (2001–   ). Arroyo attended high school at the Assumption Convent. After marrying Jose Miguel Tuason Arroyo, she graduated magna cum laude with a B.S. in commerce from Assumption College in 1968 and taught for several years. She also attended the Ateneo de Manila University, where she received an M.A. in economics in 1976, and the University of the Philippines, where she received a Ph.D in 1985. Arroyo joined the AQUINO administration as undersecretary of trade and industry. In 1992 she was elected to the Philippine Senate. In 1998 she won the vice presidency by the largest victory margin of any presidential or vice presidential candidate in history. On January 20, 2001, Arroyo advanced to the presidency when the Philippine Supreme Court unanimously declared that the position of president was vacant after the "resignation" of then president Joseph Estrada, who at that time was immersed in allegations of financial corruption and philandering.

As president, Arroyo's chief difficulty was the suppression of Abu Sayyaf, a fundamentalist Islamic terrorist group that demanded independence for those areas of the Philippines populated predominantly by Muslims. In this endeavor, she accepted aid from the U.S. and supported U.S. training of Philippine forces to defeat Abu Sayyaf. However, Arroyo endeavored to avoid accusations that she subordinated Philippine interests to U.S. policy, as she pledged to continue the efforts of her presidential predecessors to develop a Philippine foreign policy independent of its former colonial power. After her reelection in 2004, she faced allegations of corruption and calls for her resignation.

Artaud, Antonin *(1896–1948)* French playwright, poet, actor and theoretician of the theater. Artaud, who has attained a legendary status as a personification of the mad, tortured artist, ended his life in an insane asylum after a long, creative career that spanned many genres. In the 1920s Artaud won renown both as a surrealist poet, whose best work was collected in *Art and Death* (1929), and as a powerful film actor, notably in his role as a monk in *The Passion of Joan of Arc* (1928) by Danish director Carl DREYER. But Artaud was drawn first and foremost to the theater, writing several plays, including *The Cenci* (1935), as well as a theoretical work, *The Theater and Its Double* (1938), which advocated what has become known as the "Theater of Cruelty"—an impassioned, emotive style of dramatic presentation that rejects all moralizing and censorship and aims for truthful depiction of all dimensions of the human spirit.

Art Brut A name originated by the French painter Jean DUBUFFET to designate art produced by persons with no connection to the societally established worlds of art and culture. Dubuffet amassed a collection of over 5,000 works of Art Brut, which he donated in 1972 for permanent showing in the Château de Beaulieu in Lausanne, France. The creators of these Art Brut works were predominantly prisoners, hermits, psychiatric hospital residents—in short, societal outsiders. Dubuffet claimed that their works represented "pure invention" as opposed to the influence-laden techniques of officially recognized art. Dubuffet denied that Art Brut represented a form of "psychiatric art," insisting that "there is no art of the insane any more than there is an art of dyspeptics." The common threads of Art Brut, according to Dubuffet, were a disinterest in prevailing aesthetic standards and a focus on expression of vital personal crises.

Art Deco Name given to an ornately fashionable mode of interior decoration and product design that was highly popular in both America and Europe in the 1920s and 1930s. The name Art Deco arose from the Exposition Internationale des Arts Decoratifs et Industriels Modernes, held in Paris in 1925, which marked the debut of the Art Deco style. Art Deco emphasizes geometric patterns that are lavishly stylized by means of intricate tracery and ornamental details. Originally, Art Deco designs were noted for their use of rare and expensive materials such as marble, ivory, jade and lacquer. But in the 1930s Great Depression era, its focus shifted from fine material workmanship to dramatic design impact achieved with ordinary materials. Art Deco designs were most prominently used in public lobbies and railway stations of the era. The French ocean liner *NORMANDIE* was also a crowning achievement of the Art Deco style.

Art Nouveau A decorative style that was highly popular in Europe and America from the Gay Nineties era to the outbreak of World War I. Art Nouveau, which was utilized both in architecture and in product design, was distinguished by its delicate craftsmanship and its use of organic design forms such as fruits, flowers and twining leaves. It first emerged in England as an offshoot of the Arts and Crafts movement led by William Morris, although it derives its name from an 1895 exhibition held at the L'Art Nouveau gallery in Paris. The famous Tiffany lamps and stained glass windows produced in America are the most well-known examples of the Art Nouveau style. The Spaniard Antonio Gaudí is the most famous Art Nouveau architect. Art Nouveau, while predominantly influential in the applied arts, also showed itself in the fields of painting and book illustra-

tion, most notably in the works of Aubrey Beardsley.

Artois Area in northeastern France that during WORLD WAR I was a scene of heavy trench warfare. Between 1914 and 1916 three bloody, inconclusive battles were fought around the town of Arras. A ridge near Vimy was captured and recaptured three times. During the second battle French forces incurred over 3,000 casualties in 10 minutes. Between May 9 and June 18, 1915, the French lost 102,000 men. Both sides incurred heavy shelling and gas attacks.

Arts Council of Great Britain Established in 1946 by Royal Charter, the Arts Council was developed to promote high standards in the arts and to foster public appreciation and accessibility throughout Britain. The Arts Council evolved from the wartime Council of the Encouragement of Music and the Arts (CEMA). It receives its grant directly from the government and has contributed to the abolition of weekly repertory, the maintenance of relatively low-priced seats and the development of new works of writing, music and architecture. In the 1970s regional and local arts councils took more responsibility for supporting small-scale, community and young people's productions. Under the government of Prime Minister Margaret THATCHER, the Arts Council budget was severely cut, and the government suggested that the council look to corporate donations. In 1987, due largely to a noisy arts lobby and a government response to charges of philistinism, a modest increase was announced. Some critics suggested that the Arts Council should be abolished and the subsidy handed out by the Office of Arts and Libraries; arts organizations strongly oppose this idea.

Artsybashev, Mikhail Petrovich (*1878–1927*) Russian novelist, essayist and playwright. His novel *Sanin* (1907) was one of the first in Russia to include a frank discussion of sex. Other works include *Breaking Point* (1915) and *War* (1918). He left Russia following the Russian Revolution.

Aruba Island in the NETHERLANDS ANTILLES, off the northwest coast of

Venezuela; a key refining and shipping center for Venezuelan oil since 1925. In February and April 1942, during WORLD WAR II, its refineries were shelled by German submarines. In 1954 Aruba was officially recognized a part of the Netherland Antilles. Aruba seceded from the Netherland Antilles in 1986 but stopped short of full independence by becoming a self-governing member of the Kingdom of the Netherlands. In the past few decades the island's main source of revenue has been its booming tourist industry.

Arup, Sir Ove (*1895–1988*) English engineer, educated in Germany and Denmark. Arup was a consultant to Berthold Lubetkin and the Tecton group, architects, when they were designing the Highgate flats and the penguin pool at the London Zoo. Arup helped design the Sydney Opera House by Jorn Utzon. His bridge in Durham, England, is a fine example of the elegance of his work.

Arusha Declaration A 1967 call by Tanzanian president Julius NYERERE to develop TANZANIA's national economy through state ownership but locally administered village planning and for the Tanzanian people to emulate his own simple lifestyle.

Asch, Moses (*1905–1986*) U.S. record producer. He founded Folkways Records in 1947 and ran the company until his death. Folkways recordings of such artists as LEADBELLY, Woody GUTHRIE, and Brownie McGhee helped spark the U.S. folk music revival of the 1950s and 1960s. The company's catalog consisted of more than 2,000 albums that Asch kept in print. Beyond international folk music, notable titles included *Agitprop Music* and *Sounds of North American Frogs*.

Aschoff, Karl Albert Ludwig (*1866–1942*) German pathologist. Educated at Bonn, Berlin and Strasbourg, Aschoff was later professor of pathological anatomy first at Marburg (1903–06) and then at Freiburg, where he remained for the rest of his career. He carried out investigations of a number of human pathological conditions, including jaundice, appendicitis, cholecystitis, tuberculosis and thrombosis. In 1904 he described the inflammatory nodules located in the muscle of the heart and associated with rheumatism (Aschoff's bodies). He recognized the bacteria-engulfing activity of the phagocytes in various tissues and named them the reticuloendothelial system. Students from all over the world attended the pathological institute that Aschoff built up at Freiburg.

ASEAN Regional Forum (ARF)

Regional economic, political and security organization in Southeast Asia. Founded in 1994 to ensure security for Association of South-East Asian Nations (ASEAN) members in the post–COLD WAR era, ARF evolved out of an initial meeting in July 1993 by the foreign ministers of ASEAN member states. At the conclusion of that meeting, the ministers in attendance agreed to convene the following year so all nations with an interest in the Asia-Pacific area could discuss their mutual security concerns in the emerging world order. This assemblage later grew from 17 to 23 states—Australia, Brunei, Burma (1996), Cambodia (1999), Canada, China, the European Union, India (1996), Indonesia, Japan, Laos, Malaysia, Mongolia (1999), New Zealand, North Korea (2000), Papua New Guinea, the Philippines, Russia, South Korea, Singapore, Thailand, the U.S., and Vietnam (1995)—interested in preserving the security of the Asia-Pacific region. ARF has attempted to use the structure of ASEAN to elicit discussion and cooperation from its members on security issues such as the future of the Korean Peninsula, the independence movement in EAST TIMOR, the political conflict in Burma, the prohibition of nuclear testing in Southeast Asia, weapons of mass destruction (WMDs), and piracy and the illegal weapons trade. To achieve these ends, it eschews a powerful bureaucracy and instead relies on building consensus among its members to resolve international issues.

While making headway on some issues, such as securing a ban on nuclear testing in Southeast Asia, ARF failed to resolve tensions in Indonesia and over Taiwan and the South China Sea. With regard to Indonesia, ARF was prevented from having a stronger say in how that multiethnic nation responds to separatist movements against the Indonesian state. On the subject of Taiwan, ARF failed to bring to fruition the Sino-American declaration in the 1972 Shanghai Communiqué that there should be only one political entity representing mainland China and Taiwan. Finally, ARF has proven unable to resolve the competing claims of China, Vietnam, and the Philippines to the oil fields located beneath the South China Sea.

Aseyev, Nikolai Nikolayevich

(1889–1963) Russian poet. His early works include *Night Flute* (1914), *Letorey* (1915) and *Queen of the Cinema* (early 1920s). In 1923 he joined the literary LEF (Left Front); although later works, such as *The Steel Nightingale* (1922), *Twenty-Six* (1923), *The Sverdlov Storm* (1924) and *Semyon Proskakov* (1926), contained a political element, they still expressed much romanticism.

Asgeirsson, Asgeir (1894–1972)

President of Iceland (1952–68). Asgeirsson was a member of the Icelandic parliament from 1923 to 1952. While in parliament he served as minister of finance (1931–34), prime minister (1932–34) and governor of the International Monetary Fund (IMF, 1946–52).

Ashbery, John (1927–) Ameri-

can poet and art critic. Raised on a farm in upstate New York, Ashbery attended Harvard, Columbia and New York University. In 1955 he went to Paris on a Fulbright scholarship to translate French poetry. A contributor (1955–65) to *Art News* and the Paris *Herald Tribune,* he later became art critic for *Newsweek.* He was associated with the avant-garde New York School of poets. His first book, *Some Trees* (1956), won the Yale Younger Poets prize. His reputation was enhanced when *Self-Portrait in a Convex Mirror* (1975) won the PULITZER PRIZE, the National Book Award and the National Book Critics Circle Award. Later collections include *Houseboat Days, As We Know* and *A Wave* (1984). He was cowinner of the 1985 BOLLINGEN PRIZE. His playful, dreamlike and often obscure poems have often baffled readers and critics alike. In 1997 Ashbery received the American Academy of Arts and Letters' Gold Medal for Poetry. Ashbery is sometimes compared to Wallace STEVENS.

Ashcan School See the EIGHT.

Ashcroft, Dame Peggy (Edith Margaret Emily Ashcroft) (1907–1991)

British actress. One of the greatest actresses of the British theater, Ashcroft made her acting debut in James Barrie's *Dear Brutus* at the Birmingham Repertory Theatre in 1926. Many of her theatrical triumphs were in Shakespearean roles opposite Sir John Gielgud: Juliet in *Romeo and Juliet* (1935) and Beatrice in *Much Ado About Nothing* (1950), among others. Other acclaimed performances were in Chekhov's *Three Sisters* (1936–37), Goetz's *The Heiress* (1949) and Hellman's *Watch on the Rhine* (1980). A founder member and a director of the ROYAL SHAKESPEARE COMPANY, she played Margaret of Anjou in their monumental production of *The Wars of the Roses* (1963–64).

Ashe, Arthur Robert (1943–1993)

U.S. tennis player. In 1968, while still an amateur, Ashe became the first black man to win the U.S. Open title. He turned professional the following year and became a consistent winner, leading an overpowering U.S. Davis Cup team from 1968 to 1972. In 1975 he became the first black man ever to take the Wimbledon singles title, defeating the much-favored Jimmy CONNORS. Ashe retired after a heart attack in 1979 and was named captain of the Davis Cup team in 1980. He went on to a career in tennis broadcasting. Ashe remained active after retirement, protesting against South African APARTHEID. But he suffered from physical debilitation because of a 1983 blood transfusion that infected him with the HIV virus. Ashe died of AIDS-related pneumonia in February 1993.

Ashkenazy, Vladimir (1937–)

Russian pianist and conductor. Born to pianist parents in Gorki, Ashkenazy began piano lessons at six, made his debut at seven and studied at the Central Music School, Moscow, and the Moscow State Conservatory. He achieved international prominence when he won the second prize in the Chopin Competition, Warsaw, in 1956 and first prize in the Queen Elisabeth Competition, Brussels, in 1957. His busy touring schedule included an American debut in 1958. In 1963 he and his wife left the USSR. They settled in Reykjavík, Iceland, in 1968. He became a citizen of Iceland in 1972. As a pianist, Ashkenazy is noted for his sensitive, poetic yet energetic style and for a repertoire that includes Beethoven, Brahms, Mozart, RACHMANINOFF, SIBELIUS and PROKOFIEV. He made his conducting debut in Iceland in 1973 and has since turned his attention to conducting while remaining an active pianist. Ashkenazy's autobiography is titled *Beyond Frontiers*. In 1987 Ashkenazy was appointed musical director of the Royal Philharmonic Orchestra.

Ashley, Laura *(1926–1985)* Welsh-born British designer. Ashley's romantic, Victorian-inspired clothes and home furnishings have found favor with "Sloane Rangers" and romantics the world over. In 1953 she and her husband, Bernard, set up the company that bore her name by printing fabric on the kitchen table of their London home. The business grew into a global enterprise headquartered in Carno, Wales, with 4,000 employees, some 200 stores and annual sales of $130 million. Since its inception, chairman Bernard Ashley has been in charge of the business aspects of the company while Laura Ashley created its designs.

Ashton, Sir Frederick *(1906–1988)* English dancer and choreographer. Considered Britain's greatest choreographer, Ashton was born in Ecuador of English extraction and was inspired to become a dancer after seeing ballerina Anna PAVLOVA in 1917. He began to study dance in 1924 with Leonide MASSINE and Marie RAMBERT in London, and took up choreography shortly thereafter. In 1935 he joined the Vic-Wells Ballet (now the ROYAL BALLET) and began his successful association with ballerina Margot FONTEYN for whom he created leading roles in many of his ballets during the next 25 years (*Ondine* in 1958, *Marguerite and Armand* in 1963). Some of Ashton's well-known ballets are *Illuminations* (1950), *Romeo and Juliet* (1955), *La Fille mal gardée* (1960) and *Monotones I* (1965). Known for his sure poetic touch in delicately evoking scenes and moods, he helped develop a distinctly British balletic style marked by elegance, lyricism and graciousness. As a dancer he achieved his greatest acclaim in character roles, such as Carabosse in *Sleeping Beauty*. He also served as director of the Royal Ballet from 1963 to 1970. In 1950 Ashton was made a Commander of the Order of the British Empire and, in 1962, was knighted; he was also a recipient of the Legion d'Honneur.

Ashton-Warner, Sylvia Constance *(1908–1984)* New Zealand author and educator. Born in Stratford, New Zealand, she was educated at Wairapa College and the Teacher's College, Auckland. Her novels describe her experiences teaching Maori children. Her first and best-known book, *Spinsters* (1959), was the basis of a British film, *Two Loves* (1961). Other work includes the novels *Bell Call* (1964), *Three* (1970) and an autobiography, *Myself* (1967). Ashton-Warner also published poetry and short stories under the name Sylvia Henderson, her husband's surname.

Asia, Soviet Central Region of the USSR, Soviet Central Asia embraced the Kazakh SSR (Soviet Socialist Republic), the Uzbek SSR, the Turkmen SSR, the Tadzhik SSR and the Kirghiz SSR. Until 1917 Russian Central Asia was divided politically into the khanate of Khiva, the emirate of Bokhara and the governor-generalship of Turkestan. In the summer of 1919 the authority of the Soviet government became definitely established in these regions. The khan of Khiva was deposed in February 1920, and a People's Soviet Republic was set up. In August 1920 the emir of Bokhara suffered the same fate, and a similar regime was set up in Bokhara. The former governor-generalship of Turkestan was constituted an autonomous Soviet socialist republic within the Russian Soviet Federated Socialist Republic on April 11, 1921.

In the autumn of 1924 the Soviets of the Turkestan, Bokhara and Khiva republics decided to redistribute the territories of these republics on a nationality basis; at the same time Bokhara and Khiva became socialist republics. The redistribution was completed in May 1925, when the new states of Uzbekistan, Turkmenistan and Tadzhikistan and several autonomous regions were established. The remaining districts of Turkestan populated by Kazakhs were united with Kazakhstan. Kirghizia, until then a part of the Russian Soviet Federal Socialist Republic, was established as a union republic in 1936. Following the disintegration of the Soviet Union on December 25, 1991, the Soviet republics received their independence.

Asia-Pacific Economic Cooperation (APEC) Regional economic organization. Established in 1989 at the behest of Australia, APEC consists of Australia, Brunei, Canada, Chile, China, Hong Kong (later incorporated into China), Indonesia, Japan, Malaysia, Mexico, New Zealand, Papua New Guinea, the Philippines, Singapore, South Korea, Taiwan, Thailand, and the U.S.; Peru, Russia and Vietnam later joined in 1998. Since Australia suggested that nations within the Asian-Pacific area meet and discuss mutual economic issues, APEC has sought to enhance regional economic integration and free trade among those countries surrounding and in the Pacific Ocean, and its members have cooperated since 1993 to reduce tariffs, improve regional security and promote the political, economic, social and technological development of the poorer APEC members through funds loaned by other member states.

In 1996 APEC members committed themselves in principle to greater free trade. An agreement outlined later by a Japanese-led commission gained pledges from all fully industrialized APEC states to remove all trade barriers by 2010 and to extend this free-trade arrangement to all members by 2020. APEC officials also encouraged members to extend the principle of free trade to non-APEC states. The reason for this gradual introduction of the principle of free trade was the divergence of opinion among APEC members into three groups. The first faction, representing fully industrialized Asian-Pacific democracies such as the U.S. and Japan, championed the greater economic integration this agreement would produce and initially opposed any effort to make its introduction a gradual one. The second group, consisting of industrialized nations such as China, were concerned that free trade would expose their infant industries to powerful foreign competition and curb their economic growth. Finally, a third group, composed of autocratic nations such as Indonesia, expressed concern about the effects of increasing economic liberalization on the political structures of their nations.

Asimov, Isaac *(1920–1992)* Popular American writer whose more than 300 books embrace popular science, history, literary criticism, crime fiction and science fiction. His family emigrated from Russia to the U.S. when he was three years old. He grew up near New York City. Throughout most of his life he was torn between careers in science education—he was an associate professor of biochemistry at Boston University—and professional writing—his early enthusiasm for pulp magazines led to his first story sale in 1938. He was able to combine both interests in his numerous science fiction stories. Whether his subject was fact or fancy—the action of enzymes, the plays of Shakespeare or the flight of rocketships—he insisted on accuracy. "I am a working scientist," he said, "I don't want to write poetically; I want to write clearly." It is enough if his stories "stimulate curiosity and the desire to know." Two ongoing series dominated his fiction. His ROBOT stories and novels, including *I, Robot* (1950) and *Caves of Steel* (1954), brought dignity to a clichéd genre. "Metal men" stereotypes were replaced with the more thoughtful, mature images of the "positronic robots," machines that could be "the servants, friends, and allies of humanity." His Foundation novels, for which he won a Hugo Award in 1966, are a "psychohistory" of the rise and fall of future Galactic Empires.

Aslan, Ana *(1897–1988)* Romanian gerontologist who developed a controversial drug called Gerovital H3 that she claimed could restore youth. Among those rumored to have taken her treatments were such heads of state as Charles de GAULLE, Nikita KHRUSHCHEV and Indira GANDHI, and such show business luminaries as Lillian GISH and Marlene DIETRICH. Most scientists outside Romania remained unconvinced that Gerovital had any rejuvenating effect. Detractors pointed out that the drug was simply a form of procaine, which under the brand name Novocain had been in use for decades as a local anesthetic.

Asplund, Erik Gunnar *(1885–1940)* Swedish architect. Born in Stockholm, he studied architecture at the city's Academy of Art. From 1917 to 1920 he edited the influential magazine *Arkitektur*. His early neoclassical style is evident in his design of the Stockholm City Library (1924–28). Asplund's most celebrated contributions to architecture were the pavilions he designed for the Stockholm Exhibition of 1930, Sweden's first foray into the INTERNATIONAL STYLE. He is known for his spare and elegant buildings and accessories, designs that contributed greatly to the development of Swedish Modern architecture.

Asquith, Herbert Henry (earl of Oxford and Asquith, 1925) *(1852–1928)* British statesman, prime minister (1908–16). He was educated at Oxford and became a London barrister in 1876. Entering politics, he was elected to Parliament as a Liberal in 1886. Recognized as a persuasive and powerful speaker, he gained fame as a counsel to Irish nationalist Charles Stewart Parnell (1846–91) and a supporter of the South African War. Asquith served as home secretary (1892–95) and chancellor of the exchequer (1905–08). Succeeding Sir Henry CAMPBELL-BANNERMAN as prime minister in 1908, Asquith presided over a number of important social reforms. These included health and unemployment insurance, old-age pensions and trade union protection. He also set the nation on a program of naval expansion. In order to finance his programs, his government levied heavy taxes on wealthy Britons. When the House of Lords rejected his budget, Asquith ultimately fought back with the Parliament Act of 1911, which ended the Lords' veto power.

During his ministry, Asquith also faced problems with militant woman suffragists and socialists and with the Irish HOME RULE question. Asquith brought Britain into WORLD WAR I in 1914, but he did not prove a vigorous wartime leader and resigned in 1916. Succeeded by David LLOYD GEORGE, Asquith headed the waning LIBERAL PARTY until 1926, entering the House of Lords in 1925.

al-Assad, Bashar *(1965–)* President of Syria (2000–). Born in Damascus to Syrian president Hafez al-ASSAD, Bashar served as head of the Syrian army's armored division and received political training to prepare him to succeed his father. When President Hafez al-Assad died in 2000, Bashar succeeded his father as president after a national referendum. Critics of his domestic policy have pointed to the highly restricted freedom of the press within SYRIA, the continued presence of political prisoners, the harassment of dissidents by government security forces, and the government's repeated crackdown on public political meetings. In matters of foreign policy, Bashar has called for a greater and co-ordinated Arab presence in any future Middle East peace processes and has adamantly insisted that Israel return to its pre-1967 borders, thereby returning the GOLAN HEIGHTS to Syria. In 2005, in response to strong international pressure, Assad agreed to withdraw Syrian military forces from LEBANON, where they had been stationed since 1976 to preserve order during the LEBANESE CIVIL WAR OF 1975–1990.

al-Assad, Hafez *(1930–2000)* Syrian general and president. Born at Quaradah of a minority Alawite (Shiite) sect, Assad was trained as an air force pilot in the USSR. He rose to the rank of air force commander in 1964 and became defense minister in 1966. As a member of the nationalist faction off the Baath Party (pro-PLO, anti-ISRAEL and opposed to close Soviet ties), he instigated the November 1970 coup, became prime minister in 1970 and president in 1971. His attempts to merge SYRIA with IRAQ failed, and hostility developed between these two nations, especially after Saddam HUSSEIN became Iraqi president. Assad was reelected in 1978 and 1985. He also headed the Baath Party and the Syrian armed forces. The 1986 Syrian involvement in terrorism led to Great Britain's breaking off diplomatic relations and limited EUROPEAN COMMUNITY sanctions against Syria. Assad's relations with the West improved when he supported UN action against Hussein and Iraq after Iraq's 1990 invasion of KUWAIT. In 1999 Assad began conversations with Israeli prime minister Ehud BARAK, but these talks promptly ended when both sides failed to agree on the status of the GOLAN HEIGHTS. On his death in 2000, his son Bashar al-ASSAD succeeded him as president.

Assam Indian state bordered to the north by Bangladesh and to the south by Burma. The British East India Company took control of Assam in 1826, but it was not established as a separate province until 1919. It was the site of intense fighting between Japanese and Allied forces during WORLD WAR II. In 1959 it became a constituent state of India. It was invaded by Chinese troops in 1962. Rebellions on the part of various indigenous tribes led to the establishment of two separate and smaller states within Assam: Nagaland (in 1963) and Meghalaya (in 1971).

Assault *(1943–1971)* Thoroughbred racehorse. A son of Bold Venture, in 1946 Assault became the seventh Triple Crown winner in history and was named three-year-old of the year. The following year saw three of the greatest racehorses ever—Assault, Armed and Stymie—battle for top money-winning honors, a title eventually taken by the six-year-old Stymie. Never entirely sound due to injuries suffered as a yearling, he retired in 1950 with a record of 42 starts, with 18 wins and finishing out of the money only 11 times. Retired to stud at the King Ranch, he was found to be sterile but still enjoyed a lengthy retirement until his death in 1971.

Asser, Tobias *(1838–1913)* Dutch statesman, jurist and legal scholar. Asser served in a series of governmental posts in the latter half of the 19th century as a legal adviser and treaty negotiator. As a member of the Dutch Council of State, he presided over international law conferences at The HAGUE in 1893, 1894, 1900 and 1904. He was instrumental in the formation of The Hague Permanent Court of Arbitration to which he was appointed in 1900. In 1911 Asser shared the NOBEL PRIZE for peace with Alfred FRIED.

as-Suwayda Town in as-Suwayda province of Syria. First settled by the Romans, it has stood since the 10th century as the leading center of the Druze religious sect. During French Mandate rule (1921–42), it was the capital of the state of Jebel Druse. When the Druze revolted against French rule, they conducted a successful siege against as-Suwayda's French garrison, from July to September 1925, but were forced to relinquish their prize in 1926 (see DRUZE REBELLION OF 1925–1927).

Astaire, Fred (Frederick Austerlitz) *(1899–1987)* American dancer and choreographer. Immortalized in films from *Top Hat* to *Carefree,* Nebraska-born Astaire began his career in a brother-sister vaudeville act at the age of eight. With his sister Adele he appeared on the Broadway and London stage in various musicals and revues, starting with *Over the Top* in 1917 and including the GERSHWIN *Funny Face* (1927). After his sister retired in 1932, he appeared in Cole PORTER's *Gay Divorce* (1932). In 1933 Astaire made his first film, *Dancing Lady,* and then was teamed with Ginger ROGERS in RKO's film *Flying Down to Rio*—thus beginning a legendary partnership that was showcased in nine more films. In over 30 musical films Astaire sang and danced with other leading ladies, among them Judy GARLAND (*Easter Parade,* 1948), Rita Hayworth (*You Were Never Lovelier,* 1942), Cyd Charisse (*The Band Wagon,* 1953) and Audrey Hepburn (*Funny Face,* 1957).

He starred in several award-winning television specials and won acclaim as a dramatic actor in his later years, most notably in such films as *On the Beach* (1959) and *The Towering Inferno* (1974). As a singer, Astaire introduced many of the great songs of Irving BERLIN, Jerome KERN and George and Ira Gershwin, both on the stage and in movies. Considered one of the greatest dancers of the 20th century, Astaire was a perfectionist noted for his elegance and originality in choreography and his canny grasp of the movie camera's possibilities. In 1949 Astaire received a special Academy Award "for his unique artistry and his contributions to the technique of musical pictures."

Astbury, William Thomas *(1889–1961)* British X-RAY crystallographer and molecular biologist. In 1916 he won a scholarship to Cambridge University, to study chemistry, physics and mathematics, and graduated in 1921 after spending two years of the war doing X-ray work for the army. He then joined William Henry BRAGG's brilliant group of crystallographers, first at University College, London, and from 1923 at the Royal Institution. In 1928 he moved to the University of Leeds as lecturer in textile physics and by 1930 had produced an explanation of the extensibility of wool in terms of two keratin structures. A popular account of this work was given in *Fundamentals of Fibre Structure* (1933). The keratin structure established his reputation, and he quickly extended his studies to other fibers and proteins. This work laid the foundation for the X-ray structural investigations of hemoglobin and myoglobin. In 1935 Astbury began to study nucleic acids by X-ray crystallography, and in 1938 he and his research student Florence Bell produced the first hypothetical structure of DNA. In 1945 Astbury was appointed to the new chair of biomolecular structure at Leeds.

Aston, Francis William *(1877–1945)* British chemist and physicist. He was educated at Mason College, the forerunner of Birmingham University, where he studied chemistry. From 1898 until 1900 he did research on optical rotation under P. F. Frankland. He left Birmingham in 1900 to work in a Wolverhampton brewery for three years. During this time he continued with scientific research in a home laboratory, where he worked on the production of vacua for X-ray discharge tubes. This work came to the notice of J. H. Poynting of the University of Birmingham, who invited Aston to work with him. He remained at Birmingham until 1910 when he moved to Cambridge as research assistant to J. J. Thomson. He became a research fellow at Cambridge in 1920 and stayed there for the rest of his life, apart from the war years spent at the Royal Aircraft Establishment, Farnborough. Aston's main work, for which he received the NOBEL PRIZE in chemistry in 1922, was on the design and use of the mass spectrograph, which was used to clear up several outstanding problems and became one of the basic tools of the new atomic physics. Contained in Aston's work were the implications of atomic energy and destruction. He believed in the possibility of using nuclear energy and warned of the dangers. He lived just long enough to see the first atomic bomb dropped in August 1945.

Asturian Uprising of 1934 In Spain in the early 1930s political parties were polarized over powers to be granted the Roman Catholic Church. In 1934 the Socialist Party planned a nationwide general strike and various uprisings to prevent the prochurch CEDA from joining the government. On October 5, 1934, communist-oriented miners revolted in Asturias (northwestern Spain), occupying the city of Oviedo and the surrounding region, subsequently burning churches and killing about 40 people. Francisco FRANCO and another general brutally put down the uprising, killing 3,000 and capturing 35,000, who were tortured and tried in 1935. The ferocious suppression divided Spain, helping to precipitate the SPANISH CIVIL WAR (1936–39).

Asturias, Miguel Angel (1899–1974) Guatemalan novelist, poet, diplomat and journalist. As a student, Asturias was active in the overthrow of the dictator Manuel Estrada Cabrera; but in 1923 he was forced into exile. For five years he studied Mayan ethnology at the Sorbonne, meanwhile associating with SURREALISTS André BRETON and Paul ÉLUARD. *El señor presidente,* completed in 1930, was not published until 1946. Returning to Guatemala, he joined the diplomatic service and published *Hombres de maíz* (1949, *Men of Corn*). His Banana Trilogy—*Viento fuerte* (1950, *Strong Wind*), *El papa verde* (1954, *The Green Pope*) and *Los ojos de los enterrados* (1960, *The Eyes of the Interred*)—examined U.S. economic and political influence in Central America. In 1954 he again went into exile, first in Chile and Argentina, later in Italy. *Mulata de tal* (1963, *Mulata*) and *Maladrón* (1969, *Bad Thief*) described the clash between Indian and European culture. His poetry includes *Alcazan* (1940), *Bolívar* (1955) and *Clarivigilia primaveral* (1965). In 1966 he received the Lenin Peace Prize and was named ambassador to France. He was awarded the NOBEL PRIZE in literature in 1967. His work marks the beginning of El BOOM in Latin American literature.

Aswân Dam On the Nile River, about 450 miles south of Cairo. Construction of this dam was central to NASSER's industrial and agricultural development program for EGYPT. Its construction appeared thwarted when the U.S. and Britain withdrew a promise of aid on July 20, 1956. Nasser retaliated by nationalizing the SUEZ CANAL on July 26, leading to the SUEZ CRISIS and Nasser's appeal to the USSR for funds, which Egypt received until 1970. The huge lake created by the dam threatened the ancient archaeological site of ABU SIMBEL, whose massive temple and statues were moved to higher ground with U.S. aid. In June 2000 the U.S. and Egypt reached an agreement to upgrade the dam's hydroelectric facilities.

Atatürk, Mustafa Kemal (Mustafa Kemal) (1881–1938) Turkish military leader, statesman, founder and first president of the Republic of Turkey. Born in Thessaloniki (now part of Greece), Kemal graduated from the Military Academy at Constantinople and, as chief of staff of Enver Pasha (the military leader who as minister of war would bring the Ottoman Empire into World War I on the side of the German and Austro-Hungarian Empires), participated in the YOUNG TURK rebellion against the sultan ABDUL HAMID. After participating in the Ottoman Empire's disastrous wars in North Africa and the Balkans in 1911–13, Kemal distinguished himself in the empire's only successful military campaign during World War I, when British and Commonwealth forces were defeated on the beaches of the GALLIPOLI PENINSULA near the Turkish Straits. After the surrender of Ottoman forces in the fall of 1918, Sultan Mohammed VI dispatched Kemal to the eastern part of Anatolia to remove him from the center of power, but after resigning from the Ottoman army in 1919, Kemal organized a new Turkish nationalist party and created his own military force. The sultan, meanwhile, in Constantinople, remained under the control of British and French troops that occupied the Turkish Straits in preparation for carving up the Turkish remnant of the disintegrating Ottoman Empire into European spheres of influence. Operating from the city of Ankara in central Anatolia, Kemal commanded Turkish troops that expelled Greek forces from the west coast of the country in 1921–22 and then forced the British and French to evacuate Constantinople and the Turkish Straits during the CHANAK CRISIS. In 1923 his military successes obliged the Allies to replace the vindictive Treaty of SÈVRES (1920) with the Treaty of LAUSANNE (1923), which provided international recognition of the Turkish republic (of which he had been elected the first president).

In 1924 Kemal embarked on a sweeping campaign to reform the Turkish political and social system on the model of Europe. His goal was to transform the defeated, impoverished remnant of the defunct Ottoman Empire, shrunken by the loss of its Arab possessions south of Anatolia, into a modern, Westernized country. Convinced that Islam was a major source of Turkey's backwardness, he replaced the theocratic system of the empire with a strict form of secularism, including the disestablishment of Islam as the state religion through the abolition of the caliphate, the proclamation of the equality of all religions before the law, the replacement of Islamic with secular educational institutions, and the enforcement of women's right to dress in ways that were prohibited by Islamic teaching. He also replaced Islamic law with a secular form of jurisprudence. To promote the campaign of Westernization, Kemal prescribed the adoption of Western clothing, Latin script, and the Western calendar. His reforms reached every corner of Turkish society and brought about fundamental changes in the daily life of the Turkish people.

Though hailing the virtues of Western-style democracy, Kemal introduced a one-party state under his own Republican People's Party in order to prevent the emergence of opposition to the sweeping reforms that he was imposing on a conservative society for its own good. He was reelected president three times with no opposition. In recognition of his service to the country, the nation's parliament bestowed on Kemal the name "Atatürk" (father of the Turks) in 1933. Ever since his death in 1938, Atatürk has retained an almost iconic status in the minds of Turkish citizens. To some sympathetic observers inside and outside Turkey, he represents the model of the enlightened despot.

Atget, Eugène (1856–1927) French photographer. Atget was a latecomer to photography, pursuing long stints as a stage actor and as a sailor before turning to photography at age 42. Atget is today regarded by critics as one of the pioneers of artistic photographic technique. Atget was not a self-conscious artist but devoted himself primarily to commercial work. He is best remembered for his delicate, detailed renditions of the streets, parks and buildings of Paris, photographs noteworthy for their masterful use of light and their classical sense of order and proportion. A representative sampling from Atget's more than 10,000 photographs is included in *The Work of Atget,* published in three volumes (1981–83). Berenice ABBOTT wrote a biography, *The World of Atget* (1964).

Atkinson, Brooks *(1894–1984)*

American journalist, editor and theater critic. He graduated from Harvard in 1917, then served as assistant to the legendary H. T. Parker, music and drama critic for the *Boston Evening Transcript,* before moving to the *New York Times* in 1925. During his tenure at the *Times* (1925–60) he was considered "the conscience of the theater." He was also acclaimed as a foreign correspondent, receiving a Pulitzer Prize in 1947 for his articles on conditions in Moscow. Known for his wit, urbanity and candor, Atkinson declared that "to believe in the original principles of America is to be a dissenter." He was author of nearly a dozen books and an editor of the writings of Ralph Waldo Emerson and Henry David Thoreau.

Atlantic, Battle of the *(1940–1943)*

After the start of WORLD WAR II, Great Britain blockaded German-controlled Europe, but German U-boats (SUB-MARINES) disrupted the sea lanes. U-boats in the North Atlantic torpedoed and sunk many merchant ships carrying food and materiel to Britain, thus forcing the need for food rationing in the British Isles in 1940. When the U.S. began LEND-LEASE shipments, U.S. naval vessels began patrolling the western Atlantic, while British Royal Air Force planes patrolled the east. Large convoys of American merchant ships assembled west of Iceland to be escorted across the Atlantic by British warships. After the U.S. destroyer *Reuben James* was sunk by a U-boat off Iceland (October 31, 1941), the U.S. Congress repealed the Neutrality Act, and U.S. ships armed themselves and entered war zones. In 1942 and early 1943 sinkings by U-boats increased when the Germans began hunting their targets in "wolf-packs" of 15 to 20 submarines. The British, however, had invented two devices that eventually turned the tables—high-frequency direction finding and RADAR, both of which enabled the Allies to pinpoint the U-boats and sink them. So many submarines were sunk that the Germans could not disrupt shipping much after mid-1943, and the Allies soon controlled the sea lanes of the Atlantic and elsewhere. The name "Battle of the Atlantic" was coined by Winston CHURCHILL.

Atlantic Charter

A declaration of principles for a postwar world and shared democratic ideals that emerged from a meeting off Newfoundland between U.S. president Franklin D. ROOSEVELT and British prime minister Winston S. CHURCHILL on August 9–12, 1941. Among the principles agreed to by the USSR and 14 other states at war with AXIS powers in September 1941 were open seas, equal access to trade and raw materials, lives without fear and want, renunciation of force as a way of settling disputes and the creation of a means for securing world security, democratic government, the disarming of aggressors and the easing of the international arms burden.

atomic bomb development *(1942–1945)*

The American project to develop an atomic bomb—which would derive its force from the release of energy through the process of the splitting (or fission) of the nuclei of a heavy chemical element—started on August 13, 1942, and changed the world completely. Shrouded in the utmost secrecy, the project involved some of the world's top scientists laboring in a few laboratories. The great Italian scientist Enrico FERMI was in charge of a program to unleash the power of the atom at the University of Chicago. Working with Nobel scientist Arthur COMPTON and others, Fermi built a "pile" consisting of aluminum and graphite in layers. At the final experiment, scientist George Weil withdrew the cadmium-plated control rod and by this action released and controlled the energy of the atom. The first chain reaction in nuclear fission was accomplished at 3:25 P.M. on December 2, 1942. The first atomic bomb was completed in 1945 after three additional years of research and an additional cost of $2 billion. The first experimental explosion of an atomic bomb occurred on July 16, 1945, near Alamogordo, New Mexico. The first military use of the bomb came on August 6, 1945, when it was dropped on HIROSHIMA, Japan, and again on August 9, 1945, at NAGASAKI, Japan. The vast network laboring on the development of atomic energy later became known to the public by its code-name, the MANHATTAN PROJECT.

Atsugi

Town in Japan's Kanagawa prefecture; site of the airbase where U.S. troops first landed on the Japanese homeland, on August 28, 1945, after the end of hostilities in WORLD WAR II.

AT&T (American Telephone & Telegraph Company)

American telecommunications corporation, headquartered in New York City. Incorporated in 1885, AT&T grew into the largest telecommunications company in the world and one of the largest corporations in the U.S.; the firm developed a virtual monopoly on telephone service in the U.S. A government lawsuit (1974) eventually forced AT&T to divest itself of its local companies. Since then, it has had to compete against other long-distance telephone companies. AT&T is the parent company to other corporations, including

Franklin Roosevelt and Winston Churchill attending the signing of the Atlantic Charter. (LIBRARY OF CONGRESS, PRINTS AND PHOTOGRAPHS DIVISION)

Bell Laboratories, a research and development arm of the firm. In 1983 AT&T began investing in the cellular telephone industry, in an attempt to recover the revenue it lost by selling off its local telephone companies. Five years later, it laid the first transatlantic fiber optic cable. By 2002 it had deployed a fiber optic network throughout the U.S. However, in early 2005 AT&T was on the verge of being taken over by SBC Communications, a company that had originated as one of the local providers spun off from AT&T some years earlier.

Attica prison riot A 1971 riot at Attica State Prison, east of Buffalo, New York, in which 28 prisoners and nine prison guards were killed. Over 1,000 prisoners rioted and took control of one-half of the facility. They also seized over 30 guards and other employees. The head of the state prison system negotiated with the riot's leaders who demanded reforms plus total amnesty for the prisoners. Governor Nelson ROCKEFELLER refused the prisoner demands that he personally join the negotiations, and he rejected the call for total amnesty. After negotiations collapsed the prisoners displayed a number of hostages with knives held to their throats. State police stormed the prison and 28 prisoners and nine guards were killed. Although state officials initially claimed the guards had their throats slit by prisoners, a subsequent investigation revealed this to be false. In fact, all nine guards died from gunshots fired by the state police. Later investigations criticized prison officials and the governor for the entire affair, including the brutality and inadequate medical care afforded the prisoners after the riot.

Attlee, Clement Richard (first earl Attlee) *(1883–1967)* British statesman, prime minister (1945–51). Born into a middle-class family in Putney, Attlee attended Oxford University. He was admitted to the bar in 1906 and soon involved himself in social problems, lecturing at the London School of Economics and becoming a socialist in 1907. After service in WORLD WAR I, he was elected mayor of Stepney (1919–20) and became a Labour M.P. in 1922. He was a member of the Simon Commission on Indian government, visiting India in

Former prime minister of Great Britain Clement Attlee (LIBRARY OF CONGRESS. PRINTS AND PHOTOGRAPHS DIVISION)

1927 and becoming convinced of the justice of Indian independence. Attlee was a junior minister in the Labour government from 1930 to 1931 but refused to join the national government in 1931. He was elected LABOUR PARTY leader in 1935, strongly criticizing the foreign policies of the Conservative government. During WORLD WAR II he was a part of Winston CHURCHILL's coalition cabinet (1940–45). When Labour was victorious in the elections of 1945, Attlee became prime minister. Committed to radically changing the structure of British society in order to create a modicum of social equality, he instituted numerous WELFARE STATE reforms. These included the nationalization of the Bank of England, the railways, the bulk of public utilities and large industry, as well as the establishment of the NATIONAL HEALTH SERVICE. In addition, he was a leading force in granting independence to India, Pakistan, Ceylon and Burma. Maintaining Britain's alliance with the U.S., he also encouraged his nation's charter membership in NATO. After instituting an economic austerity program to deal with Great Britain's growing economic ills, he narrowly won the elections of 1950 but lost the elections of 1951. Attlee was leader of the opposition to the Conservative government until his retirement in 1955, when he was created an earl.

Atwood, Margaret *(1939–)* Canadian novelist, poet and feminist. Born in Ottawa, she published her first book of poetry, *Double Persephone,* in 1962; her first novel, *The Edible Woman,* appeared in 1969. Atwood's acute and often wry fiction reflects her concern with individual autonomy and the relations between men and women. *The Handmaid's Tale* (1986) describes a futuristic, totalitarian society in which women, ostensibly for their own protection, are relegated to specific, subservient roles; it was a highly acclaimed best seller. It was followed by *Cat's Eye.* Atwood also edited *The New Oxford Book of Canadian Verse in English* (1983). Atwood continued to publish throughout the 1990s, producing such works as *The Robber Bride* (1993), *Alias Grace* (1996), which won the 1996 Giller Prize, *The Blind Assassin* (2000), which received the Booker Prize, and *Oryx and Crake* (2003).

Auböck, Carl *(1924–)* Austrian Modern architect and designer trained in Vienna and at the Massachusetts Institute of Technology. Auböck's work includes designs for furniture, metalware, ceramics and glass, as well as industrial products and sports equipment. A metal cocktail shaker of Auböck's design is in the design collection of the MUSEUM OF MODERN ART in New York. A number of his designs are produced and distributed by the Vienna firm operated by his family.

Auchinleck, Sir Claude John Eyre *(1884–1981)* British general. He began his long army career in 1904, joining the Indian army and serving in the Middle East during World War I. In WORLD WAR II he was briefly (1940) commander of British forces at Narvik, Norway, but was soon posted as British commander in chief, first in India (1941), then in the Middle East (1941–42). While he gained ground in Libya in a 1941 offensive, he was pushed back to Egypt in ROMMEL's 1942 counteroffensive. As head of the Eighth Army, Auchinleck was victorious at the battle of El ALAMEIN (July 1–3, 1942). He resumed the post of commander in chief in India (1943–47), where he aided in the transition to independence.

Auden, Wystan Hugh *(1907– 1973)* Anglo-American poet, playwright, critic, translator and editor. The son of a physician, Auden was born in York, England. Despite an early interest in practical science, as a student at Oxford in the 1920s he declared his intention to become a great poet and became the leading member of an influential left-wing literary circle that included Christopher ISHERWOOD, Cecil DAY LEWIS, Stephen SPENDER and Louis MACNEICE. After graduating, he briefly taught school; thereafter, he spent most of his time traveling, writing and solidifying his reputation as the most brilliant poet of his generation. He collaborated with Isherwood on *The Dog Beneath the Skin* (1935) and *The Ascent of F6* (1936) and with Mac-Neice on *Letters from Iceland* (1937). In 1935 he married Erika Mann, daughter of Thomas MANN, to provide her with a British passport. His travels to Spain and China in 1937–38 yielded *Spain* (1937) and *Journey to a War* (1939). In 1939 he moved to the U.S., where he spent the years of WORLD WAR II; he was naturalized as a U.S. citizen in 1946.

During the 1930s Auden's work celebrated elements of the modern world previously considered "unpoetic," such as machinery, railways and other implements of mass living; his outlook was influenced by Marx and FREUD. In the 1940s his poems began to express a Christian existential view influenced by Kierkegaard and NIEBUHR. *The Age of Anxiety* won a PULITZER PRIZE in 1948. From 1947 to 1962 he was editor of the Yale Younger Poets series. In New York City, as at Oxford, Auden held court and was effectively the arbiter of poetic taste in the U.S. He was professor of poetry at Oxford (1956–61). The last works of the poet known in the 1930s as the conscience of his generation astonished critics with their modesty, domesticity and light comic tone. He died at Kirchstetten, Austria. A brilliant, fluent and versatile poet whose work was distinguished by a playful and mordant wit, Auden is widely considered to rank among the greatest literary figures of the 20th century.

Auerbach, Arnold Jacob "Red"

(1917–2006) American basketball coach. The Brooklyn-born Auerbach was perhaps more closely associated with Boston sports over a longer period of time than any other man. After an undistinguished college athletic career, he coached at that level before assuming the helm of the Washington Capitols for three seasons (1946–49). In 1951 he joined the Boston Celtics, leading them to 938 victories and nine championships over 16 seasons (1950–66). He was named to the Basketball Hall of Fame in 1968; in 1980 the Professional Basketball Writers' Association named Auerbach the greatest coach in NBA history. Up until his death Auerbach continued his involvement with the Celtics as president of the team.

Auger, Pierre Victor *(1899–1993)*

French physicist. Auger was educated at the École Normale Superieure, where he obtained his Ph.D. in 1926. He was later appointed to the staff of the University of Paris. After serving there as professor of physics from 1937, he became director of higher education for France in 1945. From 1948 until 1960 he was director of the science department of UNESCO; he left UNESCO to become president of the French Space Commission, but in 1964 he took the post of director-general of the European Space and Research Organization, a post he retained until his retirement in 1967.

Auger's work has mainly been on nuclear physics and cosmic rays. In 1925 he discovered the **Auger effect** in which an excited atom emits an electron (rather than a photon) when it reverts to a lower energy state. In 1938 Auger made a careful study of "air showers," a cascade of particles produced by a cosmic ray entering the atmosphere and later known as an **Auger shower.**

Aung San Suu Kyi *(1945–)*

Leader of the National League for Democracy, the most popular opposition party in Myanmar (BURMA), and recipient of the 1991 Nobel Peace Prize. Suu Kyi is the daughter of General Aung San, the Burmese nationalist who organized indigenous resistance to British colonial rule but was assassinated in July 1947, six months prior to the country's independence. Receiving her primary education in the capital of Rangoon, Suu Kyi left Burma in 1960. She spent four years in India with her mother, Burmese ambassador to India Daw Khin Kyi, and moved in a circle of friends that included Rajiv and Sanjay Gandhi, sons of the future Indian prime minister Indira GANDHI. In 1964 Suu Kyi left India for Britain, where she studied economics at Oxford University, and met Michael Aris, a professor of economics at Oxford, whom she later married.

Returning alone to Burma in August 1988 to take care of her mother, Suu Kyi joined the National League for Democracy, a movement that was protesting the repression of a prodemocracy rally in June. Within weeks, Suu Kyi became the leader of the movement and transformed the league into a political party. She traveled the country staging rallies and protests against the lack of democratic rule under the military government of General Ne Win, who had used the increasing agitation in the country to stage a coup on September 18, 1988. Suu Kyi's passionate appeals for democratic rule increased the popularity of the prodemocracy movement in Burma (renamed Myanmar in 1989). Although the Burmese government attempted to restrict the appeal of Suu Kyi by placing her under house arrest and solitary confinement in 1989, her party won 82% of the popular vote in the 1990 national elections. However, the military regime that ruled Burma refused to recognize the elections and increased its repression of the league and its members. On July 10, 1995, four years after she had won the NOBEL PRIZE for her peaceful efforts toward democratic government, the Burmese government released Suu Kyi from house arrest and began talks with her to produce a new government. However, the military government placed restrictions on her ability to travel through the country and make statements in the media, and closely followed her conversations and meetings with members of the press and league advocates. Suu Kyi was so concerned about the government's suppression of league efforts that in early 1999 she declined its offer to leave Burma in order to visit her husband, who was suffering from terminal cancer. She thought that if she indeed left Burma, she would never be allowed to return.

In September 2000 the government renewed the house arrest when Suu Kyi attempted to enter Mandalay, a city in northern Burma that was beyond the perimeter the government had established for her. However, the government permitted her to meet with league officials regularly under this second house arrest, as well as UN envoy Razali Ismail. On May 6, 2002, the junta released her from her second house arrest, and she renewed talks with the military government in an effort to establish a transition to democratic rule. Her second respite from house arrest ended in May 2003 when the military dictatorship again detained her, citing increasing conflicts between league members and government supporters.

Auric, Georges *(1899–1963)* French composer of symphonic music, film scores and ballets. Auric first came to musical prominence in the 1920s, during which he was a key member of a group of young avant-garde classical composers known as Les SIX—other members were Arthur HONEGGER, Darius MILHAUD and Francis POULENC. As a youth, Auric studied in Paris under the composers Vincent D'INDY and Albert ROUSSEL, living embodiments of the rich romanticism that had dominated late-19th-century French music. But Auric rebelled against this tradition and distinguished himself with compositions in a spare, playful manner that mocked the romantic conventions of melancholy and lush melody. In the 1920s Auric wrote a number of ballets for the Paris dance company of renowned impressario Serge DIAGHILEV. He also composed music for several films, including Jean COCTEAU's *The Blood of a Poet* (1930), *Orpheus* (1950) and *Beauty and the Beast* (1946).

Auriol, Vincent *(1884–1966)* French politician, president of France (1947–54). A member of the Socialist Party, Auriol was elected to the Chamber of Deputies in 1914. He became a leading figure in the party in the 1930s and served as finance minister in the cabinet of Léon BLUM (1936–37). An early opponent of the VICHY government established after the German defeat of France in WORLD WAR II, he was a leader of the RESISTANCE and in 1943 joined Charles de GAULLE's FREE FRENCH government-in-exile. Auriol served in the provisional government established at the end of the war and in 1946 was elected president of the national assembly. He was the first president of the Fourth Republic. He initially supported de Gaulle's presidency in 1958 but split with de Gaulle in 1960.

Auschwitz The most notorious of the Nazi CONCENTRATION CAMPS during WORLD WAR II; located near Oświęcim, Poland. Auschwitz was opened in June 1940 and was run by Heinrich HIMMLER's SS. Originally a detention and forced labor camp, in January 1942 it was designated as an extermination camp—the primary center in which the Nazis would carry out Adolf HITLER's so-called FINAL SOLUTION, the destruction of Europe's JEWS. Special gas chambers, disguised as showers, were built for the mass execution of prisoners, and crematoria (ovens) were installed to cremate the bodies of the dead. At least half of the prisoners sent to Auschwitz from various parts of German-occupied Europe—many of them women, children and elderly people—were sent immediately to the gas chambers. The remaining able-bodied were assigned to forced labor, usually at the adjacent camp of Birkenau or at another nearby camp (operated by the German industrial firm I.G. Farben), until they too were ordered to the gas chambers. The camp operated until the spring of 1945, when in the waning days of the war it was overrun and liberated by the advancing Soviet armies. Because the SS destroyed the camp records, the exact number of people killed at Auschwitz is unknown; many authorities estimate that as many as 4 million died there. After the war, Auschwitz's commandant, Rudolf Höss, was tried and convicted of war crimes at the NUREMBERG TRIALS and executed. The sheer magnitude and inhumanity of the crimes committed at Auschwitz have been the subject of much analysis, and the name of the camp has become synonymous with the darkest deeds of the 20th century. (See also HOLOCAUST; NAZISM.)

Austin, John Langshaw *(1911–1960)* British philosopher. Austin, who was educated at Oxford and taught there for over two decades, became the most important postwar proponent of the "ordinary language" approach to philosophical analysis. According to Austin, the first task of any philosopher was to consider the linguistic terminology at his disposal. This was valuable not only in order to avoid confusion and ambiguity insofar as was possible, but also because the nature of language was a worthy philosophical problem in its own

right. Austin believed that the subtle ethical and perceptual distinctions embedded in daily language usage could provide a valuable impetus to philosophical thought, which was too often based strictly on isolated intellectual analysis. Austin's methodology was one of rigorous analysis unencumbered by a priori conceptions. His major works, which are suggestive rather than conclusive, are *Philosophical Papers* (1961), *Sense and Sensibilia* (1962) and *How to Do Things With Words* (1962).

Australia (Commonwealth of Australia) Australia, the sixth-largest country on Earth, is located between the Indian and Pacific Oceans. On January 1, 1901, the British colonies of New South Wales, Victoria, Queensland, South Australia, Western Australia and Tasmania federated to form the Commonwealth of Australia. (The Northern Territory was transferred from South Australia to the Commonwealth in 1911.) The federal government was to have control of foreign affairs, defense and trade. The head of state was the governor general, appointed by the Crown, and a parliament was set up, consisting of a senate and a house of representatives. The first Commonwealth Parliament passed an Immigration Restrictions Act in 1901, which put the "white Australia" policy into effect. It was aimed in particular at keeping out Chinese immigrants, who had arrived in large numbers to work in the gold fields. The policy also caused the repatriation of Pacific Islanders. A great deal of social legislation was enacted in the years leading up to World War I. In 1902 woman suffrage was adopted by the federal government. An industrial arbitration court was established in 1906 that laid down the principle of a basic wage. Old-age and invalid pensions were brought in, along with free and compulsory education. In 1909 the first ship of the Australian navy was ordered. In 1911 territory was acquired from New South Wales to form the federal capital of Canberra, and Parliament began meeting there in 1927. In 1911 the Commonwealth Bank was established.

During WORLD WAR I Australia sent about 330,000 men to Europe to fight alongside Britain. In 1920 Australia was a founder member of the LEAGUE

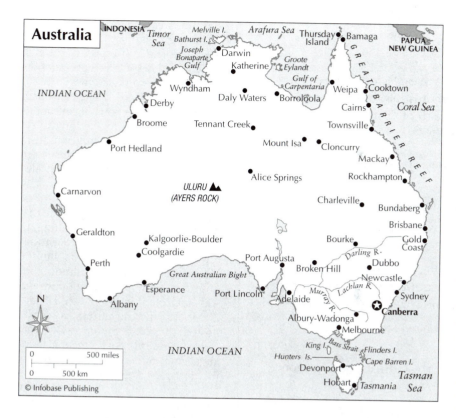

Australia

INDONESIA
Timor Sea
Arafura Sea
Melville I.
Bathurst I.
Joseph Bonaparte Gulf
Darwin
Katherine
Groote Eylandt
Gulf of Carpentaria
Thursday Island
Bamaga
PAPUA NEW GUINEA
INDIAN OCEAN
Wyndham
Daly Waters
Borroloola
Weipa
Cooktown
Derby
Cairns
Coral Sea
Broome
Tennant Creek
Townsville
Port Hedland
Mount Isa
Cloncurry
Mackay
Carnarvon
ULURU (AYERS ROCK)
Alice Springs
Rockhampton
Charleville
Geraldton
Kalgoorlie-Boulder
Coolgardie
Bourke
Bundaberg
Brisbane
Gold Coast
Darling R.
Perth
Port Augusta
Broken Hill
Dubbo
Great Australian Bight
Newcastle
Esperance
Port Lincoln
Adelaide
Murray R.
Lachlan R.
Sydney
Albany
Canberra
N
Albury-Wadonga
Melbourne
INDIAN OCEAN
King I.
Bass Strait
Flinders I.
Hunters Is.
Cape Barren I.
Devonport
Tasman Sea
Hobart
Tasmania
0   500 miles
0   500 km
© Infobase Publishing

OF NATIONS. With the passage of the STATUTE OF WESTMINSTER in 1931 Australia became a dominion within the British COMMONWEALTH. During the 1920s the Australian economy expanded, benefiting from high prices for wool and meat. Tariffs were introduced to protect new manufacturing industries, and primary producers were given subsidies. The worldwide GREAT DEPRESSION in the early 1930s caused widespread unemployment and hardship in Australia, which had an economy largely dependent on that of Britain. But it recovered more quickly than many countries, due to the rising price of wool and gold.

In WORLD WAR II Australia once again supported Britain. Australian troops fought in the Middle East between 1940 and 1942. When Japan entered the war, Australian forces returned to the Pacific theater, and the U.S. made Australia the Allied base in the Pacific. The AUSTRALIAN LABOUR PARTY (ALP) took office in 1941, after the United Australia Party lost ground in federal elections. At the end of the war there was an influx of displaced persons from Europe. In 1947 the Labour prime minister Ben CHIFLEY made a controversial attempt to nationalize the banks, which failed in the courts. A bitter coal strike was put

down with the use of troops and emergency legislation.

The ALP was voted out of office in 1949. The Liberal and the Country Parties formed a coalition government that stayed in power for the next 23 years. The new prime minister was Robert MENZIES. In 1950 the High Court prevented his government from outlawing the Communist Party. The 1950s saw the trade deficit rise, along with wages, and inflation spiraled. A secret ballot for trade union elections was introduced. Australia's foreign policy now concentrated on noncommunist Asian nations, and on strengthening ties with the U.S. Australia took a prominent part in the COLOMBO PLAN (1950), giving economic aid to underdeveloped countries of South and Southeast Asia. Australia, New Zealand and the U.S. signed the ANZUS defense treaty the following year. In 1954 it was a signatory to the South East Asia Treaty Organization, whose members pledged to help each other in the event of outside aggression. In 1952 Britain began testing atomic bombs on Australian territory and continued to do so for more than a decade. The government agreed to the establishment of an American naval communications base in Western Australia, in 1963. In

1965 Australia sent troops to support the U.S. in South Vietnam.

At home, Aborigines were given the vote in 1965 and access to social benefits, which had previously been denied them. Menzies retired as prime minister in 1966. Harold Holt took over, but died in a swimming accident the following year. John Gorton became prime minister and then in 1971, the Liberal leader William McMahon took over the premiership. The government was beset by problems of inflation and industrial unrest. It lost a general election for the House of Representatives, to the ALP, led by the charismatic socialist Gough WHITLAM. The Whitlam government ended Australia's military involvement in the VIETNAM WAR in 1972. Among the administration's domestic achievements was the introduction of a national health scheme to provide free health care for all. In 1974 Whitlam dissolved both houses of Parliament, following a conflict between the government and the Senate. On November 11, 1975, the governor general, in an unprecedented move, dismissed Whitlam and dissolved Parliament. The Liberal Party leader Malcolm FRASER was declared caretaker prime minister, pending new elections in December.

A coalition of Fraser's Liberals and the National Country Party subsequently won majorities in both houses. The coalition government was beaten in the March 1983 general elections, by the ALP under Bob HAWKE. The new prime minister immediately called an economic summit, and an accord on pay and prices was reached between the government, trade unions and employers. In 1984 a law was enacted giving greater protection to sacred Aboriginal sites. The Medicare system, providing universal health insurance, was introduced. The Australia Act (1986) gave the nation full legal independence from Britain but left the queen's status as sovereign unaltered. In 1988 Australians celebrated the bicentenary of European settlement.

In the federal elections in 1996 a Liberal-National Party coalition ousted the Labour Party, winning a landslide victory and a commanding majority in the House of Representatives. Inspired by a free-market ideology reminiscent of that of Margaret THATCHER in Great Britain, Liberal prime minister John HOWARD embarked on an

AUSTRALIA	
1901	Colonies of New South Wales, Victoria, Queensland, South Australia, Western Australia and Tasmania federate to form Commonwealth of Australia.
1902	Woman suffrage adopted.
1914–18	300,000 Australians fight alongside Britain in World War I.
1941	Australian Labour Party (ALP) takes office.
1942	Australia becomes main Allied base in the Pacific during World War II.
1949	ALP voted out of office after Prime Minister Chifley attempts to nationalize banks. Liberal and Country Parties form coalition government, remain in power for 23 years.
1950	Australia–New Zealand–United States (ANZUS) defense treaty signed.
1954	Australia joins South East Asia Treaty Organization (SEATO).
1965	Australian troops support the U.S. in Vietnam War; Aborigines given the vote.
1983	Australia wins America's Cup yachting trophy; ALP returns to power under Robert Hawke.
1984	Law passed giving greater protection to sacred Aboriginal sites.
1986	Australia Act gives full legal independence from Britain but keeps the queen as sovereign.
1987	Royal commission established to investigate high death rate of Aborigines in police custody.
1988	Bicentennial of European settlement celebrated—protested by Aborigines.
1990	Hawke returned to power for fourth time, with reduced parliamentary majority reflecting gains by Liberal-National coalition.
1992	Parliament passes the Citizenship Act, which removes the oath of allegiance to the British Crown from the requirements for Australian citizenship.
1996	A coalition of the Liberal and National (formerly Country) Parties under John Howard ousts Labour.
2000	Australia hosts the Olympic (summer) Games in Sydney.
2003	Australian troops participate in U.S.-led invasion and occupation of Iraq.
2004	John Howard wins fourth term as prime minister, his party extends gains in parliament.

ambitious campaign to reduce government expenditure during the next several years. He also pushed through a law privatizing a large portion of the state-run communications corporation Testra in 1999. The government antagonized indigenous organizations by refusing to apologize for the removal of Aboriginal children from their parents and their placement in institutions during the 1960s. It also infuriated the labor movement by seeking to abolish compulsory trade union membership and to require that unemployed workers be willing to work at assigned tasks in order to receive unemployment benefits. But the Liberal-National Party coalition continued to enjoy popular support and was reelected in 1998, 2001 and 2004. In the meantime Australia hosted the 2000 Summer Olympic Games. Howard's government also inaugurated an activist foreign policy for Australia. Australian troops led a UN peacekeeping force in EAST TIMOR after an outbreak of violence following the territory's vote in favor of independence from INDONESIA. Australia became one of the charter members of the "coalition of the willing" assembled by U.S. president George W. BUSH that toppled the regime of Iraqi dictator Saddam HUSSEIN in 2003.

Australian Labour Party (ALP)
Australian political party established in 1890. The ALP arose when trade unions sought political representation in the recessionary period at the end of the 19th century. The ALP held the balance of power in the first Commonwealth Parliament, formed minority national governments briefly in 1904 and 1908 and then won clear control of both houses in 1910. Under the leadership of William HUGHES, the party split in 1916 over the issue of conscription. Hughes left the ALP, which was out of power until 1929. From 1929 to 1931 party leader James Scullin was prime minister, but the party ruptured again over its response to the GREAT DEPRESSION. The party rose to power between 1941 and 1949 under the leadership of Prime Ministers John CURTIN and Ben CHIFFLEY when many social reforms were initiated. In the mid-1950s another split occurred when an anticommunist faction broke away and formed the Democratic Labour Party. From

1972 to 1975 ALP leader Gough WHIT-LAM was prime minister. Although his tenure ended in a constitution crisis, Labour came to power again in 1983. The HAWKE government remained in power through the 1984, 1987 and 1990 elections. In 1991 Paul Keating replaced Hawke as prime minister and retained ALP control of the government until losing the March 1996 elections.

Austria Austria is a landlocked country in central Europe, divided into nine federal states with an area of 32,368 square miles. Austria entered the 20th century as the dual monarchy of Austria-Hungary (see AUSTRO-HUNGARIAN EMPIRE). The final decades of Habsburg rule were a glorious twilight of economic, social and cultural achievement, and political corruption. Despite the introduction of universal suffrage in the Austrian half in 1907, the empire remained essentially an autocracy, inimical to its subject Slav peoples and the growing working-class movement, represented by the Social Democratic Party. Austria's annexation of BOSNIA AND HERZEGOVINA (1908) was to lead indirectly to the empire's downfall.

WORLD WAR I not only ended in defeat for Germany and Austria-Hungary but also unleashed a tide of revolutionary and national aspirations that swept away the old order in central Europe. In November 1918 the first Austrian republic was proclaimed, with Karl Renner (Social Democrat) becoming chancellor. A "Habsburg Law" (1919) barred members of the former imperial family from Austria unless they declared allegiance to the republic. Various postwar peace treaties dismembered the empire on the basis of national self-determination, and Austria was reduced to its present-day borders, being roughly the German-speaking area except South Tirol, which was ceded to ITALY. Beset by economic problems, the new republic experienced chronic strife between left and right, leading to the suspension of parliamentary government by Chancellor Englebert DOLLFUSS in 1933, Dollfuss's murder by Austrian Nazis and the suppression of the Social Democrats in 1934. Growing internal profascist agitation and pressure from Nazi GERMANY culminated in the unopposed entry of

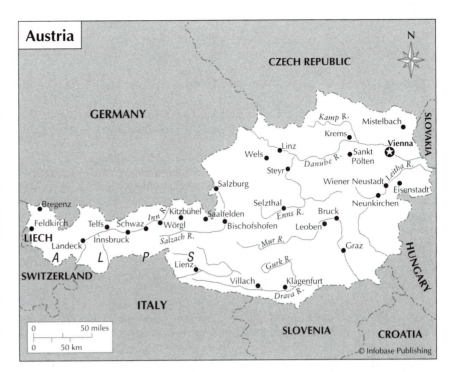

German forces in March 1938 and the ANSCHLUSS (annexation), under which Austria was fully incorporated into HITLER's Reich.

After WORLD WAR II the victorious Allies established a four-power (Soviet, U.S., British and French) occupation regime in Austria and recognized the newly declared second republic in December 1945. Economic recovery was assisted by the MARSHALL PLAN. After lengthy negotiations, the 1955 Austrian State Treaty achieved the withdrawal of all occupation forces and accorded international recognition of Austria as a sovereign, independent and democratic state within its frontiers of January 1938. The treaty specifically banned any future political or economic union with Germany and reaffirmed the 1919 Habsburg Law, while an associated constitutional law provided for Austria's permanent neutrality. The resumption of full sovereignty was followed by rapid industrialization and economic advance. A founder member of EFTA from 1959, Austria signed an industrial free-trade agreement with the EUROPEAN ECONOMIC COMMUNITY (EEC) in 1972 and applied for membership in the latter in July 1989. In 1999 the ultraconservative Freedom Party, led by Jorg HAIDER, won 27% of the popular vote, tying the conservative People's Party for sec-

ond place, and forming a coalition with the People's Party from February 2000 to September 2002. In 2004 Social Democrat Heinz Fischer was elected president.

Austria-Hungary See AUSTRO-HUNGARIAN EMPIRE.

Austrian State Treaty Treaty signed on May 15, 1955, by the U.S., USSR, Britain and France to end their joint post–World War II occupation of Austria and withdraw all troops by October 25, 1955. Austria was restored to its frontiers of 1937, and union with Germany was forbidden. The treaty raised hopes of Soviet agreement to withdraw troops from Eastern Europe.

Austro-Hungarian Empire The Compromise (Ausgleich) of 1867 united AUSTRIA and HUNGARY under the banner of the dual monarchy of Austria-Hungary. The Austro-Hungarian Empire covered much of central Europe; it included not only the Austrians and Hungarians, but a whole host of mostly Slavic peoples—Czechs, Slovaks, Serbs and Croats as well as Romanians. In the early 20th century, increasingly resentful of the predominance of the Austrians and Hungarians, these subject peoples agitated for independence. Tensions within the

---

AUSTRIA

1907	Universal suffrage introduced.
1908	Austria annexes Bosnia-Herzegovina.
1914	Gavrilo Princip assassinates Archduke Franz Ferdinand; World War I begins.
1918	Emperor Charles abdicates; Austria proclaimed a republic.
1934	Chancellor Dollfuss murdered by Austrian Nazis.
1938	"Anschluss" (annexation) of Austria by Germany.
1945–55	Austria occupied by USSR, U.S., France and Britain after World War II.
1970–83	Socialist government under Bruno Kreisky.
1986	Election of Kurt Waldheim as president stirs controversy.
1989	Austria applies for EEC membership.
1995	Austria enters the European Union.
2000	Far-right Freedom Party forms coalition with People's Party, which governs until 2002.
2002	In August torrential rain causes Danube to overflow, causing severe flooding; People's Party makes sweeping gains in general election, largely at expense of far-right Freedom Party. Coalition talks start.
2003	Coalition talks with Social Democrats and Greens fail; People's Party agrees to form government with Freedom Party.
2004	Heinz Fischer elected president.
2005	Freedom Party splits as Joerg Haider announces he is leaving to set up Alliance for Austria's Future; parliament ratifies EU constitution; floods again cause devastation as Danube overflows.

---

empire contributed to the general European unease that led up to WORLD WAR I; the assassination of the Austrian archduke FRANZ FERDINAND by a Serbian nationalist, Gavrilo Princip (June 28, 1914, at Sarajevo), was the event that sparked the great conflagration. Austria-Hungary fought alongside GERMANY; its troops were engaged mainly against the Russians in the east and the Italians in the south. Defeated in the war, the Austro-Hungarian Empire disintegrated as new countries were created from its outlying areas. The Corfu Pact of 1917 provided for a kingdom of Serbs, Croats and Slovenes; that kingdom came into being at the end of 1918, and in 1929 the new country adopted the name YUGOSLAVIA. Independent CZECHOSLOVAKIA was created in 1918, and the Treaties of St. Germain and Trianon in 1919–20 formalized the breakup of the old empire; Austria and Hungary went their separate ways as distinct nations.

Autobiography of Alice B. Toklas, The Book by Gertrude STEIN, published in 1933. It is not an autobiography at all, but rather Stein's own memoir written as if by her longtime companion and secretary, Alice B. Toklas. The book was Stein's first popular work, and describes Stein and Toklas's life together in Paris where they maintained a literary and artistic salon where Pablo PICASSO, Henri MATISSE, Ernest HEMINGWAY and many other luminaries of the time gathered. The book expresses Stein's opinions of their talent and her views on art and literature and her own "genius."

automobile Although a 19th-century invention, the automobile is a 20th-century phenomenon that transformed the way of living in much of the Western world. The automobile revolution is due in large measure to Henry FORD, who believed that every person ought to be able to own a car. Ford perfected the system of MASS PRODUCTION and in 1908 introduced his Model T, the first car available to a mass market. By the 1920s the automobile was a common means of transportation in the U.S. and much of Europe. The automobile age was encouraged as much by new roads designed for auto traffic as by the cars themselves. The German autobahn—an innovation of HITLER's Third Reich—was the first long-distance, high-speed, controlled-access highway. In 1956 U.S. president EISENHOWER signed a bill providing for the construction of an extensive interstate highway system linking virtually every region of the U.S.; in Britain, the first motorway opened in 1958.

However, nowhere more than in the U.S. did the automobile become a way of life. With more than 42,000 miles of controlled-access roads linking major cities, the interstate highway system made it possible to drive thousands of miles across country—from Portland, Maine, to Key West, Florida, or from New York City to Los Angeles, California—at high speeds, without having to use local roads. The economic boom of the 1950s and 1960s made the automobile affordable for most middle-class American families; moreover, the car was transformed from merely a means of transportation into a symbol of economic status and personal freedom, and an entire subculture was built around the automobile. The availability of plentiful and cheap gasoline had further spurred auto sales, increased the mobility of the American public and fueled a boom in the interstate trucking business. On the other hand, the proliferation of private automobiles and of highways (along with passenger airliners) spelled doom for the American railways and led to severe air pollution in many U.S. cities, most notably LOS ANGELES. The oil crises of the 1970s affected Americans' driving habits as the cost of gasoline soared. Many American drivers switched to more fuel-efficient cars; from this point into the 1990s, Japanese and other foreign imports made a significant impact on the U.S. market. By the last decade of the century, the automobile had become a universal phenomenon, traveling the roads of virtually every country in the world. The automobile industry in the 1990s displayed both a trend toward larger cars, such as the emergence of the sport-utility vehicle (SUV), as well as an increasing incorporation of safety and environmental features such as air bags and more efficient engines.

Autry, Gene (*1907–1998*) American singing cowboy and businessman. A familiar figure on the airwaves and the silver screen during the 1930s and 1940s, Autry recorded numerous "cowboy" songs and starred in over 100 B-movies with his horse Champion. After WORLD WAR II service, Autry returned to show business with such perennial song hits as "Rudolph the Red-nosed Reindeer" and "Here Comes Peter Cottontail." Autry's holdings included hotels, radio stations and the California Angels baseball club.

Avedon, Richard (*1923–2004*) American photographer known for his creative approach to fashion and portrait photography. Avedon studied with Alexey BRODOVITCH at the New School in New York, establishing his own studio in 1946. He was a regular contributor to *Harper's Bazaar* from 1945 to 1965, where Brodovitch was art director, and also was frequently published in *LIFE* and *Theater Arts* magazines. Although at first primarily a fashion photographer, his portraits, often of famous people, became equally well known, while his work became constantly more varied and

more creative. His work was often exhibited, and he published a number of books, including *Observations* of 1959 (with a text by Truman CAPOTE), a collection of his celebrity portraits up to that time. In 1991 Avedon received the Hasselblad Award, an international award given in recognition of his professional achievements.

Averoff-Tositsas, Evangelos (*1910–1990*) Greek politician. Averoff served as Greek foreign minister from 1956 to 1963 and was instrumental in negotiating the 1959 settlement that led to independence for CYPRUS. While holding the post of defense minister (1974–80), he helped oversee the restoration of democracy in GREECE in 1974, by successfully advocating the recall of President Constantine CARAMANLIS. Averoff served as the leader of New Democracy, the country's main conservative party, from 1981 until his retirement in 1984.

Avery, Fred "Tex" (*1907–1980*) American cartoon animator, producer and director. Working for WARNER BROS. in the late 1930s, he created and/or developed such classic cartoon characters as Daffy Duck (in *Porky's Duck Hunt*, 1937) and BUGS BUNNY (in *A Wild Hare*, 1940). In the latter film Avery came up with Bugs's famous greeting, "What's up, doc?" From 1941 to 1954 Avery ran his own animation unit at METRO-GOLDWYN-MAYER, where he developed the character of Droopy the Dog. During his later years he produced a number of cartoons for the Walter Lantz company. A self-styled anarchist, Avery was known for creating irreverent caricatures, outrageous spoofs and absurd situations. Avery's influence upon younger generations of animation directors, like Chuck Jones and Friz Freleng, has been enormous. Always the exponent of slapstick humor, Avery said: "Dialogue gags are a dime a dozen, but a good sight gag is hard to come by."

Avery, Milton (*1893–1965*) American painter. Born in Altmar, New York, he studied briefly at the Art Students League, New York City, traveled in Europe and settled in New York in 1925. His first one-man show was held in the

city in 1928. Working within the MATISSE tradition, he is noted for flat, figurative canvases of great boldness and originality. His mature landscapes, such as *Green Sea* (1954, Metropolitan Museum of Art, in New York Ctiy), border on pure abstract art.

Avery, Oswald Theodore (*1877–1955*) American bacteriologist. Educated at Colgate University, Avery received his A.B. in 1900 and his M.D. in 1904. After a time at the Hoagland Laboratory, New York, as a lecturer and researcher in bacteriology, he joined the Rockefeller Institute Hospital (1913–48). While investigating the pneumococcus bacteria responsible for causing lobar pneumonia, Avery found that the bacteria produced soluble substances, derived from the cell wall and identified as polysaccharides, that were specific in their chemical composition for each different type of pneumococcus. This work provided a basis for establishing the immunologic identity of a cell in biochemical terms. In 1932 Avery started work on the phenomenon of transformation in bacteria. It had already been shown that heat-killed cells of a virulent pneumococcus strain could transform a living avirulent strain into the virulent form. In 1944 Avery and his colleagues Maclyn McCarthy and Colin MacLeod extracted and purified the transforming substance and showed it to be deoxyribonucleic acid (DNA). Previously it had been thought that protein was the hereditary material. Thus Avery's work was an important step toward the eventual discovery, made nine years later by James WATSON and Francis CRICK, of the chemical basis of heredity.

aviation The 20th-century development of practical aviation has had an incalculable effect on human history. The WRIGHT BROTHERS made the first successful powered flight in December 1903, just a week after LANGLEY's failed attempt. In 1909 Louis BLÉRIOT was the first to fly across the watery perils of the English Channel. The airplane's military potential was seen in WORLD WAR I, while air-mail service began in the 1920s in the U.S. Charles LINDBERGH's solo transatlantic flight in 1927 made

AVIATION

1900	First Zeppelin airship flight.
1903	Orville and Wilbur Wright make first flight in motor-powered heavier-than-air machine.
1909	Louis Blériot makes first flight across English Channel.
1911	Anthony Fokker builds first fighter plane.
1915	Hugo Junkers produces all-metal plane.
1918	First regular air service between Kiev and Vienna, also New York and Washington.
1919	Alcock and Brown first to fly across Atlantic, also London to Australia.
1927	Charles A. Lindbergh makes first nonstop solo flight across Atlantic (New York–Paris).
1928	First flight across the Pacific.
1928–29	Dirigible *Graf Zeppelin* makes transatlantic and world flights.
1930	Amy Johnson flies solo from U.K. to Australia.
1931	Auguste Piccard ascends to stratosphere in balloon.
1932	Amelia Earhart flies solo from Newfoundland to Ireland.
1934	DC-3 enters service.
1936	Louis Breguet flies first successful helicopter; Beryl Markham makes first solo east-to-west transatlantic flight; first flight of Mitchell's Spitfire fighter plane.
1937	Frank Whittle (RAF) runs first jet engine on test bed; *Hindenburg* disaster.
1939	Pan American begins New York–Southampton flying-boat service.
1939	First turbojet test flight by Heinkel 178, Germany.
1947	Chuck Yeager breaks sound barrier in X-1 rocket plane.
1949	First passenger jet flight by British Comet.
1952	Comet jetliner enters service.
1954	First test flight of Boeing 707 jetliner.
1955	British designer Cockerell patents Hovercraft.
1958	Boeing 707 jetliner enters service.
1959	Hovercraft crosses English Channel.
1969	First flight by Concorde supersonic airliner.
1970	Boeing 747 "Jumbo Jet" enters service.
1976	Concorde enters service.
1977	Laker Airways inaugurates cheap transatlantic "Skytrain" flights.
1978	Airline deregulation in U.S.
1981	First flight of space shuttle.
2003	Last commercial flight of the Concorde.

long-distance flight acceptable. Commercial passenger service was established in the 1930s. WORLD WAR II saw warplanes that were faster, could fly farther and carry heavier payloads. The Germans introduced jet planes—but too late to do more than startle Allied pilots. RADAR, a wartime development, had a tremendous impact on postwar commercial aviation. Well into the 1950s, the piston-engine propeller airplane and the turbo-prop aircraft remained the mainstay of long-distance commercial aviation. However, the JET ENGINE (developed by British aviation engineer Frank Whittle in the 1930s) was perfected in the 1950s, and the first jet-powered commercial aircraft entered service. Aircraft such as the BOEING 707 were able to cross the Atlantic Ocean in half the previous time. Long-distance passenger aviation boomed—with dire consequences for the passenger OCEAN LINERS and the railroads. By the last decade of the 20th century, there were few inhabited places on Earth that could not be reached by airplane. The end of an era in aeronautical history took place October 24, 2003, when three Concorde aircraft landed at Heathrow Airport. This marked the end of passenger flights by the controversial Anglo-French supersonic airplane, which had run afoul of environmentalists and proved a commercial failure because of cost overruns and insufficient passenger demand, as well as safety concerns in the wake of a fiery crash near Paris in July 2000.

Axelrod, Julius (1912–2004) American neuropharmacologist. Axelrod was educated at the City College of New York. Denied a medical career by poverty during the Great Depression, Axelrod instead worked as a technician in a food-testing laboratory for 12 years. Still with an ambition for a career in scientific research, and after some years at the Goldwater Memorial Hospital and the National Heart Institute, he took a year off in 1955, obtained a Ph.D. from George Washington University and moved to the National Institute of Mental Health as chief of the pharmacology section.

Axelrod threw much light on the action of the catecholamines, the neurotransmitters of the sympathetic nervous system. For work on the catecholamines, Axelrod shared the 1970 NOBEL PRIZE in physiology or medicine with Ulf von Euler and Bernard Katz.

Axelrod also worked on the role of the pineal gland in the control of circadian rhythms and the neuropharmacology of schizophrenia. In 1984

Axelrod retired from the National Institute for Mental Health.

Axis Term used to describe the alliance among GERMANY, ITALY and JAPAN immediately before and during WORLD WAR II. The term was coined by Italian dictator Benito MUSSOLINI. On October 25, 1936, Mussolini and Adolf HITLER signed a treaty that recognized the two nations' common foreign policy goals; this alliance was reinforced when the two leaders concluded a formal military alliance, known as the "Pact of Steel," on May 22, 1939. This so-called Rome-Berlin Axis expanded to become the Rome-Berlin-Tokyo Axis on September 27, 1940, when Japan joined the two nations in the Tripartite Pact of September 27, 1940.

Axis Sally (Mildred Elizbeth Siek) (1900–1988) U.S.-born radio propagandist for the NAZIS. She was convicted of treason in 1949 for broadcasting English-language programs from Berlin to Allied troops during WORLD WAR II. She served 12 years in prison. After her release at the age of 60, she taught music at a Roman Catholic convent school in Columbus, Ohio.

Ayckbourn, Sir Alan (1939–) British playwright and theatrical director. Born in London, he is known for his numerous successful farces portraying a dark view of British middle-class life in the late 20th century. He began his career at 17 working as assistant stage manager to Donald Wolfit and supported his early writing by producing plays for the BBC. His first major success, *Relatively Speaking* (1967), is characteristic of his work with its suburban setting and bitter undertones—although the bitterness increases in his later work. Author of some 39 plays through 1989, in 1975 Ayckbourn had five plays running simultaneously in London. His work has been performed worldwide, but he did not gain the popularity in the U.S. he enjoyed in England. His works include *The Norman Conquests* (1974), *It Could Be Any One of Us* (1983), *Man of the Moment* (1989) and *The Revenger's Comedies* (1990), which depicts two suicidal people deciding instead to seek revenge on one another's enemies. Ayckbourn is artistic director of the Stephen Joseph Theatre-in-the-Round in the seaside resort town of Scarbor-

ough, where much of his work is first performed. He is admired by his contemporary Harold PINTER, who describes him as "a very serious playwright." In 1997 Ayckbourn was knighted in recognition of his services to the British theater.

Ayer, Alfred Jules (1910–1989) British philosopher. Ayer was one of the most influential philosophers of the 20th century due to his controversial definition of "truth" as applying only to logical or empirical statements. Ayer, who studied LOGICAL POSITIVISM in Vienna following his graduation from Oxford in 1932, was the first English-speaking philosopher to apply the teachings of that Continental school of philosophy to problems of language and meaning. In his first major work, *Language, Truth and Logic* (1936), Ayer argued that logical statements were empty of factual content but were true as defined by the conventional rules of mathematics and logic. As for empirical statements, they were only meaningful in so far as they could be verified by observation. This left all metaphysical and ethical statements as emotive assertions without essential meaning. Ayer developed these ideas in *The Foundations of Empirical Knowledge* (1940) and *Philosophical Essays* (1954). In *The Problem of Knowledge* (1956), however, Ayer showed that analytical skepticism had its limits—it could not disprove the possibility that certain statements could be true even if they could not be logically or empirically justified.

Aylwin, Patricio (1918–) Chilean politician and president of Chile (1990–94). Born in Viña del Mar, Aylwin became an active participant in Chilean legal and governmental affairs. After receiving his bachelor's degree in judicial and social sciences from the University of Chile in 1943, he went on to teach administrative law both at his alma mater (1946–67) and at Chile's Catholic University (1952–60). He also held positions in the Chilean National Institute and the College of Lawyers. After over two decades of teaching law at these institutions, Aylwin won election to the Chilean senate in 1965 as a member of the Christian Democratic Party. Though not a supporter of the socialist policies of President Salvador ALLENDE (1970–73), Aylwin repeatedly attempted to produce a constitutional and democratic alternative to the Augusto PINOCHET dictatorship that came to power after Allende's overthrow in 1973. He cofounded the Group of Constitutional Studies, an organization of academics that attempted to build a national consensus in favor of a return to constitutional rule; he also led a coalition that championed a 1989 referendum to reject the continuation of Pinochet's rule. Shortly after losing that referendum, Pinochet resigned, and in 1990 Aylwin became the first elected Chilean president since Allende in 1970.

Aylwin was responsible for resuming Chile's involvement in the international community and for striving to reconcile Chile to its recent past. Perhaps his greatest accomplishment in the latter endeavor was the founding of the Reparations and Reconciliation Corporation, which regularly reported on the fate of those alleged to have perished under Pinochet in violation of recognized human rights. Before the end of his term in 1994, Aylwin also reformed the Chilean civil and criminal code to improve the treatment of women, youths and ethnic minorities within his country. He also promoted environmental legislation and governmental efforts to redress socioeconomic ills in housing, health care and education.

Ayres, Lew *(1908–1996)* American screen actor. A leading man in films of the 1930s, Ayres hurt his career by declaring himself a conscientious objector in WORLD WAR II. His best-known film is *All Quiet on the Western Front* (1930). Among his other films are *Holiday* (1938), *Advise and Consent* (1961) and *The Carpetbaggers* (1964).

Ayub Khan, Mohammed *(1908–1974)* Military leader and president of Pakistan (1958–69). Educated at the Royal Military College at Sandhurst, he was commissioned in the British Indian army in 1928 and served as a battalion commander in World War II. After the creation of the Muslim state of PAKISTAN in 1947, he headed the military forces in East Pakistan (now the state of BANGLADESH) and later became Pakistani commander in chief (1951–58). He also served as defense minister from 1954 to 1956. In 1958, a military coup toppled the govern-

ment, martial law was declared and Ayub Khan proclaimed himself president. He became a field marshal in 1959, and his presidency was confirmed in a 1960 referendum. Ayub Khan began ambitious social, political and economic programs, including land reform, economic development and a system of local government councils he dubbed "basic democracies." He was reelected in 1965, the same year he led Pakistan in a one-year war with INDIA. Despite his attempts at reform, dissatisfaction with the repressiveness of his government, continued social inequalities and his lack of success in conflicts with India led to criticism, unrest and finally to riots in 1968. Ayub Khan resigned on March 26, 1969, turning the presidency over to General YAHYA KHAN.

Azaña, Manuel *(1880–1940)* President of Spain (1936–39). A distinguished liberal journalist and critic, Azaña became politically active in the early 1930s. After the flight of ALFONSO XIII in 1931, he served first as minister of war in the Republican cabinet, then as prime minister (1931–33). During his ministry, Azaña inaugurated various social, military and educational reforms. Becoming prime minister again with the victory of the Popular Front in 1936, he was soon elected president. Azaña acted as a virtual figurehead

during the SPANISH CIVIL WAR, fleeing to France in 1939 just before the collapse of the republic.

Azerbaijan Territory of the Russian Empire (1828–1918), independent nation (1918–20), Soviet socialist republic (1920–91) and republic (1991–   ). Azerbaijan was a predominantly Muslim sector of the Russia. It became an important czarist possession when oil reserves were discovered there, resulting in a large Russian migration to extract the oil. The introduction of a large Russian and Armenian minority within Azerbaijan created tension in the cities of the region, often leading to civil unrest and eventually resulting in Russian domination of regional government and the booming oil industry.

In May 1918 Azerbaijan obtained its independence as a result of the BOLSHEVIK REVOLUTION in November 1917 and the resulting RUSSIAN CIVIL WAR (1918–20). However, Russians and Armenians within the new state protested the declaration of independence, largely fearing reprisals for their earlier rule of the region, and both minorities took up arms in a series of clashes within the state's capital, Baku. Azerbaijan also fought a war with ARMENIA, in which the latter state attempted to acquire the Azerbaijani provinces of Naxçivan and Nagorno-Karabakh, which were largely inhabited by ethnic

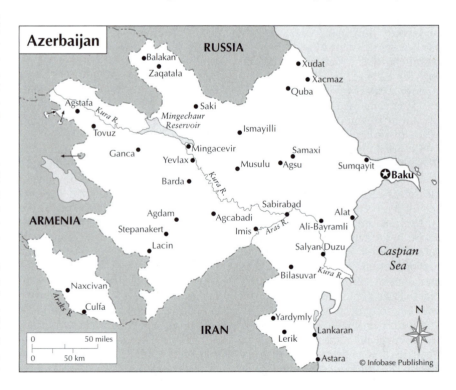

AZERBAIJAN

1917–18	Azerbaijan becomes a member of the anti-Bolshevik Transcaucasian Federation.
1918	Azerbaijan becomes an independent republic.
1920	Azerbaijan is occupied by the Red Army and subsequently forcibly secularized.
1922–36	Along with Georgia and Armenia, Azerbaijan becomes part of the Transcaucasian Federal Republic.
early 1930s	Peasants stage uprisings against agricultural collectivization; the local Communist Party conducts Stalinist purges.
1936	Azerbaijan becomes a constituent republic of the USSR.
1945	With both Armenia and Azerbaijan members of the Soviet Union, Moscow's Bureau of Caucasian Affairs awards the territory of Nagorno-Karabakh to Armenia, but Soviet leader Joseph Stalin reverses the decision, declaring Nagorno-Karabakh an autonomous region.
1988	The Azerbaijani political reawakening begins, sparked by an outbreak of ethnic violence between Azerbaijanis and Armenians over Armenian claims to the Nagorno-Karabakh region in which hundreds die; Moscow sends 5,000 troops to the region to quell the violence.
1991	Azerbaijan declares its independence from Russia; Ayaz Mutalibov wins a hastily called election that many believed was rigged by the former Communist Party; the conflict with Armenia over the disputed Nagorno-Karabakh region intensifies.
1992	Azerbaijan joins the United Nations and signs a friendship treaty with Russia.
1993	Reydar Aliyev ousts Elchibey in a bloodless coup; Azerbaijan forces launch a counteroffensive in Nagorno-Karabakh.
1994	In May Azerbaijan signs the Bisbkek Protocol, a cease-fire agreement regarding Nagorno-Karabakh, which remains in force through the 1990s.
1995	Internal Affairs Ministry militia stage an unsuccessful coup attempt in Baku.
1996	Azerbaijan signs an economic cooperation pact with the European Union.
1997	Aliyev becomes the first Azerbaijani leader to make an official visit to Washington; Azerbaijan's state-owned oil company signs agreements on oil exploration with U.S. and international companies; the Organization for Security and Cooperation in Europe brokers a draft peace proposal between Armenia and Azerbaijan.
1998	President Reydar Aliyev of the New Azerbaijan Party wins the presidential election with 77.61% of the vote.
2000	In November, Aliyev's son Ilham leads the New Azerbaijan Party to victory in disputed parliamentary elections to claim the Speaker of parliament position.
2001	Azerbaijan becomes a full member of the Council of Europe.
2005	A pipeline from Baku to carry Caspian oil to Turkey begins operation.

Armenians. However, as the Bolshevik forces defeated their opponents and established communist rule over much of the former czarist empire, the independence of Azerbaijan came to an end. In mid-1920 Bolshevik-controlled forces returned to the region and established control over Azerbaijan. Two years later the former state was forced to submerge itself in the Transcaucasian Soviet Federated Socialist Republic, one of four political entities that formed the Union of Soviet Socialist Republics (USSR) in 1922. Fourteen years later this entity disbanded and Azerbaijan became a republic in the USSR.

Under Soviet rule many Azerbaijanis joined the COMMUNIST PARTY, participated in regional government and benefited from development of their oil reserves. However, the Soviet government regularly persecuted Azerbaijani Muslims and nationalists by closing and destroying mosques and imprisoning and executing dissidents, such as Azerbaijani farmers who protested STALIN's collectivization of agriculture in the 1930s.

In 1988, as a result of the new political policy of GLASNOST instituted by Soviet premier Mikhail GORBACHEV, which called for increasing civil liberties and tolerance of noncommunist groups, Nagorno-Karabakh bred new tension between Azerbaijan and Armenia. That year, the Armenian-dominated council of Nagorno-Karabakh petitioned for transfer to Armenian control. However, authorities in Moscow, concerned that this action could fragment the USSR, blocked this action. In response, many Armenians demonstrated against that decision, leading to ethnic violence in Nagorno-Karabakh, a civil war between Armenia and Azerbaijan and a blockade by the latter against the former. Although the Kremlin sent 5,000 troops to establish martial law, ETHNIC CLEANSING continued in both Soviet republics, and the blockade remained in place. The status of Nagorno-Karabakh also led to protests from the Popular Front of Azerbaijan (PFA), a nationalist organization the Azerbaijani Communist Party refused to recognize until 1989 for fear of its strident tone over Nagorno-Karabakh's future and the conflict with Armenia. As the war continued and attacks on Armenians in Azerbaijan increased in the capital city of Baku, additional Soviet military forces arrived in January 1990. By the end of the month these troops had established martial law and outlawed nationalist groups like the PFA. To avert renewed political tension, the Azerbaijani Supreme Soviet (the regional legislature) delayed elections to the USSR's Supreme Soviet for eight months. When these elections occurred, the continued state of emergency limited opposition efforts and helped Communist candidates dominate the Azerbaijani delegation. In September 1991 the Azerbaijani presidential elections had a similar outcome—the Communist candidate, Ayaz Mutalibov, won easily because opposition elements such as the PFA had boycotted the vote. However, the Communist delegates in the Azerbaijani legislature kowtowed to nationalism after the hard-line coup against Gorbachev failed in August 1991 and voted to secede from the USSR on August 30, 1991. By November 1991 Azerbaijan had gained full independence.

As an independent nation, Azerbaijan's greatest challenge has been the fate of Nagorno-Karabakh. Not long after seceding, Azerbaijan ended that territory's autonomy, prompting a declaration of independence by its Armenian residents and a renewed conflict between Armenia and Azerbaijan. The instability caused by this dispute led to a relatively bloodless takeover of the Azerbaijani government by the PFA (with support from the Azerbaijani armed forces) in May 1992. The new president of Azerbaijan, PFA leader Aliyev Abul'faz Elchibey, was elected in June 1992 but was deposed a month later by Colonel Surat Huseinov after Elchibey had attempted to disarm his troops.

As a result of the series of short-lived governments, the Milli Majlis, the Azerbaijani legislature, appointed Heydar Aliyev, a former Communist Party official, as interim president until he was elected to that post in an October 1993 vote. The legislature also designated Colonel Husinov as prime minister, and he soon began directing military operations to gain control of Nagorno-Karabakh. Despite Husinov's efforts, the conflict ended in a draw after a series of Armenian offensives in August 1993, and the two sides opened cease-fire talks in early 1994. While a cessation of hostilities was finally achieved by the end of 1994, an effective resolution over the disputed territory remains to be achieved. In 2003 Heydar Aliyev died. His son Ilham Aliyev subsequently won a huge margin in presidential elections that drew criticism from Western observers, owing to voting irregularities. This oil-rich nation has made many deals with Western oil companies, including a pipeline from Baku to Turkey that became operational in 2005.

Azikiwe, Benjamin (*1904–1996*) President of Nigeria (1963–66). An Ibo active in nationalist politics as editor of various newspapers and executive member of the **Nigerian Youth Movement** (1934–41), he was elected member of the Eastern Region House of Assembly (1954–59) and premier, Eastern Region (1954–59). He served as governor-general of Nigeria (1960–63) and first president of the republic (1963–66). Azikiwe unsuccessfully ran for reelection in 1979 and 1983.

Aznar, José María (*1953– *) Spanish politician and prime minister of

Spain (1996–2003). Aznar was the leader of a new conservative movement in Spain that has sought to work within the structure of the Spanish constitutional monarchy. He served as a deputy from Ávila (1982–87), as general secretary of the Popular Alliance, an offshoot of the Popular Party (1982–87), as president of the federal state of Castile-León (1989) and as a member of the Spanish parliament (1989–). Aznar rose to national attention championing a fiscal conservatism and opposing corruption, while at the same time accepting the expansion of civil liberties under the Socialist prime minister Felipe GONZÁLEZ. As a result of the Popular Party's failure to unseat González and his leftist majority in the 1989 national elections, Aznar was elected to president of the Popular Party in an effort to increase the appeal of conservatism among the electorate. He promptly moved the party in a more centrist direction by emphasizing his goals of reducing the national debt, curbing inflation and corruption and reducing the scope of the national government both through increased privatization and granting greater autonomy to Spain's federal states. The last element, however, failed to satisfy the more extreme advocates of Basque separatism; Basque terrorists repeatedly targeted Aznar for assassination and almost succeeded in killing him in 1995. Although again failing to unseat González in the 1993 elections, Aznar eventually led his party to a narrow victory in 1996, when the Popular Party won 156 seats in Parliament. After reaching out to smaller parties to create a coalition government, he ensured his election as prime minister. As a consequence of the improving Spanish economy, Aznar's Popular Party won a majority of seats in Parliament in the 2000 elections. However, he suffered a decline in approval as a result of his staunch support of U.S. president George W. BUSH during the war in Iraq as part of the "coalition of the willing." Aznar decided not to seek reelection in 2004, and his party was voted out of office in favor of the Socialists amid accusations that it had misled the public about the perpetrators of a terrorist attack on a Madrid commuter train.

AZT See AIDS.

B

Baade, Wilhelm Heinrich Walter
(1893–1960) German-American astronomer. Baade was educated at the Universities of Münster and Göttingen where he obtained his Ph.D. in 1919. He worked at the University of Hamburg's Bergedorf Observatory from 1919 to 1931, when he moved to the U.S. He spent the rest of his career at the Mount Wilson and Palomar Observatories, retiring in 1958. In 1920 Baade discovered the minor planet Hidalgo, whose immense orbit extends to that of Saturn, and in 1949 he detected the minor planet Icarus, whose lopsided orbit lies within that of Mercury but can bring Icarus very close to Earth. In the 1930s he did important work with Fritz Zwicky on supernovae, with Edwin HUBBLE on galactic distances and with his old Hamburg colleague Rudolph Minkowski on the optical identification of radio sources.

Baade's most significant work began in 1942. Of German origin, he was precluded from the general induction of scientists into military research. In early 1943 Baade took some famous photographs with the 100-inch reflecting telescope of the central region of the Andromeda galaxy. He was able to distinguish stars in the inner region where Hubble had found only a blur of light. These observations allowed Baade to introduce a fundamental distinction between types of stars. The first type, Population I, he found in the spiral arms of the Andromeda galaxy. They were hot young blue stars as opposed to the Population II stars of the central part of the galaxy, which were older and redder, with a lower metal content. This distinction, now much expanded, has played a crucial role in theories of galactic evolution. Baade found that the Andromeda galaxy was 2 million light-years distant. The distance to the Andromeda galaxy had been used by Hubble to estimate the age of the universe as 2 billion years. Baade's revised figure gave the age as 5 billion years. With Baade's revision of the distance of the Andromeda galaxy—without any change in its luminosity—it became clear that its size must also be increased together with the size of all the other galaxies for which it had been a yardstick. Baade was thus able to establish that, while our galaxy was somewhat bigger than normal, it was not the largest, as Hubble's work had implied.

Baader-Meinhof Group (Red Army Faction) Post-1968 West German urban guerrillas, emerging from the radical student movement, led by **Andreas Baader** and **Ulrike Meinhof.** The group was responsible for six killings, 50 attempted killings, bombings of U.S. military installations and bank raids. Captured in June 1972, Baader and Meinhof later committed suicide while in custody.

Baath (Ba'ath) Meaning "revival" or "renaissance," an Arabic party founded in 1910 by a Syrian Christian, Michel AFLAQ. The Baath Party propounds a policy of pan-Arabism and principles of freedom, unity and socialism. It became the Baath Socialist Party in 1952 after merging with the Syrian Socialist Party. However, Baathists are not confined to SYRIA, and their pan-Arab philosophy has been influential in IRAQ, JORDAN, LEBANON and the PERSIAN GULF states. Baathists were most influential during the UNITED ARAB REPUBLIC (EGYPT and Syria) of the late 1950s, but supporters became disillusioned by the authoritarianism of Egyptian president NASSER. A military coup in 1961 was followed by Syria's withdrawal from the union the same year. The Baathist cause suffered from the failure of this experiment and from antidemocratic tendencies of Baathist governments in Iraq and Syria since 1963—tendencies displayed in the 1980s by Hafez al-ASSAD (Syria) and Saddam HUSSEIN (Iraq), both professed Baathists. In March 2003 the U.S.-led invasion of Iraq overthrew Hussein and ended the Baath Party's domination of the Iraqi government.

Babangida, Ibrahim *(1941–)* Military ruler of Nigeria (1985–93). In 1985 Babangida, a general in the Nigerian army, executed a coup against the regime of General Buhari and Brigadier Tunde Idiagbon and placed himself in control of Nigeria. Babangida functioned as Nigeria's dictator for the next eight years. In 1993 he promised that he would step down as leader and arrange for free elections to determine his successor. Those elections took place in the summer of 1993, and Mashood ABIOLA, an outspoken advocate of Nigerian democracy, won the presidency. Abiola's election, however, was anathema to Babangida and many of the country's ruling elite. In response, Babangida annulled the election results. In October 1993 Babangida himself was removed from power and replaced by an interim government headed by Ernest Shonekan, a chieftain of one of Nigeria's major ethnic groups. Shonekan was later forced from office by General Sani ABACHA. Since his forced removal from office, Babangida has attempted to regain his influence in Nigerian political affairs. Originally alleged to have sponsored the candidacy of former vice president Dr. Alex Ekwueme in the presidential elections of April 2003, he switched his support to former general and Nigerian businessman Olusegun Obsanjo, who won the elections amid numerous accusations of electoral fraud.

Babbitt, Irving (*1865–1933*) American educator and author. After attending Harvard University and the Sorbonne in Paris, Babbitt taught French and comparative literature at Harvard from 1894 until his death. He opposed the romantic movement and established a new literary movement, neohumanism, that emphasized human concerns based on studies of art and literature and the civilizations of ancient Greece and China. H. L. MENCKEN was a critic of Babbitt; early followers included T. S. ELIOT and George SANTAYANA, who later disagreed with his philosophy. His books include *Literature and the American College* (1908).

Babbitt, Milton (*1916–*) American composer. Babbitt is one of the pioneers of modern musical composition for electronic instruments. He earned his M.A. in fine arts in 1942 from Princeton University, where he studied with Roger SESSIONS. Babbitt subsequently taught at Princeton while pursuing an active and influential career as a composer. Among his most noted works are *Three Compositions for Piano* (1946–47), *Composition*

for Four Instruments (1947), *Composition for Synthesizer* (1961) and *Vision and Prayer* (1961). In many of his works, Babbitt employed a 12-tone, serialized method of composition that featured marked variations in timbre, pitch and dynamics.

Babcock, Harold Delos (*1882–1968*) American astronomer. Babcock was educated at the University of California, Berkeley, where he graduated in 1907. In 1908 he joined the staff of the Mount Wilson Observatory where he remained until his retirement in 1948, after which he continued to work for many years with his son Horace BABCOCK. When he joined the observatory Babcock's first task was to supply the basic laboratory data on the effects of strong magnetic fields on various chemical elements. Many years later, in collaboration with his son, he used their joint invention, the magnetograph, to detect the presence of weak and more generalized magnetic fields on the Sun. In 1948 they also revealed the existence of strong magnetic fields in certain stars.

Babcock, Horace Welcome (*1912–2003*) American astronomer. Babcock was the son of Harold Delos BABCOCK. Horace Babcock graduated in 1934 from the California Institute of Technology and obtained his Ph.D. in 1938 from the University of California. He worked at Lick Observatory from 1938 to 1939 and at the Yerkes and McDonald observatories from 1939 to 1941. He was engaged in war work at the radiation laboratory at the Massachusetts Institute of Technology (1941–42) and at Cal Tech (1942–45). In 1946 Babcock returned to astronomy and joined his father at Mount Wilson where they began an enormously profitable collaboration. Babcock later served from 1964 until his retirement in 1978 as director of the Mount Wilson and Palomar Observatories, which became known in 1969 as the Hale Observatories.

Babcock, Stephen Moulton (*1843–1931*) American agricultural chemist. After graduating from Tufts College in 1866, Babcock studied at Cornell and in 1879 took a Ph.D. at the University of Göttingen. He taught at Cornell in 1881 and 1882 and later worked for five years as a chemist at Cornell's agricultural ex-

periment station. He joined the University of Wisconsin faculty in 1887 as professor of agricultural chemistry and served until he retired in 1913. During this time he made possible some of the most notable advances in his field. In 1890 he invented the still-used method of testing the amount of butterfat in milk. The test helped both milk producers and sellers in quality control and thus paved the path for the modern dairy industry, especially in Wisconsin. Babcock made extensive studies in the nutritional requirements of animals. This formed the basis for the discovery of vitamin A by E. V. McCollum in 1912. Babcock never patented his discoveries, making them available to benefit all.

Babel, Isaac Emmanuelovich (*1894–1941*) Russian novelist, playwright and short story writer. Babel wrote mainly about violence and brutality, from the viewpoint of an intellectual both fascinated and repelled by his material, yet striving to be objective. He gained fame with *Odessa Tales* (1923–24), which was published by Maxim GORKY. *Red Cavalry* (1924) was written as a result of his service as a soldier in the war against POLAND. He also wrote two plays, *Sunset* (1928) and *Maria* (1935). He was arrested in 1937 or 1938 and died in a Soviet CONCENTRATION CAMP, a victim of STALIN'S GREAT PURGE.

Babi Yar Massacre In September 1941 large numbers of Ukrainian JEWS and communists in Nazi-occupied KIEV were summoned to be registered. Many were then transported to a deep gully called Babi Yar (Old woman's gully) outside the city, where they were machine-gunned in front of pre-dug graves by Nazi SS troops commanded by General Otto Rasch. The mass graves were covered over by bulldozers. Perhaps 100,000 inhabitants of Kiev, including 34,000 Jews, were massacred by the Nazis in two days.

Baby M case American court case in 1987 that considered a surrogate mother's plea for the return of the child she bore, pitting the child's natural mother against the child's adoptive parents. Mary Beth Whitehead, a married mother of two, agreed to bear a child for Mr. and Mrs. William Stern, who wanted a child but knew a pregnancy and childbirth would be dangerous because of Mrs. Stern's medical condition. Whitehead agreed in a written contract to be artificially inseminated with Mr. Stern's semen and to bear a child, which would be turned over to the Sterns. In return she received $10,000 and the Sterns paid all costs. After the delivery Whitehead refused to turn over the baby and vanished with the child. After Whitehead and the child were found the Sterns sued for breach of contract. The ensuing court battle caught the attention of the public at large and precipitated a vigorous national debate over the issue of surrogacy. The Sterns ultimately gained custody of the child, but a number of state legislatures passed laws outlawing surrogacy contracts in the future.

Bacall, Lauren (Betty Joan Persky) *(1924–)* American actress; one of Hollywood's most engaging film stars of the 1940s and 1950s. After graduating from the American Academy of Dramatic Arts, Bacall was cast—at only 19 years of age—opposite Humphrey BOGART in the film *To Have and Have Not* (1944). She married the great actor a year later and costarred with him in three more film noir classics: *The Big Sleep* (1946), *Dark Passage* (1947) and *Key Largo* (1948). Bacall's model-like figure (she was nicknamed "slim"), husky voice and cool sex appeal formed a perfect chemistry with Bogart's famed "tough" exterior. After Bogart died in 1957, Bacall's career slipped somewhat, although she continued to appear in films such as *Harper* (1966) and *The Shootist* (1976). In the 1970s and 1980s she turned more to stage work, with acclaimed performances in *Cactus Flower* and *Woman of the Year*. In the 1990s Bacall continued to make intermittent television, stage and film appearances, such as her small role in *My Fellow Americans* (1996).

Bachauer, Gina *(1913–1976)* Greek pianist. Born in Athens, Bachauer studied at the Athens Conservatory, the École Normale de Musique in Paris with Alfred Cortot and privately with Sergei RACHMANINOFF from 1932 to 1935. She made her debut as a soloist with the Athens Symphony Orchestra in 1935

and debuted with the Paris Symphony Orchestra two years later. When the Nazis invaded Greece, her immediate family was killed, and she fled to Egypt, where she performed in hundreds of concerts for the Allied troops. After the war she settled in London, making her English debut with the New London Symphony in 1946. From then on she toured the world as a high-ranking international soloist, making her first American appearance at New York City's Town Hall in 1950. Bachauer was known for her accomplished and sometimes bravura technique, her penetrating tone and liquid playing style.

Bachelet Jeria, Verónica Michelle (1951—). Chilean politician; president of Chile (2006–). Born in Santiago, she traveled extensively with her family during her father's service as an officer in the air force, including a stint in Washington, D.C., where she became fluent in English. After enrolling in medical school in 1970, Bachelet, along with her mother and father, were detained and tortured by agents of General Augusto PINOCHET, who had overthrown the left-wing government of President Salvadore ALLENDE in 1973. Her father, who had served as head of the Food Distribution Office in Allende's government, died of a heart attack during his detention and torture. In 1975 Bachelet and her mother were exiled to Australia and soon moved to East Germany, where she learned German and continued her medical studies at the Humboldt University in East Berlin. In 1979 she returned to her homeland and received a medical degree from the University of Chile in 1983. After work as a consultant to various nongovernmental organizations, Bachelet developed an interest in military strategy. She studied that subject at the National Academy of Political and Strategic Studies and then at the Inter-American Defense College in the U.S. before becoming an adviser to the Chilean minister of defense in 1998.

A longtime activist in the Chilean Socialist Party, Bachelet was named minister of health in the government of Socialist president Ricardo Lagos in 2000. Two years later she became minister of defense and won widespread praise for initiating a comprehensive program to modernize the Chilean

armed forces. After winning the Socialist Party's nomination for president, Bachelet won 40% of the vote in the first round of the presidential election of 2005 and then gained an absolute majority in January 2006, making her the first woman president of her country. A single mother with three children, she combines progressive social views with a pledge to continue the free-market economic policies of her predecessor.

Bachmann, Ingeborg *(1926–1973)* Austrian poet, short story writer, novelist, critic and dramatist. Bachmann studied law and philosophy at Graz, Innsbruck and the University of Vienna. *Die gestundete Zeit* won the Gruppe 47 prize in 1953; these pessimistic poems showed an awareness of German guilt and ambivalence. *Anrufung des grossen Baren* appeared in 1956. In 1959–60 she gave a series of lectures on the existential situation of the writer and published an essay on the philosopher Ludwig WITTGENSTEIN that addressed the "language problem." She also collaborated on libretti with composer Hans Werner HENZE. In 1964 she won the Georg Buchner prize. She ceased to write poetry in the 1960s but went on to write a novel, *Malina*, part of a trilogy left unfinished at her death, and *Simultan* (1972), a cycle of short stories. FEMINISM is a major theme of her later work.

Bach-Zelewsky, Erich von dem *(1899–1972)* German Nazi general who crushed the 1944 WARSAW UPRISING during WORLD WAR II. In putting down the uprising, his troops killed 100,000 Poles and leveled 90% of the city. Bach-Zelewsky later testified against Nazi leaders at the NUREMBERG TRIALS. He was sentenced to life imprisonment for the murder of six communists.

Backhaus, Wilhelm *(1884–1969)* German pianist. Born in Leipzig, he studied at that city's conservatory and made his concert debut there at the age of eight. He pursued further studies with Eugène d'Albert in Frankfurt. A 1900 concert tour marked the beginning of his solo career. Backhaus settled in London in 1905, becoming a professor of piano at the Royal College of Music, Manchester. He continued to tour Europe, establishing a distinguished reputation for his interpretations of

Beethoven and Brahms. He debuted in the U.S. in a concert with the New York Symphony Society in 1912. Beginning in 1909, Backhaus made a great many recordings, and he is particularly noted for his two series of Beethoven piano sonatas, the last of which he recorded at the age of 80. He was especially known for his boldness, clarity, breadth and devotion to accuracy. He and his wife moved to Lugano in 1930 and became Swiss citizens. Backhaus remained an active and admired soloist up until the time of his death.

Bacon, Francis *(1909–1992)* British painter. Bacon emerged in the postwar generation of British "pessimistic" painters that also included Graham SUTHERLAND. He earned worldwide recognition in the l960s for his strikingly bizarre canvases that probed highly charged emotional themes through the use of incongruent and violent images. One of Bacon's best-known paintings is *Three Studies for a Crucifixion* (1962), a triptych in which the Christian symbolism of death and resurrection is transformed into a series of brutal scenes of dismembered torsos locked in seemingly erotic postures. Because Bacon frequently employed nonpainted images—such as photographs—for his canvasses, he was linked by critics to the American POP ART movement, although the emotional tenor of Bacon's work was far removed from the light satire of most pop art productions.

Baden-Powell, Robert (Robert Stephenson Smyth, first baron Baden-Powell of Gilwell) *(1857–1941)* British soldier and founder of the Boy Scouts and Girl Scouts. An officer in the 13th Hussars cavalry regiment, Baden-Powell first gained fame as the defender of Mafeking during the South African BOER WAR (1899–1900). Back home, he initiated a program for boys that stressed self-reliance, resourcefulness and courage; this developed into the Boy Scouts organization in 1908. In 1909, with the help of his sister Agnes Baden-Powell, he founded the Girl Guides (which became the Girl Scouts in the U.S.). His wife, Lady Olave Baden-Powell, was the first and only World Chief Guide (1918–77). He was

created a peer with the title of baron in 1929. His many books include *Scouting for Boys* (1908) and *Scouting and Youth Movements* (1929).

Badoglio, Pietro *(1871–1956)* Italian soldier and premier (1943–44). A career officer, he served in WORLD WAR I and later became ITALY's governor of LIBYA (1929–33). He was commander in chief during the Italian conquest of ETHIOPIA (1935–36) and the failed invasion of GREECE (1940). An opponent of Italy's entry into WORLD WAR II, he became premier after the fall of MUSSOLINI and negotiated a 1943 alliance with the Allies. Badoglio resigned in 1944.

Baez, Joan *(1941–)* American folk and rock vocalist. Baez, who was one of the major figures in the widespread folk music revival of the early 1960s, was a musical star before the age of 20 by virtue of her haunting and powerful soprano voice. Her father was a Mexican-American scientist and her mother an American professor of English. Baez attended Boston University for a time but gave up her academic career to become involved in the active folk scene then based in Cambridge, Massachusetts. Baez enjoyed phenomenal success with albums including *Joan Baez in Concert* volumes I, 1962, and II, 1964, and *Daybreak* (1968). Her rendition of "We Shall Overcome" was an anthem of the 1960s CIVIL RIGHTS MOVEMENT. In the 1960s and 1970s, she toured with Bob DYLAN, with whom she was also romantically linked. Baez enjoyed hits in the 1970s with two different singles— "The Night They Drove Old Dixie Down" and "Diamonds and Rust." She remains active both in music and in libertarian politics. In 1979 Baez established Humanitas International, a human rights group designed to send immediate aid to foreign peoples living in crisis.

Baffi, Paolo *(1911–1989)* Italian financier and politician. He was one of the major economic figures in post-World War II Italy and served as governor of the Bank of Italy from 1975 to 1979, during one of the most turbulent periods in the country's recent economic history. He resigned in 1979 after he was arrested on charges

of misconduct but was later cleared and remained honorary governor of the bank until shortly before his death. It was later reported that his arrest had been prompted by angry members of the ruling Christian Democratic Party who had been upset by an investigation he had conducted into the misuse of government credit for political purposes.

Baghdad Capital city of Iraq located on both banks of the Tigris River. This ancient city was captured by British forces in 1917, during WORLD WAR I. In 1921 the British made Baghdad the capital of Iraq and saw an Arab monarchy installed. A violent revolution in 1958 toppled the monarchy after major fighting in Baghdad. The capital was a main target of U.S. bombing raids during **Operation Desert Storm** in the PERSIAN GULF WAR (January–February 1991). In 2003 Baghdad came under U.S. military occupation during the concluding combat phase of Operation Iraqi Freedom and became the headquarters for the U.S.-formed Iraqi Governing Council.

Bahama Islands (Bahamas) Nation of over 700 islands extending in a chain north of the West Indies, on a rough line from Florida to Haiti. Once a member of the British COMMONWEALTH, the Bahamas was granted independence in 1973. Its main industries are tourism and international banking; Nassau is the capital.

Bahrain Emirate state consisting of a group of islands in the Persian Gulf, off the east coast of Saudi Arabia. Key islands are Bahrain, on which the capital of Manama is located, and Muharraq. In topography they are flat and sandy, with a humid climate. Bahrain became a British protectorate in 1861; after resistance to colonial rule in the 1950s and 1960s, Britain granted independence in 1971. Bahrain is ruled by an emir of the al-Khalifah family. Its key source of income is oil, first discovered in 1931, but it is also an international banking center.

Baikonur See TYURATAM.

Bailey, Sir Donald Coleman *(1901–1985)* British civil engineer. Bai-

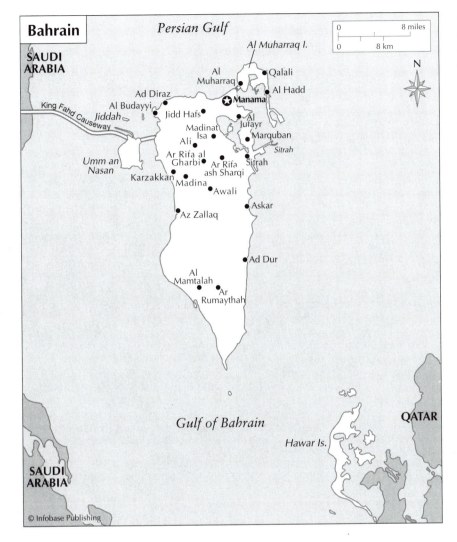

Bahrain

Persian Gulf

SAUDI ARABIA

Al Muharraq I.

Qalali

Al Muharraq

Al Hadd

Ad Diraz

Al Budayyi
Jiddah
King Fahd Causeway

Jidd Hafs

★ Manama

Al Jufayr

Madinat Isa
Ali

Marquban

Sitrah

Ar Rifa al Gharbi

Umm an Nasan

Ar Rifa ash Sharqi

Sitrah

Karzakkan
Madina

Awali

Az Zallaq

Askar

Ad Dur

Al Mamtalah

Ar Rumaythah

Gulf of Bahrain

Hawar Is.

QATAR

SAUDI ARABIA

0   8 miles
0   8 km

N

© Infobase Publishing

ley was the inventor of the portable **Bailey bridge,** a device that played a key role in the Allied victory in WORLD WAR II. The bridge, assembled from welded panels of light steel connected by pinned joints, was extremely portable and could hold loads weighing tons. It was particularly useful during the June 1944 Allied invasion of NORMANDY.

Bailey, F. Lee *(1933–)* American criminal attorney and author. A graduate of Harvard University and Boston University Law School, Bailey handled many high-profile cases during the years after World War II. He gained national notice for his defense of Sam SHEPPARD, a Cleveland doctor who had been convicted of murdering his wife. After the U.S. Supreme Court granted Sheppard a new trial on the charge, Bailey won an acquittal. A decade later Bailey was hired to defend Patty HEARST, the daughter of newspaper magnate William Randolph Hearst Jr., who after her kidnapping by an extremist group voluntarily joined the group and robbed a California bank. Because of the overwhelming evidence against her, even Bailey was unable to convince a jury of her innocence. In 1994–95 Bailey was part of the legal "dream team" that defended O. J. Simpson (see O. J. SIMPSON MURDER TRIAL) and obtained the acquittal of the former professional football player. Bailey, a celebrity in his own right, is the author of several books including *The Defense Never Rests.*

Bailey, Pearl Mae *(1918–1990)* U.S. singer. A Broadway musical star and cabaret singer, she was known for her campy, bawdy singing style and her dedication to performing. Her career began in VAUDEVILLE in the 1930s. She appeared in several films, including *Carmen Jones* (1954) and *Porgy and Bess*

(1959). She played the title role in the acclaimed all-black production of the stage musical *Hello, Dolly!* (1967–69). Among her best-known songs were "Tired," "Birth of the Blues," "That's Good Enough for Me" and "Takes Two to Tango." She won a special Tony Award in 1968 and the Presidential Medal of Freedom in 1988.

Bailey Bridge See Sir Donald Coleman BAILEY.

Bailey v. Drexel Furniture Co. *(1922)* U.S. Supreme Court decision overturning a federal law that attempted to outlaw child labor. The exploitation of children in factories was widespread in the early years of the 20th century. In response to an outcry from the public, Congress passed the Child Labor Tax Act to discourage employers from exploiting children. The law placed a 10% tax on the net profits of businesses who employed child labor. The Supreme Court declared the law unconstitutional on the grounds that, since the purpose of the tax was to regulate rather than raise revenue, the tax was an impermissible intrusion on business. The case was a major blow to reformers, and child labor remained common until World War II, when the practice was finally outlawed.

Baillie-Scott, Mackay Hugh *(1865– 1945)* English architect and designer involved with the Arts and Crafts movement. Baillie-Scott received his training while working in the office of the Bath city architect from 1886 to 1889. His commission to decorate rooms in a palace at the art colony at Darmstadt in 1898 led to his developing a reputation in Germany. He continued architectural practice and produced furniture designs for production and publication in Germany and Switzerland until his retirement from active practice in 1939.

Baird, Bill (William Britton) *(1904– 1987)* U.S. puppeteer. Baird's impish creations, including Charlemane the Lion and Slugger Ryan, delighted millions of U.S. television viewers during the 1950s. With his third wife, Cora, he staged puppet shows around the world, including some in the Soviet Union. He trained a generation of other gifted puppeteers, most notably Muppets' creator Jim HENSON.

BAHRAIN

1928	Sovereignty is claimed by Persia (Iran).
1930s	Oil is discovered, providing the backbone of the country's wealth.
1953–56	The Council for National Unity is formed by Arab nationalists but is suppressed after large demonstrations against British participation in the Suez War.
1968	Britain announces its intention to withdraw its forces. Present-day Bahrain is formed, with Qatar and the Trucial States of the United Arab Emirates, and the Federation of Arab Emirates.
1970	Iran's claims over Bahrain are referred to the United Nations; UN representatives report popular opinion as overwhelmingly in favor of independence; Iran accepts UN report.
1971	The United Kingdom withdraws from the Persian Gulf region and ends its treaty obligations to the Trucial States; Bahrain declares its independence. The sheikh of Bahrain assumes the title emir.
1973	New constitution is ratified; elections are held for the newly created National Assembly; the radical Popular Bloc of the Left gains 10 of the 30 elected seats.
1975	The National Assembly is dissolved by the emir, who promises new elections and a new electoral apparatus. Television is introduced.
1976	International Parliamentary Union expels Bahrain for its autocratic dissolution of the National Assembly.
1977	Bahrain terminates a six-year agreement permitting U.S. naval ships to be based in Bahrain.
1981	Bahrain joins the Gulf Cooperation Council.
1984	The emirate bans the Shiite Islamic Enlightenment Society, charging it with pro-Iranian subversive plots.
1988	Bahrain holds its first official talks with the USSR.
1989	Bahrain establishes diplomatic relations with the People's Republic of China.
1990	Iraq invades Kuwait; Bahrain supports UN economic sanctions against Iraq and permits the stationing of U.S. combat aircraft in Bahrain; Bahrain establishes diplomatic relations with the USSR.
1991	Bahrain sends troops and air support to Saudi Arabia; Bahrain fights alongside international troops against Iraq; Bahrain joins seven moderate Arab states in agreeing to a U.S.-backed postwar plan for collective security in the Persian Gulf region.
1992	The emir establishes an advisory council as a replacement for the National Assembly that was dissolved in 1975.
1995	Uneven economic and social conditions lead to rioting against the government of Bahrain; the State Security Law is established to suppress unrest.
1996	The government cracks down on antigovernment protests, arresting more than 600 dissenters.
1999	Emir Isa bin Salman al-Khalifa dies and is succeeded by his son Hamad bin Isa al-Khalifa; Bahrain begins negotiations with Qatar over the disputed Hawar Islands.
2000	The emir promises to restore a democratically elected parliament.
2001	The emir pardons more than 800 political prisoners and exiles; in a national referendum, 98% of voters support a proposal for a new national charter providing for free elections and restoration of the National Assembly; the emir abolishes the State Security Law.
2002	First elections in 32 years are held on May 9 to decide municipal representatives. Women vote and run for office for the first time.

Baird, John Logie (*1888–1946*) British inventor. Baird studied electrical engineering at the Royal Technical College in Glasgow and then went to Glasgow University. His poor health prevented him from active service during World War I and from completing various business enterprises in the years following the war. After a breakdown in 1922 he retired to Hastings and engaged in amateur experiments on the transmission of pictures. Using primitive equipment he succeeded in transmitting an image over a distance of a couple of feet, and in 1926 he demonstrated his apparatus before a group of scientists. Recognition followed, and the next year he transmitted pictures by telephone wire between London and Glasgow. In the same year he set up the Baird Television Development Company. He continued to work on improvements and on September 30, 1929, gave the first experimental BBC broadcast. Synchronization of sound and vision was achieved a few months later. In 1937, however, the Baird system of mechanical scanning was ousted by the all-electronic system put forward by Marconi-EMI. Baird was at the forefront of virtually all developments in television; he continued research into color, stereoscopic and big-screen television until his death.

Baj, Enrico (*1924–2003*) Italian artist. An influential figure in the Milan art world, Baj was the cofounder of the journal *Il gesto* in 1955. Working in oils, collages and graphics, he underwent a number of stylistic changes during his career. Beginning as an abstract painter, he turned to a kind of surrealist imagery in semifigurative paintings inhabited by otherworldly humanlike creatures. He is also known for his POP ART parodies of paintings by modern masters.

Bajer, Frederik (*1837–1922*) Danish author and pacifist. In the Danish army from 1856 to 1864 he became interested in social problems. He started to write newspaper articles, and in 1867 he attempted to found a peace society. In 1870 he established the Association of Scandinavian Free States, which advocated the union of Scandinavian nations. As a member of parliament (1872–95), he worked for various progressive reforms including neutrality and women's rights. From 1891 to 1907 he served as chairman of the International Peace Bureau, headquartered in Bern, Switzerland. In 1908 he was instrumental in the establishment of a Scandinavian Interparliamentary Union, and that same year he was awarded the NOBEL PRIZE for peace along with the Swedish peace advocate Klas ARNOLDSON.

Bakelite Trade name of one of the first PLASTICS to come into wide use. A phenolic invented in 1907 by chemist Leo Baekeland, the material is a good insulator against heat and electric current, can easily be molded in varied shapes and is relatively inexpensive. It has a wide application in electrical hardware, for example, for handles and enclosure elements on kitchen wares, irons and similar products. The material is brittle, making it easily damaged by impact; its color is normally limited to browns and black. The term has become a generic name for any phenolic plastic, regardless of manufacturer.

Baker, Chesney "Chet" (*1929–1988*) American JAZZ trumpeter and vocalist. Baker helped set the standard for West Coast "cool jazz" in the early 1950s, when he appeared with the Gerry Mulligan Quartet, a revolutionary, pianoless ensemble. Baker's career was blighted by heroin addiction. He was arrested repeatedly during the 1950s and 1960s on drug-related charges, both in the U.S. and in Europe. After a 1968 beating in which he lost most of his teeth, he did not play again for several years.

Baker, Ella (*1903–1986*) American CIVIL RIGHTS activist. Baker's talents as an organizer led to her becoming director of the New York branch of the NATIONAL ASSOCIATION FOR THE ADVANCEMENT OF COLORED PEOPLE during World War II. After the SOUTHERN CHRISTIAN LEADERSHIP CONFERENCE was established in 1957, she was asked to set up its national office and serve as its executive director. In 1960 she organized the conference that created the Student Nonviolent Coordinating Committee and later played a key behind-the-scenes role in that group's efforts to register black voters in Mississippi.

Baker, James Addison, III (*1930– *) U.S. government official and secretary of state. Born in Houston, Texas Baker graduated from Princeton University in 1952. After service in the U.S. Marine Corps he received his law degree from the University of Texas in 1957 and embarked on a successful career as an attorney in the Houston firm of Andrews & Kurth. He entered government service in 1975 as undersecretary of commerce in the administration of President Gerald FORD. Baker served as President Ronald REAGAN's chief of staff during his first term, 1981–85, and then as secretary of the treasury during Reagan's second term. President George H. W. BUSH named Baker secretary of state in 1989, a position he occupied until the summer of 1992 when he became Bush's chief of staff and senior counselor to the president.

While secretary of state, Baker played a major role in orchestrating the formation of the broad coalition that supported the U.S.-led military operation (Operation Desert Storm) that evicted the Iraqi army from KUWAIT in 1991. Later that year he organized the Madrid Conference, at which a delegation of Palestinians unaffiliated with the PALESTINE LIBERATION ORGANIZATION met for the first time with Israeli representatives as members of the Jordanian delegation. In 1992 Baker coordinated a complicated set of negotiations in Washington between various Arab and Israeli spokesmen in an ambitious effort to reach a comprehensive settlement of the Israeli-Palestinian problem. But these negotiations failed to produce a breakthrough, which did not come until the Oslo Accords were signed in 1993 during the administration of President Bill CLINTON.

In addition to his government service, Baker was widely regarded as a master political strategist after he managed President Reagan's successful reelection campaign in 1984. But he was blamed by some for President Bush's defeat in his 1992 reelection campaign, which he also managed. After leaving government service in 1993, Baker became a senior partner with the Houston law firm of Baker Botts and served as a senior counselor to the Carlyle Group, a merchant banking firm in Washington, D.C. He was called upon by presidential candidate George W. BUSH to manage the public relations campaign in Florida during the dispute over the outcome of the 2000 presidential election in that state. After Bush's election, he appointed Baker as special presidential envoy on the issue of Iraqi debt.

Baker, Dame Janet *(1933–   )* English mezzo-soprano. Born in York, she studied with Helene Isepp and Meriel St. Clair in London and with Lotte LEHMANN in Salzburg. She made her English debut with the Glyndebourne Festival Chorus in 1956 and her American debut with the San Francisco Symphony in MAHLER's *Das Lied von der Erde* 10 years later. Her first American recital, also in 1966, was given at New York's Town Hall. Singing in a wide range of recitals, oratorios and operas, and as a soloist with major orchestras, Baker became an international star. She is known for her vocal warmth and richness, her exquisite phrasing, her sensitive musicianship and her breadth of repertoire. A superb interpreter of lieder, she also has a broad operatic range. Baker was named a Dame of the British Empire in 1970. She retired from the opera and concert stage in the 1980s but received two important designations in the 1990s: She was named the chancellor of the University of York (1991) and also was made Companion of Honour of the British Empire.

Baker, Josephine *(1906–1975)* American dancer, singer, entertainer and CIVIL RIGHTS activist. Baker, an African American whose mother was a St. Louis washerwoman, first achieved international fame as an entertainer in the 1920s. Unable to find acceptance in her native land due to racial prejudice, Baker immigrated to Paris where in 1925, at age 18, she became a star while appearing in *La Revue Negre*. A beautiful woman with exceptional dancing and singing ability, Baker was also adept at presenting herself in a unique manner—such as walking on with her pet cheetah or having herself lowered upside down onto center stage. In the U.S., her career fared less well. While Baker appeared with the ZIEGFELD FOLLIES in the 1930s, she was barred from many segregated clubs in the 1950s. In 1963 she marched for civil rights in Washington, D.C., with Rev. Martin Luther KING, Jr. In 1937 Baker became a French citizen; her au-

tobiography, *Josephine,* was published in 1977.

Baker, Newton Diehl *(1871–1937)* U.S. secretary of war (1916–21). After graduating from Johns Hopkins University in 1892, Baker earned his law degree from Washington and Lee University and returned to Martinsburg, West Virginia, to practice law. Moving to Cleveland, Ohio, he was city solicitor (1902–12) and mayor (1912–16). Appointed secretary of war by Woodrow WILSON in March 1916, he began his service as WORLD WAR I was grinding on in Europe. During his first year in office, he was investigated by Congress for not doing much to strengthen the U.S. Armed Forces, but he was not removed from office. Baker overcame the early judgments of his administration and ended his service to the War Department with almost universal praise for his mobilization effort. Nevertheless, he remained one of the most ardent advocates of peace and continued to urge U.S. entry into the LEAGUE OF NATIONS. In 1928 President Calvin COOLIDGE appointed him to the Permanent Court of Arbitration at The HAGUE.

Baker scandal Political scandal involving President Lyndon JOHNSON's close political aide, Bobby Baker, a former Senate page. While Johnson was Senate majority leader, his aide Baker improperly used his political contacts to get contracts for his vending machine business and to amass a sizable personal fortune. When Johnson became vice president in 1961, additional accusations were raised that Baker received illegal payments and also bribed public officials. The outcry against Baker continued after Johnson became president following the assassination of President John KENNEDY. A Senate investigation raised additional accusations of wrongdoing against Baker, including financial improprieties involving Baker, President Johnson and Mrs. Johnson's Texas radio station. Although Baker himself testified, he added little damning nor exculpatory evidence. The committee found Baker had committed gross improprieties. Although Barry GOLDWATER, the Republican presidential nominee in 1964, raised the Baker scandal in his campaign, President

Johnson won reelection handily. Baker was eventually convicted of tax evasion, theft and conspiracy to defraud the government. He served time in a federal penitentiary before being paroled in 1972.

Baker v. Carr ("One Man, One Vote") *(1962)* Landmark Supreme Court case holding that citizens could challenge the makeup of state legislatures in federal courts. From the earliest days of the republic, state legislatures employed considerable ingenuity in drawing legislative district boundaries, a process referred to as "gerrymandering." Legislative district lines were also often drawn to favor rural areas: A rural district with only a few thousand voters would enjoy the same voting power as an urban area with hundreds of thousands of voters. Despite suits protesting such disenfranchisement, federal courts traditionally declined to hear such cases on the grounds that they were "political" matters. In *Baker v. Carr* the Supreme Court reversed its previous position and held that state apportionment could be challenged in the federal courts. The decision, also known as the "one man, one vote" decision, started the process of reapportionment of state legislatures in favor of urban areas, which were often populated by minority groups.

Bakhtin, Mikhail *(1895–1975)* Russian theorist and critic. Descended from the nobility, Bakhtin was born in Orel, a small town outside Moscow, and was educated at Odessa and Petersburg Universities. His complex intellectual nature led him to write literary criticism and to work in the disparate fields of theology, anthropology, philosophy, political science, linguistics and psychology. Bakhtin worked in obscurity until the last 12 years of his life, and some of his books languished unpublished for 25 years or more. He made important contributions to the development of Marxism, Formalism and Freudianism. Bakhtin's books include *Problems of Dostoevsky's Poetics, The Dialogic Imagination* and *Rabelais and His World.*

***Bakke* case** Legal case, formally known as *University of California v. Bakke,* decided by the U.S. Supreme Court in 1978. It was brought by Allan Bakke, a white applicant for admission to the medical school at the University of California at Davis. Twice-rejected, Bakke claimed that he was the victim of reverse discrimination, in that he was denied admission while various minority group members with lower scores than his had been admitted to the school. The decision was close (5-4) and complex. It upheld the principle of race-based AFFIRMATIVE ACTION PROGRAMS, while denying institutions the right to establish race-based quotas. In this case the University of California was found to have discriminated against Bakke by maintaining a 16% minority quota, and the Court ordered that Bakke be admitted. The decision was viewed by many civil rights advocates as a setback to affirmative action programs. In 2003 the Supreme Court upheld the University of Michigan School of Law's use of race as an admissions factor but declared unconstitutional the quantification of race in the university's undergraduate admissions.

Bakr, Ahmed Hassan *(1914–1982)* President of Iraq (1968–79). An army officer and a member of the BAATH Party, Bakr participated in the 1958 coup that overthrew the monarchy in Iraq. He became president after a bloodless coup in 1968. Bakr was ousted in 1979 by Saddam HUSSEIN.

Balaguer, Joaquín *(1907–2002)* President of the Dominican Republic. Balaguer served in the government of dictator Rafael TRUJILLO MOLINA before becoming vice president (1957–60). He assumed the presidency in 1961, although Trujillo held effective power until his assassination in May 1961. Unable to govern in the chaos that followed Trujillo's death, Balaguer was overthrown in a military coup in January 1962. He was elected president in 1966 and reelected in 1970 and 1974 with overwhelming majorities. Balaguer's administration restored order and promoted economic development but was subject to attempted coups from both the right and the left. Balaguer lost the election of 1978 but was returned to office in 1986. Balaguer was reelected in 1990 and 1994 but resigned in 1996 amid accusations of electoral fraud.

Balanchine, George (Georgi Balanchivadze) *(1904–1983)* Russian dancer, choreographer and ballet director. One of the greatest and most influential choreographers of the 20th century, Balanchine was born in St. Petersburg. After studying dance at the Imperial School of Ballet (1941–21) and music at the Petrograd Conservatory of Music, he organized a short-lived touring company with fellow dancers in 1923. Denounced for his experimentation in dance, Balanchine left Russia in 1924 and joined Serge DIAGHILEV's BALLETS RUSSES, for which he choreographed 10 ballets, including the seminal works *Prodigal Son* and *Apollo.* During this time he began to work with composer Igor STRAVINSKY, a collaboration that lasted over 50 years and resulted in 26 ballets, such as *Firebird* and *Orpheus.* After the company disbanded in 1929 upon Diaghilev's death, Balanchine formed associations with several other companies before Lincoln KIRSTEIN and Edward Warburg invited him to establish a ballet school (the School of American Ballet) and company (later named the NEW YORK CITY BALLET) in the U.S. As artistic director of NYCB from 1948, Balanchine choreographed dozens of ballets, including *Midsummer Night's Dream, Liebeslieder Walzer* and *Sonnambula.* His oft-repeated maxim, "Ballet is woman," led to his association with many prominent ballerinas (such as Vera Zorina, Maria TALLCHIEF, Suzanne FARRELL and Patricia McBride), who were the inspiration for many of his ballets. The hallmarks of Balanchine's choreography are his musicality, his development of the plotless ballet that emphasized the dance element, his full use of a large dance ensemble and his emphasis on the ballerina. An innovative teacher, he also set a standard for ballet pedagogy and technique rarely equaled. Balanchine also created dances for Broadway musicals (*On Your Toes,* 1936) and films (*Goldwyn Follies,* 1938).

Balch, Emily Greene *(1867–1961)* American economist and sociologist. Born in Jamaica Plains, Massachusetts, she was educated at Bryn Mawr College, Harvard Annex (later Radcliffe), the University of Chicago and the University of Berlin. In 1896 she began teaching at Wellesley College. Also interested in social reform, she was co-founder of the Boston branch of the Women's Trade Union League and worked to promote the minimum wage. Her researches in Slavic immigration resulted in her book *Our Slavic Fellow Citizens* (1910). Balch's advocacy of liberal causes and world peace brought about her dismissal from Wellesley in 1918. Secretary-treasurer of the Women's International League for peace, she spent the next 40 years promoting international peace. In 1946 she shared the NOBEL PRIZE for peace with John MOTT.

Baldwin, Faith *(1893–1978)* American popular author. During her career Baldwin wrote some 85 books of light fiction, as well as light verse. She reached the peak of her success during the GREAT DEPRESSION of the 1930s with magazine serializations and popular novels such as *Office Wife, District Nurse, Honor Bound* and *Rich Girl, Poor Girl.* Four movies were made from her books, with such stars as Henry FONDA, Jean HARLOW and Clark GABLE.

Baldwin, James *(1924–1989)* American author. Born in New York City, the son of a preacher, Baldwin felt the "rhetoric of the storefront church" to be an influence on his work, which examines racial, national, sexual and personal identity. He left home at 17 and eventually settled in Paris (1948). His first novel, *Go Tell It on the Mountain* (1953), the story of one day in the lives of the members of a HARLEM church, established him as a leading novelist of black American life and drew inevitable comparisons to his mentor Richard WRIGHT, whose work Baldwin later rejected. His second novel, *Giovanni's Room* (1956), explored a man's struggle with his homosexuality. During the American CIVIL RIGHTS MOVEMENT, he wrote *Nobody Knows My Name* (1961), essays on race relations, and *The Fire Next Time* (1963), a powerful nonfiction book. Other works include *Another Country* (1962), *The Evidence of Things Not Seen* (1985), *The Price of a Ticket: Collected Non-Fiction* (1985) and *Perspectives: Angles on African Art* (1987).

Baldwin, Roger *(1884–1981)* Founder of the AMERICAN CIVIL LIBERTIES UNION (ACLU) and self-styled political reformer. As executive director of the ACLU from its formation in 1920 until 1950, he defended such disparate clients as communists, Nazis, members of the KU KLUX KLAN, Henry FORD and SACCO AND VANZETTI, all with equal vigor and dispassion. He was widely regarded as a leftist because of his defense of radical labor unions and other left-wing groups in the 1920s and 1930s. However, he also coordinated the defense of such underdogs as John Scopes in the SCOPES TRIAL (1925), and the Jehovah's Witnesses in 1938, achieving free-press rights for that religious group. After retiring as director, he remained the ACLU's international affairs adviser until his death. In January 1981 he received the White House Medal of Freedom.

Baldwin, Stanley (Earl Baldwin of Bewdley, 1937) *(1867–1947)* British statesman, three-time prime minister (1923, 1924–29, 1935–37). Educated at Cambridge he entered the political arena as a Conservative member of Parliament, where he served from 1908 to 1937. He became parliamentary private secretary to Andrew Bonar LAW in 1916, financial secretary of the treasury in 1917 and entered the cabinet as the president of the Board of Trade in 1921. After serving as chancellor of the exchequer (1922–23), he succeeded Law as prime minister in 1923. He left office briefly in 1923, returning as prime minister from 1924 to 1929. During this tenure in office, economic distress and rising unemployment led to the GENERAL STRIKE OF 1926, a crisis that Baldwin handled with considerable firmness and skill. After losing the election of 1929, he joined the coalition government of Ramsay MACDONALD in 1931 and again assumed the prime minister's office in 1935. Opposing the marriage of King EDWARD VIII, he deftly handled the ABDICATION CRISIS of 1936. Baldwin was widely criticized for his underestimation of the NAZI threat during his last years in office. He resigned in 1937 and was made a peer later that year.

Balearic Islands (Islas Baleares) Archipelago of 16 islands in the Mediterranean Sea, east of Spain (of which they are a province). Ibiza, Minorca and Majorca are the major islands. During the SPANISH CIVIL WAR (1936–39), Ibiza and Majorca were held by insurgents from the outset, but Minorca was held until 1939 by the losing Loyalists. Since 1983 they have been an autonomous region of Spain.

Balenciaga, Cristobal *(1895–1972)* Fashion designer whose work suggested the influence of his Spanish Basque origins. Balenciaga is viewed as a "dean" of fashion design, sometimes called "the greatest of the century." At the age of 18 he established Elsa, a retail shop in San Sebastian and shortly thereafter in Madrid and Barcelona. He made regular buying trips to Paris to augment his own design productions. In 1937, in response to the SPANISH CIVIL WAR, he relocated to Paris, opening a shop there that remained in business for 30 years. His first offerings were quiet and simple, but he soon developed design directions generally independent of the trends of any particular moment. His work was characterized by a bold sense of color, use of much black, strong and stiff fabrics and rich ornament suggestive of traditional Spanish origins. Hats, scarfs and rich jewelry were frequent additions to his productions. His work had a quality of timeless elegance.

Balewa, Alhaji (Sir Abubakar Tafawa) *(1912–1966)* Nigerian political leader. A member of the northern Hausa tribe, he was a founder of the Northern People's Congress political party, entering the regional house of assembly in 1947 and the federal house of representatives in 1951. Serving in various ministerial positions, he became the first prime minister of the Federation of NIGERIA in 1957, retaining the office when Nigeria became independent in 1960. A respected statesman, knighted by the British in 1960, he was nevertheless criticized by members of western and eastern tribes for favoritism toward the north. Balewa was assassinated in a 1966 military coup.

Balfour, Arthur James (first earl of Balfour, 1922) *(1848–1930)* British statesman, prime minister (1902–05). He entered Parliament as a Conservative in 1874. Balfour gained his first international experience serving as secretary to his uncle, the third marquess of Salisbury (1830–1903) at the Congress of Berlin (1878). He first achieved prominence as chief secretary for Ireland (1887), opposing HOME RULE and championing land reform. He served as first lord of the treasury in 1891–92 and 1895–1902, and in 1902 he succeeded Salisbury as prime minister. During his

term in office, Balfour introduced educational reforms (1902) and negotiated the ANGLO-FRENCH ENTENTE (1904). When the government split in 1905 over Joseph CHAMBERLAIN's tariff proposals, Balfour resigned. He was the leader of the opposition from 1906 to 1911.

During WORLD WAR I, Balfour served as first lord of the admiralty (1915–16) and foreign secretary (1916–19). In this capacity, he issued the BALFOUR DECLARATION in 1917, a document he considered the most important achievement of his political career. Balfour was prominent in the reshaping of Europe and the promotion of international peace, serving at the VERSAILLES Peace Conference (1919), the LEAGUE OF NATIONS (1920) and the WASHINGTON CONFERENCE (1921–22). He was lord president of the council in Stanley BALDWIN's cabinet from 1925 to 1929. An outstanding actor on the world stage, Balfour was also a profound thinker and the author of a number of books on philosophy and theology.

Balfour Declaration Statement of British policy regarding ZIONISM. It was formulated in a letter of November 2, 1917, from British foreign secretary Arthur BALFOUR to Lord Rothschild, head of the British Zionist Federation. It endorsed the creation of a Jewish national home in PALESTINE, providing that the rights of non-Jewish communities in Palestine and the rights of Jews in other countries were not abridged thereby. Confirmed by the Allied governments, the declaration was written into the LEAGUE OF NATIONS mandate for Palestine (1922).

Bali Island province of INDONESIA, between the Bali Sea and the Indian Ocean. Unlike the remainder of Indonesia, which is Muslim, Bali has been a Hindu island since the seventh century. Conquered by Japanese forces during WORLD WAR II, it became a part of Indonesia upon the founding of that independent nation in 1949. In 1965 it saw fierce fighting when the Indonesian government murdered members of the nation's Communist Party. In 2002 terrorists bombed a Bali nightclub killing 202 people and injuring 209.

Balikpapan Indonesian port city on the northeast coast of the island of Borneo. Since the 20th century it has been a major oil producing and refining center. In January 1942, during WORLD WAR II, the Japanese navy met U.S. naval forces in the adjacent Makassar Strait and thereafter maintained control of it until 1945.

Balkans The Balkan Peninsula, a large, ethnically diverse region of southeastern Europe, is crossed by the borders of European and Asian nations: ALBANIA, BULGARIA, GREECE, ROMANIA, SERBIA AND MONTENEGRO, SLOVENIA, BOSNIA-HERZEGOVINA, CROATIA, MACEDONIA and TURKEY. The border between the Balkans and central Europe is generally considered to be the course of the Danube and Sava Rivers. Since ancient times the Balkans have been a violent blending pot of peoples and cultures, of migrating horsemen and invading armies, the arena for numerous battles, conquests and revolutions. From the late 14th century until WORLD WAR I, the Balkans were largely dominated by the OTTOMAN EMPIRE. In 1815 Istria and Dalmatia were ceded to the Austrian Empire. In 1867 the AUSTRO-HUNGARIAN EMPIRE included Croatia, Slovenia and Transylvania; in 1908, Bosnia and Herzegovina as well. Serbian nationalism was the spark that lit the conflagration of WORLD WAR I. Border conflicts and ethnic readjustments continued into the last decade of the 20th century. During the 1990s the map of the Balkan Peninsula changed as Bosnia-Herzegovina, Croatia, Slovenia and Macedonia obtained their independence from the former YUGOSLAVIA.

Balkan War, First *(1912–1913)* SERBIA, BULGARIA, GREECE and MONTENEGRO attacked the OTTOMAN EMPIRE soon after its defeat in the Italo-Turkish War (1911–12), with the intent of seizing its remaining Balkan possessions. The Turks were unprepared, and the Balkan allies were prevented only by Bulgarian supply problems from advancing all the way to Constantinople (now ISTANBUL). Despite an armistice and an attempted peace conference, fighting resumed. Additional Turkish losses caused the new YOUNG TURK government to accept peace terms temporarily, but fighting began again, when it rejected them. The **Second Balkan War** (1913) was largely between Bulgaria and its former allies, joined by ROMANIA, over dismember-

ment of Macedonia, with Turkey attempting to regain its territories. In the **Treaty of Bucharest** (August 10, 1913), Bulgaria ceded its gains to its former allies, and the Ottoman Empire retained Adrianople, but lost 80% of its Balkan territories.

Ball, Lucille Desiree *(1911–1989)* American actress. Ball was one of television's most popular comedians. In the 1930s and 1940s she was a contract player at the RKO movie studio, and she also performed on radio. Her greatest success came with the debut of the television series *I LOVE LUCY* in 1951. The slapstick situation comedy featured Ball as the zany, redheaded wife of a Cuban bandleader (played by her coproducer and real-life husband, Desi ARNAZ); it soon became the most popular television program in the U.S. The show was the first to be filmed in front of a live audience, thus ensuring its preservation on high-quality film (rather than by a film, or kinescope, shot off a live TV transmission). Years later, reruns continued to be shown in syndication in more than 70 countries around the world. In 1957, after the series ended, Ball and Arnaz bought out RKO and began producing other shows. After they divorced in 1960, she bought out his share of their Desilu Productions company for $3 million and eventually sold Desilu to Gulf and Western for $17 million in 1967. She also starred in two other series of her

Comedian Lucille Ball, 1948 (LIBRARY OF CONGRESS, PRINTS AND PHOTOGRAPHS DIVISION)

own, *The Lucy Show* (1962–68) and *Here's Lucy* (1968–74), as well as films, television movies and specials.

Balla, Giacomo *(1871–1958)* Italian Futurist painter. Early in his career Balla created academic paintings. While on a trip to Paris, he discovered impressionism and divisionism, and became fascinated by the interaction of light and color. He began to paint in the futurist style in 1901 and was one of the signers of the futurist manifesto in 1910 (see FUTURISM). Influenced by cubist dissections of form and by the flickering images of the cinematograph, he developed a visual language that expressed dynamic motion. He is known for his whimsical futurist work *Dog on a Leash* (1904), as well as for such later paintings as *Speeding Automobile* (1912, both in New York's Museum of Modern Art). (See also CUBISM.)

Ballard, James Graham *(1930–)* British novelist. Ballard began writing short stories for *New Worlds* in 1956 and established himself as one of the "New Wave" science fiction writers of the 1960s. His novels include *The Drowned World* (1962), *High Rise* (1975) and *Hello America* (1988). His short story collections, which are more admired, include *The Terminal Beach* (1964), *The Disaster Area* (1967) and *Vermilion Sands* (1971). Ballard was born and raised in Shanghai before returning to England to attend Cambridge; turning away from science fiction, he drew on his experiences in Japanese-occupied China in *Empire of the Sun* (1984, filmed 1988).

Ballets Russes (de Serge Diaghilev) The Ballets Russes, composed of some of the best Russian dancers of the day (such as Anna PAVLOVA and Vaslav NIJINSKY), was founded by Serge DIAGHILEV in 1909. The company's sensational debut at the Théâtre du Chatelet in Paris (1909) is regarded as the birth date of modern ballet. For the next 20 years the company dominated the international ballet scene and became known for Diaghilev's ability to integrate all aspects of dance through his collaborations with such composers as Igor STRAVINSKY, Claude DEBUSSY and Sergei PROKOFIEV, painters such as Leon Bakst, Alexandre BENOIS and Pablo PICASSO, and choreographers such as Michel FOKINE, Leonid MASSINE and

George BALANCHINE. In addition, the talents of dancers like Anton DOLIN and Tamara KARSAVINA were showcased. Notable ballets of the company include *Les Sylphides* (1909), *Le Sacre du printemps* (1913), *Tricorne* (1919) and *Prodigal Son* (1929). The company disbanded in 1929 upon Diaghilev's death.

Ballinger-Pinchot controversy

Conflict between U.S. secretary of the interior Richard Ballinger and Gifford Pinchot, head of the U.S. Forest Service, that badly split the REPUBLICAN PARTY in 1910, allowing the election of Democrat Woodrow WILSON as president in 1912. Ballinger, appointed as interior secretary by President William Howard TAFT, approved the sale of an Alaskan coal field to one of his former law clients. The same sale had been declared illegal by President Theodore ROOSEVELT's secretary of the interior, James Garfield. Pinchot, an ardent conservationist and the head of the Forest Service, opposed the sale. President Taft himself became involved, ultimately supporting the sale and his appointee Ballinger. The president fired both Pinchot and Louis Glavis, an employee of the Interior Department's land office who had opposed the sale and urged the Justice Department to intervene. Taft's strategy backfired when Pinchot and Glavis brought the matter to the public's attention. Glavis wrote an article for *Collier's* magazine that led to a congressional investigation in which Louis BRANDEIS—later to become a Supreme Court associate justice—demonstrated improprieties by both Ballinger and Taft himself. Taft's lame excuse that he "misremembered" events only worsened the situation; Roosevelt split from the Republicans and formed the Bull Moose Party, allowing Democrat Wilson to win the White House in 1912.

Baltimore, David (1938–)

American molecular biologist. Baltimore studied chemistry at Swarthmore College and continued with postgraduate work at the Massachusetts Institute of Technology and Rockefeller University, where he obtained his Ph.D. in 1964. After three years at the Salk Institute in California, he returned to MIT in 1968 and in 1972 became professor of biology. In June 1970 Baltimore and, quite independently, Howard TEMIN announced the discovery of an enzyme, later to be known as reverse transcriptase, which is capable of transcribing RNA into DNA. For this work Baltimore shared the 1975 NOBEL PRIZE in physiology or medicine with Temin and Renato DULBECCO. Earlier (1968) Baltimore had done important work on the replication of the polio virus. In 1989 Baltimore became president of Rockefeller University. In 1991 he became the center of controversy when it was revealed that he had fabricated research data in a scientific paper earlier in his career. In 1997 Baltimore accepted an appointment as president of the California Institute of Technology. He announced that he would resign his post at the end of 2006.

bamboo curtain

Term given to the physical and ideological barrier to movement across the borders of the People's Republic of CHINA. The bamboo curtain was apparently lifted with the end of U.S. embargoes on exports to China in 1971, admission of China to the United Nations, President NIXON's visit to China (February 1972) and establishment of official relations with the European communities in 1975. The bamboo curtain's importance decreased further with the fall of the Soviet Union in 1991 and the U.S.'s increasing involvement in Asia-Pacific organizations such as the ASEAN REGIONAL FORUM (ARF), and the ASIA-PACIFIC ECONOMIC COOPERATION organization, in which the U.S. sought to work with countries on both sides of this "curtain." (See also IRON CURTAIN.)

Band, The

Canadian rock band. Composed of Robbie Robertson, guitar; Garth Hudson, organ; Richard Manuel, piano and vocals; Rick Danko, bass and vocals; and the group's only American, Levon Helm on drums and vocals. Initially touring as a backup group for Ronnie Hawkins, they toured much of North America before hooking up with Bob DYLAN. Dylan, who was in the midst of his controversial transition from acoustic to electric, hired them for a world tour. Their debut album *Music from Big Pink* (1968) catapulted them to the top of the American rock scene. Other notable albums include *Stage Fright* (1970), *Moondog Matinee* (1970) and *Before the Flood* (1974). The Band's last performance is chronicled in Martin SCORSESE's *The Last Waltz* (1976).

Banda, Hastings Kamuzu (1906–1997)

President of Malawi (1966–94). After practicing medicine in the United Kingdom and Ghana, he returned to Nyasaland as president-general of the AFRICAN NATIONAL CONGRESS (ANC) in 1958. He was imprisoned in 1959–60. He became leader of the Malawi Congress Party in 1961, minister of natural resources and local government (1961–63), prime minister of Nyasaland (1963–64) and of independent Malawi (1964–66). After 1992 antigovernment riots, Banda ended one-party rule in Malawi in 1993 and unsuccessfully ran for the presidency in 1994.

Bandaranaike, Sirimavo (1916–2000)

Sri Lankan political leader. Bandaranaike became the world's first female prime minister in 1960. She was the wife of the founder of the Sri Lanka Freedom Party, S. W. R. D. BANDARANAIKE, who was prime minister from 1956 until his assassination in 1959. His widow took over leadership of the party, then as prime minister she vigorously pursued a policy of socialist economics and Sinhalese domination of culture and politics. Defeated in 1965, she returned to office in 1970 and in 1972 was instrumental in the adoption of a new constitution. She was decisively beaten in the 1977 elections and, accused of abuses while in office, was stripped of her civil rights in 1980. She ran against Premadasa in the 1988 presidential elections and lost. In 1994 her daughter, **Chandrika Kumaratunga**, was elected president. Kumaratunga immediately appointed Bandaranaike prime minister. Bandaranaike held that office until resigning in 2000 because of failing health.

Bandaranaike, Solomon West Ridgeway Dias (1899–1959)

Sri Lankan political leader and prime minister (1956–59). An Oxford-educated barrister, he returned to Ceylon (later renamed SRI LANKA) where he entered politics and was elected to the legislative assembly in 1931. From 1948 to 1951, he was minister of health and led the fight against malaria. In 1951 he resigned from the government and from the ruling United National Party, forming the socialist Sri Lanka Freedom Party. In 1956 he organized a leftist alliance, which was victorious in the elections of 1956. Becoming prime minister that year, he promoted neutralism in Ceylon's international policy and Sinhalese nationalism and language at home, while dealing with severe economic problems. He was assassinated by a Buddhist monk in 1959.

Bandung Conference Conference of 29 African and Asian states, held April 17–24, 1955. Agreement was reached on economic and cultural cooperation, opposition to Dutch and French colonialism, and the development of a specifically THIRD WORLD nonaligned and neutral political stance in the COLD WAR.

Bane, Frank B. (1893–1983) U.S. government official. A strong proponent of federal welfare policies, Bane played a prominent role in shaping the programs of Franklin D. ROOSEVELT's NEW DEAL. He was an author of the legislation that created the nation's SOCIAL SECURITY system and served as the system's first administrator from 1935 to 1938. During WORLD WAR II he played an important role in directing the rationing of goods and food. In addition to other government offices, he headed the Council of State Governments for 20 years.

Bang & Olufsen (B&O) Danish manufacturer of high-quality audio and video equipment. Peter Bang and Svend Olufsen began building wireless sets in the attic of the Olufsen family home in Struer, Denmark, in 1925. By 1929 they were operating a small factory that produced such innovative equipment as an early pushbutton tuning radio. A pick-up arm of 1965 designed by B&O staff designer E. Rorbaek Madsen was one of the first products to attract design attention to the firm. B&O products are of consistently high quality (and high price); their external designs are unique in emphasizing simplicity, unobtrusive controls, genuine wood panels, and black-finished metal, in contrast to the complex display of controls and high-tech look of most comparable equipment. In the 1990s B&O products remained popular throughout Europe, particularly in Britain.

Bangkok (Krung Thep) Capital and commercial center of THAILAND. In December 1941, during WORLD WAR II, it was conquered by the Japanese; later in the war, it was heavily bombed by the Allies. Severed into two municipalities in 1937—Krung Thep and Thon Buri—it was reunited into one city, Bangkok, in 1971. Bangkok has undergone much development since the 1960s and consequently combines the features of both First World and Third World cities—modern opulence, pollution and poverty.

Bangladesh Nation in South Asia, bound on the east, north and west by India and to the southeast by (Myanmar) Burma. Formerly known as East Pakistan, it is the most densely populated country on Earth. Located in the Bengal region, its topography is dominated by the delta created by the confluence of the Brahmaputra, Ganges and Meghna Rivers, and the land is prone to recurrent flooding. The population is 80% Muslim. From 1857 to 1947, the region was ruled as a part of British India. In 1947 it was granted independence as East Pakistan, separated (by 1,000 miles of India) from West Pakistan. The government of the new nation was located in West Pakistan, despite the East's larger population. Matters came to a head in 1970, when the Awami League of East Pakistan, led by Mujibur RAHMAN (known as Sheikh Mujib), won a majority of the parliamentary seats but was not allowed to convene. On March 15, 1971, civil war began; on the next day

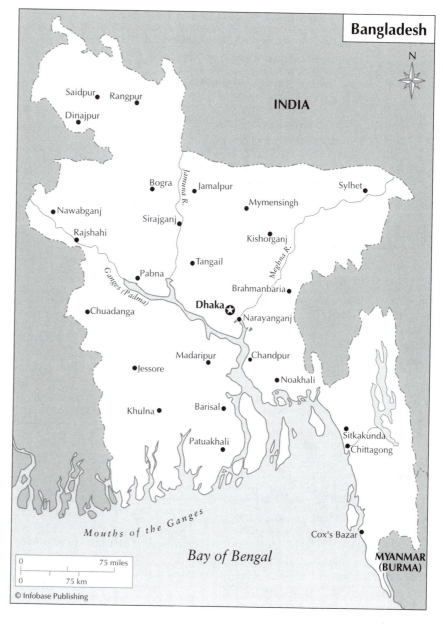

BANGLADESH

1947	Eastern region of Bengal becomes East Pakistan.
1971	East Pakistan becomes independent state of Bangladesh.
1982	Hussein Mohammed Ershad takes power in military coup; martial law imposed.
1988	Record floods leave three-quarters of Bangladesh under water and 25 million homeless.
1989	Rioting against Salman Rushdie's *Satanic Verses* kills 100 in Dacca.
1990	Ershad resigns; Awami League (AL) and Bangladesh National Party (BNP) unite to choose president.
1991	BNP wins first free elections in 20 years.
1994	In Parliament nearly 150 members of the opposition resign, hoping to force new elections.
1996	AL wins control of the government for the first time since 1975.
1997	The opposition BNP organizes a series of strikes to protest the government.
1998	Monsoons cause severe flooding, killing over 1,000 and leaving millions homeless.
2001	In parliamentary elections the BNP wins a majority of seats; Khaleda Zia becomes prime minister.

Bangladesh declared its independence. Shocking, large-scale massacres of Bangladesh civilians by the Pakistani military ensued. In December 1971 India entered the war on the side of Bangladesh, which it formally recognized as a new nation. In two weeks the Pakistani military was defeated, but PAKISTAN did not recognize the nation of Bangladesh until 1974.

Sheikh Mujib became president of the new nation, its capital in Dacca. He nationalized several banks and businesses and assumed full dictatorial control in 1975, the same year he was assassinated by army officers. Subsequent president ZIAUR RAHMAN, who took office in 1977, was assassinated in 1981, after numerous coup attempts. The following year General Hossain Mohammad ERSHAD seized power and declared martial law, which lasted until democracy was restored in

1990. Disastrous floods in 1988 put three-quarters of Bangladesh under water and left 25 million people homeless. A cyclone in 1991 caused a reported 125,000 deaths, destroyed crops and contaminated drinking water. Apart from these natural disasters, Bangladesh remains plagued by the problems of famine, overpopulation and poverty. In 1998 two-thirds of the country was ruined in the worst flood in Bangladesh's history, leading to year-long food shortages and more than 1,000 deaths. In October 2001 Khaleda Zia, widow of Ziaur Rahman and leader of the Bangladesh National Party, won a landslide election victory.

Bankhead, Tallulah (*1903–1968*) American stage and screen actress known for her sultry voice and sophisticated manner. The daughter of politician William Brockman Bankhead,

speaker of the U.S. House of Representatives in the late 1930s, Bankhead made her stage debut in New York in 1918 and spent the 1920s in London. Returning to the U.S. in 1930, she became a familiar personality and was admired for her leading performances in such plays as *Dark Victory* (1934), *Rain* (1935), *Anthony and Cleopatra* (1937) and *The Little Foxes* (1939). Her most memorable film performance was in Alfred HITCHCOCK's *Lifeboat* (1944).

Banks, Ernest "Ernie" (*1931– *) American baseball player. Known as much for his effusive personality as for his playing skills, Banks was the first black player on the Chicago Cubs. By the end of his career, which spanned 17 seasons (1954–71), he was known as "Mr. Cub." He was named Most Valuable Player in 1958 and 1959, both years in which he hit over .300. Dividing his career between shortstop and first base, his fielding skills were mediocre at the beginning of his career, but he improved enough to win a Gold Glove in 1960. He hit his 500th home run in 1970 and retired the following year. An 11-time All-Star, he was named to the Hall of Fame in 1977.

Banks, Harold Chamberlain "Hal" (*1909–1985*) American-born union leader. Banks led the Seafarers International Union of Canada in the 1950s and early 1960s. A militant anti-communist, he was at first welcomed by Canadian authorities but later accused of trying to destroy Canada's shipping industry. He returned to the U.S. as a fugitive in 1964 after conviction by a Canadian court on charges of conspiracy in an attack on a rival union leader. Canadian authorities tried unsuccessfully to have him extradited.

Bannister, Sir Roger (Gilbert) (*1929– *) English runner, physician and amateur athlete. While still a medical student Bannister became the first person to run a mile in less than four minutes. His record-setting run occurred on May 6, 1954, at Oxford; his time was 3 minutes 59.4 seconds. His record was soon broken by the Australian runner John Landy, who ran a 3:58 mile a month and a half later. Bannister came back to beat Landy at the Commonwealth Games, clocking

3:58.8 on August 7, 1954. He retired from competition shortly thereafter. Becoming a neurologist, he was knighted in 1975.

Banting, Sir Frederick Grant
(1891–1941) Canadian physiologist. Banting, a farmer's son, began studying to be a medical missionary at Victoria College, Toronto, in 1910. During his studies he concentrated increasingly on medicine and graduated an M.D. in 1916, whereupon he immediately joined the Canadian Army Medical Corps and served in France in WORLD WAR I. In 1918 he was awarded the Military Cross for gallantry in action. Banting returned to Toronto and for a time studied children's diseases before setting up practice in London, Ontario, in 1920. He also began work at the London Medical School, specializing in studies on the pancreas, particularly the small patches of pancreatic cells known as the islets of Langerhans. Earlier work had shown a connection between the pancreas and diabetes, and Banting wondered if a hormone was produced in the islets of Langerhans that regulated glucose metabolism. In 1921 he approached John Macleod, professor of physiology at Toronto University, who was initially skeptical. Feeling that Banting needed help in physiological and biochemical methods, Macleod suggested the assistance of a young research student, Charles Best. Over the next six months Banting and Best devised a series of experiments. They tied off the pancreatic ducts of dogs and made extracts of the islets of Langerhans free from other pancreatic substances. These extracts, called "isletin," were found to have some effect against diabetes in dogs. Prior to trials on humans, Macleod asked a biochemist, James Collip, to purify the extracts, and the purification method for what is now known as INSULIN was patented by Banting, Best and Collip in 1923. They allowed manufacturers freedom to produce the hormone but required a small royalty to be paid to finance future medical research.

The pharmaceutical firm Eli Lilley began industrial production of insulin in 1923, and in the same year Banting was awarded the chair of medical research at Toronto University and a government annuity of $7,000. The NOBEL PRIZE in physiology or medicine was awarded jointly to Banting and Macleod in 1923; Banting was furious that Best had not been included in the award and shared his part of the prize money with him. In 1930 the Banting Institute opened in Toronto, and under Banting's guidance this was to become the home of Canadian medical research, with work on cancer, coronary thrombosis and silicosis as well as diabetes. Banting was knighted in 1934. When war broke out in 1939 he joined an army medical unit and worked on many committees linking Canadian and British wartime medical research. His bravery was much in evidence at this time, particularly his personal involvement in research into mustard gas and blackout problems experienced by airmen. In 1941 on a flight from Gander, Newfoundland, to Britain his plane crashed, and he died in the snow.

Bao Dai *(1913–1997)* Last emperor
of VIETNAM. Enthroned in 1932 (though he succeeded as emperor in 1926), Bao Dai abdicated in 1945 under communist pressure and retired to Hong Kong, leading a playboy existence. He returned as head of state in 1949 at the request of FRANCE. When a separate **South Vietnam** came into existence in 1954, he was only a figurehead ruler, with Ngo Dinh DIEM as prime minister. In 1955 he was deposed by Diem in a referendum held while he was out of the country. The former emperor lived in exile in France until his death in 1997.

Bara, Theda (Theodosia Goodman) *(1890–1955)* A HOLLYWOOD star
of the SILENT FILM era, Bara had a short, but sensational career as the original vamp—her name, an anagram for "Arab death," was coined to describe the evil temptress characters she played. A publicity campaign describing her as a seductress who was poison to men made her a star. Bara made more than 40 films between 1916 and 1919

Barak, Ehud *(1942–)* Israeli military officer, politician and prime
minister (1999–2000). Barak distinguished himself in numerous posts within the Israeli Defense Forces (IDF). In the SIX-DAY WAR of 1967, he led a reconnaissance group in a preemptive strike against Egyptian forces; in the YOM KIPPUR WAR of 1973, he conducted a tank battalion in the Sinai that defended and later counterattacked against the invading Egyptian force. In 1982 he was promoted to major general and sent to help conduct Israeli operations in southern Lebanon. Nine years later, Barak became chief of the General Staff of the Israeli forces.

He served as minister of the interior in 1995, and then as minister of foreign affairs from 1995 to 1996. In later years he was also elected to the Knesset (the Israeli parliament), where he served on the Foreign Affairs and Defense Committee and was elevated to the chairmanship of the Labor Party. In 1999 Barak formed a coalition, and he won the 1999 elections. Barak became Israeli prime minister and minister of defense.

In 2000 Barak met at CAMP DAVID with Yasir ARAFAT, in an abortive effort to reach an agreement with the Palestinian Authority over control of the West Bank and the Gaza Strip. In the autumn of 2000, a new intifada (see INTIFADA II) began in the West Bank and Gaza Strip. In response to a continual decline in his popularity and the increasing popularity of political rivals Ariel SHARON and Benjamin NETANYAHU (both members of the conservative LIKUD Party) Barak scheduled elections early in February; Barak lost to Ariel Sharon, and in March 2001 Sharon replaced Barak as the Israeli prime minister.

Baraka, Amiri (Everett LeRoi Jones) *(1934–)* American poet, playwright,
social activist. Baraka had a middle-class childhood in Newark, New Jersey, and attended Rutgers and Howard University. In the late 1950s and early 1960s he lived in New York's Greenwich Village and associated with the BEAT GENERATION poets. After the publication of *Preface to a Twenty-Volume Suicide Note,* he became a well-known avant-garde artist. In 1964 *Dutchman* received an Obie Award for best off-Broadway play. In the mid-1960s he became a militant black spokesman and moved to Harlem. Later he returned to Newark, where he became involved with local politics. His later writing is highly revolutionary, directed primarily to blacks. As the tone of his work grew more violent, his stature in the white literary establishment dwindled, but he is still regarded as an important African-American poet. Baraka became involved

in the controversy following the terrorist attacks of SEPTEMBER 11, 2001, when
he published a poem, "Somebody Blew
Up America," in which he alleged Israeli
foreknowledge about the attacks.

Barany, Robert (1876–1936) Austro-
Hungarian physician. Barany was educated at the University of Vienna,
graduating in medicine in 1900. After
studying at various German clinics, he
returned to Vienna to become an assistant at the university's ear clinic. In
1909 he was appointed lecturer in
otology. Through his work at the clinic
he devised a test, now called the
Barany test, for diagnosing disease of
the semicircular canals of the inner ear
by syringing the ear with either hot or
cold water. For this he was awarded
the 1914 NOBEL PRIZE in physiology or
medicine. At this time he was being
held as a prisoner of war in Siberia, but
through the offices of the Swedish Red
Cross he was released and the award
presented to him. In 1917 Barany was
appointed professor at Uppsala University where he continued his investigations on the inner ear and the role of
the cerebellum in the brain in controlling body movement. Barany's pointing
test is used to test for brain lesions.

Barbados Island nation in the Windward Islands of the West Indies; formally became a British colony in 1885.
The first elections with local participation were held in 1944 and were won
by Grantly Adams's Barbados Labour
Party (BLP). Barbados was a part of the
now-defunct Federation of the West
Indies from 1958 to 1962, with Adams
as federation prime minister. Britain
granted Barbados independence on
November 30, 1966, and Earl Barrow,
leader of the Democratic Labour Party,
was the country's first prime minister.
In 1976 Adam's son, J. M. G. Tom
ADAMS, was elected and pursued a conservative, pro-American policy. Barbados has remained a parliamentary
democracy and is one of the more stable and prosperous West Indian nations. Its population is roughly 90% of
black African ancestry. Barbados contains no rivers, and its water supply is
pumped from underground caves.
Sugar, rum and molasses are its primary exports, but tourism is also a
major source of revenue. The capital is
Bridgetown. In 1994 the BLP gained

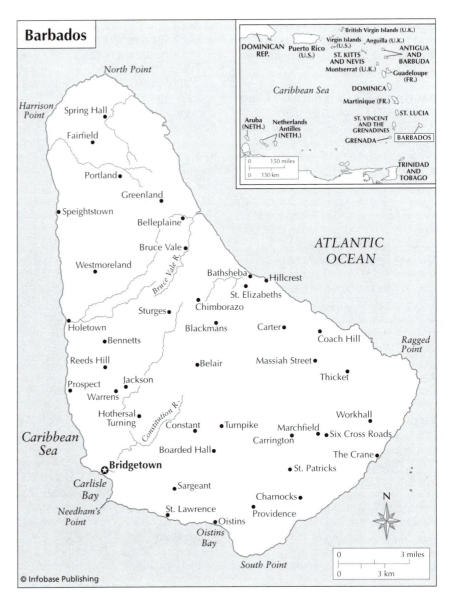

control of the country's lower house,
the House of Assembly. Since then the
BLP has continued to dominate Barbados's political life.

Barbarossa German code name for
the invasion of the USSR in 1941. "Operation Barbarossa" was approved by
Adolf HITLER late in 1940 and called for
an invasion by the following May. The
invasion aimed at creating LEBENSRAUM
("living space") for GERMANY and at the
establishment of German colonies
within Russia. German intervention in
the Balkans postponed her plans
slightly, but on June 22, 1941, 121
massed divisions crossed the Russian
frontier, attacking on a front from the
Baltic to the Black Sea. Hitler was com-

pletely confident of success in this undertaking, so convinced of early victory
that he failed to outfit his troops for
possible winter fighting. Catching the
Soviets by surprise, German troops met
with overwhelming initial success. By
the fall of 1941, Russian resistance to
the invasion began to solidify while
German resolve began to falter and their
supply lines to break down. A counteroffensive by Soviet general Georgi
ZHUKOV forced back German troops in
central Russia. The largest military undertaking in history, Barbarossa failed
largely because of Germany's underestimation of Russian resistance and Germany's inability to subdue Moscow
before the coming of winter. (See also
WORLD WAR II ON THE RUSSIAN FRONT.)

BARBADOS

1937	An outbreak of riots is followed by establishment of the Barbados Labour Party (BLP) by Grantley Adams; Barbados moves towards a more independent political system.
1951	Universal adult suffrage is introduced. The BLP wins a general election.
1954	Ministerial government is established, with BLP leader Adams as the first prime minister.
1955	A group breaks away from the BLP and forms the Democratic Labour Party (DLP).
1961	Internal independence is achieved from Britain.
1966	Barbados gains full independence, with Errol W. Barrow as prime minister.
1969	National government takes over all local parish administration.
1971	Barrow's Democratic Labor Party (DLP) wins in national elections.
1973	The Barbados dollar is introduced, replacing the East Caribbean dollar.
1976	The Barbados Labor Party (BLP) wins an upset victory in national elections, gaining 17 seats in the House of Assembly; J. M. G. ("Tom") Adams is named prime minister; Frederick Smith is elected president of the DLP.
1978	Mercenary army led by Robert Denard is reported preparing for an invasion of the island.
1979	Britain announces formation of a special force to counter Cuban influence in the Barbados region.
1983	Barbados supports U.S. invasion of Grenada.
1984	Governor-General Sir Deighton Lisle dies and is succeeded in office by Sir Hugh Springer.
1985	Prime Minister Adams dies and is succeeded in office by H. Bernard St. John.
1986	The BLP loses the 1986 elections; Barrow returns as prime minister.
1987	Barrow dies and is succeeded as prime minister by Lloyd Erskine Sandiford.
1989	The National Democratic Party (NDP) is formed by members of the DLP.
1990	Dame Nita Barrow is named governor-general.
1991	General elections are held; Sandiford is elected to a five-year term as prime minister; the DLP wins 18 of 28 seats in the House of Assembly; the BLP wins the remaining 10.
1994	The BLP wins the general election and 19 of the 28 seats in the House of Assembly; Owen Arthur becomes prime minister.
1996	Sir Clifford Husbands is appointed governor-general.
1998	A constitutional commission undertaken by former foreign minister Sir Henry Fords recommends that Barbados should remain within the Commonwealth, replace the British monarch with a Barbadian president as head of state, and establish a Caribbean or Barbadian court of appeals.
2000	The Organization for Economic Cooperation and Development (OECD) threatens trade sanctions on Barbados and 34 other territories for acting as tax havens.
2001	The 12 Caribbean Community (CariCom) countries, including Barbados, sever legal ties between the region and Britain and establish their own regional supreme court.
2002	Two years after the Organization for Economic Cooperation and Development (OECD) catalogs Barbados as one of the countries deemed to be "non-cooperative tax havens," the group removes it from the list.
2003	Owen Arthur is reelected for a third term and Bernard St. John (BLP) wins general elections.
2004	The arrest of Barbadian fishermen sparks a sea border argument between Trinidad and Tobago and Barbados, which is taken to a tribunal backed by the UN.
2005	The only prison in Barbados suffers from internal inmate uprisings and ravaging fires. The West Indies is set to host the 2007 World Cup for the first time in the history of the championship.

Barber, Samuel *(1910–1981)* American composer. Barber is one of the outstanding composers of the 20th century, especially noted for his lyrical, melodic style and mastery of modern counterpoint. In 1937 his Symphony No. 1, in one movement, became the first American work to be performed at the Salzburg Festival of Contemporary Music. He collaborated with his lifelong friend Gian Carlo MENOTTI on his first opera, *Vanessa,* which won the PULITZER PRIZE for music (1958). A second Pulitzer was awarded for his 1962 Piano Concerto. Other major works include his most popular piece, *Adagio for Strings* (1938); the Violin Concerto (1941); and the ballet score for Martha GRAHAM's *The Cave of the Heart* (1946).

Barbie trial Klaus Barbie, a former officer in the Nazi SS, was tried and convicted of crimes against humanity in a widely-publicized trial held in Lyon, France, in 1987. During WORLD WAR II, Barbie had been an SS lieutenant in charge of the German GESTAPO in Lyon, where he became known as the Butcher of Lyon for his sadistic treatment of Jewish and French RESISTANCE prisoners. After World War II, the U.S. Army employed Barbie and later assisted his secret escape to Bolivia, where he lived until his discovery in 1983.

Although Barbie had been tried in absentia years before, the statute of limitations had run out on his specific crimes, so he was tried for the more general charge of crimes against humanity. Although he appeared only briefly during the trial, he protested his innocence and any responsibility. The judges and jury, however, convicted him of deporting 842 people, resulting in the known deaths of 373 individuals. Barbie was sentenced to life imprisonment, although he was eligible to be released on parole in 1993 at age 88. He died in prison in 1991.

Barbirolli, Sir John (Giovanni Battista) *(1899–1970)* British conductor noted for his rich interpretations of 20th-century British and late-romantic composers. Born in London to a French mother and Italian father, Barbirolli studied at the Royal Academy of Music. After service in World War I, he played the cello in a London orchestra and in several string quartets. He made his conducting debut in 1925 directing his own chamber orchestra. Over the next decade he conducted various British orchestras. He succeeded Arturo TOSCANINI as director of the New York Philharmonic (1937–43); despite his generally fine performances, he inevitably suffered from comparisons to his legendary predecessor. Returning to England in 1943, he became director (1943–58) of the Halle Orchestra in Manchester and built it into an orchestra of international caliber. He later directed the Houston Symphony Orchestra (1961–67). During his last decade Barbirolli made many outstanding recordings with the Philharmonia and the London Symphony Orchestra, among others. His performances of the works of Sir Edward ELGAR, Ralph VAUGHAN WILLIAMS, Jean SIBELIUS and Gustav MAHLER were particularly acclaimed.

Barbusse, Henri *(1873–1935)* French novelist, biographer and journalist. Barbusse played an influential role in the French society of his era due to the political forcefulness of his writings. He worked as a journalist prior to WORLD WAR I, in which he served in the French army and was wounded. *Under Fire* (1916), his best-known work, is one of the major works of literature on the sober realities of warfare. In it Barbusse advocated a committed pacifism. In the 1920s Barbusse joined the Communist Party; in the 1930s he was active in various antifascist movements. Barbusse wrote biographies of Jesus (1927) and the French writer Émile Zola (1932). *I Saw It Myself* (1928) is his autobiography.

Barcelona chair Chair, together with an ottoman, designed by Ludwig MIES VAN DER ROHE in 1929 for the BARCELONA PAVILION. Its design consists of a simple X frame of steel bars supporting leather straps that carry seat and back cushions covered in leather. The Barcelona chair has become known as a modern design classic.

Barcelona Pavilion German Pavilion at the Barcelona Exhibition of 1929 that became one of the best-known and most admired works of INTERNATIONAL STYLE modern architecture by Ludwig MIES VAN DER ROHE. The building, demolished after the close of the exhibition, was reconstructed in 1986 in its original location.

Barcroft, Sir Joseph *(1872–1947)* Irish physiologist. Professor of physiology at Cambridge University (1926–37) and director of animal physiology for the Agricultural Research Council (1941–47), Barcroft carried out extensive research into human embryology, physiology and histology. He investigated the oxygen-carrying role of hemoglobin and devised (1908) an apparatus for the analysis of blood gases. Barcroft led three high-altitude expeditions—to Tenerife (1910); Monte Rosa, Italy (1911); and the Peruvian Andes (1922)—in order to study acclimatization and the effects of rarefied atmospheres on respiration. During WORLD WAR I, Barcroft was chief physiologist at the Experimental Station at Porton, Wiltshire, where he studied the effects of poisonous gases. Elected a fellow of the Royal Society in 1910 and knighted in 1935, Barcroft wrote the famous text *Respiratory Function of the Blood* (1914), as well as publications on the brain and its environment and on prenatal conditions.

Bardeen, John *(1908–1991)* American physicist. Bardeen, the son of a professor of anatomy, studied electrical engineering at the University of Wisconsin and obtained his Ph.D. in mathematical physics at Princeton in 1936. He began work as a geophysicist with Gulf Research and Development Corporation, Pittsburgh, in 1931 but in 1935 entered academic life as a junior fellow at Harvard, moving to the University of Minnesota in 1938. Bardeen spent the war years at the Naval Ordnance Laboratory, followed by six creative years from 1945 until 1951 at the Bell Telephone Laboratory, after which he was appointed professor of physics and electrical engineering at the University of Illinois. Bardeen was a unique figure in science—the only recipient of two NOBEL PRIZES in physics. The first, awarded in 1956, he shared with Walter BRATTAIN and William SHOCKLEY for their development of the point-contact TRANSISTOR (1947), thus preparing the way for the development of the more efficient junction transistor by Shockley. Bardeen's second prize was awarded in 1972 for his formulation, in collaboration with Leon Cooper and John Schrieffer, of the first satisfactory theory of superconductivity—the so-called BCS theory. (See also SUPERCONDUCTORS.)

Bardot, Brigitte (*1934– *) French film actress. Bardot began her career as a model but soared to immediate international fame as a sex symbol with the release of her first film, *And God Created Woman* (1956). The Bardot look—blond hair, catlike eyes and full, pouting lips—became the rage on both sides of the Atlantic Ocean. She went on to star in numerous sex farces, not all of which were box office successes. Nonetheless, and in spite of long inactivity on the screen, Bardot has retained a high celebrity status. Her more notable films include *Contempt* (1963) and *Viva Maria* (1965). In the 1990s Bardot came under criticism as one of the staunchest supporters of the ultra-conservative French politician Jean-Marie LE PEN. Her autobiography *A Cry in Silence* (2003) provoked the ire of French Muslim and homosexual communities for her derogatory remarks about both groups.

Barenboim, Daniel (*1942– *) Israeli pianist and conductor, considered one of the most talented and glamorous classical musicians of his generation. Born in Buenos Aires, Barenboim was a child prodigy and gave his first public piano recital at age seven. His family subsequently moved to Europe, where the young Barenboim gave frequent concerts and recitals and also studied conducting and composition (with Nadia BOULANGER, among others). During the 1960s he established his reputation as a brilliant pianist and made extensive recordings of Mozart and Beethoven. He married the celebrated British cellist Jacqueline DU PRÉ in 1967. By the late 1960s he had also become well known as a conductor in Britain, Europe and the U.S. He was named director of the Orchestre de Paris in 1975. In the late 1980s Barenboim was appointed artistic and music director of the new Bastille Opera in Paris; his abrupt firing by the board's director before the company's first season in 1989, over the issue of artistic control, caused a major artistic and political controversy in France. Barenboim succeeded Sir George SOLTI as director of the Chicago Symphony Orchestra in 1991. In 1992 Barenboim also became general music director of the Berlin Deutsche Staatsoper. Barenboim's repertoire includes relatively little 20th-century music, although he has championed the works of Sir Edward ELGAR. He has caused controversy in Israel, where he moved in 1952, by performing Richard Wagner's *Tristan and Isolde* in Jerusalem and by criticizing Israel's occupation of Palestinian territories.

Barger, George (*1878–1939*) British organic chemist. Barger, of Anglo-Dutch parentage, went to school in Holland and read natural sciences at Cambridge University, where he graduated with equal distinction in chemistry and botany. While a demonstrator in botany at the University of Brussels (1901–03) Barger discovered a method of determining the molecular weight of small samples by vapor-pressure measurements. From 1903 to 1909 he was a researcher at the Wellcome Physiological Research Laboratories, where he worked mainly on ergot, isolating ergotoxine in collaboration with Francis Carr (1906). Work on ergot by Barger and Henry Dale led to a better understanding of the nervous system and to the development of new drugs. From 1909 to 1919 Barger worked in London, as head of chemistry at Goldsmiths' College, professor of chemistry at Royal Holloway College and from 1914 as chemist with the National Institute of Medical Research. In 1919 he was elected a fellow of the Royal Society and appointed to the new chair of chemistry in relation to medicine at Edinburgh. In 1938 Barger became professor of chemistry at the University of Glasgow. He was a pioneer of medicinal chemistry, an excellent linguist and a tireless ambassador for science.

Barkan, Alexander Elias (*1909–1990*) U.S. labor leader. He served as political director of the AMERICAN FEDERATION OF LABOR AND CONGRESS OF INDUSTRIAL ORGANIZATIONS (1963–81). As director of the AFL-CIO's Committee on Political Education, he was the chief political fund-raiser and campaign operator for much of the organized labor movement and was instrumental in winning the election of sympathetic U.S. House and Senate candidates. He became disenchanted with the DEMOCRATIC PARTY in the late 1970s and retired in 1981.

Barkhausen, Heinrich Georg (*1881–1956*) German physicist. After attending the gymnasium and engineering college in Bremen, Barkhausen gained his Ph.D. in Göttingen and in 1911 became professor of electrical engineering in Dresden. Here he formulated the basic equations governing the coefficients of the amplifier valve. In 1919 he discovered the **Barkhausen effect**, observing that a slow, continuous increase in the magnetic field applied to ferromagnetic material gave rise to discontinuous leaps in magnetization, which could be heard as distinct clicking sounds through a loudspeaker. This effect is caused by domains of elementary magnets changing direction or size as the field increases. In 1920, with K. Kurz, he developed an ultra-high-frequency oscillator, which became the forerunner of microwave technology developments. After World War II he returned to Dresden to aid the reconstruction of his Institute of High-Frequency Electron-Tube Technology, which had been destroyed by bombing, and remained there until his death.

Barkla, Charles Glover (*1877–1944*) British X-ray physicist. After taking his master's degree in 1899 at Liverpool, Barkla went to Trinity College, Cambridge, but transferred to King's College to sing in the choir. At King's College he started his important research on X-RAYS. In 1902 he returned to Liverpool as Oliver Lodge Fellow and in 1909 became Wheatstone Professor at King's College, London. From 1913 onward he was professor of natural philosophy at Edinburgh University. His scientific work, for which he received the 1917 NOBEL PRIZE in physics, concerned the properties of X-rays—in particular, the way in which they are scattered by various materials. Barkla also demonstrated X-ray fluorescence. From about 1916, Barkla became isolated from modern physics, with an increasingly dogmatic attitude, a tendency to cite only his own papers and a concentration on untenable theories.

Barkley, Alben (*1877–1956*) U.S. political leader. Barkley served as a Democrat in the House of Representatives (1912–23) and in the Senate (1926–48, 1954–56), where he acquired a reputation as an ardent internationalist and supporter of progressive and NEW DEAL legislation. He was Harry S. TRUMAN's vice president from 1948 to 1953. The following year he was reelected to the Senate.

Barlach, Ernst *(1870–1938)* German playwright and sculptor. Barlach was one of the leading figures in the expressionist dramatic movement that dominated German theater in the decade following World War I. He frequently dealt with theological themes, such as the nature of the relationship between God and a troubled world, as well as with the tangled dynamics of family relationships. His major works include *The Dead Day* (1919), *The Poor Cousin* (1919) and *The Foundling* (1922).

Barmine, Alexander G. *(1899–1987)* Soviet-born U.S. diplomat. A brigadier general in the Soviet army, in 1937 he became one of the earliest high-level Soviet defectors. Three years later he arrived in the U.S., where he became a journalist and government official. He served for 16 years (1948–64) as chief of the Russian branch of the VOICE OF AMERICA and for eight years (1964–72) as senior adviser on Soviet affairs at the U.S. Information Agency.

Barnack, Oscar *(1879–1936)* Inventor-designer of the LEICA, the first successful 35mm camera. Barnack grasped the possibility of using 35mm motion picture film for still photographs and developed a light, portable instrument and the optics to make this practical. The Leica camera has become a greatly admired icon of modern technological design, sternly functional in the tradition of Leitz optical instruments, but beautiful in a way that has made it a key example of industrial design in the 20th century.

Barnard, Christiaan Neethling *(1922–2001)* South African surgeon who performed the first human heart transplant. Barnard was awarded his M.D. from the University of Cape Town in 1953 and joined the medical faculty as a research fellow in surgery. After three years at the University of Minnesota (1955–58), where he studied heart surgery, he returned to Cape Town as director of surgical research. He concentrated on improving techniques for artificially sustaining bodily functions during surgery and for keeping organs alive outside the body. On December 2, 1967, Barnard performed the first heart-transplant operation on a human patient, a 54-year-old grocer named Louis Washkansky. He received the heart of Denise Duvall, a traffic accident victim. The heart functioned, but the recipient died of pneumonia 18 days after the operation. The body's immune system had broken down following the administration of drugs to suppress rejection of the new heart as a foreign protein. Barnard subsequently performed further similar operations with improved postoperative treatment giving much greater success. His pioneering work generated worldwide publicity for heart-transplant surgery, and it is now fairly widely practiced.

Barnard, Joseph Edwin *(1870–1949)* British physicist. While working in his father's business, Barnard used his spare time to study at the Lister Institute, King's College, London, where he developed an interest in microscopy, especially photomicrography, which led to his receiving a chair at the Charing Cross Medical School. He was a fellow and three-time president of the Royal Microscopical Society and in 1920 became honorary director of the applied optics department at the National Institute for Medical Research. His research and experience in photomicrography led him to write *Practical Photomicrography* (1911), which became a standard work. Later he developed a technique for using ultraviolet radiation, which is of shorter wavelength than visible light and therefore gives greater resolution. With W. E. Gye he used this method to identify several ultramicroscopic organisms connected with malignant growths that were too small to see using standard microscopy.

Barnes, Djuna *(1892–1982)* American author. Born in Cornwall-on-Hudson, New York, Barnes later studied art in New York City and eventually settled in Paris. Her first works, *A Book of Repulsive Women* (1911) and *A Book* (1923), were collections of poems and plays. Her most enduring work of fiction, *Nightwood* (1936), a STREAM OF CONSCIOUSNESS narrative about five malevolent characters, was praised by T. S. ELIOT. Other works include *Ryder* (1928), a novel exploring the relationships of a man, his wife, mother and mistress; *Ladies Almanack* (1928), which dealt with lesbianism; and *Selected Works* (1962). Her work is characterized by a dark decadence.

Barnett, Ross Robert *(1898–1987)* American politician. A white supremacist and segregationist, Barnett was governor of Mississippi from 1960 to 1964. Elected as a Democrat, he left that party during the 1960 presidential election. In 1962, in defiance of a court order, he refused to allow a black student, James MEREDITH, to be admitted to the University of Mississippi. This incident touched off one of the great confrontations of the CIVIL RIGHTS MOVEMENT.

Baron, Salo Wittmayer *(1895–1989)* Professor of Jewish history at Columbia University, widely regarded as one of the greatest Jewish historians of the 20th century. In 1961 Baron testified in Jerusalem at the trial of former Nazi official Adolf EICHMANN, setting the historical framework for the Israeli government's case against Eichmann. Baron wrote 13 works on Jewish history, including the 18-volume *A Social and Religious History of the Jews*.

Barr, Alfred Hamilton, Jr. *(1902–1981)* American art scholar. He was director of New York City's MUSEUM OF MODERN ART (MOMA) from its opening in 1929 until 1943 and was its director of collections from 1947 until 1967. An innovative exhibition designer, he expanded the museum's collection of 20th-century art to include industrial design as well as PICASSO, avant-garde impressionists, architecture and motion pictures. Dubbed the "soul" of MOMA, he was considered by many to be the premier museum curator and tastemaker of the century.

Barragán, Luis *(1902–1988)* Mexican engineer and architect whose work combines the austerity of the INTERNATIONAL STYLE, or minimalist modernism, with a strong use of chromatic color (see MINIMALISM). Barragán was a self-taught architect, although he had some training in engineering and experience in his family's building business in Guadalajara. He traveled in Spain and was influenced by the vernacular architecture of that country as well as that of his native Mexico. His work also shows influences of LE CORBUSIER and of many artists, historic and contemporary. His own house in Mexico City (1947) and the 1954 chapel in Tlalpan, Mexico, are well-known examples of his work. His work was exhibited at the MUSEUM OF MODERN ART in New York in a 1976 retrospective, and he was the recipient of the Pritzker Prize in 1980 in recognition of his work's international reputation.

Barrault, Jean-Louis *(1910–1994)* French actor, director and theater manager. Barrault was one of the leading figures of French theater in the 20th century, having served at various times as the guiding force behind such renowned theatrical companies as the Comédie-Française, the Théâtre Marigny of Paris and the Odéon-Théâtre de France. Barrault first came into prominence as a film actor in the 1940s, most notably for his romantic lead role in *Les Enfants du paradis* (1944). Also during that decade Barrault staged numerous premieres of works by the prominent French playwright Paul CLAUDEL. In the 1950s and 1960s Barrault became a proponent of the THEATER OF THE ABSURD and directed plays by Samuel BECKETT, Jean GENET and Eugene IONESCO, among others. In 1968, having been dismissed by the Odéon-Théâtre for his support of the French student uprising in May of that year, Barrault staged his play adaptation *Rabelais* in a Montmartre wrestling arena to great critical acclaim. With his wife, the actress Madeleine Renaud, Barrault founded the renowned Compagnie Renaud-Barrault.

Barrie, Sir James Matthew *(1860–1937)* Scottish-born novelist and playwright, the creator of PETER PAN. Barrie was born at Kirriemuir in Forfarshire, Scotland. After education at the Dumfries Academy and Edinburgh University he worked as a journalist for the *Nottingham Journal* and the *St. James Gazette.* Publication of his vivid recollections of his boyhood—*Auld Licht Idylls* (1887) and *A Window on Thrums* (1889)—brought him his first public notice. Many popular books and plays quickly followed. The plays *Quality Street* (1901), *The Admirable Crichton* (1902), *Peter Pan* (1904) and *What Every Woman Knows* (1908) established him as the most popular

playwright of his time. The devoted efforts of his longtime friend, theater producer Charles Frohman, brought them to equally enthusiastic audiences in America. Today Barrie's works find a mixed reception. As a member of the so-called Kailyear School—a term applied to writers of romantic fiction utilizing the vernacular and common life of Scotland—he is without equal. However, other aspects of his work are more problematic. Barrie continued to write until the end of his life, finishing his last play, *The Boy David,* just before his death from a long illness in 1937.

Barringer, Daniel Moreau *(1860–1929)* American mining engineer and geologist. Barringer graduated from Princeton in 1879 and then studied law at Pennsylvania, geology at Harvard and chemistry and mineralogy at the University of Virginia. In 1890 he established himself as a consulting mining engineer and geologist; he was the author of the standard work *Law of Mines and Mining in the U.S.* (1907). Barringer is remembered for his investigation of the massive Diabolo Crater in Arizona, which is nearly 600 feet deep and over 4,000 feet in diameter. Barringer, finding numerous nickel-iron rocks in the area, became convinced that the remains of an enormous meteorite lay buried at the center of the crater. He began drilling in 1902 but failed to find anything of significance. After his death the crater became known as the **Barringer Meteor Crater.**

Barron, Clarence *(1855–1928)* American newspaper editor and author. Born in Boston, Barron joined the staff of the *Boston Evening Transcript* as a young man in 1875 and remained until 1884. Three years later, he established the Boston News Bureau and, in 1897, its counterpart in Philadelphia. Later in his career he edited *Barron's Financial Weekly* and served as manager of Dow Jones & Company, publisher of the WALL STREET JOURNAL. Among Barron's books are *The Audacious War* (1915) and *A World Remaking* (1920).

Barrow, Clyde See BONNIE AND CLYDE.

Barrow, Errol Welton *(1920–1987)* Barbadian statesman. Barrow helped

lead BARBADOS to independence from Great Britain in 1966 and in the process became the Caribbean island's first prime minister after 350 years of constitutional rule. He governed Barbados for three consecutive terms before being voted out of office in 1976. In 1986 he was voted back into office.

Barry, Philip *(1896–1949)* American playwright. With wry comedies such as *Holiday* in 1928 and *The Animal Kingdom* in 1932, Barry became a prominent playwright of his time. His 1939 play *Philadelphia Story* was a hit and was adapted into a classic film. He also wrote serious dramas. His other plays include *Cock Robin* (1928), *Hotel Universe* (1930), *Here Come the Clowns* (1938), *Liberty Jones* (1941), *Without Love* (1942) and *The Foolish Notion* (1945).

Barrymore America's "first family" of stage and motion picture performers. The Barrymore saga begins in the middle of the 19th century with the distinguished actors, Mr. and Mrs. John Drew. Their daughter Georgiana married Herbert Blythe, who adopted the name "Maurice Barrymore." The three children of that union were born as "Barrymores": **Lionel** (1878–1954), **Ethel** (1879–1959) and **John** (1882–1944). Each at an early age followed in the family acting tradition. Lionel was a Broadway star at age 22 and a movie actor eight years later in 1909, when he began appearing in many BIOGRAPH films directed by D. W. GRIFFITH. Ethel was a smash hit on Broadway in *Captain Jinks of the Horse Marines* (1900) and began movie acting after 1914. Handsome, rambunctious John, who was a sensation on Broadway and in London with the record-breaking *Hamlet* (1922–25), had the brightest success of the three in SILENT FILM, where he was a top star for WARNER BROS. in the 1920s, his appearance eliciting the memorable remark from Heywood Broun: "He now edges into pictures like a beautiful paper knife."

All three siblings made successful TALKING PICTURES. Lionel won an Oscar in *A Free Soul* (1931) and, after an accident that confined him to a wheelchair, played the crusty "Dr. Gillespie" in the Dr. Kildare series. Ethel won an Oscar for *None but the Lonely Heart* (1944) and appeared as a character actress in many subsequent films and television shows. John never got an Oscar but left a proud gallery of characters: the evil hypnotist in *Svengali* (1931), the disturbed father in *Bill of Divorcement,* the gentle teacher in *Topaze* (1933). Surprisingly, the three never appeared together on stage. Lionel and John costarred in the plays *Peter Ibbetson* (1917) and *The Jest* (1919) and on film in *Night Flight* (1933). John and Ethel occasionally appeared together on stage, most notably in *Clair de Lune* (1920). But the three were destined to appear together only once, on film, in MGM's *Rasputin and the Empress* (1932).

It was a brilliant, if unstable, family, full of eccentricities and temperament. For all their glitter, the Barrymores lived under a shadow. As Ethel put it, "I think that both my brothers and I were born under a dark star so that there was no such thing for us as enduring happiness." Later generations of Barrymores fared little better. John's children, John Jr. and Diana, pursued unsuccessful film careers. **Drew** Barrymore (1975–), daughter of John Jr., was a successful child prodigy in films like *Bogie* (1980), E.T. (1982) and *Irreconcilable Differences* (1985) but struggled through her teenage years, obliging her mother to commit her to a drug rehabilitation clinic, from which she escaped and attempted to commit suicide before being recommitted. In her early 20s she returned to films as a leading lady, appearing in *The Wedding Singer, Ever After,* and *Home Fries* in 1998. She formed her own production company in the same year and acted and produced in a number of films, including *Never Been Kissed* (1999), *Donnie Darko* (2001), and *A Confederacy of Dunces* (2004).

Barth, John (*1930– *) American novelist and story writer. Barth, a native of Maryland who attended Johns Hopkins University in Baltimore and taught there for many years, first rose to prominence in the 1950s when his novels *The Floating Opera* (1956) and *The End of the Road* (1958) earned him a reputation as a gifted comic writer with a keen eye for the absurdities of American pop culture. Barth then proceeded to write two epic-length novels, *The Sot-Weed Factor* (1960) and *Giles Goat Boy* (1966), that both consolidated his reputation as a satiric explorer of existential themes and won

him a broad popular readership. A book of novellas, *Chimera* (1972), earned Barth the National Book Award. Subsequent works by Barth include *Letters* (1979), *Tidewater Tales* (1987), *The Last Voyage of Somebody the Sailor* (1991), *Once Upon a Time* (1994) and the collection *On with the Story* (1996).

Barth, Karl (*1886–1968*) Swiss theologian. Barth was one of the leading Protestant theologians for the 20th century, proclaiming as his central credo that "Faith, not reason, is the basis of Christian knowledge." Barth's father was a theologian of the Swiss Reformed Church, and Barth himself, after university study in Germany, became a Reformed Church minister in the small Swiss village of Safenwil, where he remained for 10 years. In 1918 Barth published his first book, *Epistle to the Romans,* which attacked liberal Protestant theology as having produced a "God-forgetting humanism." Over the next four decades, works such as *The Word of God and the Word of Man* (1928) and *Dogmatics in Outline* (1949) established Barth as a leading existential theologian whose defense of absolute faith echoed that of the 19th-century Danish philosopher Soren Kierkegaard. Although he felt that the church should stay out of politics, Barth personally was an active opponent of the HITLER government, joining the Swiss army at age 54 in order to serve sentry duty on the Swiss-German frontier.

Barthelme, Donald (*1931–1990*) American novelist and story writer. Barthelme, who is best known for his short stories that appeared frequently in THE NEW YORKER, is often termed a POSTMODERN writer by virtue of his use of nontraditional, episodic narratives filled with black humor and absurdist irony. Barthelme, who was raised in Texas, was a gifted stylist fond of puns, neologisms and tangled literary allusions. His short story collections include *Come Back, Dr. Caligari* (1964), *Unspeakable Practices, Unnatural Acts* (1968), *City Life* (1970), *Sadness* (1972), *Guilty Pleasures* (1974), *Amateurs* (1976) and *Great Days* (1979). Barthelme also produced acclaimed novels such as *Snow White* (1967), a deadpan, disturbing retelling of the traditional fairy tale, and *The Dead Father* (1975), a fablelike account of a fa-

ther who is at one and the same time alive and a gigantic dead carcass.

Barthes, Roland (*1915–1980*) French literary critic and philosopher. Barthes was one of the most influential literary critics of his era, a proponent of the "nouvelle critique" method that brought stringent philosophical analysis into the domain of textual criticism, where traditional stylistic analysis had long prevailed. Barthes drew heavily from Marxism, Freudian psychoanalysis, EXISTENTIALISM and STRUCTURALISM in his works, as well as from the study of SEMIOTICS, a linguistics-based school of thought proposing that a structure of basic signs underlies all forms of human communication, including literary expression. A suave stylist and versatile observer of cultures as well as of literature, Barthes's major works include *Writing Degree Zero* (1953), *Mythologies* (1957), *On Racine* (1963), *Critical Essays* (1964), *The Empire of Signs* (1970), *Sade, Fourier, Loyola* (1971), *S/Z* (1971) and *The Pleasures of the Text* (1972).

Bartlett, Sir Frederick Charles (*1886–1969*) British psychologist. Bartlett earned distinction both in theoretical and applied psychology over a long academic career that saw him become the first-ever professor of experimental psychology at Cambridge University in 1931. As a theoretician, Bartlett is best known for his book *Remembering* (1932), in which he argued—contrary to the schools of behaviorism and gestalt theory, both of which argued for a passive model of memory processes—that the human mind is highly selective, reconstructive and goal-oriented in its use of memory. During WORLD WAR II, Bartlett conducted practical psychological testing to improve British army performance on gunnery and radar control systems. After the war, he became active in research on issues of industrial psychology. From 1924 to 1948 Bartlett was editor of the prestigious *British Journal of Psychology.* Bartlett was knighted in 1948.

Bartlett, Neil (*1932– *) British-American chemist. Bartlett was educated at the University of Durham, England, where he obtained his Ph.D. in 1957. He taught at the University of British Columbia, Canada, and at

Princeton before being appointed to a chemistry professorship in 1969 at the University of California, Berkeley. Bartlett was studying metal fluorides and found that the compound platinum hexafluoride is extremely active. At the time it was an unquestioned assumption of chemistry that the noble gases—helium, neon, argon, krypton and xenon—were completely inert, incapable of forming any compounds whatsoever. Further, there was a solid theory that provided good reasons why this should be so. So struck was Bartlett with the ability of platinum hexafluoride to react with other substances that he tried, in 1962, to form a compound between it and xenon. To his and other chemists' surprise xenon fluoroplatinate was produced—the first compound of a noble gas. Once the first compound had been detected xenon was soon shown to form other compounds. Krypton and radon were also found to form compounds.

Bartlett, Paul Doughty (*1907– 1997*) American chemist. Bartlett was educated at Amherst College and Harvard, where he obtained his Ph.D. in 1931. After teaching briefly at the Rockefeller Institute and the University of Minnesota, he returned to Harvard in 1934 and served there as professor of chemistry from 1948 until his retirement in 1975. Bartlett worked mainly on the mechanisms involved in organic reactions. He also investigated the chemistry of elemental sulfur and the terpenes (a family of hydrocarbons found in the essential oil of plants).

Bartók, Béla (*1881–1945*) Hungarian composer and pianist, one of the foremost figures in 20th-century music. Born in Nagyszentmiklos, Hungary, Bartók was a sickly child with precocious music talents. With the encouragement of friend and mentor Ernst von DOHNÁNYI, he went to Budapest's Royal Academy of Music in 1899. Although trained in the Germanic tradition exemplified by Franz Liszt and Richard STRAUSS, Bartók displayed a growing interest in the Magyar music and poetry of his native Hungary. Beginning in 1905 he made a series of trips across Hungary with his friend, composer Zoltán KODÁLY, to collect and record thousands of peasant folk songs. Far different from the

"gypsy" music of Liszt, these colorful melodies and strange rhythms became the basis of Bartók's mature musical expression. They freed him from classical major-minor systems and instead utilized many modes, like the pentatonic scale and so-called acoustic octaves (with their augmented fourth intervals) with which he established a system of 12 semitones that functioned tonally, as opposed to the atonality of Arnold SCHOENBERG. Examples of this new music vocabulary abound in Bartók's many sets of piano pieces, particularly the two books of *For Children* (1908–09) and the collection of 137 tiny pieces called *Mikrokosmos* (1932–37). During Bartók's tenure as professor of piano at the Royal Academy (1907–36) and later residence at Columbia University in New York (1940–42), he composed *Bluebeard's Castle* (1911), the *Dance Suite* (1923), *Music for Strings, Percussion, and Celesta* (1936), six string quartets and two piano concertos. However, living in virtual poverty in his last years, he was commissioned by Serge KOUSSEVITZKY to write what would be one of his most beloved works, the *Concerto for Orchestra* (1944), in which he quoted a theme from SHOSTAKOVICH's Leningrad Symphony. Bartók died of leukemia in 1945 before he could return to Hungary. "Bartók was not a robust man," recalled pianist and student of Bartók, Gyorgy Sandor, who premiered many of Bartók's works, including the unfinished Third Piano Concerto. "But his emotional and intellectual qualities were superb. He spoke fourteen languages and dialects. He was honest and extremely civilized. Everywhere in his music you find the most complete range and expression of human emotion."

Barton, Sir Derek Harold Richard (*1918–1998*) British chemist. Barton was educated at Imperial College, London, where he obtained his Ph.D. in 1942. After some industrial research he spent a year as visiting lecturer at Harvard before being appointed reader (1950) and then professor (1953) in organic chemistry at Birkbeck College, London. Barton moved to a similar chair at Glasgow University in 1955 but returned to Imperial College in 1957 and held the chair of chemistry until 1978, when he became director of the Institute for the Chemistry of Natural

Substances at Gif-sur-Yvette in France. In 1950 Barton published a fundamental paper on conformational analysis in which he proposed that the orientations in space of functional groups affect the rates of reaction in isomers. He confirmed these notions with further work on the stability and reactivity of steroids and terpenes. It was for this work that he shared the 1969 NOBEL PRIZE in chemistry with Odd Hassell. Barton's later work on oxyradicals and his predictions about their behavior in reactions helped in the development of a simple method for synthesizing the hormone aldosterone.

Baruch, Bernard Mannes (*1870– 1965*) American financier who acted as an adviser to every president from Woodrow WILSON to John F. KENNEDY. Born in Camden, South Carolina, he studied at City College in New York City. Starting as a Wall Street office boy, he quickly rose in the world of high finance, becoming a millionaire before he was 30. During WORLD WAR I he headed (1918–19) the War Industries Board and after the war (1919) served as a U.S. delegate to the PARIS PEACE CONFERENCE. After the election of President Franklin D. ROOSEVELT, he was offered the post of secretary of the treasury but declined the office in order to be an unofficial presidential adviser on economics and politics, a role he played until Roosevelt's death in 1945. During WORLD WAR II, Baruch was special adviser to James F. BYRNES (1942). Appointed U.S. representative to the United Nations Atomic Energy Commission in 1946, he was an important force in the attempt to control the forces of the atom. He described his life in two volumes of autobiography, *Baruch: My Own Story* (1957) and *Baruch: The Public Years* (1960).

Baryshnikov, Mikhail (*1948– *) Russian-born dancer, actor and ballet director. Considered one of the greatest male dancers of the 20th century, Baryshnikov was born in Riga, Latvia. After training in Riga and Leningrad, Baryshnikov joined the Kirov Ballet as a soloist in 1966. That same year he won international acclaim and a gold medal at the Varna ballet competition. Then in 1969 he won the gold medal at the prestigious International Ballet Competition in Moscow. But limited repertory at the Kirov proved frustrating, and in 1974 Baryshnikov defected to the West. His search for artistic freedom led to a memorable partnership with Gelsey Kirkland at AMERICAN BALLET THEATRE, which he joined in 1974. As an ABT principal and guest artist with other companies, he achieved brilliant success in a variety of roles, ranging from Albrecht in *Giselle* to the lead in the modern dance *Push Comes to Shove* created for him by Twyla THARP (1976). In 1978 he left ABT for the NEW YORK CITY BALLET and the opportunity to work with George BALANCHINE.

He returned to ABT in 1980 as artistic director. During his nine-year tenure as director, he restaged classic works, commissioned pieces in the postmodern idiom and launched many dancers' careers, while also pursuing a career as an actor in movies (*The Turning Point, White Nights*) and on Broadway (*Metamorphosis*). In addition, he has choreographed some works, most notably new versions of the *Nutcracker* and *Don Quixote*. In 1989 Baryshnikov left the ABT. A year later he formed the White Oak Dance Project, his own touring troupe of modern dancers, which offered performances until its dissolution in 2002. As a dancer, Baryshnikov is best known for his spectacular jumps and turns.

Barzani, Mustafa (*1904–1979*) General Barzani was leader of an estimated 12 million Muslim KURDS. Under his leadership, the Kurds waged guerrilla war on and off against IRAQ for more than 40 years, beginning in the 1940s. Barzani hoped to establish an autonomous Kurdistan in northern Iraq. His secessionist movement collapsed in 1975.

Barzini, Luigi (*1908–1984*) Italian author, journalist and politician. Barzini began his career as a proponent of Benito MUSSOLINI and FASCISM. However, he became disillusioned and was later jailed for his opposition. As a journalist, he covered wars in GERMANY and ETHIOPIA and wrote for such U.S. magazines as *Harper's*, THE NATION and *LIFE*. Barzini also served as a member of the Italian parliament. His books on European culture include *The Italians,* a best seller that offended many of his countrymen with its biting criticism, and *The Europeans.*

Barzun, Jacques Martin (*1907– *) American cultural historian and literary critic. Barzun was born in France but immigrated to the U.S. just after World War I. He graduated at the head of his Columbia College class in 1927 and commenced a lifelong career as a writer and teacher, ultimately becoming a professor of history at Columbia. Barzun's approach to historical and literary criticism was humanistic and eclectic, without recourse to absolute ideologies. He wrote a highly influential work on educational method, *The Teacher in America* (1945); in an essay for *LIFE* magazine (1950) he asserted that the true test of education was that the student "finds pleasure in the exercise of his mind." Other works by Barzun include *Darwin, Marx, Wagner: Critique of a Heritage* (1941), *Romanticism and the Modern Ego* (1943) and *God's Country and Mine* (1954), a book of reflections on American life. In 2000 Barzun published at the age of 93 the internationally acclaimed best seller *From Dawn to Decadence: 500 Years of Western Cultural Life, 1500 to the Present.*

Bashir, Omar Hassan Ahmed al-Bashir (*1944– *) President of Sudan (1989–). After rising to the rank of brigadier general with the Sudanese army, Bashir was named minister of defense in the government of Jaafar Nimeri, whose rule ended in 1985 as a result of widespread rioting and protests over his economic austerity measures. In 1989 a military coup overthrew the civilian Sudanese government that had ruled since 1985, and appointed Omar Hassan Ahmed al-Bashir as president of SUDAN. In March 1991, Bashir reinstituted Islamic law, or sharia, throughout the country, strengthened ties with the government of Iran and the Muslim Brotherhood movement in Egypt. The country was engulfed in a brutal civil war between the largely Muslim north and the predominantly Christian south.

Following a series of terrorist attacks in Saudi Arabia, Yemen and Somalia, Bashir expelled al-QAEDA leader Osama BIN LADEN from Sudan in May 1996. On August 20, 1998, 13 days after the U.S. embassies in Kenya and Tanzania were the target of terrorist bombings that killed 11 Americans and 212 nationals of those countries, President Bill CLINTON ordered cruise missile attacks on al-Qaeda camps in Afghanistan as well as on a pharmaceutical plant in Khartoum, Sudan, that intelligence sources claimed (wrongly as it turned out) was being used by bin Laden to produce chemical weapons. In recent years Bashir's regime has come under harsh criticism from the international community for permitting nomadic groups to terrorize inhabitants of the western region of Darfur in a campaign that human rights organizations and others labeled as genocide.

Basic Treaty A December 21, 1972, treaty of friendship and mutual recognition between the Federal German Republic (WEST GERMANY) and the German Democratic Republic (EAST GERMANY). The Basic Treaty was the culmination of West German chancellor Willy BRANDT's OSTPOLITIK and was followed by the entry of both nations into the UN in 1973.

Basie, William "Count" (*1904–1984*) American jazz legend, born in Red Bank, New Jersey. Count Basie, the seminal big band leader-pianist, forged a uniquely swinging style and subsequently achieved his initial fame and influence in the mid-1930s through national radio broadcasts from Kansas City, Missouri. His band's great appeal was based on an insistent yet subtly syncopated rhythmic pulse, a penchant for loosely sketched blues-based arrangements and a "riff" style where the brass and saxophone sections alternated repeated background motifs, punctuating the impassioned improvisations of the band's always great stable of soloists. The Count Basie Orchestra, with only a few brief hiatuses, succeeded with its big band format (generally including five saxophones, three trombones, four trumpets, piano, rhythm guitar, bass and drums) in impressing critics and jazz fans, as well as dancers. Basie's orchestra, one of the most potent incubators of jazz talent, brought to fame such fabled jazz soloists as trumpeters Harry "Sweets" Edison and Thad Jones, plus saxophonists Lester YOUNG, Eddie "Lockjaw" Davis and Frank Wess; Basie also featured arrangements by such noted composer-arrangers as Neal Hefti, Benny Carter and Quincy Jones. The Count Basie Orchestra continues to tour and record under the direction of one of its most outstanding alumni, saxophonist Frank Foster.

Baskin, Leonard *(1922–2000)* American artist and illustrator. Born in New Brunswick, New Jersey, Baskin studied at New York University and the New School and at art schools in Paris and Florence. A figurative sculptor and printmaker, he is noted for expressive figures, often of bloated, corrupt humans and powerful animals. Noted also for his dramatic, spikey line, Baskin is particularly acclaimed for his dramatic woodcuts. He illustrated several books by the British poet Ted HUGHES as well as numerous books on Jewish traditions. An articulate advocate of humanistic values in the visual arts, he was a noted teacher as a member of the faculty at Smith College since 1953. One of his best-known sculptures, *Man with a Dead Bird,* is in the collection of the Museum of Modern Art, New York City.

Basque separatist movement The Basques are a people whose homeland, in the western Pyrenees Mountains, is spread across four Spanish and three French provinces; they are a group with their own culture and language and have long sought political autonomy. Under the leadership of José Antonio Aguirre y Lecube (1904–60), the Basques supported the Republicans in the SPANISH CIVIL WAR and briefly (1936) were granted autonomy in Spain. The Basque Republic, called Euzkadi, with Aguirre as president, was destroyed with the victory of FRANCO, although a government-in-exile was maintained, first in Spain and later in France. Largely ignored by Franco, the Basques reemerged as a political force in 1959 with the formation of a militant separatist group known as the ETA. This organization became particularly active in the 1970s, causing a good deal of violence and embarking on a campaign of terrorism. In 1980 the Basques gained home rule as an entity within the Spanish state, but Basque violence and the quest for complete political autonomy continued. In 1995 the ETA began a new wave of terrorist attacks in an effort to force Spain to acknowledge Basque independence. Starting with the failed assassination attempt against Spanish Popular Party leader José María AZNAR, the campaign continued unabated, save for a 14-month cease-fire from September 1998 to November 1999. In December 2001 the EUROPEAN UNION (EU) declared the ETA a terrorist organization. In 2006 ETA leaders declared a formal cease-fire suspending the organization's violent activities.

Basra (al-Basrah) Sole port and second largest city of Iraq, located on the Shattal-Arab in the southeastern part of the country, near the Persian Gulf. Basra was occupied by British forces in 1941, during WORLD WAR II. A vital port for oil shipping, it was the site of intense fighting during the IRAN-IRAQ WAR (1980–88). During the PERSIAN GULF WAR it was bombed by the UN allies in Operation Desert Storm (1991). After the war there was fighting between forces loyal to Saddam HUSSEIN and Iraqis who opposed Hussein. Following the 2003 overthrow of Saddam HUSSEIN, British forces in the U.S.-led coalition met determined resistance in Basra from insurgents opposed to the occupation of Iraq.

Bastin, Jules *(1889–1944)* Belgian army officer. A PRISONER OF WAR during WORLD WAR I, Bastin achieved public notice for his repeated and finally successful attempts to escape captivity. He commanded the Belgian cavalry in 1939–40, at the outset of WORLD WAR II. Following the German invasion of BELGIUM in May 1940 he joined the Belgian forces in FRANCE. Commander of the Belgian Legion, he was appointed commander in chief of Belgium's underground military forces in 1942. Bastin was imprisoned in 1943 and died the following year while still in prison. He was posthumously (1946) awarded the title of general.

Bataan Peninsula On Luzon Island in the Philippines. During WORLD WAR II, U.S. forces under General Douglas MACARTHUR retreated here after Manila fell to Japanese forces. In April 1942 some 12,000 American and 64,000 Philippine soldiers surrendered to Japanese forces in Mariveles, a town on the Bataan Peninsula. It was the largest surrender of U.S. forces in history. Some Americans retreated farther to CORREGIDOR, an island off the south end of the peninsula, but these too surrendered in May 1942 after fierce resistance. The Japanese forced their U.S. and Philippine prisoners to march to northern Luzon under extremely desperate conditions; some 10,000 died and the march earned notoriety as the **Bataan Death March.** In February 1945 U.S. forces reconquered Bataan. The area of the peninsula overlooking Manila Bay to the east is today a Philippine national shrine.

Bates, Herbert Ernest *(1905–1974)* British author. Born in Northampton and educated at Kettering Grammar School, Bates later worked at a local newspaper. On the advice of publisher Edward Garnett, Bates's first novel, *The Two Sisters,* was published in 1926, followed by many short stories. He achieved great success during WORLD WAR II with his stories of wartime flying and maintained his reputation with such postwar books as *Love for Lydia* (1952), which was later adapted and televised by the BBC, and *The Darling Buds of May* (1958). Bates's work is marked by lyricism, simplicity, nostalgia for the countryside and rural traditions and insight into the lives of ordinary people. He also published an autobiography in three volumes: *The Vanished World* (1969), *The Blossoming World* (1971) and *The World in Ripeness* (1972).

Bates, Leslie Fleetwood *(1897–1978)* British physicist. Bates was educated at Bristol University and at Cambridge University, where he obtained his Ph.D. in 1922. After teaching first at University College, London, he moved to Nottingham where he served as professor of physics from 1936, apart from wartime duties on the degaussing of ships, until his retirement in 1964. Most of Bates's work was on the magnetic properties of materials. He was the author of a widely used textbook, *Modern Magnetism* (1938), which went through many editions.

Bateson, William *(1861–1926)* British geneticist. Bateson graduated in natural sciences from Cambridge University in 1883, having specialized in zoology. At Cambridge Bateson began studying variation within populations and soon found instances of discontinuous variation that could not simply be related to environmental conditions. He believed this to be of evolutionary importance and began breeding experiments to investigate the phenomenon more fully. These prepared him to accept Mendel's work when it was rediscovered in 1900, although other British scientists were largely skeptical of the work. Bateson translated Mendel's paper into English and set up a research group to investigate heredity in plants and animals. He found that certain traits are governed by two or more genes, and in his sweet pea crosses showed that some characteristics are not inherited independently. This was the first hint that genes are linked on chromosomes, but Bateson never accepted the chromosome theory of inheritance. In 1908 Bateson became the first professor of the subject he himself named—genetics. However, he left Cambridge only a year later and in 1910 became director of the newly formed John Innes Horticultural Institution at Merton, Surrey, where he remained until his death. He was the leading proponent of Mendelian genetics in Britain.

Batista y Zaldívar, Fulgencio *(1901–1973)* President (1939–44) and dictator (1952–58) of Cuba. Batista joined the army, rising to the rank of sergeant before participating in a military coup against President Gerardo Machado. He promoted himself to colonel and established a fascist-inspired corporate state (see FASCISM). Elected president after permitting the formation of rival political parties in 1939, he went into voluntary exile in 1944 when he lost to Ramón Grau San Martín in the presidential elections. Batista returned to power in 1952 after a coup d'état, but from 1956, faced by Fidel CASTRO's left-wing guerrilla movement, he lost support in the army and in January 1959 was forced to flee the country.

Batman Celebrated American comic book hero, second only to SUPERMAN in international popularity. Batman first appeared in a six-page story in *Detective Comics* (1939). Identified at first as simply "The Bat-Man," he was the creation of 18-year-old artist Bob Kane. Like Superman, Batman wore a uniform and cape, possessed a dual identity and fought against the underworld. However, he possessed no superpowers beyond his native intelligence and training in science and criminology. Batman's nemesis the Joker (one of a gallery of colorful super villains) appeared in late 1939; Batman's young assistant Robin ("the Boy Wonder") followed the next year. COLUMBIA PICTURES produced two film serials in 1943 and 1949, respectively. In 1964 the character was revived by the popular tongue-in-cheek *Batman* television series, which featured well-known actors in the roles of various villains. The hit film *Batman* (1989), starring Michael Keaton as Batman and Jack NICHOLSON as the Joker, brought the character back to its original conception.

Battle of Britain *(1940)* After France fell to the invading Germans in WORLD WAR II, the Nazis planned to bomb Great Britain into submission before invading across the English Channel. On August 15, 1940, the Luftwaffe (German air force) sent its first wave of bombers to southern England, encountering stiff resistance from British fighter planes. At first focusing on airfields, then intensively bombing London and other cities (the blitz), great damage was caused, but British morale was unbroken. The Royal Air Force (RAF) fought tenaciously, shooting down many German aircraft, and the Luftwaffe failed to establish air superiority. Germany called off the operation, and Prime Minister Winston CHURCHILL said of the RAF pilots, "never . . . was so much owed by so many to so few."

battleship See DREADNOUGHT.

Bauer, Riccardo *(1896–1982)* Italian socialist leader. He was a founder of the Action Party during the 1920s and of the underground Justice and Liberty organization that opposed MUSSOLINI during the 1930s and 1940s. During WORLD WAR II, he led guerrilla strikes against German troops occupying northern ITALY.

Bauhaus German college of architecture and applied design that became a highly influential center of the arts in the 1920s. The Bauhaus was founded in Weimar by Walter GROPIUS in 1919. Gropius, inspired in part by the aesthetic craft movement of the British writer and artist William Morris, created the Bauhaus to further the role of the artist in industrial mass production. The Bauhaus became known for an architectonic approach to design in which purely ornamental touches were eliminated in favor of a spare, geometric approach that utilized component materials with strict economy. The Bauhaus worked closely with industrial firms, and its furniture, textile and light-fixture designs were mass produced successfully. Bauhaus faculty members included painters Wassily KANDINSKY and Paul KLEE and the architect Ludwig MIES VAN DER ROHE. The Bauhaus moved from Weimar to Dessau in 1925 and then to Berlin in 1931. In 1933 it was closed down by the Nazis. The subsequent emigration of Bauhaus faculty and students contributed to its enduring worldwide influence.

Baum, Lyman Frank *(1856–1919)* American author. Born in Chittenango, New York, he worked as a journalist in South Dakota and Chicago. In 1899 he published his first book, *Father Goose: His Book,* which quickly became a best seller. His next book, *The Wonderful Wizard of Oz* (1900), was to be his most famous. This story of little Dorothy from Kansas who is transported by a "twister" to a magical realm was made into a musical comedy in 1901 and into one of America's most popular motion pictures in 1939. The tale was the first of 14 Oz books by Baum, such as *Ozma of Oz* (1907) and *The Scarecrow of Oz* (1915), and many more written by others after his death. During his career Baum wrote more than 60 books, many of them for children.

Baumeister, Willi *(1889–1955)* German painter. Born in Stuttgart, Baumeister was a student of Adolf Hoelzel. At first influenced by the postimpressionists, he turned to a CONSTRUCTIVISM strongly associated with Fernand LEGER, creating abstract paintings filled with mechanical shapes. Dismissed from his teaching post in Frankfurt in 1933 for tendencies deemed "degenerate" by the Nazis, he remained in Germany during World War II, researching color theory and archaeology. Influenced in his later works by these studies as well as by the work of Paul KLEE and Joan MIRÓ, his later work swarms with organic forms and ideographic signs.

Bavaria State in southern GERMANY; formerly an independent duchy, kingdom and republic. Its major cities are

Munich, the capital, and Nuremberg. After Germany was unified by Prussian chancellor Otto von Bismarck in 1871, Bavaria joined the German Empire. After WORLD WAR I, King Louis III, the last of the Wittelsbach royal lineage, was deposed and a socialist republic was established under the leadership of Kurt Eisner. But Eisner was assassinated a few months later, and a subsequent communist revolt was crushed by the German military. Bavaria joined the WEIMAR REPUBLIC. Munich saw the rise of HITLER and his failed Munich BEER HALL PUTSCH of 1923. When Hitler finally came to power in 1933, Bavaria became a part of the Nazi Reich. After WORLD WAR II, it was in the U.S. occupation zone and was merged into West Germany in 1949.

Bawden, Sir Frederick Charles (*1908–1992*) British plant pathologist. Bawden was educated at Cambridge University, receiving his M.A. in 1933. From 1936 to 1940 he worked in the virus physiology department at Rothamsted Experimental Station, becoming the head of the plant pathology department in 1940 and director of the station in 1958. In 1937 Bawden discovered that the tobacco mosaic virus (TMV) contains ribonucleic acid, this being the first demonstration that nucleic acids occur in viruses. With Norman Pirie, Bawden isolated TMV in crystalline form and made important contributions to elucidating virus structure and means of multiplication. Bawden's work also helped in revealing the mechanisms of protein formation. Bawden was knighted in 1967.

Bax, Arnold (*1883–1953*) British composer known for his romantic symphonic works. Bax was acquainted with the Irish poet W. B. YEATS, and his first work to gain recognition, *In the Faery Hills* (1909), was inspired by Yeats's narrative poem *The Wanderings of Oisin*. Bax's output includes seven symphonies and the tone poem *Tintagel* (1917), among numerous other works. His music is marked by rich orchestration and soaring melodies; quiet, poetic passages are frequently interrupted by rhapsodic outbursts. Bax never achieved the critical acclaim or popularity of ELGAR, VAUGHAN WILLIAMS or DELIUS, but his music has been widely performed and recorded in Britain and

has undergone something of a revival in the latter part of the 20th century.

Bayar, Celal (*1882–1986*) Turkish statesman. Bayar was one of the founding fathers of the modern Turkish republic (see YOUNG TURKS). In the 1920s and 1930s he held a number of key cabinet posts under ATATÜRK; he was prime minister from 1937 to 1939. In 1945 he founded the opposition Democratic Party, and five years later he was overwhelmingly elected president of TURKEY. Ousted in a military coup in 1960, he was condemned to death; the sentence was commuted to life in prison. He was freed during a general political amnesty in 1964 but thereafter refused to sit in the Turkish senate, although this was his right as a former president.

Bayer, Herbert (*1900–1985*) Austrian artist; one of the last major figures associated with the BAUHAUS design school. Bayer arrived in the U.S. as a refugee from NAZISM in 1938 and soon became a major contributor to the advancement of graphic and industrial design, as well as advertising and urban planning. During the 1940s he helped develop the town of Aspen, Colorado, as a cultural and resort center. From the 1960s until his death he served as art and design consultant to the Atlantic Richfield Company.

Bayliss, Sir William Maddock (*1860–1924*) British physiologist. Bayliss was the son of a wealthy iron manufacturer. In 1881 he entered University College, London, as a medical student but when he failed his second MB exam in anatomy he gave up medicine to concentrate on physiology. He graduated from Oxford University in 1888, then returned to University College, London, where he worked for the rest of his life, holding the chair of general physiology from 1912. Bayliss was elected a fellow of the Royal Society in 1903 and was knighted in 1922. He was chiefly interested in the physiology of the nervous, digestive and vascular systems, on which he worked in association with his brother-in-law, Ernest Starling. Their most important work, published in 1902, was the discovery of the action of a hormone (secretin) in controlling digestion. In 1915 Bayliss produced a standard textbook on phys-

iology, *Principles of General Physiology*, which treated the subject from a physiochemical point of view.

Baylor, Elgin Gay (*1934– *) American basketball player. In 1958 Baylor was a first-round draft pick of the then-Minneapolis Lakers and was named rookie of the year in his first professional season. He remained with the Lakers for 14 years, a tenure that might have lasted even longer had it not been for his troublesome knees. He finished his career 11th on the all-time scoring list, with 23,149 points and, in 1960, set a record for most points in a game with 71. A 10-time all-star, Baylor went on to a less-successful career as a coach in the late 1970s. He was named to the Basketball Hall of Fame in 1976. In April 1986 Baylor was hired by the Los Angeles Clippers to act as the organization's vice president of basketball operations.

Bay of Pigs invasion (*1961*) Abortive attempt by anticommunist Cuban exiles to invade CUBA and overthrow the government of Fidel CASTRO. The 1959 takeover of Cuba by Castro and his revolutionary followers prompted the exodus of many Cubans, especially to the U.S. When Castro's regime began confiscating private property and established close ties to the Soviet Union, the U.S. imposed an embargo on all exports to Cuba (except food and medicine) and broke diplomatic relations (1960–61). Anti-Castro Cuban exiles demanded that the U.S. back an invasion of their homeland to topple the government; as early as 1960 the American CENTRAL INTELLIGENCE AGENCY (CIA) began to train an exile army in Guatemala. On April 17, 1961, about 1,400 exiles invaded southern Cuba at the Bahía de los Cochinos (Bay of Pigs), but by April 20 they were totally defeated by the Cuban army. Most of the invaders were killed or taken prisoner. Critics of this failure blamed the last-minute withdrawal of naval air support by U.S. president John F. KENNEDY, but closer investigation disclosed that the CIA scheme, meant to be secret but long a matter of public knowledge, had been based on faulty intelligence information and was poorly planned and executed. The failed invasion aggravated already hostile U.S.-Cuban relations and eventually required the expenditure of $53 million in food and medicine (raised by private donors) to secure the release of 1,113 surviving captive invaders (1962–63).

Bayreuth Festival Located in the town of Bayreuth in Bavaria, Germany, where Richard Wagner built his home, the festival has given regular performances of Wagner's operas since 1892 (interrupted only by the world wars). The first festival was given in 1876 after Wagner had a theater built to house performances of his *Der Ring des Nibelungen*. Directors of the festival have all been members of the Wagner family, and no opera by any other composer has been given there. In July 2001 the festival became involved in a controversy between the opera star Plácido DOMINGO and event director Wolfgang Wagner, a grandson of Richard Wagner. The struggle led to the appointment in December 2001 of Klaus Schultz, then director of a small state-owned theater in Munich, as the festival's interim director, with Wagner retaining an advisory role.

Bazelon, David *(1909–1993)* American judge. A graduate of Northwestern University Law School, Bazelon was appointed to the powerful U.S. Court of Appeals for the District of Columbia where he helped shape criminal and administrative law for the nation. Among other notable achievements, Bazelon formulated the famous Durham rule, an insanity defense under which an accused would not be criminally responsible if a criminal act was the product of mental disease or mental defect. Although the rule was hailed as an advance, it was abandoned because it proved unworkable in practice.

Baziotes, William *(1912–1963)* American painter. Born in Pittsburgh, Pennsylvania, he studied at the National Academy of Design, New York City (1933–36) and held a number of teaching posts in the city. Influenced by CUBISM and SURREALISM, he developed a highly personal form of ABSTRACT EXPRESSIONISM in the 1940s, which he refined in the 1950s. His brooding abstract canvases, usually painted in subdued colors, are inhabited by mysterious, otherworldly and faintly organic shapes. Characteristic

works are *Dragon* (Metropolitan Museum of Art, New York) and *The Dwarf* (Museum of Modern Art, in New York).

BBC See BRITISH BROADCASTING CORPORATION.

Beach, Amy Marcy Cheney *(1867–1944)* American composer and concert pianist. A child prodigy, in 1883 in Boston she premiered as a concert pianist to critical praise. In 1892 her *Mass in E flat major* became the first woman's composition performed by the prestigious Handel and Haydn Society of Boston, as was her *Eilende Wolken* (Opus 18) for the New York Symphony. Her reputation was solidified with a commission to write the *Festival Jubilate* for the 1892 World Columbian Exposition in Chicago. Beach toured Europe to critical and popular acclaim (1911–14). Her 150 works have generally been discussed with those of the Boston classicists, well constructed, late romantic, with broad melodies and beautiful harmonies. Her *Gaelic Symphony* (Opus 32) and Browning songs are still popular.

Beach, Sylvia Woodbridge *(1887–1962)* American literary publisher, bookseller and author. Born in Baltimore, Maryland, she immigrated to PARIS, where for many years she ran the renowned book shop and lending library, Shakespeare and Company. During the 1920s and 1930s it was a gathering place for such writers as Ernest HEMINGWAY, André GIDE, T. S. ELIOT, James JOYCE, Gertrude STEIN and many other lions of the Paris literati. Beach gained additional fame when she published Joyce's ULYSSES (1922) and, with the help of Hemingway, arranged for copies of the book to be smuggled to the U.S., where it was banned until 1933. Shakespeare and Company was forced to close during the NAZI occupation of Paris in WORLD WAR II, but Beach and friends saved her vast collection of correspondence, books and memoirs from Nazi confiscation. She was detained in a CONCENTRATION CAMP for several months. In 1959 Beach presented the collection in an exposition at the U.S. embassy in Paris. Much of it was later housed at the Sylvia Beach collection at Princeton; her Joyce collection was donated to the University of Buffalo. Her memoir is *Shakespeare and Company* (1959).

Beach Boys, The American rock and roll band. The Beach Boys are one of the best-known rock groups in history. Their hit songs of the 1960s, such as "I Get Around" (1964), "Help Me Rhonda" (1965) and the classic "Good Vibrations" (1966), have never left the radio airwaves since the time of their first airings. The five white male members of the Beach Boys included three brothers, Brian, Carl and Dennis Wilson, along with Al Jardine and Mike Love. Brian Wilson, who produces, composes and plays keyboard, has been the guiding musical force behind the group since its founding in 1961. In the mid-1960s, the Beach Boys linked themselves indelibly to the California beach scene with hits such as "Surfin' U.S.A.," "Fun, Fun, Fun" and "California Girls." While the group has continued to perform and record to the present day, it is these early hits—featuring the Beach Boys' trademark lilting vocal harmonies—that have won them a worldwide following of loyal fans. The loss of Dennis Wilson to a 1983 drowning accident did not prevent the Beach Boys from generating renewed interest in the 1980s with a worldwide tour and such hit singles as their remakes of "California Dreaming" (1985) and "Wipe Out" (1987) as well as their new single "Kokomo" (1988). In 1998 Carl Wilson died after a year-long battle with cancer.

Beadle, George Wells *(1903–1989)* American geneticist. Beadle graduated from the University of Nebraska in 1926 and gained his Ph.D. from Cornell University in 1931. He then spent two years doing research in genetics at the California Institute of Technology. In 1937 Beadle went to Stanford University, where in 1940 he began working with Edward Tatum on the mold *Neurospora*. From this and similar work Beadle and Tatum concluded that the function of a gene was to control the production of a particular enzyme and that a mutation in any one gene would cause the formation of an abnormal enzyme that would be unable to catalyze a certain step in a chain of reactions. This reasoning led to the formulation of the one gene–one enzyme hypothesis, for which Beadle and Tatum received the 1958 NOBEL PRIZE in physiology or medicine, sharing the prize with Joshua Lederberg, who had worked with Tatum on bacterial genetics.

Beamon, Bob (*1946–*) American athlete who set the world record for the long jump at the 1968 OLYMPIC GAMES in Mexico City. His spectacular jump of 29 feet, 2.5 inches shattered the previous record by 1 foot, 9 inches. Some critics point out that Beamon achieved his record at high altitude and that he was helped by a tail wind; Beamon's supporters feel that he has never gotten the recognition he deserves. Beamon retired from competition before the 1972 Olympics. In 1991 Beamon's record in the long jump was broken by American athlete Mike Powell, who jumped 30 feet, 8 inches.

Bean, Alan (*1932–*) U.S. astronaut. Presently a professional artist, his paintings, like those of Russian cosmonaut-artist Alexei LEONOV, are enhanced not only by his creative imagination but also by his actual experiences; he was the fourth human to walk on the Moon. Bean's moonwalk (November 18, 1969) came after he and Commander Charles CONRAD landed the lunar module of *Apollo 12* on the surface of our nearest space neighbor. It was a near pinpoint landing, about 600 feet away from a U.S. SURVEYOR that had landed 31 months before. Curiously, among the parts of Surveyor returned to Earth, scientists found a colony of bacteria in the foam insulation of its TV camera—alive after two-and-a-half years. It can thus be said that Bean and Conrad "encountered" life on the Moon. In one of the most successful of the APOLLO missions, Bean and Conrad spent over 30 hours walking the Moon's dusty surface before returning to Earth on November 24, 1969. Bean commanded his second and last flight aboard *Skylab 3,* the second of three manned missions on America's first space station. With fellow astronauts Owen Garriott and Jack Lousma, Bean spent over 59 days (July 28–September 25, 1973) conducting experiments and making observations of the Earth and Sun. Although he was in line to command the first shuttle/Spacelab mission, Bean decided to work full time as an artist and resigned from NASA on June 26, 1981.

Beard, Charles Austin (*1874–1948*) U.S. historian and political scientist. After graduating from De Pauw University in 1898, he studied abroad for four years. From 1907 to 1917 he taught political science and history at Columbia University. During this time he became more interested in American history and economics and became an intellectual leader of the Progressive movement. Beard was named director of the Training School for Public Service in 1917, and in 1919 he founded the New School for Social Research. He continued to write on political and historical matters and is considered one of America's most influential historians. With his wife, Mary, Beard began work in 1927 on a four-part series called *The Rise of American Civilization.* His book *A Basic History of the United States* (1944) continues to be a standard text. Beard's writings include *The Development of Modern Europe* (1907), *The Supreme Court and the Constitution* (1912), *President Roosevelt and the Coming of War* (1948) and *An Economic Interpretation of the Constitution of the United States* (1913).

Beard, James Andrews (*1903–1985*) American food authority. In 1945 Beard became the first chef to give cooking demonstrations on network television. A chef, lecturer and syndicated columnist, he wrote or coauthored 24 books, most of which celebrated American food. His best-known work, *James Beard's American Cookery,* published in 1972, is considered a classic. For many years he also ran a New York–based cooking school.

Beat Generation A group of American writers and poets whose work came into international prominence in the 1950s and continues to exercise a worldwide influence. The three key figures of the Beat Generation are novelist and poet Jack KEROUAC (*On the Road,* 1957), poet Allen GINSBERG (*Howl,* 1956) and novelist William BURROUGHS (*The Naked Lunch,* 1962). The term *beat* was originally devised by writer John Clellon Holmes, a friend of Kerouac's, to connote a person who had abandoned the materialism of postwar American life in favor of a bohemian quest for worldly experience and spiritual meaning. Kerouac and Ginsberg first met in 1944 while both were still students at Columbia University; Burroughs, an older Harvard graduate who was holding various odd jobs, joined their circle and exercised a mentor's influence. In the late 1940s Neal Cassady, a brilliant and charismatic blue-collar worker from Denver, befriended Kerouac and became Ginsberg's lover. Cassady's exuberant love of life became a vital source of inspiration for both authors; the central character of *On the Road,* Dean Moriarty, is based upon Cassady.

The Beat Generation literary movement, which also included poets such as Gregory Corso, Lawrence FERLINGHETTI, Gary Snyder and Philip Whalen, celebrated intuition over intellect, impulsive passion over puritanism, and the joys of bohemian simplicity and the open road. It exercised a tremendous influence on the youth of America and helped to spur the social and political protest movements of the 1960s.

Beatles, The British rock and roll group of the 1960s. The Beatles were and remain the most popular band in the history of ROCK and roll. They were more than just a music group—they were a phenomenon, and they influenced and reflected the social history of the 1960s. The group had its origins in Liverpool, England, in the late 1950s when several teenagers got together to play "skiffle" music, a form blending JAZZ and folk music, in local nightclubs. The group performed for several years (under a number of names and with various members) in Liverpool and in Hamburg, Germany, before finally emerging as a hit group in England in 1963. By this time the Beatles had coalesced and had developed a distinctive style that placed them far above run-of-the-mill pop groups. By 1964 "Beatlemania" spread to America and then around the world. The four musicians known to the world formally as the Beatles and informally as the "Fab Four" were guitarists George Harrison (1943–2001) and John LENNON (1940–80), bassist and pianist Paul MCCARTNEY (1942–) and drummer Ringo Starr (born Richard Starkey, 1940–). Manager Brian Epstein (1934–67) and producer-arranger George Martin (1926–) also contributed substantially to the group's success. The Lennon-McCartney songwriting team is now regarded as one of the finest in the history of popular music. The Beatles still hold the record for the most number-one hits (20),

The Beatles with Ed Sullivan (center) (LIBRARY OF CONGRESS, PRINTS AND PHOTOGRAPHS DIVISION)

including "I Want to Hold Your Hand" (1964), "A Hard Day's Night" (1964), "Penny Lane" (1967), "Hey Jude" (1968) and "Let It Be" (1970). Their 1967 album, *Sgt. Pepper's Lonely Hearts Club Band,* is considered a classic. The Beatles stopped giving live performances in 1966 and thereafter devoted themselves to songwriting and recording. The Beatles disbanded in 1970, after several years of increasing tensions among Lennon, McCartney and Harrison. The four musicians went on to new solo careers. Lennon was murdered in New York City in 1980. Despite the death of Lennon and the separate projects of the remaining three members in the 1990s, the Beatles produced the 1995 single "Free As a Bird." The song was composed by combining a 1977 recording by Lennon with vocal contributions from McCartney, Harrison and Starr. It was released as a component of the Beatles' *Anthology* album, which contained 52 unreleased outtakes and demo tracks. Both *Anthology* and "Free As a Bird" fared well on the American and British popular music charts. In November 2001 the Beatles again experienced the loss of a member when George Harrison died of cancer.

Beaton, Cecil *(1904–1980)* English designer and photographer. Educated at Cambridge University, Beaton worked from 1939 to 1945 as a war photographer in the British Ministry of Information. After the war he won acclaim as a photographer in England and the U.S. He was known for his sartorial style and became the favorite photographer of the British royal family, and of the rich and famous in theater, film, ballet

and opera. Beaton's photographs have been published widely in magazines and books. Among the milestones of his career were set and costume designs for the Academy Award–winning films *Gigi* (1959) and *My Fair Lady* (1965). In 1957 he was made Commander of the Most Honourable Order of the British Empire, and in 1960 he received the Legion d' Honneur.

Beattie, Ann *(1947–)* American novelist and short story writer. Her first collection, *Distortions* (1976), established her as an acute observer of self-absorbed contemporary Americans. Her first novel, *Chilly Scenes of Winter* (1976), describes a man with 1960s sensibilities coming to terms with the 1970s. Other works include *Secrets and Surprises* (1979), a collection of short stories, and *Picturing Will* (1989), a novel. Beattie is a frequent contributor to *The NEW YORKER,* where many of her short stories first appeared.

Beaubourg See POMPIDOU CENTER.

Beauvoir, Simone de *(1908–1986)* French philosopher, novelist and essayist. Born in Paris, Beauvoir was one of France's most esteemed writers and was also well known for her left-wing political views and iconoclastic personal life. Her writing embraces EXISTENTIALISM and reflects her rejection of her religious upbringing. Her fiction includes *L'invitée* (1943, translated as *She Came to Stay,* 1949), which depicts a leftist intellectual and his two lovers; *Les Mandarins* (1954), which is based on her love affair with Nelson ALGREN and won the Prix Goncourt; and

Quand prime le spirituel (1979, translated as *When Things of the Spirit Come First,* 1982), a collection of early short fiction. She is, arguably best known for the landmark feminist essay *Le deuxième sexe* (1949, *The Second Sex,* 1953), which has enormously influenced subsequent feminist criticism. Beauvoir was an early champion of abortion rights, safety for factory workers and the rights of the elderly. In *La vieillesse* (1970, translated as *The Coming of Age,* 1972), she assails Western society's treatment of the aged. She was a lifelong companion of Jean-Paul SARTRE, about whom she wrote in *Adieux: A Farewell to Sartre* (1984).

Beaux Arts style Style characteristic of architecture, interior design and related objects (such as textiles and furniture) designed under the influence of the French École des Beaux-Arts during the second half of the 19th century. Beaux Arts design combines a concern for rational, functional planning with a florid decorative style based generally on the classic architecture of ancient Rome and the Renaissance. Many prominent American architects, including Raymond HOOD, George HOWE, Charles Follen McKim and John Russell Pope, studied at the Beaux-Arts in Paris in the late 19th and early 20th century. They introduced Beaux Arts thinking into American architectural education and into their own and their students' work. Outstanding examples of Beaux-Arts design in the U.S. include the New York Public Library by Carrere and Hastings (1897–1911) and Grand Central Station in New York by Warren and Wetmore (1907–13).

Beaverbrook, William Maxwell Aitken (first baron B eaverbrook, 1917) *(1879–1964)* British newspaper owner and political figure. Born in Canada, he was already an extremely wealthy businessman by the time he immigrated to England in 1910. There he established close ties with the Conservative leader Andrew Bonar LAW and soon was elected a Conservative member of Parliament (1910). He was minister of information in 1918 and left Parliament after World War I. He had purchased the *Daily Express* in 1916, and he founded the *Sunday Express* in 1918 and acquired the

Evening Standard in 1923. An influential man of strong prejudices and opinions, he used his newspapers to advocate free trade within the BRITISH EMPIRE and favor imperial isolationism. During the ABDICATION CRISIS, Lord Beaverbrook sided with EDWARD VIII against Stanley BALDWIN, favoring the option of morganatic marriage. He returned to public office during WORLD WAR II in the cabinet of his friend Sir Winston CHURCHILL, assuming a number of important wartime posts. He was minister of air force production (1940–41), minister of supply (1941–42), minister of production (1942) and lord privy seal (1943–45). He continued to be active in his newspapers after Churchill's defeat in 1945.

bebop Bebop, the predominant postwar jazz style, appeared in the mid-1940s largely in reaction to the limitations of big band swing. Bebop, generally a small group affair, emphasized the individual soloist and a highly interactive and dynamic rhythm section. Whereas big bands had relied largely on the contributions of the arranger, bebop, in contrast, put the spotlight on the spontaneously improvising musician. The big bands of the SWING ERA had attracted a mass following because of their danceable beats, attractive singers and entertaining novelty numbers. As the audience for jazz changed, bebop grew in popularity. It was pioneered by alto saxophonist Charlie PARKER, trumpeter Dizzy GILLESPIE, pianists Bud Powell and Thelonious MONK and the drummers Max Roach and Kenny CLARKE, who introduced new levels of virtuosity, harmonic daring and rhythmic audacity. Though bebop has been periodically eclipsed by such alternate jazz styles as the modal and fusion approaches, it has remained jazzdom's most sophisticated and demanding form. For musicians a good part of bebop's challenge comes from its reliance on a repertoire of "standards" from 1930s–40s Broadway and Hollywood shows, whose complex harmonic changes and intriguing melodies continue to constitute a litmus test for a musician's improvisatory mettle. Bebop remained somewhat popular throughout the 1990s, thanks to artists such as trumpeter Wynton MARSALIS and, in the 2000s, the emergence of Norah Jones.

Bechtel, Stephen Davison *(1900–1989)* American businessman, president of the Bechtel Corporation. In 1935 Bechtel assumed control of his family's San Francisco–based business and helped mold it into one of the world's most prominent international construction and engineering firms. Among the projects completed under his guidance were the HOOVER DAM and the San Francisco Bay Area Rapid Transit System. In the 1980s several of his top executives—notably George P. Schultz and Caspar Weinberger—served in key positions in the REAGAN administration.

Beck, Julian *(1925–1985)* American actor and director. In 1947, with his wife Judith Malina, he founded the LIVING THEATRE, which became one of the most influential of all American avant-garde theater companies. The company came to the fore in the 1960s with such landmark productions as *The Connection, The Brig* and *Antigone.* In these and other productions the company aimed for maximum audience involvement and sought to promote revolutionary political ideals. In the mid-1980s, the Becks brought the Living Theatre back to New York City after a long self-imposed exile in Europe.

Beck case Investigation and conviction of the president of the International Brotherhood of Teamsters in 1957. Dave Beck was a aggressive union leader from Seattle who rose to become president of the 1.4-million-member Teamsters' Union. In 1957 he was called before the Senate Select Committee on Improper Activities in Labor or Management, headed by Senator John McClellan of Arkansas. The committee presented evidence that Beck had become a millionaire by siphoning off union funds. Beck was expelled from the AFL-CIO after he asserted his Fifth Amendment right against self-incrimination 7,200 times during the hearings. He was convicted of filing false tax returns and served a prison sentence. After his parole in 1964 he still owed the government $1.3 million in back taxes. This debt was eventually forgiven by the NIXON administration: The Teamsters were among President Nixon's more ardent supporters.

Beckenbauer, Franz *(1945–)* German soccer player and manager—and the only man to have captained and managed a World Cup winning team, in 1974 and 1990, respectively. Beckenbauer first gained recognition as a stylish midfield player for Bayern Munich and West Germany in the 1960s, but his greatest contribution to the game came with his conversion from midfield player to "libero" in the early 1970s. His unsurpassed ability to read the game, combined with his speed and outstanding passing skills, allowed him to orchestrate offensive plays from defensive zones, a novel tactic that produced enormous success for his club and national teams. Bayern captured three European Cups (1974–76), and West Germany won the European Championship in 1972 and the World Cup in 1974, all under Beckenbauer's captaincy. Beckenbauer retired in 1983, after stints with the New York Cosmos and SV Hamburg. In 1984 he was appointed West Germany team manager. Under his guidance West Germany was runner-up in the 1986 World Cup and was the winner of the tournament in 1990.

Becker, Boris *(1967–)* German tennis player. Becker achieved instant tennis stardom when at age 17 he became the youngest competitor to win the Wimbledon men's singles title (1985). His aggressive, rough and tumble style and skinned knees made him an audience favorite. He won Wimbledon again in 1986 and 1989. Although Becker has also won the U.S. Open (1989) and Australian Open (1991), his level of play was sometimes erratic. In 1996 Becker again won the Australian Open. He retired from professional tennis in 1998.

Beckett, Samuel *(1905–1989)* Irish writer who spent most of his creative life in France. Beckett, who won the NOBEL PRIZE in literature in 1969, is closely linked to EXISTENTIALISM by virtue of his absurdist novels and plays that capture the emptiness and desperate humor of modern life, in which abiding values are lacking. Beckett studied at Trinity College, Dublin, before moving to France and establishing a friendship with James JOYCE, who served as Beckett's literary mentor. Beckett's first major work was the comic novel *Murphy* (1937), which showed the influence of Joycean punning and wordplay. In the postwar years came an important novelistic trilogy—*Molloy* (1951), *Malone Dies* (1951) and *The Unnameable* (1953)—written in French, which Beckett had adopted as his new literary language. Beckett also emerged as a master of the THEATER OF THE ABSURD with his 1953 play *WAITING FOR GODOT*, his most famous work and still widely performed. Two other important Beckett plays are *End Game* and *Krapp's Last Tape*, both written in 1958.

Beckham, David Joseph *(1975–)* British soccer star. Born in London, Beckham signed on as an apprentice to the soccer team Manchester United in 1991 and made his league debut four years later at the age of 19. For the rest of the decade he established his reputation as one of England's premier players of soccer. In the 1998–99 season Beckham led the team as a midfielder to an unprecedented "triple crown" win in the Premier League, the FA Cup and the Champions' League. During the 2002–03 season relations between Beckham and Manchester United manager Alex Ferguson deteriorated, leading to rumors that Beckham would join another team. By the time he signed a four-year contract with Spain's Real Madrid team, in June 2003, for the equivalent of more than $41 million, Beckham had scored 86 goals in 397 games for Manchester United for an average of about two goals every nine games, an extraordinary performance for a midfielder.

By the beginning of the 21st century Beckham had become an international celebrity, winning a devoted following in Asia and Latin America. Beckham continued his impressive scoring record with the Madrid team. During his career in Manchester Beckham was also a regular participant in Great Britain's team efforts to qualify for the World Cup. He helped the team to qualify for the 2002 finals by defeating Germany in Munich and then fighting to a 2-2 tie with Greece before being eliminated by Brazil.

In addition to his performance on the soccer field, Beckham gained international attention by his highly publicized marriage to **Victoria Adams**, a member of the pop group Spice Girls. In 2003 Queen Elizabeth II designated Beckham an Officer of the Order of the British Empire.

Beckmann, Max *(1884–1950)* German painter. The expressionist artist was born in Leipzig, studying at the Weimar Academy. In 1906 he moved to Berlin, where he was a member of the Berlin secession from 1908 to 1911. After terrible experiences as a medical corpsman in WORLD WAR I, his style changed from a gently realistic impressionism to a savage and symbolic depiction of the human form that grew more personal and allegorical through the years. Beckmann taught at the Frankfurt Art Institute from 1925 to 1933, when he was dismissed by the Nazis, who branded his art "decadent." He moved to Amsterdam in 1936 and spent the war years there. In 1947 he immigrated to the U.S., teaching at Washington University (1947–49) and the Brooklyn Museum School (1949–50). One of his best-known paintings is the triptych *Departure* (1932–35; Museum of Modern Art, New York City).

Becquerel, Antoine-Henri *(1852–1908)* French physicist. Becquerel's early scientific and engineering training was at the École Polytechnique and the School of Bridges and Highways, and in 1876 he started teaching at the Polytechnique. In 1899 he was elected to the French Academy of Sciences. He held chairs at several institutions and became chief engineer in the department of bridges and highways. Becquerel is remembered as the discoverer of radioactivity in 1896. Following Wilhelm RÖNTGEN's discovery of X-RAYS the previous year, Becquerel began to look for X-rays in the fluorescence observed when certain salts absorb ultraviolet radiation. His method was to take crystals of potassium uranyl sulfate and place them in sunlight next to a piece of photographic film wrapped in black paper. The reasoning was that the sunlight induced fluorescence in the crystals and any X-rays present would penetrate the black paper and darken the film. The experiments appeared to work and his first conclusion was that X-rays were present in the fluorescence. The true explanation of the darkened plate was discovered by chance. He left a plate in black paper next to some crystals in a drawer and some time later developed the plate. He found that this too was fogged, even though the crystals were not fluorescing. Becquerel investigated further and discovered that the salt gave off a penetrating radiation independently, without ultraviolet radiation. He deduced that the radiation came from uranium in the salt. Becquerel went on to study the properties of this radiation; in 1899 he showed that part of it could be deflected by a magnetic field and thus consisted of charged particles. In 1903 he shared the NOBEL PRIZE in physics with Pierre and Marie CURIE.

Bedny, Demyan *(1883–1945)* Soviet poet and propagandist. In the 1920s he was considered to be the chief proletarian poet of the USSR. Official approval was such that LENIN advised GORKY to read Bedny's fables. His RUSSIAN CIVIL WAR poems did much to spur on the fighters, but his poems of the NEW ECONOMIC POLICY period were considered lewd. The obedient puppet of STALIN, he glorified Stalin's policies. Bedny also produced pornographic and antireligious verse. The production of his play *Ancient Warriors,* in which the Orthodox Church is ridiculed, occurred just as the Communist Party proclaimed that the church had had a positive effect on the development of early Russia and brought Bedny's career to a halt. He was later allowed to continue publishing.

Beebe, Charles William *(1887–1962)* American naturalist. Beebe graduated from Columbia University in 1898 and the following year began organizing and building up the bird collection of the New York Zoological Park. After serving as a fighter pilot in WORLD WAR I he became, in 1919, director of the Department of Tropical Research of the New York Zoological Society. Beebe is noted as one of the pioneers of deep-sea exploration. His first observation capsule was a cylinder; later collaboration with the geologist and engineer Otis Barton resulted in the design of a spherical capsule (the bathysphere). Various dives were made, and in August 1934 Beebe and Barton were lowered to a (then) record depth of 3,028 feet near Bermuda. Beebe made many interesting observations, such as the absence of light at 2,000 feet, phosphorescent organisms and an apparently unknown animal estimated to be some 20 feet long. He abandoned deep-sea exploration after making 30 dives. Descents to even greater depths were subsequently made by Auguste Piccard and others.

Beecham, Sir Thomas *(1879–1961)* English orchestral and operatic conductor. The wealthy grandson of a prominent pharmaceutical manufacturer, he attended Oxford University. Instead of going into the family business, he chose a musical career and formed his own orchestra. Musically self-educated, and at first regarded as a dilettante, he gained public attention and critical respect in 1910 when he conducted at the Royal Opera House, Convent Garden; he was later the company's artistic director (1933–40). Beecham also founded two of Britain's leading orchestras, the London Philharmonic (1932) and the Royal Philharmonic (1947). A musician of strong and often idiosyncratic tastes, he championed the music of Mozart, Berlioz, Delius and Sibelius. He gave many concerts throughout Britain, Europe and the U.S.; his performances were noted for their elegance and spontaneity, and his recordings are prized by collectors. Beecham was also acknowledged as one of the great wits of the 20th century.

Beeching, Lord Richard *(1913–1985)* British scientist, businessman and railway director. In 1961, while serving as a director of Imperial Chemical Industries (ICI), one of the largest corporations in Britain, he was asked to join British Transport Commission as chairman-designate of the newly created British Railways Board. In this role, he took radical measures to increase the efficiency and profitability of British Rail. In 1963 he produced the historic and controversial Beeching Report, which called for a much smaller British railway system with far fewer employees. His plan met with much opposition from railway workers and the railway riding public. However, it was adopted and many rural lines and stations were closed. Beeching also succeeded in restructuring the railway's management before departing in 1965, after the Labour Party regained power. That same year he was made a life peer.

Beene, Geoffrey *(1927–2004)* American fashion designer known for his youthful, almost playful approach, combined with respect for traditional craftsmanship and detail. Beene was a medical student at Tulane University in New Orleans before dropping out to relocate in Los Angeles. His fashion sketches led to his enrolling at the Traphagen School in New York and then to study in Paris. In 1962 Beene opened his own firm. His work often crossed the lines between sportswear and more formal costume, using the best of materials and fine details along with generally bright and lively color. An element of humor appeared in his designs, which sometimes verged on the shocking. Beene won many awards, including a 1964 Neiman Marcus Award, eight Coty Awards, and four from the Council of Fashion Designers of America.

Beerbohm, Sir Henry Maximilian *(1872–1956)* British playwright, critic, essayist and caricaturist. Born in London, Beerbohm was educated at Charterhouse School and at Merton College, Oxford. Beerbohm entered the world of the arts and society through his elder half brother, Sir Herbert Beerbohm-Tree. Turning a gimlet eye on the social, artistic and literary personalities of the day, he produced witty caricatures, essays and also drama criticism for the *Saturday Review,* where he succeeded George Bernard Shaw. He was also author of several plays, most notably *The Happy Hypocrite* (1900). His first collection of essays was called *The Works of Max Beerbohm* (1896), followed by *More* (1899), *Yet Again* (1909) and *And Even Now* (1920). In *A Christmas Garland* (1912) he parodied the works of Henry James, H. G. Wells and Rudyard Kipling, among others. He lived primarily in Italy after 1911, but during World War II he broadcast commentaries for the BBC in London; these were collected in *Mainly on the Air* (1957).

Beer Hall Putsch Name given to Adolf Hitler's abortive attempt to overthrow the German Weimar Republic. On November 8, 1923, his Nazi Party storm troopers invaded a large political meeting in a Munich beer hall, coercing Bavarian leaders to proclaim loyalty to the Nazis. But the leaders escaped, mobilized the army against the Nazis and soon arrested Hitler. The fiasco brought him to national prominence, however. During his ninemonth imprisonment Hitler dictated *Mein Kampf,* the bible of National Socialism, to his aide Rudolf Hess.

Begin, Menachem *(1913–1992)* Prime minister of Israel (1977–83). Having emigrated from Siberia to Palestine in 1941, he led Irgun Zvai Leumi extremists. A member of the Knesset (parliament) from 1948, he was a junior minister (1967–70), leader of the right-wing Likud (Unity) Party from 1970 and prime minister on winning the 1977 elections. His premiership was marked by his tough line against the Palestine Liberation Organization (PLO) and on Israeli control of the West Bank of the Jordan, but also by relaxation of tension with Egypt, following talks with President Sadat in 1977. He was joint recipient of the Nobel Prize for peace (with Sadat) in 1978. He retired due to ill health in 1983. (See also Camp David talks; King David Hotel attack.)

Behan, Brendan *(1923–1964)* Irish playwright. Behan was born in Dublin to a lower middle-class family. Active in the Irish Republican Army (IRA) as a teenager, he was arrested in 1939 and spent several years in British borstals (reform schools) and in jail; he later recounted his experiences in the autobiography *Borstal Boy* (1958). His most popular works are *The Hostage* (1958), which showed the influence of Bertolt Brecht, and *The Quare Fellow* (1959). Both were produced in Britain by Joan Littlewood; *The Hostage* was staged in New York and Dublin as well. He also wrote a television play, *The Big House* (1957). Celebrated for his radical views, irreverent wit and public rowdiness, Behan died an alcoholic. An unfinished play, *Richard's Cork Leg,* was posthumously presented at the Abbey Theatre in 1972.

Behrens, Peter *(1868–1940)* German architect. An influential figure in the development of modern architecture, Behrens was born in Hamburg and at first studied painting. He worked as an architect and designer from 1890 to 1898. Moving to Darmstadt in 1899, he joined a leading artists' colony, designing his house and all its furnishings, which were exhibited in the 1901 Darmstadt Exhibition. Behrens made a lasting contribution to modern industrial design with the works he created as architect for the huge Berlin electrical company A.E.G. from 1907 to 1914.

His factory buildings, notably the turbine plant of 1909, are celebrated for their monumental and utilitarian clarity. His other A.E.G. designs, including furnishings, equipment, stationery and catalogs, are early examples of functional modernism. His other works include apartment blocks and workers' housing as well as the Abbey of St. Peter, Salzburg, and the German embassy, Leningrad. An influential teacher, he was a professor of architecture at the Düsseldorf Academy (1921) and director of the architecture school at the Vienna Academy (1922–36) before heading up the architecture department of Berlin's Prussian Academy in 1936. His students included LE CORBUSIER and Ludwig MIES VAN DER ROHE.

Behring, Emil Adolf von (1854–1917) German immunologist. Behring graduated in medicine at Berlin University and entered the Army Medical Corps before becoming (in 1888) a lecturer in the Army Medical College, Berlin. In 1889 he moved to Robert Koch's Institute of Hygiene and transferred to the Institute of Infectious Diseases in 1891, when Koch was appointed its chief. In 1890, working with Shibasaburo Kitasato, Behring showed that injections of blood serum from an animal suffering from tetanus could confer immunity to the disease in other animals. Behring found that the same was true for diphtheria, and this led to the development of a diphtheria antitoxin for human patients, in collaboration with Paul EHRLICH. This treatment was first used in 1891 and subsequently caused a dramatic fall in mortality due to diphtheria. Behring's success brought him many prizes, including the first NOBEL PRIZE in physiology or medicine, awarded in 1901. In 1913 he introduced toxin-antitoxin mixtures to immunize against diphtheria, a refinement of the immunization technique already in use. He also devised a vaccine for the immunization of calves against tuberculosis.

Beiderbecke, (Leon) Bix (1903–1931) American jazz cornetist, pianist and composer—one of the legends of jazz history. Beiderbecke was an astonishingly gifted cornet player who was devoted to his music but died at the young age of 28 from a combination of excessive drinking and ill health. He never achieved great public fame in his own lifetime, but he was highly esteemed among his fellow musicians. In the late 1920s he was the featured cornetist with the Paul WHITEMAN band, with which he made numerous recordings. A gifted piano player, Beiderbecke composed several pieces principally for that instrument, including "In a Mist" and "Candlelights."

Beilby, Sir George Thomas (1850–1924) British industrial chemist. The son of a clergyman, he was educated at Edinburgh University. He began work with an oil-shale company as a chemist in 1868 and increased the yield of paraffin and ammonia from oil shales by improving the process of their distillation. He also worked on cyanides, patenting in 1890 a process for the synthesis of potassium cyanide in which ammonia was passed over a heated mixture of charcoal and potassium carbonate. This had wide use in the gold-extracting industry. From 1907 to 1923 Beilby was chairman of the Royal Technical College, Glasgow, later the University of Strathclyde. He became interested in the economic use of fuel and smoke prevention, submitting evidence to the Royal Commission on Coal Supplies in 1902. In 1917 he was appointed as the first chairman of the Fuel Research Board. He was knighted in 1916.

be-in Be-in is a term that originated in the 1960s to describe a large-scale gathering of people that generally emphasized freedom, spontaneity and a lack of social and sexual inhibitions. The genesis to the be-in concept owed a great deal both to the art world conception of a HAPPENING and to the libertarian outlook that pervaded many of the prominent political and psychological theories of the era. Be-ins were usually organized in open public spaces, such as parks, and invited all comers to participate in a spirit of peace and joy. Activities were unstructured and ranged from political protest to free-form theatrical and musical events to frank sexuality to friendly, innocuous conversation.

Being and Nothingness Influential philosophical work by the French writer Jean-Paul SARTRE. Being and Nothingness (1943) was written prior to the onset, in the late 1940s, of Sartre's political commitment to Marxism, a commitment that showed itself strongly in his philosophical writings thereafter. Nonetheless, Being and Nothingness stands as Sartre's most famous work, a seminal text of EXISTENTIALISM. In it Sartre argued that there was no a priori value structure to human existence. Existence and activity alone could define the essence and meaning of one's life. Absolute freedom was thus the natural human condition—in Sartre's famous phrase, man is "condemned to liberty." Genuine "being" consists in seizing and making use of this freedom and thereby emerging from the "nothingness" that submerges the passive man who seeks to justify his life in terms of accepted bourgeois values, externally imposed philosophical systems or religious dogma.

Beirut Capital of LEBANON, located on its Mediterranean Sea coast. Conquered by French troops during WORLD WAR I, Beirut was made capital of Lebanon in 1921, pursuant to a French mandate awarded by the LEAGUE OF NATIONS. It was held by French and British forces during WORLD WAR II and was declared the national capital in 1945 when Lebanon earned its independence. In recent decades it has been the site of Palestinian refugee camps and of violent fighting between various Christian and Muslim paramilitary factions. Numerous Westerners have also been taken hostage by terrorists in Beirut. In June 1982 the city was invaded by Israeli military forces seeking to oust PALESTINE LIBERATION ORGANIZATION guerrillas who had used it as a key base of operations against Israel. In September 1982 in spite of the presence of Israeli troops, Lebanese Christian Phalangists massacred Palestinians in the SABRA AND SHATILA refugee camps. By October an international peacekeeping force had helped to restore order, but the massacre spurred major political debate in Israel. U.S. forces withdrew after several terrorist attacks on their base caused high American casualties. Devastation continued in the late 1980s in fierce fighting between rebel Christian leader General Michael Aoun and Syrian and other Muslim forces. Aoun was finally forced to surrender in October 1990, and the city assumed a semblance of calm for the first time in many years. Beirut remains a theater of conflict between Israel and Arab terrorist groups devoted to Israel's destruc-

tion, such as HEZBOLLAH. In August 2003 the Israeli army orchestrated a bombing in Beirut that killed Hezbollah militant Ali Hussein Saleh. (See also LEBANESE CIVIL WAR OF 1975–1990.)

Béjart, Maurice (Maurice Berger) *(1928–   )* French dancer and choreographer. The son of philosopher Gaston Berger, Béjart studied at the Marseille Opera Ballet School and danced with the Marseille Opera Ballet until 1945, then joined the Ballets de Roland Petit (1947–49) and the International Ballet. He first became known and celebrated as a choreographer in the 1950s for work that synthesized elements of ballet, modern, jazz and acrobatics. He formed a company of his own (Ballets Romantiques, then Ballet de l'Étoile) in 1953. In 1960 he formed the Belgium-based Ballet of the Twentieth Century, which showcased his eclectic explorations of dance in such works as *Contes d'Hoffman* (1961), *Damnation de Faust* (1966) and *Symphonie pour un Homme seul* (1971). Controversially, Béjart has staged unambiguously sexual scenes, including nudity, and characteristically works in a heroic mold. He has also worked as a director of operas, and as director of the Béjart Ballet Lausanne. In 1994 Béjart was inducted into the Académie des Beaux-Arts.

Bejerot, Nils *(1921–1988)* Swedish physician and psychiatrist. Bejerot won worldwide recognition for his investigation into the spread of drug addiction and his search to find ways of preventing that addiction. He remained a controversial figure in Sweden because of his emphasis on the prevention rather than the treatment of drug abuse. Until his retirement in 1987, he was a professor in the Department of Social Medicine at the Karolinska Institute.

Belafonte, Harry (Harold George Belafonte) *(1927–   )* American folksinger. Although he was born in New York, Belafonte spent many years in his parents' native Jamaica. There he developed a love for the calypso music of the West Indies that became his trademark. During the 1950s his calypso hits included "Jamaica Farewell" (also known as the "banana boat song"), "Matilda" and "Mary's Boy Child." Belafonte also appeared in a number of films, including *Carmen Jones* (1953)

Calypso musician, actor and human rights activist Harry Belafonte, photographed by Carl Van Vechten, 1954 (CARL VAN VECHTEN COLLECTION, LIBRARY OF CONGRESS, PRINTS AND PHOTOGRAPHS DIVISION)

and *Island in the Sun* (1957). Belafonte has since occasionally appeared in films, such as *Kansas City* (1996) by Robert Altman.

Belarus (Byelorussia, Belorussia, White Russia) Territory of the Russian Empire (1795–1917), German-controlled territory (1918), Soviet Socialist Republic (SSR) (1919–91) and independent nation (1991–   ). Brought under Russian rule through the successive partitions of Poland in the 18th century, the people of Belarus endured Russian repression of their Uniate Church (feared for its subservience to the pope in Rome) and Belarus noble houses that had served the Polish monarch in order to ensure the territory stayed under Russian control. Russian vigilantes also regularly conducted pogroms, or raids, on the large Jewish communities residing in Belarusian cities such as Minsk. In December 1917, a month after the BOLSHEVIKS came to power in Russia, they thwarted Belarusian efforts to establish a republican government. The Belarusians gained a brief respite from the Bolsheviks in March 1918, when the Treaty of BREST-LITOVSK ended the fighting between the Bolsheviks and Germany that had occurred during WORLD WAR I and made Belarus an os-

tensibly independent country but in reality a German-controlled territory. However, when Germany surrendered to the Allies in western Europe on November 11, 1918, it withdrew its forces in eastern Europe and left Belarus open to a Bolshevik invasion that occurred in January 1919 and established Belarus as an SSR of the Russian Soviet Federated Soviet Republic. Following its reabsorption by Russia, Belarus was divided further in 1921 after the Russo-Polish War, with a portion of the SSR going to Poland, and the rest remaining within Bolshevik Russia. In December 1922 this smaller Belarus SSR joined with three other SSR's to form the Union of Soviet Socialist Republics. While the cultural repression of Belarusians ended under the early Soviet rule, it began anew with the emergence of Joseph STALIN, who purged the SSR of any nationalist, religious and cultural figures independent of his control through exile, forced labor camps and executions. Repression of Jewish Belarusians increased during WORLD WAR II when Adolf HITLER gained control of the province and extracted many Jews for labor details and mass executions as part of his FINAL SOLUTION. In part because of Hitler's treatment of Belarusian Slavs and Jews, considered "inferior" by Hitler, many Belarusians waged a guerrilla war against Nazi forces and officials in the region until it was again under Soviet control in 1944. After World War II ended in 1945, Soviet development of Belarus increased and resulted in more heavy industrial factories for the production of products like automobiles in Belarusian cities, which created more jobs within the region and increased the urban population of Minsk and other such cities in which these factories were located. In order to provide these factories with power, Soviet officials built power plants, many of which produced their electricity from nuclear chain reactions controlled in nuclear reactors. In 1986 an experiment went haywire in of these reactors at the power plant in Chernobyl, in the Ukrainian SSR, which resulted in the chain reaction growing beyond the technicians' abilities to control it, leading to the entire facility's evacuation and the contamination of much of Belarus through radioactive particles that escaped the

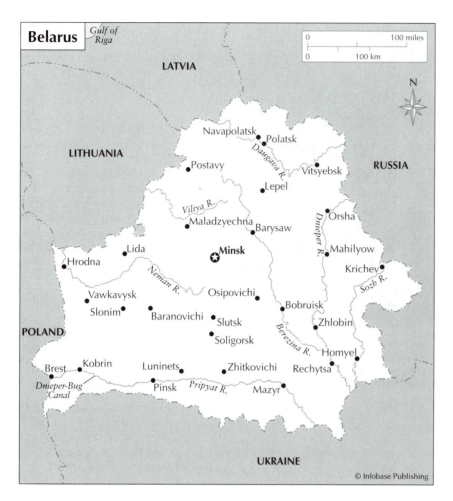

Belarus

Gulf of Riga

LATVIA

LITHUANIA

RUSSIA

POLAND

UKRAINE

Navapolatsk
Polatsk
Daugava R.
Postavy
Vitsyebsk
Lepel
Viliya R.
Maladzyechna
Barysaw
Orsha
Dnieper R.
Lida
Minsk
Mahilyow
Hrodna
Krichev
Neman R.
Osipovichi
Sozh R.
Vawkavysk
Slonim
Baranovichi
Bobruisk
Slutsk
Zhlobin
Soligorsk
Berezina R.
Kobrin
Luninets
Zhitkovichi
Homyel
Brest
Rechytsa
Dnieper-Bug Canal
Pinsk
Pripyat R.
Mazyr

N

0   100 miles
0   100 km

© Infobase Publishing

confines of the reactor and were swept by winds across Belarus and other parts of the world. Two years after the CHERNOBYL DISASTER, Belarusians took advantage of the new civil liberties permitted under Soviet leader Mikhail GORBACHEV's policy of GLASNOST, or "openness," and founded the Belarusian Popular Front (BPF), an organization dedicated to promoting Belarusian culture as distinct from Russian culture. The increasing presence of the Belarusian language, religion and other cultural aspects that resulted from the activities of the BPF inspired the Communist members of the Belarusian Supreme Soviet (Belarusia's parliament) to declare that its decisions superceded those of the Supreme Soviet (the national parliament). After the failed hard-line Communist coup in August 1991, Belarus declared its independence on August 25, and its Supreme Soviet designated Stanislau Shushevich as its new head of state. Four months after the state's creation, Shuskevich conferred with Russian president Boris YELTSIN and Ukrainian president Leonid Kravchuk and agreed to form the COMMONWEALTH OF INDEPENDENT STATES (CIS), an international federation of former

	BELARUS
1914–18	Belarus is the site of fierce fighting between Germany and Russia during World War I.
1918–19	Belarus is briefly independent from Russia.
1919–20	Poland and Soviet Russia battle over control of Belarus.
1921	West Belarus is ruled by Poland; East Belarus becomes a Soviet republic.
1930s	Agriculture is collectivized despite peasant resistance. More than 100,000 people, chiefly writers and intellectuals, are shot in mass executions ordered by the Soviet dictator Joseph Stalin.
1939	West Belarus is occupied by Soviet troops.
1941–44	The Nazi occupation results in the death of 1.3 million people, including many Jews; Minsk is destroyed.
1944	The Soviet Red Army drives Nazi forces out of Belarus.
1945	Belarus is reunited with the Soviet Union and admitted as a founding member of the United Nations.
1960s–70s	The Soviet government closes Belarusian language schools and emphasizes the Russian language.
1986	An explosion at the nuclear power station at Chernobyl, in the neighboring Soviet state of Ukraine, contaminates 20% of Belarus's territory and a large portion of its population with high-radiation fallout. Mikhail Gorbachev initiates his programs of glasnost and perestroika.

1988	The Belarusian Popular Front (BPS) is formed with the goals of restoring Belarusian culture and language and eliminating repressive Stalinist policies.
1990	The Byelorusian parliament declares that the laws of the republic take precedence over those passed by the Soviet Union.
1991	On August 19 the BSSR is renamed the Republic of Belarus . . . . seven days later, the Supreme Soviet of the BSSR suspends the Communist Party of Belarus.
1994	In March the Supreme Soviet adopts a constitution that declares Belarus a unitary, democratic, social-oriented and legal state. Alyaksandr Lukashenko is elected as the first president of Belarus.
1996	The 1994 constitution is amended to extend Lukashenko's term until 2001.
1997	The Treaty on Union of Belarus and Russia, calling for the merger of Belarus with Russia, is signed. The United States cuts off aid to Belarus because of the new authoritarian government.
1998	The United States and all 15 European Union countries ban officials from Belarus.
2000	Parliamentary elections are criticized by election observers as undemocratic. Turnout in some constituencies is so low that new elections will be necessary.
2001	Lukashenko is reelected to a second term. Opposition leaders and international electoral observers allege irregularities.
2002	President Lukashenko rejects President Putin's proposition to unite the governments of Russia and Belarus into one state adhering to the Russian parliament and constitution.
2004	The Council of Europe denounces the state of human rights advocacy in Belarus, particularly in regard to the lack of investigation following the disappearance in 1999 and 2000 of four men with links to the government's opposition party. A referendum vote scraps previous legislation that allowed a president to serve for only two terms. At the same time, opposition parties fail to place a single representative in the 110 seats in parliament. Criticism arises from the West, calling into question the fairness of the elections; in agreement, thousands of agreeing protesters invade the streets and many are arrested.
2005	Lukashenko extends an invitation to Fidel Castro to visit Belarus in the hope of developing a bilateral relationship with Cuba.

Soviet republics designed to preserve economic, military and diplomatic unity among the new states they had possessed under the Soviet Union.

After independence Belarus encountered domestic problems stemming from the Communist Party's efforts to maintain its control over the Supreme Soviet. In 1992 Communist legislators thwarted a BPF drive to call for new national elections that would have removed the Communists from office. Two years later, a Communist-led effort removed Shuskevich from office on charges that he had engaged in government corruption and replaced him with his prime minister, Vyacheslau Kebich; however, this precipitated a wave of antigovernment opposition that led to Kebich's defeat

at the hands of a young candidate named Aleksandr Lukashenko in the presidential election in July of 1994. Despite authoritarian actions by Lukashenko, such as electoral fraud, his dissolution of the Supreme Soviet in 1996 and repression of the BPF, he has enjoyed surprisingly high popularity in Belarus. As president, Lukashenko has solidified Belarus under his control and moved the country toward greater union with Russia. In 1998 he and Yeltsin arranged to create a common currency, tax base and trade policy between the two states by the end of 1999. When Vladimir PUTIN succeeded Yeltsin as Russian president, Lukashenko rejected Belarusian alignment with Russian policies.

Belasco, David (1853–1931) American playwright, producer, stage manager and theater owner whose innovations in popular melodrama and realism at the turn of the century marked an important phase of American stagecraft. Belasco was born in San Francisco to Portuguese Jews recently emigrated from England. He filled his early years with touring as an actor and collaborating as a playwright, with important writers of the time like James A. Herne and Dion Boucicault. After his arrival in New York City in 1882 as stage manager for the Madison Square Theater, he began writing and producing plays noted for their flair for, by turns, thrilling melodrama and intimate realism. By the turn of the century Belasco was one of the most

Belgium

North Sea

Zaventem

NETHERLANDS

Zeebrugge
Blankenberge   Knokke-Heist
Oostende
Brugge
(Bruges)
Nieuwpoort
De Panne   Veurne   Torhout
Diksmuide

Turnhout
Beveren   Antwerp   Mol   Lommel
Herentals
Sint-Niklaas   Geel   Hechtel
Lokeren   Hoboken   Lier
Gent   Willebroek   Beringen
(Ghent)   Mechelen   Diest   Genk
Schelde R.   Dendermonde   Demer R.   Aarschot   Hasselt
Warégem   Vilvoorde
Roeselare   Aalst   Zaventem   Louvain   Sint-Truiden
Poperinge   Oudenaarde   Brussels ✪   Overijse   Tienen   Tongeren
Ieper   Kortrijk   Waterloo
Ronse   Geraardsbergen   Halle   Wavre   Liège   Eupen
Ath   Braine-l'Alleud   Verviers
Tournai   Soignies   Nivelles   Gembloux   Meuse R.   Spa   Malmédy
Mons   La Louvière   Huy   Stavelot
Binche   Charleroi   Namur   Ourthe R.
Sambre R.   Beaumont   Dinant   Marche-en-Famenne
Philippeville   Rochefort
Chimay   Couvin   Bastogne
Neufchateau

North
Sea

FRANCE

GERMANY

LUXEMBOURG

Arlon
Virton   Aubange

N

0   30 miles
0   30 km

© Infobase Publishing

powerful and influential men of the theater. He opened two theaters of his own, the Belasco and the Stuyvesant, in an ongoing conflict with the controlling interests of the notorious New York–based Syndicate. In 1913 he turned to the new medium of the motion picture to ensure his plays could reach wider audiences. The Protective Amusement Company in association with the BIOGRAPH company released movies of his De Mille collaborations. The Jesse L. Lasky Feature Play Company, in association with director Cecil B. DE MILLE, released *The Girl of the Golden West* and *The Warrens of Virginia*, among others, in 1914. The decline of Belasco in later years was in part due to his resistance to the growing "Little Theater" movement and to emerging playwrights like Eugene O'NEILL. He is regarded today not as a great playwright but as an innovator of scenic, electrical and aural stage effects.

Belau Belau is composed of over 200 islands at the western end of the Car-

oline Islands chain in the Pacific Ocean; total land area is 177 square miles. From 1921 the territory of Micronesia, of which Belau is part, was administered by Japan under a LEAGUE OF NATIONS mandate. After withdrawal from the league in 1935, Japan constructed military installations on the islands, which became strategically important during WORLD WAR II. All of Micronesia became a UNITED NATIONS trusteeship under U.S. administration in 1947. After Belau rejected a territorial constitution in 1978, the trust territory was dissolved. With its own constitution approved in 1981, Belau signed a Compact of Free Association (1982) with the U.S., giving America the right to install military installations. However, the compact had yet to be ratified because of conflict between a ban on nuclear weapons in Belau's constitution and a clause permitting them in the compact. In 1993 a referendum amended the constitution to allow the compact to enter into force.

Belém (Santa Maria de Belém do Grao Pará) Capital of Pará state in northern Brazil and key port for the vast Amazon basin. During the rubber production boom of the late 19th and early 20th centuries, Belém expanded as a commercial center. The GREAT DEPRESSION of the 1930s brought hard times. After WORLD WAR II, Belém grew again due to increased development in the basin.

Bel Geddes, Norman (*1893–1958*) American industrial and stage designer with a prominent role in the use of STREAMLINING in the design style of the 1930s. Bel Geddes was born in Michigan and studied briefly at the Art Institute of Chicago before establishing his own office as an industrial designer. His work included Toledo scales, Philco radio cabinets and a Graham Page automobile, but his influence was greatest through the publication of unrealized, generally futuristic projects. His 1932 book, *Horizons*, described and illustrated such projects as a fully streamlined ocean liner and a huge passenger airplane with public lounges, promenade decks (in the wings) and a gymnasium. His best-known and most influential work was the FUTURAMA exhibit for GENERAL MOTORS at the 1939 NEW YORK WORLD'S FAIR in which visitors traveled above a model landscape complete with cities and highways as Bel Geddes anticipated they might be in the future. The exhibit is often credited as a major force in the development of modern superhighways.

Belgian Congo Former Belgian colony in south-central Africa, now the independent nation of Democratic Republic of CONGO (formerly ZAIRE). In the 1870s British explorer Henry M. Stanley was hired by Belgian king Leopold II to help expand Belgian power in Africa. As a result, the Congo Free State was established as a personal possession of Leopold II in 1885, with borders roughly corresponding to those of present-day Democratic Republic of Congo. The European population remained small, while native laborers were grossly exploited. This led to an international scandal in 1904, when Britain brought the extent of Congo exploitation to the world's attention. The Belgian government responded by annexing the Congo Free State in 1908 and reopening it to free trade. During WORLD WAR I, it was a base of operations against German colonial forces in Africa. Free trade led to development of natural resources; the diamond and copper deposits of the Katanga (now Shaba) region led to the Congo becoming the world's leading supplier of these commodities by 1928. During WORLD WAR II, it was a major raw material supplier for the Allied war effort. After the war the colonial economy boomed, but resistance to Belgian colonial rule culminated in riots in the capital city of Leopoldville (renamed Kinshasa in 1966) in 1959. In 1960 Belgium granted independence to the country.

Belgium Country in northeastern Europe; a highly industrialized, densely populated lowlands nation. First established as an independent state by the London Conference of 1830–31, it expanded economically under the rule of

BELGIUM	
1908	Belgium annexes the Congo.
1909	Death of King Leopold II, succeeded by Albert I.
1914	Germany invades Belgium in opening days of World War I.
1925	Locarno Pact sets aside neutrality forced on Belgium since the 19th century.
1932	Flemish language accorded equal status with French.
1934	Albert I dies in accident; Leopold III crowned.
1940	Belgium invaded after attempting to remain neutral in World War II.
1946	Belgium, Netherlands, Luxembourg sign Benelux economic pact.
1951	Unpopular Leopold III abdicates, succeeded by his son as Baudoin I.
1958	Women gain right to vote.
1962	Congo and other colonies gain independence.
1971	New constitution recognizes separate Flemish, Walloon and French cultural communities.
1986	Former prime minister Boeyants convicted of tax evasion and fraud.
1991	Belgium sends fighter planes to Turkey as part of Allied coalition against Iraq in Persian Gulf War.
1993	King Baudouin dies. His brother, Albert, becomes king.
1995	Belgium creates Flemish Brabant and Walloon Brabant from the former Brabant province.
1998	Belgium agrees to adopt the euro currency on January 1, 1999, for electronic transactions and January 1, 2002, for coin and paper money.
1999	Prime Minister Jean-Luc Dahaene's center-left coalition resigns; a new center-right coalition comes to power led by Guy Verhofstadt of the Liberal Party.
2003	Verhofstadt begins a second term as prime minister.

King Leopold II (1865–1909) and forged a valuable colonial empire in Africa (see BELGIAN CONGO). Its two major ethnic regions are Flemish-speaking FLANDERS in the north and French-speaking Wallonia in the south. In the 1960s political conflict between these two groups threatened the unity of the nation. The capital, BRUSSELS, is home to both languages and also serves as headquarters of the EUROPEAN COMMUNITY and of NATO (North Atlantic Treaty Organization). The German invasion of Belgium in WORLD WAR I was met by the British Expeditionary Force, but—except for the vicinity of YPRES—

Belgium was held by Germany throughout the war; some of the most bloody battles of that war were fought on Belgian soil. The nation was again occupied by Germany in WORLD WAR II. In 1948 Belgium joined the BENELUX economic union, with the Netherlands and Luxembourg, and was a founding member (1951) of the EUROPEAN COAL AND STEEL COMMUNITY. The 1985 decision to base U.S. CRUISE MISSILES in Belgium caused political controversy. In September 2002 Belgium decriminalized euthanasia.

Belgrade Capital of the former YUGOSLAVIA and present-day SERBIA AND MONTENEGRO. Located at the juncture of the Danube and Sava Rivers, it occupies a key position in trade routes between the BALKANS and central Europe and has also been the site of numerous battles. By 1867 the newly-independent Serbs had thrown off the centuries-long shackles of Ottoman rule, declaring Belgrade their new capital. In 1915, during WORLD WAR I, the country was conquered by the CENTRAL POWERS, which occupied Belgrade. In 1918 a new Kingdom of the Serbs, Croats and Slovenes was declared and subsequently named Yugoslavia. During WORLD WAR II Belgrade was held by German forces from 1941 to 1944. It remains the center of commerce and is well known for its elegant parks and palaces. In 1999 Belgrade came under NATO-led air strikes in an effort to force Yugoslav leader Slobodan MILOŠEVIĆ to end his suppression of the Kosovars.

Beliveau, Jean Arthur (1931–) Canadian athlete. The captain of the Montréal Canadiens hockey team during their dynastic run of the 1960s, Beliveau was known as a gentlemanly and unselfish player. A two-time Hart Trophy winner as most valuable player, he also won the Conn Smythe Trophy in 1965 as the Stanley Cup playoff's most valuable player. A gifted passer and playmaker, he finished his career with 507 goals and 712 assists. He was named to the Hockey Hall of Fame in 1972.

Belize Nation in Central America bordered on the north by Mexico and on the south and west by Guatemala; formerly known as British Honduras. The capital is BELMOPAN and the largest

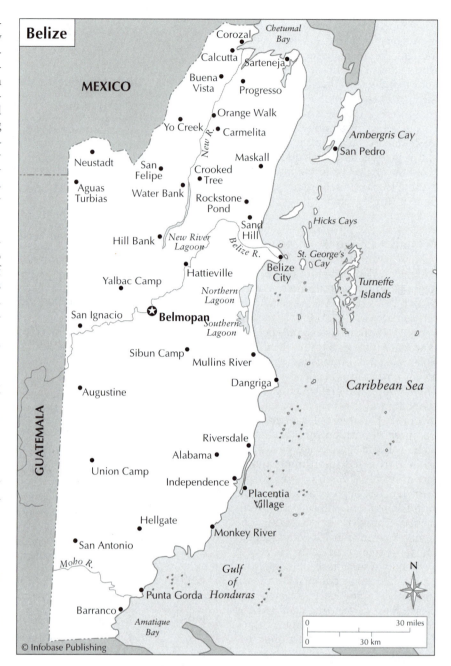

city is BELIZE. From 1862 to 1884 it was subject to the rule of British colonial authorities in Jamaica but thereafter designated as an individual colony under the name of British Honduras. In 1964 it was granted internal autonomy by Britain. In 1973 it was designated as the Colony of Belize. In 1981 it was accorded independence within the British Commonwealth. During this period Britain and Guatemala entered into a dispute over the latter's claims, stemming from an 1859 treaty, to certain of the territory of Belize. In 1992 Guatemala formally recognized Belize but in 1994 took up again its territorial claims. The population of Belize, unlike that of the rest of Central America, is English-speaking and largely of black African ancestry.

Bell, Alexander Graham (1847–1922) Inventor of the telephone, who also designed early telephone instruments and made a contribution to the development of aircraft. Born in Scotland, Bell moved to Canada in 1870 and then to the U.S. in 1872. The first telephone was demonstrated in 1876, and the first commercial

---

BELIZE

1964	Belize is granted internal self-government.
1973	The country's name is legally changed from British Honduras to Belize.
1981	Belize becomes independent
1988	The Joint Commission is established to examine territorial dispute issues. This is an unofficial recognition by Guatemala of Belize sovereignty.
1990	Belize holds official talks with Guatemala in an effort to settle their long-standing border dispute.
1991	Belize becomes a member of the Organization of American States (OAS).
1992	Guatemala formally recognizes Belize.
1994	Guatemala reasserts its territorial claims.
2000	Guatemala announces that it will pursue its claim to half of Belize through international courts.
2005	Private and public workers commence a strike to protest against tax increases and other budgeting measures, and to demand salary increases. Widespread rioting breaks out in Belmopan during surges of political protests.

---

model, a simple wood box of Bell's own design, was introduced in 1877. In 1907 Bell organized the Aerial Experiment Association (AEA) to promote work on aircraft design and was the designer of a spectacular man-lifting kite. In spite of their striking appearance, Bell's aircraft designs were not particularly successful and never equaled the earlier (1903) efforts of the WRIGHT BROTHERS.

Bell, (Arthur) Clive Heward (*1881–1962*) British critic and author. Born into a wealthy country family, Bell was educated at Marlborough College and Trinity College, Cambridge, where he met many of the people with whom he would later form the BLOOMSBURY GROUP. In 1907 he married Vanessa Stephen (see Vanessa BELL), the elder sister of Virginia WOOLF. Noted for his ability to write evocatively about the visual arts, he contributed regularly to the *New Statesman* and *Nation*. He was a friend of Roger FRY, who coined the term POSTIMPRESSIONISM, of which Bell

was a great admirer. In *Art* (1914) he attempted to develop a cohesive theory of visual art and put forth the notion of "significant form," which held that form is the most important component of visual art. In *Civilization* (1928) he reasoned somewhat ironically that civilization depends upon the leisured elite. Other works include *Poems* (1921), *An Account of French Painting* (1931) and a memoir, *Old Friends: Personal Recollections* (1956).

Bell, James "Cool Papa" (*1903–1991*) American baseball player. The greatest star of the NEGRO LEAGUES, Bell was known for his outstanding speed. He played from 1922 to 1950, including 21 seasons of winter ball, which totaled 50 seasons of pro baseball. While statistics are sketchy, he was renowned for both his fielding and his batting ability, hitting over .400 several times. He himself estimated that he once stole 175 bases in a 200-game season. He was named to the Baseball Hall of Fame in 1972.

Bell, Vanessa (Vanessa Stephen) (*1879–1961*) The elder sister of Virginia WOOLF, she married the critic Clive BELL in 1907. She is known chiefly for these associations and as a member of the BLOOMSBURY GROUP. After 1914 she lived with the painter Duncan GRANT.

Belleau Wood (Bois de Belleau, Bois de la Brigade Marine) French village northeast of Paris and northwest of CHÂTEAU-THIERRY. It was the site of a major and bloody battle between Allied and German forces from June 6 to 25, 1918, during WORLD WAR I. U.S. troops, primarily the Fourth Marine Brigade, combined with French forces to half a German offensive directed at Paris as a part of the Second Battle of the MARNE. Losses were heavy. In 1923 the battlefield was dedicated as a permanent memorial to U.S. servicemen slain during the war.

Belli, Melvin (*1907–1996*) American attorney and author who revolutionized trial practice by the introduction of physical evidence in tort claim cases. Highly visible and well known to the public, Belli was dubbed the "King of Torts" for his success on behalf of injured clients. Through his efforts, and those of ATLA—the American Trial Lawyers Association, an organization he helped to found—injured plaintiffs were able to battle large corporations and insurers on an equal basis. Indeed, the success of trial lawyers before juries in the later years of the 20th century led some states to limit the amounts that victims could recover. Belli, a graduate of Boalt Hall, was also the editor of the multivolume treatise *Proof of Facts* and the author of *My Life on Trial*. A flamboyant character both inside and outside the courtroom, he gained notoriety as the attorney for Jack RUBY, the killer of Lee Harvey Oswald, who had assassinated President John F. KENNEDY. Belli's law office, located at street level on Montgomery Street in downtown San Francisco, and filled with an eclectic collection of objects, became a well-known stop for tourists visiting the city.

Belloc, (Joseph) Hilaire Pierre (*1870–1953*) British poet and prose writer. With G. K. CHESTERTON, George Bernard SHAW and H. G. WELLS, Belloc was one of the "big four" literary figures in Edwardian England. Born in France of a French father and English mother, he graduated from Balliol College, Oxford, where he was a brilliant student. A prolific and versatile writer, he published some 150 books, including novels, histories, biographies, travel books and poetry collections. He published several collections of essays on literary, social, religious and political topics. He also edited or contributed to some of the most influential journals of the Edwardian period and served as a Liberal member of Parliament (1906–10). His staunch Roman Catholicism (which he shared with Chesterton) was evident in his many essays. He was renowned in his lifetime, particularly through the period of World War I, but his reputation later declined. Today he is best remembered for such books of light verse as *The Bad Child's Book of Beasts* (1896).

Bellow, Saul *(1915–2005)* American writer. Born Solomon Bellows in Lachine, Canada, a suburb of Montreal, to an Orthodox Jewish–Russian émigré family, Bellow moved as a child to Chicago, which was later to be the inspiration and setting for much of his work. In 1933 he entered the University of Chicago but transferred to Northwestern University, where he studied anthropology and sociology and graduated in 1937. After a brief stint in graduate school at the University of Wisconsin, Bellow abandoned his studies to pursue a career as a writer. To make ends meet, he worked for the editorial department of the *Encyclopaedia Britannica* during World War II before serving in the U.S. Merchant Marine in 1944–45. While in the Merchant Marine, Bellow completed most of the work on his first novel, *The Dangling Man* (1947), a treatment of the inner conflicts of a young man waiting to be drafted that was loosely based on Dostoyevsky's *Notes from the Underground* (1864).

Bellow first reached a wide readership with *The Adventures of Augie March* (1953), a moving portrait of a Jewish immigrant in Chicago who seeks to escape his humble beginnings to "make it" in American society, encountering a memorable cast of characters amid a richly evocative description of city life. His later works of the 1950s, *Seize the Day* (1956) and *Henderson the Rain King* (1959), established his reputation as one of America's most respected novelists. In 1962 he was appointed professor on the Committee of Social Thought at University of Chicago, where he combined an active teaching career with writing. His novel *Herzog* (1964), like *Henderson the Rain King*, received the National Book Award. During the turbulent 1960s at the University of Chicago, Bellow became disenchanted with the political Left, which had earlier exerted an important influence on him. This disenchantment was reflected in his novel *Mr. Sammler's Planet* (1970), whose protagonist, an elderly Holocaust survivor, anxiously makes his way through an unpleasant urban environment populated by lower-class pickpockets, uncultured, ill-mannered student revolutionaries and self-centered denizens of the counterculture. In 1975 Bellow visited Israel and recorded his impressions in his first important work of nonfiction, *To Jerusalem and Back* (1975).

Bellow was awarded the Pulitzer Prize and the Nobel Prize in literature in 1976 in recognition of his achievements. In his later years Bellow continued his impressive output of evocative works of fiction, such as *The Dean's December* (1982), *Him with His Foot in His Mouth* (1984) and *Something to Remember Me By: Three Tales* (1992), although they did not receive the critical acclaim that had greeted his earlier novels. In 1993 Bellow left Chicago for Boston, where he taught in Boston University's University Professors' Program.

Bellow was a master of characterization, and some of the protagonists of his novels were based on real-life persons. In his Pulitzer Prize–winning *Humboldt's Gift* (1975), the main character celebrates the memory of the deceased Von Humboldt Fleischer (modeled on the American poet Delmore Schwartz), who never lived up to his great promise but represented the best of literary culture. Bellow's novel *Ravelstein* (2002), which recounts the tale of a closet homosexual college professor who dies of AIDS without acknowledging the nature of his illness, was a thinly veiled reference to his University of Chicago colleague Allan Bloom. Another minor character in the same work was based on Paul Wolfowitz, a Bloom protégé at Chi-

cago who would later become an influential official in the U.S. Defense Department and president of the World Bank. Bellow avowed that "art has something to do with the achievement of stillness in the midst of chaos." In all of his novels he emphasized the psychological challenges that confront the individual seeking to form his identity in the impersonal world of modern industrial society.

Bellows, George Wesley *(1882–1925)* American painter. Born in Columbus, Ohio, he studied painting under Robert Henri in New York City. Inspired by his teacher's vigorous style and everyday subject matter, he developed a direct and unsentimental realism. Deeply humane in approach, his work is among the best produced by the so-called Ashcan School. Bellows was also central in the promotion of lithography as an American art form, and he produced a number of important prints. An influential teacher, he taught for many years at New York's Art Students League and was one of the organizers of the Armory Show. Among his most famous works are his dramatic boxing paintings, such as *Both Members of This Club* (1909; National Gallery of Art, Washington, D.C.) and *Stag at Sharkey's* (1909; Cleveland Museum of Art). He is also known for his landscapes and portraits.

Belmondo, Jean-Paul *(1933–)* French actor. An international film star with great personal magnetism, Belmondo is especially known for his portrayals of appealing outlaws in the vein of Humphrey Bogart. His acting style evokes the techniques of the Nouvelle Vague. International acclaim came with his performances in Jean-Luc Godard's *A Bout de souffle* (1960), *Une femme est une femme* (1961) and *Pierrot-le-fou* (1965). Other important films include *That Man from Rio* (1964) and *Le Guignolo* (1980). Belmondo's performance in the 1995 film production of *Les Misérables* also was noteworthy.

Belo, Carlos Felipe Ximenes *(1948–)* Catholic bishop and political and humanitarian activist for East Timor. Born in Wailakama in what was then the Dutch East Indies, he was educated in the Catholic school system established in the then Indonesian region of East Timor. Belo graduated from the Dare Minor seminary in 1968 after joining the Salesian Society, an order dedicated to helping the poor. Belo studied both Catholic philosophy and theology, eventually receiving his ordination in Lisbon in 1980.

The following year he returned to East Timor (which had been annexed by INDONESIA after the withdrawal of Portuguese colonial authority in 1974). He eventually became the de facto bishop of the Catholic Church in East Timor, reporting directly to Pope JOHN PAUL II instead of responding to the Indonesian Catholic officials who generally acted as intermediaries between diocesan and papal levels.

In 1989 Bishop Belo began to be involved in the emerging struggle for East Timorese independence. In November of 1991, at a funeral for a Timorese youth killed in demonstrations against the government, Indonesian troops fired upon the mourners, killing 271 people in what was later termed the "Dili Massacre." Belo quickly made his residence a sanctuary for protesters against the Indonesian government. In 1994 Belo published an open letter in which he called for a referendum on independence and an expansion of civil liberties.

Belo received the Nobel Peace Prize in 1996, along with his fellow bishop José Ramon-Horta. In September 1999 a UN-observed referendum on the fate of East Timor produced a vote of 78.5% in favor of independence and immediately led to antiseparatist riots and terrorist acts. On September 6, Belo's offices were attacked by mobs and his residence destroyed by militia members, who also killed 25 people on his staff. The following day the Indonesian military arranged for the Royal Australian Air Force to evacuate him to Darwin, Australia, until order was restored in 2000.

In 2002 Belo resigned his ecclesiastical office as a result of ill health.

Beltrán Espantoso, Pedro Gerardo *(1897–1979)* Prime minister and finance minister of Peru (1959–61). Beltrán published the Lima newspaper *La Prensa* from 1934 until it was taken over by the military government in 1974.

Bely, Andrei *(1880–1934)* Russian novelist, poet and literary critic. Bely was the son of an eminent Moscow University mathematician and "became a writer by accident." He became a guiding figure in the Russian Symbolist movement and was an intrepid literary experimentalist in the Joycean mold who, in the eyes of one Soviet critic, was "the most audacious reformer of Russian prose." He wrote many influential works of poetry, literary criticism, memoirs and, most notably, novels such as *St. Petersburg, The Dramatic Symphony, Kotik Letaev* and *The Silver Dove.*

Belyayev, Pavel *(1925–1970)* Soviet military pilot and cosmonaut. Belyayev was commander aboard *Voskhod 2* when fellow cosmonaut Alexei LEONOV made the world's first space walk (March 18, 1965). Upon its return the spacecraft ran into trouble, and Belyayev was forced to take over the controls and make a manual reentry. Although the crew landed safely, they were far off course and after the rigors of their spaceflight were forced to endure two cold days in the wilderness until a rescue team arrived to help them.

Benavente y Martínez, Jacinto *(1866–1954)* Spanish playwright and critic. Recipient of the NOBEL PRIZE in 1922, he wrote over 150 plays. He is noted for his use of satire, irony, psychological probing and social commentary. *Los intereses creados* (1907; produced in New York as *The Bonds of Interest,* 1919) and *La malquerida* (1913; produced in New York as *The Passion Flower,* 1920) are his best-known plays. In addition, he was a columnist for a Madrid newspaper from 1908 to 1912 and became Spain's foremost literary critic.

Ben Bella, Mohammed Ahmed *(1916–   )* Prime minister of Algeria (1962–66). Leader of the extremist **Algerian National Movement** in 1947, he was imprisoned by the French in 1950. He escaped in 1952 and founded the Front de Libération Nationale in 1954. He led the armed revolt against French rule and was captured and imprisoned by the French from 1956 to 1962. First prime minister of newly independent ALGERIA from 1962 to 1965, he was deposed by BOUMEDIENNE's military coup and kept under house arrest until 1979. Ben Bella returned to Algeria in 1990.

Bench, Johnny *(1947–   )* American baseball player. There is little doubt that Bench was one of the greatest catchers ever. The first catcher ever to take National League rookie of the year honors, he spent his entire 16-year major league career (1967–83) with the Cincinnati Reds. The team that became known as the "Big Red Machine" dominated its league competition throughout the 1970s, winning four pennants and two World Series. Twice named the league's most valuable player, he was first-team all-star catcher 13 times and won 10 consecutive Gold Glove awards. He retired in 1983 and was named to the Hall of Fame in 1989.

Benchley, Robert Charles *(1889–1945)* American humorist, editor and writer. Educated at Harvard University, Benchley served as writer and editor for the Curtis Publishing Company and the *New York Tribune.* He later became a regular contributor to a variety of magazines, including *LIFE* and the *NEW YORKER,* and acted in a number of feature films and short comedies. His books include *The Early Worm* (1927).

Benda, Julien *(1867–1956)* French essayist, philosopher and novelist. Benda, born of Jewish parents, was one of the most influential French thinkers of the first half of the 20th century. In the years just prior to World War I, Benda earned a reputation as a fierce polemicist for his essays in opposition to the philosophy of Henri BERGSON. Bergson emphasized creative intuition; Benda, by contrast, was a classicist who held that detached reason was the key to the development of the human spirit. Benda deplored the use of emotional appeals and political polemics. In his most famous work, *The Treason of the Intellectuals* (1927), Benda argued that the supremacy of reason was threatened by a decline in rigor and courage among philosophers. He wrote: "Once the moralist gave lessons to actuality. Now he takes his hat off to it." In the 1930s, Benda lectured at Harvard and became active in antifascist organizations. Other works by Benda include *The Ordination* (1910), a novel, and *Belphegor* (1929), an analysis of French aesthetics.

Bender, Lauretta *(1897–1987)* Child neuropsychiatrist known for the development in 1923 of the **Bender Gestalt**

visual motor test, a neurophysiological examination that became a worldwide standard. She spent many years investigating the causes of childhood schizophrenia and published studies on child suicides and violence.

Benedict XV (*1854–1922*) Roman Catholic pope. Born Giacomo della Chiesa in Pegli, Italy, Pope Benedict XV reigned from September 3, 1914, to January 22, 1922. On August 1, 1917, Benedict offered a seven-point peace plan for ending WORLD WAR I, but it was rejected by the combatant nations. He personally directed Vatican relief efforts during the war.

Benedict XVI (Joseph Alois Ratzinger) (*1927– *) Pope of the Roman Catholic Church (2005—). Born in Bavaria, Germany, in 1927, Joseph Ratzinger joined the HITLER YOUTH in 1941 (membership was required by law after 1936) and was drafted into the German army in 1944 but did not engage in combat. He was briefly interned in an Allied prisoner-of-war camp before being released after the war. He and a brother entered a seminary and were ordained in 1951. He completed a dissertation at the Ludwig-Maximilian University in Munich in 1957 and became a professor of theology at Freising College the following year. After teaching in the theology faculties of the University of Bonn and the University of Münster, Ratzinger participated in (and became a strong supporter of) the SECOND VATICAN COUNCIL (1962–1963) that had been called by Pope JOHN XXIII to institute reforms in the church. After his appointment to a chair in dogmatic theology at the University of Tübingen in 1966, Ratzinger was repelled by the reformist theories of the university's unorthodox theologian Hans KÜNG and the left-wing political activism of the student body. After moving to the University of Regensburg in 1972, Ratzinger began to speak and write about the need to preserve traditional Catholic teachings concerning contraception, ABORTION homosexuality, and other issues.

In 1977 Pope PAUL VI appointed him archbishop of Munich and Freisling and a cardinal. After the accession of Pope JOHN PAUL II in 1978, Ratzinger began a steady ascent through the upper echelons of the church hierar-chy. He became prefect of the Congregation for the Doctrine of the Faith in 1981, was named to the college of Cardinals in 1993 and became the dean of the College in 2002. During his tenure as head of the Congregation for the Doctrine of the Faith, that organization (the successor to the Inquisition) cracked down on modernist tendencies of the church in Latin America known as liberation theology. Ratzinger continued to defend the conservative brand of theology that had become the hallmark of John Paul II's papacy. On the death of John Paul II in 2005, Ratzinger's health problems (which included minor strokes and a heart ailment) dissuaded him from becoming a candidate to replace his deceased mentor. But such was his popularity among the College of Cardinals that he was persuaded to declare his candidacy and was elected as the ninth German pope. He began his papacy with a strong commitment to promoting interfaith dialogue and a determination to continue the policies of his popular predecessor.

Benedict, Ruth (*1887–1948*) American anthropologist. Benedict studied with Franz BOAS at Columbia University, receiving her Ph.D. there in 1923. She subsequently taught at Columbia until her death. Considered one of the most influential anthropologists of the 20th century, Benedict formulated a number of important theories in cultural anthropology and human behavior. She was particularly active in popularizing the notion of cultural relativism. Among her books are *Patterns of Culture* (1934), *Zuni Mythology* (1935) and *Race: Science and Politics* (1940).

Benelux Acronym for *Be*lgium, *Ne*therlands and *Lux*embourg, used as the name of a customs union created in 1948 among the three Low Countries. A treaty establishing an economic union was concluded at The Hague in the Netherlands in 1958 and came into force on November 1, 1960. This provided for free movement of goods, traffic, services and population among the three member states; a common trade policy and coordination of investment; and agricultural and social policies.

Benenson, Peter See AMNESTY INTERNATIONAL.

Beneš, Edvard (*1884–1948*) Czechoslovakian nationalist and diplomat; president of CZECHOSLOVAKIA (1935–38, 1945–48) and the Czechoslovak government-in-exile (1941–45). Beneš was born into a peasant family in Bohemia, then part of the AUSTRO-HUNGARIAN EMPIRE (now in western Czechoslovakia). He studied at the Universities of Prague, Dijon and Paris, earning a doctorate in sociology. Beneš spent World War I in exile in Paris, where he joined Tomáš MASARYK in working for Czechoslovak independence. As the landlocked country's first foreign minister (1918–35) he gave it a strong presence in international affairs. Beneš supported the LEAGUE OF NATIONS and established good relations with France and the USSR. He succeeded Masaryk as president in 1935. In 1938 Beneš was forced to accept the MUNICH PACT that HITLER dictated to British prime minister CHAMBERLAIN, giving Germany the SUDETENLAND of northwestern Czechoslovakia. He thereupon resigned and went into exile. After the German occupation he was joined in exile by other Czechoslovakian leaders, and in 1941 he formed the Czechoslovak government-in-exile, which the Allies recognized as the legitimate government of the country. At the end of the war he accompanied Ludwik SVOBODA's forces into Prague. Beneš sought to maintain democracy in Czechoslovakia despite increasing pressure from the communists. He resigned in despair after the de facto communist coup by Klement GOTTWALD and died three months later.

Benét, Stephen Vincent (*1898–1943*) American poet. Born in Pennsylvania, Benét was educated at Yale and at the Sorbonne. He began publishing poetry while still a student. He is best remembered for his epic poem about the Civil War, *John Brown's Body* (1928), and his later folk opera, *The Devil and Daniel Webster* (1939; filmed 1941), based on his 1937 short story. Benét also wrote five unmemorable novels and worked in HOLLYWOOD as a screenwriter. Other poetry includes *Ballads and Poems* (1931) and *Western Star* (1943), an epic poem published posthumously. His elder brother, **William Rose Benét** (1886–1950), was a journalist who helped found the *Saturday Review of Literature* in 1924 and a poet whose verse autobiography, *The Dust Which Is God* (1941), won a PULITZER PRIZE.

Benetton, Giuliana (*1938– *) Founder of an Italian company in 1965, a manufacturer and retailer of knitwear. With her three brothers, Benetton has built up a firm with over 2,500 shops all over the world offering clothing of simple design in attractive colors. The design of the shops and the merchandise offered are of high quality and support each other in conveying an image of bright modernity. The firm has adopted advanced computer and automation techniques in manufacturing and business management.

Bengal Ancient region in northeastern INDIA, now divided among BANGLADESH and India; a former province of British India. The British took it from the Muslims in 1757, when General Robert Clive defeated Siraj-ud-Daula in the battle of Plassey. When India was granted independence some two centuries later, Bengal was divided along religious lines, with its eastern, Muslim population becoming East Pakistan (Bangladesh). West Bengal is now an Indian state. The region has been marked by political turmoil in recent decades, due to Hindu-Muslim tensions, a large influx of Bangladesh refugees and the efforts of a Maoist group named the Naxalites.

Bengsch, Alfred Cardinal (*1921– 1979*) Roman Catholic archbishop of BERLIN and spiritual leader of 1.4 million Catholics in EAST GERMANY, East Berlin and West Berlin from 1967 until his death. Bengsch was considered a conservative theologian with impressive oratorical skill and was known for his struggle for religious freedom in East Germany.

Ben-Gurion, David (**David Green**) (*1886–1973*) Israeli statesman, considered the "father of ISRAEL." Born in Russia, he immigrated to PALESTINE in 1906. During the 1920s and 1930s he emerged as leader of the Labour Zionists and became leader of the Labour Party. In 1948 he proclaimed the restoration of the state of Israel, becoming its first prime minister. In his two terms (1948–53, 1955–63) he forged the image of Israel as a modern democratic state and consolidated its

Israeli statesman David Ben-Gurion (left) with Richard Nixon, 1960 (LIBRARY OF CONGRESS, PRINTS AND PHOTOGRAPHS DIVISION)

international position. During his premiership, over 1 million JEWS immigrated to Israel. (See also ZIONISM.)

Ben Haim, Paul (**Paul Frankenburger**) (*1897–1984*) German-born composer. After the rise of Adolf HITLER, he fled to Palestine from Germany. By the time of his death, he was Israel's leading composer. His music was late romantic in style. Ben Haim was also known for his attempts to unite Oriental and Occidental musical traditions. His orchestral piece *The Sweet Psalmist of Israel* won the 1957 Israel State Prize.

Benin Nation in West Africa, on the "Gold Coast"; bordered on the west by Togo and on the east by Nigeria. France established its colony of FRENCH WEST AFRICA in the 19th century and actively suppressed the Abomey people, exploiting the country's agricultural production—predominantly cocoa, cotton and palm tree products—until 1960, when it granted independence to "Dahomey," a name of long usage for the region. Extreme political instability followed, with 11 different regimes holding power from 1960 to 1972. A 1972 coup by Major Mathieu Kérékou had as its goal the imposition of a Marxist-Leninist socialist economy. The Kérékou regime has withstood several coup attempts, including a 1977 airborne assault that Kérékou accused France of backing.

Throughout the 1990s Benin maintained a commitment to democratic elections. In the 1999 parliamentary elections, 35 political parties sought representation in Benin's legislature. In 2001 Kérékou was reelected president.

Benn, Gottfried (*1886–1956*) German poet. Trained as an army medical officer at the Kaiser Wilhelm Academy in Berlin, Benn practiced medicine all his life. His first volumes of expressionist verse appeared in 1912–13 (see EXPRESSIONISM). His best works were written in the 1920s. Like the French surrealists (see SURREALISM), Benn attempted to write "absolute" poetry that used language for incantatory effect, dispensing with conventional structure and meaning; as a result, little of his work has been translated. Despite his initial sympathy with NAZISM, the Reich eventually banned his writing as "degenerate." However, he remained in Germany during WORLD WAR II. After 1948 he enjoyed a comeback. His reflections on his political career, *Doppelleben* (*Double Life*), were published in 1950.

Benn, Tony (**Anthony Neil Wedgwood Benn**) (*1925– *) British politician. An aristocrat by birth but socialist by inclination, Benn was a Labour M.P. from 1950 to 1960, when he had to leave the House of Commons because he succeeded his father as the second

BENIN

1914	During World War I French troops from Dahomey participate in the conquest of German-ruled Togoland to the west.
1940–44	During World War II, along with the rest of French West Africa, the country supports the "Free French" anti-Nazi resistance cause.
1960	The Republic of Dahomey is proclaimed, with Hubert C. Maga as president.
1963	Colonel Christophe Soglo leads the first of the country's six coups; Maga is placed under house arrest.
1964	The constitution of the Second Republic is approved by referendum.
1965	Soglo leads his second coup. Apithy and Ahomadegbé are dismissed, and the government is entrusted to Tairou Congacou, president of the National Assembly. Within a month Soglo leads his third coup, assumes full powers and sets up his own administration.
1967	Soglo is toppled in a coup led by Maurice Kouandete, and an interim military administration is formed under the dual leadership of Kouandete and Colonel Alphonse Amadou Alley, who is the official president.
1968	A new constitution—the country's fourth—is approved by referendum; after 74% of eligible voters abstain, the election of president-elect Moumouni Adjou is annulled; the military appoints Emile Derlin Zinsou as president, and his appointment is confirmed in a plebiscite.
1969	Kouandete unseats Zinsou in a coup but is himself ousted in an interfactional struggle in the army
1970	Maga is inaugurated as first president of the Presidential Council. A new constitution is promulgated.
1972	Maga transfers power to Ahomadegbé. Within five months Major Mathieu Kérékou seizes power in the nation's sixth coup.
1974	Kérékou proclaims a Marxist-Leninist state and nationalizes banks and major industries.
1975	Dahomey is renamed the People's Republic of Benin and the Parti de la Révolution Populaire de Bénin (PRPB) is founded as the country's sole political party and as the supreme organ of state.
1977	Government troops reportedly foil a coup attempt by "mercenaries in the pay of international imperialism"; a curfew is imposed throughout the country, and borders and airports are closed.
1984	Kérékou is reelected to a new term in office.
1987	Kérékou resigns from the army to become a civilian leader of government.
1988	After an abortive military coup, nearly 150 officers are arrested.
1989	The ANR reelects Kérékou president. Public-sector workers strike to protest economic problems and austerity programs. Kérékou announces that Benin is abandoning its Marxist-Leninist ideology.
1990	The Loi Fondamentale is abolished, and a High Council of the Republic replaces the National Revolutionary Assembly. The PRPB is abolished and replaced with a new political organization, the Union des Forces de Progrès. The nation approves a new constitution.
1991	Nicephore Soglo defeats Kérékou in the first free presidential elections in nearly 30 years.
1996	Kérékou is elected president in the country's second free election.
2001	Kérékou is reelected president.
2002	Benin becomes a member of the Community of Sahel-Saharan States.
2003	President Kérékou's political party obtains 52 out of 83 in parliamentary seats in the legislative elections.
2005	Alongside political efforts to eradicate female genital mutilation (also known as female circumcision), a practice that was outlawed and criminalized just a year before, Benin plans to host a "No More Excisions" festival.

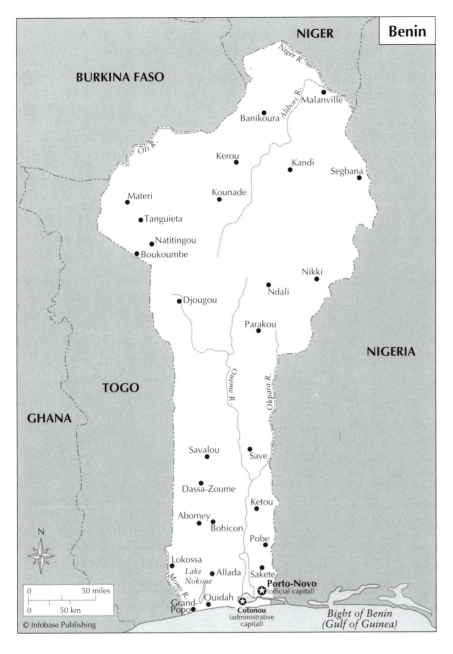

Benin

Forty Years On, in 1968. As a playwright he is known for his use of satire, irony, farce and everyday language. His many successful plays include *Getting On* (1971), *Habeas Corpus* (1973) and *Kafka's Dick* (1986). In addition, he has written several one-act plays and monologues for television. His greatest success was *The Madness of King George III* (1992), which he adapted for film as the slightly retitled *The Madness of King George* (1994), a critical and commercial success in the U.S. that earned him an Oscar nomination. Since then Bennett's creative energies have lagged, leading him to complain in 2001 of writer's block.

Bennett, (Enoch) Arnold *(1867–1931)* British author. Born in the Potteries district of Staffordshire and educated at the Burslem Endowed School and the Middle School of Newcastle-under-Lyme, he went to London in 1888 and began writing. He edited the periodical *Woman* from 1893 until 1902, when he moved to Paris. His first short stories appeared in periodicals in the 1890s; his first novel, *The Man from the North,* was published in 1898. Although he was also a successful playwright, he is best remembered for the series of novels that take place in his provincial birthplace, renamed in the books the "Five Towns." These novels include *Anna of the Five Towns* (1902), *The Old Wives Tale* (1908) and *Clayhanger* (1910). Influenced by the techniques of naturalism practiced by Émile Zola and other French writers, they are wry and yet affectionate, clear-eyed portraits of provincial personalities and their ordinary lives. Bennett returned permanently to England in 1912, continuing his prolific literary output and also contributing a weekly column on books to the *Evening Standard* until his death from typhoid. An important writer, though not a great one, he was one of the last English realists. Much admired in his time, he was later derided by the modernists, but he is still read.

Bennett, Donald Clifford Tyndall *(1910–1986)* Australian-born British aviator. During WORLD WAR II, at the age of 33, Bennett became the youngest air vice marshal in the history of the ROYAL AIR FORCE. He formed and commanded the Pathfinder Force,

Viscount Stansgate. Benn never used his title and campaigned for the right to disclaim it. This led to passage of the Peerage Act (1963), under which Benn became the first person to disclaim an inherited title. Becoming a member of Labour's National Executive Committee in 1962, Benn served in the Harold WILSON government as postmaster general (1964–66), minister of technology (1966–70) and industry secretary (1974–75). Opposed to Britain's entry into the EUROPEAN ECONOMIC COMMUNITY, he was shifted to the Department of Energy, where he served in the James CALLAGHAN government until Labour's

defeat in 1979. In 1981 Benn ran against Denis HEALEY for the deputy leadership of the LABOUR PARTY. Defeated by a narrow margin, the charismatic Benn established himself as a leader of the party's left wing. He lost his seat in 1987 but reentered Parliament in a later by-election. Benn is the author of *Arguments for Socialism* (1979).

Bennett, Alan *(1934–)* British actor and playwright. Bennett initially gained recognition as coauthor of and actor in the 1960 *Beyond the Fringe* revue. His reputation as a playwright was established with his first play, which became the spearhead of Bomber Command's mass attacks on German cities. After the war he became the first chief executive of British Overseas Airways Corp. He was also involved in politics, moving from a LIBERAL PARTY affiliation further to the right as he grew older.

Bennett, Floyd (*1890–1928*) American aviator. After becoming a pilot in the U.S. Navy, Bennett was chosen by Richard BYRD to accompany the MacMillan Expedition to Greenland. On May 9, 1926, Bennett piloted Byrd over the NORTH POLE, in the first successful flight over either Pole. Bennett was awarded the Congressional Medal of Honor as well as a medal by the NATIONAL GEOGRAPHIC SOCIETY. Also in 1926 Bennett made an 8,000-mile test flight around the U.S. to prove the viability of scheduled commercial flights. While planning a trip with Byrd to the SOUTH POLE, Bennett volunteered to rescue two downed German aviators in the Gulf of St. Lawrence. Bennett became ill during the flight and died of pneumonia in Quebec in 1928. Brooklyn, New York's first airport was named for him in 1931.

Bennett, Jill (*1931–1990*) British actress. She specialized in stylish comedy, appearing in such films as *Moulin Rouge* (1952) and *Lust for Life* (1956). She is perhaps best remembered for her role as a heavy-drinking actress in the play *Time Present*, written for her by her second husband, John OSBORNE.

Bennett, Joan (*1910–1990*) American actress; she and her sisters Constance and Barbara, all actresses, were the daughters of stage star Richard Bennett. Bennett began her film career playing ingenue roles and went on to become one of the most glamorous leading ladies of the 1930s and 1940s. Her 75 films ranged from melodramas and thrillers to comedies and included *Bulldog Drummond* (1929), *The Woman in the Window* (1944), *Scarlet Street* (1946) and *Father of the Bride* (1950). In the 1950s, after her film career began to fade, she turned to stage and television. She starred in the gothic daytime soap opera *Dark Shadows* (1966–71), which became a television cult classic.

Bennett, Michael (*1943–1987*) American dancer, choreographer and director. Bennett is best known for the landmark musical *A Chorus Line* (1975), which he conceived, choreographed and directed, with Marvin Hamlisch as composer. The musical won nine Tony Awards, a PULITZER PRIZE and the New York Drama Critics Award. Bennett began his career as a dancer in the musical *West Side Story,* then choreographed the musicals *Promises, Promises* (1968) and *Company* (1971), among other shows. He directed and choreographed the shows *Seesaw, Ballroom* and *Dreamgirls* before his untimely death.

Bennett, Richard Bedford (Viscount Bennett, 1941) (*1870–1947*) Canadian statesman and prime minister (1930–35). A successful businessman and lawyer, he became a member of the Parliament for Calgary in 1911 and leader of the Conservative Party in 1927. After the Conservative electoral victory in 1930, he became prime minister. During his tenure, Bennett advocated free trade within the empire and attempted to deal with the GREAT DEPRESSION through a broad program of social legislation. His government was defeated in 1935, and he retired to England in 1941, where he was made a viscount.

Bennett, Tony (*1926– *) American singer. Tony Bennett (born Anthony Dominic Benedetto) studied both painting and music at New York's High School of Industrial Arts and displayed his paintings in exhibits throughout London, New York and Paris. After serving in World War II, Bennett performed in clubs and lounges while studying singing at the American Theatre Wing School. He eventually became a featured signer and master of ceremonies in Pearl BAILEY's Greenwich Village revue. In 1949 his performances eventually caught the eye of comedian Bob HOPE who recruited him for Hope's Paramount television show and convinced him to change his stage name to Tony Bennett.

In 1950 Bennett signed with Columbia Records and produced several hits in the coming decade. In 1962 he achieved national prominence with his rendition of "I Left My Heart in San Francisco" as part of his act at a sold-out concert in CARNEGIE HALL.

In the 1970s Bennett ended his working relationship with Columbia and recorded for numerous labels. By the 1980s Bennett had returned to Columbia, with which he recorded *The Art of Excellence,* which included a duet with Ray CHARLES. He followed *Excellence* with *Bennett/Berlin,* which paid tribute to Irving BERLIN, a man Bennett considered America's greatest songwriter. His performances at venues in Las Vegas, London and New York continued to attract a large fan base and win critical praise.

Starting in 1993 Bennett began branching out into the alternative rock genre through duets with artists such as k. d. lang and Elvis Costello, which connected the veteran singer with a generation searching for a sound distinct from the band-oriented pop of the late 1980s. The result was an *MTV Unplugged* album that remained at the top of the U.S. jazz music charts for 35 weeks and gained two more Grammys for Bennett, bringing his career total to 10.

Bennett, Ward (*1917–2003*) American furniture and interior designer. Bennett studied art with Hans Hofmann in New York and with the sculptor Constantin BRANCUSI in Paris before working briefly for LE CORBUSIER beginning in 1938. As an interior designer, he was a consultant to SKIDMORE, OWINGS & MERRILL, for example, designing the interiors of the executive offices of the Chase Manhattan Bank in New York. He also designed office and residential projects for a number of private clients. His style was generally quiet, reserved and elegant, with an implication of luxury conveyed through simplicity. Bennett was also active as a sculptor, jewelry designer and designer of china and silver tableware.

Benny, Jack (Benjamin Kubelsky) (*1894–1974*) Born in Chicago, Benny went on to become one of America's most beloved comedians. Beginning as a violinist and singer, he was known onstage as "the Aristocrat of Humor." In 1932 he took his act to radio and gradually formed his own stock company of performers: Mary Livingston (who became his wife in 1927), sidekick Eddie "Rochester" Anderson, Dennis Day and Mel BLANC. By the mid-1930s his show had caught on, and Benny developed his trademark "stingy" character, which included the catchphrase "Now cut that out!" and his brilliantly timed pauses.

Benny continued his radio program until 1955 but was also the star of various television shows and specials from 1950 to 1965. His humor also found its way into the movies, few of them successful; his one unanimously hailed screen role was in the ahead-of-its-time black comedy *To Be or Not to Be* (1942). Benny continued to make television appearances until his death in 1974.

Benois, Alexandre *(1870–1960)* Russian designer, painter and art historian. Born the son of an architect in St. Petersburg, Benois was descended on his mother's side from the builder of the Maryinsky and Bolshoi Theaters. Benois came to view his calling as "the propagation of art." He served as artistic director and designer of Konstantin Stanislavsky's Moscow Art Theatre, but his metier was ballet. He played an important role in the Ballets Russes company led by Serge Diaghilev. Ballet productions for which his costumes or decor are well known include *Les Sylphides* (1909), *Giselle* (1910), *Petrouchka* (1911), for which he also cowrote the libretto with Igor Stravinsky, *Graduation Ball* (1940) and *The Nutcracker* (1957). Benois was also the author of several books, including *Reminiscences of the Ballets Russes* and *Memoirs*. The hallmark of his ballet design was historical accuracy combined with delicate stage settings.

Benson, Edward Frederic *(1867–1940)* British novelist. Benson's witty series of novels, such as *Dodo: a Detail of the Day* (1893), followed by other "Dodo" novels (*Dodo the Second* [1914], *Dodo's Daughter* [1914] and *Dodo Wonders* [1921]), and *Queen Lucia* (1920) and several other "Lucia" novels, were—and are—enormously popular. The "Lucia" novels were collected in *Make Way for Lucia* (1977). An extremely prolific writer, Benson was also renowned as one of the 20th century's most anthologized ghost story writers. His two brothers were also men of letters. The elder, A(rthur) C(hristopher) Benson (1862–1925), was a biographer and critic; R(obert) H(ugh) Benson (1871–1914) was a religious writer. E. F. Benson spent his later years at Lamb House in Rye, Sussex, the former home of Henry James.

Benton, Thomas Hart *(1889–1975)* American painter, illustrator and folk music collector. With other midwestern artists Iowan Grant Wood and Kansan John Steuart Curry, Benton was a leading example of the movement in the 1930s dubbed Regionalism. He was born in Missouri. His great uncle was the legendary "Thunderer," Senator Thomas Hart Benton, and his father was a member of the U.S. House of Representatives. However, young Benton preferred painting to politics and from 1908 to 1911 studied in Paris, dabbling in experimental movements like Constructivism, Cubism and, later, synchronism. After World War I, Benton became convinced that the avant-garde did not mirror the real life and history around him. Soon, he was embroiled in controversy for attacking what he called the "aesthetic drivelings" and "morbid self-concerns" of modernist styles. The 1920s and 1930s were spent painting the murals that would establish his reputation as an observer of southern, midwestern and urban American life: the "America Today" cycle for the New School in New York; the cycle of murals for the Whitney Museum; the great "Social History of Indiana" cycle; and the "Social History of Missouri" cycle for the Jefferson City statehouse. At the same time he began his annual rambles through the countryside. He sketched field hands, attended church services in the Smoky Mountains, sat in with Virginia politicians, worked with cotton pickers in central Georgia and lived with the farming families of the Texas flatlands.

By the time his self-portrait appeared on the cover of *Time* magazine in 1934, he was the most famous painter in America. He left New York City in 1935 after bickering with the art establishment to take on a teaching position at the Kansas City Art Institute. Six years later his increasingly strident attacks against art museums ("graveyards" run by "pretty boys") ran him afoul of both Kansas City's Nelson-Atkins Museum and the Art Institute. He was fired. It was at this time that his most notorious comment was voiced, that he would prefer his paintings be hung in a saloon than in a museum. (His controversial nude, *Persephone,* was subsequently hung in Billy Rose's Diamond Horseshoe Saloon in New York.) Benton's last years were spent in what his biographer Henry Adams has called "an artistic retreat" into landscapes and nostalgia. Benton's autobiography, *An Artist in America,* written in three installments in 1937, 1951 and 1968, remains an important document of Benton's times.

Bentsen, Lloyd Millard, Jr. *(1921–2006)* American politician. Born in Mission, Texas, he received a law degree from the University of Texas in 1942. Becoming a judge after World War II, he was elected to the House of Representatives in 1948. Turning to business in Texas in 1954, he reentered politics when he was elected to the Senate in 1970, defeating Republican candidate George H. W. Bush. One of the most conservative Democratic senators, he was a financial expert, a powerful advocate of the oil, banking and real estate industries of his native state and an extremely effective fund-raiser. Chosen as the vice presidential running mate of Michael Dukakis, Bentsen was defeated in the 1988 election. However, he remained an influential figure in the Senate. In 1993 Bentsen began a two-year term as secretary of the treasury in the cabinet of President Bill Clinton.

Beobandi See Deobandi.

Berchtesgaden Town in the southeast of the German state of Bavaria. A popular resort, in the 1930s and 1940s its mountaintop Berghof was the favorite retreat of Adolf Hitler. Consequently it was a target of heavy Allied bombing during World War II. Most of the Berghof was destroyed following its capture in May 1945 by the Allies.

Berdyaev, Nikolai Aleksandrovich *(1874–1948)* Russian theologian and philosopher. Berdyaev, who was born in Kiev, published his first philosophical work when he was 26 and went on to become one of the most prolific and influential Russian writers of his epoch. In his youth Berdyaev was briefly drawn to Marxism, but he soon rejected its materialist viewpoint in favor of a spiritual existentialism that emphasized the power of faith to transform human lives. After the Russian Revolution, Berdyaev was appointed to the chair of philosophy at the University of Moscow, but in 1922 he was expelled from his native land (on the charge of being an anticommunist upholder of religion) and died in exile in Paris.

Berdyaev insisted that faith could not be achieved by rational argument but was instead a matter of intuition and of the natural impulse of the soul to seek spiritual freedom. Berdyaev's major works in English translation include *Spirit and Reality* (1939) and *Slavery and Freedom* (1948).

Beregovoy, Georgy *(1921–1995)* Soviet cosmonaut and veteran of more than 100 combat missions against the Nazis in WORLD WAR II. The first Soviet test pilot to fly in space, Beregovoy was 47 (the oldest cosmonaut at the time) when he flew aboard *Soyuz 3* in October 1968. After his flight he was appointed director of the Gagarin Cosmonaut Training Center.

Berenson, Bernard *(1865–1959)* American art critic. In his lifetime Berenson established himself as a leading writer on the Italian Renaissance and as an unquestioned expert on the authenticity of Renaissance paintings. Born in Lithuania of a poor Jewish family, Berenson immigrated to Boston as a young boy. Educated at Harvard and Oxford, he published his first essays on Renaissance art in the 1890s. Berenson championed the view that form—not subject matter—is the preeminent criterion for excellence in painting. His major critical work is *Italian Pictures of the Renaissance* (1932). As an authenticator of Renaissance paintings offered for sale, Berenson acquired an legendary status among art dealers and museum curators and managed to amass a sizable personal fortune, which he used to acquire a villa on the outskirts of Florence in which he lived for most of the last six decades of his life. In *Sketch for a Self-Portrait* (1949) Berenson recounted his difficult years of hiding from the Nazis during World War II.

Berg, Aksel Ivanovich *(1893–1979)* Soviet radio engineer and pioneer of cybernetics. Berg started his career as a submarine navigator and from 1918 to 1921 commanded a submarine in the Soviet navy's Baltic fleet. He later taught advanced training courses for naval radio operators at Leningrad Naval Academy. His main work concerns theories and methods of design and calculation of tube generators. He was awarded many orders and medals and in 1946 became a member of the USSR ACADEMY OF SCIENCES.

Berg, Alban Maria Johannes *(1885–1935)* Viennese composer, influential disciple of the modern 12-tone techniques of Arnold SCHOENBERG and composer of the opera *Wozzeck*. He was born in Vienna where his association with Schoenberg overturned his enthusiasm for Wagner and led him in the direction of atonality in early works like the *Five Songs with Orchestra* (1912) and the landmark opera *Wozzeck* (begun in 1913 and completed in 1920). Unlike his colleagues Anton von WEBERN and Schoenberg, Berg achieved at least a degree of popularity in his lifetime. Major works like the *Lyric Suite* (1926), the *Chamber Concerto* (1923–25) and the Violin Concerto (1935) held an elusive appeal because of their ambiguous tonal commitments. Such traditional forms as waltzes, major-minor triads and baroque quotations (like the Bach chorale at the end of the Violin Concerto) were nostalgic reminders of a rapidly vanishing past. The emotional impact of these works was overwhelming. "Musical theories and systems never supplanted an essential humanism in Berg," writes biographer Karen Monson. On the one hand, wit and humor are everywhere. Note-ciphers, musical descriptions of himself, Schoenberg and Webern pervade the *Chamber Concerto*. On the other hand, deeply felt love and sorrow illuminate the Violin Concerto (inspired by the death of a beloved friend) and the *Lyric Suite* (expressive of Berg's clandestine love affair with Hanna Werfel-Robettin, his "one eternal love"). "I can tell you, dear friend," he wrote Schoenberg, "that if it became known how much friendship, love and how many spiritual references I have smuggled into [my music] . . . the adherents of program music . . . would go mad with joy." He died of blood poisoning on Christmas Eve, 1935, before he completed his opera *Lulu* (the entire work was finally staged in 1979). (See also SERIAL MUSIC.)

Berg, Patty *(1918–)* American professional golfer. In 1946 Berg won the first U.S. Women's Open ever held. Between 1935 and 1964 she won 83 tournaments and served as the first president of the Ladies Professional Golf Association. Chosen by the Associated Press as Athlete-of-the-Year three times, Berg was elected to the American Golf Hall of Fame in 1972.

Bergen, Edgar (Edgar Bergren) *(1903–1978)* American comedian. One of the top radio personalities for over 10 years (1937–late 1940s), Bergen initially gained fame on the VAUDEVILLE circuit as a ventriloquist. His two wooden dummies, Charlie McCarthy and Mortimer Snerd, became household names. He also toured Europe and appeared on television and in several films, including *The Goldwyn Follies* (1938).

Bergen-Belsen Nazi CONCENTRATION CAMP in northwestern GERMANY. Bergen-Belsen was opened in 1941 to house Russian PRISONERS OF WAR. In 1943 HIMMLER turned it into a concentration camp for JEWS and incapacitated victims from other camps. The lack of medical care and hygiene caused many deaths—including that of diarist Anne FRANK in March 1945. When the camp was liberated by the U.S. Army on April 14, 1945, 10,000 corpses were found. Of the 38,000 living prisoners, barely one-third survived.

Berger, Erna *(1900–1990)* German opera singer. Berger was one of the best known and most popular lyric and coloratura sopranos of the pre– and post–World War II era. She was especially noted for her performances as the Queen of the Night in Mozart's *Die Zauberfloete* and her singing of the German lieder.

Berger, John Peter *(1926–)* British art critic, novelist, social critic and screenplay writer. Berger, one of the most influential art critics of the postwar era, is noted for his Marxist-influenced insistence on placing art in the social context of its times. He was for a long period the art critic of the *New Statesman* and has appeared frequently on British television. His book *Art and Revolution* (1968) underscores the revolutionary content in much of modernist European painting. *The Moment of Cubism* (1969) reevaluates the origins of the cubist movement in terms of the social implications of its new vision. A representative sampling of his work is included in *The Look of Things: Essays* (1972). Berger has also published several novels, notably *G* (1972), and has written screenplays for several films by the French director Alain Tanner, including *Jonah Who Will Be 25 in the Year 2000* (1976).

Berghof, Herbert *(1909–1990)* Austrian-born actor, director and teacher. Among the plays he directed was the U.S. debut of Samuel BECKETT's WAITING FOR GODOT in 1956. His students included Robert DE NIRO, Al Pacino, Anne Bancroft, Matthew Broderick and Geraldine Page.

Bergman, Ingmar *(1918–)* Celebrated Swedish stage and film director. Bergman was born in Uppsala, Sweden, the son of a stern Lutheran pastor, and brought up in a household full of what he has called "misery and exhausting conflicts." He sought refuge in two interests that became lifelong passions: the theater, especially the plays of August STRINDBERG, and the movies, which he described as "a fever which has never left me." After completing his education at the University of Stockholm, he went to work as a scriptwriter for the Svenskfilmindustri studio. From 1946 to 1982 he divided his time between the theater (mostly at the Royal Dramatic Theater) and the direction of 40 films, a body of distinguished work unparalleled in modern cinema. With favorite cameraman Sven Nykvist and a stock company that included Liv Ullmann (his wife), Gunnar Björnstrand, Bibi Andersson and Max von Sydow, he worked with the precision and nuance of a master sculptor. Themes frequently overlap from film to film: the carnal comedy (*Sommarnattens Leende/Smiles of a Summer Night*, 1955); studies of women (*Autumn Sonata*, 1978); historical allegories (*Det Sjunde Inseglet/The Seventh Seal*, 1957); and his most personally-felt theme, the isolation and alienation of modern man (the 1961–63 trilogy of *Sasom i en Spegel/Through a Glass Darkly; Nattsvardsgasternal/Winter Light;* and *T Lysnaden/The Silence*). Autobiography is everywhere, especially in his final motion picture, *Fanny and Alexander* (1982). The images scattered through his oeuvre are unforgettable: the peasant by the windmill lustily saluting the dawn in *Smiles of a Summer Night;* the minister's altar rituals in an empty church in *Winter Light;* the appearance of the "spider god" in *Through a Glass Darkly;* the violent rape in *The Virgin Spring;* and the sweeping "dance of

death" at the conclusion of *The Seventh Seal.* As biographer Birgitta Steene has written, "Bergman has focused his lens on an interior landscape . . . on the progress of the soul." Bergman retired from filmmaking after *Fanny and Alexander* (1982) and worked on stage and television projects, such as *The Best Intentions*, a stage script transformed into a Billie August television production, and *Saraband,* also television, which he claimed would be his last film.

Bergman, Ingrid *(1915–1982)* Swedish-born actress, one of the most acclaimed—and controversial—film stars of her time. Trained at the Royal Dramatic Theater in Stockholm, she was brought to HOLLYWOOD to star in a 1939 remake of her earlier Swedish film *Intermezzo.* She starred in several successful films but was catapulted to stardom as Ilsa Lund in the classic *Casablanca* (1942), opposite Humphrey BOGART. She continued to be one of the most popular Hollywood stars through the 1940s, giving acclaimed performances in *For Whom the Bell Tolls* (1943), *Gaslight* (1944; ACADEMY AWARD) and Alfred HITCHCOCK's *Notorious* (1946), among others. However, she became the center of a major scandal in 1948 when she left her husband and child to marry the Italian director Roberto ROSSELLINI, and her career floundered. She returned to the U.S. in 1957 and worked intermittently; her notable later films were *Anastasia* (1957), *Indiscreet* (1957), *Murder on the Orient Express* (1974) and *Autumn Sonata* (1978), her last film. She also played Israeli prime minister Golda MEIR in a made-for-television drama.

Bergonzi, Carlo *(1924–)* Italian tenor. Born in the village of Vidalenzo, Bergonzi studied at the Arrigo Boito Conservatory in Parma. He debuted in the role of Figaro in *The Barber of Seville* in 1948. In 1951 he began singing as a tenor, performing in the title role of *Andrea Chenier.* Bergonzi made his first U.S. appearance with the Chicago Opera in 1955 and debuted with the Metropolitan Opera the following year as Radames in Verdi's *Aida.* Not a particularly robust singer, he made up for a certain lack of strength with his beautiful tone, subtle phrasing and elegant style. The nearly 70 roles in his operatic reper-

toire included Cavaradossi in *Tosca,* Rodolfo in *La Bohème,* Pinkerton in *Madama Butterfly,* Des Grieux in *Manon Lescaut* and Riccardo in *Un Ballo in Maschera.*

Bergson, Henri *(1859–1941)* French philosopher. Bergson was a rarity—a philosopher with a style so rich and evocative that he was awarded the NOBEL PRIZE in literature in 1927. Bergson is best known for his speculative concept—best articulated in *Creative Evolution* (1907)—of the *elan vital* (vital impetus), which he posited as "a current of consciousness" that penetrates matter, gives rise to all forms of life and determines the nature of their evolution. The *elan vital* is conveyed from one generation to the next through physical means of reproduction, though it remains something apart from matter in order to assure the maximum indeterminacy in physical evolutionary development. Bergson asserted that humankind was the highest creation of the *elan vital* and hence the focus of all evolution. Bergson's other major works include *Matter and Memory* (1896), *Laughter* (1900) and *The Two Sources of Morality and Religion* (1932). A Jew, Bergson died an invalid as a result of harassment from the Vichy French government.

Beria, Lavrenti *(1899–1953)* Head of the Soviet SECRET POLICE (NKVD) (1935–53). Beria organized a BOLSHEVIK group during the RUSSIAN REVOLUTION and directed the secret police in Soviet Georgia from 1921 to 1931. He was first secretary of the Georgian Communist Party and was appointed commissar for international affairs by Joseph STALIN in 1938 and head of the NKVD. After Stalin's death Beria was dismissed and executed by other leading Communists, who believed he had been planning to succeed Stalin. Along with YEZHOV and Stalin himself, Beria was one of the most feared figures in the USSR during the Stalinist era.

Berkeley U.S. city on the east side of California's San Francisco Bay; since 1873, the site of the largest campus of the University of California. In the 1960s Berkeley was the tinderbox for the FREE SPEECH MOVEMENT that influenced campus political activism nationwide.

Berkeley, Busby (William Berkeley Enos) *(1895–1976)* American choreographer and dance director and one of the few authentic geniuses of the motion picture; famous for the lavish musical extravaganzas he created for such HOLLYWOOD films as *42nd Street* (1933), *Gold Diggers of 1933* (1933) and *Easy to Love* (1953) (directed by Lloyd Bacon, Mervyn Leroy and Charles Walters), and *Strike Up the Band* (1940) and *The Gang's All Here* (1943) (directed by Berkeley himself). Berkeley, a Broadway veteran, almost immediately grasped the possibilities of the motion picture camera to liberate him from the proscenium-bound stage. Berkeley numbers were hallucinogenic extravaganzas that wandered in space and time and invited the viewer to wink at the conceit that they were being performed on a normal stage. He filled the screen with an energetic movement that was created as much by his trick photography as by the dancing, swimming or flying around of hordes of blond, brunet and redhead chorines ("350 of the most gorgeous creatures on Earth"—according to the *Dames* publicity). Berkeley had a great deal of success from the 1930s into the 1950s but began to struggle with personal problems and a declining public interest in extravagant musicals. He returned to the spotlight in 1970 as director of a successful Broadway revival of Vincent YOUMANS's *No, No, Nanette.*

Berkeley, Sir Lennox Randal Francis *(1903–1989)* British composer. He studied French, Old French and philology at Oxford University before deciding upon a career in music. Beginning in 1930 he studied with Nadia BOULANGER in Paris for five years. He completed his first major work, the oratorio *Jonah*, in 1935. During his career he composed choral, solo, chamber and orchestral music, including four symphonies as well as several operas. He was knighted in 1974.

Berkshire Festival Summer music festival held in Lenox, in western Massachusetts, one of the popular Berkshire summer resorts and summer home of the Boston Symphony Orchestra. In 1936 Tanglewood—a private estate consisting of some 200 acres—was donated to the orchestra, then under the direction of Serge KOUSSEVITZKY. Thus was born the Berkshire Festival. Each year the orchestra presents 24 weekend performances, as well as concerts by the orchestra's chamber players and guest performers. Facilities include a 6,000-seat music shed, several smaller theaters, chamber music halls and studios.

Berle, Adolf Augustus, Jr. *(1895–1971)* U.S. lawyer and public official. Berle was a member of the PARIS PEACE CONFERENCE after WORLD WAR I but resigned in protest over the terms of the VERSAILLES TREATY. He later became professor of law at Columbia University and an influential figure in President Franklin ROOSEVELT's NEW DEAL and Good Neighbor Policy. In 1945 Berle became ambassador to Brazil. He was a founder and chairman of the New York State Liberal Party and author of *Power* (1969).

Berle, Milton *(1908–2002)* Prominent American stage and screen entertainer; known as "Uncle Miltie" in the early days of television. After only middling success in VAUDEVILLE, the movies (from *The Perils of Pauline* in 1914 to *Sun Valley Serenade* in 1937), radio and nightclubs, he found his metier in television. Tuesday evenings became known as "Milton Berle Night," beginning on June 8, 1948, on NBC and extending through 1951. At a time when only 9% of homes had television sets, millions watched *The TEXACO STAR THEATER* inside taverns and in front of appliance store windows. Berle's program led a wave of variety programming at the time. But by 1952 Berle's popularity was beginning to fade, and new sponsors started "tinkering" with his on-air persona, a process that Berle described as softening the "aggressive, pushy 'Milton Berle' into a passive straight man." Also, the technical achievement of coast-to-coast network transmissions had unleashed Berle's essentially "urban" comedy on rural audiences. After a few more seasons with different sponsors in different timeslots, Berle left television, never to have his own series again. Although he did not have the enduring popularity of rivals like Jack BENNY and Jackie GLEASON, he was an essential factor in the postwar success of television.

Berlin Past and future capital of GERMANY; lying along the Spree River, it is the largest city in Germany, with a population of over 3 million and was once the capital of Prussia. By 1900 the city had a population of 2,712,000. It entered a period of social unrest after the German defeat in World War I and was the scene of the leftist SPARTACIST UPRISING in 1919 and the rightist KAPP PUTSCH in 1920. While under great economic strain, it was nonetheless a noted cultural center as capital of the postwar WEIMAR REPUBLIC. The city prospered materially but declined spiritually after it became HITLER's capital in 1933. During WORLD WAR II Berlin was severely damaged by Allied bombs and by the Soviet artillery fire that preceded the capture of the capital in May 1945. Agreements reached at the YALTA and POTSDAM CONFERENCES divided the conquered city into four occupied sectors, individually administered by the U.S., USSR, Great Britain and France.

Berlin soon became a major issue in the COLD WAR, with the USSR demanding Western withdrawal from a city that was totally within the boundaries of the Soviet occupation zone (which became EAST GERMANY). In 1948 the Soviets established a blockade between West Berlin and WEST GERMANY, which was successfully broken by an Anglo-American airlift (see BERLIN AIRLIFT). In 1949 East Berlin was made the capital of East Germany, and the three Western zones were formally unified to create West Berlin, which became a West German state in 1950. In the years that followed West Berlin was totally rebuilt, and it quickly developed into one of the most thriving cities in Europe. East Berlin, on the other hand, was much slower to rebuild and never experienced the economic rebirth of its sister city. A stream of refugees fled to West Germany from East Germany, via East Berlin, throughout the 1950s. This exodus was abruptly ended in 1961, when the East German authorities erected the BERLIN WALL, a barrier that prevented traffic between the divided cities. Allied disapproval of the wall was perhaps best crystallized in President John F. KENNEDY's 1963 visit to the divided city. Tensions were eased somewhat in 1972, when visits across the wall and access to West Berlin from West Germany were formalized in the so-called Berlin accords.

The wall remained a hated symbol of communist repression and of a divided Germany until November 1989, when, in the wake of revolutions sweeping Eastern Europe, East Germany lifted restrictions on travel between East and West Berlin. The impromptu celebration at the wall turned into a joyous occasion, with jubilant, dancing crowds picking at and hurling away chunks from the wall. A September 1990 agreement ended four-power responsibility over Berlin and pledged to unite the city. On October 3, 1990, Germany and Berlin were formally reunited. In 1999, following a series of national construction projects designed to accommodate an influx of government officials and departments, the German capital moved from Bonn to Berlin.

Berlin, Irving (Israel Baline) (1888–1989)

Russian-born American popular songwriter. His Russian-Jewish family immigrated to the U.S. when he was a few years old, and he grew up on the poor Lower East Side of New York City. He began working at age eight, first as a newspaper seller then as a street singer and as a singing waiter. He began writing songs in 1907, and in 1911 had his first hit, "Alexander's Ragtime Band." He went on to write such well-known songs as "Puttin on the Ritz," "Always," "Mammy" (for the first TALKING PICTURE, *The Jazz Singer,* 1927), "Cheek to Cheek" (for the Fred ASTAIRE–Ginger ROGERS film *Top Hat*), "Oh How I Hate to Get Up in the Morning" (featured in both a 1917 revue and in the 1943 film *This Is the Army*), "Easter Parade" and "There's No Business Like Show Business" (for the musical *Annie Get Your Gun*). Perhaps his two greatest classics were "God Bless America" and "White Christmas," which is believed to have sold more copies than any other song in history. He received a congressional gold medal and a proclamation of appreciation from President Dwight D. EISENHOWER in 1954. Altogether Berlin composed some 1,500 songs, 19 Broadway musicals and 18 movie scores, despite the fact he never learned to read or write music. His songs captured the mood of 20th-century American experience, whether it was WORLD WAR I, the GREAT DEPRESSION of the 1930s, WORLD WAR II or the postwar prosperity of the 1950s and 1960s. He died at the age of 101, still young in spirit.

Berlin Airlift (June 1948–May 1949)

With BERLIN under the four-power administration of the victorious Allies after WORLD WAR II, the USSR hoped to force the U.S., Britain and France out of the city. Alleging that the West had broken postwar agreements on German status, the Soviets imposed obstacles to road and river traffic crossing into the western (U.S., British, French) sector of Berlin. The West responded with a round-the-clock airlift of fuel, food, mail and personnel to relieve the beleaguered city.

Berlin-Baghdad Railway

Railway from the Bosporus to the PERSIAN GULF that was proposed by a German company in 1899. The idea of this project was greeted with anger by the Russians, who had their own plans for such a railway. In Britain some who wished to encourage German-Russian conflict favored the project, but many who feared a Gulf port dominated by Germany spoke out against it. By 1914 most European objections to the plan had been settled. However, the argument proved academic as only a small part of the railway line had been completed by the outbreak of WORLD WAR I, and the war caused the cessation of construction.

Berlinguer, Enrico (1922–1984)

Italian Communist politician and popular founder of eurocommunism. Berlinguer led ITALY's 1.7-million-member Communist Party—Europe's largest—from 1972 until his death. In 1973 he called for a "historic compromise" between communist and democratic parties in Western Europe. He urged Western communists to act independently of the Soviet Union, renounce the idea of violent revolution and embrace democratic coalition politics. He nearly brought his party to power in the 1976 Italian parliamentary elections, with 34.5% of the vote. Although the party's strength later declined from that high point, Berlinguer remained a dominant and respected force in Italy's political and intellectual life. His funeral in Rome was attended by more than 1 million people, the city's biggest crowd since the end of World War II.

Berlin Wall

Fortified barrier between East and West BERLIN that existed from 1961 to 1989–90. After the East Berlin riots of 1953, many East Berliners fled into West Berlin to find freedom and better living conditions. This stream of refugees continued throughout the 1950s, until August 13, 1961, when Communist authorities closed 68 border crossing points and began to erect a wall between the eastern and western zones of the city. Barbed wire, ditches and guard towers were added and became a part of the landscape. Escape attempts continued but became deadly affairs, many fewer in number and in success. On June 26, 1963, U.S. president John F. KENNEDY traveled to Berlin where he made his famous "Ich bin ein Berliner" speech denouncing the wall and communism and expressing his solidarity with the people of Berlin. Nonetheless, the wall remained for nearly three decades as a physical manifestation of the IRON CURTAIN. After a mass exodus of East Germans to the West in the summer of 1989, political demonstrations against the Communist government led to the downfall of hard-line East German leader Erich HONECKER (October 1989); the reform-minded premier Egon KRENZ announced the lifting of travel restrictions between East and West Berlin. East and West Berliners responded by mounting the wall and holding an impromptu celebration. By the end of 1990 the last remnants of the wall had been dismantled, and East and West Berlin were one—a part of a reunited GERMANY. (See also COLD WAR.)

Berlusconi, Silvio (1936–)

Italian businessman, media mogul and prime minister of Italy (1994, 2001–2006). Born in Milan, Berlusconi studied law at Milan University and upon graduation began work in the then booming construction sector in the early 1960s as a construction manager. In 1969, while designing Milano 2, a dormitory suburb on the edge of Milan, he began his first foray into the telecommunications industry when he installed a cable network throughout the development. Two years later Berlusconi began to expand his involvement in the Italian television market as a consequence of the Italian Constitutional Court's ruling that RAI, the Italian state broadcasting network, could not possess a monopoly on local programming. After several years of accumulating capital and purchasing film rights, he established a sizable film library through Finivest, his holding company. Berlusconi's agency prospered as television stations gathered an increasing share of national advertising revenues, and by the end of the 1980s the income from his marketing division, Pubitalia, comprised 70% of all funds spent on television ads in Italy. In 1977 Berlusconi used the profits from Pubitalia, along with other investment capital, to purchase local TV stations and create Canale 5 (Channel 5), a national TV network that, with Berlusconi's purchase of Italia 1 in 1982 and Rete 4 in 1984, provided him with a media empire managed under Finivest that eventually reached 45% of the Italian market. By the mid-1990s Finivest had become a conglomerate that oversaw the activities of almost 150 companies.

In 1993 Berlusconi began to express interest in entering the political arena and formed a new political party, Forza Italia (meaning "Go Italy," a crowd chant developed by fans of AC Milan, a soccer team that he had purchased). Riding a wave of anticorruption sentiment that pervaded the country, his party performed well in the 1994 national elections, and Berlusconi became prime minister in a coalition government. However, the coalition dissolved shortly after a Milan court indicted Berlusconi for tax fraud. Out of office, Berlusconi returned to his constituent base and reorganized his party so as to ensure its greater appeal in national elections. After a strong performance in the 2001 elections, Berlusconi again entered power through another coalition, called Casa della Libertà (House of Liberties), with his 1994 political partners, the National Alliance and the Northern League.

In April 2003 Berlusconi's former lawyer, Cesare Previti, was convicted of bribing a judge during one of Finivest's acquisitions. Moreover, new evidence surfaced suggesting that Berlusconi himself had bribed judges in the 1980s to prevent a business adversary from purchasing SME, a state-owned food distribution group. As a result of these charges, Berlusconi's coalition quickly enacted a new law preventing the prosecution of a sitting government official for crimes committed prior to his or her assumption of office. In 2003 Berlusconi strongly supported the U.S.-led "coalition of the willing," with Italy providing troops in the military venture designed to remove Saddam HUSSEIN from power in Iraq. In December 2004 Berlusconi was cleared of corruption charges, after a four-year trial. A political crises in 2005 brought about his resignation. Days later he formed a new government. In April 2006 general elections Berlusconi lost by a narrow margin to Romano PRODI and his left-center coalition.

Bermuda A group of islands in the North Atlantic Ocean, approximately 700 miles southeast of New York City, Bermuda covers an area of 19.3 square miles. The population of some 58,000 is approximately two-thirds black and one-third white of mainly British descent. Bermuda is a dependent territory of the UNITED KINGDOM with a constitution dating from June 1968. In the 1970s clashes between those favoring dependent status and those wanting independence, exacerbated by racial tension, resulted in the murder of the governor (1973) and riots (1977). Since 1980 the political party that endorses continued ties with Britain has been in power. Tourism is the main industry; since the 1930s Bermuda has been a popular tourist and honeymoon destination for Americans. It has managed to retain much of its old world charm and scenic beauty. In 1995 a referendum on independence resulted in nearly 75% voting to remain part of Britain. Independence reemerged as an issue in Bermuda following the 2004 decision by its prime minister, W. Alex Scott, to hold a national debate on the subject.

Bernadotte, Count Folke (*1895–1948*) President of the Swedish RED CROSS and UNITED NATIONS mediator. A Swedish soldier involved with the Red Cross in WORLD WAR I, in WORLD WAR II he arranged exchanges of sick and disabled PRISONERS OF WAR at Göteborg in 1943 and 1944. He was used by Heinrich HIMMLER in 1945 as intermediary to seek a surrender of German forces to the British and Americans, but the proposal was rejected in London and Washington. He was invited by UN secretary general Trygve LIE to serve as UN mediator in PALESTINE, where he was assassinated by Jewish terrorists in 1948.

Bernadotte, Sigvard (*1907–2002*) Leading Swedish craft and industrial designer. Bernadotte, son of the Swedish king Gustave V, began his design career in the firm of Georg Jensen, working in silver, furniture and textiles and helping to build that firm's international reputation. In 1949 he opened an industrial design office in Copenhagen, with the Danish designer Acton Bjorn, where he made a wide variety of industrially produced products. The dignified audio equipment of Bang & Olufsen is an example of distinguished work of the firm. From 1964 he was the head of his own design firm in Stockholm, serving a number of major clients.

Bernhard, Thomas (*1931–1989*) Austrian playwright and novelist. Several of his works were highly controversial. His last play, *Heldenplatz* (Heroes' Square), provoked protests in 1988 for its implicit denunciation of Austrian president Kurt WALDHEIM and Austrian ANTI-SEMITISM.

Bernhardt, Sarah (*1844–1923*) French actress. Considered one of the finest actresses of the French theater, Bernhardt was acclaimed for her distinctive voice and her tragic characterizations. Her career began at the Comédie-

French actress Sarah Bernhardt. 1917 (LIBRARY OF CONGRESS, PRINTS AND PHOTOGRAPHS DIVISION)

Française in 1862; 10 years later she had achieved an international reputation. Her most famous parts included title roles in *Phèdre* and *Hamlet* (played *en travesti*), Dona Sol in *Hernani*, Marguerite Gautier in *La Dame aux camélias* and leading roles in the melodramas of Victorien Sardou. She continued to act even after the amputation of her right leg in 1915.

Bernstein, Carl See WOODWARD AND BERNSTEIN.

Bernstein, Leonard *(1918–1990)* American composer, orchestra conductor and educator. An exuberant larger-than-life figure, Bernstein was perhaps the best-known if not the most talented American musician of the 20th century. He was the first native-born American to lead a major American orchestra (the New York Philharmonic), and much of his concert and popular stage music has become standard in the modern repertoire. Born in Lawrence, Massachusetts, of a family of Russian Jewish immigrants, he studied at Harvard after 1935 with composer Walter PISTON and at the Curtis Music Institute after 1939 with conductor Fritz REINER. He subsequently worked with Serge KOUSSEVITZKY at Tanglewood, Massachusetts. He created a sensation when in November 1943 he appeared before the New York Philharmonic Symphony Orchestra as a substitute for the ailing Bruno WALTER.

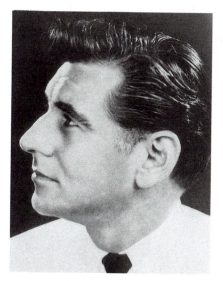

American conductor and composer Leonard Bernstein (LIBRARY OF CONGRESS, PRINTS AND PHOTOGRAPHS DIVISION)

Thereafter his activities were numerous and diverse. He composed three symphonies, ballets (*Fancy Free,* 1944), musicals (*On the Town,* 1944; *Wonderful Town,* 1953; *West Side Story,* 1957), operas (*Candide,* 1956; *Trouble in Tahiti,* 1952) and the *Mass* (1971). He appeared on the *Omnibus* television program in 1955 for the first of his more than 100 discussion/demonstrations of music. A concert pianist, he conducted and performed many major works. As music director, he led the New York Philharmonic with a flamboyant, emotionally self-indulgent style from 1959 to 1969; he later appeared often with the Vienna Philharmonic. Bernstein made several hundred recordings, including a landmark cycle of the MAHLER symphonies as well as important readings of COPLAND, STRAVINSKY, and IVES.

A political activist, he was well known for his left-wing views. In the 1960s he vigorously opposed the VIETNAM WAR; his public support of the BLACK PANTHERS led author Tom WOLFE to coin the term *radical chic.* Bernstein unashamedly embraced the credo of tonality in music, insisting that there was a "worldwide, inborn musical grammar," a tonality that "persists beyond the changes, imperturbable and immortal."

Berra, Yogi (Lawrence Peter Berra) *(1925–)* American baseball figure. Berra spent his entire playing career (1946–65) with the New York Yankees. He is primarily remembered as one of the all-time great catchers, but he also played in the outfield. Berra had a lifetime batting average of .285, with 358 home runs. He appeared in 14 all-star games and in 14 World Series (more than either Joe DIMAGGIO or Mickey MANTLE, teammates whose careers overlapped his). Berra later coached and managed various teams, including the Yankees (1964 and 1984–85) and the New York Mets (1972–75). He was elected to the Baseball Hall of Fame in 1972. In 1986 he joined the Houston Astros as a coach, until his retirement in 1992. Regarded as one of the sages of the game, he is also known for his humorous aphorisms, such as "It ain't over till it's over" and "50 percent of the game is half mental."

Berrigan brothers Daniel Berrigan (1921–) and Philip Berrigan (1923–2002), both Roman Catholic priests and political activists, became famous in the late 1960s as leaders of the American-based Catholic resistance to the VIETNAM WAR. The brothers were raised in a working-class family in Syracuse, New York. Their father, a political activist, encouraged his sons in both their Catholic vocation and their concern for social issues. Daniel became a Jesuit priest, while Philip joined the Josephite order. In 1965 the brothers became the only priests to support a "declaration of conscience"—its signatories including Dr. Martin Luther KING Jr. and Dr. Benjamin SPOCK—calling for total noncooperation with the Vietnam War effort. The most famous of the brothers' draft resistance efforts was the May 1968 break-in (with seven others) into draft board offices in Catonsville, Maryland. As members of the "Catonsville Nine," both brothers served prison terms. They remained politically active in antinuclear weapons protests throughout the 1980s. (See also ANTIWAR MOVEMENT).

Berry, Chuck (Charles Edward Berry) *(1926–)* Black American rock and roll songwriter, guitarist and vocalist. Berry is one of the seminal figures in the history of ROCK and roll. From the release of his hit single "Maybelline" (1955), Berry set a standard for songwriting that has deeply influenced every subsequent generation of rock musicians. The standard Berry song begins with a rhythmically compelling guitar solo and features witty and knowing lyrics on teenage dreams and frustrations. Berry's pure vocal range is limited, but his slyly articulate phrasing lends spirit and conviction to his songs. Berry's signature stage movement—walking quickly in a low squat while playing his guitar—is known as the "duckwalk." Born in San Diego and raised in St. Louis, Berry began his career as a blues performer in the late 1940s before creating the guitar style that made him a rock and roll star. In 1988 there appeared both his *Autobiography* and a tribute film, *Hail! Hail! Rock and Roll.* Major hits by Berry include "School Days" (1957), "Rock 'n' Roll Music" (1957), "Sweet Little Sixteen" (1958), "Johnny B. Goode" (1958), "No Particular Place to Go" (1964), "My Ding-A-Ling" (1972), and "Reelin' and Rockin" (1972).

Berry, Wendell Erdman *(1934–)* American poet, essayist, novelist and farmer. Born in a rural county northeast of Louisville, Berry earned two degrees from the University of Kentucky at Lexington, where he also taught (1964–77). After a brief sojourn in New York, he settled down on a small farm once owned by his family. He is best known as a philosophical proponent of the environmental movement. The essays of *A Continuous Harmony* (1972), *The Unsettling of American* (1977), *The Gift of Good Land* (1981) and *What Are People For?* (1990) argue for ecological responsibility and the maintenance of the integrity of the land. Berry's lyrical, psalmic poems are similarly earnest pleas for the traditional values of the farmer. His novels are forthright studies of honest country people.

Berryman, John *(1914–1972)* Major American poet and critic noted for his tragic view of life, intermingled with a razorsharp sense of humor in his works. Berryman taught at various American universities from 1939 to 1953 before becoming professor of humanities at the University of Minnesota in 1954, where he remained until his death by suicide. His intensely autobiographical poems show a marked shift in style from the earlier works, such as *The Dispossessed* (1948), to the later volumes, which include *Homage to Mistress Bradstreet* (1956) and *77 Dream Songs* (1964), for which he received the 1965 PULITZER PRIZE for poetry. He also wrote a critical biography of Stephen Crane (1950) and several critical reviews, which appeared in such publications as PARTISAN REVIEW.

Bertoia, Harry *(1915–1978)* Italian-born sculptor and designer. Bertoia was best known for his design of a chair with a padded, diamond-shaped wire web suspended in a steel cradle. He also crafted massive architectural sculptures in metal featuring honeycomb shapes and sculptures of rods in dandelion-like bursts. Bertoia worked with Charles EAMES from 1949 to 1952 and probably had some influence on Eames's designs.

Bertolucci, Bernardo *(1940–)* Italian-born motion picture director, leader of that postwar generation of filmmakers who came after Vittorio DE SICA, Federico FELLINI and Luchino VISCONTI. He was born in Parma. His enthusiasm for the movies was influenced by the politics and innovative styles of Alain RESNAIS and Jean-Luc GODARD. Bertolucci's early films were a heady mixture of leftist politics and striking imagery. *Partner* (1968) was a melodramatically charged adaptation of Dostoyevsky's *The Double; Prima della rivoluzione* (*Before the Revolution*, 1965), *La Strategia del ragno* (*The Spider's Stratagem*, 1970) and *Il Conformista The Conformist*, (1970) all dealt to a degree with radical politics and revolution in modern-day Italy. With *Last Tango in Paris* (1972), which was filmed in English, his films more openly confronted the international audience. Its candid, frequently brutal dissection of a sexual obsession challenged censorship codes. Since then, his epic vision has enlarged with the five-hour *1900* (1976); the extraordinary history of China during WORLD WAR II, *The Last Emperor;* and the spacious silences of *The Sheltering Sky* (1990). Elements of fantasy, an almost neurotic inner vision and intensity, a sprawling operatic opulence and a complete command of camera technique distinguish his finest films. Nowhere is this better demonstrated than in his masterpiece, *The Spider's Stratagem,* where a young man must confront the truth of his father's traitorous activities during the anti-fascist RESISTANCE—all of this to the strains of opera music by Verdi. Bertolucci continued to produce critically acclaimed films throughout the 1990s and into the 21st century. His *Stealing Beauty* (1996), *Besieged* (1998) and *The Dreamers* (2003) formed a kind of trilogy focusing on the theme of human isolation.

Bertone, Nuccio Giuseppe *(1914–1997)* Italian automobile body designer. Bertone was responsible for a number of distinguished automobile designs, including the Alfa Romeo Giulietta Sprint of 1954, the Lamborghini of 1966 and the CITROEN BX of 1982. His work has been central in the development of typically Italian automotive design.

Bessarabia Region of the southwestern USSR, on the western shores of the Black Sea. Annexed by Russia in 1812, Bessarabia declared itself independent in 1917, during WORLD WAR I, and was united with Romania in 1918. Romania surrendered it to the USSR in 1939 but again took control of the region during WORLD WAR II. In 1947 the USSR regained control. In 1991 it became the major part of the independent republic of MOLDOVA.

Bessell, Peter Joseph *(1921–1985)* British politician. Bessell was a LIBERAL PARTY member of Parliament (1964–70) and a key witness for the prosecution in the 1979 trial of former Liberal Party leader Jeremy THORPE. Thorpe was accused of having planned to murder Norman Scott, a male model with whom Thorpe was alleged to have had a homosexual affair. Bessell's credibility as a witness came under severe attack, and Thorpe was acquitted. Bessell returned to the U.S. where he had been working as a investment banker. He wrote his own account of the matter, *Cover-Up: The Jeremy Thorpe Affair,* which was published in the U.S. in a limited edition in 1981.

Betancourt, Rómulo *(1908–1981)* Venezuela politician, president of Venezuela (1945–48, 1959–64). He first took power as the head of a revolutionary leftist junta that in 1945 toppled the dictatorship of General Isaias Medina Angarita. Three years later, after the first democratic elections ever held in Venezuela, an army coup forced Betancourt into exile for a decade. In 1959, when the leadership again changed, he returned to Venezuela and won a free presidential election by an overwhelming margin. As president, he worked for social and political reforms.

Bethe, Hans Albrecht *(1906–2005)* German-American physicist. The son of a distinguished physiologist, Bethe was educated in Germany, where he received his doctorate in physics in 1928. He taught at various German universities but, because of his part-Jewish ancestry, fled the country in 1933. After a year in England he settled in the U.S. and joined the faculty of Cornell University, where his research into celestial energy aided scientists in developing the hydrogen bomb. From 1943 to 1946 Bethe worked on the MANHATTAN PROJECT under the direction of J. Robert OPPENHEIMER. Bethe and Oppenheimer became leading spokesmen for "finite containment" in the postwar debate over research on the hydrogen bomb. These scientists believed that a large stockpile of American nuclear arms was necessary to contain Soviet aggression. However, they maintained that further technological advances would bring the supply of weapons to dangerous levels unwarranted by strategic considerations. Declaring that the Soviet Union was "largely imitative" in its atomic energy programs, they maintained that the U.S. could forego the hydrogen weapon without incurring a serious security risk. Instead, they suggested that work on the bomb be conducted only at a theoretical level. President Harry Truman rejected their advice; reacting to recommendations of Edward Teller, he authorized production of the weapon in 1950.

During the early years of the Eisenhower administration, Bethe became a leading defender of Oppenheimer, who had been suspended from his post as an Atomic Energy Commission (AEC) consultant in 1953 as an alleged security risk. Bethe was among the many outstanding scientists who declared their confidence in Oppenheimer and testified on his behalf. Following the AEC's decision not to reinstate Oppenheimer, despite its finding that he was loyal, Bethe released a statement by the American Physical Society denouncing the ruling as based on differences over nuclear weapons policy rather than on actual security risk.

In 1956 Bethe was appointed to the President's Science Advisory Committee. Two years later he became chairman of a special panel formed to study the possible effects of a NUCLEAR TEST BAN agreement between the U.S. and the Soviet Union and to research the efficiency of various methods of detecting atomic blasts. Bethe attended the 1958 U.S.-Soviet disarmament talks in Geneva, where the two delegations agreed that any test ban accord would include acoustical, radiological, seismic and electromagnetic detection systems. Bethe continued to serve as a presidential adviser in the Kennedy administration. During his career he won many scientific honors, including the Max Planck Medal, West Germany's highest scientific honor, for his research on celestial energy. He received the AEC's Enrico Fermi Award in 1961 and the Nobel Prize in physics in 1967. Bethe

continued to teach at Cornell through the 1990s.

Bethmann-Hollweg, Theobald von
(1856–1921) German chancellor (1909–17). A career civil servant, he was Prussian minister of the interior (1905–07) and German secretary of state (1905–07). He succeeded von Bulow as chancellor of the Reich in 1909. At home, he was a moderate reformer who extended the franchise and insurance laws while granting considerable autonomy to Alsace-Lorraine and attempting to modernize the constitution. A bureaucrat who was largely inexperienced in international affairs, he was opposed to World War I but was unable to effectively challenge the army, Kaiser Wilhelm II and Admiral Alfred von Tirpitz. When the war began, he justified the German invasion of Belgium, portraying Russia as the aggressor. He attempted to restrict submarine warfare but was forced out of office in 1917 after conflicts with Generals Hindenburg and Ludendorff.

Bethune, Mary McLeod *(1875–1955)* American educator. Bethune was special adviser to President Franklin Roosevelt on the problems of minorities in the U.S. A teacher in southern schools (1895–1904), she later founded the Institute for Girls in Daytona (1904), which became the Bethune-Cookman College in 1923. During World War II she assisted the secretary of war in selecting officer candidates for the Women's Army Corps

Civil rights activist Mary McLeod Bethune (National Archives)

and was an observer for the State Department at the 1945 UN conference. From 1936 to 1944 she directed the Negro affairs division of the National Youth Administration.

Betjeman, Sir John *(1906–1984)*
British poet. Born in Highgate, London, Betjeman was educated at Marlborough and Magdalen College, Oxford, though he did not complete a degree. He taught for a time, then in 1931 began writing for *Architectural Review*. His first volumes of poems, *Mount Zion* (1933), *Continual Dew: A Little Book of Bourgeois Verse* (1937) and *New Bats in Old Belfries* (1945), had a limited readership, but his *Collected Poems* (1958, expanded 1962) was enormously popular. His work, on the surface light and witty, has been dismissed by some as facile, but his champions, including W. H. Auden and Philip Larkin, found undertones of wistfulness. Betjeman also wrote on architecture: *Ghastly Good Taste* (1933) and *First and Last Loves* (1952). He was named poet laureate in 1971.

Bettelheim, Bruno *(1903–1990)*
Austrian psychologist. Bettelheim, who immigrated to the U.S. in 1939 after having been interned in two Nazi CONCENTRATION CAMPS, Auschwitz and Buchenwald, first became renowned for his psychological writings on the meaning of the concentration camp experience. He continued to write prolifically for five decades, winning the National Book Award in 1977 for *The Uses of Enchantment* (1976), which argued that the "dark side" of children's fairy tales—occult spells, terrible bodily transformations, willful violence—was part and parcel of their value in helping children to come to recognize and to assimilate all parts of their psychological makeup. *Surviving and Other Essays* (1980) is a representative sampling of Bettelheim's writing on a variety of therapeutic themes. In *Freud and Man's Soul* (1982) Bettelheim drew upon his own psychiatric training in Vienna to argue for a flexible, non-mechanistic view of the psychoanalytic theories of Sigmund Freud.

Beuve-Méry, Hubert *(1902–1989)*
French journalist and newspaper publisher. In 1944, following the liberation of France, General Charles de Gaulle selected Beuve-Méry to establish a new

newspaper of record; the existing French newspapers were not permitted to resume publishing because of their association with the German occupation. Beuve-Méry created *Le Monde,* an austere paper that carried very few photographs but became widely respected for its independent viewpoint and its authoritative coverage of foreign and domestic news. Beuve-Méry retired in 1969 and later directed a journalism school and wrote several books.

Bevan, Aneurin *(1897–1960)* British political leader. A coal miner, he was active in the trade union movement and was elected to Parliament as a LABOUR PARTY member in 1929. He served there until his death. Minister of health (1945–52) in Clement ATTLEE's Labour government, he was instrumental in developing and administering Britain's NATIONAL HEALTH SERVICE. He resigned from the cabinet in 1951 in a dispute over health and defense costs and thereafter led the Labour Party's left wing. A fiery speaker, Bevan was Labour's foreign policy spokesman from 1956 on, strongly advocating nuclear disarmament.

Beveridge, Albert J. *(1862–1927)* U.S. historian and politician. He was a successful Republican compromise candidate for the U.S. Senate in 1899 and served in the Senate until 1911. As an Indiana senator, he was the chief spokesman for U.S. imperialism. Renominated in 1905, he was a firm supporter of President Theodore ROOSEVELT's policies. Beveridge assisted the passage of the Pure Food and the Meat Inspection Acts of 1906 and championed child labor legislation. Defeated in 1910, he joined Roosevelt's Progressive Party and gave the keynote speech in 1912. He rejoined the REPUBLICAN PARTY in 1916 but was defeated in 1922 in his attempt to return to the Senate from Indiana. After 1917 he supported the war effort but opposed U.S. participation in the LEAGUE OF NATIONS. His best-known work is a four-volume biography of Chief Justice John Marshall.

Beveridge, William Henry (first baron Beveridge) *(1879–1963)* British economist. A civil servant, Beveridge had served as lieutenant to LLOYD GEORGE in the Liberal government prior to WORLD WAR I, director of the London School of Economics from 1919 to 1937 and master of University College, Oxford, from 1937 to 1945. Beveridge created a plan for social security in 1941 that was published as *A Report on Social Insurance and Allied Services* in 1942 and came to be known as the BEVERIDGE REPORT. It served as the basis for the British postwar WELFARE STATE. Beveridge is also the author of *Full Employment in a Free Society* (1944).

Beveridge Report Popular name of *A Report on Social Insurance and Allied Services,* written by British economist Sir William Henry BEVERIDGE and published in 1942. It recommended an extensive plan for social insurance to stamp out poverty and unemployment. Although Beveridge himself was a Liberal, the report was embraced by the LABOUR PARTY. Against party leader Clement ATTLEE's wishes, some Labour members of Parliament criticized CHURCHILL's wartime coalition government for neglecting the report, causing some friction in the coalition. After the Labour Party came to power in 1945, the Beveridge Report became the basis for Britain's postwar social legislation, including the NATIONAL HEALTH SERVICE.

Bevin, Ernest *(1879–1951)* British labor organizer and politician. The uneducated son of a laborer, Bevin became an official in the Docker's Union in 1911 and was an eloquent spokesman for it. Bevin organized disparate unions into the Transport and General Workers' Union in 1922 and served as its general secretary until 1940, when he entered into the war cabinet as minister of labour. He was highly successful at maintaining industry during the war and created the "Bevin Boys," men who worked in the coal mines as war service. From 1945 to 1951 Bevin served as foreign secretary in Clement ATTLEE's Labour government and was instrumental in the acceptance of the MARSHALL PLAN and in the creation of the BRUSSELS TREATY (1948), NATO and the COLUMBO PLAN (1950).

Beyond the Fringe Popular British satirical revue of the early 1960s. *Beyond the Fringe* was conceived by and featured four Cambridge University undergraduates: Alan BENNETT, Peter COOK, Dudley MOORE and Jonathan MILLER. The revue was first presented as part of the "fringe" entertainment at the 1960 EDINBURGH FESTIVAL; the following year it moved to London's West End, where it ran for over 1,100 performances. In 1962 *Beyond the Fringe* was brought to New York City, with more than 600 off-Broadway performances; another West End run in 1964, featuring new material, saw more than 1,000 performance. At the cutting edge of comic satire, *Beyond the Fringe* had its roots in the GOON SHOW of the 1950s; it influenced the British comedy troupe MONTY PYTHON'S FLYING CIRCUS, the American television shows *SATURDAY NIGHT LIVE* and the Canadian *SCTV* television program. The four members of the troupe each went on to successful individual careers in theater and film.

Bharatiya Janata Party (BJP) Political party in INDIA. Formed in April 1980 as a result of the splinter of the JANATA PARTY, the BJP formed around individuals who sympathized with the goals of the Bharatiya Jan Sangh, a nationalist party from the 1950s that decried the iniquitous effects of Western culture and ideas on Indian society. The BJP has consistently championed a platform that calls for India to return to its Hindu cultural and religious roots, end India's experience as a secular state, revoke the separate civil code applied to the Muslim minority in autonomous regions like KASHMIR, continue to develop its nuclear deterrent and limit the amount of influence foreign investors can have on the Indian economy.

For its first 10 years the BJP exerted a strong sectional appeal within India's northern regions, particularly among Hindi-speaking, urban middle-class entrepreneurs. It engaged in the clever manipulation of religious Hindu symbols in an effort to stir popular passions. In the 1990s it began to develop a more national following and by 1996 had won a plurality of 161 of the 545 possible seats in the Indian Parliament. As the largest party in Parliament, the BJP and its leader, Atal Bihari Vajpayee, attempted to form a coalition government with Vajpayee as prime minister but failed to do so because it could not muster a majority vote of confidence. In national elections held in 1998 and

1999 as a result of the dissolution of the coalition governments formed between the BJP and other Indian political parties, the BJP retained its status as the largest party within Parliament. This time it managed to forge a successful coalition, called the National Democratic Alliance, with Vajpayee occupying the premiership.

The national success of the BJP prompted the party to tone down some of the pro-Hindu rhetoric, enabling it to gain support among the Muslim electorate. BJP leaders have described the party's new ideology as the "philosophy of integral humanism." However, a strong ultranationalist element remained within the BJP. Several of its members have been accused of participation in the outbreak of anti-Muslim violence in the Gujarat region between February and March 2002 that led to 2,000 deaths.

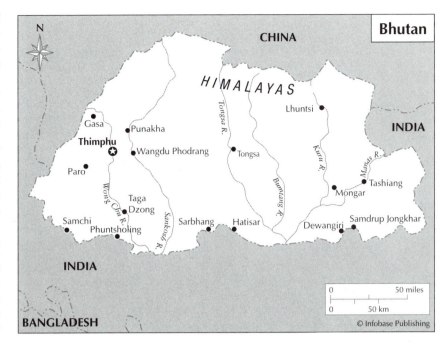

Bhopal disaster Leak of a highly toxic gas (methyl isocyanate) at the Union Carbide pesticide plant in the central Indian city of Bhopal on December 3, 1984. The leak killed over 2,000 and injured some 50,000 others out of a total population of about 800,000. The gas severely affected the functioning of the lungs, causing severe asthma, and many suffered permanent lung, kidney, liver and eye damage. The Indian government sued Union Carbide for the disaster, and in a settlement reached by the Indian Supreme Court in 1989, Union Carbide paid the country $465 million.

Bhutan (Drukyull) Nation in Central Asia, wedged between northeastern India and Tibet; the capital is Thimbu, but the traditional capital is Punaka. The Himalaya Mountains crisscross the country from north to south, with the resultant valleys serving as agricultural land for the kingdom. The population shares its ethnic heritage with Tibet, and the dominant religion is a Lamaist form of Buddhism. In 1907 the British installed Sir Ugyen Wangchuk as the first of a hereditary line of kings. In 1949 India assumed responsibility for the defense and foreign policy of Bhutan. In 1950 China took control over Tibet and made claim to Bhutan as well—a claim that India rejected. From 1953 to 1972 King Jigme Dorji Wangchuk made improvements, in-

cluding the abolition of the caste system and slavery, the emancipation of women and the partition of large landholdings. A democratization of the monarchical government took place in 1969. In 1972, JIGME SINGYE WANGCHUK was crowned as king. During the 1990s Bhutan's king came under increasing pressure from such international groups as AMNESTY INTERNATIONAL and domestic groups such as the outlawed Bhutan People's Party to establish democratic rule. The monarchy's greatest democratic concessions came in 1998, when the king handed over some political functions to the national assembly, and in 1999, when he permitted establishment of television and Internet services. In 2005 King Wangchuk announced that he would abdicate in 2008, in favor of his son the crown prince.

Bhutto, Benazir *(1953–)* Politician and prime minister (1988–90, 1993–96) of Pakistan. Bhutto graduated from Radcliffe College in 1969 and obtained a master's degree from Oxford University in 1976. She is the daughter of former Pakistan prime minister Zulfikar Ali BHUTTO, who was executed in 1979. With her mother, Begum Nusrat, she assumed the leadership of the Pakistan People's Party (PPP). She returned to Pakistan from exile in 1986 and became prime minister in December 1988. In August 1989

Pakistan president Ghulam Ishag Khan dismissed Bhutto's government amid charges of nepotism and corruption. Bhutto called the charges politically motivated and asserted she would be returned to office by the voters. She was, however, decisively defeated by the opposition Islamic Democratic Alliance in October 1990. In 1993 Bhutto returned to power following a general election but was forced from office in 1996 amid charges of corruption. In April 1999 a Pakistani court tried and convicted Bhutto and her husband in abstentia of corruption.

Bhutto, Zulfikar Ali *(1928–1979)* President (1971–73) and prime minister (1973–77) of Pakistan. A barrister Bhutto served under President AYUB KHAN from 1958 to 1966. Foreign minister from 1963 to 1966, he resigned over the Indo-Pakistan truce (see INDO-PAKISTANI WAR OF 1965). Founder of the People's Party, which won a majority of seats in the assembly in 1970, he was elected president in 1971 when Pakistan was defeated in the war with INDIA over BANGLADESH (see INDO-PAKISTANI WAR OF 1971). He led Pakistan out of the COMMONWEALTH OF NATIONS in 1972 (when Britain, Australia and New Zealand recognized Bangladesh independence). Under a new constitution introduced in 1973, he became prime minister. Accusations of ballot rigging led to riots in 1977,

---

BHUTAN

1910	The Anglo-Bhutanese Treaty is signed, placing foreign relations under the "guidance" of the British government in India.
1952	Maharaja Jigme Dorji Wangchuk ascends to the throne.
1961	Bhutan's first five-year plan is launched.
1962	Bhutan joins the Colombo Plan.
1963	The ruler of Bhutan adopts the title of *druk gyalpo* "dragon king."
1964	Prime Minister Jigme Polden Dorji is assassinated; Brigadier Bahadur Namgyal, deputy commander in chief, is implicated and arrested along with 40 other members of the military. Namgyal is executed. Lhendup Dorji is named prime minister but becomes involved in a power struggle with the *druk gyalpo* and flees to Nepal with the army commander, Brigadier Ugyen Tyangbi. The *druk gyalpo* names himself prime minister.
1968	Bhutan's first High Court is established.
1969	Bhutan holds its first census.
1971	Bhutan is admitted to the United Nations.
1972	Druk Gyalpo Jigme Dorji Wangchuk dies; his son, 17-year-old Jigme Singhye Wangchuk, ascends the throne.
1974	The ngultrum is introduced as the national currency. Jigme Singhye Wangchuk is crowned king.
1983	Bhutan becomes a founding member of the South Asian Regional Cooperation (SARC), in addition to Bangladesh, India, Maldives, Nepal, Pakistan and Sri Lanka.
1990	Alarmed by restoration of democracy in Nepal, King Wangchuk bans viewing of foreign television and orders strict enforcement of the Driglam Manzha, subjecting violators to fines and imprisonment; demonstrations are held.
1991–93	Thousand of illegal immigrants, mostly Nepali-speaking Hindus, are expelled.
1997	Nearly 80,000 Bhutanese refugees in United Nations camps in Nepal claim they were forced out of their homeland.
1998	King Wangchuk agrees to some constitutional governmental reforms, including the election of a cabinet.
1999	Bhutan releases 200 prisoners that human rights groups had identified as political detainees.
2003	Soldiers attack Indian separatist rebels in an attempt to drive them from their bases in the southern region. The rebels persistently ignore Bhutan's deadline, which required them to leave the country by 2001.
2005	A new constitution that encourages Bhutan to move toward a parliamentary democracy is unveiled. A referendum vote is awaited at the end of the year to adopt or reject the new legislation. King Wangchuk announces his intention to abdicate in 2008.

his overthrow by a military coup led by General ZIA UL-HAQ and his execution in 1979.

Biafra Region in eastern NIGERIA. Formerly a republic, it is populated by the Ibo (Igbo) tribe, as opposed to western Nigeria, which is populated by the Hausa tribe. In 1967 ethnic tensions spurred a declaration of independence by Biafra's General O. OJUKWU. Civil war resulted, and the population of Biafra was forced into starvation by the tactics of the Nigerian governmental forces. In 1970 Biafra surrendered. Since then the Nigerian government has adopted a policy of leniency.

Bicesse Accord In 1991 the Popular Movement for the Liberation of Angola (MPLA) and the National Union for the Total Independence of Angola (UNITA), the two warring factions in the Angolan civil war, signed the Bicesse Accord under pressure from their respective COLD WAR sponsors, the USSR and U.S. The accord codified a cease-fire between the MPLA government and the UNITA rebel movement, created an Angolan national army that would integrate MPLA and UNITA commanders, provided for a resolution of grievances between the two sides and scheduled UN-monitored free elections for the Angolan legislature and presidency. In the ensuing multiparty elections of 1992 the MPLA acquired a majority of seats in the legislature. The UNITA leader and presidential candidate, Jonas SAVIMBI, failed to win election in the first round of voting garnering 40% of the vote and trailing the MPLA leader and candidate, José Eduardo DOS SANTOS, who had 49%. Savimbi alleged that the elections were fraudulent and broke the cease-fire, reigniting the civil war. (See also ANGOLA.)

Bidault, Georges (1899–1983) French government official. During WORLD WAR II Bidault was active in the French RESISTANCE, and in 1943 he became president of the National Council of the Resistance. In 1944 he was named foreign minister in Charles de GAULLE's provisional government. As founder of the Popular Republican Movement, Bidault played a pivotal role in the coalition governments of the Fourth Republic, and he served in the French cabinet almost constantly from 1944 to 1954, playing a dominant role in French foreign policy during these years. A strident opponent of independence for ALGERIA, Bidault quit France to lead the underground opposition. He accepted political asylum in Brazil in 1963, eventually returning to France after the political amnesty in 1968.

Bierce, Ambrose (1842–1914?) American author. Born in Ohio, he fought in the U.S. Civil War. He subsequently worked as a journalist in California and later in London (1872–76), where he published some volumes of sketches and epigrams. He eventually settled in Washington, D.C. He is best known for his numerous short stories collected in *Tales of Soldiers and Civilians* (1891; renamed *In the Midst of Life,* 1892, revised 1898), which show the influence of Edgar Allan Poe. His fiction is darkly realistic and bitterly ironical. He also wrote *The Devil's Dictionary* (1906), a peevish and droll collection of definitions. In 1913 he traveled to Mexico and vanished mysteriously, perhaps perishing in the MEXICAN CIVIL WAR, although the actual date and cause of his death are unknown. A fictional account of his last days is given in the novel *The Old Gringo* by Carlos FUENTES.

big bands See SWING ERA.

big bang theory Theory that at one time all the matter in the universe was condensed into an area infinitesimally small and infinitesimally dense, and that a massive explosion threw this matter out into space, creating the universe as we know it. After Albert EINSTEIN published his general theory of relativity (1916), scientists began to consider various nontraditional views of the universe and its origin. Russian mathematician and physicist Alexander FRIEDMANN (1922) and Belgian astronomer Georges LEMAITRE (1927) independently proposed that the universe is not static but constantly expanding. In 1929 astronomer Edwin HUBBLE made observations that confirmed these views. Friedmann, Lemaitre and Hubble's findings pointed to the big bang theory, although not all scientists were ready to accept this theory. British astronomer Fred HOYLE and others proposed the **steady-state theory,** which posited that new matter was being created continuously. In 1970 British physicists Roger Penrose and Stephen HAWKING published a paper offering mathematical proof of the big bang theory, again on the basis of Einstein's general theory of relativity. The big bang theory has been widely accepted in the scientific community, although some scientists and mathematicians have questioned various assumptions or conclusions.

Bikini U.S.-owned atoll, a part of the Marshall Islands chain in the central Pacific Ocean. First discovered by Europeans in 1825, it was formerly known as Escholtz Atoll. From 1946 to 1958, when it was used by the U.S. as an atomic testing site, the indigenous population was forced to leave and not allowed to return until 1969 (under medical supervision). In the late 1940s it lent its name to a woman's swimsuit style.

Biko, Steve (1947–1977) South African nationalist leader. One of the founders of the **Black Consciousness** movement and president of the South African Students Organization established in 1969, he organized the Black Community Program banned by the South African government following the Durban strikes in 1973. He was arrested and died in police custody, his death sparking major international concern. (See also APARTHEID; SOUTH AFRICA.)

Bill, Max (1908–1994) Swiss architect and designer whose work is identified with the austere MODERNISM thought of as characteristically Swiss. Bill studied at the BAUHAUS and was director of the Hochschule für Gestaltung at Ulm from 1951 to 1956. His influence, through his teaching, writing and the Gute Form exhibitions that he organized, was a continuing force in favor of the functionalist ideas that stem from Bauhaus origins. His work as a painter and sculptor equalled his design production in importance and quality.

Billings-Mooney Affair In 1916, during WORLD WAR I, a patriotic parade in San Francisco was bombed. Warren K. Billings and Tom Mooney, two controversial labor organizers and agitators, were charged with the bombing. The two were convicted and imprisoned, but the case became an international cause célèbre after witnesses changed their testimony and fraudulent evidence was revealed. Both men were released from prison in 1939.

Billy Sol Estes scandal A scandal involving prominent Democrats during the administration of President John KENNEDY. Billy Sol Estes, a self-made Texas millionaire, swindled millions of dollars from commercial finance companies by mortgaging nonexistent fertilizer tanks. He also circumvented government cotton allotment price supports by selling land to farmers with unused allotments and then leasing it back to get around the allotment limit. A newspaper exposé revealed Estes's operations and precipitated a congressional investigation of his connections in the Department of Agriculture. Although the investigation found no collusion, it did find lax controls that allowed Estes to circumvent several rules. Estes was tried and convicted for mail fraud and conspiracy and served a lengthy prison sentence in addition to paying a large fine. After his release he again became involved in a fraudulent scheme and was convicted again and returned to the penitentiary. Estes was paroled in 1983.

Billy the Kid Landmark American ballet choreographed by Agnes DE MILLE that, with *FILLING STATION,* was one of the first ballets of specifically American inspiration. First performed by Ballet Caravan in Chicago on October 16, 1938, it brought together the talents of impresario Lincoln KIRSTEIN, composer Aaron COPLAND, choreographer Eugene Loring (who danced the title role) and dancers Lew Christensen, Todd Bolender and Marie-Jeanne. Its 11 episodes depict the lawless career of William Bonney. Choreographically the dancers' movements are derived from natural gesture rather than from the ballet vocabulary. Copland's music teases the ear with its elusive references to cowboy songs such as "Old Paint" and "The Old Chisholm Trail." The ballet is best known today through a suite of music for which Copland used approximately two-thirds of the ballet score.

Binet, Alfred (*1857–1911*) French psychologist. Binet was a pioneering figure in modern psychological research who played a major role in the development of biometrics and psychometrics. Binet invented, in 1905, a series of intelligence tests for children that formed the basis for much of the scholastic intelligence testing done in Europe and America for decades to come. Throughout his career, Binet argued that psychological research should closely follow the models offered by the natural sciences and physiology and include within its focus animal behavior and genetic development. In his own researches Binet established new techniques for statistical measurement, evaluation of higher mental faculties and control group comparisons. His writings include *The Psychology of Rea-*

soning (1886) and *Alterations of Personality* (1892).

Bing, Sir Rudolph (*1902–1997*) Viennese-born opera director and impresario. Bing studied at the University of Vienna but chose to work in music as an administration rather than a performer, associating himself first with a musical agency in Vienna, from 1923 to 1927, then with the Darmstadt State Theater and the Municipal Opera at Charlottenburg-Berlin. He helped to found the Glyndebourne Opera Festival in England in 1933 and became its manager from 1935 to 1939 and again from 1946 to 1949. In 1947 he helped to found the Edinburgh International Festival of Music and Drama and served as its first director. In 1950 Bing was made general manager of the Metropolitan Opera in New York City and guided the development of the Metropolitan Opera House at Lincoln Center, which opened in 1966. His memoir, *Five Thousand Nights at the Opera* (1972), tells of his time at the Met, from which he resigned in 1972. A British subject since 1946, he was knighted in 1971. Among the many opera singers that Bing presented at the Met were Maria CALLAS, Joan SUTHERLAND, Franco CORELLI and Tito GOBBI. He also presented the first black in a leading role of the Met when Marion ANDERSON sang Ulrica in Verdi's *Un Ballo in Maschera* (1955).

Bingham, Hiram (*1875–1956*) American explorer, statesman and educator. An expert on South American history, Bingham taught at Yale University from 1907 to 1923, served as a U.S. delegate to the Pan-American Scientific Congress in 1908 and made several important scientific/historical expeditions to South America between 1906 and 1915. On his most famous expedition in 1911, he discovered the great Inca ruins of Machu Picchu and Vitcos, the last Inca capital, in Peru. He also served briefly as governor of Connecticut, in 1924, then as that state's U.S. senator from 1924 to 1933.

bin Laden, Osama (*1957–　*) Head of the fundamentalist Islamic terrorist group al-QAEDA. While his early years remain shrouded in mystery, much is known of bin Laden's actions as an adult. Born into a Saudi Arabian family made wealthy through its success in

the construction business, bin Laden traveled to AFGHANISTAN as a young man to participate in the Islamic rebellion against the Soviet invasion of that country. As one of thousands of such young Muslim men participating in a jihad, or "holy war," against the Soviet forces, bin Laden received military and intelligence training from the MUJAHIDEEN, the bands of Islamic fighters that formed to carry on a guerrilla campaign against the Soviets and their allies in Afghanistan. It was during this nearly decade-long struggle that bin Laden formed Maktab al-Khidmat (MAK), an organization that solicited the participation of Muslim men across the world in this conflict.

When the mujahideen had forced the total withdrawal of Soviet forces from Afghanistan in February 1989, bin Laden and Mohammad Atef formed al-Qaeda, an umbrella group for mujahideen, based al-Qaeda along the western extremities of the Afghanistan-Pakistan border and returned to SAUDI ARABIA, where he focused his efforts on combating the increasing Western presence in the Muslim world. A follower of ISLAMISM, a fundamentalist Muslim philosophy that requires strict adherence to Islamic law and life, bin Laden became a critic of the Saudi government's close association with Western nations, particularly the visible and sizable U.S. military presence in Saudi Arabia during and after the PERSIAN GULF WAR of 1991. As a result of his activities, bin Laden was expelled from Saudi Arabia in 1991 and spent the next five years in SUDAN, where he was provided refuge by the Islamist government of President Omar BASHIR, and continued to fund the al-Qaeda training camps located in Afghanistan. However, American pressure on the Sudanese government resulted in bin Laden's second expulsion and return to Afghanistan in 1996. There bin Laden became a more visible leader of al-Qaeda, which he largely funded through his familial wealth. Bin Laden became particularly involved in al-Qaeda's support of the TALIBAN government of Afghanistan, which also espoused an Islamist ideology and applied its teachings to Afghan society. He has been connected to a variety of attacks on American targets throughout the world, such as the 1993 bombing of the WORLD TRADE CENTER, the 1998 destruction of the American embassies in Kenya and

Tanzania, the bomb attack on the USS *Cole* in 2000, and the terrorist attacks on New York City and Washington, D.C., on SEPTEMBER 11, 2001. After the U.S. invaded Afghanistan in an effort to capture bin Laden and destroy his training camps, he went into hiding in an effort to continue his efforts to "liberate" the Muslim world through terrorist attacks on the U.S.

Biograph Company One of the first important American motion picture studios. As a chief competitor to the EDISON COMPANY, founding member of the Motion Picture Patents Company and home studio to such developing talents as Edwin S. Porter and D. W. GRIFFITH, it would have enormous impact upon the course of the American movie industry. Originally named the American Mutoscope Company, it was founded in 1895 by Henry Norton Marvin to manufacture a peep-show machine called the Mutoscope. With the help of former Edison associate W. K. L. Dickson, the company made a camera that did not infringe on the Edison patents and presented its first program of short films at Hammerstein's Olympia Music Hall in New York City on October 12, 1896 (just six months after a program of Edison films was premiered). Now called the American Mutoscope and Biograph Company (later shortened to simply Biograph), in 1908–09 the company engaged in a series of court battles with Edison for control over patents of motion picture equipment. In 1909 the two rival companies formed the nucleus of the notorious Motion Picture Patents Company, which sought to monopolize the patents governing film production, distribution and exhibition in the U.S. Most Biograph films were made at a studio located at 11 East 14th Street in New York City. Former actor and playwright D. W. Griffith directed his first film for Biograph, *The Adventures of Dollie* (1908); thereafter until 1913 Griffith supervised virtually all Biograph product, personally directing some of his greatest and most influential one- and two-reel movies, including *The Lonely Villa* (1909), *Enoch Arden* (1911), *The Lonedale Operator* (1911) and *The Musketeers of Pig Alley* (1912). He also built up a stock company of players, including Mary PICKFORD, Lillian and Dorothy GISH, Mae Marsh and

Robert Harron. In 1913 Biograph signed with the Broadway firm of Klaw and Erlanger to produce feature-length adaptations of popular stage plays. However, after Griffith's departure late in 1913, Biograph began to decline. Its policy of limiting publicity for its stars and the dissolution of the Patents Company hastened its demise in 1915.

Biological and Toxin Weapons Convention (BTWC) Signed on April 10, 1972, the BTWC prohibits its 148 signatory states from developing, producing and stockpiling bacteriological and chemical weapons and requires them to destroy any biological and chemical weapons and delivery systems they had produced prior to their ratification of the convention. However, the convention failed to established any means of verifying absolute compliance with its provisions. For instance, in 1992 Russia admitted that Soviet military officials had regularly violated the BTWC during the COLD WAR by maintaining its bacteriological stockpiles; in the same year, Russia agreed to allow international inspectors unfettered access to verify its compliance with BTWC guidelines. However, the relative ease with which any scientist can produce biological weapons agents continues to make enforcement of the BTWC through inspection, detection and verification exceedingly difficult.

Birdseye, Clarence (*1886–1956*) American inventor and the father of the frozen foods industry. Although attempts to commercially freeze foods had begun as early as the 1840s, the technology was not perfected until 1917, when New York inventor and businessman Birdseye began to quick-freeze food in individual packages. Birdseye's technique, which he had seen used by the native peoples of Labrador, was the first to retain the original flavor and texture of the food; after his breakthrough, the frozen foods industry expanded rapidly. In 1929 he sold his General Seafoods Corp. for $22 million. The new owners, the Postum Co. and the investment firm Goldman-Sachs, renamed it General Foods.

Birendra Bir Bikram Shah Dev (*1945–2001*) King of Nepal (1972–2001). Born into the Hindu royal

family of Nepal, Birenda received his education at the hands of Jesuit instructors in India before heading to Britain, where he attended Eton from 1959 to 1964. After he graduated from Eton, he studied further at the University of Tokyo as well as a year at Harvard University.

In 1972, following the death of his father, King Mahendra, Birendra became the reigning monarch of Nepal. Birendra allowed greater civil liberties and designated a panel of 11 individuals charged with reforming the country's constitution. This body, called the Constitution Reforms Commission, then persuaded the king to create a national *panchayat,* or council, that would serve as a parliament. An election for the legislature led to the creation of a ministerial government that would assist the king in his governing tasks. Birendra was also known for his close association with his subjects. He regularly inspected Nepalese villages, often flying to these mountainous locations by helicopter, to observe living conditions and determine what could be done to improve their livelihood.

In November 1990 Birendra caved in to the demands of those elements within Nepal calling for a wholly parliamentary government and ceded all of his authority to a council of ministers and a prime minister. Birendra and his family then adopted a more ceremonial role, in the fashion of the royal families of European constitutional monarchies. On June 1, 2001, King Birendra, his wife of 21 years, Queen Aiswarya, and two of his children, Prince Nirajan and Princess Shruti, were shot and killed by Crown Prince Dipendra, allegedly over a dispute between the queen and the crown prince over whom the latter should marry. Shortly after killing his siblings and his parents, Dipendra committed suicide. King Birendra was succeeded by his brother, Prince Gyanendra.

Birmingham Largest city in Alabama (2000 population: 242,820) and the industrial and cultural capital of the state; site of major protests of the CIVIL RIGHTS MOVEMENT from April 3 to May 10, 1963. On April 3, 1963, the SOUTHERN CHRISTIAN LEADERSHIP CONFERENCE (SCLC), directed by Martin Luther KING Jr., began a boycott of Birmingham businesses to draw attention to the grievances of the city's blacks. Daily protest marches began on April 6, until halted by an injunction four days later. On April 12, King led another march, in defiance of the injunction, and was arrested and later convicted of criminal contempt. On April 16, King called for unity and justified civil disobedience in the face of injustice in an open letter now known as the Letter from Birmingham Jail. More than 900 youngsters between the ages of six and 16 were arrested for taking part in a children's march on May 2. On May 3 nearly 1,000 marching protesters were attacked by police with nightsticks, dogs and fire hoses.

As print and broadcast journalists documented the violent reaction of the police over the next four days, American public opinion tilted in favor of the SCLC. On May 7 two demonstrations degenerated into rioting in reaction to the actions of the police. Eager to end the escalating violence, on May 10 white leaders announced an agreement with the civil rights organizers, the key points of which included gradual integration of the city's businesses. That night, however, bombs exploded at the house of Rev. A. D. King, brother of King Jr., and at the SCLC's headquarters, sparking a night of rioting in the city. On September 15, 1963, a church in Birmingham was bombed, killing four black girls. Although white city leaders honored their promises only incompletely, the SCLC campaign in Birmingham had the effect of enhancing King's prestige within his movement and around the nation, and it moved the KENNEDY administration toward direct action on the issue of civil rights.

Birth of a Nation, The

Birth of a Nation, The Classic American silent film and among the top box-office blockbusters in history. No other motion picture has ever received more praise—and blame. It was directed by D. W. GRIFFITH and premiered at the Clunes Auditorium in Los Angeles, February 8, 1915, as *The Clansman* (the title was changed after the premiere). The story of two families separated by the Civil War and the subsequent Reconstruction was adapted from Thomas Dixon's controversial racist novel *The Clansman* (1906). The film validated the feature-length format, vaulted the American film indus-

try into the front rank of international cinema, influenced narrative techniques for the next decade and brought an expanded critical awareness to the new medium. Its use of pioneering techniques—flashbacks, parallel editing, moving camera, masked frames, close-ups and panoramas—was dazzling, prompting the remark attributed to President Woodrow WILSON, "It is like history written in lightning." However, the depiction of blacks—especially mulattos—in the Reconstruction sequences triggered black protests from the NAACP and other groups. Charges of racism dogged the film wherever it opened, precipitating riots. Attempts to censor and ban the film led to an important Supreme Court decision in 1915 (*Mutual Film Corporation v. Industrial Commission of Ohio*) denying motion pictures protection under the First Amendment—a decision not reversed until 1952. Distribution was on a states-rights basis, and *Birth of a Nation* was in almost continual release throughout the silent film period and, with synchronized music, well into the sound period—generating repeated waves of protest. And so it has been ever since. Griffith himself vigorously refuted charges of racism and, in a pamphlet he wrote in 1916 called "The Rise and Fall of Free Speech in America," argued for the movies' right to protection as a form of the press right. (Griffith had some justice on his side, since he had cleaned up considerably Dixon's racist rag of a novel.) In the final analysis, film historian Kevin Brownlow has said its reputation must reside in its importance as a cornerstone in the development of the medium: "It established the classic format of the American motion picture and separated it for all time from the stage."

Bishop, Elizabeth

Bishop, Elizabeth *(1911–1979)* American poet. Bishop's first book, *North and South* (1945), established her reputation as a gifted poet. Her second book, *A Cold Spring* (1956), won a PULITZER PRIZE. For many years she lived abroad, mainly in Brazil. Her poems deal with exile, travel and the longing for identity in an impersonal and threatening world, and her best work is characterized by a sense of the strangeness that underlies ordinary events. Although she was a member of the generation of CONFESSIONAL POETS, her treatment of per-

sonal themes is calm and understated. Her other books include *Questions of Travel* (1965) and *Geography III* (1976). She served as a consultant in poetry at the Library of Congress (1949–50).

Bishop, Ronald Eric

Bishop, Ronald Eric *(1903–1989)* British aircraft designer. Bishop was the creator of the Comet, the world's first production jet airliner, as well as the wooden DH-98 Mosquito bomber, which proved to be one of Britain's most versatile military planes in WORLD WAR II. Although the Comet won the postwar race to become the first jet-powered commercial airliner, it fell into disfavor following a series of crashes caused by structural failure induced by metal fatigue. However, Bishop continued to design civil and military aircraft until he retired from the De Havilland Aircraft Company in 1964.

Bishop, William Avery "Billy"

Bishop, William Avery "Billy" *(1894–1956)* Canadian WORLD WAR I flying ace. The top-ranking Imperial or Canadian ace of the war, the flamboyant Bishop was credited with shooting down 72 enemy aircraft. He was the first Canadian airman to win the Victoria Cross, for a single-handed attack on a German airfield.

Bismarck

Bismarck The most famous German battleship of WORLD WAR II, the *Bismarck* was completed at Hamburg toward the end of 1940. After a shakedown cruise in the Baltic Sea, the ship, one of the largest and fastest vessels of the war, sailed from Gdynia on May 18, 1941, with the cruiser *Prinz Eugen,* their mission to harass Atlantic shipping. On May 24 the *Bismarck* was intercepted at the Denmark Strait by the British battle cruiser *Hood* and the battleship *Prince of Wales.* In the fighting the *Hood* was sunk, with nearly 1,400 men killed, and the *Prince of Wales* was damaged. The *Bismarck,* also damaged, sailed toward German-occupied France, with other ships of the Royal Navy in pursuit. On the night of May 24 the German battleship was attacked by torpedo-bombers from the *Victorious.* After temporarily slipping away from the British, the *Bismarck* was assaulted again on the morning of May 26 by planes from the *Ark Royal* and on the next day by the *King George V,* the *Rodney* and the *Dorsetshire.* The *Bismarck* sank at 10:30 A.M. on May 27, with the loss of more than 2,000 crew-members. By destroying the *Bismarck,* following the 1939 sinking of Germany's *GRAF SPEE,* Britain had struck an important blow in the Battle of the ATLANTIC.

Bismarck Archipelago Archipelago northeast of the island of New Guinea. Now a part of Papua New Guinea, the archipelago includes the ADMIRALTY ISLANDS, New Britain and New Ireland. Topographically, the islands were formed by volcanic activity and support heavy forest growth. They were seized by Germany in 1884 and subsequently named after Otto von Bismarck, the German chancellor. During WORLD WAR I they were occupied by Australian forces. During WORLD WAR II they were conquered by the Japanese but regained by Allied forces in 1944.

Björling, Jussi John Jonaton *(1911–1960)* Swedish operatic tenor known for the beauty and purity of his voice and for his stylish singing in the great tenor roles of Italian opera. Björling made his operatic debut in 1930 in Stockholm, singing Don Ottavio in Mozart's *Don Giovanni.* In the next half-dozen years he sang major roles with opera companies throughout Europe. In 1937 he went to the U.S., where he quickly received public and critical acclaim. In 1938 he gave his first recital at CARNEGIE HALL and shortly thereafter was signed to a contract at the Metropolitan Opera in New York. Björling spent WORLD WAR II in Scandinavia. After the war he returned to the Metropolitan, where he remained (except for three seasons) one of the company's principal tenors until his untimely death from a heart attack. During this time he was virtually unparalleled in such leading roles as Rodolfo in *La Bohème* and Cavaradossi in *Tosca* (both by PUCCINI) and the Duke in Verdi's *Rigoletto.* Many critics consider Björling's voice comparable to that of the great CARUSO. Björling's golden tones have been captured in many distinguished recordings, including a classic record of *La Bohème* conducted by Sir Thomas BEECHAM.

Black, Davidson *(1884–1934)* Canadian anthropologist whose work expanded the knowledge of human evolution. Trained in medicine at the University of Toronto, Black went to China in 1918 to teach at a medical college in Beijing (Peking). In 1927, after the discovery of some fossilized remains at a cave near Beijing. Black classified a hitherto unknown genus and species of prehuman hominid. This he called *Sinanthropus pekinensis,* or Peking man. Peking man was dated at nearly half a million years old.

Black, Hugo Lafayette *(1886–1971)* Associate justice, U.S. Supreme Court (1937–71). A graduate of Birmingham Medical College and the University of Alabama Law School, Hugo Black grew up in rural Alabama. After abandoning medicine he studied law and became a lawyer in private practice and later a local judge. Black won an upset election as U.S. senator from Alabama in 1926. In the Senate he was a loyal and vocal supporter of President Franklin D. ROOSEVELT's NEW DEAL. Roosevelt appointed Black to the Supreme Court in 1937. The nomination was controversial because Black was a former member of the KU KLUX KLAN. However, on the Court he proved an effective champion of civil rights and continued as a strong supporter of New Deal legislation. He was later an important member of the WARREN Court. Black wrote many of the era's important decisions, including *ENGEL v. VITALE,* which banned public school prayer, and *GIDEON v. WAINWRIGHT,* which required counsel in criminal cases.

Black Consciousness See Steve BIKO.

Black Hand, The Popular name of a Serbian secret society known as "Unity or Death," which was founded in 1911 in an attempt to unite Serbs from Austria-Hungary and Turkey with those living in independent Serbia. Led by Colonel Dragutin Dimitrijević, the group has been blamed for the assassination of Archduke FRANZ FERDINAND, heir apparent to the Austro-Hungarian throne, on June 28, 1914. In 1916 Black Hand leaders were arrested by Serbian government authorities and accused of plotting to murder the Serbian prince regent. Dimitrijević and two others were tried, found guilty and executed, and the Black Hand society was disbanded. The name has also been used to designate an alleged organization held responsible for crime in the U.S. Italian community during the early 20th century. Many immigrants received extortion letters signed with a black hand, and the senders were thought to belong to an organization with links to the MAFIA. However, modern researchers doubt a criminal band was actually responsible for most of the threats and have seen the black hand as a symbol of terror, not as the signature of an organized group.

black hole Term coined by American physicist John Wheeler in 1969 to describe a star that has collapsed and become so dense that no light can escape from it. The concept of the black hole was actually originated in 1783 by a Cambridge don. In the 20th century the black hole phenomenon has been studied and verified by a number of scientists. Black holes hold fascination for scientists because matter and energy behave very differently in black holes than they do in the rest of the universe.

Black Hundreds, Raids of the *(1906–1911)* As a reaction against the RUSSIAN REVOLUTION OF 1905, the czarist government secretly sanctioned a reactionary, anti-Semitic group, **League of the Russian People,** also known as the Black Hundreds. Made up of landowners, wealthy peasants, officials and police, it attacked revolutionaries in the provinces and organized frequent, violent pogroms in more than 100 cities. In Odessa, Jews and others were slaughtered for four days before order was restored. These repressions encouraged Russia's autocratic leadership to delay enactment of the constitution of 1905. (See also ANTI-SEMITISM.)

blacklist A list of persons to be denied employment. Early in the century employers maintained blacklists of workers who were union members or sympathetic to unions; but blacklists gained their greatest notoriety in HOLLYWOOD after WORLD WAR II, at the height of the anticommunist McCarthy era. In 1946 President Truman required federal employees to sign loyalty oaths. After a private consulting firm founded by former FBI agents wrote that many broadcasters had alleged leftist leanings, hundreds of writers, directors, producers and performers were fired and blacklisted from the industry. Some of the most talented were able to work under pseudonyms but many others lost their livelihoods. The blacklisting episode eventually widened into the MCCARTHYISM hysteria that gripped the nation for a number of years.

"Black Mask School" The name of the so-called hard-boiled school of American detective fiction—and the magazine that spawned it in the 1920s and 1930s. When H. L. MENCKEN and George Jean Nathan began publishing *Black Mask* magazine in the spring of 1920, most detective stories followed the formulas laid down by 19th-century masters like Emile Gaboriau and A. Conan DOYLE. Dapper detective and shrewd policemen matched their feats of ratiocination against the enigmatic clues and ingenious puzzles of the criminal mind. However, a succession of editors of *Black Mask* including Phil Cody, Harry North and especially Captain ("Cap") Joseph T. Shaw, encouraged a new generation of writers in rather different directions. Beginning with the appearance of the Race Williams stories of Carroll John Daly, the Continental Op tales of Dashiell HAMMETT and, later in the decade, the Sam Spade adventures (also by Hammett), detective fiction developed a new "American language," as Mencken put it. The stories were told in terse, clipped diction at a racehorse gallop. Race, the Op and Spade were violent, even brutal characters who nonetheless adhered fiercely to their own highly individualistic codes of honor. "I trusted myself," said Race, "that was what counted." In a murky world bereft of values, these men knew violence was the only act of human courage and decision. Women and relationships were, as the Op put it, "nuisances during business hours." With the publication in *Black Mask* between 1927–30 of Hammett's four novels, *Red Harvest*, *The Dain Curse*, *The Maltese Falcon* and *The Glass Key*, and the appearance late in the 1930s of Raymond CHANDLER's Philip Marlowe in *The Big Sleep* (1939), the hard-boiled school reached its peak. Chandler, particularly, brought to the form a richly poetic style full of colorful similes and evocative images. Motion pictures in the 1930s and 1940s like *The Thin Man* (1934), *The Maltese Falcon* (1940), *Murder, My Sweet* (1943) and *The Big Sleep* (1946) further honed the tradition for screen tough guys like William Powell, Humphrey BOGART and Dick Powell.

Blackmun, Harry A. *(1908–1999)* Associate justice, U.S. Supreme Court (1970–94). A graduate of Harvard University and Harvard Law School, Blackmun clerked for a federal judge in Minneapolis before entering private law practice. In 1950 he became counsel to the MAYO CLINIC in Rochester, Minnesota. In 1958 he was appointed to the Eighth Circuit Federal Court of Appeals. In 1970 President Richard M. NIXON appointed Blackmun to the Supreme Court to fill the vacancy left by the resignation of Abe FORTAS. Blackmun was Nixon's third choice; the president's two previous nominees—Clement Haynsworth and Harold Carswell—had been rejected by the Senate. Blackmun was confirmed without any protest.

Blackmun, a boyhood friend of Chief Justice Warren BURGER, was originally considered a "conservative" on the bench because of his adherence to strict constructionism. The two justices were sometimes referred to as the "Minnesota twins" because of the similarity of their voting records. Over the years, however, Blackmun moved to the center and finally the liberal wing of the Court. Blackmun's best-known and most controversial opinion was the majority opinion he wrote in *ROE V. WADE* legalizing ABORTION. The decision upheld the right to an abortion as a basic medical procedure protected by the right to individual privacy implied in the Constitution. In 1994 Blackmun retired from the Supreme Court and was replaced by Steven G. Breyer.

Black Power Movement that emerged in the U.S. in the 1960s to express the dissatisfaction of black people with their position in American society. It rejected integration and asserted the intellectual and cultural equality of blacks with whites. The movement was most aggressive in the late 1960s, but improvements in the position of black people in the 1970s and the death of leaders such as George Jackson and MALCOLM X seem to have muted it.

Black September Palestinian terrorist organization founded in 1970. In February 1970 King HUSSEIN of JORDAN sought to curtail activities of the PALESTINE LIBERATION ORGANIZATION (PLO). The organization responded with violence, leading to civil war (September 17–25). Jordanian government forces eventually imposed authority. Black September, founded following these events, was responsible for the kidnap attempt that resulted in the deaths of 12 Israeli athletes at the MUNICH OLYMPICS in 1972 and for other atrocities. (See also FATAH REVOLUTIONARY COUNCIL; JORDANIAN CIVIL WAR OF 1970–1971).

Black Shirts Popular name for the Italian Fascist paramilitary group formally known as the Fasci di combattimento. These units, founded by Benito MUSSOLINI in 1919, wore distinctive black shirts as a part of their uniforms. Ultrarightists and nationalist extremists who opposed communists, socialists and moderate liberals alike, they broke up strikes, attacked trade unions and made other violent assaults on their opponents. In 1922 the Black Shirts marched on Rome and initiated Mussolini's rule. (See also MARCH ON ROME.)

Black Sox scandal The unsavory events of the 1919 World Series have passed into literary and celluloid legend as other, unsullied fall classics have not. When the heavily favored Chicago White Sox lost to the National League champion Cincinnati Reds in eight error-riddled games (in a best-of-nine series), persistent rumors of a "fix" led to an investigation by the baseball commissioner, Kenesaw Mountain LANDIS. While the details of the scheme have never come to light, one theory has gangster Arnold Rothstein as a major backer. A grand jury cleared all eight indicted players, but Landis banned them from the game for life. Although the White Sox's legendary "Shoeless Joe" Jackson admitted taking the bribe, he batted .375 in the series. Jackson was allegedly confronted by a child outside the courtroom who cried, "Say it ain't so, Joe!"

Blair, Tony *(1953–)* British politician, member of parliament (1983–) and prime minister (1997–). Born in Edinburgh, Scotland, Blair was the son of a CONSERVATIVE PARTY politician and lawyer. In 1972 he graduated from Fettes College and enrolled at Oxford

British prime minister Tony Blair (FOREIGN AND COMMONWEALTH OFFICE)

University to specialize in industrial and trade union law. Four years later he graduated from Oxford with a law degree and began practicing law. In 1983 he was elected a Labour Party M.P., representing Sedgefield. A year after he entered the House of Commons he began his service in the Labour Party's "shadow" branches of government ministries during the Conservative governments of Margaret THATCHER and John MAJOR. In 1994, Blair was elected head of the Labour Party.

In his new position as head of the opposition, Blair eliminated the more extreme socialist elements of Labour's political platform. In particular, he removed Clause 4, which had promised that an elected Labour government would place all "means of production," as well as distribution networks and exchange systems, under government control. In May 1997 Blair led the party to victory in national elections and replaced Major as prime minister, becoming the youngest British statesman to hold that office in 185 years. In June 2001 Blair scheduled national elections, and Labour retained its large majority in the House of Commons after a decisive victory in the polls.

As prime minister, Blair established regional parliaments in Scotland and Wales, although only Scotland's parliament acquired the power to enact laws and levy taxes. Additionally, he reduced the powers of the House of Lords, the largely ceremonial upper house of Parliament. In foreign affairs Blair increased British efforts to negotiate with SINN FÉIN (the political organ of the IRISH REPUBLICAN ARMY), a terrorist organization that demanded the complete British withdrawal from Northern Ireland. In April 1998, after six months of peace talks with Sinn Féin spokesman Gerry ADAMS, a power-sharing arrangement was created in which Northern Ireland was governed largely by a legislature elected by its citizens, which shared power with an executive council appointed jointly by the United Kingdom and the Republic of Ireland. Later Blair lent strong support to American efforts to combat terrorism in Afghanistan and to eliminate the regime of Saddam HUSSEIN in Iraq. In 2003 Blair came under intense domestic criticism for his involvement in the U.S.-led invasion of Iraq. When the U.S. and Britain failed to gain the approval of the UN Security Council for military action against Iraq, Blair agreed to participate in the U.S.-led invasion. He defended these actions in Parliament on the grounds that they were needed to remove the threat to the world posed by the Iraqi dictator, who, Blair claimed, was building weapons of mass destruction. After the invasion of Iraq and the fall of Hussein's regime in the spring of 2003, no nuclear weapons were found in Iraq, prompting criticisms of Blair's decision by Conservative and Labour M.P.s. In 2005 Blair was elected to a third term; he later announced that it would be his last.

Blaize, Herbert Augustus (1918–1989) Grenadan statesman. Blaize served as chief minister in 1960 and 1961 and again from 1962 to 1967, when GRENADA was still a British colony. He then became a member of the opposition in Parliament, remaining in that role once full independence was granted in 1974. He came out of retirement and was elected prime minister in 1984, following the U.S. invasion of Grenada that ousted the Marxist government that had seized power and killed Prime Minister Maurice Bishop (1983). Blaize served as prime minister until his death.

Blake, Eubie (1883–1983) American RAGTIME composer and pianist. Blake reached his centenary year as an acclaimed legend in the field of American popular music. The son of former slaves, he was born in Baltimore. His fundamentalist mother opposed Blake's interest in ragtime music, but by age 12 he had joined a vocal quartet that performed the popular music outside saloons. In 1921, along with lyricist Noble Sissle, Blake wrote music for, and starred in, *Shuffle Along,* the first all-black Broadway production to successfully draw white audiences. One of the biggest hits from this show was "I'm Just Wild About Harry," which Harry S. TRUMAN used as a theme song in his 1948 presidential campaign. In 1954, after years of neglect, a reissued recording of Blake's ragtime tunes won him a new generation of fans. In 1978 the Broadway show *Eubie*—featuring 23 of Blake's songs—began a long and critically triumphant run. In 1981 Blake was awarded the Presidential Medal of Honor.

Blake, Nicholas See Cecil DAY LEWIS.

Blakely, Colin George Edward (1930–1987) British actor. Blakely became one of the most familiar figures in British theater, films and television by giving acclaimed performances in a wide variety of mostly supporting roles. A native of Northern Ireland, he made his London debut at the Royal Court Theater in 1959. In 1963 he joined the newly established National Theatre and achieved critical and popular acclaim as a member of that company for five years. Perhaps his outstanding role was as Dr. Watson in Billy WILDER's *The Private Life of Sherlock Holmes* (1970).

Blakey, Art (Abdullah Ibn Buhaina) (1919–1990) American jazz drummer, band leader and composer. Blakey is one of the preeminent drummers in the history of JAZZ, renowned by fans and fellow musicians alike for the subtlety and force of his rhythms. He was also the founder and leader of a band, the Jazz Messengers, which endured (with numerous changes in personnel) as a musical force from the late 1940s to the late 1980s. The Jazz Messengers became known as a vital training ground for young jazz musicians who learned their craft under Blakey's expert tutelage. Trumpeters Freddie Hubbard and Wynton MARSALIS, saxophonists Jackie McLean and Branford Marsalis, and pianist Horace Silver are just a few renowned Jazz Messenger alumni. Blakey, who was born in Pittsburgh, first emerged in the BEBOP era of the 1940s, when he played in bands led by Fletcher HENDERSON and Billy ECKSTINE.

Blalock, Alfred *(1899–1964)* American surgeon. A professor of surgery for many years at Johns Hopkins University, Blalock is known for his work on the vascular system. On the eve of America's entry into WORLD WAR II, Blalock demonstrated that surgical shock is caused by blood loss and accordingly introduced the practice of transfusions during surgery. In 1944 he performed the first "blue baby operation," in which surgery is performed on a fetus in utero to correct the congenital heart condition called pulmonary stenosis.

Blanc, Melvin Jerome *(1908–1989)* American actor, famous as the voices of such notable cartoon characters as BUGS BUNNY, Duffy Duck, Porky Pig, Elmer Fudd and Woody Woodpecker. In a career that spanned more than 60 years, Blanc provided voices for 800 WARNER BROS. cartoons as well as the animated television series *The Bugs Bunny Show* and *The Flintstones.*

Blass, Bill *(1922–2002)* Leading American fashion designer. Blass was self-taught as a fashion artist, drawing inspiration from the films he watched as a boy in his hometown in the American Midwest. He studied for a time at the Parsons School of Design and then began his professional career as a sketch artist in New York in 1940. Blass established his own design house in 1970, and his name and work became well known, placing him among the leaders of current apparel designers. He was known for women's suits. He licensed the use of his name to some 35 other firms. He even designed interiors for the LINCOLN CONTINENTAL automobile. Blass won seven Coty Awards. In 1999 Blass received the inaugural Lifetime Achievement Award from the Fashion Institute of Technology.

Blaue Reiter, Der **(The Blue Rider)** The name for a group of German expressionist painters who organized themselves in 1911 in order to promote—in their paintings and critical writings—the depiction in abstract form of spiritual realities. The name of the group was derived from a painting by Wassily KANDINSKY, one of its members. Other prominent painters associated with Der Blaue Reiter were Paul KLEE, Auguste MACKE and Franz MARC. While these artists were far from uniform in their styles, they were united in emphasizing spiritual concerns that they felt had been ignored by the Impressionists. Blaue Reiter exhibitions were held throughout Germany to publicize the aims of the group. Artists outside of Germany who exhibited with the group included Georges BRAQUE and Pablo PICASSO. With the outbreak of WORLD WAR I, Der Blaue Reiter ceased its organized activities.

Blériot, Louis *(1872–1936)* French pioneer aviator and airplane designer. Blériot began his career as a manufacturer of automobile accessories but became interested in flying in 1901. His early efforts at airplane building had very limited success, but by 1907 he arrived at the general plan of a tractor (engine-in-front) monoplane, the Blériot VI, which managed a number of successful (although brief) flights. In several further steps he progressed to the Blériot XI, the design that turned out to be his masterpiece. (The design must be credited, in part, to collaboration with Raymond Saulnier.) In 1909 Blériot made the first successful flight across the English Channel in this airplane, earning fame for himself and his airplane as well. The structure was made of steel tubing, ash and bamboo with fabric covering. Power was supplied by a 25-horsepower, three-cylinder engine. The wings were without ailerons, and banking was controlled by warping the entire wing. Bicycle-type wire landing wheels and the open frame of the rear fuselage construction gave the Blériot XI a fragile, insectlike appearance of great elegance. Its form was a first step toward the development of modern aircraft types. Shortly after his triumphant Channel flight, Blériot quit flying to devote himself to commercial production of his design. By 1914 over 800 Blériot aircraft had been produced. A surviving example was restored in 1979 and is displayed in the Smithsonian National Air and Space Museum in Washington, D.C.

blitzkrieg *(German:* "lightning war") Term first used in 1939 to describe the German invasion of Poland in WORLD WAR II and, subsequently, any sudden and overwhelming strike by one country against another. Despite frantic British and French negotiations to prevent it, Adolf HITLER was determined to absorb POLAND. On September 1, 1939, a well-equipped mechanized German army swept into Poland, while the German Luftwaffe (air force) destroyed Polish air defense and transportation systems and blasted industrial centers. A second German army invaded from East Prussia, while the Soviets invaded at the eastern border. The Poles fought valiantly but ineffectually, and although Britain and France declared war, they could do nothing. Warsaw was besieged and fell on September 27, and the last Polish resistance collapsed eight days later.

Bloch, Ernest *(1880–1959)* Swiss-American composer. Born in Switzerland, he studied abroad and returned to his native country to conduct and teach, notably at the Geneva Conservatory (1911–15). Settling in the U.S. and naturalized in 1924, Bloch taught at New York's Mannes School (1917–19), later becoming director of the Cleveland Institute of Music (1920–25) and the San Francisco Conservatory (1925–30). He returned to Switzerland to pursue his activities as a composer in 1930, coming back to the U.S. in 1938 and teaching part-time at the University of California at Berkeley, beginning in 1943. Bloch is best known for his expressive classical works composed in a specifically Jewish idiom. These compositions include the rhapsody *Schelomo,* the symphonic work *Israel* (both 1916), *Trois poèmes juifs* (1918), the *Sacred Service* (1933) and *Cinq pièces Hébraïques* (1951). Bloch's intense work includes many pieces in other musical modes, including five string quartets, the opera *Macbeth* (1909), two symphonic poems and various pieces for chorus and orchestra.

Bloemfontein South African city located on a tributary of the Modder River. Bloemfontein was the site, in 1899, of the Bloemfontein Conference, which failed to prevent the outbreak of the BOER WAR; the British occupied the city in 1900. It was also the site of negotiations leading to the establishment, in 1908, of an independent Union of SOUTH AFRICA.

Blok, Alexander (*1880–1921*) Russian poet. Born to the family of a university professor in St. Petersburg, Blok began publishing his poetry at the age of 20. He studied law and philosophy at the University of St. Petersburg and published his first book, *Songs to the Beautiful Lady,* in 1904. An early convert to the Russian Symbolist movement, he altered his views with the advent of Bolshevism, seeking an association with the Communist Party. An unhappy marriage, poverty and disillusionment with life, combined with his love of Russia, influenced the themes of social protest and individual despair that dominate the later works. His best-known book is *The Twelve* (1920), which depicts the rise of the Bolshevik movement in poetic form.

Bloody Sunday January 9, 1905, massacre of peaceful demonstrators in St. Petersburg, RUSSIA, by Russian imperial guards. A workers' strike in the city at the end of 1904 had led to a lockout by employers. As a consequence, some 200,000 people, mostly workers and their families, marched to the Winter Palace to petition Czar NICHOLAS II to end the lockout and to improve working and living conditions. The demonstration was organized in part by Georgi Capon, a priest and workers' leader who, it was later believed, acted as an agent provocateur. As the marchers approached the palace they were fired on by soldiers and police and dispersed. Some 130 were killed, and many more wounded. Ironically, the majority of the marchers were not revolutionaries but loyal citizens who looked up to the czar as the father of Russia. The events of Bloody Sunday radicalized public opinion within Russia and helped set in motion the events that led to the RUSSIAN REVOLUTION of 1917.

Bloody Sunday On January 30, 1972, 13 Catholic civilians were killed by British troops in Londonderry, NORTHERN IRELAND, while demonstrating in favor of civil rights and a united Ireland. The event aroused international condemnation and led to further escalation of the fighting in the province. (See also IRISH REPUBLICAN ARMY.)

Bloom, Allan (*1930–1992*) American philosopher, educator and social critic. Bloom, a professor at the University of Chicago, won national renown with the publication of THE CLOSING OF THE AMERICAN MIND: EDUCATION AND THE CRISIS OF REASON (1987). As a result of that book, Bloom became a leading spokesman for a traditional, conservative approach to American education from grade school through college. He attacked cultural relativism—the view that each culture has a set of beliefs that hold relative truth only within the context of that culture—as a de facto assault upon the Western intellectual tradition. That tradition, according to Bloom, ought to remain the foundation of American educational efforts. Bloom also argued in favor of more strict curricula that emphasize basic reading, writing and mathematical skills.

Bloomsbury Group A disparate group of British writers, painters and political thinkers that flourished between the two world wars. The key figures in what was designated the Bloomsbury Group (after the district of London in which most of them lived) were novelists Virginia WOOLF and E. M. FORSTER, art critic Roger FRY, painter Duncan GRANT, biographer Lytton STRACHEY, political essayist Leonard Woolf and economist John Maynard KEYNES, although there were a host of additional writers and bohemian figures who figured intermittently in the social doings of the group. The "Bloomsberries," as they called themselves, were linked, not by any single express ideology, but rather by a common sense of the ultimate value of aesthetic excellence and of the superiority of the bonds of friendship and love to those imposed by law and social custom. Homosexuality and bisexuality were common among group members, in defiance of the mores of the upper-class Victorian upbringing from which most of them had emerged. The Bloomsbury Group exercised a dominant influence upon British culture between the wars, and the social and sexual doings of the group continue to fascinate biographers to the present day.

bluegrass A distinctive musical blend of COUNTRY AND WESTERN and folk styles that emphasizes acoustic instrumenta-tion, driving tempos and vocal harmonies. Bluegrass took its name from the Blue Grass Boys, a band formed in the 1930s by Grand Old Opry star Bill Monroe, which featured Monroe on lead vocals and mandolin. Monroe was the first great star of bluegrass, and his influence shows itself strongly in the playing of subsequent stars such as guitarist Lester Flatt, banjo player Earl Scruggs, the harmonizing brother duo of Ralph and Stanley Carter and current-day bluegrass singer-guitarists Ricky Skaggs and Peter Rowan. The reason often given for the acoustic sound in bluegrass is that the original bluegrass players did not have electricity in their homes. This strong sense of rural folk tradition imbues the lyrical content of bluegrass songs, which celebrate simple country living, true love and family loyalty. Acoustic instruments specially featured in bluegrass playing include the fiddle, the string bass and the dobro (a steel or "Hawaiian" guitar).

blues An American musical form created primarily by blacks living in the southern states in the early decades of the 20th century. Blues music, with its emphatic, driving beat, emotion-laden vocals and earthy themes, draws musically from two key sources: the chanting field songs of black workers (often with melodies of African origin) and the impassioned gospel music of black church worship. It was in the 1920s that so-called blues music began to make an impact with the broad American public. Its first major stars were guitarist Blind Lemon Jefferson and singer Bessie SMITH. The legendary composer-guitarist Robert JOHNSON emerged in the 1930s, when blues music aptly mirrored the concerns of depression-era America. Also at this time, blues began to exercise a major influence on JAZZ musicians such as Count BASIE and Billie HOLIDAY. In the 1940s Chicago became a vital center of blues music: vocalist-guitarist Muddy WATERS, vocalist Howlin' Wolf and composer-bassist Willie Dixon were key figures of this era. In the 1950s, when ROCK and roll first came to prominence, many of the early hits of white singers such as Elvis PRESLEY were rerecordings of old blues songs. Leading lights of the current blues scene are guitarist-vocalists Albert Collins and Robert Cray.

Bluford, Guion (*1942–   *) U.S. astronaut. As a mission specialist aboard the U.S. SPACE SHUTTLE mission STS-8 (August 30–September 5, 1983), Bluford was the first African American to go into space. He made a second flight aboard Mission 61-A/Spacelab D1 (October 30–November 6, 1985) as part of an eight-astronaut team on a mission directed by the Federal German Aerospace Research Establishment. Bluford holds a Ph.D. in aerospace engineering. He retired from the NATIONAL AERONAUTICS AND SPACE ADMINISTRATION (NASA) in 1993.

Blum, Léon (*1872–1950*) French writer and political leader, premier (1936–37, 1946). A Jewish socialist, he was a literary critic who became politically active during the Dreyfus affair. He was elected to the office of deputy in 1919 and headed the French Socialist Party in 1925. In 1936 he became premier, presiding over a Popular Front government that included Socialists, Communists and other left-wing groups. In the year he held office Blum introduced such reforms as the 40-hour work week and collective bargaining and nationalized the Bank of France. He was ousted from office in 1937, returning for a few weeks in 1938. During WORLD WAR II he was arrested by the VICHY government (1940) and tried at Riom (1942) where he defended himself brilliantly. He was imprisoned until 1945. Growing more moderate in his views toward the end of his life, Blum returned briefly as interim premier in 1946.

Blumberg, Baruch Samuel (*1925–   *) American physician. Blumberg studied physics and mathematics at Union College, Schenectady, and at Columbia where, after a year, he changed to medical studies. He received his M.D. from Columbia in 1951 and his Ph.D. in biochemistry from Oxford University in 1957. After working at the National Institutes of Health in Bethesda, Maryland, from 1957 until 1964, Blumberg was appointed professor of medicine at the University of Pennsylvania. In 1963, while examining literally thousands of blood samples in a study of the variation in serum proteins in different populations, Blumberg made the important discovery of what soon became known as the "Aus-

tralian antigen." For his work on the Australian antigen, Blumberg shared the 1976 NOBEL PRIZE in physiology or medicine with Carleton Gajdusek. In 1999 Blumberg became director of the NASA Astrobiology Institute.

Blunt, Sir Anthony (*1907–1983*) British double agent. A don at Cambridge University in the 1930s, Blunt worked for British intelligence during WORLD WAR II, was later the official art adviser to Queen ELIZABETH II and was knighted for his services to the Crown. In 1979 British writer and broadcaster Andrew Boyle published *The Climate of Treason*, in which he charged that a respected but unnamed figure in the British establishment had been the "fourth man" in the infamous Philby-Burgess-Maclean spy ring during World War II and after (see BURGESS-MACLEAN SPY CASE; Kim PHILBY). On November 15, 1979, Prime Minister Margaret THATCHER told Parliament that Blunt had been the "fourth man." Blunt had secretly confessed to British authorities in 1964 that he had recruited spies for the USSR from among his students while he was a don at Cambridge University in the 1930s, that he had passed intelligence to the Soviets during the 1940s and that he had warned Burgess and Maclean of their impending arrest. Blunt's confession was kept from the public, and Blunt was allowed to continue as the queen's art adviser until he retired in 1972. The revelation about Blunt's earlier involvement in Britain's worst spy scandal shocked the nation; the fact that Blunt's crimes had gone unpunished led to charges that the British establishment was more interested in protecting its members than in national security and justice. The Blunt exposé also led to speculation that there may have been a highly placed "fifth man"—possibly MI5's director, Sir Roger Hollis—working for the Soviets in British intelligence. (See also the APOSTLES.)

Bly, Robert Elwood (*1926–   *) American poet, editor and translator. Educated at Harvard and the University of Iowa, Bly received a Fulbright to translate contemporary Norwegian poetry. Back in his native Minnesota, he began the *Fifties* magazine (later the *Sixties* and the *Seventies*), which also

promoted the work of James Wright, Donald Hall and Louis SIMPSON. *Silence in the Snowy Fields* (1962) and *The Light Around the Body* (1967) made his reputation. The latter collection, which also contained polemical antiwar verse, won the National Book Award. Bly and his friends seek the "deep image" in poems characterized by simplicity, subjectivity and surreal imagery. Bly continues to publish, producing *Eating the Honey of Words* (1999), *The Night Abraham Called to the Stars* (2001) and a book of antiwar verse, *The Insanity of Empire* (2004). He also edited the annual anthology *Best American Poetry* in 1999.

BMW (Bayerische Motoren Werke) German firm noted for its automobile designs. Founded in 1916 by Karl Rapp and Gustav Otto as a manufacturer of aircraft engines, BMW began manufacturing motorcycles in 1923 and finally automobiles in 1929. Many of its products have been of outstanding design quality. The 2002 sedan of 1968–76, designed by BMW staff under the direction of Andreas Glas, was particularly admired for its logical and consistent design, free of meaningless ornament and with a unity of theme rare in automobile design. In 1990 BMW began to produce aircraft engines in partnership with Britain's Rolls-Royce PLC. In 1992 the company launched its first U.S. auto plant, in Spartanburg, South Carolina.

Boas, Franz (*1858–1942*) American anthropologist. Educated at the University of Kiel, Boas taught at Clark University and, in 1899, became Columbia University's first professor of anthropology, a position he held for 37 years. The dominant force in American anthropology during the first half of the century, Boas emphasized the importance of culture on human behavior and development. He was one of the first anthropologists to emphasize field research, and many of his theories are based on his own studies of the Indians of northwest Canada. Among his best known works are *The Mind of Primitive Man* (1911), *Primitive Art* (1927), *Anthropology and Modern Life* (1928) and *Race, Language, and Culture* (1940).

boat people, Vietnamese Part of the terrible aftermath of the VIETNAM

WAR was the exodus of more than a million refugees from communist oppression. While some fled overland into THAILAND, the majority attempted to escape in small boats across the South China Sea to HONG KONG, INDONESIA or the PHILIPPINES or across the Gulf of Siam to Thailand or MALAYSIA. It is estimated that some 200,000 died from exposure, drowning or attacks by pirates while making this perilous voyage.

Bob and Ray American comedy team. Bob Elliot and Ray Goulding performed on radio and television from the late 1940s through the mid-1980s. They specialized in offbeat humor and gentle satire. Among their creations were the bumbling interviewer Wally Ballou and Mary Backstage, Noble Wife (a parody of the popular 1940s soap opera, *Mary Noble, Backstage Wife*). They were perhaps best known for a series of commercials they created for Piels beer, in which they appeared as the fictional Piels brothers, Harry and Bert.

Bodenstein, Max Ernst August *(1871–1942)* German physical chemist. Bodenstein earned his doctorate at Heidelberg (1893) and worked with Wilhelm Ostwald at Leipzig before becoming a professor at Hannover (1908–23) and at the Institute for Physical Chemistry, Berlin (1923–36). He made a series of classic studies on the equilibria of gaseous reactions, especially that of hydrogen and iodine (1897). Bodenstein also worked in photochemistry and was the first to show how a chain reaction could explain the large yield per quantum for the reaction of hydrogen and chlorine.

Boeing, William Edward *(1881–1956)* Born in Detroit, Boeing founded the Pacific Nero Products Co. in Seattle in 1916. In 1929, the corporation's name was changed to Boeing Aircraft; today it is the world's largest manufacturer of commercial aircraft. In recognition of his pioneering achievement in the AVIATION industry, Boeing was awarded the Daniel Guggenheim medal in 1934. He died 22 years later, on his yacht in Puget Sound, Seattle.

Boer Uprising of 1914–1915 The Union of SOUTH AFRICA entered WORLD WAR I on the side of the Allies in 1914, but many Boers (South Africans of Dutch descent) balked, favoring Germany. Three army commanders led a Boer uprising in the Orange Free State and Transvaal, and by the end of 1914 12,000 rebels were involved. Prime Minister Louis BOTHA and Jan SMUTS, former Boer generals, opposed the rebels, and in three campaigns (October and December 1914, and February 1915) overcame the rebel forces. Botha showed unusual clemency, and all prisoners were set free by 1917. (See also BOER WAR.)

Boer War (Second Boer War; Great Boer War) *(1899–1902)* Conflict between Boers (South Africans of Dutch descent) and British forces in SOUTH AFRICA; the first major war of the 20th century. The discovery of large, rich deposits of gold in the southern Transvaal in 1886 had brought a rush mainly of Britons to the region and exacerbated longstanding British-Boer tensions. When troops protecting British mining interests failed to comply with a Boer ultimatum to withdraw, the South African Republic (Transvaal) and its ally, the Orange Free State, declared war on Great Britain (October 1899). Well-equipped Boer forces, led by Piet Joubert, Piet Cronje, Louis BOTHA and others scored initial successes, seizing Kimberly, Mafeking and Ladysmith. However, in 1900 the fortunes of war turned with the arrival of British reinforcements under Field Marshal Lord Frederick Roberts and General Lord Horatio Kitchener. Roberts advanced into the Orange Free State, seizing its capital, Bloemfontein (March 13, 1900), and soon occupying the country. The British then invaded the Transvaal and captured Johannesburg and Pretoria (May–June 1900), effectively crushing Boer resistance on the battlefield. The British formally annexed the Boer states, but it took Kitchener's forces two more years of bitter fighting to subdue guerrilla units led by such Boer generals as Jan SMUTS and Botha. Through a line of blockhouses (to split the country) and the detention of Boer women and children in CONCENTRATION CAMPS, Kitchener wore down Boer morale and systematically destroyed guerrilla units. By the Treaty of Vereeniging (May 31, 1902) the Boers recognized British sovereignty in exchange for a large indemnity and other concessions.

Boesky scandal Wall Street scandal that rocked the U.S. financial world in 1986. Ivan Boesky was a multimillionaire who had made his fortune through risk arbitrage—speculating on the stocks of corporations that are suspected to be involved in mergers. Boesky traded on behalf of many wealthy individuals and corporations in addition to himself. However, his success was largely founded on illegal insider trading. When the SECURITIES AND EXCHANGE COMMISSION prosecuted Wall Street trader Dennis Levine for insider trading, Levine revealed that Boesky had been receiving illegal tips about mergers and takeovers. Boesky eventually cooperated with the SEC and paid a fine of $50 million and a civil indemnity of an equal amount. He retained at least $200 million of his personal fortune. Boesky's disclosures implicated Michael R. Milken and his Wall Street firm DREXEL BURNHAM LAMBERT, which went bankrupt in the wake of the scandal.

Bogan, Louise *(1897–1970)* American poet and critic. Bogan's poetic output was small, and she continually revised her work throughout her career. Her collected poems *The Blue Estuaries: Poems 1923–1968* brought together a slender oeuvre of short, highly distilled, rhymed and metered lyrics that show the influence of Emily Dickinson. From 1931 to 1970 she served as poetry editor and critic for *The NEW YORKER*; her influential critical essays were published as *A Poet's Alphabet* (1970). In *Achievement in American Poetry 1900–1950* (1951) she argued that the woman poets of the 19th century were responsible for the revitalization of American poetry. Bogan won the BOLLINGEN PRIZE in 1955 and held the Library of Congress Chair in Poetry in 1945–46.

Bogart, Humphrey DeForest *(1899–1957)* Popular American motion picture actor known for his tough and cynical screen persona. The son of a prominent New York surgeon, Bogart began in the entertainment business with Broadway stage producer William A. Brady. After rising from office boy to stage manager, he began to play juvenile parts in the 1920s. (For one role he came on stage in white trousers to utter the immortal line, "Tennis anyone?") His big break came playing gangster Duke Mantee in *The Petrified Forest* in 1935, a role he repeated a year later in the film version for WARNER BROS. Despite some fine performances in subsequent movies, he almost became mired in second-rate gangster melodramas. Two superior crime thrillers changed everything: *High Sierra* (1939) and *The Maltese Falcon* (1940), a virtually perfect film debut by director-writer John HUSTON. For the next 15 years Bogart perfected the battle-scarred but vulnerable roles for which he is best known: the lovelorn Rick in *Casablanca* (1942), the crafty Phillip Marlow in *The Big Sleep* (1946), the obsessive prospector in *Treasure of the Sierra Madre* (1948), the "river rat" in *The African Queen* (for which he won an ACADEMY AWARD in 1952) and the twitchy, ball-bearings-rolling Captain Queeg in *The Caine Mutiny* (1956). He died of cancer of the esophagus in 1957.

Bogoliubov, Nikolai Nikolaevich

(1909–1992) Soviet mathematician and physicist. Bogoliubov did his graduate work at the Academy of Sciences of the Ukrainian Soviet Socialist Republic and subsequently worked there and at the Soviet Academy of Sciences. His main contribution was in the application of mathematical techniques to theoretical physics. He developed a method of distribution-function for nonequilibrium processes and also worked on superfluidity, quantum field theory and superconductivity. His work was partly paralleled by that of John BARDEEN, Leon COOPER, and John Robert Schrieffer. Bogoliubov was a prolific author, with many of his works translated into English. He was active in founding scientific schools in nonlinear mechanics, statistical physics and quantum-field theory. In 1963 he became academician-secretary of the Soviet Academy of Sciences and was made director of the Joint Institute for Nuclear Research in Dubna in 1965. The next year he was also made a deputy to the Supreme Soviet. He was honored by scientific societies throughout the world, and in his own country received the State Prize twice (1947, 1953) and the Lenin Prize (1958).

Bohm, Karl

(1894–1981) Austrian orchestral and operatic conductor. Bohm divided his early studies between law and music, taking piano lessons at Graz Conservatory and the Vienna Conservatory while studying law at the University of Graz. He served in the Austrian army in WORLD WAR I and was wounded. He received his law degree in 1919 but decided on a conducting career, even though he had no formal training. During the 1920s and 1930s he held a series of conducting posts in Germany, where he worked under Bruno WALTER and Hans Knappertsbusch. He was music director at Dresden (1934–43) before moving to the Vienna State Opera, which he also directed (1950–53) after World War II. He also frequently conducted at the Metropolitan Opera, Bayreuth, Salzburg, Berlin and London. Bohm was particularly identified with the Austrian-German repertory and specialized in the works of Mozart, Beethoven, Schubert, Wagner, Richard STRAUSS (who was a personal friend) and Alban BERG. His repertory included 150 different operas, and he made numerous recordings. A precise stylist and a purist in interpretation, his performances were less glamorous and flamboyant than those of many of his more popular colleagues. Nonetheless, he was one of the outstanding conductors of the 20th century, and the only person ever designated as Austria's General Music Director.

Bohr, Aage Niels

(1922–   ) Danish physicist. The son of Niels BOHR, he was educated at the University of Copenhagen. After postgraduate work at the University of London from 1942 to 1945, he returned to Copenhagen to the Institute of Theoretical Physics, where he has served since 1956 as professor of physics. When Bohr began his research career, Maria Goeppert-Mayer and Hans Jensen had just proposed, in 1949, the shell model of the nucleus. Almost immediately Leo James Rainwater produced experimental results at odds with the predictions derived from a spherical shell model and proposed that some nuclei were distorted rather than perfectly spherical. Bohr, in collaboration with Ben Mottelson, followed Rainwater's work by proposing their collective model of nuclear structure (1952), so called because they argued that the distorted nuclear shape was produced by a participation of many nucleons. For this work Bohr shared the 1975 NOBEL PRIZE in physics with Rainwater and Mottelson.

Bohr, Niels Hendrik David

(1885–1962) Niels Bohr came from a distinguished scientific family and was educated at the University of Copenhagen where he obtained his Ph.D. in 1911. After four productive years with Ernest RUTHERFORD in Manchester, Bohr returned to Denmark, becoming in 1918 director of the newly created Institute of Theoretical Physics. Under Bohr (after Albert EINSTEIN probably the most respected theoretical physicist of the 20th century) the institute became one of the most exciting research centers in the world. A generation of physicists from around the world were to pass through it, and eventually the orthodox account of QUANTUM theory was to be described as the "Copenhagen interpretation."

In 1913 Bohr published a classic paper, *On the Constitution of Atoms and Molecules,* in which he used the quantum of energy, *h,* introduced into physics by Max Planck in 1900, to rescue Rutherford's account of atomic structure from a vital objection and also to account for the line spectrum of hydrogen. He was able to calculate energies for possible orbits of the electron, receiving the NOBEL PRIZE in physics for this work in 1922. The Bohr theory was developed further by Arnold Sommerfeld. Bohr made other major contributions to this early development of quantum theory. The "cor-

Nobel Prize–winning physicist Niels Bohr, 1962
(LIBRARY OF CONGRESS, PRINTS AND PHOTOGRAPHS DIVISION)

respondence principle" (1916) is his principle that the quantum-theory description of the atom corresponds to classical physics at large magnitudes. In 1927 Bohr publicly formulated the "complementarity principle," which argued against continuing attempts to eliminate such supposed difficulties as the wave-particle duality of light and many other atomic phenomena. It was a principle Bohr remained faithful to, even representing it on his coat of arms in 1947 (the motto *Contraria sunt complementa* above yin/yang symbols). Together with the indeterminancy principle of Werner HEISENBERG and the probability waves of Max BORN, this principle emerged from the 1930 Solvay conference (the last one Einstein attended) as the most authoritative and widely accepted theory to describe atomic phenomena.

Bohr also made major contributions to the work on radioactivity that led to the discovery and exploitation of nuclear fission. It was Bohr who in 1939 made the crucial suggestion that fission was more likely to occur with the rarer isotope uranium 235 than the more common variety uranium 238. In 1943 Bohr, who had a Jewish mother, felt it necessary to escape from occupied Denmark; he eventually made his way to Los Alamos in America where he served as a consultant on the atomic bomb project (see ATOMIC BOMB DEVELOPMENT). He was quick to appreciate the consequences of using such weapons and in 1944 made an early approach to ROOSEVELT and CHURCHILL, proposing that such an obvious danger could perhaps be used to bring about a rapprochement between Russia and the West. Scientists were in a unique position, he argued, in having the Soviet contracts and the knowledge to make the first approach. Much of Bohr's time after the war was spent working, among scientists, for adequate controls of nuclear weapons, and in 1955 he organized the first Atoms for Peace conference in Geneva.

Bok, Bart Jan (*1906–1983*) Dutch-American astronomer. Bok studied at the University of Leiden (1924–27) and Groningen (1927–29) and obtained his Ph.D. from Groningen in 1932. He had moved to the U.S. in 1929, was naturalized in 1938 and served at Harvard from 1929 to 1957,

being appointed professor of astronomy in 1947. Dok spent 1957 to 1966 in Australia as director of the Mount Stromlo Observatory, Canberra, and professor of astronomy at the Australian National University. He returned to the U.S. in 1966 to become director of the Steward Observatory, Arizona, until 1970 and then professor of astronomy at the University of Arizona, Tucson. Bok's major interest was the structure of our galaxy, the Milky Way. With his wife, Priscilla, he published a survey of the subject. *The Milky Way* (1941). In 1947 Bok discovered small dark circular clouds visible against a background of stars or luminous gas, since known as **Bok globules.** Since they are thought to be precursors of stars, as Bok himself conjectured, they have received considerable attention in recent years.

Bokassa, Jean-Bédel (*1921–1996*) African dictator. Bokassa joined the French army in 1939 and became chief of staff of the newly formed CENTRAL AFRICAN REPUBLIC (CAR) army in 1962. In December 1965 he overthrew the government of his cousin, David DACKO. Bokassa served as president from 1966 to 1979, proclaiming and crowning himself Emperor Bokassa I in 1977. Bokassa's despotic leadership achieved worldwide infamy when 100 schoolchildren were massacred by government troops at his behest in April 1979 in Bangui, the capital, after the children protested a decree requiring them to wear school uniforms. Bokassa was overthrown in a bloodless coup in September 1979, and Dacko was reinstated as president. Bokassa was exiled to the Ivory Coast, and later lived in France before returning to the CAR in 1986. He stood trial and in 1987 was sentenced to death by firing squad. The sentence was later commuted to life imprisonment by General Kolingba. Bokassa was released in 1993 and died three years later.

Bolet, Jorge (*1914–1990*) Cuban-born pianist. He began his career as a child prodigy, noted for his mastery of such romantic-era composers as Franz Liszt. His style of playing was not popular among critics or the public for much of his adult life. A revival of interest in romantic composers won him accolades in the 1970s.

Bolger, Raymond Wallace (*1906–1987*) U.S. dancer and comic actor. His most celebrated role was as the Scarecrow in the 1939 film classic *The Wizard of Oz.* Among the many Broadway productions in which he appeared was the late 1940s *Where's Charley,* in which he created his most memorable song-and-dance number, "Once in Love with Amy." During the 1950s he had his own television show.

Bolivia Nation in west-central South America; Sucre is the constitutional capital, while La Paz is the political capital and main commercial center. Bolivia was named after the South American leader Simón Bolívar, who fought the Spanish colonial power early in the 19th century. From 1879 to 1884, Bolivia was allied with Peru against Chile in the War of the Pacific, which was triggered by a dispute over control of nitrate deposits in the Atacama (now Antofagasta) coastal province of Bolivia. In 1899 the balance of internal political power switched from conservatives to liberals, whose principal leader, Ismael Montes, served as president from 1904 to 1909 and from 1913 to 1917. In 1903, negotiations with Brazil led to Bolivia ceding the Acre rubber production region in exchange for financial and railroad interests. There was an opposition coup in 1920 and a military coup during the GREAT DEPRESSION of the 1930s. From 1932 to 1935, Bolivia and Paraguay waged war over control of the long-disputed GRAN CHACO lowlands, in which oil had been discovered. A 1938 treaty granted 75% of the region to Paraguay. In 1967 Cuban revolutionary leader Ernesto "Che" GUEVARA was captured while organizing guerrilla resistance in Bolivia and was executed. In 1969 Alfredo Ovando Candía became president and nationalized U.S. oil holdings in Bolivia. Lidia Gueiler Tejada later became the first woman president of Bolivia. Political instability has been a constant throughout the country's history. In December 2001 Bolivian farmers rejected a government plan to offer them $900 annually to eradicate all coca plants on their lands. Protests and street blockades became regular occurrences around the country during the first years of the 21st century. In 2006 coca grower and peasant leader Evo MORALES became the country's first indigenous president. He promised to

nationalize the country's oil and gas industries, to protect the rights of indigenous people, and to legalize the growing of coca.

Bolivian Guerrilla War of 1966–1967 In the mid-1960s Ernesto "Che"

GUEVARA, the Argentine-born Cuban revolutionary, believed that conditions in Bolivia made it ripe for a Cuban-type revolution. In autumn 1966 he and 15 followers clandestinely established headquarters at Nancahuazu, a wild, unsettled region of Bolivia. Local communists

failed to support them. The Bolivian army began to patrol the area, looking for a large force, and in March 1967 fighter planes strafed the area while counterinsurgency troops began an encirclement. On April 26 two couriers were captured; the army later used them

BOLIVIA

1946	President Gualberto Villarroel shot and killed by rioters; Tomás Manje Gutiérrez named provisional president.
1956	After a bloody uprising, tin miners overthrow the government; Víctor Paz Estenssoro becomes president, enacts land reform and universal suffrage and nationalizes the mines.
1964	General René Barrientos overthrows Paz Estenssoro and represses militant miners.
1967	Che Guevara captured by government forces and executed.
1982	General Luis García Meza seizes power; his government becomes notorious for violent repression and cocaine trafficking.
1985	General elections won by Paz Estenssoro; tin prices plummet and unemployed miners turn to coca production.
1989	Jaime Paz Zamora, a self-described social democrat, sworn in as president by his 81-year-old second cousin and predecessor, Paz Estenssoro.
1990	Government launches anti-cocaine program, paying farmers to destroy more than 8,400 acres of coca.
1997	Hugo Banzer's government launches program of economic austerity and coca eradication, inciting resistance from coca growers and worker-peasant unions.
2001	Jorge Quiroga Ramírez replaces Banzer as president.
2005	Indian activist and former coca farmer Evo Morales is elected president.

to arouse Bolivians against the foreign "invaders." By the fall of 1967 Guevara was retreating through the jungles with only 16 men. On October 8 his band was discovered; some were killed outright, but Guevara was captured. He was executed the next morning.

Bolivian National Revolution (1952) Although outlawed in 1946, the Movimiento Nacionalista Revolucionario (MNR) won a plurality for its presidential candidate and founder, Víctor Paz Estenssoro in the 1951 elections in BOLIVIA. To prevent Paz Estenssoro from coming to power, the president handed over power to a 10-man military junta. On April 8–11,

1952, armed workers, peasants and the national police revolted in La Paz, the administrative capital, and elsewhere, overthrew the junta and recalled Paz Estenssoro from exile. As president, Paz Estenssoro nationalized the tin mines, raised miners' wages, liquidated large landholdings, distributed land to Indians and established universal suffrage. Bolivians gained civil and political rights, but Paz Estenssoro imprisoned many of his political opponents.

Bolivian Revolt of 1946 A popular revolt (July 17–21, 1946) due to severe inflation and unemployment caused by falling mineral prices after World War II. Bolivian tin was vital to the Allies in

World War II. After Bolivia declared war on the Axis power (April 1943), dissident army officers led by Gualberto Villarroel and supported by German agents, the Argentine government and the National Revolutionary Movement staged a coup and named Villarroel president. The U.S. refused to recognize the new regime until it agreed to cooperate with the Allis. The army stood by during the revolt. Villarroel was seized and killed, and a liberal provisional government was installed.

Bolivian Revolt of 1971 The arrest of rightist demonstrators in Santa Cruz, BOLIVIA, triggered a general revolt (April 19–22, 1971). Peasants, students, miners and the air force supported leftist President Juan José Torres against rightists of the army and the middle and upper classes. The rightist rebels gained control of Santa Cruz and Cochabamba and, after the air force joined them, captured La Paz, the administrative capital. Torres fled to Peru, then Chile, while a military-civilian coalition established Colonel Hugo Banzer Suárez as head of government.

Böll, Heinrich Theodor (1917–1985) German novelist, short story writer and essayist. Böll, who won the NOBEL PRIZE in literature in 1972, is one of the major figures in postwar German literature. Born in Cologne, Böll attended school there and then was drafted into the German army despite having been one of the few boys in his class to refuse to join the HITLER YOUTH movement. He served throughout WORLD WAR II. After the war he studied at the University of Cologne and turned to writing. His first novel, *The Train Was on Time* (1949), which told of a young German soldier's horrific experiences in combat, was a critical success. Böll produced a steady stream of fictional works over the next three decades, most notably the novels *Billiards at Half Past Nine* (1959), *The Clown* (1963) and *Group Portrait with Lady* (1971), all of which dealt with Nazi decadence and the dehumanizing materialism that fueled the postwar German economic success. *What's to Become of the Boy* (1985) is his autobiography. Böll was a politically engaged writer and an active proponent of artistic freedom.

Bollingen Prize in Poetry Awarded biennially, with administrative offices maintained at Yale University, this prize is given to the best book of poetry written by an American during the two years preceding each award. Poets are nominated by jury. As of the early 2000s the cash award for the Bollingen Prize stood at $50,000.

Bollywood Bombay-located center of the film industry in INDIA; the name *Bollywood* signifies the Indian effort to create an international competitor to HOLLYWOOD. India's film industry began in 1899, when director Harischandra Bhatvadekar debuted two pictures in Bombay. However, India did not began creating films wholly written, shot and developed within its borders until 1913, when *Raja Harishchandra,* a silent film (subtitled in Hindi and English) produced by Dhundiraj Govind Phalke (also known as Dada Saheb Phalke) premiered in Bombay's Coronation Cinema. The industry gradually grew from then until the end of the 1920s. In 1931 India's motion picture industry produced its first talkie—a picture accompanied by its own soundtrack in which the audience could hear the actors' voices—titled *Alam Ara.* These talkies also tackled social issues within India and championed more humane treatment for the different members of India's social castes.

International recognition of the developing Indian cinema did not come until 1952, five years after India's independence from British colonial rule, when Bombay hosted the first International Film Festival of India to trumpet the productions of its various movie houses, as well as introduce Indian moviegoers to the pictures of other nations. Most of the films released during the 1950s and 1960s took advantage of the less expensive colorization techniques to produce films designed largely to entertain rather than to promote social and political change. By the end of the 1960s a movement called the New Indian Cinema began among several Indian directors who wanted to reduce the commercial aspects of Indian movies and return to the socially conscious films of the 1930s. By the end of the 1970s this vanguard movement effectively began to challenge the more mainstream film companies. India's film industry thereafter became well known for adult dramas and comedies produced by studios much smaller than those of Hollywood. The other major category of Indian films consists of musicals in which the musical numbers are prerecorded and the actors and actresses merely mouth the words. Because of India's larger film market and larger number of films produced annually, Bollywood has regularly generated more annual revenue than Hollywood, although Hollywood averages more income per film than its Indian counterpart.

Bolotowsky, Ilya *(1907–1981)* Russian-born sculptor and painter. He was known for his simple, highly geometric forms. In 1937 he helped found the **American Abstract Artists,** a group that included Piet MONDRIAN and Ad REINHARDT. The group's style, known as **Neo-Plasticism,** was one of pure, formal abstraction not based on natural forms.

Bolshevik Revolution Military defeats, shortages and widespread distrust of government during WORLD WAR I led to the overthrow of Czar NICHOLAS II (March 1917). When he failed to subdue rioters in Moscow and Petrograd (Leningrad), the parliament established a provisional government under Prince LVOV and forced Nicholas's abdication. Revolutionary committees (Soviets) agitated for withdrawal from the war, encouraged by Vladimir I. LENIN, leader of left-wing Russian Marxists (Bolsheviks). They attempted to seize power but failed, and Lenin fled. Alexander F. KERENSKY, a socialist moderate, became premier. He soon lost support, and Lenin returned to lead a bloodless coup in November (the OCTOBER REVOLUTION), masterminded by Leon TROTSKY. The Bolsheviks withdrew Russia from the war and consolidated power. They abolished private property and class privilege, nationalized banks and industries, and suppressed opposition with secret police. A bloody civil war followed.

Bolsheviks Those of the radical faction of the Russian Social Democratic Workers' Party when it split in 1903. The Bolsheviks, meaning "those in the majority" (MENSHEVIKS were the minority), were headed by LENIN, who believed that the revolution must be led by a single centralized party of professional revolutionaries. After the RUSSIAN REVO- LUTION (1917) the Bolsheviks succeeded in eliminating other political parties, and from 1918 until 1952 the COMMUNIST PARTY OF THE SOVIET UNION was termed Communist Party (Bolsheviks).

Bolshoi Ballet Acclaimed Russian dance company in existence since 1776. The Bolshoi is particularly noted for its dramatic ballet style. The company staged the first productions of the Petipa-Minkus ballet *Don Quixote* (1869) and the Reisinger-Tchaikovsky *Swan Lake* (1877) and presented the first ballet on a modern theme, *The Red Poppy* (1927). Under the direction of Leonid Lavrovsky, who was also chief choreographer (1944–64), the Bolshoi appeared for the first time in London (1956) and New York (1959), presenting acclaimed productions of Lavrovsky's *Romeo and Juliet* and *Giselle* and starring the legendary ballerina Galina Ulanova. Yuri Grigorovich became director in 1976. His new version of *Spartacus* (1968) and reworking of *Swan Lake* were performed on the company's world tours with great success. The affiliated ballet school has produced some outstanding dancers for the company, including Natalia Bessmertnova and Nikolay Fadeyechev. Despite the collapse of the Soviet Union in 1991, the Bolshoi Ballet has continued to operate and enjoy the sponsorship of the Russian government.

Bolton, Guy Reginald *(1894–1979)* British-born playwright and musical librettist. Bolton coauthored the books of dozens of romantic Broadway musicals in the 1920s and 1930s. These included the shows *Lady Be Good* (1924) and *Girl Crazy* (1930) with music by George GERSHWIN and *Anything Goes* (1934) with music by Cole PORTER. He also worked with Jerome KERN. Probably his most celebrated association was his lifelong collaboration with P. G. WODEHOUSE.

Boltwood, Bertram Borden *(1870– 1927)* American chemist and physicist. Boltwood was educated at Yale and the University of Munich. Apart from the period 1900–06, when he served as a private consultant, and the year 1909–10, which he spent with Ernest RUTHERFORD at the University of Manchester, England, he devoted the whole of his academic career to Yale. He occupied the chair of physics (1906–10), the chair of radioactivity (1910–18) and the chair of chemistry from 1918 until his death by suicide in 1927. Boltwood made a number of contributions to the study of radioactivity. In 1905 he demonstrated that lead was always found in uranium and was probably the final stable product of its decay. He argued that in minerals of the same age the lead-uranium ratio would be constant and that in minerals of different ages the ratio would be different. His estimates of the ages of several rocks based on accepted decay rate estimates were good. This was the beginning of attempts to date rocks and fossils by radiation measurements and other physical techniques, which have revolutionized geology and archaeology.

Bond, George F. *(1915–1983)* U.S. Navy doctor. An authority on the medial effects of deep-sea diving and undersea pressure, Bond was the pioneer of the **Sealab** program of the 1960s. Teams of Sealab "aquanauts" studied the feasibility of undersea living by spending days in a small capsule anchored to the ocean floor.

Bond, (Horace) Julian *(1940–)* American leader of the CIVIL RIGHTS MOVEMENT and government official. A native of Nashville, Tennessee, Bond was an organizer of the Committee on Appeal for Human Rights while he was a student at Morehouse College in Atlanta. In 1960 he helped to found the Student Nonviolent Coordinating Committee. In 1965 Bond was elected to the Georgia state legislature, one of eight blacks elected under court-order reapportionment. However, his fellow legislators, by a vote of 184-12, voted to bar Bond, citing his vocal criticism of the Vietnam War and his alleged encouragement of draft evasion. He was finally admitted to the legislature under a December 5, 1966, order of the U.S. Supreme Court. Bond also served in the Georgia state senate and, in an upset, was defeated in a 1986 Democratic congressional primary by John Lewis, who went on to win the election. In 1995 Bond was elected to a fourth term on the board of the NATIONAL ASSOCIATION FOR THE ADVANCEMENT OF COLORED PEOPLE (NAACP) and became chairman of the NAACP in February 1998.

Bondarchuk, Sergei *(1920–1994)* Russian actor and film director. Bondarchuk was best known as the director of the acclaimed, seven-hours-plus Soviet film *War and Peace* (1966–67), an adaptation of the classic novel by Leo Tolstoy. He was born in the Ukraine and served in the Theater of the Soviet Army during World War II. In the decade following the war, Bondarchuk distinguished himself as the leading actor in the Soviet cinema. While the range of dramatic portrayals open to him under Soviet censorship was severely limited, Bondarchuk gave life to legendary figures in Russian history, playing the title roles in *Michurin* (1948) and *Taras Shevchenko* (1951). He won international acclaim for his lead performance in a Soviet film adaptation of *Othello* (1955). Bondarchuk's debut as a director of full-length features was *Destiny of a Man* (1959), based on a novel by Nobel Prize winner Mikhail SHOLOKHOV. Subsequent Bondarchuk films included *Waterloo* (1970) and *Uncle Vanya* (1971).

Bondi, Sir Hermann *(1919–)* British-Austrian mathematician and cosmologist. Bondi studied at Cambridge University, where he later taught. In 1954 he moved to London to take up the chair in mathematics at King's College. Bondi has always been actively interested in the wider implications of science and the scientific outlook, as his membership of the British Humanist Association and the Science Policy Foundation testify. He served as chief scientific adviser to the Ministry of Defence (1971–77), chief scientist at the Department of Energy (from 1977) and chairman of the Natural Environment Research Council (from 1980). He was knighted in 1973. Bondi's most important work has been in applied mathematics and especially in cosmology. In collaboration with Thomas Gold, in 1948 he propounded a new version of the steady-state theory of the universe. Fred HOYLE had first suggested the idea of a steady-state theory to devise a model of the universe that could accommodate both the fact that the universe is the same throughout and yet is expanding. Bondi and Gold suggested that, in order to maintain the universe despite its expansion, matter is created continuously. Although it enjoyed con-

siderable popularity, Bondi and Gold's steady-state model is now considered to have been decisively refuted by observational evidence, and the BIG BANG THEORY is favored.

Bonds, Barry *(1964–)* American baseball player. Bonds is best known for his record 73 home runs set in the 2001 Major League Baseball (MLB) season. His father, Bobby Bonds, played for several MLB teams, including the San Francisco Giants, and received the MVP award for the 1973 All-Star game. His godfather was the baseball great Willie MAYS, and he is a cousin of Reggie JACKSON. At Arizona State University, Bonds compiled a .347 hitting average in the three years he played for the Sun Devils. He was named to the All-Pacific-10 baseball team in each of his three years, and in his junior year, the *Sporting News* named him to its All-America Team. Drafted by the Pittsburgh Pirates in 1985, Bonds continued to improve his game, and by 1990 he had won his first Golden Glove and been named Major League Player of the Year by *Sporting News* and the National League's Most Valuable Player by the Baseball Writers' Association. Although 1992 ended well for Bonds, with a second MVP award, the following season he hit 46 home runs, compiled a batting average of .336 and won another MVP award.

During his career Bonds has earned numerous honors—five selections as MVP, 11 All-Star appearances and eight Golden Gloves. However, his season record of 73 home runs in 2001 came under a cloud when a *Sports Illustrated* article alleged that half of MLB players were using steroids or some sort of muscle enhancement to generate impressive statistics. Eventually, Bonds admitted that, while he had not taken any steroid substance banned by the league, he had ingested Creatine, a substance designed to help individuals increase muscle mass and strength. In the spring of 2004 Bonds broke Mays's total home run record of 660, placing him third on baseball's career list (behind Babe Ruth's 714 [which he tied in May 2006] and Hank Aaron's 755). However, Bonds continued to be dogged by suspicions that steroid use had helped him attain his records. In 2006 federal investigators were looking into the possibility that Bonds lied during his 2003 grand jury testimony relating to the steroids scandal.

Bonestell, Chesley *(1888–1986)* U.S. space-astronomical artist. Recipient of a special award from the British Interplanetary Society, Bonestell was the world's best-known space artist, inspiring a generation of space enthusiasts, scientists, science fiction writers and other artists with his talent for rendering astronomical scenes that were thoroughly researched and had a photographic verisimilitude. Although trained as an architect, he never completed his studies and spent his early years working in various architectural offices in San Francisco. He later worked as an artist, doing background paintings (mats) for such motion pictures as CITIZEN KANE (1941), *Destination Moon* (1950), *When Worlds Collide* (1951) and *War of the Worlds* (1953). From the early 1940s until the 1970s he specialized in works depicting the facts and wonders of space, producing over 10 books, including his most famous, *The Conquest of Space* (1949), with text by rocket pioneer Willy LEY. A 10-by-40-foot mural he did for the Boston Museum of Science in 1950–51 was transferred to the Smithsonian's National Air and Space Museum in 1976.

Bonhoeffer, Dietrich *(1906–1945)* German theologian. Bonhoeffer has exercised an enormous influence on 20th-century Western theology by virtue of his impassioned writings on moral and political issues and the example set by his martyrdom at the hands of the Nazis. Bonhoeffer combined in his writings a practical view of human psychology and a reverential standard as to the requirements of a truly religious life. In *The Cost of Discipleship* (1937), written in response to the threat posed by the HITLER Reich, Bonhoeffer insisted that true "grace" required direct involvement in the fight against worldly evil. At the outset of WORLD WAR II Bonhoeffer was in America, but he voluntarily returned to GERMANY to work against the Nazi regime. He was arrested in 1943; *Letters and Papers from Prison* (1953) contains writings smuggled out of his prison cell. He was hanged by the Nazis in 1945 just after leading a Sunday prayer service for his fellow prisoners.

Bonnard, Pierre *(1867–1947)* French painter. Bonnard, though his name has been linked with the Nabi and fauve artistic movements, stands out as an independent visionary of 20th-century French painting (see FAUVISM). His canvases, which are frequently devoted to simple domestic and pastoral scenes, employ a radiant palette of colors and emphasize pictorial values over dramatic content or aesthetic experiment. Born near Paris, he established a close early friendship with fellow painter Edouard Villard, with whom he was active in the Nabi (Prophet) movement that was strongly influenced by the stylized, decorative qualities of Japanese woodblock prints. By 1905 Bonnard had linked himself with the fauves (including Henri MATISSE) who called for bold, expressive use of color. From 1910 until his death, Bonnard worked in relative solitude in the southern Midi region of France. In addition to painting, Bonnard made frequent use of color lithography and illustrated books by French contemporaries such as André GIDE.

Bonnefoy, Yves *(1923–   )* French poet, critic and scholar. After graduating from the University of Paris with a degree in philosophy, Bonnefoy traveled in Europe and the U.S. and studied art history. In 1954 *Du Mouvement et de l'immobilité de Douve* (translated in 1967 by Galway Kinnell as *On the Motion and Immobility of Douve*) immediately established him as a major poet. *Hier regnant desert* (1958) received the Prix de l'Express. *Pierre écrite* (1965) included essays on poets and poetry. Bonnefoy is also acclaimed as a critic for his books on Rimbaud and Joan MIRÓ, as well as for his translations of Shakespeare. In 1971 he received the Prix des Critiques. Although Bonnefoy was heavily influenced by SURREALISM and the work of Paul VALÉRY, an interest in Hegel is also evident in his work.

Bonner, James Frederick *(1910–1996)* American biologist. Bonner received a degree in chemistry from the University of Utah in 1931 but turned to biology under the influence of Theodosius Dobzhansky. He received his Ph.D. from the California Institute of Technology in 1934, which was then becoming known as the main center for molecular biology. There he became interested in developmental biology and the question of why any one cell expresses only some genes of the chromosome complement of an organism. He discovered that histone, a protein associated with chromosomes, is responsible for shutting off gene activity, and that if the histone is removed then the repressed genes become functional again. He also discovered that certain hormones act by repressing and derepressing genes. In addition, Bonner conducted research on the artificial synthesis of ribonucleic acid (RNA) and studied ribosomes and mitochondria. In 1946 he became professor of biology at Cal Tech.

Bonnie and Clyde Texas-born criminals **Bonnie Parker** (1910–34) and **Clyde Barrow** (1909–34) robbed filling stations, restaurants and banks throughout the Southwest in the early 1930s. Both were born into poverty. The two teamed up in 1930, joined by Clyde's brother Buck, his wife Blanche, gunman Ray Hamilton (who left the gang) and William Daniel Jones, who joined the group in 1932. Tireless publicity seekers, they played to the press with snapshots and Bonnie's ballads of crime, and they became popular heros to some of the poverty-stricken victims of the GREAT DEPRESSION. Their fame and popularity notwithstanding, Bonnie and Clyde were vicious criminals who murdered 12 people during their rampage. They were killed in a Louisiana police ambush on May 23, 1934. Their story formed the basis for the award-winning 1967 film *Bonnie and Clyde*.

Bonn Pact An international agreement, also known as the Bonn Convention, that provided for the end of the Allied occupation of WEST GERMANY and also made West Germany a member of the Western Alliance—in effect signalling the denazification of Germany and accepting the Western zone back into the community of nations. Signed on May 26, 1952, the Bonn Pact gave West Germany the right of complete self-determination in its domestic and foreign policies. The French, British and American troops stationed in Germany since the end of World War II would no longer be there as an occupying force but rather as a defender of Western Europe against possible Soviet aggression. Three years later, West Germany became a member of NATO.

Bonus Army Popular name for a group of some 20,000 American veterans of WORLD WAR I who marched on Washington, D.C., in the spring of 1932 to demand payment of a bonus voted to them by Congress in 1921. This bonus was payable in 1945 but the men, mainly unemployed, many destitute and some literally starving as a result of the GREAT DEPRESSION, hoped to pressure Congress into passing an alternative bill. This legislation, submitted by Representative Wright Patman, would have provided for an immediate lump-sum payment. Dubbed the Bonus Expeditionary Force, they camped at Anacostia Flats, Maryland, and peacefully demonstrated in favor of the bill. Although passed by the House, the bill was defeated in the Senate on June 17. While much of the army returned home, at least 5,000 men remained in their shantytown, demanding action. On July 28 President Herbert HOOVER, claiming that a communist conspiracy was involved, ordered federal troops under the command of General Douglas MACARTHUR to disperse the veterans. A bloody riot ensued in which the shantytown was burned to the ground and the marchers forcibly evicted from the city. Hoover was widely, although perhaps wrongly, blamed for this brutality. The episode is thought to have contributed to his defeat in the 1932 presidential elections.

Book of Common Prayer See PRAYER BOOK CONTROVERSY.

Boom, El Term applied to a creative flowering of Latin American fiction from the mid-1950s through the 1960s. El Boom, or the Boom, is a highly general label that expresses the breadth and magnitude of the fictional talent that seemed to emerge in unison from numerous Latin American countries in the mid-1950s. There were no distinct themes that unified the writers linked under the El Boom rubric, but what they did have in common was a willingness to explore both political and personal subject matter with a maximum of linguistic and narrative experimentation. The major figures in the El Boom movement included Julio CORTÁZAR, Carlos

FUENTES, Mario VARGAS LLOSA and Gabriel GARCÍA MÁRQUEZ.

Boothby, Robert (Robert John Graham, Baron Boothby of Buchan and Rattray Head) (1900–1986) British politician. An outspoken member of the CONSERVATIVE Party, Boothby spent 34 years in the House of Commons as a member representing East Aberdeenshire in Scotland, from 1924 to 1958, when he was created a life peer. He served as parliamentary private secretary to Winston CHURCHILL from 1926 to 1929, when Churchill was chancellor of the exchequer. Boothby's memoirs, published in 1978, presented a somewhat controversial portrait of Churchill.

Borah, William Edgar (1865–1940) U.S. senator. Born near Fairfield, Illinois, Borah was admitted to the bar in 1887. He was elected to the Senate as a Republican from Idaho in 1887 and served there until his death. Borah gained national attention in 1907 as prosecutor in the trial of William Haywood, accused of conspiracy to murder ex-Governor Frank Steurenberg. A political maverick, Borah's support of progressive reform was limited by his distrust of big government and devotion to states rights. He backed labor legislation, Prohibition, the income tax and direct election of senators but opposed woman suffrage. Borah led the irreconcilables opposed to the LEAGUE OF NATIONS. He supported international action as long as military sanctions were not involved and hoped to achieve peace through international law. Borah was responsible for calling the WASHINGTON DISARMAMENT CONFERENCE in 1921 and played a major role in the development of the KELLOGG-BRIAND PACT in 1924. A chairman of the Senate Committee on Foreign Relations after 1924, he exercised enormous influence on foreign policy. An isolationist, he opposed U.S. intervention in WORLD WAR II until the end of his life. Borah supported many NEW DEAL measures but was a severe critic of the NATIONAL RECOVERY ADMINISTRATION and Franklin ROOSEVELT's attempt to pack the Supreme Court.

Borden, Sir Robert Laird (1854–1937) Canadian statesman, prime minister (1911–20). A teacher and lawyer, he was elected to Parliament

from Halifax in 1896 and became leader of the Conservative opposition in 1901. When his party was victorious in the elections of 1911, he was made prime minister, a post he held throughout WORLD WAR I, and knighted in 1914. He was successful in preparing his nation for the war, sending about half a million soldiers to fight overseas. Head of a Conservative government for his first six years, he was returned to office in 1917 as the leader of a Union coalition. After the war and mainly through Borden's efforts, CANADA achieved separate representation at the PARIS PEACE CONFERENCE (1919) and in the LEAGUE OF NATIONS. He retired from office in 1920.

Bordet, Jules Jean-Baptiste Vincent (1870–1961) Belgian immunologist. Bordet graduated in medicine from Brussels University in 1892 and in 1894 joined the Pasteur Institute, Paris, where he worked under the bacteriologist Elie Metchnikoff. In collaboration with Octave Gengou, Bordet discovered that in an immunized animal the antibodies produced by the immune response work in conjunction with another component of blood (which Bordet termed alexin but which is now called complement) to destroy foreign cells that invade the body. This component, Bordet found, was present in both immunized and nonimmunized animals and was destroyed by heating to over 55°C. This work formed the basis of the **complement-fixation test,** a particularly sensitive means of detecting the presence of any specific type of cell or its specific antibody. A notable application of this was the test to detect syphilis devised by August von WASSERMANN. In 1901 Bordet left Paris to found and direct the Pasteur Institute in Brussels, and in 1907 he was appointed professor of pathology and bacteriology at Brussels University. In 1906 Bordet isolated the bacterium responsible for whooping cough, which is named after him: *Bordetella (Haemophilus) pertussis*. For his discovery of complement and other contributions to medicine, he was awarded the 1919 NOBEL PRIZE in physiology or medicine.

Borg, Björn (1956–) Swedish tennis player. Borg turned professional at the age of 14 and began winning major tournaments long before his 20th birthday. In 1975 he led Sweden to its first Davis Cup. Borg's methodical and emotionless style on play belied a competitive drive that led him to five successive Wimbledon singles championships (1976–80). His domination of the French Open was equally impressive, with four consecutive singles titles (1978–81) and six titles overall. In 1981 he won an unprecedented 41 singles matches until being defeated by a representative of tennis' next wave, John McEnroe. Borg retired to Monaco in 1983 but announced an attempted comeback in 1990. He was rumored to be experiencing financial difficulties. In 1991 Borg retired permanently from professional tennis.

Borges, Jorge Luis (*1899–1986*) Argentinian essayist, story writer and poet. Borges is one of the major figures of 20th-century literature—a master of mazelike plots and imaginative paradoxes. Born in Buenos Aires, Borges immigrated to Spain for a short time but lived most of his life in his native city. In the 1920s Borges focused on poetry. His stories and essays, for which he is best known, first began to appear in the 1930s. Much of the best of Borges's prose work can be found in two story collections, *Ficciones* (1944) and *The Aleph and Other Stories* (1949), and in a volume of selected essays, *Other Inquisitions* (1952). Many of his essays and stories take the form of an intricate commentary on another written text, real or imagined. Borges overcame the onset of blindness as a young man to become a prodigious reader and, at one time, director of the National Library of Argentina. Borges won the Prix International des Editeurs in 1961.

Borglum, John Gutzon de la Mothe (*1867–1941*) U.S. sculptor. Borglum is best known as the creator of the gigantic Mount Rushmore sculpture of Presidents George Washington, Thomas Jefferson, Theodore Roosevelt and Abraham Lincoln. Borglum was an inventor, engineer and artist of international acclaim when he visited Custer State Park in 1924 to find a suitable site for a massive sculpture. He chose Mount Rushmore in the Black Hills of South Dakota. Using five-foot models of each figure, he multiplied every measurement by 12 in order to guide his workers in removing unnecessary stones (by using dynamite). He designed a "bosun chair" to lower workmen over the edge of the mountain. He worked tirelessly to raise money for the project. He even held a one-man strike, refusing to continue his part of the work until 1938, when an additional $300,000 in federal aid was authorized. He envisaged Mount Rushmore Hall of Records as the most elaborate national archive in the world. Due to overwork and failing health, he died in Chicago from a heart attack.

Bori, Lucrezia (*1887–1960*) Spanish singer. Known for her unique operatic style and clear soprano voice, Bori made her debut in Rome as Michaela in *Carmen* (1908). She made a successful return to opera in 1919 after nodes were removed from her vocal chords. Appearing primarily with the Metropolitan Opera in New York City from 1921 until her retirement in 1936, Bori received acclaim for her performances as Mimi in *La Bohème* and Manon in *Manon Lescaut,* among other roles.

Boris III (*1894–1943*) King of Bulgaria (1918–43); as crown prince, he fought in World War I and succeeded to the throne at the abdication of his father, Ferdinand I. He was a constitutional ruler until 1935, when he formed a military dictatorship. He allied Bulgaria with the Axis in 1940 but was unwilling to declare war on the Soviet Union. An angered Adolf Hitler summoned the king to a meeting in 1943, and Boris died mysteriously a few weeks later. He was succeeded by his six-year-old son, Simeon II, who ruled under the regency of Boris's brother Prince Cyril (1895–1945).

Bork, Robert Heron (*1927– *) American jurist and Supreme Court nominee. A graduate of the University of Chicago Law School, Bork taught law at Yale University during the 1960s and served as solicitor general of the U.S. (1973–77) under Presidents Richard M. Nixon and Gerald Ford. He gained prominence during the Watergate scandal, when as acting attorney general, he obeyed Nixon's order to fire special prosecutor Archibald Cox (October 20, 1973) after Attorney General Elliot Richardson and his deputy, William Ruckelshaus, had refused to do so and resigned. Bork returned to Yale in 1977. In 1982 President Ronald Reagan named Bork to the Court of Appeals in the District of Columbia. In this post and in his writings Bork compiled a substantial record as a conservative thinker who emphasized the doctrine of "original intent" in his decisions. When Justice Lewis F. Powell resigned from the Supreme Court in 1987, Reagan was determined to appoint a conservative to fill the vacancy. He chose Bork, whom he called a "prominent and intellectually powerful advocate of judicial restraint." The controversial appointment sparked a bitter debate between liberals and conservatives throughout the country. Democratic senator Edward Kennedy and other Senate liberals led the fight against Bork's nomination, claiming that Bork was an extremist who would reverse the civil rights decisions reached by the Court under Earl Warren, as well as the 1973 *Roe v. Wade* decision on abortion. Many special interest groups also testified against Bork during his confirmation hearings. The Senate Judiciary Committee ultimately voted 9-5 to reject the nomination; the full Senate voted 58-42 for rejection. One Republican senator who voted for Bork said that he had never seen "such an unjustified and untrammeled assault on a distinguished American citizen as I have witnessed in these last few weeks," and other supporters compared the clamor against Bork to the "witch hunts" of McCarthyism.

Borlaug, Norman Ernest (*1914– *) American agronomist and plant breeder. He graduated in forestry from Minnesota University in 1937 and earned his Ph.D. in plant pathology in 1941. He then spent three years with the Du Pont Chemical Company, testing the effects of chemicals on plants and plant diseases. In 1944 he joined the newly formed International Maize and Wheat Improvement Center in Mexico and began the breeding work that was to produce the highly adaptable dwarf wheats that played so large a part in the Green Revolution of the late 1960s and early 1970s. Borlaug's high-yielding cereals increased agricultural production in the developing countries to the extent that many became self-sufficient for grain. For his major role in temporarily alleviating world famine, Borlaug was awarded the NOBEL PRIZE for peace in 1970.

Borman, Frank *(1928–)* U.S. astronaut and airline executive. As commander of *Apollo 8* (December 21–27, 1968), Borman and fellow astronauts James Lovell and William Anders made 10 orbits of the Moon, while Borman earned the dubious distinction of becoming the first U.S. astronaut to vomit in space (but certainly not the first to experience space sickness). He also found himself involved in an unusual controversy upon his return to Earth. At NASA's request, the three *Apollo 8* crewmen had read passages from the Bible on a live Christmas Eve broadcast from lunar orbit. The act drew some angry protest and even a threatened legal suit to "stop the astronauts from broadcasting religious propaganda from space." Borman's only previous spaceflight had been aboard *Gemini 7* (December 4–18, 1965), when he and copilot James Lovell joined up with *Gemini 6-A* and its crew of Wally Schirra and James Stafford for NASA's first space rendezvous; Borman and Lovell also went on to set a new space endurance record of 14 days. Borman retired from NASA in 1970 to join Eastern Airlines, becoming that firm's chairman of the board. In March 1993 he was inducted into the U.S. Astronaut Hall of Fame.

Bormann, Martin *(1900–1945)* German Nazi leader. An important figure in the inner circle of the National Socialist (Nazi) Party, Bormann was devoted to HITLER and became the Führer's personal secretary in 1942. A master bureaucrat, he was not well known to the general public but wielded great power behind the scenes. Bormann disappeared in the final days of WORLD WAR II and was condemned in absentia by the NUREMBERG TRIALS of war criminals. In 1973 a skeleton unearthed in Berlin was positively identified as Bormann's; he had committed suicide on May 2, 1945. (See also NAZISM.)

Born, Max *(1882–1970)* German physicist. Born was educated at the Universities of Breslau, Heidelberg, Zurich and Göttingen, where he obtained his Ph.D. in 1907. From 1909

until 1933 he taught at Göttingen, being appointed professor of physics in 1921. With the rise of HITLER he moved to Britain and from 1936 served as professor of natural philosophy at the University of Edinburgh, returning to Germany on his retirement in 1953. Born is noted for his role in the development of the new QUANTUM theory. Together with Pascual Jordan he developed (1925) the matrix mechanics introduced by Werner HEISENBERG. He also showed how to interpret the theoretical results of Louis de Broglie and the experiments of such people as Clinton J. DAVISSON, which showed that particles have wavelike behavior. Born shared the 1954 NOBEL PRIZE in physics with Walter BOTHE.

Borneo Third largest island in the world, north of Java and south of the Philippines. Populated in the interior by the Dyaks and in its coastal areas by Malays, the topography ranges from swampy coastal chain to mountain to jungle. From the end of 1941 to 1945, during WORLD WAR II, it was occupied by Japanese forces. The region of Brunei (an enclave on the northwest coast of Borneo) was a British protectorate and gained its independence in 1984 while Kalimantan (the major part of the island) is now a part of Indonesia (after being held by the Dutch until 1949); the regions of Sabah and Sarawak (the northern and northwestern parts of the island) are now a part of MALAYSIA (after being held by the British until 1963).

Bosch, Carl *(1874–1940)* German industrial chemist. Bosch was trained as both metallurgist and chemist and earned his doctorate under Johannes Wislicenus at Leipzig (1898). He joined the large German dyestuffs company, Badische Anilin und Soda Fabrik (BASF), in 1899. Following Fritz Haber's successful small-scale ammonia synthesis in 1909, Bosch began to develop a high-pressure ammonia plant at Oppau for BASF. The plant was opened in 1912—a successful application on a large scale of the Haber process. Bosch also introduced the use of the water-gas shift reaction as a source of hydrogen for the process. After World War I the large-scale ammonia fertilizer industry was established, and in 1923 BASF extended

the high-pressure technique to the synthesis of methanol from carbon monoxide and hydrogen. Bosch was chairman of BASF's successor, I. G. Farben (1935–40) and concurrently director of the Kaiser Wilhelm Institutes. He shared the NOBEL PRIZE in chemistry with Friedrich Bergius in 1931.

Bosch, Juan *(1909–2001)* President of the Dominican Republic (1963). Bosch lived in exile from 1937 to 1961 during the Dominican dictatorship of Rafael TRUJILLO. On Trujillo's assassination, Bosch returned home and was elected president in 1962. After seven months, however, he was removed from office by a right-wing military coup in 1963. His leftist supporters staged a counter-coup in 1963, which was quelled by U.S. troops. Bosch ran for president again in 1966 but was defeated. On May 16, 1990, he lost another bid for reelection, to longtime rival Joaquín BALAGUER; Bosch claimed fraud, although an international panel proclaimed the elections honest.

Bose, Sir Jagadis Chandra *(1858–1937)* Indian plant physiologist and physicist. He began his studies in London as a medical student. He then won a scholarship to Cambridge University, from which he graduated in natural sciences in 1884. He was appointed professor of physical science at Presidency College, Calcutta, in 1885 and retained this post until 1915. In 1917 he founded and became director of the Bose Research Institute, Calcutta. He was knighted in 1917 and in 1920 became the first Indian to be elected a fellow of the Royal Society. Bose's early research was on the properties of very short radio waves. His most famous work concerned his investigations into plant physiology and the similarities between the behavioral response of plant and animal tissue. While his experimental skill was widely admired, at the time his work did not gain universal acceptance.

Bose, Satyendra Nath *(1894–1974)* Indian physicist. Bose was educated at Presidency College, Calcutta. Among his teachers was the eminent Indian physicist Jagadis Chandra BOSE. Bose held the post of lecturer at the Calcutta University

College of Science from 1917 until he left in 1921 to become a reader in physics at the new University of Dacca in East Bengal. His work ranged over many aspects of physics, including statistical mechanics, the electromagnetic properties of the ionosphere, theories of X-ray crystallography and unified field theory. He is best known for his work in quantum statistics. Bose attracted the attention of Albert EINSTEIN and other European physicists by publishing an important scientific paper in 1924. Because of this work Bose was able to get two years' study leave in Europe. During his visit he came into contact with many of the great physicists of the day, such as Louis DE BROGLIE, Max BORN, and Einstein. Einstein's generalization of Bose's work led to the system of statistical QUANTUM mechanics now known as **Bose-Einstein statistics.**

Bosnia and Herzegovina Province of the former YUGOSLAVIA. A part of the AUSTRO-HUNGARIAN EMPIRE from 1878, the streets of the capital, SARAJEVO, witnessed perhaps the most fateful event of the 20th century. On June 28,

	BOSNIA AND HERZEGOVINA
1908	Bosnia and Herzegovina are annexed by Austrian Habsburgs in wake of Turkish Revolution.
1914	Archduke Franz Ferdinand, the Habsburg heir, is assassinated in Sarajevo by a Bosnian-Serb extremist, precipitating World War I.
1918	On the collapse of the Habsburg empire, the region becomes part of the Serb-dominated Kingdom of Serbs, Croats and Slovenes, known as Yugoslavia from 1929.
1941	Axis powers incorporate Bosnia into the independent state of Croatia, a puppet state run by the Ustaše, a Croat fascist group; the Ustaše attempts to exterminate the region's 2 million Serbs. Civil war breaks out, with the multiethnic communist Partisans, led by Josip Broz (Marshal Tito), fighting both the Ustaše and the Serb royalist Četniks.
1943	The Partisans proclaim a federation of South Slav peoples, known as Yugoslavia, with Tito as marshal and prime minister.
1945	World War II ends; Tito organizes the Yugoslavia Socialist Federation as six republics: Bosnia-Herzegovina, Croatia, Serbia, Slovenia, Montenegro and Macedonia; political representation within Bosnia-Herzegovina is strictly apportioned among the state's three constituent peoples, Croats, Serbs and Muslims.
1948	Tito breaks relations with the Soviet Union's Joseph Stalin and begins a gradual process of decentralization of Yugoslavia.
1968	Muslims are officially recognized as one of Yugoslavia's six national groups.
1980	Tito dies; Yugoslavia's economy takes a turn for the worse.

1985	Yugoslavia's economic crisis hits its nadir, with production and living standards at 1965 levels.
1988	Slobodan Milošević, the president of Serbia, embarks on a campaign to recentralize Yugoslavia.
1989	Croatia and Slovenia resist centralization and call for multiparty elections.
1990	In the first multiparty national elections since World War II, Communist candidates are easily defeated by new parties representing the three national communities of Bosnia-Herzegovina, which gain seats roughly in proportion to their populations; Alija Izetbegović, a Bosniak (Muslim), leads the resulting tripartite government and joint presidency.
1991	The Serbian Democratic Party of Bosnia-Herzegovina, led by Radovan Karadžić, boycotts joint presidential meetings and declares a Serb National Assembly in Banja Luka.
1992	In a referendum boycotted by Serbs, 97% of voters endorse independence for Bosnia-Herzegovina; in April the United States and the EU recognize Bosnia-Herzegovina; within a week the combined Serb forces of the Yugoslavian army, Serb paramilitary groups and Bosnian Serbs begin bombarding Sarajevo; Serbia and Montenegro declare themselves the Federal Republic of Yugoslavia (FRY). Serb forces begin a process of "ethnic cleansing" to clear non-Serbs from Serb-claimed areas; by mid-May Serb forces control two-thirds of Bosnia-Herzegovina.
1993	The UN imposes economic sanctions on the FRY; war breaks out between Croats and Bosniaks, formerly allied against the Serbs, over control of central Bosnia-Herzegovina; Serb ethnic cleansing is nearly complete by mid-year.
1994	Bosniaks and Croats agree to form a Bosniak-Croat federation in Bosnia-Herzegovina; a cease-fire with Serb forces is negotiated in December.
1995	Serbian forces massacre some 6,000 Muslim men in the UN-declared "safe haven" at Srebrenica; NATO carries out major air strikes on Serb positions. The United States brokers a peace agreement, the Dayton Accords, retaining Bosnia-Herzegovina's prewar boundaries but distinguishing two separate entities within it: one Serb, the other Croat-Bosniak.
1996	Voters choose candidates on essentially ethnic lines in national elections observed by the Organization for Security and Cooperation in Europe.
1998	NATO extends indefinitely its peacekeeping operations in Bosnia-Herzegovina, which were scheduled to expire in June.
2000	Non-nationalist parties gain a slim majority in national elections.
2001	Croat representative Ante Jelavić is released from his position, as his party, the Croatian Democratic Union of BiH (HDZ-BiH), threatens to declare an independent Croat republic. Bosnian Serb general Radislav Krstić is found guilty of genocide for his participation in the massacre in Srebrenica and sentenced to 46 years in prison. The SDS, the main Bosnian Serb nationalist party, votes to oust all war crimes suspects, including wartime leader Radovan Karadžić.
2002	Nationalists reclaim power during the country's presidential, parliamentary and local elections. Biljana Plavsić, the former Bosnian Serb president, pleads guilty to crimes against humanity at the UN Tribunal in The Hague. The other seven charges against her are dropped, but she is consequently sentenced to 11 years in prison.
2003	Parliament approves a new government and appoints Adnan Terzić as its leader. Naser Orić, a wartime commander, is summoned to The Hague tribunal for his role in crimes against Serbs.
2004	NATO entrusts peacekeeping duties to Eufor, a European Union-led organization. Serbian president Boris Tadić makes a public apology in Bosnia-Herzegovina to all those who suffered crimes committed in the name of the Serb people.
2005	Survivors of the Srebrenica massacre in Bosnia mark its 10th anniversary by symbolically marching for 45 miles from the Crni Vrh mass grave—where 600 bodies are buried—to Srebrenica, the city where Serbs had killed 8,000 Muslims.

1914, Serbian nationalist Gavrilo Princip assassinated the heir to the imperial throne, Austria's Archduke FRANZ FERDINAND, triggering WORLD WAR I. In 1918 the region was united by Serbia with Slovenia, Croatia and Montenegro to form the Kingdom of Serbs, Croats and Slovenes, renamed Yugoslavia in 1929. In 1946 Bosnia and Herzegovina were included within Yugoslavia as one of its six republics. In 1992 the predominantly Muslim government of Bosnia declared its independence from Yugoslavia, prompting an armed insurrection by Bosnian Serb forces backed by the central government in Belgrade. This dispute led to the outbreak of civil war in Bosnia in which Bosnian Serbs rallied behind Radovan KARADŽIĆ, and Bosnian Muslims (Bosniaks) behind the province's president, Alija IZETBEGOVIĆ. In 1995 the Bosnian, Serb and Croat leaders signed the DAYTON ACCORDS, which partitioned Bosnia into an autonomous Bosnian-Croat federation and a Bosnian Serb republic, with a central government to exercise sovereignty over the two ethnic-based entities. That same year Bosnia-Herzegovina's constitution was ratified.

Boss, Lewis (*1846–1912*) American astronomer. Boss studied at Dartmouth College where he graduated in 1870. In 1872 he was appointed assistant astronomer to the 49th parallel survey for the American-Canadian boundary, accurately locating stations from which the surveyors could work with confidence. In 1876 Boss was appointed director of the Dudley Observatory, Albany, a post he held until his death in 1912. While working on the parallel survey Boss became aware of the many errors made in the measurement of stellar positions, which caused the current star catalogs to be inaccurate. He consequently made his own observations, publishing the positions of 500 stars in 1878. In 1910 he published the *Preliminary General Catalogue* containing the position and proper motion of 6,188 of the brighter stars. His work was extended by his son, **Benjamin Boss**, who published in 1937 the *General Catalogue* containing comparable details of 33,342 stars.

Boston police strike Strike (1919) of uniformed Boston police officers in which then-Governor Calvin COOLIDGE called out the Massachusetts State Militia to keep order. In 1919 the vast majority of Boston police officers went out on strike after the police commissioner refused to recognize their right to join the American Federation of Labor (AFL). The result was a rash of crime, including near riots throughout the city. At the time, the police commissioner was appointed by the state governor, not the city's mayor. Before the walkout, the commissioner had ignored the pleas of the mayor to reach a compromise with the strikers. Governor Coolidge broke the strike by sending in the militia to restore order. All striking policemen were fired and replaced. Coolidge's forceful and well-publicized action paved the way for his selection as Republican Warren HARDING's running mate in the 1920 presidential election—and his rise to the presidency on Harding's sudden death in 1923.

Botero, Fernando (*1932–   *) Colombian artist. Botero is one of the most acclaimed Latin American painters of modern times. He has taken the bold social realism of precursor Latin American painters such as Diego RIVERA and transformed it into a wry and individualistic commentary on modern life. Botero's distinctive style features bizzare human figures who resemble overinflated dolls; these figures, often set in absurd and jangling urban situations, have a satirical, clownish impact. Botero is also renowned for his parodistic treatments of the themes of the Old Masters of the European painting tradition. Botero has lived and worked in New York and Paris, and his works are featured in private collections and museums worldwide.

Botha, Louis (*1862–1919*) South African soldier, statesman and prime minister (1910–19). An Afrikaner and originally a farmer, he fought the British in the BOER WAR, rising to become a commanding general in the Transvaal (1900) and later leading guerrilla forces. Assuming a more moderate stance after the war, he strived for reconciliation, becoming prime minister of the Transvaal from 1907 to 1910. He worked toward the creation of the Union of SOUTH AFRICA and became its first prime minister in 1910. In WORLD WAR I, Botha joined the Allies, suppressing a pro-German Boer revolt and, in 1915, sending South African troops into Germany's South-West Africa colony. Just prior to his death, Botha participated in the Paris Peace Conference (1919) and signed the Treaty of Versailles.

Botha, Pieter W. (*1916–2006*) President of SOUTH AFRICA (1984–89). Botha held various federal government offices from 1958 to 1978. He led the ruling **National Party** from 1978 to 1989. Prime minister from 1978 to 1984, he became state president when a constitutional change was introduced in 1984. Although a conservative, he introduced cautious reforms in the APARTHEID system. Caught between increasing international opposition toward South Africa and the diehard reactionaries in his party, he resigned in 1989 following a stroke and was succeeded by the more moderate F. W. DE KLERK.

Bothe, Walther Wilhelm Georg Franz (*1891–1957*) German atomic physicist. Bothe studied at the University of Berlin under Max Planck and received his Ph.D. in 1914. For the next few years he was a PRISONER OF WAR in Russia. On his return to Germany in 1920, he taught at Berlin and worked in Hans GEIGER's radioactivity laboratory. He devised the "coincidence method" of detecting the emission of electrons by X-rays in which electrons passing through two adjacent Geiger tubes at almost the same time are registered as a coincidental event. He used it to show that momentum and energy are conserved at the atomic level. In 1929 he applied the method to the study of cosmic rays and was able to show that they consisted of massive particles rather than photons. For this research he shared the 1954 NOBEL PRIZE in physics with Max BORN. By 1930 his reputation was established, and he was appointed professor of physics at Giessen. While director of the Max Planck Institute in Heidelberg, Bothe supervised the construction of Germany's first cyclotron. This work was finished in 1943. During WORLD WAR II he led German scientists in their search for atomic energy. When the war ended he was given the chair of physics at Heidelberg, which he retained until his death.

Botswana Nation in central part of southern Africa. Formerly known as Bechuanaland, it is without a seacoast and is populated primarily by the Botswana, a Bantu people who migrated there centuries ago. In 1885, to counter German power in Africa, the British claimed northern Bechuanaland as a protectorate and made southern Bechuanaland a Crown colony (which was annexed to Britain's Cape Colony in 1895). According to the constitution of independent South Africa, drafted in 1909, all of Bechuanaland was to become a part of that nation. But the British maintained their rule over Bechuanaland until 1965, when general elections were conducted and a constitution enacted. Gabarone replaced Mafeking as capital, and full independence was granted to the newly named Botswana in 1966. Its first leader was Sir Seretse Khama. Large deposits of copper, diamonds and nickel spurred the new nation's economy. While maintaining relations with white-ruled South Africa, Botswana sought to forge strong ties with its black African neighbors. On Botswana's northwest border, Rhodesia (now ZIMBABWE) became a source of tension during its own struggle for independence; Rhodesian forces invaded Botswana repeatedly during the 1970s

© Infobase Publishing

Botswana	
1895	The southern part of the Bechuanaland Protectorate is annexed by Cape Colony (South Africa).
1966	The Republic of Botswana is proclaimed, with Sir Seretse Khama as first president.
1969	Sir Seretse's Botswana Democratic Party (BDP) is returned to power in election.
1974	Sir Seretse and BDP win another term in office at the polls.
1977	Relations with Rhodesia worsen as the two countries accuse each other of armed attacks across the borders.
1979	President Khama is reelected in national elections, with increased majority for his Botswana Democratic Party.
1980	President Khama dies of cancer and is succeeded in office by Vice President Quett K. J. Masire.
1989	The ruling Botswana Democratic Party wins national elections by a landslide.
1990	Following the release of ANC leader Nelson Mandela from prison in South Africa, the government frees 16 members of South African liberation movements who had been held in detention.
1998	President Quett Masire retires and is replaced by Festus Mogae, the vice president.
2000	In an effort to battle the AIDS epidemic in Botswana, President Mogae announces that combative drugs for the disease will be distributed free of charge starting in the year 2001.
2004	President Festus G. Mogae is elected to serve a second term.
2005	Scientists at a conference in Brazil praise Botswana for its determination to fight HIV/AIDS.

in search of Zimbabwe nationalist guerrillas. In the 1990s AIDS became an increasing problem for Botswana as the country experienced a surge in foreign travel. By 2003 Botswana had the highest AIDS infection rate in the world.

Botvinnik, Mikhail Moiseyevich *(1911–1995)* Soviet chess player. Born near St. Petersburg, Botvinnik studied electrical engineering at Leningrad Polytechnic. He began playing chess at the age of 12 and won his first Soviet championship in 1931. Beginning to play in international chess tournaments in the 1930s, he became the first preeminent Soviet chess master. A wily strategist who relished difficulty, Botvinnik was world chess champion three times, from 1948 to 1957, 1958 to 1960 and 1961 to 1963, and is considered one of the chess world's all-time greats. In 1995 Botvinnik died of cancer.

Boudreau, Louis "Lou" *(1917–2001)* American baseball player. Boudreau was named playing manager of the Cleveland Indians at the age of 24, the youngest ever to hold that position. He led that team to the American League pennant and a victory in the World Series in 1948, a year in which he was also the league's Most Valuable Player, with a .355 batting average. He was named All-Star shortstop seven times and was the American League batting champion in 1944. After his retirement as a manager in 1960, he went into a successful career in broadcasting. He was named to the Hall of Fame in 1970.

Boué, Michel *(1936–1971)* French automobile designer, Boué's brief career with the French manufacturer Renault centered on the development of the Renault 5, or R5 (known in the U.S. as Le Car) in 1972, an economical front-wheel-drive compact car of simple and logical form. The design is notable for its consistency and unity, a reflection of its development by a single person of exceptional talent.

Bougainville Island In the southwestern Pacific Ocean. Created by volcanic activity, Bougainville was discovered by Europeans in 1768 and placed under German control in 1898. During WORLD WAR I it was occupied by Australian forces, and during WORLD WAR II it was conquered by the Japanese. After the war it was returned

to Australia, but after considerable secessionist activity, it became a part of Papua New Guinea when the latter became independent in 1975. Its main export is copper ore.

Boulanger, Nadia *(1887–1979)* French pianist, composition teacher and conductor. A student of Gabriel FAURÉ, she abandoned a career as a pianist to become ultimately one of the most influential teachers of musical composition, harmony and counterpoint in the 20th century. In the 1920s and 1930s, as her reputation grew, many young American composers flocked to Paris to study with her; among her most celebrated pupils were Aaron COPLAND, Roy HARRIS and Walter PISTON, as well as the British composer Lennox BERKELEY. Boulanger was the first woman to conduct the New York Philharmonic, the Boston Symphony, the Philadelphia Orchestra and London's Royal Philharmonic. She taught at the Paris Conservatory and for 30 years directed the American Conservatory of Music at Fontainebleu.

Boulanger, Pierre *(1886–1950)* French engineer who became chief of the CITROËN automobile firm in 1935. He was the person responsible for the development of the Traction Avant, 2CV, ID, and DS models that made Citroën the leader in innovative automobile design from the 1930s until recent years. It is said that Boulanger's insistence that the driver's seat of the DS accommodate him wearing a hat (and he was tall) led to the exceptionally spacious design of the car's interior.

Boulder Dam See HOOVER DAM.

Boulez, Pierre *(1925–)* French composer and conductor. Born near Lyon, he studied at the Paris Conservatoire with Olivier MESSIAEN during 1944–45 and learned the 12-tone system from René Liebowitz in 1946. A musical rebel, Boulez went beyond Arnold SCHOENBERG in the techniques of SERIAL MUSIC, which rejects traditional melody, tonality, harmony, pitch and rhythm. Rigorously intellectual, difficult to perform and often unpopular with traditional classical audiences, his avant-garde compositions include *Le Soleil des eaux* (1948), *Symphonie concertante* (1950), *Le Marteau sans maître* (1953–54), *Éclat* (1965), *Domaines*

(1968) and *Memoriales* (1975). Boulez has acted as an advocate for avant-garde music, directing Jean-Louis BARRAULT's company, organizing (1954) the "Domaine musicale" concerts in Paris, stressing avant-garde compositions throughout his career as a conductor and becoming deeply involved with electronic and computer-generated music. He has led major symphony orchestras throughout the world, serving as principal guest conductor of the Cleveland Orchestra (1970–71), as music director of London's BBC Symphony Orchestra (1971–75) and of the New York Philharmonic (1971–76) and, since 1976, as director of the Institut de Recherche et de Coordination Acoustique/Musique in Paris. In 2000 Boulez won the Israeli Wolf Prize for the Arts.

Boult, Sir Adrian Cedric *(1889–1983)* British conductor. Born in Chester, Boult studied at Oxford and in Leipzig. Returning to England in 1913, he made his conducting debut the following year. Boult conducted throughout Europe and the U.S., leading the Birmingham City Symphony (1924–30), the BBC Symphony Orchestra (1930–50) and the London Philharmonic (1950–57). He also had a distinguished teaching career at the Royal College of Music. Knighted in 1937, Boult was a tireless champion of 20th-century English music. Among the world premieres he conducted were Gustav HOLST's *The Planets* (1919), Sir Michael TIPPETT's Symphony No. 2 (1958) and several works by Ralph VAUGHAN WILLIAMS, including the *Pastoral* Symphony (1922) and three other symphonies. A modest and self-effacing conductor, Boult believed in adhering to the letter of the score and refrained from imposing his personal interpretation on any music he performed. His autobiography, *My Own Trumpet*, was published in 1973.

Boulting brothers British filmmakers. Twin brothers **Roy Boulting** (1913–85) and **John Boulting** (1913–) were a major force in postwar British filmmaking and wrote, produced and directed more than 30 films, many of them comedies. They lampooned such venerable British institutions as the armed forces (*Private's Progress*, 1955), labor unions (*I'm All Right, Jack*, 1959) and the Church of England (*Heavens Above!* 1963).

Boumedienne, Houari (*1925–1978*)
President of Algeria (1965–78). A soldier, he joined the Front de Libération Nationale in the war against FRANCE in 1955. Appointed minister of defense in 1962 by President BEN BELLA, he led a coup that overthrew Ben Bella in 1965. President of Algeria from 1965 until his death in 1978, he was responsible for the Four Year Plan (1969–73), which developed industry, reformed agriculture and nationalized French oil interests.

Bourbaki, Nicolas
French group of mathematicians. *Nicolas Bourbaki* is the collective pseudonym of a group of some of the most outstanding of contemporary mathematicians. The precise membership of Bourbaki, which changed over the years, was a closely guarded secret, but it is now known. Since 1939 Bourbaki has been publishing a monumental work, the *Elements de mathematique (Elements of Mathematics)*, of which over 30 volumes have so far appeared. In this Bourbaki attempts to expound and display the architecture of the whole mathematical edifice starting from certain carefully chosen logical and set-theoretic concepts. As the members are all working mathematicians rather than pure logicians, the influence of Bourbaki's writings on contemporary mathematicians and their conception of the subject has been immense.

Bourguiba, Habib (Muhammad Boukharouba) (*1903–2000*)
President of Tunisia (1957–87). A member of the Destour Party from 1921, he split away to form the Neo-Destour Party in 1934. Imprisoned by the French from 1934 to 1936 and from 1938 to 1943, he lived outside TUNISIA from 1946 to 1949. On his return he was again imprisoned (1952–54). Prime minister in 1956 when Tunisia became independent, he was elected president in 1957. After his deposition in 1987 his health gradually deteriorated while he remained under house arrest. He died of arteriosclerosis in 2000.

Bourke-White, Margaret (*1906–1971*)
American photographer. Bourke-White is famous for capturing in pictures many of the major events of the first half of the 20th century. Initially an industrial photographer for *Fortune* magazine (1929–33), she gained international recognition as a photographer for LIFE magazine (1936–69). Her photo-essay books include *Eyes on Russia* (1931) and *Halfway to Freedom: A Study of the New India* (1949). Briefly married to novelist Erskine CALDWELL (1939–42), she collaborated with him on several books, including *North of the Danube* (1939).

Boussac, Marcel (*1889–1980*)
French textile magnate. After World War I Boussac built a $150 million financial empire that at its peak included 65 textile mills, the fashion house of Christian DIOR, thoroughbred racing stables and the right-wing Paris newspaper *L'Aurore*. During this time Boussac was known as the "King of Cotton" in France. In the 1960s and 1970s, however, faced with increasing foreign competition and a lack of modern management and facilities, his textile empire declined.

Bouton, James (Jim "Bulldog" Bouton) (*1939– *)
American baseball player. Although Bouton enjoyed a respectable career as a pitcher, making the All-Star team in 1963 with a 21-7 record and a 2.53 ERA, he is best-known for his controversial book *Ball Four*. The book exposed baseball players as people with human foibles and, occasionally, unhealthy off-the-field habits. While it seems mild by today's standards, its 1969 publication unleashed a furor in the baseball establishment and the baseball press. Bouton's early career with the Yankees (1962–64) gave him a World Series win as well as material about some of baseball's most revered figures, including Mickey MANTLE. He converted to the knuckleball in 1968, and played with a variety of expansion teams before retiring in 1975. He tried a comeback in 1977 and finally retired in 1978.

Boutros-Ghali, Boutros (*1922– *)
Egyptian state minister (1977–91) and prime minister (1991–92), and secretary-general of the UNITED NATIONS (1992–96). Born and raised as a Christian in EGYPT, Boutros-Ghali was educated at the Sorbonne in Paris and Columbia University in New York. After working as a professor of law and a journalist, Boutros-Ghali served as a minister of state in Egyptian president Anwar al-SADAT's entourage when the latter journeyed to Israel in 1977. He also joined the Egyptian diplomatic team that, with their Israeli counterparts and American president Jimmy CARTER, produced the 1978 Camp David accords (see CAMP DAVID TALKS) and the Egypt-Israeli peace treaty the following year.

On January 1, 1992, he succeeded Javier PÉREZ DE CUÉLLAR as the UN's sixth secretary-general. As secretary general, Boutros-Ghali attempted to use his position to direct the attention of the U.S. and other leading nations to the plight of peoples and states in the Third World. For example, he was instrumental in persuading the U.S. to initiate Operation Restore Hope, which provided food and other humanitarian aid to the people of war-torn Somalia under the banner of the UN, and later sought to protect the Somali people from the warlords who were causing civil strife. Also, his 1992 "Agenda for Peace" proposed creating a permanent-standing UN peacekeeping force independent of UN member nations that could intervene rapidly in a world crisis. Some critics objected to Boutros-Ghali's efforts to shame European nations, as well as the U.S., into action in Somalia, by comparing their initial inertia toward the crisis with the Security Council's continuous efforts to end the civil war in Yugoslavia. When he came up for reelection four years later, the U.S., dissatisfied with some of Boutros-Ghali's methods and his occasional criticism of American policies, used its veto power on the Security Council to prevent his election to a second term.

Bové, José (*1949– *)
French political and agricultural activist. Raised in Berkeley, California, where his parents worked as scientists at the University of California. Bové did not permanently return to France until 1968. In 1975 Bové had moved to the town of Larzac to start an agricultural commune that largely produced wool and Roquefort cheese (which he later attempted to smuggle into the U.S. to protest its trade barriers and those codified by GATT and the WORLD TRADE ORGANIZATION. The following year Bové left France to train at a "direct action"

camp in Libya, where he studied under instructors provided by Libya's ruler, Muammer QADDAFI.

In 1987 Bové returned to France to found the Confédération Paysanne, a leftist union of French peasant farmers advocating traditional methods and bigger government subsidies for farmers. In the mid-1990s Bové expanded his activist repertoire when he sailed on the *Rainbow Warrior,* a GREENPEACE vessel that attempted to prevent French atomic testing by sailing into areas designated for testing.

By 1997 Bové embarked on a foray against the forces of globalization and genetically modified (GM) crops. He also participated in protests against the WTO, such as the one staged at its Seattle meeting in 1999, and in the destruction of a McDonald's in his native France. While many antiglobalization and anti-GM forces applauded Bové's actions, he has drawn criticism for his willingness to espouse violent methods.

Bovet, Daniel (*1907–1992*) Swiss-Italian pharmacologist who was responsible for developing many of the medical drugs taken for granted in the 20th century. Educated at the University of Geneva, Bovet worked at the Pasteur Institute in Paris in the 1930s and was able to isolate sulfanilamide, which destroys streptococcal bacteria both in the body and in laboratory cultures. This led to the production of the first "wonder drug" that worked directly against the cause of a disease. Bovet later synthesized many drugs derived from sulfanilamide, creating an entire family of sulfa drugs. He also developed the first antihistimine; his work in this field laid the groundwork for virtually all the antihistimines that are now available. Bovet moved to Rome in 1947 and became an Italian citizen. He next worked on the drug curare, a muscle relaxant derived from plants in the South American jungles. He helped to develop synthetic curare for use in surgery. For this work, Bovet was awarded the 1957 NOBEL PRIZE in physiology or medicine. During the 1960s Bovet investigated the possible chemical causes and treatments of mental illness. In addition to his Nobel Prize, Bovet received numerous other awards and honors.

Bow, Clara (*1905–1965*) HOLLY-WOOD film star who personified the in-dependent, 1920s JAZZ AGE woman, or "flapper." Known as the "It" girl because of her sexual appeal; Bow's clothes, hairstyle and makeup were copied by women everywhere. In films such as *Mantrap* (1926), *It* (1927) and *Roughhouse Rosie* (1927), she played a madcap emancipated woman in search of money, a handsome man and a good time. A scandal in the early 1930s involving adultery, bribery and drugs brought an early end to her career.

Bowen, Elizabeth (Dorothea Cole) (*1899–1973*) Anglo-Irish author. Born in Dublin, Bowen spent much of her early childhood in County Cork and was educated at Downe House School in Kent, England. Orphaned at 13, she was shuttled between relatives in England and Ireland; her resulting sense of displacement is reflected in her fiction. In 1918 she moved to LONDON, which is a moody, vividly described, additional "character" in much of her later work. A prolific short story writer, her first collection, *Encounters,* was published in 1923. Of her novels, perhaps best known are *The Death of the Heart* (1938), the story of an orphaned young woman sent to live with relatives in London, where she has her first experience with love, and *The Heat of the Day* (1949). Wartime London served as inspiration to some of her best work, and in the introduction to *The Collected Stories of Elizabeth Bowen* (1981) novelist Angus Wilson called her one of "two English writers who convey what life in blitzed London was like."

Bowen, Ira Sprague (*1898–1973*) American astronomer. Bowen graduated from Oberlin College in 1919 and earned his Ph.D. from the California Institute of Technology in 1926. He taught physics at Cal Tech from 1921 to 1945, serving from 1931 as professor. In 1946 he was made director of the Mount Wilson Observatory and, in 1948, of the newly opened Palomar Observatory, posts he held until his retirement in 1964.

Bowers, Claude (*1878–1958*) U.S. diplomat, journalist and historian. He performed editorial duties for newspapers in Indianapolis, Terre Haute and Fort Wayne, Indiana. He delivered the keynote address to the 1928 Democra-tic convention in Houston, Texas. He was appointed ambassador to SPAIN in 1933, but resigned his position in 1939 when the U.S. recognized Francisco FRANCO's regime. He was appointed as ambassador to CHILE, where he served until his retirement in 1953. His writings include *The Party Battles of the Jackson Period* (1922), *The Tragic Era, a History of Reconstruction* (1929) and *Chile Through Embassy Windows* (1958).

Bowie, David (*1947–*) British ROCK and roll musician and actor. Bowie has maintained a steady popularity with rock and roll listeners for two decades, largely through his ability to create a range of fascinating styles and stage personae. Bowie was one of the first new rock stars to emerge in the 1970s. A 1972 album, *The Rise and Fall of Ziggy Stardust and the Spiders from Mars,* coupled with a promotional concert tour, portrayed Bowie as an orange-haired, beglittered, androgynous, alien rock and roller. Bowie borrowed from disco for his 1975 *Young Americans* album, which included his first number one hit, "Fame." The title track of his 1983 album *Let's Dance* also climbed to number one on the charts. By 1990 Bowie's musical image was that of a gaunt, jaded rock aristocrat. He has appeared in a number of films, notably *The Man Who Fell to Earth* (1976), and also starred in a 1980s Broadway run of *The Elephant Man.* In 1993, a year after he married supermodel Iman, Bowie resumed his solo career, producing such albums as the R&B-influenced *Black Tie, White Noise* (1992), the instrumental soundtrack *The Buddha of Suburbia* (1994), the heavy metal album *Outside* (1995), *Earthling* (1997) and *Heathen* (2002). Bowie was inducted in the Rock and Roll Hall of Fame in 1996.

Bowles, Chester Bliss (*1901–1986*) U.S. public official. Bowles held high posts in four Democratic administrations and personified the liberal wing of the DEMOCRATIC PARTY in the 1950s and 1960s. He came to public service after a successful career in advertising, having been a founding partner of the Benton & Bowles agency. During World War II, after serving as head of the Connecticut Office of Price Administration, Bowles was made director of the national Office of Price Administration (1943). After the war he served briefly as director of the Office of Economic Stabilization. In 1948 he was elected governor of Connecticut but was defeated in 1950. The following year he was appointed ambassador to INDIA, where he served until 1953. From 1959 to 1961 he served in the U.S. House of Representatives. As chairman of the Democratic platform committee during the 1960 presidential race, he led the fight for a strong civil rights plank and for a vigorous policy of foreign aid. In 1961 President John F. KENNEDY appointed Bowles undersecretary of state. From 1963 to 1969 he was again ambassador to India. Bowles wrote several books, including *Ambassador's Report* (1954).

Bowles, Jane *(1917–1973)* American novelist, story writer and playwright. Bowles, who was born in New York, lived abroad—primarily in Tangiers, Morocco, with husband Paul BOWLES—for most of her creative career. Bowles first gained a reputation in avant-garde literary circles with her experimental novel *Two Serious Ladies* (1943), which concerned two women, one prosperous and conventional, the other sensuous and defiant, whose lives touch obliquely on two occasions. This novel showed the influence of Gertrude STEIN. Bowles's play *In the Summer House* (1954) received critical acclaim during its New York run. *Plain Pleasures* (1966) is a representative selection of Bowles's stories. A posthumous collection, *Feminine Wiles* (1976), includes stories, sketches and letters.

Bowles, Paul *(1910–1999)* American novelist, short story writer and composer. Bowles, an expatriate who lived in Morocco for four decades, is regarded as one of the finest short story writers of the 20th century, a master of an incisive style that depicts psychological horror with absolute precision. Born on Long Island, Bowles studied musical composition as a young man with Aaron COPLAND. Throughout the 1930s Bowles devoted himself to music (including numerous theater scores) and music criticism. In the 1940s he turned to fiction and won critical acclaim for his first novel, *The Sheltering Sky* (1949), and a story collection, *The Delicate Prey* (1950). The themes examined in these works—the impersonal cruelty of nature, and the gulf between Western cultural values and the stark realities of North African life—remained dominant in Bowles's subsequent works, which included forays into travel writing, autobiography and translation. His *Collected Stories* (1976) contains much of the best of Bowles's work. His wife, Jane BOWLES, was also a highly regarded fiction writer. Paul Bowles was cofounder of the literary journal *Antaeus*.

Boxer, Mark (Marc) *(1931–1988)* British editor, cartoonist and satirist. Boxer's witty, savage cartoons, which he drew under the pen name Marc, appeared in nearly all British newspapers, including the *Times,* the *Guardian,* the *Observer* and the *Daily Telegraph.* A cartoonist in the tradition of Max BEERBOHM and Oscar Lancaster, he was famous for his creation of a social-climbing couple, the Stringalongs. The first editor of the *Sunday Times* magazine, he was later editor of *Tatler* and editorial director of Condé Nast Publications Ltd.

Boxer Uprising *(1899–1901)* A secret organization in the Chinese government, the Society of the Righteous Harmonious Fists (Boxers) led an uprising against foreign missionaries and their converts. Britain, France, Italy, Germany, Russia and the U.S. sent military forces to Tianjin (Tientsin) and Beijing (Peking) to protect their legations. China's empress dowager Cixi (Tz'u Hsi), supporting the Boxers, ordered death to all foreigners. An international expedition subdued the Boxers and captured Peking and the Imperial City, sending the empress dowager fleeing, while the Russians occupied southern Manchuria. The

Painting by Sargent John Clyme depicting scenes from the Boxer Rebellion (LIBRARY OF CONGRESS, PRINTS AND PHOTOGRAPHS DIVISION)

Boxer Protocol, signed by China, the Western nations and Japan, compelled Chinese reparations payments and established "extraterritorial" rights for foreign powers in China.

Boycott, Geoffrey (*1940–*) English cricket player. A controversial cricketer, Boycott scored more runs than any other Englishman in Test cricket but piled up as many critics as he did runs. Noted for his strict discipline at the wicket, Boycott built his innings slowly. He was often accused of playing for himself and that his slow scoring rate was detrimental to the team. Boycott's career statistics place him in the uppermost echelon of batsmen. His 8,114 runs from 108 Tests lead all Englishmen and place him third all-time. During his first-class career (1962–86), he scored 48,426 runs at an average of 56.83. He was one of the few men to have scored 100 centuries, accomplishing the feat in a Test versus Australia on his home ground at Headingley. Boycott played his entire county career for Yorkshire, captaining the side for eight seasons.

Boyd, William Clouser (*1903–1983*) American biochemist. Boyd was educated at Harvard and Boston University where he obtained his Ph.D. in 1930 and later taught in the medical school, serving as professor of immunochemistry from 1948 until his retirement in 1969. Karl Landsteiner's discovery of blood groups in 1902 and subsequent studies of their global distribution permitted a far more accurate estimate of racial types than had previously been possible. To this end Boyd began the systematic collection and analysis of blood samples from all over the world. Eventually, in the 1950s in such works as *Genetics and the Races of Man* (1950) he began to present evidence for the existence of 13 races— early European, northern and eastern European, Lapp, Mediterranean, African, Asian, Dravidian, Amerind, Indonesian, Melanesian, Polynesian and Australian aborigine.

Boyd Orr, John (first baron Boyd Orr) (*1880–1971*) British nutritionist, agricultural scientist and educator. Born in Scotland, he attended the University of Glasgow and was a professor of agriculture at the University of Aberdeen from 1942 to 1945. He was the author of a number of influential books on nutrition including *The National Food Supply* (1934), *Food, Health and Income* (1936) and *Food and the People* (1943). Boyd Orr served as the first director general of the United Nations Food and Agriculture Organization, playing a leading role in dealing with post–World War II famine. His UN work was largely responsible for his being awarded the 1949 NOBEL PRIZE for peace. Boyd Orr was knighted in 1935 and made a baron in 1949. Vitally concerned with world food problems, he was also an ardent internationalist who favored world government and served as president of the World Federalist Movement.

Boyer, Charles (*1897–1978*) French-born actor and movie star, known as "the Great Lover" because of his romantic appeal. Boyer acted in romantic films opposite most of HOLLYWOOD's leading ladies in the 1930s and 1940s. A graduate of the Sorbonne and the Paris Conservatory, he established his reputation on the French stage in the 1920s. He also appeared in some films at this time. His first films in Hollywood in the early 1930s were unsuccessful. However, his films later in the 1930s won larger audiences. He became a star in America in *Algiers* (1938), the film in which he supposedly uttered the line, "Come with me to the Casbah." (In fact, he never said this.) In 1945 he had the highest salary of any star at WARNER BROS. For many years American audiences regarded Boyer as the archetypal romantic Frenchman, charming, elegant and sophisticated. Later in his career he turned to character roles and continued to act in films until 1976. He committed suicide two days after his wife died.

Boyer, Herbert Wayne (*1936–*) American biochemist. He was educated at St. Vincent College in Latrobe, Pennsylvania, and the University of Pittsburgh, where he obtained his Ph.D. in 1963. He joined the faculty of the University of California, San Francisco, in 1966 and has served since 1976 as professor of biochemistry. Much of Boyer's work has been concerned with developing some of the basic techniques of recombinant DNA, known more popularly as GENETIC ENGINEERING. In 1973 he succeeded with Robert Helling, and independently of the work of Stanley Cohen and Annie Chang, in constructing functional DNA from two different sources. By 1976 Boyer and others realized that recombinant DNA could be used to produce such important proteins as INSULIN, INTERFERON and growth hormone in commercial quantities. Consequently, in 1976 he joined with financier Robert Swanson to invest $500 each to form the company Genentech, which went public in 1980. In 2001 Boyer was inducted into the National Inventors Hall of Fame.

Boyington, Gregory "Pappy" (*1912–1988*) U.S. Marine, WORLD WAR II flying ace. Boyington began the war with the FLYING TIGERS in China. From September 1943 to January 1944 he commanded Fighter Squadron 214, known as the Black Sheep, in the SOLOMON ISLANDS. During the war he downed 28 Japanese warplanes, a marine pilot record. He was shot down over New Guinea in January 1944 and spent the rest of the war in Japanese captivity. For his exploits he was awarded the Medal of Honor and the Navy Cross. His 1958 autobiography, *Baa Baa Black Sheep,* was the basis of a 1970s television series.

Boyle, William Anthony "Tony" (*1904–1985*) American labor leader. Born in Bald Butte, Montana, Boyle was, like his father, a coal miner in the American West. Joining the United Mine Workers of America (UMW) in 1922, he rose quickly in the ranks. International vice president of the UMW from 1960 to 1963 and a protégé of the powerful John L. LEWIS, he became union president in 1963. For the remainder of the decade he maintained dictatorial control over the burgeoning union and was widely charged with corruption and nepotism. In the 1969 election he was challenged by "Jock" YABLONSKI. Two weeks before the election the Labor Department issued a damning report regarding the UMW's finances. When Boyle was reelected, Yablonski charged vote rigging. Shortly thereafter he, his wife and daughter were murdered. After the killings, the Department of Labor and the FBI began extensive investigations. In 1972 the Labor Department invalidated the 1969 election. The following year Boyle was convicted of illegal use of union funds, and in 1975 he was sentenced to life in prison for conspiring to murder the Yablonski family.

Boys Town Also known as Father FLANAGAN's home for homeless boys. Established in 1917 by Father Edward J. Flanagan, it started in an old house in Omaha, Nebraska, but soon moved to the larger German Civic Center. Fund-raising led to the purchase of the present land, where wooden shelters were built. The home was incorporated as a village in 1936. The name of the institution spread with the popular 1938 motion picture *Boys Town.* Today most of the buildings on the 320-acre facility are of sturdy red brick construction. Over 10,000 boys may be counted as "alumni." The place now gives shelter to both boys and girls.

Brachet, Jean-Louis-Auguste *(1909– 1988)* Belgian cell biologist. Brachet was educated at the Free University of Brussels where his father, an embryologist, was rector. After earning his M.D. in 1934 he joined the faculty as an anatomy instructor and in 1943 was appointed professor of general biology. Brachet began his career by studying the then poorly understood nucleic acids. In 1933 he demonstrated that DNA and RNA occur in both plant and animal cells. In 1942 he proposed the important hypothesis that ribonucleoprotein granules could be the agents of protein synthesis. Later experiments, in which Brachet removed the nucleus from the cell, showed that although protein synthesis continued for a while, the amount of RNA in the cytoplasm decreased until there was none left. This indicated that RNA production occurs in the nucleus and that it is then transported from the nucleus to the cytoplasm.

Bracken, Brendan *(1901–1958)* British politician. Bracken was educated at Sedbergh and was later publisher of the *Financial Times* and other periodicals. He entered Parliament as a Conservative in 1929 and became minister of information in 1941. During WORLD WAR II Bracken was one of Winston CHURCHILL's closest advisers, and in 1945 he served briefly as first lord of the admiralty.

Bradbury, Ray Douglas *(1920–)* American fantasy and science fiction writer whose work is characterized by poetic impulse and allegory rather than hard technology. Born in Waukegan, Illinois, in 1934 Bradbury moved with his family to Los Angeles. His enthusiasm for science fiction led to the creation of his own magazine, *Futuria Fantasia* (1939), and his first story sales in 1941. He soon published stories in such quality magazines as *Colliers* and *The Saturday Evening Post.* His short story collection *Dark Carnival* (1947) and subsequent books—*The Martian Chronicles* (1950), *Fahrenheit 451* (1953) and *Dandelion Wine* (1957)—established his reputation with readers and critics alike. These remain his most important works, although his later output, while uneven, continues unabated. An author of screenplays (notably *Moby Dick* for John HUSTON, 1957), poetry collections and musical plays, he also hosted his own television anthology program, *The Ray Bradbury Theater.* His work has appeared in over 800 anthologies, and his name has become synonymous with the modern weird tale. His main themes may be grouped around two frequent locations for his works—Green Town, Illinois (a fictional reworking of his hometown), and the planet Mars. The former is the abode of childhood nostalgia and terror; the latter is the arena where the technology and poetry of humankind clash in an ongoing struggle. Bradbury's prose shows a distinctive flair for unusual metaphors and symbolic imagery, although in his later works it tends to become inflated. He himself prefers *Dandelion Wine* to all his works. Its deeply felt emotion and wonder about childhood may be taken as autobiographical. In 2000 Bradbury received a National Book Foundation medal in recognition of his contributions to science fiction.

Braddock, James J. *(1905–1974)* American boxer. Born and raised in New York City, Braddock began his professional career in 1926 and for three years was undefeated until he lost the light-heavyweight title to Tommy Loughran in 1929. He then suffered several years of defeats and retired in 1933 after breaking both hands in a match. After two years as a dockworker, he attempted a comeback and in 1935 defeated the favorite Max Baer for the heavyweight title. This upset earned him the nickname "Cinderella Man." In 1937 he lost the title to a young Joe LOUIS.

Bradlee, Benjamin *(1921–)* American journalist and editor. Born in Boston, Bradlee graduated from Harvard University in 1942 and served in the navy during World War II. An appointment as press attaché in the American embassy in Paris was followed by a post as European correspondent for *Newsweek* magazine from 1953 to 1957. Bradlee then went to *Newsweek's* Washington, D.C., bureau where he was named bureau chief in 1961. Four years later he joined the *Washington Post,* where he was appointed executive editor in 1968. He presided over major investigative stories, including the *Post's* epoch-making coverage of the WATERGATE scandal by WOODWARD AND BERNSTEIN. Known for his tough, exacting editorial standards, Bradlee is also the author of *That Special Grace* (1964) and *Conversations with Kennedy* (1975). In 1996 he published his memoir, *A Good Life.*

Bradley, Francis Herbert *(1846– 1924)* British philosopher. Bradley was one of the most influential British philosophers of the Idealist school, which allowed an ultimate reality to nonmaterial concepts. As a metaphysician, Bradley was greatly influenced by German Idealist thought, most notably the works of Georg Hegel. A fellow of Merton College, Oxford, Bradley's works include *Ethical Studies* (1876), *Appearance and Reality* (1893) and *Essays on Truth and Reality* (1914). The poet and critic T. S. ELIOT devoted his youthful master's thesis at Harvard University to Bradley. Eliot later acknowledged that Bradley had greatly influenced his own prose style.

Bradley, Jenny *(1886–1983)* Belgian-born literary agent. During the 1920s and 1930s she was an agent for such eminent authors as James JOYCE, Gertrude STEIN and F. Scott FITZGERALD. She and her husband acted as a liaison between authors and publishers in New York City and Paris, acquiring options on leading French writers including André GIDE, André MALRAUX and Antoine de SAINT-EXUPERY for American publishers.

Bradley, Omar Nelson *(1893– 1981)* U.S. Army general. After graduating from West Point, he served in WORLD WAR I. In 1943 he took command of the Second Corps and played an important role in the invasions of North Africa and Sicily. EISENHOWER chose him to lead the Allied invasion of NORMANDY in 1944. Later the same year he was placed in command of the Twelfth Army, the largest ever to be led by a single American field commander. In 1945 he received the four stars of a full general. He was the principal figure in Allied operations in the battle to take GERMANY. He served as army chief of staff from 1948 to 1949 and became first chairman of the Joint Chiefs of Staff, from 1949 to 1953. In 1950 he was promoted to the five-star rank of general of the army. He retired to a business career in 1953. Among the many commendations earned by Bradley were the Distinguished Service Medal, Silver Star, Bronze Star, Presidential Medal of Freedom and Grand Cross Legion of Honor.

Bradman, Sir Donald (1908–2001) Australian cricketer, widely regarded as the greatest batsman in cricket history. Bradman holds the record for the highest batting average in Test matches, 99.94 (6,996 runs in 70 innings). He played 52 Tests for Australia from 1928 to 1948, captaining the side 24 times (1936–48). Among his many other batting feats, Bradman holds the record for the fastest double century in Test cricket: 214 minutes from 259 balls, scored on July 11, 1930, for Australia v. England. In this innings he went on to score 334 runs, the fifth highest score in Test history. In Australia, Bradman played state cricket for New South Wales and South Australia (1927–49). Following his retirement, he was knighted for his services to cricket.

Bradshaw, Robert (1917–1978) Prime minister of the British-associated West Indies state of SAINT KITTS–NEVIS from its formation in 1967 until his death in 1978.

Brady Plan U.S. government financial plan (1989) to address the problem of excessive international indebtedness. Devised by U.S. secretary of the treasury Nicholas Brady to alleviate the debt crisis among lesser-developed countries (LDCs), the Brady Plan addressed a problem that had plagued LDCs since 1982. In 1989 numerous LDCs, particularly in Latin America, fell deeply into debt on account of both the lower prices on the commodities these countries sold on the world market and the high interest rates on the loans their governments had subscribed to in an attempt to promote economic growth. The result was that these states had insufficient foreign exchange to pay the interest, let alone the principal, on their foreign loans. Several LDCs teetered on the brink of default because they could not repay the hundreds of billions of dollars they owed. This further complicated their economic outlook, as these LDCs depended on a regular influx of loans to sustain their economic and fiscal structures.

The solution to the crisis proposed by Brady represented a compromise between the LDCs and their foreign creditors. The Brady Plan benefited the LDCs in that it required the banks to reissue the existing bonds at a lower interest rate. It benefited the lending institutions in that they were guaranteed repayment of their loans by the WORLD BANK, the International Monetary Fund and the national banks of the world's more industrialized and economically stable nations. Furthermore, the LDCs had to take steps to stabilize their economies and currencies in order to qualify for the aid offered under the Brady Plan. Through the Brady Plan, the U.S. alone issued over $160 billion in bonds to countries throughout Eastern Europe, Latin America, Africa and Asia. The result has been the recovery and reform of the economies of many of these nations and the survival and prosperity of the institutions that lent them funds in the 1970s and early 1980s. However, continued economic instability in some recipients of Brady bonds, such as Nigeria, serves as a reminder of the acute financial difficulty that plagued the world in the 1980s.

Bragg, Sir William Henry (1862–1942) British physicist. Bragg graduated in 1884 from Cambridge University and after a year's research under J. J. Thomson took the chair of mathematics and physics at the University of Adelaide, Australia, in 1886. He returned to England as professor of physics at Leeds University in 1909, moving from there to University College, London, in 1915. In Australia Bragg concentrated on lecturing. There he started original research late in life (in 1904), working first on alpha radiation, investigating the range of the particles. Later he turned his attention to X-RAYS. He constructed (1915) the first X-ray spectrometer to measure the wavelengths of X-rays. Much of his work was on X-ray crystallography, in collaboration with his son, William Lawrence BRAGG. They shared the NOBEL PRIZE in physics in 1915. During WORLD WAR I Bragg worked on the development of hydrophones for the admiralty. In some ways his most significant work was done at the Royal Institution, London, where he was director from 1923.

Bragg, Sir William Lawrence (1890–1971) British physicist. The son of William Henry BRAGG, Bragg was educated at the University of Adelaide, Australia, and Cambridge University, where he became a fellow and lecturer. In 1919 he was appointed professor of physics at Manchester University. After a short period in 1937 as director of the National Physical Laboratory, he succeeded Ernest RUTHERFORD in 1938 as head of the Cavendish Laboratory and Cavendish Professor at Cambridge. In 1953 he became director of the Royal Institution, London, a post his father had held previously and which he held until his retirement in 1961. Success came early to Bragg, who shared the NOBEL PRIZE in physics with his father in 1915. Following Max von Laue's discovery of X-ray diffraction by crystals in 1912, Bragg in the same year formulated what is now known as the Bragg law. Bragg collaborated with his father in working out the crystal structures of a number of substances. He later worked on silicates and on metallurgy and set up a program to determine the structure of proteins.

Brahimi, Lakhdar (1934–) Algerian foreign minister (1991–93), UNITED NATIONS special envoy to Afghanistan (1997–99) and UN special representative for Afghanistan (2001–). Born in Algeria when it was still a possession of France, Brahimi studied law and political science in Paris before joining the NATIONAL LIBERATION FRONT (FLN), an Algerian organization that waged a rebellion against France to achieve independence (1954–62). In 1963 he became the newly independent country's permanent representative to the ARAB LEAGUE. After seven years in this position, Brahimi served as ambassador to Britain from 1971 to 1979. After advising the president on foreign affairs, Brahimi became undersecretary general of the League of Arab States in 1984. From 1989 to 1991 he attempted in vain to produce a diplomatic settlement to the Lebanese civil wars and then served as minister of foreign affairs (1991–93).

Brahimi served at the UN in 1994 as its special representative to Haiti and South Africa, helping to pave the way for the return of the democratically elected Haitian president Jean-Bertrand ARISTIDE and leading the international supervision of South Africa's first free national elections. In July 1997 UN secretary-general Kofi ANNAN appointed Brahimi as his special envoy to Afghanistan. However, he resigned this post in October 1999, citing repeated frustration dealing with the ruling TALIBAN's practice of ISLAMISM and its support for terrorist groups such as al-QAEDA. On October 3, 2001, he returned to Afghanistan as Annan's special representative to direct the UN's role in whatever government emerged after the American military operation in that country.

As Afghanistan's special representative, Brahimi coordinated international aid to the war-torn country, worked on the development of a plan for its infrastructure's reconstruction and supported the efforts of Hamid KARZAI to create a stable national government for the country. In the spring of 2004 Brahimi represented the UN in an effort to arrange for the transfer of political authority from the U.S.-led Coalition Provisional Authority to an Iraqi government.

Braine, John Gerald (1922–1985)

British novelist. Born in Bradford, Yorkshire, he served in the navy during WORLD WAR II. After the war he worked as a librarian in the north of England, settling in London in the late 1950s. One of the ANGRY YOUNG MEN of the 1950s, his successful first two novels, *Room at the Top* (1957; filmed 1958) and *Life at the Top* (1962; filmed 1965), tell the story of Joe Lampton, a disillusioned lower-middle-class Yorkshireman who cynically marries for money and social standing although he is in love with a married woman. Braine's later works, among them *The Queen of a Distant Country* (1975), *The Pious Agent* (1976) and *Waiting for Sheila* (1980), show a departure from the radical, anti-establishment views of his youth.

brain trust Nickname given to the group of informal advisers who helped President Franklin D. ROOSEVELT plan his NEW DEAL program. During his successful 1932 presidential campaign, FDR relied heavily on three professors from Columbia University—Adolf A. BERLE Jr., Raymond MOLEY and Rexford Guy TUGWELL, as well as Harry HOPKINS—to help him in conceptualizing his economic reform program. The brain trust designed a program that was radical in conception, based on massive government intervention in the economy. The program was implemented as FDR's New Deal, and it forever changed the role of the federal government in the U.S. Although the names of these advisers have faded, their work lives on.

Brambell, Francis William Rogers (1901–1970)

British zoologist. Brambell earned both his B.A. and Ph.D. from Trinity College, Dublin, and then worked successively at University College and King's College, London. In 1930 he became professor of zoology at Bangor University, remaining there until his retirement in 1968. Brambell's work on prenatal mortality in wild rabbits led to his discovery that protein molecules are transferred from mother to fetus, not through the placenta as previously supposed, but by the uterine cavity and fetal yolk sac. He further found that this process is selective; for example, the gamma globulins are transferred more readily than other serum proteins. Such work is important in studies of resistance to disease in the newborn and of hemolytic diseases of infants. For this work Brambell received the Royal Medal of the Royal Society of London in 1964.

Brancusi, Constantin (1876–1957)

Romanian sculptor who spent most of his creative life in Paris. Brancusi is among the most revered figures of 20th-century art, a sculptor who belonged to no particular school but whose work is universally admired. After studying art in Bucharest, Vienna and Munich, Brancusi settled in Paris in 1904, where he endured years of poverty and obscurity. In 1906 the great sculptor Auguste Rodin offered to take on Brancusi as an assistant; Brancusi declined with this famous explanation: "No other trees can grow in the shadow of an oak tree." Around 1910. Brancusi turned to highly stylized sculptures made of bronze and other metals that captured the essential forms of birds and other natural fauna. These won him international fame. In 1937 he completed, for the public park at Tirgu Jiu near his birthplace, an immense sculpture called *Endless Column* (over 30 meters high). That same year he designed a Temple of Meditation for the maharajah of Indore in India. Jacob EPSTEIN and Henry MOORE are just two of the many major sculptors who have acknowledged the influence of Brancusi. A re-creation of Brancusi's studio is now housed in the POMPIDOU CENTER in Paris.

Brandeis, Louis Dembitz (1856–1941)

American jurist, associate justice of the U.S. Supreme Court (1916–39). Born in Louisville, Kentucky, Brandeis graduated from Harvard Law School in 1877. As a private attorney in Boston (1879–1916), he established a brilliant liberal record, initiating (1907) Massachusetts savings-bank insurance and defending the public interest in such areas as labor law, utility and railroad rates, consumerism and conservationism. His "Brandeis brief," introduced in his Supreme Court argument in *Muller v. Oregon* (1908), revolutionized legal practice by introducing sociological and economic data into legal discourse. A critic of big banks, he was the author of the best-selling *Other People's Money, and How the Bankers Use It* (1914). Also a staunch opponent of corporate monopoly, he strongly influenced Woodrow WILSON, and his views were reflected in the Wilson administration's strong antitrust legislation. In 1916 Wilson appointed "the people's attorney" to the Supreme Court, and Brandeis became the first Jewish justice in U.S. history. During his distinguished career on the bench, he maintained his liberal positions, often dissenting from the opinions of the Court's conservative majority. After the election of Franklin D. ROOSEVELT in 1933, Brandeis became a supporter of NEW DEAL policies, again finding himself often in the Court's minority. After retirement in 1939, Brandeis, a committed Zionist (see ZIONISM), spent much of his time working for the cause of a Jewish homeland.

Brando, Marlon, Jr. *(1924–2004)* American stage and screen actor; acclaimed as the most magnetic and influential American actor of the postwar era. Trained in the 1940s, in the method school of acting by teachers Stella Adler and Elia KAZAN, Brando began his Broadway stage career in 1944 with minor roles but achieved major stardom with his portrayal of Stanley Kowalski in the Tennessee WILLIAMS play *A Streetcar Named Desire* (1947). Brando played the same role in the successful film adaptation of *Streetcar* (1951) and from that point on devoted himself to film work. His early film successes included *Viva Zapata!* (1952) and *The Wild One* (1954), but his most brilliant role—for which he won an ACADEMY AWARD as best actor—came as boxer Terry Malloy in *On the Waterfront* (1954). Other films featuring Brando include *Guys and Dolls* (1955); *One-Eyed Jacks* (1960), a western in which he directed himself; *The Godfather* (1972), for which he won another best actor Oscar for his portrayal of Don Corleone; *The Missouri Breaks* (1976); and *Apocalypse Now* (1979). More recently Brando starred in *A Dry White Season* (1989), a look at South African apartheid, and *The Freshman* (1990), an offbeat comedy. Although Brando appeared in several later films, such as *Don Juan DeMarco* (1995) and *The Island of Dr. Moreau* (1996), his performances there failed to equal those of the 1960s and 1970s.

Brandt, Bill *(1905–1983)* One of the leading British photographers of the 20th century. In the late 1920s Brandt served as an assistant to the American Surrealist photographer Man RAY in Ray's Paris studio, and the influence of SURREALISM persisted in his work. But Brandt went on to more socially conscious work in documenting British poverty during the GREAT DEPRESSION of the 1930s. He also earned renown for his moody photographs of London during the blackouts of WORLD WAR II. His later work included experimental studies of the human body, published in the collection *Perspective of Nudes* (1961). Other major volumes of photographs include *Literary Britain* (1951) and *Shadow of Light* (1977).

Brandt, Willy (Herbert Ernst Karl Frahm) *(1913–1992)* German political leader. Born in Lübeck, as a teenager he became a socialist in the European democratic tradition. He opposed HITLER in the early 1930s and fled to Norway in 1933. There he changed his name to Willy Brandt, a pseudonym he had used in earlier writings, became a Norwegian citizen, attended Oslo University and began a career as a journalist. When the Germans invaded Norway in 1940 he escaped to Sweden, where he acted as a link between the Scandinavian and German RESISTANCE movements. After the war he was appointed Norwegian press attaché to Berlin and soon resumed relations with the Social Democratic Party (SPD). He regained German citizenship in 1947 and subsequently (1949–57) served as an SPD member of the West German Bundestag. In 1957 Brandt was elected to the highly visible post of mayor of BERLIN. Becoming SPD chairman in 1964, he was appointed foreign minister in 1966. When the SPD was victorious in the 1969 federal elections, Brandt became chancellor and worked tirelessly to promote reconciliation with Eastern European countries and EAST GERMANY. This policy, known as OSTPOLITIK, earned him the 1971 NOBEL PRIZE for peace. Brandt was pressured into resigning in 1974 after an East German spy was discovered among his close advisers. From 1976 he served as chairman of the Socialist International, a confederation of worldwide Social Democratic parties. He continued to speak on national and international issues.

Brandt Report A report of February 1980 generated by the Brandt Commission, headed by former West German chancellor Willy BRANDT. The Brandt Report—*North-South: A Program for Survival*—advocated a restructuring of the world economy and financial institutions and the development of plans to stimulate growth, trade and confidence—in order to divert the divisions between North (the industrialized First World) and South (the developing THIRD WORLD) that threatened an eventual crisis.

Brans, Carl Henry *(1935–)* American mathematical physicist. Brans graduated in 1957 from Loyola University and earned his Ph.D. in 1961 from Princeton. He returned to Loyola in 1960 and in 1970 was appointed professor of physics. Brans has worked mainly in the field of general relativity. He is best known for his production with Robert Dicke in 1961 of a variant of EINSTEIN's theory in which the gravitational constant varies with time. A number of very accurate measurements made in the late 1970s have failed to detect this and some of the other predictions made by the **Brans-Dicke theory.**

Braque, Georges *(1882–1963)* French painter and cofounder, with Pablo PICASSO, of CUBISM. After graduation from the École des Beaux-Arts in Paris in 1900, Braque became actively involved in the FAUVE school of painting that called for the use of bright colors and pure pigments. But in 1907 Braque's style changed dramatically as a result of his study of the geometrically structured late landscapes of Paul Cézanne. Also in that year, Braque was introduced to Picasso, and the two began to work together actively to formulate an abstract cubist style that fractured and reconstructed traditional pictorial forms. While Braque and Picasso soon went their separate ways, Braque continued to show a cubist influence throughout his career while experimenting with new techniques. Braque's *The Portuguese* (1911) was the first modern painting to employ stenciled lettering. Braque also frequently employed papier collé—molded surfaces made of papier-mâché and other materials—in his paintings. In his final decades Braque devoted himself primarily to stylized still-lifes, in flat hues, of simple objects such as plants, fruits, bowls and vases.

Brasília Capital of Brazil; in Goias province. The site was selected in 1956 as the new capital of Brazil, in place of Rio de Janeiro. It was built with an eye to contemporary architectural innovation and was formally instituted as the capital in 1960.

Brassai (Gyula Halasz) *(1899–1984)* Hungarian photographer. Brassai is renowned for his candid and revealing portraits of urban life, and it is his remarkable series of black and white photos of what he called "the secret Paris" of the 1930s—its bars, bordellos and street life—that constitute his best-remembered legacy. Born in Hungary, Brassai immigrated to PARIS in 1924 to take part in the thriving artistic community then centered in Montparnasse. The photographs of Brassai have a relaxed, snapshot quality, but they also display a studied, dramatic use of light and shadow. *Picasso and Company* (1966) contains photographs of Brassai's numerous artist friends. *The Secret Paris of the 30's* (1976) is a collection of night-life photographs accompanied by his autobiographical reminiscences. Brassai's work is featured in the collections of museums around the world.

Brattain, Walter Houser *(1902–1987)* American physicist. Brattain, brought up on a cattle ranch, was educated at Whitman College, the University of Oregon and the University of Minnesota, where he earned his Ph.D. in 1929. He immediately joined the Bell Telephone Company where he worked as a research physicist until his retirement in 1967. After leaving Bell, Brattain taught at Whitman College. Brattain's main field of work was the surface properties of SEMICONDUCTORS. He was particularly interested in using them to amplify signals. Working with John BARDEEN, he investigated various arrangements for achieving this—originally studying silicon in contact with electrolytes but later using germanium in contact with gold. Their first efficient point-contact TRANSISTOR (1947), consisting of a thin wafer of germanium with two close point contacts on one side and a large normal contact on the other, had a power amplification of 18. For their development of the transistor, Bardeen and Brattain shared the 1956 NOBEL PRIZE in physics with William SHOCKLEY.

Braudel, Fernand Paul *(1902–1985)* French historian, widely considered to have been one of the great historians of the 20th century. For many years he was the foremost representative of the influential Annales school of historiography, which focused on the daily lives of ordinary people rather than the deeds of those in power. Braudel's two major works were *The Mediterranean and the Mediterranean World in the Age of Philip II* (1949), written from memory while he was in a German prison camp, and a trilogy, *Civilization and Capitalism, 15th–18th Century* (1979).

Braun, Karl Ferdinand *(1850–1918)* German physicist. Braun studied at Marburg and received a doctorate from the University of Berlin (1872). He taught in various university posts. In 1885 he became professor of experimental physics at Tubingen, and in 1895 he became professor of physics at Strasbourg. In 1874 Braun observed that certain semiconducting crystals could be used to convert alternating to direct currents. At the turn of the century he used this fact to invent crystal diodes, which led to the crystal radio. He also adapted the cathode-ray tube so that the electron beam was deflected by a changing voltage, thus inventing the oscilloscope and providing the basic component of a television receiver. His frame comes mainly from his improvements to MARCONI's wireless communication system, and in 1909 they shared the NOBEL PRIZE in physics. Braun's system, which used magnetically coupled resonant circuits, was the main one used in all receivers and transmitters in the first half of the 20th century. Braun went to the U.S. to testify in litigation about radio patents, but when the U.S. entered World War I in 1917 he was detained as an alien. He died in New York a year later.

Braun, Wernher von *(1912–1977)* Pioneer German-American rocket engineer and controversial genius behind the early days of the U.S. space program. Von Braun was responsible for America's first space success, the satellite *EXPLORER 1,* launched January 31, 1958, a few months after the Soviet Union's SPUTNIK satellite rocked the Western scientific establishment. Born in Germany and educated in Switzerland and Berlin, he became interested in rocketry and the idea of space travel after reading a book by Hermann OBERTH. Joining the German Rocket Society in 1930, he aided in the firing of over 80 experimental rockets. When the society disbanded in 1932, some members began working on rocketry for the German army while others dropped out of what was clearly becoming a military project. Undeterred by politics, von Braun stayed on to pursue his all-consuming interest in rockets. By the time HITLER assumed power in 1933, the young von Braun had become one of Germany's most influential rocket pioneers.

Working under the command of Walter DORNBERGER on the Baltic Sea island of PEENEMUNDE when WORLD WAR II broke out, von Braun joined the Nazi Party in 1940. Although he had developed a "V-2" prototype in 1938, it was not until 1943 that von Braun and his fellow engineers and scientists began full-scale development of rockets for military purposes—becoming pioneers not only in spaceflight but also in the more deadly art of the guided missile. The V-2 missile was capable of carrying its own fuel and oxygen and of reaching a height of 60 miles. The V-2 was developed too late to rescue the German army from defeat, but in its short history the V-2 terrorized London, killing more than 2,500 people, and was also used against advancing Allied troops after D day. U.S. intelligence officers later calculated that more than 3,000 people, used as slaves by the Nazis to build the missiles, may have died of mistreatment or in accidents.

Fleeing from advancing Russian troops near the end of the war, von Braun and his team surrendered to the U.S. Army, deciding that they would get better treatment from the U.S. than the USSR, whose countryside the Nazis had ravaged. Von Braun and his group were secretly smuggled into the U.S. under a government program known as OPERATION PAPERCLIP and began working openly and with few restrictions on the fledgling American rocket program. As vocal an American advocate for space exploration and colonization as he had been in Germany in his youth, von Braun went on to become a driving force behind the Saturn 5 rocket that took the first humans to the Moon, as well as a popular author and speaker in defense of America's space program.

Brautigan, Richard *(1935–1984)* American novelist, story writer and poet. In the late 1960s Brautigan, a writer with great lyric and imaginative gifts, became a best-selling hero of the COUNTERCULTURE. His novel *Trout Fishing in America* (1967), a wry, picaresque tale of love and simple bohemian pleasures, was greeted with both popular and critical acclaim and, in its numerous translations, made the California-based Brautigan one of the best-known American writers of his generation. Other important Brautigan works of this epoch include a volume of poems, *The Pill Versus the Springhill Mine Disaster* (1968); a novel, *In Watermelon Sugar* (1968); and a volume of stories, *The Revenge of the Lawn* (1972). While Brautigan continued to write throughout the 1970s and early 1980s, his novels—although retaining Brautigan's unique, stylish whimsy—fell out of critical favor, and some have speculated that this decline was a factor leading to his suicide.

Brave New World Novel by the British writer Aldous HUXLEY. *Brave New World* (1932) is by far the most famous of the works of Huxley. It stands alongside *1984*, by George ORWELL, as the most influential vision of a future dystopia in 20th-century literature. The setting of *Brave New World* is the 7th Century AF (After Ford), so designated in honor of the man who set civilization on a scientifically controlled course in which eugenics and imposed social conformity reign supreme. Human beings are assigned caste status according to intelligence—manual workers being lowest on the scale. To maintain the caste populations, genetically planned infants are birthed from incubators and brought up in communal schools. The plot revolves around Bernard Marx, a Britisher with a high Alpha-Plus status, who is dissatisfied with the bland conditioning of his world and so brings a Savage from a New Mexican Reservation to live in London. The Savage soon develops a repugnance for the new society's lack of spontaneity and warmth. The Savage confronts Mustapha Mond, the World Controller, who insists on the ultimate goods of peace and order and deprives the Savage of his last hope for freedom. Huxley wrote a sequel, *Brave New World Revisited* (1958), in which he argued that his 1932 novel remained a plausible scenario, given the dire growth of both totalitarian power and the scientific means of behavior control.

Bray, John R. (*1929–1978*) American inventor of the animated cartoon process used by almost all early animators, including Walt DISNEY. Bray also pioneered the use of motion picture training films for WORLD WAR II draftees and syndicated many cartoon strips, including *Out of the Inkwell*. (See also ANIMATED FILM.)

Brazil (**Federative Republic of Brazil**) South American country, bordered on the east by the Atlantic Ocean and abutting all other South American countries save Chile and Ecuador. Brazil is the fifth largest country in the world and the largest in South America. Ruled by an emperor from 1822 until a republic was established in 1889, Portuguese is Brazil's national language. Due to profitable coffee and rubber industries, Brazil enjoyed a wave of prosperity in the late 19th and early 20th centuries, and many Europeans and others immigrated there. Its population more than tripled between 1850 and 1920. During WORLD WAR I, Brazil joined the Allies and declared war on Germany in 1917. Following the war demand for rubber and other Brazilian exports sharply dropped as did the price of coffee. The resulting unemployment led to social unrest and political upheaval during the 1920s. In 1930 a military coup ousted the newly elected president Julio Prestes and replaced him with Getúlio Vargas, a former governor of Rio Grande do Sul. Vargas wrought many popular reforms in a new constitution adopted in 1934, including increased power to labor unions and giving women the right to vote, but Brazil, like the rest of the world, remained in the grips of economic depression. In 1937 he wrote yet another constitution, which gave him absolute powers as a dictator. Brazil again joined the Allies in WORLD WAR II, declaring war on the Axis and taking part in the invasion of Italy, the first time any South American forces had fought on another continent. The

BRAZIL	
1930	Getúlio Vargas establishes right-wing dictatorship following major revolt.
1942	Brazil declares war on Germany and Italy, becoming first South American country to send troops to another continent.
1945	Vargas overthrown in military coup.
1960	Brasilia, a new city on an inland jungle plateau, replaces Rio de Janeiro as capital.
1976	Death-squad victims are found.
1977	Divorce is legalized.
1985	Civilian government is restored; Nazi Joseph Mengele's remains are exhumed and examined.
1988	Rubber-tapper labor leader and environmentalist Chico Mendes is murdered.
1990	President Fernando Collor de Mello supports "debt-for-nature" swap to preserve Amazon.
1998	Economy in depression; IMF provides loans to stabilize the country's financial system.
2002	After losing to a U.S.-backed opponent in the elections of 1998, leftist labor leader Luis Ignacio Lula da Silva is elected president.

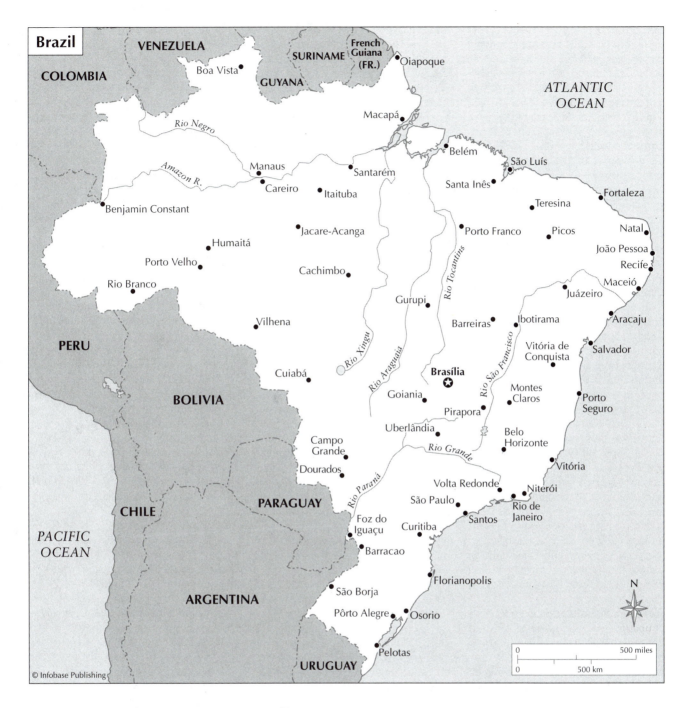

war also brought about an increased demand for rubber. In 1945 the army forced Vargas to resign and General Eurico Dutra assumed the presidency. Dutra introduced a new constitution restoring some civil rights and creating an elected legislature. When Vargas was reelected in 1950, Brazil was again facing economic disaster and extreme inflation, which his corrupt government was unable to mitigate. In 1954, after another military coup, Vargas committed suicide. In 1956 Juscelino Kubutschek was elected president. To encourage economic re-covery, Kubutschek promoted development of Brazil's interior and began construction on the planned city of Brasilia, which replaced Rio de Janeiro as capital in 1960. In 1961 Jasnio Quadros became president, but quickly resigned and was succeeded by his vice president, João Goulart, who was deposed in a bloodless coup in 1964 when General Castelo Branco established himself as dictator. His right-wing military regime was maintained by a succession of like-minded presidents. In 1985 Tancredo Neves was elected, the first civilian president since 1964. The 75-year-old Neves was in ill health and died shortly after his election. He was succeeded by his vice president, José Sarnay. Sarnay amended the constitution to permit direct presidential elections and introduced other reforms. Faced with 600% inflation, Sarnay also declared a wage and price freeze in 1985. In 1989 the conservative governor Fernando Collor de Mello was elected and vowed to reconstruct the economy, but his political career was ruined by allegations of corruption. Brazil has increasingly become a focus of attention due to the destruction of the Amazon rain forest, much of which lies within its borders, which has contributed to GLOBAL WARMING and the worldwide GREENHOUSE EFFECT. In 1998 the Brazilian economy experienced a brief depression following the collapse of the Asian stock markets. In response, the International Monetary Fund (IMF) provided a series of short-term loans to stabilize the national economy. After several years of financial instability and social unrest, the Brazilian Workers' Party won the elections in 2002. The leader of the Workers' Party, longtime union activist Luis Ignacio LULA DA SILVA became president and launched an ambitious program of socioeconomic reform.

Brazilian Revolt of 1964 On March 25, 1964, 1,400 sailors and marines, organized by the Sailors and Marines Association supporting President João Goulart, seized a trade union building to protest the arrest of their association's president. After refusing to surrender to the minister of the navy, two days later they yielded to army troops and were pardoned. Military leaders accused Goulart of undermining discipline and staged a revolt against him on March 31, 1964. A general strike staged by the General Confederation of Workers failed to prevent military takeover, and Goulart fled to Uruguay. The new government instituted a purge of all leftists, including officials of Goulart's Labor Party.

Brazilian Revolution of 1930 Suffering from the GREAT DEPRESSION and the collapse of the coffee market, Brazilians were discontented even before President Washington Luis Pereira de Souza broke with expected practice to name fellow native of São Paulo, Júlio Prestes, his conservative successor in the upcoming election, instead of someone from Minas Gerais. The leaders of Minas Gerais supported Getúlio Dornelles Vargas, governor of Rio Grande do Sul. When Prestes was declared winner (March 1930), his opponents made preparations for overturning the results. Vargas called for a revolt, promised economic and political reforms, gathered loyal troops and in a bloodless revolution (October 1930) seized the presidency, marking the end of the old, or first, republic.

Brazzaville Declaration Statement of January 1944 that defined the post–World War II relationship between FRANCE and its overseas colonies. It was the result of a 1944 meeting between the FREE FRENCH, headed by Charles de GAULLE, and representatives of various French colonies, and was held in Brazzaville, capital of FRENCH EQUATORIAL AFRICA and center for Free French forces. The declaration guaranteed French citizenship to colonial peoples, reaffirmed the colonial unity of France and its colonies and recommended a measure of autonomy for those colonies. It did not, however, address the issue of colonial independence. The document was largely rejected as too stringent by nationalists in ALGERIA and elsewhere and as overly moderate by many French settlers.

Brecht, Bertolt (Eugen Bertolt Friedrich Brecht) *(1898–1956)* German playwright, stage director and theoretician, and poet. Brecht is one of the seminal figures of 20th-century drama. He wrote his first play, *Baal* (1918), while studying medicine in Munich but began his theater career in earnest in the early 1920s as an assistant director to Max REINHARDT in Berlin. *A Man's a Man* (1926) was his first play to incorporate a Brechtian dramatic trademark—an epic view of history that overlays the action of the individual characters. *The Threepenny Opera* (1928), with Kurt WEILL composing the music (sung by Lotte LENYA) for Brecht's acerbic text, remains one of the most influential musical plays of the century. Brecht became a socialist in 1927. In 1933 he and his wife fled Nazi GERMANY. While in exile in the U.S., Brecht wrote most of his best plays, including *Mother Courage and Her Children* (1941) and *The Caucasian Chalk Circle* (1945). He returned to East Germany in 1949, where he founded the Berliner Ensemble. *Little Parables for the Theater* (1949) is his major theoretical work.

Breit, Gregory *(1899–1981)* Russian-American physicist. Born in Russia, Breit moved to the U.S. in 1915 and became a naturalized citizen in 1918. He studied at Johns Hopkins University, earning his Ph.D. in 1921. From 1921 until 1924 he worked at the University of Leiden, Harvard and University of Minnesota, before joining the Carnegie Institution, Washington, D.C. (1924–29). At Carnegie he worked in the department of terrestrial magnetism as a mathematical physicist. There, with Merle A. TUVE, he conducted some of the earliest experiments to measure the height and density of the ionosphere. Their technique was to transmit short bursts of radio waves and analyze the reflected waves received. Their work was a significant step in the historical development of RADAR. Besides his pioneering work on the ionosphere, Breit researched quantum theory, nuclear physics and quantum electrodynamics. Between 1929 and 1973 Breit held professorial posts at the universities of New York, Wisconsin, and Yale, and the State University of New York, Buffalo.

Brel, Jacques *(1929–1978)* Belgian-born singer and composer. In the U.S. he was best known for a musical based on his lyrics, *Jacques Brel Is Alive and Well and Living in Paris.* He stopped giving concerts in 1966 and devoted himself to acting and directing. In 1973, when he learned he had cancer, he settled in the South Pacific. He returned to France in 1977 to record *Brel,* which sold a million advance copies.

Brennan, William J., Jr. *(1906–1997)* Associate justice, U.S. Supreme Court (1956–90). Brennan, the son of Irish immigrants, graduated with distinction from the University of Pennsylvania and Harvard Law School. Before and after service in WORLD WAR II, Brennan was a labor lawyer in private practice in Newark, New Jersey. He was appointed as a justice of the New Jersey Superior Court and eventually rose to the state's supreme court. Appointed to the U.S. Supreme Court by President EISENHOWER, Brennan was known as a strong advocate of civil rights on the WARREN court of the 1960s. Brennan remained the leader of the liberal minority after 1970, and his ability to build consensus positions preserved and often extended the liberal decisions of the Court even after the appointment of a number of conservatives. Brennan was accused by critics of legislating from the bench because he normally interpreted the Constitution flexibly rather than literally. In 1990 Brennan resigned from the

Supreme Court because of failing health and was replaced by David SOUTER.

Brenner, Sydney *(1927–)* South African–British molecular biologist. Brenner, the son of a Lithuanian exile, was educated at the Universities of the Witwatersrand and Oxford, where he earned his D.Phil. in 1954. In 1957 he joined the staff of the Medical Research Council's molecular biology laboratory in Cambridge. Brenner's first major success came in 1957 when he demonstrated that the triplets of nucleotide bases that form the genetic code do not overlap along the genetic material (DNA). A greater triumph followed in 1961 when Brenner, in collaboration with Francis CRICK and others, reported the results of careful experiments with the bacteriophage T4, which clearly showed that the code did consist of base triplets that neither overlapped nor appeared to be separated by "punctuation marks." Also in 1961 Brenner, in collaboration with Francois Jacob and Matthew Meselson, introduced a new form of RNA, messenger RNA (mRNA). With this came one of the central insights of molecular biology—an explanation of the mechanism of information transfer whereby the protein-synthesizing centers (ribosomes) play the role of nonspecific constituents that can synthesize different proteins, according to specific instructions, which they receive from the genes through mRNA. After such early successes in the pioneering days of molecular biology, Brenner became involved in a major investigation into the development of the nervous system of nematodes. In 2002 Brenner won the 2002 NOBEL PRIZE in physiology or medicine for his discoveries relating to the genetic regulation of organ development and cell death.

Brenner Pass Alpine mountain pass between Innsbruck, Austria, and northeastern Italy; an ancient, major trade route between central Europe and Italy. From 1940 to 1943, during WORLD WAR II, it was a site for recurrent meetings between Axis leaders Adolf HITLER and Benito MUSSOLINI.

Bresson, Robert *(1907–1999)* French film director. Bresson is regarded by film critics as the ultimate directorial auteur—one who carefully creates and controls every aspect of the finished film, from script to cinematography to the casting of nonprofessional actors so as to use, in Bresson's words, "not what they do but what they are." While Bresson wrote screenplays in the 1930s, it was his first full-length film, *Angels of the Streets* (1943), that brought him to international prominence. During WORLD WAR II Bresson was a PRISONER OF WAR under the Nazis; he drew from this experience to make *A Man Escaped* (1956). While not a prolific filmmaker, virtually all of Bresson's finished work is highly regarded. His other films include *Diary of a Country Priest* (1951), *The Trial of Joan of Arc* (1962) and *Lancelot of the Lake* (1974). His *Notes on Cinematography* (1977) emphasizes the importance of attention to minute detail and the use not of "beautiful" images but of "necessary" ones.

Brest-Litovsk, Treaty of Treaty, signed on March 3, 1918, by the CENTRAL POWERS of Germany and Austria and the newly formed Soviet Union, that created a separate World War I peace for Russia. Hard-pressed by advancing German troops, the fledgling government of the UNION OF SOVIET SOCIALIST REPUBLICS was forced to accede to extremely harsh provisions, giving up the Ukraine, Finland, the Baltic provinces, the Caucasus, White Russia and Poland, and obliged to pay a large indemnity as well. The treaty was invalidated upon the signing of the general armistice that ended the war on November 11, 1918.

Breton, André *(1896–1966)* French poet, essayist and novelist. In his early poems Breton revealed the marked influence upon him of the lyricism of Guillaume Apollinaire and of dadaism. But in 1924, with the publication of his first Surrealist Manifesto, Breton became the unquestioned leader of SURREALISM, a literary movement that extolled the value of dreams and of uncensored, automatic writing from the depths of the human psyche. Breton composed two more Surrealist Manifestos (1930, 1942) as well as a book of essays, *What Is Surrealism?* (1934), and remained an active proponent of surrealist theories unto his death. Breton scored a major critical success with his evocative prose fantasy, *Nadja* (1928), in which Paris is evoked through meetings with a mysterious woman. He collaborated with his fellow surrealist poet Paul ÉLUARD on *Immaculate Conception* (1930). In *Arcane 17* (1945), Breton explores occult themes. *Poems* (1948) was a major collection of his verse over three decades.

Brett, George *(1953–)* American baseball player. Throughout his playing career, Brett wore the uniform of one team, the Kansas City Royals. However, his early years with the team were anything but impressive. In 1973, his first year in the major leagues, Brett only managed to hit .125. But in 1975 he began an impressive 11-year consecutive run in which he hit over .300, and continually improved his defensive play at third base.

In 1980 Brett mounted a serious challenge to Ted WILLIAMS's .406 season batting average of 1941. He eventually finished the year at .392, along with sustaining a 37-game hitting streak, winning the MVP award for the American League, leading the Royals to the American League pennant. However, despite good numbers from Brett—a .375 average with one home run and three RBIs—they lost the World Series to the Philadelphia Phillies four games to two. Five years later Brett earned some consolation for the 1980 loss when he led the Royals to victory over the St. Louis Cardinals in the World Series by hitting .370, giving Kansas City its only world championship. In 1993, after a career with 3,154 hits, a .305 batting average and 13 All-Star appearances, Brett retired from the Royals and moved into their front office, becoming Kansas City's vice president in charge of baseball operations. Five years later he headed an association of investors that purchased the Royals from the estate of its former owner, Ewing Kauffman. The following year Brett was voted into baseball's Hall of Fame.

Bretton Woods Conference International conference held in July 1944 to establish a structure for international monetary and economic cooperation in the postwar world. The Bretton Woods Conference was called by U.S. president Franklin D. ROOSEVELT, who saw a need to prevent a recurrence of the economic crises (notably the GREAT DEPRESSION) that had troubled the world during the 1920s and 1930s. Held in the resort town of Bretton Woods, New Hampshire, the conference was attended by representatives of 28 Allied nations. Treasury Secretary Henry MORGENTHAU Jr. headed the U.S. delegation and greatly influenced the conference. The Bretton Woods Conference laid the groundwork for the establishment of the International Monetary Fund (see WORLD BANK).

Breuer, Marcel Lajos *(1902–1981)* Hungarian-born architect and designer. Breuer introduced architectural MODERNISM to the U.S. and later helped create and establish the INTERNATIONAL STYLE. He was trained under Walter GROPIUS at Germany's famous BAUHAUS in the 1920s. While there he designed the now-ubiquitous Wassily and Cesca chairs, curved, steel-framed tensile structures that created a revolution in furniture design. In 1937 he fled Nazi Germany and immigrated to the U.S., joining Harvard's Graduate School of Design. There he taught some of the 20th century's preeminent architects. Breuer's later conceptions made extensive use of concrete as a prime building material and were more massive and austere than his earlier designs. Among his creations of the 1950s and 1960s were such buildings as New York's Whitney Museum and Pan Am Building and the Paris headquarters of UNESCO.

Breytenbach, Breyten *(1939–)* South African poet, prose writer and painter. He writes in Afrikaans. Breytenbach left the University of Cape Town to travel to Europe. He settled in Paris in 1961, where he gained a reputation as a painter. His early anti-APARTHEID poetry *Die Ysterkoi Moet Sweet* (The iron cow must sweat) and *Katastrofes* (Catastrophes) established him as a writer. In 1975, on an illegal visit to SOUTH AFRICA, he was arrested under the Terrorism Act. Charged with being a founder of Okehela, a white wing of the AFRICAN NATIONAL CONGRESS, he was sentenced to nine years in prison. Some of his finest poems and *Mouroir: Mirror-notes of a Novel* (tr. 1984) were written in prison. Under pressure from the French government, South Africa released Breytenbach in 1982, and he returned to Paris.

Brezhnev, Leonid Ilyich *(1906–1982)* Soviet political leader. Born in Dneprodzerzhinsk in the Ukraine, Brezhnev was educated at the Dneprodzerzhinsk Metallurgical Institute and later became deputy chief of the Urals regional land department. In 1935–36 he served in the Soviet army. From 1937 to 1939 he was chief of a department in the Dnepropetrovsk regional party committee. A political officer in the army from 1941 to 1946, in 1944 he was made major general. The first secretary of the central committee of the COMMUNIST PARTY in Moldavia in 1950–52, Brezhnev was made a member of the central committee of the CPSU in 1952. His political career continued to climb: In 1956 he was made a member of the Politburo, and from 1956 to 1960 he served as secretary of the central committee of the CPSU. Chairman of the Presidium of the Supreme Soviet of the USSR from 1960 to 1964, and also from 1977, in 1963 he was appointed as secretary of the central committee of the CPSU and general secretary from 1966. In 1976 he was made marshal of the Soviet Union and in 1977 became president of the Presidium of the Supreme Soviet. He died on November 10, 1982. Yuri ANDROPOV succeeded him.

Soviet political leader Leonid Brezhnev (LIBRARY OF CONGRESS, PRINTS AND PHOTOGRAPHS DIVISION)

French statesman Aristide Briand (LIBRARY OF CONGRESS, PRINTS AND PHOTOGRAPHS DIVISION)

Brezhnev Doctrine An assertion by Soviet Communist Party first secretary BREZHNEV of the legitimacy of the intervention of one socialist state in the affairs of another, when the central role of the COMMUNIST PARTY itself appeared threatened. The doctrine was demonstrated in the WARSAW PACT invasion of CZECHOSLOVAKIA (August 20–21, 1968), which ended the liberal PRAGUE SPRING.

Briand, Aristide *(1862–1932)* French statesman, 11-time premier. A socialist lawyer, he entered the Chamber of Deputies in 1902 and was known for his work in separating church and state (1905). He became premier in 1909, between that year and 1929 holding the office 11 separate times. Briand is best remembered, however, for his post–WORLD WAR I efforts in promoting international reconciliation and peace through arbitration. As foreign minister, Briand was the driving force behind the LOCARNO PACT of 1925, and the following year he shared the NOBEL PRIZE for peace with Germany's Gustav STRESEMANN. He went on to help formulate the KELLOGG-BRIAND PACT (1928), which attempted to eradicate war altogether, and in 1929–30 advocated a United States of Europe. He retired in 1932 after running unsuccessfully for the presidency.

Brice, Fanny (Fanny Borach) *(1891–1951)* One of the great legends of burlesque, vaudeville and Broadway, Brice began her career at age 14 when she won a singing contest at Keeney's Theater in Brooklyn, New York. Working both the VAUDEVILLE circuit and Broadway (in revues such as the ZIEGFELD FOLLIES), she developed a popular routine consisting of physical comedy, jokes in Jewish dialect, and a wide assortment of humorous songs, including "Sadie Salome," "Oh How I Hate That Fellow Nathan" and "Mrs. Cohen at the Beach." After her marriage to producer Billy ROSE ended in divorce in 1938, Brice became popular for her regular radio programs, which included *Good News of 1938* and the *Baby Snooks Show* (named after her famous character) in 1944. Before Brice had a chance to prove herself in the new medium of television, she died in 1951, several days after suffering a stroke. Her life story has been told, sometimes with names disguised, in several films, including the Barbra STREISAND vehicles *Funny Girl* (1968) and *Funny Lady* (1975).

Bricktop (Ada Beatrice Queen Victoria Louise Virginia Smith) *(1894–1984)* African-American entertainer, singer and nightclub owner. Like many black artists of her day, Bricktop did not gain wide recognition until she moved abroad. Her nightclub in Paris, also called Bricktop, was a gathering place during the 1920s for members of café society and for such prominent American expatriate writers as Ernest HEMINGWAY and F. Scott FITZGERALD. During the 1940s she presided over clubs in Rome and Mexico City. Cole PORTER wrote his song "Miss Otis Regrets" in her honor. Her protégés included Josephine BAKER, Mabel MERCER and Duke ELLINGTON.

Brico, Antonia *(1902–1989)* American orchestra conductor. Brico led her own orchestras in New York in the 1930s and helped lead the fight to overturn prejudice against female conductors around the world. She was the subject of the 1974 documentary film *Antonia: Portrait of a Conductor.*

Bridges, Alfred Renton Bryant "Harry" *(1901–1990)* Australian-born U.S. labor leader. Bridges organized the International Longshoremen's and Warehousemen's Union in 1933 and served as its president from 1934 to 1977. The union staged a strike in May 1934 that led to a general strike that virtually shut down the city of San Francisco for three days. Long accused of being a communist, Bridges denied the charge, although he willingly accepted financial aid from the Communist Party. He was the target of repeated attempts to deport him to his native Australia in the 1940s and 1950s. Upon Bridges's death, San Francisco's mayor ordered all city flags to be flown at half-mast in his honor. (See also *BRIDGES V. CALIFORNIA.*)

Bridges, Robert Seymour *(1844–1930)* English poet. Educated at Eton and Corpus Christi College, Oxford (1863–67), Bridges worked as a physician in London until 1881. His first book appeared in 1873, but it was the publication of *Shorter Poems* in 1890 that earned him a reputation as a master of the lyric form. A technically accomplished metricist, he was named poet laureate in 1913. Bridges has been blamed for delaying the publication of the more innovative poems of his friend Gerard Manley Hopkins until 1918. Although his diction is now regarded as stilted and cold, he is remembered for *The Testament of Beauty* (five volumes, 1927–29) and some fine, short lyric poems, such as "London Snow."

Bridges v. California *(1941)* U.S. Supreme Court decision involving the First Amendment; brought against union leader BRIDGES. At the start of WORLD WAR II, when the U.S. government was stepping up its war effort, Bridges, the left-wing leader of the West Coast Longshoreman's Union, was held in contempt by a California state court. While his trial was in progress, Bridges issued a press release threatening to tie up all shipping from West Coast ports in the event he was convicted. Two California state courts held Bridges in contempt of court, but he appealed to the Supreme Court, arguing that the action violated his First Amendment right to free speech. Despite the wartime setting the Supreme Court threw out the contempt conviction. Applying the clear and present danger test, the Court held that the state court's contempt order had violated Bridges's free speech rights.

Bridgman, Percy Williams *(1882–1961)* American physicist. The son of a journalist, Bridgman was educated at Harvard, where he earned his Ph.D. in 1908. He immediately joined the faculty, leaving only on his retirement in 1954 after serving as professor of physics (1919–26), professor of mathematics and natural philosophy (1926–50), and a Huggins Professor (1950–54). Most of Bridgman's research was in the field of high-pressure physics. When he began, he found it necessary to design and build virtually all his own equipment and instruments. In 1909 he introduced the self-tightening joint. With the appearance of high-tensile steels, he could aim for pressures well beyond the scope of earlier workers. Bridgman used such pressures to explore the properties of numerous liquids and solids. In the course of this work he discovered two new forms of ice, freezing at temperatures above 0°C. In 1955 he transformed graphite into synthetic diamond. Bridgman was awarded the 1946 NOBEL PRIZE in physics for his work on extremely high pressures. He was also widely known as a philosopher of science. While in his 70s Bridgman developed Paget's disease, which caused him considerable pain and little prospect for relief. He committed suicide in 1961.

Brightman, Edgar Sheffield *(1884–1953)* American philosopher. Brightman was the leading American proponent of personalism—the view that each individual human consciousness creates a unique reality that is not subject to objective verification or dispute. Brightman argued that these individual realities were unified by the conscious will of God, who creates individuals and cooperates with them in the creation of a cosmic reality. The most controversial position taken by Brightman concerned the nature of evil, which he called "the Given" and held to be a nonrational aspect of reality that was neither created nor approved by God, but that God was capable of holding in check. Brightman taught for several decades at Boston University. His chief works include *Introduction to Philosophy* (1925), *The Problem of God* (1930), *Moral Laws* (1933) and *Nature and Values* (1945).

Brightman, Sarah *(1960–)* British singer and theatrical performer. Born in Berkhampstead, England, Brightman began her career as a dancer in the London theater and on a British television series. After turning to singing, she produced her first hit with the single "I Lost My Heart to a Starship Trooper," in 1978. Two years later she played the role of Jemima in Andrew LLOYD WEBBER's musical extravaganza CATS. In 1984 she married Lloyd Webber. Brightman played the role of Christine Daaé in Lloyd Webber's blockbuster musical *The Phantom of the Opera,* which opened in 1986 and became one of the most successful stage musicals in history. Although the couple divorced in 1990, they remained on good terms, and Brightman went on tour in *The Music of Andrew Lloyd Webber: A Concert Spectacular.* Throughout the 1990s and into the 21st century she recorded best-selling solo albums, such as *As I Come of Age* in 1993, *Fly* in 1995, *Eden* in 1998, *Encore* in 2001 and *Harem* in 2003.

Brighton bombing On October 12, 1984, during the 1984 CONSERVATIVE PARTY conference in Brighton, England, a bomb exploded at the hotel where party leaders, including Prime Minister Margaret THATCHER and cabinet members, were staying. Five people were killed and 32 wounded, including top party official Norman Tebbitt and his wife. The Provisional IRISH REPUBLICAN ARMY claimed responsibility for the blast. Thatcher herself narrowly escaped injury. The blast occurred a few hours before the party's debate on Northern Ireland policy. The bombing was denounced by British and international leaders. In 1986 a London jury found a Belfast man guilty of the bombing, along with four codefendants. Charges against some codefendants were later dropped.

Brinkley, David McClure *(1920–2003)* American news commentator. He helped develop documentary television techniques for NBC with the *Huntley-Brinkley Report* (1956–71), which won Peabody, Sylvania and Emmy awards. In the 1980s he hosted an influential weekly political discussion program from Washington, D.C., *This Week with David Brinkley,* on ABC. Brinkley was noted for his terse, dry sense of humor. In 1992 Brinkley received a Presidential Medal of Freedom, the nation's highest civilian honor, from President George H. W. BUSH. Four years later Brinkley retired from *This Week.*

brinksmanship In foreign affairs, the policy of forcing a rival power to reach agreement by deliberately creating the risk for nuclear war. In 1956 U.S. secretary of state John Foster DULLES told *LIFE* magazine that "if you are scared to go to the brink you are lost."

Brinks Robbery Robbery on January 17, 1950, of the Brinks Security company's North Terminal Garage in Boston. In 15 minutes 11 middle-age Bostonians, who had carefully planned the caper, stole some $2.7 million in cash, checks and securities. The robbers had intended to maintain low profiles until the seven-year statute of limitations ran out. However, one of their number, Joseph "Specs" O'Keefe, felt cheated. Fearing that he might turn informer, the others unsuccessfully tried to have him killed. After the attempt on his life, O'Keefe did talk with the authorities, and eventually eight of the Brinks thieves were tried, convicted and sentenced to life imprisonment. The Brinks Robbery was one of the largest and most highly publicized of all 20th-century crimes. It was the subject of a 1980 film, *The Brinks Job.* (See also GREAT TRAIN ROBBERY.)

British Antarctic Territory A vast territory that lies south of 60 degrees south latitude, stretches to the South Pole and is bounded by longitudes 20 degrees and 80 degrees West. About 659,828 square miles in area, the territory includes the South Orkney Islands, the South Shetland Islands, Palmer Land and Graham Land on the Antarctic Peninsula, the Filcher and Ronne ice shelves and Coats Land. The territory was formed in 1908 when the various areas were grouped together; they are administered by a British high commissioner based in the Falkland Islands. The first permanent settlement was established on the South Shetland Islands in the early 20th century; scientific bases followed in the 1940s. Both CHILE and ARGENTINA have territorial claims to parts of the territory. Clashes between Argentina and Britain occurred in 1952 and again in 1982 when Britain expelled Argentina from its occupation of the South Shetland Islands during the FALKLAND ISLANDS WAR.

British Broadcasting Corporation (BBC) The state-owned broadcasting service of the UNITED KINGDOM. Established as a private company in 1922, the BBC was converted by royal charter to a public corporation in 1927. Its first director-general (1922–38) was the legendary John Reith, who established strict guidelines and a tone of high moral seriousness. Since 1932 the BBC's headquarters have been in Broadcasting House in Portland Place, London. During WORLD WAR II the BBC served as the "voice of Britain" and broadcast war news to Britain and to occupied Europe. It also relayed coded messages to RESISTANCE fighters in FRANCE and other occupied countries. Television broadcasting began in 1936, was suspended at the beginning of the war (1939) and resumed in 1946. The BBC is now responsible for four national radio stations (Radio 1, contemporary pop and ROCK and roll; Radio 2, pop standards, JAZZ and light music; Radio 3, classical music and drama; Radio 4, news, quiz and game shows and information and educational programs). It also operates several regional services, the world service and two national television services (BBC 1 and BBC 2). It is financed by fees from annual television licenses (for domestic services) and the government (for the world service). A board of 12 governors (appointed by the crown) oversees its operations and appoints a governor-general, the corporation's chief executive. While the British government has power over technical and related matters and final review of programming, the BBC theoretically has independent control over the content of programming. In the 1980s and 1990s the establishment of a fourth independent television network (Channel 4), the advent of cable television, and Prime Minister THATCHER's emphasis on "free-market values" as well as government attempts to censor certain news and documentary programs posed a serious challenge to the BBC's traditional role as a public service committed to excellence. The BBC has played a major and controversial role in weakening the hold of regional accents and spreading "standard English" (also known as "BBC English") throughout the United Kingdom. Over the years the BBC has provided a livelihood for many distinguished writers, actors, directors, musicians and other personalities. In the U.S., the BBC is known as a purveyor of quality programs to American public television stations. In 1996 the BBC

World Service closed its Arabic TV station. Most of its employees were soon hired by a new Arabic news station, al-JAZEERA. In 2003 the BBC was plunged into a row with the government of Prime Minister Tony BLAIR over the broadcasting service's reporting of the government's policy during the U.S.-led invasion of Iraq.

British Council An organization established in 1934 and incorporated by Royal Charter in 1940 dedicated to promoting British culture abroad. It established a specialist drama department in 1939, incorporating dance in 1980, and organizes overseas tours of British companies and writers as well as arranging visits to Britain by foreign theatrical dignitaries. The council also publishes a continually updated series, *British Writers,* and runs libraries and English-language schools around the world.

British Ecology Party See GREENS.

British Empire A collection of colonies, settlements, protectorates and outposts throughout the world that were administered by, or owed their loyalty to, the UNITED KINGDOM. Dating from the Age of Discovery, the British Empire grew throughout the Victorian era and reached its zenith early in the 20th century—from which point it almost immediately began a decline that turned into a dismantling after WORLD WAR II. Some of the colonies—notably INDIA, the jewel in the imperial crown—had never been settled by large numbers of Britons but were administered by an efficient British-organized civil service. India, along with various other colonies and/or protectorates in Asia (such as BURMA [Myanmar] and Malaya [now MALAYSIA]) and Africa (such as EGYPT, NIGERIA and Rhodesia [now ZIMBABWE]) were viewed mainly as sources of raw materials and markets for British manufactured goods or as military outposts, buffers against potentially hostile states. On the other hand, CANADA, AUSTRALIA and NEW ZEALAND were populated largely by British émigrés and their descendants who outnumbered the native populations (American Indian in Canada, Aborigine in Australia, Maori in New Zealand); these self-governing dominions (notwithstanding a significant number of French Canadians) remained loyal to the British Crown while evolving their own particular national identities and institutions.

Some historians have asserted that the far-flung empire was held together by bluff, bluster, pomp and circumstance, rather than overwhelming military force; there is more than a grain of truth to this. There was also a good deal of racism in British attitudes toward the empire's non-British subjects. In some parts of the empire, local movements for independence (most notably in India) gained momentum in the first four decades of the century. Britain, though a victor in WORLD WAR II, had been pauperized by the long and costly struggle and was in no position to contest an empire. After India was granted independence in 1947, the empire began to unravel; Britain's humiliation in the SUEZ CRISIS (1956) demonstrated that the United Kingdom was no longer an unchallenged world power. A large number of colonies gained independence in the late 1950s and early 1960s. Despite guerrilla movements in KENYA (see MAU MAU) and Malaya, the dismantling of the British Empire was generally a peaceful and orderly affair. Most former colonies continued their association with Britain as members of the COMMONWEALTH OF NATIONS.

British Indian Ocean Territory Island colony in the southwestern Indian Ocean. In 1965 the territory was created by the unification of Aldabra, Destoches and Farquhar Islands (formerly with SEYCHELLES) and the Chagos Archipelago (formerly with MAURITIUS). In 1976, when the Seychelles were granted independence, the above three islands were restored to it, leaving only the Chagos Archipelago within the Indian Ocean Territory. The major island, Diego Garcia, became in 1972 a communications and defense base for British and U.S. forces. At that time the extant population—primarily copra plantation workers—were moved elsewhere.

British Legion A British organization to aid war veterans and their dependents. The legion was created largely by Douglas HAIG in 1921, was recognized by royal charter in 1925 and became the Royal British Legion in 1971. Much of its funding is generated by its disabled members selling Flanders poppies on Remembrance Sunday, when Britain honors the dead of WORLD WAR I.

British Library Built in 1857 as part of the British Museum, the famous domed reading room was planned by the librarian Sir Antonio Panizzi. In 1963, due to the huge increase in the library's collection, much of which was being stored in various locations around London, plans were first laid to build a new headquarters. After much delay and difficulty with financing, the first phase of construction of the new library designed by Colin St. John Wilson began, but throughout the 1980s the project was still beset by financial woes due to construction cost inflation.

The library is home to many treasured first editions and manuscripts, such as the manuscript of Jane Austen's *Juvenilia,* which it acquired in 1988. In 1990 it acquired an important collection of manuscripts by major 20th-century writers from the British publisher Macmillan. It also serves a function similar to that of the Library of Congress in the U.S., holding a copy of every book published in the United Kingdom. In the 1990s the British Library's finances improved, and its physical structure was amended as part of the Millennium Commission's 2000 renovation of the British Museum. The library's holdings were moved to the new, completed building in London, and the old domed reading room at the British Museum was opened to tourists.

British Telecom British telecommunications company. Prior to 1980 British Telecom was a nationalized service, part of the Post Office; it was privatized in 1984 as part of Margaret THATCHER's program of PRIVATIZATION. It operates radio and television broadcasting, the telephone system and Britain's viewdate network, Prestel. Formerly a monopoly, British Telecom faces increasing competition from other commercial suppliers. In 1993 the British government completely privatized British Telecom, thereafter known as BT.

British Union of Fascists See Oswald MOSLEY.

British Volunteer Programme Since 1966, an umbrella organization overseeing associations such as Voluntary

Service Overseas (VSO) that send British volunteers to work in developing countries. VSO served as a model in the creation of the U.S. PEACE CORPS.

Brittain, Vera Mary *(1894–1970)* British author, pacifist and feminist. Brittain interrupted her studies at Somerville College, Oxford, to serve as a nurse during WORLD WAR I. *Testament of Youth* (1933) draws on her experiences and reflects her beliefs. She returned to Oxford after the war where she became close friends with the like-minded Winifred HOLTBY, about whom Brittain wrote in *Testament of Friendship* (1940). Brittain also wrote poetry and essays as well as fiction. She was married to the political scientist Sir George Catlin (1896–1979); their daughter, Shirley WILLIAMS, was a prominent LABOUR PARTY politician in the 1970s and cofounded the SOCIAL DEMOCRATIC PARTY (1981).

Britten, Benjamin *(1913–1976)* One of Britain's most important 20th-century composers, Britten was born at Lowestoft, Suffolk. Displaying early musical talent, he was a pupil of the composer Frank BRIDGE and studied at the Royal College of Music, London, with John IRELAND. His early work consists mainly of instrumental music written to accompany films, dramas and plays. Britten achieved early fame with his choral work *A Boy Was Born* (1933) and his Fantasy Quartet for Oboe and Strings (1934). He excelled at vocal works, many of them written for his friend, the English tenor Peter PEARS. His song cycles and choral works include a setting of Rimbaud's *Illuminations* (1940), *Seven Sonnets of Michelangelo* (1942), *A Ceremony of Carols* (1942) and the *War Requiem* (1962). Also a superb operatic composer who often explored themes of innocence and corruption, Britten is particularly noted for *Peter Grimes* (1945). His other operas include *The Turn of the Screw* (1954) and *Death in Venice* (1973). A traditionalist in style with an enormous lyrical gift, Britten was also a noted conductor.

Broad, Charlie Dunbar *(1887–1971)* British philosopher and essayist. Broad is one of the best-known and most eclectic of modern British philosophers. In the course of a long academic career as a fellow at Trinity College, Cambridge, Broad wrote on subjects as diverse as epistemology, the philosophy of science, psychical research and ethics, and wrote analyses of the works of thinkers Francis Bacon and Immanuel Kant, both of whom exercised a strong influence on Broad's skeptical but open-minded approach to philosophical issues. Broad is best known for his writings on the scope and limits of scientific knowledge, especially *The Mind and Its Place in Nature* (1925) and *Religion, Philosophy and Scientific Research* (1953). In these works Broad argued for a skeptical empiricism that distinguished between persistent substances (with consistently perceived shape, mass, position and the like) and sense-qualified occurrents (such as mirages and other light reflections) that are seen because of the unique perceptual capabilities and limitations of human beings.

broadband Multimedia information transfer technology, and the system it supports. In the mid-1990s, as the INTERNET market expanded, numerous companies looked for ways to develop technologies that would capitalize on the transfer of images, sound and text over this new medium. Broadband was one such technology. It represented a service provided generally by cable companies that utilized the same technology that transferred live performances and sporting events nationally and globally via satellite. Instead of broadcasting television or cable entertainment, broadband was used to transmit Web pages and their text, graphics, video and audio clips both to personal computers and to TV sets equipped to function as computers. The secret to the rapid transfer of all this information was the nature of cable companies' information transfer system. Unlike telephone companies, which needed to make certain that the cables they used to transmit telephone conversations and Internet hookups were light enough to be carried on telephone poles, cable companies began investing in a large subterranean piping network that spread throughout cities. This larger and heavier network (in which broadband connections were made by more fiber-optic fibers than could be supported by standard telephone cables) allowed for a more rapid transfer of information over the cable network than a telephone network by offering substantially more fiber optic cables with which to transfer the information, thereby increasing the speed of Internet and cable interaction. Broadband technology and new broadband networks are being developed by both cable and telephone companies as a promising source of communication and commercial.

Broch, Hermann *(1886–1951)* Austrian novelist, essayist and poet. Broch turned to writing at the relatively late age of 41, after having devoted two decades to working in the textile business. But the novels he produced thereafter established him as one of the modern literary masters in the German language. *Die Schlafwandler* (*The Sleepwalkers*), which appeared in three volumes (1930–32), dealt with political apathy and social cynicism in the WORLD WAR I era. This was followed by *Die unbekannte grosse* (1933; *The Unknown Quantity,* 1935). Shortly thereafter Broch immigrated to the U.S. after being detained by the Nazis. *Der Tod des Bergil* (1945; *The Death of Virgil*), Broch's most famous work, drew parallels between the decline of modern Europe and that of the ancient classical era as symbolized by the death of the Roman epic poet Vergil. It, along with *Die Schuldlosen* (1950; *The Guiltless,* 1974), was published posthumously. In addition to his novels, Broch wrote poems, dramatic works and literary criticism.

Brock, Louis Clark "Lou" *(1939–)* American baseball player. Best remembered for his years with the St. Louis Cardinals, Brock began his career with the Chicago Cubs in 1961. He joined the Cardinals during the 1964 stretch drive and batted .348 while leading the team to an eventual World Series victory. He led the league in batting in 1967 and batted an astonishing .414 during the World Series, with seven steals, as the "Cards" won another title. Always at or near the top in stolen bases, his 118 thefts in 1974—at the age of 35—broke the old record of 104. Never known as a fielder, he led the National League in errors seven times. His basepath speed and batting prowess, however, won him a place in the Hall of Fame in 1985. In 1991

Brock's record of 938 total stolen bases was broken by Rickey Henderson.

Brockway, Lord (Archibald) Fenner *(1888–1988)* British socialist and pacifist; a leader of the anticolonial movement and a founder of the nuclear disarmament movement (see Campaign for Nuclear Disarmament [CND]). In 1964, after many years as a militant Labour Party MP in the House of Commons, Brockway reluctantly accepted a life peerage from Queen Elizabeth II. He thus became a member of the House of Lords, a body he had sought to abolish throughout his career.

Brod, Max *(1884–1968)* Czech biographer, novelist, poet and dramatist. Brod, best remembered today for his biography of his close friend Franz Kafka, was born of Jewish parents in Prague, then within the Austro-Hungarian Empire. Brod earned a law degree but soon thereafter devoted his energies exclusively to journalism and literary writing. He first befriended Kafka in 1908. In 1912 Brod became a Zionist. At the outset of World War II, Brod fled to Tel Aviv, where he became the director of the renowned Habimah Theater. But Brod's greatest contribution to world literature came in 1924, following the death of Kafka, when Brod ignored his friend's express wish that all of his manuscripts be destroyed. Instead, Brod, who was convinced of Kafka's genius, edited and arranged for the publication of many of Kafka's classic novels and stories.

Brodie, Bernard Beryl *(1909–1989)* American pharmacologist. Brodie was educated at McGill University in Montreal, Canada, and at New York University, where he earned his Ph.D. in 1935. He worked at the medical school there from 1943 to 1950 when he moved to the National Institutes of Health at Bethesda, Maryland, where he served as chief of the chemical pharmacology laboratory until 1970. Brodie has worked in a wide variety of fields including chemotherapy, anesthesia, drug metabolism and neuropharmacology. In 1955 Brodie and his colleagues produced some results that once more raised the possibility of a chemical basis of mental disease. The speculations arising from Brodie's work have turned out to be surprisingly difficult to confirm or reject.

Brodkin, Herbert *(1912–1990)* U.S. television producer. He helped create such innovative programs as *The Defenders* (1961–65) and *Playhouse 90*. After forming an independent production company in the 1960s, he went on to create a series of highly acclaimed, often controversial made-for-television movies and mini-series. Among the most notable were *Holocaust* (1978), *Skokie* (1981) and *The Missiles of October* (1981).

Brodovitch, Alexey *(1898–1971)* Russian-born art director, graphic designer and teacher with major influence in the U.S. Born in Ogolitchi, Russia, Brodovitch came to the U.S. in 1930 to take up a design career. From 1934 to 1956 he was art director of *Harper's Bazaar* magazine, a post in which his own design and his influence on other designers and photographers were extensive. His use of strong photographic images, emphatic typography and simple layout with generous white space characterized his innovative style. He continued in practice as a consultant after leaving *Harper's Bazaar* until his retirement in 1967. Classes he conducted in design and photography were attended by many younger designers and photographers, who looked toward him as their mentor. The character of the American fashion magazine and of modern fashion photography was largely molded by Brodovitch.

Brodsky, Joseph *(1940–1996)* Russian-born poet and critic. Brodsky quit school after the eighth grade. As a young man, he befriended the elderly Anna Akhmatova and began writing poetry of lyric intensity and metaphysical inwardness. He was arrested and tried by Soviet authorities for "social parasitism" in 1964 and as a result served 20 months of hard labor, during which time he began studying English seriously. In 1972 he was asked to leave the USSR permanently; he settled in the U.S. where he took up a series of academic appointments at the University of Michigan, Mt. Holyoke College and elsewhere. He received a National Book Critics Circle award for criticism in 1986 and the Nobel Prize in literature in 1987. Brodsky's books include *Selected Poems* (1973), *Less Than One: Selected Essays* (1986) and *To Urania* (1988). He was characterized by poet W. H. Auden as "a traditionalist" who "shows a deep respect and love for the past of his native land" but appears to be irrevocably estranged from it.

Broglie, Louis-Victor-Pierre-Raymond de (prince and seventh duke de Broglie) *(1892–1987)* French physicist. Educated at the Sorbonne as a historian, de Broglie's interest in science was aroused in World War I when he was posted to the Eiffel Tower as a member of a signals unit. He pursued this interest after the war and obtained a doctorate in physics from the Sorbonne in 1924. He taught there from 1926, serving as professor of theoretical physics at the newly founded Henri Poincaré Institute (1928–62). De Broglie is famous for his theory that particles (matter) can have wavelike properties. At the start of the 20th century physicists explained phenomena in terms of particles (such as the electron or proton) and electromagnetic radiation (light, ultraviolet radiation, etc.). Particles were "matter," discrete entities forming atoms and molecules; electromagnetic radiation was a wave motion involving changing electric and magnetic fields. In 1905 two papers by Albert Einstein began a change in this conventional view of the physical world. His work on the special theory of relativity led to the idea that matter is itself a form of energy. More specifically, he explained the photoelectric effect by the concept that electromagnetic radiation (a wave) can also behave as particles (photons).

In 1924 de Broglie, influenced by Einstein's work, put forward the converse idea—that, just as waves can behave as particles, particles can behave as waves. Experimental support was obtained independently by George Thomson and Clinton J. Davisson, and the wavelike behavior of particles was used by Erwin Schrodinger in his formulation of wave mechanics. Wave-particle duality—the fact that particles can behave as waves, and vice versa—has caused intense debate as to the "real" nature of particles and electromagnetic radiation. De Broglie took the view that there is a true, deterministic physical process underlying quantum mechanics—that is that the current indeterminate approach in terms of probability can be replaced by a more fundamental theory. He based his ideas on the concept of particles that are concentrations of energy guided through space by a real wave and exchanging energy with a "subquantum medium." De Broglie received the 1929 NOBEL PRIZE in physics for his "discovery of the wave nature of the electron."

Bronk, Detlev Wulf *(1897–1975)* American physiologist. The son of a Baptist minister, Bronk came from Dutch stock; the family name survives in the Bronx borough of New York City. He was educated at Swarthmore College and the University of Michigan, where he earned his Ph.D. in 1922. Bronk spent some time in England working with Edgar ADRIAN in Cambridge before accepting, in 1929, the post of director of the Johnson Institute, attached to the University of Pennsylvania, where he was already serving as professor of biophysics and director of the Institute of Neurology. In 1949 Bronk became president of Johns Hopkins University but left there in 1953 to take the presidency of the Rockefeller Institute (later Rockefeller University) in New York, where he remained until his retirement in 1968. Bronk established an early reputation with his fundamental work with Adrian on nerve impulses (1928–29). They demonstrated that both motor and sensory nerves transmit their messages by varying the number of impulses sent rather than by using impulses of different intensities. By careful experiments they established that the range of the impulses is between five and 150 per second, with greater stimuli producing higher frequencies. In the 1930s Bronk worked mainly on the autonomic nervous system. He is, however, mainly remembered for his crucial role in organizing the institutional structure of American science.

Bronowski,   Jacob *(1908–1974)* Polish-born philosopher of science. Bronowski immigrated to Britain and earned a Ph.D. in mathematics at Cambridge University. He subsequently pursued the career of a 20th-century Renaissance man; as well as a mathematician, he was a poet, playwright and inventor and held various government, administrative and academic posts. Shortly before his death, Bronowski gained wide public recognition when he hosted *The Ascent of Man.* This series, produced by the BRITISH BROADCASTING CORPORATION

(BBC), surveyed the history of Western civilization.

Bronsted, Johannes Nicolaus *(1879–1947)* Danish physical chemist. He studied at the Polytechnic Institute, Copenhagen, from 1897, earning degrees in engineering (1899) and chemistry (1902) and a doctorate (1908). The same year he became professor of chemistry there. Bronsted worked mainly in thermodynamics, especially in the fields of electrochemistry and reaction kinetics. In 1923 he proposed, concurrently with Thomas Lowry, a new definition of acids and bases. This, the **Lowry-Bronsted theory,** states that an acid is a substance that tends to lose a proton, and a base is a substance that tends to gain a proton.

Brook, Peter Stephen Paul *(1925–)* British theatrical director. Brook has been one of the most influential British theatrical directors of the post–World War II era. He made his mark as a prodigy with his successful direction, at age 18, of *Doctor Faustus* by Christopher Marlowe at the Torch Theatre in London. Brook went on to direct an acclaimed production of Shakespeare's *Love's Labour's Lost* (1946) at Stratford-upon-Avon. In 1950 he directed the renowned British actor Paul Scofield in *Ring Around the Moon* by Jean ANOUILH. In 1962 Brook was named codirector of the new Royal Shakespeare Company. He achieved great success with that company in productions of Shakespeare's *King   Lear*   (1962)   and *Marat/Sade* (1964) by Peter WEISS. Brook's production of Shakespeare's *A Midsummer Night's Dream* (1970) featured intricate stage acrobatics and a white stage setting. He founded the International Centre of Theatre Research in 1970 and there directed a 10-hour stage adaptation of the Indian epic *Mahabharata*. In 1988 Brook staged a revival of Anton CHEKHOV's *The Cherry Orchard* in New York City.

Brooke,   Edward   William,   III *(1919–)* U.S. senator. Born in Washington, D.C., Brooke attended Howard University and the Boston University Law School. After practicing law during the 1950s, Brooke, a liberal Republican, began his political career as attorney general of Massachusetts (1963–66). In 1966 he became the first black since Re-

construction to be elected to the Senate, and the first black in history to be elected to that office by popular vote. He was a senator from 1967 to 1979, serving (1967) on the President's Commission on Civil Disorders, which looked into urban race riots; advocating a strong civil rights policy; initiating housing legislation that resulted in the 1970 Housing and Urban Development Act; and breaking (1973) with the NIXON administration over WATERGATE. Brooke was defeated by Democrat Paul Tsongas in the 1978 election. He was awarded the Presidential Medal of Freedom in 2004.

Brooke, Rupert Chawner *(1887–1915)* British poet. Brooke was born at Rugby, where his father was a master, and was educated at Cambridge. He published his first collection of poetry, *Poems,* in 1911, and his work was featured in *Georgian Poetry,* the periodical he was instrumental in founding along with his friend, editor Sir Edward Marsh (see the GEORGIANS). Brooke served in WORLD WAR I in the Royal Naval Division and was acclaimed for his War Sonnets, which appeared in *New Numbers* in 1915. He died of blood poisoning en route to the Dardanelles and was buried in Scyros. His War Sonnets presented a dreamy, patriotic and heroic view of the war that went out of fashion as the war dragged on and the appalling carnage of the trenches became apparent. Nonetheless, his tragic early death made Brooke seem the romantic embodiment of an age that was about to end. He is now chiefly remembered for his higher verse and for his Elizabethan scholarship.

Brookner, Anita *(1928–)* British novelist and art historian. Born in London and educated at King's College, London, and the Courtauld Institute of Art in London, where she later taught, Brookner became the first female Slade Professor at Cambridge in 1968. An authority on 18th- and 19th-century art, she has written books on Watteau and Greuze, among others. Her fiction includes *Hotel du Lac* (1984, Booker Prize), *Family and Friends* (1985), *A Friend from England* (1987) and *Lewis Percy* (1990). Her delicate, inward novels explore the themes of family and loneliness; they are peopled with neurotic characters and written with an ironic wit.

Brooks, Cleanth *(1906–1994)* American critic. Brooks first met the southern FUGITIVES AND AGRARIANS, who laid the groundwork for NEW CRITICISM, at Vanderbilt University (1924–28). After receiving an M.A. from Tulane (1929), he studied at Exeter College, Oxford, on a Rhodes scholarship. With Robert Penn WARREN, he taught at Louisiana State, where he was an editor of the influential *Southern Review.* Together they wrote *Understanding Poetry* (1938), which emphasized close reading rather than subjective response to poetry. In 1946 he moved to Yale where he was associated with the critics Rene Wellek, William K. Wimsatt and Maynard Mack. His major theoretical work, *The Well-Wrought Urn,* appeared in 1947. He collaborated with Wimsatt on *Literary Criticism: A Short History* (1957). He is also known for two key works on FAULKNER and as the critic whose classic essay made T. S. ELIOT's *WASTE LAND* accessible.

Brooks, Garth *(1963–)* American country musician. Born in Tulsa, Oklahoma, Brooks attended Oklahoma State University on an athletic scholarship for his skills as a javelin thrower, but he began to sing in local clubs. After graduating with a degree in advertising in 1984, Brooks tried and failed to sign with a record company. In 1987 he moved to Nashville and after a year of auditions, performances and producing demonstration tapes, Capitol Records signed Brooks in 1988. Brooks's first self-titled album debuted in 1989, and its first released single "Much Too Young" reached the Top 10 of the country music charts. In the fall of 1990 he released his second album, *No Fences,* which sold well over 10 million copies within three years. The next year, he released *Ropin' the Wind,* which debuted at the top of the country and pop music charts and sold over 10 million albums. In 1992 his single "We Shall Be Free" from his forthcoming album *The Chase* generated criticism from traditional country music fans for its gospel music sound. However, despite *Chase's* premiere at number one in October 1992 and sale of over 5 million copies, it performed well below *Fences,* which led Brooks to exhibit more of a country sound in his

fifth album, *In Pieces* (1993). His seventh album, *Sevens* (1997), became a bona fide hit on the same level as *Fences,* in large part due to the huge marketing campaign created by Capitol Records, which included a concert in New York's Central Park.

In 1998 Brooks began to branch out beyond country music. In 1999 he won the role of rock star Chris Gaines in a movie project called *The Lamb* and began to invent a history of the character beyond that of the film, even recording *The Life of Chris Gaines,* an album containing the fictional singer's "greatest hits," in an effort to generate interest in the film for its scheduled 2000 premiere. However, *Chris Gaines's* pop music sound and Brooks's thinner appearance as the rock star led to a poor performance for the record after its September 1999 release, leading to the eventual shelving of *The Lamb.*

Brooks, Gwendolyn *(1917–2000)* American poet and playwright. Born in Topeka, Kansas, Brooks graduated from Wilson Junior College (1936) and worked for the NAACP Youth Council in Chicago during the 1930s. *A Street in Bronzeville* (1945) won her wide acclaim and several grants and fellowships. Her second book, *Annie Allen,* was awarded a PULITZER PRIZE in 1950. In 1968 she ended a 28-year relationship with her New York publisher in favor of a black-owned firm in Detroit. In 1969 she was made poet laureate of Illinois. She also had a varied teaching career and received numerous honorary degrees. Whereas her early work was largely a realistic portrayal of urban ghetto life, her later work became more overtly prolemical and sociopolitical. Her work has set the highest standards for African-American literature.

Brooks, Louise *(1906–1985)* American actress. Brooks's most memorable performances were in the German SILENT FILM classics, *Pandora's Box* and *Diary of a Lost Girl,* directed by Austrian G. W. Pabst. Spurned by HOLLYWOOD, Brooks made her last film in 1938 and began contributing articles to various film journals. Her memoir, *Lulu in Hollywood,* was published in 1982 to wide critical acclaim.

Brooks, Mel (Melvin Kaminsky) *(1926–)* American comedic film di-

rector, writer, actor and producer. Brooks is one of the best-known figures in American comedy of the second half of the 20th century. He first emerged as a major talent in the 1950s when, as a young man, he became one of the leading writers for the hit Sid CAESAR television program *Your Show of Shows.* Brooks enjoyed further success with the comedy album *2,000 Years with Carl Reiner and Mel Brooks* (1960), in which Brooks played a 2,000-year-old man with cranky attitudes and a poor memory. Brooks was also a key creator of the *Get Smart* television comedy series in the 1960s. But he has made his greatest mark as a film director. He won an ACADEMY AWARD for best animated short subject with *The Critic* (1964), then achieved both popular and critical success with *The Producers* (1967), a classic black comedy with a plot that includes the ultimate bad taste musical, *Spingtime for Hitler.* Other hit films by Brooks include the western parody *Blazing Saddles* (1974), the horror film spoof *Young Frankenstein* (1974), the Alfred HITCHCOCK send-up *High Anxiety* (1977) and *Spaceballs* (1987), a satirical rewrite of *Star Wars.* Brooks has also produced films including the acclaimed drama *The Elephant Man* (1980). His wife of more than 40 years, the actress **Anne Bancroft,** died in 2005. In March 2001 Brooks's stage musical adaptation of *The Producers* premiered on Broadway, which won a record-breaking 12 Tony Awards.

Brooks, Van Wyck *(1886–1963)* American critic. After a brief flirtation with poetry at Harvard, Brooks worked as a literary journalist to support his critical writing. *The Wine of the Puritans* (1908) introduced his theme of the schism in American culture between idealism, or transcendentalism, and commercialism; *America's Coming of Age* (1915) employed the terms *highbrow* and *lowbrow* to describe the same dialectic. His critical trilogy (1920–32) examined the careers of Mark Twain, Henry JAMES and Emerson; and his five-volume *Makers and Finders: A History of the Writer in America, 1800–1915* (1936–52) presented an anecdotal, impressionistic view of the American literary scene. *The Flowering of New England* won a 1936 PULITZER PRIZE and was a best seller. In the 1940s his vision came under fire from adherents of the NEW CRITICISM, the PARTISAN REVIEW group and other academics.

Broom, Robert *(1866–1951)* British–South African morphologist and paleontologist. Broom graduated in medicine from Glasgow University in 1889. He traveled to Australia in 1892 and in 1897 settled in South Africa where he practiced medicine, often in remote rural communities, until 1928. He also held posts as professor of geology and zoology (1903–10) at Victoria College, now Stellenbosch University, South Africa, and curator of paleontology at the Transvaal Museum, Pretoria, from 1934 until his death. Apart from studies of the embryology of Australian marsupials and monotremes, Broom's major contributions to science have been concerned with the evolutionary origins of mammals, including humans. He excavated and studied the fossils of the Karroo beds of the Cape and in the 1940s discovered numbers of Australopithecine skeletons in Pleistocene age quarries at Sterkfontein, Transvaal. These latter have proved of considerable importance in investigations of human ancestry. Broom's account of their discovery is given in *Finding the Missing Link* (1950).

Brophy, Brigid Antonia *(1929–1995)* British author. An eccentric, prolific writer of catholic tastes, Brophy was a novelist, critic, biographer and dramatist as well as an advocate of animal rights and a successful campaigner for the Public Lending Right, which provides that authors are paid when their works are borrowed from libraries. Her first collection of short stories was *The Crown Princess and Other Stories* (1953). *Hackenfeller's Ape* (1959), which she considered her best work, won the Cheltenham Literary Festival First Prize for a first novel. Other works include *Mozart the Dramatist: A New View of Mozart, His Operas and His Age* (1964) and *The Adventures of God in His Search for the Black Girl: A Novel and Some Fables* (1973). In the early 1980s Brophy was stricken with multiple sclerosis, which she eloquently described in *Baroque and Roll and Other Essays* (1987).

Brouwer, Dirk *(1902–1966)* Dutch-American astronomer. Brouwer studied at the University of Leiden where he earned his Ph.D. under Willem de Sitter in 1927. He then moved to the U.S. to do postdoctoral research at the University of California, Berkeley. He joined the Yale faculty in 1928, serving from 1941 until his death as professor of astronomy and director of the Yale Observatory. Brouwer worked mainly in celestial mechanics, particularly in the analysis of observations concerning orbiting bodies, and on planetary theory, providing new methods by which the motion of a planet could be determined and by which the very long term changes in orbits could be calculated. He collaborated with Gerald CLEMENCE and W. J. Eckert to write in 1951 a basic paper to give the accurate orbits of the outer planets. He introduced new techniques and initiated programs for the measurement of stellar positions, especially in the southern sky. He was also involved in the decision to adopt a new time scale, known at Brouwer's suggestion as **Ephemeris Time** (ET). This became necessary when the rotation rate of the Earth, on which time measurements had been based, was found to vary very slightly. Ephemeris Time is derived from the orbital motions of the Moon and the Earth and is perfectly uniform. It is only used by astronomers, however; more general timekeeping now involves atomic clocks.

Brouwer, Luitzen Egbertus Jan *(1881–1966)* Dutch mathematician and philosopher of mathematics. Brouwer studied at the University of Amsterdam, where he became professor in the mathematics department. From 1903 to 1909 he did important work in topology, presenting several fundamental results, including the fixed-point theorem. Brouwer's best-known achievement was the creation of the philosophy of mathematics known as **intuitionism.** The central ideas of intuitionism are a rejection of the concept of the completed infinite and an insistence that acceptable mathematical proofs be constructive; that is, they must not merely show that a certain mathematical entity (for example, a number or a function) *exists* but must actually be able to construct it. This view leads to the rejection of large amounts of widely accepted classical mathematics and one of the three fundamental laws of logic, the law of excluded middle (a proposition is either true or not true). Brouwer was able to reprove many classical results in an intuitionistically acceptable way, including his own fixed-point theorem.

Browder, Earl *(1891–1973)* Long-time American Communist leader. Browder, a native of Kansas, became active in the tiny American Communist Party in 1920 and journeyed to Moscow where he met LENIN. At the start of WORLD WAR II, Browder and the party were opposed to U.S. involvement. After Germany invaded the Soviet Union, Browder and the party were ardent supporters of the U.S. war effort. After the war Browder had a philosophical dispute with the leaders of the U.S. party and was ousted from membership. During the anticommunist McCarthy period he was called to testify before a Senate Foreign Relations subcommittee investigating communist infiltration of the State Department. Although he was jailed when he refused to answer certain questions, his conviction was overturned because he had the right to refuse to answer irrelevant questions. Although many considered him the elder statesman of the American Left, he never resumed any formal affiliation with the Communist Party.

Brown, Archie *(1911–1990)* U.S. labor leader. West Coast leader of the International Longshoremen's Union, he had been convicted in 1962 under a provision of the 1959 Landrum-Griffin Act that barred communists from serving in official union positions. He won a landmark Supreme Court decision in 1965, which found the previous ruling unconstitutional and upheld the right of communists to so serve.

Brown, Sir Arthur Whitten See ALCOCK AND BROWN.

Brown, Christy *(1932–1981)* Irish author and painter. Born in Dublin, the 10th of 22 children, Brown was afflicted from birth with cerebral palsy. Almost completely disabled, Brown had the use of his left foot and trained himself to paint and to type with it. His first book, an autobiography, *My Left Foot* (1954; reissued as *The Childhood Story of Christy Brown*, 1972; filmed 1989), describes his efforts to cope with his disability. His next book, *Down All the Days* (1970), is a fictionalized autobiography with a bawdy depiction of life in Dublin slums. Other work includes *Come Softly to My Wake: The Poems of Christy Brown* (1971), *Of Snails and Skylarks* (1977) and the novel *Wild Grow the Lilies* (1976).

Brown, Clarence (*1890–1987*) American film director. Brown spent his formative years as an assistant director to filmmaker Maurice Tourneur, from whom he inherited a crisp, pictorial eye, a solid craftsmanship and an intelligent sensibility for story and character. Establishing himself with the Rudolph VALENTINO vehicle *The Eagle* (1925), Brown then became a leading director for METRO-GOLDWYN-MAYER with a series of films starring Greta GARBO, including *Flesh and the Devil* (1927), *Anna Christie* (1930) and *Anna Karenina* (1935) as well as three others. A six-time ACADEMY AWARD nominee, he directed many splendid character studies that are now regarded as classics, including *Of Human Hearts* (1938), *Edison the Man* (1940), *National Velvet* (1944) and *The Yearling* (1946). His *Intruder in the Dust* (1949), adapted from William FAULKNER's book, was a pioneering indictment of racial prejudice in the American South. In 1971 he established the Clarence Brown Theatre for the Performing Arts at his alma mater in Knoxville, Tenn.

Brown, Clifford (*1930–1956*) American jazz trumpeter, a pivotal figure of 1950s jazz. While consolidating the BEBOP virtuosity of Dizzy GILLESPIE and Fats Navarro with the moody lyricism of Miles DAVIS, Brown pointed the way for such modern trumpet stylists as Lee Morgan and Freddie Hubbard. As he studied mathematics and music in college in the late 1940s, Brown began sitting in at Philadelphia jazz clubs with such major improvisers as Charlie PARKER and Gillespie and Navarro, who encouraged his musical ambitions. Key engagements with pianist Tadd Dameron, vibraphonist Lionel HAMPTON and drummer Art BLAKEY brought international recognition and further refinements in an extraordinary approach that combined a big brash sound, a crisp percussive attack and consistently inspired improvisatory flights based on the bebop lexicon coined by Parker and Gillespie.

Brown's zenith came in 1954–56 when he co-led the Clifford Brown–Max Roach Quintet, a justly celebrated 1950s jazz group noted for its "hard bop" edge, featuring Roach's aggressive drumming and Brown's dazzling yet lyrical and finely structured solos. Brown's genius was cut short at the age of 25 when an automobile accident claimed his life.

Brown, Edmund Gerald "Jerry," Jr. (*1938– *) American politician; governor of California (1975–82). Brown, son of California governor Pat Brown, received his B.A. from the University of California at Berkeley (1961) and his law degree from Yale (1964). In the late 1960s Brown became active in the ANTIWAR MOVEMENT and in the campaign to unionize migrant workers. In 1970 he was elected secretary of state of California, in which office he conducted some highly publicized reform campaigns that won him wide popularity. In 1974 he was elected governor of the state by a narrow margin. As governor, Brown quickly gained national attention with his quirky style, his commitment to limited government and the austerity measures he implemented. In 1976 he made a run for the Democratic presidential nomination, losing to Jimmy CARTER. He was re-elected governor in 1978, and in 1980 he made another unsuccessful attempt at the Democratic presidential nomination. In 1982, by which time he had acquired a reputation for being mercurial and was widely known as "Governor Moonbeam," Brown ran for the U.S. Senate but was defeated by Pete Wilson. That year he was succeeded as governor by George Deukmejian, who defeated Democrat Tom Bradley. In 1992 Brown campaigned for the Democratic presidential nomination but eventually lost the contest to Bill CLINTON. Since 1998 he has served as Mayor of Oakland, California.

Brown, George Scratchley (*1918–1978*) American military officer. A graduate of West Point (1941), Brown served in the U.S. Eighth Air Force in Europe in WORLD WAR II. He won the Distinguished Service Cross for his role in the Allied bombing of the oil refineries at PLOESTI, Romania (August 1943). During the KOREAN WAR he was director of operations for the Fifth Air Force. In 1968 he became head of U.S. Air Force

operations in VIETNAM (see VIETNAM WAR). In 1973 President Richard M. NIXON named him air force chief of staff. He was later chairman of the Joint Chiefs of Staff (1974–78). His years as America's top-ranking military officer were marked by controversy over his often blunt public statements. Brown blamed South Vietnam's defeat (1975) on congressional cutbacks in military aid to the South.

Brown, Harrison Scott (*1917–1986*) American chemist. Brown played a key role in producing plutonium for the first atomic bomb (see ATOMIC BOMB DEVELOPMENT). He later emerged as a leading opponent of nuclear weapons development. His varied career included long service as foreign secretary of the National Academy of Sciences. He was also involved in analyses of meteorites for clues to their origin and the promotion of birth control. He was editor of the *Bulletin of Atomic Scientists*. From 1951 to 1977 he was professor of geochemistry at the California Institute of Technology.

Brown, Helen Gurley (*1922– *) American author and editor. Brown worked as a secretary and award-winning advertising copywriter before becoming editor in chief of *Cosmopolitan* magazine in 1965. In that role she parlayed a bold and brassy view of American women to readers, glamorizing power (often sexual power) and freedom as prime goals for young, professional and primarily unmarried women. Brown also wrote two books: *Sex and the Single Girl* (1962) and *Having It All* (1982). She received the Distinguished Achievement Award in journalism from Stanford University in 1981. In 1996 Brown retired from *Cosmopolitan*.

Brown, Herbert Charles (*1912–2004*) American chemist. Brown moved from England to Chicago with his family when he was two years old. Brown left school to help support his mother and three sisters. When he finally did enter Crane Junior College, it was forced to close in 1933 for lack of funds. He eventually went to the University of Chicago where he earned his doctorate in 1938. Brown then worked at Wayne University, from 1943 until 1947, when he moved to Purdue University, where he served as professor of inorganic chemistry until his retirement in 1978. Brown was noted for his work on compounds of boron. He discovered a method of making sodium borohydride, used extensively in organic chemistry for reduction. He also found a simple way of preparing diborane by reacting diborane with alkenes (unsaturated hydrocarbons containing a double bond). He produced a new class of compounds, organoboranes, which are also useful in organic chemistry. Brown also used addition compounds of amines with boron compounds to investigate the role of steric effects in organic chemistry. He received the 1979 NOBEL PRIZE in chemistry.

Brown, H(ubert) "Rap" *(1943–)* Militant American leader of the CIVIL RIGHTS MOVEMENT. Brown was born in Baton Rouge, Louisiana. In the 1960s he attracted wide attention for his militant views, and in 1967 he assumed the chairmanship of the Student Nonviolent Coordinating Committee. Brown had frequent brushes with the law during these years and was charged with inciting riot, transporting weapons across state lines and arson. In 1971, after living as a fugitive for 17 months, he was wounded in a shootout with New York City police during the holdup of a tavern. He was convicted of the crime and on May 10, 1973, was sentenced to five to 15 years in prison. He was paroled on October 21, 1976. During his stay in prison, Brown converted to Islam. In March 2000 Brown was charged with the murder of a Fulton County, Georgia, sheriff's deputy and the attempted murder of another deputy. In March 2002 he was sentenced to life in prison.

Brown, James *(1928–)* American singer-songwriter. The flamboyant Brown combined gospel, soul, funk and flat-out showmanship to become a music legend. Early hits included "Papa's Got a Brand New Bag" (1965) and "I Got You (I Feel Good)" (1965). His popularity surged with the emergence of the 1960s BLACK POWER movement and with such hits as "Say It Loud, I'm Black and Proud" (1968), "Super Bad" (1970) and "Soul Power" (1971). He continues to record such hits as "Living in America" (1986) and is a charismatic live performer. Jailed

for tax evasion in 1990, Brown resumed recording upon his release. In 1993 Brown received a Grammy Award for his lifetime achievements in music.

Brown, James Nathaniel "Jim" *(1936–)* American football player. A combination of athletic ability and grace under pressure made Brown the most exciting ball carrier in the history of professional football. A star at Syracuse University, he won three letters in addition to football. He was the NFL's 1957 rookie of the year, with a total of 942 yards rushing, and in 1960 was named the best back of the previous decade. The first back ever to surpass 10,000 yards rushing, over a nine-year career he gained a total of 12,312 yards and scored a record 126 touchdowns. In 1965 Brown retired to pursue a career in acting. He was named to the Pro Football Hall of Frame in 1971. In 1999 Brown combined both his football and movie careers when he appeared as an assistant coach in the Oliver Stone film *Any Given Sunday*.

Brown, Robert Hanbury *(1916–2002)* British radio astronomer. Brown was educated at the City and Guilds College, London. From 1936 to 1942 he worked on the development of RADAR at the Air Ministry Research Station, Bawdsey. This was followed by three years in Washington with the British Air Commission and two years with the Ministry of Supply. By the late 1940s Brown was keen to enter academic research and persuaded Bernard LOVELL to admit him as a research student at the Jodrell Bank radio observatory. Brown later served there as professor of radio astronomy from 1960 to 1963 when he was appointed to a professorship in physics at the University of Sydney. In 1950 Brown plotted the first radio map of an external galaxy, the spiral nebula in Andromeda. He later identified emissions from four other extragalactic nebulae.

Brown, Sterling Allen *(1901–1989)* American poet and teacher of black American literature. As a professor at Howard University (as was his father), he introduced the school's first course in Afro-American literature. Among his students were the writers Amiri BARAKA

and Toni MORRISON, psychologist Kenneth B. CLARK and actor Ossie Davis. Brown's own work helped to lay the foundation for studies in African-American literature. His collected poems were published in 1983. Brown also wrote the study *A Negro in American Fiction*.

Browning, John Moses *(1855–1926)* U.S. inventor of the Browning automatic rifle. Browning was born in Ogden, Utah, the son of a Mormon gunsmith. Beginning in 1879 he designed a number of firearms, including some automatic and repeating models, for different firms; he manufactured guns at his own company as well. Many of his designs were purchased by the U.S. military, including his "Peacemaker" machine gun. In 1918 he introduced the Browning automatic rifle (BAR), which became a standard shoulder weapon of the U.S. Army for the next four decades.

Brown Shirts See Ernst ROEHM.

Brown v. Board of Education *(1954)* Landmark U.S. Supreme Court case that set the groundwork for the racial desegregation of schools throughout the U.S. Despite the Civil War amendments to the U.S. Constitution guaranteeing legal rights to black citizens, segregated school systems and accommodation persisted for a century after the end of the war. The 1896 Supreme Court case *Plessy v. Ferguson* had legalized SEGREGATION under the "separate but equal" doctrine. Under this doctrine a state could legally maintain one set of schools for whites and one set of schools for blacks under the guise of their being separate but equal. In fact, the black school systems were nearly always radically inferior to the white school systems.

In the *Brown* decision, written by Chief Justice Earl WARREN, the Supreme Court held that the maintenance of two separate school systems was inherently unequal and a violation of the Fourteenth Amendment's equal protection clause. Despite the ruling, many states refused to comply, which led to forced desegregation of public schools by the federal government—accompanied by violence and bloodshed. The tide turned in favor of public school desegregation only after President Dwight D. EISENHOWER threatened to desegregate the LITTLE ROCK, Arkansas, public schools using federal troops. The desegregation of public universities, which came later, was also marked by violence and enforcement by federal troops. The ruling in the case outlawing "separate but equal" schools was later extended to other state-supported facilities. Private facilities were later desegregated by the CIVIL RIGHTS ACT OF 1964. Because of its importance, the *Brown* case is sometimes simply referred to as "the school desegregation case."

Brubeck, Dave (*1920– *) In the 1950s, pianist-composer Brubeck rose to the top of the jazz world with the "classic" David Brubeck Quartet, featuring the significant contributions of alto saxophonist Paul Desmond, bassist Eugene Wright and drummer Joe Morello. Brubeck's success, especially with college audiences, was signaled in 1954 when he appeared on the cover of *TIME* magazine and was signed by Columbia Records; in 1959 Brubeck enjoyed the distinction of having the first million-selling jazz instrumental recording (Desmond's "Take Five" on one side, Brubeck's "Blue Rondo a la Turk" on the reverse). In 1967 Brubeck dissolved his highly visible and very successful quartet to focus on composition, a decision influenced by early studies with prominent 20th-century composers Darius MILHAUD and Arnold SCHOENBERG. Though he has continued to assemble engaging foursomes through the years, Brubeck's transcendent period was in the 1950s in company with the exceptional Desmond, Wright and Morello. In the 1990s Brubeck received additional recognition for his contributions to music, including the National Medal of Arts in 1994 and the National Academy of Recording Arts and Sciences Lifetime Achievement Award in 1996.

Bruce, Sir David (*1855–1931*) British bacteriologist. A one-time colleague of Robert Koch in Berlin, Bruce spent the greater part of his career as a military physician. Educated at Edinburgh University, he was assistant professor of pathology at the Army Medical School, Netley (1889–94), and then commandant of the Royal Army Medical College, Millbank, where he was also director of research on tetanus and trench fever (1914–18). He undertook royal commissions of inquiry into various diseases of humans and domestic animals in Malta and central Africa. In Malta he was able to trace the cause of Malta fever (brucellosis or undulant fever found in the milk of goats) to a bacterium later named after him as *Brucella melitensis*. Bruce also investigated the cause of nagana, a disease of horses and cattle in central and southern Africa, and found it to be transmitted by a trypanosome parasite carried by the tsetse fly. This work was of great help in his later research on sleeping sickness (trypanosomiasis), which he also proved to be transmitted by the tsetse fly. The recipient of many honors for his humanitarian work, Bruce was chairman of the War Office's Pathological Committee during WORLD WAR I. He was knighted in 1908.

Bruce, Lenny (**Leonard Alfred Schneider**) (*1925–1966*) American stand-up comedian. Bruce, who drew considerable hostility and attention from government authorities due to his use of so-called dirty words in his nightclub comedy act, was a brilliant satirist who dramatically expanded the style and subject matter of stand-up comedy. Bruce served in the navy during World War II. He first drew national attention in the mid-1950s when his daring style of satire, in which Bruce probed taboo subjects such as racial fears, sexual fantasies and Jewish-Christian tensions, won him an admiring audience and made his act a cause célèbre in liberal literary circles. In 1961 Bruce was imprisoned on obscenity charges. In 1963 his show was banned both in England and in Australia. Bruce published an autobiography, *How to Talk Dirty and Influence People* (1965). In his later years he became addicted to heroin. He died of an overdose in 1966.

Bruhn, Erik (*1928–1986*) Danish-born ballet star regarded as one of the greatest classical dancers of the 20th century. For nearly two decades (1953–72) Bruhn was principal dancer with the AMERICAN BALLET THEATRE. He also appeared in major roles with most of the world's other major companies, partnering a notable succession of great ballerinas, including the Italian dancer Carla FRACCI. Bruhn was also distinguished as a choreographer, directing the Royal Swedish Ballet from 1967 to 1972. In 1983 he assumed the position of artistic director of the National Ballet of Canada.

Brunei (State of Brunei Darussalam) The sultanate is located on the northwestern coast of the island of Borneo and covers an area of 2,225

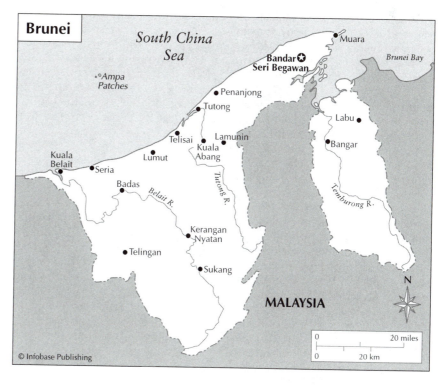

BRUNEI

1906	Brunei becomes a British dependency.
1929	Oil is discovered.
1941–45	Brunei is occupied by Japan.
1971	Brunei is given full internal self-government.
1975	A United Nations resolution calls for independence for Brunei.
1984	Brunei becomes an independent nation in accordance with its 1979 treaty with the United Kingdom.
1996	Brunei successfully limits its economic dependence on oil revenue with nearly two-thirds of GNP coming from other diversified sources.
2004	Sultan Hassanal Bolkiah reestablishes a parliament and elections.

square miles. A British residency from 1906 and 1971, Brunei was ruled by a sultan who was advised by a British resident on all matters except religion and culture. This residency was interrupted from 1941 to 1945 when Japan occupied the country. In 1971 a new United Kingdom–Brunei treaty was signed under which Britain retained control of Brunei's external affairs only. In 1984 Brunei achieved full independence from Britain; it is currently ruled by Sultan Hassanal Bolkiah. In August 2000 the Brunei government began a program to train 20% of its workforce for jobs outside the oil industry, such as in tourism.

Brunhes, Jean (1869–1930) French geographer. Brunhes came from an academic background—both his father and brother were professors of physics. He was educated at the École Normal Superieure, Paris (1889–92), and taught at the University of Fribourg from 1896 until 1912, when he moved to the Collège de France, Paris, as professor of human geography. His most important work was his three-volume Géographie humaine (1910), which was translated into English in 1920. Following his teacher, Vidal de la Blache, he argued against the geographical determinism implicit in the work of Friedrich Ratzel. Instead, he was more interested in revealing the complicated interplay among humans, society and the environment.

Brüning, Heinrich (1885–1970) German chancellor (1930–32). A member of the Catholic Center Party and an expert in economics, he was appointed chancellor (1930) by President HINDENBURG in hopes that he would stabilize finances and lessen the appeal of the rising NAZI movement. His program of taxation and budget-cutting was defeated in the Reichstag, but Brüning continued to govern under emergency decrees from Hindenburg, thus helping to undermine parliamentary powers. As GERMANY's economic crisis deepened, he was forced to resign in 1932 and was replaced by Franz von PAPEN. A strong opponent of Adolf HITLER, Brüning fled Germany in 1934 and settled in the U.S., where he taught at Harvard University from 1939 to 1951. He returned to Germany in 1951, assuming a teaching post at the University of Cologne.

Brunner, Emil (1889–1966) Swiss theologian. The writings of Brunner are often closely linked to those of his Swiss contemporary, Karl BARTH. Both men began their careers as ministers in the Swiss Reformed Church and both emphasized, in their writings, the dependence of the human soul on a divine grace that could be achieved only by faith. Brunner, who spent most of his productive years as a professor of practical theology at the University of·

Zurich, emphasized in works such as The Word and The World (1931), Justice and the Social Order (1945), Christianity and Civilization (1948) and The Christian Doctrine of Creation and Redemption (1952) that Christianity is founded not on human reason or observation but rather in a divine revelation that supersedes all questioning. Brunner further held that the church ought to play a definite but limited role in social and political issues; this was necessary in order to fend off totalitarian policies that would constrict the dignity of the human soul.

Brussels, Treaty of A 50-year mutual guarantee (March 17, 1948) among Belgium, Britain, France, Luxembourg and the Netherlands of military and other assistance in the event of an attack. With the adherence of West Germany and Italy in May 1955, the **Western European Union** was formed, intended to further West European unity.

Brustein, Robert (1927–) American actor, playwright, stage director and drama critic. Since 1959 he has served as the drama critic for the New Republic. Along with reviewing stage theater productions, between 1965 and 1979, Brustein served as dean of the School of Drama at Yale University, where he oversaw more than 200 productions, directed 12 plays, and on eight occasions even acted in the performances arranged by his department. He founded the Yale Repertory Theater in 1966. After he left Yale in 1979 he joined the faculty at Harvard University, where he served as a professor of English and helped found the American Repertory Theater. In addition to his academic duties at Harvard and Yale, Brustein also published 13 books on the role of theater in society, a few of which (Dumbocracy in America) focused on the diminished importance of theater in the country. Brustein also composed his own plays, such as Demons (1993), Six Characters in Search of an Author (1996) and Nobody Dies on Friday (1998), as well as such shorter works as Poker Face, Chekhov on Ice and Divestiture, all of which premiered at the Boston Playwrights' Theater at Boston University. For his contributions to the performing arts Brustein has received numerous honors, including the George Polk

Award in Journalism, the Elliot Norton Award for Professional Excellence in Theater within the Boston community, the Annual Award for Outstanding Creative Achievement in American Theatre by the New England Theater Conference (1985), the American Academy of Arts and Letters Award for Distinguished Service to the Arts (1995) and a commendation from the Egyptian government for his unique contribution to theater across the globe.

Brutalism (New Brutalism) Term first used in the 1950s by British architectural critics to describe an aspect of modern architectural design that emphasizes massive forms, usually constructed of reinforced concrete with its rough surfaces left exposed. Much of the later work of LE CORBUSIER is often referred to as brutalist. The term is applied to the work of such architects as Paul Rudolph in the U.S. and Kenzo Tange in Japan that display similar characteristics.

Bryan, William Jennings *(1860–1925)* U.S. politician, often called "the Great Commoner" because of his advocacy of the common man. He studied law at Chicago and practiced in Jacksonville, Illinois (1883–87). He moved to Lincoln, Nebraska, in 1887 to practice law but left it for politics. Democrat Bryan was elected to Congress in 1890 and reelected in 1892. He was particularly known in the Congress as an advocate for farm interests. Later he started a career as a newspaper editor in Omaha, Nebraska, and soon became a sought-after public speaker. After his speech at the Democratic convention in 1896, he was the Democratic presidential candidate. Although unsuccessful, he stressed the "sectional struggle between Wall Street and the 'toiling masses.'" He became known for his constant support of silver as the basis for U.S. currency. Nominated again for president in 1900, he lost to incumbent President MCKINLEY. Nominated by the Democrats again in 1908, he was defeated. Later Bryan worked to elect Woodrow WILSON and served as Wilson's secretary of state from 1912 and 1915. He made his last political appearance at the Democratic convention of 1924. His greatest publicity came when he acted for the prosecution at the trial of J. T. Scopes in 1925

(for teaching of evolutionary theory, see SCOPES TRIAL). Five days after the trial ended, Bryan died in his sleep. His memoirs were unfinished, but they were completed by his wife and published in 1925.

Brynner, Yul *(1915–1985)* American actor of Swiss-Mongolian descent, best known for his portrayal of the king in the musical play *The King and I* by Richard RODGERS and Oscar HAMMERSTEIN II. Brynner shaved his head for his Broadway debut as the king in 1951 and continued to do so for the rest of his career. He received an ACADEMY AWARD as best actor in 1956 for his appearance in the film version of *The King and I*. Other notable performances were in such films as *Anastasia* and *The Ten Commandments*. Toward the end of his life, when he was terminally ill with lung cancer, he made a series of television commercials warning of the dangers of cigarette smoking.

Bryusov, Valery Yakovlevich *(1873–1924)* Russian symbolist poet and writer. Bryusov's early work was largely misunderstood and ridiculed. By 1906, however, symbolism was recognized, and Bryusov was hailed as the foremost Russian poet. His *Stephanos* (1906) was warmly received, although his poetic talents were on the wane. Bryusov also wrote stories and plays, translated poetry, reviewed books and became an expert on Armenian poetry. After the Russian Revolution (1917) he became a Communist and worked as the head of censorship, but he was not felt to be sufficiently reliable and was replaced.

Buber, Martin *(1878–1965)* Austrian-born Jewish theologian, philosopher and social critic. Buber is one of the best-known theologians of the 20th century, primarily due to the pervasive influence—in fields as diverse as clinical psychology, social work and existential philosophy—of his classic book *I and Thou* (1923). In this work Buber argued for the primacy of an immediate, unstructured and personal relationship between man and God that must, at times of crisis, supersede the dogma of organized religious faith. Buber, born in Vienna, studied philosophy at the Universities of Vienna, Zurich, and Berlin. As a young man he

was politically active as a Zionist and worked with both Theodore HERZL and Chaim WEIZMANN. In the 1930s he immigrated to Israel and taught at the Hebrew University in Jerusalem. Buber's translations of the folktales of the Hasidic Jews of eastern Europe served as the first popular introduction of Hasidism to the West. His major works include *Moses* (1946), *Eclipse of God* (1952), *Kingship of God* (1956) and *The Origin and Meaning of Hasidism* (1960).

Buchenwald Nazi CONCENTRATION CAMP located in the Buchenwald forest near Weimar, Germany. Buchenwald was established in 1937 ostensibly as a camp for "rehabilitation and labor." Initially it housed Germans—JEWS and Gypsies who were persecuted by the Nazis, as well as socialists and others who opposed Hitler's program of ANTI-SEMITISM. After the outbreak of WORLD WAR II, Buchenwald became a death camp as Hitler tried to implement his FINAL SOLUTION.

Buchner, Eduard *(1860–1917)* German organic chemist and biochemist. Buchner studied chemistry under Adolf von Baeyer and botany at Munich, earning his doctorate in 1888. He was Baeyer's assistant until 1893. In 1897, while associate professor of analytical and pharmaceutical chemistry at Tubingen, he observed fermentation of sugar by cell-free extracts of yeast. Following Pasteur's work (1860), fermentation had been thought to require intact cells. Buchner's discovery of zymase was the first proof that fermentation was caused by enzymes and did not require the presence of living cells. Buchner also synthesized pyrazole (1889). He was professor of chemistry at the University of Berlin from 1898 and won the NOBEL PRIZE in chemistry in 1907 for his work on fermentation. He was killed in Romania while serving as a major in World War I.

Buck, Pearl Comfort Sydenstricker *(1892–1973)* American novelist. The daughter of American missionaries, Buck was born in West Virginia but spent most of her early life in China, learning to speak Chinese before she spoke English. Buck returned to the U.S. to attend Randolph Macon Women's College in West Virginia but returned to China to teach in 1921.

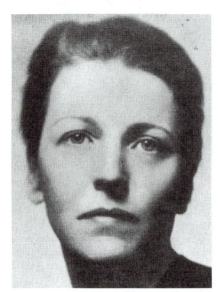

American author Pearl S. Buck, winner of the 1938 Nobel Prize in literature (LIBRARY OF CONGRESS, PRINTS AND PHOTOGRAPHS DIVISION)

There she later met and married the missionary John Lossing Buck. Her most important novels are set in China and address the broader themes of the cyclical quality of life and the need for tolerance. These include *East Wind; West Wind* (1930); *A House Divided* (1935); *The Good Earth* (1931), which won the PULITZER PRIZE; and the biographies of her father and mother, *Fighting Angel* (1936) and *The Exile* (1936). Buck also translated Chinese literature into English. She was awarded the NOBEL PRIZE in literature in 1938.

Buckley, William Frank, Jr. *(1925–)* American political writer, essayist, television interviewer and novelist. Buckley is perhaps the best-known conservative political analyst in the post–World War II U.S., due largely to the success of his television interview program *Firing Line* (1966–99), which earned an Emmy Award in 1969. Raised in a wealthy Roman Catholic family, Buckley was educated in private schools in England, France and the U.S. In 1944 he studied for a year at the University of Mexico and also gathered information for the CENTRAL INTELLIGENCE AGENCY, an experience Buckley would later draw on in writing a series of spy novels—beginning with *Saving the Queen* (1976)—that featured CIA operative Blackford Oakes as their protagonist. During WORLD WAR II Buckley served in the U.S. Army and earned the rank of sec-

ond lieutenant. He graduated from Yale University in 1950 and shortly thereafter won acclaim for *God and Man at Yale* (1951), a vituperative lambasting of the liberal policies of his alma mater. *McCarthy and His Enemies* (1954) was a vigorous defense of MCCARTHYISM. Buckley founded the NATIONAL REVIEW in 1955, beginning his long tenure as the magazine's editor. A candidate for mayor of New York City in 1965, he served as a member of the American delegation to the United Nations in 1973, an experience he chronicled in *United Nations Journal* (1973). After Buckley retired as editor in chief of the *National Review* in 1990, President George H. W. BUSH awarded him the Presidential Medal of Freedom, the nation's highest civilian honor. Buckley published his memoirs, *Miles Gone By: A Literary Autobiography,* in 2004 and transferred his shares in the company controlling *National Review* to a group of loyal associates. His older brother, **James Buckley** (1923–), was a U.S. senator from New York (1971–77). (See also CONSERVATISM.)

Budenny, Semyon Mikhailovich *(1883–1973)* Russian military leader and marshal of the USSR. Having served in the 48th Cossack Regiment in the Far East, Budenny was involved in revolutionary activity early in 1917. In 1918 he organized a cavalry unit to combat White forces. A member of the COMMUNIST PARTY from 1919, he took an active role in the RUSSIAN CIVIL WAR. He pursued a highly successful military and political career; in 1939 he was deputy commissar for defense and in 1940 was first deputy. Despite a setback to his career in WORLD WAR II, in 1953 he was made inspector of cavalry. From 1939 to 1961 he was a full member of the Communist Party central committee.

Budge, (John) Donald *(1915–2000)* American tennis player. Budge had a major impact on the game of tennis as he transformed the backhand from a defensive stroke into a formidable offensive weapon. He played on four U.S. Davis Cup teams, leading the team to its first victory in a decade. In the late 1930s his domination of the game was absolute, as he twice won both the Wimbledon singles title (1937–38) and the men's and mixed doubles. He duplicated the feat at For-

est Hills, winning the U.S. Open singles and doubles titles four times from 1936 to 1938. In 1938 he became the first amateur to win the Grand Slam, encompassing the championships of the U.S., Great Britain, Australia and France. He turned professional in 1939 and also published his book *Budge on Tennis*. Budge was named to the National Lawn Tennis Association Hall of Fame in 1964.

Buea (Bouea) Town in western Cameroon. It was the capital of Germany's Kamerun colony from 1884 to 1919. In 1922 Buea was designated as headquarters of the British commissioner for the Southern Cameroons.

Buffet, Bernard *(1928–1999)* French painter. An extremely precocious artist, Buffet was well known in Parisian art circles by the mid-1940s and was awarded a major French critical prize in 1948. Much influenced by the Misérablisme movement, his early work is somber in nature, boldly outlined in black, with drab colors and a distinctive angular signature. He is known for his earlier religious paintings and for later views of London, Paris and New York. Buffet's work became increasingly popular in the 1960s but was dismissed by many critics as mawkish and sentimental.

Buganda Former kingdom of southern Uganda, located on the north shore of Lake Victoria. Its capital was Kampala, and as an independent kingdom it exercised considerable power in the 19th century. In 1900, pursuant to the Buganda Agreement, it was made a British protectorate. Following the independence of UGANDA, tensions between the former kingdom and the new nation rose to such a point that the political entity of Buganda was formally abolished.

Bugatti, Ettore *(1881–1947)* Italian designer primarily known as a designer of automobiles. Bugatti, at one time or another, built cars in Italy, Germany and France. His product included both racing and sports cars and luxury sedans, such as the legendary Type 41 Royale, a massive vehicle of great elegance. Bugatti's greatest contribution was in the technical and engineering design of engines, but the appearance of many of his cars—even the appearance of their mechanical components—was remarkably sophisticated. A picture of a Bugatti motor appears in LE CORBUSIER's *Vers une architecture* of 1923.

Bugatti, Jean *(1909–1939)* Italian-born designer and son of Ettore BUGATTI, who joined his father's career as a designer of sport and luxury automobiles. The Type 57 Bugatti of 1934, built in both sedan and open touring versions, is largely his work. His streamlined railcars for the French state railways (also of 1934) are among the earliest examples of modern railroad equipment produced in Europe. Bugatti died in an accident while testing a streamlined version of the Type 57.

Bugs Bunny Celebrated American animated cartoon character and star of many WARNER BROS. "Looney Tunes." Bugs, who turned 60 in 2000, is second only to Walt DISNEY's MICKEY MOUSE in name recognition and popularity among cartoon stars. The "wabbit" (as arch-foe Elmer Fudd called him) was the joint creation of a team of young animators—Ben Hardaway, Chuck Jones, Fritz Freleng and Tex AVERY—working at the Warners animation unit in Burbank in the late 1930s. He first appeared in 1938 as an unidentified white rabbit in Hardaway's *Porky's Hare Hunt*. He was soon refined in Jones's *Elmer's Candid Camera* and Avery's *A Wild Hare* (both 1940), acquiring a name ("Bugs" was Hardaway's nickname), a voice (courtesy of Mel BLANC), and a trademark salutation, "What's up, doc?" (courtesy of Avery). Since then the brash rabbit from Brooklyn has been all over the map. He's played every position on a baseball team, gone to other planets, fought in the bullring, sung grand opera and won an ACADEMY AWARD (in Freleng's *Knighty Knight, Bugs*, 1958). His star was installed on HOLLYWOOD's Walk of Fame in 1985 and his television series in television history. In contrast to the Disney characters, the humor of Bugs and friends Daffy Duck, Yosemite Sam and the others was really for adults, quite sophisticated and full of double entendres.

Buhler, Karl Ludwig *(1879–1963)* German psychologist. Buhler remains best known for his early writings on the psychology of perception, which contributed to the development of GESTALT theory. In contrast to the contemporary Gestalt school of psychologists, he held that gestalts were merely hypothetical possibilities, not proven realities. Buhler earned a medical degree from the University of Freiburg and a doctorate in psychology from the University of Strasbourg. In the 1920s, he operated a psychological institute in Vienna and wrote *The Mental Development of the Child* (1927). In 1938 Buhler was briefly arrested by the Nazis. Upon his release, he immigrated first to Norway and then to America, where he taught at several institutions, including the University of Southern California medical school.

Buick, David Dunbar *(1854–1929)* Scots-born American auto manufacturer. After starting out in the plumbing supply business, Buick founded the Buick Motor Company in 1903 to build automobiles. In August 1904 the company produced its first model in its plant in Flint, Michigan. Later that same year Buick's investors invited William C. Durant to assume management of the company, and in 1908 Buick resigned from the firm, which continued to bear his name. Although Buick was paid at least $100,000 to step down, he lost the money in a series of bad business ventures, and he died virtually penniless on March 6, 1929.

Bukharin, Nikolai Ivanovich *(1888–1938)* Russian Communist leader and Marxist theoretician. In 1908 Bukharin was made a member of the Moscow Bolshevik committee. He was imprisoned and deported by the czarist government. After the 1917 RUSSIAN REVOLUTION he returned to Russia, edited *PRAVDA* (1917–29) and in 1919 was elected to the executive committee of the COMINTERN. The following year he published *The Economy of the Transitional Period*. A member of the Politburo from 1924, Bukharin supported STALIN but distrusted him. In 1928 he disagreed with Stalin over the latter's collectivization and industrialization policy and was expelled from the Politburo in 1929, although he remained on the Central Committee. A victim of the GREAT PURGE, in 1938 he was charged with treason, tried (along with YAGODA and Krestinsky) and shot. His reputation was officially rehabilitated during the GLASNOST period of the late 1980s. (See also KULAKS.)

Bukowski, Charles *(1920–1994)* American poet. Born in Germany. Bukowski immigrated to the U.S. in 1922. As a young man, he worked as an unskilled laborer, emerging on the literary scene in Los Angeles in the early 1960s. Although prolific, he remained a literary outsider who published his work with small presses, primarily on the West Coast. His work is marked by a sordid and brutal realism sometimes tempered with a vein of sentimentality. His confessional persona is that of a tough, skid-row, hard-drinking womanizer; his rough, gritty work portrays the underbelly of urban life, populated with bums and criminals; his tone is by turns matter-of-fact, despondent and bored. Frequent subjects include suicide, depression and the loneliness of one-night stands.

Bulgakov, Sergei Nikolayevich *(1871–1944)* Russian philosopher, economist and theologian. Bulgakov first emerged as an important Marxist economic thinker in 1897, with the publication of *Markets in Capitalist Production*. His work *Capitalism and Agriculture* (1900) revised accepted notions of the role of agrarian production in a Marxist society. Bulgakov shifted his focus from economic to philosophical questions in *Problems of Idealism* (1902) and *From Marxism to Idealism* (1903). After the 1905 revolution, Bulgakov joined the Constitutional Democrats reform party. As a result of a religious conversion, Bulgakov became a priest of the Russian Orthodox Church in 1918 and was ultimately expelled from his native land in 1922 for alleged anti-Soviet activities. *Quiet Thoughts* (1918) is representative of his theological writings. Bulgakov died in exile in Paris.

Bulganin, Nikolai *(1895–1975)* Prime minister of the USSR (1955–58). Bulganin joined the COMMUNIST PARTY at the time of the RUSSIAN REVOLUTION (1917). He was chairman of the Moscow soviet (in effect, mayor of Moscow) from 1931 to 1937. He succeeded STALIN as minister of defense in 1946, after World War II. On Stalin's death in 1953 Bulganin initially appeared to share power with KHRUSHCHEV, but Khrushchev rapidly took the ascendancy, ousted Bulganin in 1958 and became prime minister himself.

Bulgaria Nation in southeastern Europe, its boundaries corresponding roughly to those of the ancient countries of Moesia and Thrace. In 1908, following a revolt within the neighboring OTTOMAN EMPIRE (longtime and former master of Bulgaria), Prince Ferdinand declared himself czar over all Bulgaria. The country engaged in two brief wars with other Balkan nations in 1912 and 1913 (see the BALKANS), prevailing in the first but losing in the second—and thus was forced to cede land under the 1913 Treaty of Bucharest. During WORLD WAR I, it sided with the CENTRAL POWERS, including GERMANY. Defeat led to the 1919 Treaty of Neuilly, pursuant to which Bulgaria ceded land to both GREECE and YUGOSLAVIA and also paid reparations. In 1934 BORIS III created a military dictatorship; during WORLD WAR II he allied Bulgaria with the Nazis. Following that defeat, Bulgaria came under Soviet control as part of the Eastern bloc. Communist Georgi DIMITROV served as leader from 1946 to 1949. In 1954 Todor ZHIVKOV became party secretary

and in 1962 prime minister. He was finally ousted in 1989 due to worsening domestic conditions and a general wave of anticommunist feeling throughout Eastern Europe. In the 1991 elections the Communist Party lost to the opposition party, the Union of Democratic Forces (UDF). The following year the UDF's leader, Zhelyu Zhelev, became the country's first popularly elected president. In 2004 Bulgaria was admitted to the NORTH ATLANTIC TREATY ORGANIZATION.

Bulge, Battle of the As a last desperate gamble to win WORLD WAR II, Adolf HITLER, GERMANY's leader, ordered an offensive in the Ardennes Forest in Luxembourg and southern Belgium. On December 16, 1944, three German armies attacked the line held by four inexperienced U.S. divisions. The Germans, aided by bad weather, advanced 50 miles along a 50-mile front in a week (the bulge). When the skies cleared Allied air forces attacked, stiffening American resistance. U.S. general George S. PATTON

rushed in the Third Army, and on December 26, 1944, the Germans began a slow retreat, pushed back to their starting line by January 28, 1945. Both sides suffered heavy losses in personnel and materiel, the Germans losing over one and a half times as much as the Allies.

Bullard, Sir Edward Crisp (1907–1980) British geophysicist. Bullard was educated at Cambridge University. After war service in naval research he returned to Cambridge as a reader in geophysics before accepting a post as head of the physics department of the University of Toronto (1948) and visiting the Scripps Institute of Oceanography in California (1949). After a five-year spell as director of the National Physical Laboratory, he returned to Cambridge as a reader and, in 1964, professor of geophysics and director of the department of geodesy and geophysics. There he remained until his retirement in 1974. Bullard made a number of contributions to the revolution in the Earth sciences that took

	BULGARIA
1908	Bulgaria declares independence from Turkey; Ferdinand crowned czar.
1912	Allied with Greece against Turkey in First Balkan War.
1913	Loses Macedonia as Greece allies with Turkey in Second Balkan War.
1914	Allied with Turkey and other Axis power in World War I.
1918	Loses Thrace after defeat of Central Powers; Ferdinand forced to resign; Boris II crowned.
1920	Agrarians under Prime Minister Stambolisky begin sweeping land reforms.
1922	Death of Ivan Vasov, national poet who recorded struggles for freedom.
1923	Stambolisky assassinated; centrist coalition forms government.
1934	Putsch by fascist Zuevno movement briefly drives out the king; he returns to rule as a royal dictator until 1943.
1941	Bulgaria joins Axis powers in World War II.
1944	Soviet troops enter Sofia; communist Fatherland Front forms government.
1948	Industries nationalized, farms collectivized under new constitution.
1954	Todor Zhivkov named Communist Party chief.
1962	Zhivkov consolidates power, adds prime minister's title.
1985	"Bulgarianization" drive launched against ethnic Turks.
1989	Zhivkov ousted by massive protests; Maldsnov assumes presidency.
1991	Communist Party loses to opposition Union of Democratic Forces (UDF).
1992	UDF leader Zhelyu Zhelev becomes country's first popularly elected president.
2004	Bulgaria admitted to the North Atlantic Treaty Organization (NATO).

place in the 1950s and 1960s. He carried out major work on the measurement of the heat flow from the Earth. In 1965 Bullard studied continental drift using a computer to analyze the fit between the Atlantic continents. He found an excellent fit for the South Atlantic at the 500-fathom contour line. However, a reasonable fit could be made for the North Atlantic only if a number of assumptions, such as deformation and sedimentation since the continents drifted apart, were taken into account. Later, independent evidence for these assumptions gave powerful support for the theory of continental drift. Bullard was knighted in 1953.

Bullen, Keith Edward *(1906–1976)* Australian applied mathematician and geophysicist. The son of Anglo-Irish parents, Bullen was educated at the universities of Auckland, Melbourne and Cambridge, England. He began his career as a teacher in Auckland and then lectured in mathematics at Melbourne and Hull, England. In 1946 he became professor of applied mathematics at the University of Sydney. Bullen's chief contributions to science were his mathematical studies of earthquake waves and the ellipticity of the Earth. In 1936 he gave values of the density inside the Earth down to a depth of 3,100 miles. He also determined values for the pressure, gravitation intensity, compressibility and rigidity throughout the interior of the Earth. From the results on the Earth's density he inferred that the core was solid. He applied his results to the internal structure of the planets Mars, Venus and Mercury and to the origin of the Moon. Bullen conducted some of his early work on earthquake travel times in collaboration with Harold Jeffreys. This resulted in the publication of the Jeffreys-Bullen (JB) tables in 1940.

Bulow case, von *(1982)* Criminal trial of socialite Claus von Bulow, a noted Danish-born aristocrat alleged to have poisoned his wife, Sunny, who had previously inherited $75 million. A few years after their marriage, Sunny twice fell into a mysterious coma. She never emerged from the second coma but remained at a hospital in a persistent vegetative state. The couple's maid suspected foul play and alerted Sunny's children from a prior marriage of her suspicions. Claus von Bulow stood to gain millions on his wife's death. He was ultimately tried for attempted murder and convicted based on circumstantial evidence, including a black bag that contained a hypodermic syringe. During the trial it was revealed that he maintained a mistress while his wife was in a coma. The conviction was thrown out because the black bag was illegally seized evidence. A retrial followed, but after a hard-fought trial, the jury acquitted von Bulow. Sunny continues in a coma.

Bultmann, Rudolf *(1884–1976)* German theologian and biblical historian. Bultmann became a center of controversy in Christian theological circles by virtue of his advocacy of a "de-mythologizing" approach to biblical interpretation. Bultmann adopted as a starting point the disparity in consciousness between the scientific 20th century and the New Testament period, when the possibility of miracles was readily embraced. Bultmann argued that Christian faith could best survive by embracing the "mythic" teaching aspects of the Gospels and refusing to be caught up in debates over the historical reality of such events as the Resurrection. For Bultmann, the Bible retains its human value as a source of inspiration and wisdom capable of pointing one to an existentially authentic personal existence. Bultmann's major works include *History and Eschatology* (1957), *Jesus Christ and Mythology* (1958) and a volume of selected essays, *Existence and Faith* (1961).

Bunche, Ralph (*1904–1971*) American statesman. A graduate of UCLA, Bunche earned a master's and a Ph.D. in government from Harvard in 1934. He did postdoctoral study in anthropology and colonial policy at Northwestern University, the London School of Economics and the University of Capetown, South Africa. Under Rosenwald and Social Science Research Council fellowships, he studied in Africa, Europe, Malaya and the Netherlands Indies (now Indonesia). Bunche was a member of the political science department at Howard University from 1928 to 1950. His diplomatic career begin in 1944 when he joined the Department of State. He helped found the UNITED NATIONS and served as a UN undersecretary from 1955 to 1971. Bunche received the Spingarn Medal of the NAACP in 1949 and the Presidential Medal of Freedom in 1963. He was awarded the NOBEL PRIZE for peace in 1950 for his mediation of the Armistice of Rhodes, which formally ended the ARAB-ISRAELI WAR OF 1948–1949.

Bund (General Union of Jewish Workers) Active in Russia and Poland, the Bund was a socialist political movement founded in Vilna in 1897. Its aims were an end to anti-Jewish discrimination (see POGROMS) and a reorganized, federal Russian empire. By 1900 it was the most powerful socialist body in Russia. In conflict with LENIN over its emphasis on Jewish interests, it seceded from the Russian Social Democ-

rat Party (1906) and supported the MENSHEVIKS. In 1920 it was divided. The majority of members joined the COMMUNIST PARTY of the Soviet Union; the minority continued as a separate group until suppressed by the government.

Bundy, McGeorge (*1919–1996*) U.S. government official. Bundy graduated from Yale in 1940 and served in the army during World War II. He joined the Harvard faculty in 1949. From 1953 to 1961 he was the dean of the faculty of arts and sciences. Bundy served as special assistant to the president for national security affairs in both the KENNEDY and JOHNSON administrations (1961–66). As special assistant, he played a major role in formulating and directing foreign policy. One of Kennedy's inner circle, he helped determine administration action in the CUBAN MISSILE CRISIS. Under Johnson he strongly advocated escalating the VIETNAM WAR. Bundy resigned in 1966 to accept the presidency of the Ford Foundation (1966–79). In 1968 he came out in support of deescalation of the war.

Bunin, Ivan Alexeyevich (*1870–1953*) Russian poet, short story writer and novelist. After his early publication of nature poetry in the classical style of Pushkin, Bunin turned to prose. *The Village* (1910) was a pessimistic prose poem that recounted the decline of the rural peasantry after the RUSSIAN REVOLUTION OF 1905. A volume of stories published in 1917 included his best-known work, "The Gentleman from San Francisco," a fantasy-satire of bourgeois Western society. After the BOLSHEVIK REVOLUTION (1917), Bunin left Russia and lived as an expatriate, mainly in France. His semiautobiographical novel, *The Life of Arsenyev: The Well of Days* (1933), earned him the NOBEL PRIZE in literature. He was also a translator of such writers as Byron, Longfellow, Tennyson and Alfred de Musset. During his lifetime he was regarded as a leading Russian writer, but his reputation later declined.

Bunshaft, Gordon (*1909–1990*) American architect who was the partner in the large firm of SKIDMORE, OWINGS & MERRILL credited with the design of a number of that firm's most distinguished glass wall and steel buildings. Trained at MIT, Bunshaft worked briefly for Edward Durrell STONE before

joining Skidmore, Owings & Merrill, where he became a partner in 1949. He was the partner in charge of design for such major SOM projects as Lever House (1951–52), the Pepsi-Cola Building (1959) and the Chase Manhattan Bank headquarters (1961), all in New York; the U.S. Air Force Academy (1956–62) at Colorado Springs; and the Beinecke Rare Book Library (1964) on the Yale campus in New Haven, Connecticut. The Bunshaft aesthetic was generally austere and mechanistic; seemingly he drew on Ludwig MIES VAN DER ROHE as a major inspiration. His role in raising SOM's work to a high level of design quality was much praised in the 1950s and 1960s, although by the 1980s it was also criticized for a certain coldness and monotony.

Buñuel, Luis (*1900–1983*) Spanish-born filmmaker. An iconoclastic and scathing critic of bourgeois society, Buñuel was internationally acclaimed for his pioneering surrealistic work. He achieved notoriety with his first short firm, *Un chien andalou* (1928), made with the surrealist artist Salvador DALÍ, and *The Age of Gold* (1930). Buñuel went into exile in the 1930s and ultimately settled in Mexico City in 1947. His career did not revive until *Los olvidados* (1950), for which he received the best director prize at the 1951 Cannes Film Festival. Other well-known Buñuel films included *Viridiana* (1961), *Diary of a Chambermaid* (1964), *Tristana* (1970), *The Discreet Charm of the Bourgeoisie* (1972) and *That Obscure Object of Desire* (1977). His memoirs were published as *My Last Sigh* (1983).

Burbank, Luther (*1849–1926*) American plant breeder. Burbank was brought up on a farm and received only an elementary education. He began breeding plants in 1870, when he bought a seven-hectare plot of land. After about a year he had developed the Burbank potato, which was introduced to Ireland to help combat the blight epidemics. By selling the rights to this potato he made $150, which he used to travel to California, where three of his brothers had already settled. He established a nursery and experimental farm in Santa Rosa, where the climate was especially conducive to fruit and flower breeding—his occupa-

Luther Burbank (LIBRARY OF CONGRESS, PRINTS AND PHOTOGRAPHS DIVISION)

tion for the next 50 years. He worked by making multiple crosses between native and introduced strains, using his remarkable skill to select commercially promising types. These were then grafted onto mature plants to hasten development so that their value could be assessed rapidly. In this way he produced numerous new cultivated varieties of plums, lilies and many other ornamentals and fruits.

Burbige, Eleanor Margaret (Margaret Peachey) (1922–   ) British astronomer. Burbidge studied physics at the University of London. After graduation in 1948 she joined the University of London Observatory where she earned her Ph.D. and served as acting director (1950–51). She then went to to the U.S. as a research fellow, first at the Yerkes Observatory of the University of Chicago (1951–53) and then at the California Institute of Technology (1955–57). She spent 1953–55 in highly productive work at the Cavendish Laboratory in Cambridge, England. She returned to Yerkes in 1957, serving as associate professor of astronomy from 1959 to 1962 and then transferred to the University of California, San Diego, where she was professor of astronomy from 1964 and also served from 1979 as director of the Center for Astrophysics and Space Sciences. In 1948 she married Geoffrey BURBIDGE a theoretical physicist and began a highly productive partnership. They collaborated with Fred HOYLE and William Fowler in 1957 in publishing a key paper on the synthesis of the chemical elements in stars. Their *Quasi-Stel-*

lar Objects (1967) was one of the first comprehensive works on quasars. She had earlier recorded the spectra of a number of quasars with the 120-inch Lick reflector and discovered that their spectral lines displayed different red shifts, probably indicating the ejection of matter at very high speeds. The first accurate estimates of the masses of galaxies were based on Margaret Burbidge's careful observation of their rotation. Burbidge received the National Medal of Science from U.S. president Ronald REAGAN. After 1990 Burbidge became an emeritus professor at the University of California, San Diego.

Burbidge, Geoffrey (1925–   ) British astrophysicist. Burbidge graduated in 1946 from the University of Bristol and earned his Ph.D. in 1951 from the University of London. From 1950 to 1958 he held junior university positions at London, Harvard, Chicago, Cambridge (England) and the Mount Wilson and Palomar Observatories in California. He became associate professor at Chicago (1958–62) before being appointed associate professor (1962), then professor of physics (1963) at the University of California, San Diego. In 1978 Burbidge accepted the post of director of the Kitt Peak National Observatory, Arizona. Burbidge began his research career studying particle physics; after his 1948 marriage to Margaret Peachey (see Eleanor Margaret BURBIDGE), who was to become one of the world's leading optical astronomers, he turned to astrophysics and began a productive research partnership with his wife. The Burbidges worked on the mysterious quasars, first described by Allan Sandage in 1960, and produced in their *Quasi-Stellar Objects* (1967) one of the earliest surveys of the subject. Burbidge was reluctant to accept without reservation the BIG BANG THEORY on the origin of the universe. In 1971 he published a paper in which he maintained that we still do not know whether the big bang occurred and that much more effort must be devoted to cosmological tests. Although such views found little favor, Burbidge continued to be highly productive, rich in new ideas, and yet outside and somewhat skeptical of prevailing cosmological and astrophysical orthodoxy.

Burchfield, Charles (1893–1967) American painter. Born in Ashtabula,

Ohio, Burchfield studied at the Cleveland School of Art and was a wallpaper designer from 1921 to 1929. Painting mainly in watercolors, he is best known for his evocative portrayals of ghostly midwestern towns, replete with Victorian houses and crumbling wooden shacks in wintry snows, blustery storms or bright sunshine. In the early and late phases of his career, Burchfield also painted lyrical nature studies. Typical of his work are *Night Wind* (1918, Museum of Modern Art, New York City), *Ice Glare* (1933, Whitney Museum of American Art, New York City) and *Freight Cars Under a Bridge* (Detroit Institute of Arts).

Burden, William Douglas (1898–1978) American naturalist and explorer. Burden established the Department of Animal Behavior at the American Museum of Natural History in New York. In 1926 he led an expedition to the Dutch East Indies. On this expedition he captured the Komodo dragon, the world's oldest and largest lizard. This exploit inspired the film *King Kong* (1933).

Burgee, John (1933–   ) American architect known for his partnership with Philip JOHNSON. Burgee received his architectural education at Notre Dame University Indiana and worked for the Chicago firms of Holabird and Root and Naess-Murphy before collaborating with Johnson on a 1965 project. The relationship led to a partnership in 1967. Many major projects often viewed as Johnson designs are in fact the work of this partnership—for example, Pennzoil Plaza in Houston, Texas (1972–76), the AT&T Building in New York (1985) and the elliptical office tower at 53rd Street and Third Avenue in New York (often called the Lipstick building, in reaction to its shape). Since 1987 the firm has been called John Burgee Architects to reflect Johnson's current role as design consultant while Burgee, with two partners, has primary responsibility for the firm's operation.

Burger, Warren (1907–1995) Chief justice, U.S. Supreme Court (1969–86). The son of immigrant parents, Burger worked his way through two years of the University of Minnesota and the St. Paul College of Law (later Mitchell College of Law). He then spent about 20

years in private practice. An active Republican, Burger was appointed assistant attorney general in charge of the civil division of the Justice Department. He first gained national attention when he supported the federal government's prosecution of John Peters for disloyalty after the U.S. solicitor general had refused to prosecute. Burger was appointed as a judge of the important U.S. Court of Appeals for the District of Columbia. Appointed by President Richard M. NIXON to succeed Earl WARREN as chief justice of the Supreme Court, Burger was known as a strict constructionist. Although the Burger court proved more conservative than the Warren court, the Court was judicially active. During Burger's term the Court delivered several controversial opinions that led to liberalized ABORTION laws. After resigning from the Court, Burger served as head of the U.S. Bicentennial Commission.

Burgess, Anthony *(1917–1993)* British novelist, critic and dramatist. Burgess is one of the most prolific and versatile British writers of his generation, having worked in genres as diverse as journalism, screenplay and television writing, theatrical adaptations and a 1970 biography of Shakespeare. But he is best known as a novelist. His most famous work is *A Clockwork Orange* (1962), a dire futuristic vision of street violence, repressive government and high-technology mind control, which was adapted into an evocative 1971 film by Stanley KUBRICK. Other notable Burgess novels include his Malayan Trilogy on British colonial life—*Time for a Tiger* (1956), *The Enemy in the Blanket* (1958) and *Beds in the East* (1959)—and *Earthly Powers* (1980), which mingles real and imagined characters to chronicle the events of the 20th century. Burgess was a prolific book reviewer and wrote a full-length study of James JOYCE.

Burgess, W. Starling *(1878–1947)* American naval architect and designer of sailing yachts known for his successful designs for racing craft, including several winners of America's Cup races. He was, in 1910, the designer of the first successful airplane built in New England and, shortly after, of the first successful flying boat. His design for the 59-foot schooner *Nina* of 1928

was a great success in racing in both American and British waters and established his reputation as a master designer of fast sailing craft. His most famous designs were *Enterprise* (1930), *Rainbow* (1934) and *Ranger* (1937), the last designed in collaboration with Olin STEPHENS. All three were America's Cup winners. Burgess was largely responsible for establishing the characteristic design of the modern racing sailboat.

Burgess-MacLean spy case On May 26, 1951, two officials of the British foreign office slipped out of England on a ferry bound for France and vanished; it was later learned that they had defected to the USSR. **Guy Burgess** had been an attaché at the British embassy in Washington, D.C.; **Donald MacLean** had been chief of the Foreign Office's American section. MacLean had had access to high-level Anglo-American diplomatic, military and intelligence secrets. The two finally surfaced in Moscow in 1956 and admitted that they had become communists while they were students at Cambridge in the 1930s. They had disagreed with British and American foreign policy and believed that the USSR offered the most reasonable hope for world peace; while serving in the Foreign Office, they had passed British and American secrets to Soviet

agents. In 1950 or 1951, British and U.S. counterintelligence had become suspicious of the two and placed them under surveillance. However, Burgess and MacLean were tipped off by a "third man" in the spy ring who knew that they were about to be arrested. The "third man" turned out to be the high-ranking British diplomat and intelligence agent Kim PHILBY, who had been MacLean's superior in Washington. Philby himself defected to the USSR in 1963.

Burkina Faso Landlocked republic in West Africa, lying south of the Sahara; its total area of 105,811 square miles is divided into 30 provinces. More than 90% of the population is rural based, yet only 8%–10% of the republic's land is arable; soil conditions are poor. The area came under French rule at the end of the 19th century, when it was incorporated into the colony of the French Sudan, which itself formed part of the Federation of FRENCH WEST AFRICA. In 1920 the area became a separate colony known as Upper Volta, but in 1932 it was divided among the neighboring colonies of French Sudan, Niger and the Ivory Coast; in 1947 it reemerged as a separate administrative unit in its current boundaries. Throughout the colonial period Upper Volta was a backwater of France's West African empire. There

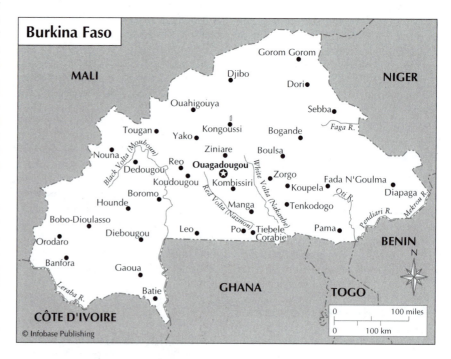

BURKINA FASO

1960	Country becomes independent from France as Upper Volta with Maurice Yaméogo, leader of Union Democratique Voltaïque (UDV), as president.
1966	Following a general strike, mobs attack the national assembly; army chief of staff Sangoulé Lamizana removes Yaméogo and assumes power.
1973	Drought of unprecedented severity hits the Sahel.
1981	Lamizana, elected president in 1978, is overthrown in a military coup led by Colonel Saye Zerbo.
1982	Zerbo ousted in army coup led by Jean-Baptiste Ouedraogo.
1983	Thomas Sankara ousts Ouedraogo and sets up left-leaning regime, "National Council of the Revolution."
1984	Upper Volta renamed Burkina Faso, meaning "country of honest men."
1987	Sankara assassinated, replaced by Blaise Compaoré.
1992	Compaoré is reelected without opposition for a seven-year term.
1998	Facing opposition candidates for the first time, Compaoré wins by a large majority.
2005	Campaoré is reelected.

was little investment, and many inhabitants worked in the coffee plantations of neighboring Ivory Coast (to which it was linked by a railway started before World War I but not completed until 1954). After World War II the Mossi king was a pro-French conservative influence in opposition to the more radical Rassemblement Démocratique Africain (RDA), which campaigned for independence for the whole of French West Africa as a single state. The country became independent as Upper Volta on August 5, 1960, with Maurice Yaméogo, leader of the Union Démocratique Voltaïque (UDV), as president. Yaméogo soon moved to one-party state but was deposed in a 1966 coup led by Lt. Col. Sangoulé Lamizana. A new constitution, providing for a return to civilian rule, was approved in a June 1970 referendum. Severe hardship caused by the Sahelian drought combined with political ineptitude led to another military intervention, with Lamizana resuming power on February 8, 1974. During the 1970s the trade unions became the principal mouthpiece for opposition politics. Full party politics were restored in assembly and presidential elections in April and May 1978 in which the UDV again won a majority of the votes, and Lamizana was confirmed as president. His regime was overthrown in a 1980 military coup that installed Colonel Saye Zerbo as president; he was overthrown in November 1982 in a coup of junior officers led by Captain Thomas Sankara. Sankara's new government, the People's Salvation Council, had a radical reform program closely modeled on policies pursued in GHANA by Flight Lieutenant Jerry Rawlings. On August 3, 1984, Upper Volta was renamed Burkina Faso, or "country of honest men." War broke out with neighboring Mali in December 1985, when Burkinabe troops crossed the disputed border and were driven back by superior Malian air power; relations were normalized the following year.

Sankara's drive against corruption and his authoritarian policy of forcing city-dwellers to return to the countryside caused resentment against the urban elite; on October 15, 1987, he was assassinated. Blaise Compaoré, his replacement, had been one of his closest friends but was not thought to have been directly involved in the assassination. With one of the lowest GNPs in the world, Burkina Faso is increasingly dependent upon foreign aid for its survival. In 1992 the political party founded by Campaoré, the Organization for Popular Democracy-Labor Movement, won a parliamentary majority in Burkina Faso's first free elections since 1978. In 1998 and 2005 Campaoré won in the country's presidential elections.

Burleigh, Harry Thacker (1866–1949) African-American art song composer, best known for his many arrangements of Negro spirituals. During his boyhood in Erie, Pennsylvania, Burleigh heard the Negro folk songs as well as the songs of Stephen Foster from his blind grandfather, Hamilton E. Waters, a former slave. In 1892 he enrolled in the National Conservatory in New York, where he worked as a copyist for its director, Antonín Dvorák. His singing of spirituals for Dvorák—especially "Swing Low, Sweet Chariot"—resulted in the composer's incorporation of them into his famous "New World" Symphony. In 1894 Burleigh gained the important post of baritone soloist at St. George's Church, the only black man in an otherwise white congregation. He held the post for the next 50 years. His arrangements of spirituals and folk songs included the *Six Plantation Melodies for Violins and Piano* (1901), *From the Southland* (1914), *Jubilee Songs of the United States of America* (1916) and *Old Songs Hymnal* (1929). The popularity of "Deep River" and "Go Down, Moses," for example, may be attributed to his efforts. He also had a profound impact upon the next generation of black composers, including Duke ELLINGTON. "He was America's first great black composer of art songs," says biographer Jean Snyder. "This helped create the audience and the acceptance among white singers of the artistic value of the arrangements of the spirituals as well." Today his life and work are enjoying a great revival in interest and popularity.

Burma (**Myanmar Naingngan, Union of Myanmar**) Nation of Southeast Asia, located on the western side of the Indochina Peninsula, with a lengthy coastline on the Bay of Bengal and the Andaman Sea. Its landward borders dominated by mountains, Burma developed as an isolated nation with a unique culture, lying athwart the ancient overland trade route between India and China. In 1885, following its defeat in the third Anglo-Burmese war, Burma was annexed as a province of British India. Under British exploitation it became a major rice exporter but suffered from a degeneration of its own culture. Nationalist movements became recurrent; a serious rebellion against British rule broke out in 1931 and was quashed after two years of violent struggle. During WORLD WAR II, it was occupied by Japanese forces and was forced to support Japan through 1943, but Burmese troops fought for the Allies in 1945. In 1947 Burma was granted independence by Britain, on January 4, 1948. It has since maintained a neutral stance in international affairs. In 1962 a military coup established General NE WIN as a socialist dictator, through 1973, when a new constitution was enacted and civilian rule restored, although Ne Win remained a powerful figure behind the scenes. After another period of intense turmoil (1987–88), the military again assumed power and used terror to crush any opposition. Since 1989 the military government has tried to get other countries to recognize the name Myanmar, but many (including the U.S.) refuse to do so. The military government has tried to repress the National League for Democracy (NLD) in its efforts to bring democratic government to the country and has on occasion tolerated NLD dissension, as when it briefly released NLD leader and Nobel Peace Prize recipient AUNG SAN SUU KYI in 1995 and 2002 before returning her to house arrest. In November 2005 the capital was moved from Yangon to Pyinmana.

Burma Campaign (*1943–1945*) The Japanese occupied BURMA in 1942, closing the BURMA ROAD, the only supply route from northern Burma to China. British, Gurkha and Burmese guerrillas maintained resistance, while a joint American-Chinese army trained and led by General Joseph "Vinegar Joe" STILWELL attacked from the north, traversing extremely rugged terrain

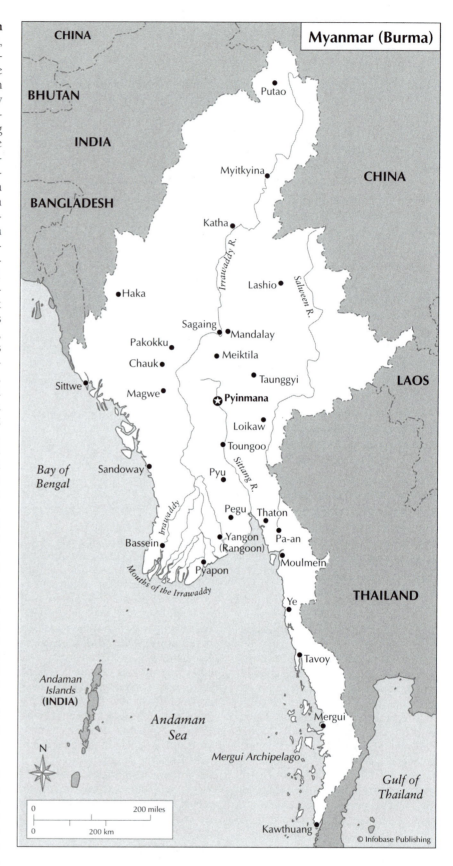

and fighting experienced Japanese troops. Joined by 3,000 volunteers ("Merrill's Marauders") recruited by Stilwell aide Frank Dow Merrill, the combined forces seized Myitkyina airfield in northern Burma (May 17–18,

BURMA (MYANMAR)

1937	Burma separates from India to become British dependency.
1942	Japan invades Burma.
1948	Union of Burma becomes independent.
1949	Karen nationalists capture Mandalay with the help of communist guerrillas.
1962	General Ne Win seizes power, publishes *The Burmese Way to Socialism*, combining Buddhist thought with Marxist theory, as the nation's official policy.
1964	All political parties banned.
1981	Ne Win steps down as president but maintains influence.
1989	Official name of Burma changed to Myanmar; Rangoon becomes Yangon; Aung San Suu Kyi arrested for first time.
1990	World Resources Institute study finds that 1.7 million acres in Burma have been lost to deforestation.
2002	Military regime briefly releases dissident leader Aung San Suu Kyi before returning her to house arrest.
2004	Prime Minister Khin Nyut is replaced and put under house arrest.
2005	Seat of government is moved to Pyinmana.

1944) after much hardship, permitting reinforcements and supplies to be flown in. After fierce fighting the Japanese surrendered the city of Myitkyina on August 3, while the Chinese moved against them at Lun-ling on the Burma Road. Much bloody fighting continued into 1945 before the road was opened, marking the only Chinese victory against the Japanese in eight years of war.

Burma Road Road running north-south between central Burma (Myanmar) and southern China; it was built from 1937 to 1939. During the SINO-JAPANESE WAR, it was utilized as a supply route into China but was closed in 1942, during WORLD WAR II, when Japanese forces took control of its southern terminus at Lashio. At present, it serves as a trade route between Chongqing in China and Rangoon in Burma. (See also BURMA CAMPAIGN.)

Burmese Guerrilla War of 1948– The establishment of the Union of BURMA in 1948 provoked minorities to rebel, demanding autonomous states. Aided by communists in south-central Burma, separatists seized Mandalay and besieged the government in Rangoon. A separate independent state was proclaimed at Toungoo (1949); the city was retaken by the government (1950); and the main communist center, Prome, was also seized, but fighting continued. Chinese Nationalist forces fleeing the Chinese Communist takeover moved into eastern Burma, resisting Burmese control until evacuated to Taiwan under United Nations auspices (1953–54). About that time Burmese troops under General NE WIN gained control of most of the country. U Ne Win established a military dictatorship in 1962 to prevent a communist takeover, but separatist and communist resistance continued. General U San Yu succeeded U Ne Win as president in 1981, holding Burma together despite continued strong rebel opposition. The rebellion against the government continued sporadically into the 21st century.

Burnet, Sir (Frank) Macfarlane *(1899–1985)* Australian microbiologist and virologist. Burnet shared the 1960 NOBEL PRIZE in medicine with British scientist Peter MEDAWAR. The two were honored for their independent work in the discovery of acquired immune tolerance, a discovery that led to major advances in organ transplantation. Burnet also did pioneering work in the field of viral genetics that formed the basis for current theories about viruses as cancer-causing agents. After his retirement in 1965 as professor of experimental medicine at the University of Melbourne, a post he held for more than 20 years, he wrote 16 books dealing mainly with science and medicine in a nontechnical manner.

Burnett, Frances Eliza Hodgson *(1849–1924)* Anglo-American author. Born in Manchester, England, Burnett moved to Tennessee with her family in 1865. She began writing for periodicals and published her early short stories in *Scribner's* beginning in 1872. Although she also wrote fiction for adults, Burnett is chiefly remembered for her popular and successful children's books, which include *Little Lord Fauntleroy* (1886) and *The Secret Garden* (1911).

Burnham, James *(1905–1987)* American conservative activist. Burnham was founding editor of NATIONAL REVIEW magazine (1955), and his warnings about the dangers of COMMUNISM had a profound impact on U.S. political debate. In his 20s he was a follower of Leon TROTSKY, but switched to CONSERVATISM after concluding that Marxism would lead to totalitarian despotism. He wrote a number of books, among them two that sparked great debate because of their prediction of an inevitable clash between the U.S. and the USSR—*The Struggle for the World* (1947) and *The Coming Defeat of Communism* (1950). He worked briefly for the CENTRAL INTELLIGENCE AGENCY in the 1950s, organizing anti-communist intellectual movements abroad. In 1983 he was awarded the Presidential Medal of Freedom for his contributions to conservative thought in the U.S.

Burns, Arthur F. (Arthur Frank Burnzelg) *(1904–1987)* American economist. Burns taught at Columbia University for two decades, until in 1953 he was chosen by President Dwight D. EISENHOWER to head the Council of Economic Advisers. Burns held the post for three years before returning to academia and a 10-year stint as president of the National Bureau of Economic Research. He returned to government service in 1969 as economic counselor to President Richard M. NIXON. One year later Nixon named him to the first of two four-year terms as chairman of the Federal Reserve Board. From 1981 to 1985 he was U.S. ambassador to West Germany.

Burns and Allen From the early days of VAUDEVILLE and RADIO to movies and TELEVISION, Burns and Allen were America's most popular husband-and-wife comedy team. **George Burns** (Nathan Birnbaum, 1896–1996) and **Gracie (Ethel Cecile Rosalie) Allen** (1902–64) first teamed in 1923. Burns—already a veteran vaudeville performer in various acts—elected to be the "comedian," while his partner Allen (then in secretarial school) was the "straight man." The act didn't quite work, as Allen began to get more laughs than her partner. The duo switched roles and found success: Burns became the wisecracking straight man and Allen the silly, often air-headed comic focus. The Jewish Burns and Irish-Catholic Allen were happily married in 1926. Burns and Allen subsequently worked the Palace in the early 1930s and starred in a series of short films. In 1932 they became national stars over the radio waves, continuing for 18 years until they brought their tremendous appeal to the new medium of television. They also appeared in a number of feature films, including *International House* (1933), *College Holiday* (1936), *The Big Broadcast of 1937* (1937), *College Swing* (1938) and *The Gracie Allen Murder Case* (1939). Allen's retirement from the entertainment world in 1958—and her death six years later—were tragic blows to her adoring fans. Burns pressed on, with limited success; HOLLYWOOD considered him worthless without Allen, in spite of the fact that for years he had supplied most of the team's jokes. But in 1975—at the age of 79—he made a comeback with his ACADEMY AWARD–winning performance

in *The Sunshine Boys*. This was followed by another movie hit, *Oh God* (1977), and other films. The "grand old master of comedy" continued to make television and film appearances until his death in 1996.

Burpee, David (*1893–1980*) American horticulturist and seed merchant. Burpee headed the world's largest mail-order seed company, W. Atlee Burpee Co., for 55 years. He developed hundreds of new varieties of flowers and vegetables, created many successful merchandising methods and sent out as many as 4 million seed catalogs annually.

Burroughs, Edgar Rice (*1875–1950*) American writer of fantastic novels and stories, creator of the character of TARZAN OF THE APES. Born in Chicago, Burroughs led a life full of failures. He flunked entrance exams for West Point. He tried to be a clerk, cowboy, railroad policeman, gold miner and shop owner. Finally, in 1911 at the age of 35, surrounded by a growing family and debts, he began his first successful story, "Dejah Thoris, Princess of Mars" (first published in *All-Story* magazine in 1912 as "Under the Moons of Mars"; later published in book form in 1917 as *A Princess of Mars*). The 11 Mars books (the planet is called "Barsoom" in the series) chronicled the adventures of an earthling, Captain John Carter, on a hostile but savagely beautiful planet. A few months later in 1912 appeared Burroughs's biggest success, *Tarzan of the Apes*. In a total of 24 books the ape-man roamed an unlikely but exotic and dangerous jungle, discovered lost races, penetrated to the Earth's core and fought in two world wars. Other series flowed from Burroughs's incredibly prolific pen—the Carson of Venus books, the Pellucidar tales (located at the center of the Earth), the Land That Time Forgot trilogy (located on an unknown continent in the South Seas); a trilogy of books located on the Moon; and many other titles. Most of Burroughs's works could not be called science fiction because their science is inconsistent and implausible. Rather, they blend the color and sheer storytelling exuberance of such 19th-century masters as H. Rider Haggard with the more modern zest for science and space travel of H. G. WELLS. While criticized as repetitious and frequently

clumsily written, Burroughs's works display superb pacing and an unflagging imagination. They have never been out of print and continue to be adapted to radio, comic strips and movies. *The Gods of Mars* (1913), *Tarzan of the Apes* (1912) and *The Moon Maid* (1926) will likely endure as narrative masterpieces. Burroughs died of a heart ailment after serving as a war correspondent in WORLD WAR II.

Burroughs, William Seward (*1914–1997*) American novelist and essayist. Burroughs was a highly controversial yet critically acclaimed author whose best-known work, *The Naked Lunch* (1959), sparked a well-publicized obscenity trial in the U.S. upon its first publication. Burroughs, the scion of a wealthy St. Louis family, was educated at Harvard. But he rejected his background and instead plunged into an alternative lifestyle that included travel, odd jobs, bisexualty and drug addiction; he also accidentally shot his wife. In the mid-1940s in New York, he befriended younger writers Allen GINSBERG and Jack KEROUAC, with whom he would be linked—in the 1950s—as key figures in the BEAT GENERATION. With painter Brion Gysin, Burroughs developed a "cut-up" system of prose composition that employed cutting and blending of several random texts into one hybrid narrative. Burroughs's works include *Junky* (1953), *The Soft Machine* (1961), *Nova Express* (1964) and *The Western Lands* (1987).

Burstyn, Ellen (*1932–   *) U.S. film and television actress who won an ACADEMY AWARD for best actress for the film *Alice Doesn't Live Here Anymore* (1974). She also won a Tony Award for *Same Time Next Year* in 1978. Burstyn was also nominated for an Academy Award for *The Exorcist* (1973) and *The Last Picture Show* (1971). Burstyn continued to appear in supporting roles throughout the 1990s in such films as *How to Make an American Quilt* (1995) and *The Spitfire Grill* (1996).

Burton, Harold Hitz (*1888–1964*) Associate justice, U.S. Supreme Court (1945–58). A graduate of Bowdoin College and Harvard University Law School, Burton first entered private practice in Ohio before working in Utah and Idaho. After service in World

War I, he resumed private law practice in Cleveland. An active Republican, Burton was elected mayor of Cleveland, vowing to rid the city of racketeers and gangsters. An extremely popular mayor, he was next elected to the U.S. Senate (1941), where he took a leadership role. In 1945 Burton was nominated to the Court by President Harry S. TRUMAN, who had been under pressure to name a Republican to the overwhelmingly Democratic Court. Burton generally took a conservative approach to civil liberties cases but was impartial and open-minded, judging each case on its own merits and often basing his decisions on technical rather than philosophical grounds. He gained a reputation as a conciliator between the more contentious justices. He served on the Court for 13 years before retiring for health reasons.

Burton, Philip *(1926–1983)* American politician. A Democrat from California, Burton served in the U.S. House of Representatives from 1964 until his death. In 1976 he came within one vote of being elected House Democratic majority leader. A champion of liberal causes, he helped pass legislation that established a cost-of-living adjustment for Social Security recipients, raised the minimum wage and improved benefits for the disabled and elderly and miners with black lung disease. He also introduced the largest national parks bill in history, which established more than 100 parks around the U.S.

Burton, Richard Walter (Richard Walter Jenkins) *(1925–1984)* Welsh-born actor, noted for his intense performances and his stormy life. Widely regarded as one of the most talented actors of the 20th century, Burton is remembered for his spectacular failures as well as his considerable successes. One of 13 children of a Welsh coal miner, he spoke only Welsh before the age of 10. His schoolteacher-mentor, Philip Burton, recognizing the boy's talent, adopted him and gave the boy his own name. He made his stage debut in *The Devil's Rest* (1943) by playwright-actor Emlyn Williams, who further encouraged Burton's career. By the early 1950s, Burton had emerged as one of Britain's finest Shakespearean actors, appearing at Stratford and the Old Vic. He soon

moved on to films, making his breakthrough as Jimmy Porter in John OSBORNE's *Look Back in Anger* (1959). He became an international star in the HOLLYWOOD spectacle *Cleopatra* (1963), playing opposite Elizabeth TAYLOR, whom he subsequently married. Burton's stormy relationship with Taylor, whom he later divorced and then remarried, was well publicized and earned the couple considerable notoriety. Of his more than 40 films, *Becket* (1964), *The Spy Who Came in from the Cold* (1965) and *Who's Afraid of Virginia Woolf* (1966) are the most notable. Burton was the most-nominated actor never to win an ACADEMY AWARD. His Broadway performances in *Hamlet, Camelot* and *Equus* were also acclaimed. However, he also appeared in many inferior films. Critics have explained Burton's inability to sustain his early promise in terms of his womanizing, his heavy drinking and the debilitating demands of fame. His last appearance was

in a movie adaptation of George ORWELL's *1984* (1984).

Burundi In east-central Africa, just south of the equator and across the Nile-Congo watershed, Burundi is a landlocked country with an area of 10,744 square miles. Twa (Batwa) pygmies were the earliest peoples of the Burundi forests. Hutu (Bahutu) cultivators settled in the 14th century but over the next two centuries were swept aside by Tutsi (Batutsi) herders, who made virtual serfs of the majority Hutu. Germany took control as a colonial power after 1884, merging Burundi with Rwanda (1899) and making Ruanda-Urundi part of German East Africa. Troops from the adjoining Belgian Congo occupied Ruanda-Urundi during WORLD WAR I, after which Belgium administered it under a LEAGUE OF NATIONS mandate and, from 1946, a UNITED NATIONS trusteeship. In 1959 Rwanda and Burundi were separated.

BURUNDI

1916	The region is occupied by Belgium during World War I.
1923	Belgium is granted a League of Nations mandate to administer Ruanda-Urundi.
1962	Burundi achieves independence.
1964	Rwanda withdraws from the Rwanda-Burundi currency union; fighting breaks out in the interior between Hutu and Tutsi, with the government supporting the Tutsi.
1965	In legislative elections Hutu win a majority in both houses but the king refuses to appoint a Hutu prime minister, dissolving the National Assembly and declaring an absolute monarchy; both Tutsi and Hutu groups attempt coups.
1966	Prince Charles deposes his father and is enthroned as Ntare V but is deposed after 89 days; Prime Minister Micombero becomes president of the newly proclaimed Republic of Burundi, with UPRONA as the sole official party.
1972	Ntare V is killed; fighting escalates into civil war between the poorly armed Hutu and government forces; an estimated 100,000 to 250,000 Hutu are killed, and approximately 400,000 refugees flee; Albin Nyamoya, a Tutsi, is named prime minister;.
1973	Hutu-Tutsi strife breaks out in neighboring Rwanda; Hutu begin guerrilla warfare against the Burundian army; Burundi receives aid from Libya; relations with Tanzania are strained as Burundian troops cross the border to attack Hutu camps there.
1976	Micombero is overthrown in a coup led by Lieutenant Colonel Jean-Baptiste Bagaza, who suspends the constitution of 1974, dissolves the National Assembly, and vests executive and legislative powers in a Supreme Revolutionary Council.
1987	President Bagaza is overthrown in a coup led by Pierre Buyoya.
1988	Renewed tribal disputes lead to the death of over 1,000 Tutsi and 100,000 Hutu.
1992	A new constitution is adopted.
1993	Melchior Ndadaye is elected the country's first Hutu president; a failed coup kills several ministers, and violence erupts between Tutsi and Hutu factions.
1996	The army seizes power in an attempt to restore peace; Major Pierre Buyoya is installed as president; the civil war between the Tutsi and Hutu continues.
2000	The government of Burundi and three Tutsi groups agree to a cease-fire, but the two major Hutu groups refuse to cooperate.
2001	Talks brokered by Nelson Mandela lead to the installation of a transitional, power-sharing government backed by a South African peacekeeping force carrying a UN mandate.
2005	Pierre Nkurunziza, a former Hutu rebel leader, is elected president.

The Parti de l'Unité et Progès National (UPRONA) won UN-supervised elections in September 1961, and Prince Louis Rwagasore became prime minister; he was assassinated less than a month later.

Burundi became an independent kingdom on July 1, 1962. By October 1965, when an attempted coup was crushed and thousands were killed, two more prime ministers had been assassinated. An army coup in November 1966 overthrew the monarchy, and Burundi became a republic under President Michel Micombero. The exiled former king, Mwami Ntare V, was killed in 1972 during an abortive coup attempt, which was blamed on the Hutu. About 100,000 Hutu died in the subsequent Tutsi crackdown, and thousands more fled (see BURUNDIAN CIVIL WAR OF 1972). Another military coup ousted Micombero in 1976, and Jean-Baptiste Bagaza became president, introducing some pro-Hutu reforms, although Tutsi dominance continued. Fellow Tutsi Pierre Buyoya deposed Bagaza in a September 3, 1987, coup; up to 20,000 Hutu were massacred by the Tutsi in August 1988, when ethnic fighting again flared up, resulting in many deaths and a (temporary) mass exodus of refugees, mostly Hutu, to Rwanda. Despite the creation of a new multiparty constitution in 1992 and the election of the first Hutu president, Melchior Ndadaye, in June 1993, Burundi was beset by more political disorder following the October 1993 assassination of Ndadaye and the 1994 death of his successor, Cyprien Ntaryamira, in a plane crash that also claimed the life of Rwanda's president. In 1995 the massacre of Hutu refugees in Rwanda helped precipitate the overthrow of Burundi's government by Pierre Buyoya, who established a transitional constitution in 1998 and continued to rule Burundi until April 2003, when Domitien Ndayizeye succeeded him. In 2005 Pierre Nkurunziza, a former rebel leader, was elected president.

Burundian Civil War of 1972

War between the Tutsi and Hutu ethnic groups in BURUNDI. They very tall Tutsi had long ago conquered the medium-height Hutu peasant farmers in east-central Africa. The Tutsi became the aristocratic ruling minority and held the Hutus in serfdom. When Burundi (which had been governed under a UN mandate since 1946) gained independence in 1962, a Tutsi monarchy was established. A struggle for power resulted in a military coup (1966), deposing the monarch and creating a republic, but with the Tutsi still in control. In 1970 the Hutu rebelled, massacring many Tutsi; most Hutu leaders were eventually executed. After a failed coup by the deposed monarch (1972), the Hutu attacked the Tutsi throughout Burundi. The government slaughtered over 100,000 Hutu to suppress the rebellion. About 10,000 Tutsi died, but they regained firm control of the country and put down another Hutu rebellion in 1973.

Busch, August Anheuser, Jr.

(1899–1989) American brewery and baseball executive. In 1946 Busch took control of his family's small, financially ailing St. Louis brewing firm, Anheuser-Busch and built it into the largest brewing operation in the world. The company's several brands included the world's top-selling beer, Budweiser. In Busch's 29 years as head of the company, Anheuser-Busch increased its production more than 12-fold and eventually became a major sponsor of sporting events worldwide. After his retirement in 1975, Busch remained active as president of the St. Louis Cardinals baseball team, which Anheuser-Busch had purchased in 1953. He was also a breeder of Clydesdale horses.

Busemann, Adolf (1901–1986)

German-born aerospace engineer. Busemann's design of the swept wing for aircraft helped make supersonic flight possible. After settling in the U.S. in 1947, he worked for the forerunner of the NATIONAL AERONAUTICS AND SPACE ADMINISTRATION and later for NASA itself. He designed a rotating space station for NASA and recommended the use of ceramic titles as heat shields on the SPACE SHUTTLE.

Bush, George Herbert Walker

(1924–   ) Forty-first president of the United States (1989–93). Bush was born into a prominent Connecticut family; his father, Prescott Bush, served as a U.S. senator (1952–63). Bush attended Phillips Academy in Andover, Massachusetts, before joining the navy in 1942. The youngest American pilot during WORLD WAR II, he was based on a carrier in the Pacific, saw combat and was shot down once. Bush won three Air Medals and the Distinguished Flying Cross. Discharged in 1945, he entered Yale University, where he completed his bachelor's degree in economics in two-and-a-half years and won Phi Beta Kappa honors. In 1948 Bush and his wife, Barbara Pierce Bush, moved to Texas, where he worked in the oil industry and eventually founded a number of successful businesses that made him wealthy. Bush entered politics in 1964, running unsuccessfully for a U.S. Senate seat, but in 1966 he won election to the U.S. House of Representatives. In his two consecutive terms in the House he compiled a generally conservative record and favored stringent environmental protection measures. In 1968 Bush was reportedly considered as a vice presidential running mate by Richard M. NIXON; he was apparently considered again in 1973, after the resignation of Vice President Spiro AGNEW; and again in 1974, when Gerald FORD had to name his own successor after Nixon resigned the presidency.

George Herbert Walker Bush, 41st president of the United States (LIBRARY OF CONGRESS, PRINTS AND PHOTOGRAPHS DIVISION)

Following his defeat (by Lloyd BENTSEN) in a second bid for the Senate (1970), Bush was appointed U.S. ambassador to the UNITED NATIONS. After the 1972 elections he was named chairman of the Republican National Committee. In September 1974 President Ford named Bush to head the U.S. Liaison Office in Beijing; although the U.S. and China did not have full diplomatic relations at the time, Bush was in effect ambassador. From late 1975 to January 1977, Bush headed the CIA and was credited with improving the agency's professionalism. Out of government during the CARTER administration, Bush was chairman of a Houston, Texas, bank. He announced his candidacy for the Republican presidential nomination in May 1979 and remained in the race longer than any of front-runner Ronald REAGAN's rivals. Bush caused a stir during one televised debate when he criticized Reagan's economic proposals as "voodoo economics." Nonetheless, Reagan chose Bush as his vice presidential running mate at the convention, and Bush served as vice president throughout Reagan's two presidential terms (1981–89).

Bush won the Republican presidential nomination in 1988 and defeated Democrat Michael DUKAKIS for the presidency after a bitter campaign. Bush promised to work for "a kinder, gentler nation" and urged a new spirit of public service and volunteerism. In office he largely continued Reagan's conservative policies but proved more willing to compromise with Congress. Domestically, much of his attention was devoted to dealing with the effects of the SAVINGS AND LOAN SCANDAL, which had caused many banks to collapse. Drugs, crime and education were also priorities on Bush's domestic agenda. However, the huge budget deficit and a new recession made his task difficult.

When IRAQ invaded and occupied KUWAIT in August 1990, Bush condemned Iraqi president Saddam HUSSEIN and acted decisively to counter this aggression. He announced **Operation Desert Shield**, sending more than 200,000 U.S. troops to Saudi Arabia to deter an Iraqi invasion of that country, but promised that the U.S. would not repeat the mistakes of the VIETNAM WAR. In November 1990 Bush doubled the number of U.S. personnel in the region, achieving a U.S. offensive capability. He rallied the UN to impose tough sanctions on Iraq and to declare a deadline (January 15, 1991) for Iraq's withdrawal from Kuwait. A UN resolution gave him a supranational authority to use force against Iraq after the deadline. When Iraq refused to comply, Bush ordered **Operation Desert Storm** to dislodge the Iraqis (see PERSIAN GULF WAR). On March 6, 1991, Bush addressed Congress and nation and proclaimed victory in the Gulf. He also announced a four-point plan for restoring peace and stability to the region, including a proposal that ISRAEL give up land in return for peace. At the end of the Gulf War, national polls put Bush's approval rating at over 90%—the highest ever recorded for any U.S. president. However, Bush's job approval ratings declined in 1991 and 1992 as the economy entered a minor recession. These economic woes, along with the unusually strong third-party candidacy of H. Ross PEROT, contributed to Bush's loss in the 1992 election to the Democratic nominee, Bill CLINTON. In 2000 Bush played a minor role on the campaign trail of his son George W. BUSH, in the latter's successful effort to gain the Republican nomination for president and win the election against Democrat Al GORE. In 2005 he was recruited to head, with former president Clinton, U.S. relief efforts for victims of the December 2004 tsunami that devastated the Indian Ocean basin.

Bush, George Walker (1946–) American politician, governor of Texas (1995–2001) and 43rd president of the United States (2001–). Born in Connecticut to George Herbert Walker BUSH and Barbara Bush, Bush did not exhibit an immediate interest in public office. After graduating from Yale University in 1968 with a B.A. in history, he signed up with the Texas Air National Guard to fulfill his military service during the VIETNAM WAR. However, his record as an Air Guardsman was mixed. While some superiors remarked favorably on his performance at Lackland Air Force Base (AFB) in San Antonio, Texas, and Moody AFB in Valdosta, Georgia, others claimed he was not particularly effective. After he left the Air National Guard in 1973, Bush enrolled in the Harvard Business School, where he received an M.B.A. in 1975. He then returned to Texas and worked in the oil industry as a "landman," a coordinator of oil exploration. Two years later he married Laura Welch and began an unsuccessful bid for a Texas seat in the U.S. House of Representatives. Following the defeat Bush focused on his career in the oil industry but failed repeatedly to sustain the several oil companies he founded (such as Arbusto Energy) or chaired (such as Spectrum 7), which purchased Arbusto (later renamed Bush Exploration) in 1984. It was not until 1986, when he joined Harken Energy Corporation as a consultant, that he began to have sustained success in the oil business. In the same year his wife confronted him about his addiction to alcohol and inspired her husband to curtail his drinking and adopt the Methodist faith. In 1987 Bush and his family moved to Washington, D.C., to work on his father's upcoming bid for the presidency. Bush functioned as an intermediary between the campaign staff and the Christian groups that the elder Bush relied on to capture the Republican nomination. After George H. W. Bush defeated Michael DUKAKIS, Bush worked on the transition team that assembled his father's prospective administration. When his father entered the Oval Office in 1989, Bush returned to Texas and became a minority owner and president of the Texas Rangers baseball franchise. He regularly served as a liaison between the Christian coalition that had supported his father's campaign and the first Bush administration (1989–93). When his father ran for reelection in 1992, George W. Bush again worked on his staff, resuming his role as intermediary with Christian political groups.

Following George H. W. Bush's defeat by Arkansas governor Bill CLINTON, Bush began to consider a bid for the governorship of Texas. After repeated conversations with business leaders and high-profile Republicans in the state, he announced his intention to take on Democratic governor Ann Richards in 1994. Despite Richards's receiving the endorsement of Texas billionaire and 1992 independent presidential candidate H. Ross PEROT, Bush won the election. Along with his efforts to build bipartisan support for such policies as welfare reductions and deregulation of Texas schools, the governor gained national attention for his support of the death penalty despite appeals on behalf of Karla Faye Tucker from Pope JOHN PAUL II and Christian televangelist Pat Robertson to spare a pickax murderer's life. In his reelection campaign in 1998, he defeated Democrat Garry Mauro with 69% of the popular vote largely due to his plan to increase teacher salaries and his aggressive courting of the Latino vote.

In June 1999, barely eight months after his reelection, Bush announced he would seek the Republican nomination for the 2000 presidential election. In a field of nine candidates, it soon became clear that only Arizona senator John MCCAIN possessed enough popular appeal to threaten Bush's candidacy. McCain soundly defeated Bush in the first head-to-head test in the New Hampshire primary. However, McCain withdrew from the race after Bush won primaries in California and other states, and at the Republican National Convention in July all his former primary opponents endorsed him. For his vice presidential running mate, Bush chose Dick CHENEY, who had been secretary of defense in his father's cabinet. In the campaign against the Democratic ticket of Al GORE and Joseph LIEBERMAN, Bush narrowly won the electoral vote and became the nation's 43rd president, despite losing the popular vote (see FLORIDA BALLOT CONTROVERSY, 2000). As president, Bush has been best known for his prosecution of the "war on terrorism" following the terrorist attacks on New York City and Washington, D.C., on SEPTEMBER 11, 2001. Bush organized an international coalition to destroy the training facilities of the terrorist group al-QAEDA, kill or capture its leaders and topple the TALIBAN government of AFGHANISTAN that harbored the group. In his 2002 State of the Union speech Bush vigorously denounced what he termed the "Axis of Evil"—the states of IRAQ, IRAN and NORTH KOREA, that were allegedly developing weapons of mass destruction (WMDs). In 2003 he led a coalition in an invasion of Iraq to overthrow Saddam HUSSEIN, citing the Iraqi dictator's links to al-Qaeda and his possession of WMDs. He also accelerated work on the creation of a missile defense system to protect the U.S. against missiles launched by "rogue states" such as North Korea. On domestic issues Bush has experienced more difficulties than in his prosecution of the war on terrorism. His proposal in 2001 for government funding of "faith-based initiatives"—social welfare programs organized by religious institutions—failed to gain congressional support. Also, his efforts to stimulate the economy following the stock market decline of 2000–01 through tax cuts created a large federal budget deficit while the unemployment rate remained at higher levels than previously until spring 2006. By the spring of 2004, opinion polls revealed a drop in public support for his policy in Iraq as he geared up for the presidential campaign. Bush defeated the Democratic candidate, Senator John KERRY of Massachusetts. At the outset of his second term, with a revamped cabinet, Bush pledged to work to bring democracy and freedom to Iraq and the Middle East and to reform SOCIAL SECURITY and the tax system domestically, but his approval rating continued to decline steadily, the public losing confidence with his handling of Hurricane KATRINA and the ongoing war in Iraq.

Bush, Vannevar *(1890–1974)* American engineer and public official. Bush earned his B.S. and M.S. degrees from Tufts College in 1913 and received his Ph.D. in engineering jointly from Harvard and the Massachusetts Institute of Technology in 1916. The following year he worked in a special navy antisubmarine laboratory. Bush joined MIT's faculty in 1919, becoming the institute's vice president and dean of the school of engineering in 1932. A prolific inventor, he designed a number of advanced mathematical analyzing instruments, including the differential analyzer, a forerunner of the computer. In 1939 he became president of the Carnegie Institution of Washington. In 1940 Bush served as chairman of the National Defense Research Committee (NDRC), formed at his suggestion to direct war-related scientific research. The following year he became chairman of the Office of Scientific Research and Development (OSRD), which included the NDRC.

Bush made no technical contribution to the war effort, but as an administrator he was responsible for the development of an array of new weapons, including RADAR, amphibious vehicles and the atomic bomb (see ATOMIC BOMB DEVELOPMENT). In June 1945 he advised President Harry S. TRUMAN to use the atomic bomb against Japan without prior warning. After the war Bush continued to serve on government policy committees. He prepared recommendations on ways in which wartime research could be applied to peace; "Science, the Endless Frontier," urged massive government support for basic research. His recommendations resulted in the establishment of the National Science Foundation in 1950. Bush opposed the development of the HYDROGEN BOMB and urged negotiations to end the arms race.

In the 1950s Bush was a vocal critic of abuses in security investigations, which he thought had retarded weapons research by undermining scientists' morale. He was particularly alarmed by the 1954 OPPENHEIMER security hearings. Because of Oppenheimer's prewar involvement with leftist groups and his postwar reservations about the development of the hydrogen bomb, President Dwight D. EISENHOWER ordered his security clearance suspended in late 1953 pending a hearing. Bush objected to the charges, urging that they be "redrafted in such a way as to remove all implication that Oppenheimer was being tried for his opinions." Bush declared that "useful men" were "denied the opportunity to contribute to our scientific efforts because of their youthful indiscretions." In an apparent reference to Senator Joseph R. MCCARTHY, he accused "ruthless, ambitious men" of using "our loyalty procedures for political purposes."

In 1957 Bush became chairman of the MIT Corporation and in 1959 its honorary chairman. He continued to write and lecture on national defense through the 1960s. In 1970 he and James CONANT received the Atomic Pioneers Award from the AEC.

Bushuyev, Konstantin D. *(1914–1978)* Soviet space scientist. Bushuyev was the director of the historic 1975 U.S.-Soviet APOLLO-SOYUZ TEST PROJECT, in which American astronauts and Soviet cosmonauts linked their spacecraft in orbit above the earth.

Busia, Kofi *(1913–1978)* Prime minister of Ghana (1969–72). Following Ghana's independence (1957), Busia was a leader of conservatives and a strong critic of the socialist prime minister Kwame NKRUMAH. He went into exile in the early 1960s. In September 1969 the military government that had deposed Nkrumah turned power over to Busia and his Progress Party. However, he was unable to solve Ghana's social and economic problems and was himself overthrown by the army while he was out of the country in January 1972. Busia went into exile in Great Britain.

Busignies, Henri Gaston *(1905–1981)* French-born electronic engineer and inventor. Busignies's 140 patented inventions included the first automatic direction finder for aircraft. His many innovations in aerial navigation, RADAR and other areas contributed significantly to the Allied military capability during WORLD WAR II. After the war he became chief scientist with the International Telephone and Telegraph Corporation (ITT).

busing Local government policy in the U.S. to promote racial integration by transporting schoolchildren by bus from predominantly white or black neighborhoods to racially mixed schools. Ordered by court decisions in the 1960s and 1970s, the policy has proven controversial and has attracted much hostility from members of both races.

Busoni, Ferrucio Benvenuto (1866–1924) Italian composer, pianist and music critic. Born of an Italian father and a German mother who were both musically gifted, Busoni was a piano prodigy who made his debut in Vienna at age eight. In addition to his acclaimed status as a concert performer throughout Europe and America, Busoni earned a reputation as a gifted composer who combined both classicism and romanticism in his works. His major compositions include *Piano Concerto* (1904) and *Indian Fantasy* (1913). Busoni also wrote *Sketch of a New Esthetic of Music* (1907), one of the earliest critical pieces to point toward the new compositional techniques that would emerge with Igor STRAVINSKY and his fellow modernists.

Bustamante, Sir (William) Alexander (1884–1977) Jamaican political leader and prime minister (1962–67). Taken to Spain as a child, he traveled extensively before returning to JAMAICA in 1932. There he became active in the trade union movement, making a name for himself with his fiery oratory. Jailed in 1941–42 for his union activities, he founded the Jamaican Labour Party, a relatively moderate political group, in 1943. Chief minister from 1953 to 1955, he was knighted in 1955, became prime minister in 1962 and welcomed Jamaican independence later that year. The voluble and flamboyant leader instituted ambitious public works and agrarian reform programs before his retirement in 1965.

Bustamante y Rivero, José Luis (1894–1989) Peruvian political leader. Bustamante was elected president of PERU in 1945 but was ousted three years later in a military coup. Following the coup, he taught law and served as a judge at the International Court of Justice in The HAGUE; he served as president of the court from 1967 to 1970.

Butenandt, Adolf Friedrich Johann (1903–1995) German organic chemist and biochemist. Butenandt took his first degree in chemistry at the University of Marburg and earned his doctorate in 1927 under Adolf Windaus at Göttingen, where he remained until 1933. Following the work of Windaus on cholesterol, Butenandt investigated the sex hormones and in 1929 isolated the first pure sex hor-

mone, estrone. (The compound was also discovered independently by Edward Doisy.) A search for the male sex hormone resulted in the isolation in 1931 of androsterone. In 1933 he became professor of organic chemistry at the Danzig Institute of Technology. There he demonstrated the similarities between the molecular structure of androsterone and cholesterol. His proposed structure for androsterone was confirmed by Leopold Ruzicka in 1934. Butenandt and Ruzicka synthesized the male hormone testosterone only months after its isolation in 1935. They were jointly awarded the NOBEL PRIZE in chemistry in 1939, but Butenandt was forbidden to accept it by the Nazi government. Butenandt was also the first to crystallize an insect hormone, ecdysone, and found that this too was a derivative of cholesterol. Later he led research on the isolation and synthesis of the pheromones. From 1936 to 1945 Butenandt was director of the Max Planck Institute for Biochemistry at Tubingen and from 1945 to 1956 professor of physiological chemistry there. He retained these posts when the institute moved to Munich in 1956, and in 1960 he succeeded Otto HAHN as president of the Max Planck Society.

Buthelezi, Mangosuthu Gatsha (1928–) Chieftain of the Buthelezi tribe, member of the South African parliament, and president of the INKATHA Freedom Party, a political party largely representing ethnic Zulus in SOUTH AFRICA. In 1953 he inherited the position of chieftain of the Buthelezi tribe. In 1970 the Assembly of KwaZulu, a political entity created by the APARTHEID South African government to increase the appearance of political agency among black South Africans, unanimously invited Buthelezi to assume the duties of chief executive officer of the Zulu Territorial Authority. In 1975 Buthelezi helped found and became president of the Inkatha Freedom Party, an anti-apartheid and pro-Zulu organization that served as an alternative to the AFRICAN NATIONAL CONGRESS (ANC). In 1976 he was selected as chief minister (the equivalent of a prime minister) of KwaZulu.

In the 1980s Buthelezi used his position as head of Inkatha and KwaZulu (also referred to as Zululand) to criti-

cize the apartheid system in South Africa. However, he also condemned the guerrilla tactics the ANC used in its struggle against the South African government and denounced the ANC's call for a multiethnic single state on the basis of "one man, one vote." Instead, Buthelezi advocated greater autonomy for the various ethnic groups throughout South Africa.

When apartheid rule ended in South Africa, Buthelezi became an important force in South African politics. As the head of the Inkatha Freedom Party, the second largest black-dominated party in South Africa, Buthelezi represents approximately 22% of South Africa's citizens. In recognition of his political power he was appointed minister of home affairs in 1994, and he has repeatedly served as acting president of South Africa. However, his past association with the KwaZulu Assembly and apartheid governments have subjected him to harsh criticism from the ANC.

Butler, Nicholas Murray (1862–1947) American educator who was awarded, jointly with Jane ADDAMS, the NOBEL PRIZE for peace in 1931. Butler, who was born in New Jersey and received a doctoral degree in philosophy from Columbia University in 1884, became one of the guiding voices of American education in the first half of the 20th century. He became president of Columbia University in 1901 and was the first to introduce education as a distinct field of study there. Butler became a major lobbying force behind the unified administration of public education in New York State. In 1910 he was instrumental in convincing steel magnate Andrew Carnegie to establish the Carnegie Endowment for International Peace. A conservative Republican, Butler became a controversial figure during World War I when he fired two Columbia faculty members in 1917 for their opposition to the Conscription Act. In the 1930s Butler was critical of American neutrality and urged economic unity for Europe.

Butler, Pierce (1866–1939) Associate justice, U.S. Supreme Court (1923–39). A graduate of Carleton College, Butler was admitted to the bar after reading law at a law firm. He was in private practice in St. Paul, Minnesota, when the federal government enlisted him to prosecute several antitrust cases. Butler's success enhanced his reputation, and in 1922 President Warren G. HARDING followed the advice of Chief Justice William Howard TAFT and nominated Butler to the Supreme Court. Selected at least in part, because he was a Roman Catholic, Butler's nomination had been challenged because of his close association with large railroads while he was in law practice. On the Court Butler did prove to be a supporter of big business and a foe of government regulation.

Butler, Richard Austen "Rab" (Baron Butler of Saffron Walden) *(1902–1982)* British statesman. He was a leading politician in Britain for half a century and the most influential figure in the reconstruction of the CONSERVATIVE PARTY after WORLD WAR II. During his career he served in top ministerial posts in seven Conservative governments. He was chancellor of the exchequer (1951–55), leader of the House of Commons (1955–61), home secretary (1957–62), foreign secretary (1963–64) and deputy prime minister (1962–63). He was first elected to Parliament in 1929. He was largely responsible for the India Act of 1935, which established greater constitutional freedom for INDIA by creating provincial legislatures. He supported Neville CHAMBERLAIN's MUNICH PACT with Adolf HITLER (1938). As minister of education (1941–45) he was responsible for the Education Act of 1944, which restructured secondary education in Britain and secured the right of free education for British children. A leading contender for prime minister in 1957 and 1963, he was defeated by Harold MACMILLAN and Alec DOUGLAS-HOME, respectively. He was made a life peer in 1965 and served as master of Trinity College, Cambridge (1965–78).

Butor, Michel *(1926–)* French novelist, literary critic and philosophical essayist. Butor came to prominence in the 1950s as one of the NOUVEAU ROMAN (new novel) school of postwar French novelists—also including Marguerite DURAS and Alain ROBBE-GRILLET—who had abandoned the traditional space-time plot conventions of the novel in favor of episodic disjunctions and philosophical explorations of the consciousness of the fictional characters. Butor's first novel was *Passage to Milan* (1954); other notable novels include *The Modification* (1957), *Degrees* (1960) and *Intervalle* (1973). He has also been active as a literary critic, producing a psychological study of 19th-century French poet Charles Baudelaire, *Histoire Extraordinaire* (1961), as well as analyses of Proust and of the nature of artistic creation. Beginning in 1963 Butor published several volumes of *Illustrations*, an ongoing "journal in-time."

Button, Richard Totten "Dick" *(1929–)* American figure skater. Button brought the first breath of athleticism to figure skating and was the first to perform a triple loop jump. He dominated the sport as no other had before him, holding the U.S. title from 1946 to 1952 and winning the world title five times from 1948 to 1952. He turned professional in 1953 and skated for some years with the Ice Capades. He later became known throughout the world as an insightful figure skating commentator.

buzz bomb See V-1 AND V-2 ROCKETS.

Byalik, Chaim Nachman *(1873–1934)* Russian-born Hebrew poet, essayist and story writer. Byalik's poem "Into the City of Slaughter" (1905) was written in reaction to the Kishinev POGROM; it is a moving account of human suffering and an admonition to the JEWS for their passivity under oppression. In 1924 Byalik settled in Palestine, where he was the leader of a cultural revival. He translated Shakespeare's *Julius Caesar* and Cervantes's *Don Quixote* into Hebrew and is regarded as the greatest modern Hebrew poet.

Byatt, A. S. See Margaret DRABBLE.

Bykova, Yelizaveta Ivanovna *(1913–1989)* Soviet chess player and economic planner. The women's world chess champion (1953–56 and 1958–62), she became an international chess master in 1953 and an honorary master of sport of the USSR.

Bykovsky, Valery *(1934–)* Soviet cosmonaut who made space history in June 1963, when he spent nearly five days alone in the *Vostok 5* spacecraft, the longest solo spaceflight up to that date. Bykovsky later commanded *Soyuz 22* (1976) and *Soyuz 31* (1978), both scientific missions.

Byrd, Harry Flood *(1887–1966)* Byrd was the scion of a Virginia line dating back to 1674. He left school at the age of 15 to restore his father's newspaper, the *Winchester Star,* to solvency, and at age 20 established his own newspaper in Martinsburg, West Virginia. In 1915 Byrd entered the Virginia state senate and within a decade was the dominant figure in Virginia politics. A master political technician, he served as Virginia's governor from 1926 to 1930. Appointed to the Senate in 1933 at the urging of President Franklin D. ROOSEVELT, Byrd ironically became one of the most bitter opponents of the NEW DEAL.

In the 1950s Byrd was one of the Senate's most influential members. He sat on the powerful Armed Services Committee and became chairman of the Finance Committee in 1955. In the presidential election of 1952 he refused to endorse the Democratic ticket headed by Adlai STEVENSON. In 1960 he opposed federal aid to education, federal aid for areas beset by chronic unemployment and an increase in the minimum wage and Medicare.

In the wake of the Supreme Court's 1954 ruling banning school SEGREGATION, Byrd moved to the forefront of the southern crusade to maintain segregation and STATES' RIGHTS. In March 1956 he helped mobilize the signing of the "Southern Manifesto," a rhetorical defiance of the Court signed by 101 southern members of Congress. A national symbol of unbudging resistance to integration, deficit-spending and the WELFARE STATE, Byrd received support in the presidential elections of 1956 and 1960. Byrd resigned from the Senate in November 1965; his son, Harry F. Byrd Jr., was appointed his successor.

Byrd, Richard Evelyn *(1888–1957)* American pilot, military officer and explorer. A member of Virginia's famous Byrd family, and brother of Harry Flood BYRD, Richard Byrd graduated from the U.S. Naval Academy in 1912 and served in WORLD WAR I. Forced in 1916 to resign from the navy with an injured leg, he joined its fledgling air arm. After the end of World War I he became interested in polar aviation. He joined the MacMillan expedition to the Arctic in 1924 and, with Floyd BENNETT, made the first flight over the NORTH POLE on May 9, 1926. Byrd then became interested in Antarctic exploration, leading his first expedition there in 1928. He established a based camp, Little America, on the Ross Ice Shelf and, in 1929, flew over the SOUTH POLE. The Antarctic was the largest unmapped and unexplored area of the world, and Byrd contributed greatly to opening up and mapping the continent. A more extensive expedition was undertaken in 1933–35, during which Byrd spent five months alone at an Antarctic weather station; there were three more expeditions, the last in 1955–56. A large section of the Antarctic was named Marie Byrd Land, after his wife.

Byrds, The American folk-country-rock band. The original band lineup was Roger McGuinn, vocals, guitar; Gene Clark, vocals, percussion, guitar; Christ Hillman, bass, mandolin, vocals; Michael Clarke, drums; and David Crosby, guitar, vocals. The band's pedigree, via various members, included the Limelighters, the Scottsville Squirrel Barkers, the Hillmen and the New Christy Minstrels. In 1965 they hit number-one on both sides of the Atlantic with a cover of Bob DYLAN's "Mr. Tambourine Man." The group charted with two other covers, "All I Really Want to Do" and "Turn, Turn, Turn." By 1966 the group's personnel began to shift, with Clark departing. Crosby left the following year, which also saw the release of *Younger Than Yesterday*. Gram Parsons was part of the Byrds for the 1968 albums *Notorious Byrd Brothers* and *Sweetheart of the Rodeo*. The group dissolved for good in 1973, having introduced a shot of country music into mainstream rock. McGuinn, Clark and Hillman would resurface in 1979 as the group McGuinn, Clark and Hillman.

Byrnes, James Francis (*1879–1972*) American lawyer, politician and government official. A leading Democrat, Byrnes had a long and distinguished career at the highest levels of government. He served as U.S. representative from South Carolina (1911–25), U.S. senator (1931–40), South Carolina state supreme court justice (1941–42), director of war mobilization (1942–45), U.S. secretary of state (1945–47) and governor of South Carolina (1951–55). President Franklin D. ROOSEVELT described the powerful Byrnes as "assistant president" during WORLD WAR II. He attended the YALTA CONFERENCE (1944) and the POTSDAM CONFERENCE (1945). However, his tenure as secretary of state was stormy. Byrnes was often at odds with the TRUMAN administration and Congress on foreign and domestic policy and on the way he handled his job. As governor of South Carolina, he championed STATES' RIGHTS, favored school segregation and opposed the Supreme Court's decision In BROWN V. BOARD OF EDUCATION (1954).

C

Cabaret Long-running Broadway musical show and ACADEMY AWARD–winning motion picture. The songs, by John Kander and Fred Ebb, and the book, by Joe Masteroff, signaled a shift from the conventional musicals of the 1950s to the edgy and raffish style of the 1960s. "It mocked emotion and emphasized decadence and immorality in its depiction of the mood of pre-Nazi Germany," writes historian Abe Laufe; but it intrigued theater-goers and had "a morbid fascination for others." The source was John VAN DRUTEN's adaptation of a number of stories by Christopher ISHERWOOD about a young writer, Clifford, living in Berlin during the pre-Hitler era. Van Druten's *I AM A CAMERA* opened on Broadway in 1951 with Julie Harris in the leading role of Clifford's pregnant girlfriend, Sally Bowles (a nightclub entertainer). Kander and Ebb's musical version, *Cabaret,* opened on November 12, 1966, at Broadway's Broadhurst Theater. It ran for a total of 1,166 performance and garnered 10 Tony Awards as well as the Critics' Circle Award as best musical for 1966–67. The cast included Grey as the Master of Ceremonies, Jill Haworth as Sally, Bert Convy as Cliff, Jack GILFORD as Schulz and Lotte LENYA as Fraulein Schneider. Grey repeated his role in the Bob FOSSE film adaptation (1972), which starred Liza Minnelli as Sally and received eight Oscars.

Cabinda (Kabinda) District and town on the Atlantic Ocean, in an enclave north of the Congo River; sequestered from the rest of Angola by a span of Zaire's (now Democratic Republic of Congo) coastline. Cabinda actively supported the Angolan effort for independence from Portugal (see ANGOLAN WAR OF INDEPENDENCE). After liberation in 1975, some local residents wanted Cabinda to become a separate nation so that it could retain its copious oil reserves.

Caesar, Sid *(1922–)* American comedian and actor. Born in Yonkers, New York, he initially displayed an interest in the music performing industry when he joined the Shep Fields Band as a teenager and studied saxophone at New York's prestigious Julliard School of Music. His music studies ended when he enlisted in the U.S. Coast Guard during WORLD WAR II. During his service with the Coast Guard, he participated in efforts to entertain the servicemen and-women by appearing in a 1945 stage show called *Tars and Spars;* Caesar also appeared in the film version of the show the following year.

At the end of the war Caesar worked in various nightclubs in which he performed his comedy and music routine. In 1949 he developed a television variety show—a program composed of many short performances and skits—for NBC called *Admiral Broadway Revue* that starred Imogene Coca. In 1950 the show was renamed *Your Show of Shows;* it ran for four additional years featuring comics like Coca, Woody ALLEN and Mel BROOKS. In 1952 Caesar earned a Best Actor Emmy for his performance as lead on the show. However, after the show ended in 1954, Caesar's career declined despite the appearance of another television variety program called *Caesar's Hour* between 1955 and 1957. Seeking another outlet for his talents, Caesar began to appear in motion pictures, such as *It's a Mad, Mad, Mad, Mad World* (1963), *Grease* (1978) and *The History of the World Part I* (1981). In 1985, in recognition of his contribution to television comedy, Caesar entered the Television Hall of Fame.

Caetano, Marcello *(1906–1980)* Prime minister of Portugal (1968–74). A minister under Antonio de Oliveira SALAZAR in the 1940s and 1950s, Caetano retired from politics in 1959 to become rector of the University of Lisbon. He was recalled as prime minister on Salazar's retirement in 1968. He was more inclined than his predecessor to favor social change; however, his conservative pace for implementing reforms led to a left-wing military coup in 1974 that sent him into exile in Brazil and brought an end to Portugal's colonial empire in Africa. (See also ANGOLAN WAR OF INDEPENDENCE.)

Cage, John Milton *(1912–1992)* American composer, self-styled Zen philosopher, social anarchist and tinkerer in sounds. The son of an inventor, Cage was born in Los Angeles. In 1934, at age 22, he went to the University of California, Los Angeles, to study with composer Arnold SCHOENBERG.

Experiments in the 12-tone (see SERIAL MUSIC) techniques led to such early works as the "Six Short Inventions" (1933). Other influences included the concepts of "organized sound" of Edgard VARESE and the tone clusters of Henry Cowell. After teaching at the Cornish School in Seattle, Cage began presenting concerts of his works in the 1940s. Renown and notoriety followed him everywhere. He developed the "prepared piano," attaching metal and fiber objects to the strings in order to produce new and unusual sounds ("Sonatas and Interludes," 1946–48). He scored music for unlikely sound-producing artifacts. "Imaginary Landscape, No. 4" (1951) was scored for 12 radios and 24 "players." "Water Music" (1952) instructed the pianist to use a radio, whistle, water containers and a deck of cards during the performance. Cage attached microphones to house furniture. He even experimented with producing no sounds at all. His famous "Four Minutes 33 Seconds" (1952) presented a pianist sitting motionless before a closed piano for the prescribed period of time. Throughout the 1960s he presented multimedia HAPPENINGS, interfacing audience and performers. After numerous appointments and honors, including membership in the National Institute of Arts and Letters (1968) and the chair of Charles Eliot Norton Professor of Poetry at Harvard (1988–89), Cage continued his radical reorganization of traditional concepts of creativity and expression. His "change" music short-circuits the composer's intent and substitutes spontaneous operations as determinates of the sequencing of sounds. This he derived from studying the *I Ching* (the Chinese *Book of Changes*).

Cagney, James *(1899–1986)* American actor of Irish decent, Cagney rose from the streets of New York City to become one of the greatest stars of HOLLYWOOD's Golden Age. He became an overnight sensation with the 1931 release of *The Public Enemy,* in which he portrayed a gangster. He followed that film with a series of gangster films interspersed with musicals. He won his only ACADEMY AWARD for the 1942 musical *Yankee Doodle Dandy,* in which he portrayed songwriter George M. COHAN. Other memorable roles were in *Angels with Dirty Faces* (1938), *White Heat*

(1949) and *Mister Roberts* (1955). After appearing in more than 60 films, he retired from the screen in 1961. He came out of retirement in 1981 to appear in Milos FORMAN's *Ragtime*. His last appearance was in the television movie *Terrible Joe Moran* (1984).

Cahiers du cinéma The most influential journal of film criticism in the 20th century, founded in 1951 by the French film critics André Bazin, Jacques Doniol-Valcroze and Lo Duca. Edited primarily by Bazin until his death in 1958, *Cahiers* broke with the traditional approach of film criticism that habitually valued "art" films over "commercial" HOLLYWOOD productions. Instead, *Cahiers* proclaimed the directorial genius of certain commercial filmmakers, especially Alfred HITCHCOCK. Another critical approach championed by *Cahiers* was the "auteur" theory that directors—not actors, scriptwriters or producers—are the governing force in the making of a film. *Cahiers* also featured the critical writings of a number of young French film enthusiasts—such as Claude CHABROL, Jean-Luc GODARD, Eric ROHMER, and François TRUFFAUT—who would shortly thereafter emerge as leading directors in the French Nouvelle Vague (New Wave) cinema of the 1960s.

Cahn, Sammy (Samuel Cohen) *(1913–1993)* American lyricist and librettist. Cahn first gained success in the 1940s writing for films and Broadway (for example, *High Button Shoes,* 1947) with composer Jule STYNE. He also collaborated with Johnny Burke and Jimmy van HEUSEN. Cahn won ACADEMY AWARDS for his lyrics to "Three Coins in the Fountain," "All the Way" and "High Hopes"—the latter was used as John F. KENNEDY's campaign theme in 1960. Frank SINATRA recorded many Cahn songs, such as "Saturday Night Is the Loneliest Night of the Week." The Broadway show *Words and Music* (1974) was a retrospective devoted entirely to Cahn's lyrics.

Caillaux, Joseph-Marie-Auguste *(1863–1944)* French statesman. A tax inspector and son of a former cabinet minister, he was elected to the Chamber of Deputies in 1898. He was soon made minister of finance (1899) and

served in that post at various times over the next 36 years. Among his financial reforms was an extremely unpopular income tax. During his brief tenure as premier (1911–12), Caillaux reached a settlement with GERMANY over MOROCCO that was as unpopular as his tax proposals and led to his resignation. While again serving as finance minister, he was involved in a scandal when his wife assassinated a Parisian newspaper editor in 1914. A pacifist, he was imprisoned by the CLEMENCEAU government after the outbreak of WORLD WAR I and was deprived of his civil rights. After a 1924 amnesty he served as minister of finance under Paul Painlevé (1925) and Aristide BRIAND (1925), serving in that post for the last time in 1935. Losing his seat in the Chamber of Deputies in 1919, he was elected to the Senate in 1925, remaining there until his death.

Cain, James Mallahan *(1892–1977)* American novelist. Cain stands alongside Raymond CHANDLER and Dashiell HAMMETT as one of the great American writers of mystery and thriller fiction. Cain's novels were both widely read and critically acclaimed and were frequently adapted into Hollywood films. Cain was particularly noted for his extremely spare and hard-boiled style. His best-known novel is *The Postman Always Rings Twice* (1934), which was adapted into a 1946 film starring John Garfield and Lana Turner. A 1981 remake starred Jessica Lange and Jack NICHOLSON. Other novels by Cain include *Double Indemnity* (1936), *Serenade* (1937), *Mildred Pierce* (1941), *The Butterfly* (1947), *The Moth* (1948), *Root of His Evil* (1954), *Magician's Wife* (1965) and *Rainbow's End* (1977).

Caine, Sir Michael (Maurice Joseph Micklewhite) *(1933–)* British film actor. Born into a poor Cockney family, Caine played small roles in over 30 films from 1956 to 1963. Although he received attention from a supporting role in *Zulu* (1963) and the starring role of Harry Palmer in *The Ipcress File* (1965), it was his portrayal of the charming, self-centered *Alfie* (1966) that made him a star. Despite the box-office failure of many of his films, Caine is praised by critics for his versatility and craft. He received ACADEMY AWARD nominations for *Alfie* and *Sleuth* (1972)

British actor Michael Caine (PHOTOFEST)

and won as best supporting actor for *Hannah and Her Sisters* (1986) and *The Cider House Rules* (1999). Other memorable films include *The Man Who Would Be King* (1976), *Dressed to Kill* (1980), *Death Trap* (1982) and *Educating Rita* (1983). In 2001 Caine was knighted by Queen Elizabeth II.

Cairo Conference Conference of Allied leaders in Cairo, Egypt, November 22–26, 1943, during WORLD WAR II to discuss the war in Asia. After the conference U.S. president Franklin D. ROOSEVELT, British prime minister Winston CHURCHILL, and Chinese leader CHIANG KAI-SHEK issued a declaration on December 1 demanding JAPAN's unconditional surrender to end the war in Asia. Japan was to be forced back to its 1894 boundaries; Formosa was to be restored to CHINA and the Japanese presence in KOREA and MANCHURIA was to be ended.

Calder, Alexander *(1898–1976)* American sculptor. Calder received a degree in mechanical engineering at Hoboken, New Jersey's Stevens Institute of Technology (1919) and later studied at the Art Students League, New York (1923–26). Traveling widely in the U.S., Latin America, India and Europe, he arrived in Paris in 1928 and was influenced by the constructivism of Naum GABO, the severe structure and primary colors of Piet MONDRIAN, the organic forms of Jean ARP and the playfulness and coloristic bravura of Joan MIRÓ. Forsaking the fanciful representational wire sculpture typical of his early work (such as the small 1925 *Zoo* now at New York's

Museum of Modern Art), he created a new form of sculpture—christened "mobiles" by Marcel DUCHAMP. First shown in 1932, these sheet-metal and wire constructions mingled the principles of mechanics with the images of abstract art. Calder's mobiles are brightly-colored or black sheet-metal cutouts in organic shapes, attached by wires, finely balanced and set in motion by currents of air. From the 1950s on, he also produced a series of monumental "stabiles," constructed of sheet metal, in soaring but firmly ground-based sculptures. Calder was also a gifted printmaker and book illustrator and created a number of notable stage sets.

Caldwell, Erskine *(1903–1987)* American author and journalist. Although he had gained a modest reputation from his early short stories, Caldwell achieved notoriety with the successful staging in 1935 of his first novel, *Tobacco Road* (1932). He continued writing stories and novels about the lives of poor black and white farmers in the deep South, which include *God's Little Acre* (1933; filmed 1958), *The Sure Hand of God* (1947) and the memoir *Deep South: Memory and Observation* (1980).

Caldwell, (Janet Miriam) Taylor *(1900–1985)* Anglo-American novelist who also wrote under the pseudonyms Marcus Holland and Max Reiner. A prolific author of popular fiction, Caldwell's first novel, *Dynasty of Death* (1938), a family saga rife with intrigue and romance, is typical of her work. Though some praise her narrative ability, she has never received critical acclaim for her literary style. Other titles include *Captains and the Kings* (1972), *Bright Flows the River* (1978) and *Answer as a Man* (1981).

Calkins, Mary Whiton *(1863–1930)* American philosopher and psychologist. A graduate of Smith College (1885), Calkins taught Greek at Wellesley College. Later she studied at Clark University and Harvard and returned to Wellesley to teach philosophy and psychology (1890–1926). Her experimental research and publications in both fields revolved around her interpretations of the psyche and reality. She published more than 100 articles

and several books, the most influential of which were *The Persistent Problems of Philosophy* (1907) and *The Good Man and the Good* (1918).

Callaghan, (Leonard) James (baron Callaghan of Cardiff) *(1912–2005)* British prime minister (1976–79). The son of a naval chief petty officer, Callaghan was educated at Portsmouth and joined the Inland Revenue in 1929. He served in the navy throughout World War II and was elected as a Labour member of Parliament in 1945. He served as parliamentary secretary in the Ministry of Transport (1947–50) and as financial secretary to the Admiralty (1950–51). In 1963 he was defeated by Harold WILSON for leadership of the LABOUR PARTY. Callaghan went on to become chancellor of the exchequer (1964–67) and home secretary (1967–70). As foreign secretary (1974–76) he renegotiated Britain's membership in the EUROPEAN ECONOMIC COMMUNITY. When Wilson retired, Callaghan narrowly defeated Michael FOOT as head of the Labour Party and served as prime minister from 1976 to 1979. Economic instability and widespread strikes in 1978 and early 1979 (the so-called Winter of Discontent) caused the House of Commons to force an election in May 1979, when Callaghan was defeated by Margaret THATCHER. Callaghan resigned the Labour Party leadership in 1980 and in 1985 declared he would not run again for Parliament. Following his retirement from the House of Commons in 1987, Callaghan was awarded a life peerage.

Callas, Maria *(1924–1977)* American opera singer. Considered one of the great sopranos of the post–World War II era, Callas was especially noted for her precise diction, musical phrasing and dramatic intensity in the bel canto operas of Donizetti, Bellini, and Rossini. Of Greek heritage, she studied at the Royal Conservatory in Athens and joined the Royal Opera in 1942, making her debut in *Tosca.* Her first great success was in *Tristan and Isolde* in Venice (1947). She married businessman Giovanni Battista Meneghini in 1949 and joined La Scala Opera in Milan in 1950. She made her Metropolitan Opera debut in 1956 in *Norma,* one of her most famous roles. She also gained renown for her heroines

Lucia di Lammermoor and PUCCINI's *Tosca.* A celebrity even among the non-opera-going public, Callas was known for her fiery temper and her stormy personal relationships.

Calles, Plutarco Elías *(1877–1945)* Mexican politician and president (1924–28). An active figure in the complex Mexican politics of the 1910s–30s, Calles began as a revolutionary. He was governor of the state of Sonora (1915–19) and secretary of the interior (1920–24). He played an important role in the MEXICAN CIVIL WAR OF 1920 and was subsequently secretary of the interior in the revolutionary government of Alvaro Obregón. As president, Calles's actions against the Roman Catholic Church led to the MEXICAN INSURRECTIONS OF 1926–1929. He became increasingly conservative and remained a powerful figure even out of office. He was exiled in 1936 but allowed to return to Mexico in 1941.

Calley, William L. See MY LAI MASSACRE.

Calloway, Cabell "Cab" *(1907–1994)* American bandleader, singer and composer. Born in Rochester, New York, Calloway worked as a singer, musician and bandleader in Baltimore, Chicago, New York and elsewhere before becoming leader of the band the Missourians in 1930. In New York, Calloway's band played at the Savoy and the Cotton Club, scoring a hit in 1931 with "Minnie the Moocher." The band began to tour, and their hits during this period included the 1939 million-seller "Jumpin' Jive." Calloway quit the big band in 1948. In 1952 he sang the role of Sportin' Life in a revival of *PORGY AND BESS,* then toured with the production for many years. He appeared in Broadway shows and in films and entertained in other capacities through the 1980s.

Calvin, Melvin *(1911–1997)* American biochemist. Calvin studied chemistry at the Michigan College of Mining and Technology and earned his B.S. degree in 1931. After obtaining his Ph.D. from the University of Minnesota in 1935, he spent two years at the Victoria University of Manchester, England, working with Michael Polanyi. There he became interested in chlorophyll and its role in the photosynthetic process in plants. In 1937 Calvin began a long association with the University of California, Berkeley. From 1941 to 1945 he worked on scientific problems connected with the war, including two years on the MANHATTAN PROJECT. In 1946 Calvin became director of the Bio-organic Division of the Lawrence Radiation Laboratory at Berkeley, where he used the new analytical techniques developed during the war to investigate the "dark reactions" of photosynthesis—those reactions that do not need the presence of light. This work earned Calvin the NOBEL PRIZE in chemistry in 1961. Calvin remained at Berkeley as director of the Laboratory of Chemical Biodynamics (1960–63), professor of molecular biology (1963–71) and professor of chemistry (1971).

Calvino, Italo *(1923–1985)* Italian novelist and short story writer. Calvino was widely considered one of the major figures in contemporary world literature. His earliest published stories, which were in a realistic mode, appeared shortly after World War II. He later made increasing use of allegory and fantasy, his reputation largely accruing from his work as an experimental writer. His best-known works were *Cosmicomics* (1965), *Invisible Cities* (1972) and *Italian Folktales* (1956), a retelling of traditional stories.

Cambodia Located in the southwest of INDOCHINA, in Southeast Asia, Cambodia covers 69,880 square miles. A French colony, Cambodia was occupied by Japanese forces in late 1940, who left the pro-VICHY colonial administration intact. In April 1941 the French authorities placed 18-year-old Prince Norodom SIHANOUK on the Cambodian throne. In early 1945 the Japanese attempted to foster local support by offering limited independence to Cambodia, VIETNAM and LAOS. A few weeks later Sihanouk was pressured into proclaiming his country's independence. After Japan's surrender in 1945, the French returned to Cambodia, and in 1946 the absolute monarchy was abolished. A constitution was introduced in 1947 that permitted popular political activity. However, by 1950 anti-French rebels controlled large areas of the countryside. Sihanouk abolished the National Assembly and declared martial law in early 1953 before embarking on a "royal crusade for independence." The French, facing an increasingly stiff military test in Vietnam and Laos conceded Cambodia's independence (No-

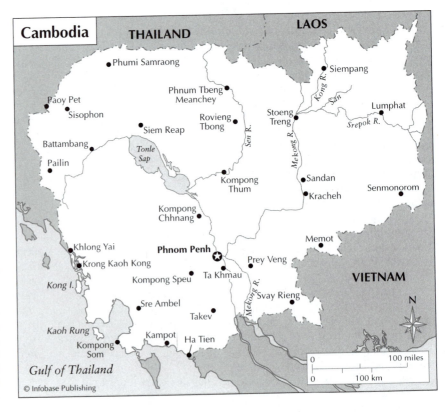

CAMBODIA

1940	Japanese occupy Cambodia.
1941	Prince Norodom Sihanouk assumes throne.
1945	Sihanouk proclaims Cambodian independence.
1953	France recognizes Cambodian independence.
1970	Right-wing coup by Marshal Lon Nol.
1975	Khmer Rouge forces capture Phnom Penh.
1975–78	Pol Pot's reign of terror kills millions of Cambodians.
1978	Vietnam invades Cambodia; pro-Vietnamese government installed.
1989	Vietnamese withdraw from Cambodia.
1991	Peace agreement ends civil war and sets timetable for national elections.
1993	Elections are held; Prince Sihanouk resumes the throne at the head of a coalition government.
1997	Co-prime minister Hun Sen ousts rival, Prince Norodom Ranariddh, in a coup.
1998	The last of the Khmer Rouge holdouts surrender to the government; Pol Pot dies while under house arrest; Hun Sen wins parliamentary elections and is sworn in as prime minister.
2001	The Senate passes a law requiring the creation of a tribunal to bring genocide charges against Khmer Rouge leaders.
2004	Norodom Sihanomi is crowned king; the Cambodian People's Party (CPP) and Funcinpek form coalition and take control of the national assembly.

vember 9, 1953). Sihanouk's royal government was accorded international recognition at the 1954 Geneva Conference. To avoid constitutional constraints on his rule, Sihanouk abdicated in 1955. His newly created political party won an overwhelming victory in national elections that year.

As head of state Sihanouk attempted to preserve Cambodia's neutrality during the VIETNAM WAR. He approved both the establishment of Vietnamese communist sanctuaries in eastern Cambodia and America's clandestine bombing of these bases. Eventually, external pressures destabilized Sihanouk's government. In March 1970 LON NOL and Sirik Matik led a right-wing coup and renamed the country the Khmer Republic. In response, Sihanouk forged an alliance with his former communist enemies, the radical KHMER ROUGE, and formed a government-in-exile in Beijing. In April 1975 PHNOM PENH fell to the Khmer Rouge.

Severing the country's links with the outside world (except China and North Korea), the new government embarked on an economic and social experiment modeled on China's GREAT LEAP FORWARD of the late 1950s. The experiment failed and hundreds of thousands of people died from brutal treatment, starvation and disease. In 1978 an ultranationalist faction led by POL POT and Ieng Sary gained full control of the revolution. Villages and communes previously under Pol Pot opponents were subjected to ferocious purges; the population of Phnom Penh was forcibly removed to the countryside in order to work on the land.

Border clashes between Cambodia and Vietnam broke out in May 1975. After organizing anti–Pol Pot refugees into a United Front, Vietnamese troops swept into Cambodia in late December 1978; Pol Pot's forces were driven toward the Thai border. On January 10, 1979, the People's Republic of Kampuchea (PRK) was proclaimed by members of the United Front and other (Hanoi-based) Khmer exiles. Western pressure ensured that Pol Pot's regime retained its UN seat, but unease over his genocidal record led to the formation of the Coalition Government of Democratic Kampuchea (CGDK) in 1982, once again bringing together the Khmer Rouge and Sihanouk. The CGDK guerrilla forces on the Thai border were routed by Vietnam in 1984–85. In late 1987 Sihanouk and PRK premier Hun Sen held talks in France. In late 1989 Vietnam withdrew the last of its armed forces from the country. The withdrawal heralded a period of increased fighting between the various Khmer protagonists. In 1991 an agreement ended the conflict between factions supporting the continued rule of Hun Sen and those supporting the return of Sihanouk. Two years later a coalition government emerged, in which Sihanouk's son, Prince Norodom Ranriddh, served as prime minister, and Hun Sen of the Cambodian People's Party (CPP) as deputy prime minister. The coalition disintegrated in 1997 when Hun Sen overthrew Ranriddh and tried him in absentia. In the same year the Khmer Rouge tried and sentenced Pol Pot to life imprisonment, but he died of natural causes the following year. The royalist party Funcinpec and the CPP have since remained rivals for political power in Cambodia. Norodom Sihamoni, also a son of Sihanouk, is the constitutional monarch.

Cambodian Civil War of 1970–1975
Cambodia became involved in the VIETNAM WAR when its ruler, Prince Norodom SIHANOUK, tolerated communist infiltration and permitted North Vietnam to supply its forces in South Vietnam through the port of Sihanoukville and the HO CHI MINH TRAIL.

When Sihanouk closed the port in 1970, North Vietnamese troops began to aid the KHMER ROUGE in their fight against him. A pro-Western coup led by General LON NOL overthrew Sihanouk when he was abroad in March 1970. Lon Nol demanded North Vietnamese withdrawal. In support, American and South Vietnamese forces attacked enemy sanctuaries in Cambodia, and U.S. bombing raids increased. Nevertheless, North Vietnamese and Khmer Rouge control advanced steadily; PHNOM PENH, the capital, was frequently shelled and besieged between 1972 and 1975 and fell to the Khmer Rouge on April 16, 1975. Cambodia was renamed Democratic Kampuchea. The new government evacuated inhabitants from Phnom Penh in a terror campaign that left about 1 million dead from executions, starvation and forced marches. (See also POL POT.)

Cambon brothers Jules (Martin) Cambon (1845–1935) and **(Pierre) Paul Cambon** (1843–1924) were French diplomats. Brilliant practitioners of statecraft, the Cambon brothers played major parts in the international politics of their day. Both were born in Paris. Jules was governor general of Algeria (1891–96), where he helped to promote Algerian autonomy. He then served as ambassador to U.S. (1897–1902), where he was important in beginning the peace process that ended the Spanish-American War. He subsequently assumed ambassadorial posts to Madrid (1902–07) and Berlin (1907–14). A delegate to the PARIS PEACE CONFERENCE in 1919, from 1920 to 1922 he was chairman of one of the key commissions that enforced the provisions of the Treaty of VERSAILLES. Paul Cambon began his career as resident minister to Tunis in 1882. He was ambassador to Madrid (1886–91), Constantinople (1891–98) and London (1898–1920), where he encouraged English cooperation with France and Russia and helped to engineer the ANGLO-FRENCH ENTENTE of 1904 and the Anglo-Russian agreement of 1907. Both Cambon brothers were known as diplomats of the utmost subtlety and skill.

Camel News Caravan One of the first nightly news programs in American television, the 10-minute show began on NBC in 1948 as *Camel Newsreel Theatre* (the name was changed within a year), with a boutonniered John Cameron Swayze as news anchor. Adapting the formula of the standard theatrical newsreel, it contained several filmed items from FOX Movietone crews stationed in principal news centers. Swayze kept the pace brisk with his famous: "Now, let's go hopscotching the world for headlines!" Within the next four years the standard formula of the nightly newscast had taken shape. Correspondents reporting from other cities were added (a device borrowed from radio news formats), and NBC organized its own film crews. As influential as the program was, writes historian Erik Barnouw, it also represented a diminution of the coverage that had been standard in radio: "The camera, as arbiter of news value, had introduced a drastic curtailment of the scope of news . . . Analysis, a staple of radio news in its finest days, was being shunted aside as non-visual." Further, the sponsor, Camel Cigarettes, influenced the show; for example, it forbade the depiction of "No Smoking" signs and personages who smoked cigars. Swayze and the program were dropped when the *Huntley-Brinkley Report* took over on NBC in October 1956.

Cameron, Sir Gordon Roy (*1899–1966*) Australian pathologist. The son of a Methodist minister, Cameron studied medicine at Melbourne University, graduating in 1922. He worked first at the university and then at the Walter and Eliza Hall Institute before leaving for Europe in 1927 to do postgraduate work at Freiburg. Shortly afterward he was appointed to the staff of University College Hospital, London, where he served as professor of morbid anatomy from 1937 until his retirement in 1964. Cameron worked on a wide range of problems including pulmonary edema, inflammation and the pathology of the spleen and liver. His *Pathology of the Cell* (1952) was a major survey of all aspects of the field.

Cameron, James (*1911–1985*) British journalist and television commentator. Cameron was perhaps the best-known British foreign correspondent of his era. One of his first major assignments was to cover the first postwar atomic bomb test at BIKINI atoll in the Pacific Ocean (see ATOMIC BOMB DEVELOPMENT). The experience prompted him to become a founding member of the CAMPAIGN FOR NUCLEAR DISARMAMENT (CND). An avowed socialist, he was the first Western correspondent to tour North Vietnam after the U.S. began bombing the country in 1965 (see VIETNAM WAR). His reports from Hanoi, published simultaneously in the London *Evening Standard* and the *New York Times,* helped fuel the ANTIWAR MOVEMENT of the 1960s.

Cameroon (*French:* Cameroun; *German:* Kamerun)** Republic on the Bight of Biafra, southeast of Nigeria. During the 19th century Britain exercised commercial control over the coastal area but was later deposed by Germany. Germany's colony was occupied during WORLD WAR I by France and Britain; in 1919 the territory was taken from Germany, assigned to Great Britain and France as a mandate under the LEAGUE OF NATIONS and was split into French and British districts. The French district became independent on January 1, 1960. In 1961 the northern division of the British district joined with NIGERIA, while the southern division fused with the self-governing Cameroon. Ahmadou AHIDJO served as president from 1961 to 1982. There was much political unrest during the 1980s. In a bizarre natural disaster, as many as 2,000 people were killed when toxic gas spewed from a volcanic lake on August 21, 1986. In 1994 and 1996 repeated border clashes between Cameroonian and Nigerian forces over the Bakasi Peninsula led to UN mediation that resulted in an August 2003 decision by Nigeria to cede the peninsula to Cameroon. Paul Biya, president since 1982, has been criticized as being a strongman, but was reelected to a seven-year term in 2004, despite claims of electoral fraud.

Campaign for Nuclear Disarmament (CND) Movement to promote the abandonment of nuclear weapons and a reduction in British defense spending. The CND was founded in Great Britain in 1958 by philosopher Bertrand RUSSELL and Canon L. John Collins. The movement reached its peak in 1960–61, when it attracted many thousands of adherents, and it

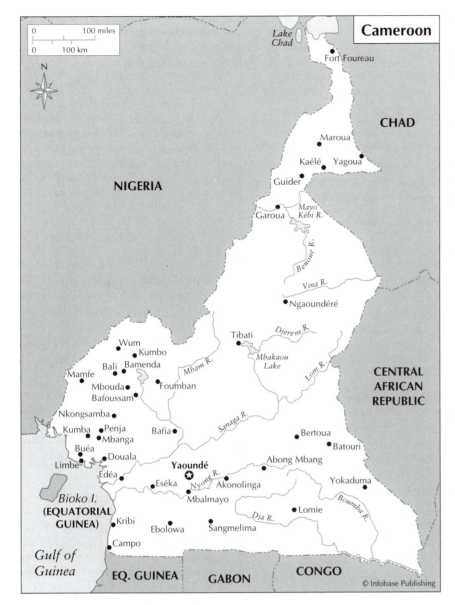

Cameroon

sponsored a number of mass demonstrations against nuclear weaponry, notably those in Trafalgar Square. The CND helped to spawn similar movements in the U.S., France and Australia. CND groups were again active in the early to mid-1980s, when they protested the U.S. decision to base CRUISE MISSILES with nuclear warheads in Britain and other NATO countries.

Campana, Dino *(1885–1932)* Italian poet. Campana abandoned the study of chemistry at the University of Bologna to travel in Europe and the U.S., where his jobs included doorman and triangle player. The onset of schizophrenia led to his imprisonment (1903) and institutionalization (1906,

1909), and he was rejected for service in WORLD WAR I. His reputation is based on *Canti Orfici* (1914; reissued with additions, 1928), translated as *Orphic Songs*. In 1918 he entered a mental asylum where he remained until his death. His fragmentary, nihilistic and intensely personal poetry was largely ignored at first, but several of his lyrics—including "The Chimera," "Autumnal Garden," "The Glass Window" and "Journey to Montevideo"—are counted among the most beautiful of the 20th century. As a poetic innovator, Campana's work marks a transition from the traditionalism of CARDUCCI to the MODERNISM and hermeticism of MONTALE, QUASIMODO and UNGARETTI.

Campanella, Roy "Campy" *(1921–1993)* American baseball player. After nine years in the NEGRO LEAGUES, Campanella became the first black catcher in Major League Baseball upon signing with the Brooklyn Dodgers. During the Dodgers' glory years in the late 1950s, he was named Most Valuable Player three times. His most outstanding year was 1953, when he hit .312 with a league-leading 142 runs batted in. His career, always plagued by injuries, came to an end when he was paralyzed by an automobile accident in January 1958. In 1969 the Baseball Writers Association of America elected Campanella to the Baseball Hall of Fame.

Campbell, Joseph *(1904–1987)* American writer on mythology and comparative religion. Campbell, who gained considerable posthumous fame by virtue of a 1988 Public Broadcasting System series of television interviews with Bill Moyers, was both an erudite scholar and a gifted writer capable of popularizing the key discoveries of comparative religion and the psychology of Carl Gustav JUNG. Campbell began his writing career as a literary critic, coauthoring *A Skeleton Key to Finnegans Wake* (1944), a study of the final novel of James JOYCE. He then turned his attention to explicating the great myths of the world's religions in terms of the Jungian concept of the collective unconscious—an innate mental stratum to be found in all peoples that shows itself in their common mythic symbols. *The Hero with a Thousand Faces* (1948), *The Mythic Image* (1983) and the multivolume *Historical Atlas of World Mythology* (1989) are his major works. Campbell was a longtime member of the faculty of Sarah Lawrence College.

Campbell, Roy *(1901–1957)* South African poet and translator. Campbell was a paradoxical poet, combining a flamboyant romanticism with a highly conservative approach to aesthetics and politics. Raised in South Africa, Campbell briefly attended Oxford but failed to pass the required examinations. His peripatetic life during the 1920s and 1930s included stints of running a fishing boat on the Mediterranean and working as a professional steerthrower in the Provence region of France. Campbell's first volume of poems, *The*

CAMEROON	
1900	Following the invasion of the Fulani tribe from the north during the 19th century, adjustments and migrations among the area's 200 ethnic groups continue.
1904	Sporadic revolts against German colonial authorities.
1916	British and French forces end German rule.
1919	Divided into British and French protectorates under League of Nations (and, later, United Nations).
1930	European plantation companies continue to dominate local economy.
1948	Union des Populations en Cameroun founded to seek reunification and independence.
1955	Unsuccessful revolt by UPC.
1957	Disturbances continue despite grant of limited self-government by French.
1960	French Cameroon gains independence; Ahmadou Ahidjo is first president.
1961	Part of British Cameroon absorbed into Nigeria; remainder joins former French territory to create Federal Republic of Cameroon.
1962	University of Yaounde founded.
1972	Ahidjo consolidates power of presidency under new constitution; pursues repressive policies to stifle tribal forces and still-active UPC.
1983	Struggles between Ahidjo and his protégé, Paul Biya; Ahidjo flees.
1984	Biya elected president, begins reported "liberalization programs"; popular unrest continues.
1986	1,200 people killed by release of natural toxic gas from Lake Nyos.
1988	Biya reelected.
1992	First multiparty elections held. Biya becomes president.
2003	Nigeria cedes Bakasi Peninsula to Cameroon.

Flaming Terrapin (1924), was hailed by influential critics. Subsequent volumes won less praise, though Campbell did establish himself as a masterful translator of St. John of the Cross and Federico GARCÍA LORCA. In 1935, while living in Spain, Campbell declared himself a fascist and later fought on the side of FRANCO's troops in the SPANISH CIVIL WAR. During WORLD WAR II Campbell served as a private in the British army and saw action in North Africa. His *Collected Poems* appeared in 1949.

Campbell-Bannerman, Sir Henry *(1836–1908)* British statesman, prime minister (1905–08). A Liberal, he was elected to Parliament in 1871 and served there for 40 years. He was secretary of the admiralty (1882–84), secretary of state for Ireland (1884) and secretary of war (1886 and 1892–95); knighted in 1895, he was elected leader of his party in 1899. "C-B" was opposed to the BOER WAR, and after his appointment as prime minister in 1905 he granted self-government to the Transvaal (1906) and the Orange Free State (1907). In England he favored a number of liberal reforms, most of which were vetoed by the House of Lords. Ill health forced him to resign in 1908 just weeks prior to his death.

Camp David Official retreat of the U.S. president and his family, located in the Catoctin Mountains about 70 miles from Washington, D.C. This 200-acre complex was acquired by President Franklin ROOSEVELT in 1942 and was originally named "Shangri-La." In 1953 President Dwight D. Eisenhower renamed the retreat Camp David after his grandson. The complex, featuring both entertainment and meeting areas, is under the jurisdiction of the office of the military assistant to the president and is patrolled by the U.S. Marine Corps. Notable among the important international meetings held here were the 1978 talks that resulted in the Camp David Peace Accords between Israel and Egypt, in 1979. In 2000 President Bill CLINTON unsuccessfully met with Israeli prime minister Ehud BARAK and PALESTINIAN AUTHORITY president Yasir ARAFAT in an attempt to produce a final settlement between the two parties.

Camp David Conference *(2000)* Diplomatic conference among U.S. president Bill CLINTON, Israeli prime minister Ehud BARAK, and PALESTINIAN AUTHORITY (PA) president Yasir ARAFAT. Beginning on July 11, 2000, the conference sought to resolve the dispute between the Israeli and PA leaders over the future political status of the WEST BANK and the GAZA STRIP. At the summit Barak offered to support the creation of a Palestinian state that included the Gaza Strip territory already administered by the PA, as well as nearly all of the Palestinian-inhabited territory in the West Bank. However, despite the offers of Barak and the urging of Clinton, Arafat rejected the Israeli offer. On July 25 the conference ended with all sides jointly issuing a trilateral statement that committed the two states and the PA to continued negotiations to achieve a settlement of the Israeli-Palestinian dispute based on UN Security Council Resolutions 242 and 288. However, in early 2001, in part because of statements from Arafat indicating his lack of interest in further trilateral negotiations, a second intifada (see INTIFADA II) broke out in Israel, led by HAMAS and Islamic Jihad.

Camp David talks Peace talks of September 5–17, 1978, among Egyptian president Anwar el-SADAT, Israeli premier Menachem BEGIN, and U.S. president Jimmy CARTER. The talks resulted in a treaty (known as the Camp David Peace Accords) signed in Washington on March 25, 1979, opening Egyptian-Israeli economic and diplomatic relations and returning the occupied SINAI PENINSULA to EGYPT. Hopes of developing an autonomous Palestinian state on the WEST BANK foundered in the face of Israeli internal opposition and PALESTINE LIBERATION ORGANIZATION (PLO) antagonism to the treaty. Arab nations publicly denounced Egypt for its role in the talks, but privately many moderate Arabs approved. Carter's role in sponsoring the talks and mediating differences between Begin and Sadat is widely regarded as the most significant foreign policy achievement of his administration. For their part, Begin and Sadat shared the NOBEL PRIZE for peace (1978). (See also ARAB-ISRAELI WAR OF 1973; ISRAEL.)

Campora, Hector J. (*1909–1980*) Argentinian politician. In 1973 Campora served as president of Argentina for 49 days before resigning to allow the election of Juan PERÓN. During his presidency he released more than 500 jailed leftist guerrillas, thereby angering the country's military. After living in the Mexican embassy in Buenos Aires for three and a half years, in 1979 he was granted safe conduct to Mexico, where he lived in exile.

Camranh Bay (**Kamranh Bay, Vinh Cam Ranh**) Harbor and port on the South China Sea north of Phan Rang,

VIETNAM. Captured by the Japanese in 1941, during WORLD WAR II it served as a major Japanese naval base. Located in South Vietnam when the country was partitioned, Camranh Bay was a major U.S. base during the VIETNAM WAR. In May 2002 Russia returned the naval base at Camranh Bay to Vietnamese control.

Camus, Albert (*1913–1960*) French novelist, essayist and story writer. Camus, who won the NOBEL PRIZE in literature in 1957, was one of the most influential writers of the 20th century, a champion of individual freedom and of an existential philosophy that extols the courage of socially committed political action. Born in Algiers, Camus published his first philosophical essays in the late 1930s. But it was with the appearance of his novel *The Stranger* (1942), the story of an inadvertent murderer who arrives at a kind of happiness by embracing the absurdity of both his crime and his punishment, that Camus first came to international attention. During WORLD WAR II Camus, who had immigrated to France, was active in the RESISTANCE. Camus's other novels include *The Plague* (1948) and *The Fall* (1956); *Exile and the Kingdom* (1957) contains a selection of his stories. His major philosophical works are *The Myth of Sisyphus* (1942) and *The Rebel* (1954). For a time Camus was a close friend of Jean-Paul SARTRE, but Camus broke with Sartre over the

French philosopher and author Albert Camus, 1957
(LIBRARY OF CONGRESS, PRINTS AND PHOTOGRAPHS DIVISION)

latter's support of Stalinist policies in the early 1950s. Camus died in an auto accident.

Canada Covering 40% of the North American continent, Canada occupies a total area of some 3,850,790 square miles and is geographically the second largest country in the world. An influential member of Britain's COMMONWEALTH OF NATIONS, especially after World War I, Canada also has close economic ties to the neighboring U.S. Liberal prime minister William Lyon Mackenzie KING, the country's longest-serving leader in this century, gave Canada strong leadership in the 1920s, 1930s and 1940s. After World War II, Canada helped establish the NORTH ATLANTIC TREATY ORGANIZATION (NATO). During Pierre TRUDEAU's first terms as prime minister (1967–79) the separatist cause of French-speaking Quebec mushroomed as the PARTI QUÉBECOIS, led by Rene LEVESQUE, pushed for secession from Canada. During the 1970s terrorist bombings and murders were associated with the movement, but a 1980 referendum in Quebec defeated the separatist plan. The Canada Act of 1982 officially recognized Canada's multicultural heritage, but the defeat of the Meech Lake Accord (Accord du lac Meech) (1990), which would have given Quebec special status within Canada, led to further talk of secession. Prime Minister Brian MULRONEY succeeded in negotiating a free-trade agreement with the U.S. in 1988. In 1993 Liberal Party leader Jean CHRÉTIEN became prime minister. He used his office to advocate greater Canadian participation within the proposed Western Hemisphere trading bloc and to reduce separatist agitation in Quebec. Chrétien retired in 2003 and was succeeded by Paul Martin. In the national parliamentary elections of 2006, the Conservative Party won a plurality of seats, and its leader, Stephen Harper, formed a government and became prime minister.

Canaris, Wilhelm (*1887–1945*) German admiral. A career officer, Canaris served in the German navy during WORLD WAR I and in the postwar era. The conservative officer was appointed chief of German's military intelligence agency, the ABWEHR, in

© Infobase Publishing

1935. At first a supporter of HITLER, Canaris came to oppose the führer's brutality and to fear the war that seemed inevitable with Hitler as Germany's leader. Under Canaris's direction, the Abwehr became an important part of an anti-Hitlerite movement. After the failed attempt to assassinate Hitler in July 1944, Canaris was arrested and, although he was never directly implicated in the plot, was hanged by the GESTAPO in April 1945.

Canaveral, Cape Cape, located in Brevard County on the east-central coast of Florida; part of a system of barrier islands paralleling the coast of the U.S. and projecting into the Atlantic Ocean. Longtime site of a lighthouse, part of the cape also became a U.S. Air Force installation for launching missiles, the first missile being launched in 1950. The base was called the Kennedy Space Center, after President KENNEDY's assassination, and in 1969 was the launching site of the first spacecraft to send men to the Moon, land them and bring them back. For a short time after the president's death the entire cape was known as Cape Kennedy.

Candler, Asa Griggs (1851–1929) U.S. pharmacist and soft-drink manufacturer. A student of medicine and a successful wholesale drug manufacturer, he bought the formula for Coca-Cola in 1887, developed a method of manufacture and engineered its worldwide success. In 1919 he received $25 million for the rights to the industry he had created. Much of his fortune was given to develop the medical school of Emory University, Atlanta, Georgia.

Canetti, Elias (1905–1994) Bulgarian-born novelist, essayist and sociologist. Canetti, who received the NOBEL PRIZE in literature in 1981, came to great prominence as a writer only after decades of obscurity. A Jew raised and educated in Vienna, Canetti immigrated to London in 1938 to escape the Nazi regime. The novel for which he is best known, *Auto da Fe* (1936), did not receive widespread critical attention until it was reprinted in the 1960s, by which time its existential tale of an isolated, bookish intellectual who is frightened of the mass manipulations of society was seen to have universal relevance. Canetti explicitly analyzed the nature of FASCISM and of mass action in a sociological work, *Crowds and Power* (1960). Canetti was a prominent literary critic as evidenced by his full-length study *Kafka's Other Trial* (1969). He also wrote travel books and a multivolume autobiography. In 1992, two years before his death, Canetti published *Pain of Flies*, his last work.

Cannes Film Festival An annual international celebration of films that takes place in the spring in Cannes,

CANADA

1926	Commonwealth Conference of 1926 accepts principle of equality of status; curtailment of the powers of the governor general follow.
1936	Reciprocity Treaty increases economic links with U.S.
1957	Long Liberal rule ends as John Diefenbaker of the Progressive Conservative Party is chosen prime minister.
1963	Lester B. Pearson leads Liberals back into office.
1967	Charles de Gaulle visits Canada, fueling French nationalism; the Parti Québecois led by René Levesque is formed and demands complete separation from the government.
1968	Pearson is succeeded by Pierre Trudeau.
1970	Members of the separatist movement kidnap British diplomat James Cross.
1970	War Measures Act is passed to deal with francophone terrorist activity in Quebec.
1974	Quebec declares French to be its official language.
1979	Conservatives form minority government under Joe Clark.
1980	Liberals, led by Trudeau, resume power.
1982	Constitution Act of 1982 and Charter of Rights and Freedoms are passed.
1984	Trudeau resigns and is replaced by Liberal leader John Turner; Brian Mulroney of the Conservatives is elected prime minister.
1986	Canada proclaims sovereignty over the Arctic region, including interisland channels, despite objections from the U.S.
1989	The Canada-United States free-trade agreement comes into force.
1990	Meech Lake Accord (a series of constitutional amendments meant to persuade Quebec to ratify the 1982 constitution) fails when it is rejected by the provinces of Newfoundland and Manitoba.
1993	Liberal Party leader Jean Chrétien becomes prime minister.
1994	Canada joins the U.S. and Mexico in the North American Free Trade Agreement (NAFTA).
1999	A large region of the Northwest Territories becomes the separate territory of Nunavut, with a majority indigenous population.
2003	Paul Martin succeeds Chrétien as prime minister.
2006	Stephen Harper of the Conservative Party is sworn in as prime minister.

France; first held in 1946. Each country enters feature-length and short films in the competition. Awards are presented for best director, actor, actress and best film (the Palme d'Or, or Golden Palm Award). Awards are sometimes given for such aspects as set design, and the judges may award a Special Jury Prize to deserving films. Much of the festival revolves around publicity for the films and their stars.

Cannon, Annie Jump (1863–1941) American astronomer. The daughter of a Delaware state senator, Cannon was one of the first women from Delaware to attend university, studying at Wellesley College from 1880 to 1884. After spending a decade at home, where she became deaf due to scarlet fever, she entered Radcliffe College in 1895 to study astronomy. In 1896 she was appointed to the staff of the Harvard College Observatory, as it was the practice of the observatory, under the direction of Edward Pickering, to employ young well-educated women as computers. She worked there for the rest of her career, serving from 1911 to 1932 as curator of astronomical photographs. In 1938, after nearly half a century of distinguished service, she was appointed William Cranch Bond Astronomer. One of the main programs of the observatory was the preparation of the *Henry Draper Catalogue* of a quarter-million stellar spectra. Stars were originally to be classified into one of the 17 spectral types, A to Q, which were ordered alphabetically in terms of the intensity of the hydrogen absorption lines. Cannon saw that a more natural order could be achieved if some classes were omitted, others added and the total reordered in terms of decreasing surface temperature. Her classification scheme has since been altered only slightly.

Cannon developed a phenomenal skill in cataloging stars, and at the height of her power it was claimed that she could classify three stars a minute. Her classification of over 225,000 stars brighter than ninth or 10th magnitude and the compilation of the *Catalogue* took many years. It was finally published, between 1918 and 1924, as volumes 91 to 99 of the *Annals of Harvard College Observatory.* She continued the work unabated, later publications including an additional 47,000 classifications in the *Henry Draper Extension* (*Annals*, vol. 100, 1925–36). Even as late as 1936, when she was over 70, she undertook the classification of 10,000 faint stars submitted to her by the Cape of Good Hope Observatory.

Cannon, Joseph Gurney (*1836–1926*) U.S. congressman, considered the most domineering speaker of the U.S. House of Representatives. He was elected to the House as a Republican in 1872, and again in 1892, but was defeated for reelection in 1912. He returned in 1914 and remained until 1923. He served as Speaker from 1903 to 1911. As Speaker he began an arbitrary and partisan control of House procedures that became known as "Cannonism." As chairman of the House Rules Committee, he and his committee members could block almost any measure they opposed and carry any measure they approved. He could block important legislation, such as civil rights. A combination of insurgent Republicans and Democrats managed to pass a resolution that stripped House Speaker Cannon of much of his power—an action that became known as the "Revolution of 1910."

Cannon, Walter Bradford (*1871–1945*) American physiologist. Cannon graduated from Harvard in 1896 and was professor of physiology there from 1906 to 1942. His early work included studies of the digestive system, in particular the use of X-RAYS to study stomach disorders. Most of his working life, however, was spent studying the nervous system, particularly the way in which hormones regulate various body functions. As early as 1915 he showed the connection between secretions of the endocrine glands and the emotions. In the 1930s he worked on the role of epinephrine in helping the body to meet fight-or-flight situations. He also studied the way hormonelike substances are involved in transmitting messages along nerves.

Canton Atoll (formerly Mary Island) Coral group in the west-central Pacific, southwest of Hawaii; part of the Phoenix Islands group. In the 1930s the islands served as an important stopover place for transpacific flights. After a quarrel concerning ownership, they were placed under mutual U.S.-British supervision. During WORLD WAR II the islands served as a key Allied air base.

Cantor, Eddie (Isidore Itzkowitz; Edward Israel Iskowitz) (*1892–1964*) Cantor was a successful VAUDE-VILLE, revue, musical comedy and Broadway and film comedian who was known not for great comic skills, but for an overpowering, enthusiastic stage persona that was every bit as formidable as Al JOLSON's. Cantor's parents died before he was two years old. Raised by his grandmother, Cantor quit school to perform in contests, on the street and ultimately on the vaudeville circuit. He worked with other performers with limited success, until he was signed for *The Ziegfeld Follies* in 1917. The show led to superstar status in the 1920s, climaxing with the ZIEGFELD smash hit *Whoopee,* in 1928. Moving into films such as *Whoopee* (1930), *Roman Scandals* (1933) and *Kid Millions* (1934), Cantor's bulging eyes and cheerful demeanor became a trademark, and his high tenor voice made instant hits out of songs such as "Potatoes are Cheaper, Tomatoes are Cheaper, Now It's Time to Fall in Love" and "Makin' Whoopee." In the 1950s Cantor spoke openly against ANTI-SEMITISM and lost some of his popular appeal. In 1956 he was given an honorary ACADEMY AWARD, but health problems caused him to limit his public appearances. After his death in 1964, Cantor's reputation plummeted, as comedians and writers such as Milton BERLE, Steve ALLEN and George S. KAUFMAN remarked that he lacked natural comic ability and had to "struggle for his laughs."

Cantos, The The major work of Ezra POUND's poetic career, this epic cycle of poems, begun in 1925, was originally planned to include 100 cantos, or chapters, but that number was surpassed before 1960. Hugely ambitious in compass, the cycle's complex structure borrows from Dante's *Divine Comedy,* Ovid's *Metamorphoses* and Homer's *Odyssey*; the cantos also weave together myth and legend, Oriental poetry and philosophy, troubadours' ballads and political and economic theory to reconstruct the history of human civilization. Most famous are Canto XLV, on "usura," or usury, and the "Pisan Cantos," which describe Pound's imprisonment by the U.S. Army in Italy at the end of WORLD WAR II. Despite their influence on modern poetry, in his embittered old age Pound declared them "a failure." They remained unfinished at his death.

Capa, Cornell (*1918–*) American photographer. The brother of photographer Robert CAPA, he was born in Hungary and began his photography career in Paris during the 1930s. He fled to the U.S. in 1937, worked for the photo intelligence section of the air force during WORLD WAR II and joined the staff of *LIFE* magazine in 1946. Becoming a well-known photojournalist, he contributed many photo essays to the magazine, even after leaving it to join his brother's photo agency, Magnum, in 1954. In 1974 he became the founder and director of the International Center of Photography in New York City. His deep political and social concerns are evident in his study of Latin America, *Margin of Life* (1974).

Capa, Robert (*1913–1954*) American photographer. Born in Hungary, Capa was active in Paris in the 1930s along with such other photographers as CARTIER-BRESSON and David Seymour. Renowned for his portrayals of humanity at war, he became well known for his superb photographs of the 1936 SPANISH CIVIL WAR and is particularly famous for his classic photo of a Loyalist soldier's "Moment of Death." He traveled throughout Africa, Italy and Sicily for LIFE magazine during WORLD WAR II, contributing powerful battlefield photos, and participated in the landing at NORMANDY. In all, Capa covered five wars, producing a profoundly moving body of work. In 1946 he cofounded the photojournalist agency Magnum. He was killed by a landmine while covering the FRENCH INDO-CHINA WAR. His books include *Death in the Making* (1938) and *Images of War* (1964).

Capecchi, Mario *(1937–   )* American molecular geneticist and biologist. He is known primarily for his 1977 discovery of homologous recombination, a cellular technique that regulates the arrangement of DNA molecules in a nucleus, and which reveals how specific genes produce physical changes in successive generations. Over the next 12 years, Capecchi attempted to utilize this cellular process to identify or "target" DNA sequences that led to specific genes. By altering the process of homologous recombination within the nucleus, he attempted to produce a specific mutation within that gene. By 1989 he had used this technique to produce several mice with such targeted genetic mutations that were similar to genetic diseases found in humans. The goal of his research has been to discover how the mutation that leads to such diseases occurs and is passed down through generations, and also to use this "gene targeting" to identify and correct such mutated genes.

Cape Esperance, Battle of On October 1–12, 1942, one of six WORLD WAR II naval engagements that occurred during the fighting at GUADALCANAL. It involved a Japanese naval bombardment force and convoy under the command of Rear Admiral Aritomo Goto and a U.S. task force under Rear Admiral Norman Scott. Mainly a nighttime battle, it pitted a Japanese force of four cruisers and two destroyers against a U.S. force of four cruisers and five destroyers that had been escorting an American regiment. During the encounter, in which Goto was killed, a Japanese heavy cruiser and a destroyer were sunk, while the Americans lost one destroyer, USS *Duncan,* and sustained damage to two other ships. In daytime fighting, the Japanese lost an-

other two destroyers to U.S. air forces. While considered an American victory, the battle did not utterly destroy the Japanese bombardment force nor prevent the convoy from getting through, and the furious battle at Guadalcanal continued. (See also WORLD WAR II IN THE PACIFIC.)

Čapek, Karel *(1890–1938)* Czechoslovakian novelist and playwright. Čapek is one of the leading Czech writers of the 20th century. He achieved international prominence between the two world wars by virtue of his distinctive satiric plays set in imagined future worlds that incorporated elements of pulp science fiction. Notable among his plays are *R.U.R.* (1920), which featured a robot as a central character, and *The Insect Play* (1921). In the 1930s Čapek devoted his primary energies to fiction writing in a philosophical vein. His novel *War with the Newts* (1936), which satirically de-

picted the rise of a totalitarian regime in a disintegrating society, achieved a wide readership. Politically Čapek was a liberal democrat who wrote an admiring biography of Czech president Tomáš MASARYK.

Cape Kennedy U.S. government space center, in Brevard County, Florida. The term is used to refer to the Kennedy Space Center located on the part of Cape CANAVERAL that has been used for launching U.S. research missiles. For a time the entire cape was named for the late president John F. KENNEDY, but the local name, Cape Canaveral, has prevailed for the geographical area.

Cape Verde, Republic of **(Portuguese: Republica de Cabo Verde)** Island nation in the Atlantic Ocean, off the west coast of Africa. Located approximately 385 miles west northwest of Dakar, SENEGAL, the republic

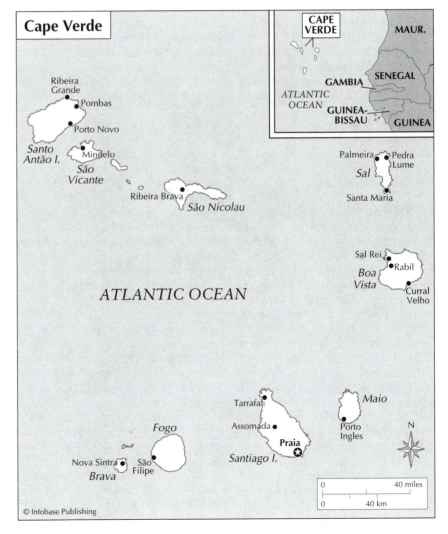

CAPE VERDE

1951	Cape Verde becomes an overseas territory of Portugal.
1975	Cape Verde is granted independence by Portugal and is proclaimed a republic, with Aristides Pereira as president.
1986	President Pereira is reelected for another five-year term.
1991	Antonio Mascarenhas Monteiro defeats Pereira in the presidential election.
2001	Pedro Pires wins the presidency by a margin of 17 votes.
2006	Pires narrowly wins another term as president.

consists of 10 main islands with a population of some 358,000 people. São Tiago is the capital. The islands began the 20th century as a colony of PORTUGAL and were granted overseas province status in 1951. An independence movement led by Amilcar Cabral began an armed rebellion in Cape Verde and Portugese Guinea in 1961. Cape Verde was granted independence on July 5, 1975. Aristides Pereira became the first president and remained in power until 1991 when António Mascarenhas Monteiro became the first freely elected president of Cape Verde. He helped inaugurate a new constitution and a multiparty political system the following year. In the 2001 and 2006 elections, Pedro Pires won as president.

capitalism Economic system in which the means of production and distribution of goods and services are privately owned and operated; also known as "private enterprise" or "free enterprise." In the 20th and into the 21st century capitalism has been diametrically opposed to COMMUNISM. The UNITED STATES has long been seen as the showcase of capitalism (although GERMANY and JAPAN have developed highly successful capitalist economies); the UNION OF SOVIET SOCIALIST REPUBLICS was and CHINA has been strongholds of communism. Advocates of capitalism argue that it is the only economic system that can guarantee personal and political freedom, because only in a capitalist system are individuals free to choose their jobs and to spend their money as they wish. Capi-

talists believe that prices and levels of production should be determined by "market forces," not by government planning. Competition (in order to achieve higher profits and, sometimes, to remain in business) is considered a cornerstone of traditional capitalism, encouraging efficiency and progress. Critics of capitalism point to unemployment, homelessness, unfair business practices and inequitable salaries and wages as its inevitable by-products. In many parts of the world, private enterprise mixed with some government ownership and regulation is seen as an alternative to both capitalism and communism. The movement toward market economies in Eastern Europe in the late 1980s was seen by many as the victory of capitalism over communism. In 1991 Pope JOHN PAUL II cautiously endorsed capitalism while calling for greater attention to spiritual and humanitarian values in capitalist societies. With the formation in 1993 of the WORLD TRADE ORGANIZATION (WTO), an international organization dedicated to reducing trade barriers through multilateralism, almost every country in the world, including the People's Republic of China, had adopted the principle (if not the practice) of the free market as the most effective means of promoting economic growth. However, some countries, such as France and Japan, have adopted protectionist policies and have refused entry to items such as U.S.-grown GENETICALLY MODIFIED FOODS.

capital punishment The use of the death penalty in U.S. criminal cases

was one of the most controversial legal issues of the 20th century. Although implementation of the death penalty had waned, by 1971 the penalty still existed in a great majority of the states. In 1972 the U.S. Supreme Court cast doubt on the constitutionality of the death penalty. The Court ruled that when the penalty was imposed in an arbitrary manner it amounted to unconstitutional cruel and unusual punishment. However, supporters of the death penalty made capital punishment a national issue, and a majority of Americans seemed to favor it. Because of these concerns, no convicts were executed in the U.S. for over 10 years. In 1976 the Supreme Court made clear that capital punishment was not inherently cruel and unusual so long as it was imposed consistently with ample procedural protections for the accused. By 1980 executions had resumed in a number of states, although capital punishment is still outlawed in many other states. In 2005 the Supreme Court declared the execution of juveniles unconstitutional. Overseas, 85 nations have banned capital punishment for all crimes.

Capone, Alphonse (1899–1947) American gangster. Born and raised in Brooklyn, New York, Capone became a small-time criminal early in life, earning the nickname "Scarface" for the razor slash across his face. Settling in CHICAGO in 1920s, he quickly moved up in the crime syndicates, ruthlessly eliminating his competition and gaining control of bootleg liquor traffic dur-

Chicago mob boss Al Capone (LIBRARY OF CONGRESS, PRINTS AND PHOTOGRAPHS DIVISION)

ing PROHIBITION. Terrorizing Chicago during the 1920s, he extorted money from businessmen and politicians and gained control of such lucrative illicit activities as prostitution and gambling. By the end of the 1920s Capone was estimated to have an annual income of over $20 million. His ruthless slaughter culminated in the ST. VALENTINE'S DAY MASSACRE of 1929, in which his henchmen machine-gunned seven members of the "Bugs" Moran gang. After a decade of corrupting the Chicago police and eluding prosecution, Capone was finally indicted (1931) by a federal grand jury for tax evasion. He was released from prison late in 1939. Racked by terminal syphilis, he retired to his Florida estate, where he died.

Capote, Truman (*1924–1984*) American author. As famous for his witty conversation on the television talk show circuit as for his evocative, disciplined prose style, Capote provoked controversy from the debut of his first novel, *Other Voices, Other Rooms* (1948), with its homosexual theme. He had already received attention with his "Southern Gothic" stories, such as "Miriam" (1945; winner of the O. Henry Memorial Award, 1946). In his novels *The Grass Harp* (1951; dramatized, 1952) and *Breakfast at Tiffany's* (1958; filmed, 1961) he shed the gothicism for a lighter, wittier approach. His most famous work is the 1966 nonfiction work *In Cold Blood* about multiple murders. His 1956 short story "A Christmas Memory" became an acclaimed television show (1967). His last novel was *Music for Chameleons* (1980).

Capp, Al (Alfred Gerald Caplin) (*1909–1979*) American cartoonist, creator of the satirical comic strip *L'il Abner*. Capp created the fictional community of Dogpatch and filled it with frolicsome hillbilly characters who lampooned the foibles of the high and the mighty in newspapers for 43 years. The comic strip gained a following of tens of millions of readers, inspired a Broadway musical, two movies and a television show, and earned Capp $500,000 a year at its peak.

Capra, Frank (*1897–1991*) American motion picture director whose films include several HOLLYWOOD classics. Born in Sicily, Capra immigrated

to the U.S. with his family in 1903. He worked as a chemical engineer, army ballistics instructor, laborer and salesman before becoming a gag writer for Mack SENNETT in Hollywood (1925), then teamed up with slapstick comedian Harry LANGDON (1926) to make his first important films. His association with producer Harry COHN and COLUMBIA PICTURES (1928–39) resulted in some of his best-known films, including *It Happened One Night* (1934), for which he won the first of his three ACADEMY AWARDS for best director, *Mr. Deeds Goes to Town* (1936), *Lost Horizon* (1937) and *Mr. Smith Goes to Washington* (1939). These pictures contain Capra's hallmarks—the topsy-turvy class mixtures of the screwball comedy; optimistic faith in democracy and the values of simplicity and honesty (called "Capra-corn" by critics); rapid pacing and snappy dialogue; and Capra's own insistence that his vision shape the entire picture. In 1940 he resigned as president of the Academy of Motion Picture Arts and Sciences and was commissioned as a major in the Army Signal Corps, where he made an important series of documentaries and training films, *Why We Fight;* these contributed to U.S. morale in WORLD WAR II. His postwar years were marked by numerous independent projects, most notably *It's a Wonderful Life* (1946), which eventually became perhaps his most popular film. He also produced a series of science films for Bell Telephone (1952–56). His last features were *A Hole in the Head* (1959) and *A Pocketful of Miracles* (1961).

Capucine (Germaine Lefèbvre) (*1933–1990*) French actress. A glamorous movie star of the 1960s Capucine starred in such films as *Walk on the Wild Side* (1962), *The Pink Panther* (1964), *What's New Pussycat* (1965) and *Fellini Satyricon* (1969). She took her name from the French word for the nasturtium flower.

Caradon, Lord (Hugh Mackintosh Foot) (*1907–1990*) British diplomat. He served as governor of CYPRUS from 1957 to 1960, and was credited with bringing together the governments of GREECE and TURKEY to forge a compromise that established Cyprus as a nation. He joined the

UNITED NATIONS in 1961 as Britain's representative to the Trusteeship Council but resigned 15 months later in protest against the white government of RHODESIA's repression of black nationalists. Appointed a life peer in 1964, he was named by Britain's Labour government as its chief UN representative. He held the post until the Conservatives' return to power in 1970.

Caramanlis, Constantine (*1907–1998*) Greek political leader, premier (1955–63, 1974–80), and president (1980–85, 1990–95). Born in Macedonia, he attended the University of Athens and was first elected to parliament in 1936. After entering the cabinet as minister of labor in 1946, Caramanlis served in a succession of posts until he was named premier in 1955. The following year he was founder of a right-wing political party, the National Radical Union. During his first term in office he supported the NORTH ATLANTIC TREATY ORGANIZATION, came to an accord with TURKEY and Great Britain regarding CYPRUS (1959) and in the early 1960s conceived and implemented a five-year agricultural and industrial reform plan. He resigned in 1963 and went into exile in France. Opposing the military junta that ruled GREECE in the interim, he returned to the premiership when the military government fell in 1974. Founding another new party, New Democracy, he remained in office until 1980, when he was elected president. In 1990 Caramanlis was again elected to the presidency for five years and in 1995 was succeeded by Kostis Stepanopoulos.

carbon-14 dating See Willard LIBBY.

Cardiff (Welsh: Caerdydd) Situated on the Bristol Channel, 130 miles west of London, Cardiff has been the official capital of Wales since 1955. Cardiff began the 20th century as the world's largest coal exporting port, but its coal business suffered a severe setback as the century progressed. During WORLD WAR II, the Luftwaffe bombed the city, causing extensive destruction.

Cardin, Pierre (*1922–*) French fashion designer (born in Venice) who has expanded his activities into a wide variety of design fields with licensing to some 500 firms in 93 countries. He was apprenticed to a tailor before World War II and after the war worked for several Paris fashion houses before spending three years with the House of DIOR. He opened his own firm in 1953. His early work focused on traditional suits and coats, but by the 1960s he had become an innovator, using big patterns with references to the OP ART of the day. He has been a key figure in turning the concept of haute couture into a commodity for the mass market, applying a name and monogram to a range of goods. Perfumes, luggage, men's fashions and wigs, among other items, all bear his label. His work has included interior design for restaurants and aircraft along with a continuing flow of fashion apparel products. Throughout the 1990s Cardin served as a goodwill ambassador of the UNITED NATIONS EDUCATIONAL, SCIENTIFIC AND CULTURAL ORGANIZATION (UNESCO) and became involved in its efforts to establish a UNESCO cultural center in Egypt. He also began to host a summer opera festival at an 11th-century chateau once owned by the marquis de Sade in the medieval village of Lacoste in Provence.

Cardozo, Benjamin N. *(1870–1938)* Associate justice, U.S. Supreme Court (1932–38). Cardozo is recognized as one of the giants of modern jurisprudence. A graduate of Columbia University, he served as a judge in New York. His father, also a judge, resigned after being implicated in Tammany Hall corruption in New York City. The younger Cardozo never married. While he was chief judge of New York's highest court, Cardozo's judicial opinions set new standards for legal analysis. He wrote a number of landmark business opinions that are still carefully studied by law students and that still carry great weight with jurists, perhaps the most famous being *Palsgraf v. Long Island R. R.* His books, including *The Nature of the Judicial Process* (1921), established him as one of the great legal theorists of the century.

After Oliver Wendell HOLMES resigned from the Supreme Court, Cardozo was the favored nominee, although President Herbert HOOVER at first resisted the nomination because three New Yorkers already sat on the Court. However, Hoover nominated Cardozo after Chief Justice Harlan Fiske STONE threatened to resign unless Cardozo was appointed. A supporter of Franklin D. ROOSEVELT'S NEW DEAL legislation, Cardozo was known as a champion of liberal causes. He served only six years before his death. His legal writings and lectures established him as a leading legal intellectual.

Carducci, Giosue *(1835–1907)* Italian poet and critic. The son of a member of the Carbonari who later embraced Roman Catholicism, Carducci was known for his own mercurial politics. He was alternately pro- and anti-republican. A professor of literature at the University of Bologna from 1860 to 1904, he was a scholar, an editor, an orator and a patriot. He was generally regarded as Italy's unofficial poet laureate. His historical verse, *Odi barbari* (1878–89), attempted to capture the spirit of the classical world by emulating ancient Greek and Latin poetry. His personal poetry includes *Rime nuove* (New lyrics, 1861–87). He received the NOBEL PRIZE in literature in 1906. Carducci's work reflects the spirit that infused the Risorgimento; it avoids the excesses of romanticism in favor of a restrained and classical style.

CARE Acronym for Cooperative for American Relief Everywhere, a nonprofit volunteer agency in the U.S. that provides assistance to people in developing nations. To the general public the agency is best known for its "CARE packages" sent to needy people around the world during natural emergencies. CARE was founded in 1945 at the end of WORLD WAR II to provide donations of food and clothing to the people of war-torn Europe. It subsequently developed into a full-time service agency that coordinates relief efforts in Africa, Asia and Latin America. CARE's activities are funded by private donations.

Carlton, Steve *(1944–)* American baseball player. Born in Miami, Florida, Carlton began his baseball career in 1964 when the St. Louis Cardinals signed him to a minor league contract. The following year he joined the Cardinals. In 1969 he gained attention throughout the National League when he struck out 19 New York Mets batters. In 1972 the Cardinals traded Carlton to the Philadelphia Phillies. Although Philadelphia ended the season at the bottom of the National League, Carlton had won an impressive 27 games for his new team, accounting for nearly half of Philadelphia's win total that year. That statistic, along with his 1.98 earned run average and 310 strikeouts in 1972, resulted in his being selected as the winner of the Cy Young Award that year. While with Philadelphia, Carlton won the Cy Young three additional times, in 1977, 1980 and 1982. The year after his fourth Cy Young Award, the Phillies released him from their roster, and Carlton began a five-year journey around the National League that was plagued by a series of injuries. When he retired in 1988 Carlton held National League records for the most games started as a pitcher (577) and most consecutive starting assignments as a pitcher (577), and his 4,136 career strikeouts trailed only Nolan RYAN. In 1994 he was inducted into the Baseball Hall of Fame.

Carmichael, Hoagland "Hoagy" *(1899–1981)* U.S. composer and actor. He first encountered jazz music as a student at Indiana University, when his song "Riverboat Shuffle" was given to Bix BEIDERBECKE for recording. Carmichael formed a band of his own, but continued with his studies and earned a law degree in 1926. He practiced law for a while but finally moved to New York City in 1929. His most popular song, "Stardust," established him as a composer. "Rockin' Chair" and "Georgia on My Mind" were published in 1930. In 1931 he assembled a band that included Jimmy DORSEY, Benny GOODMAN, Beiderbecke and Gene KRUPA. The group was called the most impressive jazz ensemble ever gathered together. Carmichael's "Lamplighter's Serenade" was the first song recorded by Frank SINATRA. He also appeared in feature films and had popular radio and television programs. He won an ACADEMY AWARD in 1951 for his song "In the Cool, Cool, Cool of the Evening." In 1971 he was one of the first 10 popular composers elected to the Songwriters' Hall of Fame.

Carmichael, Stokely *(1941–1998)* Leader of the U.S. CIVIL RIGHTS MOVEMENT. Carmichael was born in Port-of-Spain, Trinidad. He attended Howard

University, graduating in 1964. Both during his college years and later Carmichael worked with the CONGRESS OF RACIAL EQUALITY (CORE) and the Student Nonviolent Coordinating Committee, participating in protest and voter registration drives in southern states. In 1966, he was named head of the SNCC, and shortly afterward he took part in James MEREDITH's Freedom March in Mississippi. Carmichael was active in the BLACK PANTHERS beginning in 1967; he was prime minister of the group before his resignation in 1969.

Carnap, Rudolf *(1891–1970)* German-American philosopher and logician. Carnap had a rigorous scientific and philosophical education, which was reflected in the style and content of all his later work. He studied mathematics, physics and philosophy at the Universities of Jena and Freiburg (1910–14) and obtained a doctorate from Jena with a thesis on the concept of space in 1921. In 1926 Carnap was invited to take up a post at the University of Vienna, where he became a major figure in the Vienna Circle—a group of philosophers and mathematicians founded by Moritz Schlick. This group had an empiricist outlook (all our ideas, concepts and beliefs about the external world derive from our immediate sensory experience). Out of this evolved the logical empiricist or LOGICAL POSITIVISM school of thought, which states that the meaningful statements we can make are just those that have logical consequences that are observably verifiable. That is, meaningful statements must be testable by experience; those that are not, such as the propositions of metaphysics and religion, are, strictly, meaningless.

Throughout his life Carnap used the tools of symbolic logic to bring a greater precision to philosophical inquiry, including investigations into the philosophy of language and into probability and inductive reasoning. He produced his first major work in 1928, *Der Logische Aufban der Welt*, translated into English in 1967 as *The Logical Structure of the World*. In this he developed a version of the empiricist reducibility thesis, holding that scientific theories and theoretical sentences must be reducible to sentences that describe immediate experiences, which are ob-

servably verifiable. His other works included *Logishe Syntax der Sprache* (1934) and *Logical Foundations of Probability* (1950). He immigrated to the U.S. in 1936, becoming professor of philosophy at Chicago until 1952 and at UCLA until 1961. (See also A. J. AYER; Ludwig WITTGENSTEIN.)

Carné, Marcel *(1909?–1996)* French film director; came to prominence in the 1930s and 1940s for a series of films on which he collaborated with French poet and performance artist Jacques PRÉVERT, who wrote the screenplays. These films include *Port of Shadows* (1938), *Daybreak* (1939) and the internationally acclaimed *Children of Paradise* (1943), which featured French actor Jean-Louis BARRAULT. *Children of Paradise,* set in the 19th century and concerning a romance between an actor and an actress, was shot during the German occupation of France in WORLD WAR II. Carné is highly regarded by film critics for his moody, evocative style and lush romantic sensibility.

Carnegie, Dale *(1888–1955)* American salesman, lecturer and author who developed and taught the arts of self-confidence and public speaking. Carnegie was the first of the "how-to" authors. His 1936 book *How to Win Friends and Influence People* became a publishing phenomenon and instant bestseller; by the time of his death some 5 million copies had been sold worldwide, a number that has now doubled. Carnegie founded the Carnegie Institute for Effective Speaking and Human Relations. He also wrote the popular book *How to Stop Worrying and Start Living* (1948).

Carnegie Hall Legendary concert hall in NEW YORK CITY. Opened in 1891, Carnegie Hall has been a venue for cultural events of the highest order. The long list of personalities who have appeared there is a who's who of the modern era. Early in the 20th century, lectures were given by Winston CHURCHILL, Theodore ROOSEVELT, Woodrow WILSON, Sigmund FREUD and W. B. YEATS. Classical musicians who have graced the hall's stage include conductors Gustav MAHLER, Wilhelm FURTWANGLER, Arturo TOSCANINI, Leopold STOKOWSKI, Bruno WALTER, Thomas BEECHAM, Leonard BERNSTEIN, Carlo Maria GIULINI, George SOLTI and Herbert

von KARAJAN; pianists Sergei RACHMANI-NOFF, Josef and Rosina LHEVINNE, Vladimir HOROWITZ, Arthur RUBINSTEIN, Emil GILELS, Rudolf SERKIN, Van CLIBURN and Vladimir FELTSMAN; violinists Jascha HEIFETZ, David OISTRAKH, Yehudi MENUHIN and Itzhak PERLMAN; cellists Pablo CASALS, Gregor Piatagorsky, Mstislav ROSTROPOVICH and Jacqueline DU PRÉ; operatic and concert singers Marian ANDERSON, Maria CALLAS, Leontine PRICE, Janet BAKER, Joan SUTHERLAND, Luciano PAVAROTTI, Plácido DOMINGO, Dietrich FISCHER-DIESKAU; JAZZ, big band and popular music performers Benny GOODMAN, Fats WALLER, Ella FITZGERALD, Sarah VAUGHAN, Duke ELLINGTON, Count BASIE, Paul WHITEMAN and Frank SINATRA; folk singers Woody GUTHRIE, Burl IVES, the WEAVERS, Pete SEEGER and Bob DYLAN; ROCK and roll groups such as the BEATLES and the ROLLING STONES.

In the late 1950s Carnegie Hall was threatened with demolition in order to make room for a new office building; a group of music lovers, led by violinist Isaac STERN, intervened to save it. In 1986 Carnegie Hall was renovated; despite new amenities, many musicians and critics claim that its accoustics, hitherto near-perfect, were adversely affected. The hall celebrated its centennial in 1991–92 with a series of gala events.

Carol II *(1893–1953)* King of Romania (1930–40); the son of King FERDINAND I and Queen Marie (1875–1938), as crown prince his first marriage, a morganatic union, was dissolved, and he married Princess Helen of Greece in 1921. Carol became infamous for his liaison with Magda Lupescu, and when his father forced him to renounce his rights to the throne (1925), he settled in France with his mistress. On Ferdinand's death, the throne was assumed by Carol's six-year-old son Michael under a regency. Divorcing Queen Helen in 1928, Carol returned from exile and was proclaimed king in 1930. Ruling at first under a parliamentary system, Carol assumed dictatorial powers in 1938. After the outbreak of WORLD WAR II, he was obliged to cede territory to Hungary, Bulgaria and the USSR and came into violent conflict with ROMANIA's fascist Iron Guard. When Ion ANTONESCU formed a government in 1940, Carol was forced to flee and Michael again became king. Carol married Lupescu in Brazil in 1947 and died in exile in Portugal six years later.

Caroline Islands A group of several hundred small islands in the western Pacific Ocean, north of the equator. Although uninhabited in modern times, ruins show that there was life here several centuries ago. Germany bought the islands in 1899 following the Spanish-American War; JAPAN seized them in 1914 and reinforced them during WORLD WAR II. The islands became U.S. trust territories in 1947.

Carothers, Wallace Hume (1896–1937) American industrial chemist. Carothers earned a B.S. degree from Tarkio College, Missouri. (1920), after working his way through college. He gained his Ph.D. in 1924 from the University of Illinois and was an instructor in chemistry at Illinois and Harvard before joining the Du Pont company at Wilmington, Delaware, as head of organic chemistry research in 1928. Carothers's early work was in the application of electronic theory to organic chemistry, but at Du Pont he worked on polymerization. His first great success was the production of the synthetic rubber neoprene (1931). In a systematic search for synthetic analogs of silk and cellulose he prepared many condensation polymers, especially polyesters and polyethers. In 1935 one polyamide proved outstanding in its properties and came into full-scale production in 1940 as Nylon 66. But Carothers did not live to see the results of his achievements; despite his brilliant successes, he suffered from fits of depression and took his own life at the age of 41.

Carpenter, Scott (1925–) U.S. astronaut. "Spectacular, like a very brilliant rainbow" was how Carpenter described his first sunset viewed from Earth orbit aboard *Mercury 7* (May 24, 1962), his only spaceflight. The second American astronaut to orbit the Earth, Carpenter circled three times but used up too much fuel and fell behind schedule. He was forced to reenter Earth's atmosphere under manual control and splashed down 250 miles from his re-

covery ship. He was safely retrieved 40 minutes after splashdown, but not before some television newscasters announced to their nervous viewers that America might have "lost an astronaut." Critical of Carpenter's performance during the flight, some NASA officials held him responsible for the anxious moments surrounding his recovery. In 1965, taking a leave of absence from NASA, he participated in the navy's *Sealab 2* experiment, spending 30 days living and working in another alien environment, the challenging depths of the ocean floor. After retiring from NASA he continued with the Sealab experiments and served as assistant for aquanaut operations for *Sealab 3*. In 1969 he retired from the navy with the rank of commander and became an engineering consultant and wasp breeder. (See also MERCURY PROGRAM.)

Carr, Edward Hallett (1892–1982) British historian known for his 14-volume *History of Soviet Russia*. Written over a period of 30 years, this work was considered one of the most comprehensive studies of the development of the USSR and Soviet COMMUNISM.

Carr, John Dickson (1906–1977) American crime and detective story writer best known for his mastery of the "locked room" school of fiction. Born in Uniontown, Pennsylvania, Carr began writing his first detective short stories while a student at Haverford College. After the success of his first novel, *It Walks by Night* (1930), which introduced French police magistrate Henri Bencolin, Carr moved to England. For the next 15 years he introduced a series of fictional detectives. Dr. Gideon Fell, a Scotland Yard consultant, first appeared in *Hag's Nook* (1933); Sir Henry Merrivale, a barrister, debuted in *The Plague Court Murders* (1934); and Colonel March, chief of the "Department of Queer Complaints," came along in a volume of short stories under that name in 1940. Writing under his own name or the pseudonym Carter Dickson, Carr emerged the preeminent master of the "locked room" form. In a number of classics, like *The Crooked Hinge* (1938) and *The Problem of the Wire Cage* (1939), the operative question was not *who*-dunnit, but *how*-dunnit. Not locked doors, sealed rooms or trackless sands

seemed to daunt the incredible ingenuity of his criminals. It was to Carr's credit, however, that the triumph of reason over superstition rarely disappointed the reader. Carr's later years after World War II were increasingly devoted to historical novels with crime/detection themes, such as *The Bridge of Newgate* (1950) and *The Devil in Velvet* (1951).

Carra, Carlo (1881–1966) Italian painter. Carra was one of the leading Italian painter to be influenced by FUTURISM as articulated by Italian poet F. M. MARINETTI. A major painting from Carra's futurist period is *The Funeral of the Antichrist Galli* (1911). In 1917 Carra met fellow Italian painter Giorgio de CHIRICO. Together they became the key proponents of the Scuola Metafisica (Metaphysical School) movement in painting. This new movement called for the pictorial evocation—through clearly defined geometrical constructions—of disquieting states of mind that pierced through the illusion of objective, impersonal existence. Carra and de Chirico soon quarreled over who had originated the movement. In his later years Carra turned to a neoclassical painting style.

Carrel, Alexis (1873–1944) French surgeon. Carrel received his medical degree from the University of Lyon in 1900. In 1902 he started to investigate techniques for joining (suturing) blood vessels end to end. He continued his work at the University of Chicago (1904) and later at the Rockefeller Institute for Medical Research, New York (1906). Carrel's techniques, which minimized tissue damage and infection and reduced the risk of blood clots, were a major advance in vascular surgery and paved the way for the replacement and transplantation of organs. In recognition of this work, Carrel was awarded the 1912 NOBEL PRIZE in physiology or medicine. During WORLD WAR I Carrel served in the French army. With the chemist Henry Dakin he formulated the Carrel-Dakin antiseptic for deep wounds. Returning to the Rockefeller Institute after the war, Carrel turned his attention to methods of keeping tissues and organs alive outside the body. With the aviator Charles LINDBERGH he devised a so-called artificial heart that could pump physiological fluids through large organs, such as the heart or kidneys. In *Man, the Unknown* (1935) Carrel published his controversial views about the possible role of science in organizing and improving society along authoritarian lines. During WORLD WAR II he founded and directed the Carrel Foundation for the Study of Human Problems under the VICHY government, in Paris. Following the Allied liberation, Carrel faced charges of collaboration but died before a trial was arranged.

Carreras, José *(1946–)* Spanish opera singer. Carreras was born in Barcelona, where he received his musical training. His rise as an operatic superstar was meteoric. A tenor, he made his professional debut in Spain in 1970, won first prize at the International Verdi Competition in Italy in 1971 and appeared in the U.S. in 1972 to wide acclaim. He first sang at New York's Metropolitan Opera in 1974, at La Scala in 1975 and at the SALZBURG FESTIVAL in 1976 (at the invitation of Herbert von KARAJAN). He made numerous recordings, telecasts and live appearances throughout the world. However, his large number of engagements and choice of some unsuitable roles seemed to affect the quality of his voice and his interpretations. In 1987 Carreras became seriously ill with leukemia. After intensive treatment he went into remission and returned to the stage in 1988. Critics noted a new vocal refinement and musical depth in his performances. To welcome him back to the profession after his life-threatening illness, the operatic greats Plácido DOMINGO and Luciano PAVAROTTI joined Carreras in a 1990 concert in Rome entitled "The Three Tenors." In 1998 Carreras won plaudits from the critics for his title role in Wolf-Ferrari's *Sly.*

Carrizal Village and battlefield in Chihuahua State, 85 miles south of Ciudad Juárez, Mexico. On June 21, 1916, Mexican troops routed an American expeditionary force under command of General John J. PERSHING, who was in pursuit of Pancho VILLA after the revolutionary's raid on an American border town.

Carson, Sir Edward Henry *(1854–1935)* Irish political leader. A Dublin lawyer, he was elected to the British Par-

liament in 1892; a superb trial lawyer, he was solicitor general 1900–05. Carson led Irish Protestant opposition to HOME RULE, and in 1912 he raised an army of some 80,000 men in an attempt to defeat it. The threat of civil war led Parliament to concede NORTHERN IRELAND to the Protestants in 1914. Carson was attorney general (1915), first lord of the admiralty (1916–17) and a member of the cabinet during WORLD WAR I (1917–18). Knighted in 1900 and made a baron in 1921, he served as lord of appeal from 1921 to 1929.

Carson, Johnny *(1925–2005)* U.S. radio and television talk show host and comedian. After spending his early years in Iowa, he moved to Nebraska with his family. Initially Carson entertained with magic, card tricks and ventriloquism. His WORLD WAR II service took him to duty in the Pacific on the USS *Pennsylvania,* where he often entertained his shipmates with tricks and humor. He graduated from the University of Nebraska in radio and drama (1949) and finally moved to Los Angeles, where in 1951 he had a comedy show called *Carson's Cellar.* He also started writing for the comedy stars. He was offered *The Johnny Carson Show* by CBS in 1955. After the show closed he moved to New York in 1957 to host ABC's *Who Do You Trust?* for five years. A hit as a substitute on NBC's *THE TONIGHT SHOW* in 1958, he later became host of the show and one of the best-known personalities in American television. In 1992 Carson retired from *The Tonight Show* and was replaced by his longtime guest host, comedian Jay Leno.

Carson, Rachel *(1907–1964)* American biologist, environmentalist and writer. Following postgraduate research in zoology at Johns Hopkins University (1932), Carson joined the U.S. Fish and Wildlife Service as an aquatic biologist; she was later the service's editor in chief of publications. In 1952 she received the National Book Award for *The Sea Around Us.* Her most important book was *Silent Spring* (1962), which warned of the dangers of pesticides, particularly DDT; the book virtually launched the environmental movement and prompted regulatory legislation. Although the chemical industry attacked Carson's findings, President KENNEDY's Science Advisory Committee confirmed them in

1963. In addition to receiving numerous awards from CONSERVATION and animal welfare societies, Carson was elected to the American Academy of Arts and Letters. In 1980 she was posthumously awarded the Presidential Medal of Freedom.

Cartan, Elie Joseph *(1869–1951)* French mathematician. Cartan is now recognized as one of the most powerful and original mathematicians of the 20th century, but his work became widely known only toward the end of his life. He studied at the École Normale Supérieure in Paris and held teaching posts at the Universities of Montpellier, Lyon, Nancy and, from 1912 to 1940, Paris. Cartan's most significant work was in developing the concept of analysis on differentiable manifolds, which now occupies a central place in mathematics. He began his research career with a dissertation on Lie groups, a topic that led him on to his pioneering work on differential systems. The most important innovation in his work on Lie groups was his creation of methods for studying their global properties. The global approach also distinguished his work on differential systems. One of his most useful inventions was the "calculus of exterior differential forms," which he applied to problems in many fields, including differential geometry, Lie groups, analytical dynamics and general relativity. Cartan's son Henri was also an eminent mathematician.

Carter, Howard *(1873–1939)* English archaeologist and Egyptologist. A draftsman with the Egyptian Exploration Fund from 1891 to 1899, Carter was trained in the then-current techniques of archaeological excavation. He became inspector general of the Egyptian government's antiquities department in 1899 and supervised various excavations in Luxor's Valley of the Kings in 1902–03. Associated with Lord Carnarvon from 1906 on, he excavated many tombs, including those of Amenophis I and Queen Hatshepsut. He is famous for his discovery of the tomb of Tutankhamen in November 1922. Carter described the excavation of this world-renowned site in a three-volume work written with A. C. Mace, *The Tomb of Tutankh-Amen* (1923–33).

Jimmy Carter (left) meets with Egyptian president Anwar el-Sadat at Camp David, 1978. (HULTON ARCHIVE)

Carter, Jimmy (*1924– *) Thirty-ninth president of the UNITED STATES (1977–81). Born in Plains, Georgia, Carter attended the U.S. Naval Academy, graduating in 1946. He served in the navy as a nuclear engineer until 1953, when he returned to Georgia to head his family's successful peanut business. Carter entered political life as a state senator (1962–66), ran unsuccessfully for governor of Georgia in 1966 and attained the governor's office in 1970. He ran a vigorous campaign for the presidential nomination in 1975 and narrowly defeated President Gerald FORD in the election of 1976. Carter was something of a phenomenon as president: an amiable but tough outsider, a southerner, a moralist and a fundamentalist Christian. On the domestic front Carter attempted to implement new national energy policies and to reform the income tax system.

However, his status as a Washington outsider circumscribed his power with Congress, and his attempts to pass legislation met largely with failure. Moreover, the economy suffered during his presidency, experiencing high interest rates, inflation and, later, recession. In foreign affairs he was both praised and censured for the two PANAMA CANAL

treaties of 1977 that gave control of the canal to PANAMA. Carter's lack of power with the Congress was mirrored in his 1979 failure to gain ratification of a U.S.-Soviet arms control treaty. He scored his main foreign policy success in 1979 when he engineered and presided over the Camp David peace treaty between Israel and Egypt. His popularity tumbled after Muslim militants took over the U.S. embassy in Teheran in November 1979, holding a group of U.S. citizens hostage (see IRAN HOSTAGE CRISIS). The failure of a rescue mission in April 1980 added to his unpopularity, and Carter was easily defeated by Ronald REAGAN in the 1980 elections. Carter managed to secure the release of the hostages in the last month of his presidency, and he retired to private life in 1981—a private life of selfless volunteerism that has set him apart from the postpresidential activities of other former chief executives. In January 1994 Carter headed an unofficial American mission to North Korea, where he negotiated a deal with KIM IL SUNG (which subsequently fell through) calling for North Korea to cease its nuclear program in exchange for American oil. Eight months later Carter traveled to Haiti, where he persuaded

General Raoul CÉDRAS to end military rule in Haiti and permit the return of President Jean-Bertrand ARISTIDE to power. In October 2002 he received the Nobel Peace Prize for his many efforts "to find peaceful solutions to international conflicts."

Carter, "Mother" Maybelle (*1909–1978*) American country music singer. Carter was the matriarch of the Original Carter Family, the first group named to the Country Music Hall of Fame. Her guitar style changed that instrument's role in country music. She was identified with such songs as "Wabash Cannonball," "Will the Circle Be Unbroken" and "Wildwood Flower." (See also BLUEGRASS; COUNTRY AND WESTERN MUSIC.)

Carter, William Hodding, Jr. (*1907–1972*) American journalist. In 1938 he became editor and publisher of the *Delta Democratic-Times* in Greenville, Mississippi. He won the 1945 Pulitzer Prize for his editorials against racial segregation in the South and was called "the spokesman for the New South." His son **Hodding Carter III** was a prominent adviser to President Jimmy CARTER.

Carter v. Carter Coal Co. *(1936)* U.S. Supreme Court decision that declared one of President Franklin D. ROOSEVELT'S NEW DEAL programs illegal. An important part of the New Deal program to revive the U.S. economy, the Bituminous Coal Conservation Act allowed mine operators to set work and hour standards for workers. The Supreme Court declared that the federal government could not regulate mining because mining was not interstate commerce. The Supreme Court also declared illegal the act's requirement that mine operators collectively bargain with the mineworkers' unions. This case followed the Supreme Court's rejection of FDR's AGRICULTURAL ADJUSTMENT ACT and amounted to a serious roadblock to FDR's economic reform program and also led to FDR's COURT-PACKING ATTEMPT, when he sought to add additional justices to the Court who were more sympathetic to his New Deal programs.

Cartier-Bresson, Henri *(1908–2004)* French photojournalist. He began his career as a photographer in 1930 and became a cinematographic assistant to Jean RENOIR in 1936. Widely exhibited throughout the world, he was one of the founders of the photographic agency Magnum in 1947. Cartier-Bresson photographed around the globe, employing black and white and refusing to crop his images. His expressive compositions are considered among the most effective of all documentary photographs. His numerous books of photographs include *The Decisive Movement* (1952), *China in Transition* (1956), *The World of Henri Cartier-Bresson* (1968), *About Russia* (1974) and *Henri Cartier-Bresson: Photographer* (1979). In spring 2003 Cartier-Bresson, Martine Franck, and their daughter Mélanie established the Henri Cartier-Bresson (HCB) Foundation in Paris, which sponsors three exhibitions of promising artists and bestows an annual HCB Award for Creativity.

Cartland, Dame Barbara Hamilton *(1901–2000)* British novelist. A writer of popular romantic fiction, Cartland was notable for her extraordinary output. Between the mid-1920s and the late 1980s she wrote literally hundreds of books, all following a basic plot formula; she is listed in the *GUINNESS BOOK OF RECORDS* as the best-selling author in the world. Cartland, who claimed to write a novel in seven days, also published under her married name, Barbara McCorquedale. In 1991 Cartland was made a Dame of the British Empire by Queen Elizabeth II.

Caruso, Enrico *(1873–1921)* The legendary Caruso is commonly regarded as the greatest operatic tenor—if not the greatest singer—of the 20th century. He was certainly the most famous singer of his lifetime, and 70 years after his death his name remains a household word, even in households where opera is never heard. Caruso was born in the slums of Naples, the 18th of 21 children. His father intended him to become a mechanic; however, Caruso discovered his musical gifts at an early age and ran away from home at 16 to pursue his vocation. His professional operatic debut was in 1894 in Naples; over the next few years he sang at provincial opera houses throughout Italy, building his repertoire and his reputation. He debuted at Milan's La Scala in 1900 (as Rodolfo in PUCCINI'S *La Bohème*) and made his first appearance at the Metropolitan Opera in New York in 1903 as the Duke in *Rigoletto*. For the next 17 seasons he was the leading Italian tenor at the Met, singing over 600 performances at that house. He also sang frequently in Europe and toured Latin America. Among his many famous roles were Alfredo in *La Traviata,* Manrico in *Il Trovatore,* Canio in *Pagliacci* and Des Grieux in *Manon Lescaut.* Before the end of the century's first decade, Caruso had become an international celebrity, known as much for his zest for life and his sense of humor as for his singing.

Part of Caruso's fame during his lifetime stems from the fact that he took full advantage of the new recording technology. If recordings helped to secure Caruso's fame, his voice helped to establish the record industry. His rendition of "Vesti la giubba" was the first recording ever to sell 1 million copies. Caruso's contemporaries, including many other celebrated singers, acknowledged the greatness of his voice. Much has been written about that voice: It has been called warm, powerful, beautiful and golden; it was (and is, even in the primitive acoustic recordings of his time) instantly recognizable. Caruso died at the peak of his career from bronchial pneumonia.

Carvel, Tom (Thomas Andreas Carvelas) *(1906–1990)* Greek-born inventor and entrepreneur. He invented a machine to make soft ice cream, later known as frozen custard. With a $15 loan from his future wife, he started a business that grew into the Carvel Corp., the nation's third-largest chain of ice cream stores. He sold the chain to Investcorp in 1989 for more than $80 million. He became known to millions of people with his gravel-voiced radio and television advertisements, asking listeners to "please visit your local Carvel store."

Carver, George Washington *(1864–1943)* U.S. agricultural scientist. Born to a black farm family in Missouri, he and his mother were stolen and taken to Arkansas, where his mother was sold and he was traded for a race horse. After he returned to his former home in Missouri, he worked his way through high school and college and graduated in 1894. He was elected to the faculty of Iowa State University, where he devoted himself to bacterial laboratory work in botany. After gaining his master's degree in 1896, he was named chairman of the department of agriculture at Tuskegee Institute in Alabama, where he devoted the rest of his life to agricultural research. He won international recognition for discovering industrial uses for such agricultural products as peanuts, sweet potatoes and soybeans, as well as cotton wastes. His discovery of 300 by-products of the peanut gave hope for a crop to replace the sagging cotton economy of the South.

Carver is noted for his work to elevate the position of fellow blacks. He was chosen a member of the Royal Society of Arts in London in 1916. In 1939 he received the Roosevelt medal for his valuable contribution to agricultural science. During World War II he developed many dyes to replace those that could no longer be imported from Europe. January 5 has been designated George Washington Carver Day by the U.S. Congress. The George Washington Carver National Monument was established on the Missouri farm where he was born.

Carver, Raymond *(1938–1988)* American short story writer. Carver was widely regarded as the laureate of America's working poor. Writing in short, declarative sentences, he portrayed the hard underside of blue-collar life in the Pacific Northwest, where he spent his childhood. Among his most highly regarded works were *Will You Please Be Quiet, Please?* (1976), *What We Talk About When We Talk About Love* (1981), *Cathedral* (1984) and *Fires* (1983). Married twice, he spent much of his life struggling with alcohol and poverty.

Cary, (Arthur) Joyce Lunel *(1888–1957)* Anglo-Irish novelist. Born in Londonderry, Northern Ireland, of an old Anglo-Irish family, Cary studied art at Edinburgh Art School and law at Trinity College, Cambridge. He served in the BALKAN WAR OF 1912–1913 and in WORLD WAR I in Nigeria, returning to England in 1920. His first novel *Aissa Saved,* appeared in 1932 when he was 44. His first seven novels feature Nigerians and Irish peasants and children. *A House of Children* (1941) was based on his own youth. His greatest achievements were two trilogies (1941–44 and 1952–55) on the subjects of art and politics in 20th-century England; a third trilogy, on religion, remained unfinished at his death. Each volume is narrated by a different protagonist, thus allowing three points of view for each story. Most famous is *The Horse's Mouth* (1944), narrated by the scoundrel Gully Jimson.

Casablanca Conference Meeting on January 14, 1943, between U.S. president Franklin D. ROOSEVELT and British prime minister Winston CHURCHILL in CASABLANCA, MOROCCO, during WORLD WAR II. The Allied leaders reiterated their insistence on the unconditional surrender of the AXIS powers, decided to invade ITALY through Sicily and to intensify the bombing of GERMANY before mounting an invasion of occupied FRANCE, and agreed that more British forces should be sent to the Asian theater following victory in Europe.

Casadesus, Robert *(1899–1973)* French pianist and composer. Born in Paris, he was a member of a family of eminent 20th-century musicians. He studied at the Paris Conservatory, began his distinguished concert career in 1922 and continued to travel and concertize for the rest of his life. Casadesus moved to the U.S. in 1940, returning to France to become director of the American Conservatory at Fontainebleau (1945–49). A pianist with a limpid and lyric style, he was particularly noted for his performance of French music and often appeared with his wife, pianist **Gaby Casadesus.** A gifted teacher and composer, he wrote seven symphonies, numerous piano and violin concertos, songs and other orchestral and piano works.

Casals, Pablo *(1876–1973)* Spanish cellist and conductor. A prodigy, Casals first studied violin, then adopted the cello as his primary instrument at the age of 12. He began giving concerts in 1891, touring Europe and the U.S. to great acclaim. He, the violinist Jacques THIBAUD and the pianist Alfred CORTOT formed a chamber trio in 1905. He began conducting in 1908 and founded the Orquestra Pau Casals in Barcelona in 1919. In 1939 Casals went into self-imposed exile in the south of France in protest against Spain's FRANCO regime. After organizing many music festivals in France, in 1956 he settled in Puerto Rico, where he again put together many successful musical events. Famed for his interpretations of the Bach suites for unaccompanied cello, he was an adored public figure and one of the greatest musicians of the 20th century as cellist, conductor, composer, pianist and teacher.

Casement, Sir Roger David *(1864–1916)* Irish revolutionary leader. In the British consular service early in his career, he exposed atrocities in the rubber plantations of the Congo in 1903–04 and in South America in 1910–12 and was knighted in 1911 for these achievements. A committed Irish nationalist, he retired from the consular service to further the nationalist movement. After the outbreak of World War I, Casement traveled to the U.S. and then to Germany (1914) in search of aid for an Irish uprising. Securing only promises, he was landed in IRELAND by a German U-boat in 1916 on the eve of the EASTER REBELLION. Arrested by the British, he was tried for treason, convicted and hanged. In order to lessen his credibility, British agents circulated his diaries, which contained homosexual passages. Nonetheless, Casement was considered an Irish martyr and continues to be revered by Irish nationalists.

Casimir, Hendrik Brugt Gerhard *(1909–2000)* Dutch physicist. Casimir studied at the Universities of Leiden, Copenhagen and Zurich, and held various research positions between 1933 and 1942. He published many papers in the fields of theoretical physics, applied mathematics and low-temperature physics. His most notable work has been in the theory of the superconducting state. Following the work of W. Meissner, Casimir and his colleague Cornelis Gorter advanced a "two-fluid" model of superconductivity in 1934. They were successful in explaining the high degree of interrelationship between the magnetic and thermal properties of superconductors. After 1942 Casimir pursued a highly successful career with the Philips company, becoming director of the Philips' Research Laboratories in 1946 and a member of the board of management (1957–72). He supervised Philip's research activities in several countries.

Caspersson, Torbjörn Oskar *(1910–1997)* Swedish cytochemist. Caspersson earned his M.D. from Stockholm University in 1936. He then joined the staff of the Nobel Institute, where he was appointed professor of medical cellular research and genetics in 1944. In the late 1930s Caspersson spent a few years working on DNA. In 1936 with the Swiss chemist Rudolf Signer he made fundamental measurements of the molecule. These measurements showed nucleic acids to be larger than protein molecules. Further important data were collected by a photoelectric spectrophotometer developed by Caspersson. This work showed that protein synthesis in the cell was associated with an abundance of RNA. Despite this Caspersson remained committed to the orthodox view that genes were proteins and believed nucleic acids to be a structure-determining supporting substance.

Cassatt, Mary *(1845–1926)* American painter. Born in Pittsburgh, she studied at the Pennsylvania Academy of the Fine Arts (1861–65) and at the

Academy of Parma, Italy (1872), before settling in Paris. Spending most of her life in France, she was a friend of such artists as Manet and Degas, who became important influences on her work. Associated with the French Impressionists and the only American to exhibit with them, she was also influenced by the color and pattern of Japanese prints. Taking motherhood as her most frequent subject, Cassatt was an accomplished painter, pastel artist and etcher. Her images are intimate and colorful, very personal interpretations of the Impressionist esthetic. Included in many of the world's most important public collections, her best-known paintings in American museums include versions of *Mother and Child* in the Metropolitan Museum of Art, New York City, and the Museum of Fine Arts, Boston, as well as *Morning Toilette* (1886) and *The Boating Party* (1893), both at the National Gallery of Art, Washington, D.C. In 2003 the U.S. Postal Service issued a series of stamps that reproduced four of her paintings.

Cassavetes, John *(1929–1989)* American actor, screenwriter and film director. Cassavetes starred in such films as *Rosemary's Baby* and *Edge of the City;* in 1967 he was nominated for an ACADEMY AWARD for his performance as a psycopathic soldier in *The Dirty Dozen.* His own films, which he financed through his acting, were distinguished by a quirky, improvisational quality; several of them starred his wife, actress Gena Rowlands, and his friends actors Ben Gazzara and Peter Falk. Although his work was never popular with mass audiences, Cassavetes garnered Academy Award nominations in 1968 for his screenplay *Faces* and in 1974 for directing *A Woman Under the Influence.*

Cassin, René *(1887–1976)* French jurist. Cassin served in WORLD WAR I before becoming a professor of international law. Deeply interested in veterans' affairs, he founded and ran the Federal Union of Associations of Disabled and Aged War Veterans. Secretary of defense for the French government-in-exile during WORLD WAR II, he directed the military activities of the FREE FRENCH. After the war he became one of France's most prominent jurists,

serving on numerous boards and commissions. Cassin became an important figure in the human rights movement as a delegate to the United Nations Commission on Human Rights, the author of its Universal Declaration of Human Rights and later as its chairman. He was a founder of the UNITED NATIONS EDUCATIONAL, SCIENTIFIC AND CULTURAL ORGANIZATION (UNESCO) and president of the International Institute of Human Rights. In 1968 Cassin was awarded the Nobel Peace Prize.

Cassino Town, monastery and battleground in Frosinone province, Italy. During WORLD WAR II the monastery, in a key location on a hill (HILL 516), was a part of the German Gustav Line that blocked the Allied road to Rome. Some of the fiercest fighting of the war occurred here from February to May 1944, when the town and monastery were destroyed. Both were subsequently reconstructed. (See also WORLD WAR II ON THE ITALIAN FRONT.)

Cassirer, Ernst *(1874–1945)* German philosopher. Cassirer became renowned as one of the leading exponents of neo-Kantian philosophy in the 20th century. As a professor at the University of Hamburg, he was an influential philosopher in his native land. Due to his Jewish heritage, he was forced to leave Nazi Germany in 1933 and subsequently taught at Oxford University in England and at Yale University in the U.S., where he died in 1945. The key philosophical issues to which Cassirer devoted himself were the history of scientific theory, the epistemological problem of the nature of human knowledge and the structure of mythic thought. As a neo-Kantian, Cassirer stressed the need for symbolic representations to interpret reality. His major works include the three-volume *Philosophy of Symbolic Forms* (1923–29), *Language and Myth* (1925), *An Essay on Man* (1944) and *The Myth of the State* (1946).

Castaneda, Carlos *(1925?–1998)* American anthropologist and spiritual philosopher. Castaneda created a sensation both in America and in Europe with his first book, *The Teachings of Don Juan: A Yaqui Way of Knowledge* (1968), which was originally submitted as an academic thesis by Castaneda while he was a graduate student in an-

thropology at the University of California at Santa Cruz. The book detailed the life of a Yaqui Indian shaman living in Mexico who taught Castaneda, in part through the use of peyote and other hallucinogenic plants, of the existence of an alternative mode of reality in which humans and nature merged and communication with nonhuman life forms and energies was possible. Since its publication, a scholarly controversy has arisen as to whether Castaneda fictionalized the character of Don Juan in part or in whole; no definitive answer has been reached. Whether regarded as anthropology or literature, the works of Castaneda have exercised a major influence on the NEW AGE MOVEMENT. His other books include *Tales of Power* (1974), *The Fire from Within* (1984) and *The Power of Silence* (1987).

Castelnuovo-Tedesco, Mario *(1895–1968)* Italian-American composer. Born in Florence, Castelnuovo-Tedesco was educated there under Ildebrando Pizzetti. He undertook commissions for such performers as Andrés SEGOVIA, Jascha HEIFETZ and Gregor Piatigorsky beginning in the mid-1920s. By the 1930s he was one of the most frequently performed contemporary Italian composers. When anti-Semitic laws were promulgated in Italy in 1938, Castelnuovo-Tedesco, who was Jewish, immigrated to the U.S. (1939), where he became an American citizen and an influential music teacher. Known for their delicacy and refinement, his numerous compositions include film scores, songs, operas, orchestral music, chamber pieces, oratorios, concertos and piano music.

Castle, Barbara Anne *(1911–2002)* British politician. Castle was elected to Parliament in 1945 and became a member of the LABOUR PARTY national executive committee in 1950. She served as minister of overseas development from 1964 to 1965, minister of transport from 1965 to 1968, secretary of state for employment and productivity from 1968 to 1970 and secretary of state for social services from 1974 to 1976. In 1979 Castle was elected a member of the European Parliament. In 1993 Castle published her political autobiography, *Fighting All the Way.*

Castle, Irene and Vernon Irene Castle (1893–1969, born Irene Foote) and Vernon Castle (1887–1918, born Vernon Castle Blythe) were noted exhibition ballroom dancers and teachers. British-born Vernon married New Yorker Irene in 1911, and they became one of the most successful and influential ballroom dance teams of their day. Noted for their elegant style, the Castles introduced such dances as the Castle walk and the Castle polka and created a new style for ballroom dancing by popularizing such dances as the tango and the hesitation waltz. Together they wrote *The Modern Dance* in 1914. When Vernon was killed in an air crash in 1918, Irene retired from dancing and wrote *Castles in the Air* in 1958. Fred ASTAIRE and Ginger ROGERS starred in the 1939 film of their lives, *The Story of Vernon and Irene Castle.*

Castro Ruz, Fidel (*1926– *) Cuban revolutionary and premier (1959–1976) and president (1976–) of Cuba. As a young lawyer, Castro was an outspoken critic of the regime of Fulgencio BATISTA, which he toppled on January 1, 1959, after two previous, unsuccessful attempts. Initial American support for Castro eroded as he broadened his ties with the Soviet Union. In December 1961, shortly after the disastrous American-backed BAY OF PIGS INVASION, Castro declared himself to be a Marxist-Leninist. The CUBAN MISSILE CRISIS (1962) added to international tensions, as U.S. president John F. KENNEDY demanded that the Russians withdraw their offensive missiles from Cuban soil. The Russians complied, but the world lay on the brink of war throughout the crisis. Castro's domestic policies—especially his nationalization of the economy—have been brought into question by such crises as the failed sugar harvest of 1970, while Cuban military involvement in Africa and elsewhere has drawn strong condemnation. With the end of the COLD WAR, as Eastern European nations turned from communism in 1989–90, and the defeat of the Marxist Sandinista regime in Nicaragua, Castro became increasingly isolated. However, he continued to espouse his belief in revolutionary Marxism. In 1998 Castro permitted Pope JOHN PAUL II to visit Cuba and make contact with the Catholic Church hierarchy within that country.

Castroviejo, Ramón (*1904–1987*) Spanish-born eye surgeon. Castroviejo was one of the first surgeons to perform successful cornea transplants. In 1938 he made a public appeal to Americans to will their eyes to science to help restore the eyesight of others. His appeal helped led to the creation of present-day eye banks. He was based in New York for most of his career.

Cather, Willa Sibert (*1876–1947*) American novelist. Born in Virginia, she was raised in Nebraska and later attended the University of Nebraska. She taught, worked as a journalist and published her first volume of poetry, *April Twilight,* in 1903, followed by a collection of short stories, *The Troll Garden* (1905). In 1906 she moved to New York, working on the staff of *McClure's Magazine* until 1912, when she published her first novel, *Alexander's Bridge.* With *O, Pioneers!* (1913), the story of Swedish immigrants in Nebraska, she found her characteristic voice and themes. *My Ántonia* (1918) tells the story of an immigrant girl from Bohemia in Nebraska; the convincing first-person narrative is written from a male character's viewpoint. Other works include *The Song of the Lark* (1915); her best-known book, *Death Comes for the Archbishop* (1927), a historical novel set in a New Mexico mission; *Lucy Greyheart* (1935), in which a music student is torn between traditional values and those of the artistic world; and *Not Under Forty* (1936).

Cats Musical play created by Andrew LLOYD WEBBER. Based on T. S. ELIOT's child-oriented book of poems, *Old Possum's Book of Practical Cats,* Lloyd Webber's musical premiered in London on May 11, 1981; it began its 18-year run in the U.S. the following year. It continued playing to London audiences until May 11, 2002, when its 8,949 performances made it the longest-running musical in history; on May 12, 1989, it surpassed the previous record of 3,358 performances held by another production of Lloyd Webber, *Jesus Christ, Superstar.* In September 2000, after becoming the longest-running musical in Broadway history, *Cats* ceased production. During its production by stationary musical companies in London and New York and by touring companies, *Cats* generated more than $2 billion in revenue worldwide.

CAT scan Popular name for computerized axial tomography, a merger of computer and X-RAY technology that can be used to diagnose problems in any internal organ of the body, including the brain. Invented in 1961, introduced in 1972 and widely available since the mid-1970s, the tomograph focuses X-rays 100 times more sensitive than ordinary X-rays on specific planes of the body by rotating a scanner around the body. The X-ray beams are picked up by a detector and fed into a computer, which then creates an analysis of the information provided on tissue density. This analysis is converted into cathode-ray-tube pictures of detailed cross-sections of these complicated structures. By allowing doctors to examine the body and brain without invasive procedures, this painless procedure has created a revolution in the diagnosis of tumors, blood clots, cysts, abscesses and other disorders.

Catton, Bruce (*1899–1978*) American journalist and historian. Catton wrote 13 volumes on the American Civil War and won the PULITZER PRIZE (1954) for his book *A Stillness at Appomattox.* He was also senior editor of *American Heritage* magazine.

Caucasia (Caucasus) Area of the the former Soviet Union between the Black Sea and the Caspian Sea, on the west and east, and southwestern Russia and the Caucasus Mountains, on the north and south. A blend of various peoples, it was under Russian domination in the 19th century following wars with Turkey and Persia; but Russian control was rigorously challenged by the Muslims of Azerbaijan. Oil-rich Caucasia was critically important to the USSR in WORLD WAR II, and a German attack was aimed at the area in July 1942. The initial assault was triumphant, but the Germans were driven back by a counteroffensive in January 1943. In December 1991 the Soviet Union disintegrated, and the peoples of the Caucasus were divided among the former Soviet Socialist Republics such as ARMENIA and AZERBAIJAN.

Cauthen, Steve (*1960– *) American jockey. Born in Texas, Cauthen was licensed to ride professionally at age 16. The 1977 jockey of the year, Cauthen set the American racing world on fire, riding AFFIRMED to the TRIPLE CROWN one year later. The crush of publicity that attended his every move contributed to his decision in 1979 to move his career to England. The first American in nearly 80 years to win the Epsom Derby, he is the only jockey to have ridden winners in both the Epsom and Kentucky Derbies. The first jockey to win over $6 million, he had already ridden more than 1,000 winners before the end of 1990. In 1993 Cauthen retired from jockeying.

Cavafy, Constantine Peter (1863–1933) Greek poet. Except for a few years in Liverpool and Constantinople, Cavafy spent most of his life in the cosmopolitan, half-oriental city of Alexandria. Scion of a wealthy merchant family, he worked intermittently as a journalist, broker and civil servant but generally lived a sybaritic existence. Though only a few of his poems were privately printed in his lifetime, he was nonetheless celebrated as the greatest Mediterranean poet of modern times. His main themes were homosexual love, art and politics. His political poems are set in the Levantine provinces and the Eastern Roman and Byzantine Empires. His poetry is devoid of imagery, written in a mixture of demotic and pure Greek that is remarkable for its simultaneous ordinariness and lyrical beauty. *Complete Poems of C. P. Cavafy* (1961) and *Passions and Ancient Days* (1971) were published posthumously. Cavafy is also known as the "poet of the city" in Lawrence DURRELL'S ALEXANDRIA QUARTET.

Cavallero, Ugo (1880–1943) Italian general. A successful industrialist and an undersecretary of war during the 1920s, Cavallero served as head of Italian forces in West Africa from 1936 to 1937. He headed the Italian campaign in Greece and was appointed chief of the general staff late in 1940. Displeased with a number of defeats Cavallero had suffered in Africa and with his increasing closeness with the Germans, MUSSOLINI replaced him with General Ambrosio in 1943. After Mussolini's fall later that year, Cavallero was arrested on orders from premier Pietro BADOGLIO. He committed suicide on September 12, 1943.

Cavalli-Sforza, Luigi Luca (1922–) Italian geneticist. He was educated at the University of Pavia, where he earned his M.D. in 1944. After working on bacterial genetics at Cambridge (1948–50) and Milan (1950–57), he held chairs in genetics at Parma (1958–62) and Pavia (1962–70). In 1970 he was appointed professor of genetics at Stanford University in California. Cavalli-Sforza specialized mainly in the genetics of human populations. He also did much to show how genetic data from current human racial groups could be used to reconstruct their past separations. This reconstruction, based on the analysis of 58 genes, yields an evolutionary tree with Caucasian and African races in one branch and Orientals, Oceanians and Amerinds in the other. The main division appeared, according to Cavalli-Sforza, some 35,000 to 40,000 years ago.

Cavell, Edith (1865–1915) English nurse. Appointed head of a Brussels hospital in 1907, she remained there after the German occupation in 1914. She was arrested by the Germans in 1915, admitted to aiding Allied soldiers to escape to Holland and was executed by firing squad. Her death caused a furor in Great Britain and was used for anti-German propaganda throughout WORLD WAR I.

Cayman Islands The Cayman Islands (Grand Cayman, Little Cayman and Cayman Brac) cover a total area of 100 square miles in the Caribbean. Currently a dependent territory of the United Kingdom and a member of the COMMONWEALTH, the islands were a dependency of JAMAICA until 1962. Administered by a governor and a partially elected executive council, the islands are noted for their offshore banking and financial services, which developed in the 1960s and 1970s. In 1992 the islands' government sought to reform the banking institutions of the Bank of Credit and Commerce International (BCCI), which had falsified its balance sheets and provided secret tax exemptions. An additional banking scandal occurred in 1996 when the U.S. captured a Mexican drug trafficker who used the Cayman Islands to launder money en route to Switzerland.

CBS American TELEVISION and RADIO network, one of the three major broadcasting networks in the U.S. The company was founded in New York in 1927 by impresario Arthur JUDSON as United Independent Broadcasters, Inc. In 1929 William S. PALEY bought a controlling interest in the company. During the GREAT DEPRESSION the CBS radio network broadcast a wide variety of programs, including radio dramas, serials, comedy and variety shows and news. During WORLD WAR II the network broadcast regular reports from Britain by Edward R. MURROW, perhaps the most famous of all broadcast journalists. Murrow brought other distinguished journalists into the broadcast medium via CBS; after the war he originated such documentary programs as *Hear It Now* and *SEE IT NOW* on the network.

CBS made a successful transition into television broadcasting in the postwar era. Comedy and variety shows of this period established entertainers like Lucille BALL, Milton BERLE, Jackie GLEASON and Ed SULLIVAN as masters of the new medium. In the 1960s CBS news was renowned for its coverage of political conventions, the space program and the VIETNAM WAR; anchorman Walter CRONKITE achieved a reputation as perhaps the most trusted man in the U.S. In the 1970s CBS presented situation comedies with a social message; foremost among these programs were *ALL IN THE FAMILY* and *M*A*S*H*. Like the other networks, CBS was challenged in the 1980s by the advent of cable television and alternate forms of home entertainment. In 1999 CBS was purchased by the entertainment corporation Viacom.

Ceauşescu, Nicolae (1918–1989) Communist dictator of Romania (1965–89). Born into a large peasant family, Ceauşescu joined the illegal Communist Party youth organization in 1933 and was jailed by King CAROL II's government for his political agitation prior to World War II. After the war he rose rapidly in the now-ruling Communist Party. He became a full member of the Central Committee in 1952 and by 1957 was second only to his mentor, party leader Gheorghe GHEORGHIU-DEJ. Upon the death of Gheorghiu-Dej (1965), Ceauşescu became the party's first secretary. In 1968 he assumed the title of president, moved his relatives into important government and party positions and made himself the center of a cult of personality rivaled in Eastern Europe only by the late Soviet leader Joseph STALIN. However, Ceaușescu followed a foreign policy independent of the USSR; he maintained good relations with ISRAEL, condemned the SOVIET INVASION OF CZECHOSLOVAKIA and did not join the East-bloc boycott of the 1984 summer OLYMPIC GAMES. Ceaușescu's maverick stance irritated the Kremlin but gained him favor among both Western and developing nations.

While he was feted abroad, many Romanians regarded him as a ruthless tyrant. As Romania's economy faltered in the late 1980s, Ceaușescu pressed ahead with grandiose, disastrous schemes. He created severe shortages at home with the wholesale export of food and fuel to pay off Romania's foreign debt. He destroyed many rural villages and forcibly displaced their populations to make way for agricultural-industrial complexes that were never built. He steadily opposed any reforms in Romania, as communist governments began to topple elsewhere in Eastern Europe. After a massacre of unarmed protesters in Timișoara (December 17, 1989), armed rebellion broke out, with much of the army joining the people against the dreaded Securitate, Ceaușescu's elite paramilitary secret police. Ceaușescu and his wife fled the presidential palace on December 22 but were apprehended the following day. A tribunal of the provisional government tried and convicted the couple of genocide, abuse of power, undermining the economy and theft of government funds; they were executed on December 25.

Cech, Thomas (1947–) American scientist, winner of the NOBEL PRIZE in chemistry (along with Sidney Altman) in 1989 for research that confirmed RNA's function as a catalyst for cells. Born in Chicago, Cech grew up in Iowa City, Iowa. In the fourth grade he exhibited his first interest in science when he began a rock collection and started studying about the formation of mineral deposits, often going to the geology department at the University of Iowa to ask professors questions and to see their crystal structural models. He earned a B.S. in chemistry at Grinnel College (1970) and entered graduate school at the University of California, Berkeley, graduating from

that institution in 1975. After completing his postdoctoral assignment at MIT, Cech accepted an invitation in 1978 to join the University of Colorado. There he began to focus his research on RNA.

By 1982 Cech's experiments on RNA led to his discovery of a large sequence of noncoding DNA called an "intron" in a protozoan life form called a Tetrahymena. In his efforts to remove the intron from the RNA of the Tetrahymena, Cech discovered that he could splice the segment out of the produced RNA without injecting splicing enzymes into the cell. This led Cech to conclude that RNA contained its own splicing mechanism, which it could use to splice itself into segments that would produce proteins needed for cell functions. Cech termed this RNA a ribozyme. Initially, Cech's discovery was greeted by skepticism among the scientific community, as it was the first study to suggest that RNA's function was not completely dependent on the arrival and interaction of external enzymes. However, a 1983 experiment and report by Sidney Altman posted similar conclusions on the function of RNA as an enzyme.

Cech's experiments at Colorado and his growing prestige among scientists eventually led the university to designate him as a professor of chemistry, biochemistry and cell and developmental biology. Cech also obtained the position of professor of chemistry at the Howard Hughes Medical Institute in 1988 and became president of that institution in 1999. In 1989 Cech and Altman both received the Nobel Prize in chemistry for their contribution to the understanding of RNA and the development of cellular life. Additionally, he has received honorary doctorates from Grinnell (1987) and the University of Chicago (1991). In 1987 Cech joined the Howard Hughes Medical Institute as an investigator and continued to do research on RNA. He became president of the institute in 2001.

Cecil, (Edgar Algernon) Robert Gascoyne (Viscount Cecil of Chelwood) (1864–1958) British statesman. A son of the marquess of Salisbury, Cecil was educated at Eton and Oxford and became a London barrister. A Conservative, he was elected to Parlia-

ment in 1906 and became known for his progressive views on free trade, women's suffrage and internationalism. During WORLD WAR I he was active with the International Committee of the RED CROSS. In 1919 he and U.S. president Woodrow WILSON drafted the Covenant of the LEAGUE OF NATIONS. In 1923 he was created a viscount. Cecil remained a leading figure in the league until it dissolved in 1946. For his league work, Cecil was awarded the 1937 NOBEL PRIZE for peace. His autobiography, *All the Way,* was published in 1949.

Cédras, Raoul (1950–) Haitian military officer, leader of Haiti (1991–94). In September 1991 Lieutenant General Cédras led a military coup that overthrew HAITI's first popularly elected president, Jean-Bertrand ARISTIDE, and established himself in control of a military junta that ran the small Caribbean state. Aristide, however, escaped to the U.S., where he spent three years in exile. In September 1994 an independent mission composed of former U.S. president Jimmy CARTER and former U.S. chairman of the Joint Chiefs of Staff Colin POWELL traveled to Haiti to persuade Cédras to step down and permit the return of Aristide. Both Carter and Powell convinced Cédras that U.S. president Bill CLINTON would keep his promise to use military force to return Aristide to power and overthrow the junta. The following month Cédras and several of his closest associates left Haiti in exile, and U.S. troops restored Aristide to the executive mansion in Haiti.

Célan, Paul (Paul Antschel) (1920–1970) German poet. Célan was born in a German-speaking area of ROMANIA and largely educated there. In 1942 his Jewish parents were deported to a CONCENTRATION CAMP, but he managed to escape. In 1948 he immigrated to Paris, eventually becoming a French citizen. His poems began to appear in periodicals in the late 1940s. His second book, *Mohn und Gedachtnis* (Poppy and memories, 1952), established his reputation as an important poet of the HOLOCAUST. His most famous poem, "Todesfugue" (Death fugue), describes the Jewish experience under NAZISM. Its dark images and tragic themes recur throughout his subsequent collections. Readers occasionally find Célan's innovative diction difficult; he described his poetry as "a message in a bottle." In 1960 he received the Georg Buchner Prize. He committed suicide in 1970 at the age of 49.

Celibidache, Sergiu *(1912–1996)* Romanian composer and conductor. Celibidache studied in Paris and Berlin and acted as the permanent conductor of the Berlin Philharmonic Orchestra from 1945 to 1952, introducing many avant-garde works to its repertoire. He later directed the Munich Philharmonic but rarely appeared with other major orchestras because he insisted on extensive rehearsal time. Because of this and his refusal to make recordings, Celibidache reached a limited audience but became something of a cult figure. He was noted for his discipline, accuracy and finesse, as well as for his eccentric musical theories and his personal elusiveness. His own compositions include four symphonies, a piano concerto and an orchestral suite, *Der Taschengarten*.

Céline, Louis-Ferdinand (pen name of Louis-Ferdinand Destouches) *(1894–1961)* French novelist. Educated at Rennes Medical School, Céline practiced medicine throughout his life in addition to writing, working from 1925 to 1928 at the Rockefeller Foundation in New York. Céline's first novel, *Voyage au bout de la nuit* (1932; translated as *Journey to the End of Night*, 1934), is a sordid story of a ruthless doctor working in the slums following WORLD WAR I. The relentless misanthropy of Céline's work, combined with his later expressions of ANTI-SEMITISM and FASCISM, thwarted much critical or popular praise for it. However, his writing is nightmarishly evocative, and his powerful use of language has been praised. His writing has been likened to that of James JOYCE and Marcel PROUST and compared to the paintings of Goya and Dürer. Others of his many novels include *Mort à crédit* (1936; translated as *Death on the Installment Plan*, 1938); *Ballet sans personne, sans musique, sans rien*, (A ballet without anyone, without music, without anything, 1959), and *Nord* (North, 1960).

Celler, Emanuel *(1888–1981)* American politician. A Democrat from New York, Celler served in the U.S. House of Representatives for half a century (1922–72). Known for his liberal views, he chaired the influential House Judiciary Committee for a record 22 years (1949–53, 1955–72). He supported key programs of the NEW DEAL and the FAIR DEAL and opposed the HOUSE UN-AMERICAN ACTIVITIES COMMITTEE. He was credited with authoring and handling the passage of the landmark Civil Rights Acts of 1957, 1960 and 1964 (see CIVIL RIGHTS ACT OF 1964). He also left his mark on major antitrust, labor and immigration legislation. He gained a reputation as a combative, colorful debater.

cellular telephone A mobile telephone that enables audio and computer communication through the transmission of low-power radio waves instead of through wire-bound connections arranged through local or national telephone companies. Commercially, cellular telephones (or cell phones) were first successfully tested in the late 1970s by Illinois Bell. By the mid-1980s local and regional carrier services for these cell phones began to spring up across the nation. Broadcasting at frequencies between 800 and 900 megahertz, these carriers generally operated off of a single radio antenna located in the city or region in question, with each cell phone assigned a specific frequency over which it alone could operate; this in turn led to a high monthly fee for such cell phone use. Early cell phone users encountered additional problems from local radio stations, whose signals would occasionally interfere with those of the cell phones, and from the unwieldy size of the early phone models. Despite these problems there was a high consumer demand for cell phones, leading the Federal Communications Commission in the mid-1990s to increase the number of permitted telephone service providers per service area from one to six. Learning from the constraints created by the single-antenna early years of the cell phone industry, these companies soon developed networks of cellular towers. Instead of erecting metal towers across cities, however, these companies searched throughout towns for already existing high-rise buildings, church towers and other such tall structures, and then attached equipment onto them that would repeat and relay cell phone signals as subscribers moved throughout the service area. The result was a greater clarity of the phone signal and a lesser chance that the customer would lose his or her connection. By 1999 the cell phone industry encompassed 76 million subscribers in the U.S. alone. The increase was in large part due to the development of personal communication services (PCS), a cell phone technology that transmits information digitally, instead of the analog signals used by earlier cell phones, for more efficient communication. The greater speed in communication made possible by PCS has allowed contemporary cell phones to connect to the INTERNET, receive e-mail and even transmit photo images.

Cendrars, Blaise (pen name of Frédéric Sauser-Hall) *(1887–1961)* French novelist and poet. Cendrars was born, educated and died in Paris; he first ran away from home at the age of 15. He traveled to Siberia, Panama, China, Persia, Mongolia and America and visited most of Europe, working variously as a filmmaker, journalist, art critic, horticulturist and businessman. His semiautobiographical works feature resilient heroes, rich images and striking effects. During WORLD WAR I he served with the French Foreign Legion. His best-known works include *L'or* (1925; translated as *Sutter's Gold*, 1926), *L'Homme foudroye* (1945; translated as *The Astonished Man*, 1970) and *Le Panama; ou Les Aventures de mon sept oncles* (1918; translated as *Panama; or The Adventures of My Seven Uncles*, 1931). His poetry, which influenced APOLLINAIRE, includes *Dix-neuf poèmes elastiques* (1919) and *Du monde entier* (1919).

Central African Empire Formal name of the CENTRAL AFRICAN REPUBLIC during the period from December 1976 to September 1979. This name was proclaimed by the country's self-styled emperor, Jean-Bédel BOKASSA, who was overthrown in 1979.

Central African Federation A British attempt to protect the interests of the white minority population and to encourage economic development by uniting the African territories of Nyasaland, Northern Rhodesia and Southern Rhodesia. The federation was established on September 3, 1953. Unpopular with the predominantly black population, it collapsed in 1963.

Central African Republic (CAR)

Landlocked country in Africa, bordered by Chad to the north, Sudan to the east, Democratic Republic of Congo and the Republic of Congo to the south and Cameroon to the west. At the end of the 19th century the French occupied the CAR and organized it as the colony of Ubangi-Shari. In 1906 Chad was linked with the colony, and in 1910 the two were joined with Congo and Gabon to form FRENCH EQUATORIAL AFRICA. Despite occasional rebellions, the CAR supported the French RESISTANCE forces in WORLD WAR II. Following the war a rebellion forced the French to allow the establishment of a territorial government and parliament. In 1958 the CAR took its current name and voted to become an independent republic of France. Barthélémy Boganda, a founder of the Movement for the Social Evolution of Black Africa (MESAN), became its first prime minister. Upon his death in an airplane accident in 1969, his nephew, David DACKO, assumed power, becoming president in 1960 when the CAR achieved complete independence. In December 1965 Dacko was ousted by a military coup, and Colonel Jean-Bédel BOKASSA took power. Bokassa established himself as president-for-life in

CENTRAL AFRICAN REPUBLIC (CAR)	
1911	France secures complete control.
1960	CAR achieves full independence with David Dacko as president.
1966	Dacko overthrown by his cousin Colonel Jean-Bédel Bokassa.
1977	Bokassa spends $20–30 million to have himself crowned emperor in imitation of Napoleon.
1979	Amnesty International charges Bokassa in the massacre of 80 schoolchildren.
1979	With the aid of French paratroopers, Bokassa is exiled, and Dacko is restored to the presidency.
1986	Bokassa escapes from France and returns to CAR expecting an enthusiastic reception; captured and sentenced to life imprisonment.
1993	Ange-Félix Patassé elected president.
1999	Patassé reelected.
2003	After a coup, General François Bozizé becomes president.
2005	Bozizé wins presidential election.

1972, marshal of the republic in 1974 and, in an ostentatious and expensive ceremony in 1976, emperor of the Central African Empire. Bokassa's increasingly brutal and repressive regime achieved worldwide notoriety in 1979 when government troops murdered approximately 100 schoolchildren who had protested mandatory school uniforms made by a Bokassa family company. Dacko reassumed power in a bloodless coup later that year and restored the republic. In 1981 yet another coup deposed Dacko, and army chief of staff General André Kolingba took power. Kolingba's regime voided the constitution and banned political parties. Opposition to the regime received some French support, and French president MITTERRAND visited the country to influence Kolingba. There was some evidence of a loosening of Kolingba's autocratic control of the CAR in 1985, when a new constitution was proposed and some civilians were admitted into the government. In 1993 the CAR held free elections in which Ange-Félix Patassé became the first elected president in 12 years. Patassé won reelection in 1999 and in May 2001 survived a coup attempt by Kolingba. However, during a foreign trip in March 2003 Patassé was overthrown by rebel leader François Bozizé.

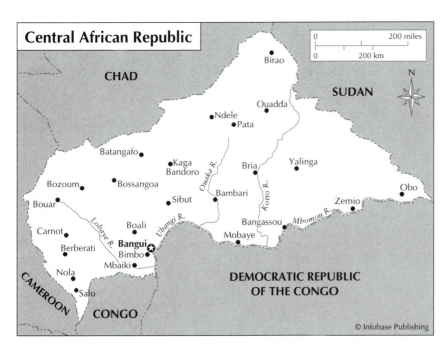

General Bozizé won a democratic election in 2005 and remained in power.

Central American Common Market (CACM)

Regional economic association among Central American states. The CACM was the product of a 1960 treaty among Guatemala, El Salvador, Honduras and Nicaragua designed to create among the signatories a free-trade zone and common tariff policy, integrate and develop their economies, coordinate their foreign and domestic policies and improve the quality of life of their citizens; Costa Rica joined the CACM in 1962. A decade after its founding the CACM had largely proven successful in increasing economic intercourse among its members, generating a 900% increase in intrabloc trade since 1960 and producing a common tariff policy for almost all CACM trading partners. Moreover, member countries had coordinated their approach to various WORLD TRADE ORGANIZATION requirements and succeeded in developing a transportation and public utilities infrastructure that fostered economic, urban and rural growth and improvement. In part because of its success and in the hopes of generating future prosperity, CACM members agreed in 1967 that they would attempt to merge with the Latin American Free Trade Association (LAFTA), a similar though less economically successful organization, in an effort to create a common market throughout Central and South America. However, continued political and military instability in CACM states such as Nicaragua and LAFTA states such as Colombia, and the absence of complementary economic resources between CACM and LAFTA states, repeatedly thwarted the achievement of this goal. Moreover, CACM encountered intra-organizational troubles throughout its existence. In 1969 a war broke out between two of its member states, El Salvador and Honduras, leading Honduras to levy import dues on CACM products and thereby reducing overall trade within the economic bloc. CACM was equally unsuccessful in achieving its goal of political unification. Despite repeated efforts, its member states failed to develop greater interstate coordination on domestic and foreign issues or to produce any notable interstate structures on the EUROPEAN UNION model.

Central Committee of the Communist Party

The highest organ of the COMMUNIST PARTY OF THE USSR between congresses. Its function was to direct all party activities between congresses. From 1917 to 1934 it acted as a quasi-parliament. In order to free himself from dependency on majority support in the central committee, STALIN liquidated 70% of the members between the 17th and 18th party congresses (1934–39). During the period of "collective leadership" after Stalin's death, leaders again had to win the support of the various factions of the central committee. Wider in scope than the Supreme Soviet, the central committee was the main tool of the government until the late 1980s, when GORBACHEV began to alter the Soviet system of government.

Central Intelligence Agency (CIA)

U.S. government agency established in 1947 to coordinate and analyze foreign intelligence. The CIA reports to the U.S. president, to whom alone it is responsible. Under the directorship of Allen DULLES in the 1950s, the CIA moved into more active involvement in foreign affairs, initiating a series of "covert operations" designed to eliminate anti-American interests in such countries as GUATEMALA and IRAN. The 1961 Bay of Pigs debacle forced a reassessment of the CIA's function (see BAY OF PIGS INVASION), and subsequent scandals and alleged domestic civil rights abuses led to further calls for accountability and reform. Despite criticism, the agency maintained its controversial dual role of overseas intelligence source and coercive arm for American interests. In 2003 the CIA came under domestic and foreign criticism for allegedly producing misleading reports for President George W. BUSH that IRAQ possessed weapons of mass destruction, which Bush used as part of his justification for invading Iraq in March 2003.

Central Powers

The nations that fought against the Allies in WORLD WAR I. They included Germany, Austria-Hungary, the Ottoman Empire (Turkey) and Bulgaria.

Century of Progress Exhibition

Chicago's World's Fair of 1933–34; a major showcase of both ART DECO and MODERNISM in architecture and industrial design. Its role as the first publicly accessible showcase for modernist directions was of major significance. Although it occurred at a low point in the GREAT DEPRESSION, the Century of Progress Exhibition included many elements pointing toward future optimism. Architecturally, the fair leaned on established figures. Also present were many more adventurous, smaller projects such as the *House of Tomorrow*, a steel-and-glass octagon complete with airplane hangar for the predicted family plane. Buckminster FULLER's DYMAXION automobile and the Burlington Zephyr railroad train were first seen at this fair. Critics from the historicist Ralph Adams CRAM to the still-controversial modernist Frank Lloyd WRIGHT tended to offer negative comments, finding the fair either too advanced or not advanced enough.

Cerf, Bennett

(1898–1971) American publisher. Born in New York City, he was a lifelong resident; he founded the publishing companies Modern Library (1925) and Random House (1927), where he served as president until 1966. Involved in censorship issues, he fought in the courts to publish James JOYCE's *Ulysses* in the U.S., succeeding in 1933. A witty and punning commentator, he wrote a variety of newspaper columns and several books but became a recognized public figure in the U.S. through his regular appearances on the television show *What's My Line?* (1952–66).

Cernan, Eugene

(1934–) U.S. astronaut. Neil ARMSTRONG had been the first astronaut to walk on the Moon. Cernan is the last—to date. Along with fellow crewman geologist Harrison SCHMITT, Cernan spent more than 22 hours on the Moon, while the third member of the *Apollo 17* (December 7–19, 1972) crew, Ronald Evans, orbited overhead. Humankind's last official words from the Moon lacked much poetry but were simple and heartfelt. Cernan said, "As we leave the Moon at Taurus-Littrow, we leave as we came and, God willing, as we shall return, with peace and hope for all mankind. God bless the crew of Apollo 17." In his two previous spaceflights, Cernan had been pilot of *Gemini 9–A* (June 3–6, 1966) and lunar module pilot of *Apollo*

10 (May 18–26, 1969), which had flown to within 10 miles of the Moon in a test flight. A former navy pilot, Cernan resigned from NASA to enter private industry.

Černík, Oldřich (*1921–1994*) Prime minister of Czechoslovakia (1968–70). Černík held various posts in the Communist Party and government from 1948 to 1968. He became associated with Alexander DUBČEK, who as first secretary introduced reform programs. (See PRAGUE SPRING.) After the SOVIET INVASION OF CZECHOSLOVAKIA in 1968, Černík continued in office until 1970, when, along with many other progressives associated with Dubček, he resigned and was suspended from the Communist Party.

Cernuda, Luis (*1904–1963*) Spanish poet. Cernuda was born in Seville and studied at its university with Pedro Salinas. A member of the GENERATION OF 1927, he was associated with GARCÍA LORCA, ALBERTI and ALEIXANDRE. During the SPANISH CIVIL WAR, he fought with the Loyalists; after 1938 he went into exile in England, the U.S. and Mexico, where he took up permanent residence in 1952. *Perfil del aire* (1927, The air in profile), *Un río, un amor* (1929, A river, a love) and *Los placeres prohibidos* (1931, Forbidden pleasures) show the influence of symbolism and SURREALISM; *Donde habite el olvido* (1934, Where forgetfulness dwells) was inspired by his reading of Holderlin. His collected poems, *La realidad y el deseo* (1936, 1940, 1958, 1964, Reality and desire), run a gamut of styles from traditionalism to free verse. His poetry is also notable for its frank homosexual themes.

Césaire, Aimé Ferdinand (*1913– *) West Indian poet, dramatist and essayist. Though born in poverty in Martinique, in 1931 Césaire went to Paris to study. At the Sorbonne he specialized in Latin, Greek and French literature. There he met the poet Léopold Sédar SENGHOR, later president of Senegal; together they formed the group known as the NÉGRITUDE poets. The négritude movement was based on a revitalization of black and African culture and a rejection of the rationalism of Western white society. After his return to Martinique in the late 1930s,

Césaire met André BRETON, then a refugee from occupied France, and was influenced to write surrealist poetry to free himself from conventional "white" language (see SURREALISM). In the 1950s and 1960s he wrote plays on the theme of black liberation, including *Une Saison au Congo* (A season in the Congo, 1967), based on the struggle of Patrice LUMUMBA.

Cesca chair Design classic of the BAUHAUS era by Marcel BREUER. This metal tube cantilever design was derived from various prototypes of a year or two before. Mart Stam developed a similar design as early as 1926, which resulted in bitter debate over credit for origination of the design concept. As it is now produced, the Cesca chair, with or without arms, is clearly Breuer's design. Its popularity and broad acceptance in modern contexts are a tribute to the long life of a design that was originally ahead of its time.

Cessna, Clyde Vernon (*1879–1954*) U.S. aircraft manufacturer. He built the first cantilever airplane and in 1927 founded the Cessna Airplane Company in Wichita, Kansas. The company supplied some of the first commercial passenger planes to an early airline, the **Curtiss Flying Service** (see Glenn CURTISS). The company was famous for its small single-engine aircraft sold to recreational flyers and businesses.

Ceylonese Rebellion of 1971 Sirimavo BANDARANAIKE, widow of independent Ceylon's first prime minister, became leader of the Sri Lanka Freedom Party (SLFP) upon his assassination in 1958. In 1960 she became prime minister, heading a strongly leftist, pro-Singalese government. After being out of power from 1965, she again became prime minister in 1970, heading a coalition of the SLFP and Marxist parties. The extreme left, impatient for reform, attempted a takeover of Columbo, the capital, and other cities (April–May 1971). Ceylon received military aid from the USSR, India, Pakistan and Britain, suppressing the rebels in the cities and then by mid-June in the rural areas. In 1972 Bandaranaike proclaimed a republic, a new constitution and a new name for the country: SRI LANKA, meaning "re-

splendent land" in Sinhalese, language of the majority.

Chabrol, Claude (*1930– *) French film director. Chabrol first earned recognition as a film critic who contributed to the renowned journal CAHIERS DU CINÉMA in the 1950s. With Eric ROHMER, a fellow critic who would also go on to achieve fame as a director, Chabrol wrote *Hitchcock* (1957), which examined the work of Anglo-American director Alfred HITCHCOCK from a moral perspective. Chabrol's directorial debut, *Le Beau Serge* (1959), is considered to be the first film of the French cinematic New Wave that also included Alain RESNAIS and François TRUFFAUT. Chabrol's former wife, the French actress Stéphane Audran, frequently stars in his films. Chabrol is a versatile director whose work ranges from light comedies to intensive examinations of bourgeois morality. Other films by Chabrol include *Killer!* (1969), *Ten Day's Wonder* (1971) and *Nada* (1974). In 1991 Chabrol released his adaptation of *Madame Bovary*, which did well in France and earned praise in foreign markets.

Chaco Boreal Region of South America, in the fork of the Paraguay and Pilcomayo Rivers. Located primarily in northwest Paraguay, this 100,000-square-mile area was long disputed by BOLIVIA and PARAGUAY. In December 1928 Paraguay attacked Bolivia, and the fighting lasted until 1935. In 1938 a peace treaty was signed that gave the larger section to Paraguay and a small, western section to Bolivia.

Chaco War (*1932–1935*) Paraguayan ownership of the GRAN CHACO region was long disputed by Bolivia, which sought an outlet to the Atlantic. In 1928 there was sporadic fighting between the countries. After launching a major offensive, Paraguay declared war on May 10, 1933. The larger Bolivian army seized northern and central parts of the Chaco, precipitating Paraguayan mobilization in defense of its homeland. In a major offensive led by Colonel José Félix Estagarribia, Paraguayan forces recaptured most of the Chaco in 1934 and advanced into eastern Bolivia in early 1935 before being pushed back. The U.S. and five South American nations arranged a truce on June 12, 1935. The two nations signed the **Treaty of Buenos Aires** (July

21, 1938) giving Paraguay most of the Chaco but granting Bolivian access to the Atlantic.

Chad Central North African country, bounded to the north by Libya, to the east by Sudan, to the south by the Central African Republic and to the west by Cameroon, Nigeria and Niger; the capital is N'Djamena, formerly called Fort-Lamy. The French began exploring the region late in the 19th century. In 1913 Chad became a part of FRENCH EQUATORIAL AFRICA; in 1958 it became an autonomous state, with François Tombalbaye as its prime minister. In 1960, Chad gained full independence and Tombalbaye became the first president. Since independence Chad has been torn by disputes between the Muslim north, which aligns itself with the Arab nations, and the Christian south. As early as 1963 the northern, Libya-backed Chadian National Liberation Front (Frolinat) began a violent revolt, quelled in 1968 with military assistance from the French. In 1975 Tombalbaye was killed during a coup led by Félix Malloum, a former army chief of staff. Malloum became president, but his government was still threatened by Frolinat. In an effort to achieve unity, Malloum named Hissène Habré, a former leader of Frolinat, as prime minister in 1978, but the two could not reconcile their differences.

Meanwhile, Libya had occupied a Chadian border area known as the Aouzou Strip—thought to contain uranium—and continued its backing of Frolinat, which had increased the territory under its influence through the leadership of General Goukouni Oueddei. In 1979 intense fighting forced Malloum to leave the country. A provisional government (GUNT) established Oueddei as president, with the approval of Libya. Meanwhile, Habré and the Army of the North (FAN) continued to oppose the Libya-backed government, and in 1980 civil war broke out. The Organization for African Unity (OAU) intervened and set up a peacekeeping force. Libyan troops withdrew, Habré and FAN gained control and Oueddei fled to the north. In 1983 the OAU recognized Habré's regime, but Libyan-backed Oueddei still fought. Habre received 3,000 French "instructor"

troops and American financial aid and arms. A 1983 cease-fire divided the country in half between north and south.

In 1984 Libya's colonel QADDAFI proposed that all foreign troops withdraw from Chad. France did so, but some Libyan forces remained in the north. By 1985 fighting had again intensified between the two factions. In 1986, there was a rift between Qaddafi and Oueddei, whose forces defected.

Habré, with French assistance, retaliated against the Libyans; in 1987 France, Chad and Libya agreed to another cease-fire called for by the OAU. In 1996 the leader of the Patriotic Salvation Movement, Idriss Déby, won Chad's first multiparty presidential election. Two years later a former Déby cabinet member, Youssouf Togoimi, formed the Movement for Democracy and Justice in Chad (MDJT), a rebel organization devoted to Déby's over-

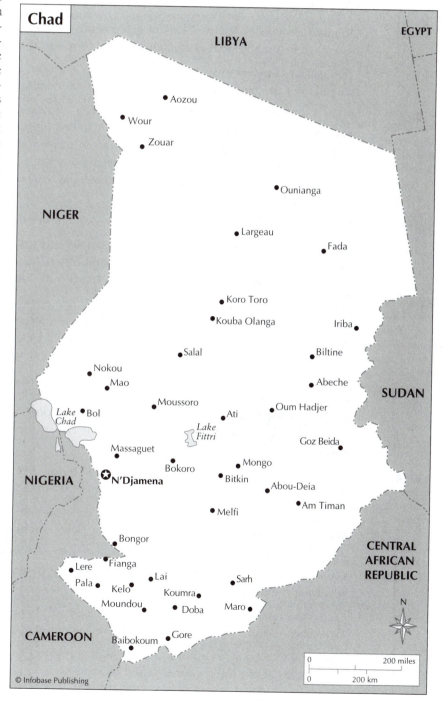

CHAD

1960	Chad becomes an independent member of the French Community, with François Tombalbaye as president.
1961	Tombalbaye's Parti Progressiste Tchadien (PPT) merges with the main opposition party, Parti Nationale Africaine (PNA).
1962	New constitution is promulgated. All political parties except the PPT are banned. Northern insurgent organization Front de Libération Nationale de Chad (FROLINAT) is founded.
1965	Open revolt breaks out in the northern prefectures as secessionist movement gathers strength among Muslims.
1968	Tombalbaye invokes Franco-Chadian agreement of 1960 for military assistance against the rebels; French troops join in campaign against the insurgents.
1975	Tombalbaye is overthrown in a swift coup; Félix Malloum is named the new president and chairman of the Supreme Military Council; the National Assembly is dissolved.
1978	Chad breaks diplomatic relations with Libya after accusing its northern neighbor of occupying a 78,000 sq km (30,000 sq mi) territory in the Tibesti region believed to hold uranium deposits. FROLINAT launches major attack against government forces at Faya-Largeau; government concludes cease-fire with the Armed Forces of the North (FAN) led by Hissène Habré and later appoints Habré prime minister; the Malloum regime and Habré engage in a bloody but inconclusive confrontation.
1979	French forces are flown into N'Djamena as Malloum flees the country.
1980	Fighting resumes and more than 700 die as violence escalates; Congo withdraws its troops; factional fighting breaks out between FAN and other FROLINAT rebel groups. Libya moves into northern Chad and concludes defense treaty with President Oueddei.
1981	Libya invades Chad, and Libyan troops occupy the capital; Libya and Chad announce a decision to "achieve full unity"; after OAU condemns the merger plan and sends a peacekeeping force, President Oueddei repudiates the merger plan; FAN takes N'Djamena and eventually controls most of the country; Oueddei flees the capital and sets up a rival government in the town of Bardai, near the Libyan border.
1982	Habré is sworn in as president; Oueddei forces regroup and advance to the south, taking strategic cities; France intervenes and stations its troops along the "Red Line" of the 16th parallel, which marks the division between the Habré-controlled south and the Oueddei-controlled north.
1984	Libya and France reach a mutual accord for withdrawal of troops from Chad; French troops evacuate the country, but Libya maintains a clandestine presence.
1986	Habré announces release of 122 political prisoners; Libyan-backed GUNT forces resume hostilities by attacking government positions; at Habré's request France again intervenes.
1987	OAU mediation culminates in cease-fire between Chad and Libya on September 11; fighting breaks out again in November, and the UN General Assembly declares OAU responsible for resolving the dispute.
1988	Diplomatic relations between Chad and Libya, severed in 1982, are restored in October; in December, military clashes resume near the Sudanese border.
1989	Libya and Chad sign an accord on August 31 agreeing to submit their border dispute over the Aozou Strip to the International Court of Justice.

1990	Habré is overthrown in a military coup on December 1; rebel leader Idriss Déby, a former Habré aide, declares himself president and promises a multiparty democracy.
1996	Déby wins the nation's first multiparty presidential election.
1998	The Movement for Democracy and Justice in Chad (MDJC) begins an armed rebellion against the government led by Déby's former defense minister, Youssouf Togoimi.
2001	President Idriss Déby is elected for a second five-year term.
2003	MDJT rebels and officials from the Chadian government sign a peace deal. Chad agrees to a U.S.-funded pipeline connecting its oil fields with port outlets in Cameroon's coast. The project is expected to boost Chad's revenue by $2 billion in the next 25 years.
2004	Close to 10,000 refugees from Sudan escape fighting in the Dafur region by fleeing to Chad. The number swells to 200,000 by 2006. Although they settle deep within the national border, the fighting from Dafur spills over into the country, instigating an encounter between Chadian troops and the pro-Sudanese government militia.
2005	A majority vote on a referendum changes the presidential term limit from two terms to three, allowing current president Déby to run in 2006.
2006	Rebels attack N'Djamena but are repulsed. Déby retracts statement indicating Chad might turn back Sudanese refugees.

throw. A December 2003 peace accord was reached, leaving Déby in power.

Chadwick, Sir James (*1891–1974*) British physicist. Chadwick was educated at the University of Manchester, where he graduated in 1911 and remained as a graduate student under Ernest RUTHERFORD. In 1913 he went to Leipzig to work under Hans GEIGER. In 1914 he was interned near Spandau as an enemy alien. There he remained for the duration of the war, cold and hungry but permitted, with the help of Walther Nernst, to carry out rudimentary research. On his return to England in 1919 he was invited by Rutherford to Cambridge University, where he served as assistant director of research at the Cavendish Laboratory (1922–35). In 1932 Chadwick made his greatest discovery—the neutron. Before this, physicists had accepted the existence of only two elementary particles: the proton (p) with a positive charge and the electron (e) with a negative charge. All physicists recognized that these two particles could not account for the atomic phenomena observed. In 1920 Rutherford had introduced the possibility of "an atom of mass 1 which has zero nuclear charge." Chadwick attempted unsuccessfully to discover such a particle in the 1920s by bombarding aluminum with alpha particles (helium nuclei). More promising, however, was the report in 1930 that the bombardment of beryllium with alpha particles yielded a very penetrating radiation. In 1932 Irène and Frédéric JOLIOT-CURIE found that this radiation could eject protons with considerable velocities from matter containing hydrogen. They thought such radiation consisted of gamma rays—electromagnetic radiation of very short wavelength. Chadwick showed that the gamma rays would not eject protons but that the result was explained if the particles had nearly the same mass as protons but no charge—neutrons. It was for this work that Chadwick was awarded the 1935 NOBEL PRIZE in physics. In 1935 Chadwick accepted the offer of the chair of physics at Liverpool University. There he built Britain's first cyclotron and was on hand at the outbreak of World War II to support the claims made by Otto Frisch and Rudolph Peierls on the feasibility of the atomic bomb. Chadwick consequently spent most of the war in the U.S. as head of the British mission to the MANHATTAN PROJECT. For this service he was knighted in 1945. He returned to Cambridge in 1958 as master of Gonville and Caius College, an office he held until his retirement in 1958.

Chadwick, Lynn (*1914–2003*) English sculptor. Trained as an architect, Chadwick worked in architecture until the outbreak of WORLD WAR II, when he became a pilot in the Royal Air Force. After the war he turned to sculpture, at first producing mobiles influenced by Alexander CALDER. He had his first one-man show in 1950. Around 1955 he began to create stationary figures whose roughly textured surfaces are wielded of iron, steel, copper or bronze. These brooding abstract pieces were built on geometric forms and suggest totemic personages. His later work maintained an angular menace while making more direct references to human and animal forms.

Chafee, Zechariah, Jr. (*1885–1957*) U.S. legal scholar. A graduate of Harvard, Chafee taught at the Harvard Law School as a professor for 40 years, beginning in 1916. Noted for his advocacy of civil liberties, he wrote *Freedom of Speech* (1920), an extended version of which became a leading text of U.S. libertarian philosophy. He was considered a leading authority on equity and unfair business competition.

Chagall, Marc (Moyshe Shagall) (*1887–1985*) Russian-born artist. Born into a poor Orthodox Jewish family in czarist RUSSIA, Chagall became one of the most famous artists of the 20th century. He moved to Paris in 1910 thanks to a rich patron and, during his four years there, produced a series of paintings that marked him as a forerunner of SURREALISM. He returned to Russia in 1922 and briefly held the postrevolutionary position of cultural commissioner before returning to France (1922), where he lived for most of his life. His subject matter was drawn largely from Jewish life and folklore, with flowers, birds and animals among his favorite motifs. In addition to producing numerous easel paintings and a great many theatrical designs and books illustrations, he created some of the best-known public art of the century.

Chain, Ernst Boris (1906–1979)
German-British biochemist. Chain graduated in 1930 from the Friedrich-Wilhelm University with a degree in chemistry. He left Germany for England in 1933 and, after two years' research at Cambridge University, joined Howard Florey at Oxford. There his brilliance as a biochemist was put to good use in the difficult isolation and purification of PENICILLIN—work Alexander FLEMING had been unable to carry out. He shared the 1945 NOBEL PRIZE in physiology or medicine with Florey and Fleming for this work. After 1945 he was professor of biochemistry at the Superior Institute of Health in Rome, returning to England in 1961 for the chair of biochemistry at Imperial College, London. During this time he discovered penicillinase, an enzyme that some bacteria can synthesize and so destroy the drug.

Chakravarti Rajagopalachari, Rajaji (1878–1972)
Indian political leader. He joined Mohandas K. GANDHI's nonviolent movement against British rule in 1919. After INDIA gained independence (1947), he served as the country's first governor-general (1948–50). He split with the CONGRESS PARTY and formed his own Swatantra Party in 1959. In 1971, at the age of 92, he organized a right-wing coalition to oppose Indira K. GANDHI but was defeated. Upon his death, the government declared a seven-day period of mourning.

Chaliapin, Feodor (1873–1938)
Russian singer. Acclaimed for his beautiful basso voice and electrifying acting, Chaliapin became the first Russian singer to gain international stature. While with Mamontov's Opera in Moscow (1896–98), he was the premier interpreter of such roles in the Russian repertory as Ivan the Terrible in Rimsky-Korsakov's opera of the same name. Chaliapin first achieved fame outside Russia as Boris in Serge DIAGHILEV's production of Boris Godunov (1908). This became his most famous role; as a result of his exciting performances as Boris the opera was included in the standard repertory of many companies. He triumphed as Boris at the Metropolitan Opera in New York City (1921) and appeared with the company until 1929. He also made several classic recordings, toured the U.S. in recital and made a world tour in 1926. Other outstanding roles included Mephistofeles in both Gounod's Faust and Boito's Mephistofele and the title role in Massenet's Don Quichotte, which he first created in 1910.

Challe, Maurice (1905–1979)
French career army officer, Challe served as chief of staff of the French armed forces (1955), commander in chief of French forces in ALGERIA (1958–60) and commander of the European Sector of NATO (1960–61). He led the

Opera singer Feodor Chaliapin, 1924 (LIBRARY OF CONGRESS, PRINTS AND PHOTOGRAPHS DIVISION)

unsuccessful coup attempt against French president Charles de GAULLE in 1961, for which he was sentenced to 15 years in prison. He was subsequently pardoned. (See also ALGERIAN WAR OF 1954–1962; ORGANIZATION DE L'ARMÉE SECRÈTE.)

Challenger disaster
January 28, 1986, explosion of the U.S. space shuttle *Challenger*, with the loss of all seven astronauts aboard. The *Challenger* exploded 74 seconds after it was launched from Cape Canaveral, Florida, on its 10th mission. The disaster was witnessed by a crowd of ground observers and by millions of people watching on television. The launch had been highly publicized because one of the crew, Christa McAULIFFE, was a high school teacher who had been selected as the first citizen in space. The disaster—the first time U.S. astronauts had been killed on a space mission—stunned the nation and resulted in the grounding of all manned missions for two year. A presidential commission comprised of current and former astronauts as well as distinguished scientists and public figures was appointed to investigate the tragedy. The investigation revealed that NASA had disregarded many safety considerations because of pressure to maintain the launching schedule. It also concluded that the explosion had been caused when hydrogen leaked through a faulty seal in one of the booster rocket joints.

Chamberlain, Sir (Joseph) Austen (1863–1937)
British political leader; half brother of Neville CHAMBERLAIN. A Conservative, he was elected to Parliament for the first time in 1892. Chamberlain served in a number of important posts, including chancellor of the exchequer (1903–05 and 1919–21), secretary of state for India (1915–17), member of the war cabinet under LLOYD GEORGE (1918–19) and lord privy seal (1921–22). He became leader of the CONSERVATIVE PARTY in 1921. As foreign secretary under Stanley BALDWIN from 1924 to 1929, he was instrumental in the creation of the LOCARNO PACT in 1925, a year in which he was knighted and awarded the NOBEL PRIZE for peace (along with U.S. vice president Charles G. DAWES). Chamberlain remained an important member of Parliament until his death.

Chamberlain, Houston Stewart
(1855–1927) Anglo-German writer. Son of a British admiral, he settled in Germany, marrying the daughter of composer Richard Wagner (1908) and becoming a naturalized German citizen (1916). His best-known work, *The Foundations of the Nineteenth Century* (1899), became one of the 20th century's most influential racist polemics. In it Chamberlain celebrated the so-called Aryan race and vilified the JEWS. The book was important in shaping the thought of Adolf HITLER and other Nazi leaders.

Chamberlain, (Arthur) Neville
(1869–1940) British statesman, prime minister (1937–40); half brother of Sir Austen CHAMBERLAIN. A successful Birmingham businessman, he became the city's mayor from 1915 to 1916. Elected a Conservative member of Parliament in 1918, he was chancellor of the exchequer (1923 and 1931–37) and minister of health (1923 and 1924–29). An able administrator, he initiated a number of reforms in social services, helped to systemize local government and aided in the rebuilding of Britain's economy in the late 1930s. His domestic successes led to his appointment as prime minister in 1937, but he was ill prepared to cope with the foreign crises that soon engulfed him. Faced with the aggression of Adolf HITLER, Chamberlain opted for negotiation and followed a policy of APPEASEMENT, signing the MUNICH PACT in 1938 and proclaiming "peace in our time." With the continuation of German advances in 1939, Chamberlain altered his views and led his nation into WORLD WAR II. After the German occupation of Norway in 1940, he was forced to resign, and Sir Winston CHURCHILL succeeded him as prime minister. He served as lord president of the council in Churchill's coalition cabinet until shortly before his death.

Chamberlain, Owen *(1920–)* American physicist. The son of a prominent radiologist, Chamberlain followed his father's interest in physics. He graduated from Dartmouth College in 1941 and earned his doctorate in physics from the University of Chicago in 1949. From 1948 until 1950 he was an instructor in physics at the University of California at Berkeley, becoming associate professor

in 1954 and professor in 1958. WORLD WAR II interrupted his university studies, and he spent the years 1942–46 under the leadership of Emilio Segrè working on the MANHATTAN PROJECT at LOS ALAMOS. There he investigated spontaneous fission of the heavy elements and nuclear cross sections. Later he worked with Enrico FERMI on neutron diffraction by liquids. At Berkeley, Chamberlain experimented with the bevatron particle accelerator of the Lawrence Radiation Laboratory, and in 1955 (with Segrè, C. Weigand and T. Ypsilantis) discovered the antiproton. For their discovery Chamberlain and Segrè received the 1959 NOBEL PRIZE in physics. Chamberlain's later work was on the interaction of antiprotons with hydrogen and deuterium, the production of antineutrons from antiprotons and the scattering of pions.

Chamberlain, Wilton ("Wilt") Norman *(1936–1999)* American basketball player. An outstanding offensive center even in high school, Chamberlain was recruited by scores of colleges before deciding on the University of Kansas in 1956. He left the school after only two years and signed on with the Harlem Globetrotters. He played 16 years in the pros: with the Warriors in both Philadelphia and San Francisco (1959–65), the Philadelphia 76ers (1965–68) and the Los Angeles Lakers (1968–73). In 1962, while with the Warriors, he became the only NBA player to score 100 points in a single game. In later years his defensive and playmaking skills caught up with his offense, and he came to be regarded as one of the game's greatest players. He retired in 1973 with career totals of 31,419 points scored and a game point average of 30.1. He published his autobiography, *Just Like Any Other 7-Foot Black Millionaire Who Lives Next Door,* in 1973 and was named to the Basketball Hall of Fame in 1978. In 1992 Chamberlain's memoir, *A View from Above,* was released.

Chamberlin, Thomas Chrowder
(1843–1928) American geologist. Chamberlin came from a farming background. His discovery of fossils in a local limestone quarry aroused his interest in geology, which he pursued at the University of Michigan.

From 1881 until 1904 he was in charge of the glacial division of the U.S. Geological Survey. After a period as president of the University of Wisconsin (1887–92), he became professor of geology at the University of Chicago (1892–1918). Apart from his work on geological surveys, Chamberlin's most significant work was in the field of glaciation. Early work on glaciation had assumed that there had been one great ice age, but James Geikie collected evidence that there had been several ice ages separated by nonglacial epochs. Chamberlin went on to establish four major ice ages, named the Nebraskan, Kansan, Illinoian, and Wisconsin after the states in which they were most easily studied. Together with the astronomer Forest Moulton, in 1906, Chamberlin formulated the planetismal hypothesis on the origin of the planets in the solar system. Chamberlin and Moultin supposed that a star had passed close to the Sun causing matter to be pulled out of both. Within the gravitational field of the Sun, this gaseous matter would condense into small planetismals and eventually into planets. The theory was published in *The Two Solar Families* (1928), but it has little support today as it cannot account for the distribution of angular momentum in the solar system.

Chambers, Whittaker See HISS-CHAMBERS CASE.

Chaminade, Cécile Louise-Stéphanie
(1857–1944) French composer and pianist. Chaminade was one of the most esteemed pianists of her era and was especially popular for her moving performances of salon pieces. As a youth she studied piano in Paris under Benjamin Godard. Her compositions include *Les Amazones,* a lyric symphony for orchestra and chorus, as well as other orchestral works and solo pieces for the piano. In her later years Chaminade performed frequently in Britain, where she became a special favorite of concert audiences.

Chamorro, Violeta Barrios de
(1930–) President of Nicaragua (1990–97). Born into an upper-class Nicaraguan family, Chamorro married Pedro Joaquín Chamorro Cardenal in

1950, who became a newspaper publisher and a guerrilla fighter during the rule of the SOMOZA family. He was assassinated in 1978. Chamorro was later a publisher of *La Prensa* and a member of the junta that took power in Nicaragua after the Sandinista revolution in 1979, but she resigned in 1980 in disagreement with the Sandinistas' increasingly dictatorial policies. Although Chamorro was not a member of any political party, she was chosen by the 14 parties in the National Opposition Union (UNO) as their presidential candidate in 1989, after the Sandinistas agreed to hold free elections. In February 1990 she was elected president with Virgilio Godoy Reyes, a member of the Independent Liberal Party and a former labor minister, as her running mate. Chamorro's surprise upset of the Sandinista regime was widely hailed as a victory for democracy in Nicaragua. However, as president, Chamorro faced considerable political and economic problems. Chamorro advocated the country's return to a completely free-market economy and helped guide the country as it emerged from Daniel ORTEGA's rule. Chamorro left office in 1997 and was succeeded by Arnoldo Alemán.

Chamoun, Camille Nimer (*1900–1987*) Lebanese political leader. A powerful Maronite Christian leader, he was a wealthy businessman, lawyer, parliamentarian and holder of many cabinet posts since 1938. He served as president of LEBANON from 1952 to 1958. At the time of his death he was finance minister in Lebanon's caretaker cabinet. He was an outspoken critic of SYRIA, the PALESTINE LIBERATION ORGANIZATION and the pro-Iranian Shiite Muslim militia factions. He survived at least three major assassination attempts.

Champassak Former empire of southern LAOS along the Mekong River. Founded in 1713, it was one of the three Laotian kingdoms. Its western lands were assimilated by Siam (modern THAILAND) in the 19th century. Franco-Siamese treaties reestablished the empire in 1904 and 1905. During WORLD WAR II, Thailand repeated its occupation of the western portion, and in 1946 Prince Boun Oum of Champassak abdicated his reigning territorial rights for a united Laos.

Champion, Gower (*1919–1980*) Broadway stage choreographer, musical director and dancer. Champion began his career in VAUDEVILLE and achieved national prominence in the 1950s for his work with his wife, **Marge Champion,** in television variety shows and HOLLYWOOD film musicals. On Broadway he directed such hits as *Hello Dolly, Carnival, Bye Bye, Birdie* and *42nd Street.*

Chanak Crisis Crisis in Anglo-Turkish relations (September–October 1922) arising from Turkey's victory over Greece at Smyrna. Great Britain feared that Turkey, under the leadership of Kemal ATATÜRK, would attack Allied troops near Constantinople. British prime minister LLOYD GEORGE was in favor of reinforcing the British garrison at Chanak (now Canakkale). A convention held on October 12, 1922, between British and Turkish representatives eased the crisis by pledging the return of some European territory to Turkey provided Turkey accepted the neutrality of the Dardanelles and Bosporus; this was the basis of the Treaty of LAUSANNE (1923). The crisis precipitated the fall of Lloyd George's government, when Conservative leaders, fearing war as the outcome of his actions, pulled out of Britain's coalition government.

Chance, Britton (*1913– *) American biophysicist. Chance, an engineer's son, was educated at the University of Pennsylvania, where he earned his Ph.D. in 1940 and where, in 1949, he was appointed to the E. R. Johnson Professorship of Biophysics. In 1943 he carried out a spectroscopic analysis that provided firm evidence for the enzyme-substrate complex whose existence biochemists had confidently assumed since the beginning of the 20th century. Chance also contributed to one of the great achievements of modern biochemistry, namely the unraveling of the complicated maze through which energy is released at the cellular level. His studies led to a better understanding of how glucose is used in the body.

Chandigarh City in northwestern INDIA, 150 miles north of Delhi; capital of Punjab and Haryana. When India was granted independence and divided in 1947, Lahore, formerly the capital of the Punjab, joined with PAKISTAN. The Indians wanted to erect a brand new capital city and commissioned the renowned French architect LE CORBUSIER for the project. In 1951 he undertook his challenging work on a site that was noted for its beneficial climate and bountiful water supply. Le Corbusier designed Chandigarh in 36 rectangular sections, 30 of which were residential. The government buildings are in one area, the industrial in another; he also designed an artificial lake. Jullundur was the provisional capital of the Punjab during the construction of the new capital.

Chandler, Albert Benjamin "Happy" (*1898–1991*) American politician and baseball commissioner. He was governor of Kentucky (1935–39, 1955–59), as well as U.S. senator (1939–45). He resigned as senator to become commissioner of organized baseball and served until 1951.

Chandler, Raymond (*1888–1959*) American motion picture screenwriter and author of detective fiction. Born in Chicago, Chandler grew up in England, where he attended Dulwich College. Back in America he worked in the oil business. When he lost his job during the GREAT DEPRESSION he began writing stories for *Black Mask* magazine, a publication noted for its "hard-boiled" crime fiction that also spawned Dashiel HAMMETT. Chandler's first story, "Blackmailers Don't Shoot" (1933), established the tough but honest protagonist who eventually would evolve into the archetypal Chandler detective, Philip Marlowe. In seven novels, including *The Big Sleep* (1939), *The Little Sister* (1949) and *The Long Goodbye* (1953), Marlow prowled the "mean streets" of Los Angeles, "looking for," in the words of historian Philip Durham, "ladies to rescue, for the little fellow who needed help, for the big man who deserved a shot of old-fashioned justice." Chandler's prose was full of colorful similes: "As a bluff, mine was thinner than the gold on a week-end wedding ring." There was "the hard-boiled redhead" who sings "in a voice that could have been used to split firewood." And there was the beer that's as "tasteless as a roadhouse blonde." Chandler wrote a number of screenplays, most notably the FILM NOIR thrillers *Double Indemnity* (1944) and *The Blue Dahlia* (1946). Marlowe has been portrayed on screen by an assortment of actors, including Humphrey BOGART (*The Big Sleep*, 1946) and Elliott Gould (*The Long Goodbye*, 1973), but perhaps the definitive interpretation was Dick Powell's in the Edward Dmytryk classic *Murder, My Sweet* (1943).

Chandrasekhar, Subrahmanyan *(1910–1995)* Indian-American astrophysicist. Chandrasekhar studied at the Presidency College, Madras, earning his M.A. in 1930. He then went to Cambridge University, England, where in 1933 he earned his Ph.D. and was elected to a fellowship. In 1936 he moved to the U.S. and worked since 1937 at the University of Chicago and the Yerkes Observatory. He became a U.S. citizen in 1953. Chandrasekhar's major fields of study were stellar evolution and structure and the processes of energy transfer within stars. He showed that when a star has exhausted its nuclear fuel, an inward gravitational collapse will begin. The star will shrink into an object so dense that a matchbox of it would weigh many tons. Chandrasekhar showed that such a star would have the unusual property that the larger its mass, the smaller its radius. There will therefore be a point at which the mass of a star is too great for it to evolve into a white dwarf. He calculated this mass to be 1.4 times the mass of the Sun. This has since become known as the **Chandrasekhar limit.** A star lying about this limit must either lose mass before it can become a white dwarf or take a different evolutionary path. In support of Chandrasekhar's theoretical work, it has been established that all known white dwarfs fall within the predicted limit.

Chanel, Gabrielle "Coco" *(1883–1971)* Leading French fashion designer. A British admirer encouraged Chanel to set up a Paris shop in 1910. Chanel's social reputation as a favorite of the Paris avant-garde added to her fame as she designed costumes for COCTEAU's *Antigone* (which also had sets by PICASSO) and for STRAVINSKY's ballet *Le Train bleu.* Chanel's characteristic style was established during the 1920s, a style based on simplicity and neatness of a timeless sort. She was a designer of jewelry, both real and costume, often of massive and flamboyant form. Her Paris shop was closed during World

War II but reopened in 1954 and has continued to emphasize the same themes of style without undue pretension. Chanel was the winner of a Neiman Marcus Award in 1957. The famous perfume Chanel No. 5, with its simple and elegant packaging (and high price), remains one of the best-known products bearing her name.

Chaney, Lon (Alonzo Chaney) *(1883–1930)* American film actor. Chaney, dubbed the "Man of a Thousand Faces" due to his penchant for appearing in elaborate physical disguises in his films, stands as one of the premier actors of the horror film genre. He began his career as a comic and dancer on the VAUDEVILLE circuit and came to HOLLYWOOD in 1914, where he played bit parts in a number of films until 1919, when his portrayal of a man who feigns to be a cripple in *The Miracle Man* won him acclaim and larger roles. Chaney achieved international fame in the 1920s when he teamed with director Tod BROWNING on a number of successful horror films including *The Unholy Three* (1925), *The Black Bird* (1926), *The Road to Mandalay* (1926), *The Unknown* (1927), *London After Midnight* (1927) and *Where East Is East* (1929). Chaney was slated to play the lead role in Browning's *Dracula* (1931) but died of throat cancer. His son Lon Chaney Jr. appeared in a number of horror films in the 1930s and 1940s.

Chang, Min Chueh *(1908–1991)* Chinese-American biologist. Chang was educated at the Tsinghua University in Beijing and at Cambridge University, England, where he earned his Ph.D. in 1941. He immigrated to the U.S. in 1945 and joined the Worcester Foundation in Shrewsbury, Massachusetts. In 1961 he became professor of reproductive biology at Boston University. Chang carried out a number of major research projects from which emerged not only greater understanding of the mechanisms of mammalian fertilization but also such practical consequences as oral contraceptives and the transplantation of human ova fertilized in vitro (by Robert Edwards and Patrick STEPTOE in 1978).

Channel Islands (French: Îles Normandes) A cluster of islands that in-

cludes Aldernay, Guernsey, Jersey and Sark, situated 80 miles south of the British coast at the opening to the Gulf of St. Malo in the English Channel; part of the UNITED KINGDOM. The islands were the only section of Britain occupied by Germany during WORLD WAR II (from June 30, 1940, to May 9, 1945).

Channing, Edward *(1856–1931)* American historian. In 1925 Channing won the PULITZER PRIZE for the sixth volume of his *History of the United States.* The series ranks high in American historical writing for its inclusive chronological coverage, original research and range of interpretation. A teacher at Harvard (1883–1929), his unique insight brought clarity to obscure historical situations. Channing's emphasis on national union as opposed to localism and the effects of urbanization and transportation provided a contrast to the emphasis on frontier exploration.

Chapayev, Vasily Ivanovich *(1887–1919)* Soviet hero of the RUSSIAN CIVIL WAR. Originally a laborer, he commanded a division in the Urals during the civil war. He has remained popular in Soviet lore as a result of Dmitry FURMANOV's book about him (1923) and the film *Chapayev* (1934) about his civil war exploits.

Chapaygin, Alexei Pavlovich *(1870–1937)* Soviet writer. He worked first as a shepherd and then as a decorator in St. Petersburg. His first work was published in 1903. His novel *The White Monastery* (1913) depicts life on the eve of the RUSSIAN REVOLUTION OF 1905. He also wrote short stories and sketches, including the autobiographic tale *My Life* (1929). His historical novel *Stepan Razin* was warmly received in Soviet Russia, particularly by Maxim GORKY.

Chaplin, Charlie (Sir Charles Spencer Chaplin) *(1889–1977)* British-born film actor and director; one of the most revered figures in the history of the cinema. Chaplin's screen alter ego of the Little Tramp, with a black mustache, bowler hat and baggy pants, remains one of the archetypal figures of comedy and an icon of popular culture. Chaplin began his career working as a British music hall performer in the years prior to World War I. He made his HOLLYWOOD

Charlie Chaplin and Jackie Coogan in The Kids (LIBRARY OF CONGRESS, PRINTS AND PHOTOGRAPHS DIVISION)

film debut in *The Little Tramp* (1915) and at once became an international star. Chaplin wrote and directed, as well as starred in, his classic films, which successfully spanned both the silent and sound eras and include *Easy Street* (1917), *The Kid* (1921), *The Gold Rush* (1925), *City Lights* (1931), *Modern Times* (1936), *The Great Dictator* (1940) and *Limelight* (1952). In 1952 adverse public reaction to Chaplin's leftist politics and sexual scandals led to a self-imposed exile from America for 20 years. Chaplin wrote an *Autobiography* (1964) and returned to America for a gala Hollywood tribute in 1972.

Chapman, Sydney *(1888–1970)* British mathematician and geophysicist. Chapman entered Manchester University in 1904 to study engineering. After graduating in 1907, his interest was diverted into more strictly mathematical areas, and he went to Cambridge to study mathematics, graduating in 1910. His first post was as chief assistant at the Royal Observatory, Greenwich. His work there sparked his lasting interest in a number of fields of applied mathematics, notably geomagnetism. In 1914 Chap-

man returned to Cambridge as a lecturer in mathematics, and in 1919 he moved back to Manchester as professor of mathematics. From 1924 to 1946 he was professor of mathematics at Imperial College, London. After working at the War Office during WORLD WAR II he moved to Oxford to take up the Sedleian Chair in natural philosophy, from which he retired in 1953. He continued teaching and research for many years at the Geophysical Institute in Alaska, and at the High Altitude Observatory at Boulder, Colorado The two main topics of Chapman's mathematical work were the kinetic theory of gases and geomagnetism. Highlights of Chapman's work on geomagnetism include his work on the variations in the Earth's magnetic field. In collaboration with one of his students, in 1930, he also developed what has become known as the **Chapman-Ferraro theory** of magnetic storms.

Chappaquiddick incident Accident in 1969, and its aftermath, involving **Senator Edward M. Kennedy**, a leading Democratic politician and brother of the late president John F. KENNEDY and the late senator Robert F.

KENNEDY. On the night of July 18, 1969, Kennedy left a party on Chappaquiddick Island, Massachusetts, presumably to drive secretary Mary Jo Kopechne home. The senator mistook turns on a country road and accidentally drove his car off the Dike Bridge into Poucha Pond. Kennedy escaped, but Kopechne drowned. Kennedy's actions were widely questioned, and he later pleaded guilty to leaving the scene of an accident. The incident followed Kennedy for the rest of his career and proved a serious impediment to his seeking higher political office.

Chapultepec Fortress and hill, three miles southwest of Mexico City's historic center, inside Mexico's Federal District. From the 1860s to the 1940s the presidents of MEXICO officially resided here. The nations of the Western Hemisphere signed the **Act of Chapultepec** in March 1945, acknowledging the perimeters of American states. Modern Chapultepec is noted as a cultural and recreational center of the capital.

Char, René *(1907–1988)* French poet. A native of the Vaucluse region, Char first visited Paris after the publication of his first book, *Le Marteau sans maître* (1934, *Hammer without a Master*). There he met Paul ÉLUARD and André BRETON and was closely associated with the surrealist movement (see SURREALISM). Thereafter he divided his time between his country home and the capital. He broke with the surrealists in 1937. *Placard pour un chemin des écoliers* (1937) focused on social issues, specifically the victims of the SPANISH CIVIL WAR. *Seuls demeurent* (1945) and *Feuillets d'Hypnos* reflected his experiences in the French RESISTANCE during WORLD WAR II. His postwar poetry again moved away from social issues. Later works included *Poèmes des deux années* (1955), *Fureur et mystère* (1967) and *Dans la pluie giboyeuse* (1968).

Chareau, Pierre *(1883–1950)* French designer and architect whose work of the 1920s and 1930s forms a link between ART DECO and the more purist architectural MODERNISM of the INTERNATIONAL STYLE. Chareau's best-known work is a Paris house of 1929–31 called *Maison de Verre* (House of glass) designed in collaboration with Dutch architect Bernard Bijvoet. It uses steel framing and glass block in a way that seems to anticipate high-tech of recent years. Furniture Chareau designed is used along with tapestries by Jean LURCAT.

As editor of the 1929 publication *Meules,* he played a significant role in publicizing the work of many of the leading modernists of the time. Chareau came to the U.S. in 1939 and continued work in a generally Art Deco style that never received wide recognition.

Chargaff, Erwin *(1905–2002)* Austrian-American biochemist. Chargaff earned his Ph.D. from the University of Vienna in 1928 and then spent two years at Yale University. He returned to Europe, working first in Berlin and then at the Pasteur Institute, Paris, before returning permanently to the U.S. in 1935. He then joined the staff of Columbia University. Initially Chargaff's work covered a range of biochemical fields, including lipid metabolism and the process of blood coagulation. Later his attention became concentrated on the DNA molecule, following the 1944 announcement by Oswald AVERY that pure DNA is the factor causing the heritable transformation of bacteria. Chargaff reasoned that, if this is so, there must be many more different types of DNA molecules than had been believed. He examined DNA using the recently developed techniques of paper chromatography and ultraviolet spectroscopy and found its composition to be constant within a species but to differ widely between species. This led him to conclude that there must be as many different types of DNA as there are different species. However, some interesting and very important consistencies emerged. First, the number of purine bases (adenine and guanine) is always equal to the number of pyrimidine bases (cytosine and thiamine); second, the number of adenine bases is equal to the number of thiamine bases and the number of guanine bases equals the number of cytosine bases. This information, announced by Chargaff in 1950, was of crucial importance in constructing the Watson-Crick model of DNA.

Charles (Prince Karel van Vlaanderen) *(1903–1983)* Prince of BELGIUM. He served as regent from 1944 through 1950 while his brother, King LEOPOLD III, was in exile. Prince Charles helped restore Belgium after the German occupation of the country in WORLD WAR II. He was credited with having saved the Belgian monarchy.

Charles I *(1887–1922)* Last emperor of Austria (reigned 1916–18) and king of Hungary (as Charles IV); son of Archduke Otto, grandnephew and successor of Emperor FRANZ JOSEPH II. After his accession to the throne, he vainly attempted to secure peace negotiations, secretly contacting Great Britain and France through Prince Sixtus of Bourbon-Parma, brother of his wife, Empress ZITA. After World War I he was forced to abdicate and in 1921 twice failed to regain the throne.

Charles, prince of Wales *(1948–)* Charles Philip Arthur George Windsor-Mountbatten, eldest son of Queen ELIZABETH II and Prince Philip; heir to the British throne. Educated at Gordonstoun school in Scotland, he became the first member of the royal family to receive a university education when he attended Trinity College, Cambridge (1967–70). During the 1970s he served in both the Royal Navy and the Royal Air Force, commanding a ship and also qualifying as a pilot. His investiture as prince of Wales at Carnarvon Castle (July 1, 1969) was a ceremony of great pomp, as was his wedding to his distant cousin Lady Diana Spencer at St. Paul's Cathedral, London, in 1981 (see DIANA, PRINCESS OF WALES). Although his royal responsibilities and authority were strictly defined by the constitution, he took an active and sometimes controversial role in many areas of public life. Outspoken in his criticism of modern architecture, he publicly urged a return to more humane . styles; his views prompted much debate in the late 1980s and into the 1990s. He also spoke out in favor of rehabilitating Britain's inner cities and sponsored several programs that provided educational and economic opportunities for young people. Prince Charles's marriage to Diana grew increasingly strained in the early 1990s, as allegations of infidelity on both parts surfaced, leading to their separation in 1992 and divorce in 1996. His reputation suffered in the wake of Diana's sudden death in 1997. In 2005 he married **Camilla Parker-Bowles,** now H.R.H. the duchess of Cornwall.

Charles, Ray (Ray Charles Robinson) *(1930–2004)* American pianist and popular singer. Born in Albany, Georgia, Charles moved to Greenville, Florida, and at age six began to lose his sight from glaucoma. While at a school for the blind he learned to play the piano and to read music in braille. After his mother's death when Charles was 15, he began playing in traveling bands across Florida and then moved to Seattle, Washington, in 1948. There he formed the Maxim Trio and began to bring out rhythm-and-blues songs with a small record company. His big break came in 1952, when Atlantic Records bought his recording contract. He added gospel music to his blues performances, producing such hits as "It Should Have Been Me," "The Things I Used to Do" and "I Got a Woman." He also experimented with jazz and became a pioneer in the growing movement of soul music with "What I Say." After moving to ABC-Paramount Records in 1959, Charles's succession of hits such as "Georgia on My Mind," "Hit the Road Jack" and "Unchain My Heart" firmly established his reputation as one of America's most versatile singers and paved the way for many popular songs during the 1960s. In the mid-1960s Charles was arrested for drug possession, which interrupted his successful career and caused him to wage a successful battle to cure his heroin addiction. In the 1980s Charles branched out into country music, collaborating with country singers such as Willy Nelson and Hank WILLIAMS. In 2004, the year of his death, Charles was portrayed in the critically acclaimed film *Ray,* which dealt with his remarkable musical career as well as his long struggle with heroin addiction.

Charleville-Mézières Capital city of Ardennes department, on the Meuse River in northeastern France; the two towns were joined in 1966. Both had succumbed to the Germans, in 1914 and 1940, and during WORLD WAR II they were the site of the German high command headquarters for Western Europe. Mézières, which was rescued by the Allies in 1918, was the last major campaign of WORLD WAR I.

Charlotte von Nassau-Weilburg, Grand Duchess *(1896–1985)* Charlotte was constitutional ruler of LUXEMBOURG from 1919 until 1964, when she abdicated in favor of her eldest son, Jean. After GERMANY invaded her country in May 1940, she went into exile in London but continued to address her subjects by radio. When she returned home in April 1945, she received a tumultuous welcome. She was later praised for her efforts in rebuilding the country.

Charlton, Sir Robert "Bobby"
(1937–) One of England's greatest soccer players, Charlton played 106 times for England (1958–70) and was the star of the 1966 World Cup winning side. Charlton joined Manchester United in 1954 and played on two League Championship teams (1964–65, 1966–67) and one F.A. Cup winning side (1963). In 1969 he scored two goals in Manchester United's emotional 4–1 defeat of Benfica in the European Cup. In 1956 Charlton had survived the Munich air crash that had taken the lives of the majority of the United team, returning from a European Cup game; the 1969 victory reinforced United, and Charlton's, position in the folklore of the English game. Noted for his "thunderbolt" shot, Charlton scored a record 49 goals for England. In 1966 he was awarded both the English and European Player of the Year awards. He was awarded the CBE for services to soccer. In 1994 Charlton was knighted by Queen Elizabeth II.

Charpentier, Gustav *(1860–1956)*
French composer. Charpentier was deeply influenced by the musical tradition of romanticism that dominated French composition in the latter half of the 19th century. His major works were in the genres of opera and the orchestral suite. Charpentier remains best known for his opera *Louise* (1900), which continues to be frequently performed. Other compositions include *Didon* (1887), *The Life of a Poet* (1888–89) and *Coronation of the Muse* (1897). Charpentier devoted much of the final decades of his life to teaching.

Charter 77
Organization formed in PRAGUE, CZECHOSLOVAKIA, in 1977 by the country's leading dissident intellectuals to monitor the Czechoslovak government's adherence to the UN Declaration of Human Rights, the HELSINKI ACCORD and UN covenants on civil, political, economic, social and cultural rights. The group's initial manifesto was signed by 242 members; the total membership was reportedly over 1,000. Playwright Václav HAVEL was a cofounder and leading spokesman for the group. Many members were imprisoned for their activities.

Chase, Lucia *(1897–1986)*
American dancer and ballet director. Although Chase began her career as a dancer with the Mordkin Ballet (1938–39), she is best known as a founder of AMERICAN BALLET THEATRE (1940, originally known as "Ballet Theatre") and as a company director for 40 years. She was the primary force in making ABT a major U.S. ballet company with an international reputation. As a dancer she created the roles of the Nurse in Antony TUDOR's *Romeo and Juliet* and the Eldest Sister in Tudor's *Pillar of Fire.*

Chase, Stuart *(1888–1985)*
American economist. Chase was a member of Franklin D. ROOSEVELT's BRAIN TRUST, the group of advisers who helped shape the NEW DEAL economic programs during the GREAT DEPRESSION of the 1930s. It was believed that the source of the term *new deal* was Chase's book *A New Deal,* published in 1932. He was the author of many other books on topics ranging from ecology to semantics.

Château-Thierry
Town on the Marne River, in the Aisne department of northeastern France. In 1918, Château-Thierry was the deepest location reached by the last German offensive of WORLD WAR I.

Chatichai, Choonhavan *(1922–1998)*
Chatichai became prime minister of THAILAND in late July 1988 when former Prime Minister Prem Tinsulanonda declined a fourth term. Chatichai's colorful lifestyle, which earned him the title "playboy minister," contrasted sharply to that of the mild-mannered Prem. Chatichai was a former army major general, serving in Indochina in 1940–41 and as part of the first Thai expeditionary force to Korea in 1950–52. His army service abruptly ended in 1958 when the regime, of which his father was deputy prime minister, was toppled in a military coup. For the next 15 years Chatichai served in various ambassadorial postings in Latin America and Eu-rope. In 1973 he returned to Bangkok to serve as deputy foreign minister and held senior government posts thereafter. He became deputy premier under Prem but was not expected to be able to exert the same degree of influence over the military as his predecessor. In 1991 a coup ousted Chatichai from power and replaced him with Anand Panyarachun. Chatichai died in 1998 while in London undergoing treatment for liver cancer.

Chávez, Carlos *(1899–1978)*
Mexican composer and conductor. Widely considered the foremost Mexican composer of the 20th century, he began writing music in his youth and composed his first symphony at the age of 20. In 1928 he founded the Mexican Symphony Orchestra, conducting it until 1949. He also became director of the National Conservatory of Music, guiding its development from 1928 to 1934. As a composer Chávez often employed Mexican Indian elements. Two of his best-known works in this idiom are the *Sinfonía india* (1936) and *Xochipilli macuilxochitl* (1940), both of which incorporate native Indian instruments. Often influenced by Mexican folk music, Chávez's music is usually powerfully rhythmic. His many other compositions include the ballet *HP* (Horsepower, 1927), *Sinfonía antígona* (1933), the choral work *La paloma azul* (1940), the string trio *Invention* (1965), as well as several symphonies, concertos and pieces for chamber ensemble and piano.

Chavez, Cesar Estrada *(1927–1993)*
American labor leader. The son of migrant farm workers, Chavez was born near Yuma, Arizona. Having attended more than 30 elementary schools up through the seventh grade, he was mainly self-taught. After service in the navy (1944–45), in 1952 he joined a Mexican-American self-help group, the Community Service Organization, becoming its general director in 1958. Four years later he left the group to found the National Farm Workers Association (NFWA) and, against strong opposition from growers, attempted to organize migrant workers in California. In 1966 the NFWA merged with an AFL-CIO agricultural affiliate to form the United Farm Workers (UFW). Through a series of long and

bitter strikes, marches and national boycotts of grapes, wine and lettuce, Chavez brought pressure on the growers and was able to obtain a number of contracts between growers and the UFW. The union became a part of the AFL-CIO, with Chavez as president, in 1972. Jurisdictional disputes with the International Brotherhood of Teamsters plagued Chavez and his union during the 1970s. Nonetheless, he continued to head the UFW, which, by 1990, claimed a membership of 100,000.

Chávez Frías, Hugo *(1954–   )* Venezuelan soldier, politician and president of Venezuela (1998–   ). In 1992 Chávez gained national and international attention when, as a colonel in the Venezuelan army, he led the Revolutionary Bolivarian Movement, a covert group he helped form in the 1980s, in an unsuccessful coup against then president Carlos Andrés Pérez. Sentenced to life imprisonment after his capture, Chávez left jail in 1994 as the recipient of a presidential pardon. He then worked to transform the Revolutionary Bolivarian Movement into a national political party titled the Movement of the Fifth Republic. By 1998 Chávez was elected president of Venezuela on a platform that promised to revolutionize Venezuelan society and prevent the abuse of the income generated by oil sales. He won the presidency despite the fact that all other Venezuelan political parties had united in support of his opponent. However, his promised "rev-

olution" in Venezuelan life failed to cure the chronic poverty and unemployment that continued to plague much of the citizenry. This led to a fall in his popularity from a peak of 80% soon after his election to 30% five months after he was reelected president in July 2001. On April 12, 2002, shortly after the beginning of a general strike in opposition to Chávez's attempts to replace managers of the state-owned oil company, during which military snipers fired into a protesting crowd of 150,000, killing 11 and injuring 80, the Venezuelan army forced Chávez's resignation. However, two days later throngs of Venezuelan poor marched throughout the streets of Caracas, Venezuela's capital, and successfully demanded Chávez's return to office.

In contrast to his domestic endeavors, Chávez's foreign policy has proven somewhat successful. Through cordial visits with Fidel CASTRO of Cuba and Saddam HUSSEIN of Iraq, alleged involvement with leftist Colombian rebels, territorial claims asserted against Guyana and, most important, increasingly hostility toward the U.S., Chávez dramatically shifted the direction of Venezuela's international orientation. He seemed intent on reducing U.S. influence in Venezuela in particular and Latin America in general.

Chayevsky, Sidney "Paddy" *(1923–1981)* American playwright and screenwriter. Beginning as a writer of domestic dramas during television's "golden age" in the 1950s, he later wrote naturalistic plays and films whose satiric slant bordered on SURREALISM. He characterized his own specialty as the portrayal of "characters caught in the decline of their society." His three ACADEMY AWARDS as best screenwriter were for *Marty* (1955), the story of a lonely butcher; *Hospital* (1971), a satirical and frightening account of daily life in a city hospital; and *Network* (1976), a satirical look at network TV through the eyes of a disillusioned news anchorman. Chayevsky had three Broadway successes (including *The Tenth Man*, 1959) before suffering a failure with *The Passion of Josef D.*, a play about STALIN. After this he refused to return to the theater but wrote exclusively for television and film.

Chechaouen (Xauen; Shaf Shawan) Holy city in northern Morocco, estab-

lished by Moors ousted from Spain in the 15th century as a shelter from Christian Ceuta. Non-Muslims were not allowed entrance until 1920, when it came under the control of SPAIN. The Spanish evacuated the city during the Rif revolt, from 1924 to 1926.

Chechen-Ingush Autonomous Soviet Socialist Republic Caucasus-area subdivision of the Russian Soviet Federated Socialist Republic (RSFSR). Its name is derived from the Chechen and Ingush people, who largely populate the area and who vigorously opposed the efforts of czarist Russia to control them. Following the RUSSIAN REVOLUTION, the BOLSHEVIKS asserted control of the area in 1918. Counterrevolutionary forces under Anton I. DENIKIN chased them out in 1919, but they regained control in 1921. The Chechen and Ingush oblasts were united in 1924, and they became a self-sufficient republic in 1936. In WORLD WAR II, when the Germans tried unsuccessfully to capture the area's oil fields, the Chechen and Ingush collaborated with the Nazis. The victorious Soviets terminated the republic and expatriated the people to Central Asia. In 1956 they were permitted to come back, and the following year the republic was restored. Following the Soviet Union's collapse in 1991, a Chechen rebellion began with the goal of obtaining independence from the Russian state that now controlled the autonomous republic (see CHECHNYA).

Chechens Caucasian-speaking people in CHECHNYA. They fought both the Cossacks and the Bolsheviks during the RUSSIAN CIVIL WAR and continued to oppose the Communists by means of guerrilla warfare in the mountains. In 1943, as a result of their anticommunist uprising, they were all deported to Kazakhstan and West Siberia, but they were rehabilitated in 1957. They are Sunni Muslims. Following the collapse of the Soviet Union in December 1991, Chechen rebels waged a guerrilla war and organized terrorist attacks, against Russia in the hopes of obtaining independence for Chechnya.

Chechnya Territory of the Russian Empire (1858–1917), territory of the USSR (1922–91) and territory within

Hugo Chávez (EMBASSY OF VENEZUELA)

the Russian Federation (1991–   ). Russia acquired Chechnya in 1858 after defeating the Caucasus domain of the Islamic resistance leader Iman Shamil. It remained under Russian rule until the Bolshevik Revolution created chaos in Russia and allowed Chechnya to establish a brief period of independence in late 1917. However, by 1922 the BOLSHEVIKS had defeated their opponents in the RUSSIAN CIVIL WAR, ended the RUSSO-POLISH WAR and reestablished their control throughout Russia, including Chechnya. It later became part of the Russian Soviet Federated Socialist Republic (RSFSR), one of four political entities that comprised the UNION OF SOVIET SOCIALIST REPUBLICS (USSR) in December 1922. In 1936 Chechnya gained a degree of autonomy within the USSR when it was incorporated into the CHECHEN-INGUSH AUTONOMOUS REPUBLIC within the RSFSR. Six years later, when Adolf HITLER's invading German forces had reached the Caucasus region, the area briefly gained its independence from Moscow; however, that ended by 1943, when the Soviet army expelled the German forces from the region. Soviet dictator Joseph STALIN then labeled many of the Chechens as collaborators with the Nazi military forces and deported them to his labor camps in Siberia and Central Asia. Those who survived the rigors of these camps were allowed to return to Chechnya in 1957, four years after Stalin's death, under the leadership of Soviet premier Nikita KHRUSHCHEV.

When the Soviet Union ceased to exist in December 1991, Dzhokhar Dudayev, a native Chechen and former officer in the Soviet air force, established himself as leader of Chechnya and declared the autonomous republic's independence from Russia. In response, Russian president Boris YELTSIN dispatched several hundred Russian troops by airplane to repress the separatist sentiment; when the planes landed, the Russian forces were immediately opposed by Chechen rebels who disarmed the troops, boarded them on buses and sent them back to Russia. This led to the start of the Russian-Chechen conflict. In 1994 Russia sent forces into Chechnya for the second time in what turned out to be a poorly organized assault that failed to destroy the rebel organization established by Dudayev and his associates. Instead of a rapid victory promised

by Yeltsin, urban guerrilla warfare broke out in the Chechen capital of GROZNY. After two years of fighting in which both sides suffered over 40,000 casualties, a peace accord was negotiated by Yeltsin's security chief, Aleksandr Lebed. Based on Lebed's plan (also called the Khasavyurt Accords), Chechnya gained greater autonomy within Russia, but this fell short of total independence. The pause in fighting also allowed multiparty presidential elections to occur in 1997, in which the Chechen chief of staff, General Aslan Maskhadov, defeated Dudayev and other candidates. However, Maskhadov could not bring all Chechen rebels under his control, particularly those who advocated ISLAMISM through the creation of an Islamic state and the purging of all non-Muslim elements from Chechnya. Dudayev and Maskhadov also proved ineffective in capturing the leaders of the Chechen mafia that emerged after the state's declaration of independence. In August 1999, three years after the end of hostilities, Chechen rebels under Shamil Basayev (1965–2006) entered the nearby autonomous Russian republic of Dagestan, declared solidarity with those within Dagestan wanting to establish an Islamic state in Dagestan and Chechnya, and championed a JIHAD, or holy war, against Russia. The new Russian prime minister, Vladimir PUTIN, later dispatched fresh Russian military troops that swiftly and powerful repressed the rebels. Putin also withdrew Russian recognition of Maskhadov, which led to the replacement of with Akhmad Kadyrov, who had fought against Russia between 1994 and 1996, but condemned the Chechen rebel entry into Dagestan. After Maskhadov's dismissal the Chechen rebel effort to gain independence relied on terrorist attacks on Russian targets, such as the seizure of Moscow theatergoers as hostages in October 2002, as well as an elementary school in Beslan in October 2004. Casualties for both attacks exceeded 500 killed, with many more wounded.

Checkers speech See Richard M. NIXON.

Cheers Television sitcom (situation comedy) that ran on NBC from 1982 to 1994. The series' storyline revolved around the life of Sam Malone (Ted Danson), a former baseball player who

purchases a bar in Boston named Cheers, his employees Nora (Rhea Pearlman), Diane (Shelly Long) and Rebecca (Kirstie Alley) and his regular customers such as Norm (George Wendt), Frasier (Kelsey Grammer) and Cliff (John Ratzenberger). Running for 217 episodes, Cheers received 27 Emmy Awards and regularly won Nielsen battles for NBC against its competition on ABC and CBS. It also led to a spin-off series, FRASIER, which explored the life of Frasier Crane after he moved from Boston to Seattle.

Cheever, John (1912–1982) American novelist and short story writer. While a student at Thayer Academy, the 16-year-old Cheever was expelled. This experience was the nucleus of his first published story, "Expelled" (1930). Many of his short stories, most of which appeared in The NEW YORKER, dealt with the constricting pressures of suburbia. Among his novels is The Wapshot Scandal (1964), which earned the Howells Award from the American Academy of Arts and Letters. The Stories of John Cheever (1978) won the PULITZER PRIZE for fiction, the National Books Critics Circle Award and an American Book Award. Other short story collections include The Enormous Radio, and Other Stories (1953) and The World of Apples (1973).

Cheka (acronym for Chrezvychaynaya Kommissiya) All-Russia extraordinary commission for fighting counterrevolution and sabotage, established on December 7, 1917. It was in operation until 1922, when it became the GPU. It was headed by Felix DZERZHINSKY. Although its sphere of work was wider than mere political repression (it also dealt with speculation and abuse of authority, for example), it did not hesitate to use terror as a means of eliminating inefficiency and opposition. It established CONCENTRATION CAMPS and internal security camps, as well as censorship of the press. The KGB took over many of the functions of the Cheka, and KGB agents were often referred to as chekisty.

Chekhov, Anton (1860–1904) Russian playwright and short story writer. While Chekhov produced the bulk of his writings in the 19th century, his enormous influence on 20th-century literature sets him within the modern

Russian novelist Anton Chekhov, 1904 (LIBRARY OF
CONGRESS. PRINTS AND PHOTOGRAPHS DIVISION)

era. Chekhov spent his childhood in
Taganrog, a country village in southern
Russia, and first went to Moscow in
1879 to study medicine. While attending the university, Chekhov began producing humorous sketches and short
stories to sell to supplement his meager
income. His stories were an immediate
success, and Chekhov went on to pursue dual careers as a physician and a
writer. In 1887 Chekhov's first full-
length play, *Ivanov,* was produced in
Moscow. In 1900, with his health failing, Chekhov moved to Yalta in the
Crimea, where he befriended Leo Tolstoy and Maxim GORKY. In the final
years of his life Chekhov wrote four
classic plays—*The Seagull* (1898), *Uncle
Vanya* (1900), *Three Sisters* (1901) and
The Cherry Orchard (1903)—that continue to be performed frequently.

**Chemical Weapons Convention
(CWC)** The CWC is a 1992 agreement adopted by the UN General Assembly to prevent the production,
acquisition and use of chemical
weapons. It requires all signatories to
destroy all chemical weapons in their
possession. It also established a means
by which its members could appoint
inspectors certified by the UN to verify
the compliance with the CWC by dis-
patching an inspection team to states

suspected of violating the convention.
The Chemical Weapons Convention
has been signed by at least 175 and ratified by at least 157 states.

Chemin des Dames Highway and
battlefield north of the Aisne River between Craonne and Fort Malmaison in
northeastern France. The area was repeatedly and savagely contested during
WORLD WAR I.

Chen Boda (Ch'en Po-ta) *(1905–
1989)* Chinese Communist political
figure. He joined the Communists in
1937 and soon became a leading ideol-
ogist and secretary to MAO ZEDONG
(Mao Tse-tung), whom he served in
this capacity for more than 30 years.
He was believed to have ghostwritten
many of Mao's speeches and articles.
He rose to public prominence in 1968,
when Mao appointed him leader of the
Central Cultural Revolution Group,
which ran the day-to-day operation of
the PURGES that swept China at this
time. He fell into disgrace in the early
1970s and eventually stood trial in
1980 with the GANG OF FOUR who had
led the CULTURAL REVOLUTION. He was
sentenced to an 18-year prison term
but was released a year later for medical reasons.

Cheney, Richard "Dick" *(1941–)*
American politician, secretary of defense (1989–93), and vice president of
the UNITED STATES (2001–). Born in
Lincoln, Nebraska, Cheney moved
with his family to Wyoming, where he
spent much of his childhood and
young adult life. After three semesters
at Yale University on a scholarship,
Cheney returned to Wyoming, where
he briefly began work with the local
electric company. Later, he enrolled in
the University of Wyoming, where he
earned his B.A. and M.A. degrees in political science. He then pursued additional graduate studies at the University
of Wisconsin where he qualified for a
congressional fellowship in 1968–69
that brought him to Washington.

He later worked as a member of the
Cost of Living Council in the administration of Richard NIXON. In this post
he reported to the director of the Office
of Economic Opportunity, Donald
RUMSFELD. After Nixon resigned in
1974, Cheney worked for the Gerald
FORD administration on the transition

team and later as deputy assistant to
the president. The following year Ford
designated Cheney as chief of staff and
promoted him to full assistant to the
president. When the Ford administration ended in 1977, Cheney returned
to Wyoming and in 1978 won a seat in
the House of Representatives and
worked his way up to the seat of House
Minority Whip (1988). In 1989 he became secretary of defense under President George H. W. Bush. While
secretary of defense, Cheney oversaw a
number of American military operations, including Operation Just Cause
in Panama (1989), Operations Desert
Shield and Desert Storm in the Middle
East (1990–91) and Operation Restore
Hope in Somalia (1992–93). He suffered three minor heart attacks before
the age of 50 and underwent quadru-
ple bypass surgery in 1998.

When the first Bush administration
ended in 1993, Cheney left politics. In
1995 he began work as the president
and chief executive office of Halliburn-
ton, a Texas construction and engineering firm specializing in servicing
oil companies. In 2000, after then
Texas governor George W. BUSH had secured the Republican nomination for
president, Cheney agreed to chair
Bush's search committee for a vice
presidential candidate. When the committee failed to agree on a choice from
the available pool of candidates, Cheney himself accepted the designation
and joined the Bush ticket. After winning the election, Cheney was sworn in
as vice president on January 20, 2001.
In that position he played an influential role in promoting a vigorous U.S.
response to the terrorist attacks on SEP-
TEMBER 11, 2001, and was a leading advocate of unilateral U.S. military action
to overthrow the Iraqi regime of Saddam HUSSEIN. However, Cheney's connections to the business community
prior to becoming vice president generated claims that Halliburton was unfairly benefiting from government
contracts to reconstruct postwar Iraq.
Cheney remained on the ticket for the
2004 elections and, following Bush's
reelection, began his second term as
vice president in January 2005.

Chennault, Clair See FLYING TIGERS.

Chen Shui-bian *(1950–)* President of the Republic of China (TAIWAN)

(2000–   ). Born to tenant farmers in the township of Kuantien, Taiwan, Chen studied law at National Taiwan University from which he graduated in 1973.

In 1981 Chen successfully ran for a seat on the Taipei city council, where he campaigned vigorously against government corruption and civic injustice. In 1986 he was sentenced to eight months in prison after his conviction for libel against the government. Chen was released from jail in 1987. After joining the Democratic Progressive Party (DPP) with his wife, Chen served as her assistant after she was elected to the Taiwanese Parliament (Yuan) in 1986. In 1990 he won his own seat in the Yuan and became first executive director of the DPP, developing DPP positions on issues such as a declaration of independence and full statehood by Taiwan. In 1999, after serving in the legislature and as mayor of Taipei, he received the DPP's nomination as its candidate for the Taiwanese presidency. He won the presidential election on March, 18, 2000, the first time that a non-Kuomintang (KMT) candidate had achieved that position. He was reelected president in 2004 by a razor-thin margin of some 30,000 votes against his KMT opponent, Lien Chan.

Chen Yonggui (Ch'en Yung-kuei) *(1913–1986)* Chinese politician. Chen originally became known throughout CHINA as the leader of a model agricultural commune in his home village of Dazhai. He was brought to Beijing by Chairman MAO ZEDONG (Mao Tse-tung) in 1973 and installed as a member of the ruling Politburo. From 1975 to 1980 he served as deputy premier, although many of his accomplishments came to be questioned after Mao's death in 1976. He was dropped from the Politburo in 1982.

Cherenkov, Pavel Alekseyevich *(1904–1990)* Soviet physicist. Cherenkov came from a peasant family. He was educated at the University of Voronezh, where he graduated in 1928. In 1930 he became a member of the Lebedev Institute of Physics in Moscow and later (1953) became professor of experimental physics. In 1934 Cherenkov was investigating the absorption of radioactive radiation by water when he noticed that the water

was emitting an unusual blue light. At first he thought it was due simply to fluorescence. He was forced to reject this idea when it became apparent that the blue radiation was independent of the composition of the liquid and depended only on the presence of fast-moving electrons passing through the medium. In 1937 Ilya FRANK and Igor Tamm showed that the radiation was caused by electrons traveling through the water at a speed greater than that of light in water (though not greater than that of light in a vacuum). This **Cherenkov radiation** can be produced by other charged particles and can be used as a method of detecting elementary particles. Cherenkov, Frank and Tamm shared the NOBEL PRIZE in physics in 1958.

Chernenko, Konstantin *(1911–1985)* Soviet COMMUNIST PARTY official and leader. Chernenko began his political career in the USSR when he joined the Communist Party in 1931. After working his way up through the ranks of the Communist Party, he was transferred to Moldavia (MOLDOVA) in 1948 to coordinate propaganda and agitation activities within that recently acquired region. While in Moldavia, Chernenko encountered Leonid BREZHNEV, who eventually arranged for Chernenko's transfer to Moscow in 1956 to lead the Central Committee of the Communist Party's department on propaganda and agitation.

In 1965 after Brezhnev assumed the leadership of the Soviet Communist Party, he made Chernenko head of the party's General Department. The following year, Chernenko was elected to the Central Committee. In 1976 he was appointed secretary of the Central Committee and member of the Politburo (a panel of elite Soviet leaders that selected the leadership of Soviet government). Chernenko was seen by many as the heir to the aging Brezhnev. However, when Brezhnev died in 1982, opposition to Chernenko emerged within the KGB and anti-Brezhnev factions on the Central Committee and the Politburo. The result was that Yuri ANDROPOV, seen as a reformer of the Communist Party in the mold of Nikita KHRUSHCHEV (and who also served as a mentor for Mikhail GORBACHEV), won election as general secretary of the Communist Party, becoming the effec-

tive head of the Soviet Union on November 12, 1982.

In the 15 months Andropov ruled, Chernenko replaced seven dead Politburo members with individuals who would support his candidacy once Andropov died. When Andropov died on February 9, 1984, the more conservative Politburo quickly voted Chernenko as general secretary four days later, and on April 11, he was elected chairman of the Supreme Soviet Presidium.

At the age of 72, Chernenko, like his predecessor and much of the Politburo whose vacancies he filled, was constantly in poor health. On March 10, 1985, Chernenko died; he was soon succeeded by Andropov's protégé, Gorbachev.

Chernobyl disaster Catastrophic explosion and fire in April 1986 at a Soviet light-water nuclear reactor in the Ukrainian city of Chernobyl. The accident spewed clouds of radiation that spread into the atmosphere over parts of the USSR and other European nations. According to Soviet authorities, who at first downplayed the disaster, 26 people were killed, as many as 1,000 suffered from radiation poisoning and over 90,000 were evacuated from the area as immediate results of the accident. About 100,000 Ukranians were considered at risk of developing cancer from the Chernobyl fallout, and other Europeans in the path of the radioactive cloud were also deemed to be at risk. Farm animals as far away as Scandinavia and Britain were exposed to the radiation and were subsequently destroyed. The disaster caused a reevaluation of nuclear power plants throughout the USSR and in other nations, as well as a rethinking of the whole issue of nuclear power.

Chernovtsy (German: Czernowitz; Romanian: Cernauti) Town and battlefield in the Ukraine, 140 miles southeast of Lviv on the Prut River. A battlefield from 1915 to 1917, it was transferred to ROMANIA at the end of WORLD WAR I and to the USSR in 1940.

Chervenkov, Vulko *(1900–1980)* Premier of Bulgaria (1950–56). Nicknamed "Little STALIN" by Russian admirers before World War II, Chervenkov rose rapidly within the Communist Party ranks in the late 1940s to become head of the Bulgarian Communist Party. As party chief and premier, he followed a Stalinist policy (see STALINISM). However, following Nikita KHRUSHCHEV's denunciation of Stalin at the TWENTIETH PARTY CONGRESS in the USSR (1956), Chervenkov was ousted from his post and from the party.

Chessman case Caryl Chessman, a convicted rapist, was executed in California's San Quentin Penitentiary after 12 years of appeals. Chessman had confessed to being the notorious "Red Light Bandit," a robber who approached victims in lonely spots, flashing a red light that resembled the one used on a police car; sometimes the robber drove off with women, forcing them to perform sexual acts. Chessman later claimed innocence and that his confession was coerced through police torture. However, he was convicted under California's "little Lindburgh Law," received a mandatory death penalty and was moved to Cell 245, Death Row. Chessman's new prison address became internationally famous after he used it as the title for a best seller penned in his prison cell. He followed with three more books, whose manuscripts were smuggled out of the prison. Chessman escaped death for 12 years by appealing his sentence, but he was finally executed in 1960 despite worldwide pleas for mercy. Ironically, Chessman would have received one last hearing and stay of his execution, but the call to stop the execution came just moments too late.

Chesterton, Gilbert Keith (*1874–1936*) British writer, artist, lecturer and broadcaster. With George Bernard SHAW, Hilaire BELLOC and H. G. WELLS, Chesterton was one of the big four Edwardian men of letters. Born in London, he attended University College and the Slade School of Art. In 1899 he embarked on a career in journalism, and for the rest of his life he worked steadily as an essayist, editor and pamphleteer for such publications as *The Speaker, The Daily News, The New Witness* and *G.K.'s Weekly.* His enthusiasms and causes were numerous, as were his books. The novel *The Napoleon of Notting Hill* (1904) and his biography of Chaucer (1932) celebrated the Middle

Ages. *The Thing,* a collection of essays (1929), examined his own conversion to Roman Catholicism. Other essay collections such as *What's Wrong with the World* (1910), and short story volumes, including *Takes of the Long Bow* (1925), propounded social and political theories of the movement known as Distributism. His love of detective stories produced probably his best-known creation, the mild-mannered priest FATHER BROWN, who cared more about saving souls than solving crimes. He appeared in five collections of short stories from 1911 to 1935. Chesterton's love of paradox was constant—and notorious, although he preferred to think his juxtaposition of contradictions produced revelation rather than confusion. His colorful bearing and appearance—boxcape, swordstick, and slouch hat surmounting his enormous bulk—was lovingly satirized by detective novelist John Dickson CARR in his Gideon Fell mysteries. Today his reputation is growing again after a post–World War II decline, largely thanks to the efforts of the Chesterton Society in Canada.

Chetniks (Četniks) Serbian guerrilla force. The original Chetniks operated from 1907 into the BALKAN WARS and WORLD WAR I and attempted to liberate their homeland from the Turks. Relatively inactive between the wars, the group was revived in 1941 and placed under the leadership of Yugoslav general Draža MIHAJLOVIĆ, who had fought with them earlier. They resisted the German occupation, engaged in acts of sabotage and helped downed Allied airmen. However, with

a Serbian rather than a Yugoslav allegiance and a strongly anticommunist ideology, they also collaborated with AXIS forces against TITO and his followers. Greatly reduced in number by the end of WORLD WAR II, they were largely eliminated by Tito's government and by the Soviet troops that occupied Yugoslavia after the war.

Chevalier, Maurice (*1888–1972*) French singer and comic actor. Chevalier was the son of an alcoholic house painter. Struggling at first as an acrobat and street performer, he became mildly successful in French music halls. After confinement in a PRISONER OF WAR camp during WORLD WAR I, Chevalier became a film star in light bedroom comedies directed in the U.S. by Ernst LUBITSCH, such as *The Love Parade* (1929), *One Hour with You* (1932) and *The Merry Widow* (1934). Chevalier's activities during WORLD WAR II caused much controversy; his performances in Germany brought charges that he was a collaborator. After several years of lost popularity in the 1940s, Chevalier returned with even greater success in the late 1950s in Billy WILDER's *Love in the Afternoon* (1957) and Vincente MINNELLI's *Gigi* (1958), which featured his famous rendition of Alan J. LERNER and Frederick LOEWE's "Thank Heaven for Little Girls."

Chiang Kai-shek (Jiang Jieshi) (*1887–1975*) Chinese president and nationalist general. After serving in the Japanese army for several years, Chiang returned to CHINA in 1911 to help SUN YAT-SEN establish a republican army. Chiang consolidated his power

Chiang Kai-shek with Madame Chiang Kai-shek and General Joseph W. Stilwell. 1942 (LIBRARY OF CONGRESS, PRINTS AND PHOTOGRAPHS DIVISION)

after Sun's death and became president of the Chinese Republic in 1928. Conflicts with Communists, autocratic warlords and periodic army rebellions culminated in Chiang's kidnapping in 1936 (see XI'AN INCIDENT). He was released contingent upon ending his campaign against the Communists and stopping Japanese encroachments. After WORLD WAR II Chiang's party, the KUOMINTANG (Guomindang), resumed its Japan-interrupted civil war with the communists (see CHINESE CIVIL WAR OF 1945–1949). In 1949 he resigned as president of China, after the Communists captured Beijing, and moved his followers to the island of TAIWAN. There he established the Republic of China, serving as president until his death.

Chiapas rebellion On January 1, 1994, several members of a group called the Zapatista National Liberation Army, or EZLN (named after Emiliano ZAPATA, a peasant leader in the MEXICAN CIVIL WAR of 1911 and 1914–1915), seized control of four towns in the southern Mexican state of Chiapas. Originally, the Zapatistas, as they came to be called, claimed they would continue to control the towns and eventually march on Mexico City, the capital, until the Mexican government agreed to end oppression of its own citizens, particularly economic oppression, which the Zapatistas claimed was resulting from the NORTH AMERICAN FREE TRADE AGREEMENT (NAFTA). Other demands included greater autonomy for Chiapas State, greater rights for the indigenous Mayan population and the return of land in Chiapas that the Zapatistas claimed the government had illegitimately seized from the Maya and redistributed to Mexican farmers to increase the agricultural yield. The Mexican government's response was twofold. It began military operations to evict the EZLN from the towns they controlled. In a battle that lasted 12 days, government forces eventually drove EZLN forces from their positions and freed those local policemen, officials and ranchers the EZLN had taken hostage. The Mexican government also entered into negotiations with EZLN representatives, with whom they reached an agreement in November 1995 that granted greater autonomy to the Maya

of Chiapas. These accords however, were never approved by Congress. In March 2001 the EZLN staged a protest march from Chiapas to Mexico City to pressure the newly elected Mexican president, Vicente FOX, and Congress to accept the accords and grant greater autonomy and rights to the indigenous peoples of the country. Congress passed an altered version of the accords.

Chicago 7 trial Highly publicized 1968 trial of political protesters. In 1968 the Democrats held their national party convention in Chicago. Protesters opposed to the VIETNAM WAR staged a violent demonstration that erupted into a riot, and many protesters were injured when the Chicago police moved to subdue them. Eight protesters were charged with conspiracy to incite a riot. The trial, which got international attention, was presided over by a crusty 74-year-old federal judge, Julius Hoffman, who was openly hostile to the defendants and their attorneys and made a number of unusual rulings, including trying to jail four defense attorneys who had participated in the early stages of the trial. Bobby SEALE, a leader of the radical BLACK PANTHER Party who was later dropped from the trial, was initially tied up in the courtroom. The defendants and their attorneys, including William KUNSTLER, used the trial to publicize their radical views and opposition to the Vietnam War. A divided jury eventually reached a compromise verdict that acquitted the defendants on the more serious charges.

Chichester, Sir Francis (1901–1972) English sailor and adventurer. Chichester won international fame in 1966 when he became the first person to make a solo nonstop voyage around the world. He accomplished the feat in 226 days in his 54-foot ketch, the *Gipsy Moth IV.*

Chieftains, The Band of Irish musicians who helped revive and popularize the traditional music of IRELAND in the 1960s–90s. The Chieftains' membership has varied slightly over the years; Matt Molloy and Paddy Moloney are generally regarded as the group's guiding spirits. They began performing traditional music with the Irish composer Sean O'Riada and have since per-

formed all over the world; they tour the U.S. annually and have even performed in the People's Republic of China. They have made over a dozen albums and have recorded the scores for several films and television programs. The Chieftains played before a crowd of more than 1 million people—the largest audience ever—when they performed for Pope JOHN PAUL II in Phoenix Park, Dublin, on the pope's visit to Ireland in September 1979.

Chifley, (Joseph) Benedict (1885–1951) Australian statesman and prime minister (1945–49). A prominent New South Wales trade unionist, he entered Parliament in 1928 as a Labour member. He was minister of defense (1929–31), later serving as John CURTIN's treasurer (1941) and minister in charge of planning postwar reconstruction (1942). As prime minister, he proposed banking reforms, expanded social services and led postwar economic growth. Chifley was defeated by a Liberal-Country Party coalition under Sir Robert MENZIES in the election of 1949.

Chile (Republic of Chile) The Spanish-speaking nation stretches for some 2,700 miles along the Pacific coast of South America. In 1904 ARGENTINA and Chile celebrated an end to old boundary feuds by erecting a statue, the Christ of the Andes, on a mountaintop on their mutual border. In 1914 Chile temporarily merged with Brazil and Argentina (as the ABC Powers) to settle an argument between the UNITED STATES and MEXICO. The worldwide GREAT DEPRESSION caused much suffering during the 1930s, and antigovernment sentiments increased. In 1938 a league of democrats and leftists achieved control. Nazi sympathizers pushed for ties with Germany during WORLD WAR II, but in 1943 Chile severed diplomatic ties with the Axis powers and in 1945 went to war with Japan.

During the 1950s and 1960s inflation soared, and Chile's economy wavered. In 1964 Eduardo FREI MONTALVA of the Christian Democratic Party was elected president, and his government took control of foreign-owned corporations and allocated land to small farmers. Salvador ALLENDE GOSSENS won by a narrow margin in the election of 1970, becoming the first democrati-

Chile

PERU
BOLIVIA
Arica
Iquique
PACIFIC
OCEAN
Tocopilla
Oyahue
Calama
Baquedano
Antofagasta
Taltal
Pueblo
Hundido
Caldera
Copiapó
Huasco
La Serena
Coquimbo
Viña del Mar
San Felipe
Valparaíso
Santiago
San Antonio
Rancagua
Constitución
Talca
Talcahuano
Chillán
Concepción
Temuco
Valdivia
ARGENTINA
Osorno
Puerto Montt
Castro
Puerto Aisén
Coihaique
ATLANTIC
OCEAN
Puerto Natales
N
Punta Arenas
Manantiales
Tierra del
Fuego
0   250 miles
Puerto Williams
0   250 km
© Infobase Publishing

CHILE

1906	Massive earthquakes rock Chile.
1910	Opening of trans-Andes railway to Buenos Aires; nitrate boom peaks as Chile exports 64% of world's nitrogen fertilizer.
1920	Nitrate boom subsides; labor unrest and political confusion follow; foreign-owned copper mines assume new importance.
1924	Parliamentary republic ends in military coup.
1932	Rebellious colonels group founds socialist republic lasting 13 days.
1938	Despite violent opposition of Nacisti (Chilean Nazis), Popular Front composed of radicals, socialists and communists forms government.
1939	Earthquakes kill 8,000 to 15,000.
1948	Radical president Videla, in line with U.S. cold war policies, breaks with communists, then bans party.
1960	Earthquakes kill 2,500.
1964	President Frei attempts limited reforms with U.S. backing, satisfying neither right nor left.
1970	Marxist Salvador Allende elected president.
1971	While serving as ambassador to France, poet Pablo Neruda wins Nobel Prize in literature; Allende nationalizes American copper holdings.
1973	With U.S. backing, General Augusto Pinochet overthrows Allende, suspends political parties and civil liberties; Allende and Neruda die during coup.
1974	Mass arrests and torture of Pinochet opponents continue.
1976	Former defense minister Orlando Letelier killed by a bomb in Washington, D.C.
1981	Pinochet's experiment with free-market economy fails, producing record 14% drop in GNP the following year; popular and labor movements resurface with support of the Catholic Church.
1989	Patricio Aylwin elected president, but Pinochet remains as commander in chief of military.
1991	Commission on Truth and National Reconciliation documents torture and murder under Pinochet.
1998	General Pinochet arrested in Great Britain but returned to Chile in 2000.
2001	Chilean court rules Pinochet unfit to stand trial.
2006	Socialist Michelle Bachelet is elected Chile's first woman president.

cally elected Marxist leader in the Western Hemisphere. Allende's policies were not universally admired, and he was killed during a bloody military revolt on September 11, 1973. He was succeeded by General Augusto PINOCHET, who headed a repressive right-wing regime. In 1988 Pinochet permitted a referendum on his continued leadership; he lost. In December 1989 Patricio AYLWIN, the candidate of the opposition Coalition for Democracy, was elected president, ending 17 years of military rule. In 1998 Pinochet, then a lifetime senator, was arrested while in Britain undergoing medical treatment. Although the British government of Tony BLAIR attempted to extradite Pinochet to Spain on murder charges, he was returned to Chile in March 2000, following the January 16 election of Ricardo Lagos Escobar to the presidency. In 2000 similar attempts were made by the Chilean Supreme Court, but anti-Pinochet forces' efforts stalled when an appellate court ruled that Pinochet was unfit to stand trial because of declining health in July 2001. In 2006 Michelle BACHELET became Chile's first woman president.

Chilean Revolution of 1973

In 1970 Salvador ALLENDE GOSSENS, an avowed Marxist, was elected president of CHILE. He began to establish democratic socialism by freezing prices and raising wages, nationalizing U.S.-owned copper mines and heavy industries and breaking up large plantations to distribute land to peasants. These actions antagonized foreign countries, the middle and upper classes and right-wing parties. The economy worsened as food shortages developed, strikes cut production, foreign loans were refused and inflation rose. A two-month strike of trucking industry owners resisting nationalization crippled the nation, and on September 11, 1973, the armed forces staged a successful coup d'état. Allende apparently committed suicide. Reportedly, the U.S. CIA helped plan and finance the takeover. A four-man military junta headed by Augusto PINOCHET took power.

China (People's Republic of China)

China encompasses 3,704,427 square miles of central and east Asia and is the most populous nation on Earth. The BOXER UPRISING of 1900 attempted to oust foreigners but was suppressed by a British-led, six-nation foreign army. Manchu (Qing, or Ch'ing) dynasty rule was overthrown during the CHINESE REVOLUTION of 1911–1912, and China became a republic in 1912. SUN YAT-SEN is regarded as the father of modern China. In 1916 civil war erupted between rival warlords, leading to conflict

CHINA

1900	Boxer rebellion: failed attempt to expel foreigners.
1911	British Parliament bans opium trade.
1912	China becomes a republic, which lasts until the death of its leader Yuan Shikai in 1916.
1916	Shikai's followers set up government in Beijing; rival government established in Canton by Sun Yat-sen's Kuomintang (Guomindang), sending the country into civil war.
1921	Chinese Communist Party established.
1927	Chiang Kai-shek attacks Communists at their base in Shanghai.
1931	Japan occupies Manchuria.
1934–35	Mao Zedong leads Communists in "Long March" to Yenan.
1936	Chiang is kidnapped and agrees to halt his campaign against the Communists.
1937	Japan launches full-scale invasion.
1945	Japan surrenders; the Nationalists take over areas formerly held by the Japanese; U.S. attempts to mediate between Nationalists and CCP.
1949	Peoples' Liberation Army captures Beijing; People's Republic of China formally established; Nationalists under Chiang flee to Taiwan.
1950	Chinese troops intervene in Korean War, push UN troops back into South Korea; China invades Tibet.
1954	Soviet-style collective farms established.
1958	Chinese crush Tibetan revolt.
1960	China breaks relations with the USSR.
1962	Sino-Indian war erupts over Chinese occupation of areas in northern Kashmir.
1964	China successfully tests atomic bomb.
1966	Cultural Revolution begins.
1971	People's Republic of China is seated at the UN, Republic of China (Taiwan) is expelled.
1972	U.S. president Richard Nixon visits Beijing.
1976	Death of Mao.
1981	Gang of Four is convicted.
1982	Deng Xiaoping emerges as paramount ruler, begins economic reforms.
1984	Sino-British agreement is signed on reversion of Hong Kong to China in 1997.
1989	Prodemocracy demonstrators in Tiananmen Square in Beijing are violently crushed by the army.
1990	China abstains from UN vote to use force against Iraq.
1993	Jiang Zemin becomes head of state.
1997	Hong Kong returned to Chinese sovereignty.
2002	China joins the World Trade Organization.
2003	Hu Jintao becomes state president. Strict quarantine measures are enforced to cope with an outbreak of the Sars virus. China's first manned spacecraft is launched.
2004	Former president Jiang Zemin resigns as army chief three years before term expires. Trade agreement reached with 10 Southeast Asian nations could eventually unite 22% of the world's population in a free-trade zone.
2005	Relations with Japan deteriorate, sparked by a Japanese textbook that China claims glosses over Japan's World War II record. Taiwan's National Party leader, Lien Chan, visits China, the first meeting between Nationalist and Communist Party leaders since 1949. China and Russia conduct joint military exercises for the first time.

between two major political factions: the KUOMINTANG (Guomindang), led by CHIANG KAI-SHEK (Jiang Jieshi), and the Chinese Communist Party (CCP), led by MAO ZEDONG (Mao Tse-tung) (see CHINESE CIVIL WAR OF 1930–1934; LONG MARCH). After the Japanese occupation (1937–45), the Communists gained control, and the People's Republic of China was established on October 1, 1949 (see CHINESE CIVIL WAR OF 1945–1949). The KMT was left in control of TAIWAN and several offshore islands. In 1951 Tibet became an autonomous region of China. From 1950 to 1976 a central council under the chairmanship of Mao Zedong held absolute power. China supported NORTH KOREA during the KOREAN WAR (1950–53), and Chinese troops fought against U.S. and UN forces during the conflict. The CULTURAL REVOLUTION (1966–76) brought violence and chaos as the RED GUARDS tried to eliminate old customs, revive the Maoist revolutionary spirit and suppress "revisionism." U.S. envoy Henry KISSINGER's secret visit to Beijing in 1971, followed by President NIXON's visit in 1972, began an era of dialogue between China and the U.S.—after more than 20 years of mutual antipathy. Upon Mao's death in 1976, the GANG OF FOUR led by Mao's widow, JIANG QING, tried to seize power but failed; they were tried and jailed.

New leader DENG XIAOPING initiated a decade of reform in 1978, attempting to modernize the economy and forging new trade ties with the West. A new constitution was established in 1982. China seemed poised to turn away from its isolationist, communist past. Student-led prodemocracy demonstrations occurred in April 1989 but were quelled when the army killed hundreds in Beijing's TIANANMEN SQUARE in June. The Communist government has since tightened its control in China, cracking down on dissidents and making it clear that economic reforms would not mean the introduction of democratic government. In 1993 JIANG ZEMIN became president of China. Under his administration China sought greater inclusion in the global market through the ASEAN REGIONAL FORUM and the WORLD TRADE ORGANIZATION, which it joined in 2002. China also repeatedly insisted on the return of Taiwan to Beijing rule. In 1997 the former British

Crown colony of HONG KONG was restored to Chinese sovereignty. By the early 21st century, China was well on its way to becoming a major economic power in the world, achieving annual growth rates double those of other industrial powers and recording huge trade surpluses with the U.S. In 2002 Hu Jintao was named chairman of the Chinese Communist Party and became state president the following year. In 2002 a string of mysterious deaths was attributed to a then unknown virus later known as SARS, a highly contagious respiratory syndrome whose symptoms resemble the flu. The Chinese government was criticized for its slowness in acknowledging the epidemic, which was declared over in 2003 by the World Health Organization. In 2003 China became the third country to put a human in space.

Chinese Civil War of 1930–1934

Although the KUOMINTANG (Guomindang), or Nationalist, armies had reunited CHINA in 1928 (see NORTHERN EXPEDITION), the problems of turning China into a modern state were enormous and complex. It could not be done in a few years, and discontent smoldered all over the country as former warlords tried to regain power and the peasants suffered the ravages of floods and famines. Revolts were put down in one province, and a fresh one broke out in another. However, the Kuomintang's Generalissimo CHIANG KAI-SHEK considered his chief enemies to be the Communists, who had been driven from the large cities and found refuge in the Jinggang Mountains in the south. Five times between 1930 and 1934 Chiang's troops tried to encircle their strongholds. The first two efforts and the fourth failed. In the third campaign of 1931 a furious battle was fought at Goaxing with heavy losses on both sides. Chiang claimed a victory, but the Red (Communist) Army was not annihilated and moved its bases farther south. By 1933 Chinese Communist communes had been set up in four other remote provinces. The fifth campaign started in October 1933 with a 700,000-man Nationalist army. This time, with the coaching of a German general and the aid of modern planes and artillery, the Nationalist troops adopted a scorched-earth policy to starve the enemy into submission. Pill-

boxes, forts and checkpoints on all roads discouraged the Communists' usual aggressive guerrilla methods, and the peasants were exterminated. The ruthless campaign continued for a year until the Communists in the southern mountains of China were finally dislodged and began their long trek to a new base (see LONG MARCH).

Chinese Civil War of 1945–1949

After Japan's defeat in WORLD WAR II (see WORLD WAR II IN CHINA; WORLD WAR II IN THE PACIFIC) and the expulsion of its troops from mainland China, both the Communists in the north and the KUOMINTANG (Guomindang), or Nationalist, armies in the south rushed to seize the Chinese areas formerly occupied by the Japanese. American planes airlifted thousands of Kuomintang troops to Shanghai, Nanjing (Nanking) and other major Chinese cities; U.S. general George C. MARSHALL was sent to negotiate a peace between the opposing Chinese sides. MAO ZEDONG, the Communist leader, seemed willing to bargain, but CHIANG KAI-SHEK, the Nationalist leader, refused to talk with the Communists. Marshall warned Chiang that China's faltering economy would collapse if negotiations were not conducted, but Chiang would not listen. Marshall reported that his mission had failed and returned home in early 1947. U.S. troops were also withdrawn, but U.S. military and economic aid continued. Meanwhile, whole divisions defected to the Communists, Kuomintang commanders quarreled among themselves and refused to take the offensive and rampant inflation and government corruption discredited the once popular Kuomintang. In October 1948, 300,000 Nationalist troops surrendered to the Communists in Manchuria, and two months later 66 Nationalist divisions were surrounded and captured—or they deserted—in north-central China. The following April the Communists crossed the Yangtze River and spread throughout the south. Shanghai fell to them in May, Canton in October and the former capital of Chongqing (Chungking) in November. In December 1949 Chiang, his Nationalist government and their followers fled to the island of Formosa (Taiwan), where Chiang set up the Republic of China (1950). Millions of Chinese died in this civil war, and millions more were impoverished by the runaway inflation. U.S. aid to the Kuomintang created anti-American sentiment among much of China's population. The Communists had triumphed and proclaimed the People's Republic of China (1949), with their capital at Beijing (Peking) and Mao as chairman; soon they would chart a completely new social, economic and political course for China. (See also SINO-JAPANESE WAR OF 1937–1945.)

Chinese Revolution of 1911–1912

Although the Manchu (Qing, or Ch'ing) dynasty (1644–1911) had ruled CHINA for more than 260 years, many Chinese still considered the Manchu (who originated in Manchuria) foreigners and hated them as much as they hated and feared the Western foreigners who had gained control of the coastal ports and had been granted concessions to build railroads, roads and mines. Throughout the first decade of the 20th century, China seethed with unrest and turmoil, revolutionary societies sprang up everywhere, new public and private schools graduated students who wanted a better life for themselves and their countrymen, and overseas Chinese sent money home to finance reform and resistance movements. The weak Manchu emperor made some attempts at reform, but these were abruptly canceled by the dowager empress, who was out of touch with the realities in the country. On October 8, 1911, an explosion in the city of Hangzhou (Hangkow) revealed the presence of a revolutionary group whose leaders were promptly arrested and executed. Soldiers in Wuchang (part of Wuhan) across the Yangtze River from Hangzhou knew of the group's plot and, fearing to be implicated, mutinied on October 10, sacked the governor's residence, took control of the city and declared a rebellion against the Manchu. This date, celebrated as the "Double Ten," sparked similar uprisings all over the country. Soon all the provinces in the Yangtze valley and southern and northwestern China were in rebel hands. They proclaimed their territory a republic. There was comparatively little bloodshed because most Chinese officials and military leaders realized the days of the Manchu were numbered. In desperation, the prince-regent recalled the Assembly, an advisory body of appointed and elected members, which elected YUAN SHIKAI (Yüan Shih-k'ai) prime minister, a post he reluctantly accepted. Yuan had organized China's modern army. A capable leader not strongly devoted to the Manchu, Yuan wanted mainly to direct China's development as a strong modern nation. His army retook several cities from the revolutionaries, and then Yuan ordered the revolution to halt. Meanwhile SUN YAT-SEN hurried home from the U.S. where he had been lecturing and raising funds for the revolution. On his return to China, he was offered the position of provisional president and was inaugurated on January 1, 1912, at the provisional capital in Nanjing (Nanking). Sun knew he had no military support and no government experience; he was chiefly a theorist and democratic idealist. Thus, when the young emperor, Xuantong (Hsuan-t'ung), abdicated on February 12, bringing the Qing dynasty to an end, Sun resigned. The newly formed National Assembly then elected Yuan provisional president, and the north and south of China were reunited as a republic.

Chinh, Trong (1908–1988) Vietnamese politician; one of the last of the original group of Vietnamese Communist revolutionaries who governed VIETNAM from the 1940s through the 1980s. He served as general secretary of the Communist Party from 1941 to 1956 and again for six months in 1986 before being replaced. His attempt at radical agrarian reform in the mid-1950s caused the widespread dispossession of families and the killing of as many as 50,000 people. In the fight against the U.S., he advocated guerrilla and political warfare rather than the throwing of North Vietnamese troops into battle.

Chin Hills Special Division In Burma, northwest of Magwe division and southeast of the Indian border. This region was established in 1948 to acknowledge the Tibetan descent of the Chins. Massive fighting occurred here from 1942 to 1944 during the WORLD WAR II Japanese operation against Manipur.

Chirac, Jacques (1932–) French politician and president of France (1995–). A graduate of the Institut

Jacques Chirac (EMBASSY OF FRANCE)

d'Études Politiques, Chirac served as an armored cavalry officer in the French army during the ALGERIAN WAR from 1954 to 1957. He graduated from the École Nationale d'Administration (ENA), the prestigious institution that trains high-level civil servants, in 1959.

While serving Gaullist prime minister Georges POMPIDOU, who appointed him undersecretary of state for social affairs in 1962, Chirac focused his attention on reforming France's unemployment insurance system. He won election to the National Assembly in 1967.

The following year student riots broke out in Paris in protest against classroom overcrowding and quickly plunged the entire city into anarchy after the major labor unions launched a general strike. Chirac was a member of the government's negotiating team that sought to resolve the conflict. On de Gaulle's resignation in 1969, Pompidou appointed Chirac as secretary of state for the economy and finance and, later, minister of the interior.

When Valéry GISCARD D'ESTAING was elected president in 1974, he chose Chirac as his prime minister, a position Chirac held until 1976 and later occupied (1986–88) under the presidency of the Socialist François MITTERRAND. Perhaps more important to his political career, Chirac was elected mayor of Paris in 1977 and reelected in 1988. In 1981 he covertly worked against Giscard's bid for reelection, and Mitterrand was elected president.

During the Mitterrand presidency, Chirac emerged as the leader of a center-right French political coalition. Although he failed to unseat Mitterrand in the 1988 elections, Chirac persevered and proved successful in 1995, winning the presidency in the second round of elections over his Socialist opponent, Lionel Jospin. In 2002, as a result of the fragmentation of the left and the emergence of several leftist candidates for the presidency, Chirac faced a runoff election with the ultra-conservative Jean-Marie LE PEN, whom he defeated easily to win reelection with the support of leftist voters.

In 2002 and 2003 Chirac gained international attention as he led European efforts to prevent U.S. military action in Iraq. Chirac also attempted to use his close relationship with German chancellor Gerhard SCHRÖDER to steer the EUROPEAN UNION toward a foreign policy that clashed with that of the U.S. on such issues as the "war on terrorism" and the Middle East peace process. Chirac faced a domestic crisis in 2005, when riots led by alienated immigrants broke out in the suburbs of Paris, and again in 2006, when protesters took to the streets over a youth employment law.

Chirau, Jeremiah (*1923–1985*) Zimbabwean chief and politician. As head of the ZIMBABWE United People's Organization in what was then RHODESIA, in 1978 he helped negotiate a settlement with Prime Minister Ian SMITH for the transfer of power to the country's black majority. He was part of the joint leadership (with Bishop Abel MUZOREWA and Ndabaningi Sithole) that governed the country briefly and was widely seen as a puppet government controlled by the white minority. In any event, Chirau lacked the broader political base enjoyed by his colleagues and by their more radical rivals, Joshua NKOMO and Robert MUGABE, and his influence quickly waned.

Chirico, Giorgio de (*1888–1978*) Italian painter. Born in Volos, Greece, he studied at Athens and Munich. Moving to Italy in 1909, he began to create his Enigma paintings, dreamlike canvases in which anonymous figures stand in starkly lit piazzas often marked by classical statues or great towers. Working in Paris 1911–15, he became acquainted with CUBISM, struck up a friendship with the poet Guillaume APOLLINAIRE and further developed his enigmatic imagery. Returning to Italy in 1915, he settled in Ferrara. Inspired by the city's architecture and continuing to explore strangely juxtaposed figurative images, he developed the movement he termed METAPHYSICAL PAINTING, and in 1920, along with the artist Carlo CARRA, he founded the magazine *Pittura metafisica*. Chirico's works characteristically include architecturally constructed mannequins, statues or still-life elements placed in shadowed and mysteriously empty spaces influenced by classical perspective. These lonely and symbolic images were important precursors of SURREALISM. Chirico moved to Paris in 1924. In 1930 he abandoned his earlier style, and his later works are widely considered academic and imitative.

Chisholm, Shirley (*1924–2005*) U.S. congresswoman. Born in Brooklyn, New York, Chisholm attended Brooklyn College and Columbia University, obtaining a degree in childhood education in 1952. From 1953 to 1964 she was a child care specialist and educational consultant in New York and was active in various civil rights organizations. In 1968, Chisholm, a Democrat, became the first black woman to be elected to the U.S. House of Representatives. In the House, she proved herself a skilled politician and an effective advocate of the rights of minorities, the urban poor and women. She was also an outspoken opponent of the VIETNAM WAR (see ANTIWAR MOVEMENT). She briefly sought the Democratic nomination for president in 1971. An extremely popular legislator, Chisholm served seven terms and retired in 1982. In 1993 Chisholm was appointed U.S. ambassador to Jamaica by President Bill CLINTON, but declined the nomination because of her severe eye ailments.

Chissano, Joaquim Alberto (*1939– *) President of Mozambique (1984–2005) and of the FRELIMO political party (1986–). Educated in Mozambique and Portugal, Chissano left his studies at Lisbon University and secretly made his way to France in order to study medicine while remaining involved in the nationalist movement of his homeland that was seeking independence from PORTUGAL. He joined the Mozambique Liberation Front (FRELIMO) in 1962, became a member of its central committee a year later and joined FRELIMO's Political-Military Committee in 1968. While coordinating the Mozambiquan effort to end Portuguese colonial rule, Chissano also taught physical education, geography and history at the FRELIMO Secondary School and the Cadre Training center at Bagamoyo, Tanzania. He served as prime minister in the transitional national government that prepared Mozambique for self-rule during 1974–75. When Portugal finally accorded Mozambique its independence in 1975, Chissano served in a variety of positions in the new FRELIMO government, including minister of foreign affairs from 1975 to 1986 while serving as a delegate to the People's Assembly. In 1984 he was elected by the FRELIMO Central Committee (the executive board that developed the policies of the political party that controlled the country) to succeed the late Samora Machel as president of Mozambique. Chissano was reelected to that position in 1989. During the postcolonial era Chissano helped transform FRELIMO from a liberation movement into a political party. He supervised its activities as a member of its political bureau, eventually winning the presidency of the party in 1986. In 1994 Chissano organized the country's first multiparty elections for the presidency of Mozambique and won reelection handily. He left office in 2005.

Chomsky, Noam (*1928– *) American linguistics theorist and political and social critic. Chomsky is one the leading thinkers of the 20th century in the field of linguistics. Son of a Hebrew language scholar, Chomsky earned his doctorate in linguistics at the University of Pennsylvania and has taught at the Massachusetts Institute of Technology since 1955. Chomsky single-handedly created a theoretical revolution in linguistics with the publication of his first major work, *Syntactic Studies* (1957), which asserted that language and grammatical structures were learned primarily through innate structures within the human brain as opposed to cultural conditioning. Chomsky elaborated this theory in *Aspects of a Theory of Syntax* (1965). In the 1960s he emerged as a prominent left-wing libertarian critic of U.S. foreign and domestic policies, most notably the VIETNAM WAR. He was also critical of U.S. military involvement in the Middle East after IRAQ's invasion of KUWAIT (1990). His writings on politics include *American Power and the New Mandarins* (1969), *At War with Asia* (1970), *Towards a New Cold War* (1982) and *The Fateful Triangle* (1983). In the aftermath of the terrorist attacks of SEPTEMBER 11, 2001, Chomsky generated controversy with comments disapproving of the policies of President George W. BUSH in the "war on terrorism" against al-QAEDA, and later against Saddam HUSSEIN.

Chongqing (Chungking, Ch'ung-ch'ing, Tchongking) City on the Yangtze River in Sichuan (Szechwan) province, central CHINA. The city, remote from the invading Japanese, was headquarters of the KUOMINTANG (Guomindang) and capital of Nationalist China from 1938 to 1946 and again in 1949, until it was seized by the Communists. During WORLD WAR II it was also a U.S. air base, from 1944 to 1945.

Chrétien, Jean *(1934–)* Prime minister of Canada (1993–2003). From 1963 until 1986, Chrétien served as a representative in the Canadian House of Commons for the Saint-Maurice–Laflèche district and held a variety of ministerial posts in the Canadian government. After a four-year respite from politics, Chrétien was elected leader of the Liberal Party and then returned to the House of Commons. After leading the Liberal opposition for almost four years, he was sworn in as prime minister in 1993 when the Liberals gained a majority. Chrétien won a second term in 1997 and a third term in 2000.

Chrétien dealt with a variety of domestic issues during his long tenure in office. Economically, he had to balance his party's traditional concern for employment security for Canada's working class with his government's commitment to free-trade practices in the NORTH AMERICAN FREE TRADE AGREEMENT (NAFTA) and the WORLD TRADE ORGANIZATION, and to reduce the national deficit through reduced government expenditures. In 1995, when it appeared that the residents of the Canadian province of Quebec would vote for independence, Chrétien's promise of a veto of future amendments to the Canadian constitution helped keep Quebec within Canada. Chrétien supported efforts in 2003 to sanction civil unions between gay and lesbian couples and to consider the legalization of marijuana.

In foreign affairs, Canada under Chrétien sought to distinguish itself from its ally to the south, particularly in the "war on terrorism." While Chrétien supported the right of the U.S. to prevent terrorist groups like al-QAEDA from staging additional attacks on American soil, he criticized the Bush administration's treatment of the alleged members of al-Qaeda held at Guantánamo Bay, Cuba, as well as the justifications the government of George W. BUSH offered for the invasion of Iraq in March of 2003. Chrétien retired in December 2003 and was succeeded by former finance minister Paul Martin.

Chrétien, Jean-Loup *(1938–)* French "spationaut." Serving as a researcher aboard the Soviet *Soyuz T-6* (June–July 1982), Chrétien was the first Western participant in the Soviet space program. Spending eight days in space, including seven aboard the space station *Salyut 7*, Chrétien supervised the operation of a specially built heart monitoring system for use in space health studies. He made his second spaceflight aboard *Soyuz TM-7*, visiting the *Mir* space station from November 26 to December 21, 1988. Chrétien was accompanied by Soviet cosmonauts Alexander Volkov and Sergei Krikalov. During his stay aboard *Mir*, he became the first West European to perform a space walk. Chrétien was also backup for French spationaut Patrick Baudry aboard U.S. space shuttle mission 51-G, flown in May 1985, and trained with him in Houston.

Christian X *(1870–1947)* King of Denmark (1912–47). During his reign the Danish government passed a wide variety of reform legislation, including social security laws. In 1915 Christian signed a new constitution granting women the franchise and ending the special rights of the upper classes. A symbol of national resistance to Nazi occupation during WORLD WAR II, he defied German authority and was placed under house arrest after open opposition to the occupation broke out in 1943.

Christian Democratic Union (CDU) Founded in 1945 as the postwar successor of the Catholic Center Party, the CDU (led in the 1980s by Helmut KOHL) was WEST GERMANY's major conservative party. A coalition headed by the CDU and including two smaller parties, the Christian Social Union and the Free Democratic Party, held office under Kohl's chancellorship from 1982 into the 1990s. The CDU was victorious in the national elections held shortly after the reunification of GERMANY (October 3, 1990). The CDU's predominance in German politics ended in 1998 when the Social Democratic Pary (SDP) formed a coalition government with the Green Party and replaced Kohl with Gerhard SCHRÖDER.

Christie, Dame Agatha *(1890– 1976)* English detective fiction writer. The most acclaimed of all British mystery writers, she is best known for two characters: the sly and egotistical Belgian detective Hercule Poirot, who first appeared in *The Mysterious Affair at Styles* (1920), and the implacable village spinster and snoop, Jane Marple, who was introduced in *Murder at the Vicarage* (1930). Married to archaeologist Sir Max Mallowan, Christie assisted him in a number of Middle Eastern digs and used the locale for some of her most famous mysteries: *Death on the Nile* (1937), which became the play *Murder on the Nile* (1946) and a film (1978); *Murder in Mesopotamia* (1936); and *Appointment with Death* (1938). Among the best known of her almost 100 other novels are *The Murder of Roger Ackroyd* (1926), *Murder on the Orient Express* (1934; U.S. title *Murder in the Calais Coach;* film, 1975), *Ten Little Niggers* (1939; retitled *Ten Little Indians;* U.S. title *And Then There Were None;* films, 1945, 1965, 1975) and *The Pale Horse* (1962). Also an extremely successful playwright, she was the author of such works as *Witness for the Prosecution* (1954; film, 1958) and *The Mousetrap* (1952). She was made a Dame Commander, Order of the British

Empire, in 1971. Her autobiography was published in 1977.

Christie, Julie *(1940–)* With her striking beauty and cool sexuality, Christie was Britain's leading actress in American films in the 1960s and early 1970s. Born in Chukua, Assam, India, she made her film debut in 1962 as a stripper in the British film *Crooks Anonymous.* Thereafter she starred predominantly in dramas and big-screen epics, such as *Billy Liar* (1963), *Doctor Zhivago* (1965), *Far from the Madding Crowd* (1967), *Petulia* (1968), *The Go-Between* (1971) and *Shampoo* (1975), although she was equally appealing in science fiction and suspense, such as *Fahrenheit 451* (1967), *Don't Look Now* (1973) and *Demon Seed* (1977). In 1965 Christie won the ACADEMY AWARD for best actress for her performance in the satire *Darling.* After an absence, she returned to the screen in the mid-1980s in *Heat and Dust.* In 1998 Christie earned an Academy Award nomination for best actress for her performance in *Afterglow* (1997).

Christmas Island Island in the Indian Ocean, about 186 miles south of Java; 52 square miles in area. The island was apparently uninhabited until 1888, when it was claimed by Britain. In 1891 it was leased to John Clunies-Ross (who also held the COCOS ISLANDS) and Sir John Murray, who ran the island as a private concession and brought in Malay and Chinese workers to mine the local phosphate. Australia and New Zealand acquired the mining interests in 1948. Christmas Island is now a self-governing dependency of Australia. The population in 2004 was slightly over 400. Another island of the same name, in the Pacific, is part of Kiribati. To protest the resumed nuclear tests in French Polynesia, the island suspended formal relations with France in 1995. Four years later it was admitted to the United Nations.

Christo (Christo Javacheff) *(1935–)* Bulgarian artist. Known for wrapping objects, a technique that at once mocks modern packaging and gives objects new and mysterious presence, he began in Paris during the 1950s, wrapping small objects such as bottles or chairs in plastic. By the 1960s he was wrapping whole buildings in temporary projects that turned commonplace

structures into ambiguous entities. He turned to environmental pieces in 1969, wrapping a mile of Australian coastline in polypropylene sheeting. His best-known environmental pieces are *Valley Curtain* (1972), a drape across a Colorado mountain valley, and *Running Fence* (1976), a 5.5-mile-long curtain constructed in northern California. Both these projects were subjects of documentaries by the MAYSLES brothers. While Christo's "spectacles" are ephemeral by nature, they are carefully planned in drawings and meticulously recorded. In 1995 Christo was responsible for wrapping the Reichstag (the German legislative building) in canvas as part of an artistic tribute to the reunified state.

Christopher, Warren *(1925–)* U.S. sectary of state (1993–97). A year after receiving his B.A. from the University of Southern California in 1945, Christopher enrolled at Stanford Law School, where he graduated in 1949. After a successful law career in Los Angeles, he was appointed deputy attorney general by President Lyndon JOHNSON in 1967. He became deputy secretary of state under President Jimmy CARTER in 1977. As the second-ranking member of the State Department, Christopher played a pivotal role in resolving several of the more contentious issues of the Carter administration, such as obtaining the release of 52 Americans taken hostage by Iranian revolutionaries in 1979, normalizing U.S. relations with China and assuring Congress's ratification of the Panama Canal treaties, which returned the canal to Panamanian control in 1999. With the end of the Carter administration in 1981, Christopher again returned to private practice.

In 1992 Christopher headed the vice presidential nominee search committee for the Democratic candidate, Arkansas governor Bill CLINTON, and soon settled on Tennessee senator Al GORE as the Democratic running mate. After Clinton won the November 1992 presidential election, Christopher led the president-elect's transition team. Clinton selected Christopher as his secretary of state, and he was sworn in to that post on January 20, 1993.

As secretary of state, Christopher's major achievement was assuring the implementation of the 1993 OSLO ACCORDS between Israel and the PALESTINE LIBER-

ATION ORGANIZATION (PLO). He also attempted to use the U.S.'s international influence to end the ongoing Yugoslav civil war involving Serbia, Bosnia and Herzegovina, and Croatia. This U.S. diplomatic intervention resulted in the DAYTON ACCORDS, which brought an end to the fighting in the Balkans. After Clinton's reelection in 1996 Christopher resigned his post to return to his Los Angeles law firm. In the U.S. presidential election of 2000, he was sent on behalf of Al Gore to supervise the recount of the contested Florida vote.

Chrysler, Walter P. *(1875–1940)* U.S. auto manufacturer and founder of the Chrysler Company. Chrysler initially worked as a machinist's apprentice, but by 1912 he was manager of the BUICK Motor Company. By 1916 he was appointed president and general manager. He was put in charge of operations for GENERAL MOTORS in 1919. In 1920 he became vice president of the Willys-Overland Company and president of the Maxwell Motor Corporation. In 1925 he launched his own company, the Chrysler Corporation, and in 1928 took control of the DODGE Company and merged it into Chrysler. The Chrysler Corporation introduced the high compression engine and torsion bar suspension to the automobile industry. Chrysler ranked among the top three American automobile manufacturers. In 1998 it was purchased by the German company Daimler-Benz and became DaimlerChrysler.

Chrysler Building New York skyscraper, a key monument of the ART DECO phase of American architecture. A 1930 design of architect William Van Alen, the Chrysler Building was, until the EMPIRE STATE BUILDING was constructed in 1931, the tallest building in the world, with a height of 1,048 feet. Its ornamentation with "gargoyles" fashioned after automobile radiator caps; its spectacular Deco lobby spaces with rich materials, geometric ornamentation and decorative lighting; its setback forms and its stainless steel spike top make it a striking example of the Art Deco architectural design of its time as well as one of New York's most famous landmarks.

Chuikov, Marshal Vasily Ivanovich *(1900–1982)* Soviet general and hero of WORLD WAR II who led the defense of STALINGRAD. Chuikov joined the Red Army in 1919 and was later military attaché to CHIANG KAI-SHEK. He commanded the Soviet forces at Stalingrad (consisting of the 62nd Army) and held off German forces for five months; the result of the bloody battle was a decisive German defeat (see STALINGRAD, SIEGE OF). Under General ZHUKOV, he led a Soviet army into Poland and Berlin, where he accepted the German surrender (May 1, 1945). After the war he became a member of the Central Committee of the Communist Party. He was commander in chief of the Soviet occupation force in Germany until 1953 and rose to commander of all Soviet land forces and deputy minister of defense.

Church, Frank Forrester (1924–1984)

U.S. senator (1957–81). An Idaho Democrat known as the "boy orator" of the Senate, Church came to national prominence when he delivered the keynote address at the 1960 Democratic National Convention. A spokesman for liberal and conservationist causes, he broke with the JOHNSON administration and called for a halt in the U.S. bombing of VIETNAM in 1966. As a leading member of the ANTIWAR MOVEMENT, Church later sought to end all American military involvement in Southeast Asia. As chairman of the Senate Select Committee on Intelligence, he led an investigation of U.S. intelligence agencies in 1975–76 that uncovered an array of civil rights abuses. His investigation resulted in closer monitoring of the agencies.

Churchill, Sir Winston Leonard Spencer (1874–1965)

British statesman, widely considered the greatest political figure in 20th-century Britain. Born at Blenheim Palace, in Oxfordshire, Winston Churchill was the third son of conservative politician Lord Randolph Churchill and his American wife, Jennie Jerome, and was descended from the first duke of Marlborough. He attended Harrow and Sandhurst and in 1894 was commissioned in the Fourth Hussars. He served in Cuba, where he was also a reporter for a London daily, and in India and the Sudan, where he fought at the battle of Omdurman (1898). The following year he resigned his commission and was assigned to cover the BOER WAR by a London newspaper. Captured and imprisoned by the Boers, he engineered a daring escape, which made him an overnight celebrity and hero. Churchill was first elected to Parliament in 1900 as a Conservative, switching to the LIBERAL PARTY in 1904 after disputes over the Conservatives' high-tariff policy. He served as undersecretary for the colonies (1906–08), president of the Board of Trade (1908–10) and home secretary (1910–11). Appointed lord of the admiralty in 1911, he helped to prepare Britain's naval forces for war. After the outbreak of WORLD WAR I, he supported the DARDANELLES CAMPAIGN; he was widely blamed when the campaign failed and was forced to resign from the government. In 1917, after active service in France, he was appointed LLOYD GEORGE's minister of munitions, subsequently becoming the state secretary for war and air (1918–21). As colonial secretary (1921–22), he helped to support the Irish Free State (see IRELAND) and affirmed PALESTINE as a Jewish homeland while recognizing Arab rights (see BALFOUR DECLARATION). He left Parliament in 1922, returning to the House as a Conservative two years later and subsequently serving as chancellor of the exchequer (1924–29) under Prime Minister Stanley BALDWIN. Out of office after the Conservative defeat in 1929, he wrote a four-volume biography of his ancestor, Lord Marlborough, and spent much of his time warning the nation about the looming Nazi threat in GERMANY and roundly condemning British APPEASEMENT of HITLER.

He returned to the government as first lord of the admiralty under Neville CHAMBERLAIN upon the outbreak of WORLD WAR II (September 3, 1939). He immediately took action against German SUBMARINE warfare. When the GERMAN INVASION OF NORWAY toppled Chamberlain's government, Churchill became prime minister on May 10, 1940. His first report to Commons promised Britain's total devotion to the defeat of Germany and contained the famous phrase "I have nothing to offer but blood, toil, tears and sweat." Churchill's superb oratory, his courageous spirit and his absolute refusal to consider British defeat helped to rally Great Britain in the dark years of 1940 to 1942 and to unite the nation throughout WORLD WAR II (see BATTLE OF BRITAIN). Establishing close ties with U.S. president Franklin D. ROOSEVELT, he secured badly-needed LEND-LEASE aid and urged U.S. entry into the war. He also met several times with Joseph STALIN and supported the USSR after the German invasion in 1941. Attending a series of conferences in CASABLANCA, QUEBEC, Cairo, Teheran, YALTA and POTSDAM, he helped to plan wartime strategy and to unite the Allied countries.

Emerging from the war as a national hero, he was nonetheless replaced as prime minister in the 1945 elections, as a nation yearning for social and economic change voted in the LABOUR PARTY of Clement ATTLEE. Out of office for several years, he led the Conservative opposition, wrote the magisterial

Winston Churchill, 1941 (LIBRARY OF CONGRESS, PRINTS AND PHOTOGRAPHS DIVISION)

six-volume work *The Second World War* (1948–54) and continued to be politically active, warning a 1946 audience of the dangers of the new communist IRON CURTAIN. He again became prime minister in 1951 and was knighted in 1953. The author of dozens of works of history, political analysis, biography and autobiography, Churchill was awarded the 1953 NOBEL PRIZE in literature. In ill health, he reluctantly resigned from the prime minister's office in 1955. After his retirement he published the monumental *A History of the English-Speaking Peoples* (4 volumes, 1956–58). His death marked the end of an era in the history of the UNITED KINGDOM and the Western world.

CIA See CENTRAL INTELLIGENCE AGENCY.

CIAM (International Congress of Modern Architects) Organization founded in 1928 at Château de la Sarraz by a group of first-generation modernists to advance the cause of MODERNISM within the architectural profession. Twenty-four leading architects, including LE CORBUSIER and Walter GROPIUS, were CIAM's founders, while Swiss historian Sigfried GIEDION acted as a spokesman for the organization in building up the now widely accepted history of the modern movement. From time to time organizational conferences served to maintain some degree of unity among the members from different countries despite many debates and conflicts. Urban planning was a subject of particular interest, but one that produced theoretical differences that were impossible to resolve. The organization dissolved after the 1956 meeting in Dubrovnik, Yugoslavia. Attempts by a group designated Team X to take over and carry on the work of CIAM have had only limited success.

Ciano, Count Galeazzo (*1903–1944*) Italian political leader. A Fascist diplomat, he married the daughter of Benito MUSSOLINI in 1930. Foreign minister from 1936 to 1943, he negotiated the AXIS pact with Germany in 1936. He was appointed ambassador to the VATICAN in 1940. Dissatisfied with the progress of WORLD WAR II, he voted for Il Duce's dismissal in 1943. Blamed by HITLER for Mussolini's downfall, Ciano was arrested by the Germans, tried for treason by Italian Fascists and executed. (See also FASCISM; ITALY.)

Ciardi, John Anthony (*1916–1986*) American writer. A poet, critic and essayist, Ciardi was the author of some 40 books, including many volumes of children's verse and an internationally acclaimed translation of Dante's *Divine Comedy* (1954). He was poetry editor of the *Saturday Review* magazine from 1956 to 1972 and from 1980 until his death produced a weekly feature on word origins for NATIONAL PUBLIC RADIO.

Cines Important early Italian motion picture studio that helped vault Italy's films to world prominence in the years before WORLD WAR I. An outgrowth of Italy's very first studio, the Alberini-Santoni Studio in Rome, it produced numerous short comedies and action pictures before leading the way toward the feature-length format with the landmark *Quo Vadis* (1913). This historical epic set the standard not only for subsequent Italian epics, such as *Cabiria* (1914), but for the feature-length aspirations of American director D. W. GRIFFITH. During a time of recession in the European film industry after 1907, Cines assumed leadership in the Congres des Dupes, a collective of the principal manufacturers and producers of Europe. Although Cines ceased operation in 1921, the name was resurrected in 1929 and again in 1949. Today it designates a studiocombine under part ownership of the state.

CIO See AMERICAN FEDERATION OF LABOR AND CONGRESS OF INDUSTRIAL ORGANIZATIONS.

Cisco Systems INTERNET network company known for its repeated enhancement of Internet protocol (IP), the basic language required for computers and servers to communicate with each other over the Internet as well as within private networks. Begun in 1984 by several Stanford University computer scientists, Cisco branched out into the production of hardware and software to enable voice and video transmissions, create wireless Internet and computer technology, permit storage networking, allow clients to route and change servers if they encounter communication and interface problems, and to enhance Internet security both for those hosting a Web site server and for those accessing and transmitting information over the Internet. When the Internet became a global rather than simply an American phenomenon, Cisco enhanced its presence throughout the world with offices in Europe, Asia and Latin America. By 2003 it had a workforce of more than 34,000 people.

Citation (*1945–1970*) Thoroughbred racehorse. Two-year-old of the year in 1947, this versatile Calumet Farms bay colt could win at any length and under any conditions. The 1948 Triple Crown winner, he went on that year to win 19 of 20 starts, including the Jockey Club Gold Cup. He scored a rare walkover in the Pimlico Special, as no other stable sent a horse to challenge him. Injuries forced him to skip his campaign as a four-year-old, and he ran unevenly the following year, some saying he was still unsound. His owner, Warren Wright, obsessed with making Citation the first million-dollar winner, continued to race him at the age of six. He achieved that mark as he won the Hollywood Gold Cup and was immediately retired to stud. His career saw him start 45 times, winning 32 and finishing out of the money only once.

Citizen Kane Motion picture directed in 1940 by Orson WELLES; regarded by many critics and viewers as the greatest film ever made. "Everything that matters in cinema since 1941," said François TRUFFAUT, "has been influenced by *Citizen Kane*." Fresh from his triumphs on radio in the late 1930s, Welles and his Mercury Theater staff—including composer Bernard HERRMANN, producer John HOUSEMAN and 15 actors (Agnes Moorehead, Joseph Cotten, Everett Sloane)—came to the RKO studios. There Welles forged an alliance with noted cinematographer Gregg Toland, hammered out a screenplay with Herman MANKIEWICZ and for $686,033 created a masterpiece. It was filmed at RKO between July 30 and October 23, 1940.

The story concerns the efforts of a newsreel reporter named Thompson (William Allan) to ferret out the private life of dead newspaper tycoon Charles Foster Kane, and the narrative consists of this "framing" story and a series of interviews with figures in Kane's life, an interplay between gothic melodrama and tabloid journalism. As the stories intertwine and sometimes contradict each other, the reporter feels that he has failed to penetrate to the truth behind Kane—although the audience may have arrived at its own conclusions. The story's similarity to the saga of newspaper tycoon William Randolph HEARST and Hearst's relationship with his mistress Marion Davies was enough to bring pressure against the film's distribution and exhibition. The scheduled premiere at Radio City in New York was canceled, and subsequent showings that year were limited to RKO-owned theaters. Nominated for nine ACADEMY AWARDS, *Kane* received only one, for best screenplay.

Proper "authorship" of *Citizen Kane* is still disputed, with the honors divided among Mankiewicz, cameraman Toland and director Welles. Critic Pauline Kael suggests that Mankiewicz was slyly making Welles the real target of the screenplay. Even the dying Kane's reference to the mysterious "Rosebud" has been open to interpretations different from the one offered at the end of the picture.

Citroën French automobile manufacturer noted for its innovative technology and design. The firm was founded before World War I as an arms manufacturer, but after the war it turned to production of cars, introducing the Type A in 1919, the first popular mass-produced automobile in Europe, designed by Jules Saloman. In 1934 Citroën introduced the first front-wheel-drive car, the Traction Avant model 7A, ahead of its competition in both engineering and design by many years. Pierre BOULANGER is credited with the design of the 2CV of 1939, a highly economical and practical four-seat car. This design, with various improvements, remained in production until 1990 and enjoyed enormous popularity in Europe where it was the only major competition for the popular VOLKSWAGEN. In 1957 the extraordinary DS19 appeared, combining front wheel drive with a hydropneumatic suspension that eliminated springs and shock absorbers while offering superior comfort and handling characteristics. More recent models retained many innova-

tive features but never attained the remarkable advanced status of earlier Citroen products.

Civilian Conservation Corps (CCC) U.S. government program, part of President Franklin D. ROOSEVELT'S NEW DEAL during the GREAT DEPRESSION of the 1930s. The CCC was designed to provide work for unemployed young men. CCC work crews, organized along military lines, were assigned to conservation projects throughout the country. They planted trees and did other work to prevent erosion and protect the environment.

Civil Rights Act of 1964 Landmark legislation granting equal public accommodations to all, regardless of race, religion or national origin. For almost 90 years after the Civil War the southern U.S. was a largely segregated society. Private businesses often excluded African Americans, and the states ran two, so-called separate but equal school systems. Although the 1954 Supreme Court case BROWN V. BOARD OF EDUCATION ruled segregated school systems illegal, the decision did not affect private businesses. The CIVIL RIGHTS MOVEMENT of

the 1960s, characterized by both peaceful protest and armed conflict and the use of troops, culminated in federal legislation outlawing both public and private discrimination. The Civil Rights Acts of 1964 and 1968 and the VOTING RIGHTS ACT OF 1965 made illegal any discrimination in providing public accommodations, admission to schools, employment or voting.

Civil Rights movement Name given to an American movement that struggled for the civil rights of black citizens in the 1950s and 1960s. It was led by such groups as the CONGRESS OF RACIAL EQUALITY (CORE), NATIONAL ASSOCIATION FOR THE ADVANCEMENT OF COLORED PEOPLE (NAACP), URBAN LEAGUE, Student Nonviolent Coordinating Committee and the SOUTHERN CHRISTIAN LEADERSHIP CONFERENCE, headed by the movement's most charismatic leader, Dr. Martin Luther KING, Jr. Highlights of judicial and legislative attempts to provide for civil rights in the 1950s include the 1954 Supreme Court decision in BROWN V. BOARD OF EDUCATION of Topeka, which prohibited SEGREGATION in public education, and the Civil Rights Acts of

Civil rights protest (LIBRARY OF CONGRESS, PRINTS AND PHOTOGRAPHS DIVISION)

1957 and 1960, which provided a federal agency to deal with the denial of equal rights. When these measures provoked riots over desegregation in LITTLE ROCK, Arkansas, in 1957 and a general lack of compliance in the South, civil rights forces mobilized. The many demonstrations by blacks and their supporters included sit-ins at segregated lunch counters, Freedom Rides on interstate buses and other forms of direct action. These culminated in the massive MARCH ON WASHINGTON of August 1963 and the dramatic march from SELMA to MONTGOMERY, Alabama, in 1965, both led by King. The demonstrations helped to prod Congress into passing the CIVIL RIGHTS ACT OF 1964 and 1968 and the VOTING RIGHTS ACT OF 1965. Together they prohibited discrimination in employment, public accommodations, housing, education and voting. Toward the end of the 1960s the movement became increasingly fractured, with some factions supporting a more militant and sometimes violent approach. While the movement was weakened, it had created revolutionary legislation and contributed to enormous gains by some U.S. black Americans. However, by the end of the 20th century, African Americans remained among the nation's poorest citizens and racial prejudice was still a fact of life in the U.S.

Clair, René **(Rene-Lucien Chomette)** *(1898–1981)* French screen-writer and film director who was one of the acknowledged masters of the French cinema in the first half of the 20th century. Born in Paris, he began acting in movies after suffering a back injury during service in WORLD WAR I. Dissatisfied with contemporary cinema, he experimented with techniques of DADAISM and SURREALISM in his first two films, *Paris qui dort* (1923) and *Entracte* (1924). Their freewheeling camera effects, absurd juxtapositions of images and bizarre humor would all be incorporated into his later mature work. Another important influence, evident particularly in his first masterpiece, *Un Chapeau de paille d'italie* (*The Italian Straw Hat*) in 1928, were the slapstick chases of the American comedy master Mack SENNETT. Clair described these chases as "a world of light in which the law of gravity seems to be replaced by the joy of movement." In 1929–31 he secured his world fame and

reputation with three successful pioneering efforts in the creative use of synchronized sound—*Under the Roofs of Paris, Le Million* (1931) and *À Nous la liberté* (1931). For the next 15 years he made films in England and in HOLLYWOOD. Back in France after World War II, he made one of his last authentic masterpieces, the fantasy *Les Belles de nuit* (*The Beauties of the Night*) in 1952. Clair's films are striking blends of comic slapstick and subtle beauty and romance.

Clancy, Tom *(1923–1990)* Irish folk singer and actor. Although Tom Clancy and his brother Liam began their careers as actors, they achieved fame through the **Clancy Brothers** folk group, which they formed with **Tommy Makem.** They started singing and recording traditional Irish folk songs in America in the late 1950s and had a major influence on the folk music revival of the 1960s. Clancy went on to act in several American television shows.

Clancy, Tom *(1947–)* American author. Clancy began his writing career with *The Hunt for Red October* (1984), a novel that described the attempt of the commander of a secret Soviet submarine, the *Red October,* to defect to the U.S. with his vessel. The principal character is Jack Ryan, a CIA analyst who eventually helps the *Red October's* officers reach asylum in America; the novel eventually became a *New York Times* best seller and was made into a movie by Paramount Pictures. Since then Clancy has written 12 other fictional works, most of them covering the rise of Jack Ryan from CIA agent to president of the U.S. via international crises ranging from COLD WAR conflicts and nuclear terrorist attacks to the war on drugs and the changing international balance of power involving China, Russia, Japan and the Islamic world. In addition to *Red October,* three other Clancy books have been made into movies: *Patriot Games* (1988), *Clear and Present Danger* (1989) and *The Sum of All Fears* (1991). Clancy also helped create the general concepts behind the fictional book series Op Center and Net Force, although he wrote none of the books in either series; *Net Force* became a TV miniseries in 1998.

In the mid-1990s Clancy began branching into nonfiction by describ-

ing the daily experiences of soldiers, sailors and airmen in the branches of the U.S. Armed Forces in such books as *Submarine* (1993), *Armored Cav* (1994), *Fighter Wing* (1995), *Marine* (1996), *Airborne* (1997) and *Carrier* (1999). In addition to writing and serving as a creative consultant in the book publishing, movie and video game industries—one of his books, *Rainbow Six* (1998), became the subject of a video game, and Clancy served as a creative consultant for another game called *Ghost Recon*—Clancy has served as a consultant to several government agencies, including the CIA and the National Space Council.

Clapton, Eric *(1945–)* British guitarist. After working with various London bands in the early 1960s, Clapton joined bassist Jack Bruce and drummer Ginger Baker to form in 1966 the band Cream, which combined blues and rock music with a psychedelic tone popular in the late 1960s. Releasing four albums, including the platinum *Wheel of Fire* and *Goodbye* (which reached number two on the U.S. charts), the band eventually dissolved in 1968 as a result of growing conflicts between Clapton and Bruce. Despite a burgeoning solo career Clapton formed a new group in 1970, Derek and the Dominos, which toured Britain that year and recorded a double album entitled *Layla and Other Love Songs.* In the late 1970s Clapton slipped into a 15-year slump, in part due to his tumultuous 11-year marriage (1977–88) to and then divorce from Patti Harrison, former wife of George Harrison, and to troubles with heroin and alcohol. In 1991 the accidental death of his five-year-old son, Connor, inspired him to write and perform "Tears in Heaven" for the movie *Rush.* The song reignited Clapton's singing career, leading to a 1992 appearance on the acoustic program *MTV Unplugged* and to an album from that performance, *Eric Clapton Unplugged. Unplugged* sold more than 7 million copies in the U.S. and won Clapton six Grammys in 1993. He later won four Grammy for such albums, as the techno–hip-hop compact disc *Retail Therapy* (1997) and the blues-guitar collaborative work *Riding with the King* (2000), produced jointly with B. B. KING. In 2001, during the promotional tour of his last album, *Reptile* (2001), Clapton announced he would no longer perform tours but would continue to write and record music.

Clark, Dick (Richard Augustus Clark) (1929–)

American TV host and entrepreneur. The ageless Clark, America's "oldest teenager," began his career in radio with a pop music show called *Bandstand*. The show became a Philadelphia hit after its move to television and became *American Bandstand* when national network ABC began carrying it. The program became a showcase for new musical talent, particularly of the teen idol variety, including Frankie Avalon, Fabian and Bobby Rydell. The format included dance regulars and took on the air of a soap opera as viewers watched real-life teenage romances blossom and fade in a matter of weeks. Clark ran into difficulty in payola investigations, losing $8 million but managing to emerge with his squeaky-clean image intact. *Bandstand* survived in a variety of forms into the 1980s and was a forerunner of such shows as *Soul Train* and *Hullaballoo*. Clark has diversified into game shows and is a millionaire many times over.

Clark, James Beauchamp "Champ" (1850–1921)

U.S. politician. Settled in Missouri in 1876, he began a career as a newspaper editor, city and county prosecuting attorney, state legislator and member of the U.S. House of Representatives (1893–95, 1897–1921). His philosophy was progressive. As Democratic leader in the House, Clark led a successful fight against the dictatorial control of speaker Joseph G. CANNON. He served as Speaker of the House from 1911 to 1919. Clark was a candidate for the Democratic presidential nomination in 1912.

Clark, Joe (1939–)

Prime minister of Canada (1979–80) and secretary of state for external affairs. Clark, from the province of Alberta in western Canada, was first elected to the Canadian Parliament in 1972. He was elected leader of the opposition PROGRESSIVE CONSERVATIVE PARTY in 1976. His party unseated the government of Liberal prime minister Pierre Elliott TRUDEAU in 1979, only to lose control of the government to Trudeau and the Liberals the following year. He was subsequently replaced as Progressive Conservative Party leader by Brian MULRONEY (1984) but reentered the government as foreign minister in the Mulroney administration, after the Progressive Conservatives' election victory in 1984. Clark briefly retired from politics in 1993 but returned in 1998 for a five-year term as head of the Progressive Conservative Party.

Clark, Kenneth Mackenzie (Baron Clark of Saltwood) (1903–1983)

British art historian and author. Born in London to a wealthy Scottish family, Clark was educated at Winchester and at Trinity College, Oxford. He later worked with the art historian and philosopher Bernard BERENSON. Clark published his first book, *The Gothic Revival* (1928), at age 26. By the time he was 30 he was appointed director of London's National Gallery. He later served as chairman of ARTS COUNCIL OF GREAT BRITAIN (1953–60). Clark's numerous works on the arts include *Leonardo Da Vinci: An Account of His Development as an Artist* (1939), the notable *The Nude: A Study of Ideal Art* (1953), *Introduction to Rembrandt* (1978), and *The Art of Humanism* (1983). To nonacademics, he is perhaps best known for creating the BBC television series *Civilization,* which was published as a book, *Civilization: A Personal View,* in 1969. Clark wrote two volumes of autobiography, *Another Part of the Wood: A Self Portrait* (1974) and *The Other Half: A Self Portrait* (1977).

Clark, Mamie and Kenneth B.

American psychologists. Mamie (1917–83) and Kenneth (1914–2005) did important research on the effects of school desegregation on black children. Their joint writings were used extensively in the U.S. Supreme Court's landmark decision in BROWN V. BOARD OF EDUCATION (1954). Mamie Clark founded the Northside Child Development Center in New York in 1946, remaining as director until 1980. Kenneth Clark exerted a powerful influence on a succession of mayors of New York City and governors of New York State, who often consulted him on racial issues such as school housing and housing discrimination. His important books include *Dark Ghetto* (1965), *A Relevant War Against Poverty* (1969) and *Pathos and Power* (1974).

Clark, Mark Wayne (1896–1984)

A graduate of the U.S. Military Academy at West Point (1917), Clark commanded an infantry battalion in FRANCE during WORLD WAR I. At age 46 he became the youngest three-star general in the U.S. Army and was General Dwight D. EISENHOWER's deputy in the World War II European theater of operations (see WORLD WAR II IN EUROPE). He helped plan the Allied invasion of North Africa (1942). Promoted to full (four-star) general, he led the U.S. Fifth Army throughout the Italian campaign and the capture of Rome in 1944. After the war he served as the Allied high commander in occupied Austria. During the KOREAN WAR Clark succeeded General Matthew B. RIDGWAY as supreme commander of the UNITED NATIONS forces in KOREA (1952). He signed the Korean armistice in 1953. After retiring from the army, he was president of the Citadel military college in Charleston, South Carolina (1954–65).

Clark, (William) Ramsey (1927–)

American lawyer and political figure. A graduate of the University of Texas and the University of Chicago Law School, Clark was the son of Supreme Court justice Tom CLARK. After graduating from law school, the younger Clark practiced law in Dallas before becoming an assistant attorney general in the U.S. Justice Department. He became deputy attorney general in 1965 and was appointed U.S. attorney general in 1967, serving in that post until 1969. A prominent liberal, Clark, was an active opponent of the VIETNAM WAR when that stance was considered radical. He was also involved in controversial left-wing causes and was a leading U.S. opponent of the U.S. bombing of Iraq in 1991. He is a recipient of the Gandhi Peace Award. After government service he returned to law practice in New York and also taught at Brooklyn Law School. He is the author of *Crime in America.* Clark is a member of the defense team in the war criminal trial of the former Iraqi president Saddam Hussein.

Clark, Septima Poinsette (1898–1987)

American civil rights activist. The daughter of a slave, she became a teacher and a pioneer in the CIVIL RIGHTS MOVEMENT. As early as 1918 she campaigned for the hiring of black teachers in South Carolina. In the

1950s she organized citizenship schools through the Deep South to train blacks to pass voter literacy tests. The schools were later incorporated into Martin Luther KING, Jr.'s SOUTHERN CHRISTIAN LEADERSHIP CONFERENCE. She accompanied King to Norway in 1964 when he was awarded the NOBEL PRIZE for peace.

Clark, Tom Campbell (1899–1977) Associate justice of the U.S. Supreme Court (1949–67). A native of Dallas, Clark was a graduate of the University of Texas and its law school. After law school he joined his politically influential father in law practice. He held a number of state and federal posts. Clark actively championed Harry S TRUMAN's vice presidential ambitions, and when Truman became president he appointed Clark as attorney general. As attorney general, Clark prosecuted a number of antitrust cases but is best-remembered for his vigorous pursuit of alleged communists and other so-called subversives during the early postwar era. In 1949 Truman appointed Clark to the Supreme Court, where he was generally a centrist. He resigned in 1967 when his son, Ramsey CLARK, became attorney general in Lyndon B. JOHNSON's administration. Clark remained active in public affairs until his death in 1977.

Clark, Wesley (1945–) American army officer, supreme commander of the NORTH ATLANTIC TREATY ORGANIZATION (NATO; 1997–2000). A resident of Little Rock, Arkansas, in his youth Clark attended West Point (1963–67), graduating at the top of his class. Clark continued his education at Oxford University, where as a Rhodes Scholar he earned a master's degree in politics, philosophy and economics. Throughout his service in the U.S. Army, which included military experience in the Vietnam War, Clark repeatedly distinguished himself, winning citations such as the Purple Heart. In 1995 Clark was responsible for handling military aspects of the Dayton negotiations that successfully ended the 1992–95 war in Bosnia. Once the DAYTON ACCORDS had been signed, Clark was assigned to be commander in chief of the U.S. Southern Command, a position he held for two years. In July 1997 President Bill CLINTON ap-

pointed Clark supreme allied commander in Europe, making him the military head of NATO and commander of all U.S. forces on the European continent. Clark entered the international spotlight when he supervised the NATO bombing campaign against Serbia during the 1999 Kosovo War. Though NATO eventually succeeded in forcing an end to the Serbian killing of Kosovar Albanians, the air campaign was not without mishaps (such as the mistaken bombing of the Chinese embassy in Belgrade). In July 1999, as a result of differences of opinion about how to prosecute the war in Kosovo, Clark agreed to retire from his position in April of the following year, three months ahead of schedule. He later became a frequent commentator on television news programs during the U.S.'s military campaigns in Afghanistan and Iraq and conducted a campaign for the Democratic nomination for president in 2004, which he lost to John Kerry.

Clarke, Arthur C. (1917–) British author. A graduate of King's College, London, with honors in physics and mathematics, Clarke is a past chairman of the British Interplanetary Society and a member of the Academy of Astronautics and the Royal Astronomical Society. The author of over 50 books, his work has been translated in more than 30 languages, and he has been the recipient of prizes in both the science and science fiction fields. One of the most influential of modern science fiction writers and author of the seminal *Childhood's End* (1953), Clarke is best known to the general public for his science fiction writing, including the popular novel and later hit motion picture *2001, A Space Odyssey*. His now-famous 1945 technical paper describing geostationary orbits helped form the basis of today's communications satellite system. Clarke joined newscaster Walter CRONKITE as part of the televised coverage of many of the U.S. APOLLO missions, sharing his insights with television viewers of the historic Moon flights. In 1989 Clarke was named a Commander of the British Empire (CBE) by Queen Elizabeth II.

Clarke, Austin (1896–1974) Irish poet, playwright and prose writer. Clarke was educated at Belvedere Col-

lege and University College, Dublin. His early work, influenced by YEATS and the other IRISH LITERARY REVIVAL poets, was largely drawn from Irish folklore and legends. Later he focused on the stultifying influence of religious parochialism in IRELAND. His prose romances and many of his verse plays and poems are set in the Celtic-Romanesque period from the fifth to the end of the 12th centuries. His later works, after 1955, are more personal and contemporary, focusing on the realities of modern Ireland. In his poems Clarke skillfully and subtly adapted Celtic rhythms and speech patterns to the English line. He also worked as a book reviewer in London from 1923 to 1937 and was a founding member (1932) and president (1952–54) of the Irish Academy of Letters.

Clarke, Sir Cyril Astley (1907–2000) British physician. Clarke was educated at the University of Cambridge and Guy's Hospital, London, where he qualified in 1932. He remained at Guy's until 1936 when he engaged in life insurance work before spending the war years in the Royal Navy. Clarke worked as a consultant physician in Liverpool from 1946 until 1958, when he joined the staff of the university. There he later served as professor of medicine from 1965 to 1972 and also, from 1963 to 1972, as director of the Nuffield unit of medical genetics. Clarke was also a skilled amateur lepidopterist. In 1952 he became interested in the genetics of the wing colors of swallowtail butterflies and began a collaboration with Philip Sheppard, a professional geneticist who later became a colleague at Liverpool University. In particular, they worked on the inheritance of mimicry in the wing patterns of certain swallowtails. They noted that the gene controlling the wing pattern is actually a group of closely linked genes behaving as a single unit—a supergene. They also found that even though the males also carry such supergenes, the patterns show only in the females. Clarke was struck by certain striking parallels between the inheritance of swallowtail wing patterns and human blood types, which aroused his interest in Rhesus babies. This condition arises when an Rh-negative mother (a woman whose blood lacks the Rh factor or antigen) and an Rh-positive father produce an Rh-positive child. Occasionally the fetus's blood leaks from the placenta into the mother's blood and stimulates the production of Rh antibodies. This will cause her body to destroy the red cells of any subsequent Rh-positive babies she may carry. Clarke and Sheppard puzzled over how to prevent the mother from producing the destructive Rh antibodies. The answer eventually came from Clarke's wife, who in an inspired moment told him to inject the Rh-negative mothers with Rh antibodies. As this is what destroys the blood of the fetus in the first place, the answer initially sounds absurd. However, the Rh antibodies should destroy incompatible Rh-positive cells before the woman's own antibody machinery can act, that is, before the woman can become sensitized to Rh-positive blood. In 1964 Clarke and his colleagues were able to announce a major breakthrough in preventive medicine. Since then thousands of women have received injections of Rh antibodies with only a few failures.

Clarke, Edith (*1883–1959*) U.S. electrical engineer. A graduate of Vassar and MIT (M.S., 1919), Clarke worked for American Telephone & Telegraph in New York City (1912–18), taught at Constantinople Woman's College in Turkey (1921) and was employed as an engineer by General Electric (1922–45). At GE she pioneered systems analysis for large power networks. She also taught at the University of Texas, Austin (1947–56). Her *Circuit Analysis of A-C Power Systems* (2 vols., 1943–50) is a standard. She was the first woman elected to membership in the American Institute of Electrical Engineers (1948).

Clarke, Kenny "Klook" (*1914–1985*) American JAZZ drummer. In the 1940s Clarke made a major contribution to the development of the complex rhythmic patterns of what came to be known as BEBOP. During this time he performed with such jazz greats as Charlie PARKER and Dizzy GILLESPIE. In 1952 he became a founding member of the Modern Jazz Quartet, in which he played until 1955. Thereafter he settled in France and pursued his career in Europe.

Claude, Albert (*1898–1983*) Belgian-American cell biologist. Claude was educated at the University of Liège where he obtained his doctorate in 1928. In 1929 he joined the staff of the Rockefeller Institute in New York and in 1941 became a U.S. citizen. Claude returned to Belgium in 1948 to serve as director of the Jules Bordet Research Institute, a post he retained until his retirement in 1972. For 20 years (beginning in the 1930s), using electron microscopes as well as improved centrifuges, Claude began to chart the constitution of the cell protoplasm. For his work in opening up the study of cell structures, Claude shared the 1974 NOBEL PRIZE in physiology or medicine with George PALADE and Christian de Duve.

Claude, Georges (*1870–1960*) French chemist. Claude was educated at the École de Physique et Chimie, after which he worked as an engineer in various industries. He made a number of important contributions to technology, including a method of liquefying air (1902), which he used for the large-scale production of nitrogen and oxygen. In 1910 he introduced neon lighting, using neon gas at low pressure excited by an electric discharge to emit a bright red light. The latter part of his life was, however, less successful. From 1926 onward he worked on new sources of energy. In particular, he tried to show how energy could be extracted from the temperature difference between the surface and the bottom of the sea. His argument was sound but he never overcame the formidable engineering difficulties. Although 75 when WORLD WAR II ended, Claude was imprisoned as a VICHY sympathizer.

Claudel, Paul-Louis-Charles-Marie (*1888–1955*) French poet and dramatist. Claudel underwent a spiritual epiphany that led to his conversion to Roman Catholicism, which he eloquently championed in his later writing. A career diplomat, Claudel lived in the U.S., South America and the Orient. His poetic dramas, such as *L'Annonce faite à Marie* (*The Tidings of Mary,* 1912) and *Le Soulier de satin* (*The Satin Slipper,* 1925) so effectively proselytized for the Roman Catholic Church that Claudel was publicly honored by Pope PIUS XII in 1950. His plays were collected into *Oeuvres complètes* (13 volumes, 1950–59). His poetry, which includes *Cinq grandes odes* (1910) and *La Cantate à troix voix* (1913), evidences the influence of the symbolist poets. Claudel also wrote essays on metaphysics, poetry and religion, and later in life concentrated on studying and interpreting the Bible, writing commentary endorsing its symbolic interpretation.

Clay, Lucius DuBignon (*1897–1978*) American army officer and diplomat who played a prominent role in the reconstruction of Germany after WORLD WAR II and in two major crises of the COLD WAR. Clay came from a distinguished southern family: His father was a U.S. senator, and he was descended from the 19th-century American statesman Henry Clay. Graduating from West Point in 1918, Clay served in the Army Engineering Corps until 1942. Known for his organizational ability and leadership qualities, for much of World War II he was head of the army's procurement program (1942–44). He saw action in France briefly after the Invasion of NORMANDY (1944). At the end of the war he was appointed commander of U.S. forces in Europe and military governor of Germany. In these roles he was directly involved in the denazification of Germany, in German reconstruction and in implementing the MARSHALL PLAN. In response to the Soviet blockade of West Berlin (1948–49), he ordered and supervised the successful massive airlift of supplies (see BERLIN AIRLIFT).

After retiring from the army he entered business as chairman of the Continental Can Co. He campaigned for Dwight D. EISENHOWER in the presidential election of 1952. When Communist authorities erected the BERLIN WALL (1961), Clay returned to Berlin as the personal representative of President John F. KENNEDY, with the rank of ambassador (1961–62). He was later a senior partner of the investment banking firm Lehman Brothers (1963–73) and served on the boards of numerous other corporations.

Cleaver, (Leroy) Eldridge (*1935–1998*) American black activist leader. Born in Wabbaseka, Arkansas, Cleaver was raised in Los Angeles's Watts section. Involved in various crimes, including rape, he was sentenced to a number of reformatories and jails. While in Folsom Prison, he became a

Black Panther leader and activist Eldridge Cleaver, 1968 (LIBRARY OF CONGRESS, PRINTS AND PHOTOGRAPHS DIVISION)

Black Muslim and began writing. On his release in 1966, he joined the BLACK PANTHERS. *Soul on Ice* (1968), a collection of his powerful and immensely personal prison writings, became one of the best-known radical works on the black experience in the U.S. In 1968 Cleaver's parole was revoked, and he fled to Algeria, remaining in exile there until 1975. Returning to the U.S., he was converted to Christianity and CONSERVATISM, subjects he discussed in lectures and the book *Soul on Fire* (1978).

Clemence, Gerald Maurice *(1908–1974)* American astronomer. Clemence studied mathematics at Brown University. After graduating, in 1930 he joined the staff of the U.S. Naval Observatory where he remained until 1963, serving as head astronomer and director of the *Nautical Almanac* from 1945 to 1958 and science director of the observatory from 1958. In 1963 he was appointed senior research associate and lecturer at Yale, becoming professor of astronomy in 1966, a post he held until his death. Clemence's work was primarily concerned with the orbital motions of the Earth, Moon, and planets. In 1951, in collaboration with Dirk BROUWER and W. J. Eckert, Clemence published the basic paper *Coordinates of the Five Outer Planets*

1653–2060. This was a considerable advance on the tables for the outer planets calculated by Simon Newcomb and George W. Hill 50 years earlier. Clemence and his colleagues calculated the precise positions of the outer planets at 40-day intervals over a period of 400 years. It was the first time that the influence of the planets on one another was calculated at each step; the prevailing custom was to assume that the paths of all except one were known in advance. Such an ambitious scheme was made possible only by the emergence of high-speed computers, one of which was made available to them by IBM from 1948. For each step some 800 multiplications and several hundred other arithmetical operations were required. Clemence said they would have taken a human computer 80 years if he could have completed the work without committing any errors en route. Clemence also conceived the idea that Brouwer named **Ephemeris Time,** by which time could be determined very accurately from the orbital positions of the Moon and the Earth. Ephemeris Time came into use in 1958, although it has been superseded for most purposes by the more accurate atomic time scale.

Clemenceau, Georges *(1841–1929)* French statesman, an ardent republican and two-time premier (1906–09, 1917–20), nicknamed "the Tiger." Trained as a doctor, he was a journalist and teacher. He began his stormy political career as mayor of Montmartre (1870), after the fall of Napoleon III. Elected as a Radical member of the chamber of deputies in 1876, he served until 1893 when he was unjustly implicated in the Panama Canal scandal. Clemenceau devoted the next nine years to journalism, returning to the political arena when he passionately defended Alfred Dreyfus. He became a senator in 1902 and served as premier for the first time from 1906 to 1909. During that period he strengthened the alliance with Great Britain and approved the ANGLO-RUSSIAN ENTENTE of 1907 that led to the TRIPLE ENTENTE. At home he battled labor unrest; his harsh treatment of strikers caused a rift with the Radicals and his fall from office. Resuming his journalistic activities, Clemenceau lashed out at Germany and called for French military strength.

In November 1917 he again became premier, forming a coalition government. An indomitable leader, he almost single-handedly rallied national morale, helping his nation weather the German onslaughts of 1918 and ultimately leading it to victory. As leader of the French delegation at the PARIS PEACE CONFERENCE of 1919, he came into conflict with the idealistic American president Woodrow WILSON. He fought for buffer states on the Rhine and demanded German reparations, ultimately feeling that the Treaty of VERSAILLES did not adequately protect France. Although his attitude was the harshest of any of the Allies, many in his country accused him of leniency, and he was defeated in the elections of 1920. In retirement the fallen "Tiger" continued to warn of future German threats to Europe.

Clemens, Roger *(1962–)* American baseball player. Born in Dayton, Ohio, Clemens attended college at the University of Texas, where he played baseball for the Texas Longhorns, amassed a 28-7 record in two years of collegiate pitching and pitched the Longhorns to victory in the championship game of the 1983 College World Series. Following his junior season he left college and signed as a starting pitcher with the Boston Red Sox of the American League (AL). Despite poor performances in 1984 and 1985, the Sox kept Clemens in their starting rotation. In the 1986 season he had a 24-4 record and stuck out 20 batters in one game; because of his dominance as a pitcher and his role in helping the Sox make it to the World Series, Clemens won both the AL Cy Young Award, and the AL Most Valuable Player award for 1986. He repeated as the Cy Young winner the following season with a 20-9 record, followed later by his third award in 1991 for recording a league-leading 2.62 earned run average (ERA). In 1997 Clemens became a free agent and left Boston for the Toronto Blue Jays. In his first year with the Blue Jays he led all AL pitchers in three categories—wins (21), strikeouts (292) and ERA (2.05)—the so-called triple crown, and won his fourth Cy Young Award. The next year Clemens won a second consecutive triple crown with 20 games won, 271 strikeouts thrown

Pitcher Roger Clemens playing for the Boston Red Sox (PHOTOFEST)

and an ERA of 2.65, for which he won his fifth Cy Young Award.

In 1999 the Blue Jays traded Clemens to the New York Yankees. With the Yankees Clemens won his only two World Series titles, in 1999 and 2000. Clemens's performance in the 2000 World Series against the New York Mets of the National League (NL) caused problems for the Yankee organization when he threw a broken bat at Mets catcher Mike Piazza. In 2001, despite failing to win a third consecutive World Series with the Yankees Clemens won his sixth AL Cy Young Award with a record of 20-3, an ERA of 3.51 and 213 strikeouts. On June 13, 2003, Clemens scored his 300th major league victory in a game against the St. Louis Cardinals of the NL. Clemens announced that the 2003 baseball season would be his last in professional baseball. However, after playing with the Yankees in the 2003 World Series, he pushed back his retirement by signing a $5 million one-year contract with the Houston Astros, his hometown team.

Clemente, Roberto *(1934–1972)* Puerto Rican–American baseball player.

One of the greatest outfielders ever to play the game, Clemente won 12 Gold Gloves during his Pittsburgh Pirate career. From 1960 through 1968 his batting average never fell below .300, and he was named to 12 All-Star teams during the late 1960s and early 1970s. During that time he also led the National League in batting four times. In 1971, he was named World Series MVP, as his .414 batting average and brilliant fielding led Pittsburgh to the championship. He hit his 3,000th base hit in 1972. Clemente died later that year in the crash of a plane bringing relief supplies to Nicaraguan earthquake victims. He was named to the Hall of Fame in 1973, when the five-year waiting period was waived in his honor.

Cliburn, Van (Harvey Lavan Cliburn, Jr.) *(1934–)* American pianist. One of the great piano virtuosos of his time, Cliburn was catapulted to international fame in 1958 when, at the height of the COLD WAR, he became the first American (and first non-Soviet) to win the prestigious Tchaikovsky Piano Competition in Moscow. Born in Shreveport, Louisiana, Cliburn gave his first public performance at the age

of four. Shortly thereafter the Cliburn family settled in Kilgore, Texas, where Cliburn studied with his mother, a concert pianist and piano teacher. He later attended the Juilliard School of Music in New York, where he studied with Rosina LHEVINNE and Olga SAMAROFF. He made his solo concert debut with the Houston Symphony Orchestra (1947) and first performed at CARNEGIE HALL in 1948 as a winner of the National Music Festival Award. Graduating from Juilliard in 1954, he won the Leventritt Competition in New York that same year. For the next few years he gave concerts throughout the U.S. When his career began to falter, Lhevinne and Cliburn's manager, Arthur JUDSON, decided to enter him in the 1958 Tchaikovsky Competition. Cliburn's victory has become legendary; he made world headlines and became an instant celebrity. Gala receptions, parades, concert tours, television appearances, a recording contract and a Grammy Award (1959) followed. In 1962 a piano competition, named in his honor, was organized in Fort Worth, Texas At the height of his powers, Cliburn was particularly known for his interpretation of Tchaikovsky's Piano Concerto No. 1 and RACHMANINOFF's Piano Concerto No. 3. In 1976 Cliburn retired from the concert stage and the recording studio. He began a "comeback" in 1989, although his repertoire was limited to the few works that had made his initial reputation. Cliburn was inducted into the American Classical Music Hall of Fame in 2001. Two years later he received the Presidential Medal of Freedom from President George W. Bush.

Clift, Montgomery Edward *(1920–1966)* American theater and film actor. Although Clift made only 17 films, he received four ACADEMY AWARD nominations in recognition of his intense and brilliant acting style. Clift began his career as an acclaimed stage actor in the 1940s, appearing in a number of Broadway productions, most notably *The Skin of Our Teeth* (1942) by Thornton WILDER and *You Touched Me* (1945) by Tennessee WILLIAMS. He made his Hollywood debut in *The Search* (1948) and followed up with a role in the classic western *Red River* (1948), in which he was directed by Howard HAWKS and starred alongside John WAYNE. Other notable films featuring Clift include *The Heiress* (1949), *A Place in the Sun* (1951), *From Here to Eternity* (1953), *The Young Lions* (1958), *Suddenly Last Summer* (1959), *The Misfits* (1961) and *Judgment at Nuremberg* (1961). Clift suffered a severe auto accident in 1957, which left him with lingering pain and led him to alcohol and drug abuse, which is thought to have contributed to his early death by a heart attack.

Clinton, Hillary Rodham (*1947– *)

First lady of the United States (1993–2001) and U.S. senator from New York (2001–). Born Hillary Rodham in Chicago, she graduated from Wellesley College in 1969 and enrolled at Yale University's law school, where she met her future husband, Bill CLINTON. In 1974 she served as a House legal counsel on a panel established by the U.S. House of Representatives to investigate whether the actions of President Richard NIXON were grounds for his impeachment. When the panel dissolved in 1974 she moved to Arkansas where she joined Bill Clinton as an instructor for the Arkansas Law School; the two married the following year and had a daughter, Chelsea, in 1980. In 1977 Hillary Clinton left the staff of the University of Arkansas to work as a lawyer for the Rose law firm, where she handled law cases relating to patent infringements.

In 1993 Clinton became first lady of the U.S. after her husband won election as president. Shortly after President Clinton's inauguration, she headed a presidential commission assigned to develop a national health insurance system. However, the House and Senate ultimately rejected the first lady's proposal. As first lady she again took up the cause of child advocacy and the role of society in the molding of children, which she discussed in her 1996 book *It Takes a Village*.

In 2000, a year after New York senator Daniel Patrick MOYNIHAN announced he would not seek reelection to his position, Clinton established her legal residency in New York State and announced she would run for the vacant seat. In November 2000 Clinton defeated U.S. congressman Rick Lazio (who had replaced New York City mayor Rudolph GIULIANI as her Republican opponent after Giuliani withdrew from the race for treatment

for colon cancer) and became a senator. She has continually denied rumors that she will use her position in the Senate as a springboard for a run at the White House but has not completely ruled out a run for the presidency in 2008.

Clinton, William Jefferson "Bill"

(*1946– *) American politician, governor of Arkansas (1979–81 and 1983–93) and president of the UNITED STATES (1993–2001). Born William Jefferson Blythe IV, after his birth father, who died in a car crash several months before Clinton's birth, the future president changed his last name when his mother remarried. After graduating from high school in 1964, Clinton entered Georgetown University, where he majored in international affairs, and served as an intern for Senator J. William FULBRIGHT, chairman of the Senate Foreign Relations Committee. Graduating from Georgetown with a B.A. in 1968, Clinton received a Rhodes Scholarship to study at Oxford University. After two years at Oxford he returned to the U.S. and enrolled in the Yale University Law School; it was at Yale that he met his future wife, Hillary Rodham CLINTON, a fellow law student. After graduating from Yale in 1973 Clinton served as an instructor at the University of Arkansas Law School. Two years later Clinton married Rodham, with whom he had one daughter, Chelsea, in 1980.

In 1974 Clinton ran as a Democrat against Republican John Hammerschmidt for a seat in the U.S. House of Representatives but lost in a closely contested election. However, his candidacy gave Clinton statewide exposure, which helped him to secure the Democratic nomination and win the election for attorney general of Arkansas two years later. As attorney general, Clinton became well known for attacking utility companies for their high rates and their environmentally unfriendly practices. In 1978, two years after becoming attorney general, Clinton successfully ran for governor when the sitting governor, David Pryor, left the position to run for a vacant U.S. Senate seat. During his two-year term as governor he continued to trumpet environmental issues and combat utility companies. In the 1980 gubernatorial elections Clinton was defeated by Republican businessman Frank White. He then entered a corporate law practice and prepared to challenge White in 1982. Clinton won back the governorship, which he retained by winning elections in 1984, 1986 and 1990. (During his third term, the governor's term in office was extended to four years.) In his second term as governor Clinton focused on currying the favor of powerful business interest such as Tyson Foods while also attempting to improve the state's education system and to attract technology-based businesses to Arkansas with state-sponsored loans for starting businesses.

Bill Clinton, standing between Hillary Rodham Clinton and their daughter, Chelsea, takes the oath of office, January 1993. (LIBRARY OF CONGRESS, PRINTS AND PHOTOGRAPHS DIVISION)

In 1991 Clinton announced that he would be running for the Democratic presidential nomination. Clinton benefited from his reputation in the South as an innovative governor, his position as chairman of the Democratic Leadership Council from 1990 to 1991 and his national exposure from delivering a keynote address at the 1988 Democratic National Convention. In 1992 Clinton defeated his opponents for the nomination and began campaigning against incumbent Republican president George H. W. BUSH and independent candidate H. Ross PEROT. Clinton criticized Bush for his poor handling of the economy, advocated creating a national health care system and suggested that he would employ the U.S. military in more humanitarian missions. To reduce criticisms of his marital infidelity while governor and his avoidance of military service during the VIETNAM WAR, Clinton chose Al GORE, Jr., well known as a family man and for his service in Vietnam, as his running mate. In a tightly contested election Clinton and Gore won the White House and entered office in January 1993.

As he pursued his domestic agenda Clinton encountered stiff opposition from congressional Republicans. His first national budget barely passed the House and Senate, with all Republicans and several Democrats voting against it. Also, Clinton's proposal for a national health care system failed to gain congressional approval in 1994, in large part because of a plethora of competing plans proposed by Democrats and Republicans. Clinton's task grew increasingly complicated when Republicans gained control of the House and Senate in the midterm elections of 1994. As a result of losing control of Congress, Clinton regularly vetoed Republican legislation that threatened to reduce funding to the programs he sponsored, such as his national youth service program AmeriCorps. The situation also necessitated compromise with Republican leadership, such as in 1996 when Clinton supported a Republican-passed welfare reform law that reduced the income assistance welfare recipients could receive from the federal government. Despite the combative Congress, Clinton successfully ran for reelection against Republican Bob Dole and Perot

(this time a candidate of the Reform Party) because of the booming American economy. However, a year after defeating Dole, Clinton came under increasing investigation for allegedly lying about an affair with a White House intern, Monica Lewinsky, while under oath. On December 19, 1998, the House of Representatives impeached Clinton for his statements, making Clinton the second president since Andrew Johnson to be impeached. However, the Senate did not convict Clinton.

In foreign affairs Clinton expanded the use of U.S. military forces in humanitarian missions. He continued the humanitarian aid begun under Bush to Somali victims of that country's civil war and briefly increased the scope of Operation Restore Hope to include targeting one of the Somali warlords, Mohammad AIDEED. However, Clinton reduced U.S. involvement after 15 servicemen died in an abortive attempt to capture Aideed. Clinton also dispatched U.S. forces to Bosnia and KOSOVO to restore peace to the former YUGOSLAVIA and continued the U.S.'s efforts to reduce Iraqi president Saddam HUSSEIN's ability to destabilize the Middle East. In negotiations between Palestinian and Israeli leaders Clinton played a pivotal role in getting official recognition of Israel by Jordan and in encouraging the implementation of the 1993 Oslo Accords between the PALESTINIAN AUTHORITY (PA) and ISRAEL. However, he failed in his efforts at the CAMP DAVID CONFERENCE (2000) to produce a settlement between Israel and SYRIA over the GOLAN HEIGHTS, and between Israel and the PA over the future of a Palestinian state composed of the WEST BANK and GAZA STRIP. Finally, Clinton actively promoted the increasing globalization of the world's economies. He supported the creation of the NORTH AMERICAN FREE TRADE ASSOCIATION (NAFTA), regularly advocated increasing the scope of the agreement to include all the nations of the Western Hemisphere and championed similar organizations such as the ASEAN REGIONAL FORUM and the ASIA-PACIFIC ECONOMIC COOPERATION.

clones and cloning A clone is an organism produced by asexual reproduction that, at the time this reproduction occurs, is genetically identical to

its "parent" organism. Clones can occur naturally; textbook cellular mitosis, identical twins, dandelions and an asexually reproduced Hydra are all examples of plants, animals and cellular organisms produced by naturally occurring cloning processes. However, in the late 20th century, the term *cloning,* and clones in general, have largely come to refer to an artificially induced process in order to duplicate perfectly an organism or, in some cases, a portion of an organism's genetic code. While scientists have been able for many years to induce cloning in simple organisms like bacteria and yeast in order to produce such medical products as insulin, the artificial production of an animal clone remained a difficult task. This was largely due to the manner in which animals formed out of a fertilized egg. Early on in the reproductive process, animal embryonic cells contain coded information that enables future cellular development to produce various organs and components needed for a functioning body. However, it had been theorized that, once these cells began to form particular organs or limbs, a cell taken from the embryo could no longer be used to construct a clone, as it had lost the information necessary to the production of all aspects of the organism. The problem impeding animal cloning therefore became determining the precise moment when the cells produced from a fertilized egg still contained enough information so that, if separated, they could form a fully functioning identical animal organism.

In 1996 Scottish scientists initially appeared to have found a way to produce a clone of an adult animal. Taking skin cells from the udder of one sheep, they injected the skin cell into an unfertilized egg from another sheep from which they had removed its nuclear material. They then implanted the egg in the womb of a third sheep. The result was the birth of a sheep in February 1997 that the scientists named Dolly. As studies later revealed, however, Dolly was not a perfect clone of the sheep that provided the skin cells. Despite the removal of the egg's original nucleus, several genes from the egg's cytoplasm incorporated themselves into Dolly's genetic structure. Also, as Dolly aged it became apparent that her biological age was not that of a young sheep, but rather that of an aging sheep, leading to speculation that the skin cell sample used to produce Dolly contained some sort of biological clock that caused Dolly's organs to age prematurely. Dolly's deteriorating physical condition led her caretakers to put her to sleep in 2003. Another claim of animal cloning emerged in December 2002, when a religious cult named the Raelian Movement announced that one of its members had given birth to a perfect clone of herself with the help of a firm called CloneAid. However, the repeated failure of the cult to provide samples of DNA or even to allow an inspection of the infant by scientists led many to dismiss the incident as a fraud.

Since the birth of Dolly raised the possibility of human cloning, efforts to prohibit any application of the techniques derived from Dolly's creation to human beings have moved forward in several countries. Australia, Austria, Britain, France, Slovakia, South Africa and other countries have passed legislation prohibiting the use of such technology to produce a human clone. Many others, such as Canada and the U.S., have considered similar legislation.

Close, Glenn (*1947– *) American film and stage actress. Her work on stage also resulted in offers for motion picture roles. While performing in the theater production of *Barnum,* the film director George Roy Hill saw Close perform and cast her in *The World According to Garp* (1982). The following

Actress Glenn Close backstage during a production of Death and the Maiden. *1992* (Photographed by Stewart Shining, Photofest)

year she appeared in *The Big Chill* (1983) playing a young urban professional, or yuppie, and received her first nomination for best actress from the Motion Picture Academy of America. Close received additional nominations for her appearance as Robert Redford's love interest in *The Natural* (1984), as Michael Douglas's seductress in *Fatal Attraction* (1987) and as a scheming French aristocrat in *Dangerous Liaisons* (1988). She later appeared in Steven Spielberg's *Hook* (1991), Tim Burton's *Mars Attacks!* (1996) and the Disney family films *101 Dalmations* (1996) and *102 Dalmations* (2000).

She has earned three Tony Awards (the theatrical equivalent of the Oscar) for her performances in Tom Stoppard's *The Real Thing* (1984) and *Death and the Maiden* (1992) and Andrew Lloyd Webber's musical *Sunset Boulevard* (1994).

Closing of the American Mind: Education and the Crisis of Reason, The Book by American philosopher and educator Allan Bloom. *The Closing of the American Mind* (1987) has been one of the most discussed works of social criticism to be published in the U.S. in recent years. In it Bloom raises the highly controversial argument that the trends toward cultural relativism and curricula innovation, which began in the 1960s and continued through the 1980s, have sapped the strength of the Western intellectual tradition, which ought to remain the primary foundation of American educational efforts. Bloom identifies the Western intellectual tradition as commencing with Socrates and Plato and extending through the great philosophical tradition of Machiavelli, Hobbes, Rousseau and Nietzsche, all of whom utilized reason to critique and enlarge upon societal values. Because students are no longer trained in this tradition, they cannot appreciate the value of liberal education as offered by American colleges, which seeks to instill techniques of rational analysis as a means of guiding public and private decision making. *The Closing of the American Mind* has become a seminal text for those advocating a more conservative approach to education in America.

Clubb, Oliver Edmund (*1901–1989*) U.S. diplomat. Clubb was the last U.S. diplomat stationed in China

after the Communists took control in 1949. He returned to the U.S. in 1950, but the following year he became one of several State Department officials to have his career wrecked by Senator Joseph McCarthy's anticommunist "witch hunts." McCarthy accused him of being a communist sympathizer, and Clubb was suspended as head of the State Department's China section. He fought the suspension and was cleared but quit after being reassigned because he felt the government had been disloyal to him.

Club Méditérranée (Club Med) An empire of vacation villages, founded by Belgian Gerard Blitz in 1950. Club Med began as a nonprofit association in which travelers would pay a set fee in exchange for a tropical, get-away-from-it-all vacation in which no money was required. Billed as an "antidote to civilization," Club Med grew into one of the world's largest tourism groups.

Club of Rome An international organization of scientists, industrialists and economists founded in Rome, Italy, in 1968 by Italian business executive Aurelio Peccei. The club studied problems of industrialization, population growth and depletion of natural resources. In 1972 it published *The Limits to Growth,* which predicted the collapse of society within 100 years if current trends continued. The book's conclusions were based on a computer model.

Clurman, Harold Edgar (*1901–1980*) American theater director, drama critic, author and teacher. Clurman's stage productions and scholarship influenced the American theater for nearly 50 years. He founded the Group Theater in 1931, which became known for landmark stage productions in the 1930s. He directed numerous plays there. He also served as drama critic for *The Nation* and wrote several books, including *All People Are Famous* (1974).

Clyde River and Firth of Clyde River and its estuary, the most prominent in Scotland. Shipbuilding leads all other industry in this heavily populated area. Glasgow, on the river's bank, is Scotland's largest city, seaport and industrial and shipbuilding hub but was faltering late in the 20th century. The famous OCEAN LINERS *Queen Mary* and *Queen Elizabeth* were constructed here in the 1930s. Another city on the Clyde is Hamilton, close to where Rudolf HESS, the Nazi leader, landed after he fled Germany in a small airplane in May 1941.

Coates, Wells (*1895–1958*) English architect and industrial designer, one of the first practitioners of MODERNISM in Great Britain. Coates was born in Japan and studied engineering at McGill University in Montreal, Canada. In 1929 he moved to London where he took up architectural practice. His Lawn Road Flats of 1934 in London is his best-known building in the INTERNATIONAL STYLE. In 1931 he founded Isokon with Jack Pritchard to manufacture furniture and other products of modern design in plywood. In 1933 he was among the founders of the Mars group, the English chapter of CIAM. As an industrial designer, he became known for furniture design using tubular steel and plywood in a BAUHAUS-related style. His best-known work is an Ekco radio (Model ADD65) of 1934, a cylindrical table model of ART DECO character with a case of BAKELITE plastic. He was also the designer of a variety of other Ekco electrical products, of BBC radio studio interiors and of aircraft interiors for British Overseas Airways Corporation.

Cobb, Arnett Cleophus (*1918–1989*) American jazz saxophonist. Cobb first came to prominence after he joined the Lionel HAMPTON Orchestra in 1942. An automobile accident in 1956 temporarily halted his performing career; after he returned, he performed on crutches for the remainder of his life. His frail appearance contrasted with the robust sound of his tenor sax playing.

Cobb, Tyrus Raymond (*1886–1961*) Legendary American baseball outfielder. In 22 seasons with the Detroit Tigers, Cobb had the highest lifetime batting average (.367) and, until recent years, the most hits (4,191) and the most stolen bases (892). Manager of the Tigers from 1921 to 1926, he was inducted into the Baseball Hall of Fame in 1936. While venerated as an icon of the game, Cobb has also been criticized for his racism and his violent temper.

Coblentz, William Weber (*1873–1962*) American physicist. Coblentz was educated at the Case Institute of Technology and at Cornell, where he earned his Ph.D. in 1903. In 1904 he joined the National Bureau of Standards in Washington and in the following year founded the radiometry section of the bureau, where he remained until his retirement in 1945. Coblentz worked mainly on studies of infrared radiation. At the Lick Observatory he began, in 1914, a series of measurements aimed at determining the heat radiated by stars. He was also one of the pioneers of absorption spectroscopy in the infrared region as a technique for identifying compounds.

CoBrA International arts movement (1948–51), an acronym of its founders' home cities: *Co*penhagen (painter Asger Jorn), *Br*ussels (Belgian writer Christian Dotremont) and *A*msterdam (Dutch artists Karel Appel, Constant [A. Nieuwenhys] and Corneille [Guillaume van Beverloo]). Among the other artists associated with CoBrA was the Belgian painter Pierre Alechinsky. Formed in reaction against the formalism of the School of Paris, the movement stressed a spontaneous expressionism, a bold use of color and a dramatic visual vocabulary of figures and symbols.

Coburn, Alvin Langdon (*1882–1966*) American photographer. Born in Boston, Coburn started experimenting with photographs at the age of eight. He joined the American PHOTO-SECESSION Group in 1902 and the British Salon of the Linked Ring the following year. Moving to London, Coburn became widely known for his probing portraits of literary and artistic figures, photographs that were collected in the two volumes of *Men of Mark* (1913, 1922). He also created notable landscapes, city scenes and seascapes, as well as the so-called vortographs, the first completely abstract photographs. His autobiography, *Photographer*, was published in 1966.

Coca, Imogene (*1908–2001*) American dancer and comedian. Born in Philadelphia, Coca received early theatrical training in piano, voice and dance lessons from her father, an opera conductor, and her mother, a vaudeville performer. By age 13 she had become an accomplished tap and ballet dancer and acrobat, displaying her skills at vaudeville performances throughout Philadelphia. By 1923 she had traveled to New York and won an audition for the chorus line of *When You Smile*. Her abilities on stage made her a regular for more than 30 years in New York revues and endeared her to audiences at the Rainbow Room, the Silver Slipper and the café society.

Coca's emergence as a comedic performer came during a 1934 performance choreographed by Leonard Stillman. During one performance the heating broke down in the theater, and Stillman sent Coca, actor Henry FONDA and other performers on stage to improvise and distract the audience while the thermostat problem was fixed. To keep Coca warm Stillman offered her his large greatcoat, which she wore during her improvised movements on stage. Stillman and the audience grew amused by Coca's actions and appearance, and Stillman thus made it a regular part of his revue, which soon became popular with audiences and critics. Coca's reputation as a comedian-dancer led to her being paired in performances with such similarly talented individuals as Danny KAYE and Carrol Channing. By far, however, her greatest success as a performer came from her regular appearances on the NBC 1949 television show *Admiral Broadway Revue* with Sid CAESAR. Coca and Caesar worked so well together that in 1950 NBC selected her to be a costar on *Your Show of Shows*, a variety television program hosted by Caesar, on which she performed until 1954. In 1951 Coca won an Emmy for her performances as a comedian on the program. During their four years on screen Coca and Caesar developed a potent rapport, especially in their skits as married couple Charlie and Doris Hickenlooper. In 1954 Coca launched her own show on NBC, *The Imogene Coca Show*, but it was dropped after one season when it failed to generate the same revenue as, and capture the audience base of, *Your Show of Shows*. After the cancellation of her program Coca appeared sporadically in other television projects. In addition to her television appearances, Coca performed on the silver screen; her best-known screen role was Aunt Edna in the 1983 spoof *National Lampoon's Vacation*.

Coca-Cola Brand name of an American soft drink that in the 20th century became one of the most widely-consumed beverages worldwide. Although closely identified with the 20th century, Coca-Cola was invented in the 19th century (1866). The formula was later purchased by Asa Griggs CANDLER. Coca-Cola is made almost exclusively of sugar and water; early in the century, COCAINE was reputedly an ingredient. The drink's popularity spread after World War II, helped by a massive advertising campaign and by the emergence of the U.S. as the leading free-world power. In the 1980s the company changed the formula and introduced "the new Coke," but there was such an outcry that the company was forced to bring back the old formula, under the name "Coke Classic." In many places Coke is now made with fructose. The drink's main rival is Pepsi-Cola.

cocaine Powerfully stimulative alkaloid-based drug derived from the leaves of coca plants (grown mainly in Colombia, Peru and Bolivia). For many years coca leaves were chewed by Indians in the Andes Mountains to counteract the effects of altitude. Cocaine became known in the West in the late 19th century and (in a refined and more potent powder form) was used for a number of medical purposes. Realization of its dangerous physical and psychological effects ended most medicinal use. Cocaine resurfaced in the 1970s as the so-called recreational use of illicit drugs expanded; cocaine acquired the reputation of a "glamour" drug and use soared. In the mid-1980s a new, cheap, smokable form of cocaine known as **crack** became available. Crack produces an even more intense (but shorter-lived) "high" in the user, followed by a period of deep depression. Crack also causes erratic, often violent behavior and is instantly addictive. By the late 1980s the widespread use of cocaine and crack had become a major social problem in the U.S. By the end of the 1990s cocaine usage had declined from an estimated 5.7 million Americans to 3.6 million, while heroin use had increased substantially.

Cochran, Jackie (*1906 or 1910–1980*) Pioneer American flier. Cochran learned to fly in her early 20s and went on to set more than 200 aviation records. She held more speed, distance and altitude records than any other flyer of her era. During WORLD WAR II she was director of the Woman's Air Force Service Pilots, a program that trained over 1,200 female pilots. In 1953 she became the first woman to break the sound barrier, and in 1964 she set another speed record of some 1,425 miles per hour.

Cockcroft, Sir John Douglas (*1897–1967*) British physicist. Cockcroft entered Manchester University in 1914 to study mathematics but left the following year to join the army. After WORLD WAR I he was apprenticed to the engineering firm Metropolitan Vickers, which sent him to study electrical engineering at the Manchester College of Technology. He later went to Cambridge University, graduated in mathematics, and joined Ernest RUTHERFORD's team at the Cavendish Laboratory. Cockcroft soon became interested in designing a device for accelerating protons and, with E.T.S. Walton, constructed a voltage multiplier. Using this the two bombarded nuclei of lithium with protons and, in 1932, brought about the first nuclear transformation by artificial means. For this work Cockcroft and Walton received the 1951 NOBEL PRIZE in physics. During WORLD WAR II Cockcroft played a leading part in the development of RADAR. In 1940 he visited the U.S. as a member of the Tizard mission to negotiate exchanges of military, scientific and technological information. In 1944 he became director of the Anglo-Canadian Atomic Energy Commission. He returned to Britain in 1946 to direct the new Atomic Energy Research Establishment at Harwell and remained there until 1959, when he was appointed master of Churchill College, Cambridge, a new college devoted especially to science and technology. Cockcroft was knighted in 1948.

Cocos Islands (Keeling Islands) Australian territory comprising a chain of islands in the Indian Ocean, about 580 miles southwest of Java. During WORLD WAR I, on November 9, 1914, the German cruiser *Emden* was demolished by the Australian cruiser *Sydney* off the Cocos Islands. In 1886 Britain granted the islands to the Clunies-Ross family. Australia took possession of the islands in 1955 and purchased most of the Clunies-Ross's interest in 1978. The islanders have the rights of Australian citizens and are represented in the Australian parliament. Only two of the islands are inhabited; the population—Cocos Malays and inhabitants of European descent—numbers only 600.

Cocteau, Jean (*1891–1963*) French poet, dramatist, novelist, playwright, literary critic and film director. Cocteau was perhaps the most versatile writer of the 20th century, scoring critical successes in virtually every literary genre and earning the friendship of great contemporaries such as painter Pablo PICASSO and composer Igor STRAVINSKY. While he was loosely associated with CUBISM and SURREALISM, Cocteau ultimately remained free of all artistic schools, pursuing his own unique blend of imaginative myth and elegant wit. Cocteau published his first volume of poems when he was 17 but dated his real emergence as a writer with *Le Potomak* (1919), a prose fantasy. In 1917 he wrote the ballet *Parade* for a score by Erik SATIE. In the 1920s he turned to the psychological novel with *Thomas the Impostor* (1923) and *Les Enfants terribles* (1929). His successful plays of the 1920s and 1930s include adaptations of *Antigone* (1928) and *The Infernal Machine* (1934). His path-breaking films include *The Blood of a Poet* (1931) and *Beauty and the Beast* (1945).

Coetzee, John M. (*1940–   *) South African author. Coetzee was educated at the University of Cape Town and the University of Texas, and after working in Britain, he returned to the University of Cape Town, where he eventually became professor of general literature. His work, which examines the themes of the abuse of power and moral conscience in contemporary SOUTH AFRICA, includes *Dusklands* (1974), *The Life and Times of Michael K.* (1983, Booker Prize), *Foe* (1986) and *White Writing: On the Culture of Letters in South Africa* (1988). He later wrote two fictionalized memoirs, *Boyhood* (1997) and *Youth* (2002). He published a collection of his literary essays titled *Stranger and Shores* (2001). Coetzee immigrated to Australia in 2002. He received the Booker Prize in 1983, the Prix Femina

Étranger in 1985 and the Nobel Prize in literature in 2003.

Coffin, Henry Sloan *(1877–1954)* American religious leader. Coffin, who was ordained as a Presbyterian minister in 1900, became the pastor of the Madison Avenue Church in New York City in 1905 and served there for over 20 years. His sermons drew considerable public attention due to their emphasis on social issues and contemporary Christian ethical dilemmas. Coffin went on to become the president of the Union Theological Seminary in New York City from 1926 to 1945. *Memory of the Cross* (1931) is noteworthy among his many works.

Coffin, William Sloane, Jr. *(1924– 2006)* American Presbyterian minister; well-known in the 1960s for his fervent involvement in the ANTIWAR MOVEMENT during the VIETNAM WAR. Coffin's background made this involvement particularly ironic: He had served as an intelligence officer during WORLD WAR II and worked for the CENTRAL INTELLIGENCE AGENCY (CIA) in the early 1950s before graduating from the Yale Divinity School in 1956. Subsequently, he served as chaplain for Yale University, and it was while holding this position that he was charged, in 1968, with criminal conspiracy to violate federal draft laws. The charges were overturned in 1970. Coffin became a minister at the interdenominational Riverside Church in New York City in 1977. *Once to Every Man* (1977) is his autobiography.

Coggan, Donald *(1909–2000)* Archbishop of Canterbury and spiritual leader of the Anglican Church. Coggan, who served as archbishop of Canterbury from 1974 to 1979, was best known for his break with longstanding Anglican tradition by advocating the right of women to become ordained as priests. He also suggested a reconciliation with the Roman Catholic Church through intercommunion—the receiving of the sacrament of communion by and between priests of both the Anglican and Catholic Churches. Prior to his election as archbishop, Coggan had taught theology at Wycliffe College in Toronto and at the London School of Divinity and had served as bishop of Bradford.

Cohan, George M(ichael) *(1878– 1942)* U.S. actor, composer, playwright and producer. He started performing with his family and later played comedy roles in vaudeville and on the stage. In 1893 he began writing skits and songs for vaudeville shows, and in 1901 his first full-length play opened in New York. His musicals include *Little Johnny Jones* (1904), *The Talk of New York* (1907) and *The Song and Dance Man* (1923). He wrote numerous songs, including "Give My Regards to Broadway" and "Over There," for which Congress awarded him a special medal in 1940. His career was the subject of an enduring movie classic, *Yankee Doodle Dandy* (1943).

Cohen, Benjamin Victor *(1894– 1983)* American attorney. A member of President Franklin D. ROOSEVELT's BRAIN TRUST, Cohen was one of the principal architects of the NEW DEAL legislation enacted during the GREAT DEPRESSION of the 1930s. Along with his close associate Thomas G. CORCORAN, Cohen was credited with writing such key measures as the **Securities and Exchange Act,** the first Wage and Hours bill, and the Public Utilities Holding Company act. He later held a number of political posts, most notably delegate to the UNITED NATIONS (1948–52).

Cohen, Seymour Stanley *(1917–)* American biochemist. Cohen was educated in New York, at the City College and at Columbia, where he earned his Ph.D. in 1941. He joined the University of Pennsylvania in 1943, serving as professor of biochemistry from 1954 until 1971, when he moved to the University of Denver as professor of microbiology. Cohen returned to New York in 1976 to take the chair of pharmaceutical sciences at the State University, Stony Brook. In 1946 Cohen began a series of studies in molecular biology using radioactive labeling. Cohen used this technique in a number of experiments in the late 1940s that suggested rather than demonstrated the vital role of DNA in heredity. It was not until 1952, when Alfred Hershey and Martha Chase used Cohen's labeling technique, that more substantial results were available.

Cohn, Harry *(1891–1958)* Cofounder, president and head of production at COLUMBIA PICTURES in HOLLYWOOD. Said to have been the most tyrannical of the old-guard studio barons, Cohn came from an immigrant family on New York's Upper East Side. He worked in vaudeville and as a songwriter before forming the C.B.C. Film Sales Company with his brother Jack in 1920. Cohn relocated to Hollywood as production chief, and four years later the studio was renamed Columbia Pictures. From humble beginnings, Columbia became one of Hollywood's most successful studios in the 1930s and 1940s. After a long power struggle with his brother, Cohn became president of the studio in 1932—and the only production chief in Hollywood to double as president of his company. To director Frank CAPRA, an important Cohn discovery, he was one of a breed of "tough, brassy, untutored buccaneers . . . indigent, hot-eyed entrepreneurs, gamblers who played longshots." Cohn was obsessed with movies, maintaining absolute control of studio operations down to the last detail. Some hunches, such as the discovery of Rita HAYWORTH in the mid-1930s, paid off; others, such as the dismissal of Marilyn MONROE in 1949, did not. After a "last hurrah" of several successful pictures, including *On the Waterfront* (1954), Cohn died following hernia surgery.

Cohn, Roy *(1927–1986)* Controversial American attorney who first gained notoriety for his role in the ARMY-MCCARTHY HEARINGS. Cohn served as council for Senator Joseph MCCARTHY's committee investigating alleged communists in the U.S. government in the late 1940s and early 1950s. He gained national prominence during the committee's televised hearings in which McCarthy denounced numerous people as communists or dangerous "fellow travelers." Cohn was also a prosecutor in the famous ROSENBERG TRIAL. In later years Cohn turned to private practice where he earned a reputation as a combative lawyer and was often accused of being abrasive and relying on intimidation. Cohn, a friend of many in New York's society, became a minor celebrity. He also had a running battle with the Internal Revenue Service and was audited annually. He was tried and acquitted three times on bribery, extortion, blackmail and obstruction of justice charges. Even the true cause of his death proved controversial. He claimed to be suffering from liver cancer, but the White House was said to have moved him ahead of other patients waiting to receive experimental treatments for AIDS.

Colani, Luigi *(1928–)* German industrial designer known for his aggressively futuristic approach to design. Colani was educated in Berlin and Paris in painting, sculpture, and, later, aerodynamics. His drawings of futuristically streamlined cars led to his development of a variety of racing and sports cars built as prototypes but never actually produced. Only the Colani T Spider, a two-seat sports body for a VOLKSWAGEN chassis, was produced as a do-it-yourself FIBERGLASS kit. About 500 were sold from 1950 to 1960. More recent projects have included furniture designs, a design for a small TV set and various designs for cars, trucks and boats.

cold war Protracted state of tension between countries falling short of actual warfare. The term was first used in the U.S. Congress to describe deteriorating post–World War II relations between the U.S. and the USSR. It especially describes the period of tension between 1946 and the early 1970s, marked by such international crises as the GREEK CIVIL WAR, the construction of the BERLIN WALL and the CUBAN MISSILE CRISIS. The division between the West and the Communist world was formalized by the creation of NATO (1949–50) and the WARSAW PACT (1955). The momentous events of 1989–90 in Eastern Europe, marking the transition from Communist to noncommunist governments, severely weakened the international position of the Soviet Union. On December 25, 1991, the Soviet Union disintegrated, marking the definitive end of the polar system that had operated during the cold war.

Cole, Nat "King" **(Nathaniel Adams Coles)** *(1919–1965)* Black American JAZZ and popular music vocalist and pianist. Cole began his career as a jazz pianist. He founded his own jazz group, the King Cole Trio, in the late 1930s, but within a decade his playing had been overshadowed by his distinctive vocal talent—soft and smooth, yet emotionally compelling—which made him a star. Major hits by Cole in the 1940s and 1950s include "Mona Lisa," "Nature Boy" and "Too Young." He also hosted his own radio and television shows. Cole was a major breakthrough figure as a black performing for mainstream white audiences. As such, he was a major influence on the next generation of black vocalists, especially Sam Cooke and Marvin GAYE.

Coleman, Ornette *(1930–)* American alto saxophonist and composer. Coleman is one of modern jazz's most enigmatic figures. Though reflecting influences from the 1940s' BEBOP revolution spawned by Charlie PARKER and Dizzy GILLESPIE, Coleman also has drawn from the collective improvisational approach of the New Orleans tradition and the raw emotion of Mississippi BLUES. For some, Coleman has "liberated" jazz from its dependence on predetermined harmonic patterns and the convention of melodic variation; for others, including modern jazz giants Miles DAVIS and Charles MINGUS, Coleman's collective "music" is primitive, a cacophonous collage lacking either form or substance. Depending on one's point of view, the controversy stirred by Coleman's radical style can be seen as pitting "freedom" against "anarchy." In the U.S. the impact of Coleman's approach—with its emphasis on group rather than virtuosic solo improvisation—has waned since its heyday in the 1960s; however, it continues to be a force in European FREE JAZZ circles. Coleman's most inspired playing and writing came in the late 1950s and 1960s; "Blues Connotation" and "Lonely Woman" are among the tunes Coleman has contributed to the repertory of "jazz standards." Overall, Coleman's greatest influence may have been in provoking—like John CAGE in conservatory music—broadly based questions on the very nature of jazz, its basic assumptions, materials and improvisational procedures.

Colette (Sidonie-Gabrielle Colette) *(1873–1954)* French novelist. Colette spent her childhood in the countryside of Burgundy, which inspired a responsiveness to nature apparent in her later work. In 1983 she married the writer Willy (Henry Gauthier-Villars), who encouraged her to write about her childhood and to make the stories as risqué as possible. This resulted in the Claudine series: *Claudine à l'école* (1900; translated as *Claudine at School,* 1930) *Claudine à Paris* (1901; translated as *Claudine in Paris,* 1958) *Claudine en ménage* (1902; translated as *Claudine Married,* 1960) and *Claudine s'en va* (published in English as *Claudine and Annie,* which Willy usurped and first had published under his name between 1900 and 1903). The marriage was an unhappy one, and Colette left Willy in 1906, working as a dancer and a mime in music halls while continuing to write novels, including *La Vagabonde* (1911). Her writing is rich, sensuous and sensitive to the influence of nature. Her later works evocatively depict the phases in a woman's life. Colette married twice more and was the first woman to be elected to the Goncourt Academy as well as the first to be honored by a state funeral. Other important novels include *Mitsou; ou, Comment l'esprit vient aux filles* (1919, translated as *Mitsou, or How Girls Grow Wise*), *Chéri* (1920) and *Gigi* (1944), which inspired a musical film of the same name in 1958.

collage Technique of creating art or graphic works by assembling various material fragments and pasting them on a flat surface. Collage became a widely used technique for the production of abstract works of modern art during the 1920s and has continued as a significant alternative to painting used by many artists. Typical collage materials are colored papers, fragments of cloth, wood or other materials, and bits of printed material or actual objects, often cut or torn before being combined in a finished work. Collage was developed, to an exceptional degree, by the German artist Kurt Schwitters, an important figure in the DADA movement. The technique was taken up and used by many leading modern artists including Henri MATISSE, Georges BRAQUE and Pablo PICASSO.

collective unconscious See Carl Gustav JUNG.

collectivization Policy first carried out in the UNION OF SOVIET SOCIALIST REPUBLICS under Joseph STALIN. The

COLD WAR

1945	Franklin D. Roosevelt, Winston Churchill and Joseph Stalin meet at Yalta Conference to plan postwar division of Europe; end of World War II.
1947	U.S. secretary of state George C. Marshall proposes European Recovery Program (Marshall Plan).
1948	Communist takeover of Czechoslovakia.
1948–49	Soviet blockade West Berlin; U.S. and Allies respond with Berlin Airlift.
1949	Communists defeat Nationalists in Chinese Civil War, proclaim People's Republic of China; pro-Western forces defeat Communists, ending Greek Civil War; U.S. and its Western allies form NATO alliance; USSR successfully tests atomic bomb.
1950–53	Korean War.
1951	U.S. successfully tests first hydrogen bomb.
1953	Julius and Ethel Rosenberg executed for passing U.S. atomic secrets to the USSR.
1955	Warsaw Pact formed by USSR and its Eastern bloc satellites.
1956	Hungarian uprising—rebellion against Communist rule crushed by Soviet invasion.
1957	USSR launches first artificial satellite, *Sputnik 1*.
1960	U2 incident—Soviets shoot down U.S. spy plane over USSR, convict pilot Gary Powers of spying.
1961	Berlin Wall erected; anti-Castro Cubans land in Cuba in abortive Bay of Pigs invasion.
1962	Cuban missile crisis.
1968	Soviet invasion of Czechoslovakia ends Prague Spring reforms.
1972	U.S. and USSR sign SALT-1 strategic arms limitation treaty.
1975	Vietnamese Communists capture Saigon (Ho Chi Minh City), Vietnam unified under Communists; Andrei Sakharov wins Nobel Peace Prize.
1983	U.S. invasion of Grenada deposes Communist government; U.S. president Ronald Reagan denounces USSR as "evil empire," proposes Strategic Defense Initiative.
1985	Mikhail Gorbachev becomes leader of USSR, ushering in period of glasnost and perestroika.
1986	Reykjavík summit between Gorbachev and Reagan; Reagan rejects Gorbachev plan to eliminate all nuclear weapons by 2000.
1988	U.S. president Reagan and Soviet leader Gorbachev hold summit meeting in Moscow.
1989	Tiananmen Square massacre—Chinese troops crush reform movement in China.
1989–90	Downfall of Communist governments in Czechoslovakia, East Germany, Hungary, Poland, Romania; opening and dismantling of Berlin Wall.
1990	Reunification of Germany under democratic government; Lech Wałęsa elected president of Poland.
1991	Soviet troops use force to quell independence movements in Lithuania and Estonia; Soviet republic of Georgia declares independence from USSR; USSR disintegrates, and Gorbachev resigns as president.

collectivization of agriculture was part of Stalin's plan to give the Communist state complete control of the economy. In his first FIVE-YEAR PLAN (1928–33), Stalin attempted to consolidate small peasant farms into large **collective farms.** By abolishing privately owned farms, the government, not the farmers, could set food prices. In theory collective farms were to be a source of cheap and plentiful grain with which to feed the nation and sustain the revolution. The KULAKS (prosperous peasant farmers) opposed collectivization; many were executed or deported to Siberian labor camps, and their property was seized by the government. By the early 1930s the Soviet collectivization policy was well under way. However, contrary to Stalin's wishes, production did not increase; rather, it plummeted. The ensuing famine in the UKRAINE—traditionally the breadbasket of Russia—resulted in several million deaths during the early 1930s.

Collier, John *(1901–1980)* British novelist, screenwriter, poet and modern master of the wickedly macabre short story. Perhaps only SAKI at the turn of the century and Roald DAHL more recently have rivalled his gleefully diabolical touch. Although he worked as a literary critic for the *London Telegraph,* poetry editor for *Time and Tide,* novelist (*His Monkey Wife,* 1930) and screenplay writer in HOLLYWOOD (sharing scenario credit with James AGEE for *The African Queen,* 1951), it is upon his remarkable short stories that his fame must ultimately reside. Originally appearing in magazines like *The New Yorker,* they have been collected in *Presenting Moonshine* (1941), *Fancies and Goodnights* (1951) and *Pictures in the Fire* (1958). The tales range from the gruesome (a man-eating orchid in "Green Thoughts") to the whimsical (the nightlife among department store mannequins in "Evening Primrose"), the naughty (the erotic fables "Bottle Party" and "The Chaser") and the most outrageous degree of grand guignol (the cheerfully grisly "Another American Tragedy"). They are, in the words of Anthony Burgess, "quaint, precise, bookish, fantastic." All the same, they bite, frequently snatching up hapless readers in the jaws of a double-take.

Collins, Joseph Lawton *(1896–1987)* U.S. general. Collins was a U.S. combat leader in WORLD WAR II and subsequently army chief of staff. He earned the nickname "Lightning Joe" when he commanded a division early in the war on the Pacific island of GUADALCANAL. Later, on the European front, he led the Army 7th Corps to the capture of Cherbourg. He led one of the two army corps that landed at NORMANDY on D day to the capture of Aachen and Cologne, and thence to a meeting with the Soviets at Dessau. As army chief of staff from 1949 to 1953, he was at the head of that service throughout the KOREAN WAR.

Collins, Judy *(1939–)* American folk and popular music vocalist and songwriter. Collins emerged as a major folk music star with her very first album, *Maid of Constant Sorrow* (1961), which featured her trademark, bell-clear vocals and affecting lyrical delivery. Two other successful albums followed during this period of peak popularity for Collins— *In My Life* (1966) and *Wildflowers* (1967), the first album to feature songs written by Collins herself. During the 1960s Collins was politically active in support of civil rights and in opposition to the VIETNAM WAR. She was also the inspiration for the Crosby, Stills & Nash hit song "Judy Blue Eyes" (1970). Subsequent albums by Collins, which have been less commercially successful, include *Judith* (1975) and *Hard Times for Lovers* (1979).

Collins, Michael *(1890–1922)* Irish revolutionary leader. After working in England (1907–16), he returned to Ireland and participated in the EASTER REBELLION of 1916. A member of SINN FÉIN and a leader of the IRISH REPUBLICAN ARMY, he was one of the organizers of

Colombia

Netherlands Antilles (NETHERLANDS)
Aruba (NETH.)
Caribbean Sea
Santa Marta
Ríohacha
Barranquilla
Cíenaga
Cartagena
Valledupar
Tolu
Sincelejo
Montería
Turbo
Cúcuta
Pamplona
Medellín
Bucaramanga
Arauca
Quibdo
Barbosa
Paz de Río
Tunja
Manizales
Bogotá
El Yopal
Pereira
Armenia
Ibagué
Villavicencio
Buenaventura
Girardot
Puerto López
Cali
Neiva
San José del Guaviare
Popayán
Tumaco
Florencia
Pasto
Mocoa
Ipiales
Mitú
PANAMA
PACIFIC OCEAN
VENEZUELA
Puerto Carreño
Puerto Inírida
Río Atrato
Río Cauca
Río Magdalena
Río Meta
Río Orinoco
Río Guaviare
Río Guainía
Río Vaupés
Río Caquetá
Río Putumayo
ECUADOR
PERU
BRAZIL
Leticia
N
0　200 miles
0　200 km
© Infobase Publishing

the Dáil Eireann in 1919 and became a member of that assembly. Three years later he helped formulate the treaty that created the IRISH FREE STATE. Serving briefly as finance minister in the government of Arthur GRIFFITH, he was assassinated by extremists in 1922.

Collins, Michael *(1930–)* U.S. astronaut. "O.K., Eagle . . . You guys take care." With those words, Collins watched Neil ARMSTRONG and Edwin "Buzz" ALDRIN maneuver the *APOLLO 11* (July 16–24, 1969) lunar module away from the command module and begin their historic descent to the Moon. During the next 24 hours Collins continued to circle the Moon while his crewmates made history on its surface. This was Collins's second spaceflight; as pilot of *Gemini 10* (July 18–21, 1966) he had made two space walks during the three-day rendezvous and docking mission. Son of an army major general, Collins was born in Rome and is the author of *Carrying the Fire,* a book of memoirs, *Flying to the Moon and Other Strange Places,* a children's book, and *Liftoff: The Story of America's Adventure in Space.*

Colombia Nation at the northwestern edge of South America, bordering on both the Caribbean Sea and the Pacific Ocean. Liberated from Spanish control, the 19th century saw political friction between right and left blocs and intermittent civil war. In 1878 Colombia granted a French firm a concession to construct a canal across the Isthmus of Panama, but the venture floundered. The **Hay-Herrán Treaty** of 1903 consigned this right to the U.S.; in exchange, Colombia was to collect $10 million and an annuity of $250,000. The Colombian senate denied the ratification of the treaty, but a Panamanian uprising on November 3, assisted by the U.S., made PANAMA a separate country. In 1921 Colombia acknowledged Panamanian autonomy after a U.S. payment of $25 million.

In 1932 a rift with PERU occurred over ownership of Leticia and its region; the LEAGUE OF NATIONS granted it to Colombia in 1934. From the late 1940s to the late 1950s bloody civil turmoil ran rampant—La Violencia (see COLOMBIAN REVOLT OF 1948). In 1957 fatigued liberals and conservatives joined forces to reduce disorder. In 1978 liberal Julio César Turbay Ayala was elected president; his government took credit for destroying the main guerrilla circle, but disorder extended into the 1980s. Conservative Party candidate Belisario Betancur Cuartas was elected president in 1982. In the late 1980s Colombia was besieged by the brutality of criminal cocaine traffickers (see MEDELLÍN CARTEL); many police officers, judges and government officials were bribed, intimidated or assassinated. When a prominent politician, Carlos Galán, was murdered during a campaign rally (August 1989), President Virgilio Barco Vargas declared war on the drug cartels. The government subsequently made progress against the cartels, arresting many top figures. In the 1990s the Colombian government continued its efforts against the Medellín Cartel, killing the cartel's leader, Pablo ESCOBAR, in December 1993. With the strong support of the U.S., Colombia has also sought to suppress the insurgency mounted by the leftist FUERZAS ARMADAS REVOLUCIONARIAS DE COLOMBIA (FARC) but has been unable to restore peace and stability to the country. In 2002 right-wing candidate Álvaro Uribe Vélez was elected president by a landslide and also won the 2006 election. In 2002 an upsurge of violence by FARC ended the peace talks that had begun in 1999. Colombia's capital and largest city is Bogotá; other cities include Medellín, Cali and Barranquilla.

Colombian Guerrilla War of 1976
In 1976 the Colombian government instituted a state of siege against left-wing guerrillas, but leftist violence continued leading to a "security statute" (1978) that curtailed individual liberties. On January 1, 1979, geurrillas of the

COLOMBIA	
1903	Panama secedes from Colombia with U.S. backing.
1940	Colombia's oil pipelines are destroyed, allegedly by German fifth columnists.
1948	Bogotá mayor Jorge Eliecer's assassination begins "La Violencia," 10 years of lawlessness.
1957	First vote on basis of universal suffrage.
1985	22,000 people are killed in volcanic disaster at Armero.
1989	Medellín cocaine traffickers kill presidential candidate Luis Carlos Galán.
1990	Medellín drug cartel issues declaration of surrender.
1993	Pablo Escobar, leader of Medellín drug cartel, is killed by government forces.
1998	Peace talks between government and Colombia Revolutionary Armed Forces (FARC) begin.
1998	Liberals retain majority in parliamentary elections.
2002	Right-wing candidate Álvaro Uribe Vélez wins landslide victory in presidential elections; end of peace talks and upsurge of violence
2006	President Álvaro Uribe is reelected.

Movement of April 19 (M-19) captured more than 5,000 weapons from the Bogotá arsenal, inducing violent government reprisals. Another left-wing group, the Colombian Revolutionary Armed Forces (FARC), simultaneously increased its attacks, while M-19 seized 15 diplomats in 1980, demanding a ransom and release of political prisoners. A settlement was reached after 61 days. Many M-19 leaders were killed or captured in a shootout with the army (March 18, 1981), but M-19 and FARC activities continued, while right-wing paramilitary groups engaged in reprisals. An amnesty (1982–83) had little success. Successive governments have attempted to improve living conditions and induce guerrillas to join the peaceful political process, but guerrillas and right-wing death squads continue to terrorize Colombia.

Colombian Revolt of 1948 Colombia, plagued by economic and social problems, was also embroiled in a political feud between Liberals and Conservatives. When popular left-wing Liberal Jorge Eliecer Gaitán (1902–48) was assassinated on April 9, 1948, long repressed tensions overflowed in violence. This initiated a period called "La Violencia" (1948–58), a state of constant insurrection and criminality. Over 200,000 people were killed and billions of dollars of damage was done. Archconservative Laureano Eleuterio Gómez (1889–1965) served as president from 1950 until ousted in 1953 by army chief of staff General Gustavo Rojas Pinilla. Rojas ruled as dictator until his corrupt rule was ended by a military junta (1957). In 1958 democracy returned with a National Front government, a Liberal-Conservative coalition, under newly elected president Alberto LLERAS CAMARGO, who slowly stabilized the country.

Colombo Plan An international plan for economic development aid to countries of South and Southeast Asia. First proposed in 1950, at a meeting of British COMMONWEALTH OF NATIONS foreign ministers in COLOMBO, Ceylon (now Sri Lanka), the Colombo Plan was intended for regional Commonwealth nations only. Australia's prime minister Robert Gordon MENZIES foresaw its potential to counter communism in the region, and U.S. backing was sought.

The program is now administered through headquarters in Colombo. Regional members include most nations from IRAN east to FIJI, excepting Vietnam, China, North Korea and Brunei. Nonregional members are AUSTRALIA, CANADA, the UNITED KINGDOM, JAPAN, NEW ZEALAND and the U.S. Regional members plan their own development programs. Nonregional members contribute financially and provide training, research and consultative services. The U.S. has provided a large share of the funding.

Colonels, Greek Military junta that seized power in GREECE on April 21, 1967. The coup was led by two colonels, George PAPADOPOULOS and Stylianos Pattakos, who suspended the democratic constitution. The regime collapsed in July 1974, following its intervention in CYPRUS. (See also Greek-Turkish CYPRIOT WAR OF 1974.)

color-field painting Style of painting that originated with one wing of ABSTRACT EXPRESSIONISM. Using pure color in two-dimensional space on enormous canvases, such painters as Mark ROTHKO and Barnett Newman created a unified color field of closely valued color. The technique was used in new ways by painters of the next generation, such as Friedel DZUBAS, Morris Louis, Kenneth NOLAND and Jules Olitsky, who also used monumentally scaled canvases (sometimes shaped), two-dimensional space and their own configurations of pure color. The work of this second group of painters was dubbed "post-painterly abstraction" by the critic Clement Greenberg.

Coltrane, John *(1926–1967)* Tenor and soprano saxophonist; arguably the most influential jazz innovator of the 1960s. Coltrane's earliest professional experiences were in rhythm-and-blues, then with jazz stalwarts Dizzy GILLESPIE and Johnny Hodges. Initially obsessed with pushing the boundaries of BEPOP chord progressions to the limit, Coltrane developed an unparalleled virtuosity in articulating scalular and arpeggiated patterns with a steely sound aptly described by critic Ira Gitler as "sheets of sound." These successful, if then controversial, experiments were explored by Coltrane in the late 1950s as a key

Jazz saxophonist and innovative musician John Coltrane, 1960 (LIBRARY OF CONGRESS, PRINTS AND PHOTOGRAPHS DIVISION)

member of the highly visible Miles DAVIS Quintet. In 1960 the tenorman formed the pivotal John Coltrane Quartet, whose seminal edition included pianist McCoy Tyner, bassist Jimmy Garrison and drummer Elvin Jones. He also added soprano saxophone to his arsenal; though the soprano was considered a relic from the 1920s, Coltrane developed a singularly muscular approach that proved the instrument a potent jazz voice and by 1970 a virtually mandatory "double" for all tenorists. While best known for his unprecedented up-tempo harmonic explorations, Coltrane was also a consummate interpreter of ballads. In the mid-1960s Coltrane's relentless quest led him to controversial explorations of the avant-garde but with the deep spirituality that marked each phase of his career. In addition to his enormous influence as a stylistically innovative player, Coltrane left a number of now-standard jazz compositions, including "Giant Steps," "Impressions" and "Naima."

Colum, Padraic *(1881–1972)* Irish-American poet. Born in Ireland, he was an important figure in the IRISH LITERARY REVIVAL and helped to found the ABBEY THEATRE (1902) and the *Irish Review* (1911). In 1912 he married the Irish literary critic and short story writer Mary Maguire (1880?–1957), and they settled in the U.S. in 1914. His volumes of poetry include *Wild Earth* (1907), *Creatures* (1927) and *Collected Poems* (1953). Colum also wrote a number of plays and stories for children based on Irish folktales.

Columbia Basin Project Launched on the Columbia River in the northwestern U.S. in 1948, a U.S. government irrigation, hydroelectric power and flood-control plan, with Grand Coulee Dam as its major facility.

Columbia Broadcasting System See CBS.

Columbia Pictures One of HOLLYWOOD's "Little Three" production companies (along with UNITED ARTISTS and UNIVERSAL PICTURES) and the only studio to transcend its "Poverty Row" origins to become a major corporation. The driving force behind Columbia was the colorful, indomitable Harry COHN, who personally supervised all studio production until his death in 1958. Cohn and his brother Jack had been producing cheap westerns and comedies since the early 1920s for their C.B.C. Film Sales Corporation in Hollywood. In 1924 they changed the company name to Columbia and in 1926 released their first feature-length film, *Blood Ship*. The arrival of director Frank CAPRA a year later had an enormous impact on the studio's rising fortunes. For the next 10 years his remarkable comedies and dramas, including *It Happened One Night,* which walked off with every major ACADEMY AWARD for 1934, vaulted the studio into the front rank. However, the 1940s saw primarily the production of formula programmers, except a handful of big-budget pictures such as *Gilda* (1946), *The Jolson Story* (1947) and *Born Yesterday* (1950). Unlike the other studios Columbia was not adversely affected by government antitrust actions after 1948 and the advent of television. Columbia owned no theaters, so the government-enforced divorcement of theaters had no impact. At the same time, the formation of Screen Gems in 1952 allowed Columbia to become the first studio to produce programs for TV. Profits from sales of Columbia films to TV were channeled into new film production. In 1968 the studio was reorganized as Columbia Pictures Industries. In 1972 it left its original studios at Sunset Boulevard and Gower in Hollywood to share the WARNER BROS.'s new Burbank Studios. Several corporate takeovers have ensued. Coca-Cola Corp. acquired the studio in 1981, and Sony Corporation purchased it in 1989. Some of the more recent successes have included *Easy Rider* (1969), *Five Easy Pieces* (1970) and *Tootsie* (1985).

Columbine High School massacre On April 20, 1999, two senior students at Columbine High School in Littleton Colorado, Eric Harris and Dylan Klebold, entered the school's amphitheater and cafeteria area and began shooting and killing other students. They then moved into the classroom buildings, throwing 30 pipe bombs in the hallways and entering classrooms, where they shot and killed several students and one teacher. When police arrived at the high school, they found the bodies of Harris and Klebold (apparently suicides), along with 12 dead students, one dead teacher and 24 wounded students throughout the building. When police had evacuated the high school and investigated the homes of both Harris and Klebold, they found detailed plans of the assault in the diaries of both individuals, along with additional plans to have hijacked an airplane and crashed it into the center of Littleton. The motive for the attacks has been attributed to many factors: both students' participation in a clique called the "Trenchcoat Mafia" and exclusion from other more popular cliques at the school, fascination with violent film scenes in *The Basketball Diaries* and *The Matrix,* violent songs by artists like Marilyn Manson and violent video games such as the Doom game series; however, it has not been established whether Harris or Klebold gave any specific reason for the rampage in their writings. In 2002 the school's plan to create a memorial to the 13 victims designed by Columbine students drew controversy when school officials prohibited one of the tiles in the memorial from containing the words *Jesus wept.* Several parents of the students filed a lawsuit to include the tile; in January 2003 the suit was decided in favor of the school.

Colville, Sir John Rupert *(1915– 1987)* British political secretary and principal private secretary to Winston CHURCHILL during most of Churchill's tenure as British prime minister. Colville also served briefly as secretary to two other prime ministers, Neville CHAMBERLAIN and Clement ATTLEE. From 1947 to 1949 he was secretary to Princess ELIZABETH before she became queen. After leaving government service in 1955, he became a merchant banker. Colville was knighted in 1974.

Comaneci, Nadia *(1961–)* Romanian gymnast. Her career began at the age of six, when Comaneci was discovered by the sport's most influential coach, Bela Karolyi. She began winning multiple gold medals as a junior competitor during the 1970s, and, in her first senior event, dethroned five-time European champion Lyudmila Turishcheva. At the 1976 Montreal OLYMPIC GAMES, she became the first gymnast to be awarded a perfect 10 in international competition, receiving seven perfect scores as she won gold medals for the uneven bars and the balance beam. Dark and petite, her gravity and intensity contrasted sharply with the winning ways of the previous Olympic star, Olga KORBUT. Comaneci retired from competition in 1984 and defected to the U.S. in November 1989. In April 1996 she married American gymnast Bart Conner.

Comden and Green American librettists and lyricists. **Betty Comden** (1919–) and **Adolphe Green** (1915– 2002), a celebrated team, wrote with equal success for the Broadway stage and the Hollywood musical. Among their most celebrated theatrical works are *On the Town* (with Leonard BERNSTEIN, 1944), *Two on the Aisle* (1951), *Peter Pan* (with Jules Styne, 1954), *Bells Are Ringing* (1956), *Subways Are for Sleeping* (1961) and *Applause* (1970). Their film successes include *Singin' in the Rain* (1952) and *The Band Wagon* (1953). Beginning in 1958 they toured in a musical autobiography entitled *A Party,* a dual performance of their songs and lyrics that they continued into the 1990s.

Cominform Communist information agency formed in 1947 and dissolved in 1956. Its members were the Communist Parties of Bulgaria, Czechoslovakia, France, Hungary, Italy, Poland, Romania, the USSR and Yugoslavia (expelled in 1948), though membership was not obligatory for Communist Parties. It sought to promote party unity through dissemination of information.

Comintern (Communist International)

Also known as the Third International, the Comintern was founded by LENIN and the Russian COMMUNIST PARTY in 1919. The organization was intended to give the Russian Communists control of the communist movement throughout the world; under the Comintern's "Twenty-one Conditions" (1920), the USSR prohibited Communist cooperation with noncommunist socialist parties. ZINOVIEV was the Comintern's first president. The Comintern was viewed with alarm in many Western countries, but it had little practical influence. The German-Japanese ANTI-COMINTERN PACT (1936) was designed to counter the world influence of the Comintern. The Comintern was dissolved in 1943.

Commentary

American periodical. Founded as a liberal Jewish journal in 1945, *Commentary* lapsed into what was considered boring stagnancy in the late 1950s. When editor Eliot Cohen died in 1960, he was replaced by Norman Podhoretz, who revolutionized the magazine. Expanding its coverage to include a wide spectrum of ideas as well as political and social concerns, Podhoretz published material from a variety of well-known authors and critics. During the mid- and late 1960s, *Commentary* increasingly became a journal of right-wing opinion. Among its editorial positions are opposition to government spending programs, affirmative action plans and university quotas as well as strong support of Israel. Widely respected for the intellectual rigor of its content and often criticized for the CONSERVATISM of its outlook, *Commentary* continues, under Podhoretz's influence as an editor at large, to be an important journal of American neoconservative thought.

Committee of One Million

See Gerald L. K. SMITH.

Common Foreign and Security Policy (CFSP)

A component of the 1991 MAASTRICHT TREATY that called for intergovernmental cooperation among the states of the EUROPEAN UNION (EU) to produce a single foreign and defense policy for the organization's member states. The treaty did not require any EU state to cede control of its foreign policy to the CFSP, since all decisions on EU-wide foreign or security policy require unanimous consent of all EU members. In foreign policy this approach has borne some limited success, such as the European cooperation under the auspices of NATO that produced the truce in the 1999 KOSOVO War. However, the CFSP failed to produce a consensus on a common defense policy for the EU. Countries such as France and Germany favored the creation of an integrated European military force by the union of the largely Franco-German Eurocorps and the Western European Union (WEU), the multinational defensive organization that allowed West Germany to rearm and join NATO during the COLD WAR. Other members opposed the creation of a European military force independent of NATO that would duplicate NATO activities and prompt criticism from the U.S.

Common Market

See EUROPEAN ECONOMIC COMMUNITY.

Commonwealth of Independent States (CIS)

Intergovernmental organization formed among the states of BELARUS, RUSSIA and UKRAINE—all former constituent republics of the USSR—on December 8, 1991. Within two weeks these three founding nations were joined in the CIS by eight other former Soviet republics: ARMENIA, AZERBAIJAN, KAZAKHSTAN, KYRGYZSTAN, MOLDOVA, TAJIKISTAN, TURKEMENISTAN and UZBEKISTAN. The former Soviet republic of GEORGIA joined the CIS in 1993. The Baltic republics of ESTONIA, LATVIA and LITHUANIA were the only former Soviet republics that elected not to join the organization.

Created in the aftermath of the failed Soviet coup of August 1991, the CIS initially represented an attempt to reduce the power of the central Soviet government over the constituent Soviet Socialist Republics (SSR). This struggle between the constituent republics and the central government was personified by the postcoup friction between Soviet president Mikhail GORBACHEV and Russian president Boris YELTSIN. During the coup, in which Gorbachev was held captive in a southern dacha, Yeltsin led the Russian efforts to overthrow the conspirators who had seized power. After the latter were toppled, Yeltsin used his popularity with the Russian people to minimize Gorbachev's power over his republic. Yeltsin also wanted to ensure that a stronger, more independent Russian state would retain all the benefits it had enjoyed as the most powerful republic in the USSR. The CIS represented the creation of a new political, economic and military arrangement among many of the constituent Soviet republics independent of Gorbachev.

Since its inception the goals, structure and problems of the CIS have resembled those of other intergovernmental organizations, such as the EUROPEAN UNION. Economically it sought to preserve a common market and a common currency among its members to preserve the business practices that had developed over the 69 years the USSR existed. It also sought to prevent the emergence of 12 separate currencies and the reduction in trade among the republics that would then result. Politically it required the cooperation and coordination of all participants on issues such as immigration, travel, the environment and international crime. On the issue of military defense, the CIS briefly held an edge over the European Union. Unlike its European counterpart's Common Foreign and Security Policy, all nations within the CIS pledged in 1992 to place their armed forces under a joined CIS command should a threat emerge to their collective security. The chief of the CIS armed forces also briefly shared joint jurisdiction with Yeltsin in any decision to use the strategic weapons of the former USSR.

While the principle of a joint military command produced unity among CIS states, it also deepened political divisions. Claiming that the Soviet Black Sea fleet was stationed in its territorial waters, Ukraine attempted to obtain sole possession of this sizable naval force, eventually resulting in its split between both Ukraine and Russia. By 1993 similar disputes between the central authority of the CIS and the emerging militaries of the new states led to the abolition of the joint military command. Thereafter Russia exercised total control over all strategic nuclear weapons the CIS inherited from the USSR. In 2003 the security component of the CIS suffered further damage when Russia was designated an observing member of NATO, whereas other CIS members such as Ukraine failed to obtain such privileged status.

The CIS has experienced other setbacks in its efforts to produce a coordinated policy. In economic matters it failed to ensure that all member states maintained the ruble as their official currency. In 1993 the republic of Kyrgyzstan began to print its own currency, the som, leading other states to follow suit in an effort to develop their own economies at the expense of trade with fellow CIS members.

Finally, the CIS failed to keep the peace among its member states. Civil wars broke out inside Georgia, Moldova and the North Caucasus region of Russia and Tajikistan. Two of its members—Armenia and Azerbaijan—have fought each other on several occasions. As a result of these problems the hope of a close-knit military, political and economic association has vanished among CIS members.

Commonwealth of Nations
Voluntary group of self-governing nations and dependencies of the UNITED KINGDOM, embracing certain affiliated states whose foreign activities are managed by the United Kingdom; formerly known as the British Commonwealth. The commonwealth is an offshoot of the BRITISH EMPIRE and includes members from all hemispheres. It developed out of the Statute of Westminster, an act of the British Parliament, passed in 1931, that acknowledged the right of self-rule for those states with dominion status within the British Empire. A free association, the commonwealth is constrained only by loyalty to the British Crown. The legislatures of the jurisdictions are equal to that of the British Parliament. The statute was considered an extension to the group of Imperial Conferences, begun in 1887, which were originally known as the Colonial Conferences. WORLD WAR I pushed the advancement of autonomy within the empire, and WORLD WAR II completed the procedure. Meetings are held on a regular basis for consultation, but no binding motions are made; the U.K., however, still plays an active role. Economic ties and trade agreements are emphasized.

The 53 members of the commonwealth are Antigua and Barbuda, Australia, Bahamas, Bangladesh, Barbados, Belize, Botswana, Brunei, Cameroon, Canada, Cyprus, Dominica, Fiji, Gambia, Ghana, Grenada, Guyana, India, Jamaica, Kenya, Kiribati, Lesotho, Malawi, Malaysia, Maldives, Malta, Mauritius, Mozambique, Namibia, Nauru, New Zealand, Nigeria, Pakistan, Papua New Guinea, Saint Kitts and Nevis, Saint Lucia, Saint Vincent and the Grenadines, Samoa, Seychelles, Sierra Leone, Singapore, Solomon Islands, South Africa, Sri Lanka, Swaziland, Tanzania, Tonga, Trinidad and Tobago, Tuvalu, Uganda, United Kingdom, Vanuatu, Zambia.

communism (Marxism, Marxism-Leninism)
Political, economic and social ideology formulated in the 19th century by Karl Marx and Friedrich Engels; it was embraced and "refined" in the 20th century by V. I. LENIN, MAO ZEDONG and numerous other theorist-practitioners. Communism has been one of the most powerful and pervasive ideologies of the 20th century, and also the most controversial. Its proponents insist that it presents the only rational and comprehensive program for correcting social ills and achieving an equitable society. Opponents point to the vast human suffering that has been inflicted in the name of communism.

In practical terms, 20th-century communism has emphasized the state ownership of all means of production, central planning of the economy and the guiding role of the COMMUNIST PARTY in all facets of society. Communism has also flourished in many places as a revolutionary movement dedicated to the overthrow of colonial, right-wing, authoritarian or democratic governments. Communism regards the party and the state as more important than the individual. The main features of 20th-century communism have been a totalitarian form of government, the use of terror and coercion to stifle political opposition or deviation, and the support of revolutionary movements throughout the world.

Communism gained hold first and foremost in Russia, where Lenin's BOLSHEVIK REVOLUTION (or October Revolution, 1917) eventually led to the Communist Party's domination of virtually every aspect of life in the country (see UNION OF SOVIET SOCIALIST REPUBLICS). According to Lenin, the "dictatorship of the proletariat" was to be simply one phase in the revolutionary transition to a purely communist society; however, this dictatorship proved to be a prevalent feature of communism. Lenin favored the spread of revolutionary communism to other nations. His successor, Joseph STALIN, adhered to a policy of communism "in one nation," consolidating his power and that of the party in the USSR.

After WORLD WAR II, however, communist regimes seized power in most countries of Eastern Europe. Many of these regimes were installed by the Soviets, whose army had occupied the region at the end of the war. A few (YUGOSLAVIA and, later, ALBANIA and ROMANIA) followed a policy independent from the USSR but generally employed similar methods in maintaining power (see STALINISM). Communism was also adopted in CHINA under Mao (see CHINESE CIVIL WAR OF 1945–1949), and communist revolutionary movements spread to many of the European colonies in Asia and Africa. The COLD WAR between (primarily) the USSR and the UNITED STATES was seen as a worldwide competition between communism and democracy.

Forty years of communism in Eastern Europe (and 70 years in the USSR) failed to bring about the transformation of society. By the late 1980s communism was being openly challenged in a number of Eastern European nations that had been under Communist governments since the end of World War II. In 1989–90, Communist governments were deposed or reformed in POLAND, CZECHOSLOVAKIA, HUNGARY, EAST GERMANY and ROMANIA. Elections in NICARAGUA also resulted in the ouster of the communist-oriented government of Daniel ORTEGA and the Sandinistas. In the USSR, Mikhail GORBACHEV's economic reforms (PERESTROIKA) and policy of openness (GLASNOST) signalled a departure from orthodox Soviet communism. Although Gorbachev's policies were intended to reform communism rather than destroy it, they indirectly led to the disintegration of the Soviet Union in December 1991. In Asia communist parties continue to dominate one-party states such as VIETNAM, NORTH KOREA and China. However, China developed a thriving capitalist economic system on its Pacific coast even as the Communist Party maintained its monopoly on political power.

Communist Party of the USSR

Following the RUSSIAN REVOLUTION (1917) the BOLSHEVIKS under LENIN emerged as the single, dominant party and adopted the name Communist Party (Bolsheviks). Under STALIN the party grew from a relatively small, elite group to a ruling bureaucracy with a much larger membership. In 1952 *Bolsheviks* was dropped from the party's official name. According to the rules adopted by the 22nd Congress of the party on October 31, 1961, the Communist Party of the Soviet Union "unites, on a voluntary basis, the more advanced, politically more conscious section of the working class, collective-farm peasantry and intelligentsia of the USSR," whose principal objects are to build a communist society by means of gradual transition from socialism to communism, to raise the material and cultural level of the people, to organize the defense of the country and to strengthen ties with the workers of other countries.

The party remained the sole and overwhelmingly dominant political force throughout the regimes of BREZHNEV and his short-lived successors, ANDROPOV and CHERNENKO. However, under GORBACHEV in the late 1980s, the party's structure and its role in Soviet society underwent profound changes. The constitution of the USSR was revised, the government structure was reformed and noncommunist politicians were elected to the new Congress of People's Deputies. Although the Communist Party remained a strong force, at the beginning of 1991 its future direction seemed unclear.

Up to the Gorbachev era, the party was built on the territorial-industrial principle. The supreme organ was the party congress; ordinary congresses were convened not less than once in four years. The congress elected a central committee, which met at least every six months, carried on the work of the party between congresses and guided the work of central Soviet and public organizations through party groups within them. The central committee formed a political bureau to direct the work of the central committee between plenary meetings, a secretariat to direct current work and a commission of party control to consider appeals against decisions about expulsion. Similar rules hold for the regional and territorial party organizations.

By the late 1970s over 398,340 primary party organizations existed in mills, factories, state machine and tractor stations, and other economic establishments; in collective farms and units of the Soviet army and navy; in villages, offices, educational establishments and so forth, where there were at least three party members. On January 1, 1978, nearly 42% of the members were industrial workers; 13% were collective farmers; and 44% were office and professional workers. Women accounted for 25.1% of all members. In 1981 the Communist Party had 17.5 million members; membership of the Young Communist League was 37.8 million in 1978. In December 1991, following the disintegration of the USSR, the Communist Party of the USSR dissolved into a series of parties within each former Soviet Socialist Republic, the largest and most influential being the Communist Party of the Russian Federation.

Comoros (Union of the Comoros [since 2002])

Four major, and several smaller, islands located in the Mozambique Channel of the Indian Ocean, 300 miles northeast of MADAGASCAR. In the 19th century FRANCE saw the strategic worth of the island of Mayotte and assumed control after negotiating a treaty with the ruling sultan. France claimed the remaining islands of Grand Comoro, Anjouan and Moheli to squelch imperial German development. By 1961 the Comoros had acquired internal self-control, and independence was claimed in 1975. Mayotte chose to remain French, but the new government opposed this and was supported by the UN General Assembly in 1979. Ahmed Abdallah was president from 1975 to 1989, except for a period (1975–78) when he was temporarily deposed by a left-wing coup. Abdallah was assassinated in 1989, and the country was run briefly by his top adviser, the French mercenary Bob Denard. After

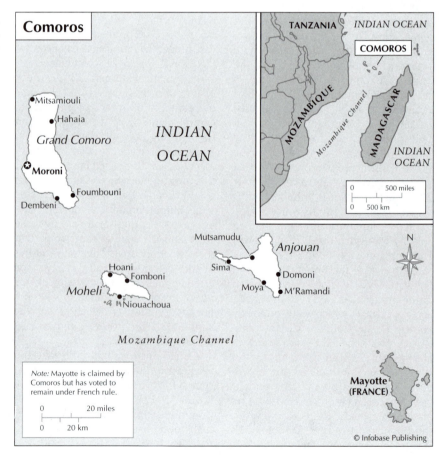

COMOROS

1912	Grande Comore and Anjouan, the main islands, join Mohéli to become a French colony, which is attached to Madagascar from 1914.
1961	Comoros achieves internal autonomy under a special statute.
1975	Chamber of Deputies votes a unilateral declaration of independence and proclaims Republic of the Comoros. President Abdallah is overthrown in coup. Comoros is admitted to the United Nations.
1976	Island of Mayotte rejects union with Comoros in two referendums.
1978	President Soilih is ousted in coup led by a French mercenary named Bob Denard and is killed as he tries to flee the country; former president Ahmed Abdallah and former vice president Mohammed Ahmed are installed as coleaders of the new government.
1984	Abdallah is reelected for a second six-year term.
1989	Abdallah is assassinated. Said Muhammad Djohar is named interim president.
1990	Djohar is elected president.
1996	In elections, Mohamed Taki Abdoulkarim is elected president in a contest of 15 candidates.
1997	The Organization of African Unity (OAU; later African Union) must come to the aid of the Comoros to put down an armed insurrection on the island of Anjouan; the rebels sought re-unification with France.
1998	In March, President Mohamed Taki Abdulkarim is reelected head of state and M. Ahmed Abdou is elected prime minister; in November, Abdulkarim dies and Tajiddine Ben Said Massounde assumes presidency.
1999	Anjouan representatives refuse to sign an OAU agreement proposing central administration of the three islands; Colonel Assoumani Azali takes control of the government in a bloodless coup.
2001	The OAU brokers a deal between the government and the secessionist islands of Anjouan and Mohéli.
2002	The presidential election for the Union of Comoros is marred by violence. Azali Assoumani is elected overall president of the reunited Comoros.
2003	Leaders and officials of Anjouan, Mohéli and Grande Comore sign a power-sharing deal.

Denard's departure, Said Mohammed Djohar became acting president, but the political situation remained uncertain. While some thought the peaceful election of Mohamed Abdulkarim Taki as president in 1996, as well as the establishment of Islamic law as national law, would lead to stability within Comoros, instability has plagued the archipelago state, leading to a coup in 1999 and a movement toward autonomy. In 2002 Colonel Azali Assoumani, the leader of the 1999 coup, was elected president. While Mayotte remains independent, the remaining islands of Anjouan, Mohéli, and Grande Comore signed a constitution in 2003 that allows them greater autonomy.

Comprehensive Test Ban Treaty (CTBT) A multilateral treaty signed by the U.S., Britain, China, France, and Russia, as well as 190 other nations, on September 24, 1996. According to the CTBT each participant agreed not to conduct any nuclear test or to encourage any other nation to conduct such a test. However, because of the manner in which the CTBT was written, it could only go into effect if all countries possessing or deemed capable of producing nuclear arms had signed and ratified the treaty. In 1999 the U.S. Senate dealt the first blow to the treaty when it voted 51-48 against ratifying it. Since the Senate's decision China, India, Israel and Pakistan (all known nuclear powers) have postponed ratification of the treaty.

Compton, Arthur Holly (1892–1962) American physicist. Compton came from a distinguished intellectual family. His father, Elias, was a professor of philosophy at Wooster College while his brother, Karl, also a physicist, became president of the Massachusetts Institute of Technology. Compton was educated at Wooster College and at

Princeton, where he earned his Ph.D. in 1916. He began his career by teaching at the University of Minnesota. After two years with the Westinghouse Corp. in Pittsburgh, he returned to academic life. In 1920 he was appointed professor of physics at Washington University, St. Louis. He spent most of his career at the University of Chicago, where he served as professor of physics from 1923 to 1945. Compton then returned to Washington University first as chancellor and then as professor of natural philosophy (1953–61). Compton is best remembered for the discovery and explanation in 1923 of the effect named for him for which, in 1927, he shared the NOBEL PRIZE in physics with Charles T. R. Wilson. His work on X-RAYS provided the first hard experimental evidence for the dual nature of electromagnetic radiation, that is, that it could behave both as a wave and a particle. This would be developed much further in the 1920s as one of the cornerstones of the new quantum physics. In the 1930s Compton concentrated on a major investigation into the nature of cosmic rays. During World War II he was an important figure in ATOMIC BOMB DEVELOPMENT and a member of the committee directing research on the MANHATTAN PROJECT. He also set up the Metallurgical Laboratory, in Chicago, which acted as a cover for the construction of the first atomic pile under the direction of Enrico FERMI and took responsibility for the production of plutonium. The book *Atomic Quest* (1956) is Compton's full account of this work.

Compton, Denis Charles Scott (*1918–1997*) English cricket player. Noted for his batting technique, entertaining style and courage, Compton established himself as one of English cricket's all-time greats. Despite losing six years of his career to World War II and being hampered by a series of knee injuries, Compton was the dominant batsman of his day. He made his county debut with Middlesex in 1936 and played for England the following year at age 19. In 1947 Compton scored 3,816 runs, 18 of them centuries. Overall Compton played 78 Test matches, scoring 5,807 runs and 17 centuries. He retired from first-class cricket in 1964 having scored 38,942 runs. Although best known as a cricketer, Compton also played soccer at the professional level. His soccer career was curtailed by his knee ailments, but he did gain an FA Cup winners medal with Arsenal in 1950.

Compton-Burnett, Dame Ivy (*1884–1969*) British novelist. Educated at Holloway College, Compton-Burnett received a degree in classics, which influenced her later work. Her first novel, *Delores* (1911), was an unsuccessful imitation of the work of George Eliot. Deeply affected by the tragedy of WORLD WAR I, she suffered a physical and emotional collapse and did not produce her first serious novel, *Pastors and Masters*, until 1925. It began an extraordinary series of 18 chilling—but not humorless—novels depicting late Victorian upper-class families and their dependents. Written almost entirely in dense, sometimes cryptic dialogue, her work explores the corrupting influence of power within families and the dark themes of incest, child abuse, murder and fraud. Later works include *A House and Its Head* (1935), *Manservant and Maidservant* (1947) and *A God and His Gifts* (1963). Defying conventional literary classification, her individualistic fiction has been described as the literary counterpart of POSTIMPRESSIONISM.

computers In the second half of the 20th century, the computer not only revolutionized business but also had a profound impact on personal life. The early stages of computer development were slow and painstaking. Vannevar BUSH designed a mechanical computer in 1930, and several other models were introduced during the 1930s. The first truly digital electronic computer, ENIAC, was invented in 1946; it was followed in 1951 by UNIVAC. The invention of the TRANSISTOR did away with the need for vacuum tubes and allowed for the miniaturization of computers. In 1959 IBM (International Business Machines) introduced its first fully transistorized computer. Many businesses began utilizing computers for accounting and recordkeeping, but it was not until the 1970s that the most significant computer revolution occurred. The perfection of the silicon microchip, which could hold thousands of miniaturized computer circuits, led to the invention of the **personal computer.** The APPLE II, designed by Steven Jobs and Stephen Wozniak, two young American entrepreneurs and computer wizards, was the first widely accepted personal computer. Entering the market in 1977, it revolutionized not only the entire computer industry but also the way in which individuals used computers. In less than a decade, the personal computer became a common tool in homes, schools and offices. Personal computers became increasingly popular with the emergence of the INTERNET as a commercial, communication and leisure network for individuals during the 1990s. In the meantime, the portable computer, or **laptop,** gradually replaced the desktop computer as the machine of choice for individual consumers. After the development of the first laptop by Osborne computers in 1981, IBM brought out the 5155 portable computer in 1984, and Apple released the first Macintosh portable (which later evolved into the Powerbook) in 1989. In 1993 the first Personal Digital Assistants (pen-based, handheld computers) reached the market.

Conant, James Bryant (*1893–1978*) American chemist. Conant studied at Harvard, earning his Ph.D. in 1916. He was professor of chemistry there (1919–33) and then president (1933–53). He had a multifaceted career as a research chemist, administrator, diplomat and educationalist. In the research phase he worked on organic reaction mechanisms and also showed that oxyhemoglobin contains ferrous iron (1923). During WORLD WAR II he was head of the National Defense Research Committee and deputy head of the Office of Scientific Research and Development; he played an important role in the ATOMIC BOMB DEVELOPMENT. On retiring from Harvard he became commissioner and then ambassador to Germany (1953–57) and wrote many controversial books on education.

concentration camps Places for confining political prisoners and prisoners of war. While the term *concentration camp* is most associated with the notorious prisons in NAZI GERMANY, the first concentration camps were established by Lord Kitchener and the British army during the BOER WAR in SOUTH AFRICA around 1900. After 1928, during the rule of Joseph STALIN in the USSR, millions of people were confined in labor camps for "reeducation," but many perished, particularly

Confessional Poets Although none of the major poets yoked together under the confessional heading would call themselves a formal group with a shared agenda, this term is used particularly to describe John BERRYMAN, Robert LOWELL and Lowell's protégés, notably Sylvia PLATH and Anne SEXTON. This piercingly subjective poetry is tinged with suffering and self-revelation. Its seminal work was Lowell's *Life Studies* (1959). In the 1970s the popularity of the Confessional Poets led to a spate of self-indulgent imitators, who saw such deeply personal statements as a means of approaching the human condition. At their best, the Confessional Poets established a new mode of discourse by making art from subject matter that had previously been taboo.

Congo, Democratic Republic of the Located in central equatorial Africa, the Democratic Republic of the

Survivors of a Nazi concentration camp. 1945 (LIBRARY OF CONGRESS, PRINTS AND PHOTOGRAPHS DIVISION)

in camps in the brutal arctic region. The Japanese also confined prisoners in harsh prison camps in wartime. The Nazis began establishing camps in 1933, DACHAU being among the first. The camps initially were used to confine communists and other political opponents; later homosexuals, Gypsies, JEWS and anyone deemed unsuitable by the Nazis were arrested. By the time WORLD WAR II began there were 22 camps where inmates were brutalized and used as slave labor. In 1941 Adolf HITLER conceived of the FINAL SOLUTION, a plan to exterminate all European Jews, and many camps were outfitted with gas chambers for mass murder. Victims' hair and bodies were collected for use in manufacturing. At some camps doctors performed medical experiments, usually on women and children, who were often killed. Many others were shot or starved. Between 7 and 11 million people were killed in the Nazi concentration camps. Some of the infamous camps include AUSCHWITZ, BERGEN-BELSEN, BUCHENWALD and TREBLINKA.

Conference on Security and Cooperation in Europe See HELSINKI ACCORDS.

ZAIRE/DEMOCRATIC REPUBLIC OF THE CONGO

1960	Belgium grants independence to the Congo; Patrice Lumumba becomes first prime minister; Province of Katanga, led by Moise Tshombe, breaks away, receiving support from Belgium; Lumumba government receives help from the UN to restore order.
1961	UN forces become involved in the fighting at Elisabethville to help end the Katanga secession, four months before they are given UN authority to use force.
1965	After renouncing the secession of Katanga and having gone into exile, Tshombe is invited to return and become prime minister; General Joseph Mobutu seizes power.
1971	Congo renamed Zaire.
1982	Attempt to form second political party is crushed.
1983	Katanga secession ends.
1990	At least 12 are murdered by a masked commando unit during a raid on student dissidents; Belgian foreign aid is subsequently frozen.
1993	Rival pro- and anti-Mobutu governments are created.
1996–97	Tutsi rebels capture much of eastern Zaire while Mobutu is abroad for medical treatment; rebels capture Kinshasa and rename the country Democratic Republic of Congo; Laurent Désiré Kabila is installed as president.
1998	Rebels backed by Uganda and Rwanda advance on Kinshasa, take control of much of the eastern part of the country; Zimbabwe, Angola and Namibia side with Kabila.
1999	Six African countries sign a cease-fire accord in Lusaka, Angola.
2001	President Kabila is assassinated by a member of his bodyguard; Joseph Kabila succeeds his father.
2002	Peace talks are held in South Africa; Kinshasa signs a power-sharing deal with Uganda-backed rebels; the presidents of Congo and Rwanda sign a peace accord under which Rwanda agrees to withdraw troops, and Congo agrees to disarm and arrest Rwandan Hutu gunmen blamed for killing millions of Tutsi in Rwanda's 1994 genocide; a peace deal is signed in South Africa between the government and main rebels.
2003	Kabila signs a transitional constitution, under which an interim government is to rule for two years, and he names a transitional government.
2004	Gunmen attack a military base in Kinshasa in an apparent coup attempt; rebels occupy Bukavu for a week.
2005	A new constitution, with text agreed to by warring factions, is adopted by the National Assembly.

Congo occupies an area of 905,328 square miles. First known as the Congo Free State (1885–1908) and ruled directly by King Leopold II of Belgium; subsequently called the BELGIAN CONGO (1908–60) and ruled by the Belgian government, the country achieved independence in 1960 and became the Republic of the Congo. Almost immediately, Katanga province, under its governor Moise TSHOMBE, seceded, and UNITED NATIONS troops arrived to help restore order. Intense fighting and controversy surround the events of the next few years. In 1965 General Joseph MOBUTU took control of the republic, changing the country's name to Zaire and Africanizing all place-names. From neighboring ANGOLA, exiled Katangese rebels invaded Zaire in 1977 and 1978, and Western and African countries sent troops to help quell the rebellion. The Katanga secession ended in 1983. During the 1980s Zaire experienced student protests and riots (1988–89) and charges of human-rights violations by its military. In 1997 Laurent KABILA led a multinational African force into Zaire, overthrew Mobutu and renamed the country the Democratic Republic of the Congo. The following year his former allies of RWANDA and UGANDA turned against him and invaded the country, sparking a bloody war with Kabila's forces and their African allies, ANGOLA, NAMIBIA and ZIMBABWE. In 2001 Kabila was assassinated; his son Joseph Kabila succeeded him as president. After waging war against the rebels for two years, Kabila signed a peace accord with the DROC and the MLC to end the fighting and establish a national unity government.

Congo, Republic of the (Congo-Brazzaville)

A nation of west-central Africa, densely covered by equatorial forest and marshland; formerly, the Middle Congo. In the late 19th century French colonial ambition was turned toward the interior of central Africa. The area covered by present-day Congo eventually became part of French Equatorial Africa and was governed by business interests as a private concession. By 1907 international anger compelled France to exercise some authority over rapacious private enter-prises, but the indigenous population and local economy (in the form of the ivory and rubber trade) had already suffered immensely. The Africans of the Congo were also exploited as workers to build the Congo-Ocean railway after WORLD WAR I; approximately 17,000 people died during its construction.

During WORLD WAR II the capital city of Brazzaville was a headquarters of the FREE FRENCH. In 1958 the Congo became an autonomous republic within the French Community; it gained full independence on August 15, 1960. Fulbert YOULOU, a former Catholic priest, was the first president. Marien Ngouabi grabbed power after a military coup in 1968 and allied the Congo with the USSR. He was assassinated in 1977, and the new military regime quickly renewed diplomatic ties with the U.S. and the West, although continuing a Marxist-Leninist state with close Soviet and Chinese affiliations. Political tensions between northern and southern tribes continued. In 1990 the Congolese Workers Party (PCT) abandoned Marxism, and two years later it sanctioned a new constitution that allowed for multiple political parties. However, these reforms failed to avert a civil war that began in 1993 and raged until April 2001, beginning anew in March 2002 and halted by a 2003 peace agreement.

Congress of Industrial Organizations

See AMERICAN FEDERATION OF LABOR AND CONGRESS OF INDUSTRIAL ORGANIZATIONS.

Congress Party

Indian political party established in 1885. The National Congress, initially an association to inculcate Indians into government service, was supported by the British viceroys prior to George CURZON whose 1905 splitting of Bengal brought about violent opposition by Congress and a rift between its more radical leader, Bal Gangadhar Tilak, and the more moderate, Western-influenced G. K. Kokhale. Mohandas K. GANDHI became its primary leader in 1920 and retained an enormous influence until his assassination in 1948. He established the doctrine of nonviolent civil disobedience to effect political change. The Congress Party took office in six provinces in 1937, but its leaders refused to support entry into WORLD WAR II, because the British neglected to check Indian opinion on the issue. Congress leaders were subsequently interned from 1942 to 1945. Following independence in 1947, the Congress Party came to power under Prime Minister Jawaharlal NEHRU with sustaining, broad-based support. He was succeeded by Lal Bahadur SHASTRI in 1964, but Shastri died suddenly in 1966. At that time a group of party bosses known as the Syndicate were vying for control of the party, but Indira GANDHI became the dominant figure of the party following the 1971 elections, and she remained so until her assassination in 1984. Although she and the Congress Party were out of power between 1977 and 1980, her role was so strong that the party is now labeled Congress (I) for Indira Congress, to distinguish it from other offshoots of the party. Congress (I) remained India's dominant party under the leadership of

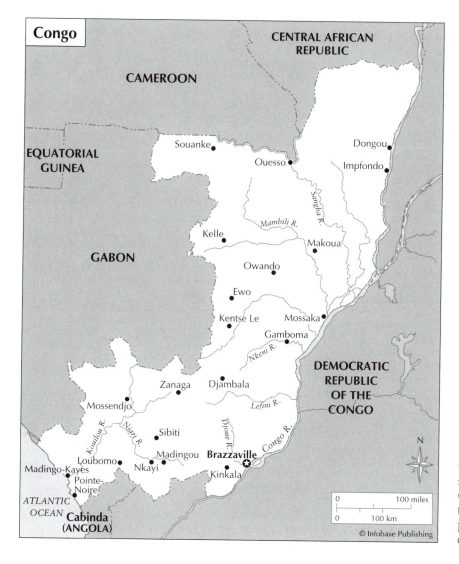

Congo

REPUBLIC OF THE CONGO

1960	The Republic of the Congo becomes an independent republic under President Fulbert Youlou.
1963	Youlou resigns office in the wake of mass demonstration and riots; Alphonse Massamba-Débat is named president.
1964	Mouvement National de la Révolution (MNR) is organized as the sole political party in the Congo, with its youth wing, Jeunesse du Mouvement National de la Révolution (JMNR), as a paramilitary force.
1968	Army seizes power following army-JMNR confrontation; Marien Ngouabi, the army commander in chief, replaces Massamba-Débat as president.
1969	Parti Congolais du Travail (PCT) replaces the MNR as the sole political party of the country; Republic of the Congo is renamed People's Republic of the Congo as the nation continues its leftward course.
1971	Student riots erupt in Brazzaville.
1973	New constitution, independent Congo's fourth, is approved in nationwide referendum; elected National Assembly is revived. Congo withdraws from French Community.
1977	President Ngouabi is assassinated by a four-man commando squad. Joachim Yhombi-Opango assumes the presidency as head of an 11-member military committee. Constitution is suspended and the National Assembly is dissolved. Former president Massamba-Débat is executed for plotting assassination. Diplomatic relations are reestablished with the United States.
1979	President Yhombi-Opango steps down and is replaced by Denis Sassou-Nguesso. The constitution of 1973 is readopted and is overwhelmingly approved in a national referendum; the National Assembly is reestablished.
1984	President Sassou-Nguesso is reelected with expanded powers. Former president Yhombi-Opango is released from prison.
1987	The government suppresses a coup by military officers. Yhombi-Opango is imprisoned for complicity with the rebels.
1991	Congo officially becomes a multiparty state.
1992	In free presidential elections, Pascal Lissouba defeats General Sassou-Nguesso.
1993	Franc zone currencies are devalued by 50%, spurring 61% inflation in Congo; bloody fighting erupts between Lissouba government forces and supporters of Sassou-Nguesso over disputed parliamentary elections.
1994	A cease-fire is established between government and opposition forces.
1997	Following outbreak of a civil war, General Sassou-Nguesso proclaims himself president with the support of the military; Lissouba goes into hiding in Burkina Faso.
1999	Sassou-Nguesso and Lissouba sign a peace treaty providing for integrated military forces and demilitarized political parties.
2002	Sassou-Nguesso runs unopposed in the country's second presidential elections. Fighting erupts between the Congolese government and "Ninja" rebels, who name themselves after the famous Japanese warriors, and thousands of civilians are driven from their homes in the Pool region. One hundred people are killed.
2003	The government signs a peace agreement with "Ninja" warriors to end hostilities in the Pool region. Rebel leader Pastor Ntumi consents to the return of governmental law to the area.
2004	Kimberley Process, a world diamond trade supervisory body, drops Congo from its list of countries recognized as dealing lawfully in the gem trade, thereby forbidding the country from doing business with member nations of the organization.
2005	The World Bank Board of Executive Directors awards Congo an Economic Recovery Credit worth $30 million in support of efforts made by the government to spur economic growth and alleviate poverty.

Rajiv GANDHI until his defeat in 1990. Following Rajiv Gandhi's assassination in 1991, no individual became a dominant force in the party, leading to political infighting that contributed to its fall from power in 1996. In 1998 Sonia Gandhi, the Italian-born widow of Rajiv Gandhi, assumed control of the party. Although she increased its support among Muslims and impoverished Indians, the party fared poorly in the 1999 elections. In May 2004 Gandhi led the Congress Party to victory over the BHARATIYA JANATA PARTY (BJP)–led coalition but declined to accept the office of prime minister in the new government.

Connally, John Bowden (1917–1993)
U.S. politician. Connally was twice elected governor of Texas (1963–69) and was secretary of the navy under President John F. KENNEDY. He was seriously wounded in Dallas during the shooting that claimed President Kennedy's life in 1963. Originally a conservative Democrat, he joined the REPUBLICAN PARTY in 1975, having served as President Richard M. NIXON's secretary of the treasury in 1971–72. Connally retired to private life in 1976. His investments in real estate toppled during the decline of Texas oil fortunes in the 1980s, and he entered bankruptcy in 1988.

Connally, Thomas "Tom" (1877–1963)
American politician. A Texas Democrat, Connally entered the House of Representatives in 1917 but resigned to serve in WORLD WAR I. After the war he returned to the House, gained a seat on the Foreign Affairs Committee and began a lifelong interest in diplomacy. Supporting Woodrow WILSON, he campaigned for U.S. involvement in the LEAGUE OF NATIONS. During the 1920s he represented the U.S. at several international conferences. Elected to the Senate in 1928, he later opposed Franklin D. ROOSEVELT's NEW DEAL but supported the president's foreign policy. After Harry S. TRUMAN became president, Connally was a frequent adviser on foreign affairs and led the fight for ratification of the UNITED NATIONS charter. With Republican senator Arthur VANDENBURG, he championed the TRUMAN DOCTRINE and the MARSHALL PLAN, but he expressed reservations about NATO. He supported the TAFT-HARTLEY ACT and opposed civil rights legislation. He retired from the Senate in 1952.

Connery, Sir Sean Thomas (1929–)
Popular Scottish actor known for his suave and manly roles in adventure and suspense films. Born in Edinburgh, Scotland, Connery at age 15 enlisted in the Royal Navy in World War II, and on his return to England he became a physical fitness addict. In the 1950s his muscular build and dashing good looks led to a career in modeling and then to theater and television work. He played bit parts and featured roles in several poorly received films (both British and American), until he landed the title role in a low-budget spy thriller Dr. No (1962). Based on Ian FLEMING's internationally famous secret agent, JAMES BOND (007), it became a mega-hit and boosted Connery to stardom. He continued his debonair but gritty portrayal of Bond in From Russia with Love (1963), Goldfinger (1964), Thunderball (1965), You Only Live Twice (1967), Diamonds Are Forever (1971) and, 12 years later, Never Say Never Again. Connery was equally larger than life in The Hill (1965), The Molly Maguires (1970), The Man Who Would Be King (1975) and Indiana Jones and the Last Crusade (1989). In 1987 Connery received the best supporting actor ACADEMY AWARD for his performance in The Untouchables. In July 2000 Connery was knighted by Queen Elizabeth II.

Connolly, Cyril Vernon (1903–1974)
British critic, editor and author. Born in Coventry, Connolly was educated at Eton and at Balliol College, Oxford, where he was acquainted with Graham GREENE. He began working as a journalist and critic and was soon contributing regularly to The New Statesman. In 1939 he and Stephen SPENDER founded the literary magazine Horizon, which Connolly edited until its demise in 1950. He also served as literary editor of the Observer from 1942 to 1943 and from 1951 until his death was a book reviewer for The Sunday Times. His sole novel, The Rock Pool (1936), is a clever satire about a smug British stockbroker attempting to gain entrée into an artistic colony on the French Riviera. Other important works include Enemies of Promise (1938), a partly autobiographical collection of essays; The Unquiet Grave (1944), a collection of thoughts and aphorisms published under the pseudonym Palimurus (the drowned Trojan pilot in the Aeneid); and The Evening Colonnade (1973), essays.

Connolly, James (1870–1916)
Irish labor leader and revolutionary. A socialist, Connolly spent some time in the U.S. at the beginning of the 20th century and was an organizer for the radical Industrial Workers OF THE WORLD (IWW). He returned to IRELAND to lead the dockworkers in Belfast. In Dublin he and union leader James Larkin organized the powerful Irish Transport and General Workers Union. During a 1913 lockout of the workers, he organized a citizen army. Connolly did not share the romantic nationalist fervor of Patrick PEARSE and other anti-British rebels, but he joined them as a leader of the EASTER RISING in 1916. He was wounded during the fighting; after the rebellion was suppressed, he was one of 16 rebels executed by the British.

Connolly, Maureen Catherine (1934–1969)
American tennis player. At 16, "Little Mo" Connolly was the youngest woman in nearly half a century to win the U.S. title; she was also the first woman ever to win the U.S., British, French and Australian championships in a single year (1953). Her string of victories continued with U.S., French and Wimbledon titles in 1954. After suffering a serious injury in a horseback riding accident, she was forced to retire from tennis at the age of 20. She embarked upon a successful coaching career, cut short when she died of cancer at the age of 35.

Connors, James Scott "Jimmy" (1952–)
American tennis player. Connors's heart and spirit revolutionized how the world viewed the genteel sport. Connors cursed on court, challenged umpires and drove himself mercilessly. One of the dominant players of the 1970s, he had his best year in 1974, when he won three of the Big Four tournaments—the U.S. and Australian Opens and Wimbledon. That year he entered into a much-publicized engagement with the women's champion, Chris EVERT, but both went on to marry others. A perennial favorite at the U.S. Open, he won that title five times, the last in 1983. He played in

occasional tournaments into the 1990s, vowing to compete as long as he continued to enjoy the sport. In 1998 Connors was inducted into the International Tennis Hall of Fame.

Conrad, Charles "Pete" *(1930–1999)* U.S. astronaut. In his four NASA missions—from his first flight on *Gemini 5* in August 1965 until his last flight on *Skylab 2* in May–June 1973—Conrad logged approximately 1,180 hours in space, including 14 hours of EVA (extravehicular activity). In between he commanded *Gemini 11* (September 1966), which established a world altitude record at that time of 850 miles, and, as commander of *Apollo 12* (November 1969), landed on the Moon and spent over 30 hours romping over its surface.

Conrad, Joseph (Jósef Teodor Konrad Nalecz Kozeniowski) *(1857–1924)* Polish-British novelist. Conrad was born in the Ukraine to Polish parents. His father's anti-Russian political views caused the family to be exiled to northern Russia. Conrad's mother died there when he was seven. Following their return to Poland, Conrad's father died when he was 11 and his uncle, Thaddeus Bobrowski, became his guardian and mentor. In 1874 he went to Marseille and became a sailor; he was essentially educated at sea. His experiences and travels provided him with the raw material for the best of his later work. Conrad became a British subject in 1886, continuing his seafaring career until 1894, when he settled in England, married and turned to writing. Although Conrad did not learn to speak English until he was 20, he eventually became one of the most renowned 20th-century English-language novelists. His first two novels, *Almayer's Folly* (1895) and *An Outcast of the Islands* (1896), demonstrate his unfamiliarity with both the English language and the craft of writing, but by *The Nigger of the Narcissus* (1897), *Lord Jim* (1900) and THE HEART OF DARKNESS (1902), he had found his characteristic voice. These three works are now among his best known, but Conrad did not realize much popular success until the publication of *Chance* in 1913. Many consider his finest novel to be *Nostromo* (1904), a profound study of the corrupting effects of colonialism and

greed in a small South American town; *The Secret Agent* (1907), about anarchist revolutionaries in turn-of-the-century London, and *Under Western Eyes* (1911), about the political and spiritual state of contemporary Russia, have also been highly praised. Conrad's work has been described as impressionistic, and while it takes place in varied (often exotic) locations, it all reflects his fundamental concern with man's physical and moral weakness. Early in his career Conrad collaborated with Ford Maddox FORD on *The Inheritors* (1900) and *Romance* (1903), but personal disagreements ended their association. Conrad's writing was admired by Arnold BENNETT, Henry JAMES and John GALSWORTHY, but during his lifetime his serious work never found a large audience. He is now considered, along with James, as the most important transitional figure between 19th-century realism and 20th-century MODERNISM. His work has had a significant influence on such later writers as Graham GREENE, John LE CARRÉ, V. S. NAIPAUL and Paul Theroux.

Conroy, Jack (John Wesley Conroy) *(1899–1990)* American novelist and poet. The son of a union organizer, Conroy was born in a coal mining camp in Missouri and spent much of his early life traveling the country as a migrant worker. Conroy edited the verse collection *Unrest* (1929) and served as editor of *Rebel Poet* from 1931 to 1932, *Anvil* from 1933 to 1937 and *New Anvil* from 1939 to 1941. In these journals he published the early works of Nelson ALGREN and Richard WRIGHT, among others. Conroy is best known for his novel *The Disinherited* (1933), which received little attention when it was first published but was critically acclaimed when it was rereleased in 1963. Conroy's writing reflected his left-leaning, proletarian politics, which, unlike many other young rebels, he maintained throughout his life. Conroy's work was collected in *The Jack Conroy Reader* (1980); he also wrote children's books and some works under the pseudonyms Tim Brennan, Hoder Morine and John Norcross.

conservatism Political and social philosophy, or set of attitudes, contrasted to LIBERALISM. Like liberalism,

20th-century conservatism has its roots in 18th-century thought. Irish statesman Edmund Burke, economist Adam Smith and several founding fathers of the U.S. (notably Alexander Hamilton) were forerunners of modern conservatism. Broadly speaking, conservatism is marked by respect for tradition, suspicion of social change and of movements that advocate radical change, and a cautious if not pessimistic view of human nature. Many conservatives also believe that political power should be held by an educated elite. In the course of the 20th century these tenets have often been simplified, distorted or misused both by proponents and critics. Conservatism has sometimes been obscured by particular issues of the moment and confused with authoritarianism, racism and even FASCISM.

In the U.S., political conservatism is generally associated with the REPUBLICAN PARTY, although there have been liberal Republicans and conservative Democrats and many who did not follow strict conservative or liberal views on all issues. Prominent conservative U.S. presidents include William Howard TAFT and Herbert HOOVER. Calvin COOLIDGE was also conservative in that he took a laissez-faire stance on most issues. Richard M. NIXON took some conservative positions, but his reliance on public expenditure in domestic welfare programs and, more significantly, his blatant disregard of constitutional principles in the WATERGATE scandal were uncharacteristic of classical conservatism. Like Nixon, Ronald REAGAN shared an active opposition to COMMUNISM—a fundamental feature of 20th-century conservatism—but both were pragmatic in their dealings with Soviet and Chinese Communist leaders. Reagan's conservatism introduced a new radical emphasis on "free-market" economics, called "Reaganomics" by its detractors. Other notable American conservatives include Russell KIRK, William F. BUCKLEY, Jr., George WILL and 1964 Republican presidential candidate Barry GOLDWATER. A more radical and activist form of conservatism, often embraced by former liberals and socialists who have rejected their earlier beliefs, is known as **neoconservatism.**

In the United Kingdom, conservative principles found a natural home in the CONSERVATIVE PARTY. Stanley BALD-WIN and Harold MACMILLAN were main-stream conservatives, but no one more embodied the central values of conservatism than Winston S. CHURCHILL, who rallied the British people against Adolf HITLER and NAZISM in the darkest days of WORLD WAR II. Churchill's conservatism was manifested in his faith in British political and social institutions as they had evolved over the centuries and in his uncompromising opposition to TOTALITARIANISM, whether in the form of German Nazism or Soviet communism. Churchill's conservatism was also colored by his imperialism and by his belief in the natural superiority of Western civilization and especially of the English-speaking peoples. Margaret THATCHER, who governed Britain throughout the 1980s, revived many of the features of Churchill's conservatism but, like Reagan, added an emphasis on market economics and a determination to uproot all traces of the WELFARE STATE. Some traditional conservatives (see WETS) felt that Thatcher's determined assault on established British institutions was contrary to the main tenets of conservatism, which stress the preservation of existing institutions. In 1997 the Conservative Party's long period in power ended when John MAJOR lost to Labour leader Tony BLAIR. In the U.S. conservatives continued to stress traditional values as well as tax reduction and welfare reform.

Conservative Party British political party, established in 1832. The well-organized Conservative Party has constituency committees in all districts in Great Britain and Northern Ireland joined at the national level by the National Union of Conservative and Unionist Associations, which holds an annual rallying conference. The party maintains a well-financed Central Office as well as 11 area offices in England and Wales. Current Conservative policy is distinguished by the party's commitment to monetarist economics (see MONETARISM). Its domestic policies generally coincide with those of conservative Republicans in the U.S. Additionally, the Conservative Party favors British rule in Northern Ireland, a strong military defense, firm allegiance to NATO, and membership in the EUROPEAN ECONOMIC COMMUNITY.

Conservatives were in power at the turn of the century and until 1905, when Prime Minister BALFOUR left office and the party went into eclipse. In 1912 a faction of the LIBERAL PARTY opposed to Irish HOME RULE allied itself to the Conservatives, and the word *Unionist* replaced *Constitutional* in the National Union of Conservative and Constitutional Associations, the party's formal name. The party came to power again in 1922 under the leadership of Bonar LAW, who was succeeded by BALDWIN, Neville CHAMBERLAIN and Winston CHURCHILL. The LABOUR PARTY came to power after WORLD WAR II and instituted many social welfare policies (see WELFARE STATE). Conservatives returned to power in 1951 with Churchill as prime minister until 1955, when EDEN took office. Following the SUEZ CANAL crisis, Eden's government was disgraced, and he left office in 1957. Under the leadership of Harold MACMILLAN, the Conservatives won the 1959 elections. A dispute over his successor and the appointment of Lord Home (see Alec DOUGLAS-HOME) led to the adoption in 1965 of the party's current balloting system of choosing its leader. The Conservative Party remained in power until 1974, when labor conflicts brought about its defeat. In 1975 Margaret THATCHER became leader of the party and became Britain's first female prime minister when the Conservatives returned to power in 1979. She oversaw a sweeping Conservative victory in 1983. While Thatcher was criticized for her dogmatic policies and inability to lower unemployment, she remained in office longer than any prime minister in the preceding 150 years. She stepped down in 1990 and was succeeded by her protégé, John MAJOR. In the 1997 national elections, the Conservatives lost their parliamentary majority, and Labour leader Tony BLAIR became the new prime minister.

Constantine I (King of the Hellenes) (*1868–1923*) Married to Sophia, sister of Germany's kaiser WILHELM II, he came to the throne after the assassination of his father, George I, and reigned from 1913 to 1917 and 1920 to 1922. He was opposed to the pro-Allied policies of Greek premier Eleutherios VENIZELOS and in 1917 was forced to abdicate in favor of his son, Alexander. After

Alexander's death in 1920, a plebiscite restored him as monarch. When Greece was defeated by the Turks in 1922, the king was widely held accountable and was again forced to abdicate. He was succeeded by his son, George II.

Constantine II (King of the Hellenes) (*1940– *) King of Greece (1964–73). He succeeded to the throne upon the death of his father, King Paul. After a military junta staged a coup in 1967, Constantine unsuccessfully sought to overthrow the new government. He fled to Italy, and in 1973 a republic was declared and he was formally deposed. A 1974 national referendum opposed his return to the throne. In 1994 the Greek government stripped Constantine of his citizenship.

Constantinople Agreements Secret accords provided to RUSSIA by Great Britain and France in the spring of 1915. The Constantinople Agreements promised that the city of Constantinople (Istanbul), parts of the Bosphorus Strait and the Dardanelles would be ceded to the Russian Empire upon an Allied victory in WORLD WAR I. The agreements provided long sought-after territory to Russia as an inducement to Czar NICHOLAS II not to conclude a separate peace with Germany. After the RUSSIAN REVOLUTION, the Bolsheviks repudiated czarist agreements, and in 1918 they angered Turkey, Britain and the U.S. by publishing the secret Constantinople treaties.

constructivism Abstract art movement that was originated in Russia in 1913 by the artist Vladimir TATLIN. Major figures in the movement included Naum GABO, Antoine PEVSNER and Alexander RODCHENKO. The works of the constructivists emphasized abstract geometric shapes that were inspired by modern machine technology. The constructivists denied that art required a socially useful purpose, but they did advocate the use in works of art of modern, nonclassical materials such as glass and plastic. Constructivism was condemned by the Soviet government in 1922. Most of the artists in the movement immigrated to other parts of Europe. As a result, constructivism exercised a substantial influence upon the de STIJL movement in

Holland and the teachings of the BAUHAUS in Germany.

consumer price index (CPI) The consumer price index, also known as the cost of living index, is a monthly U.S. government index that measures consumer prices; it is widely used to set wage increases and other price-level changes. The index, maintained by the Bureau of Labor Statistics, attempts to present a picture of the average household's costs of living and has been compiled for many years, which allows yearly comparisons of price changes. Currently, prices are represented as a percentage of the prices in the base year of 1967. In other words, the index for 1967 is 100, and later years are all in excess of 100.

The bureau carefully selects and weights purchases of goods and services, like food, clothing and transportation, to typify average household expenditures. The CPI is also tabulated for major metropolitan areas, for commodity and service groups and for individual items.

contras Rebel force in NICARAGUA opposed to the left-wing Sandinista regime of Daniel ORTEGA SAAVEDRA. Many of the contras had been members of the Nicaraguan National Guard during the SOMOZA regime; others had fought in the revolution against Somoza but were disillusioned with Ortega's Marxist methods. Operating from bases in HONDURAS and sometimes inside Nicaragua itself, the contras received U.S. military aid until June 1984, when the U.S. Congress voted to cut their funding. U.S. president Ronald REAGAN was a strong supporter of the contras, hailing them as freedom fighters. The Reagan administration's zeal to aid the contras helped lead to the 1986 IRAN-contra scandal. Later in the decade the contras entered into negotiations with the Sandinista regime; they laid down their arms in return for a promise of amnesty and free elections. The upset election of Violeta CHAMORRO and the defeat of Ortega in 1989 was widely viewed as a political vindication of the contras' cause.

Coogan, Jackie *(1914–1984)* Coogan was the first child star in movie history. In 1919, at age four, he starred in Charlie CHAPLIN's *The Kid* and became an overnight success. In 1923 he led

Rudolph VALENTINO and Douglas FAIRBANKS Sr. in box-office popularity. At age 21 he discovered that his mother and stepfather had squandered the more than $2 million he had earned. This incident prompted the passage of a California law requiring that the earnings of juvenile actors be deposited in court-administered trust funds. In all, Coogan appeared in more than 100 movies and 800 television programs.

Cook, Bill *(1896–1986)* Canadian hockey player. Before the advent of Gordie HOWE, he was regarded as the premier right winger in the National Hockey League. He was with the New York Rangers for 12 years, captaining the team from its inception in 1926 until his retirement after the 1936–37 season. He led the Rangers to two Stanley Cup championships. He was elected to the Hockey Hall of Fame in 1952.

Cook, Frederick *(1865–1940)* American physician and discredited explorer. Cook served as a surgeon on Robert PEARY's exploratory arctic expedition of 1891–92 and took part in a Belgian expedition in ANTARCTICA in 1897–99. In 1909 he announced that he had reached the NORTH POLE in 1908, a year before Peary's successful expedition. Cook described his feat in *My Attainment of the Pole* (1909) and for a short time enjoyed worldwide fame. However, he was unable to prove that he had reached the Pole, and after his own journey Peary challenged Cook's claims. Cook's claim that he had scaled Alaska's Mt. McKinley in 1906 was also questioned, and he was eventually declared a fraud. However, he continued to insist that he had told the truth about his expeditions. In 1923 Cook was convicted of mail fraud in a crooked investment scheme and spent 10 years in prison before he was pardoned by President Franklin D. ROOSEVELT in 1933. He died in poverty. In 1988, when the NATIONAL GEOGRAPHIC SOCIETY found that Peary may have missed the North Pole by as much as 60 miles, some support for Cook's claims resurfaced, although many scholars believe that neither man reached the North Pole at all.

Cooke, (Alfred) Alistair *(1908–2004)* Anglo-American journalist, commentator and author. Born in Manchester, Cooke was educated at Jesus College, Cambridge, and at Yale

and Harvard. He went to the U.S. in 1932 to study drama at Yale with the intention of becoming a theater director but became interested in the larger theater of America itself. Cooke became an American citizen in 1941. He had been a film critic for the BBC, but in 1936 he began a radio commentary about the U.S. that became *Letters from America* in 1946 and thus started his career as an interpreter of the U.S. for the British. His broadcasts, conversational and keenly observed, became enormously popular, and the program is listed in *THE GUINNESS BOOK OF RECORDS* as the longest-running radio talk show in the world. Cooke's early writing, such as *Garbo and the Night Watchman* (1937), reflect his interest in acting. His numerous articles and commentaries have been collected in such works as *One Man's America* (1952) and *The Americans: Fifty Talks on Our Life and Times* (1979). Cooke was well known to Americans as the host for the television programs *Omnibus* (1952–61), *International Zone* (1961–67) and *Masterpiece Theatre* (1971–92). His varied other work included *Return to Albion: American in England 1760–1940* (1979), *The Patient Has the Floor* (1986) and *America Observed: The Newspaper Years of Alistair Cooke* (1988), a collection of his journalism.

Cook Islands (Hervey Islands) Nation comprised of 15 scattered islands in the Pacific Ocean, 2,000 miles northeast of NEW ZEALAND. The islands were acquired by New Zealand in 1901 and became autonomous in 1965. In 1986 the prime minister declared the Cook Islands a neutral country; the nation is also part of the South Pacific Nuclear Free Zone. The population, mostly of Polynesia descent, numbers approximately 21,000.

Coolidge, Calvin *(1872–1933)* Thirtieth president of the UNITED STATES (1923–29). After studying law and graduating from Amherst College in 1895, Coolidge settled in Northampton, Massachusetts. Elected to the state legislature in 1912, he quickly rose through political ranks. Elected governor of Massachusetts in 1919, he gained national fame for his stern handling of a Boston police strike in that year. He was nominated for the vice presidency by the Republicans on the Warren HARDING

Calvin Coolidge, 30th president of the United States

ticket of 1920. Harding died in office, and Coolidge was sworn in as president on August 2, 1923. Coolidge's administration coincided with an era of great prosperity that preceded the GREAT DEPRESSION of the 1930s. His administration succeeded in reducing the national debt, and he was elected by a landslide in 1924. Although eligible for a second, full term, Coolidge declined the opportunity in 1928.

Coolidge, William D. (*1873–1975*) American inventor. Coolidge was a researcher for General Electric for nearly 40 years (1905–44). While at GE he developed a ductile tungsten filament (1908), which is still used in electric lightbulbs. In 1913 he invented the X-RAY tube that became the prototype for modern X-ray tubes.

Cooper, Lady Diana (dowager viscountess Norwich, Diana Olivia Winifred Maud Manners) (*1892–1986*) British actress and socialite. Lady Diana Cooper was a legendary beauty and glittering social personality of British high society in the 1920s and 1930s. After a brief career in silent films, she was offered the part of the Madonna in Max REINHARDT's theatrical pageant *The Miracle*. From 1923 to 1935 she toured with the production on and off on both sides of the Atlantic. She became one of the world's most photographed women, and her income enabled her to further the po-

litical ambitions of her husband, Alfred Duff Cooper. After his death in 1954, she published three witty volumes of memoirs. She was the model for Mrs. Stitch in Evelyn WAUGH's comic novel *Scoop*.

Cooper, Gary (Frank J. Cooper) (*1901–1961*) American movie actor, born in Montana to English parents; from the late 1920s through the 1950s Cooper may have had more successes and fewer failures than any other Hollywood actor. After working as an extra in such silent westerns as *The Thundering Herd* (1925), Cooper became an established star only a year later, with his featured role in *The Winning of Barbara Worth*. Equally adept at westerns, comedies and dramatic films, his magnetic appeal as "the strong, silent type"—and a genuine acting ability—made box-office hits of *The Virginian* (1929), *Morocco* (1930), *City Streets* (1931), *Design for Living* (1934), *For Whom the Bell Tolls* (1943) and many others. His legendary status and continuing reputation rest on such classics as *Mr. Deeds Goes to Town* (1936), *Beau Geste* (1939), *Meet John Joe* (1941), *Ball of Fire* (1941), *The Pride of the Yankees* (1942), *Love in the Afternoon* (1957) and his ACADEMY AWARD–winning roles in *Sergeant York* (1941) and *High Noon* (1952). Cooper died of cancer at only 60 years of age, but in his brief lifetime he produced an impressive body of work that earned him a special Academy Award in 1960.

Cooper, Gordon (*1927– *) U.S. astronaut. Youngest of the original "Mercury Seven" astronauts selected by NASA in 1959, Cooper made the sixth and last flight in the MERCURY series (May 15–16, 1963). He orbited the Earth 22 times, at that time a record exceeding the combined total of all previous Mercury missions. The self-assured and thrill-seeking Cooper, who had made NASA officials nervous by his love for fast cars and boats, took his first mission so much in stride that he fell asleep inside the spacecraft during one of the mission's almost inevitable "holds." Cooper's second and final mission was *Gemini 5* (August 21–29, 1965), with fellow astronaut Pete CONRAD. The two spent eight days in space and set a record at that time of 120 revolutions around the Earth. Cooper, who once said "I'm *planning* on getting to the Moon, I *think* I'll get

to Mars," didn't get a chance to visit either; he retired from NASA in July 1970 to enter private industry.

Cooper, Irving S. (*1922–1985*) American brain surgeon. Cooper pioneered in the development of surgical techniques, including cryogenic surgery, for treating Parkinson's disease and other neurological disorders. He also developed a "pacemaker" brain implant of benefit to epileptics, stroke victims and victims of cerebral palsy.

Cooper, Leon Neil (*1930– *) American physicist. Cooper was educated at Columbia where he earned his Ph.D. in 1954. After brief spells at the Institute for Advanced Study at Princeton, the University of Illinois and Ohio State University, he moved in 1958 to Brown University and was later (1962) appointed to a professorship of physics. Cooper's early work was in nuclear physics. In 1955 he began work with John BARDEEN and John Robert Schrieffer on the theory of superconductivity. In 1956 he showed theoretically that at low temperatures electrons in a conductor could act in bound pairs (now called **Cooper pairs**). Bardeen, Cooper and Schrieffer showed that such pairs act together with the result that there is no electrical resistance to flow of electrons through the solid. The resulting BCS theory stimulated further theoretical and experimental work on superconductivity and won its three authors the 1972 NOBEL PRIZE in physics. Cooper has also worked on the superfluid state at low temperatures and, in a different field, on the theory of the central nervous system.

Copeau, Jacques (*1879–1949*) French theatrical director, actor and critic. Copeau was a leading force in French theater in the first decades of the 20th century. He was best known for his insistence that the tenets of realism were unnecessarily constricting for theatrical productions. Copeau, whose troupe of actors at the Théâtre du Vieux-Colombier in the 1910s included Charles DULLIN and Louis Jouvet, emphasized a focus on the play itself as opposed to elaborate set design. His productions of Molière, Shakespeare and others featured strong acting, dramatic lighting and a simplified-Elizabethan style stage. In 1924 Copeau formed a highly regarded troupe of actors—called Les Copiaus—whom he trained in mime and other techniques. In 1936 he became a director of the prestigious Comédie-Française.

Copland, Aaron *(1900–1990)* Dean of modern American composers, whose popular works include the ballet *Rodeo* and *The Fanfare for the Common Man.* Copland was born of Russian immigrant parents (originally named Kaplan) and grew up in Brooklyn, New York, where he studied piano with his sister. Later in Paris at the Fontainebleau School of Music he became Nadia Boulanger's first student and met conductor Serge Koussevitzky, who subsequently commissioned three of Copland's most important works, *Music for the Theatre* (1925), the *Piano Concerto* (1927) and the *Third Symphony* (1946). Copland's best-known music is full of characteristic "Americanisms," most notably the quotations from cowboy songs and folk tunes in the ballets *Billy the Kid* (1938), *Rodeo* (1942) and *Appalachian Spring* (1945), for which he won a Pulitzer Prize. He also wrote music for movies—including *The Red Pony* (1948), which brought Bronx inflections to cowboy music, and *The Heiress* (1949), for which he won an Academy Award—and for the theater—including the Orson Welles production in New York of *Five Kings* (1939). More sophisticated, purely abstract works include the *Symphonic Ode* (1929), the dodecaphonic *Inscape* (1967) and several piano works that rank among the keyboard masterpieces of the century—the complex *Piano Variations* (1930) and the extraordinary *Piano Sonata* (1939–41). An important critic (*Copland on Music,* 1963) and force in modern music (the "Copland-Sessions Concerts" and organizer of the American Composers Alliance), Copland left an indelible stamp on every phase of American music.

Coppola, Francis Ford *(1939–)* American motion picture director, producer and screenwriter, most celebrated for his *Godfather* films. After attending the UCLA Film School in the early 1960s, he began a valuable association with low-budget film master Roger Corman. This experience produced two successful pictures, *Dementia 13* (1963), a horror film set in Ireland, and *You're a Big Boy Now* (1967). Despite the lackluster box office of his next pictures, the lavish musical, *Fin-*

ian's Rainbow (1968), and the deeply felt *The Rain People* (1969), Coppola established his own company, the San Francisco–based Zoetrope Studio, whose vicissitudes took him in and out of bankruptcy. Although Coppola has profited little from his films, his achievements have been impressive. The *Godfather* trilogy won nine Academy Awards, and Coppola is one of only four people ever to have won Oscars for best picture, director and screenplay. *Apocalypse Now* (1979) and *Tucker* (1988) were exhilarating blends of razzledazzle technique and sumptuous period detail (the Vietnam War and the 1940s). But it is the *The Conversation* (1974) that best demonstrates what biographer Diane Jacobs suggests is his main theme: "freedom versus privacy." Its depiction of a professional eavesdropper—a man as obsessed with invading the privacy of others as he is of guarding his own—concludes with the chilling (and perhaps autobiographical) realization that he himself cannot escape the prying eyes of others.

Coral Sea Southwest arm of the Pacific Ocean; site of World War II naval battle between the American and Japanese navies. The battle of the Coral Sea, May 7–8, 1942, marked the beginning of the U.S.'s Pacific counteroffensive after the bombing of Pearl Harbor. It is also noteworthy as the world's first large-scale aircraft carrier conflict; the battle was fought entirely by carrier-based planes, and during its progress no surface ships came within sight of the enemy. On the American side, the carrier *Lexington* was sunk and the carrier *Yorktown* damaged; on the Japanese side, the light carrier *Shoho* was sunk and the carrier *Shokaku* badly damaged; the Japanese lost 43 planes, the Americans 33. The battle of the Coral Sea checked the southward progress of Japanese forces in the Pacific. In addition, by reducing the number of ships available to the Japanese for the impending battle of Midway, the conflict in the Coral Sea may have played a crucial role in the other, critical battle. (See also World War II in the Pacific.)

Corcoran, Thomas G. *(1900–1981)* American lawyer and lobbyist. Corcoran was instrumental in pushing President Franklin D. Roosevelt's New Deal

legislation through Congress during the Great Depression. A deft backstage strategist with countless influential allies, he helped write the Securities and Exchange Act of 1934 and the Fair Labor Standards Act of 1938. After his efforts to aid Roosevelt in enlarging the Supreme Court and dislodging certain congressmen failed, he went into private practice. He represented many powerful corporate clients, provoking four congressional inquiries on charges of influence-peddling. The charges were never proved. (See also Brain Trust.)

Corea, Chick *(1941–)* Pianist-composer; one of modern jazz's most influential and versatile personalities. As a child, Corea learned the basics of jazz from his father and by listening to the recordings of Charlie Parker and Dizzy Gillespie. Following important engagements with the Latin bands of Mongo Santamaria and Willie Bobo, Corea worked with trumpeter Blue Mitchell; at the same time, he was absorbing the latest developments of pianists Bill Evans and McCoy Tyner. Corea joined Miles Davis's electronic jazz-rock unit of 1968–70 but departed to pursue freer forms of improvisation, largely within acoustic contexts. In the 1970s Corea successfully "crossed over" to the various jazz-Latin-rock combinations in three editions of his group Return to Forever. Unlike many who have scored big with commercial jazz, Corea has regularly returned to pure, bebop-based formats, most prominently in duo associations with fellow pianist Herbie Hancock and vibraphonist Gary Burton. In 1985 he formed the popular Elektric Band with electric bassist John Patitucci and drummer Dave Weckl; with the same personnel but playing acoustic versions of their electric instruments, Corea also established the highly regarded Akoustic Band. Among his many attractive and romantic compositions are "Spain," "Windows" and "Crystal Silence."

Corelli, Franco *(1923–2003)* Italian tenor. Born in Ancona, he was relatively untrained but possessed a strong, natural voice. Corelli made his operatic debut at the Spoleto Festival in 1952, singing Don Jose in Bizet's *Carmen.* Two years later he appeared at La Scala for the first time opposite Maria Callas in Spontini's *La Vestale.*

With a growing reputation, Corelli first appeared outside Italy at Covent Garden, London, in 1957, and he made his Metropolitan Opera debut in 1961 as Manrico in Verdi's *Il Trovatore,* one of his finest roles. Corelli continued to be a featured singer at La Scala and the Metropolitan, as well as at other important opera houses around the world. A handsome man with fine stage presence, he was noted for his passionate style and for the golden brilliance of his voice. Among his other important roles were Calaf in PUCCINI's *Turandot,* Cavaradossi in *Tosca* and the title part in *Don Carlo.*

Corey, Elias James *(1928–)* American chemist. Corey was educated at the Massachusetts Institute of Technology where he earned his Ph.D. in 1951. He immediately joined the staff of the University of Illinois and was appointed professor of chemistry there in 1955. In 1959 he moved to a similar chair at Harvard. Corey made a number of organic syntheses and was particularly successful in synthesizing a variety of terpenes, a family of hydrocarbons found in natural plant oils and important precursors of several biologically active compounds. In 1968 Corey and his colleagues announced they had synthesized five of the prostaglandin hormones. In 1990 Corey received the NOBEL PRIZE in chemistry for his theoretical work on the process of organic synthesis of chemical compounds.

Corfu Greek island in the Ionian Sea, off the coasts of Greece and Albania. The **Pact of Corfu,** signed here on July 20, 1917, created the new Serb, Croat and Slovene state that later became YUGOSLAVIA. ITALY controlled Corfu for one month in 1923; this so-called **Corfu Incident** was settled through the new LEAGUE OF NATIONS in its first practical test. During WORLD WAR II Corfu was controlled by the Italians and Germans (1941–44).

Cori, Carl Ferdinand *(1896–1984)* Czech-American biochemist. Cori was educated at the gymnasium in Trieste, where his father was director of the Marine Biological Station, and the University of Prague Medical School. He graduated in 1920, the year he married Gerty Radnitz, a fellow student who was to become his lifelong collaborator (see Gerty Theresa Radnitz CORI). The Coris

moved to the U.S. in 1922, taking up an appointment at the New York State Institute for the Study of Malignant Diseases in Buffalo. In 1931 they both transferred to the Washington University Medical School, where Cori was successively professor of pharmacology and then of biochemistry until his retirement in 1966. In the mid-1930s the Coris began work to find out how the complex carbohydrate glycogen is converted to glucose in the body. (Glucose provides energy for the body.) Through their researches they discovered that an enzyme called phosphatase is responsible. The value of the Coris' work is undeniable. Above all they pointed the way to the crucial role of phosphates in the provision of cellular energy, the details of which were soon to be worked out by Fritz Lipmann. For their work the Coris shared the 1947 NOBEL PRIZE in physiology or medicine with Bernardo Houssay.

Cori, Gerty Theresa Radnitz (Gertrude Radnitz) *(1896–1957)* Czech-American biochemist. She graduated from the Medical School of Prague University in 1920, the year in which she married her lifelong collaborator, Carl CORI. She moved with him to the U.S., taking a post in 1922 at the New York State Institute for the Study of Malignant Diseases in Buffalo. In 1931 she went with her husband to the Washington University Medical School, where she became professor of biochemistry in 1947. That year the Coris and Bernardo Houssay shared the NOBEL PRIZE in physiology or medicine for their discovery of how glycogen is broken down and resynthesized in the body.

Cormack, Allan Macleod *(1924–1998)* South African–born physicist. Cormack was educated at the University of Cape Town. He became interested in X-ray imaging at the Groote Schuur Hospital in Johannesburg, where he worked as a physicist in the radioisotopes department. In 1956 he moved to the U.S., where he became a professor at Tufts University. Cormack was the first to analyze theoretically the possibilities of developing a radiological cross section of a biological system. Independent of the British engineer Godfrey HOUNSFIELD, he developed the mathematical basis for the technique of computer-assisted X-ray tomography

(CAT), describing this in two papers in 1963 and 1964, and provided the first practical demonstration. X-ray tomography is a process by which a picture of an imaginary slide through an object (or the human body) is built up from information from detectors rotating around the body. The application of this technique to medical X-ray imaging was to lead to diagnostic machines that could provide very accurate pictures of tissue distribution in the human brain and body. Hounsfield was unaware of Cormack's work when he developed the first commercially successful CAT SCANS for EMI in England. Cormack also pointed out that the reconstruction technique might equally be applied to proton tomography or to gamma radiation from positron annihilations within a patient and investigated these as possible imaging techniques. Cormack shared the 1979 NOBEL PRIZE in physiology or medicine with Hounsfield for the development of CAT.

Corman, Roger *(1926–)* American motion picture producer and director; his ability to churn out low-budget productions earned him the title "King of the Bs." Corman divided his time in the 1940s as messenger boy and story analyst for 20TH CENTURY–FOX and student in English literature at Oxford. He hit his stride at American-International in the 1950s, directing and/or producing many forgettable cheapies such as *The Monster from the Ocean Floor* (1954) and *Viking Women and the Sea Serpent* (1957), as well as a few minor masterpieces, notably *Little Shop of Horrors* (1960). Corman's quickness is legendary: *War of the Satellites* (1958) appeared only two months after the Russians launched their first Sputnik satellite. After setting his sights and budgets higher with a series of successful Edgar Allan Poe adaptations (such as *The Masque of the Red Death,* 1964), Corman formed New World Pictures in 1970 as a kind of training school for soon-to-be prominent directors. Among his discoveries were the young Francis Ford COPPOLA and Martin SCORSESE. In the early 1970s Corman branched out into distribution and handled the American release of several BERGMAN and FELLINI films. In 1983 Corman sold New World Pictures, but soon thereafter he founded Concorde–New Horizons, which also functioned as an independent film clearinghouse.

Cornell, Joseph *(1903–1972)* American artist. Born in Nyack, New York, Cornell was self-taught and had his first exhibition in 1932. During World War II he came to know Max ERNST and other expatriate surrealists. The influence of SURREALISM is strong in his best-known works, shallow glass-fronted wooden shadow boxes that contain three-dimensional collages. In these works, everyday objects, photographs, old engravings and other elements are arranged and juxtaposed to create delicate, evocative, mysteriously symbolic and strangely haunting images. Reclusive and bookish, Cornell often made visual references to other works of art or artists, as in *Medici Slot Machine* and *A Pantry Ballet for Jacques Offenbach* (both 1942). Never a part of the New York art scene, Cornell lived in an unfashionable suburb of the city and joined no movements. His intensely personal style made him an important figure in contemporary American art, and his work is in the collections of many prominent museums, for example, *Hotel du Nord* (1953) at the Whitney Museum, New York City.

Corner, Edred John Henry *(1906–1996)* British botanist. Corner graduated from Cambridge University in 1929. He then spent 20 years overseas, first as assistant director of the Gardens Department of the Straits Settlements (Singapore) and from 1947 to 1948 as a field officer for UNESCO in Latin America. Corer returned to Cambridge in 1949 and later, from 1966 until his retirement in 1973, served as professor of tropical botany. Although he originally began as a mycologist, so little was known about tropical plants that he specialized there. He produced a large number of books on the subject; his *Life of Plants* (1964) and *Natural History of Palms* (1966) are widely known.

Cornforth, Sir John Warcup *(1917–)* Australian chemist. Cornforth was educated at the universities of Sydney and Oxford, England, where he earned his D.Phil. in 1941. He spent the war in Oxford working on the structure of PENICILLIN before joining the staff of the Medical Research Council in 1946. In 1962 Cornforth moved to the Shell research center at Sittingbourne in Kent to serve as director of the Milstead Laboratory of Chemical Enzymology. In 1975 he accepted the post of Royal Society Research Professor at Sussex University. In 1951 the American chemist Robert Woodward had succeeded in synthesizing the important steroid cholesterol; Cornforth was interested in how the molecule is actually synthesized in the living cell. Using labeled isotopes of hydrogen, he traced out in considerable detail the chemical steps adopted by the cell to form cholesterol from the initial acetic acid. It was for this work that he shared the 1975 NOBEL PRIZE in chemistry with Vladimir Prelog.

Corregidor Island fortress in Manila Bay, the Philippines, at the southern end of Luzon Island's Bataan Peninsula. Originally an 18th-century Spanish fortress, it became a U.S. military base in 1900. In 20th-century history, the name Corregidor is synonymous with the island's heroic defense against the numerically superior Japanese invaders after the fall of BATAAN, at the beginning of WORLD WAR II. It succumbed on May 6, 1942, after five months of battle; it stood alone for those last 27 days, when the rest of the Philippines had been captured. The surviving U.S. defenders of Corregidor became PRISONERS OF WAR. The American commander, Lieutenant General Jonathan WAINWRIGHT, survived his captivity and was present when the Japanese signed their surrender aboard the battleship USS *MISSOURI* in 1945.

Correns, Karl Erich *(1864–1933)* German botanist and geneticist. Correns was the only child of the painter Erich Correns. He studied at Tübingen University, where he began his research on the effect of foreign pollen in changing the visible characters of the endosperm (nutritive tissue surrounding the plant embryo). His later research concentrated on establishing how widely Mendel's laws could be applied. In 1909 he obtained the first conclusive evidence for cytoplasmic, or non-Mendelian, inheritance, in which certain features of the offspring are determined by the cytoplasm of the egg cell. Other contributions to plant genetics include his proposal that genes must be physically linked to explain why some characters are always inherited together. Correns was also the first to relate Mendelian segregation (the separation of paired genes, or alleles) to meiosis and the first to obtain evidence for differential fertilization between gametes. From 1914 until his death he was director of the Kaiser Wilhelm Institute for Biology in Berlin.

Corrigan, Mairead *(1944–)* Irish peace activist. Raised as a Catholic in Belfast, Corrigan witnessed the violence and brutality of the conflict between Catholics and Protestants in NORTHERN IRELAND through her voluntary work for the Catholic welfare organization the Legion of Mary. In 1976 an IRA member was killed at the wheel of his van by British soldiers. The uncontrolled van struck Corrigan's sister and killed three of her children. The event, witnessed by **Betty Williams**, a Protestant, galvanized the two women to action against the internecine terrorism in Belfast. Williams began collecting signatures for a peace petition, and Corrigan appeared on television denouncing the IRA and announcing a peace march. At the march 10,000 Protestant and Catholic women appeared, and Corrigan and Williams were motivated to form the Community of Peace People, which grew into a worldwide organization demonstrating and acting for peace. In 1975 groups in Norway raised money and presented it to Corrigan and Williams as a Peoples Peace Prize. The following year Corrigan and Williams received the NOBEL PRIZE for peace. Corrigan continues to live in Belfast, promoting the integration of Catholics and Protestants.

Cortazar, Julio *(1914–1984)* Argentinian novelist and short story writer. Born in Brussels, Cortazar attended Buenos Aires University and held dual citizenship in Argentina and (after 1981) France. A popular as well as critical success, *Rayuela* (1963; translated in 1966 as *Hopscotch*), an avant-garde circular, was the first great novel of El BOOM in Latin American literature. Other experimental works include *62: Modelo para armar* (1968; translated in 1972 as *62: A Model Kit*), *Libro de Manuel* (1973; translated in 1978 as *A Manual for Manuel*) and *Queremos tanto a Glenda* (1980; translated in 1983 as *We All Love Glenda So Much*). His short story "Las babas del diablo," from the 1959 *Las armas secretas*, was the basis for Michaelangelo

ANTONIONI's 1966 film *Blow Up*. His work tends to be playful, fantastic and socially committed; it attempts to jolt the reader out of traditional ways of viewing reality. His final years were devoted to political activism. Cortazar was a supporter of the Cuban and Nicaraguan revolutions.

Cortot, Alfred Denis *(1877–1962)* French pianist and conductor. Born in Switzerland, Cortot studied piano at the Paris Conservatory and made his concert debut in Paris in 1896. He taught piano at the Paris Conservatory from 1907 and was a cofounder (1919) and director of the École Normale de Musique, Paris. Also active in chamber music, he was particularly noted for his trio work with cellist Pablo CASALS and violinist Jacques THIBAUD. Touring Europe and the U.S. as a performer and a conductor, he became a popular fixture of the classical music scene between the two world wars and was especially known for his performances of Chopin, Schumann and Liszt. Accused of collaboration with the Nazis because of his ties with the VICHY government's musical establishment, Cortot was arrested and released in 1944. He then settled in Lausanne, Switzerland, and made far fewer concert appearances.

Corvette GENERAL MOTORS (Chevrolet) automobile designed as an American rival to European sports cars. GM vice president Harley J. EARL is viewed as the motive power behind the decision to produce a two-seater car with advanced body design, which first appeared in 1953. The FIBERGLASS body was a blend of functional STREAMLINING and somewhat gross styling elements. In 1956 the design was changed and a V-8 engine substituted for the original 6. Debate about the merit of the Corvette centered on whether it was a "true" sport car or merely a typically American consumer product disguised to appeal to a special audience. The redesigned Stingray model of 1963 was a striking visual form that brought new popularity to the Corvette. Since that time the Corvette has become something of a cult object, valued, collected and displayed by ardent devotees.

Cosby, Bill *(1937–)* Specializing in warm, wholesome family humor, Cosby was the most successful comic television performer of the 1980s and 1990s. Although the Philadelphia-born comedian began his career as a popular stand-up comedian—garnering a record six straight Grammy Awards (1964–69) for his albums, more than a dozen of which became certified Gold best sellers—as early as 1965 he was making history of another kind, as the black costar of Robert Culp on the successful TV drama *I Spy* (1965–68), for which he won three Emmy Awards. In the 1970s Cosby appeared in several films, including *Hickey and Boggs* (1972), *Uptown Saturday Night* (1974) and *Mother, Jugs and Speed* (1976). It was on television, however, that his brand of down-to-earth observational comedy struck home. In the 1970s he had success with several different formats, on shows such as *The Bill Cosby Show* (1969–71), *The New Bill Cosby Show* (1972–73), *Cos* (1976) and an animated kiddie-show *Fat Albert and the Cosby Kids*. But his greatest achievement was his television sitcom *The Cosby Show* (1984–92), rated as the number-one show in America through most of its first six years.

Costa-Gavras **(Kostantinos Gavras)** *(1933–)* Greek film director. Costa-Gavras, who was educated at the Sorbonne, began his film career in the 1950s as an assistant to the French film director René Clement. His first solo directorial effort was *The Sleeping Car Murder* (1965), a mystery thriller. But Costa-Gavras, with the patronage of French actor and singer Yves MONTAND, soon turned his attention to more politically involved filmmaking. *Z* (1969), which starred Montand, Irene Papas and Jean-Louis Trintignant, grippingly portrayed the murder of a Greek peace movement leader at the orders of a right-wing terrorist group tied to the ruling Greek junta (see GREEK COLONELS). *The Confession* (1970), with Montand and Simone SIGNORET, was set in 1952 and explored the psychological breakdown of a Communist Party bureaucrat who is forced by his Stalinist superiors into giving a false confession. Other films by Costa-Gavras include *State of Siege* (1972) and *Missing* (1982).

Costa Rica **(Republic of Costa Rica)** Central American country bordered on the north by Nicaragua, on the south by Panama, on the east by the Caribbean

COSTA RICA

1900	Boundary dispute with Panama (then part of Colombia); arbitrated by president of France, but dispute continues.
1913	United Fruit Company develops plantations along the Atlantic coast; bananas for a time surpass coffee as leading export.
1916	Costa Rica claims that Betan-Chamorro Treaty (U.S.-Nicaragua) ignores its rights to San Juan River.
1917	Federico Tinoco installs revolutionary government that lasts for two years.
1921	With U.S. backing, Costa Rica occupies area disputed with Panama.
1936	National Republican Party (PRN) comes to power; begins moderate reforms.
1945	United Fruit Company builds plantation on Pacific coast, imports workers from Jamaica.
1948	PRN defeated at polls; refuses to abide by election and vacate presidency; civil war ensues; PRN strongman Calderón driven from country.
1949	As a result of civil war, new constitution adopted banning national army in perpetuity; Catholicism made official religion.
1955	Calderón and supporters reinvade but are defeated despite help from regional strongmen Somoza, Trujillo and Batista.
1963	Costa Rica joins Central American common market.
1968	Arenal volcano's first eruption in centuries kills many.
1979	Costa Rica supports Sandinista rebellion against Nicaraguan dictator Somoza.
1983	Basing of anti-Sandinista contra rebels in Costa Rican territory causes friction with Nicaragua.
1985	United Fruit (now United Brands) sells Costa Rican plantations.
1987	President Óscar Arias's Nicaraguan peace plan adopted by other nations of the region; Arias wins Nobel Peace Prize.
1989	Arias plan is basis of regional agreement leading to free elections in Nicaragua in 1990, disbanding of contras.
1990	Ángel Calderón, son of former strongman and opponent of Arias's peace plan, elected president with help of U.S. media consultant Roger Ailes; Costa Rican judge seeks extradition from U.S. of John Hull, CIA operative in Iran-contra affair; earthquake leaves 14,000 homeless; Guatemala, El Salvador, Honduras, Nicaragua and Costa Rica agree to integrate their economies for a six-year period.
1998	Miguel Ángel Rodríguez, a conservative, is elected president.
2006	Arias is elected anew as president.

Sea and on the west by the Pacific Ocean; capital is San José. Since 1838 and with few exceptions, Costa Rica has remained one of the most stable and prosperous of Central American countries. In a bloodless coup d'état in 1917, Federico Tinoco established a junta government but was deposed in 1919. In 1948 a six-week civil war followed an election dispute. In 1949 a new constitution was adopted, abolishing the army in favor of a Civil and a Rural Guard. José FIGUERES, who had led the anti-government forces in the brief war, became president and was reelected in 1953. He was a cofounder of the National Liberation Party (PLN) and instituted social reforms such as nationalized banks and a social security system. Subsequent leaders drifted toward conservatism and overrode some of the PLN reforms. In 1974 PLN candidate Daniel Oduber Quirós was elected president, reinstituting social programs. In 1978 Rodrigo Carazo Odio, a conservative of the Unity Coalition (CU), was elected. During his presidency Costa Rica was brought to the verge of economic collapse, and he was accused of illegal arms trafficking. In 1982 Luis Alberto Monge Álvarez, another cofounder of the PLN, won a landslide victory and managed to salvage the economy. At issue in the 1986 elections was Costa Rica's neutrality. The U.S. had been pressuring Monge to condemn the Nicaraguan Sandinistas and to reestablish an army. However, Óscar Arias Sánchez won the election with a neutral platform and implemented a policy to prevent the U.S.-backed contras' presence in Costa Rica. In 1987 Arias won the Nobel Peace Prize for his efforts to end the Nicaraguan conflict. Economic readjustment led to a massive strike against the government in 1989, and a devastating earthquake in 1990 left 14,000 homeless. In 1998 a conservative, Miguel Ángel Rodríguez Echeverría, was elected president. In 2000 Nicaragua and Costa Rica agreed to jointly regulate navigation on the San Juan River, which separates the two countries. In 2006 Arias was again elected president.

Costa Rican Civil War of 1948

COSTA RICA's election of 1948, won by Otilio Ulate was invalidated by the

Congress on March 1, 1948. Civil war broke out between Ulate's followers, led by Colonel José "Pepe" FIGUERES FERRER, and the government and supporters of the defeated candidate, Rafael Calderón Guardia. In six weeks of fighting Figueres's forces ousted the government, despite Calderón's receiving outside aid from Nicaragua and Honduras. On May 8, 1948, Figueres established a military junta, which dissolved the army, outlawed the communists, nationalized banks and began civil service reform. Resistance by armed Calderonist rebels invading from Nicaragua was repulsed, and in early 1949 a Costa Rican constitutional assembly met, confirmed Ulate's election and drafted a new constitution. On November 8, 1949, Figueres turned over the government to Ulate.

Costa Rican Rebellion of 1955

José "Pepe" FIGUERES FERRER, a moderate socialist was elected president of Costa Rica in 1953. Nicaragua's dictatorial president Anastasio Somoza García (1896–1956) claimed that Figueres's election supporters had plotted against him. To retaliate, Somoza backed disgruntled former Costa Rican president Rafael Calderón Guardia (1900–70) to lead a rebel force into northern Costa Rica. Figueres appealed to the Organization of American States, whose investigation revealed the rebels' Nicaraguan backing, resulting in Somoza's withdrawal of support. The rebels, no match for the popular government forces, were driven out, and in early 1956 Costa Rica and Nicaragua agreed to cooperative border surveillance.

Costa Rican Revolution of 1917

The proposed reforms of Alfredo González Flores, elected president of Costa Rica in 1913, were opposed by General Federico Tinoco Granados, who overthrew González and set up a military dictatorship. Insurrections broke out, and the U.S., which had refused to recognized Tinoco, threatened intervention. Tinoco resigned in May 1919, and a month later U.S. Marines landed to protect U.S. interests. In 1920 a democratic government was restored under newly elected president Julio Acosta García.

Costello, Elvis (Declan Patrick McManus) (1955–   ) English singer-songwriter. Costello emerged on the

British punk scene as it was evolving into NEW WAVE, and he remains the genre's most enduring figure. He signed with the legendary Stiff label in 1977, joining a stable of talent that included Ian Dury, Wreckless Eric and Nick Lowe. His first hit, "Watching the Detectives," showcases the influence of reggae on his work, as well as his unusually cerebral and literate lyrics. His 1979 *Armed Forces* was his best-selling album and included the singles "Oliver's Army" and "Accidents Will Happen." *Almost Blue,* a dense and lovely homage to the country genre, included the 1981 hit "A Good Year for the Roses." His albums and singles continued to sell well through the 1980s and included his first top-40 hit "Everyday I Write the Book." Despite his success, Costello portrays himself as a bitter and angry man. In the 1990s Costello continued his writing and recording, occasionally developing songs for motion pictures, such as the single "God Give Me Strength" for *Grace of My Heart* (1996), and "I'll Never Fall in Love Again" for *Austen Powers: The Spy Who Shagged Me* (1999). He is married to singer Diana Krall.

Costello, Lou See ABBOTT AND COSTELLO.

Coster, Dirk (1889–1950) Dutch physicist. Coster was educated at the University of Leiden where he earned his doctorate in 1922. From 1924 to 1949 he was professor of physics at the University of Groningen. In 1923, in collaboration with Georg van Heyesy, he discovered the element hafnium (named for Hafnia, an old Roman name for Copenhagen the home of Niels BOHR, who had suggested that the new element would most likely be found in zirconium ores).

Côte d'Ivoire (Ivory Coast) Situated on the west coast of Africa, Ivory

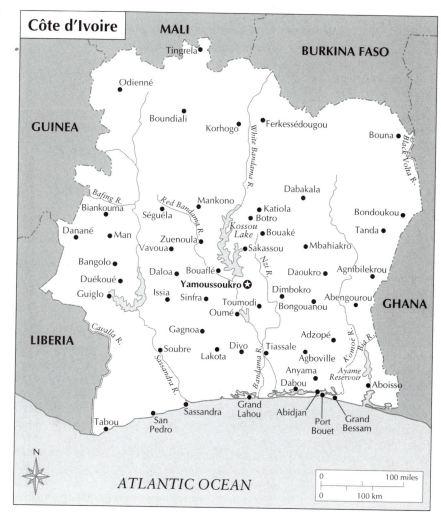

CÔTE D'IVOIRE

1904	Ivory Coast becomes member of the Federation of French West Africa.
1960	The Republic of the Ivory Coast declares independence from France, with Houphouët-Boigny of the Parti démocratique de la Côte d'Ivoire (PDCI) as president.
1964	Polygamy, bride price and matrilineal inheritance are abolished.
1969	Relations with the USSR are broken.
1971	President Houphouët-Boigny calls for dialogue with South Africa as an alternative to confrontation.
1973	Military coup plot uncovered, seven officers sentenced to death.
1975	5,000 political prisoners granted amnesty; Houphouët-Boigny reelected to a fourth five-year term.
1986	The nation is given its French appellation—Côte d'Ivoire.
1990	Austerity measures imposed in February provoke nationwide unrest, are rescinded.
1990	Implementation of multiparty system is begun; Houphouët-Boigny reelected for a seventh five-year term, making him Africa's longest-serving leader.
1993	President Houphouët-Boigny dies in office; succeeded by Henri Konan Bédié.
1999	President Bédié overthrown in bloodless coup.
2002	Coup attempt ushers in period of violence and political instability.
2003	The rebels and the government sign a cease-fire in May, but resume hostilities several months later.
2004	French forces invade after nine French soldiers are killed in an attack.
2005	Ivorian political leaders meet and sign the Pretoria Agreement, declaring an end to hostilities.

Coast covers a total area of 124,471 square miles. In 1904 the Ivory Coast became a member of the federation of FRENCH WEST AFRICA; it gained representation in the French National Assembly after World War II. Opposition to colonial representation led to the formation of the Parti démocratique de la Côte d'Ivoire in 1945. The party leader, Félix HOUPHOUËT-BOIGNY, became Ivory Coast president when the country declared its independence in 1960. The country was quite stable politically, except for brief periods of unrest in the early 1970s. The nation's name was officially changed to Côte d'Ivoire in 1990. A 1999 coup overthrew the government of President Henri Bédié, who had been in power since 1993. However, the coup's leader, Robert Guei, failed to restore order. While some hope was kindled with a March 2003 accord in which all opposition forces agreed to participate in a new coalition government, by September that coalition had disintegrated. In 2004 hostilities continued, including the invasion of French forces in response to the killing of nine French troops. In 2005 political leaders signed the Pretoria Agreement, which called for an immediate end to the war.

Cottrell, Sir Alan Howard (*1919– *) British physicist and metallurgist. Cottrell studied at the University of Birmingham, earning his B.Sc. in 1939 and Ph.D. in 1949. After leaving Birmingham in 1955, he took the post of deputy head of the metallurgy division of the Atomic Energy Research Establishment at Harwell until 1958, when he became Goldsmiths Professor of Metallurgy at Cambridge University. From 1965 he held a number of posts as a scientific adviser to the British government. In 1974 he became master of Jesus College, Cambridge, and subsequently vice-chancellor of the University of Cambridge (1977–79). Cottrell's most notable research has been in the study of dislocations in crystals. He also worked on the effect of radiation on crystal structure— work that was important in design changes to the fuel rods in early nuclear reactors.

Coughlin, Charles Edward (*1891– 1979*) Canadian-born American Catholic "radio priest" ("the fighting priest") of the 1930s. He started his own radio show in Detroit to crusade against injustice, but his views became increasingly extreme. During the GREAT DEPRESSION he was a leading critic of President Franklin ROOSEVELT. On radio and at mass rallies he preached against the banks, COMMUNISM, the NEW DEAL, the JEWS and Wall Street. In the late 1930s his National Union for Social Justice, renamed the Christian Front, took on fascist overtones. The Catholic Church ended his broadcasts in 1942. A forerunner of the televangelists, Coughlin was among the first to use radio to reach a mass audience; at the height of his popularity, he was heard by 40 million Americans each week. (See also DEMAGOGUES; FASCISM; Huey LONG; Gerald SMITH.)

Coulson, Charles Alfred (*1910– 1974*) British theoretical chemist, physicist and mathematician. Coulson was educated at Cambridge University, where he earned his Ph.D. in 1935, and afterward taught mathematics at the universities of Dundee and Oxford. Coulson then held appointments as professor of theoretical physics at King's College, London (1947–52), Rouse Ball Professor of Mathematics at Oxford (1952–72) and, still at Oxford, professor of theoretical chemistry from 1972 until his death in 1974. As a physicist Coulson wrote the widely read *Waves* (1941) and *Electricity* (1948). His most creative work, however, was as a theoretical chemist. Later he turned to theoretical studies of carcinogens, drugs and other topics of biological interest. Coulson was also one of the leading Methodists of his generation and, from 1965 to 1971, chairman of the charity Oxfam. He produced a number of works on the relationship between Christianity and science of which *Science and Christian Belief* (1955) is a typical example.

counterculture Term that first emerged in the U.S. in the 1960s. At that time, the word referred specifically to the HIPPIES, who rejected middle-class American values and advocated drug use, "free love" and an "alternative lifestyle" in general. It is now widely used to refer to the cumulative societal impact exercised by disaffected political and social groups and the artistic avant-garde. The counterculture is the collective embodiment of ideals and values that are not highly valued by mainstream culture. Members of the counterculture act as political, social and artistic gadflies, calling attention to issues that might otherwise be overlooked in the mainstream consensus. Over time, certain counterculture ideals may become accepted by the mainstream, and the counterculture moves on to emphasize different issues. There is, therefore, an ongoing dialectical interaction between the mainstream and the counterculture; both can be viewed as necessary to overall societal functioning and development.

country and western music Popular American musical form that originated in the South among rural whites. In the 19th century, a folk music tradition derived from British roots combined with Afro-American and other ethnic sources and took a new twist in the form of what came to be called "hillbilly" music, in the mountainous Appalachian region of the South. At first the music was performed at county fairs, churches and other local occasions. The music was given a great boost during the 1920s by the arrival of radio and the popularity of groups such as the Carter Family and Jimmie Rodgers (1897–1933), often dubbed "the father of country music."

The mainstream of country music received a major boost in 1927 with the establishment of the Grand Ole Opry, a music show that made Nashville, Tennessee, the mecca for country music. A variation on the country theme appeared in the 1930s with the rise of western music, popularized by Gene AUTRY, Tex Ritter and Roy ROGERS. Western was but one of a variety of allied forms ranging from the folk traditions of Woody GUTHRIE to the banjo instrumentals of bluegrass music. The postwar era has seen a widespread growth in the popularity of country and western music, although it is strongest in the South and Southwest, which still supply most of the performers. While it has been influenced by other forms, notably rock music, the tradition has been maintained by such artists as Johnny Cash, Willie Nelson, Loretta Lynn, Merle Haggard, Kenny Rogers, Dolly Parton and Barbara Mandrell. In the 2000s singers like Garth BROOKS and Faith Hill and groups like the Dixie Chicks crossed over into mainstream popular music.

Country Party Australian political party established in 1920. The Country Party arose from a group of farmers from New South Wales who, in 1913, began supporting Conservative politicians who would represent agricultural interests. In 1920 these politicians within the federal parliament were organized by W. J. Williams into the Country Party. Under the leadership of Sir Earle Page, the Country Party won 14 seats by 1922 and could influence the LABOUR and Nationalist Parties. Under the leadership of Stanley Bruce, the Nationalist Party formed a coalition with the Country Party and shared power from 1922 to 1929, 1934 to 1941 and 1949 to 1971. Sir Arthur Fadden, Country Party leader, was prime minister for the coalition gov-

ernment briefly in 1949. On April 6, 1974, the Country Party voted to change its name to the National Party.

Cournand, André Frédéric (1895–1988) French-born physician and physiologist; a professor of medicine at Columbia University for many years. While there, Cournand teamed with Dickinson Richards in researching the practical uses of the heart catheter, invented by Werner FORSSMANN of Germany in 1929. In 1956 the three men shared the NOBEL PRIZE in medicine or physiology.

Courtauld Institute of Art Museum and art school in London. The Courtauld was established in 1931 under the auspices of the University of London when **Samuel Courtauld** (1876–1947) donated his collection of Impressionist and postimpressionist paintings and Home House to quarter it. Subsequent additions to the collection include the Lee and Gambier-Perry collection of Old Masters, the Roger FRY collection of early 20th-century French and English painting and the Spooner collection of English landscape watercolors and drawing. The institute encourages the study and research of art history, and many prominent art historians, including Anita BROOKNER, have taught on its staff. In 1990 the Courtauld was relocated to Somerset House in London.

Court-packing attempt by FDR An unsuccessful attempt by President Franklin D. ROOSEVELT to add six extra members to the U.S. Supreme Court, which had struck down a number of key NEW DEAL acts as unconstitutional. During his first term Roosevelt did not have the opportunity to fill a single vacancy on the Court. Some of the justices were openly hostile to FDR's program, which seemed radical at the time. On February 5, 1937, frustrated at the aged justices' opposition to his New Deal legislation, FDR proposed a plan to allow him to appoint one additional justice to the Court for every sitting justice over the age of 70. The plan was harshly criticized as a blatant attempt to influence the Court, and the proposal was never voted upon by the full Congress. However, for whatever reason, after the unsuccessful plan to pack the

Court, the justices were less hostile to FDR's New Deal legislation. Because of advancing age and a more generous pension plan, eight of the nine justices retired during the next six years, and FDR was able to fill the vacancies with appointees more sympathetic to his New Deal program.

Cousins, Norman (1915–1990) American magazine editor, author and educator. Cousins was best known for his highly successful tenure as editor of *The Saturday Review,* a general interest magazine on the arts, education, science and other topics. Educated at Columbia University, Cousins became editor of *The Saturday Review* in 1940 and gradually increased its circulation from 20,000 to a high of 600,000. Under Cousins, the magazine became a major liberal voice in American culture, calling for restrictions on nuclear armaments and increased power for the United Nations. Forced to resign his editorship in 1971 due to a change of ownership, he returned in triumph two years later and edited *The Saturday Review* until 1977, when he resigned to devote himself to teaching and writing. In his book *Anatomy of an Illness: As Perceived by the Patient* (1979), Cousins argued— based on his own experience with a life-threatening form of arthritis— that emotional attitudes of the patient can play a vital role in healing. This theme was taken up again in Cousins's last book, *Head First: The Biology of Hope* (1989).

Cousteau, Jacques-Yves (1910– 1997) French oceanographer, explorer, inventor, filmmaker and author. Cousteau studied at the École Navale in Brest and on graduation entered the French navy. During WORLD WAR II he served in the French RESISTANCE and was awarded the Legion d'Honneur and the croix de guerre. During the war he also made his first two underwater films and, despite German occupation of France, designed and tested an aqualung. For this he adapted a valve (hitherto used by Émile Gagnan to enable car engines to work with cooking gas) to make an underwater breathing apparatus. Using compressed air, the **Cousteau-Gagnon aqualung** allows long periods of underwater investiga-tion at depths of more than 200 feet and frees the diver of the need for a heavy suit and lifeline. In 1946 Cousteau became head of the French navy's Underwater Research Group and the following year set a world record of 300 feet for free-diving. In 1951–52 he traveled to the Red Sea in a converted British minesweeper, the *Calypso,* and made the first underwater color film to be taken at a depth of 150 feet. Later he helped Auguste PICCARD in the development of the first bathyscaphes. Cousteau also designed and worked on a floating island off the French coast that enabled long-term study of marine life. He is the designer of an underwater diving saucer capable of descents to more than 600 feet and able to stay submerged for 20 hours. More significantly, he worked on the future exploitation of the seabed as a living environment for humans, conducting various experiments on short-term undersea living. Cousteau made more significant contributions to undersea exploration and study than any other individual. His work was brought to a wide audience by means of cinephotography and television, and a number of his films, for example, *The Silent World,* have won ACADEMY AWARDS. His many books and his television documentaries in the series *The Undersea World of Jacques Cousteau* captured the imagination of millions.

Cousy, Bob (1928–) American basketball player, considered one of the all-time greats of the game. A guard for the Boston Celtics of the NBA, Cousy played from 1950 to 1963, including 13 straight NBA all-star games. He led the NBA in assists for eight straight seasons and helped the Celtics win six NBA championships. After his retirement he coached basketball at Boston College (1963–69) and subsequently returned to the NBA as head coach of the Cincinnati Royals.

Coward, Sir Noel Pierce (1899– 1973) British playwright, director, actor and songwriter. Known for his sophisticated wit, he was perhaps the foremost writer of the English comedy of manners in the 20th century. He made his stage debut at age 10, and by 1920 was appearing regularly in West End comedies and writing songs, sketches and plays. His most successful plays, frequently revived, included *Hay Fever* (1925), *Private Lives* (1930), *Design for Living* (1933) and *Blithe Spirit* (1941). He wrote the book and score for the 1929 operetta *Bitter Sweet* and also wrote the screenplays for the World War II film *In Which We Serve* (1942), which he directed and starred in, and for *Brief Encounter* (1946), directed by David LEAN; both are considered classics. His work appealed less to postwar tastes, but he continued to enjoy success in films and on the stage in Britain and the U.S. until his retirement shortly before his death.

Cowles, Henry Chandler (1869– 1939) American botanist. Cowles did pioneer ecological studies of dune vegetation, the floral balance in the Chicago area and the use of trees as indicators of earlier environmental conditions. He taught at the UNIVERSITY OF CHICAGO from 1902 to 1934. Author of several publications on the subject of botany, Cowles edited the *Botanical Gazette* (1925–34).

Cowley, Malcolm (1898–1989) American literary critic, author and editor. Cowley was a member of the so-called LOST GENERATION of American writers who settled in Paris in the 1920s, and which he later chronicled in *Exile's Return.* As editor at the *New Republic* magazine in the 1930s and at Viking Press from 1944 to 1985, Cowley championed the cause of such post–World War I writers as John DOS PASSOS and William FAULKNER. Cowley's edition of *The Portable William Faulkner* (1946) brought about renewed interest in Faulkner's work and led to his receiving the NOBEL PRIZE. Cowley's other work includes *Thinking Back on Us: A Contemporary Chronicle of the 1930's* (1964) and the memoirs *And I Worked at the Writer's Trade* (1963) and *The Dream of the Golden Mountain: Remembering the 1930's* (1980). *The Selected Correspondence of Kenneth Burke and Malcolm Cowley, 1915–1981* was published in 1988.

Cox, Archibald (1912–2004) American lawyer, law school professor and author. Cox, a graduate of Harvard University, left a private law practice in Boston to work first with the U.S.

Justice Department and then the Labor Department during World War II. After the war he returned to Boston as a professor of law at Harvard, although he interrupted his teaching to act as U.S. solicitor general during the early 1960s. Cox is best remembered as the special prosecutor appointed to investigate the WATERGATE scandal that rocked the administration of President Richard M. NIXON. After the Supreme Court upheld Cox's demand for tapes of Nixon's White House conversations, Nixon ordered his attorney general, Elliot Richardson, to fire Cox. Instead, Richardson and his deputy, William Ruckelshaus, resigned. Subsequently, Solicitor General Robert BORK, then acting attorney general, fired Cox in what became known as the Saturday Night Massacre. Cox's dismissal intensified calls for Nixon's impeachment and helped lead to the president's eventual resignation.

Cox, Harvey Gallagher (*1929– *) American Protestant theologian and sociologist. Cox rose to national prominence in the 1960s due to widespread acclaim for his first book, *The Secular City* (1965), which examined the difficulties of maintaining religious faith in a secularized American society. Cox, who was educated at Yale and Harvard, taught church history and sociology for nearly three decades at Harvard. His other works include *God's Revolution and Man's Responsibility* (1965), *The Feast of Fools* (1969), *The Seduction of the Spirit: The Use and Misuse of People's Religion* (1973) and *Turning East: The Promise and Peril of the New Orientalism* (1977).

Cox, James Middleton (*1870–1957*) U.S. newspaper journalist and politician. Cox started his newspaper career at the *Cincinnati Enquirer* and later bought the *Dayton Daily News* (1898). He subsequently bought several other newspapers in various states. Beginning in 1909, he served two terms in the U.S. House of Representatives. He supported the political philosophy of President Woodrow WILSON. Cox was strongly in favor of Wilson's international policies, such as freedom of the seas, arms reduction, freedom of trade and, particularly, some kind of union of nations. In 1920 he was nominated for the

presidency by the DEMOCRATIC PARTY, with F. D. ROOSEVELT as his running mate, but was defeated by Warren G. HARDING.

Cozzens, James Gould (*1903–1978*) American novelist and short story writer. Cozzens was educated at Kent School in Connecticut, which he would later portray in short stories and the novel *The Last Adam* (1933, published in England as *a Cure of Flesh;* filmed as *Doctor Bull* in 1933), and at Harvard University, although he did not complete a degree there. Cozzens published his first novel, *Confusion* (1924), at the age of 19. Although not well received, it expressed one of Cozzens's recurrent concerns, that of a gifted youth finding her destiny. Cozzens moved to Canada and then to Cuba, where he taught children of American mill employees and gleaned the material for his next two novels, *Cock Pit* (1928) and *The Son of Perdition* (1929). After returning to New York in 1927, Cozzens met and married Bernice Baumgarten, a literary agent who subsequently managed his career. Although he produced many novels and short stories between 1927 and 1948, Cozzens's best-known work is *Guard of Honor* (1948), which is based on his experiences while stationed in Washington, D.C., during WORLD WAR II and on the detailed diaries he kept. The novel won a PULITZER PRIZE in 1949. Cozzens was often criticized for his cranky iconoclasm and controversial elitism. Many critics feel that his work has not received the attention that its complexity merits. Among his many other works are *By Love Possessed* (1957; filmed 1961), *Morning, Noon and Night* (1968) and the short stories *Children and Others* (1964).

Crabbe, Buster (Clarence Linden Crabbe) (*1907–1983*) American athlete and actor. During an impressive swimming career in the 1920s and early 1930s, Crabbe broke five world records. He placed third in a race in the 1928 OLYMPICS and captured the gold medal in the 400-meter freestyle event in the 1932 Olympics. He then parlayed his impressive physique and rugged looks into a career in HOLLYWOOD "B" movies in the 1930s and 1940s. He first played TARZAN in *King of the Jungle* (1932), but he was most

familiar to audiences for his starring roles in the serials *Flash Gordon* and *Buck Rogers.*

Craig, Edith Geraldine Ailsa (*1869–1947*) British theatrical actress and director. Craig, daughter of the legendary British actress Ellen Terry, did not equal her mother's achievements as an actress, but she did win renown as a director. Early in her career Craig appeared in plays with both her mother and the famous actor Sir Henry Irving. After managing an American tour by her mother in 1907, Craig turned to the study of music in Berlin and London. She then returned to the theater, directing over 100 plays for the Pioneer Players in London from 1911 to 1921. Her brother, Gordon CRAIG, was a well-known theatrical set designer and dramatic theorist.

Craig, (Edward Henry) Gordon (*1872–1966*) British stage designer, dramatic theorist, actor and director. Craig, the son of the legendary British actress Ellen Terry, achieved great renown both as a set designer and as a theorist on dramatic presentation. After beginning his career as an actor, Craig turned to directing in the early 1900s, including a production of Shakespeare's *Much Ado About Nothing* that featured his mother. Craig then focused on stage design for numerous plays including *Venice Preserv'd* (1904), *Hamlet* (1911) and *The Pretenders* (1926). Craig, who articulated his stage design theories in his book *On the Art of the Theatre* (1911), was best known as an advocate of nonrepresentational design. His sister, Edith CRAIG, was a prominent actress and director.

Craig, Lyman Creighton (*1906–1974*) American biochemist. Craig was educated at Iowa State University where he earned his Ph.D. in 1931. After two years at Johns Hopkins University he moved to Rockefeller University, New York, where he was appointed professor of chemistry in 1949. Craig concentrated on devising and improving techniques for separating the constituents of mixtures. His development of a fractional extraction method named countercurrent distribution (CCD) proved to be particularly good for preparing pure forms of several antibiotics and hormones. The method also established that the molecular weight of insulin is half the weight previously suggested. Craig also used CCD to separate the two protein chains of hemoglobin. During work on ergot alkaloids Craig, with W. A. Jacobs, isolated an unknown amino acid, which they named lysergic acid. Other workers managed to prepare the dimethyl amide of this acid and found the compound, LSD, to have considerable physiological effects.

Cram, Donald James (1919–2001)
American chemist. Cram, a lawyer's son, was educated at Rollins College and the University of Nebraska. After working for Merck and Company on streptomycin and PENICILLIN, he entered Harvard, where he earned his Ph.D. in 1947. He then joined the University of California at Los Angeles, becoming professor of chemistry there in 1956. Cram coauthored with George Hammond a standard textbook, *Organic Chemistry* (1959). He also produced *Fundamentals of Carbanion Chemistry* (1965), the first general work on the subject. In 1987 Cram shared the NOBEL PRIZE in chemistry with Jean-Marie Lehn and Charles Pedersen for their development of molecules that, due to their structure, would identify each other and form predictable compounds.

Cram, Ralph Adams (1863–1942)
American architect known for his achievements in eclectic Gothic Revival work, primarily in religious and academic buildings. Cram studied art in Boston and was an art critic for a time before forming an architectural partnership with Charles Wentworth in 1889. In 1892 Bertram G. Goodhue joined the firm, which became, in 1913, Cram, Goodhue, & Ferguson. Among the many Gothic buildings designed by the firm are the East Liberty Presbyterian Church in Pittsburgh, the Swedenborgian Cathedral at Bryn Athyn, Pennsylvania, and St. Thomas Church (1914) in New York. In 1911 Cram took over design of the then-partly-built Cathedral of St. John the Divine in New York, revising the design from Byzantine to Gothic style. The Gothic buildings of Princeton University are the result of his role as supervising architect for that institution. Cram was an energetic propagandist for the gothic style and was the author of a number of books, such

as his *Church Building* of 1901, which offers "good" and "bad" examples, including a number of Cram's early works in the former category. Other books include *The Ruined Abbeys of Great Britain* (1906), *The End of Democracy* (1937) and *Black Spirits and White,* a renowned collection of ghost stories.

Crane, Barry (Barry Cohen) (?–1985)
U.S. television director and bridge player. Crane was one of the world's foremost tournament bridge players. The winner of more titles than anyone else in history, he had accumulated nearly 35,000 master points in tournament play, some 11,000 points more than his nearest rival.

Crane, Hart (1899–1932)
American poet. The son of a midwestern candy manufacturer, Crane was largely self-educated. At 16 he left home to make a career in New York as a writer. There his literary friends included Vachel LINDSAY, Sherwood ANDERSON and Malcolm COWLEY, and he contributed to *The Little Review* and *Poetry.* However, he was dogged by the necessity of earning a living and by frequent bouts of depression. His first volume, *White Buildings,* appeared in 1926. The banker Otto Kahn then provided him with funds to work on *The Bridge* (1930). In 1931 he received a Guggenheim grant to go to Mexico and write a long poem, but a year later he committed suicide by jumping overboard from the ship on which he was returning to New York. A poetic innovator who was greatly underestimated and misunderstood in his lifetime, Crane is now regarded as one of the giants of 20th-century American poetry.

Cranko, John (John Rustenburg) (1927–1973)
South African–born dancer, choreographer and ballet director. After studying at the Cape Town University Ballet School in South Africa and the Sadler's Wells School in London, Cranko joined the Sadler's Wells Ballet in 1947, quickly moving from dancer to choreographer. He created several ballets for the company, including *Pineapple Poll* (1951), and works for other companies as well, before becoming director of the Stuttgart Ballet in 1961. He built the Stuttgart into one of the leading ballet companies in the world, particularly noted

for its large, diversified repertory and the strong commitment of such dancers as Marcia HAYDEE and Richard Cragun to his artistic vision. Full-length dramatic works such as the popular *Romeo and Juliet* (1962), *Onegin* (1965) and *Taming of the Shrew* (1969) were his forte. He also served as principal choreographer for the Bavarian State Opera in Munich (1968–71). After Cranko's untimely death in 1973, Glen TETLEY became director of the Stuttgart until Haydee succeeded him in 1976.

Crater, disappearance of Judge
In 1930 a New York judge abruptly vanished. Joseph Crater had maintained a very successful commercial law practice in New York City. Despite being married, he was also a man-about-town who had numerous affairs with a succession of models and show girls. Crater had been appointed a New York supreme court justice for only a short time when he mysteriously disappeared without a trace. After vacationing with his wife at their summer home in Maine, he planned a short trip to his Manhattan office and promised to return in a few days to celebrate her birthday. Crater gathered various papers and $5,000 from his office, had dinner with friends, then took a taxi and was never to be seen again. News of Crater's disappearance made headlines nationwide, with many reported sightings of the missing judge. Although never firmly established, Crater's disappearance may have been linked to an investigation of graft and corruption in Tammany Hall.

Crawford, Joan (Lucille le Sueur) (1906–1977)
An enormously popular American film actress, Crawford became famous for her brilliant portrayals of the "ruthless working woman." Starting out in local talent shows and contests, Crawford appeared as a chorus girl on Broadway, then as a contract player at MGM in the final days of silent movies (*Our Dancing Daughters,* 1928) and finally as a star in such early talkies as *Grand Hotel* (1932). In the 1930s and early 1940s she starred in several sensationally successful melodramas of the "modern woman" (with Clark GABLE, among others) that won her a huge and adoring female audience; of these roles perhaps only

The Women (1939) stands out as more than a star turn. It wasn't until she left MGM and made the film noir classic *Mildred Pierce* (1945) that she became recognized as one of Hollywood's most talented actresses. Subsequent hits included *Humoresque* (1946), *Possessed* (1947), *Daisy Kenyon* (1947) and *Flamingo Road* (1949). In the 1950s and 1960s her career slipped, and *Whatever Happened to Baby Jane?* (1962) was one of her few successes. Although the Crawford mystique has continued and she is almost always ranked among the top actors of her time, revelations about her character and personal life have cast a shadow on her career.

Craxi, Benedetto (Bettino Craxi)

(1934–) Italian politician, prime minister of Italy (1983–87). A native of Milan, Craxi joined the Socialist Party at an early age. He was elected to the Italian Chamber of Deputies in 1968 and became party leader in 1976. In 1983 Craxi became the country's first Socialist premier, presiding over a five-party coalition government. A moderate in both his foreign and domestic policies, Craxi broadened the base of the Socialist Party, advocated cooperation with the U.S., introduced austerity measures to control inflation, fought organized crime and abolished Catholicism as Italy's official religion. He resigned in March 1987, after three years and seven months in office—the longest tenure of any Italian premier since World War II. In February 1993 Craxi was forced out of the Socialist Party's leadership on allegations of corruption.

Creedence Clearwater Revival

American band cofounded by brothers Tom and John Fogerty. The band blended basic rock, country and rhythm and blues. The bank had six gold records and eight Top 10 singles between 1968 and 1972, including "Suzie Q," "Proud Mary," "Bad Moon Rising" and "Traveling Band." Tom Fogerty left the group in 1971.

Creel, George Edward *(1876–1953)* U.S. journalist. He began his career as a news reporter for the *Kansas City World* (1894). Later, when he established his own newspaper, the *Kansas City Independence* (1899), his reputation as a dedicated investigative

reporter was firmly established. In 1917 President Woodrow WILSON appointed him head of the U.S. Committee on Public Information. Creel ran unsuccessfully against novelist Upton SINCLAIR for the Democratic nomination for governor of California in 1934. He published more than a dozen books, including *War Criminals and Punishment* (1944).

Creeley, Robert White *(1926–)*

American poet and fiction writer. Educated at Harvard (1943–46), Black Mountain College (B.A., 1955) and the University of New Mexico (M.A., 1960), Creeley was influenced by the colloquial language of William Carlos WILLIAMS, the Projectivism of Charles OLSON and the freewheeling and far-ranging compositions of Robert Duncan. His central theme is love, marriage and the relationship between men and women. His verse tends to be terse and typographically slender. His output has been prolific; starting with his first book in 1952, he has published more than a book a year.

Cret, Paul-Philippe *(1876–1945)*

French-born architect who was active and influential in American architecture in the first half of the 20th century. Cret was a graduate of the Paris École des BEAUX-ARTS and was invited to America in 1903 to become the principal teacher and critic at the architectural school (School of Fine Arts) of the University of Pennsylvania in Philadelphia. Under his leadership, the school became preeminent in American architectural education. Particularly well known as a teacher, Cret numbered Louis KAHN among his many distinguished students. Cret also had an active practice. He designed the Pan American Union Building of 1903, the Folger Shakespearean Library of 1930–32 and the Federal Reserve Office Building of 1935–37, all in Washington, D.C. Cret accepted such commissions as the design of the Hall of Science at the Chicago CENTURY OF PROGRESS EXPOSITION of 1933 and the interiors of the Burlington Zephyr railroad train of 1934.

Cretan Uprising of 1935 In early March 1935 the antiroyalist followers of Cretan-born Eleutherios VENIZELOS, Greek premier six times between 1910

and 1933, leader of the Liberal Party and a founder of the republic, rebelled against the government of royalist Panayoti Tsaldaris in protest of the imminent restoration of the monarchy. Government forces under General George Kondylis defeated the rebels, who held out longest in Crete; Venizelos fled to France. In 1935 Kondylis engineered a coup against Tsaldaris, became premier and prompted parliament to recall Greece's exiled King George II. George was enthroned by nearly unanimous plebiscite on November 25, 1935.

Crichton, (John) Michael *(1942–)*

American author and screenwriter. Educated as a doctor and scientist at Harvard University, Crichton has brought his training to bear in such critically acclaimed best-selling suspense novels as *The Andromeda Strain* (1969; filmed 1971), *The Terminal Man* (1972) and *Westworld,* (1974), for which he wrote the screenplay. Other screenplays include *Coma* (1977) and *The Great Train Robbery* (1978), which he adapted from his novel of the same name. Crichton has also written popular thrillers under the pseudonyms John Lange and Jeffrey Hudson and nonfiction, including *Five Patients: The Hospital Explained* (1970) and *Electronic Life: How to Think About Computers* (1983). Other works include *Sphere* (1987), *Travels* (1988) and *Jurassic Park* (1990), the last of which provided the basis for three popular motion pictures. In 1994 Crichton helped develop the medical drama *ER* for NBC.

Crick, Francis Harry Compton

(1916–2004) British molecular biologist. Crick graduated from University College, London, and during WORLD WAR II worked on the development of RADAR and magnetic mines. Later he changed from physics to biology and in 1947 began work at the Strangeways Research Laboratory, Cambridge, transferring to the Medical Research Council unit at the Cavendish Laboratory in 1949. Crick received his Ph.D. in 1953. In 1951 a young American student, James WATSON, arrived at the unit. Watson suggested to Crick that it was necessary to find the molecular structure of the hereditary material DNA (deoxyribonucleic acid) before its function could be properly understood. Much was already known about

the chemical and physical nature of DNA from the studies of such scientists as Phoebus Levene, Erwin CHARGAFF, Alexander Todd and Linus PAULING. Using this knowledge and the X-ray diffraction data of Maurice Wilkins and Rosalind FRANKLIN, Crick and Watson had built, by 1953, a molecular model incorporating all the known features of DNA. Fundamental to the model was their conception of DNA as a double helix. The model served to explain how DNA replicates—by the two spirals uncoiling and each acting as a template—and how the hereditary information might be coded—in the sequence of bases along the chains. Ten years' intensive research in many laboratories around the world all tended to confirm Crick and Watson's model. For their work, which has been called the most significant discovery of the 20th century, they were awarded, with Wilkins, the 1962 NOBEL PRIZE in physiology or medicine. Crick, in collaboration with Sydney Brenner, made important contributions to the understanding of the genetic code. He also suggested that in protein synthesis, small adaptor molecules act as intermediaries between the messenger RNA template and the amino acids. Such adaptors, or transfer RNAs, were identified independently by Robert Holley and Paul Berg in 1956. Crick is also known for his formulation of the central dogma of molecular genetics, which assumes that the passage of genetic information is from DNA to RNA to protein. David BALTIMORE was later to show that in certain cases, information can actually go from RNA to DNA. In 1966 Crick published the book *Of Molecules and Men,* reviewing the recent progress in molecular biology. He remained in Cambridge until 1977, when he took up a professorship at the Salk Institute in San Diego. Crick died of colon cancer in 2004.

Crippen, Robert (1937–   ) U.S. astronaut. The first person to pilot a manned U.S. SPACE SHUTTLE launch (STS-1, April 12–14, 1981), Crippen, with Commander John Young, began the historic two-day journey aboard Columbia on the 20th anniversary of humankind's first spaceflight, by Soviet cosmonaut Yuri GAGARIN (April 12, 1961). An experienced pilot, Crippen had served aboard carriers in the Pacific and worked as an instructor for the Aerospace Research Pilot School commanded by Chuck YEAGER. Trained for military spaceflight in the U.S.A.F. Manned Orbiting Laboratory (MOL) Program, which was canceled in 1969, Crippen joined NASA and worked as a team leader and member of the astronaut support crew for all three SKYLAB missions and the APOLLO-SOYUZ TEST PROJECT before being transferred to the Shuttle development program. Crippen also commanded shuttle mission STS-7 (June 18–24, 1983), which included Sally RIDE, America's first woman in space, as well as missions 41-C (April 6–13, 1984) and 41-G (October 5–13, 1984). Logging over 23 days and 14 hours in his four space voyages, Crippen is NASA's "old pro" of the post-Apollo, post-Skylab era. Crippen retired from NASA in 1991.

Cripps, Sir (Richard) Stafford *(1889–1952)* British statesman. A brilliant lawyer, he was knighted in 1930 and was made solicitor general (1930–31). A radical socialist in the 1930s, he was a Labour MP but was expelled from the party in 1939 for advocating an alliance with the communists in a united front. He was CHURCHILL's ambassador to the USSR from 1940 to 1942 and later served as lord privy seal, leader of the House of Commons and minister of aircraft production. In 1945 Cripps was readmitted to his party and became president of the board of trade (1945–47) and chancellor of the exchequer (1947–50) in Clement ATTLEE's postwar Labour government. He is remembered best for the tight controls of the austerity program that he instituted while guiding Britain's economic life. Cripps retired in 1950.

Croatia A former constituent republic of YUGOSLAVIA, bordering on the northeastern shore of the Adriatic Sea; encompasses Slavonia, Dalmatia and most of Istria, as well as Croatia

CROATIA	
1918	On dissolution of Habsburg empire, Croatia joins Serbia, Slovenia and Montenegro in the "Kingdom of Serbs, Croats and Slovenes," under the Serbian Karageorgević dynasty.
1929	The kingdom of Yugoslavia is declared. Croatia continues its campaign for autonomy.
1930s	Ustaša, a Croat terrorist organization, begins a campaign against non-Catholic Serb dominance of Yugoslavia.
1941	Germany and Italy set up the so-called Independent State of Croatia, run by the Croat Ustaše regime of Ante Pavelić; the Ustaše begin the expulsion and extermination of Serbs, Jews, Gypsies, and antifascist Croats, killing more than 500,000; the communist Partisans, led by ethnic Croat Josep Broz (later, Marshal Tito), organize resistance against the Ustaše and their Axis supporters.
1944	Partisan control of Croatian territory, except for the major cities, is nearly complete; Partisans retaliate against anti-Partisan Croats, slaughtering tens of thousands.
1945	Both World War II and the Croatian civil war end; the Yugoslavia Socialist Federation is formed, led by Marshal Tito, consisting of six republics: Croatia, Slovenia, Bosnia-Herzegovina, Serbia, Montenegro and Macedonia.

1948	Tito breaks relations with the Soviet Union and Tito replaces Croatian-nationalist members of the Croatian Communist Party with centralist officials of his own choosing.
1969	Efforts at decentralization by the Yugoslavian federal government fuel a cultural flowering in Croatia known as the "Croatian Spring," a movement that gained nationalist momentum under the reformist leadership of Miko Tripalo and Savka Dabcević-Kucar.
1971	Tito responds to calls for greater Croatian autonomy by dismissing and/or imprisoning numerous intellectual and cultural leaders, including Tripalo, Dabcević-Kucar and members of the cultural organization Matica Hravatska.
1974	Yugoslavia adopts a new republican constitution but undermines the autonomy nominally granted to Croatia by continuing to exercise centralized control of the Croatian Communist Party.
1989	Croatia, along with Slovenia, resists centralization and calls for its own multiparty elections.
1990	In the first multiparty national elections since World War II, the Communist Party is defeated by the Croatian Democratic Union (HDZ), a conservative nationalist party led by Franjo Tudjman; President Tudjman's administration begins to purge Serbs from positions of authority, prompting fear among Serbs of a reprise of the ethnic cleansing campaigns of the 1940s.
1991	Serb-dominated Krajina in the southwest secedes from Croatia to join with Serbia; Croatia declares independence; civil war breaks out in Krajina between ethnic Serbs and ethnic Croats; the government of Yugoslavia declares war on Croatia, bombs the cities of Vukovar and Dubrovnik, and occupies about one-third of Croatian territory.
1992	The UN dispatches 14,000 peace-keeping troops to Croatia; the European Community and the United States recognize Croatia's independence; Croatia supports Croats against Serbs and Muslims in the war in Bosnia-Herzegovina; Tudjman is reelected to a five-year term as president of Croatia.
1995	Tudjman, Milošević and President Alija Izetbegović of Bosnia-Herzegovina sign a peace accord in Dayton, Ohio, ending the war in Bosnia-Herzegovina; Croatia reasserts control over Krajina, leading to a mass exodus of Croatian Serbs; the HDZ dominates legislative elections but loses seats.
1997	Tudjman is reelected, but independent election monitors criticize his control over the media and curtailed minority suffrage.
1998	After two years under UN supervision, eastern Slavonia and Baranja are returned to Croatian control.
1999	Tudjman dies and is succeeded by Vlatko Pavletić as acting president.
2000	Stjepan Mesić, leader of the Croatian People's Party, is elected president, ending HDZ rule.
2001	General Mirko Norac faces the international war crimes tribunal in The Hague on charges of killing Serb civilians in Gospić in 1991. Two years later, the tribunal sentences him to 12 years in jail.
2002	The Croatian government refuses to turn in General Janko Bobetko to The Hague tribunal, citing health reasons. The extradition controversy, which escalates during the course of the year, ends when Bobetko dies in 2003.
2003	Croatian Democratic Union (HDZ) representative Ivo Sanader is appointed prime minister.
2004	The Hague tribunal sentences Croatian Serb leader Milan Babić to 13 years in jail for his role in war crimes against non-Serbs in the Krajina Serb Republic.
2005	President Stjepan (Stipe) Mesić is elected for a second term. The European Union defers Croatia's induction into the organization due to the country's failure to indict General Ante Gotovina, who is wanted by The Hague tribunal on charges of war crimes.

Croatia

AUSTRIA

SLOVENIA

HUNGARY

– – – Republic border

Drava R.

Varaždin
Koprivnica

Zagreb   Bjelovar

Daruvar   *Drava R.*   Beli Manastir

Karlovac   Našice   Osijek

Buje   Rijeka   Sisak   Nova   Dakovo   Vukovar
                            Gradiska   Vinkovci

Krk   Krk   Senj   Slavonski   SERBIA
Pula   Brod

Cres   Slunj

Rab

Pag   Gospić

Dugi Otok   Gracać   BOSNIA-
                  Zadar   HERZEGOVINA
            Knin

Adriatic Sea   Šibenik

N   Ugljane

Šolta   Split
Brač   Markarska
Vis   *Hvar*   Ploče

SERBIA AND MONTENEGRO

Korčula
Lastovo   *Mljet*   Dubrovnik

MONTENEGRO

0 ——— 50 miles
0 ——— 50 km

© Infobase Publishing

itself. In 1867, with the establishment of the Austro-Hungarian dual monarchy, Croatia proper was incorporated into Hungary with Zagreb as its capital. When the AUSTRO-HUNGARIAN EMPIRE collapsed after WORLD WAR I, Croatia affiliated itself with the realm of the Serbs, Croats and Slovenes, named Yugoslavia in 1929; but until WORLD WAR II some Croat loyalists still fought for independence. In 1941 the Nazi conquest of Yugoslavia put the area under German and Italian rule until 1945, when Yugoslavian sovereignty was reinstated. During WORLD WAR II many Croatians joined the anticommunist CHETNIKS. The Croatians never fully accepted their status as part of Serbian-dominated Yugoslavia, and with the fall of Communist governments throughout Eastern Europe at the end of the 1980s, Croatian demands for independence increased. On June 25, 1991, Croatia declared its independence from Yugoslavia and began a four-year civil war with Serbian-led Yugoslav forces. Croatian independence was internationally recognized, and the independent nation joined

the UN in 1992. In 1995 Croatia was one of several nations to sign the DAYTON ACCORDS and agree to reestablish relations with the Serbian remnant of Yugoslavia. In February 2000 Stipe (or Stjepan) Mesić, leader of the Croatian People's Party, was elected president. He was reelected in 2005.

Croce, Benedetto (*1866–1952*) Italian philosopher, historian and statesman. After studying in Rome and Naples, Croce founded a critical review, *La Critica,* in 1903. His philosophy emphasized reconciliation between human activities and an aesthetic theory. Croce was minister of education from 1920 to 1921. He resigned from his professorship at Naples when MUSSOLINI came to power in 1922. Croce strongly attacked TOTALITARIANISM in his work *History as the Story of Liberty* (1941), and with the fascist regime's downfall (see FASCISM) promoted LIBERALISM through his writings. He also wrote critical studies of Dante, Ariosto and Corneille as well as an autobiography.

Cronin, Archibald Joseph (*1896–1981*) British novelist. Educated at

Glasgow University Medical School, Cronin worked as a medical inspector of mines and as a general practitioner in Wales and in London, experiences that figure in his work. His extremely popular, though not particularly literary, novels include *Hatter's Castle* (1931), the success of which allowed him to give up practicing medicine in favor of writing, *The Citadel* (1937; filmed 1938), *The Judas Tree* (1961), and *A Question of Modernity* (1966). Much of his work has been adapted for films or television programs.

Cronin, James Watson (*1931– *) American physicist. Cronin was educated at the Southern Methodist University and at Chicago, where he earned his Ph.D. in 1955. After a period at the Brookhaven National Laboratory he moved to Princeton in 1958 and later served as professor of physics from 1965 until 1971, when he was appointed to a comparable chair at the University of Chicago. Cronin and Val FITCH shared the 1980 NOBEL PRIZE in physics for their work.

Cronin, Joseph Edward (*1906–1984*) American baseball player and executive. A shortstop, Cronin played principally with the Boston Red Sox. He was manager (1934–45) and general manager (1945–58) of the Red Sox, and president of the American League (1959–73). He was inducted into the Baseball Hall of Fame in 1956.

Cronkite, Walter (*1916– *) American radio and television journalist. Cronkite became a trusted and ubiquitous figure in postwar America through his preeminent role with CBS television news. From 1962 to 1981 he was the anchorman of the *CBS Evening News.* His trademark sign-off line, "And that's the way it is," was familiar to millions of devoted viewers. In a 1973 public opinion poll, Cronkite was voted the most trusted man in America. Among the major stories he covered were the 1963 assassination of President John F. KENNEDY (during which Cronkite openly wept on camera), the 1969 U.S. Moon landing, WATERGATE and the VIETNAM WAR. Cronkite was born in Missouri and educated at the University of Texas, which he left in his junior year to become a reporter for the *Houston Post.* He covered WORLD

WAR II for United Press and joined CBS in 1950.

Crosby, Bing (Harry Lillis Crosby) *(1901–1977)* American JAZZ and popular music singer and film actor. Crosby enjoyed outstanding success both as a vocalist and as a HOLLYWOOD star. Born in Tacoma, Washington, he began his career as a singer with various jazz bands in the 1920s, most notably the big band led by Paul WHITEMAN. In the early 1930s Crosby hosted his own radio program and gained national popularity both as an entertainment personality and as a singer. His mellifluous baritone led to ultimate record sales of over 30 million, with "White Christmas" (1942), heading the list as the most enduringly popular single in the history of the recording industry. He was a success in Hollywood as well, making numerous films from the early 1930s through the 1960s, including *The Road to Singapore* (1940) and six other "Road" comedies in which he was memorably teamed with Bob HOPE. Crosby could also play dramatic parts, as an ACADEMY AWARD for best actor for his role as a priest in *Going My Way* (1944) testifies.

Crosby, Harry *(1897–1929)* American poet, essayist and small press publisher. Crosby was raised in a wealthy Boston family and attended Harvard University but rejected a banking career for the life of a poet and bohemian. He married Caresse Crosby, who also wrote poetry and held a patent for having invented the strapless brassiere. Together, the two financed their own small literary enterprise, the Black Sun Press, an avant-garde fixture in Paris during the 1920s. Crosby books published by the press include *Shadows of the Sun* (1922) and *Chariot of the Sun* (1927). Solar imagery reoccurs obsessively in Crosby's verse. With his illicit lover of the time, Crosby committed suicide in 1929.

Crosby, Stills, Nash and Young American ROCK AND ROLL band originally formed in 1968. The original members of the group—three singer-guitarists—were David Crosby, Graham Nash and Steven Stills. All had enjoyed success with prior bands—Crosby with the BYRDS, Nash with the Hollies and Stills with Buffalo Spring-field. Their first album, *Crosby, Stills & Nash* (1969), combined sensitive songwriting with pleasing vocal harmonies and featured a hit single, "Marrakesh Express." Shortly thereafter another Buffalo Springfield alumnus, Neil Young, joined the band to contribute to its second album, *Deja Vu* (1970), which spawned three hit singles, "Woodstock," "Teach Your Children" and "Ohio." The band broke up in 1971 but has since enjoyed several reunions in its original trio grouping, without Young.

Crosland, Anthony *(1918–1977)* British politician. A member of the LABOUR PARTY, Crosland was a leading theorist of democratic socialism. He held six ministerial posts in Labour governments between 1964 and his death. From 1976 until his death he was foreign secretary.

Cross, Charles Frederick *(1855–1935)* British industrial chemist. Cross studied chemistry at King's College, London, in Zurich and at Owens College, Manchester, where he met Edward Bevan, whose partner he became and with whom he developed the viscose process of rayon manufacture. Cross was subsequently involved in the industrial development of this process. He wrote several books on cellulose and papermaking.

Crossfield, Scott *(1921–2006)* U.S. test pilot, the first person to fly at twice the speed of sound. After earning his navy pilot wings at the Naval Aviation Cadet School in 1942, Crossfield spent World War II as a flight instructor in Texas and after the war attended the University of Washington, receiving a master's degree in aeronautical engineering. In 1950 he joined NACA, the National Advisory Committee for Aeronautics, which would later become NASA, the NATIONAL AERONAUTICS AND SPACE ADMINISTRATION. NACA was doing work in experimental aircraft, and Crossfield signed on as a test pilot. Working out of Edwards Air Force Base deep in the Mojave Desert of California, Crossfield quickly established a reputation as one of America's top test pilots.

Flying such advanced aircraft as the X-1, America's first rocket plane, Crossfield developed a friendly rivalry with Charles "Chuck" YEAGER, the first human being to fly at the speed of sound. The rivalry led to an undeclared race between Crossfield and Yeager to see who would be the first to break Mach 2 (twice the speed of sound). In November 1953 Crossfield reached that speed, not in the specially developed X-1 but in a Douglas D-558-1 Skyrocket test plane hastily upgraded for the purpose. Leaving NACA for North American Aviation in 1955, Crossfield became instrumental in the development of America's most advanced rocket plane, the X-15. As engineer and test pilot he was inseparable from the plane, the pride of North America until it was turned over to NASA in 1960. During that time Crossfield had flown the X-15 in 14 of its 30 test flights for North American, including its first "captive flight" attached to the wing of a B-52 "mother ship," its first glide flight and its first powered flight.

Crothers, Rachel *(1878–1958)* The most important female playwright in American theater during the early decades of the 20th century. She was born in Bloomington, Illinois. Her mother was a physician, rather unusual in those days, and perhaps that kind of family background inspired her to concentrate upon women's issues in her subsequent work. After several years writing and staging one-act plays for the Stanhope-Wheatcroft School of Acting in New York, she turned to full-length works. *The Three of Us* (1906) was her first successful Broadway production. Her most important plays examined "women's themes"—subjects such as prostitution, the double standard, birth control, new professions. *A Man's World* (1910) and *He and She* (1912) were her first fully developed examples. In the first, heroine "Frank" Ware stubbornly refuses to sacrifice her independence for a man. In the second, Ann Herford, a sculptress, tragically relinquishes a career in art for the sake of harmony in a marriage. Later plays such as *Young Wisdom* (1914), *Nice People* (1921), *Mary the Third* (1923), *When Ladies Meet* (1932) and *Susan and God* (1937), her most acclaimed play, all deal with aspects of women's search for freedom in a male-dominated society. "Most of the great modern plays are studies of women," she said in 1912. "If you want to see the signs of the times, watch women. Their evolution is the most important thing in modern life." She was more than a mere polemicist, however, and her chosen subject of the tensions between men and women (not to mention an astute sense of stagecraft) make much of her work relevant today.

Crowe, Russell *(1964–   )* Film actor. Born in New Zealand, Crowe has lived in Australia since his childhood. After a career as a child star on Australian television, a lead singer and guitarist in a pub rock band and an actor in two films for Australian companies, Crowe broke into the American film market with *The Quick and the Dead* (1995) and *Virtuosity* (1995), a science fiction production starring Denzel Washington. His third Hollywood film, *L.A. Confidential* (1997), catapulted him to star status and led to major cinematic successes such as *The Insider* (1999), *Gladiator* (2003), for which he won the Academy Award for best actor, and *A Beautiful Mind* (2001).

Crowley, Aleister Edward Alexander *(1875–1947)* English writer and occult figure, popularly known as "the Great Beast" and "the wickedest man in the world." He was educated at Cambridge University. Rejecting his strict Christian upbringing, he became notorious as a "black magician" because of his anti-Christian writings, his drug-taking, his hedonism and his public pagan celebrations. During his lifetime he published numerous volumes of poetry, fiction and essays. *Magick in Theory and Practice* (1929), a brilliant and stylish guide to occult self-development, is his masterwork. His writings influenced the NEW AGE MOVEMENT of the 1980s and 1990s.

Crown Film Unit The most important documentary film production company in the history of the British cinema. It grew out of the Film Unit formed by John GRIERSON for the Empire Marketing Board in 1930. For the next three years, from its location in Oxford Street in London, the unit was staffed by rising young filmmakers who, shielded by Grierson and sponsor Sir Stephen Tallents from bureaucratic interference, produced a

group of minor masterpieces lumped under the catchphrase "Bring the Empire alive!" In 1933 the unit was taken over by the General Post Office, and in 1939 it was transferred to the Ministry of Information, where it was renamed the Crown Film Unit. When the Conservatives returned to power in 1951, the unit was dismantled. Brash young Harry Watt made *Night Mail* (1936), a glorious tribute to the mail trains running between London and Edinburgh, with verse narrative by W. H. AUDEN and music by Benjamin BRITTEN. (Britten's *Young Person's Guide to the Orchestra* was written for the unit's *Instruments of the Orchestra*, 1946.) Basil Wright and Alberto Cavalcanti's *Song of Ceylon* (1934) transmuted into visual poetry the incursion of the British tea trade into that country. During WORLD WAR II, Humphrey Jennings produced *Listen to Britain* (1943), a sensitive masterpiece about the British homefront. Other major figures in the unit included Paul Rotha (the group's historian), Edgar Anstey, Stuart Legg and John Taylor. Through theatrical and 16mm distribution these films celebrated the British working person.

Crucible, The Play by American playwright Arthur MILLER. *The Crucible* (1953), which deals with the impact of panic and persecution when society allows them free rein, was written at the height of the anticommunist blacklistings being conducted by Senator Joseph MCCARTHY in the early 1950s. These blacklistings were often termed *witch hunts* by critics who opposed McCarthy's slanders and excesses. Miller borrowed the metaphor quite literally, setting *The Crucible* in Salem, Massachusetts, during the late 17th century in an attempt to cast a comparative historical light on the McCarthy era. The plot concerns two adolescent girls who are obsessed with dark, erotic fantasies that they repress and project by means of accusing other, innocent persons in Salem of heresy and witchcraft. Jean-Paul SARTRE adapted *The Crucible* into a screenplay for a 1956 French-German film version. *The Crucible* continues to be widely performed and is regarded as a classic of the post–World War II American theater.

cruise missile An accurate, low-flying and virtually undetectable missile with first-strike capability. The U.S. deployment in 1983 of cruise missiles with nuclear warheads in Western Europe encouraged a growth in antinuclear agitation, particularly in Britain, West Germany and the Netherlands. Medium-range cruise missiles, carrying conventional warheads, were used for the first time in the PERSIAN GULF WAR (1991). They were launched by the U.S. against strategic targets in IRAQ with great effectiveness.

Crumb, George *(1929–   )* American composer. Crumb, who won the PULITZER PRIZE in 1968 for his composition *Echoes of Time and the River,* is one of the major American composers of the postwar era. Educated at the Universities of Illinois and Michigan, as well as at the Berlin Hochschule für Musik, Crumb has held a series of academic teaching posts since the 1950s while producing a broad range of compositions. Crumb's musical style is distinctly unpretentious and idiosyncratic, falling into none of the prevailing schools of composition of his era. At the same time Crumb is not at all simplistic in his approach, drawing from the tonal techniques of Anton von WEBERN as well as from the romanticism of 19th-century masters such as Claude DEBUSSY. Other works by Crumb include *String Quartet* (1954), *Night Music I* (1963) and *II* (1964), and *Songs, Drones, and Refrains of Death* (1968).

Cry, the Beloved Country Novel by South African writer Alan PATON. The 1948 book tells the story of Rev. Stephen Kumalo who searches for and finds his sister, Gertrude, and son Absolom in Johannesburg, SOUTH AFRICA. Circumstances have forced her into prostitution, and Absolom has murdered the son of a white farmer, James Jarvis. Absolom is sentenced to death for the crime, but the novel ends on a hopeful note as Jarvis and Kumalo are reconciled, and Jarvis commits himself to the struggle of the impoverished blacks of Johannesburg. The novel is not only an eloquent plea for racial equality but also examines how a squalid and deprived environment can thwart and pervert the human spirit. An American film, for which Paton

Cuba

Gulf of Mexico

THE BAHAMAS

Havana
Matanzas
Corralillo
Sagua la Grande
San-Cristóbal
Artemisa
Cárdenas
Colón
Santa Clara
ATLANTIC OCEAN
Los Arroyos
Pinar del Río
Pedro Betancourt
Santo Domingo
Caibarien
Guane
Cienfuegos
Sancti Spiritus
Ciego de Avila
Morón
Esmeralda
Nueva Gerona
Nuevitas
La Fe
Florida
Isle of Juventud
Camagüey
Jesus Menéndez
Trinidad
Crucero
Las Tunas
Sagua de Tánamo
Caribbean Sea
Santa Cruz del Sur
Holguín
Moa
N
Manzanillo
El Salvador
Baracoa
Niquero
Bayamo
Guantánamo
Yucatán Channel
Santiago de Cuba
Guantánamo Bay U.S. Naval Base
Windward Passage

Cayman Islands
(UNITED KINGDOM)

0   150 miles
0   150 km

© Infobase Publishing

wrote the screenplay, appeared in 1951. (See also APARTHEID.)

Cuba The largest island and nation of the West Indies, flanked by the Caribbean Sea on the south, the Atlantic Ocean on the northeast and the Gulf of Mexico on the northwest; the nation includes a few other islands of which the Isle of Youth (Isle of Pines until 1978) is the largest. Connections with the UNITED STATES have played a significant role in Cuban affairs for over a century. Active American attention dates to the Spanish-American War of 1898, provoked by the explosion of the U.S. battleship *Maine* in Havana harbor. On May 20, 1901, a Cuban government independent of Spain assumed control, although an act of the U.S. Congress, the Platt Amendment, granted the U.S. the power to intercede in Cuban matters—a right exercised in 1906 and not relinquished until 1934. Fulgencio BATISTA Y ZALDÍVAR, an unscrupulous dictator who had seized power in 1933, was ousted in 1959 by rebels led by Fidel CASTRO.

Castro instituted extensive social and economic changes. He quickly aligned Cuba with the USSR and got in return monetary and military aid. In 1961 Castro proclaimed himself a Marxist-Leninist. On April 14, 1961, a force of anti-Castro Cubans, trained by the U.S., landed at the island's BAY OF PIGS and was utterly crushed (see BAY OF PIGS INVASION). In the summer of 1962 a U.S. air survey discovered that the USSR was erecting missile sites in Cuba. In a tense COLD WAR face-off, the U.S. imposed a naval blockade of Cuba; the Russians capitulated and removed their missiles (see CUBAN MISSILE CRISIS).

In 1976 Castro deployed large numbers of Cuban troops abroad, chiefly to ANGOLA, to bolster Soviet-backed governments or rebels; by 1978 approximately 50,000 Cubans were in Africa. In 1980 Castro temporarily withdrew an embargo on emigration, and by September nearly 125,000 Cubans had sought sanctuary in the U.S. (see MARIEL BOATLIFT). The U.S. has leased a naval base at GUANTÁNAMO Bay, on Cuba's southeastern coast, since 1903. Relations have yet to fully normalize between Cuba and the U.S. Following the fall of Communist governments in Eastern Europe in 1989–90 and political and economic reforms in the USSR, Castro repeatedly insisted that Cuba would continue to develop as a Marxist-Leninist state. Although Cuba's economy suffered when the Soviet Union collapsed in December 1991 and the U.S. intensified its trade embargo after Cuba shot down two civilian aircraft piloted by Cuban exiles in 1996, Cuba did benefit from increased attention when Pope JOHN PAUL II visited the country in 1998.

Cuban leader Fidel Castro (foreground). 1960 (LI-BRARY OF CONGRESS, PRINTS AND PHOTOGRAPHS DIVISION)

CUBA

1902	Independence from U.S.; U.S. retains right to intervene and retains naval bases.
1933	Military revolt brings army sergeant Fulgencio Batista to power.
1944	Batista retires after official four-year term as president.
1952	Batista returns to power in bloodless coup.
1953	Radical group led by Fidel Castro attacks army barracks; Castro is captured but later released and exiled.
1956	Castro lands in Cuba at head of small revolutionary group, begins guerrilla campaign against Batista government.
1959	Castro's guerrillas force Batista to flee Cuba; Castro assumes power.
1960	Castro nationalizes U.S. business interests in Cuba.
1961	U.S.-sponsored anti-Castro émigrés land of Bay of Pigs; invasion fails.
1962	Soviet missiles are withdrawn following U.S. naval blockade.
1980	125,000 Cuban "marielitos" land in Florida.
1990	38,000 of 50,000 troops pulled out of Angola; Castro denounces anticommunist reforms in Eastern Europe, pledges to maintain socialism in Cuba.
1991	Collapse of USSR deprives Cuba of economic aid; Soviet troops withdraw from the island.
1996	Cuba shoots down two airplanes piloted by Cuban exiles; U.S. tightens embargo.
1998	Pope John Paul II visits Cuba and calls for greater freedom within Cuba, as well as a lifting of the U.S. embargo.
1999	Head of the U.S. Chamber of Commerce Thomas Donahue visits Cuba to look at potential business ties, the first such visit in 40 years; Cuba demands return of Elián González, a refugee who lost his mother and other companions after the boat they were traveling on to Florida sank; relatives in Miami were caring for the boy, but his father remains in Cuba.
2000	U.S. federal agents take Elián González from his relatives' home in Miami and return him to his father; U.S. courts uphold the custody rights of Elián's father, and father and son return to Cuba to a rapturous welcome.
2002	The U.S. exports food to Cuba for the first time in more than 40 years to help it cope with the devastation caused by Hurricane Michelle. In June National Assembly enacts legislation to make socialism in Cuba "permanent and untouchable."
2005	Hurrican Dennis causes widespread destruction.

Cuban missile crisis Confrontation of October 1962 between the U.S. and the USSR, resulting from a Soviet attempt to base nuclear missiles in CUBA and U.S. insistence that the missiles be removed. When American reconnaissance flights over Cuba confirmed allegations that the USSR was constructing ballistic missile-launching sites, President John F. KENNEDY issued (October 22) a public denunciation of the Soviet action. He announced a U.S. naval blockade of Cuba to prevent any further shipments and demanded withdrawal of all Soviet missiles from the island. On October 26 the Russians countered with an offer to remove their missiles from Cuba if all NATO missiles were withdrawn from Turkey. The U.S. refused, tension mounted and war seemed imminent until October 28 when Soviet premier Nikita KHRUSHCHEV agreed to withdraw the missiles and dismantle the launching sites providing the U.S. lifted the naval blockade and promised not to invade Cuba. With these assurances from the U.S., the naval blockade ended on November 20 and Soviet missiles were withdrawn. Kennedy's stand during this crisis is widely regarded as a significant U.S. victory in the

COLD WAR. A secret agreement was later revealed between Kennedy and Khrushchev in which the U.S. also promised to remove its Jupiter missiles from Turkey.

Cuban Revolt of 1917 Mario García Menocal, CUBA's incumbent conservative president, was reelected in 1916, but the opposition liberals claimed fraud, a protest upheld by Cuba's supreme court, and new elections were scheduled for February 1917 in several provinces. However, liberals rose in revolt, García Menocal assembled an army and blocked them, while U.S. Marines landed in Santiago to restore order. Within weeks García Menocal's forces, supported by the U.S., had crushed the rebels, and García Menocal was inaugurated president on May 20, 1917. To maintain order, García Menocal asked for and received U.S. troops; they remained until 1923.

Cuban Revolts of 1930–1933 After securing a constitutional amendment providing for a six-year term, President Gerardo Machado y Morales was reelected president of Cuba in 1928. Students at the University of Havana opposed his dictatorial policies, and the university was closed in 1930. While the army easily defeated a band of revolutionaries landing at Gibara in August 1931, Cubans continued to resist with terror and sabotage, organizing secret societies such as ABC, estimated to have 30,000 to 40,000 members. Government reprisals were murderous, but mediation by U.S. ambassador Sumner Wells in June 1933 did not prevent a general strike and a clash between police and citizens. The army rebelled, forcing Machado from office on August 12, 1933; Carlos Manuel de Céspedes y Quesada became provisional president but was ousted on September 5 in an army coup staged by Sergeant Fulgencio BATISTA Y ZALDÍVAR, who installed professor Ramón Grau San Martín as president and himself as commander in chief of the army and virtual dictator.

cubism Important movement in painting and other arts during the first two decades of the 20th century. Cubism was largely based in France. The painters Georges BRAQUE and Pablo PICASSO are commonly accorded joint status as the creators of cubism by way of their 1907–08 collaborative efforts in Paris. Cubism sought to project standard visual realities onto randomly intersecting planes, producing an effect resembling that of a broken mirror. Cubist theory held that a new and intense aesthetic significance could be achieved by recombining ordinary aspects of daily life in this manner. *Les Demoiselles d'Avignon* (1907) by Picasso, which portrays five nude women in highly varied styles, is regarded as the first cubist painting. Subsequent painters influenced by cubism include Marcel DUCHAMP, Juan GRIS, Fernan LÉGER and Francis Picabia. The poet Guillaume APOLLINAIRE championed cubism in his critical writings and adopted its tenets to verse. Other cubist-influenced poets included Jean COCTEAU and Pierre REVERDY.

Cugat, Xavier (Francisco de Asís Javier Cugat Mingall de Bru y Deulofeo) *(1900–1990)* Spanish-born band leader. He began his musical career in Cuba and helped popularize Latin American dance music in the U.S. in the 1930s and 1940s. He and his band, the Gigolos, appeared in many of the U.S.'s top nightclubs, as well as in such films as *A Date with Judy* (1948) and *Neptune's Daughter* (1949). He was married five times, and his wives included singers Abbe Lane and Charo.

Cukor, George *(1899–1983)* American motion picture director, best known for his sensitive direction of actors and of "women's theme" pictures. His career spanned more than 50 years, in which he directed some 50 films. After some success as a Broadway director, he moved to HOLLYWOOD where, working with David O. SELZNICK at RKO and METRO-GOLDWYN-MAYER, he directed several 1930s classics, including an adaptation of Dickens's *David Copperfield* (1935). During this time he made a notable series of pictures with Katharine HEPBURN and guided Greta GARBO through one of her best films, *Camille* (1937). He was chosen to direct *GONE WITH THE WIND* (1939) but was fired by Selznick. His subsequent movies included *The Philadephia Story* (1940) and *Adam's Rib* (1949, both with Hepburn), *Gaslight* (1944, with Ingrid BERGMAN), *A Star Is Born* (1954, with Judy GARLAND), *Born Yesterday* (1950) and *My Fair Lady* (1964), for which he won his only ACADEMY AWARD.

Cullen, Countee *(1903–1946)* American poet. Educated at New York University (B.A., 1925) and Harvard (M.A., 1926), Cullen was a major figure of the HARLEM RENAISSANCE. His early works—*Color* (1925), *Copper Sun* (1927), *The Ballad of the Brown Girl* (1927) and *The Black Christ* (1929)—explored racial themes but were criticized for their romanticism and absence of black rhythms and idiom. *The Medea and Some Poems* (1935) included a translation of Euripides. Cullen also published a novel about HARLEM life (*One Way to Heaven*, 1932), an anthology of black verse (*Caroling Dusk*, 1932) and books for children.

Cultural Revolution Directed at young people, a new political campaign (1966–69) known as the Great Proletarian Cultural Revolution was launched by MAO ZEDONG (Mao Tsetung), China's Communist leader. Mao, whose power base was in the Chinese army, wanted to regain control from the bureaucracies that had grown up in education, industrial management and agricultural and economic development and to encourage the continuation of the revolution in Chinese cultural life. Free rail passes were issued, and hundreds of thousands of militant young men and women flocked to Beijing, China's capital, to march in massive parades reviewed by Mao in Tiananmen Square. These Communists or RED GUARDS vied with each other to express their patriotism and devotion to Mao. They covered walls with posters denouncing Mao's enemies and traveled around China spreading the doctrines contained in Mao's "little red book." This endeavor to re-create and experience the fervor of the Red Army's LONG MARCH of 1934–35 soon got out of hand, however. Bands of Red Guards destroyed works of art and historical relics, denounced intellectuals, burned books and attacked those they considered elitists or anti-Mao. Schools and universities were closed and the economy almost came to a standstill. Red Guards fought one another over ideological differences, and armed Chinese factions clashed in most provinces, especially in the south. Gradually the violence and chaos waned as new Revolutionary Committees, made up of representatives of the army, the more responsible Red Guards and peasants and workers, were organized to restore order and stamp out factionalism. In the spring of 1969 schools were reopened, but the universities did not reopen until September 1970. According to some accounts, the Cultural Revolution did succeed in eliminating many of the age-old differences between rich and poor and city and country, but it did so at enormous cost and loss.

Cummings, Edward Estlin (1894–1962) American poet, prose writer and painter. After graduating from Harvard, Cummings served as a volunteer ambulance driver in France during WORLD WAR I. *The Enormous Room* (1922) is a novelistic account of his brief internment there. His first collection, *Tulips and Chimneys* (1923), contrasted the evils of war to the "sweet spontaneous earth." In 1925 he won the Dial prize. His series of Norton Lectures at Harvard were published as *i: six non-lectures* (1953). In 1955 Cummings received a special citation from the National Book Award committee for *Poems, 1923–1954,* and in 1957 he won the BOLLINGEN PRIZE. Despite its typographical eccentricities, Cummings's work is in many respects quite traditional. It has always been popular with readers, and his innovations have influenced numerous American poets although many critics have found his romantic lyrics somewhat cloying.

Cummings, (Charles Clarence) Robert Orville (1908–1990) American actor. Cummings starred in dozens of films and four television series. He won an Emmy Award for his 1954 portrayal of a conscientious juror in the original television drama *Twelve Angry Men.* He starred in the series *My Hero* (1952–53), *The Bob Cummings Show*

(1955–59), *The New Bob Cummings Show* (1961–62) and *My Living Doll* (1964–65). His film work included Alfred HITCHCOCK's *Saboteur* (1942), *King's Row* (1942) and *Dial M for Murder* (1954).

Cunningham, Glenn (1909–1988) American athlete. As the top U.S. miler of the 1930s, Cunningham set six world records for the mile and the 1,500 meters, and another record at 1,000 yards. In 1979 he was named the greatest track athlete in the history of New York City's Madison Square Garden.

Cunningham, Imogen (1883–1976) American photographer. Born in Portland, Oregon, she began her career in photography at the age of 18. She studied abroad and opened her own photographic studio in Seattle in 1910. A leading member of the West Coast photographers' Group f/64, she is probably best remembered for her powerful portraits. Cunningham is also known for the sensuous studies of flowers she began in the late 1920s, such as *Magnolia Blossom (Tower of Jewels)* (1925), and for her innovative multiple and negative images.

Cunningham, Merce (1919–) American dancer and choreographer. The much-honored Cunningham, whose iconoclastic work in the modern dance idiom was at one time considered "a unique audio-visual torture technique," studied tap, folk and ballroom dancing in his native Washington State before performing with modern dancer Lester Horton. He joined the Martha GRAHAM company in 1939, where he remained as a soloist until 1945, inspiring Graham to create many leading roles for him in such works as *Appalachian Spring.* Since 1944 he has choreographed over 100 dances, including such well-known works as *Summerspace* (1958), *Winterbranch* (1964) and *Rainforest* (1968). Also in 1944 Cunningham began his lifelong collaboration with American composer John CAGE, a fellow experimentalist. Other collaborations with noted painters, sculptors and designers such as Andy WARHOL, Robert RAUSCHENBERG and Jasper JOHNS, are a hallmark of Cunningham's approach to dance. He employs "chance" methods as his favored compositional device,

virtually eliminating narrative from dance, combines everyday actions and gestures with more formal movements, and casts performers of independent mind with a strong foundation in ballet and modern. His dance company was founded in 1952.

Curie, Marie (Maria Skłodowska) (1867–1934) Polish-born chemist whose work on the sources and uses of radioactivity helped set the foundation for 20th-century atomic science. She was the first woman to receive a NOBEL PRIZE and the first person to be awarded the prize twice. Raised in Warsaw, Skłodowska developed an early interest in science (particularly chemistry) and in Polish nationalism. Prohibited from attending the University of Warsaw because she was a woman, she moved to Paris and entered the Sorbonne; she spent most of the remainder of her life in France. She graduated in 1893 at the top of her class with the equivalent of a master's degree in physics. The following year she also obtained a degree in mathematics, placing second in her class. That same year (1894) she met the French physicist Pierre CURIE, whom she married in 1895. Inspired by Henri BECQUEREL's discovery that uranium emits radiation, she began her experiments on radioactivity. For several years she and her husband worked painstakingly to discover and isolate the source of radioactivity in pitchblende, a radioactive ore. They finally isolated and analyzed the element in 1902, naming it radium. In 1903 Curie presented her findings in her doctoral dissertation; that year, she and her husband gained international recognition when, with Becquerel, they were awarded the Nobel Prize in physics. Curie continued her research into radium and radioactivity and suggested that radiation might be used to treat tumors. She received a second Nobel Prize in 1911, this time "for her services to the advancement of chemistry." During WORLD WAR I she directed the basic research division of the Radium Institute (established by the University of Paris and the Pasteur Institute). She taught army medical staff how to use X-RAYS to find bullets and shrapnel in wounded soldiers, and also worked

to ensure that wartime ambulances carried portable X-ray equipment. Throughout the 1920s she worked to promote the medical use of radiation, advising many students and researchers on the new technology she had helped to create. She died at the age of 66 from leukemia caused by her long exposure to radiation. Her daughter, Irène JOLIOT-CURIE (1897–1956), won the Nobel Prize in chemistry the year after Curie's death.

Curie, Pierre (*1859–1906*) French physicist. The son of a physician, Curie was educated at the Sorbonne, where he became an assistant in 1878. In 1882 he was made laboratory chief at the School of Industrial Physics and Chemistry, where he remained until he was appointed professor of physics at the Sorbonne in 1904. In 1895 he married Maria Skłodowska, with whom he conducted research into the radioactivity of radium and with whom he shared the NOBEL PRIZE in physics in 1903. Curie's scientific career falls into two periods, the time before the discovery of radioactivity by Henri BECQUEREL, when he worked on magnetism and crystallography, and the time after, when he collaborated with his wife, Marie CURIE, on this new phenomenon. In 1880, with his brother Jacques, he had discovered piezoelectricity. The brothers used the effect to construct an electrometer to measure small electric currents. Marie Curie later used the instrument to investigate whether radiation from substances other than uranium would cause conductivity in air. Pierre Curie's second major discovery was in the effect of temperature on the magnetic properties of substances, which he was studying for his doctorate. In 1895 he showed that a substance at a certain temperature specific to it will lose its ferromagnetic properties; this critical temperature is now known as the **Curie point.** Shortly after this discovery he began to work intensively with his wife on the new phenomenon of radioactivity. Two new elements, radium and polonium, were discovered in 1898. The rays these elements produced were investigated and enormous efforts were made to produce a sample of pure radium.

Pierre Curie received little recognition in his own country. He was initially passed over for the chairs of physical chemistry and mineralogy in the Sorbonne and was defeated when he applied for membership of the Académie in 1902. (He was, however, admitted in 1905.) The only reason he seems eventually to have been given a chair at the Sorbonne (in 1904) was that he had been offered a post in Geneva and was seriously thinking of leaving France. Partly this may have been because his political sympathies were very much to the left and because he was unwilling to participate in the science policies of the Third Republic. Curie may have been one of the first people to suffer from radiation sickness. No attempts were made in the early days to restrict the levels of radiation received. He died accidentally in 1906 in rather strange circumstances—he slipped while crossing a Paris street, fell under a passing horse cab and was kicked to death. The Curies' daughter Irène JOLIOT-CURIE carried on research in radioactivity and also received the NOBEL PRIZE for work done with her husband, Frédéric.

Curley, James Michael (*1874–1958*) American politician. A Democrat, Curley began his public career in 1902 in the Massachusetts legislature and subsequently served as congressman (1911–14, 1943–45), Boston mayor (1914–18, 1922–26, 1930–34, 1946–50) and governor (1935–37). In 1946 he was convicted of mail fraud and served five months in prison before President Harry TRUMAN pardoned him—and he returned to complete his last term as mayor.

Curragh, the Plain in County Kildare, Ireland, where the yearly Irish Derby is held. The Curragh is at the center of the Irish racing industry; horse races have been run at this ancient site since the first century A.D. In 1914 the CURRAGH INCIDENT involved British officers who rebelled against the HOME RULE Act.

Curragh Incident As Ulster opposition to Irish HOME RULE mounted in early 1914, the British government considered sending troops to Northern Ireland. However, in March 1914 the government informed officers stationed at the Curragh, near Dublin, that they might resign their commissions and be dismissed from the army if they were unwilling to fight the Ulstermen. Of the 71 officers in the Third Cavalry Brigade, 58 of them, including the commander, said they would resign if ordered north. British military officials responded by assuring the officers that they would not be ordered to force Home Rule on Ulster, and the officers withdrew their resignations. The incident was an unusual case of military officers influencing the government away from an unpopular policy.

Curtin, John Joseph Ambrose (*1885–1945*) Prime minister of Australia (1941–45). Curtin, who had become a socialist in 1906, began his career as a secretary to the Victorian timber worker's union in 1911. From 1917 to 1928 he was editor of the *Westralian Worker,* meanwhile working to promote the LABOUR PARTY, and was a Labour member of Parliament from 1928 to 1931 and from 1934 to 1945. He became leader of the party in 1935 and in 1941 became prime minister. Curtin was an asset to the Allies during WORLD WAR II, offering full support to Britain in the war against HITLER and joining with the U.S. in the Pacific war against JAPAN. (See WORLD WAR II IN THE PACIFIC.) However, when a joint defense with the U.S. was set up under General Douglas MACARTHUR, Curtin sought an increased British naval presence to counteract MacArthur's growing authority. Curtin was reelected in a landslide victory in 1943 and died in office five weeks before the end of the war in Asia.

Curtis, Cyrus H. K. (*1850–1933*) American publisher. A self-made man, Curtis began his publishing career as a newspaper delivery boy in his hometown of Portland, Maine. At 15 he launched *Young America,* a weekly paper, and four years later moved to Boston to work as an ad salesman for the *Boston Times.* Along with a partner he established a newspaper, *The People's Ledger,* which he moved to Philadelphia in 1875. With the editorial aid of his wife, Curtis founded in 1883 the instantly popular *Ladies' Home Journal* as a monthly supplement to another Philadelphia paper, *The Tribune and Farmer.* This success and others led him to expand his business, forming the Curtis Publishing Company a decade later. In 1897 he bought the *Saturday Evening Post,* which had been started by Benjamin Franklin in 1728 as *The Pennsylvania Gazette,* and in 1911 Curtis acquired *The Country Gentleman.* Curtis said of his chosen profession, "I edit the editors."

Curtis, Heber Doust *(1872–1942)* American astronomer. Curtis earned his A.B. (1892) and A.M. (1893) from the University of Michigan, where he studied classics. He moved to California in 1894, where he became professor of Latin and Greek at Napa College. There his interest in astronomy was aroused. After earning his Ph.D. from the University of Virginia, in 1902 he joined the staff of the Lick Observatory, where he remained until 1920 when he became director of the Allegheny Observatory of the University of Pittsburgh. In 1930 he was appointed director of the University of Michigan's observatory. Curtis's early work was concerned with the measurement of the radial velocities of the brighter stars. From 1910 on, however, he was involved in research on the nature of "spiral nebulae" and became convinced that these were isolated independent star systems. In 1917 he argued that the observed brightness of novas he and George Ritchey had found on photographs of the nebulae indicated that the nebulae lay well beyond our galaxy. He also maintained that extremely bright novas (later identified as supernovas) could not be included with the novae as distance indicators. He estimated the Andromeda nebula to be 500,000 light-years away. Curtis's view was opposed by many, including Harlow SHAPLEY, who proposed that our galaxy was 300,000 light-years in diameter, far larger than previously assumed, and that the spiral nebulae were associated with our galaxy. In 1920, at a meeting of the National Academy of Sciences, Curtis engaged in a famous debate with Shapley over the size of the galaxy and the distance of the spiral nebulae. The matter was not settled until 1924, when Edwin HUBBLE redetermined the distance of the Andromeda nebula and demonstrated that it lay well beyond our galaxy.

Curtiss, Glenn Hammond *(1878–1930)* American aviation and inventor. Curtiss, who began his career as a bicycle mechanic, designed the motor for the first American dirigible balloon in 1904. In 1908 he gained renown for the first one-kilometer public flight in the U.S., flying at an average speed of 40 miles an hour in his plane, the *June Bug.* Curtiss invented the aileron in 1911, the same year he developed the first practical seaplane. During WORLD WAR I Curtiss's factories produced military planes, including the NC-4 flying boat that made the first transatlantic flight in 1919.

Curzon, Sir Clifford *(1907–1982)* British concert pianist. A child prodigy, at the age of 12 Curzon became the youngest student ever admitted to the Royal Academy of Music. He became the academy's youngest professor at the age of 19. Unlike many prodigies, however, he continued to mature as an artist and at the height of his powers was considered one of the finest pianists in the world. His repertoire included more than 50 concertos. He was best known for his performances of works by Mozart, Beethoven and Schubert. He was knighted in 1977.

Curzon, George Nathaniel (Baron Curzon of Kedleston) *(1859–1925)* British statesman. Curzon distinguished himself at Balliol College, Oxford, and became a Conservative member of Parliament in 1886, serving as undersecretary of state of India from 1891 to 1892 and undersecretary for foreign affairs from 1895 to 1898. He was appointed viceroy to India in 1899. His viceroyalty was marked by substantial administrative reforms, but his imperious manner grated on Indian sensibilities. In 1904 his tenure was extended, but in 1905, after a clash with Lord Kitchener, the commander in chief in India, over their spheres of authority, Curzon resigned. From 1907 on he was chancellor of Oxford University, and in WORLD WAR I he was a member of LLOYD GEORGE's war cabinet and foreign secretary from 1919. When Bonar LAW resigned in 1923, Curzon was disappointed not to be chosen prime minister. However, he served BALDWIN well as foreign secretary and, from 1924, as lord president of the Council. Again, his hauteur may have cost him the prime ministry, as Law considered him out of touch with public opinion. Curzon was among the last of the British imperialists. He was created baron in 1898, earl in 1911, and marquis in 1921. (See also CURZON LINE.)

Curzon Line Line proposed as a possible boundary between Poland and the USSR. Suggested by England's Lord Curzon (see George Nathaniel CURZON) during the Polish-Russian War of 1919–20, it would run south from Grodno through Brest-Litovsk, along the Bug River to Sokal, then west and south past Przemysl to the Carpathian Mountains. It was the basis for the post–World War II boundaries put in place after the YALTA CONFERENCE of 1945.

Cushing, Harvey Williams *(1869–1939)* U.S. surgeon. Cushing received his M.D. from Harvard School in 1895 and joined Massachusetts General Hospital, Boston, before moving to Johns Hopkins Hospital, Baltimore, where he progressed to associate professor of surgery. In 1912 he was appointed professor of surgery at Harvard. Cushing's specialty was brain surgery, and he pioneered several important techniques in this field, especially in the control of blood pressure and bleeding during surgery. From his many case histories he distinguished several classes of brain tumors and made great improvements in their treatment. Cushing also demonstrated the vital role of the pituitary gland in regulating many bodily functions. He was the first to associate adenoma (tumor) of the basophilic cells of the anterior pituitary with the chronic wasting disease now known as **Cushing's syndrome.** This syndrome is now known to be caused by any of several disorders that result in the increased secretion of corticosteroid hormones by the adrenal glands. Cushing had a lifelong interest in the history of medicine and wrote the *Life of Sir William Ogler,* (1925), which won him a PULITZER PRIZE. He donated his large collection of books and papers to the Yale Medical Library.

Cushman, Robert E., Jr. *(1914–1985)* U.S. military leader. Cushman was one of the most highly decorated U.S. officers in WORLD WAR II, winning the Navy Cross for Valor in the liberation of GUAM and citations for bravery at BOUGAINVILLE ISLAND and IWO JIMA. In 1957 he was named assistant for U.S. security affairs to Vice President Richard NIXON. In 1967 he became commanding general of the third Marine Amphibious Force in Vietnam, the largest combined combat unit ever led by a marine. He was responsible for the defense of KHE SAHN and the recapture of HUE following the TET OFFENSIVE (see VIETNAM WAR). President Nixon appointed Cushman deputy director of the CENTRAL INTELLIGENCE AGENCY (CIA) (1969–72) and U.S. Marine Corps commandant (1972–75).

Cutting, C. Suydam *(1889–1972)* U.S. explorer and naturalist, reported to be the first white Christian to visit the forbidden city of Lhasa in TIBET (1935).

Cypriot War of 1963–1964, Greek-Turkish The Republic of CYPRUS was established on August 16, 1960, to avoid annexation by either Greece or Turkey. Its population was three-fourths Greek and one-fourth Turkish. Its president, Greek archbishop MAKARIOS III, foreswore union with Greece. However, both Greeks and Turks influenced their Cypriot compatriots to acts of violence. Turkish Cypriots, thinking their rights threatened by Greek constitutional changes, began fighting in late 1963. The UNITED NATIONS sent a peacekeeping force in March 1964. Despite the UN force and the U.S. preventing a Turkish invasion, fighting continued between Greek and Turkish Cypriots. In August 1964 Turkish warplanes attacked Greek Cypriots, and Makarios sought help from Egypt and the USSR, but

the UN arranged a cease-fire. Later tensions were reduced when the government passed laws abolishing de facto abuse of Turkish rights.

Cypriot War of 1974, Greek-Turkish The shaky peace established in 1964 between Greek and Turkish Cypriots was broken by violent clashes, and in mid-July 1974 the Greek Cypriot National Guard, led by Greek officers, overthrew President MAKARIOS III, seeking union with Greece. Since the UNITED NATIONS and a London conference of involved parties failed to act, Turkish forces invaded. The Turks won 37% of the island, where the inhabitants voted to form a separate state. The UN sponsored two cease-fires. The second, on July 30, 1974, established a UN buffer area between Greek and Turkish zones. The guarantors of the Cypriot constitution (Britain, Greece and Turkey) arranged another cease-fire on August 16, 1974, with the Turks. Makarios returned in late 1974, recognizing Turkish autonomy but not partition.

Cyprus *(Greek:* **Kypros;** *Turkish:* **Kibris)** Island in the eastern Mediterranean, 40 miles south of Turkey and 60 miles west of Syria. At the beginning of the 20th century the population was about 80% Greek and

20% Turkish, with the Greek faction demanding ENOSIS (union) with GREECE. Violence broke out in 1955; the military-political EOKA, directed by Colonel George GRIVAS, backed the Greek cause. The British banished Archbishop MAKARIOS III, symbol of Greek-Cypriot nationalism, in an attempt to keep the peace. The U.K., Greece and TURKEY all eventually consented to an independent Cyprus, with balanced representation for Greeks and Turks. The new nation materialized in 1960 with a returned Makarios as its president. In 1964 dissension erupted again, and UN troops were brought in to keep the peace. Violence did not subside, and in 1974 a coup overthrew Makarios. Turkey attacked Cyprus and grabbed nearly 37% of the island. The Turkish faction proclaimed its freedom from the Greek-held region, effecting a divided nation and a standoff that continued through the 1980s. Although the government of Cyprus remained in power into the 21st century, the situation remained tense on the island despite the efforts of the EUROPEAN UNION (EU) and UN secretary general Kofi ANNAN to produce mutually acceptable peace plan between the Greek and Turkish factions. In 2004 Cyprus was admitted into the EU. (See also CYPRIOT WAR OF 1963–1964; CYPRIOT WAR OF 1974.)

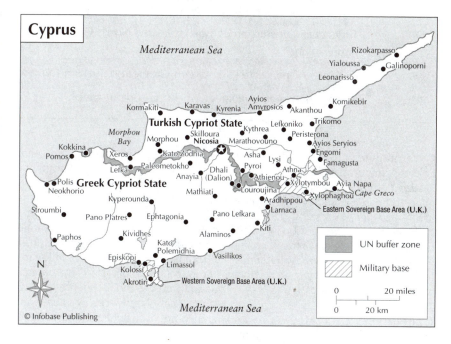

CYPRUS

1900	Mixed population of Greeks and Turks is governed as a protectorate by British following pullout of former Ottoman rulers.
1914	Annexed by Britain when Turkey declares war.
1925	Made British Crown colony.
1931	Enosis movement begins; Greek Cypriots riot for union with Greece; British respond with policies that drive Turkish and Greek Cypriots further apart.
1935	Law passed governing treatment and export of antiquities.
1940	Cypriot regiment fights in British army.
1943	Local elections held; British announce possibility of self-government.
1955	EOKA begins pro-Enosis guerrilla war; Archbishop Makarios leads anti-British demonstrations.
1956	Makarios deported.
1959	Britain, Turkey and Greece agree to a Cypriot republic set up within British Commonwealth; all three will have a military presence on the island.
1960	Republic established with Makarios as president and Kutchuk (a Turk) as vice president.
1963	Turks withdraw from government; ethnic violence is widespread.
1964	UN peacekeeping force arrives.
1968	Provisional government formed by Kutchuk in Turkish northern Cyprus.
1974	Pro-Enosis coup (backed by Greek military government) against Makarios; in response, Turkey invades the island in strength.
1975	Greek Cypriots flee the northern territory; Turkish Federated State of Cyprus proclaimed there.
1983	Turkish Federated State declares independence, renames itself Republic of North Cyprus, recognized only by Turkey.
1988	Leaders of Greece and Turkey meet in Geneva to discuss Cyprus.
1989	Turks claim jurisdiction of waters around North Cyprus; confrontation between Greek and Turkish fighter planes.
1997	Collapse of peace talks between Greek and Turkish Cypriot leaders.
2004	Cyprus becomes a member of the European Union.

Cyrankiewicz, Józef (1911–1989) Polish Communist political leader. He headed the Polish government as premier from 1947 and 1970, with a break between 1952 and 1954. In 1970 he signed an accord with West Germany that established POLAND's western border; a few days later his regime was toppled by violent riots over food price increases.

Czechoslovakia Much-abused country in central Europe; a conglomeration of Czechs, Slovaks and other nationalities, it was carved from the death throes of the AUSTRO-HUNGARIAN EMPIRE. In 1916, during WORLD WAR I, the Czechs and Slovaks joined in a national council directed by Tomáš MASARYK to lobby with the Allies for a Czechoslovak national state following the war. In October 1918 the council announced the independence of their state, whose boundaries eventually included not only Bohemia and Moravia and Slovakia, but also part of the duchy of Teschen and Ruthenia. Czechoslovakia's broad constitution of 1918 assured minority rights, but this disparate collection of peoples soon demonstrated its instability.

President Masaryk and Edvard BENEŠ, who replaced him in 1935, managed to lead the state through the minefield of its early years and into the GREAT DEPRESSION of the 1930s. During that decade German upheaval in the SUDETENLAND of Bohemia, led by Konrad Henlein and

Czechoslovakia/Czech Republic

1918	Independent Czechoslovakia founded with Tomáš Masaryk as president.
1935	Edvard Beneš becomes president.
1938	Czechoslovakia cedes Sudetenland to Germany under Munich Pact.
1939	Independent, pro-German Slovak state declared; Germany occupies Prague, declares Protectorate of Bohemia-Moravia.
1941	Beneš's Czech government-in-exile in London recognized by Allies.
1942	Czech resistance assassinates Heydrich; Germans destroy Lidice.
1945	Creation of National Front government; Soviet troops liberate Prague.
1946	Communist Klement Gottwald becomes prime minister in coalition government.
1948	Communist takeover of Czechoslovakia under Gottwald; death of Foreign Minister Jan Masaryk; death of Beneš.
1952	Slansky trial; purge of Communist Party.
1953	Death of Gottwald.
1960	New Soviet-style constitution introduced.
1968	Alexander Dubček becomes first secretary of Communist Party, initiates "Prague Spring" reforms; Soviet invasion of Czechoslovakia.
1977	Charter 77 group formed calling for human rights.
1988	Anticommunists demonstrate in Prague on anniversary of Soviet invasion.
1989	Mass anticommunist demonstrations lead to fall of Communists; noncommunist government elected under Václav Havel.
1991	Czechoslovakian troops join Allies in Saudi Arabia as part of Operation Desert Shield/Desert Storm.
1993	Czechoslovakia divided into Czech Republic and Slovakia.
1998	Havel is reelected president.
1999	Czech Republic joins NATO.
2003	Václav Klaus is elected president.
2004	Czech Republic joins the European Union.

backed by Germany's Adolf HITLER, critically endangered the nation. After his annexation of AUSTRIA in March 1938, Hitler insisted that any part of Czechoslovakia whose population was more than half German be under German authority. Unwilling and unready to go to war, Great Britain and France sanctioned the German land-grab—a practice that became known as APPEASEMENT. In a pact signed at MUNICH on September 29, 1938, the Sudetenland was given to GERMANY. POLAND insisted on and

received Teschen; Ruthenia and a section of Slovakia went to HUNGARY. In March 1939 Hitler invaded the rest of the country, transforming Bohemia and Moravia into a German protectorate and setting up a German puppet state in Slovakia. German rule during WORLD WAR II was savage, more so after the assassination of Reich protector Reinhard Heydrich in May 1942; in revenge all male citizens in the town of LIDICE were killed.

The expelled Czech government came under Soviet influence, and

when prewar boundaries were restored, Ruthenia became part of the USSR. Klement GOTTWALD, a Communist, was named prime minister in 1946. By February 1948 Communist control was absolute. A Soviet-style state was organized with concentrated and strict control of political and economic affairs, and the party was purged in the early 1950s. By the mid-1950s some efforts were being made to combat a growing dissatisfaction, but unrest persisted and erupted in the PRAGUE SPRING of 1968. The Soviet

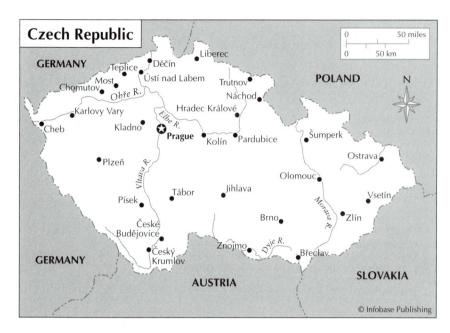

Czech Republic

GERMANY

Liberec

Teplice   Děčín
Most   Ústí nad Labem   Trutnov
Chomutov   Ohře R.   Náchod
Karlovy Vary   Hradec Králové

Cheb   Kladno   Elbe R.
Prague   Pardubice
Kolín   Šumperk

Plzeň   Vltava R.   Ostrava

Olomouc   Vsetín

Písek   Tábor   Jihlava   Morava R.   Zlín

Brno

České
Budějovice   Znojmo   Dyje R.   Břeclav
Český
Krumlov

GERMANY

AUSTRIA   SLOVAKIA

POLAND   N

0   50 miles
0   50 km

© Infobase Publishing

Union, feeling itself to be threatened, led a WARSAW PACT assault on the country on August 20. The military installed Gustav HUSÁK as premier, succeeding the reformist Alexander DUBČEK. Strict party rule was restored, and Czechoslovakia again became one of the enslaved nations in the Eastern bloc. But by 1989 the people of Eastern Europe had had enough of Communist governments, and mass demonstrations were held in Prague and in other Czech cities. The Communists were forced out; free elections were held for the first time in over 40 years, and playwright Václav HAVEL was elected president; Dubček was elected speaker of parliament. While a majority of Czechoslovaks sought to preserve the unity of the country, a movement to dissolve Czechoslovakia gained momentum, particularly among Slovak politicians. On January 1, 1993, after both Czech and Slovak states voted to secede, the Czechoslovak state was dissolved and replaced by the CZECH REPUBLIC and SLOVAKIA.

Czechoslovakia, Soviet Invasion of Early in 1968, the Slovak leader Alexander DUBČEK became first secretary of the Communist Party of CZECHOSLOVAKIA. A brief period of liberalization—labeled the PRAGUE SPRING—began, during which Dubček attempted to democratize Czechoslovakia by lifting press censorship, establishing ties to the West, promising increases in consumer goods, seeking autonomy for Slovakia within the larger state and planning a new constitution that allowed individual liberties. The Soviet Union, used to governing Czechoslovakia and its other satellites rigidly, was alarmed, and a Soviet-Czech conference was held in the Slovak town of Cierna (July 29–August 1, 1968), from which the Soviet officials departed amicably. But their views changed, for on the night of August 20–21, 1968, Soviet forces, aided by WARSAW PACT

troops from Bulgaria, Hungary, Poland and East Germany, invaded Czechoslovakia, overcame minor resistance and occupied the country (the invaders numbered at least 600,000). Dubček and other Czechoslovak leaders were arrested, taken to Moscow, forced to make concessions and then returned home; a pro-Soviet Communist regime was established firmly in Czechoslovakia. By April 1969 all of Dubček's reforms (except Slovak autonomy) had been invalidated, and Dubček was out of office. Justifying their action under the so-called BREZHNEV DOCTRINE, the Soviets ordered arrests, union purges and religious persecutions in 1970 to rid Czechoslovakia of its liberal tendencies.

Czech Republic A state created with the dissolution of CZECHOSLOVAKIA into separate and independent Czech and Slovak republics on January 1, 1993. The decision to dissolve Czechoslovakia came as a result of an agreement brokered in late 1992 between Václav Klaus, the prime minister of the Czech portion of Czechoslovakia, and his counterpart in SLOVAKIA, Prime Minister Vladimír Mečiar. In response to this accord, the president of Czechoslovakia, Václav HAVEL, resigned in protest; however, he was later elected to a five-year term as president of the Czech Republic and was reelected in 1998. In March 2003 Klaus succeeded Havel as president of the Czech Republic.

Since its creation the Czech Republic has achieved many important political milestones. It has succeeded in privatizing nearly all government industries created during Czechoslovakia's period of Communist rule. In 1999 the Czech Republic, Poland and Hungary gained admission into the NORTH ATLANTIC TREATY ORGANIZATION (NATO). In 2004 it gained admission to the EUROPEAN UNION.

D

Dacca City and area of central BANGLADESH, 80 miles northeast of Khulna. From 1905 to 1912 the city of Dacca was the capital of the British jurisdiction of Eastern Bengal and of Assam. It was the capital of East Pakistan from 1956 to 1971. Following INDIA's victory over PAKISTAN in the INDO-PAKISTANI WAR OF 1971, it emerged as the capital of the new nation of Bangladesh. The American architect Louis I. KAHN designed the National Assembly and other government buildings in Dacca.

Dachau Bavarian town, 11 miles northwest of Munich, Germany. In 1933 Dachau became the site of one of the first CONCENTRATION CAMPS built by the new Nazi regime. Here JEWS and other minorities, along with political inmates and Russian PRISONERS OF WAR, were exploited for slave labor and for so-called medical research. A mass extermination of prisoners also occurred here. It was liberated by the Allies on April 29, 1945, and 32,000 surviving prisoners were set free.

Dacko, David (*1930–2003*) President of the Central African Republic (CAR; 1960–66, 1981). Dacko served as minister of agriculture from 1957 to 1958 in the Central African government council and from 1958 to 1959 as minister of the interior. Following the death of the CAR's first leader, Boganda, in 1959 Dacko, his nephew, became prime minister, and in 1960 he became the first president of the country. In 1966 Dacko's government

was overthrown by Jean-Bédel BOKASSA, and Dacko was put under house arrest, later serving as an adviser to Bokassa. In 1979 Bokassa was deposed, and Dacko was reinstated as president. Dacko won a presidential election in 1981, but a faltering economy forced him to retire that same year. He was replaced by General Kolingba. Dacko unsuccessfully ran for president of the CAR in 1992 and 1999.

dada International artistic and literary movement that flourished in the 1910s and remains highly influential today. It was formed in 1916 in Zurich by a disparate group of European artists and poets including Jean ARP, Hugo Ball, Richard Huelsenbeck, Marcel Janco, and Tristan TZARA. The word *dada* literally means "wooden horse" in French. But as it was employed by artists and writers, *dada* became a cacaphonic nonsense term that was used to shout down all bourgeois artistic pretensions and to embrace the absurdity of modern life. Dada was, in essence, a movement of negation. It posed no positive theories of artistic creation and in part was a nihilistic response to the horrors of WORLD WAR I. Dadaists composed nonsense poems and cabaret skits and displayed artistic works with satirical themes and an informal, even random, approach to form and composition. For the most part, dadaists avoided manifestos and ideological commitments of any sort. The dada movement became a major influence on SURREALISM.

Dahl, Roald (*1916–1990*) British writer of Welsh and Norwegian parentage, author of popular fantasies, wicked parables and outstanding children's books. After injuries in action with the British Royal Air Force in WORLD WAR II, he was assigned as an air attaché to Washington, D.C., where he began his first volume of short stories, *Over to You* (1945). Dahl's finest stories appeared in two collections, *Someone Like You* (1953) and *Kiss Kiss* (1960). Their blend of keen-edged satire, dark humor, occasional horror and morbid subjects have been rivaled only, perhaps, by the work of John COLLIER and SAKI. Some, such as "Lamb to the Slaughter" and "Man from the South," were presented on Alfred HITCHCOCK's television series; others were adapted for a television series in the early 1960s hosted by Dahl himself, *Way Out*. After the publication of *James and the Giant Peach* (1961), Dahl increasingly turned to children's books—without sacrificing much of the bite of his more adult books. At the same time his later adult fables, such as the collection *Switch Bitch* (1974) and the novel *My Uncle Oswald* (1979), smack overmuch of scatological jokes and bathroom humor. He also wrote two volumes of an autobiography—*Boy* (1984) and *Solo* (1986). Dahl was married to the American actress Patricia Neal from 1953 to 1983.

Dahlberg, Edward (*1900–1977*) American novelist, essayist and poet. Dahlberg is a highly individualistic figure in American letters. In the course of his long writing career he underwent a decisive transformation from being a proletarian writer concerned exclusively with social issues to the adaptation, in the 1940s and after, of a neoclassical aesthetic. Dahlberg, an illegitimate son, was raised for a time in Kansas City by his mother, a barber. Thereafter he spent some years in an orphanage in Cleveland. These experiences are movingly recounted in Dahlberg's masterful autobiography, *Because I Was Flesh* (1964). In 1929 Dahlberg published his first novel, *Bottom Dogs,* which featured a glowing introduction by D. H. LAWRENCE. Other novels of his proletarian period include *From Flushing to Calvary* (1932) and *Those Who Perish* (1934). In *Can These Bones Live* (1941, revised 1960), Dahlberg explored the course of American literature in a series of stylish, insightful essays. Other of his works include *The Sorrows of Priapus* (1957), on the mind-body split in Hebraic, Hellenic and other cultures and the autobiographical *Confessions of Edward Dahlberg* (1971).

Daiches, David *(1912–2005)* Scottish literary critic and author. Educated at Balliol College, Oxford, Daiches served in several academic posts both in Britain and the U.S. A prolific author of nonfiction on a variety of subjects, Daiches is perhaps best known for his definitive biographies, *Virginia Woolf* (1942), *Robert Louis Stevenson* (1947), and *Robert Burns* (1950), and for his literary criticism, including *Critical History of English Literature* (four volumes, 1960). Other works include *Scotch Whiskey* (1969); three volumes of autobiography, *Two Worlds* (1957), *A Third World* (1971) and *Was; a Pastime from Time Past* (1975); and *God and the Poets* (1984).

Dáil Éireann *(Irish Gaelic; "assembly of Ireland")* House of representatives, lower chamber of the Irish parliament (Oireachtas), with 166 members elected for five years by adult suffrage on a system of proportional representation. Often abbreviated to Dáil, it is IRELAND's main legislative body, the upper house (**Senaad Éireann,** or Senate) being largely consultative and ceremonial.

Daily News New York City tabloid founded in 1919. The *Daily News* was begun by Captain Joseph M. Patterson, who co-owned the paper with Colonel Robert R. McCormick of the *Chicago Tribune.* The *News,* with its sensationalist reporting, comics, snappy headlines and abundant photography, was an immediate success. When Patterson died in 1946, McCormick took over the paper; while continuing to highlight sex and scandal, the *News* maintained a conservative, antiunion, anticommunist, pro-American stance. It began to lose readers in the liberal 1960s and by 1970 was in serious difficulties. It attempted to reshape itself and accommodate changing readership patterns, presenting more straight news and introducing style and business sections, but to little avail. In 1981 the *Tribune* announced that the *Daily News* had lost $11 million that year and was for sale. In 1982 Joe L. Albritton, owner of several other papers and television and radio stations, took an option to buy the *News* but relinquished it a month later. The *Tribune* continued to publish the *News,* but in 1990 the paper's workers began a long strike. The *News* was acquired by British publishing magnate Robert MAXWELL in 1991. Maxwell died in November 1991, shortly after purchasing the paper. Because of the financial insolvency of Maxwell's media group, the Mirror Group, the *Daily News* and other publications owned by Mirror Group were offered for sale. In 1993 Mortimer Zuckerman, owner of the *Atlantic* and *U.S. News and World Report,* purchased the *Daily News.*

Dainton, Frederick Sydney (Baron Dainton of Hallam Moors) *(1914–1997)* British physical chemist and scientific administrator. Dainton was educated at the universities of Oxford and Cambridge. After World War II he remained in Cambridge until 1950, when he was appointed professor of physical chemistry at the University of Leeds. Apart from a brief period (1970–73) as professor of physical chemistry at Oxford, most of Dainton's time since 1965 was spent as an administrator. Dainton's early work in physical chemistry was on the kinetics and thermodynamics of polymerization reactions. From about 1945 he turned his attention to studies of radiolysis—chemical changes produced by high-energy radiation (alpha, beta or gamma rays). In particular he studied the properties and reactions of hydrated electrons in liquids. From 1965 he was a member of the Council for Scientific Policy and was its chairman from 1969. While holding this office he was influential in decisions made about the way British academic research is financed. He served as chancellor of the University of Sheffield and was created a life peer in 1986.

Dakar Harbor and capital of SENEGAL, West Africa, on the south end of the Cape Verde peninsula. It was established by the French in 1857. Dakar became a French naval base and in 1902 was named capital of FRENCH WEST AFRICA; between 1924 and 1946 the city and encompassing areas were self-governing. It was restored to Senegal in 1946 and made capital of the new nation in 1956.

Daladier, Édouard *(1884–1970)* French politician, three-time premier (1933, 1934, 1938–40). A radical socialist teacher, he entered the chamber of deputies in 1919 and served in successive cabinets beginning in 1924. He was premier for 10 months in 1933 and two months in 1934. He began service as minister of war in 1936, the year that he aided in forming a Popular Front coalition of radicals, socialists and communists. Daladier became premier again in 1938 and, following a policy of APPEASEMENT toward Nazi aggression, was a cosigner of the MUNICH PACT in that same year. A weak and vacillating leader, he was forced to step down as premier in 1940 after FRANCE failed to come to the aid of Finland when that country came under attack from the USSR. Replaced by Paul REYNAUD, he continued in the post of minister of war, later becoming foreign minister. After the fall of France, he was arrested by the VICHY government (1940), tried at Riom (1942) and imprisoned in Germany (1943–45). Elected to the National Assembly in 1946, he served there until 1958.

Dalai Lama *(1935–)* In 1940, at age five, Tenzin Gyatso was enthroned as the 14th Dalai Lama—the spiritual reincarnation of Buddha and political leader of TIBET. In 1950 Communist CHINA invaded Tibet and seized power from the Dalai Lama. He attempted to mediate between the Chinese government and the Tibetan people, but increasing Chinese repression sparked an unsuccessful uprising in 1959. The failure of the revolt led him and 100,000 other Tibetans to seek asylum in India. The Dalai Lama later settled in the town of Dharmsala in the Himalayas, where he continued to call for an end to Chinese control over Tibet and to advocate nonviolent protest. He received the 1989 NOBEL PRIZE for peace; China denounced the award and called it politically motivated.

Dale, Sir Henry Hallett (*1875–1968*) British physiologist. Educated at Cambridge University and St. Bartholomew's Hospital, Dale became, in 1904, director of the Wellcome Physiological Research Laboratories. His work there over the next 10 years included the isolation (with Arthur Ewins) from ergot fungi of a pharmacologically active extract—acetylcholine—which he found had similar effects on various organs as to the parasympathetic nervous system. Otto Loewi later showed that a substance released by electrical stimulation of the vagus nerve was responsible for effecting changes in heartbeat. Following up this work, Dale showed that the substance is in fact acetylcholine, thus establishing that chemical as well as electrical stimuli are involved in nerve action. For this research, Dale and Loewi shared the 1936 NOBEL PRIZE in physiology or medicine. Dale also worked on the properties of histamine and related substances, including their actions in allergic and anaphylactic conditions. He was the chairman of an international committee responsible for the standardization of biological preparations and from 1928 to 1942 was director of the National Institute for Medical Research.

Dalen, Nils Gustaf (*1869–1937*) Swedish engineer. In 1896 Dalen graduated in mechanical engineering from the Chalmers Institute in Göteborg and then spent a year at the Swiss Federal Institute of Technology in Zurich. For several years he researched and improved hot-air turbines, compressors and air pumps, and from 1900 to 1905 he worked with the engineering firm Dalen and Alsing. He then became works manager for the Swedish Carbide and Acetylene Company, which in

1909 became the Swedish Gas Accumulator Company with Dalen as managing director. Dalen is remembered principally for his inventions relating to acetylene lighting for lighthouses and other navigational aids, and in particular an automatic light-controlled valve, for which he received the 1912 NOBEL PRIZE in physics. The valve, known as "Solventil," used the difference in heat-absorbing properties between a dull black surface and a highly polished one to produce differential expansion of gases and thus to regulate the main gas valve of an acetylene-burning lamp. The lamp could thus be automatically dimmed or extinguished in daylight. This allowed buoys and lighthouses to be left unattended and less gas to be used. The system soon came into widespread use and is still in use today. Another of Dalen's inventions was a porous filler for acetylene tanks that prevented explosions. It was ironic that in 1912 he was himself blinded by an explosion during the course of an experiment. This did not, however, deter him from continuing his experimental work up to his death.

Daley, Richard Joseph (*1902–1976*) U.S. politician and mayor of CHICAGO from 1955 to 1976. Working in the stockyards of Chicago, Daley studied law at night and took his degree from Loyola University in 1933. He was elected to the Illinois house of representatives in 1936, and later also served in the Illinois senate. Running for sheriff of Cook County, he suffered the only defeat of his career in politics. In 1950 he was appointed clerk of Cook County. His selection as chairman of the Democratic county organization in 1953 brought him major political power. He used harsh measures to quell rioters protesting the VIETNAM WAR during the 1968 DEMOCRATIC PARTY convention. Daley was reelected in 1975 to an unprecedented sixth term as mayor. He was an adviser to Presidents KENNEDY and JOHNSON. His administration reorganized Chicago's scandal-ridden police department, stressed urban renewal and encouraged construction of major downtown buildings. Scandals during his term of office never involved Daley personally.

Dalglish, Kenneth (*1951– *) Scottish soccer player and manager. An in-

telligent forward noted for his goal-scoring skills and ability to create space. Dalglish is Scotland's most capped player with 102 appearances, and shares the all-time goal-scoring record at 30. Unique among British soccer players, Dalglish has won the full array of domestic championships in both Scotland and England, starring for Glasgow Celtic in Scotland and Liverpool in England. Dalglish joined Celtic in 1970 and gained four league championships in seven years, scoring 112 goals in 204 games. In August 1977 he joined Liverpool and embarked on a period of unremitting success with the team. Liverpool won seven championships in nine years and three European Cups, 1978, 1981 and 1984. In May 1985, 39 fans were crushed during a riot by Liverpool fans at the European Cup Final. In the wake of this tragedy Dalglish was appointed player-manager of Liverpool. The team was banned from Europe, but Dalglish led the team in its continued dominance of English soccer. In 1986 and 1988 he was named English Manager of the Year. Although his success in British soccer is unparalleled, Dalglish will always be remembered for his leadership following the HILLBOROUGH STADIUM DISASTER (April 1989), when 95 Liverpool fans were crushed to death at the English F.A. Cup semifinal. Dalglish led the city in mourning, and his influence was credited with restoring the shaken image of the game in England. Dalglish resigned as Liverpool manager in March 1991.

Dalí, Salvador (**Salvador Domingo Felipe Jacinto Dalí Domenech**) (*1904–1989*) Spanish-born surrealist. Dalí was one of the best-known and most controversial artists of his day; his paintings and other work explored the subconscious mind with images of fantasy, dreams and hallucinations. Dalí's lifestyle was as dramatic and well publicized as his art, and he was a well-known figure with his waxed, pointed mustache and silver-handled cane. His career began in 1928, when he visited Paris and was welcomed into the surrealist group (see SURREALISM). During the next several years he produced some of his best-known work, including the painting *The Persistence of Memory* (1931), with its drooping watches and barren landscape. He also collaborated with Luis BUÑUEL on the scenario for the surrealist film *Un Chien andalou*. In 1934 the surrealists expelled him from their movement for having developed what they considered an unhealthy interest in money. Dalí fled Europe at the outbreak of World War II and eventually settled in the U.S., where he worked on films, plays, ballets, paintings and other projects. After returning to Spain in 1949 he became reconciled with the Catholic Church and began a series of large-scale religious paintings. His last years were marred by a forgery scandal, in which Dalí was said to have signed thousands of blank sheets of paper to be filled in later by others and sold as Dalí originals. After the death (1982) of his wife of nearly 50 years, Gala, Dalí spent most of his time in seclusion.

Dalkon Shield controversy Involving the safety of an IUD birth control device. The A. H. Robbins pharmaceutical company developed and in 1971 marketed an intrauterine device (IUD), called the Dalkon Shield, for birth control. Because it was marketed as a safe alternative to birth control pills, nearly 5 million were sold worldwide. Only three years later the U.S. Food and Drug Administration asked the company to cease marketing the product on the grounds that it was neither safe nor effective. Reportedly, the company had known of potential problems with the IUD and knowingly exposed women to severe medical consequences. Many users experienced serious pelvic inflammatory disease that often led to chronic pain and illness and even death. More than half of the women who did become pregnant lost their babies while other women became infertile. When confronted with thousands of lawsuits Robbins aggressively fought each case but eventually filed for a bankruptcy reorganization. Ultimately Robbins moved much of its assets to a trust fund for the victims and was acquired by American Home Products Corporation.

Dallapiccola, Luigi (*1904–1975*) Italian composer and pianist. He was trained at the Conservatory of Florence and later taught there. His difficult personal life—he was interned in an Austrian detention camp in WORLD WAR I and was persecuted by the Italian government during WORLD WAR II be-

cause his wife was Jewish—was a profound influence on his music, which often deals with themes of suffering and freedom. The first Italian composer to employ the 12-tone scale, he is noted for his vocal music, which includes the choral works *Songs of Captivity* (1938–41) and *Songs of Liberation* (1955), the operas *The Prisoner* (1944–48) and *Odysseus* (1968), the oratorio *Job* (1950) and the *Christmas Cantata* (1957). Dallapiccola also composed numerous orchestral and instrumental works as well as several ballets. An influential teacher, he taught in American universities throughout the 1950s and early 1960s.

Dalmatia Ancient region on the Adriatic coast of the Balkans; it became a part of YUGOSLAVIA's constituent republic of CROATIA. In 1915 part of Dalmatia was pledged to Italy by the Allies, who in return wanted Italy on their side in WORLD WAR I. However, in 1918 most of Dalmatia joined with the new kingdom of the Serbs, Croats and Slovenes, renamed Yugoslavia in 1929. In WORLD WAR II Italy controlled Dalmatia for a brief period, but in 1945 the area was given back to Yugoslavia. In 1991 it became part of the independent republic of Croatia. Today Dalmatia's coast is brimming with lush scenery and fashionable resorts.

d'Amboise, Jacques (*1934–   *) American dancer. One of the outstanding interpreters of George BALANCHINE's choreography, d'Amboise joined NEW YORK CITY BALLET in 1950 and created roles in such Balanchine works as *Western Symphony* (1954), *Stars and Stripes* (1958) and *Who Cares?* (1970). He is especially known for his interpretation of Balanchine's *Apollo*. In addition, he has appeared in several movies and television productions, taught at the School of American Ballet and choreographed many works (since 1963). Currently he serves as director of the National Dance Institute, which he founded in 1976, and works to involve young people in dance activities. D'Amboise has been the recipient of numerous honors, including the Capezio Award (1990), the Award for Distinguished Service to the Arts from the American Academy of Arts and Letters (1993) and the National Medal of Arts (1998).

Dance Theatre of Harlem The major, classically oriented, predominantly black American ballet company, Dance Theatre of Harlem made its debut in 1971. Founded by NEW YORK CITY BALLET principal dancer Arthur Mitchell, the dance school was established first in 1968, followed by the formation of the company under the direction of Mitchell and Karel Shook (formerly ballet master of the Dutch National Ballet). Since 1974 the company has had regular seasons in New York City and became the first black ballet company to have a season at Covent Garden in London (1981). Influenced primarily by the neoclassical style of George BALANCHINE, the company performs many of his works in addition to ballets created by Mitchell and other contemporary choreographers. In 1988 Dance Theatre of Harlem served as part of a cultural exchange program between the U.S. and the USSR and became the first U.S. ballet company to appear in the Soviet Union, where it performed before sold-out audiences in Moscow and Leningrad. (See also HARLEM.)

Daniel, Yuli M. (Nikolai Arzhak) (*1925–1988*) Soviet dissident satirist and poet. He was arrested in 1965 and served five years in prison and labor camp for illegally publishing his work abroad. The criminal charge was one of the first ever brought against an intellectual for literary criticism of the Soviet system.

Daniels, Farrington (*1889–1972*) American chemist. Daniels was educated at the University of Minnesota and at Harvard, where he earned his Ph.D. in 1914. He moved to the University of Wisconsin in 1920, spending his whole career there and serving as professor of chemistry from 1928 until his retirement in 1959. Daniels worked on a wide variety of chemical problems. In addition to a textbook, *Outlines of Physical Chemistry* (1931), he wrote on photochemistry, nitrogen fixation and thermoluminescence. He was also interested in the utilization of **solar energy**, publishing a book on the subject, *Direct Use of the Sun's Energy* (1964), and organizing a symposium on it in 1954, many years before the discussion of solar energy had become fashionable.

Daniels, Josephus (1862–1948) U.S. cabinet member. Born in Washington, D.C., Daniels had a successful career as a newspaper editor, becoming the chief spokesman for Progressive reform in North Carolina and the Upper South. He served on the Democratic National Committee beginning in 1896 and was in charge of publicity for the 1908 and 1912 campaigns. Daniels served as secretary of the navy through Woodrow WILSON's two terms. Regarded as a great secretary, he was initially criticized for pacifist tendencies and failure to prepare the navy for possible entry into WORLD WAR I. However, he helped push through Congress the greatest naval building program to that date and improved the conditions and opportunities for enlisted men. Daniels returned to newspaper publishing in 1921. He opposed the KU KLUX KLAN, championed child labor laws and supported U.S. entry into the LEAGUE OF NATIONS and the World Court. As ambassador to MEXICO (1933–41). he was influential in improving relations between the two countries.

Danilova, Alexandra (1906–1997) Russian ballerina. After training at the Russian Imperial and Soviet State ballet schools in Leningrad. Danilova worked at the Maryinsky Theater. She left the Soviet Union in 1924, joined DIAGHILEV and the BALLETS RUSSES and worked with them from 1925 to 1929. Her most important roles included *Le Pas d'Acier, Apollon Musagetes* and *The Gods Go a'Begging*. From 1933 to 1937 she was a member of Colonel de Basil's company, and from 1938 to 1958 she was prima ballerina of MASSINE's Ballet Russe de Monte Carlo. For many years she taught and lectured on ballet. In 1975 she choreographed *Coppelia* with George BALANCHINE for the New York City Ballet, and she made her screen debut in *The Turning Point* in 1977.

Danish Modern Term identifying the MODERNISM developed in post–World War II Denmark by such designers as Kay Bojesen, Finn Juhl, and Hans Wegner. Danish design of the 1930s had developed a cautious modernism based on craft traditions. In the 1950s Danish design developed in a strongly functionalist direction, but always with a certain sense of craft tradition that led to qualities of warmth and softness, which aided the growth of worldwide popularity for Danish design. At a time when modernism was still somewhat new and frightening to American consumers, Danish Modern became a popular compromise, often called "contemporary" or "transitional" to distinguish it from the more mechanistic qualities of BAUHAUS-inspired functionalism. Economic developments in recent years have made Danish products less economical than they were in the 1950s, a tendency that, combined with changing taste, has limited the importance of Danish design in current markets.

D'Annunzio, Gabriele (1863–1938) Italian poet, novelist, patriot and adventurer. Born in Pescara on the Adriatic, he departed for Rome in 1881 and was soon established as a literary figure. His first poems, such as those in *Canto nuovo* (1882), were lyrical, colorful and idyllic. His earliest fiction, exemplified by the short stories in *Terra vergine* (1882), were realistic tales of his native Abruzzi region. D'Annunzio came under the influence of the French symbolists and decadents toward the end of the 19th century and produced a number of rather superficial novels that celebrate the joys of sensuality. These include *Il piacere* (1889; translated as *The Child of Pleasure,* 1898) and *Il trionfo della morte* (1894; translated as *The Triumph of Death,* 1896). During this period D'Annunzio also began the romantic liaisons that made him one of the most controversial figures of his time. He married Duchess Maria Hardouin di Gallese in 1883 and in the mid-1890s began a celebrated affair with the actress Eleonora DUSE, a relationship erotically dissected in his roman à clef, *Il fuoco* (1900; translated as *The Flame of Life*). The affair also prompted him to write 18 plays, including *La città morta* (1898; translated as *The Dead City,* 1902), *Francesca* (1902; translated as *Francesca da Rimini*) and *La figlia di Iorio* (1904; translated as *The Daughter of Jorio,* 1907). The poetry of the early 20th century, including the patriotic *Laudi* poems (1903–12) and the lushly sensuous *Alcione* (1904), are regarded as his most successful verse.

D'Annunzio lived in Paris from 1910 to 1915, returning home to urge his country to join WORLD WAR I on the Allied side. During the war (1915–18), he fought with distinction as a flyer. In 1919 he led 1,000 troops in a raid on the Adriatic port of Fiume, ruling the city until 1921 (see D'ANNUNZIO'S WAR), while wearing the black shirts and using the Roman salute that were later adopted as Fascist emblems. The flamboyant D'Annunzio was an admirer of MUSSOLINI and the Fascist movement, but he did not take part in their development and retired from politics after the Fiume adventure. His works continue to be admired for their linguistic skill, and he remains a romantic figure in European history.

D'Annunzio's War (1919–1920) Italy and Yugoslavia both claimed the city of Fiume (RIJEKA) at World War I's end. Italian soldier-poet Gabriele D'ANNUNZIO (1863–1938), believing it was Italy's, led an expedition of black-shirted troops into Fiume, September 12, 1919, and occupied it. His autocratic rule was opposed by Italy. The Treaty of RAPALLO between Italy and Yugoslavia (November 12, 1920) established Fiume as a free state, causing D'Annunzio to declare war on Italy. He was forced to evacuate by an Italian bombardment, December 27, 1920, and turmoil ensued until a Fascist coup overthrew the local government in 1922. Then Italian troops occupied the city. In 1947 Fiume was awarded to Yugoslavia.

Dansgaard, Willi (1922–   ) Danish meteorologist. Dansgaard was educated at the University of Copenhagen, earning his Ph.D. in 1961. He has studied the applications of environmental isotopes to meteorological, hydrological and glaciological problems and in particular to the climate of the last 100,000 years. In the early 1960s the U.S. Army drilled down into the Greenland icecap, producing an ice core 4,600 feet (1,400 m) long and with a 100,000-year history. Dansgaard realized that by making careful measurement of the core's varying oxygen-18 level he should be able to reconstruct the climatic history of the last 100,000 years. The most recent ice age, ending 10,000 years ago, was clearly marked, as was evidence of a weather cycle during the last 1,000 years. In 1996 Dansgaard won the Tyler Prize for Environmental Achievement in recognition for his work in using glacier ice as a barometer for environmental pollution.

Danzig corridor   See GDAŃSK.

Dardanelles (Hellespont) Strait running southwest to northeast between Europe and Asia, uniting the Aegean Sea with the Sea of Marmara and the Bosporus. It is strategically and commercially prominent because, with the Sea of Marmara and the Bosporus, it joins the Black and Mediterranean Seas and has been the entrance to Istanbul (Constantinople) for Westerners. Its perennial strategic prominence grew as Russia came to dominate the Black Sea region in the 18th century, while the Ottoman Empire began its ultimately fatal decline. A compact of July 1841, reasserted by the Peace of Paris after the Crimean War in 1856, forbade alien warships from entering the strait without Turkish consent. But in 1914, at the beginning of WORLD WAR I, Admiral Carden led an Anglo-French armada that attempted to occupy the Dardanelles preparatory to attacking the enemy Turks at Constantinople. The postwar Treaty of SÈVRES in 1920 demilitarized and internationalized the straits area. In 1923 the Treaty of LAUSANNE substantiated the demilitarization but restored the strait to Turkish authority; the 1936 Montreux Convention accepted the refortification of the strait, which Turkey had already accomplished covertly. Further adaptations were made during WORLD WAR II to allow the Allies to carry supplies to the USSR. After the war the Soviets tried to acquire more advantages but failed. The strait continues under Turkish control.

Dardanelles Campaign (Gallipoli Campaign) Military campaign waged in 1915, during WORLD WAR I, between the Allies and the Turks. Britain and France wanted to control the straits of the Dardanelles and ISTANBUL so that they could supply their wartime ally, Russia. After naval attacks failed to dislodge the Turks in February 1915, the Allies (mainly Australian and New Zealand forces) launched a land attack, including naval bombardment, on the Gallipoli Peninsula, landing at two points north and south. The Turks, firmly entrenched and aided by German artillery and officers, could not be dislodged. Three bloody battles waged

Australian soldier carries a wounded comrade out of harm's way in the Dardanelles. 1915 (LIBRARY OF CONGRESS, PRINTS AND PHOTOGRAPHS DIVISION)

between April and June 1915 gained and lost the Allies a few thousand yards, and another assault in August was also futile. In December 1915 the Allied high command, acknowledging the hopelessness of the campaign, evacuated their disease-ridden troops. First Lord of the Admiralty Winston CHURCHILL was made a scapegoat for the failed campaign that he had urged and was forced to resign from the British government.

Darfur   See SUDAN.

Darío, Rubén (Félix Rubén García Sarmiento) *(1867–1916)* Nicaraguan poet, novelist and journalist. Significant as the architect of Spanish MODERNISM, Darío, whose work is relatively unknown in the U.S., is critically acclaimed as among the foremost writers in the world. Darío worked as a correspondent for various South and Central American newspapers and spent much of his life traveling and living outside of Nicaragua. His most important works are the collections of poetry and short stories *Azul* (1888), *Prosas profanos, y otros* (1896, translated as *Prosas profanos and Other Poems*) and *Cantos de vida y esperanza* (1905; "Songs of life and hope"),

which evidence a shift away from the romantic tradition.

Darkness at Noon Novel by Arthur KOESTLER, published in England in 1941. An indictment of communist TOTALITARIANISM, which Koestler had rejected in 1938, the novel depicts the crushing regime of "No. 1" and its arrest and eventual execution of N. S. Rubashov. Rubashov is Koestler's fictional amalgamation of the victims of the show trials that took place during the GREAT PURGE in the USSR. The book, originally written in German, exposes Joseph STALIN's betrayal of the Russian Revolution.

Darlan, Jean-François *(1881–1942)* French admiral and political figure. A career officer, he was a naval commander in WORLD WAR I, executive head of the French navy from 1933 to 1939 and, after that date, commander in chief. His service was the only one in the French military that did not surrender to Germany in 1940. A collaborator, Darlan became foreign minister and vice premier in PÉTAIN's VICHY government and was slated to be the elderly marshal's successor. However, after Pierre LAVAL returned to power in 1942, Darlan was sent to North Africa as French military commander. In Algiers during the Allied landings in November of that year, he again shifted his loyalties, coming to an agreement with U.S. general Mark CLARK and ordering the end of French resistance. He was assassinated in 1942.

Darling, J. N. "Ding" *(1876–1962)* U.S. political cartoonist and "Father of Conservation." He gained fame drawing political cartoons that depicted national events and human weaknesses. He won the PULITZER PRIZE for editorial cartooning twice, in 1923 and 1943. Darling began his career as a reporter but turned to cartooning in 1901. In 1906 he joined the staff of the *Des Moines Register* where he remained until 1949 (except for 1911–13 when he worked for the *New York Globe*). His cartoons went into syndication in 1917 and appeared in as many as 135 papers. A leader in America's conservation movement, he worked for the establishment of wildlife preservation laws, migratory waterfowl refuges and soil conservation. Among the best collections of his work is the one maintained by the University of Iowa in Iowa City.

Darrow, Clarence Seward *(1857–1938)* American criminal attorney, best remembered for his defense of John Scopes in the famous SCOPES TRIAL, also known as the Monkey Trial (1925). Darrow was perhaps the most celebrated trial attorney of his day, defending both mobsters and businessmen. His most famous client was Eugene DEBS, the Socialist labor leader. He also successfully defended the notorious killers LEOPOLD AND LOEB, winning them life sentences instead of the death penalty. Darrow's methods of cross-examination and his appeals to juries were legendary. Darrow volunteered to help the AMERICAN CIVIL LIBERTIES UNION (ACLU) defend John Scopes, a Tennessee teacher who agreed to challenge the state's law prohibiting the teaching of the theory of evolution. The trial gained international attention, pitting Darrow against three-time Democratic presidential candidate William Jennings BRYAN, who railed against Darwin and his theory.

Dart, Raymond Arthur *(1893–1988)* Australian-born anatomist. Dart revolutionized the study of human origins when, in 1924, he discovered the first early human fossil to be found in Africa. Prior to that time, evolutionists had believed that humans developed in Asia. Dart's theory was not widely accepted until Louis LEAKEY confirmed the African origin of humankind with a series of discoveries after World War II. Dart served for many years as professor and dean of the medical school at the University of Witwatersrand in South Africa.

Dashnaktsutyun The "Confederacy" party, commonly called Dashnaks, was a national revolutionary grouping founded in Turkish Armenia in 1890. The party started out to recruit Russian Armenians, with the aim of establishing an independent state of Great Armenia. When Czar NICHOLAS II closed many Armenian schools, libraries and newspaper offices in 1903 and took over the property of the Armenian Church, the Dashnaks carried out a policy of civil disobedience in RUSSIA in 1903–05. They supported the provisional government but were opposed to the Bolshevik Revolution Party in the independent Armenian republic of 1918–20, which became the chief party. Even today the party is in existence and aims at achieving an independent ARMENIA.

Dassault, Marcel (Marcel Bloch) *(1892–1986)* French aircraft designer. His career as a designer and builder of both civil and military aircraft spanned most of the 20th century. The best known of all his planes was probably the Mirage, the delta-winged jet fighter that gained world attention when it was used by the Israeli air force during the SIX-DAY WAR in 1967. Twice his manufacturing operations were nationalized by French left-wing governments, and, as a Jew, he was stripped of his business interests during WORLD WAR II. Despite this, at the time of his death he was one of the richest men in France. He was also the oldest member of the French parliament, having served almost uninterrupted since 1951.

Daudet, Léon *(1867–1942)* French novelist, memoirist and journalist. Daudet, who was the son of the renowned 19th-century story writer Alphonse Daudet, wrote several novels and plays as well as an autobiography (1925), but he never came close to equaling the literary success of his father. Daudet did succeed, however, in making his mark as a political journalist. In 1908 Daudet took over the editorship of the right-wing journal *L'Action française,* in which he called for a restoration of the French monarchy and published vehemently anti-Semitic essays (see ACTION FRANÇAISE and ANTI-SEMITISM). Daudet, who served on the Chamber of Deputies from 1919 to 1924, was a severe critic of the democratic French Third Republic in the years between the two world wars.

Daugherty, Harry M. *(1860–1941)* American politician who was reputedly involved in the infamous TEAPOT DOME SCANDAL that rocked the reputation of the administration of President Warren HARDING. Daugherty, a Cleveland lawyer and member of the Ohio legislature with Harding, was a longtime Harding supporter and managed Harding's successful nomination and campaign for the presidency. In gratitude, Harding named Daugherty as his attorney general. Rumors of corruption quickly arose, and Daugherty was accused of benefiting from a less-than-vigorous enforcement of PROHIBITION regulations; he was already unliked for his vigorous antilabor stance and for packing the Justice Department with questionable men. After Harding's sudden death, Daugherty refused a congressional investigation's efforts to see his department's files. President COOLIDGE dismissed Daugherty from his post in March 1924. Two 1927 trials for conspiring to defraud the government ended in hung juries. He died in 1941.

Dausset, Jean *(1916–)* French physician and immunologist. Dausset, the son of a doctor, earned his M.D. from the University of Paris in 1945 following wartime service in the blood transfusion unit. He was professor of hematology at the University of Paris from 1958 and professor of immuno-hematology from 1968. In 1977 he was elected professor of experimental medicine at the Collège de France.

Dausset's war experience stimulated his interest in transfusion reactions, and in 1951 he showed that the blood of certain universal donors (those of blood group O), which had been assumed safe to use in all transfusions, could nonetheless be dangerous. This was because of the presence of strong immune antibodies in their plasma, which develop following antidiphtheria and antitetanus injections. Donor blood is now systematically tested for such antibodies. In the 1950s Dausset noticed a peculiar feature in the histories of patients who had received a number of blood transfusions: They developed a low white blood cell (leukocyte) count. He suspected that the transfused blood might have contained antigens that stimulated the production of antibodies against the leukocytes. With insight and considerable courage Dausset went on to claim that the antigen on the blood cells, soon to be known as the HLA, or human lymphocyte antigen, was the equivalent of the mouse H-2 system described by George Snell.

The significance of Dausset's work was enormous. It meant that tissues could be typed quickly and cheaply by simple blood agglutination tests as opposed to the complicated and lengthy procedure of seeing if skin grafts would take. Such work made the technically feasible operation of kidney transplantation a practical medical option, for at last the danger of rejection could be minimized by rapid, simple and accurate tissue typing. Dausset shared the 1980 NOBEL PRIZE in physiology or medicine with Snell and Baruj Benacerraf. In the 1990s Dausset collaborated with geneticists around the world in an effort to map the human genome.

Davenport, Charles Benedict *(1866–1944)* American zoologist and geneticist. Davenport earned a Ph.D. in zoology at Harvard in 1892, where he taught until 1899. From 1901 until 1904 he was curator of the Zoological Museum at the University of Chicago and from 1904 until 1934 was director of the Carnegie Institution's Department of Genetics at Cold Spring Harbor, New York. In 1910 Davenport founded the Eugenics Record Office, directing it until 1934. Davenport carried out early studies of animal genetics, using chickens and canaries, at the turn of the century. He was among the first to accept Gregor Mendel's rediscovered theory of heredity. He later turned his attention to humans, and in *Heredity in Relation to Eugenics* (1912) offered evidence for the inheritance of particular human traits, suggesting that the application of genetic principles to human breeding might improve the race (eugenics). From 1898 Davenport was assistant editor of the *Journal of Experimental Zoology;* he was also editor of both *Genetics* and the *Journal of Physical Anthropology.*

Davidson, Jo *(1883–1952)* American sculptor. Born in New York City, Davidson studied at the Art Students League there and at the École de Beaux-Arts, Paris. He was a consummate portraitist who worked in an expressive and naturalistic style, mainly in bronze, to capture the personalities of his sitters. Davidson portrayed many of the most celebrated people of his time, diverse figures that included Woodrow WILSON, George Bernard SHAW, Mohandas K. GANDHI, Franklin D. ROOSEVELT, Albert EINSTEIN, Benito MUSSOLINI, Will ROGERS, Rabindranath TAGORE and Gertrude STEIN. His philosophy of sculpture and his encounters with the

celebrated are detailed in his 1951 autobiography, *Between Sittings.*

Davie, Donald Alfred *(1922–1995)* English poet and critic. Born in Yorkshire, Davie studied at Cambridge (B.A., 1947; M.A., 1949; Ph.D., 1951), where he came under the influence of F. R. LEAVIS. He served in the Royal Navy in World War II and thereafter taught at a number of British and American universities. Davie was a literary traditionalist who believed the poet was responsible "for purifying and correcting the spoken language." Among his collections are *Brides of Reason* (1955), *A Winter Talent* (1957), *Essex Poems* (1969) and *In the Stopping Train* (1977). His poems tend to be erudite, abstract, philosophical and highly precise in their use of language. His criticism includes studies of Scott, HARDY, POUND, the Augustans and Boris PASTERNAK.

Davies, Sir Peter Maxwell *(1934–)* British composer and conductor. Born in Manchester, England, Davies attended the Royal Manchester College of Music and Manchester University. While studying composition in Rome he won the Olivetti Prize (1958). In the early 1960s he studied with Roger SESSIONS at Princeton University. In 1967 in England he formed a chamber ensemble, The Fires of London, to perform his works. In the early 1970s Davies went to live in the Orkney Islands, off the northernmost tip of Scotland. Much of the music he has written since then reflects the rugged landscape, seascape and local traditions of this isolated region. One of the most gifted and accessible British composers of his generation, Davies has written many works on commission. His compositions include *Ave Maris Stella* (1975), eight symphonies and numerous concertos, orchestral works and chamber pieces. Davies continued to compose throughout the 1990s, developing the operas *The Doctor of Myddfai* (1996) and the orchestral piece *The Jacobite Rising* (1997).

Davies, (William) Robertson *(1913–1995)* Canadian author. Davies was born in Ontario and educated at Upper Canada College, Toronto University, Queen's University (Kingston) and Balliol College, Oxford. He began his career as an actor and teacher with the

Old Vic Company, London, and subsequently worked in Canada as an editor, publisher and professor of English. Davies's first three novels, *Tempest-Tossed* (1951), *Leaven of Malice* (1959) and *A Mixture of Frailties* (1960), known as the Salterton Trilogy, were well received, but he achieved both critical and popular success with the Deptford Trilogy: *Fifth Business* (1970), *The Manticore* (1972) and *World of Wonders* (1976), which follow the lives of three men connected by an incident in their childhood home of Deptford. Davies's writing, which some say is theatrical, explores the choices between good and evil and evidences his interest in Jungian psychology (see Carl JUNG). While contemporary, his fiction is rich in myth and folklore and is often very funny. Other fiction includes *The Rebel Angels* (1982), *What's Bred in the Bone* (1985) and *The Lyre of Orpheus* (1989). Davies also wrote numerous plays, including *Questions Time* (1975) and *Pontiac and the Green Man* (1977), and newspaper articles under the pseudonym Samuel Marchbanks.

Davis, Angela Yvonne *(1944–)* Black American radical political activist. Davis studied philosophy with Herbert MARCUSE and became involved in radical Marxist politics and the BLACK POWER movement in California in the 1960s. She joined the Communist Party (1968) and was hired by the philosophy department at the University of California in Los Angeles (1969). A furor ensued, and her contract was not renewed at the end of the year. Davis next became involved in a case involving the "Soledad brothers," three black convicts in California. Using guns that Davis owned, a brother of one of the convicts entered a courtroom and seized five hostages. A shootout ensued, in which the gunman, the judge and two inmates were killed. Because she owned the guns, Davis was indicted on charges of murder, kidnapping and conspiracy. She went into hiding and was placed on the FBI's 10-most-wanted list. She was arrested in October 1970, and her trial finally began in March 1972. She was acquitted but remained a focus of controversy. In many ways her case was a microcosm of the political and racial tensions of the late 1960s and early 1970s in the U.S. Davis was a lecturer in African-American and women's studies at Claremont College and San Francisco State University. In 1980 and 1984 she was the Communist Party's vice presidential candidate.

Davis, Benjamin Oliver, Sr. *(1877–1970)* U.S. military officer. After studying at Howard University (1897), Davis became a lieutenant of volunteers in the Spanish-American War. In 1899 he enlisted in the regular army as a private and rose to the rank of lieutenant in the Philippine service. Davis served as military attaché in Liberia (1909–12). He taught at several universities until 1938 when he was given his first independent command, the 369th New York National Guard Infantry Regiment. Despite much criticism based on race and politics, Davis became the first black general in the U.S. Army in 1940 and assistant to the inspector general of the army in 1941. He served in Europe in WORLD WAR II as an adviser on race relations; he retired in 1948. Davis is the father of air force general Benjamin Oliver DAVIS, Jr.

Davis, Benjamin Oliver, Jr. *(1912–2002)* U.S. military officer. The first African-American graduate of West Point (1936), Davis served as an in-

Brigade General Benjamin O. Davis Sr. the first African-American general in the U.S. Army. on duty in France during World War II. 1944 (LIBRARY OF CONGRESS, PRINTS AND PHOTOGRAPHS DIVISION)

fantry officer before joining the U.S. Air Force. A distinguished combat pilot during WORLD WAR II, he led the all-black 99th Fighter Squadron (known as the "Tuskegee Airmen") in combat over North Africa and Italy and played a key role in the air war at the battle of Anzio. After leading an integrated fighter force in the KOREAN WAR, Davis became the first black general in the U.S. Air Force in 1954. (In 1940 his father, Benjamin Oliver DAVIS, Sr., had become the first black general in the U.S. Army.) In 1961 Davis was appointed director of airpower and organization in the USAF. He commanded the 13th Air Force during the VIETNAM WAR. He retired in 1970 as a three-star general. In 1998 President Bill Clinton awarded him a fourth star, raising him to the rank of full general. In 1971 he was named assistant secretary of transportation for environment, safety and consumer affairs. He published his autobiography, *Benjamin O. Davis Jr.: American,* in 1991.

Davis, Bette (**Ruth Elizabeth Davis**) *(1908–1989)* Legendary American HOLLYWOOD movie star. Born in Massachusetts, Davis worked in small theater companies in New England until she broke into the Broadway theater in the late 1920s. She quickly moved on to Hollywood; although her screen test with Samuel GOLDWYN's studio failed to impress, she played bit roles in pictures at UNIVERSAL, then signed a contract with WARNER BROS., where she remained from 1930 to 1949. There she established a reputation for playing tough, independent women who defied convention. Among her best-known films were *Of Human Bondage* (1934), *The Private Lives of Elizabeth and Essex* (1939), *Dark Victory* (1941), *All About Eve* (1950) and *What Ever Happened to Baby Jane?* (1962). She also appeared in several stage roles and, later in her career, in made-for-television movies. Altogether, she made more than 80 films, was nominated for 11 ACADEMY AWARDS, and won the best actress award twice, for *Dangerous* (1935) and *Jezebel* (1938).

Davis, Elmer *(1890–1958)* U.S. broadcast journalist and author. A writer of international note, Davis was a teacher at the Franklin Indiana High School (1909–10) and part of the editorial staff first at the legendary all-

fiction pulp magazine *Adventure* (1913–14) and then at the *New York Times* (1914–24). He was a news analyst for CBS (1939–42) when he became director of the Office of War Information, for which he received the Medal of Merit. He worked at ABC as a news analyst, from 1945 to 1956. His famous works include *But We Were Born Free* (1953) and *Two Minutes Till Midnight* (1955).

Davis, John William *(1873–1955)* U.S. lawyer and politician. Davis received both his bachelor (1892) and law (1895) degrees from Washington and Lee University. After election to Congress from West Virginia (1910), he resigned to become solicitor general of the U.S. (1913), simultaneously serving as counselor for the RED CROSS. In 1918 Davis served at a conference in Switzerland concerned with the treatment of World War I PRISONERS OF WAR and then served as ambassador to Great Britain (1918–21). After election to the presidency of the American Bar Association (1922), he won the Democratic presidential nomination (1924) but was soundly defeated in the election by Calvin COOLIDGE. Davis then returned to private practice. He took 140 cases to the Supreme Court, often without a fee.

Davis, Miles *(1926–1991)* Trumpeter and band leader; perhaps the single most influential figure in postwar jazz due to his introduction and popularization of such significant styles as cool jazz, MODAL JAZZ, jazz-rock and FUSION. Originally inspired by the BEBOP revolutionary and alto saxophonist Charlie PARKER, Davis left his hometown of East St. Louis, Illinois, in 1944 to find his idol in New York City. Parker took the youngster under his wing, and Davis appeared in live and recorded performances with Parker in 1945–48. In 1959 Davis collaborated with arranger Gil Evans in a seminal set of recordings issued as *Birth of the Cool,* thus establishing the "cool" sensibility as one of the dominant styles of the 1950s. Davis turned his back on the movement and instead organized a fiery bop-based quintet. This group, with some modifications, recorded "Kind of Blue" (1959), setting the pace for the modal approach, a dominant force in 1960s' modern jazz. By the early 1970s Davis had discarded standard tunes such as "Bye Bye Blackbird," a staple of his

Jazz trumpeter and composer Miles Davis during his legendary performance at Carnegie Hall. 1961 (PHOTOFEST)

repertory for nearly two decades, in favor of an evolving style that amalgamated elements from funk, rock and modality; there was an increased reliance on electronic instruments as well. Davis's more recent work continued in his fusionistic vein. In addition to his status as a stylistic innovator, Davis helped introduce such pivotal contemporary musicians as keyboardists Herbie HANCOCK and Chick COREA, saxophonist Wayne Shorter, guitarist John SCOFIELD and drummer Tony Williams.

Davis, Sammy, Jr. *(1925–1990)* American entertainer. Davis's energy and versatility as a singer, dancer, actor and nightclub entertainer made him one of the first black performers to win widespread acclaim from white audiences. He began his career in a family VAUDEVILLE group at age three and became the group's star performer. A car accident in 1954 led to the loss of his left eye and his widely publicized conversion to Judaism. He appeared in the 1959 film version of *PORGY AND BESS,* and starred in the Broadway shows *Mr. Wonderful* (1956) and *Golden Boy* (1964). In the 1960s he became a member of, and often

performed with, the "Rat Pack," a group of fast-living, hard-drinking, womanizing HOLLYWOOD performers led by Frank SINATRA. He wrote two autobiographies, *Yes I Can* (1965) and *Why Me?* (1989).

Davis, William Morris *(1850–1934)* American physical geographer. Davis was educated at Harvard, where he returned to teach in 1877 after a period as a meteorologist in Argentina and as an assistant with the North Pacific Survey. He became professor of physical geography in 1890 and of geology in 1898. Davis is acknowledged as the founder of the science of geomorphology, the study of landforms. He introduced what later became known as the Davisian system of landscape analysis. His aim was to provide an explanatory description of how landforms change. His most important contribution to this was his introduction of the "cycle of erosion" into geographical thought. He proposed a complete cycle of youth, maturity and old age to describe the evolution of a landscape. Davis also produced an influential work, *Elementary Meteorology* (1894), which was used as a textbook for over 30 years,

and in 1928 published *The Coral Reef Problem.*

Davisson, Clinton Joseph *(1881–1958)* American physicist. Davisson was educated at the University of Chicago and at Princeton, where he earned his Ph.D. in 1911. After working for a short period at the Carnegie Institute of Technology in Pittsburgh, Davisson joined the Bell Telephone Laboratory (then Western Electric) in 1917 and remained there until his retirement in 1946. In 1937 he shared the NOBEL PRIZE in physics with George Thomson for "their experimental discovery of the diffraction of electrons by crystals."

Dawes, Charles Gates *(1865–1951)* American lawyer and banker; vice president of the UNITED STATES (1925–29). During WORLD WAR I, Dawes served as the head of procurement for the U.S. forces in Europe (1917–18). In the early 1920s he was the chief architect of the DAWES PLAN to reschedule GERMANY's postwar reparations, thereby helping Germany to survive an economic crisis. For this Dawes received the 1925 NOBEL PRIZE for peace. A Republican, he was chosen as Calvin COOLIDGE's vice presidential running mate in 1924 and was elected to that office. During Herbert HOOVER's administration, Dawes was the U.S. ambassador to Britain.

Dawes Plan In 1924 American banker Charles DAWES (later vice president of the U.S.) presented a plan to ease GERMANY's WORLD WAR I reparations payments. The London Schedule of Payments (1921) had set Germany's reparations at $33 billion; however, postwar inflation and other problems confronting the young WEIMAR REPUBLIC resulted in great economic hardship. The Dawes Plan provided for an international loan, set fixed payments and reorganized the German state bank in order to stabilize the currency. The mark, which had inflated to 4.2 trillion to the dollar, was replaced by the rentenmark (4.2 to the dollar). The plan was superseded by the YOUNG PLAN in 1929, but Germany defaulted on its debts during the GREAT DEPRESSION.

Dawidowicz, Lucy Schildkret *(1915–1990)* U.S. historian. Her 1975 book *The War Against the Jews* was considered a pioneering study of Nazi genocide. The book argued that the extermination of the JEWS had been one of the central aims of the Nazi program, not merely a secondary development. She also clashed with other historians of the HOLOCAUST in refusing to blame Jews for passivity in the face of the Nazi threat.

Dawkins, Richard *(1941–)* British ethologist. Dawkins was educated at Oxford University where he worked for his doctorate under Niko TINBERGEN. He initially taught at the University of California, Berkeley, before returning to Oxford in 1970 as lecturer in animal behavior. In *The Selfish Gene* (1976) Dawkins did much to introduce the work of such scholars as William Hamilton, Robert L. Trivers and John Maynard Smith to a wider public. He tried to show that such apparently altruistic behavior as birds risking their lives to warn the flock of an approaching predator can be seen as the "selfish gene" ensuring its own survival (by ensuring the survival of the descendants and relatives of the "heroic" bird). In 1997 Dawkins was elected a fellow of the Royal Society of Literature.

Day, David Talbot *(1859–1925)* American chemist. Day was educated at Johns Hopkins University, earning his Ph.D. in 1894. He started his career as a demonstrator in chemistry at the University of Maryland but left to become head of the Mineral Resources Division of the U.S. Geological Survey in 1896. Day investigated the reasons for the differences found in the composition of various petroleum deposits. He did much to stimulate the growth of the petroleum industry and in 1922 produced one of its basic texts, *Handbook of the Petroleum Industry*. From 1914 to 1920 he was a consultant chemist with the Bureau of Mines.

Day, Dorothy *(1897–1980)* American Catholic social activist. A founder of the Catholic Worker Movement in 1933, Day influenced a generation of American priests, intellectuals and laypeople. A devout Roman Catholic, she was also a nonviolent social radical who embraced a philosophy of voluntary poverty and care for the destitute through direct involvement. Her phi-

losophy looked to the individual rather than to mass action to transform society. Active in the church for more than 50 years, she founded many homes for the poor and homeless.

Dayan, Moshe *(1915–1981)* Israeli military hero and politician. Born in PALESTINE and educated at the Hebrew University in JERUSALEM, he joined the Jewish defense force HAGANAH in the late 1930s. Imprisoned by the British (1939–41), he subsequently fought against Axis forces in Syria during WORLD WAR II, losing his left eye. After ISRAEL became independent (1948), he fought in the ARAB-ISRAELI WAR OF 1948–1949, and as chief of staff (1953–58) he directed the successful Sinai campaign in the ARAB-ISRAELI WAR OF 1956. He entered politics in 1958 and served in the cabinet of David BEN-GURION. Named defense minister several days before the SIX-DAY WAR (1976), he launched the attacks that brought speedy victory against EGYPT, JORDAN and SYRIA. Criticized after Israeli reverses in the YOM KIPPUR WAR (1973), he left the cabinet after a dispute with the Labor prime minister, Golda MEIR (1974). He was named foreign minister by Menachem BEGIN in 1978 but resigned in 1979. A charismatic figure and a brilliant general, Dayan remained a legend even after the setbacks of his later years.

Day Lewis, Cecil *(1904–1972)* British poet, fiction writer, editor and translator. Day Lewis's decade of triumph was the proletarian 1930s when, along with AUDEN, SPENDER and (to a lesser degree) MACNEICE, he was a poet-propagandist for socialism in England. However, disillusioned by the events of WORLD WAR II and thereafter, he later returned to writing neo-Georgian verse (see the GEORGIANS). Although he also wrote criticism and children's books, edited anthologies and translated Vigil and VALÉRY, between 1935 and 1968 he supported himself primarily by producing detective fiction under the pseudonym **Nicholas Blake.** He also lectured at Oxford, Cambridge and Harvard. He was made C.B.E. (Commander, Order of the British Empire) in 1950. In 1968 he succeeded John Masefield as poet laureate of England. His son **Daniel**

Day-Lewis established a reputation as an accomplished film actor in the late 1980s, winning an ACADEMY AWARD as best actor in 1990.

Dayton Accords (Dayton Agreement, General Framework Agreement) The name given to the peace agreement among ethnic Croat, Muslim and Serb factions fighting one another in BOSNIA AND HERZEGOVINA. It was initialed in Dayton, Ohio, on November 21, 1995. Sponsored by the U.S. and the European Union (EU), the agreement provided a formal and final settlement of the conflict that had plagued the former YUGOSLAVIA since 1991. In June of that year, residents of the largely Catholic province of CROATIA and the predominantly Muslim region of Bosnia and Herzegovina declared independence from the Serbian-dominated Yugoslav state. In response, ethnic Serbs in both Croatia and Bosnia launched a guerrilla war against both governments in 1991 and 1992, respectively. As these ethnic Serbs fought Croats and Bosniaks (Muslim Bosnians), they received military support from Serbian president Slobodan MILOŠEVIĆ. Further complicating the situation, Croatia and Bosnia began fighting each other over territory each state claimed at the expense of the other. The fighting in Croatia stopped in 1992 when a ceasefire was negotiated between the Croatian government and its ethnic Serbian minority. Two years later an agreement signed in Washington ended the conflict between Croatia and Bosnia and produced a Muslim-Croat federation that cooperated militarily against the ethnic Serbs. By mid-1995, this coalition had recaptured several Serbian-controlled cities in Bosnia. These events, in conjunction with efforts by NATO to negotiate an end to the conflict, prompted Milošević, Bosnian president Alija IZETBEGOVIĆ and Croatian president Franjo Tudjman to agree to meet with American, British, French, German, Italian, Russian and EU diplomats in Dayton, Ohio, to seek a resolution of the conflict.

The accords produced at Dayton created two political entities within the state of Bosnia. One, the Federation of Bosnia and Herzegovina (dominated by the Muslim-Croat federation created in 1994) would administer

51% of Bosnian territory; the other, consisting of the remaining 49%, would come under the authority of the Bosnian Serbs. Although both entities would possess their own governmental structures, they would remain under the authority of a national president and legislature and a Bosnian constitution that ensured civil liberties to all ethnic Croats, Bosniaks and Serbs (including free transit throughout Bosnia and the right of war refugees to return to their original residences). To ensure that the Dayton agreement was honored by all parties, NATO created an Implementation Force (IFOR) in 1996 to protect demilitarized zones and enforce the continuation of the cease-fire. When IFOR's NATO mandate expired in 1997 it was succeeded by a Stabilization Force (SFOR) that continued to maintain the cease-fire and demilitarized zones established in 1995.

DC-3 Douglas DC-3 airplane of 1934, which proved to be one of the most successful aircraft designs ever developed. Its predecessors, the DC-1, DC-2, and DST, were steps toward the development of the DC-3, all twin-engine, low-wing monoplanes of clean, streamlined form with retractable landing gear and a 21-passenger seating capacity. The success of the DC-3 made passenger air transportation reliable, practical and widely available. The basic design of the DC-3 established the norm for passenger aircraft and became the basis for many similar designs by other manufacturers and for the gradually larger four-engine transport airplanes that succeeded it. Even modern jet aircraft owe much of their basic form to the DC-3. Including the

military version (C-47), some 11,000 DC-3s were built. A surprising number remain in service, particularly in out-of-the-way locations where only short-runway airfields are available.

D-day See Invasion of NORMANDY.

DDT Dichlorodiphenyltrichloro-ethane, an insecticide developed by Swiss scientists in 1939–40. DDT was first heralded as a wonder insecticide that would destroy agricultural pests and thus help farmers increase their crop production. During the 1950s and 1960s it was routinely sprayed on crops. However, many insects developed a resistance to DDT. Moreover, it was discovered that DDT entered the food cycle and poisoned birds and other animals, as well as contaminating freshwater supplies. The dangerous effects of DDT on the environment were chronicled by Rachel CARSON in her book *Silent Spring* (1962).

Deakin, Alfred (*1856–1919*) Australian statesman, three-time prime minister (1903–04, 1905–08, 1909–10). A noted lawyer, he served in the Victoria legislature from 1880 to 1899 and pressed for social, labor, tariff and agricultural reform. An advocate of the federation of Australian states, he became the Commonwealth of AUSTRALIA's attorney general in 1901. As prime minister, he initiated important health and old-age pension legislation.

Dean, Arthur Hobson (*1898–1987*) American lawyer. While head of the prestigious New York law firm Sullivan & Cromwell, Dean served four U.S. presidents in various diplomatic and advisory capacities. During the Franklin D. ROOSEVELT administration he helped

draft landmark securities laws. During the EISENHOWER administration he negotiated for seven weeks in 1953 on behalf of the U.S. and the UNITED NATIONS at talks in Panmunjom that tried to achieve a permanent political settlement to the KOREAN WAR. He conducted important disarmament negotiations during the KENNEDY administration. He later played a key role during the VIETNAM WAR, persuading President JOHNSON to stop the bombing of North VIETNAM in 1968 and not to seek reelection.

Dean, Christopher See TORVILLE AND DEAN.

Dean, James (*1931–1955*) American actor; burst into sudden HOLLYWOOD stardom in the 1950s and died at age 24 in an automobile crash. Dean remains an icon of American popular culture in much the same manner as a contemporary Hollywood figure, Marilyn MONROE. He starred in only three films: *East of Eden* (1954) (based on the novel by John STEINBECK), *Rebel Without a Cause* (1955) and *Giant* (1956). In each film Dean portrayed an archetypically rebellious American young man with thick, swept-back hair, piercing eyes and a sneer that could transform suddenly into a vulnerable smile. It is more as an image—one that has graced millions of posters and postcards—than as an imitated actor that Dean has survived in American popular culture to this day.

Dean, Jay Hanna "Dizzy" (*1911–1974*) American baseball player. Dean joined the world champion "Gas House Gang" St. Louis Cardinals in 1932. An outstanding all-around player, he led the National League in strikeouts his first year and was a stellar fielder and a solid hitter with a .258 average. He won 102 games over four seasons. His brother Paul ("Daffy") joined the club in 1934, and the two combined for 49 wins. Dizzy led the team to the pennant and finished the season with two World Series wins. He was traded to the Cubs in 1938 and posted a 7-1 record. He was beloved by fans not only for his skill but also for his colorful personality and cocksure ways. After his retirement he was a TV commentator for more than 20 years.

Dean, John Wesley, III (*1938–   *) A minor functionary in the NIXON

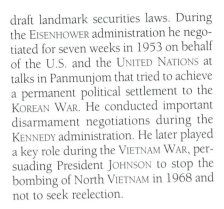

The Douglas DC-3, the most widely used aircraft in aviation history (LIBRARY OF CONGRESS, PRINTS AND PHOTOGRAPHS DIVISION)

White House, Dean played a key role in the WATERGATE scandal. As counsel to President Richard M. Nixon from July 1970 to April 1973, he became deeply involved in the coverup. However, fearing prosecution for his own role in the affair, he began to cooperate with federal prosecutors in April 1973. The star witness of Senator Sam ERVIN's Watergate Committee, he was the first administration official to accuse Nixon of direct involvement. Dean testified that, under the direction of Nixon aides H. R. Haldeman and John Ehrlichman, he had managed the day-to-day coverup of the affair and supervised payments of "hush money" to the convicted Watergate burglars. Dean also revealed that the White House kept an "enemies list" of prominent administration critics whom it wished to discredit. Dean received a mild sentence for his part in the affair and served only four months in prison.

De Andrade, Mario Pinto (1928–1990)
Angolan writer and historian. He was one of the founders of the Angolan nationalist movement. As the first head of the Popular Movement for the Liberation of Angola, from 1960 to 1974, he helped the country's struggle against Portuguese rule. He became disillusioned with the movement's authoritarian tendencies and split from it a year before ANGOLA gained its independence in 1975.

Death in Venice
Classic 1911 novella by German author Thomas MANN. The fictional protagonist is Gustave von Aschenbach, a famous but aging author with impeccable work habits who has resolved to take a restful vacation in Venice for the sake of his health. But von Aschenbach is soon distracted by Tadzio, a beautiful boy of 14, with whom he falls chastely in love. The central theme of *Death in Venice* is the painful clash between disciplined artistic creation and wayward passion, which ultimately undermines all values and beckons toward nothingless by virtue of its mindless intensity. While von Aschenbach resists overt advances toward Tadzio, he becomes obsessed by the boy and loses the will to return to the ordered pattern of his previous life. At the end of the novella, the heartsick von Aschenbach dies in a cholera epidemic that sweeps through Venice.

Death of a Salesman
Classic drama by American playwright Arthur MILLER, regarded by many critics as the greatest American play of the 20th century. Miller intended it as a new kind of tragedy: "I believe that the common man is as apt a subject for tragedy in its highest sense as kings were." The basic plot concerns the decline of Willy Loman, a onetime bustling salesman who was inspired by the American Dream of success. Now forsaken by his employer, Loman (note the allegorical last name) is alternately pitied and disrespected by his two sons, Biff and Happy. Only his wife, Linda, remains loyal, but she cannot save him from his descent into escapist fantasy and ultimate despair. Loman ultimately kills himself in a car accident so his family can have the insurance money. *Death of a Salesman* opened on Broadway on February 10, 1949, directed by Elia KAZAN, with Lee J. Cobb as Loman. The action roams freely through time and space; at Miller's instructions, designer Jo Mielziner created a set—Willy's house—whose rooms could instantly be transformed into other locations—hotel room, office, cemetery. The play is both realistic in its study of a man's professional decline and expressionistic in its projection of a psychological crisis. Frederick March played Willy in the 1951 film version. Perhaps the most memorable of the many stage revivals was one starring Dustin HOFFMAN (1984); it was filmed for television in 1985 by German director Volker Schlondorff. *Death of a Salesman* has become a staple play in the repertoire of theater companies around the world and was revived on Broadway in 1999, the play's 50th anniversary.

de Beer, Sir Gavin Rylands (1899–1972)
British zoologist. De Beer graduated from Oxford University, where he was a fellow from 1923 to 1938. He served in both world wars; during WORLD WAR II he landed in Normandy in 1944, where he was in charge of psychological warfare. He was professor of embryology at University College, London (1945–50) and then director of the Natural History Museum in London (1950–60). In an early publication, *Introduction to Experimental Biology* (1926), de Beer finally disproved the germ-layer theory. He also did work to show that adult animals retain some of the juvenile char-acters of their evolutionary ancestors (pedomorphosis), thus refuting Ernst Haeckel's theory of recapitulation. De Beer also carried out research into the functions of the pituitary gland. In the field of ancient history, de Beer applied scientific methods to various problems, for example, the origin of the Etruscans and Hannibal's journey across the Alps. His other books include *Embryology and Evolution of Chordate Animals* (1962, with Julian HUXLEY), *The Elements of Experimental Embryology* (1962) and a biography of Charles Darwin (1961). He was knighted in 1954.

Debierne, André-Louis (1874–1949)
French chemist. Debierne was educated at the École de Physique et Chimie. After graduation he worked at the Sorbonne and as an assistant to Pierre and Marie CURIE, finally succeeding the latter as director of the Radium Institute. On his retirement in 1949 he in turn was succeeded by the Curies' daughter, Irène JOLIOT-CURIE. Debierne was principally a radiochemist; his first triumph came in 1900 with the discovery of a new radioactive element, actinium, which he isolated while working with pitchblende. In 1905 he went on to show that actinium, like radium, formed helium. This was of some significance in helping Ernest RUTHERFORD to appreciate that some radioactive elements decay by emitting an alpha particle (or, as it turned out to be, the nucleus of a helium atom). In 1910, in collaboration with Marie Curie, he isolated pure metallic radium.

Deborin, Abram Moiseyevich (pseudonym of Abram Moiseyevich Ioffe) (1881–1963)
Russian historian and philosopher. Deborin became a BOLSHEVIK in 1903, went over to the MENSHEVIKS in 1907 but eventually joined the COMMUNIST PARTY in 1928. He was editor of the chief Marxist philosophical journal, *Under the Banner of Marxism* and secretary of the department for history and philosophy in the Academy of Sciences (1935–45). His writings argued against mechanical materialism, but he was condemned as a "Menshevik idealist." His works included *Introduction to the Philosophy of Dialectical Materialism* (1916), *Dictatorship of the Proletariat and the Theory of Marxism* (1927), *Dialectical Material-*

ism (1929) and *Lenin and the Crisis of Modern Physics* (1930).

Deboyne Islands Volcanic island group in the Louisiade Archipelago, 110 miles southeast of New Guinea in the southwestern Pacific Ocean; a part of Papua New Guinea. A lagoon in the middle of this island chain held a Japanese seaplane base during WORLD WAR II. U.S. forces annihilated it after the battle of the CORAL SEA in May 1942.

Debs, Eugene V. *(1855–1926)* U.S. labor leader and Socialist Party presidential candidate. A locomotive fireman, he helped establish the first local lodge of the Brotherhood of Locomotive Firemen. Between 1880 and 1884 he was city clerk of Terre Haute, Indiana, and in 1885 he became a member of the lower house of the Indiana legislature. Debs soon came to criticize social conditions, oppose unionization along craft lines and form the American Railway Union—an organization open to all railroad workers. The union's strike against the Pullman Company resulted in violence in Chicago and federal intervention. As a result, the union was destroyed, and Debs and several associates were sent to jail for six months on contempt of court charges. In 1896 Debs supported William Jennings BRYAN for president. He organized the Social Democratic Party of America the next year. Debs was the Socialist Party candidate for president four times successively, between 1900 and 1912, and again in 1920. In 1912 he received 6% of the total vote, the highest total ever gained by a Socialist. Indicted under the Espionage Act in 1918 for his opposition to entry of the U.S. into WORLD WAR I, he was sentenced to 10 years in prison but was pardoned in 1921. Debs had remained a Socialist when the communists broke with the Socialist Party in 1919.

Debus, Kurt Heinrich *(1908–1983)* German-born electrical engineer and rocket pioneer. During WORLD WAR II he worked with Werner von BRAUN at PEENEMUNDE, Germany, to develop the V-2 rocket. After the NAZI defeat, he was brought to the U.S. In the 1950s he worked on the Redstone Ballistic program, developing the U.S. Army's first

missile equipped with a nuclear warhead. He became a U.S. citizen in 1959. In 1952 he became director of operations at what later became the Kennedy Space Center. He directed the launch of the first American Earth satellite and presided over the first American landing on the Moon (see APOLLO 11). He also oversaw the three SKYLAB missions in the early 1970s.

Debussy, Claude-Achille *(1862–1918)* French composer and critic considered the prime architect of modern music in the 20th century. With Béla BARTÓK, Igor STRAVINSKY and Charles IVES, Debussy liberated tonality and rhythm from the straitjacket of 19th-century musical practice. He was born in Saint-Germain-en-Laye near Paris. He entered the Paris Conservatory at age 11 and for the next 11 years confounded colleagues and teachers with his unorthodox experiments and improvisations. Contacts with symbolist poets such as Mallarme and Impressionist painters such as Monet led to an "impressionist" music of his own. Such orchestral works as *Printemps* (*Spring*, 1887) and *Prélude à l'après-midi d'un faune* (*Prelude to the Afternoon of a Faun*, 1894), his landmark opera *Pelléas et Mélisande* (1902), the piano *Images* (1907) and the ballet *Jeux* (1913) all aroused virulent hostility for their presumed "vagueness" and veiled atmospheres. Reclusive and bitter—one of his few lasting friends was his mentor, Erik SATIE—Debussy lived out his last years suffering from depression, poverty and, ultimately, the cancer that took his life during a German bombardment of Paris in 1918. He was the great tone painter of the ineffable—of silences, foot tracks in the snow, fogs and clouds, and drowsy fauns. On the other hand, he reveled in the buoyant RAGTIME rhythms of the music hall, the modal strains of the Far East and sensuous thrummings of Spain. He had the courage to look beyond the standard conceptual and performance trappings of music. "I believe that music has until now rested on false principles," he wrote, anticipating later, oddly similar pronouncements by John CAGE. "We do not listen for the thousands of natural sounds which surround us. This, to my mind, is the new path. But, believe me, I have but caught a glimpse of it."

Decline of the West, The A two-volume (1918, 1922) analysis of the nature of the growth and decline of world cultures by the German historian Oswald SPENGLER. *The Decline of the West* provoked passionate international debate as to the validity of Spengler's central thesis that all cultures, from classical Greece to the Europe of Spengler's own era, go through an organic evolution from youthful vigor to sterile decay. Spengler insisted that true cultural creativity and religious fervor could only emerge early on in the development of a civilization. In the later period of its decline (as in the case of the modern West), the fitting goal of its members was to consolidate and expand its power rather than to cast about futilely for renewed spiritual meaning, which could only come from a newly emerging culture elsewhere. Spengler thus viewed a commitment to imperialism and warfare as symptoms of a civilization's decline rather than as evidences of its ongoing vitality. But the Nazis distorted Spengler's views, casting them falsely as a glorification of their own obsession with militarism.

deconstruction Theory of literary criticism that denies that works of literature have any meaning in and of themselves and that sees meaning as imposed by the reader, not the writer. Deconstruction is largely the invention of French critic Jacques DERRIDA, who introduced the concept in the late 1960s. The deconstructive analysis is arcane and abstract, but deconstruction has gained a substantial following in the academic community. Nonetheless, many writers, readers and scholars have denounced deconstruction for making the analysis of a text more important than the text itself and for denying that a literary work—a novel, poem or story—has any reference to the outside world and any inherent moral value.

Defferre, Gaston *(1910–1986)* French politician. A Socialist and vigorous anticommunist, Defferre was mayor of Marseilles for 33 consecutive years, where he built a political machine that dominated much of southern FRANCE. He first emerged as a hero of the French RESISTANCE during WORLD WAR II. Under the Fourth Republic, he held a number of ministries and, as minister for France overseas, was the architect of a law that gave autonomy to the African colonies and paved the way for their independence. He played a major role in the regrowth of France's Socialist Party and was a candidate for the presidency of France in 1965 and 1969. As President François MITTERRAND's minister of the interior in 1981–82, he set in motion the Socialist master plan for decentralization of some powers from France to the regions.

De Forest, Lee *(1873–1961)* American inventor whose many creations contributed to the development of radio, motion pictures and television. His most important invention was the Audion Three-Electrode Amplifier Tube (U.S. Patent No. 841,386) in 1907. It was an amplification device for the improved reception of radio broadcasting. In 1912 he used the device to pioneer the development of TALKING PICTURES. Rejecting sound-on-disc processes, he sought a method of transforming sound waves to electrical energy, which in turn could be translated into light waves and recorded on the edge of a film strip. The film projector, correspondingly, contained an incandescent lamp and photoelectric cell, which changed the optical track back into sound. After many experiments he made his first talking picture in 1921. A year later he founded the De Forest Phonofilm Corporation and afterward made hundreds of short sound films of stage entertainers like Eddie CANTOR, DeWolf Hopper and Sir Harry LAUDER. But HOLLYWOOD was underwhelmed and would wait several years before taking on the new technology, by which time associates and competitors were poaching on his inventions. De Forest spent many frustrating years in legal disputes. Though the U.S. courts upheld his patents in 1935, proclaiming him the true inventor of the sound-on-film system, he was broke and forgotten. He had made a bold prophecy in 1923 about the sound film: "I think it will add brains to the movies." The jury is still out.

De Gasperi, Alcide *(1881–1954)* Italian statesman, prime minister (1945–53). Born in Pieve Tesino in the Austrian-held Trentino, he attended Vienna University. Involved in Austrian politics from 1911, he became a member of the Italian parliament when his native region became a part of ITALY in 1919, after World War I. That same year he was a cofounder of the Catholic Popular Party. De Gasperi served in parliament and as secretary-general of his party until 1925, when nonfascist parties were banned; the following year he was imprisoned by MUSSOLINI. After 16 months he was released and took refuge in the Vatican. There he began to organize a new version of the Popular Party, the Christian Democratic Party. After the liberation of all of Italy in 1945, De Gasperi organized a centrist government with himself as premier. He continued in this office through seven more coalition cabinets. A staunch anticommunist and a supporter of the EUROPEAN COMMUNITY, he brought Italy into the EUROPEAN COAL AND STEEL COMMUNITY, the Council of Europe and the NORTH ATLANTIC TREATY ORGANIZATION.

DeHoffmann, Frederic *(1924–1989)* American nuclear physicist. While still in his teens, DeHoffman worked on the MANHATTAN PROJECT for ATOMIC BOMB DEVELOPMENT during WORLD WAR II. He later went on to direct the Salk Institute for Biological Studies, building it into one of the world's largest centers of biological research (see Jonas SALK). He died of complications from AIDS acquired through a blood transfusion.

de Klerk, Frederik Willem *(1936–)* South African politician, president of South Africa (1989–96). Born in Johannesburg into a well-established political family, de Klerk studied law at Portchefstroom University, where he graduated in 1958. In 1972 de Klerk began his political career when he was elected to Parliament as a National Party candidate. By 1982 his performance as a parliamentary delegate and a loyal supporter of the National Party and his family name helped him win the presidency of the National Party. Seven years later, when South African president Pieter W. BOTHA resigned from his post for health-related problems, de Klerk succeeded him.

As South Africa's president, de Klerk immediately tackled the problems created by the nation's system of APARTHEID, which segregated South Africans based on the color of their skin. In 1990 de Klerk legalized the AFRICAN NATIONAL CONGRESS (ANC), a black-organized South African political organization that had combatted apartheid, and ended the 38-year prison term of one of its leaders, Nelson MANDELA. In 1992 two-thirds of South Africans participating in a nationwide referendum (then an all-white affair) gave their support to de Klerk's dismantling of apartheid; for his desegregation of South Africa, de Klerk shared the 1993 NOBEL PRIZE for peace with Mandela. After winning the referendum de Klerk and Mandela both agreed to create a "one-man, one-vote" policy with a three-member presidency, in order to prevent one faction from dominating South African affairs. The elections for South Africa's government held in April 1994 resulted in victory for the ANC, though de Klerk's National Party had enough of a showing to guarantee him one of the two deputy presidencies under the new chief executive, Mandela. Two years later, when South Africa adopted a new constitution that did not guarantee that minority parties in Parliament would be able to designate a deputy president, de Klerk pulled his National Party out of the government in protest. In 1997 de Klerk ended his political career and resigned as president of the National Party.

de Kooning, Willem *(1904–1988)* American painter. Born in Rotterdam, Holland, de Kooning studied in Amsterdam (1916–24) and immigrated to the U.S. in 1926, settling in New York City. Like many painters of the period, he worked on the Federal Arts Project and executed murals from 1935 to 1939. His early figural murals enhanced a number of public buildings, including the 1939–40 World's Fair. De Kooning's style became increasingly abstract, especially after his meeting with Arshile Gorky. His mature style evolved from the 1940s to the 1950s, and de Kooning became one of the foremost exponents of ABSTRACT EXPRESSIONISM. Perhaps his best-known cycle of paintings is the ferociously brushstroked *Woman* series of the 1950s–60s. In these monumentally sized works, such as *Woman I* (Museum of Modern Art, New York City), an elemental figure emerges from slashing strokes and expressive color. De Kooning's other typical paintings are completely abstract. These huge canvases are the quintessence of the highly energetic gestural spontaneity that marks abstract expressionism and are also characterized by a lush color range. De Kooning taught at Black Mountain College (1948) and Yale University (1950–51), and his work influenced and inspired a generation of American artists.

de la Mare, Walter *(1873–1956)* English poet and novelist. Of Huguenot descent, he worked as an accountant for many years until a government pension allowed him to concentrate on his writing. His poetry and prose often take place in a fantasy world, and much of his verse was written for or about children. De la Mare's poetry includes *Songs of Childhood* (1902), *the Listeners and Other Poems* (1912), *Peacock Pie* (1913), *Poems for Children* (1930) and *Memory and Other Poems* (1938). Among his fictional works are *Henry Brocken* (1904), *Memoirs of a Midget* (1921), *Broomsticks and Other Tales* (1925) and *On the Edge* (1930).

de la Renta, Oscar *(1932–)* New York–based fashion designer known for ornate and amusing design, often based on exotic themes and cultures. De la Renta was born in the Dominican Republic and studied art in Madrid. He began his professional career in Paris with a job with Cristobal BALENCIAGA before moving to New York to take over couture design for Elizabeth Arden. In 1965 he began work for Jane Derby Ltd., taking over the firm in 1967 and giving it his name. De la Renta's reputation as a celebrity of the social world has supported the growing reputation of his work as a designer. He was the winner of a 1968 Coty Award for his Russian- and Gypsy-inspired collection of that year, of a Neiman Marcus Award in 1968 and of a Coty Hall of Fame Award in 1973. In 1977 perfumes were introduced under the de la Renta name, and various other products have been added to his lines, including bathing suits, bed linens and jewelry.

Delaunay, Robert *(1885–1941)* French painter. Delaunay was deeply influenced by the emergence of CUBISM in 1907, but he went on to establish himself as a unique artistic visionary who associated with a variety of aesthetic movements but was hidebound by none of them. He first earned critical praise for a series of paintings commenced in 1910, each of which was titled *Window on the City*. The paintings moved from representational cityscapes bathed in light to abstract, grid-like patterns. In 1912 Delaunay painted a new series of canvases, titled *Simultaneous Windows,* that were abstract and dominated by a startling use of brilliant, clashing colors. This series linked Delaunay to "simultaneism," while poet and art critic Guillaume APOLLINAIRE coined the term *Orphism* to describe the Delaunay's new style. Delaunay himself wrote at this time that "Color alone is form and subject." Delaunay, who married the painter Sonia Stern (see Sonia DELAUNAY) in 1910, continued to paint in a style dominated by color in the remaining decades of his life.

Delaunay, Sonia (Sonia Stern) *(1885–1979)* Russian-born French artist and designer, considered among the foremost painters of her time. A leading figure in the Paris art world by the time of World War I, she was influenced by folk art, Gauguin, van Gogh and Matisse. She married the artist Robert DELAUNAY in 1910; the couple exerted a stimulating influence on each other and on the modernist movement in art in general (see MODERNISM). In the 1920s she became increasingly interested in costume design and branched out into other design fields. She was particularly influential in creating new designs for fabrics, ceramics and household goods. Equally capable in virtually all media, she also illustrated books and wove an important series of tapestries at Aubusson.

Delbruck, Max *(1906–1981)* German-born molecular geneticist. Delbruck began his scientific career as a physicist, receiving his Ph.D. in physics from the University of Göttingen (1930). After Adolf HITLER came to power, Delbruck immigrated to the U.S. (1937) and joined the staff of Vanderbilt University (1940–47). In 1947 he moved to the California Institute of Technology, where he remained until his retirement in 1977. In the U.S., Delbruck turned his attention to biology and genetics. At Vanderbilt he studied a group of viruses called bacteriophages, which were important for understanding the genetic controls that govern the reproduction of living cells. With Dr. Salvador E. LURIA, Delbruck proved that viruses were able to undergo spontaneous mutations and attack cells that were normally resistant to viral invasion. This conclusion was confirmed independently by Alfred Hershey. For this work Delbruck, Luria and Hershey received the 1969 NOBEL PRIZE in physiology or medicine.

Delderfield, Ronald Frederich *(1912–1972)* British novelist and playwright. Born in London, he later settled in the West Country of England, the setting for such novels as *God Is an Englishman* (1971) its sequel *Theirs Was the Kingdom* (1971), and *To Serve Them All My Days* (1972). Though not critically acclaimed, these books were enormously popular, particularly in the U.S.; several were adapted for television. His plays include *A Worm's Eye* (1945), which ran in the West End of London for more than five years.

Deledda, Grazia *(1871–1936)* Italian novelist. Deledda wrote in the 19th-century verismo Italian literary tradition, a movement related to naturalism. Her best-known novels include *Elias Potolu* (1900; translated as *The Woman and the Priest,* 1928), *Canne al Vento* (1913), *Reeds in the Wind* (1937) and the autobiographical *Cosima* (1939). Deledda was awarded the NOBEL PRIZE in literature in 1926.

Delius, Frederick *(1862–1934)* English composer. Born in Bradford of German parents, he left England at the age of 20 to become an orange grower in Florida, later teaching piano in Virginia. Returning to Europe, he studied at the Leipzig Conservatory (1886–88), where his romantic impressionism was influenced by his friend Edvard Grieg. His work proved more popular in Germany than in his native country. His suite *Florida* (1886) was first performed there in 1888, followed by performances of such works as the chorale *Sea Drift* (1903) and the opera *A Village Romeo and Juliet* (1907). In England, Delius's reputation began to grow, largely due to the efforts of the conductor Sir Thomas BEECHAM, who performed his choral *A Mass of Life* (1904–05) in 1909. Delius spent the latter part of his life at his home near Fontainebleau. In the 1920s his health failed, and he became blind and paralyzed. Nonetheless, he continued to compose with the aid of a secretary, **Eric Fenby.** His finest compositions include the choral works *Mass of Life* and *A Song of the High Hills* (1912) and the orchestral pieces *Brigg Fair* (1907), *On Hearing the First Cuckoo in Spring* (1912) and *North Country Sketches* (1913–14).

Del Monaco, Mario *(1915–1982)* Italian opera singer. Del Monaco was an impressive dramatic tenor in Italian roles in the 1940s and 1950s—a period that included such outstanding Italian tenors as Carlo BERGONZI, Franco CORELLI and Giuseppi DI STEFANO. He made his debut in a provincial performance of *Cavalleria Rusticana* in 1939. After his appearing at La Scala in Milan in 1941 in PUCCINI's *Madama Butterfly,* his career soared. From 1951 to 1959 he was a leading tenor at the Metropolitan Opera in New York and was acclaimed for the intensity of his performances in such operas as *Otello* and *Tosca.* He also made numerous recordings.

Delon, Alain *(1935–)* French movie actor. One of France's major actors, Delon has earned an international reputation. He is often cast as the romantic leading man but has received his greatest acclaim for more offbeat roles in such films as Jean-Pierre Melville's *La Samourai* (1967) and his own production of the comic film *Borsalino* (1970). Among the more than 84 films in which he has starred are *L'Eclisse* (1961), *Is Paris Burning?* (1966) and *The Investigator* (1974). Delon directed, produced and starred in the film *Dance Machine* in 1990.

DeLorean, John Z. *(1925–2005)* Flamboyant American would-be automobile manufacturer whose venture collapsed in bankruptcy after he was implicated in selling drugs. DeLorean had been a successful executive at General Motors, perhaps in line to head the world's largest manufacturer, when he left GM to head a firm of his own that planned to build an innovative sports car in Northern Ireland with government financing. The venture floundered, and DeLorean resorted to smuggling millions of dollars of COCAINE into the U.S., which he planned to resell to save his company. However, the FBI stepped in, and he was arrested. Despite videotaped evidence, DeLorean was acquitted of drug charges by a jury that may have felt the FBI was overzealous. DeLorean beat government tax charges and a number of civil lawsuits despite evidence of financial improprieties. Even the bankruptcy of DeLorean Motors was relatively painless to its founder—while creditors received little more than a token repayment of their debts. In September 1999 DeLorean declared bankruptcy.

Delors, Jacques *(1925–)* French economist and politician, president of the European Commission (1985–95). Born in Paris, Delors was employed by the Banque de France 13 years. In 1957 Delors left the Banque and became a researcher for the French Confederation of Christian Workers (CFTC). An adherent of Social Catholicism, Delors helped the organization chart a middle ground between the leftist goals championed by the French Communist Party and the more conservative objectives of the Gaullists and other parties on the right. Delors became an adviser to Gaullist governments as they attempted to reconcile the student radicals and their allies in the labor movement who had initiated the general strike in 1968. In 1974 Delors formally joined the French Socialist Party, and five years later he was elected a French Socialist representative to the newly established European Parliament. He joined the parliament's Monetary Affairs Committee, which oversaw efforts aimed at producing common monetary policies among EUROPEAN COMMUNITY (EC) members. Under the Socialist president François MITTERRAND, Delors served as minister of finance and economics from 1981 to 1984.

In 1985, a year after Mitterand had declined to designate Delors as prime minister and Delors resigned as minister of finance, he was appointed president of the European Commission, the executive organ of the EC. In this position Delors launched a campaign to negotiate a new treaty that would increase the power of the EC's governing institutions and create total integration of all EC members' economies. Delors was the moving force behind the Single European Act (SEA) of 1986, which provided for the removal of all trade barriers among the signatory states and the creation of single market for the European Community by the beginning of 1993. In the meantime he began to solicit support for expanding the economic integration called for in the founding treaty of the EC. This initiative culminated in the 1991 Treaty of MAASTRICHT, which called for total monetary integration of all EC members by the end of the 20th century and proposed the creation of a new monetary unit (later named the euro). In January 1995 Delors stepped down as president of the European Commission.

Del Ponte, Carla *(1947–)* Chief prosecutor for The HAGUE WAR CRIMES TRIBUNAL FOR THE FORMER YUGOSLAVIA (1999–). Born in Lugano, Switzerland, Del Ponte studied law at Bern and Geneva as well as in Britain, obtaining her law degree in 1972. In 1981 she left her private practice when she was appointed a Swiss magistrate, an investigator of alleged crimes. She investigated and uncovered a money laundering operation in Switzerland designed to conceal funds from an Italian drug cartel, which in 1988 attempted to assassinate her by blowing up her house. In 1994 Del Ponte became attorney general of Switzerland. Prior to her appointment as a chief prosecutor for The Hague in 1999, she served briefly in the same capacity at the UN-led war crimes trials in RWANDA. However, the Rwandan government requested her removal when Del Ponte asked to investigate an alleged link between the Rwandan Patriotic Army and the deaths of over 30,000 Hutus. In response, UN secretary general Kofi ANNAN transferred Del Ponte to the same position as a UN prosecutor of alleged war criminals from the former Yugoslavia. When The Hague War Crimes Tribunal began its permanent operations on March 11, 2003, Del Ponte became the chief prosecutor of the new court, which placed her in charge of prosecuting alleged Serb war criminals such as former Serbian president Slobodan MILOŠEVIĆ.

demagogues Politicians or other public figures who gain power by using oratory that plays on people's fears. During the 20th century, the new mass media of radio, film and television made it possible for demagogues to manipulate the public with great effectiveness. Demagogues flourished in times of crisis and uncertainty, such as the GREAT DEPRESSION of the 1930s, by promising popular but simplistic and fanatical solutions to complex social problems. American demagogues included Charles COUGHLIN, Huey LONG, Joseph McCARTHY and Gerald K. SMITH. Benito MUSSOLINI, Adolf HITLER, Joseph GOEBBELS and Juan PERÓN also used demogogic techniques to attain their ends. (See also PROPAGANDA.)

Demerec, Milislav *(1895–1966)* Yugoslavian-American geneticist. Demerec graduated from the College of Agriculture in Križevci, Yugoslavia, in 1916 and after a few year's work at the Križevci Experimental Station, moved to the U.S. He earned his Ph.D. in genetics from Cornell University in 1923 and then worked at the Carnegie Institution, Cold Spring Harbor, New York, where he remained for most of his career, becoming director in 1943. Demerec was concerned with gene structure and function, especially the effect of mutations. He found that certain unstable genes are more likely to mutate than others and that the rate of mutation is affected by various biological factors, such as the stage in the life cycle. He also demonstrated that chromosome segments that break away and rejoin in the wrong place may cause suppression of genes near the new region of attachment. Demerec's work with the bacterium *Salmonella* revealed that genes controlling related functions are grouped together on the chromosome rather than being randomly distributed through the chromosome complement. His radiation treatment of the fungus *Penicillium* yielded a mutant strain producing much larger quantities of PENICILLIN— a discovery of great use in WORLD WAR II. He showed that antibiotics should be administered initially in large doses so that resistant mutations do not develop and should be given in combinations, because any bacterium resistant to one is most unlikely to be resistant to both.

Demerec greatly increased the reputation of Cold Spring Harbor while director there and also served on many important committees. He founded the journal *Advances in Genetics* and wrote some 200 scientific articles.

Demichelli, Alberto *(1896–1980)* President of Uruguay (1976). A lawyer by profession, Demichelli was a member of the liberal Colorado Party. He was one of a group of political leaders who agreed to cooperate with the Uruguayan armed forces in a 1973 coup that dissolved Congress, banned political and union activities and imposed stiff censorship on all news organization. In 1976 he was chosen president with the approval of the military; however, he governed for only 80 days.

De Mille, Agnes *(1909–1993)* American dancer and choreographer known for her innovative ballets. De Mille used American subjects in her work and transformed American musical theater by integrating dance sequences into the unfolding plot in the landmark show *Oklahoma!* (1943). She first gained fame as a dancer with Ballet Rambert and touring Europe as a solo performer (1929–40). Her first major choreographic works, *Black Ritual* (1940) and *Three Virgins and a Devil* (1941), were for the AMERICAN BALLET THEATRE and were followed by the popular *Rodeo* (1942) and *Fall River Legend* (1948). Other musicals she choreographed include *Carousel* (1945), *Brigadoon* (1947) and *Paint Your Wagon* (1951). In 1973 she founded the Heritage Dance Theatre at the North Carolina School of the Arts. In addition, she worked in film and television, served as a dance consultant and wrote several books on dance, including *Dance to the Piper* (1952), *The Book of the Dance* (1963) and *America Dances* (1981).

DeMille, Cecil B(lount) *(1881–1959)* American film director and producer. DeMille enjoyed a long and successful career that spanned both the silent and the talkie film eras. He codirected the very first HOLLYWOOD feature, a western called *The Squaw Man* (1913). In conjunction with Samuel GOLDWYN and Jesse Lasky, DeMille produced numerous silent films in the 1910s but made his primary mark as a director of action-filled biblical spectacles such as *The Ten Commandments* (1923) and *The King of Kings* (1926). He continued to work in this vein in the sound era, enjoying blockbuster successes with *The Sign of the Cross* (1932), *Samson and Delilah* (1949) and a remake of *The Ten Commandments* (1956), starring Charlton HESTON. Other films by DeMille include *The Greatest Show on Earth* (1952), an extravaganza focusing on circus life. DeMille was one of the few Hollywood directors of his era to enjoy a marquee billing more prominent than that of his actors, a true mark of his popularity with audiences.

Demirel, Suleyman *(1924–)* Turkish statesman. Demirel was director of water works from 1955 to 1961. One of the founders of the right-wing Justice Party (1961), he was its chairman in 1964. Demirel was prime minister of TURKEY from 1965 to 1971 but was ousted by military intervention. As leader of a coalition, he was again prime minister from 1975 to 1980 when removed in a military coup. Together with other former opposition leaders, he was forced to renounce political activity in 1983. Demirel returned to the premiership for two years during 1991–93, followed by seven years as Turkish president (1993–2000). Demirel used his positions during the 1990s to promote greater economic growth and foreign investment in Turkey, particularly in its industrial sectors.

Democracy Movement Political movement in the People's Republic of CHINA, led by students and supported by many Chinese workers in 1989. The Democracy Movement occurred at the same time that Eastern Europeans were pressing for reforms in the Communist-dominated Eastern bloc, but the Chinese movement proved to be less successful in the short run. It was marked by mass demonstrations, especially in the center of Beijing. The students called for an end to government corruption, reform of the Communist Party and public participation in decision making. The Chinese government at first tolerated the movement but repeatedly warned that the demonstrations must stop. While the movement apparently had widespread enthusiastic support, it was poorly organized, and its specific goals were unclear. The movement was crushed in the TIANANMEN SQUARE MASSACRE (June 3–4, 1989) in Beijing and subsequent crackdowns on pro-democracy students throughout China as the Communist Party under DENG XIAOPING reasserted its authority. Many students and workers were arrested and imprisoned, while others went into hiding or fled China.

Democratic Party American political party, founded in 1828. Along with the REPUBLICAN PARTY, the Democratic Party is one of two major U.S. political parties. While each party encompasses a broad range of opinions, generally speaking the Democratic Party is more apt to favor welfare programs, government intervention in the economy, federally funded social programs and a lower military profile abroad. The liberal sector of the party has traditionally embraced the CIVIL RIGHTS MOVEMENT, the WOMEN'S MOVEMENT and labor unions. Southern Democrats tend to be more conservative. The Democratic National Committee is comprised of a chairperson and representatives from each state and coordinates the party's national conventions and fund-raising for Democratic candidates.

Woodrow WILSON was the first Democratic president of the 20th century. His success in the 1912 elections was partly due to opposition to monopolistic trusts that emerged during the prior Republican administration. The modern Democratic Party arose with Franklin D. ROOSEVELT's election in 1932. His NEW DEAL policy of federal programs to offset the GREAT DEPRESSION established the basis for subsequent Democratic administrations. In the following 50 years Democrats controlled the presidency for 32 years and the House and Senate for 44. While the Republicans won the presidential elections in 1968 and 1972, the Democrats retained control of Congress. In 1976 Democrat Jimmy CARTER of Georgia was elected president, but Republicans returned to office in 1980 when Ronald REAGAN was elected on a platform of reduced government spending and strengthened national defense. Reagan's enormous personal popularity and internal dissension and disorganization within the Democratic Party were widely cited as reasons for the party's

apparent decline in the 1980s. Many voters also felt that the national party was controlled by left-wing elements, and the party's presidential candidates in 1980, 1984 and 1988 were perceived as weak and ineffectual. However, the Democratic Party continued to enjoy successes at the local and state levels. The Democratic Party returned to power in 1992 with the election of Bill CLINTON as president and for two years held control of both houses of Congress as well as the White House. However, an anti-Clinton backlash in 1994 led to a loss of control in both houses that continued until 2001 when Vermont senator Jim Jeffords left the Republican Party and became an independent. The party suffered further losses in the election of 2004 with the defeat of its presidential candidate, John KERRY, and continued its relegation to minority status in both houses of Congress.

Democratic Republic of the Congo See Democratic Republic of the CONGO.

Dempsey, William Harrison "Jack" *(1895–1983)* World heavyweight boxing champion from 1919 to 1926. Known as the "Manassa Mauler" (after his hometown, Manassa, Colorado), he worked as a mucker in Colorado mining camps, where he first fought professionally in 1912. Dempsey knocked out Jess Willard in 1919 to win the title he eventually lost in 1926 to Gene TUNNEY, in the controversial **"long count"** match.

Dempster, Arthur Jeffrey *(1886– 1950)* Canadian-American physicist. Dempster was educated at the University of Toronto. He immigrated to the U.S. in 1914, attended the University of Chicago, earned his Ph.D. in 1916 and began teaching in 1919. In 1927 he was made professor of physics. He is noted for his early developments of and work with the mass spectrograph (invented by Francis W. ASTON). In 1935 he was able to show that uranium did not consist solely of the isotope uranium 238, for seven out of every 1,000 uranium atoms were in fact uranium 235. Niels BOHR later predicted that this isotope was capable of sustaining a chain reaction that could

release large amounts of atomic fission energy.

Demy, Jacques *(1931–1990)* French film director. A director of musical comedies, his best-known film was *Les Parapluies de Cherbourg* (*The Umbrellas of Cherbourg,* 1964). His other films include *Les Demoiselles de Rochefort* (1966), *Lola* (1960), *Peau d'âne* (1970) and *Trois places pour le 26* (1988).

Deneuve, Catherine (Catherine Dorléac) *(1943–)* French movie actress. The daughter of actor Maurice Dorléac and sister of actress Françoise Dorléac, Deneuve is considered one of the most beautiful women in the world, as well as an accomplished actress. Working with some of the major directors in the world, she has shown her versatility and craftsmanship in such films as Roman POLANSKI's *Repulsion* (1965), Luis BUÑUEL's *Belle de Jour* (1966), and François TRUFFAUT's *La Sirène de Mississipi* (1969). She won the French Film Academy's best actress award for her performance in Jacques DEMY's *The Umbrellas of Cherbourg* (1964). In 1993, for her role in the French film *Indochine* (1992), Deneuve was a best actress contender for the Golden Globes and the Academy Awards.

Deng Xiaoping *(1904–1997)* A member of the Chinese Communist Party since the early 1920s, Deng Xiaoping emerged as the leading political personality in CHINA in the late 1970s. He was twice purged for his views: first during the CULTURAL REVOLUTION, when he was designated the "number-2 capitalist roader" in 1966 and forced to undergo public self-criticism in 1968, and then in 1976, when he was blamed for public demonstrations in April of that year. Eulogizing the recently deceased ZHOU ENLAI after the defeat of the GANG OF FOUR, Deng returned to the political limelight and thereafter largely shaped Chinese politics, even though he held no major, formal position. In 1987 he retired from the politburo of the party but retained his post as chairman of the Central Military Commission until November 1989. Diminutive in stature, he has been praised by foreign leaders for his pragmatism but lost face internationally when in June 1989 he supported the army's massacre of prodemocracy students throughout China, then blatantly lied to the country and the world about what had occurred. (See also DEMOCRACY MOVEMENT; TIANANMEN SQUARE MASSACRE.)

Denikin, Anton Ivanovich *(1872–1947)* Distinguished Russian general of WORLD WAR I who rose from the ranks. After the RUSSIAN REVOLUTION, Denikin was imprisoned for supporting KORNILOV's attempted revolt against KERENSKY's socialist government but escaped to raise an army in the south. Meanwhile (November 1917) the BOLSHEVIKS under Lenin had seized power and Denikin's "White" army, with Allied support, occupied the Ukraine and North Caucasus. As Bolshevik power grew, the Red Army gradually forced the Whites back to the Crimea, and in 1920 Denikin abandoned the struggle. He died in exile in France.

De Niro, Robert *(1943–)* American film and theater actor. De Niro is perhaps the most critically acclaimed film actor of his generation. He began his career as a stage actor in New York but soon turned his primary focus to film work. In the 1960s he appeared in student films by the emerging director Brian DE PALMA. But De Niro first attracted the attention of critics—as well as an ACADEMY AWARD for best supporting actor—with his role as a dying catcher in the baseball film *Bang the Drum Slowly* (1973). He won further acclaim for his searing portrayal of a violent youth in *Mean Streets* (1973), directed by Martin SCORSESE. De Niro and Scorsese went on to collaborate on several brilliant films, including *Taxi Driver* (1976); *Raging Bull* (1979), for which De Niro won a best actor ACADEMY AWARD for his portrayal of boxer Jake La Motta; *The King of Comedy* (1983); and *GoodFellas* (1990). De Niro reunited with De Palma in *The Untouchables* (1987), in which he played Al CAPONE. His other films include *The Deer Hunter* (1978), *True Confessions* (1981) and the comedy *Midnight Run* (1988). In the 1990s and into the 21st century De Niro continued to appear in dramas such as *Heat* (1995) and *Casino* (1995), as well as in comedies such as *Meet the Parents* (2000), *Analyze This* (1999) and *The Adventures of Rocky and Bullwinkle* (2000).

Denis, Maurice *(1870–1943)* French decorator and painter. Denis was, in his youth, influenced by the symbolist movement and by the theories of the Nabis, who emphasized the technical importance of painting as a two-dimensional depiction of three-dimensional reality. A noted early canvas by Denis was *Hommage à Cézanne* (1900), a still-life tribute to French painter Paul Cézanne. Later in his career Denis became well-known as a theatrical set designer. In 1912, with Georges Desvallières, Denis founded the Atelier d'Art Sacré, a studio that taught techniques of painting works with religious themes.

Denmark Denmark occupies the Jutland Peninsula, which runs into the North Sea from north-central Europe; the islands of Sjaelland, Funen, Lolland, Falster and Bornholm in the Baltic Sea; and 480 smaller islands—for a total area of 16,629 square miles. A monarchy since the 14th century, the country has been governed since 1972 by Queen Margrethe II, who shares authority with a parliament. Denmark, which remained neutral during World War I, saw egalitarian reforms and a welfare-state system introduced after the Social Democratic Party gained power in 1929. Danish attempts to remain neutral during WORLD WAR II were thwarted when Germany occupied the country (1940–45). After the war Denmark became a founding member of the NORTH ATLANTIC TREATY ORGANIZATION (NATO) in 1949 and joined the EUROPEAN COAL AND STEEL COMMUNITY (ECSC) in 1973. In 1982 the first conservative-led

DENMARK

1915	Universal adult suffrage enacted.
1920	Schleswig votes 3-1 in favor of return to Danish rule.
1929	Social Democratic Party comes to power and implements welfare-state legislation.
1940	Germans occupy Denmark during World War II.
1948	Denmark grants home rule to Faeroe Islands.
1949	Denmark joins NATO.
1953	Royal succession opened to females.
1966	Odense University is founded.
1969	Pornography legalized.
1972	King Frederick IX dies; his daughter succeeds to the throne as Queen Margrethe II.
1973	Denmark joins EEC.
1976	Government razes "Free City" hangout of drug users and counterculturists.
1979	Greenland granted home rule.
1989	Legislation passed allowing civil marriage between homosexuals—the first legislation of its kind among the 12 members of the EC.
1992	Referendum rejects Maastricht Treaty on European Union after gaining legislative approval; negotiations allow Denmark to opt out of European plans for a common defense, common citizenship, border controls and common currency; longest suspension bridge in Europe is completed to link Sjaelland with Jutland.
1993	Scandal over an immigration case causes formation of a Social Democrat–led government under Poul Nyrup Rasmussen; new referendum approves Maastricht Treaty with the opt-out provisions.
1994	Parliamentary elections confirm Rasmussen team in office with a coalition of Social Democrats, Social Liberals and Center Democrats.
1999	Danes reject adoption of the euro as their national currency.
2001	Anders Fogh Rasmussen becomes prime minister.
2006	Furor erupts in the Muslim world over cartoons published in a Danish newspaper the previous year insulting to the prophet Muhammad, leading to boycotts of Danish products and violence against some of its embassies and consulates in Muslim countries when the Danish government refuses to apologize.

government since 1901 was elected. In 1992 Denmark complicated the goal of European economic and political unification when it rejected the MAASTRICHT TREATY but approved the treaty the following year when greater autonomy was accorded to the peninsular state. In 1999 Denmark continued to assert its independence vis-à-vis the EUROPEAN UNION when a national referendum rejected adopting the euro as the national currency. In early 2006 the Danish government came under intense criticism from Muslim countries for refusing to apologize for cartoons published in a Danish newspaper in 2005 that depicted the prophet Muhammad in an unfavorable light.

Denmark Strait Channel between southeastern GREENLAND and ICELAND, 180 miles wide and 300 miles long;

links the Arctic Ocean with the North Atlantic Ocean. On May 24, 1941, during WORLD WAR II, the British battleship *Hood* was sent to a watery grave by the German battleship *Bismarck* in this strait.

Dennis, Nigel Forbes *(1912–1989)*
British novelist, playwright and critic. Dennis's best-known novel was *Cards of Identity* (1955), a cult hit among young

Britons because of its black humor and satire of social pretensions. His other works included the play *The Making of Moo* (1958), the biography *Jonathan Swift* (1964) and the novel *A House in Order* (1966). He also worked as a book and drama reviewer for the *Sunday Telegraph,* The NEW REPUBLIC, and TIME magazine.

Dennis v. United States *(1951)* McCarthy-era U.S. Supreme Court decision upholding a conviction of U.S. Communist Party leaders under the SMITH ACT. The Smith Act, passed in 1940, made it illegal to advocate the violent overthrow of the U.S. government or to belong to a group that advocated such overthrow. In 1950 Dennis and 10 other U.S. Communists were prosecuted under the law. At the trial, the defendants had argued that the provisions of the law were contrary to the Free Speech protections guaranteed by the First Amendment. However, a divided Supreme Court upheld their convictions. Six years later the Warren court largely limited the application of this case by limiting convictions to instances where the speaker incited actual "activity."

Densmore, Frances *(1867–1957)* U.S. music historian. She made a career of preserving the American Indian heritage. She began studying the music of American Indians in 1893 and, starting in 1907, made special researches into American Indian music for the Bureau of American Ethnology. The Smithsonian-Densmore collection contains sound recordings of American Indian music made between 1941 and 1943. Her writings include *American Indians and Their Music* (1926), *Teton Sioux Music* (1918) and many more books on the various Indian tribes and groups. In 1940 Densmore received the National Association of Composers and Conductors award for service to American music.

Deobandi (Beobandi) Founded in 1866 in the Indian town of Deoband, Deobandi is a branch of the Sunni sect of Islam whose adherents are generally located in southern Asia (particularly along the Afghanistan-Pakistan border) and follow the general precepts of ISLAMISM, which calls for the literal application of the Koran (Qur'an) and other

holy Muslim works to Islamic societies and opposition to non-Muslim institutions and people. Current practitioners of Deobandi follow the teachings of Abu Hanifa Niaa Caaa, their imam, or religious teacher, who articulated the manner in which the strict application of Islamic law is to occur in areas controlled by Deobandi followers. Its institutions of religious instruction located in Deoband, called Darul Uloom ("the House of Knowledge"), constitute the largest focal point for the study of Islam outside Cairo, Egypt. Many of these institutions' graduates found employment in the religious schools, or madrassas, in Pakistan and Afghanistan, with others serving as Muslim scholars and clerics in Saudi Arabia, Malaysia, China, Afghanistan and Pakistan. Among the elements for which the movement is known is its strict code of conduct for women. According to Deobandi teachings, women must be completely veiled, should have no formal education beyond their eighth year, should avoid mingling with men in public areas and should defer to men in all matters. While it did defend the actions of the TALIBAN in destroying two 1,500-year old statues of Buddha in March 2001, Deobandi practitioners are not encouraged openly to acts of violence against non-Muslim cultures or even the different sects of Islam.

In political affairs the Deobandi movement exercised particular influence over the Taliban, a political-religious movement that held power over much of Afghanistan from 1995 until 2001, as well as al-QAEDA, an Islamic terrorist group then operating within the territory controlled by the Taliban. Not long after the terrorist attacks on U.S. soil on SEPTEMBER 11, 2001, a religious edict, or fatwa, came from Deobandi clerics in Darul Uloom that blamed Israeli secret forces for the destruction in New York City and Washington, D.C.

deoxyribonucleic acid (DNA) See CRICK, Francis Harry Compton; FRANKLIN, Rosalind; and WATSON, James.

De Palma, Brian *(1940–)* American film director. De Palma has inspired both admiration and controversy for his films that so often depict—in a vivid montage style—extreme violence. De Palma has acknowledged the great

influence of thriller specialist Alfred HITCHCOCK upon his directorial approach. De Palma began his career with short student films in the 1960s that featured future stars Jill Clayburgh and Robert DE NIRO. He went on to direct a number of features but enjoyed his first great success with *Carrie* (1976), which starred Sissy Spacek and was based on the Steven KING novel. *Dressed to Kill* (1980) was a critically and commercially successful thriller, but numerous other De Palma films of the early 1980s were box office failures. He enjoyed two later successes with *The Untouchables* (1987), starring Kevin Costner and De Niro, and *Casualties of War* (1989), a VIETNAM WAR drama. In the 1990s De Palma's films continued to be marked by the director's distinctive approach to violent scenes; among them were *Carlito's Way* (1993), *Mission: Impossible* (1996) and *Femme Fatale* (2002).

Depardieu, Gérard *(1948–)* French movie actor. One of the most popular and acclaimed actors of the French cinema, Depardieu has shown his dramatic range and depth in such internationally recognized films as François TRUFFAUT's *The Last Metro* (1980), *The Return of Martin Guerre* (1982), *Jean de Florette* (1985), *Camille Claudel* (1989) and *Cyrano de Bergerac* (1990). His first American-made film, the comedy *Green Card* (1990), was very successful. Depardieu continued to make English-language films, such as *1492: Conquest of Paradise* (1992), *My Father the Hero* (1994), *The Count of Monte Cristo* (1998), *102 Dalmatians* (2000) and *Chicken Run* (2001). In October 2003 he opened a restaurant in Paris.

depression of 1900 Economic depression in Russia following the great industrial expansion of the previous decade. During this period there was considerable political agitation, culminating five years later in the RUSSIAN REVOLUTION OF 1905.

De Priest, Oscar *(1871–1951)* U.S. congressman. De Priest, from Chicago, Illinois, was the first black elected to the U.S. House of Representatives from the North. As a member of the Republican Party, he voted against Franklin D. ROOSEVELT's NEW DEAL concepts—a fact that eventually cost him his seat in

1934. His most notable victory was his amendment to the bill creating the CIVILIAN CONSERVATION CORPS; it barred discrimination because of race, color or creed. He called upon the government to live up to its promises to the Indians and introduced a measure to have the government pay a pension to an estimated 100,000 ex-slaves.

De Rochemont, Louis (*1899–1978*) Documentary film producer. De Rochemont was the originator and producer of the *March of Time* film series (1934–43). Among his numerous films were the documentaries *The Fighting Lady* and *Windjammer* and the documentary-style *House on 92nd Street* and *Martin Luther.*

Derrida, Jacques (*1930–2004*) French literary critic and philosopher; gained international attention as the leading spokesperson of the critical school of DECONSTRUCTION, which seeks to evade the metaphysical belief structures of writers and concentrate instead on the inner psychological dynamic mirrored in the creative writing process itself. Derrida was born in Algiers in a Sephardic Jewish family. He immigrated to France and became a contributor to the leading philosophical quarterly *Tel Quel* in the 1960s. His writings show the influence of such disparate thinkers as Hegel, Nietzsche, Sigmund FREUD and Martin HEIDEGGER. Derrida's major works include *Of Grammatology* (1967; second edition, 1998), *Writing and Difference* (1967), *Dissemination* (1972), *Margins of Philosophy* (1972) and *Who's Afraid of Philosophy?* (2002).

Déry, Tibor (*1894–1977*) Hungarian novelist, story writer and playwright. Déry, a politically committed writer, was a radical activist who was involved in the HUNGARIAN REVOLUTION of 1918–19 and joined the Communist Party in 1919. Due to his political beliefs, he spent several years in exile from Hungary. Most of his literary works were not published in his native land until after World War II. These include a three-volume novel, *The Unfinished Sentence* (1947); a two-volume novel, *Response* (1950–52); and the novel *Niki, the Story of a Dog* (1956). *The Portuguese Princess and Other Sto-*

ries (1966) is an English translation of his best tales.

Desai, Anita (*1937– *) Indian novelist. Desai was born in Mussoorie and educated at Delhi University. She writes in English, and her work is known for its realistic portrayal of contemporary India, often focusing on the grittier aspects of urban life. Her novels include *Cry the Peacock* (1963), *Fire on the Mountain* (1977) and *Baumgartner's Bombay* (1990). Desai has also written short stories and books for children.

Desai, Shri Morarji Ranchhodji (*1896–1995*) Indian prime minister (1977–79). Active in the civil disobedience movement led by Mohandas K. GANDHI in the 1930s, he emerged as one of the leaders of the CONGRESS PARTY after independence (1947) and held many senior government offices. Increasing conflict with Indira GANDHI led to his imprisonment (1975–77). Leading the **Janata Party** (an electoral alliance of noncommunist parties against Gandhi) to victory in 1977, he inflicted the first defeat on the Congress Party since independence. Factionalism within the coalition led to his defeat in an election in January 1980.

descamisados (**Spanish:** "the shirtless ones") The urban poor in ARGENTINA, who supported Juan Domingo PERÓN and whose demonstrations in 1945 helped win his release from prison.

Desch, Cyril Henry (*1874–1958*) British metallurgist. Desch was educated at King's College, London. He taught in Glasgow from 1909 until 1920, then served as professor of metallurgy at the University of Sheffield from 1920 to 1930. He next moved to the National Physical Laboratory at Teddington, Middlesex, where he was in charge of the metallurgy department until his retirement in 1939. Desch is mainly known for his publication in 1910 of *Textbook of Metallography,* a work that served as the standard account of the subject for the first half of the 20th century.

De Sica, Vittorio (*1902–1974*) Italian motion picture director, best known for his post–World War II neorealist

style. After two decades of success as a leading man on the stage and in films, De Sica turned to filmmaking in the early 1940s. He hit his stride with his fifth film, *I Bambini ci guardano* (*The Children Are Watching Us,* 1943), a poignant tale of a child's suicide. This was the first of several memorable collaborations with screenwriter Cesare Zavattini, all consistent in their deeply felt observation of contemporary life: the interlocking stories of street children in postwar Italy (*Sciuscia/Shoeshine,* 1946); the Academy Award–winning tale of a man looking for a stolen bicycle (*Ladri di biciclette/The Bicycle Thief,* 1948); the fantasy parable (*Miracolo a Milano/Miracle in Milan,* 1950); and the daily activities of an unwanted, elderly man (*Umberto D,* 1952). When his directorial fortunes sagged in the late 1950s, De Sica fell back upon his acting experience; his performance in *General della Rovere* (1959), a wartime story of an Italian traitor, was acclaimed as one of the best character portrayals in the modern cinema. Shortly after directing the Oscar-winning *The Garden of the Finzi-Continis* (1971), De Sica died of complications from lung surgery.

de Sitter, Willem (*1872–1934*) Dutch astronomer and mathematician. De Sitter studied mathematics and physics at the University of Groningen, where his interest in astronomy was aroused by Jacobus Kapteyn. After serving at the Cape Town Observatory in South Africa from 1897 to 1899 and, back at Groningen, as assistant to Kapteyn from 1899 to 1908, he was appointed to the chair of astronomy at the University of Leiden. He also served as director of Leiden Observatory from 1919 to 1934. De Sitter is remembered for his proposal in 1917 of what came to be called the "de Sitter universe" in contrast to the "EINSTEIN universe." The contrast was summarized in the statement that Einstein's universe contained matter but no motion while de Sitter's involved motion without matter. The Russian mathematician Alexander FRIEDMANN in 1922 and the Belgian George Lemaitre independently in 1927 introduced the idea of an **expanding universe** that contained moving matter. It was then shown in 1928 that the de Sitter universe could be transformed mathematically into an expanding universe, the

"Einstein–de Sitter universe." De Sitter also worked on celestial mechanics and stellar photometry. He spent much time trying to calculate the mass of Jupiter's satellites.

Desnos, Robert *(1900–1945)* French poet. Desnos was one of the most gifted poets to be drawn to SURREALISM. He first emerged as a major voice in French letters in the 1920s, when his youthful love lyrics were championed by André BRETON. Desnos's poems featured strikingly disjointed and bizarre imagery but nonetheless managed to convey a romantic and melancholy tone. He employed automatic writing techniques by which he sought to evade conscious control over his use of language while evoking the power of dreams and unconscious longings. Desnos's best-known volume of poems was *Liberty or Love* (1927). In the 1930s he devoted much of his energies to radio and film scripts. Following the fall of FRANCE in WORLD WAR II, Desnos, a Jew, was arrested by the Nazis and sent to the Theresienstadt CONCENTRATION CAMP, where he died in 1945.

De-Stalinization Name given to official policy that undermined STALIN's hitherto uncontested infallibility. In February 1956, at the Twentieth Congress of the Communist Party of the USSR, KHRUSHCHEV attacked the cult of Stalin's personality and drew attention to the injustices of Stalin's regime. After the Twenty-second Party Congress, the central committee of the party published a decree condemning the "cult of the individual" and stressing the need for collective leadership. In 1961 Stalin's body was removed from LENIN's side in the mausoleum on Red Square, and numerous busts and pictures of Stalin were destroyed. Places named after Stalin had their names changed, a number of prisoners were released, a freer intellectual atmosphere ensued and the excesses of forced assimilation were condemned. De-Stalinization also stimulated a process of change in Eastern European countries.

détente Attempts at relaxing or easing tension, particularly between the countries of Eastern and Western Europe. Intense hostility between the U.S. and the USSR ended in 1953 after STALIN's death. After 1963, and the CUBAN MIS-SILE CRISIS, both superpowers became aware of the need to prevent nuclear warfare. Accordingly, in 1967 the Outer Space Treaty and in 1968 the Treaty on the Non-Proliferation of Nuclear Weapons worked toward this goal, as did the normalization of relations between East and West Germany, the Treaty of Non-Aggression between the USSR and West Germany in 1970, the Four Power Agreement on Berlin in 1971 and the Seabed Arms Control Treaty, also of 1971. In 1971–72 the U.S.'s decision to end its military intervention in VIETNAM enabled the Kremlin to feel more able to seek détente, although the Sino-American rapprochement made the Soviet leaders apprehensive that the U.S. would curry favor with MAO ZEDONG, thus providing Beijing with technological aid. In 1972, after his visit to Moscow, President NIXON proclaimed the end of the COLD WAR and the beginning of Soviet-American détente. Such events as the invasion of Afghanistan and the nuclear arms debate did not enhance détente. In the late 1980s, during GORBACHEV's reign, U.S.-Soviet relations improved markedly, beyond the expectations of those who had earlier sought détente. Following the collapse of the Soviet Union in December 1991, the U.S. continued to pursue friendly relations with the Russian successor state.

Deutsch, Helene Rosenbach *(1884–1982)* Austrian-born psychoanalyst. A follower of Sigmund FREUD, Deutsch was the first female psychoanalyst to be analyzed by him. She founded the Vienna Psychoanalytic Institute (1923), remaining its director until 1935, when she immigrated to the U.S. where she helped spread Freudian psychoanalysis. Her important work in personality disorders foreshadowed later research into narcissism. She was also known for her major book, *The Psychology of Women* (1944).

Deutscher Werkbund German association founded in 1907 to promote excellence in design and design-related craft and manufacturing. In its early years the Werkbund carried forward craft traditions somewhat in the manner of William Morris's Arts and Crafts movement. The orientation turned toward a more clearly modernist direction with the 1914 exhibition in Cologne housed in buildings designed by Walter GROPIUS. Among the personalities associated with the organization were Peter BEHRENS, Ludwig MIES VAN DER ROHE, Hermann Muthesius, Richard Riemerschmidt and Henry Van de Velde. The organization grew to a membership of over 3,000 and had direct connections with its Austrian counterpart. A 1927 exhibition included the building of a model suburb, Die Weissenhof Siedlung at Stuttgart, that included buildings by many of the major European modernists of the time. The organization was dissolved in 1934 in response to the growing pressure against MODERNISM generated by the rise of the Nazi regime. A revival of the Werkbund began in 1947.

De Valera, Eamon *(1882–1975)* Irish revolutionary and political leader, prime minister of Ireland (1932–48, 1951–54, 1957–59) and president (1959–73). De Valera was the dominant force in Irish politics from the 1920s through the 1950s. Born in New York City, the son of a Spanish father and an Irish mother, he moved to Ireland at the age of two after the death of his father. Despite his poor background, he became a mathematician and a teacher. He became involved in the Irish-language movement, then joined the Irish Republican Brotherhood (forerunner of the IRISH REPUBLICAN ARMY) and the paramilitary Irish Volunteers. He participated in the 1916 EASTER RISING, commanding 125 men who seized Westland Row railway station and Boland's Bakery in DUBLIN. Captured by the British, he was sentenced to be executed along with the other 16 leaders of the uprising but was spared ultimately because he held American citizenship. Instead he received a life sentence, but served only one year in prison before being released (1917). He then became president of the revolutionary SINN FÉIN nationalist movement. Elected to the British parliament (1919), he refused to take his seat but instead joined other nationalists in forming the Irish assembly, the DÁIL ÉIREANN, whose leader he became. He opposed the compromise Anglo-Irish Treaty of 1921, rejecting the partition of Ireland into the 26-county Free State and the six-county NORTHERN IRELAND. Founder of the FIANNA FÁIL Party (1926), De Valera became prime minister in 1932. He followed a nationalist policy, instituting a new constitution (1937) that transformed the country from the Irish Free State to Eire; he later declared IRELAND a republic (1947) and formally withdrew the country from the British COMMONWEALTH (1949). He kept Ireland neutral during WORLD WAR II. He also forged strong ties between the state and the Catholic Church and generally followed conservative domestic and social policies.

Devereux, James P. S. *(1903–1988)* U.S. military hero. In the marines, Devereux won fame as the commander of a 522-man detachment that defended WAKE ISLAND, along with 1,200 U.S. construction workers, when the Japanese invaded three days after their attack on PEARL HARBOR. Defending the island against overwhelming odds for 15 days, he reportedly sent out the message "Send us more Japs." Devereux was captured and interned in a Japanese prisoner of war camp for four years. A four-term Republican member of the House of Representatives, he favored public school desegregation.

Devil's Island (Île du Diable) One of the Safety Islands off the Atlantic coast of French Guiana. A tiny island, it was organized in 1852 and used as a penal colony, particularly for French political prisoners; the most famous one was Alfred Dreyfus. The French started closing the prison in 1938 but were interrupted by WORLD WAR II. By 1948 all prisoners were returned to their countries of origin. However, the lore of Devil's Island as a place of no escape has continued to hold the imagination.

Devlin, Denis *(1908–1959)* Irish poet, diplomat and translator. Born in Scotland, Devlin returned with his family to Ireland when he was 10. After a year in a seminary, he turned to the study of languages at University College, Dublin, Munich University and the Sorbonne. His best poetry was marked by religious fervor. He joined the diplomatic corps in 1935, and his first book, *Intercessions,* appeared in 1937. From 1940 to 1947 he was posted to the U.S., where he met Robert Penn WARREN, who championed his work in *The Southern Review.*

Lough Derg, his masterpiece, was published in 1946. After 1950 he resided in Italy, publishing only sporadically. *Collected Poems* came out in Dublin in 1963; *Selected Poems* (1963) was edited for the U.S. by Warren and Allen TATE. He translated St. John PERSE, APOLLINAIRE, QUASIMODO and Goethe.

Dewar, Michael James Stewart *(1918–1997)* British-American chemist. Dewar was educated at Oxford University, where he earned his D.Phil. in 1942. After research at Oxford he worked in industry as a physical chemist until his appointment in 1951 as professor of chemistry at Queen Mary College, London. In 1959 Dewar moved to the U.S. and served successively as professor of chemistry at the University of Chicago and from 1963 at the University of Texas. Dewar is noted for his contributions to theoretical chemistry. In his *Electronic Theory of Organic Chemistry* (1949) he argued strongly for the molecular-orbital theory introduced by Robert MILLIKEN. He did much to improve molecular-orbital calculations and by the 1960s was able to claim that he and his colleagues could rapidly and accurately calculate a number of chemical and physical properties of molecules.

Dewey, John *(1859–1952)* U.S. philosopher and educator. After graduating from the University of Vermont and Johns Hopkins University he taught at several universities and in 1904 was permanently appointed at Columbia University. In philosophy Dewey was the most important heir to the school of American philosophical pragmatism founded by William JAMES. Like James, he challenged all absolute theories of reality and truth. In their place he espoused a theory of truth that stressed the use of human ideas and hypotheses as limited but necessary instruments for creation of workable truths. To this philosophy he gave the name *instrumentalism.* In education Dewey was a prominent proponent of experimentation, or "learning by doing." His most important writings include *Psychology* (1886), *The School and Society* (1900) and *Problems of Man* (1946).

Dewey, Thomas Edmund *(1902–1971)* American attorney, politician, and Republican presidential candidate

Governor Thomas E. Dewey (LIBRARY OF CONGRESS. PRINTS AND PHOTOGRAPHS DIVISION)

(1944, 1948). Dewey graduated from the University of Michigan in 1923, took a law degree from Columbia in 1925 and began to practice law in New York City. He gained national fame as special prosecutor between 1935 and 1937 and was elected the district attorney of New York County in 1937. The following year he ran for governor of New York, losing by a narrow margin to Democrat incumbent Herbert Lehman. In 1940 he sought the Republican presidential nomination, losing to Wendell WILLKIE. Dewey was elected governor of New York in 1942 and reelected in 1946 and 1950. He took a moderate stance on most issues but was renowned for his opposition to the NEW DEAL of President Franklin D. ROOSEVELT. Dewey unsuccessfully challenged Roosevelt for the presidency in 1944. Nominated again in 1948, Dewey chose California governor (later Supreme Court chief justice) Earl WARREN as his running mate. Many polls predicted a Dewey victory over President Harry S. TRUMAN, but Truman's aggressive campaigning led to Dewey's surprise defeat. After retiring as governor in 1954, Dewey remained active in Republican national politics. He was the author of *The Case Against the New Deal* (1940) and *Journey to the Far Pacific* (1952).

DEW Line Radar terminals of the Distant Early Warning network, near

69 degrees North latitude and extending from northwestern ALASKA to northeastern CANADA—their purpose to give an alert at the approach of unfriendly aircraft. The DEW Line, constructed and run by the UNITED STATES and Canada, began operations in 1957. It was expanded to the ALEUTIAN ISLANDS in 1959 and across GREENLAND in 1961.

de Wolfe, Elsie (Lady Mendl) *(1865–1950)* American interior decorator and designer, often viewed as the originator of modern professional interior design. After an early career as an actress, de Wolfe took on a total renovation (c. 1910) of her New York townhouse. Notables who visited the house spread word of the de Wolfe style and brought professional commissions. Stanford WHITE, the noted architect, asked her to deal with the interiors of the Colony Club (1905–07), a project that further advanced her vocabulary of light color tones and simple forms. She became a spokesperson for the "good design" direction of its day, giving lectures and writing a popular and influential book of 1913, *The House in Good Taste*. She continued to conduct a successful practice in New York, in Paris (where she became Lady Mendl with her 1926 marriage to Sir Charles Mendl) and finally in Beverly Hills. Although never an advocate of modernism as that term is now understood, de Wolfe moved the decorator's profession toward the modern world with her emphasis on professionalism and with her advocacy of simplicity and common sense in design.

Dexter, John *(1925–1990)* British theater and opera director. Dexter began his career at the Royal Court Theatre in London in the late 1950s. Later asked by Laurence OLIVIER to become associate director of the National Theatre, he staged such major plays as Peter SHAFFER's *Equus* (1974) and David Henry Hwang's *M. Butterfly* (1988). He won Tony Awards in New York for best director for both plays. He also staged operas for the Paris Opera and the Metropolitan Opera in New York.

Deyneka, Alexander Alexandrovich *(1899–1969)* Russian painter and sculptor. When SOCIALIST REALISM was imposed by the Soviet au-

thorities, he managed to preserve some of his earlier style in his works, which included sports, industrial and military scenes. Many of his murals decorated Moscow Underground stations.

Diaghilev, Serge Pavlovich *(1872–1929)* Russian ballet impresario, born in Novgorod. In pursuit of his goal of introducing Russian art to western Europe, in 1908 Diaghilev presented the bass Feodor CHALIAPIN in a season of Russian opera in Paris. He followed this up with his famous BALLETS RUSSES, presented in Paris (1909) and London (1911), in the conviction that in ballet he could form a union of all the arts. To this end he secured the services of dancers of outstanding skill—PAVLOVA, NIJINSKY, KARSAVINA and LOPOKOVA— and choreographers such as FOKINE and MASSINE; he commissioned BENOIS, BAKST, MATISSE, PICASSO, BRAQUE and others to design the decor, and DEBUSSY, RAVEL, STRAVINSKY and PROKOFIEV to compose ballet scores. The revolution broke his links with Russia, but with Paris as its headquarters his company continued to enjoy the highest reputation.

Dial, The American periodical. *The Dial* was founded in Chicago in 1880 and later moved to New York. It began as a conservative literary magazine but in 1916 evolved into a journal of radical opinion. By 1920 it was an influential champion of modern art and literature. Contributors to the *The Dial* included Sherwood ANDERSON, George SANTAYANA, D. H. LAWRENCE, T. S. ELIOT and Gertrude STEIN. *The Dial* published portions of Oswald SPENGLER's *The Decline of the West* in 1924–25 and Thomas MANN's *DEATH IN VENICE* in 1924. Marianne MOORE served as its editor for the last four years of its existence, but it folded in 1929 from lack of finances.

Diamond, I.A.L. *(Iţec Dominici)* *(1920–1988)* Romanian-born HOLLYWOOD screenwriter. A longtime collaborator of director Billy WILDER, with whom Diamond made such films as *Love in the Afternoon* (1957), *Some Like It Hot* (1959), *Irma la Douce* (1963), *Kiss Me, Stupid* (1964) and *The Private Life of Sherlock Holmes*. Diamond won an ACADEMY AWARD for *The Apartment* (1960).

Diana, princess of Wales *(1961–1997)* Born the third of four children to Viscount Althorp (later Earl Spencer in 1975), Lady Diana Spencer received her primary education in Riddlesworth Hall in Norfolk and then attended West Heath Boarding (secondary) School in Kent from 1974 to 1977. After leaving West Heath, Diana spent a year at the Institut Alpin Videmanette, a finishing school in Rougemont, Switzerland. After that she moved to London, where she briefly served as a nanny as well as a kindergarten teacher at the Young England School.

In 1980 Diana began dating Prince CHARLES, the son of Queen ELIZABETH II of England and heir to the throne. On July 29, 1981, Diana married Charles in St. Paul's Cathedral in London. Diana gave birth to the couple's first son, Prince William, on June 21, 1982, followed two years later by his younger brother, Harry, on September 15, 1984. On the surface Diana appeared to enjoy a happy life, but rumors surfaced about affairs between Charles and Camilla Parker Bowles (whom Charles married in April 2005) and between Diana and Major James Hewitt of the British army. In December 1992, after tabloids had printed numerous allegations of infidelity on both sides, Diana and Charles separated.

After their separation Diana promptly became an international ambassador of goodwill for Britain, raising funds for neglected and abused children and for the British Red Cross and campaigning regularly for an international accord

Diana, princess of Wales, and Prince Charles at their wedding. 1981 (BETTMAN/CORBIS)

banning the use of land mines. She also began to discuss openly the more unseemly aspects of the British royal family. In 1996 Charles and Diana obtained a divorce. Just prior to their divorce, she publicly began to date again and was regularly seen in the company of Dodi al-Fayed, the son of a wealthy Egyptian family. Early on the morning of August 31, 1997, Diana, Dodi and their driver (who was later found to have been intoxicated) were killed when their speeding limousine crashed in a tunnel in Paris. Diana's death and her subsequent funeral sparked a worldwide wave of sympathy and adulation for the princess.

Díaz, Porfirio (*1830–1915*) Mexican general and dictator. Díaz's long career straddled the 19th and 20th centuries. Born into a poor mestizo family, he changed his studies from the priesthood to law, but in 1854 joined the revolutionary forces of Benito Juárez. He rose in the military, achieving the rank of general in 1861 and becoming a federal deputy that same year. Díaz fought against France and Maximilian from 1861 to 1867 and was promoted to army commander. In 1871 he unsuccessfully revolted against the Juárez government and lost a presidential bid, and in 1876 he again was defeated in the presidential elections. However, he rebelled again, this time against Juárez's successor, Sebastián Lerdo de Tejada, and succeeded in overthrowing the government. Díaz assumed the presidency in 1877 and, while he was not president from 1880 to 1884, he effectively ruled MEXICO for the next 35 years. He proved a stern dictator, suppressing opposition and almost eliminating the previously prevalent countrywide banditry. He opened Mexico to foreign development, notably by U.S. business interests, bringing enormous revenue into the country and ensuring economic growth. This policy enriched Díaz and his followers but left the peasantry in wretched conditions with diminished landholdings and the workers as poor as ever with a government-opposed labor movement. In 1909 Díaz proclaimed a reinstatement of democracy, but when he again engineered reelection (1910) and showed no evidence of fulfilling his pledge, his regime was overthrown by a 1911 revolution led by Francisco Madero. He fled to Paris, where he died in exile.

Dibelius, Martin (*1883–1947*) German Protestant theologian. Dibelius became a professor of theology at the University of Heidelberg in 1915 and taught there for most of his adult life. He was known as an interdisciplinary thinker who drew from literature and folkloric oral traditions in his theological works. Dibelius was especially interested in the history of early Christianity. His major books include *Die Formgeschichte des Evangeliums* (1919) and *Geschichte der Unchristlichen Literatur* (1926).

Dick, George Francis (*1881–1967*) American physician. Dick and his wife, **Gladys Rowena Henry Dick** (*1881–1963*), also a physician and medical researcher, were renowned for their work on the prevention and treatment of scarlet fever. Until their work, scarlet fever was an endemic and often fatal or crippling childhood disease.

A graduate of Rush Medical College (1905), Dick studied pathology at the Universities of Vienna and Munich. Returning to the U.S. in 1909, he joined the faculty of the University of Chicago, where he eventually became professor of pathology and head of the department of medicine. Gladys Henry obtained her M.D. from Johns Hopkins University School of Medicine (1907) and did postgraduate work in several fields at Johns Hopkins and the University of Berlin. Meeting in 1911 at the University of Chicago, where they were both research pathologists, they were married in 1914.

Collaborating in their research, in the early 1920s the Dicks discovered that hemolytic streptococci bacteria cause scarlet fever. They developed the first test for determining a person's susceptibility to scarlet fever—the Dick test. They also did important work on immunization. However, they became the subject of international controversy because they patented their techniques of toxin and antitoxin development used in the test. In 1935 the LEAGUE OF NATIONS declared that these patents restricted further research into scarlet fever immunization or treatment.

Dick, Philip Kindred (*1928–1982*) American novelists and short story writer. Dick enjoyed a steadily increasing reputation as one of the most original and visionary American fiction writers of the second half of the 20th century. Within the science fiction field, in which he produced most of his best work, he is regarded by peers such as Ursula LE GUIN and Stanislaw LEM as the finest writer in that genre. Dick, who lived in California for nearly all his life, began his career as a prolific short-story writer in the 1950s, contributing to a wide range of science fiction pulp magazines. He first emerged as a major science fiction novelist with *Eye in the Sky* (1956), which was followed by numerous acclaimed works including *The Man in the High Castle* (1962), which won the Hugo Award for best novel, *The Three Stigmata of Palmer Eldrich* (1965) and *Ubik* (1969). *Valis* (1981) is a fictionalized account of Dick's mystical experiences in the final decade of his life. *The Transmigration of Timothy Archer* (1982) is considered Dick's best mainstream fiction novel.

Dickey, James Lafayette (*1923–1997*) American poet, novelist and critic. Born in Georgia, Dickey attended Vanderbilt University and began his career as an advertising copy writer. His first volume, *Into the Stone*, appeared in 1960; his fourth, *Buckdancer's Choice*, won the National Book Award in 1965. He is best known for his novel *Deliverance* (1970), an adventure story about four businessmen on a hunting trip in rural Georgia, which became a best seller and was made into a movie. *The Zodiac* (1976) is a long poem in 12 parts. The title work of *The Strength of Fields* was written for President CARTER's inauguration. *Puella* (1982) describes a girl's coming of age. Dickey is also known for his outspoken criticism of his contemporaries, collected in *The Suspect in Poetry* (1964), *Babel to Byzantium* (1968), *Self-Interviews* (1970) and *Sorties* (1971). Dickey's *The Whole Motion* (1992) is considered to be his most comprehensive volume. Other later works include *The Eagle's Mile* (1990) and *Falling, May Day Sermon, and Other Poems* (1982).

Dick Tracy The world's most popular detective comic strip, by Chester Gould (1900–85), *Dick Tracy* was first syndicated on October 12, 1931, and is still enjoyed by millions. Over the years the incorruptible Tracy has used his two-way wrist radio and other high-tech gadgets to do battle with a host of underworld types, including Pruneface, the Mole, Flyface, Itchy and Ugly Christine. Gould retired on Christmas Day 1977, after which the strip was taken over by Max Allan Collins and Rick Fletcher; after Fletcher's death in 1983, Dick Locher was added. The feature-length motion picture *Dick Tracy,* directed by and starring Warren Beatty, was released in 1990.

Didion, Joan *(1934–)* American author. Born in Sacramento, California, which she evokes in much of her work, Didion was educated at the University of California at Berkeley. She went to New York and worked for *Vogue* magazine for eight years, during which time she published her first novel, *Run River* (1963). Returning to California, she wrote a series of essays for the *Saturday Evening Post,* which were collected in the acclaimed *Slouching Towards Bethlehem* (1968). The title essay, a portrait of HIP-PIES in the Haight Ashbury district of SAN FRANCISCO, established her as a leading practitioner of the NEW JOURNALISM, with its subjective point of view and detailed impressions. In the best-selling novel *Play It as It Lays* (1970, filmed 1972), she established her unique fictional style, taut, precise and flat. Her writing evidences her fundamentally bleak and hopeless view of life. Other works include *The White Album* (1979), essays; *Salvador* (1983); *Democracy: A Novel* (1984); and *Miami* (1987). Didion was married to the writer **John Gregory Dunne,** with whom she collaborated in the writing of screenplays. One of their collaborative efforts was the film *Up Close and Personal* (1996), which starred Robert REDFORD and Michelle Pfeiffer. Her book *The Year of Magical Thinking* (2005), is about her husband's death, grief and mourning, was a 2005 National Book Awards winner.

Didrikson, Mildred "Babe" *(1913– 1956)* American athlete. Didrikson became a professional athlete after the 1932 OLYMPIC GAMES in Los Angeles, in which she set two world records. She excelled in a variety of sports, including basketball, baseball, billiards and swimming. In 1947 she began her career as a professional golfer, winning every possible women's title at least once during the next decade and was named outstanding

American athlete and Olympian Babe Didrikson (LIBRARY OF CONGRESS, PRINTS AND PHOTOGRAPHS DIVISION)

woman athlete of the first half of the 20th century by an Associated Press poll. Her autobiography, *The Life I've Led,* was published in 1955, a year before her death from cancer.

Die Brücke (The Bridge) German artistic movement that was heavily influenced by EXPRESSIONISM. The young German painters who initially founded Die Brücke were all, at the time, studying architecture at the Dresden Technical School. These artists, who included Ernst-Ludwig KIRCHNER and Fritz Bleyl, were especially drawn to anti-classical forms from non-European cultures, such as African and Oceanic sculpture. Their pictorial style featured intense distortions intended to emphasize spiritual freedom and a shattering of accepted artistic definitions. Die Brücke never formulated a developed and consistent artistic manifesto, but it did create a sense of mission—declaring itself as the bridge to the art of the future. Emil NOLDE was among the painters who associated themselves for a time with the movement, which ultimately disbanded in 1913.

Diefenbaker, John George *(1895– 1979)* Prime minister of Canada (1957–63). Diefenbaker was first elected to Canada's House of Commons in 1940 and served 13 terms as a representative for Saskatchewan. In 1958 he led his PROGRESSIVE CONSERVATIVE PARTY to the largest electoral victory in Canada's history. His administration was noted for its ambitious efforts to unlock the natural resources of the Canadian north and to increase independence from the U.S. A tireless critic of the opposition LIBERAL PARTY governments that succeeded him, Diefenbaker often demonstrated an acerbic humor and eloquent oratory in debate in the House of Commons.

Diels, Otto Paul Hermann *(1876– 1954)* German organic chemist. The son of Hermann Diels, a famous classical scholar, Diels earned his doctorate under Emil FISCHER in Berlin (1899) and became professor there in 1906. From 1916 until his retirement in 1948 he was professor at Kiel. In 1906 he made an unexpected discovery, that of a new oxide of carbon, carbon suboxide. Diels's second major discovery was a method of removing hydrogen from steroids by means of selenium. He used this method in research on cholesterol and bile acids, obtaining aromatic hydrocarbons that enabled the structure of the steroids to be deduced. In 1928 Diels and his assistant Kurt ALDER discovered a synthetic reaction in which a diene (compound containing two double bonds) is added to a compound containing one double bond flanked by carbonyl or carboxyl groups to give a ring structure. The reaction proceeds in the mildest conditions and is of general application and hence of great utility in synthesis. It has been used in the synthesis of natural products such as sterols, vitamin K, cantharides and synthetic polymers. For this discovery Diels and Alder were jointly awarded the NOBEL PRIZE in chemistry in 1950.

Diem, Ngo Dinh *(1901–1963)* South Vietnamese leader. Born in Annam, Diem was a member of an important Roman Catholic family, an ardent nationalist and a strong anti-communist. Repeatedly declining offers of political office, he finally became prime minister of South VIET-NAM under BAO DAI in 1954 after the partition of his country. Victorious in the presidential elections of 1955, he declared South Vietnam a republic the following year. Strongly supported by the U.S., Diem consolidated his power but became increasingly unpopular due to his nepotism, his dictatorial control and his favoring of Catholics over Buddhists. Under Diem the South Vietnamese position in the VIETNAM WAR worsened and American support waned. He was assassinated during a 1963 military coup.

Dien Bien Phu (Dienbienphu) Site of the climactic battle that effectively ended the war between FRANCE and the VIET MINH (1946–54). It was a small village on the border between Laos and North Vietnam. About 180 miles from the nearest French post, it was fortified by some 16,000 French troops, including soldiers of the French Foreign Legion and Vietnamese, Laotians and Cambodians fighting on the French side. The French hoped to draw the Viet Minh into a set-piece battle in which French firepower would destroy them. But the French underestimated their enemy. Viet Minh general VO NGUYEN GIAP entrenched artillery in the surrounding mountains and massed five divisions totaling about 60,000 troops. The battle began with a massive Viet Minh artillery barrage on March 13, 1954, and was followed by an infantry assault. At the height of the battle the French requested military support from the U.S., but diplomatic and domestic U.S. political considerations caused President EISENHOWER to deny the request. Fighting raged until May 7, 1954, when the French were overrun. The shock of the fall of Dien Bien Phu led France, already plagued by public opposition to the war, to agree to the independence of VIETNAM at the GENEVA CONFERENCE in 1954.

Dieppe Port city on the English Channel north of Rouen, in France's Seine-Maritime department. Dieppe was held by the Germans from 1940 to 1944. On August 19, 1942, during WORLD WAR II, the city was stormed by Allied commandos who were reconnoitering German defenses. The Germans retaliated and inflicted many fatalities on the Allies (who put the experience to good use during the NORMANDY invasion of 1944). Several structures damaged during the war have been reconstructed.

Diesel, Rudolph Christian Carl *(1858–1913)* German engineer and inventor, designer of the diesel engine. After graduating from the Munich Institute of Technology, Diesel worked as a mechanic for two years in Switzerland and then worked in Paris as a thermal engineer. He was a devout Lutheran and a dedicated pacifist, believing in international religious liberation. In 1893 he demonstrated his first engine, and although the first few attempts failed, within three years he had developed a pressure-ignited heat engine. The engine named for him is now used universally, for example, in powering boats and in running generators.

By 1898 Diesel was a millionaire, but his fortune soon disappeared. He toured the world giving lectures and visited the U.S. in 1912. His health was bad; he suffered from gout and was depressed by the buildup to WORLD WAR I. On the ferry returning to Paris from London in 1913, after dining with a friend, he disappeared and was assumed to have drowned in the English Channel.

Dietrich, Marlene (Maria Magdalena von Losch) *(1901–1992)* German-born film actress. Dietrich, whose primary film triumphs were in the 1930s, has become one of the enduring femme fatale figures of the cinema. Born in Berlin, she studied as a youth for a career as a concert violinist before an injured wrist deflected her into an acting career. After studying at the Max Reinhardt Drama School, she was discovered by film director Josef VON STERNBERG, who made Dietrich an international star through her roll as the alluring dance-hall chanteuse Lola-Lola in *The Blue Angel* (1930), a film shot in Germany. Von Sternberg then directed Dietrich in a number of classic HOLLYWOOD films, including *Dishonored* (1931), *Shanghai Express* (1932), *Blonde Venus* (1932) and *The Scarlet Empress* (1934). Dietrich shed von Sternberg's heavy dramatic burden and had a comedy hit alongside James STEWART in *Destry Rides Again* (1939). She made relatively few films in the remaining decades of her life, but her supporting roles in *Witness for the Prosecution* (1958) and *Touch of Evil* (1958) were memorable. Maximilian Schell made a biographical documentary, *Marlene,* in 1984.

Diffrient, Niels *(1928–)* American industrial designer best known for his development of chairs based on ERGONOMICS. Diffrient studied at Cranbrook Academy in the 1940s and worked with the SAARINEN office from 1946 to 1951. From 1951 to 1952 he was with the office of Walter B. Ford and thereafter in New York in the office of Henry Dreyfuss, where he became a partner in 1956. His work there included aircraft interiors, road and farm machinery, and studies in ergonomics. After leaving the Dreyfuss office in 1981, Diffrient became an independent designer concentrating on furniture. His chairs and his office systems furniture are his best-known recent projects.

digital divide Term describing the gap between those individuals who possess access to modern means of electronic communication and those who lack such access. Within the U.S. the term has signified the gap between white Americans and minorities over access to the INTERNET. The term became popular during the administration of President Bill CLINTON, who himself regularly mentioned the dangers that such a racial division would cause in American society. In the technology intensive sectors of the U.S.

economy, the digital divide has also come to refer to the general paucity of ethnic minorities (African, Hispanic and Native Americans) within this sector's workforce.

Dillard, Annie *(1945–)* American essayist. Dillard was educated at Hollins College and was married to the poet and novelist Henry Dillard and later to the novelist Gary Clevidence. Her first book of poetry, *Tickets for a Prayer Wheel,* was published in 1974. That same year her prose reflections in *Pilgrim at Tinker Creek* were published to great acclaim. Compared to Thoreau's *Walden Pond,* the book won the PULITZER PRIZE in 1974. The book presents Dillard's lyrical reflections on nature, humanity and theology. Dillard has contributed to *Atlantic Monthly, Poetry, Harper's* and many other periodicals and has taught poetry and creative writing. Other works include *Holy the Firm* (1978) and the autobiographical *An American Childhood* (1987). Dillard continues to write, producing such works as *Teaching a Stone to Talk* (1988), *The Writing Life* (1989), *The Living* (1991), *Mornings Like This* (1996), *For the Time Being* (1999) and others. She is an adjunct professor of English at Wesleyan University.

Dillinger, John Herbert *(1903–1934)* American bank robber. A petty thief during his childhood in Indianapolis, Indiana, Dillinger graduated to serious crime in 1924, when he attempted to rob a grocery store. Apprehended, he served nine years in prison where he became a confirmed criminal. After he was released in 1933, his spectacular bank-robbing career lasted a mere 11 months. During that time he and his two successive gangs held up approximately 20 midwestern banks; he was captured and escaped jail twice; and he was responsible for 16 murders. While the robbery spree was in progress, Dillinger became something of a popular figure to many depression-era Americans who appreciated his courtesy to individuals and his hatred of banking institutions. Named public enemy number one by the FBI, Dillinger was the object of an intensive manhunt. Apparently betrayed by a female friend, he was killed by FBI agents as he left the Biograph Theater in Chicago on July 22, 1934.

Dillon, Clarence *(1882–1979)* American financier. In 1925 his firm, Dillon, Read & Co., won a hard-fought battle for control of DODGE BROTHERS Automobile Company. Shortly thereafter, Dillon arranged a merger of Dodge and CHRYSLER, which resulted in Chrysler Corp. becoming the nation's third-largest auto maker. Dillon's son, **C. Douglas Dillon,** held various posts in the EISENHOWER administration and served as secretary of the treasury (1961–65) under presidents KENNEDY and JOHNSON.

DiMaggio, Joe (Joseph Paul Di-Maggio) *(1914–1999)* American baseball player. Immortalized in song and story, DiMaggio's reputation has reached legendary status. He joined the New York Yankees in 1936 and remained with the team through their "dynasty" years, which included nine world championships. Perhaps the game's all-time best natural hitter, his 1941 56-game hitting streak is one of his more memorable feats. He was an All-Star during each of his major league seasons and was named Most Valuable Player three times. His career was interrupted by World War II, but he was still a considerable factor in four postwar World Series championships and led the league in home runs in 1948. His legendary status was perhaps fueled by the fact that he was for a time married to another American legend, Marilyn MONROE. His two brothers, Dom and Vince, also played in the majors. DiMaggio retired in 1951 and was named to the Hall of Fame in 1955.

Dimitrov, Georgi *(1882–1949)* Bulgarian Communist leader. An early trade unionist, Dimitrov was organizing strikes by 1905. Elected to the Bulgarian National Assembly (1913), he was imprisoned in 1915 for his opposition to BULGARIA's entry into WORLD WAR I. From 1917 to 1923 he secretly led the nation's Communist Movement and, in 1923, a Communist uprising against Alexander Tsankov. When it failed, Dimitrov fled the country. In Berlin (1933) he was accused of complicity in the REICHSTAG FIRE but was acquitted. Settling in the USSR, Dimitrov served as secretary-general (1935–43) of the COMINTERN. In 1945 he returned to a newly liberated Bulgaria, where he headed the Communist Party and became prime minister in 1946. During his tenure in office, he followed an unswerving Communist line but showed signs of growing independence from the USSR. He died in Moscow in 1949 while undergoing medical treatment.

Dinesen, Isak (Karen Blixen) *(1885–1962)* Danish author. Dinesen, who wrote primarily in English, is best known for the acclaimed memoir *Out of Africa* (1937, filmed 1985), which recounts her life on a coffee plantation in Kenya with her philandering husband and her lover. Dinesen was born to an upper-class family and, after studying art in Paris, married her cousin, Baron Bror Blixen-Finecke, in 1914. They immediately moved to Africa, but following their divorce and the eventual failure of the plantation, she returned to Denmark and began writing in earnest. Her first important work, *Seven Gothic Tales* (1934), was praised for its use of fantasy and evocative description; it aroused much curiosity about the unknown author. Dinesen continued to produce successful and esteemed stories and memoirs, though she suffered ill health as the result of syphilis contracted from her husband. Her works include *Out of Africa* (1937), *Winter's Tales* (1942), *Last Tales* (1957) and the essay collection *Shadows in the Grass* (1961).

Ding Ling (Jiang Bingzhi) *(1904–1986)* Chinese writer. She was a feminist whose writings were primarily concerned with the impact of CHINA's communist revolution on the lives of peasant women. After the Communist victory in 1949, she held a number of key literary and cultural posts. A political purge in 1957 led to her banishment from public life and the banning of her works. She was imprisoned for a number of years and was not officially rehabilitated until 1977.

DioGuardi, John (Johnny Dio) *(1915–1979)* American organized-crime leader. DioGuardi was believed to have specialized in labor racketeering and was allegedly associated with Teamster official Jimmy HOFFA in the 1950s. He was indicted for arranging the 1956 acid-throwing incident that blinded labor columnist Victor Riesel, but he never came to trial for that crime. DioGuardi served several prison terms for tax evasion, extortion and fraud, and died in prison.

Dion, Céline (*1968–   *) French-Canadian singer. In 1981 Dion released her first album, *La voix du Bon Dieu* (The voice of God), which did well in Canada. Two years later her second album, *Les chemins de ma maison* (The Roads of my house), became the first record produced by a Canadian singer to go gold in France.

By 1989 Dion had begun singing in English, which paved the way for *Unison* (1990), her first English-language album. While *Unison* produced several hit singles, most notably "Where Does My Heart Beat Now," it was not until Dion recorded the title duet with Peabo Bryson for the Disney animated film *Beauty and the Beast* (1991) that she had a song in the top 10 pop charts in the U.S. Dion and Bryson received a 1992 Academy Award for best song as well as a Grammy.

Since her breakthrough year in 1992 Dion has recorded some dozen albums, among them *The Colour of My Love* (1993), *Falling into You* (1996), *Let's Talk About Love* (1997) and *A New Day Has Come* (2002). Her recording of "My Heart Will Go On" in the movie soundtrack *Titanic* (1997) won her a second Academy Award for best song.

Dior, Christian (*1905–1957*) French fashion designer best known for his 1947 line, with its long skirts and hint of a backward turn toward the austere style of the WORLD WAR I era. Dior studied in PARIS with the intention of becoming a career diplomat but in 1927 opened a small Paris art gallery showing the works of avant-garde artists such as Salvador DALÍ and Jean COCTEAU. The GREAT DEPRESSION closed the gallery, leading Dior to turn to fashion design in 1935. In 1947 his firm launched with overwhelming success the style that became known as the New Look. His annual lines thereafter, each with a central theme, were popular and widely copied in the production of ready-to-wear manufacturers. Practicality and a look that was both soft and architectural were typical themes of Dior's designs. His firm was taken over briefly by Yves SAINT LAURENT and then by Marc Bohan after Dior's death. Gianfranco Ferré, John Galliano and Hedi Slimane were successive design directors. As the House

of Dior, the organization has continued to grow with divisions devoted to hats, furs, shoes, perfumes and jewelry. The New York branch alone employed a staff of about 1,200 by 1948. Dior was the recipient of a 1947 Neiman Marcus Award and a Parsons Medal in 1956.

Diori, Hamani (*1916–1989*) First president of the independent nation of NIGER. He held several government posts during the years when Niger was an autonomous French territory and was chosen by the French to became president when the nation was granted independence in 1960. His regime was plagued by widespread corruption, and the government's problems were compounded by a severe drought that hit sub-Saharan Africa in the late 1960s and early 1970s. Diori was overthrown by a military coup in 1974. After spending 13 years in prison and under house arrest, he was freed in 1987. He then moved to Morocco.

Dirac, Paul Adrien Maurice (*1902–1984*) British mathematician and physicist. After graduating in 1921 in electrical engineering at Bristol University, Dirac went on to read mathematics at Cambridge, where he obtained his Ph.D. in 1926. He lectured for several years in America, then was appointed (1932) to the Lucasian Professorship of Mathematics at Cambridge, a post he held until his retirement in 1969. In 1971 he became professor of physics at Florida State University. Dirac is acknowledged as one of the most creative theoreticians of the early 20th century. In 1926, slightly later than Max BORN and Pascual Jordan in Germany, he developed a general formalism for QUANTUM MECHANICS. In 1928 he produced his relativistic theory to describe the properties of the electron. The wave equations developed by SCHRÖDINGER to describe the behavior of electrons were nonrelativistic; a significant deficiency was their failure to account for the electron spin discovered in 1925 by GOUDSMIT and George Uhlenbeck. Dirac's rewriting of the equations to incorporate relativity had considerable value, for it not only predicted the correct energy levels of the hydrogen atom but also revealed that some of those levels were no longer single but could be split into two. It is just such a splitting of spectral lines that is characteristic of a spinning electron.

Dirac also predicted from these equations that there must be states of negative energy for the electron. In 1930 he proposed a theory to account for this that added a new dimension of matter to the universe—antimatter. It was soon appreciated that Dirac's argument was sufficiently general to apply to all particles. Above all else a quantum theorist, in 1930 Dirac published the first edition of his classic work *The Principles of Quantum Mechanics*. In 1933 he shared the NOBEL PRIZE in physics with Schrödinger for his work on electron theory.

dirigible See ZEPPELIN.

Dirksen, Everett McKinley (*1896–1969*) American political leader. Born in Pekin, Illinois, Dirksen served in WORLD WAR I, returned to his hometown, practiced law and won election to the House of Representatives as a Republican in 1932. He served as a member of the House until 1948 and was elected to the Senate in 1950, remaining a senator until his death. A popular and colorful conservative, he became party whip in 1957 and minority leader two years later. Dirksen maintained a conservative stance regarding foreign and domestic affairs and supported Senator Joseph MCCARTHY. Moderating his positions in the 1960s, he helped President KENNEDY secure the passage of a NUCLEAR TEST BAN TREATY in 1963. He was an enthusiastic supporter of President

Senator Everett Dirksen (LIBRARY OF CONGRESS, PRINTS AND PHOTOGRAPHS DIVISION)

Lyndon JOHNSON's civil rights program and aided in the passage of landmark civil rights legislation.

Disney, Walt (Walter Elias Disney)

(1901–1966) American motion-picture producer and amusement-park entrepreneur whose work has become synonymous with family entertainment. Born in Chicago, Disney spent his boyhood on a farm in nearby Marceline, Missouri and his later school days in Kansas City, Missouri, where he first experimented with cartooning and animation. In 1923 he moved to Los Angeles, intending to market his first series of ANIMATED FILMS, *Alice in Cartoonland*, which blended live-action characters with animated backgrounds. The appearance of MICKEY MOUSE in a synchronized-sound cartoon called *Steamboat Willie* in 1928 saved his studio from certain ruin and set the course for future success. With his brother Roy and assistants like the brilliant Ub Iwerks, Disney dominated animation for the next 40 years. *Snow White and the Seven Dwarfs* (1938) demonstrated the viability of a feature-length format. Shorts like *The Old Mill* (1937) and features like *Pinocchio* (1940) pioneered the three-dimensional effects of the multiplane camera technology. For FANTASIA (1941) he developed a stereophonic sound system; he was also the first filmmaker to contract exclusively with the new Technicolor system. After World War II Disney turned his attention to other interests. *Treasure Island* (1950) inaugurated a successful series of live-action adaptations from children's classics. Several television series, beginning in 1954 with *Disneyland* for ABC, showcased not only the Disney movies, but the new theme parks as well. The DISNEYLAND park opened in Anaheim, California, in 1955. The Disney World project in Orlando, Florida, was well into the planning stages when Disney died in 1966 of an acute circulatory collapse. During his career he amassed 39 ACADEMY AWARDS and hundreds of other awards and honors.

Disneyland and Disney World

These two American amusement parks were inspired by animator and film producer Walt DISNEY and are famous throughout the world. Disneyland, located in Anaheim, California, was launched by Disney himself in 1955.

The second park, Walt Disney World, was opened outside Orlando, Florida, in 1971, with a companion park, Epcot Center, opening in 1982. Disney's approach was to create specific themes within each park, such as Fantasyland and Tomorrowland. The first Disney theme park outside the U.S. opened in Tokyo, Japan, in 1983 (Tokyo Disneyland). In April 1992 EuroDisney (now Disneyland Paris) opened for business. Designed to appeal to adults as well as children, the parks are known for their friendly employees, cleanliness and lavish, innovative attractions that utilize the latest in technology. The Walt Disney Corporation also built Disneyland Hong Kong just outside the Chinese city. It opened in 2005.

Di Stefano, Giuseppe *(1921–)*

Italian tenor. Born near Catania, Sicily, Di Stefano studied privately and made his debut at Reggio Emilia in 1946 as Des Grieux in *Manon Lescaut*. His La Scala debut occurred a year later, and this theater became his European home base. He first performed in the U.S. at the Metropolitan Opera in 1948, singing the Duke in *Rigoletto*. He remained at the Metropolitan for the next five years, singing there again from 1955 to 1956 and 1964 to 1965. Noted for the pure lyricism of his voice, Di Stefano appeared at most of the world's leading opera houses, singing the major tenor parts in the Italian and French repertoires. Di Stefano gave his last performance in 1992 at the Caracalla Theater in Rome.

Di Stéfano Laulhé, Alfredo *(1926–)*

Argentine-born soccer player. Renowned for his achievements with Real Madrid of Spain in the 1950s and 1960s, Di Stéfano began his career in Argentina with the famous River Plate club. In 1949 he joined the exodus to Colombia, where higher salaries were luring the cream of South America soccer. In 1953 FIFA ruled the Colombian system illegal and forced the release of all non-Colombian players. Di Stéfano moved to Spain and embarked upon the golden period of his career and that of Spanish soccer. Real Madrid dominated Spanish domestic competition and helped forge the popularity of the newly created inter-European competitions. Led by Di Stéfano, Real won the first five European Cups (1956–60) and the first World Club

Championship held in 1960. The forward line of Francisco Gento, Ferenc Puskas and Di Stéfano became the most famed and feared in soccer history. Their master reached its peak at the 1960 European Cup Final when Real crushed Eintracht Frankfurt 7-3, Puskas and Di Stéfano scoring the goals created by Gento's brilliant wing play. Di Stéfano played seven times for Argentina and 31 times for Spain.

Dix, Dom Gregory (George Eglington Alston) *(1901–1952)*

Anglican priest and theologian. Dix was one of the leading figures in the Anglican Church in the 20th century. He was noted both for his personal charm and leadership abilities and for his insightful writings on the history and meaning of the Anglican liturgy. Educated at Oxford, he was ordained as an Anglican priest in 1925 and took his final vows in 1940 after a period of monastic life at Nashdom Abbey. In 1946 Dix was named Select Preacher for the University of Cambridge. In 1948 he became the Prior of Nashdom Abbey. His major works include *A Detection of Aumbries* (1942) and *The Shape of the Liturgy* (1945).

Dix, Otto *(1891–1969)*

German painter. Born in Gera, he studied at art schools in Dresden and Düsseldorf. A soldier in WORLD WAR I, he was horrified by the fighting and returned to Düsseldorf to create a series of harrowingly realistic paintings and the cycle of 50 powerful etchings entitled *War* (1925). He lived in Berlin (1925–27), moving to Dresden in 1927 to teach at that city's academy. Branded a decadent by the Nazis, he was removed from his post in 1933. Although he was arrested in 1939 for plotting against HITLER, he was drafted into the German army in 1945 and was later a French prisoner of war. Dix is known for his bitingly satirical German expressionist works. In these paintings the personalities of the WEIMAR REPUBLIC—often prostitutes, beggars and criminals—are forcefully portrayed in harsh colors and expressively distorted forms. His later paintings were largely religious in subject matter.

Dixieland jazz

Synonymous with "traditional jazz," although the two terms continue to evoke significant polemical resonances. *Dixieland* derived from the ORIGINAL DIXIELAND JAZZ BAND, the white New Orleans group that became an international sensation through its tours and recordings. Since such groups were regarded as essentially imitative of the style developed by black musicians in New Orleans, *Dixieland* become associated with white groups like the ODJB and New Orleans Rhythm Kings, with the terms *traditional* and *New Orleans* reserved for the music of the black originators and their followers. But the distinction has lost much of its original specificity, and the terms can now be considered interchangeable. Stylistically, Dixieland involves a collective approach to improvisation, with the trumpet generally assigned the melody and with counterpoint provided by a clarinet and trombone; the typical rhythm section consists of drums, banjo (or piano or guitar) and tuba (later, often replaced by the double bass). Today, Dixieland is typically rendered with celebratory gusto and, in groups like the Dukes of Dixieland, with great virtuosity and polish.

Dixon, Thomas F. *(1916–1998)* U.S. rocket design pioneer. Dixon got in on the ground floor of what would later become the Rocketdyne Division of North American Aviation, where he served as vice president of research and engineering from 1955 to 1961. After briefly interrupting his career in the rocket industry to serve as deputy associate administrator of NASA, he returned to the private sector in 1963. Dixon was awarded the Robert H. Goddard Memorial Award by the American Rocket Society in 1957.

Djemal, Ahmed *(1872–1922)* Turkish general and statesman. Djemal, as a staff officer in Salonika (now Thessaloniki, Greece), was the first officer to join the "Society [later Committee] of Union and Progress," also known as YOUNG TURKS. This organization, with military support, overthrew the reactionary government led by Sultan ABDUL HAMID II in 1909 and dominated Ottoman politics until the empire's defeat in WORLD WAR I (1918). Djemal served as military governor of Constantinople, minister of marine and Turkish governor of SYRIA during World War I. After TURKEY's defeat, he became military adviser to AFGHANISTAN.

Djibouti Republic located on the northeastern coast of the Horn of Africa, fronting the Strait of Bab el Mandeb; the volcanic, mostly infertile country covers a total area of 8,938 square miles. The bulk of the population inhabits the comparatively fertile coastal strip bordering the Gulf of Tadjoura. The port of Djibouti was an important coal-bunkering station on the SUEZ CANAL route and became the capital of French Somaliland in 1892; a railway to ADDIS ABABA was completed in 1917. In response to the majority Somali community's calls for independence, a referendum was held in March 1967. Although the territory voted to retain its association with France, the Somali community contested the validity of the result. After nearly a decade of Somali agitation and pressure from the ORGANIZATION OF AFRICAN UNITY, the territory acceded to independence in June 1977. A Somali, Hassan Gouled, was elected president, and an Afar, Ahmed Dini, appointed prime minister. In December 1977 Ahmed Dini and four other Afar ministers resigned, alleging discrimination against Afars. As part of a policy of detribalization, the Rassemblement Populaire Pour le Progres (RPP) party was formed in 1979; in November 1981 Djibouti became a one-party state. President Gouled was reelected in 1982 and 1987 but stood as sole candidate on both occasions. Ethnic tensions between rival Somali-speaking groups led to serious violence in 1989, when security forces also moved to suppress unrest among the Afar majority. In 1999 Omer Gelleh was elected president. In 2000 the government reached an agreement with northern rebels of the FRUD (Front for Restoration of Unity and Democracy) and put an end to civil war. In response to the U.S.-led war on terror after SEPTEMBER 11, 2001, Djibouti has attempted to remain friendly with the U.S. while not alienating nearby Arab countries. For instance, it has refused to serve as a

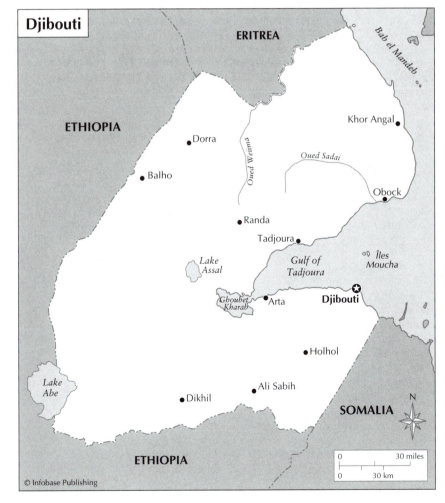

DJIBOUTI

1946	French Somaliland becomes a French overseas territory.
1967	The territory, now renamed Territory of the Afars and the Issas, is granted a semiautonomous executive, headed by a president and a council of eight members.
1976	Ali Arif resigns the presidency.
1977	The Territory of the Afars and the Issas gains independence under the name of Djibouti. Ahmed Dini Ahmed resigns along with four cabinet members following Afar-Issa strife.
1979	Popular Rally for Progress (Rassemblement Populaire pour le Progrès, RPP) is formed.
1981	Legislation is enacted making RPP the country's only legal political party.
1987	Gouled is reelected unopposed.
1989	Somali refugees escaping their country's civil war flee to neighboring Djibouti.
1999	Ismael Omar Gelleh is elected president.
2000	The government and the radical faction of FRUD sign a peace agreement, putting an end to the civil war.
2002	Full multiparty democracy is implemented. Because of its location and ocean access in the Horn of Africa, Djibouti becomes a strategic place for American bases monitoring terrorist activities in the Middle East.
2003	The Union for Presidential Majority, the coalition supporting President Guelleh, wins all 65 seats in parliament. This is the first free multiparty election since the country acquired independence in 1977.
2005	Incumbent president Guelleh runs unopposed in April elections, which are boycotted by the opposition.

base for attacks upon another state but allowed 900 U.S. troops to establish a support base in Djibouti for their operations in AFGHANISTAN. In 2002 multiparty elections were made possible after the law allowing only four political parties expired. The party supporting President Gelleh won Djibouti's first free multiparty election in 2003, while in 2005 Gelleh ran unopposed and won another term as president.

Djilas, Milovan (1911–1995) One-time Yugoslav party and government official, Marxist intellectual, chief propagandist and closest friend of TITO.

Djilas was born of peasant origins in Montenegro. After studying at Belgrade University he joined the illegal Communist Party of YUGOSLAVIA in 1932, in 1938 was made a member of the central committee by Tito and in 1940 was made a member of the Politburo. During WORLD WAR II Djilas was a member of Tito's supreme headquarters and for a while led partisan forces in Montenegro. After Tito had fallen from Moscow's favor in 1948, Djilas was blamed by Moscow for being responsible for "revisionist heresies." Denouncing STALINISM, Djilas assisted Tito in creating Yugoslavia's "self-management socialism."

After publishing a series of articles in which he stressed the need for greater freedom, Djilas was brought to trial. He continued to write articles criticizing the regime, and although he was released from prison in 1966, he was forbidden to publish in Yugoslavia. As a critic of authoritarian rule, Djilas welcomed the end of the Communist Party's monopoly in Yugoslavia. However, before his death he repeatedly expressed concerns about and criticism of the Serbian and Croatian nationalism that had emerged in 1991. His publications include *The New Class* (1957), *Conversations with Stalin* (1962), *Memoirs of a Revolutionary* (1973) and *Of Prisons and Ideas* (1986).

Dniester Republic (1990–1994) An area that proclaimed its independence from the Soviet Socialist Republic of MOLDOVA, a state within the disintegrating USSR, in September 1990. Officially titled the Trans-Dniester Autonomous Soviet Socialist Republic, the political entity continued the anti-Moldovan actions that began in the ethnically Russian local administrative unit of Tighina in 1989. That year, in response to greater civil liberties permitted by USSR leader Mikhail GORBACHEV under his policy of GLASNOST, the Tighina soviet (government council) coordinated an effort by other likeminded soviets to reject Romanian as the official language of the Moldovan Soviet Socialist Republic (SSR) and began a campaign of civil disobedience against the ethnically Romanian province in an effort to ensure that Russians within Moldova would not come under the rule of ethnically Romanian Moldovans. In 1990 these soviets began to promote the creation of a new Soviet republic centered in Tighina that would be independent of Moldovan control, for which they received paramilitary and military assistance from their populations. When a referendum for the Dniester area resulted in a vote for independence, the Dniester region declared its independence as an Autonomous Soviet Socialist Republic. No foreign country recognized the Dniester Republic after the disappearance of the USSR and the independence of the Republic of MOLDOVA in December 1991. In 1994 the conflict between the Dniester Republic and the Republic of Moldova was terminated by a peace accord between the Dniester separatists and the Moldovan government. The agreement ended the Dniester Republic but ensured that the region would retain autonomy within Moldova.

Döblin, Alfred *(1878–1957)* German novelist. Döblin was one of the most important German writers to participate in the modernist movement that dominated European literature in the two decades following World War I. His most famous novel is *Berlin Alexanderplatz,* (1929), which employs multiple viewpoints to create a complex, teeming narrative that mirrors the disjointed style of life in modern urban areas. Three different film versions of this novel have been produced. A Jew, Döblin fled Nazi Germany in 1933 and ultimately established himself in exile in the U.S. His other novels include the four-volume *Men Without Mercy* (1935) as well as *Citizens and Soldiers* (1939), *A People Betrayed* (1948), *Karl and Rosa* (1950) and *Tales of a Long Night* (1956).

Dobrovolsky, Georgi *(1928–1971)* Soviet cosmonaut. At age 43, Lieutenant Colonel Dobrovolsky was in command of the Soviet *SOYUZ 11* mission when he and fellow cosmonauts Viktor Patsayev and Vladislav Volkov became the first travelers to be killed in space. He and his crew had successfully completed more than three weeks aboard the world's first space station, *SALYUT 1,* and were returning home when tragedy struck. *Soyuz 11* had successfully disengaged from the space station and was preparing to separate from its instrument module when a malfunction in the charges used for the separation caused all the charges to fire at once, rather than sequentially. The explosive shock tore open a seal inside one of the craft's pressure-equalization valves, causing the spacecraft's oxygen-nitrogen atmosphere to be sucked out into space. Dobrovolsky and his crew, confident of success, had flown without space suits. The three men gasped for breath and indications were that they attempted to reach the valve and close it manually, but in less than a minute *Soyuz 11* was a vacuum chamber, silent and lifeless. Dobrovolsky, buried in the Kremlin wall, is the subject of a 1977 biography, *The Flight Continues.*

Doctorow, Edgar Laurence *(1931–)* American novelist. E. L. Doctorow was educated at Kenyon College and at Columbia University and began his career reading scripts for Columbia Pictures. Doctorow's first novel, *Welcome to Hard Times* (1960, filmed 1967), is a western that addresses Doctorow's recurrent philosophical concern of the correlation between man and evil. Doctorow frequently places notable figures of recent history in fictional situations, to the chagrin of some critics. *The Book of Daniel* (1971), for example, examines the Rosenberg TRIAL of the 1950s. *Ragtime* (1971, filmed 1981), arguably Doctorow's most popular novel, includes appearances by J. P. Morgan, Harry HOUDINI, and Henry FORD, among others. Other works include *World's Fair* (1985), *Billy Bathgate* (1989) and the play *Drinks Before Dinner* (1978). After *Billy Bathgate,* Doctorow published *Waterworks* (1994), *City of God* (2000), *Reporting the Universe* (2004), and *The March,* winner of the 2006 PEN/Faulkner Award for fiction and the National Book Critics Circle Award.

"Doctor's Plot" Alleged plot by some Moscow doctors to kill well-known government officials. The "conspiracy" was fully reported in the press in January 1953. The doctors, many of whom were Jewish, were said to have murdered Andrei ZHDANOV (1896–1948), head of the Leningrad Party Organization. This was probably the pretext for starting another great purge and was part of STALIN's anti-Semitic policy, but the death of Stalin in March 1953 saved the country from this. All but two of the doctors survived their ordeals and were released, and later KHRUSHCHEV stated that there had been no plot whatsoever and that it all had been engineered by Stalin.

Doctor Who From 1963 to 1989, a television series produced by the BRITISH BROADCASTING CORPORATION. *Doctor Who* was a phenomenally popular science fiction program that was syndicated in over 100 countries. Sets and costumes were resoundingly low budget in look, but outrageous scripts and characters conveyed an appealing blend of arch comedy and blatant melodrama. The central character, Doctor Who, is a 750-year-old native of the planet Gallifrey who—for convenience's sake—assumes human form for adventures that take him through-out the universe. Doctor Who was played by more than 10 actors during the show's long run. Novelizations of the teleplays have also been big sellers.

Doctor Zhivago Novel by Boris PASTERNAK, written during the 1940s and 1950s. The novel follows the life of Zhivago, a Moscow physician and poet, as he attempts to come to grips with the tumultuous changes brought by WORLD WAR I, the RUSSIAN REVOLUTION, the RUSSIAN CIVIL WAR and the policies of LENIN and STALIN. Although it does not directly criticize COMMUNISM or the revolution, the book's philosophical and spiritual outlook ran counter to the official doctrine of SOCIALIST REALISM, and Pasternak was refused permission to publish it in the Soviet Union. The manuscript was smuggled out and published in Italy in 1957 and in other Western countries soon thereafter. After Pasternak was awarded the 1958 NOBEL PRIZE in literature, he was denounced by Soviet authorities and forced to refuse the award. The book was not published in the USSR until 1987, under GORBACHEV's policy of GLASNOST. It was adapted as a motion picture by David LEAN (1965).

Dodd, Charles Harold *(1884–1973)* British theologian. Dodd was a highly influential figure in biblical studies in the 20th century, both as a general director of a major new translation of the New Testament (1966) and as a theological interpreter of the Gospels. Dodd was educated at Oxford and went on to teach there as well as at the universities of Manchester and Cambridge. In three major works—*The Parables of the Kingdom* (1935), *The Apostolic Preaching and Its Developments* (1936) and *History of the Gospel* (1938)—Dodd posed his theory of realized eschatology in which he argued that the coming of the Kingdom of God had already been fulfilled through the Incarnation of Christ and its historical impact upon human civilization. Other works by Dodd include *The Authority of the Bible* (1928), *The Epistle to the Romans* (1932), *The Bible and the Greeks* (1935) and *The Interpretation of the Fourth Gospel* (1953).

Dodd, Thomas *(1907–1971)* U.S. senator from Connecticut, censured for his misuse of campaign donations.

Before entering the Senate Dodd served in the federal government and was a prosecuting attorney at the NUREMBERG WAR CRIMES TRIALS following World War II. A Democrat, Dodd was elected to the House of Representatives in 1952, serving until his election to the U.S. Senate in 1958. Dodd generally supported liberal Democratic domestic programs and was known as a strong anticommunist. As senator, Dodd conducted hearings on the possible relation between crime and violence on television and its possible impact on juvenile delinquency; he charged that the television industry lacked imagination and responsibility. Dodd also favored strong gun-control legislation.

Between 1965 and 1967 columnists Drew PEARSON and Jack ANDERSON revealed that Dodd had used for personal purposes funds earmarked for his election campaign. A Senate investigation followed in 1966–67 and substantiated the allegations against Dodd. The Senate formally censured Dodd in 1967, but he was not expelled. He failed to win reelection to his Senate seat in 1970. His son **Chris Dodd** was later elected senator from Connecticut.

Dodecanese Islands Island chain in the Aegean Sea, southeast of the Greek mainland, between Crete and Asia Minor. It comprises most of an island area called the Southern Sporades, consisting of about 20 islands. The Turks forfeited the islands to ITALY in the Italo-Turkish War of 1911–12. The Germans gained control from their faltering Italian allies in 1943 during WORLD WAR II, but the Allies took over the islands in 1945; on March 31, 1947, by treaty, they were given to Greece.

Doderer, Heimito von (*1896–1966*) Austrian novelist. Doderer was educated as a historian in Vienna and served in the German air force in WORLD WAR II. Initially a Nazi sympathizer, he was stripped of his illusions about that ideology during the war, as his diaries of the time, published as *Tangenten* (1964, *Tangents*) indicate. Doderer is best known for his expansive novel *Die Dämonen* (1956; *The Demons*, 1961), which he began in 1931 and published on his 60th birthday. The novel, which depicts the nine months leading up to the burning of the Austrian supreme court in 1927, was praised as a masterpiece upon its

publication in German-speaking countries. It has never received the same acclaim in the U.S., although it was praised by Thornton WILDER. Doderer's other works include *Die Strudlhofstiege* (1951), *Grundlagen und Funktion des Romans* 1959) and *Die Merowinger* (*The Merowingians*, 1962).

Dodge, Raymond (*1871–1942*) American educator and experimental psychologist. Best known for his studies of the brain and the motor movements of the eye during the act of reading, Dodge began his academic career at Wesleyan University, where he taught from 1898 to 1924. He was also a member of the Institute of Psychology at Yale. His studies of eye movement were applied directly to gunners during WORLD WAR I. He also studied extensively the psychological effects of alcohol on humans. His written works include *Conditions and Consequences of Human Variability* (1931) and *The Craving for Superiority* (1931).

Dodge brothers American automobile manufacturers. **Horace E. Dodge** (*1868–1920*) and **John Dodge** (*1864–1920*) began their careers by making bicycles and stove parts. Soon they were manufacturing engines and auto parts for Ford Motor Company and Olds Motor Works. On November 14, 1914, the first Dodge automobile was produced, and the brothers started their own auto manufacturing business. They built one of the first all-steel American cars, and Horace Dodge invented many improvements for the industry. Both of the Dodge brothers died in 1920, and their company was taken over by the Chrysler Corporation in 1928.

Doe, Samuel (*1951–1990*) Military ruler of Liberia (1980–90). Born into the Krahn tribe, Doe began his military career in 1969 when he enlisted in the Liberian army, eventually rising to the rank of master sergeant. In April 1980 Doe led an attack by rebel soldiers on the Liberian capital of Monrovia. The rebels eventually seized the city and assassinated President William Tolbert Jr. and 13 key members of his administration. Following this coup Doe, who assumed the rank of general, formed the People's Redemption Council. The council elected him president of LIBERIA, a post he held for the next 10

years. In 1985 Doe ran for president in what he claimed were open and free elections. After Doe was elected, international observers labeled the election fraudulent. As leader of Liberia, Doe failed to bring about a peaceful resolution of the conflict between the indigenous African population of the Liberian state and the descendants of those 19th-century African-American émigrés from the U.S. who had founded the republic. He also failed to reverse the economic decline of Liberia that began under his rule. In efforts to quell resistance to his rule and to put a stop to the periodic assassination attempts against him, Doe repeatedly turned to the Krahn tribe for assistance in suppressing his domestic opposition.

In 1989 Doe's opponents launched a rebellion against his government. Headed by Charles TAYLOR and his National Patriotic Front of Liberia (NPFL), the insurgents managed to gain control of all parts of the country save the capital by July 1990. In September of that year, while evading attacks by the NPFL, Doe was assassinated by the Independent National Patriotic Front of Liberia, a faction that had split from the NPFL.

Doenitz, Karl (*1891–1980*) German admiral. Born in Prussia, Doenitz entered the Imperial German Navy and specialized in SUBMARINE warfare from 1916 onward. The architect and commander of GERMANY's submarine campaign against Allied shipping, he was appointed commander in chief of the navy in 1943. He succeeded Adolf HITLER as leader of Nazi Germany after the Führer's death in May 1945 and surrendered to the Allies six days later. Doenitz was among those tried and convicted of war crimes at the NUREMBERG TRIALS, and he served 10 years in Berlin's SPANDAU PRISON.

Doesburg, Theo van (**C. E. M. Küpper**) (*1883–1931*) Dutch architect and designer, a major figure in the de Stijl movement of the 1920s. Van Doesburg began his career as a painter but was drawn toward architecture through collaboration with J. J. P. Oud and Jan Wils beginning in 1916. In 1917 he founded the magazine *De Stijl*. He taught briefly at the BAUHAUS in 1922. His reputation rests on his paintings and in large measure on drawings and models for works never executed.

His only completed projects were an entertainment group at the Aubette in Strasbourg, France, of 1928 (since demolished) and a house at Meudon of 1931. A kit for a paper model of the "Maison d'Artiste," reproducing the model van Doesburg and Cornelis van Eesteren designed in 1923 for an exhibition in Paris, is currently available.

Dogger Bank Incident International incident on October 21, 1904, during the RUSSO-JAPANESE WAR. On its way to the Far East, a Russian fleet under the command of Admiral Zinovy Rozhdestvensky encountered vessels believed to be Japanese torpedo boats on the Dogger Bank, North Sea sandbanks located between Great Britain and Denmark. The Russians fired on the boats, killing two crew members and sinking one vessel. However, the boats were really English fishing trawlers, and fury in Great Britain over the attack was so great the incident almost led to war. Compensation claims for the attack were ultimately paid to Britain by Russia.

Dohnányi, Ernst von (*1877–1960*) Hungarian composer, pianist and conductor. Studying at Budapest's Royal Academy (1894–97), he was later its director. He made his piano debut in Berlin in 1897, touring Europe and America to considerable acclaim until 1908, when he began teaching at the Berlin Hochschule. He remained there until 1915 and became associate director of Hungary's Franz Liszt Academy in 1919. Dohnányi conducted the Budapest Philharmonic Orchestra from 1919 to 1944. He left Hungary after World War II and settled in the U.S. in 1949, teaching first at Ohio State University, then at Florida State University, where he remained until his death. Greatly influenced by Brahms, his compositions include *Variations on a Nursery Song* (1913) and *American Rhapsody* (1954) as well as many other orchestral works, songs, piano pieces, chamber music and three operas. He was the grandfather of conductor Christoph von Dohnányi.

Dole, Bob (**Robert Joseph Dole**) (*1923– *) American political leader. A native of Kansas, Dole was seriously wounded in Italy during World War II. After receiving a law degree from Washburn University in 1952, he served as a county attorney until he was elected to the House of Representatives as a Republican in 1960. After serving four terms in the House, Dole was elected to the Senate in 1968. He was chairman of the Republican National Committee from 1971 to 1973, including the early part of the Watergate scandal that eventually led to the resignation of President Richard NIXON. He was President Gerald FORD's vice presidential running mate during his unsuccessful presidential campaign in 1976. Serving as Senate majority leader in 1985–87 and 1995–96, Dole became the legislative spokesman for the Republican Party. After unsuccessful campaigns to win his party's nomination for president in 1980 and 1988, Dole won the nomination in 1996 but lost the election to President Bill CLINTON. He married **Elizabeth Hanford Dole**, who was elected to the Senate in 2002.

Dolin, Sir Anton (**Sydney Francis Patrick Chippendall Healey-Kay**) (*1904–1983*) The first male British ballet dancer to gain an international reputation. Dolin's work with Serge DIAGHILEV's BALLETS RUSSES in the 1920s helped launch his career. He then formed a highly acclaimed partnership with Alicia MARKOVA, which lasted more than two decades. During the 1940s Dolin worked as ballet master, choreographer and premier danseur with Ballet Theater, the forerunner of the AMERICAN BALLET THEATRE. In 1950 he helped organize the London Festival Ballet.

Dollfuss, Engelbert (*1892–1934*) Austrian political leader. A WORLD WAR I hero and devout Catholic, Dollfuss became a member of the Christian Social Party and a leader in the Farmers' League. He was an effective minister of agriculture and forestry (1931–32) during the GREAT DEPRESSION and was appointed chancellor in 1932. Dollfuss suspended parliamentary government in 1933 and subsequently quelled a socialist revolt in 1934. Allied with HORTHY in Hungary and MUSSOLINI in Italy, he promulgated a new fascist constitution in 1934 but opposed ANSCHLUSS with GERMANY in his support of an independent AUSTRIA. He was assassinated by Austrian Nazis during their attempt at a coup d'état.

Dolly (*1997–2003*) A sheep born in Scotland in 1997 as a result of an attempt at artificially producing an animal clone. Because of health complications brought on by prematurely aged organs and other physical ailments, Dolly was put to sleep on February 14, 2003. (See also CLONES AND CLONING.)

Domagk, Gerhard (*1895–1964*) German biochemist. Domagk graduated in medicine from the University of Kiel in 1921 and began teaching at the University of Greifswald and later at the University of Munster. At this time he carried out important research into phagocytes—special cells that attack bacteria in the body. He became interested in chemotherapy and in 1927 was appointed director of research in experimental pathology and pathological anatomy at the giant chemical factory I. G. Farben at Wuppertal-Elberfeld. Pursuing the ideas of Paul EHRLICH, Domagk tested new dyes—produced by the Elberfeld chemists—for their strength against various infections. In 1935 he reported the effectiveness of an orange-red dye called prontosil in combating streptococcal infections. For the first time a chemical had been found to be active in vivo against a common small bacterium. Earlier dyes used as drugs were active only against infections caused by the much larger protozoa. The work was followed up in research laboratories throughout the world. Alexander FLEMING even neglected his experiments with PENICILLIN to study prontosil in the early 1930s. The most significant ramifications of his work were discovered by Daniel BOVET and his coworkers. Prontosil and the sulfa drugs that followed were effective in saving many people from death, including Franklin D. ROOSEVELT, Winston CHURCHILL and Domagk's own daughter. In 1939 Domagk was offered the NOBEL PRIZE in physiology or medicine. The Nazis forced him to withdraw his acceptance because HITLER was annoyed with the Nobel Committee for awarding the 1935 Peace Prize to Carl von OSSIETZKY, a German whom Hitler had imprisoned. In 1947 Domagk was finally able to accept the prize. In his later years he undertook drug research into cancer and tuberculosis.

Domingo, Plácido (*1941– *) Spanish-born opera singer. Since the 1960s

Domingo has been regarded as one of the great dramatic and lyric tenors of his generation. He began his professional career as a baritone in his family's zarzuela (Spanish operetta) company and made his opera debut in 1961 with the Baltimore Civic Opera. That same year he changed his vocal range to tenor and sang the role of Alfredo in *La Traviata*. In 1962 he married soprano Marte Ornelas, and together they appeared with the Hebrew National Opera. He joined the New York City Opera in 1965 and achieved star status after singing the title role in the American premiere of *Don Rodrigo*. He made his Metropolitan Opera debut in 1968, subsequently becoming one of that company's principal tenors. Domingo has performed worldwide and sung a wide range of roles, including Hoffman in *The Tales of Hoffman* and the title roles in *Don Carlo* and *Otello* (also appearing in Franco ZEFFIRELLI's film version of the latter). He has also recorded popular music and has branched out into opera conducting. Throughout the 1990s Domingo performed and recorded several classical opera pieces on *Opera Classics* (1993) and *Opera Gala* (1996). In 1994 he began to exhibit his interest in Latin American songs and released *From My Latin Soul* (1994), which contained renditions of popular Latin tunes.

Dominica Small island nation in the Windward Islands of the West Indies, north of MARTINIQUE and south of GUADELOUPE. In 1833 Great Britain incorporated Dominica with the Leeward

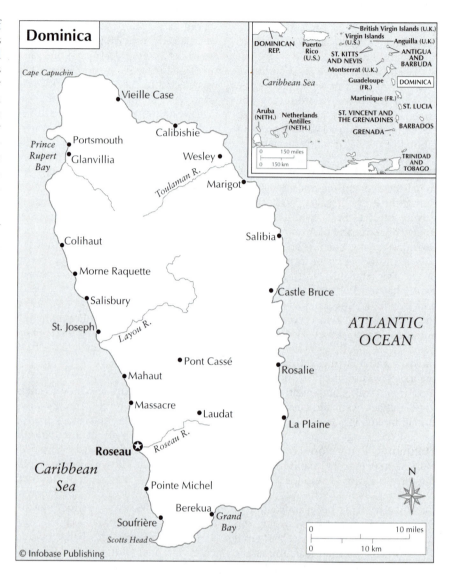

DOMINICA	
1940	The island is transferred to the British Windward Islands federation.
1958–62	Dominica becomes part of the West Indies Federation.
1967	Dominica is granted separate, semi-independent status.
1978	Dominica achieves full independence within the Commonwealth.
1980	Mary Eugenia Charles becomes the first female prime minister in the Caribbean
1989	Hurricane Hugo causes severe damage to the island and its banana industry.
1995	After 15 years in office, Prime Minister Charles resigns. Edison James becomes prime minister
2000	Pierre Charles is elected prime minister.
2004	Roosevelt Skerrit becomes prime minister after the death of Charles.

Islands, and in 1940 administration was switched to the Windward Islands. The island was a member of the short-lived WEST INDIES FEDERATION from 1958 to 1962, was given internal self-government in 1967 and achieved independence in 1978. The 1995 election victory of the United Workers Party (UWP) resulted in Edison James's appointment as prime minister. Under James, Dominica began an effort to become a principal provider of offshore financial services for the global market. Dominica has remained committed to this objective despite the defeat of the UWP in the 2000 general elections, a deep recession that began in 2002 and several hurricane disasters.

Dominican Republic Island nation in the West Indies, inhabiting the eastern two-thirds of the island of Hispaniola, southeast of Cuba. Political upheavals, governmental changes and burgeoning financial difficulties abounded until the early 20th century. It went bankrupt in 1905 when European nations threatened force in col-

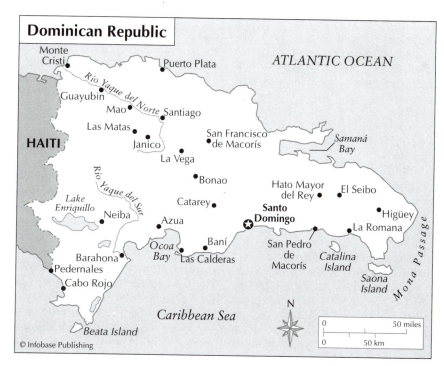

lecting money they were owed. U.S. president Theodore ROOSEVELT stepped in, and the U.S. assumed management

of customs receipts. The financial picture improved, but the U.S. dominated the country. Unrest persisted, and in

DOMINICAN REPUBLIC

1905	The United States takes over the near-bankrupt republic's debts.
1916–24	The Dominican Republic is temporarily occupied by U.S. forces.
1930	Rafael Leonidas Trujillo overthrows Horacio Vásquez and begins a three-decade-long dictatorship.
1937	Following Haiti's discovery of Dominican spies on its soil, Trujillo orders slaughter of 10,000 to 20,000 Haitian immigrants.
1961	Trujillo assassinated.
1962	Juan Bosch of leftist Dominican Revolutionary Party (PRD) elected president.
1963	Bosch overthrown in military coup.
1965	Uprising by Bosch supporters succeeds temporarily; civil war ensues with rightist military officers; United States intervenes decisively in support of rightists.
1966	Balaguer, leading right-wing Reformist Party, wins election.
1978	PRD wins power under Silvestre Antonio Guzmán Fernández.
1982	Guzmán commits suicide; PRD retains presidency as Salvador Jorge Blanco is elected.
1990	Balaguer reelected by slim margin over Bosch
1994	Balaguer wins sixth term as president
1996	Leonel Fernández Reyna elected president with barely 51% of vote in runoff.
2000	Hipólito Mejía of PRD elected president.

1916 the U.S. Marines began keeping the peace. They stayed until 1924, but customs management continued until 1941. In 1930 Rafael TRUJILLO MOLINA began a 31-year dictatorial reign, one of the most inhumane in history. In 1937 Dominican troops attempting to prevent Haitians from entering the country stormed Haiti and slaughtered thousands.

Trujillo was murdered in 1961, and the first free elections since 1924 were held in December 1962. Leftist Juan BOSCH was elected president but was overthrown by a right-wing military revolt. An effort was made in April 1965 to reinstate Bosch, sparking a civil war that was followed by the arrival of U.S. troops sent by U.S. president JOHNSON. The ORGANIZATION OF AMERICAN STATES organized a peacekeeping force that eventually supplanted the U.S. troops, and in September both groups accepted Héctor García Godoy as interim president. OAS forces were removed, but the Dominicans continued to be cursed by political upheaval and economic problems, despite the 1966 election of President Joaquín BALAGUER and his 15-year improvement plan. In May 1978 the army interrupted voting when it appeared that Balaguer would lose a re-election attempt. U.S. president CARTER intervened with a forcefully worded diplomatic note, and the army was obliged to allow the election of leftist President Antonio Guzmán, who committed suicide after his term in August 1982. His successor, Dr. Jorge Salvador Blanco, was later convicted of corruption and sentenced to 20 years' imprisonment (1988). For several years sugar has been the leading export, and in recent times its low price has caused hardship. Santo Domingo is the capital. In 1996 the leftist candidate Leonel Fernández Reyna of the Dominican Liberation Party (PLD) was elected president. Fernández oversaw some privatization of state-owned companies. In 2000 Hipólito Mejía of the Dominican Revolutionary Party (PRD) was elected president.

Domino, Antoine "Fats" *(1928–)* African-American ROCK and roll singer and pianist. Domino is one of the distinctive vocal stylists in rock-and-roll history. He has also enjoyed incredible popularity, selling over 65 million records—all featuring his warm, bluesy singing voice—accompanied by his pounding, boogie-woogie piano. Domino was born in New Orleans into a musical family: His father was a well-known violinist, and his brother-in-law later became lead guitarist in Domino's band. Domino recorded his first successful single, "The Fat Man" (1950), when he was 21. Over the next two decades came classic hits including "Ain't It a Shame" (1955), "Blueberry Hill" (1956), "I'm Walkin'" (1957), "Whole Lotta Loving" (1958), "I'm Ready" (1959), "Walkin' to New Orleans" (1960) and "Let the Four Winds Blow" (1961).

domino theory Theory used by several U.S. presidents as a rationale for U.S. presence and military intervention in Southeast Asia. The domino theory argued that if the U.S. did not make a stand in South VIETNAM, then the rest of the nations of Southeast Asia and beyond—CAMBODIA, LAOS, THAILAND, MALAYSIA, BURMA, INDONESIA, the PHILIPPINES—would accommodate to communist power and eventually topple one after the other like a stack of dominoes. It is true that with American abandonment of South Vietnam in 1975, the Laotian and Cambodian "dominoes" fell in rapid succession. But the almost quarter century of U.S. involvement in Vietnam gave other nations an opportunity to resist communist expansion and build their own defenses. Indonesia fell toward the West in 1965, and Thailand successfully repelled communist attacks on its eastern borders in the 1980s.

Dong, Pham Van See PHAM VAN DONG.

Donleavy, James Patrick *(1926–)* Irish author. Born in New York of Irish parents, Donleavy was educated at Trinity College, Dublin, and became an Irish citizen in 1967. His first novel, *The Ginger Man* (1955), is a bawdy and scatological tale of a law student in Dublin. The book was refused by many publishers as obscene; Donleavy was finally able to have it published in Paris. The book, comic in tone, shows the influence of James JOYCE. Critics cited it as his most important work, despite the greater success of his later novels, which include *Schultz* (1979) and *Are You Listening Rabbi Loew* (1987, a sequel to *Schultz*). Donleavy has also written the plays *Fairy Tales of New York* (1961, based on his book of the same title), *A Singular Man* (1964) and others based on his fiction.

Donnan, Frederick George *(1879–1956)* British chemist. He was educated at Queen's College, Belfast, and the Universities of Leipzig and Berlin, where he obtained his Ph.D. in 1896 and acquired some of the German expertise in physical chemistry. On his return to England he worked at University College, London, with William Ramsay from 1898 until 1904, when he accepted the post of professor of physical chemistry at the University of Liverpool. In 1913 Donnan returned to succeed Ramsay at University College and remained there until his retirement in 1937. Donnan is mainly remembered for the Donnan membrane equilibrium (1911)—a theory describing the equilibrium that occurs when ions pass through membranes.

Donoso, José *(1924–1996)* Chilean novelist and short story writer. Born in Santiago, Donoso received a B.A. from Princeton in 1951. His realist works, *Veraneo y otros cuentos* (1955, Summertime and other stories) and *Coronación* (1957; translated in 1965 as *Coronation*), were published only after Donoso guaranteed sales of 100 copies by subscription. He also peddled his books on street corners. His reputation is based on *El obsceno pájaro de la noche* (1970; translated in 1973 as *The Obscene Bird of Night*), an experimental, hallucinatory novel full of freaks and monsters and narrated by a deaf-mute. His *Historia personal del "Boom"* (1972; translated in 1977 as *The Boom in Spanish American Literature*) traces the rise of the Latin novel during the 1960s, focusing on the emergence of such writers as BORGES, FUENTES, VARGAS LLOSA and Donoso himself.

Donovan, William "Wild Bill" *(1883–1959)* Director of the U.S. OFFICE OF STRATEGIC SERVICES, the WORLD WAR II forerunner of the CENTRAL INTELLIGENCE AGENCY. Born in Buffalo, New York, Donovan attended Columbia University and Columbia Law School. After serving in the army in WORLD WAR I, Donovan became active in New York State Republican politics and served as U.S. district attorney in the state and as assistant U.S. attorney general; he also ran unsuccessfully for lieutenant governor of New York in 1922 and for governor in 1932. Donovan conducted several sensitive fact-finding missions in Europe for the U.S. government during the early years of WORLD WAR II. In mid-1941, he urged President Franklin D. ROOSEVELT to establish an American intelligence agency comparable to Britain's Secret Intelligence Service; in June 1942 the OFFICE OF STRATEGIC SERVICES (OSS) was formed. During the war the OSS proved extremely useful to the Allied cause, and in July 1947 the CIA was established as its peacetime successor. After acting as an aide during the NUREMBERG TRIALS, Donovan retired from the military as a major general. From 1953 to 1954 he served as U.S. ambassador to Thailand.

Doodson, Arthur Thomas *(1890–1968)* British mathematical physicist. Doodson was educated at the University of Liverpool. After working at University College, London, from 1916 to 1918 he joined the Tidal Institute, Liverpool, in 1919 as its secretary. Doodson remained through its reformation as the Liverpool Observatory and Tidal Institute as assistant director (1929–45) and as director until his retirement in 1960. Much of Doodson's early work was on the production of mathematical tables and the calculation of trajectories for artillery. Proving himself an ingenious, powerful and practical mathematician, he found an ideal subject for his talents in the complicated behavior of the tides. He made many innovations to achieve more accurate computations about them and, with H. Warburg in 1942, produced the *Admiralty Manual of Tides*.

Doolittle, Hilda (H.D.) *(1886–1961)* American poet. Born in Bethlehem, Pennsylvania, she moved to England in 1911 and married fellow poet Richard ALDINGTON in 1913. Heavily influenced by Ezra POUND, she became an important member of the imagist group. Her free-form verse is characterized by both vividness and precision. H.D.'s volumes of poetry include *Sea Garden* (1916), *Collected Poems* (1925 and 1940), *The Walls Do Not Fall* (1944) and *Bid Me to Live* (1960).

Doolittle, James Harold *(1896–1993)* American aviator. Born in Alameda, California, he served as a flyer in WORLD WAR I and, after the war, was an aeronautic specialist, civilian test pilot and airborne racer. In 1922 he became the first pilot to cross North America within 24 hours. Recalled to the U.S. Army Air Corps in 1940, Doolittle gained worldwide recognition as the commander of the bold bombing RAID ON TOKYO on April 18, 1942. Subsequently, he commanded the 12th Air Force during the landing in North Africa, headed the Anglo-American Strategic Air Force in the the Mediterranean (1944) and led the Eighth Air Force in Europe (1944) and the Pacific (1945). Awarded the Medal of Honor, he resigned from the army as a lieutenant general in 1945.

Doors, The American rock and roll band. The Doors, featuring lead singer Jim Morrison, remain one of the most popular rock bands to emerge from the psychedelic era of the 1960s. Hits such as "Light My Fire" (1967) and "Hello, I Love You" (1968) are still played regularly on radio stations. The band first formed in Los Angeles in the mid-1960s. Other band members included keyboard player Ray Manzarek, guitarist Robbie Krieger and drummer John Densmore. Morrison, a charismatic figure who abused both drugs

Lieutenant General James Doolittle. 1942 (LIBRARY OF CONGRESS, PRINTS AND PHOTOGRAPHS DIVISION)

and alcohol, died of a heart attack in 1971, at age 27.

Dorati, Antal *(1906–1988)* Hungarian-born conductor. During a career that spanned more than 60 years, Dorati served as principal conductor for more than a dozen organizations, including the Dallas Symphony, the Minneapolis Symphony, the Stockholm Philharmonic and the Royal Philharmonic. He led the National Symphony in the inaugural concert at the John F. Kennedy Center for the Performing Arts in Washington in 1971. Of the more than 500 recordings Dorati made during his lifetime, his interpretations of the Haydn symphonies were particularly praised.

Dorn, Friedrich Ernst *(1848–1916)* German physicist. Dorn studied at Konigsberg and in 1873 was made professor of physics at Breslau. In 1886 he transferred to a professorship at Halle and started working with X-RAYS. He is noted for his discovery, in 1900, that the radioactive element radium gives off a radioactive gas, which Dorn called radium emanation. The gas was isolated in 1908 by William Ramsay, who named it niton. The name radon was adopted in 1923. Dorn's discovery is the first established demonstration of a transmutation of one element into another.

Dornberger, Walter *(1895–1980)* German-born rocket engineer. When Germany decided to develop experimental rockets in the 1920s, Dornberger, then an army officer, was named to head the project. His team produced Germany's first rocket engine (1932) and its first launches (1934). During WORLD WAR II, working with Werner von BRAUN, he headed the development of the German V-2 rocket bomb at PEENEMUNDE. A lieutenant general, he directed the firing of more than 1,000 deadly rockets on London and its suburbs in the last years of the war. At the end of the war, he was working on a rocket bomb designed to reach New York from German territory. Along with Kurt DEBUS and von Braun, he surrendered to the U.S. Army rather than to Russians at the end of the war. Following his de-Nazification, he immigrated to the U.S. and became an American citizen. He served as an adviser to the U.S. Air Force and worked for military industries in the U.S. (See also OPERATION PAPERCLIP.)

Dors, Diana (Diana Fluck) *(1931–1984)* British actress, once billed as Britain's answer to Marilyn MONROE. Dors was known as the "blond bombshell" of films from the early 1950s to the 1960s. When she was 25 years old she was Britain's highest-paid actress, with a contract valued at more than £500,000. Her films were less than memorable, but she held the public's interest with revelations about her colorful private life and three marriages. Before her death she appeared as a television advice columnist.

Dorsey brothers Tommy Dorsey (1905–56) and **Jimmy Dorsey** (1904–57) Dorsey were jazz instrumentalists and big band leaders whose Dorsey Brothers Orchestra, one of the premier jazz big bands of the 1930s, lasted only one year, from 1934 to 1935. But both brothers went on to even greater success with their separate big bands from the 1930s and into the 1950s—and became jazz legends. Jimmy, who played alto saxophone and clarinet, and Tommy, who played trombone, had been renowned sidemen in the 1920s and early 1930s, when they were featured with numerous bands and in the Broadway musical *Everybody's Welcome* (1931). With the founding of the Dorsey Brothers Orchestra, they and their theme song "Sandman" became nationally famous. After quarreling in 1935, the brothers went their separate ways for over a decade before working together on the Hollywood biographical film *The Fabulous Dorseys* (1947). From 1953 to 1956 the Dorsey brothers again performed together in a big band led by Tommy.

Dos Passos, John Roderigo *(1896–1970)* American novelist. After graduating from Harvard University, Dos Passos traveled to Spain intending to study architecture. WORLD WAR I intervened, and he volunteered for the French ambulance corps, later becoming a private in the U.S. Army medical corps. His first two books, *One Man's Initiation—1917* (1920) and *Three Soldiers* (1921), bitterly portray the effects of war on the three main characters. By 1925 in *Manhattan Transfer,* he had arrived at his unique style combining naturalism and STREAM OF CONSCIOUSNESS. Perhaps his best-known work is the trilogy *U.S.A.,* which is an expression of his radical approach to life and consists of *The 42nd Parallel* (1930), *1919* (1932) and *The Big Money* (1936). These traced the first three decades of the 20th century, in which he found absurdity, moral deterioration and helplessness—all reflected in the lives of his characters. He incorporated fragments of the era's popular culture into the novels, juxtaposing his characters against prominent Americans of the time. His later work became more conservative, and he eventually expressed disillusion with liberal and radical movements. Later novels include *The Great Days* (1958) and *MidCentury* (1961). He also wrote biographies and works on travel and history.

dos Santos, José Eduardo *(1942–)* Angolan politician. Born in Luanda, dos Santos joined the Soviet-backed Popular Movement for the Liberation of Angola (MPLA) in 1961 and went into exile that same year. Sent to the USSR by the MPLA in 1963, he returned to Africa and graduated from college with an engineering degree in 1969. He fought for Angolan independence from 1970 to 1974, assuming various party offices during the 1970s. He served as planning minister from 1978 to 1979 and became head of the MPLA and president of ANGOLA after the death of Agostinho NETO in 1979. In 1992 dos Santos was elected Angolan president over UNITA candidate Jonas SAVIMBI.

Double Eagle II, flight of the First transatlantic crossing by balloon—August 17, 1978. Three Americans—Max Anderson, Ben Abaruzzo and Larry Newman—successfully completed the trip in the *Double Eagle II* when they landed in a wheat field 60 miles west of Paris. They had departed from Presque Isle, Maine, on August 11 and had set an endurance record of 137 hours, 18 minutes aloft, during which they had withstood icy conditions and extreme cold over the Atlantic. Abaruzzo and Anderson had attempted the journey in 1977 in the *Double Eagle I* but had been forced down five miles off the coast of Iceland.

Doubrovska, Felia (Felizata Dluzhnevska) *(1896–1981)* Russian ballerina. Doubrovska was trained at the Imperial Academy in St. Petersburg. After graduating (1913) she joined the Maryinsky Theater there and with that troupe remained through the RUSSIAN REVOLUTION. In 1920 she fled to Paris and joined Serge DIAGHILEV's BALLETS RUSSES, dancing in many principal roles choreographed by the legendary George BALANCHINE. After moving to the U.S., she became prima ballerina of the Metropolitan Opera Ballet (1938) but retired from the stage the following year. She subsequently joined the faculty at the School of American Ballet at Balanchine's invitation and in a long second career became one of the most highly regarded ballet teachers in the U.S. Doubrovska was known as the archetypal Balanchine dancer.

Douglas, Aaron *(1899–1979)* American painter. A native of Kansas, Douglas studied in New York and Paris. He was a leading artist during the HARLEM RENAISSANCE of the late 1920s. He was the first African-American artist recognized for incorporating African iconography into American art. He was known for his murals and his illustrations of books by black American authors.

Douglas, Donald Wills, Sr. *(1892–1981)* American pioneer aircraft designer, engineer and manufacturer. Founder of the DOUGLAS AIRCRAFT CO., Douglas built airplanes that helped bring about the era of mass commercial air travel. While in his 20s he learned about aircraft design by working on the development of a heavy bomber for Glenn Martin's company. In 1920 he set up his own company with backing from a wealthy investor. He designed the first aircraft (*Cloudster*) that could carry a load heavier than its own weight. He also designed and developed the airplane that made the first flight around the world in the early 1920s. His company, which dominated the aviation industry during the period when airplanes were driven by propellers, was perhaps best known for the twin-engine DC-3, introduced in 1935. This classic and reliable craft became a familiar sight around the world, hauling passengers, cargo and military loads; DC-3s were still in service 50 years after the first one taxied down a runway. Douglas also produced military aircraft used by the U.S. during WORLD WAR II (including the C-47 military transport and the A-20 attack bomber) and the KOREAN WAR. In 1958 the company introduced the DC-8 passenger jetliner, which (with the Boeing 707) helped revolutionize airline travel. Douglas's fortunes declined in the 1960s. In 1967 the company merged with the McDONNELL Aircraft Corp. to form McDonnell Douglas Corp. In 1997 it became part of Boeing.

Douglas, Helen Gahagan (Helen Gahagan) *(1900–1980)* American actress, concert singer and politician. A liberal Democrat from California, she served in the U.S. House of Representatives (1944–50). She won national recognition during a bitter election campaign for the U.S. Senate in 1950, in which she was defeated by Representative Richard M. NIXON. During the campaign, Nixon accused her of being a communist sympathizer. Gahagan was married to the actor Melvyn DOUGLAS.

Douglas, Kirk (Issur Danielovitch Demsky) *(1916–)* American actor; son of an illiterate Russian ragpicker and junkman, Douglas grew up to become one of Hollywood's legendary "tough guy" stars in the 1940s and 1950s. After graduating from the American Academy of Dramatic Arts, he starred on Broadway in shows such as *Spring Again* (1941), then enlisted in the navy. In 1946 he made his film debut in *The Strange Love of Martha Ivers*, but it wasn't until his eighth film—*Champion* (1949)—that he became a recognized star. His dynamic, powerhouse performances can be found in such films as *Ace in the Hole* (1951), *Detective Story* (1951), *The Bad and the Beautiful* (1952), *Lust for Life* (1956), *Paths of Glory* (1957), *Lonely Are the Brave* (1962) and many others. Douglas was also the producer of several films in which he acted, including *The Vikings* (1958) and *Spartacus* (1960), for which he courageously hired the blacklisted writer Dalton Trumbo. In 1988 Douglas earned praise for his autobiography, *The Ragman's Son;* he has also written fiction. Douglas's son **Michael Douglas** (by his first wife, Diana Douglas) is also a respected film actor and has won acclaim

for his roles in *Fatal Attraction* (1987) and *Black Rain* (1989). In 2003 Kirk Douglas starred with his son Michael and his grandson Cameron in the comedy *It Runs in the Family.*

Douglas, Melvyn (Melvin Edouard Hesselberg) *(1901–1981)* Melvyn Douglas began his career as a leading man in HOLLYWOOD romantic films of the 1930s and 1940s, playing opposite some of the leading female stars of the day; he later shifted to character roles on stage and screen. He appeared in 77 films and won two ACADEMY AWARDS for best supporting actor (1963, 1980).

Douglas, Thomas Clement *(1904–1986)* Scottish-born Canadian political leader. Douglas set up the first socialist government in North America after being elected premier of the province of Saskatchewan in 1944 on the Cooperative Commonwealth Federation slate. During the 16 years that he served as premier, he introduced a host of social and economic reforms and laid the groundwork for North America's first medicare plan. He resigned in 1961 to become the first national leader of the NEW DEMOCRATIC PARTY, a socialist coalition of farmers, intellectuals and trade unionists. He led the party through four general elections and represented it in Parliament from 1962 to 1968 and again from 1969 to 1979.

Douglas, William Orville *(1898–1980)* Associate justice of the U.S. Supreme Court. With a law degree from Columbia University in 1925, he taught at the university between 1925 and 1928. After serving in various federal posts, he was made chairman of the Securities and Exchange Commission in 1937 and was appointed to the Supreme Court in 1939. Generally considered a liberal, Douglas defended individual liberties throughout his career and was one of the most controversial figures in the recent history of the Court. He retired from the Court in 1975 but continued an active public life. An aggressive outdoorsman, Douglas wrote several books, including *Men and Mountains* (1950), *A Wilderness Bill of Rights* (1965), *The Bible and the Schools* (1966) and *Points of Rebellion* (1969).

Douglas Aircraft Co. Leading American airplane builder whose 1930s products are credited with having made air transportation practical as a form of mass transport. The firm was founded in 1920 by Donald Wills DOUGLAS and developed the pioneer low-wing, twin-engined monoplanes, the DC-1 and DC-2, predecessors of the famous DC-3, one of the most successful airplanes ever produced. Later Douglas products, beginning with the DC-4, introduced tricycle landing gear and moved to four engines. The DC-8 was a highly successful four-engined jet transport. The successor company, McDonnell Douglas, continued production of the modern DC-9 and DC-10 jet transport aircraft. In 1997 Boeing and McDonnell Douglas merged.

Douglas-Home, Sir Alec (Alexander Frederick Douglas-Home; Baron Home of the Hirsel) *(1903–1995)* British politician and prime minister (1963–64). Born into a titled family, he was educated at Eton and Oxford. A member of the CONSERVATIVE PARTY, he entered the House of Commons in 1931. Parliamentary private secretary to Prime Minister Neville CHAMBERLAIN from 1937 to 1939, he succeeded his father as 14th earl of Home in 1951 and resigned from his seat in the Commons, moving automatically to the House of Lords. He served as minister of state from 1951 to 1955, minister for commonwealth relations (1955–60), leader of the House of Lords (1957–60) and foreign secretary (1960–63). Following Harold MACMILLAN's resignation in October 1963, Douglas-Home disclaimed his peerage to become prime minister as Sir Alec Douglas-Home (winning a by-election to return to the House of Commons). Following his defeat by Harold WILSON in the October 1964 general election, he became leader of the opposition until 1965, when he stood down, being replaced by Edward HEATH. In 1970 he was appointed foreign secretary by Heath. Following the Conservative defeat in 1974, he was created a life peer. His brother, William Douglas-Home, was a noted playwright.

Douglass, Andrew Ellicott *(1867–1962)* American astronomer and dendrochronologist. Douglass came from a family of academics, and his father and grandfather were college presidents. He graduated from Trinity College, Hartford, Connecticut, in 1889 and in the same year was appointed to an assistantship at Harvard College Observatory. In 1894 he went with Percival Lowell to the new Lowell Observatory in Flagstaff, Arizona, and became a professor of astronomy and physics at the University of Arizona in 1906.

Initially Douglass was interested in the 11-year sunspot cycle. While trying to trace its history he was led to the examination of tree rings in the hope that he would find some identifiable correlation between sunspot activity and terrestrial climate and vegetation. Soon tree rings became the center of his studies. Douglass found that he could identify local tree rings with confidence and use them in dating past climatic trends. He thus founded the field of dendrochronology. By the late 1920s he had a sequence of more than a thousand tree rings having six thin rings, presumably records of a severe drought that correlated with the end of the 13th century. In 1929 he found some timber that contained the six thin rings and plus a further 500. This took him to the eighth century and over the years he managed to get as far as the first century. This was extended still further and by careful analysis scholars have now established a sequence going back almost to 5000 B.C. The dated rings of Arizona and New Mexico, however, were found not to correlate with sequences from other parts of the world: The tree-ring clock was a purely local one. The search for a more universal clock continued, while the method of **radiocarbon dating** was developed by Willard LIBBY in 1949.

Dover British port on the English Channel, 71 miles southeast of London, in Kent. A key crossing point between Britain and France, it served as a naval base in WORLD WAR I and was heavily shelled by German guns in WORLD WAR II. The British end of the ENGLISH CHANNEL TUNNEL is near Dover.

doves Term originally used to describe Americans advocating negotiation or reduction of U.S. involvement in VIETNAM in the 1960s and 1970s. The term came to be applied to politicians taking moderate stances on foreign policy issues and opposed to the use of military force in general. (See also HAWKS; VIETNAM WAR.)

Dovzhenko, Alexander Petrovich *(1894–1956)* Film director. Of a Cossack family, Dovzhenko was appointed People's Artist of the Russian Soviet Federated Socialist Republic in 1950. He started in films in 1926, having previously been a teacher and a painter. His *Arsenal* (1929) and *Earth* (1930), in which he used a variety of techniques, all infused with poetic lyricism, brought him fame but were denounced by official critics as counterrevolutionary. *Shchors,* made in 1939, is the story of a Ukranian Red Army hero. Among his other films were *Battle of the Ukraine* (1943), an important war documentary made by giving personal instruction to 24 different cameramen distributed along a battle front; the color film *Michurin* (1949); and *Poem of the Sea,* completed in 1958 after his death.

Dow, Herbert H. *(1866–1930)* U.S. chemist and industrialist. His college thesis at the Case School of Applied Sciences (1888) was about extracting minerals from the brines underlying much of Ohio. Encouraged by his teachers, he studied the vast underground resources of brines also found in nearby states and presented his studies at a meeting of the American Association for the Advancement of Science in 1888. In 1889 he discovered and patented an inexpensive method of extracting bromine, chromium and lithium from brine by electrolysis. He founded Dow Chemical Company in 1897 at Midland, Michigan. Dow was the first U.S. company to manufacture indigo and phenol, a compound used in explosives. During WORLD WAR I, the company manufactured mustard gas for troops in Europe. A major industrial enterprise of the day, the company has continued as a producer of a wide variety of chemicals.

Dowell, Anthony *(1943–)* British dancer. One of the great classical male dancers of his generation, Dowell is famous for his elegance and flawless technique. He joined Britain's ROYAL BALLET in 1961 and quickly received acclaim dancing the leading classical roles. He created roles in Frederick ASHTON's *The Dream* (1964) and *A Month in the Country* (1976) and in Anthony TUDOR's *Shadowplay* (1967), among others. From 1978 to 1980 he was a principal dancer with AMERICAN BALLET THEATRE. He served as the artistic director of the Royal Ballet from 1986 to 2001. Dowell was elevated to the rank of Knight Bachelor in 1995.

DO-X Giant flying-boat airplane built by the German firm of Dornier and first flown in 1929. The DO-X had been preceded with some success by the flying boats Dornier WAL and Super-WAL, the latter operating on a regular schedule between Europe and South America. Each carried eight to 10 passengers and mail. The huge DO-X, however, carried up to 150 passengers and was intended to provide a regular transatlantic passenger service. It had three decks and provided spacious passenger accommodation somewhat in the manner of a ship. Twelve engines mounted above the single wing, six facing forward and six facing aft, were required to power it. A flight to New York was made, but because the DO-X was underpowered and unable to gain safe altitude, its use was discontinued.

Doyle, Sir Arthur Conan *(1859–1930)* British writer and physician, best known for his stories about the greatest of all consulting detectives, SHERLOCK HOLMES. Born in Edinburgh and educated at Stonyhurst College and Edinburgh University, Doyle took up his medical practice as an eye specialist near Portsmouth in 1882. He began supplementing his income by writing, and in 1887 the first Sherlock Holmes novel appeared, *A Study in Scarlet,* followed by a spectacularly popular series of Holmes short stories in *The Strand Magazine* (1891–92). Although his fame would ultimately rest on his detective stories, Doyle preferred other literary pursuits. His most cherished projects were historical novels such as *Micah Clarke* (1889) and *The White Company* (1891). His patriotic fervor fueled works like *The War in South Africa: Its Cause and Conduct,* a defense of the British involvement in the BOER WAR (1902); his scientific background led to the creation of Professor George Edward Challenger in *The Lost World* (1912) and *The Poison Belt* (1913)—stories that blended scientific fact with fantastic romance. His growing interest in spiritualism after World War I led to such books as *The Coming of the Fairies* (1922), in which he supported the existence of what he called the little people. Doyle devoted most of the decade of the 1920s and more than a million dollars to this cause. Holmes remained a skeptic to the last story *The Case-Book of Sherlock Holmes* (1927). While Doyle's output was prodigious and diverse, his contributions to the modern detective story and to the new field of science fiction remain his most important literary legacies.

Drabble, Margaret (*1939– *) British novelist. Born in Sheffield, Drabble was educated at Victoria University of Manchester. She achieved success with her first novel, *A Summer Bird-Cage* (1962), which, like her other early works, depicts intelligent young women facing career and marriage decisions. Leaving behind the almost breathless tone of her early work, Drabble's increasingly complicated novels reflect her earnest concern with contemporary social themes, although some critics have attacked her for her turgid prose and for taking a sociologist's rather than a novelist's view of life. *The Realms of Gold* (1975) depicts archaeologist Francis Wingate—a successful, divorced mother. *The Ice Age* (1977) describes the economic crises of England in the mid-1970s and the social damage wrought by unchecked real estate development. Later works, notably *The Radiant Way* (1987) and its sequel, *A Natural Curiosity* (1989), express her discontent with England under Margaret THATCHER. An outspoken feminist and socialist, Drabble has also written a biography of Arnold BENNETT and edited the *Oxford Companion to English Literature* (1985, fifth edition). She is married to the biographer Michael Holroyd. Her sister **A. S. Byatt** is also a noted novelist. More recent novels by Drabble are *The Gates of Ivory* (1992), *The Witch of Exmoor* (1997), *The Peppered Moth* (2001) and *The Seven Sisters* (2002).

Drake, Frank Donald (*1930– *) American astronomer. Drake graduated in 1952 from Cornell University and obtained his Ph.D. in 1958 from Harvard. He worked initially at the National Radio Astronomy Observatory (NRAO), West Virginia (1958–63), and at the JET PROPULSION LABORATORY, California (1963–64), before returning to Cornell and being appointed professor of astronomy in 1966. Although Drake has made significant contributions to radio astronomy, including radio studies of the planets, he is perhaps best known for his pioneering search for extraterrestrial intelligence. In April 1959 he managed to gain approval from the director of NRAO, Otto Struve, to proceed with his search, which was called Project Ozma, from the Oz stories of L. Frank BAUM. Drake began in 1960, using the NRAO 26-meter radio telescope to listen for possible signals from planets of the sunlike stars Tau Ceti and Epsilon Eridani, both about 11 light-years away. No signals were received. In July 1960 the project was terminated to allow the telescope to be used for other purposes. Drake revived the project in 1975, in collaboration with Carl SAGAN, when they began using the Arecibo 100-foot. radio telescope to listen to several nearby galaxies on frequencies of 1420, 1653 and 2380 megahertz. No contact was made; nor was it likely, for as they declared: "A search of hundreds of thousands of stars in the hope of detecting one message would require remarkable dedication and would probably take several decades."

Draper, Charles Stark (*1901–1987*) U.S. engineer and physicist. In 1939 Draper helped found the Massachusetts Institute of Technology Instrumentation Laboratory. His work there on gyroscopic systems broke new ground in such developments as gunsights for WORLD WAR II battleships and guidance systems for intercontinental ballistic missiles. Known as the father of inertial navigation, he developed the navigation system that guided the APOLLO astronauts to the Moon and back.

Draper, Dorothy (*1889–1969*) American interior decorator known for her designs for hotels, restaurants, clubs and other public spaces. She founded her own firm in 1925 and produced early work in a version of the popular ART DECO idiom of the time. In the 1930s her work took on more eclectic, traditional elements, often in overscaled, exaggerated form. Her book of 1939,

Decorating Is Fun! sums up the Draper approach with its energetic, somewhat flamboyant, commercial emphasis. The redecoration of the Pompeiian restaurant of New York's Metropolitan Museum of Art is a highly visible (although now altered) example of the florid Draper style.

dreadnoughts Class of "all-big-gun" battleships; derived from HMS *Dreadnought,* a British battleship launched in 1906. The first such ship powered by steam turbines, it carried 10 12-inch guns and five torpedo tubes, giving it about twice the firepower of its predecessors. With heavy armor plate made of Krupp steel and able to reach a cruising speed of 21 knots, the ship outranged and outpaced every other such vessel and immediately became the most powerful ship in the world. Representing a revolution in naval design, the *Dreadnought* provided a model and a name for the battleship that were to render previous capital ships obsolete. Dreadnoughts had a prominent place in WORLD WAR I, but the only engagement in which opposing dreadnoughts faced each other occurred at the battle of JUTLAND in 1916. Limitations were placed on the dreadnoughts by the postwar WASHINGTON CONFERENCE, and their importance was lessened by the growth of air forces and underwater weaponry.

Drees, Willem (*1886–1988*) Dutch politician. Premier of the NETHERLANDS from 1948 to 1958 (the longest premiership in Dutch history), he was the architect of the nation's comprehensive welfare system. Under his stewardship the Netherlands reemerged into prosperity as it recovered from five years of German occupation during WORLD WAR II. Drees, who helped found the Dutch Labor Party after the war, quit the party in the early 1970s, as he felt it was moving too far to the left. His son, Willem Jr., founded the Dutch Democratic Socialist Party.

Dreiser, Theodore (*1871–1945*) American author who was a major force in the development of modern literary realism. He was born the 11th child to a poor German immigrant family in Terre Haute, Indiana. He came to New York an ambitious journalist in 1894, the same year that critic Hamlin

Garland proclaimed that city the "literary center of America." Six years of struggle and privation before the publication of his first novel, SISTER CARRIE (1900), introduced him to many of the greatest young realists of the time—the painter Everett SHINN, photographer Alfred STIEGLITZ, and novelists William Dean Howells, Stephen Crane and Frank Norris. However, the poor reception accorded *Sister Carrie* caused Dreiser to withdraw into seven years of depression and hospitalization. Back on his feet and encouraged by the successful republication of the novel in 1907, he plunged into a series of 21 books in the next 21 years: *Jennie Gerhardt* (1911), *A Traveller at Forty* (1913), *The "Genius"* (1915), the three Frank Cowperwood novels (*The Financier,* 1912; *The Titan,* 1914; and *The Stoic,* published posthumously in 1946) and his most important novel, *AN AMERICAN TRAGEDY* (1925).

Despite frequent complaints from his contemporaries that his prose was clumsy, his method ponderous and his subjects sordid, Dreiser managed to secure a lasting reputation as a major novelist. His was a mind, according to colleague H. L. MENCKEN, that was "packed to suffocation with facts directly observed." His greatest characters—Carrie Meeber, Hurtswood, Clyde Griffiths—are superbly realized and, as Dreiser himself put it, "pit their enormous urges" against the limitations "of their pathetic equipment."

Dresden German city, on the Elbe River in Saxony. Renowned for its music and art collections, its singular architecture and its Dresden china, which has been crafted in nearby Meissen for the past two centuries. Dresden was devastated in WORLD WAR II by Allied firebombing in February 1945. In its ferocity and the destruction it caused, the bombing of Dresden, in which thousands of German civilians died, is considered third only to the atomic bombing of HIROSHIMA and NAGASAKI. Dresden was part of EAST GERMANY from 1949 to 1990. Most of the city has been reconstructed and revitalized.

Drexel, Mother Katharine (*1858–1955*) American nun. Drexel was born into a wealthy and socially prominent banking family of Philadelphia. She donated her share of the family's fortune to the order she created in 1891, the Sisters of the Blessed Sacrament for Indians and Colored People. At its height, the order (now known as the Sisters of the Blessed Sacrament) maintained 66 schools in 23 states, including the predominantly black Xavier University in New Orleans. In 1988 Mother Drexel was beatified by Pope JOHN PAUL II, leaving her one step from sainthood. The pope praised Mother Drexel as someone who "would stand up for the rights of the oppressed."

Drexel Burnham Lambert scandal
Financial scandal involving so-called junk bond king Michael R. Milken of Drexel Burnham Lambert, a large Wall Street brokerage firm. During the 1980s American business went through a period of merger mania characterized by "hostile takeovers." At the center of the action was the once obscure investment banking house of Drexel Burnham Lambert, which garnered the limelight when one of its partners, Milken, pioneered the use of high-yielding junk bonds to finance corporate takeovers. Both Milken and his firm grew immensely wealthy from these transactions. However, the bubble burst in 1986 when Ivan BOESKY, a multimillionaire who had made his fortune through risk arbitrage, implicated both Milken and Drexel in illegal insider trading. The federal government prosecuted both Milken and the firm. Drexel, which only a year before had been the most successful firm on Wall Street, went bankrupt in the wake of the scandal.

Dreyer, Carl Theodor (*1889–1968*) Danish film director. Dreyer was one of the most critically acclaimed directors of the 20th century. Many of his films, which span the transition from silent films to the "talkies," are widely regarded as classics. Dreyer, an orphan, was raised by a Lutheran family. He worked as a journalist and as an editor before turning to the cinema in 1919. During his peripatetic career, he made a total of 14 films in Scandinavia, France and Germany. Perhaps his best-known work is *The Passion of Joan of Arc* (1928), a highly dramatic black-and-white SILENT FILM that featured the French playwright Antonin ARTAUD as a monk. Other films by Dreyer include *Vampyr* (1932) and *Day of Wrath* (1943), a story of religious persecution, which Dreyer courageously shot in Denmark during the Nazi occupation. *Ordet* (1955) deals with the themes of love and faith, and *Gertrude* (1964) concerns the quest of a woman for absolute love. His writings include *Dreyer in Double Reflection* (1973).

Dreyfuss, Henry (*1904–1972*) American industrial designer. Born in New York City, Dreyfuss began his career in stage design, working on Broadway productions from 1921 to 1929. In 1929 he opened his own studio, and from then on he produced a wide variety of industrial designs. Function and ease of use were prime considerations to Dreyfuss in his creation of designs for such products as Bell telephones (1930), Hoover vacuum cleaners (1934), passenger cars for the New York Central Railroad (1941), RCA television sets (1946), refrigerators, hearing aids, typewriters, farm machinery, airplanes, ships, printed materials and myriad other objects. A founder of the American Society of Industrial Design, he expressed his design philosophy in *The Measure of Man* (1959) and an autobiography, *Designing for People* (1955). He and his wife committed suicide in California.

Drickamer, Harry George (*1908–2002*) American physicist. Drickamer was educated at the University of Michigan, where he earned his Ph.D. in 1946. He then joined the staff of the University of Illinois, Urbana, serving first as professor of physical chemistry and, after 1953, as professor of chemical engineering. He specialized in the study of the structure of solids by means of high pressures, producing in the course of his research pressures on the order of some 500,000 atmospheres.

Dries Right-wing members of the British CONSERVATIVE PARTY during Margaret THATCHER's tenure in office. They supported monetarist policies and opposed increases in public expenditure to alleviate social problems. They also supported PRIVATIZATION, curtailment of trade union influence and a vigorous defense policy. (See also WETS.)

Driesch, Hans Adolf Eduard *(1867–1941)* German biologist. Driesch held professorships at Heidelberg, Cologne and Leipzig and was visiting professor to China and America. A student of zoology at Freiburg, Jena and Munich, he was for some years on the staff of the Naples Zoological Station. Driesch carried out pioneering work in experimental embryology. He separated the two cells formed by the first division of a sea-urchin embryo and observed that each developed into a complete larva, thus demonstrating the capacity of the cell to form identical copies on division. He was also the first to demonstrate the phenomenon of embryonic induction, whereby the position of and interaction between cells within the embryo determine their subsequent differentiation. Driesch is perhaps best known for his concept of entelechy—a vitalistic philosophy that postulates the origin of life to lie in some unknown vital force separate from biochemical and physiological influences. This also led him to investigate psychic research and parapsychology.

Drinkwater, John *(1882–1937)* British poet, playwright and actor. Drinkwater was a competent Georgia poet and a founding member of the Birmingham Repertory Theatre, where he was a longtime actor and manager. His early poetic dramas, the most successful of which was *X = O; a Night of the Trojan War* (1917), were followed by such acclaimed plays as *Abraham Lincoln* (1919) and the comedy *Bird in Hand* (1927) as well as several historical dramas. (See also the GEORGIANS.)

Drummond de Andrade, Carlos *(1902–1987)* Brazilian poet. He was a leader of Brazil's modernist movement in literature. Aside from Fernando PESSOA of Portugal, he was perhaps the foremost Portuguese-language poet of the 20th century. According to the *Times* of London, he was also "perhaps the most successful humorous poet of really major stature in this century."

Drury, Allen Stuart *(1918–1998)* American journalist and novelist. Drury worked as a journalist for 20 years—including a stint at United Press International as a Washington correspondent—before the publication of his first novel, *Advise and Consent* (1959, filmed 1962). The book was an immediate success, largely because it was assumed it was a roman à clef depicting the political and sexual intrigues of prominent Washington figures of the time. It won a PULITZER PRIZE in 1960. Drury wrote several sequels following the careers of the characters of *Advise and Consent*, including *A Shade of Difference* (1962), *That Summer* (1965), *Capable of Honor* (1966) and *Preserve and Protect* (1968). Other works include *A Senate Journal 1942–1945* (1972), *Egypt the Eternal Smile: Reflections on a Journey* (1980) and *Pentagon* (1986).

Druze Rebellion of 1925–1927 The Druze, a small Islamic sect in French mandated Syria, protested their tyrannical treatment by the governor and rebelled under Sultan al-Atrash in July 1925. They soon controlled much of the countryside. Syrian nationalists joined them, forcing the French to withdraw from Damascus. The French unleashed artillery and bombing attacks, but the rebellion, which had spread to southern Lebanon, continued until June 1927. The Druze then accepted peace. (Lebanon had been declared a republic by the French on May 23, 1927.)

Dryden, Hugh L. *(1898–1965)* U.S. research scientist and administrator. Although he had never flown an airplane, Dryden was one of the world's great authorities in aeronautics. A graduate of Johns Hopkins University in 1917, he pioneered a series of high-speed flight phenomena projects for the National Bureau of Standards in the mid-1930s and by 1938 had become chief physicist of the agency. After leaving the Bureau of Standards in 1947, that same year he became director of aeronautical research for NACA (the National Advisory Committee on Aeronautics); when that agency became NASA in 1958, Dryden was named deputy administrator. Over a long career he published more than 100 papers on aeronautics research and was the recipient of many awards, including the Daniel Guggenheim Medal in 1950 and the Wright Brothers Memorial Trophy in 1955. The Dryden Flight Research Center (formerly known as the High Speed Flight Station) at Edwards Air Force Base in California is named in his honor.

Duarte Fuentes, José Napoleón *(1926–1990)* Salvadoran politician, president of El Salvador (1980–82, 1984–89). A centrist, Duarte helped found El Salvador's Christian Democratic Party in 1961. He ran for the presidency in 1972 and was leading in votes when the military government stopped the count and declared its candidate the winner. Following an unsuccessful coup by military officers who supported him, Duarte was arrested and finally exiled. In 1979 he returned to the country as part of a military-civilian junta. Appointed president in 1980, he was looked on as a force for Central American democracy by the REAGAN administration. He served during most of the 1980s, but large amounts of U.S. aid did not help bring peace. Although himself a man of integrity, his government came to be viewed as inept and riddled with corruption. Ill with cancer, he was forced from office in a 1989 election.

Dubasov, F. V. *(1845–1912)* Dubasov was the general responsible for the suppression of the RUSSIAN REVOLUTION OF 1905 in Moscow. Initially unsuccessful because the loyalty of his troops was uncertain, he was given reinforcements in the form of the Semenovsky Guards, who ruthlessly quelled the revolt in a few days.

Dubček, Alexander *(1921–1992)* Czechoslovak political leader and reformer. Dubček joined the Communist Party in 1939, fought with the Slovak RESISTANCE against the Germans (1944–45) and studied political science in Moscow (1955–58). He became principal secretary of the Slovak Communist Party in 1958 and first secretary—in effect, the leader of CZECHOSLOVAKIA—on January 5, 1968. In the following months he introduced economic and political reforms designed to create what he called "socialism with a human face" (see PRAGUE SPRING). Although he assured the USSR that he intended to keep Czechoslovakia in the WARSAW PACT, Soviet leader BREZHNEV ordered the SOVIET INVASION OF CZECHOSLOVAKIA (August 20–21, 1968) to crush the reform movement and restore a hard-line Communist government; Dubček was briefly arrested. He remained first secretary until 1969 but was expelled from the party in 1970 and vanished from public life. When the democractic reform movement swept Czechoslovakia in late 1989, he reemerged to popular acclaim and was unanimously elected Speaker of the Czechoslovak parliament in December of that year. He lived to see the fall of communism in his country in 1989 but died in an automobile accident after the division of Czechoslovakia into the Czech Republic and Slovakia.

Dubinsky, David *(1892–1982)* American union leader. A major figure in the U.S. labor movement during the middle third of the 20th century, he was president of the International Ladies Garment Workers Union from 1932 to 1966. Under his leadership the union membership grew tenfold, from 45,000 to 450,000. He took the union from near bankruptcy and built up assets of $500 million. Dubinsky largely eliminated sweatshops in the industry and drove communists out of leadership positions in the union. He pioneered the union role in granting health insurance, housing, severance pay, retirement benefits and a 35-hour workweek. He also helped found New York State's Liberal Party and served as its vice chairman. He advised many presidents—from Franklin ROOSEVELT to John F. KENNEDY.

DuBois, William Edward Burghardt *(1868–1963)* Pioneering black American civil rights leader. Born in Great Barrington, Massachusetts, DuBois attended Fisk University and in 1895 became the first African American to receive a Harvard Ph.D. He taught history and economics at Atlanta University from 1897 to 1910 and from 1932 to 1944. In the early part of the 20th century, DuBois was the leading black figure in the fight against racial discrimination. Demanding equal rights, he opposed Booker T. WASHINGTON's credo that hard work alone would improve the status of African Americans. In some 20 books and scores of articles he made great contributions to the historical and sociological understanding of black life in America. His liberationist ideology was eloquently ex-

Civil rights leader W. E. B. DuBois (LIBRARY OF CONGRESS, PRINTS AND PHOTOGRAPHS DIVISION)

pressed in the classic work *The Souls of Black Folk* (1903). In an attempt to fight racial discrimination he founded (1905) the NIAGARA MOVEMENT, a forerunner of the NATIONAL ASSOCIATION FOR THE ADVANCEMENT OF COLORED PEOPLE (NAACP), which he cofounded four years later. In addition, he edited the organization's influential journal *The Crisis* from 1910 to 1934. Also concerned with colonialism and the international status of blacks, he participated in a number of Pan African Congresses, meeting Kwame NKRUMAH and Jomo KENYATTA at one of these (1945). Impatient with what he felt was the NAACP's timid approach to the civil rights struggle, he resigned from the organization in 1948. Increasingly radical, DuBois came to view COMMUNISM as the best way to achieve black liberation, and he joined the Communist Party in 1961. That same year he moved to Ghana, becoming a Ghanaian citizen just before his death.

Dubos, René Jules *(1901–1982)* French-born bacteriologist and author. Graduated from France's National Agronomy Institute (1921) with a degree in agricultural science, Dubos worked briefly at the International Institute of Agriculture in Rome and immigrated to the U.S. in 1924. After earning his Ph.D. for research on soil

microorganisms (Rutgers University, 1927), he joined the staff of Rockefeller University in New York. There he devoted his career to the study of bacteria and antibacterial substances. He was also a tireless crusader against environmental pollution. The author of more than 20 environmental and scientific works, he received many major scientific awards. He won the 1969 PULITZER PRIZE for nonfiction for his book *So Human an Animal.*

Dubuffet, Jean *(1901–1985)* French painter and sculptor. Dubuffet was regarded by many as the most important artist to emerge from FRANCE at the end of WORLD WAR II. Supporting himself as a wine merchant, he did not begin his artistic career in earnest until he was in his 40s. Opposed to respectability in art, he reveled in simplicity and created works in a primitive, childlike idiom with a caricatural quality. He was the recipient of a number of large-scale sculptural commissions in the U.S. He also wrote widely on art and other subjects and was considered a master of French prose.

Duchamp, Marcel *(1887–1968)* French painter and art theorist; in spite of his relatively slim production, one of the most important figures in 20th-century art—an avant-garde icon. The brother of Raymond DUCHAMP-VILLON and half brother of Jacques Villon, he was born in Blainville and painted his first pictures in an Impressionist style around 1908. Soon thereafter he produced works influenced by the formal brilliance of Paul Cézanne and the color of FAUVISM. Duchamp quickly developed a style of his own, a merging of CUBISM and FUTURISM that represented form and motion in a series of overlapping planes. This style was manifested in his famous work *Nude Descending a Staircase* (1912), which scandalized a conservative American public when it was shown in the 1913 ARMORY SHOW. Around this time he began to develop the ideas that crystallized in 1915 in the DADA movement. Duchamp also created the first "readymades," everyday objects—such as bottle rack, bicycle wheel, urinal—exhibited out of context as works of art, which would strongly influence the adherents of POP ART.

He moved to New York City in 1915, became the center of a group of dada artists and writers and began work on his magnum opus, a symbol-laden composition of painted foil and wire held between two sheets of plate glass and entitled *The Bride Stripped Bare by Her Bachelors, Even* (1915–23). Duchamp is also well known for his mustache-decorated Mona Lisa called *L.H.O.O.Q.* (1919). Although he executed a number of sketches and created his last work, *Etant Donnes* (1949), in the 1940s, Duchamp, who vowed never to repeat himself, officially retired from painting in 1923 and largely devoted himself to the game of chess. Many of his works are in the collection of the Philadelphia Museum of Art.

Duchamp-Villon, Raymond *(1876–1918)* French sculptor. Duchamp-Villon, who was markedly influenced by CUBISM and was one of the first sculptors to apply its theories to his medium, was also a member of an important artistic family. His brother was the renowned painter and theorist Marcel DUCHAMP, while his half brother was painter Gaston Duchamp. Duchamp-Villon produced the bulk of his major sculptures in the years just prior to World War I, including *Seated Woman* and *Horse*. He was singled out for praise by French poet and art critic Guillaume APOLLINAIRE as a sculptor who went beyond mere modeling from nature to enlarge and glorify the human spirit.

Dudinskaya, Natalya Mikhailovna *(1912–2003)* Soviet ballerina. She joined the Leningrad Academic Theater Opera and ballet troupe and within a year was dancing the main roles. She participated in the creation of new Soviet ballets such as *The Flame of Paris, Laurensya* and *The Bronze Horseman.*

Dudintsev, Vladimir Dmitriyevich *(1918–1998)* Soviet author. Trained as a lawyer, during WORLD WAR II he served as defense counsel with a Siberian tribunal (1942–45). He began writing seriously in 1946 as a contributor to *Komsomolskaya Pravda,* the newspaper of the Communist Party's youth organization (see KOMSOMOL; *PRAVDA*). His most successful work, *Not by Bread Alone* (1957), was a frank description of the Soviet social and political system; it was censored by the authorities.

Dufek, George J. *(1903–1977)* American naval officer. He commanded the U.S. Navy's **Operation Deep Freeze** Antarctic expeditions (1955–59) and was the first American to set foot on the SOUTH POLE (1956). He retired with the rank of rear admiral.

Dufy, Raoul *(1877–1953)* French painter. Dufy was strongly influenced by the Impressionists early in his career in Massachusetts but emerged in the 1900s as a practitioner of FAUVISM, a school of painting that emphasized the dynamic use of bright color to create emotional and spiritual impact. Dufy crafted woodcut illustrations for the *Bestiare* (1911) of French poet Guillaume APOLLINAIRE, who was a critical supporter of Dufy's art. Dufy later turned his attention to artistic mass production of woodblock print, textiles, pottery and tapestries. He also designed theatrical sets and public works displays.

Duggar, Benjamin Minge *(1872–1956)* American plant pathologist. Duggar devoted his career to studying plant diseases and while professor of plant physiology at Cornell University wrote *Fungus Diseases of Plants* (1909), the first publication to deal purely with plant pathology. He is known for his work on cotton diseases and mushroom culture, but he made his most important discovery after retiring from academic life. In 1945 he became consultant to the American Cyanamid Co. and soon isolated the fungus *Streptomyces aureofaciens.* Three years' work with this organism resulted in Duggar extracting and purifying the compound chlortetracycline, (marketed as Aureomycin), and first of the tetracycline antibiotics. This drug was on the market by December 1948 and has proved useful in combatting many infectious diseases. Duggar was one of the foremost coordinators of plant science research in America and was editor of many important publications.

Dukakis, Michael Stanley *(1933–)* American politician and Democratic presidential candidate (1988). Born in Brookline, Massachusetts, Dukakis attended Swarthmore College and received a law degree from Harvard University. He served in the Massachusetts legislature (1963–70) and was elected governor of the state in 1974. Defeated in 1978, he taught at Harvard (1979–82) before regaining the statehouse in 1982; he was reelected in 1986. Due largely to the economic successes in Massachusetts, Dukakis emerged as the front-runner in the Democratic presidential primaries of 1988, besting such better-known challengers as Senator Al GORE, Representative Richard Gephardt and Jesse JACKSON. Capturing the nomination, Dukakis led his Republican rival, George H. W. BUSH, in many polls in the summer of 1988. Dukakis, however, was often perceived as a cold and cautious technocrat, and he generated little enthusiasm among the majority of voters. He was resoundingly defeated by Bush. Dukakis completed his term as Massachusetts governor but, burdened by a failing economy, family problems and growing unpopularity in his home state, he declined to run again in 1990. In 2001 Dukakis joined the political science faculty at Northeastern University.

Dukas, Paul *(1865–1935)* French composer best known for his orchestral scherzo *L'apprenti sorcier* (1897; *The Sorcerer's Apprentice*), which is considered a masterpiece of modern music. Initial recognition as a composer came with his overture to Corneille's drama *Polyeucte* (1892). Among Dukas's most important works are the opera *Ariane et Barbe-Bleue,* with libretto by Maurice Maeterlinck (1907), the ballet score *La Peri* (1912), and the piano Sonata in E Flat Minor (1901). He also was a music critic for several journals, most notably the *Gazette des beaux-arts,* and taught at the Paris Conservatory (from 1918) and the École Normale de Musique.

Duke, Charles *(1935–)* U.S. astronaut. *Apollo 16* was Duke's only spaceflight, but on that mission he became the 10th human to walk on the Moon. As lunar module pilot, Duke, along with Commander John YOUNG, spent almost three days exploring the Moon's surface by foot and on the specially built Lunar Rover vehicle.

Duke, James Buchanan *(1856–1925)* American entrepreneur and philanthropist. Duke was born in North

Carolina, the son of a tobacco processor. In 1890, after expanding his father's company into the largest tobacco corporation in America, Duke joined with four competitors to form the American Tobacco Company, which would dominate the industry for two decades, until dissolved by the U.S. Supreme Court in 1911. Duke University in Durham, North Carolina, is named after Duke, who contributed heavily to the institution.

Dukhonin, Nikolai Nikolayevich
(1876–1917) Russian general. He was commander in chief of all Russian forces when the OCTOBER REVOLUTION broke out. Having helped several senior officers to escape, he refused to obey an order to open truce negotiations with the Germans. He was shot by mutinous troops in November 1917.

Dulbecco, Renato (1914–) Italian-American physician and molecular biologist. Dulbecco obtained his M.D. from the University of Turin in 1936 and taught there until 1947, when he moved to the U.S. He taught briefly at Indiana before moving to California in 1949. He served as professor of biology (1952–63) at the California Institute of Technology. Dulbecco then joined the staff of the Salk Institute, where—apart from a period (1971–74) at the Imperial Cancer Research Fund in London—he has remained.

Beginning in 1959 Dulbecco introduced the idea of **cell transformation** into biology. In this process special cells are mixed in vitro with such tumor-producing viruses as the polyoma and SV40 virus. With some cells a productive infection results, where the virus multiplies unchecked in the cell and finally kills its host. In other cells, however, this unlimited multiplication does not occur; instead, the virus induces changes similar to those in cancer cells: The virus alters the cell so that it reproduces without restraint and does not respond to the presence of neighboring cells. A normal cell is thus transformed into a cancer cell in vitro. The significance of this work was to provide an experimental set-up where the processes by which a normal cell becomes cancerous can be studied in a relatively simplified form. It was for this work that Dulbecco was awarded the NOBEL PRIZE in physiology or medicine in 1975, sharing it with Howard TEMIN and David BALTIMORE.

Dulles, Allen Welsh (1893–1969)
U.S. foreign service officer; director of the CIA. Dulles was born in Watertown, New York, and graduated from Princeton University in 1914. In 1916, after earning a master's degree at Princeton, he joined the foreign service, with which he served first in Vienna then in Switzerland during WORLD WAR I; in 1919 he was on the American delegation to the peace conference in Paris. In 1926 Dulles received a law degree from George Washington University and resigned from the State Department to enter private practice. During WORLD WAR II he worked for the OFFICE OF STRATEGIC SERVICES (OSS), first as head of the New York City office and, from November 1942, as director of the office in Bern, Switzerland. Dulles's group made a significant contribution to the war effort, discovering, among other things, that the Nazis were working to develop the V-1 and V-2 rockets and that Germany had broken the American diplomatic code in use in Europe. In 1946, after the war, Dulles became president of the private Council on Foreign Relations. In 1951 he was appointed deputy director of the CIA, and in 1953 he became the agency's director, about the same time that his brother, John Foster DULLES, was appointed secretary of state. During Dulles's tenure, the CIA was involved in many covert operations, including coups in Iran and Guatemala, U-2 surveillance flights over the Soviet Union (see U-2 INCIDENT) and the BAY OF PIGS INVASION of Cuba. In 1961, after the failure of the latter, Dulles resigned his position at the CIA. In 1964 he was a member of the Warren Commission, which investigated the assassination of President John F. KENNEDY.

Dulles, John Foster (1888–1959)
American statesman, secretary of state (1953–59). Born in Washington, D.C., Dulles was the grandson and nephew of previous secretaries of state. He attended Princeton, the University of Paris and George Washington University before becoming a prominent international lawyer. He was a representative to the PARIS PEACE CONFERENCE of 1919, where he was the chief American spokesman on the question of reparations. He subsequently attended a variety of international conferences held between the wars. An adviser to the

U.S. delegation at the 1945 conference that founded the UNITED NATIONS, he served as a U.S. delegate to the UN from 1945 to 1949. In 1951 he negotiated the final peace treaty with Japan. Dulles' long experience in international affairs caused President Dwight D. EISENHOWER to appoint him secretary of state in 1953. Serving in this office until 1959, he became the main architect of America's COLD WAR stance, expanding the anticommunist policies of Dean ACHESON, whom Dulles denounced as too soft on COMMUNISM. He was important in forming a number of anticommunist alliances, such as SEATO and CENTO (Central Treaty Organization), and played a central role in the strengthening of NATO. In his unyielding opposition to communism, which he viewed as an absolute moral evil, Dulles initiated a policy of BRINKSMANSHIP and encouraged the development of nuclear weapons that could be used in a "massive retaliation" against any Soviet aggression. Dulles was a strong backer of the Nationalist Chinese and of the DIEM regime in South Vietnam. However, he strongly opposed the French and British intervention against Egypt in the ARAB-ISRAELI WAR OF 1956 (see SUEZ CRISIS). In ill health, he resigned from his post only five weeks before his death. Dulles's political philosophy was enunciated in his books War, Peace, and Change (1939) and War or Peace (1950).

Dullin, Charles (1885–1949) French theatrical actor and producer. Dullin began his career as an actor working under Jacques COPEAU in the Vieux-Colombier theater company. In 1919 Dullin founded an experimental theater company, which he ultimately located at his Théâtre de l'Atelier Paris. It was one of the leading avant-garde troupes of the 1920s, producing plays by notables including Jean COCTEAU and Luigi PIRANDELLO. Dullin was named a director at the prestigious Comédie Française in 1936. While there, he provided tutelage to actor Jean-Louis BARRAULT.

duma The elected legislative assemblies that, with the State Council, made up the Russian legislature from 1906 to 1917, and which were established in response to the 1905 revolution. The czar could rule absolutely when the duma was not in session, and he could dissolve it at will. The first state duma, elected by universal male suffrage but

with limited power over financial and other matters, met for 73 days in 1906 and the second met in 1907 for 102 days. The first and second dumas were unsuccessful in that, although it was expected that the representatives would be conservative, they were mainly liberal and socialist, and their demands for reform were totally unacceptable to the government. The franchise was then restricted, and the third duma ran its full five-year term (1907–12) and gave support to the government's agrarian reforms and military reorganization. The fourth duma sat from 1912 to 1917, but it gradually became opposed to the government's war policy and increasingly critical of the imperial regime. On the abdication of Czar NICHOLAS II the provisional committee established by the duma asked Prince LVOV to form a provisional government.

After the dissolution of the Soviet Union in 1991, the parliament of the Russian Federation was called the Duma.

du Maurier, Dame Daphne (1907–1989)

British novelist. Daughter of the noted actor-manager **Sir Gerald du Maurier** and granddaughter of novelist **George du Maurier,** Daphne was born in London and educated in Paris. A writer of popular romantic fiction, she published her first novel, *The Loving Spirit,* in 1913. Like much of her fiction, her best-known work, *Rebecca* (1938, filmed 1940), takes place in Cornwall—where she lived much of her life. Du Maurier also wrote lesser-known historical fiction. Other works include *Jamaica Inn* (1938), *Frenchman's Creek* (1941), *My Cousin Rachel* (1951), *The Breaking Point* (1959) and *The Flight of the Falcon* (1965). Du Maurier wrote plays as well as nonfiction books about the Brontës, Cornwall and her family's history.

Dumbarton Oaks conferences

From August 21 to October 7, 1944, representatives of China, the USSR, the U.S. and Great Britain met at Dumbarton Oaks, a mansion in Georgetown, Washington, D.C., to formulate proposals for an organization the eventually became the UNITED NATIONS. Paragraph four of the Moscow Declaration of 1943 had stressed the need for such a postwar organization to succeed the LEAGUE OF NATIONS. The Dumbarton Oaks proposals for the establishment of a general international organization did not establish the voting procedures or qualifications for membership; these were settled at the YALTA CONFERENCE in February 1945, at which a trusteeship system was agreed upon to replace the league mandates. The final proposals formed the basis of negotiations at the San Francisco Conference in 1945, from which the Charter of the United Nations was published.

Dunand, Jean (1877–1942)

Swiss designer. Born near Geneva, he trained as a sculptor and designer in his native city and in Paris, where he settled in 1897. He was particularly well known for his vases, which he began producing in 1903. His styles ranged from ART NOUVEAU, to ART DECO, CUBISM and naturalism. Beginning to work in hammered metal, he became well known for his elegant lacquer works, particularly for the panels he executed for the luxury OCEAN LINERS *Île de France* (1928), *L'Atlantique* (1931) and *NOR-MANDIE* (1935). He was also known for his furniture designs.

Dunayevskaya, Raya (1910–1987)

Ukrainian-born Marxist philosopher. Raised in the U.S., she is considered the founder of a philosophy called Marxist humanism, on which she wrote four books. From 1937 to 1939, she was secretary to Russian Communist revolutionary Leon TROTSKY during his Mexican exile.

Dunayevsky, Isaak (1900–1955)

Soviet composer. He worked as a conductor and composer in Moscow, Kharkov and Leningrad. In 1932 he began to compose for films. His works include the operettas *The Golden Valley* (1937), *The Road to Happiness* (1941) and *The Son of the Clown* (1950). He was one of the first composers in the USSR to use JAZZ forms.

Dunbar, Paul Laurence (1872–1906)

U.S. poet, novelist and one of the country's first black poets to gain international fame. Although from a poor family and the only black in his Dayton, Ohio, class, by the time he reached high school he had been chosen president of the school literary society and editor of the school newspaper. His first poems were published in Dayton newspapers, and his first volume of verses, *Oak and Ivy* (1893), was also published in Dayton. He won wide recognition for his *Lyrics of a Lowly Life* (1896) and took a literary trip to London in 1897. Despite his fame and frail health, Dunbar supported himself and his mother by running a Dayton elevator and by writing in his meager spare time. For the last seven years of his short life, he took no time out to treat the tuberculosis that killed him at the age of 34. His writings include seven volumes of poetry, two volumes of short stories and two novels. The *Ohio State Guide* declared, "Dunbar became the idol of his race and an artist admired by many other Americans, establishing a tradition that undoubtedly encouraged . . . Countee CULLEN, Claude McKay and Langston HUGHES." A 10-cent U.S. stamp honoring him was issued in the American Poets series, and his house in Dayton has been preserved as a state museum (1938).

Duncan, Isadora (1877–1927)

Legendary American dancer. A pioneer of modern dance, Duncan rebelled against the constraints and conventions of classical ballet, adopting a more natural, emotionally inspired dance movement. Her choreography was largely improvisational and based on her ideas of classic Greek drama and her emotional response to the music of such great composers as Beethoven, Chopin and Schubert. Her performances, in which she danced barefoot in a diaphanous tunic, often reflected the passions and tragedies of her unconventional lifestyle. Duncan's dancing shocked American sensibilities, so in 1899 she left for Europe where she remained for most of her life. Her first European performances in Vienna, Paris, Berlin and Budapest (1900–02) were triumphs. She even appeared at the BAYREUTH FESTIVAL in 1904. Her dancing style during her first Russian tour (1904) influenced the balletic reforms of Mikhail FOKINE and Serge DIAGHILEV. She danced in Egypt, Greece and South America and returned to the U.S. for performances in 1908 and 1914, then toured the new Soviet Union (1921, 1923). In addition, she founded several short-lived dance schools in Germany, France and the Soviet Union. Duncan gave her last recital in Paris in 1927, shortly before she was killed when her lengthy scarf caught in the wheelspokes of a car. Her personal magnetism and role as representative of a new dance movement made her the dominant dance influence of her time.

A pioneer of modern dance. Isadora Duncan shocked American audiences by dancing barefoot in a flowing tunic. (Library of Congress, Prints and Photographs Division)

Not only did she inspire innumerable later dancers and choreographers (including Frederick Ashton and Kenneth MacMillan), she also influenced other arts—the drawings and designs of Gordon Craig, the photographs of Edward Steichen and the poetry of Sergei Esenin, to whom she was briefly married (1922–23).

Duncan, Robert Edward *(1919–1988)* American poet. A prolific lyric poet, Duncan was influenced by Charles Olson and his work is included in the Black Mountain School of poetry as well as associated with the works of the Beat Generation. His poetry reflects his homosexuality and often deals with the nature of poetry itself. His many works include *The Opening of the Field* (1960), *Roots and Branches* (1964), both poetry; *The*

Truth & Life of Myth: An Essay in Essential Autobiography (1968) and *Fictive Certainties: Essays* (1985). Some of his poetry was first published under the pseudonym Robert Edward Symmes. Early in his career, Duncan served as editor of *Experimental Review, Phoenix* and *Berkeley Miscellany*. Duncan was the first recipient of the National Poetry Award and is responsible for San Francisco's role as a center of poetry in the U.S.

Duncan-Sandys, Lord (Duncan Edwin Sandy) *(1908–1987)* British politician and a leading figure in British political affairs for nearly four decades. He was elected a Conservative member of Parliament in 1935 and that same year married Winston Churchill's eldest daughter, Diana. He directed key military actions as a junior member of Churchill's cabinet during World War II. He lost his seat in Parliament in 1945 but was reelected in 1950 and served uninterruptedly until 1974. During that time, he served successively as minister of supply, minister of housing and local government, minister of defense and minister of aviation. As secretary of state for Commonwealth relations from 1960 to 1964, he helped negotiate the independence of 11 British colonies. After resigning from the House of Commons in 1974, he was elevated to the House of Lords.

Dunham, Katherine *(1909–2006)* American dancer, choreographer, teacher and director. Dunham received an M.A. and a Ph.D. in anthropology from the University of Chicago. After extensive study of Negro dances in the West Indies, she worked with the Federal Theatre Project in Chicago (1938), then became director of the Labor Stage in New York City (1939). The first New York concert featuring her choreography was in 1940, and she danced in the Broadway musical *Cabin in the Sky* that same year. After performing in and/or choreographing several Hollywood films, most notably *Stormy Weather* (1943), she toured the U.S. and Europe with her own dance company. In 1945 she established a dance school, which became the focal point for Afro-American dance until 1955. Her works, such as *Choros* (1943), combine elements of classical ballet, modern and Afro-Cuban dance and are based on her ethnological studies. She became director of the Per-

forming Arts Training Center at Southern Illinois University, East St. Louis Campus. Dunham has received 10 honorary doctorates and the Presidential Medal of Arts, the Kennedy Center Honors, the French Legion of Honor, the Grand Cross of Haiti and other awards and honors.

Dunkirk, evacuation of After German armies overran Belgium at the start of World War II, they focused on seizing the English Channel ports, bombarding them heavily. Hundreds of thousands of British, French, Belgian and other Allied troops were trapped between the sea and German lines. The British and French navies, merchant fleets and private yachts and trawlers came to rescue the troops off the beaches of Dunkirk. From May 26 to June 4, 1940, more than 1,200 ships sailed back and forth across the channel, despite German bombing and strafing, evacuating about 340,000 troops to the safety of England. Many Allied vessels, including six destroyers, were sunk and all equipment abandoned.

Dunkirk, Treaty of An Anglo-French agreement of March 4, 1947, to provide mutual assistance against any future German aggressive threats, together with consultation over economic relations, symbolizing French reemergence as a major European power.

Dunne, Irene Marie *(1898–1990)* U.S. actress. She was noted for her patrician appearance and an ability to play roles ranging from screwball comedy to sentimental drama. Although she never won an Academy Award, she was nominated for her work in *Cimarron* (1931), *Theodora Goes Wild* (1936), *The Awful Truth* (1937), *Love Affair* (1939) and *I Remember Mama* (1948). She also starred in *Roberta* (1935), in which she introduced the song "Smoke Gets in Your Eyes," *Show Boat* (1936) and *Anna and the King of Siam* (1946).

Dunning, John Ray *(1907–1975)* American physicist. Dunning was educated at Wesleyan University, Nebraska and at Columbia University, New York, where he earned his Ph.D. in 1934. He took up an appointment at Columbia in 1933 and was made professor of physics in 1950. Dunning was one of the key figures in the Manhattan Project to build the first atomic bomb.

Dunsany, Edward John Moreton Drax Plunkett, Lord *(1878–1957)* Anglo-Irish author. Born in London of Irish parents, Lord Dunsany was the 18th baron of Dunsany Castle in County Meath, Ireland. A prolific writer, Dunsany is perhaps best remembered for his mythological tales, such as *The Gods of Pegana* (1905), *The Book of Wonder* (1912) and *The Blessing of Pan* (1927). Although politically aligned with the BRITISH EMPIRE in the question of HOME RULE and other Irish matters, Dunsany is associated with the IRISH LITERARY REVIVAL and was acquainted with Lady GREGORY and W. B. YEATS. Dunsany's first play, *The Glittering Gate,* was performed at the ABBEY THEATRE in 1909. Other plays include *The Gods of the Mountain* (1911) and *A Night at an Inn* (1916). Dunsany also wrote a popular series of story collections beginning with *The Travel Tales of Mr. Joseph Jorkens* (1931) and a series of autobiographies.

DuPont, Clifford W. *(1905–1978)* First president of Rhodesia (1970–75). A British-born soldier and lawyer, DuPont was appointed head of state following RHODESIA's Unilateral Declaration of Independence (UDI) from Britain in 1965. He held the post until his election as president in 1970. DuPont's roles were largely ceremonial, with Prime Minister Ian SMITH holding the effective decision-making power for the rebellious colony.

Du Pré, Jacqueline *(1945–1987)* English cellist. Noted for her intense, romantic playing, Du Pré had come to be recognized as one of the world's leading cellists when her career was cut short in the early 1970s by the onset of multiple sclerosis. She and her husband, pianist and conductor Daniel BARENBOIM, had appeared frequently together on concert stages throughout the world and were regarded as the most prominent husband-and-wife musical team of their generation. By the mid-1970s Du Pré was virtually paralyzed, though she continued to teach and work for the cause of the victims of multiple sclerosis. Her story became the basis of a play, *Duet for One.* Du Pré left a number of fine recordings.

Durand, William Frederick *(1859–1958)* American engineer. Durand worked mainly on problems connected with the propeller, both marine and, after 1914, aeronautical. He was general editor of an important standard work, *Aerodynamic Theory,* produced in six volumes (1929–36). He also served on the National Advisory Committee for Civil Aeronautics (NACA) from 1915 to 1933 and, in 1941, was recalled to advise the government on the construction of an American jet-propelled airplane.

Durant, Will and Ariel American historians and writers. William James Durant (1885–1981) was born in North Adams, Massachusetts. After graduating from St. Peter's College in Jersey City in 1907, he taught at Seton Hall and attended the seminary there for two years before moving to New York City and teaching at the Francisco Ferrer Modern School. There he met Ida Kaufman (1898–1981), a Ukrainian immigrant, who was 15 years old when they were married in 1913. "Ariel" was her husband's pet name for her, which she legally adopted after their marriage. Both Durants attended Columbia University, and Will received a doctorate from the school in 1917. In 1926 he published *The Story of Philosophy,* which sold over 2 million copies in three years. From 1935 to 1975, the Durants labored on their masterwork, *The Story of Civilization,* an 11-volume history of human achievement spanning 11,000 years; Ariel was credited as coauthor from volume seven on. Criticized by some academic historians but extremely popular among general audiences, the highly readable series has been a perennial best seller since its publication. Volume 10, *Rousseau and Revolution,* won the PULITZER PRIZE in 1968. While hospitalized, Will Durant died of a heart attack on November 8, 1981, apparently unaware that Ariel had died of natural causes two weeks before, on October 25.

Durante, Jimmy (James Francis Durante) *(1893–1980)* American vaudeville, nightclub, television and film comedian. Durante gained national popularity in the 1920s in the song-and-dance vaudeville trio of Clayton-Jackson-Durante, performing in PROHIBITION-era speakeasies. In the 1930s he appeared in many Broadway stage shows and in numerous movies for METRO-GOLDWYN-MAYER, where he supplanted Buster KEATON as the studio's top comedian. The Schnozzola, as he was known because of his bulbous nose, extended his fame in the mid-1940s on radio and later on television. He ended his programs with his celebrated sign-off, "Goodnight, Mrs. Calabash, wherever you are." In addition to his nose, his trademarks included a raspy voice, battered hat, butchered diction (with many malapropisms thrown in) and honky-tonk style of piano playing. His last film, *It's a Mad, Mad, Mad, Mad World* (1963), capped a career that spanned half a century.

Duras, Marguerite *(1914–1996)* French novelist, playwright and screenwriter. Duras was born in Indochina, now Vietnam, and came to Paris in 1932. She published her first of many novels, *Les impudents,* in 1943. Her experimental fiction, which includes *Blue Eyes, Black Hair* (1977), *The Lover* (1984) and *Emily L.* (1987), is highly esteemed in France. Duras never enjoyed the same success in the U.S., though her later works gained more notice. In the States, she is better known for her screenplays, which include *Hiroshima mon amour* (1959). Her plays, which are generally associated with the THEATER OF THE ABSURD, include *L'Eden Cinéma* (1977) and *Savannah Bay* (1984).

Durkheim, Emile *(1858–1917)* French social theorist; a seminal influence on 20th-century sociology. Through his many writings, he established a scientific framework and methodology for the measurement of societal beliefs, dynamics and change. Durkheim, the son of an Alsatian rabbi, was educated at the École Normale Superieure. In 1887 he taught the first ever university course on sociology in France. As a social theorist, Durkheim emphasized the need for stable political and religious institutions. In *Suicide* (1897), a classic study, Durkheim demonstrated that the per capita suicide rates of various countries were related to the strength of the ongoing social ties in those countries. In *The Elementary Forms of Religious Life* (1915) Durkheim proposed that the major function of religion was to enhance social bonds and that schismatic movements were symptomatic of societal unrest.

Durocher, Leo "the Lip" *(1905–1991)* American baseball player and manager. An average hitter, Durocher was an outstanding fielder who appeared in three All-Star games over a

17-year playing career. However, he is better known for his long and colorful managerial career, immortalized in his statement "Nice guys finish last." He managed the Brooklyn Dodgers through most of the 1940s, often feuding with owner Branch RICKEY but winning the pennant in 1941. His temper cost him frequent ejection, and he was indicted for assaulting a fan in 1945. Fired by the Dodgers in 1948, he was quickly signed by the rival Giants and led them to a pennant in 1951 and a World Series victory in 1954. He became a TV commentator in 1955 but returned to manage the Chicago Cubs from 1966 until 1972 and the Houston Astros in 1973. One of the most successful managers in baseball history, he retired with 2,010 wins.

Durrell, Lawrence George *(1912–1990)* British author. Born in India, Durrell was educated at the College of St. Joseph, Darjeeling and St. Edmund's School in Canterbury. He traveled widely, living with his family in Corfu and in Paris in the 1930s. He spent much of his life in the eastern Mediterranean region, which figures in his poetry and fiction as well as his travel writing. Although he had written an earlier collection of poetry and a novel,

Durrell first achieved recognition as a poet with collections including *A Private Country* (1943), *On Seeming to Presume* (1948) and *The Tree of Idleness* (1955). His sensuous writing explores the nature of love and knowledge. His first important novel, *The Black Book: On Agon* (1938), was an erotic pastiche that shows the influence of Henry MILLER and James JOYCE. Durrell is best known for the ALEXANDRIA QUARTET, which consists of the novels *Justine* (1957), *Balthazar* (1958), *Mountolive* (1958) and *Clea* (1960). The work shows Durrell's departure from realism; he goes farther in this direction in his later novels, including *Nunquan* (1970), *Monsieur* (1974) and *Constance* (1982). His travel writing includes *Prospero's Cell* (1945), *Reflections on a Marine Venus* (1953) and *Bitter Lemons* (1957). Durrell's brother, **Gerald Durrell** (1925–95), was a prominent zoologist and writer.

Durrenmatt, Friedrich *(1921–1990)* Swiss playwright, screenplay writer, novelist and story writer. Durrenmatt rose to prominence in the 1950s, when his absurdist drama *The Visit* (1956) was performed worldwide to critical and popular acclaim. *The Visit* debuted on Broadway in 1958, starring Alfred LUNT and Lynn

FONTANNE, and won the New York Drama Critics Award. Other plays by Durrenmatt, whose pessimistic social vision is thematically linked to the THEATER OF THE ABSURD, include *The Physicists* (1962) and *The Execution of Justice* (1989). He also wrote prose fiction, notably the novel *Justice* (1985), and coscripted (with actor Maximilian Schell) the film *End of the Game* (1976).

Duse, Eleanora *(1859–1924)* Italian actress. Duse was considered by many (including George Bernard SHAW) to be the greatest actress of the late 19th and early 20th centuries. Unlike her rival Sarah BERNHARDT, who performed in the florid 19th-century style of acting, Duse was known for the subtlety and naturalness of her performances. This style of acting, developed at the same time in Russia by STANISLAVSKY, replaced the earlier "tragic" style and became the standard for the 20th century. Poet-playwright Gabriele D'ANNUNZIO wrote several plays, including *Francesca da Rimini* (1902), especially for her.

Dust Bowl The worst droughts in U.S. history. At their peak in the late 1930s, they devastated an overall area of 25,000 square miles in the Central

The American Central West was devastated by droughts and dust storms during the Great Depression. (LIBRARY OF CONGRESS, PRINTS AND PHOTOGRAPHS DIVISION)

West. As the rain practically ceased the soil dried to dust and unusually high winds created vast dust storms, turning much of the area into a "dust bowl." The plight of the people of Oklahoma gained special attention in such works as john STEINBECK's *The Grapes of Wrath* (1939). In South Dakota, from 1933 to 1936, high winds carried choking clouds of dust. In North Dakota one-third of the state's lakes dried up and never refilled.

Great areas of the Central West had been plowed to grow grain for the WORLD WAR I food effort. Much of this land should have been left in its original condition. The dust storms carried off enormous amounts of topsoil—unprotected by roots of the original prairie grasses. The drought added to the hardships of the GREAT DEPRESSION, with banks foreclosing on thousands of farm mortgages.

Gradually the rains returned to the region. The drought taught many conservation lessons. A "shelter belt" of trees was planted from north to south across much of the area to restrain the "dust busting" winds. Vast reservoirs were created in the Dakotas, Oklahoma and elsewhere to provide more moisture. Subsequent periods of low rainfall have caused substantially less damage, because of the precaution taken. The drought of the summer of 1988 was one of the most severe since the great drought, as many farmers once again faced foreclosure because of the total failure of their crop.

Du Toit, Alexander Logie (*1878–1949*) South African geologist. Du Toit studied at the South Africa College, now the University of Cape Town; the Royal Technical College, Glasgow; and the Royal College of Science, London. After a short period of teaching at Glasgow University (1901–03) he returned to South Africa and worked with the Geological Commission of the Cape of Good Hope (1903–20), during which time he explored the geology of South Africa. For the next seven years he worked for the Irrigation Department and produced six detailed monographs on South African geology. He also served as a consulting geologist to De Beers Consolidated Mines (1927–41). Following a visit to South America in 1923, Du Toit became one of the earliest supporters of Alfred WEGENER's theory of continental drift, publishing his observations in *A Geological Comparison of South America with South Africa* (1927). He noted the similarity between the continents and developed his ideas in *Our Wandering Continents* (1937), in which he argued for the Wegener's theory of the separation of Pangaea into the two supercontinents, Laurasia and Gondwanaland.

Dutschke, Rudi (*1940–1979*) German radical student leader and Marxist scholar. Known as "Red Rudi," at the Free University of West Berlin, Dutschke was at the forefront of the student revolt in Western Europe in the late 1960s. A fiery orator, he called for the radicalizing of society and the solidarity of workers and students. He moved to Britain in December 1968 for medical treatment of head wounds he suffered from an assailant in Berlin. He attempted to remain for academic studies but was expelled from the country in 1971 when a British government tribunal ruled that his "meetings and associations have far exceeded normal social activities." Thereafter, he took up a teaching post at Aardhus University in Denmark.

Duvalier, François (Papa Doc) (*1907–1971*) Haitian dictator (1957–71). Trained as a physician, and a specialist in tropical medicine, Duvalier was popularly known as "Papa Doc." During the 1940s he was an important figure in medicine in the rural parts of HAITI and became involved in various nationalist cultural groups. He served as director of public health (1946–48) and secretary of labor (1949–50) in the regime of President Dumarsais Estimé, but was ousted and forced to flee upon Paul Magloire's coup in 1950. After Magloire's resignation, Duvalier was elected president in 1957, in an election believed to have been fraudulent. At first enormously popular, he became increasingly brutal and dictatorial and in 1964 had himself declared president for life. Duvalier's long reign was marked by poverty, fear and terror, with all signs of opposition suppressed by the dread Tontons Macoutes, his private army of civilian enforcers. On his death in 1971, he was succeeded by his son, **Jean-Claude Duvalier** (known as "Baby Doc"), who was overthrown in a popular revolt in 1986.

Dwan, Allan (Joseph Aloysius Dwan) (*1885–1981*) Canadian-born pioneer motion picture director. Educated at Notre Dame as an electrical engineer, Dwan began providing new lamps for movie lighting to HOLLYWOOD studios in 1909. He was soon writing and editing scripts for silent movies, and in 1911 he directed his first film, a one-reel western. He learned about filmmaking from D. W. GRIFFITH, and created the "dolly shot" by mounting a camera on a moving car—an innovation that revolutionized moviemaking. He discovered Lon CHANEY and Ida Lupino and directed Douglas FAIRBANKS in many films. During the sound era he worked for 20TH CENTURY–FOX in the 1930s, Republic Pictures in the 1940s and RKO in the 1950s. According to his own account, he made about 1,850 films. Among the best known were *The Iron Mask* (1929), *Heidi* (1937), *Rebecca of Sunnybrook Farm* (1938), *Suez* (1938), *The Three Musketeers* (1939) and *The Sands of Iwo Jima* (1949).

Dylan, Bob (Robert Zimmerman) (*1941– *) American folk singer and composer. He adopted the given name of Dylan THOMAS, the Welsh poet. He taught himself guitar and other musical instruments at the age of 10 and ran away from home several times. After leaving home for good, he rode

Songwriter and musician Bob Dylan. 1967 (LIBRARY OF CONGRESS. PRINTS AND PHOTOGRAPHS DIVISION)

freight trains around the country and wrote songs, many inspired by Woody GUTHRIE. In 1961, after occasional coffeehouse appearances, his first record album was released. Dylan is considered the musical symbol of protest by Americans who began to develop their social conscience in the 1960s. His best-known works, like "Blowin' in the Wind" (1962), "The Times They Are A-Changin'" (1963) and "Like a Rolling Stone" (1965), are focused on social injustice. Dylan continued to record and tour throughout the 1990s, winning Grammy Awards in 1994 for best traditional folk album (*World Gone Wrong*) and in 1998 for album of the year (*Time out of Mind*). In 2001 Dylan's single "Things Have Changed" for the *Wonder Boys* (2000) soundtrack won the artist an Academy Award for best original song.

Dymaxion Word coined by Buckminster FULLER to describe a number of his projects. The word is made up of dynamic and maximum and is intended to define Fuller's aims toward "maximizing" performance through recognition of "dynamic" forces. The first Dymaxion House of 1927, developed in a model but never constructed, was a hexagonal living space suspended one story above the ground by tension cables radiating from a central vertical mast. His Dymaxion automobile of 1933, a radical, truly streamlined design, was built in three prototype examples but never accepted for production. The second Dymaxion House of 1946, a domed cylinder, was built as a prototype at Wichita, Kansas, and attracted wide notice, but once again, production was never undertaken because of technical and financial difficulties that made such a radical solution to housing problems seem to be too advanced for its day.

Dyson, Sir Frank Watson (*1868–1939*) British astronomer. After first working as chief assistant at the Royal Observatory at Greenwich from 1894

to 1905, he was Astronomer Royal for Scotland from 1905 to 1910 and then returned to Greenwich as Astronomer Royal, serving from 1910 to 1933. He was knighted in 1915. Dyson's early observational work was done in collaboration with William G. Thackeray: They measured the positions of more than 4,000 circumpolar stars that had first been observed by Stephen Groombridge at the beginning of the 19th century. They were thus able to determine the proper motions of the stars. Dyson observed the total solar eclipses of 1900, 1901 and 1905, obtaining spectra of the atmospheric layers of the Sun. He also organized the detailed observations of the total solar eclipse in 1919, sending expeditions to Príncipe in the Gulf of Guinea and Sobral in Brazil. The measured positions of stars near the Sun's rim during the eclipse provided evidence for the bending of light in a gravitational field, as predicted by EINSTEIN in his theory of general relativity; these measurements were the first experimental support for that theory.

Dyson, Freeman (*1923–*) English-American physicist. Graduating from Cambridge in 1945, Dyson became an American citizen in 1951 and taught at Cornell University before joining the Institute for Advanced Study at Princeton in 1953. A freewheeling, adventurous thinker, Dyson has done major work in quantum electrodynamics but is best known for his challenging speculations on space science and the possibility of super-intelligent extraterrestrials. Always thought-provoking and often controversial, Dyson's carefully reasoned ideas, although sometimes appearing to be "outlandish," command serious attention and debate.

Dzerzhinsky, Felix Edmundovich (*1877–1926*) Communist politician, of Polish noble descent. During the reign of Czar NICHOLAS II he was imprisoned for revolutionary activities several times. After the RUSSIAN REVOLUTION he was the first head (1917–

24) of the secret police (CHEKA) and of its successors, the OGPU and the GPU.

Dzhanibekov, Vladimir (*1942–*) Soviet cosmonaut and veterans of five different space missions from 1978 to 1985, Dzhanibekov is unquestionably one of the brightest and most experienced Soviet cosmonauts. His expert piloting of Soyuz spacecraft accounted for five out of five docking successes at a time when the Soviet space program was haunted with a one-in-four failure rate. Dzhanibekov's most spectacular success was docking the *SOYUZ T-13* craft with the dead *SALYUT* 7 space station in 1985. The tricky and exacting mission required unusual expertise, and Dzhanibekov and flight engineer Viktor Savinykh got the job. After a June 6, 1985, launch and two days chasing the dead station, they were able to link up and succeeded within a few days in repairing the station's onboard systems. On August 2, in a 6.5-hour space walk, they installed new solar panels, and within a few weeks *Salyut* 7 was operable again. Praised by French spationaut Jean-Loup CHRÉTIEN for his calm during a serious docking problem in an earlier flight aboard *Soyuz T-6* in 1982, Dzhanibekov also piloted *Soyuz* 27 in 1978, *Soyuz* 39 in 1981 and *Soyuz T-12* (attempting to repair the *Salyut* 7 power system in a space walk with Svetlana Savitskaya) in 1984. He also served as a deputy in the Uzbek soviet before the breakup of the Soviet Union. He later became an amateur painter and balloonist.

Dzubas Friedel (*1915–1994*) German-American painter. Born in Berlin, Dzubas was a student of Paul KLEE (1933–36) in Düsseldorf before immigrating to the U.S. in 1939. His first one-man show was held in New York City in 1952, but his mature style did not develop until the 1960s. Dzubas was a leading figure in COLOR-FIELD PAINTING, using large areas of color in allover patterns on huge canvases.

E

Eagleton, Thomas Francis *(1929–)* American politician. Born in St. Louis, Missouri, Eagleton attended Amherst College and Harvard Law School; he was admitted to the bar in 1953. After serving as St. Louis's circuit attorney (1957–60), state attorney general (1961–65) and lieutenant governor (1965–68), he was elected to the U.S. Senate as a Democrat in 1968. His liberal views were important to Democratic presidential nominee George McGovern, who chose Eagleton as his 1972 vice presidential running mate. Shortly afterward, however, rumors surfaced that Eagleton had been hospitalized for depression three times in the 1960s and had undergone electric shock therapy. Eagleton acknowledged this and withdrew from the campaign. The Eagleton affair proved embarrassing to McGovern, whose judgment was called into question. McGovern subsequently selected Sargent Shriver as his running mate. Eagleton was reelected to the Senate in 1974 and 1980 but retired from political life in 1986.

Eaker, Ira Clarence *(1896–1987)* U.S. Air Force general. An aviation pioneer between the world wars, he made the first blind transcontinental flight (entirely with instruments). He commanded U.S. air forces in Europe during World War II and then played a key role in the establishment of the U.S. Air Force as a separate military service. He retired from the air force in 1947 and until the late 1970s was a business executive and syndi-

cated newspaper columnist. In 1985 he was promoted to full general on the retired list.

Ealing Studios British film studio associated with some of the most successful movies in the post–World War II period. The "Ealing comedy" became the standard worldwide for the British style of tasteful yet irreverent entertainment. Established in 1929 under the name Associated Talking Pictures, the studio borrowed the name Ealing in the late 1930s from the London borough where it was located. Under the guidance of Sir Michael Balcon, it functioned during its peak period (1946–58) as a relatively small-scale business enterprise that encouraged the individual creativity of its members—notably actors Alec Guinness and Stanley Holloway, writers T. E. B White and William Rose, and directors Alberto Cavalcanti, Michael Crichton, Alexander Mackendrick and Robert Hamer. Dry wit, picturesque locations and a sympathy for the "little man" infused the callous black comedy of *Kind Hearts and Coronets* (1949), the grandtheft hijinks of *The Lavender Hill Mob* (1951) and *The Lady Killers* (1955) and the stinging social satire of *Tight Little Island* (1949), to name only a few representative films. Perhaps the masterpiece from this studio was *The Man in the White Suit* (1951), a tragicomedy about a meek little chemist (Guinness) whose invention of an indestructible fabric nearly brings about, ironically, his own destruction. Ealing suffered

its own mortal blows when it dissolved in the late 1950s under a burden of debts.

Eames, Charles *(1907–1978)* American industrial designer and filmmaker best known for a molded plywood chair he designed in 1940 with Eero Saarinen. The chair was later mass-produced in plastic. He and his wife designed a luxurious leather-and-rosewood lounge chair and ottoman in 1952. Charles Eames made over 50 educational movies, many using a multimedia projector approach.

Eames, Ray (Ray Kaiser) *(1915–1988)* U.S. designer. One of the most influential furniture and industrial designers of the post–World War II era, she was founder and partner in the Venice, California, design firm Office of Charles and Ray Eames. Eames and her husband, Charles, designed the Eames chair, two pieces of molded plywood connected by stainless steel tubing. Their work was known for infusing mass production with a high sense of style and comfort.

Earhart, Amelia *(1898–1937?)* Pioneer American aviator. Earhart was the first woman to fly across the Atlantic Ocean, from Trepassey Bay, Newfoundland, to Burryport, Wales. In 1928 she wrote about that epic journey in her book entitled *20 hrs., 40 min.* In 1931 she married publisher George Putnam. She flew alone across the Atlantic once again in 1932. In 1935 she was the first woman to fly to the mainland of the U.S. from Honolulu, Hawaii, and was the first woman to fly successfully across the U.S. alone in both directions. On a planned around-the-world trip, Earhart vanished near Howland Island in the Pacific Ocean. After her last contact on March 17, 1937, no confirmed report of her fate has ever been made.

Earl, Harley J. *(1893–1954)* American design executive responsible for the styling of GENERAL MOTORS cars from 1927 until his retirement in 1959. Earl was born in California, the son of a builder of custom auto bodies. After joining General Motors, he exerted a constantly increasing influence in favor of design as a major ingredient in sales success. His 1927 LaSalle, dignified and elegant with its narrow hood and simple radiator grille, is viewed as his first major success. Over the years, particularly after World War II, the styling of General Motors cars became gradually more exaggerated, introducing excess CHROMIUM trim, oversized bodies, wraparound windshields, and, ultimately, tailfins. The concept of forced obsolescence is often associated with the constantly changing body designs developed under Earl's direction and imitated by other American automobile manufacturers.

Easter Rebellion (Easter Rising) *(April 1916)* Radical members of SINN FÉIN and the older Irish Republican Brotherhood (later known as the IRISH REPUBLICAN ARMY [IRA]) called for rebellion during WORLD WAR I, while vainly sending Sir Roger CASEMENT to Germany for help. Loosely organized, the planned uprising was confined to Dublin and included only 2,000 Irish volunteers and a 200-citizen army. Seizing the General Post Office as headquarters on Easter Monday, April 24, 1916, Patrick PEARSE and James CONNOLLY and their rebels proclaimed a republic. The British, losing about 460 men, put down the uprising in a week. Many Dubliners condemned the rebellion, but when 16 rebel leaders were executed, the rebels became martyrs and the Irish parliamentary party was ruined. Sinn Féin continued under Eamon DE VALERA, and the IRA became a guerrilla underground. (See also IRELAND; IRISH CIVIL WAR.)

Eastland, James Oliver *(1904–1986)* U.S. politician. A Mississippi Democrat, Eastland served in the U.S. Senate for more than 36 years. A wealthy plantation owner, he was best known during his years in the Senate as a segregationist and militant anticommunist. He was often at odds with the national DEMOCRATIC PARTY and frequently criticized the U.S. Supreme Court. He left this party during the 1948 presidential election to support the Dixiecrat STATES' RIGHTS ticket. Often sharply critical of President Lyndon B. JOHNSON's GREAT SOCIETY program, he was nonetheless respected and liked by Senate liberals. When he retired in 1979, Eastland had been chairman of the Senate Judiciary Committee for 22 years and president pro tem of the Senate for six.

Eastman, George *(1854–1932)* American inventor. Eastman began his career in banking and insurance but turned from this to photography. In 1880 he perfected dryplate photographic film and began manufacturing it. He produced a transparent roll-film in 1884 and in the same year founded the Eastman Dry Plate and Film Co. In 1888 he introduced the simple handheld box camera that made popular photography possible. The Kodak camera with a roll of transparent film was cheap enough for all pockets and could be

used by a child. It was followed by the Brownie camera, which cost just $1. Eastman gave away a considerable part of his fortune to educational institutions, including the Massachusetts Institute of Technology. He committed suicide in 1932.

East Pakistan See BANGLADESH.

East Timor (Timor-Leste) Portuguese possession (until 1975), Indonesian territory (1975–2002) and independent state (2002–). From the 17th century until 1975, East Timor was a possession of the Portuguese empire, which introduced the Roman Catholic faith to the population of the territory. In 1975 the new democratic government of PORTUGAL announced its intention to withdraw from East Timor and began preparing the territory for independence. However, a few months after East Timor became an independent nation, a conflict erupted between the Catholic majority in the country and the Muslim minority, which demanded that East Timor join the predominantly Muslim state of INDONESIA. As this internal dispute intensified, evidence surfaced that the Indonesian government was funding those East Timorese groups advocating unification with Indonesia. On December 7, 1975, Indonesian forces invaded the country and instituted martial law.

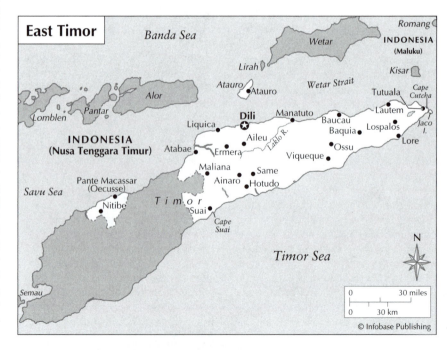

Seven months later Indonesia annexed East Timor. Dissident groups in East Timor rejected Indonesian rule and rallied around leaders such as Bishop Carlos BELO and José RAMOS-HORTA, a government minister who had been abroad petitioning the UN Security Council at the time of the invasion. Between 1975 and 1999 Indonesian forces conducted what they termed the *pacification* of East Timor in order to eradicate secessionist elements within the territory. During this period an estimated 200,000 East Timorese died as a result of repression or famine throughout the province.

In November 1991, during a funeral service for several East Timorese nationalists at a Catholic cemetery in Dili, Indonesian paramilitary forces opened fire on the mourners, massacring several hundred men, women and children. The assault sparked outrage in the international community and helped Horta persuade the American and British governments to suspend the delivery of weapons and military advisers to Indonesia. However, the independence movement was dealt a setback when in November 1992 Indonesian troops captured Xanasa Gusmao, the leader of the most prominent guerrilla movement, and sentenced him to life in prison. In June 1998, a month after the overthrow of Indonesian dictator SUHARTO, the new Indonesian president, B. J. HABIBIE, announced his willingness to consider holding a referendum on East Timor's status. A year later Indonesia and Portugal brokered an agreement in which the UN would administer the referendum to ensure a free and fair process. Despite repeated interference from paramilitary forces allegedly sponsored by Indonesia, the referendum was conducted on August 30, 1999. It produced a massive 78.5% vote in favor of independence. Shortly after the UN announced the result, paramilitary forces opposing East Timorese independence launched a brief military campaign in the province that burned several villages to the ground, forced an estimated 200,000 refugees to flee their homes and led the UN to approve the dispatch of an Australian-led peacekeeping force to enter the province and restore order. A week after the vote, Indonesia released Gusmao from jail in an effort to placate rebel sentiments

within East Timor and announced that the Indonesian troops would completely leave the province by November 1. In late October 1999 the UN established a transitional administration in East Timor to prepare the province politically and economically for independence. In the inaugural presidential elections held in April 2002, Gusmao won a clear majority of the popular vote. He has since devoted himself to gaining international acceptance of the new parliamentary regime, in which the Revolutionary Front for an Independent East Timor (FRETILIN) has emerged as the ruling political party. The UN maintained its mission of support in East Timor until May 2004.

Eastwood, Clint (*1930– *) American film actor and director; a dominant box-office star since the mid-1960s. Eastwood began his acting career in the 1950s and first achieved success with his cowboy role on the television series *Rawhide* (1959–66). Real stardom came with his portrayal of the fearsome, gunslinging "man with no name" in a trio of Italian-made "spaghetti" westerns: *A Fistful of Dollars* (1964), *For a Few Dollars More* (1965) and *The Good, the Bad, and the Ugly* (1967). Eastwood's other continuing character (in five films) is ultimate enforcer-cop Harry Callahan, whose "Make my day!" in *Dirty Harry* (1971) became a national catchphrase. Other successful films include *Play Misty for Me* (1971, also his first directing effort), *Tightrope* (1984) and *Heartbreak Ridge* (1986).

In recent years, he has concentrated on producing and directing films, such as *Bird* (1988), based on the life of jazz great Charlie PARKER. Eastwood's direction of the film *Unforgiven* (1992) added a new dimension to his Hollywood career. The film proved popular with critics and moviegoers and earned Eastwood two Academy Awards, for best picture and best director. While Eastwood's success with *Unforgiven* inspired him to increase his time behind the camera with such films as *A Perfect World* (1993), *Absolute Power* (1997), *Midnight in the Garden of Good and Evil* (1997), *True Crime* (1999) and *Space Cowboys* (2000), he continued to star in such blockbuster pictures as *In the Line of Fire* (1993). He also directed and starred in *Million Dollar Baby*

(2004), for which he received another Academy Award for best director.

Eaton, Cyrus Stephen (*1883–1979*) American financier and industrialist. Born in Nova Scotia, Canada, Eaton was a "self-made man." He invested in rubber, steel, coal and utilities. In 1930 he founded the Republic Steel Corporation (1930). Although a champion of U.S. capitalism, he was also an early advocate of trade with communist nations. He was a friend of Soviet premier Nikita KHRUSHCHEV and other high Soviet officials. In 1955 he established the first of the Pugwash Conferences, annual meeting attended by scientists and scholars from the Eastern and Western blocs designed to lessen international tension. In 1960 the Soviet Union awarded Eaton the Lenin Peace Prize.

Ebashi, Setsuro (*1922– *) Japanese biochemist. Ebashi received his M.D. (1944) and his Ph.D. (1954) from the University of Tokyo. He became professor of pharmacology in 1959 and, since 1963, has held the chair of biochemistry. Ebashi has for many years been one of the leading workers in the field of muscle contraction. His work has thrown considerable light on the identity and workings of the so-called relaxing factor. In 1999 Ebashi won the International Prize in biology for his research on naturally occurring muscle relaxants in animals.

Ebro River River that rises in the Catabrian Mountains and flows southeastward for 565 miles to a delta on the Mediterranean Sea, between BARCELONA and Valencia, Spain. During the SPANISH CIVIL WAR the Loyalists suffered a major defeat here (August–November 1938). Hydroelectric power plants in the Ebro system now provide nearly 50% of Spain's hydroelectricity.

Eccles, Sir John Carew (*1903– 1997*) Australian physiologist. Eccles was educated at the University of Melbourne and in England at Oxford University, working at Oxford with Charles Sherrington on muscular reflexes and nervous transmission across the synapses (nerve junctions). For a time he taught in Australia and New Zealand, and in 1966 he began working at the Institute for Biomedical Research in

Chicago. While professor of physiology at the Australian National University Canberra (1951–66), Eccles carried out work on the chemical changes that take place at synapses, pursuing the findings of Alan Hodgkin and Andrew HUXLEY, with whom he subsequently shared the 1963 NOBEL PRIZE in physiology or medicine. Eccles showed that excitation of different nerve cells causes the synapses to release a substance that promotes the passage of sodium and potassium ions and effects an alternation in the polarity of the electric charge. It is in this way that nervous impulses are communicated—or inhibited—by nerve cells.

Ecevit, Bülent (*1925– *) Turkish statesman and writer. After a career in government and journalism, Ecevit became a member of TURKEY's parliament in 1957. He was minister of labor (1961–65) and chairman of the Republican People's Party (1972). He was briefly prime minister of a coalition government in 1974, again holding that office in 1978–80. After the 1980 military coup, Ecevit was imprisoned and banned from public life in 1983. He voluntarily renounced political activities in 1987 but became chairman of the Democratic Left Party in 1989. Ecevit returned to the premiership in 1999 following the outbreak of a financial crisis and attempted to restore the Turkish economy while preserving its secular status. However, opposition from conservative nationalists within his coalition and a plummeting lira in 2001 led to his ouster in November 2002.

Eckstine, Billy (William Clarence Eckstine) (*1914–1993*) American bandleader, singer and trumpeter. Eckstine was born in Pittsburgh, Pennsylvania, and attended Washington University. He began his career as a jazz vocalist and from 1939 to 1943 was a vocalist and trumpeter with the Earl HINES band. In 1944 he formed his own band and was a pioneer in the development of BEBOP. Jazz greats such as Dizzy GILLESPIE, Charlie PARKER, Miles DAVIS and Sarah VAUGHAN gained valuable experience performing with the band. After the band broke up in 1974, Eckstine continued his career as a solo performer and recording artist. He continued to perform in cabarets until the 1970s.

eclecticism Term used in design and architecture to refer to the practice of borrowing from various historic styles, sometimes in combination. From about 1900 until World War II, most architecture and interior design was eclectic, using the styles of ancient Greece and Rome, the Middle Ages and the Renaissance as the taste of architects and clients might suggest. Such buildings as New York's old Pennsylvania Railroad terminal, built in imitation of Roman baths, the Woolworth Building, constructed in the style of a Gothic cathedral tower, and many lesser buildings are typical of the eclectic phase of American architecture. Interiors were similarly designed in imitative styles. Manufacturers of furniture, lighting devices and similar items produced designs to match the popular periods and styles. Although eclecticism was largely displaced by MODERNISM, in survives in the continuing manufacture of antique reproductions and is currently being revived in a modified form as an aspect of POSTMODERNISM.

Eco, Umberto (*1932– *) Italian novelist and philosopher. Eco achieved best seller status in Europe and the U.S. with the publication of his medieval mystery novel, *The Name of the Rose* (1984). A professor of semiotics—the study of human signs and symbols—at the University of Bologna, Eco has written extensively in the fields of philosophy and literary criticism on subjects including Saint Thomas Aquinas and James JOYCE. But he emerged as an important novelist in the 1980s through his ability to combine erudite and esoteric themes, such as Christian scholasticism and Jewish kabbalah, with fast-paced plots set in a historical past that interweave crime and passion with the spiritual quest for

meaning in life. *The Name of the Rose*, which is set in a labyrinthine medieval monastery in which a series of murders have taken place, was adapted into a 1986 film starring Sean CONNERY. Eco's second novel was *Foucault's Pendulum* (1988).

Economic Community of West African States (ECOWAS) Regional economic organization consisting of 15 nations in West Africa, created in May 1975. ECOWAS sought to increase economic integration among its members with the ultimate goal of producing a West African version of the EUROPEAN COMMUNITY (EC). It also encouraged its members to adopt a more international outlook, rather than pursue purely nationalist policies. In 1976 the Nigerian and Togo governments proposed that all ECOWAS members establish a collective defense arrangement among themselves. While this did not lead to a West African version of the NORTH ATLANTIC TREATY ORGANIZATION (NATO), it did lead to a nonaggression pact among some ECOWAS members in 1978, a mutual defensive arrangement among members in 1981 and the adoption of the nonaggression pact by all members in 1986. In 1978 ECOWAS members also agreed to refrain from intervention in the internal affairs of other members in order to prevent one ECOWAS state from capitalizing on the internal disorder of another by supporting a rebel faction.

Since 1991 the mutual defense principles established by ECOWAS have been applied in many cases throughout West Africa, although not with uniform success. In October 1991 ECOWAS brokered a deal with the rebel National Patriotic Front of Liberia (NPFL) that called for its disarmament and the creation of an interim government; however, the deal collapsed when the NPFL rearmed in the face of continued aggression by the Liberian government, and the Liberian civil war continued for another five years. The principles of ECOWAS were put to more effective use 12 years later when Liberian president Charles TAYLOR resigned and Nigerian peacekeeping forces entered Liberia to restore order until an interim government took office.

Ecuador Nation on the Pacific coast of northwestern South America, with Colombia to the north and PERU to the south and east; the equator, from which the country takes its name, crosses Ecuador near its capital city of Quito. The anticlerical Flavio Eloy Alfaro ruled for nearly 15 years after 1895. From the 1920s to the 1940s there were continual changes of president, a dozen serving between 1931 and 1940. José María VELASCO IBARRA, a liberal, was elected president five times from 1934 to 1972 but served only one full term. Galo Plaza Lasso served as a liberal president from 1948 to 1952. Camilo Ponce Enríquez was elected in 1956 as the first conservative president in 60 years.

Ecuador's long border dispute with Peru began in 1860 and involved the Oriente, a section east of the Andes Mountains, at the headwaters of the Amazon. The two nations battled in 1941, and the following year Ecuador was compelled to relinquish a large

ECUADOR	
1912	President Eloy Alfaro killed by proclerical faction.
1925	"July Revolution" introduces period of reform.
1931–48	Twenty-two governments hold temporary office.
1960	José María Velasco Ibarra elected president for the sixth time.
1972	General Guillermo Rodríguez Lara overthrows President Velasco; Rodríguez threatens oil contracts and investments of more than 30 foreign companies.
1980	Freedom House lists Ecuador as free country; death of Velasco Ibarra.
1989	Leftist guerrilla group lays down arms after nine-year struggle; two U.S. environmental groups absorb Ecuadoran debt in exchange for rain forest preservation.
1997	Some 2 million workers stage a general strike in February; more than 10,000 protesters surround the Congress, which dismisses President Abdalá Bucaram Ortíz for "mental incapacity."
1998	Leaders of Ecuador and Peru sign treaty confirming long-disputed border between the two countries.
2000	Ecuador adopts the U.S. dollar as its national currency; President Jamil Mahuad is forced out of office after massive demonstrations.
2003	Lucio Gutiérrez elected president.
2005	Gutiérrez's vice president, Alfredo Palacios, appointed president after congress removes Gutiérrez after a week of unrest.

section of Peru, only to have President Velasco Ibarra condemn the treaty in 1960. The 1960s and 1970s brought numerous revolts and different presidents; from 1961 to 1963, however, Carlos Julio Arosemena Monroy's practices enhanced the financial situation. Following several years of government by military junta, Jaime Roldós Aguilera was installed as president in 1979 in a quiet shift of command. When Aguilera died in a plane crash in May 1981, control was transferred quietly to Vice President Osvaldo Hurtado, who carried on Aguilera's reform program. In January 1981 war erupted again over the Peru-Ecuador border; in March, however, both sides started to negotiate. Ecuador's economy surged after the discovery of oil in 1971, but falling oil prices in the 1980s, combined with high inflation, ensured that the standard of living remained low for the average Ecuadoran. Ecuador's economic woes continued into the 1990s despite efforts to stimulate the economy by producing more oil in 1992 and by adopting the U.S. dollar as its national currency in 2000. Quito is the capital and Guayaquil the largest city.

Eddington, Sir Arthur Stanley
(1882–1944) British astrophysicist and mathematician. Eddington graduated from Owens College (now the University of Manchester) in 1902 and from Cambridge University in 1905. From 1906 to 1913 he was chief assistant to the Astronomer Royal at Greenwich, after which he returned to Cambridge as Plumian Professor of Astronomy. He was knighted in 1930. Eddington was the major British astronomer of the interwar period. His early work on the motions of stars was followed, from 1916 onward, by studies of the interiors of stars—about which he published his first major book, *The Internal Constitution of the Stars* (1926). He showed that for equilibrium to be maintained in a star, the inwardly directed force of gravitation must be balanced by the outwardly directed forces of both gas pressure and radiation pressure. He also proposed that heat energy was transported from the center to the outer regions of a star not by convection, as thought hitherto, but by radiation. It was in this work that Eddington gave a full account of his discovery (1924) of the mass-to-

luminosity relationship, which shows that the more massive a star is the more luminous it will be. The value of the relation is that it allows the mass of a star to be determined if its intrinsic brightness is known. Eddington realized that there was a limit to the size of stars. Relatively few would have masses exceeding 10 times the mass of the Sun, and any exceeding 50 solar masses would be unstable because of excessive radiation pressure. Eddington wrote a number of books both for scientists and for a lay readership. His more popular books, including *The Expanding Universe* (1933), were widely read, went through many editions and opened new worlds to many inquiring minds of the interwar years. It was through Eddington that EINSTEIN's **theory of general relativity** reached the English-speaking world. Eddington was greatly impressed by Einstein's theory and was able to provide experimental evidence for it. He observed the total solar eclipse of 1919 and submitted a report that captured the intellectual imagination of his generation. It stated that a very precise and unexpected prediction made by Einstein in his general theory had been successfully observed. He had seen the very slight bending of light by the gravitational field of a star—the Sun. Further support came in 1924 when Einstein's prediction of the reddening of starlight by the gravitational field of the star was tested. Eddington thus did much to establish Einstein's theory on a sound and rigorous foundation and gave a very fine presentation of the subject in his *Mathematical Theory of Relativity* (1923). Eddington also worked for many years on an obscure but challenging theory, which was only published in his posthumous work *Fundamental Theory* (1946). Basically, he claimed that the fundamental constants of science, such as the mass of the proton and mass and charge of the electron, were a "natural and complete specification for constructing a universe" and that their values were not accidental. He then set out to develop a theory from which such values would follow as a consequence, but he never completed it.

Eden, Anthony (first earl of Avon)
(1897–1977) British Conservative party statesman, prime minister of the United Kingdom (1955–57). Eden entered the

British statesman Anthony Eden (LIBRARY OF CONGRESS, PRINTS AND PHOTOGRAPHS DIVISION)

House of Commons in 1923 and served three times as foreign secretary (1935–38, 1940–45 and 1951–55). He was a leading figure in Winston CHURCHILL's coalition cabinet during WORLD WAR II. Heir-apparent to Churchill for many years, he was deputy prime minister in Churchill's second period in office (1951–55) and succeeded Churchill as prime minister in 1955. Eden's main interests were always in foreign affairs. His ministry was marked by increasing tensions in the Middle East. Eden's hostility toward NASSER's Egypt tempted him to support Anglo-French military intervention and led to the SUEZ CRISIS (1956). This divided the country, lost Eden the support of most Commonwealth leaders and aroused the ire of U.S. secretary of state John Foster DULLES. The Suez Crisis contributed to a collapse of Eden's health and his resignation in January 1957. He was created earl of Avon in 1961.

Ederle, Gertrude "Trudy" *(1906–2003)* American swimmer, considered one of the greatest athletes of the 1920s. In the 1924 OLYMPIC GAMES, Ederle won a gold medal as a member of the U.S. women's 400-meter relay team. In 1926 she became the first woman to swim across the English Channel; she made the 35-mile swim in 14.5 hours, two hours faster than the previous record, held by a man. At

the peak of her amateur career, Ederle held 29 national or world swimming records.

Edgerton, Harold Eugene "Doc"
(1903–1990) American inventor. A professor at the Massachusetts Institute of Technology, Edgerton is credited with inventing the electronic flash for use in photography. His repeating strobe unit, developed in 1931, made high-speed photography possible by "freezing" action. He also devised a flash technique that was used to take nighttime reconnaissance photos prior to the Allied Invasion of NORMANDY on D day in 1944. An interest in deep-sea exploration led him to develop an underwater camera for explorer Jacques COUSTEAU. He developed a sonar device that in 1973 helped locate the sunken American Civil War ironclad *Monitor.* The device was less successful in 1976 in an attempt to find the Loch Ness monster.

Edinburgh Festival
Held annually for a three-week period in August–September in Edinburgh, Scotland, the festival is an international celebration of the arts, with an emphasis on music and, more recently, theater, dance and film. Founded in 1947, the festival was first directed by Rudolph BING. Since 1992 Sir Brian McMaster has been director. A special feature of the festival is the Fringe, a subfestival composed of hundreds of events, often innovative and experimental, that are outside the official program but often command much attention. Such distinguished opera companies as La Scala have performed there as well as such famous musicians as opera singer Plácido DOMINGO and conductor Zubin Mehta.

Edison, Thomas Alva *(1847–1931)*
One of the most productive of American inventors of the late 19th and early 20th centuries. His invention of the phonograph ("talking machine") in 1877 and of the electric lightbulb in 1878 established his reputation as a key figure in the development of modern technology. As with many inventors, Edison combined invention with design through the necessity of giving form to his original prototypes. Although many Edison designs seem crude, others, such as the incandescent bulb, were so well conceived as to be-

American inventor Thomas Edison with his phonograph (LIBRARY OF CONGRESS, PRINTS AND PHOTOGRAPHS DIVISION)

come the norm, surviving with little change to the present. Edison was a prolific inventor of many electrical devices and systems and played an important role in the development of modern, near-universally available electrical power distribution systems.

Edison Company
America's first motion picture studio, named after Thomas Alva EDISON. A facility called the Black Maria was constructed in West Orange, N.J., in 1891. It was a large structure, covered inside and out with tar paper, with only a removable part of the roof allowing sunlight inside. Utilizing the Edison devices of the **kinetophone** (a device that synchronized film with a sound cylinder) and the **kinetograph** camera, Edison's assistant, W. K. L. Dickson, produced numerous short motion picture strips on the newly developed EASTMAN celluloid film. At first these movies were merely brief actualities of vaudeville acts, strongmen and prize fights; but after April 23, 1896, when the first public performance of Edison's films took place at Koster and Bial's Music Hall in New York's Herald Square, production grew more ambitious. A stock company of players was developed, including Viola Dana, Mary Fuller and Charles Ogle. At a new studio facility in New York, director Edwin S. Porter made many narrative films of one-reel duration (approximately eight to 12 minutes), including *The Great Train Robbery* (1903). An itinerant actor named D. W. GRIFFITH arrived in 1907 and appeared as a player in *Rescued from an Eagle's Nest.* Later at the rival studio, American Mutoscope and Biograph Company, Griffith would revolutionize filmmaking techniques and effects (see BIOGRAPH COMPANY). After a bitter battle over motion picture equipment patent rights between Edison and Biograph, the two cooperated in the formation (1909)

of the notorious Motion Picture Patents Company. The period from 1908 to 1912 saw Edison's peak of success. Several factors, however, caused his business to decline rapidly. There was a disastrous fire at the new Edison studio in the Bronx. Edison was slow to exploit the popular trend toward feature-length movies after 1914. The Patents Company, moreover, was dissolved by the Supreme Court in 1915 in an antitrust action. The Edison Company disbanded in 1918. Its last film was a feature called *The Unbeliever,* directed by Alan Crosland—who 10 years later would direct the seminal synchronized-sound film *The Jazz Singer* for WARNER BROS.

Edlen, Bengt *(1906–1993)*
Swedish physicist. Edlen studied at the University of Uppsala, where he gained his Ph.D. in 1934 and also served on the faculty from 1928 until 1944. He was then appointed professor of physics at the University of Lund, a post he retained until his retirement in 1973. Edlen is recognized for his research on atomic spectra and their applications to astrophysics. In the early 1940s he carried out important work on the emission lines in the Sun's corona. Edlen succeeded in showing (1941) that the coronal lines were caused mainly by iron, nickel, calcium and argon atoms deprived of 10 to 15 of their electrons, that is, by highly charged positive ions. The implications of such extreme ionization were not lost on Edlen, who was quick to point out that it must indicate temperatures of more than a quarter of a million degrees in the solar corona.

Edrich, W. J. "Bill" *(1916–1986)*
English cricketer whose career stretched from 1934 to 1958. Edrich's greatest achievement came in 1947 when he scored 3,539 runs and, with

Dennis COMPTON, set an English Test record of 370 for the third wicket. The following year he and Compton had an unbroken stand of 424 against Somerset, a Middlesex and Lord's record.

Edsall, John Tileston *(1902–2002)*

American biochemist. Edsall was educated at Harvard and at Cambridge University, England. He joined the Harvard faculty in 1928 and from 1951 to 1973 served there as professor of biochemistry. From 1956 to 1967 he edited the *Journal of Biological Chemistry*. Edsall's work focuses mainly on protein chemistry. He spent much time establishing basic data on the constitution and properties of numerous proteins—information that has since been reproduced in innumerable textbooks. With Edwin Cohn he was the author of the authoritative work *Proteins, Amino Acids and Peptides* (1943). In later years Edsall turned his attention to the history of biochemistry; his book in this field included *Blood and Hemoglobin* (1952).

Edsel

Brand name of an automobile introduced by the Ford Motor Company in 1958. The Edsel has become a legend of the failure of a giant company in developing, designing and marketing a product so badly matched to consumer preferences that it faced almost total public rejection. The Edsel (named for Henry FORD's son) was developed with the aid of consumer preference studies of the time and was designed with heavily exaggerated styling elements of the kind that had become popular in the early 1950s. By the time the Edsel appeared, however, public taste had changed, turning away from such styling toward a slightly more conservative look. The Edsel therefore seemed a caricature of over-design, the subject of derision rather than admiration. The model was discontinued after a very brief production run. Ironically, surviving examples have become collectors' items.

Edward VII *(1841–1910)*

King of Great Britain and Ireland (1901–10). The eldest surviving son of Queen Victoria and Prince Albert, he did not accede to the throne until he was 59. As Prince of Wales, he traveled widely, was the center of a fashionable social

King Edward VII. 1902 (LIBRARY OF CONGRESS, PRINTS AND PHOTOGRAPHS DIVISION)

circle and was a noted patron of the arts. He married ALEXANDRA of Denmark in 1863, and the couple had six children. After the death of Albert in 1861, Edward represented the Crown at most official functions. However, he was widely regarded as a playboy, and his libertine ways were roundly disapproved of by his mother, who gave him virtually no political responsibility. He became king after Victoria's death in 1901, and his urbane and genial demeanor made him a popular, if little-experienced, monarch. Edward advanced British foreign policy by his many trips abroad, and he supported the ANGLO-FRENCH ENTENTE of 1904. At home he favored the policies of the LIBERAL PARTY and was a reluctant participant in ASQUITH's attempt to limit the power of the House of Lords. He died in 1910 and was succeeded by his son GEORGE V. In Britain, the first decade of the 20th century is generally known as the **Edwardian** period.

Edward VIII, duke of Windsor

(1894–1972) King of the United Kingdom of Great Britain and Ireland (1936) who gave up the British throne to, as he said, "marry the woman I love." The eldest son of GEORGE V and Queen Mary, he was proclaimed Prince of Wales in 1911. He served in the Royal Navy in WORLD WAR I. During the 1920s and early 1930s the handsome prince lived the life of a charming playboy and sophisticated trendsetter. He was also a goodwill ambassador for Britain around the world. Much admired by the British people, during the GREAT DEPRESSION he visited working-

class areas throughout Britain and expressed genuine concern for the unemployed. Groomed for kingship, he ascended to the throne upon the death of George V (January 20, 1936) but was never formally crowned. By this time, he was involved with Mrs. **Wallis Warfield Simpson,** an American who had been divorced from her first husband and was still married to her second. When Mrs. Simpson obtained her second divorce, the king's decision to marry her provoked the ABDICATION CRISIS (November 1936). Many people felt that as an American and a divorcée, she would be an unsuitable wife for the king. In a moving radio address to the nation (December 11, 1936), Edward announced and explained his decision to abdicate. He was succeeded by his younger brother, GEORGE VI. Taking the title duke of Windsor, Edward married Mrs. Simpson in France the following year. He was governor (1940–45) of the Bahamas during World War II. The couple then settled in France and rarely visited England.

Edwards, Douglas *(1917–1990)*

U.S. broadcaster. He began his broadcast career in radio and in 1947 became the first major radio announcer to switch to television. The next year, he became the first American news anchorman, as CBS made him the host of its first nightly news program, *Douglas Edwards with the News*. He was one of the first television news anchors to do on-the-scene reporting, covering such events as the 1956 sinking of the *ANDREA DORIA*. He was replaced by Walter CRONKITE in 1962 but continued to work for the network until his retirement in 1988.

Egas Moniz, António Caetano de Abreu Freire) *(1874–1955)*

Portuguese neurologist and political activist. Egas Moniz was educated at the University of Coimbra, where he gained his M.D. in 1899. After postgraduate work in Paris and Bordeaux he returned to Coimbra, becoming a professor in the medical faculty (1902). He moved to Lisbon in 1911 to a newly created chair of neurology, a post he retained until his retirement in 1944. At the same time he pursued a successful political career, being elected to the National Assembly in

1900. He served as ambassador to Spain in 1917 and in the following year became foreign minister, leading his country's delegation to the PARIS PEACE CONFERENCE. Egas Moniz achieved his first major success in the 1920s in the field of angiography (the study of the cardiovascular system using dyes that are opaque to X-rays). In collaboration with Almeida Lima, he injected such radio-opaque dyes into the arteries enabling the blood vessels of the brain to be photographed. In 1927 he was able to show that displacements in the cerebral circulation could be used to infer the presence and location of brain tumors; he published a detailed account of his technique in 1931.

Egas Moniz is better known for his introduction in 1935 of the operation called **prefrontal lobotomy.** It was for this work, described by the Nobel authorities as "one of the most important discoveries ever made in psychiatric therapy," that they awarded him the 1949 NOBEL PRIZE for physiology or medicine. The operation consisted of inserting a sharp knife into the prefontal lobe of the brain. It required the minimum of equipment and lasted less than five minutes. The technique was suggested to Egas Moniz on hearing an account of a chimpanzee that became less aggressive after its frontal lobes had been excised. Egas Moniz believed that a similar surgical operation would relieve severe emotional tension in psychiatric patients. He claimed that 14 of the first 20 patients operated upon were either cured or improved. The operation generated much controversy, since the extent of the improvement in the patients' symptoms was not easy to judge and the procedure often produced severe side effects.

Egk, Werner *(1901–1990)* German composer. Born in Bavaria, he became a respected conductor, often directing the Berlin State Opera. Egk was also a teacher of music and became director of the Berlin Hochschule in 1950. Strongly influenced by Igor STRAVINSKY in his use of harmony, instrumentation, rhythms and musical irony, he is principally known for his operas, particularly his first, *Die Zaubergeige* (1935), and his second, *Peer Gynt* (1938). Egk's output also included orchestral and chamber works and ballets.

Egypt (Arab Republic of Egypt) Nation on the Mediterranean coast of northeastern Africa, surrounding the fertile valley of the Nile River. Occupied by the British in 1882, it became a British protectorate in 1914 when the OTTOMAN EMPIRE allied itself with England's enemy, GERMANY, in WORLD WAR I. Made an independent kingdom in 1922, it was the site of fierce tank battles between British and German forces in its western deserts during WORLD WAR II. Egypt became a republic in 1953, after Gamal Abdel NASSER led a military coup against King FAROUK; Nasser became president in 1954. Hostility toward the new state of ISRAEL has been a key factor in modern Egypt's history, as it assumed the mantle of major champion of nonaligned Arab solidarity. Although it suffered a military defeat in the ARAB-ISRAELI WAR OF 1956, Egypt won wide respect in the Arab world (see SUEZ CRISIS).

In 1958 SYRIA, YEMEN and Egypt briefly united to create the UNITED ARAB REPUBLIC (UAR)—a venture that ended in 1961. During the SIX-DAY WAR of 1967 Israel solidly defeated Egypt as it outpaced Egyptian, Syrian and Jordanian forces and captured the SINAI PENINSULA and GAZA STRIP; the SUEZ CANAL was closed. Nasser died in 1970 and was succeeded by Anwar al-SADAT. In 1973 war again broke out with Israel, and a section of the Sinai was recaptured by Egypt. Israel withdrew following negotiations, and in 1975 the canal was reopened. U.S. president Jimmy CARTER encouraged Sadat to form cordial relations with Israel, thus distancing Egypt from the rest of the Arab world. Sadat was murdered by a fundamentalist Arab faction in 1981, and Hosni MUBARAK became president. Egypt censured IRAQ's assault on KUWAIT in 1990 and actively participated in the UN's allied coalition against Iraq in the ensuing PERSIAN GULF WAR. In the 1990s Mubarak experienced increased opposition to his continued rule from Islamic fundamentalists, escaping an assassination attempt in June 1995 while at an ORGANIZATION OF AFRICAN UNITY summit in Addis Ababa, Ethiopia. To curb some of these fundamentalist criticisms,

EGYPT	
1900	Nominally autonomous within the Ottoman Empire, Egypt is controlled by the British consul-general.
1902	First dam at Aswân to control flooding of the Nile; spread of irrigation to promote cotton as a cash crop.
1914	Declared a British protectorate.
1918	Nationalist movement under Saad Zaghlul.
1922	Britain grants independence but retains military control and possession of Suez Canal; discovery of Tutankhamen's tomb sparks new fashion styles in the West.
1942	British stop Rommel's drive toward the Suez Canal at El Alamein.
1948	Rioting in Cairo after Egypt's defeat in attack on new state of Israel; assassination of pro-Western leaders.
1952	Free Officers' movement forces abdication of King Farouk; proclaims republic.
1954	Colonel Gamal Nasser takes power; reorganizes nation, pursues pan-Arab socialism and closer ties with USSR.
1956	Nasser nationalizes Suez Canal, prevents British and French forces from reclaiming it before UN imposes cease-fire.
1958	Egypt joins Syria to form United Arab Republic.
1961	Syria withdraws from UAR.
1966	Ancient monuments at Abu Simbel are moved to protect them from waters of immense new flood control dam at Aswân.
1967	Egypt attacks Israel; Egyptian forces crushed in Six-Day War; Egypt loses Gaza Strip.
1970	Death of Nasser; Anwar Sadat begins rapprochement with the West.
1976	Free multiparty elections.
1978	Camp David Accord signed with Israel; Sadat wins Nobel Peace Prize.
1979	Peace treaty with Israel; other Arab states break off relations with Egypt.
1981	Sadat killed by Islamic fundamentalists; succeeded by Hosni Mubarak.
1984	Jordan becomes first Arab state to reestablish ties.
1987	Mubarak reelected president.
1989	Egypt reaccepted into Arab League at Casablanca summit.
1991	Egypt contributes troops to anti-Iraq coalition in Persian Gulf War.
1993	Mubarak reelected president.
1997	Assassination attempt against Mubarak at Organization of African Unity meeting in Addis Ababa, Ethiopia.
1999	Mubarak begins fourth term in office.
2005	Mubarak announces the country's first "free and fair" elections, is reelected.

Egypt downgraded its relations with Israel after Israeli prime minister Ariel SHARON placed Palestinian leader Yasir ARAFAT under house arrest. In 2005 pressure from the administration of U.S. president George W. BUSH induced Mubarak to promise "free and fair" elections in Egypt. Mubarak was reelected.

Ehrenburg, Ilya Grigorovich *(1891–1967)* Writer, of Jewish origin, who spent much of his life in Paris. A symbolist poet at the start of his career, Ehrenburg was a skillful master of all the genres. His works include *A Street in Moscow* (1932), *Out of Chaos* (1934) and *European Crossroad* (1934). A one-time member of the Supreme Soviet, he was a pioneer of the DE-STALINIZATION of literature and wrote the influential novel *The Thaw* (1954–56). While permitted to strive for the rehabilitation of victims of the Terror, such as Osip MANDELSTAM, at the same time he had to make considerable concession to the authorities.

Ehricke, Krafft A. *(1917–1984)* German rocket scientist. Ehricke studied rocket engineering at the Technical University of Berlin, but his studies were interrupted by WORLD WAR II, and he was drafted to work on the V-2 rocket project at PEENEMUNDE. After the war he was brought to the U.S. along with Werner von BRAUN and other German rocket scientists. He subsequently worked on the Redstone, Atlas and Centaur rockets. While heading a committee of the American Rocket Society, Ehricke urged government officials to establish a civilian space agency, which evolved into NASA. He was also an adviser on the development of the APOLLO spacecraft and the SPACE SHUTTLE.

Ehrlich, Paul *(1854–1915)* German physician, bacteriologist and chemist. Ehrlich studied medicine at the Universities of Breslau, Strasbourg and Freiburg, gaining a physician's degree at Breslau in 1878. For the next nine years he worked at the Charite Hospital, Berlin, on many diseases, including typhoid fever, tuberculosis and pernicious anemia. As a result of his laboratory work he contracted tuberculosis and was not restored to health until 1890, when he set up his own small research laboratory at Steglitz on the outskirts of Berlin. When Robert Koch announced the discovery of tuberculin (1890) and suggested its use in preventing and curing tuberculosis, he asked Ehrlich to work on it with him at the Moabit Hospital in Berlin. Ehrlich accepted and for six years studied TB and cholera. In 1896 he accepted the post of director of the new Institute for Serum Research and Serum Investigation at Steglitz and in 1899 moved to the Institute of Exper-

imental Therapy in Frankfurt. Here he investigated African sleeping sickness and syphilis. In 1908 he was awarded the NOBEL PRIZE in physiology or medicine for his work on immunity and serum therapy. Two years later he announced his most famous discovery, **Salvarsan,** a synthetic chemical that was effective against syphilis. Until the end of his life he worked on the problems associated with the use of this compound of arsenic in treating patients. Ehrlich is considered to be the founder of modern chemotherapy because he developed systematic scientific techniques to search for new synthetic chemicals that could specifically attack disease-causing microorganisms.

Eichmann, Adolf *(1906–1962)* Nazi SS official who oversaw the deaths of millions of JEWS and others during WORLD WAR II. Eichmann rose with GERMANY's Nazi Party to be head of the GESTAPO's Jewish section. After the **Wannsee Conference** (January 1942), he was responsible for the deportation and incarceration of Jews in CONCENTRATION CAMPS throughout Europe. Millions of Jews were ultimately killed in the camps. When the war ended, Eichmann was able to escape to Argentina with the unwitting help of the VATICAN. Although furiously pursued, he eluded detection because he had destroyed all photos of himself. However, Israeli agents traced him to Argentina after his wife rejoined him in Buenos Aires. In 1961 Israeli agents apprehended him and secretly transported him to Israel, where he was tried for crimes against the Jews. He was convicted and hanged.

Eigen, Manfred *(1927–)* German physical chemist. Eigen was educated at the University of Göttingen, where he obtained his Ph.D. in 1951. He joined the staff of the Max Planck Institute for Physical Chemistry at Göttingen in 1953 and became its director in 1964. Eigen introduced (1954) the so-called relaxation techniques for the study of extremely fast chemical reactions (those taking less than a millisecond). Eigen's general technique was to examine a solution in equilibrium for a given temperature and pressure. If a short disturbance was applied to the solution the equilibrium would be very briefly destroyed and a new equilibrium quickly reached. Eigen studied exactly what happened in this very

short time by means of absorption spectroscopy. He applied disturbances to the equilibrium by a variety of methods, such as pulses of electric current, sudden changes in temperature or pressure, or changes in electric field. For this work Eigen shared the 1967 NOBEL PRIZE in chemistry with George Porter and Ronald NORRISH. Eigen later applied his relaxation techniques to complex biochemical reactions. He also became interested in the origin of nucleic acids and proteins.

Eight, the A popular reference to a group of eight young American painters working and exhibiting in the cause of realism during the first decade of the 20th century. More derisively, they were also branded the Black Gang, the Apostles of Ugliness and the Ashcan School. In contrast to the prevailing taste of establishments such as the National Academy of Design in New York, these artists—Robert HENRI, Everett SHINN, George Luks, John SLOAN, Arthur B. Davies, William GLACKENS, Ernest Lawson and Maurice PRENDERGAST—observed and painted the relatively squalid conditions of contemporary American urban sprawl. Since most of them were trained as newspaper illustrators—they had been employed by newspapers like the *Philadelphia Press* and the *New York World* to provide on-the-spot sketches of breaking news stories—they had developed a quick, incisive, unblinking attitude toward the world around them. They knew the police beat, the slums, the ragpickers. When some of them presumed to present their work for gallery viewing at the National Arts Club in 1904, they were roundly denounced. Three years later several of them were rejected for exhibition at the National Academy. Stung, they decided—under the unofficial leadership of Robert Henri—to exhibit their work collectively in the winter of 1908. The Macbeth Gallery show subsequently became not only the most famous exhibition of the Eight but also the first important event in modern American painting. The titles of some of the works on display tell the story: *Street Scene, The Shoppers* and *Sixth Avenue and Thirtieth Street.* Two years later some of the artists, headed by Sloan and Henri, exhibited in another important modern show: The Independent Artists Exhibition. The way had been prepared for the famous Armory Show of 1913, when work by the Eight rubbed easels, as it were, with modern works by Cézanne, Picasso, Matisse and other famous artists. Apart from their common vision of contemporary American life, there were no philosophical or political bonds among the Eight. They soon disbanded, and some even grew suspicious of the modernist trends they had helped to encourage.

Eijkman, Christiaan (1858–1930)

Dutch physician. Eijkman earned a medical degree from the University of Amsterdam in 1883. He served as an army medical officer in the Dutch East Indies from 1883 to 1885, when he was forced to return to Holland to recuperate from a severe attack of malaria. In 1886 he returned to the East Indies as a member of an official government committee to investigate beriberi. After the completion of the committee's work, Eijkman remained in Batavia (now Djakarta) as director of a newly established bacteriological laboratory. In 1896 he took up the post of professor of public health at the University of Utrecht.

Eijkman was responsible for the first real understanding of the nature of and possible cure of beriberi. For this work he shared the 1929 Nobel Prize in physiology or medicine with Frederick Gowland Hopkins. He failed to conclude, however, that beriberi is a deficiency disease. Although Eijkman had clearly demonstrated how to cure and prevent beriberi, it was left to Hopkins to identify its cause as a vitamin deficiency. It was not until the early 1930s that Robert Williams identified the vitamin as B1 (thiamine).

Einstein, Albert (1879–1955)

German-born physicist and humanist. Einstein is widely considered one of the greatest and most original thinkers of the 20th century. Although not easily understood by the layperson, Einstein's theories of time, space, matter and the nature of the universe radically changed our view of the world. The son of nonreligious German Jewish parents, Einstein taught himself mathematics and physics at an early age. He was far from being an outstanding student, but his intellectual independence and creativity soon brought him into conflict with the strict regimentation of

German physicist and 1921 Nobel Prize winner Albert Einstein (Library of Congress, Prints and Photographs Division)

the German Catholic schools to which his parents sent him. While attending the Zurich Federal Institute of Technology from 1896 to 1900, he applied for and received Swiss citizenship. Upon graduation from the institute, Einstein took a job at the Swiss Patent Office, pursuing scientific studies in his spare time. In 1905 he published four important papers. One of these, *Über einen die Erzeugung und Verwandlung des Lichtes betreffenden heuristichen Gesichtspunkt* (On a heuristic point of view about the creation and conversion of light), introduced quantum theory into physics to explain the nature of electromagnetic radiation.

The most famous of the four papers of 1905—*Zur Electrodynamik bewegter Körper* (On the electrodynamics of moving bodies)—introduced his revolutionary **special theory of relativity**, showing that space and time, once thought to be absolutes, are actually relative to the observer; the only constant is the speed of light. Einstein's special theory of relativity also states that matter behaves differently as it approaches the speed of light, and that classical Newtonian physics does not apply at these speeds.

In a third paper (only two pages long), *Ist die Trägheit eines Körpers von seinem Energieinhalt abhängig?* (Does the inertia of a body depend on its energy content?), Einstein concluded that matter is really concentrated energy, a most important consequence of relativity. This discovery led directly to

Atomic bomb development nearly four decades later.

In 1907 Einstein further developed his ideas about gravity and inertia and predicted that light moving through a gravitational field would be curved. This theory, known as the **general theory of relativity**, was later confirmed when the astronomer Arthur Eddington observed during an eclipse that starlight was indeed curved as it passed near the Sun.

As his work gained recognition in scientific circles, Einstein received his doctorate from the University of Zurich in 1909 and then taught in Zurich, Prague and Leyden. He became director of the Kaiser Wilhelm Institute of Sciences in Berlin in 1913. In 1916 he further refined his general theory of relativity in the paper *Die Grundlagen der allgemeinen der Relativitatstheorie* (The foundation of the general theory of relativity). This work proposed that space itself is curved. In 1921 Einstein received the Nobel Prize for his work in atomic physics.

The suffering of European Jews after World War I led Einstein to become an active Zionist, traveling extensively during the 1920s to raise money for Jewish settlement in Palestine. (Years later, following the death of Chaim Weizmann in 1952, Einstein was asked to become president of Israel, but he declined.) In 1933 he fled Nazi Germany and accepted a professorship at Princeton's Institute for Advanced Study. Appalled by Nazi tyranny and the rearming of Germany, Einstein reversed his lifelong pacifist views in 1933, warning European countries to arm against Hitler's threat.

In 1939 scientists proved the possibility of releasing the atom's energy through a nuclear chain reaction. Acting on the belief that the Germans were close to developing an atomic bomb, Einstein addressed a letter to President Franklin D. Roosevelt, describing the destructive potential of the new weapon and urging an accelerated research program so that the U.S. would be the first nation with the bomb. This letter spurred Roosevelt's decision to institute an ultimately successful crash program for the manufacture of the weapon.

With the creation of the first bomb in 1945, Einstein, along with many of the scientists working on the project, began to fear that the U.S. would use the bomb offensively against Japan, thus initiating an atomic arms race. Hoping to preclude the bomb's use, Einstein signed a letter to Roosevelt, warning that any momentary military advantage the bomb might give the U.S. would be offset by grave political and strategic disadvantages. FDR died before receiving the letter. The TRUMAN administration disregarded the warning and dropped atomic bombs on HIROSHIMA and NAGASAKI.

After the war Einstein became a passionate spokesman for the "control" school of thought—those scientists who felt that the only hope for peace was to place all control of nuclear power in a supranational government. In 1945 he organized the Emergency Committee of Atomic Scientists to educate the public about the possibilities and dangers of atomic power. In numerous speeches, broadcasts and letters, he warned against the physical danger and cultural repression that would result from an arms race. He deplored the U.S.'s postwar policy of nuclear rearmament, warning, "We must realize that we cannot simultaneously plan for war and peace." In 1948 he joined in a denunciation of universal military training and in 1950 signed a protest against the penetration of the civilian educational system by the military establishment. He opposed the production of the HYDROGEN BOMB, stating in 1950 that an arms race was the worst method of preventing conflict and advocated the Gandhian tactic of "nonparticipation in what you believe is evil." He also supported physicist J. Robert OPPENHEIMER against charges that he was a security risk.

In 1953 Einstein completed his last great piece of scientific work, the **unified field theory,** which related his work in quantum mechanics to the theory of relativity. In the year of his death, 1955, he and Bertrand RUSSELL made a world appeal against the dangers of thermonuclear war. This statement, signed by six other Nobel Prize winners, led to the Pugwash Conference, a movement to utilize the internationalism of science as a force for peace.

Although his theories challenged traditional views of the universe, Einstein perceived a rational rather than random force behind creation. "God does not play dice with the universe," he asserted. "He may be subtle, but he is not malicious."

Eire See IRELAND.

Eisenhower, Dwight David *(1890–1969)* American general and 34th president of the UNITED STATES (1953–61). Born in Denison, Texas Eisenhower grew up in Abilene, Kansas, where his family had moved in 1892. He graduated from West Point in 1915, then commanded an army tank corps training camp during World War I, becoming a leading exponent of mobile armored vehicles. He served in the Panama Canal Zone (1922–24), later attending the Command and General Staff School. After a tour on the Battle Monuments Commission, he attended the Army War College and served in the office of the assistant secretary of war (1929–33) and in the Philippines with General Douglas MACARTHUR (1935–40). After the outbreak of WORLD WAR II in Europe, he served in a number of posts before becoming chief of staff of the Third Army in 1941 and leading it successfully in large-scale war games. This performance led directly to his posting as chief of operations under General George C. MARSHALL in Washington, D.C.

Winning Marshall's confidence and friendship, Eisenhower was named U.S. commander in Europe in 1942. He quickly amassed a string of successes, commanding the invasion of North Africa (November 1942), con-

American military leader and president Dwight D. Eisenhower. 1945 (LIBRARY OF CONGRESS. PRINTS AND PHOTOGRAPHS DIVISION)

quering Sicily (July–August 1943) and invading Italy (September 1943). In December 1943 Eisenhower was named supreme commander of the Allied Expeditionary Force. A warm and plainspoken man, he was particularly adept at winning cooperation among the Allies and at achieving a successful integration of the various branches of the armed forces into a fighting machine that could win the struggle for Europe. Under Eisenhower the Invasion of NORMANDY of June 6, 1944, was successfully planned and mounted, and the Allies pushed into France, driving out German forces. His slow advance allowed the Allied setback at the battle of the Ardennes, but Eisenhower pushed forward, reaching the Elbe in April 1945. Germany's surrender on May 8, 1945, left Eisenhower, a five-star general since December 1944, one of the great heroes of the war.

Afterwards he served as army chief of staff, wrote his war memoirs (*Crusade in Europe,* 1948) and was president of Columbia University. In 1951 he returned to Europe as military commander of NATO, further enhancing his international standing. Eisenhower resigned from the army in 1951 to seek the Republican presidential nomination in 1952; he won the nomination by a close margin over Senator Robert TAFT. That year much of the country adopted the slogan "I Like Ike," and he won a landslide victory over Governor Adlai STEVENSON; he was reelected by an even larger margin four years later.

Early in his first term Eisenhower fulfilled a campaign promise by securing an armistice ending the KOREAN WAR, in July 1953. Along with his secretary of state, John Foster DULLES, he continued the TRUMAN administration policy of containing COMMUNISM, while also working to ease some COLD WAR tensions. On the homefront, he maintained a business-oriented middle-of-the-road policy, initiating little legislation but overseeing an improved highway and seaway system and taking firm action on Civil Rights in the 1957 school desegregation of LITTLE ROCK, Arkansas, and in legislation (1957, 1960) (see CIVIL RIGHTS MOVEMENT).

Shortly before leaving office, Eisenhower warned the nation about the growing power of what he termed the *military-industrial complex.* He supported the unsuccessful presidential candidacy of his vice president, Richard M. NIXON, in the 1960 election that was won by Democrat John F. KENNEDY. After retiring to his Gettysburg, Pennsylvania, farm in 1961, Eisenhower resumed writing. Among his books were *Mandate for Change* (1963) and *Waging Peace* (1965).

Eisenhower, Milton Stover *(1899–1985)* U.S. educator and public servant, brother of Dwight D. EISENHOWER. Milton Eisenhower was an adviser to every president from Franklin D. ROOSEVELT to Richard M. NIXON. He became perhaps the most important presidential adviser in the nation's history during the administration of his brother. He began his government career in 1926 with the Department of Agriculture. During WORLD WAR II he directed the resettlement of refugees in North Africa after the 1942 Allied invasion. He left government service in 1943 to become president of Kansas State College. In 1950 he was named president of Pennsylvania State University, a post he held for six years. From 1956 to 1967 and again from 1971 to 1972, he was president of Johns Hopkins University. During those years he held a number of major part-time government posts and served on 12 major government commissions.

Eisenhower Doctrine Policy promulgated by President Dwight D. EISENHOWER in 1957 during his second term in office. It provided for the use of American military force and economic aid in the protection of Middle Eastern states from internal or external communist aggression. The doctrine was applied in July 1958, when 10,000 U.S. Marines were sent to LEBANON to ensure stability after the pro-Western monarchy of Iraq was overthrown. The doctrine proved unpopular in the Middle East and lapsed after the death of Secretary of State John Foster DULLES in 1959.

Eisenstaedt, Alfred *(1898–1995)* American photographer, considered the father of PHOTOJOURNALISM. He introduced the techniques of the photo-essay and news reporting using candid-camera shots. His career began in his native Germany, where he produced candid documentaries (1929–35). Immigrating to the U.S. in 1935, he gained fame for his picture story on the Italian invasion of ETHIOPIA. In 1936 he became one of the original staff photographers for LIFE magazine. He is known for his expressive candid portraits of such people as Albert EINSTEIN (1947) and Marilyn MONROE (1953) and for his evocative photo-essays, such as those from Japan (1945–46). Among his many books is *Witness to Our Time* (1966).

Eisenstein, Sergei Mikhailovich *(1898–1948)* Russian filmmaker and theoretician. With colleagues Lev KULESHOV, Vsevelod PUDOVKIN and Dziga VERTOV, Eisenstein stood at the center of the great decade of Soviet filmmaking in the 1920s. He was born in Riga, Latvia, and at an early age displayed interests and talents in subjects as diverse as architecture, Japanese culture and theater. As an assistant to the great stage entrepreneur and innovator Vsevelod MEYERHOLD in the early 1920s, he was vitally influenced by the tenets of **constructivism**, which held that theater and acting were essentially machinelike assemblies of stylized elements in gesture, design, language and light. Eisenstein carried such ideas forward into his great films of the rest of the decade. *Stachka* (*Strike*, 1924), *Bronenosets Potemkin* (*The Battleship Potemkin*, 1925), *Oktiabr* (*October*, 1927) and *Generalnaya Linya* (*The General Line*, 1929) helped vault the Soviet cinema into international prominence. Although nominally about such standard Soviet subjects as revolution and collective agriculture, they were more significant as demonstrations of Eisenstein's theories of montage of discrete attractions (his term for the editing together of pieces of film). As opposed to Pudovkin's theory that editing was essentially a linkage process, Eisenstein insisted that it was a dialectic, a collision and contrast of shots. Metaphors could be created with the collision of elements within the shot ("potential montage"), in the juxtaposition of shots ("metric" and "tonal" montage) and in the combinations of image and synchronized sound ("vertical" montage). This "series of explosions," as he cryptically called them, would "drive forward the total film" like an internal combustion engine. Such theories ran him afoul of the STALIN regime in the 1930s and 1940s. Eisenstein completed only two more projects before his death from a heart attack in 1948—*Alexander Nevsky* (1938) and the two parts of *Ivan Groznyi* (*Ivan the Terrible*, 1944). His theoretical writings have been collected into two volumes: *The Film Sense* (1942) and *The Film Form* (1948).

Eisner, Michael *(1942–)* American television and film executive. After working at the Columbia Broadcasting Service (CBS) to plan the layout of the commercials it showed during children's programs, Eisner became assistant to the national programming director at the American Broadcasting Corporation (ABC), in 1966. After being promoted to vice president of daytime programming in 1971, Eisner helped develop hit ABC primetime shows such as *Happy Days, Welcome Back Kotter, Barney Miller* and *Starsky and Hutch*. In 1976 Eisner joined Paramount Pictures as president and chief operating officer. After approving several successful feature films, Eisner left Paramount eight years later to become chairman and chief executive officer of the Walt Disney Company, where he helped develop the animated musical feature format that produced such blockbuster hits as *The Little Mermaid, Beauty and the Beast, Aladdin, The Lion King* and *Pocahontas*. In 2004 about 43% of Disney's shareholders voted to oppose his reelection to the corporation's board because of dissatisfaction with his policies and management style; the board subsequently stripped Eisner of his role as chairman while retaining him as chief executive officer. He retired in 2006.

Ekman, Vagn Walfrid *(1874–1954)* Swedish oceanographer. Ekman was educated at the University of Uppsala, graduating in 1902. He worked at the International Laboratory for Oceanographic Research in Oslo (1902–08) before he moved to Lund, Sweden, as a lecturer in mathematical physics, being made a professor in 1910. Ekman's fundamental paper, *On the Influence of the Earth's Rotation on Ocean Currents* (1905), originated from an observation made by the explorer Fridtjof NANSEN that in the Arctic, drift ice did not follow wind direction but deviated to the right. Ekman showed that the motion, now known as the Ekman spiral, is produced as a complex interaction between the force of the wind on the water surface, the deflecting force due to the Earth's rotation (Coriolis force) and the frictional forces within the water layers. Ekman also studied the phenomenon of dead water—a thin layer of freshwater from melting ice spreading over the sea, which could halt slow-moving ships. This, he established, resulted from the waves formed between water layers of different densities. The **Ekman current meter**, which he invented, is still in use.

ELAS (Ellenikos Laikos Apeleutherotikos Stratos, Hellenic People's Army of Liberation) Organization founded by the communist resistance in GREECE during WORLD WAR II. ELAS wished to achieve a communist government in postwar Greece along the lines of TITO's PARTISANS. Opposing them, Britain and the U.S. had supported promonarchist groups since 1943, and Britain sent troops to Greece in 1944 to prevent civil war, which eventually broke out following the return of the king in 1946. The **Democratic Army**, successor to ELAS, was defeated in 1949 by the royalists, backed by the U.S. and Britain. (See also GREEK CIVIL WAR.)

Elat Israeli port city at the head of the Gulf of Aqaba, about 120 miles south of Beersheba. Following its occupation of the area at the conclusion of the ARAB-ISRAELI WAR OF 1948–49, ISRAEL established this modern city to secure its access to the Red Sea, the Far East and Africa. The port was temporarily put out of commission by Egyptian blockades of the Gulf of Aqaba in the 1956 and 1967 Arab-Israeli wars but was expanded after hostilities ceased. The population rose from 529 in 1959 to over 14,000 by the 1970s.

Elath, Eliahu (Eliahu Epstein) (1903–1990) Ukrainian-born journalist and diplomat. In 1934 he was named head of the political department of the Jewish Agency for PALESTINE, a precursor of the Israeli government. A force in the founding of ISRAEL, he was named that country's ambassador to the U.S. in 1948 and later its ambassador to Great Britain. He played a major role in negotiations surrounding the 1956 invasion of SUEZ by Britain, France and Israel.

Elbe River River that rises in northwestern Czechoslovakia and courses through Germany past DRESDEN, then northwest through Hamburg and into the North Sea at Cuxhaven. A prominent river of central Europe, it is about 725 miles long and is linked by canal with BERLIN, with the RUHR area, with the Oder and RHINE Rivers and with the Baltic Sea. Toward the end of WORLD WAR II, on April 25, 1945, U.S. and Soviet army units met at Torgau on the Elbe. From 1949 to 1990 a section of the river formed part of the border between East and West Germany.

Eldjarn, Kristjan (1916–1982) President of Iceland (1968–80). An archaeologist by profession, Eldjarn served as curator of the National Museum of Iceland (1947–68) before his election to the country's presidency.

Eldridge, (David) Roy (1911–1989) U.S. jazz trumpeter. A flamboyant and innovative performer, Eldridge was often regarded as the link between Louis ARMSTRONG's pioneering trumpet solos of the 1920s and the instrumental virtuosity of Dizzy GILLESPIE's BEBOP style of the 1950s. Although he performed with his own band in the 1930s, Eldridge did not gain national attention until he performed with white bandleader Gene KRUPA in 1941. He also played with Artie SHAW, Benny GOODMAN, and the Jazz at the Philharmonic series. Heart problems forced him to give up trumpet playing in 1980.

electronic mail (e-mail) Electronic means of communicating data, text and audio, visual and program files through an intranet (a network of computers within an organization) and, later, over the INTERNET. Mobile units such as personal digital assistants (PDAs) and advanced CELLULAR TELEPHONES also developed the capability of transmitting and receiving e-mail. As a method of communication, e-mail increased exponentially since the mid-1990s, when companies such as America Online (AOL) began to offer consumers the ability to connect to the Internet and possess an e-mail account. Governmental agencies, companies, colleges and universities, and nonprofit organizations also established e-mail accounts to ensure the rapid dissemination of information to their employees and public.

The destination of each piece of e-mail is determined by the specified e-mail address, which contains components designating the recipient's username within the network, the domain or company to whom the e-mail address is registered and, in some cases, the country in which the domain or company resides. After the message has been composed and text, program or audio and visual files have been attached to the e-mail, it is converted into binary language and transmitted from a computer modem to a network server, also referred to as a message transfer agent (MTA), which eventually routes the message to its intended recipient.

As more individuals obtained e-mail addresses through companies such as AOL, Juno, NetZero and Microsoft, the proliferation of e-mail to these recipients has created the phenomenon of Internet junk mail, often referred to as spam. In 2003 Utah and other states passed legislation making it illegal for companies to send unsolicited e-mails to e-mail addresses, in an effort to reduce the spam received by their residents and to protect them against fraudulent e-mail inquiries (called phishing) designed to elicit Social Security numbers, credit card numbers, bank account details or any other information that could be used to rob or otherwise defraud individuals. In 2003 Congress passed the Can-Spam Act to reduce the flow of junk e-mail, but the legislation proved largely ineffective.

electron microscope The electron microscope is one of the scientific miracles of the 20th century and represents a huge advance over the conventional light microscope. Using beams of electrons to magnify objects that are invisible to the naked eye, the electron microscope can magnify particles up to 1 million times. Especially valuable in medical research, it allows researchers to study bacteria and viruses; the most powerful electron microscopes can make individual atoms visible.

Elgar, Sir Edward (1857–1934) The first British composer of international stature since Henry Purcell, Elgar is generally regarded as the foremost British composer of the 20th century. He was born into a middle-class

British composer Edward Elgar (LIBRARY OF CONGRESS, PRINTS AND PHOTOGRAPHS DIVISION)

Catholic family in Worcestershire, where his father owned a music shop. Largely self-educated, Elgar held various minor posts (including that of bandmaster in the local insane asylum, 1879–84) before becoming organist at St. George's Church, Worcester (1895). During this time he composed steadily but received little recognition until his *Enigma Variations* (1899) and the oratorio *The Dream of Gerontius* (1900) established him as Britain's leading composer. He went on to compose two large-scale symphonies (1908, 1911), the introspective Violin Concerto (1910) and Cello Concerto (1919), several tone poems and the five popular *Pomp and Circumstance* marches, among other works. Although influenced by Brahms and by Richard STRAUSS, his compositions were unmistakably English in character. Distraught over the death of his wife, Alice, the horrors of WORLD WAR I and the advent of MODERNISM, Elgar composed little during his later years but continued to enjoy both popular and official acclaim as England's greatest living composer. When Elgar died in 1933, he left behind sketches for a third symphony. In 1997 an elaboration of these sketches by composer Anthony Payne was premiered to favorable reviews. It is frequently performed worldwide.

Eliade, Mircea *(1907–1986)* Romanian-born historian of religion and fiction writer. Eliade was one of the preeminent interpreters of world religion in the 20th century. A prolific writer, he drew upon the myths and beliefs of virtually all cultures. In his analyses

Eliade synthesized these myths into enduring themes of human spirituality, such as the golden age at the beginning of time, the cyclical functioning of nature and the hierarchical structure of being from divine emanation to earthly matter. As a young man, Eliade spent three years in study at the University of Calcutta in preparation for his first book, *Yoga: Essay on the Origins of Indian Mysticism* (1936). In the 1930s and 1940s he published several works of fiction with a supernatural tone. He joined the faculty of the University of Chicago in 1956 and remained there until his death. His other major works include *Patterns of Comparative Religion* (1949), *Myths, Dreams, and Mysteries* (1957), *Shamanism* (1968) and the three-volume *A History of Religious Ideas* (1976, 1978, 1983).

Elion, Gertrude Belle *(1918–1999)* American biochemist. Born in New York City, she attended Hunter College and Brooklyn Polytechnic Institute. At first a high school teacher, she became a researcher during World War II. She joined the laboratory staff of Burroughs Wellcome, Tuckahoe, New York, in 1944, beginning her long association with George H. HITCHINGS. Together the two worked on the comparative study of normal and cancer cells, bacteria and viruses. Working with the staff at New York's Sloan Kettering Institute, they developed the first effective chemotherapy to fight leukemia. She and Hitchings investigated the method by which nucleic acids are formed and analyzed their chemical composition, with a focus on purine and pyrimidine. Most important, they developed chemotherapies to inhibit nucleic acid formation in diseased cells without damaging normal cells. This discovery led to various advances in drug research, notably the development of AZT, which is used to fight AIDS. In 1988 she, Hitchings and Sir James Black were awarded the NOBEL PRIZE in physiology or medicine.

Eliot, Thomas Stearns *(1888–1965)* Anglo-American poet, critic and playwright. Born in St. Louis, Missouri, he studied literature and philosophy at Harvard, the Sorbonne and Oxford. In 1914 he settled in London, where he worked briefly as a teacher and then as an officer at Lloyd's Bank; during this

time he also wrote and published literary criticism. His first poetry collection, *Prufrock and Other Observations* (1917), attracted some attention, but it was *The WASTE LAND* (1922) that established his reputation as a leading modernist poet (see MODERNISM; EZRA POUND). In 1925 he joined the publishing firm of Faber & Gwyer (later FABER & FABER) as an editor, later becoming a director. From 1922 to 1939 he also edited *The Criterion*, an influential literary journal. In 1927 he became a British subject and a member of the Church of England; soon after, he declared himself "an Anglo-Catholic in religion, a classicist in literature, and a royalist in politics." These views are evident in *Ash Wednesday* (1930) and in *FOUR QUARTETS* (1943), his last and perhaps his greatest poetic work. In his later years, he attempted to revitalize verse drama in such works as *Murder in the Cathedral* (1935), *The Family Reunion* (1939) and *The Cocktail Party* (1949). In 1948 he received the NOBEL PRIZE in literature and the British Order of Merit. Eliot is widely regarded (along with W. B. YEATS) as one of the most significant poets in the English language in the 20th century. His critical theories have also had an enormous influence on other writers.

Elizabeth II *(1926–)* Queen of the United Kingdom of Great Britain and Northern Ireland (1952–). Born in London, Elizabeth became the heir presumptive upon the accession to the throne of her father, GEORGE VI, in 1936 after the abdication of his brother, EDWARD VIII. She married Philip Mountbatten, duke of Edinburgh, in 1947. The two have four children—Prince CHARLES, Princess Anne, Prince Andrew and Prince Edward. Elizabeth inherited the throne on the death of George VI (February 6, 1952), and her coronation took place in Westminster Abbey on June 2, 1953. An active constitutional monarch, Elizabeth celebrated her Golden Jubilee, the 50th anniversary of her accession to the throne, in 2002. Her eldest son, Prince Charles, the prince of Wales, is heir apparent.

Elkin, Stanley *(1925–1986)* U.S. writer. His mystery novels and short stories have been translated into many languages. In some countries, including France, he is regarded as a major literary figure. Such directors as Claude CHABROL and Joseph LOSEY have made films based on his work. In 1981 the Mystery Writers of America honored him with their Grand Master Award for lifetime achievement.

Ellington, Edward Kennedy "Duke" *(1899–1974)* Composer-bandleader-pianist; one of jazzdom's (and American music's) transcendant figures. In 1923, after developing rudimentary musical skills in his native Washington, D.C., Ellington settled in New York City, where he became a respected bandleader-entertainer at such venues as the Hollywood and Kentucky clubs on Broadway, and then at the fabled Cotton Club in HARLEM (1927–31). Ellington's tremendous productivity as a composer (he is credited with well over 2,000 separate titles) can be attributed to his ability to organize and sustain a relatively stable performing ensemble; indeed, Ellington's orchestra was a veritable workshop in which its leader explored a wide variety of forms, exotic colors and textures, often exploiting the attributes of such individual soloists as baritone saxophonist Harry Carney, alto saxophonist Johnny Hodges and valve trombonist Juan Tizol. Ellington's work of the 1930s to early 1940s is regarded as his most significant. There were popular songs ("I Let a Song Go Out of My Heart," 1938), atmospheric "jungle" pieces ("Jungle Nights in Harlem," 1934), ballads ("In a Sentimental Mood," 1935), swing tunes (including the SWING ERA anthem, "It Don't Mean a Thing If It Ain't Got That Swing," 1932) and the first of Ellington's extended concert pieces ("Black, Brown and Beige," 1943). Ellington achieved international popularity during the postwar period with frequent tours of Europe and Asia; he also collected an array of honors, including the Presidential Medal of Honor in 1969.

Elliott, Thomas Renton *(1877–1961)* British physician. Elliott was educated at Cambridge University and University College Hospital, London, where he later served as professor of clinical medicine from the end of World War I until his retirement in 1939. It was as a research student under John Langley at Cambridge that Elliott made his greatest discovery. In 1901 Langley had injected animals with a crude extract from the adrenal gland and noted that the extract stimulated the action of the sympathetic nerves. **Adrenaline** (epinephrine) had earlier (1898) been isolated by John ABEL at Johns Hopkins University. Elliott decided to inject adrenaline into animals to see if he got the same response as Langley had with the adrenal gland extract. He did indeed achieve increases in heartbeat, blood pressure and so on—characteristics of stimulation of the sympathetic nervous system. Elliott is remembered for his subsequent suggestion that adrenaline may be released from sympathetic nerve endings—the first hint of neurotransmitters.

Ellis, (Henry) Havelock *(1859–1939)* British psychologist. Ellis was a true pioneer in establishing a modern, scientific approach to the study of sex. While Ellis did earn a medical degree, he devoted most of his life to writing. His magnum opus was the seven-volume *Studies in the Psychology of Sex* (1897–1928), which explored sexual relations from a multicultural perspective and emphasized the importance of sexuality for mental and physical well-being. The *Studies* were initially declared obscene by a British judge; in the U.S. they were for many years made legally available only to physicians. Ellis was an iconoclast who advocated woman suffrage and birth control at a time when such views were far from respectable (see WOMEN'S MOVEMENTS). *My Life* (1940) is his autobiographical summation of his years of research and political involvement.

Ellis Island A small, nearly rectangular island of about 27 acres in upper New York Bay, just north of the Statue of Liberty, about a mile southwest of the Battery and some 1,300 feet east of Jersey City, New Jersey. Owned by the U.S. government since 1808, it was the site of an early fort and arsenal. It became famous when it served (1892–1943) as the principal immigration port for the U.S. During its peak years (1892–1924) some 16 million prospective Americans passed through Ellis Island, where they were given physical examinations and questioned about such matters as political beliefs, job prospects and final destinations in the U.S. Largely a port of entry for poor immigrants (the wealthier arrivals were inspected aboard their ships), Ellis Island was the first taste of the New

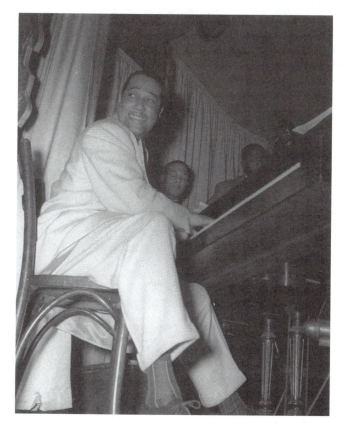

Jazz musician and orchestra leader Duke Ellington (LIBRARY OF CONGRESS, PRINTS AND PHOTOGRAPHS DIVISION)

Newly arrived immigrants have their eyes examined at Ellis Island. (LIBRARY OF CONGRESS, PRINTS AND PHOTOGRAPHS DIVISION)

World for the ancestors of about 100 million present-day Americans. After its buildings were vacated by the Coast Guard in 1955, they fell into disrepair and dilapidation. Administered by the National Park Service and a part of the Statue of Liberty National Monument since 1965, the island was restored during the late 1980s to its former imposing appearance. It became the site for a number of permanent exhibitions when it was formally opened as the Ellis Island Immigration Museum in 1990.

Ellison, Harlan Jay (*1934– *) American writer. Although Ellison has published essays as well as short stories about contemporary life, he is known primarily for his gut-wrenching science fiction stories dealing with urban angst, alienation and regimentation. Among his best-known short works are "I Have No Mouth, and I Must Scream," "'Repent, Harlequin,' Said the Ticktockham" and "A Boy and His Dog." Collections of his stories include *The Beast That Shouted Love at the Heart of the World* and *Deathbird Stories.* His novels include *Doomsman* and *The Man with Nine Lives.*

Ellison, Ralph (*1914–1994*) American writer. Born in Oklahoma City, he attended Tuskegee Institute (1933–36). Moving to New York City, he became part of the FEDERAL WRITERS' PROJECT and contributed short stories and nonfiction to various periodicals. His literary reputation rests largely on his first novel, *INVISIBLE MAN* (1952), a wrenching tale of a nameless black protagonist who loses his sense of identity in a world of prejudice and hostility. The novel won the National Book Award in 1953. Ellison is also known for his collection of essays *Shadow and Act* (1964). He taught at Bard College, Rutgers, the University of Chicago and New York University.

Ellmann, Richard (*1918–1987*) American literary scholar and biographer. One of the foremost authorities on 20th-century Irish literature, Ellmann was the author of a 1959 biography of James JOYCE that is considered the definitive work on the Irish novelist. He also wrote important books on W. B. YEATS and Oscar Wilde. Ellmann had taught at a number of U.S. universities before joining the faculty of Oxford University in 1970. He later became Goldsmiths' professor emeritus of English literature at Oxford.

Ellsworth, Lincoln (*1880–1951*) American explorer. Born in Chicago, he was left a fortune by his father and became the financial backer and associate of Roald AMUNDSEN. Together, they undertook the Polar Flying Expedition in 1925. Joined by Umberto NOBILE, they accomplished (1926) a transpolar mission in the dirigible *Norge,* flying from Spitzbergen over the NORTH POLE to Alaska. Ellsworth became the first man to fly over ANTARCTICA (1936); three years later he completed an aerial expedition that photographed vast sections of the Antarctic and claimed them for the U.S. His books include *Our Polar Flight* (1925) and *First Crossing of the Polar Sea* (1927), written with Amundsen, as well as *Search* (1932) and *Beyond Horizons* (1938).

Elman, Mischa (*1891–1967*) Russian-American violinist. Born near Kiev, Elman began studying the violin as a young child and at the age of 11 became a student of Leopold Auer at the St. Petersburg Conservatory. He debuted in that city in 1904 and, on a subsequent tour of Germany and England, became an enormous popular success. He made his U.S. debut in New York in 1908, thereafter touring the world as a soloist with major symphony orchestras and as a chamber player and a recital artist. Elman became an American citizen in 1923. He was known for his sensuous and opulent tone, his expressive playing and his technical mastery of the violin.

El Salvador (Republic of El Salvador) The smallest and most densely populated of the Central American countries, El Salvador stretches for 208 miles along the Pacific coast and covers

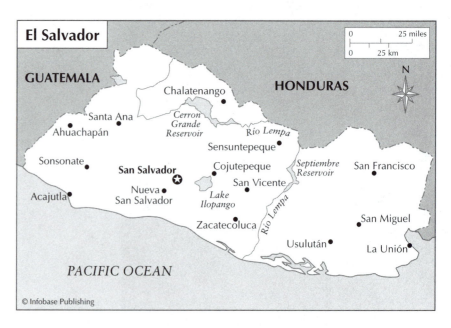

EL SALVADOR

1932	Army crushes popular insurrection led by Agustín Farabundo Martí, killing an estimated 30,000 civilians (mostly Indian peasants).
1969	Riots during a soccer game in San Salvador escalate into armed conflict between Honduras and El Salvador.
1972	Jose Napoleón Duarte, a member of the Nationalist Democratic Union, narrowly loses his presidential bid, accuses the government of massive election fraud and attempts a coup; is arrested and exiled.
1980	Duarte returns from exile and joins the Revolutionary Government Junta.
1981	Civil war breaks out when the Farabundo Martí National Liberation Front (FMLN) launches its first major military offensive.
1984	Duarte defeats the extreme right-wing major Roberto d'Aubuisson of the Nationalist Republican Alliance (ARENA).
1989	Alfredo Cristiani of ARENA wins 53.8% of the presidential vote; peace negotiations break down, the FMLN launches military offensive; government declares the capital, San Salvador, under a state of siege; seven Jesuit priests killed by the military.
1990	Death of Duarte.
1991	Rebels call cease-fire for national election; ruling ARENA party claims victory amid charges of fraud.
1992	A cease-fire brokered by the United Nations terminates the civil war; the FMLN became an opposition party.
1998	Hurricane Mitch devastates El Salvador.
1999	ARENA candidate Francisco Flores elected president.
2004	Antonio Saca of the ARENA party elected president.

an area of 8,259 square miles. Independent since 1821, El Salvador had its political stability shattered in 1932 when the army crushed a popular insurrection led by Agustín Farabundo Martí. The subsequent repressive regime of General Maximiliano Hernández Martínez lasted until 1944. The army retained power until 1972, when political and social unrest led to the formation of popular organizations and guerrilla groups. Civil war broke out in 1981. The moderate José Napoleón DUARTE was elected president in 1984 and, with U.S. support, tried to negotiate a peace with the left-wing guerrilla group the FARABUNDO MARTÍ NATIONAL LIBERATION FRONT (FMLN). However, his successor Alfredo Cristiani (elected 1989) opposed negotiation. Increased guerrilla warfare led to declaration of a state of siege in the capital of San Salvador in 1989, and political violence continued. Leftists scored gains in the national election of March 1991. In 1991 the FMLN and the conservative government signed a UN-sponsored peace accord that allowed the rebel organization to function as a political party. Since the accord, the FMLN has steadily improved its representation in El Salvador's parliament; however, the country continued to be governed by leaders of the conservative Nationalist Republic Alliance (ARENA): Dr. Armando Calderón Sol, elected in 1994, Francisco Flores, elected in 1999, and Antonia Saca, elected in 2004.

Elsasser, Walter Maurice (1904–1991) German-American geophysicist. Elsasser was educated at the University of Göttingen, where he obtained his doctorate in 1927. He worked at the University of Frankfurt before leaving Germany in 1933 following HITLER's rise to power. He taught at the Sorbonne, in Paris, before immigrating to the U.S. (1936), where he joined the staff of the California Institute of Technology. He became professor of physics at the University of Pennsylvania (1947–50) and at the University of Utah (1950–58). In 1962 he became professor of geophysics at Princeton; later he was appointed research professor at the University of Maryland from 1968 until his retirement in 1974. Elsasser made fundamental proposals about the origin of the Earth's magnetic field. He proposed that the molten liquid core contains eddies set up by the Earth's rotation. These eddies produce an electric current that causes the familiar terrestrial magnetic field. Elsasser also made predictions of electron diffraction (1925) and neutron diffraction (1936). His works include *The Physical Foundation of Biology* (1958) and *Atom and Organism* (1966).

Elton, Charles Sutherland (1900–1991) British ecologist. Elton graduated in zoology from Oxford University in 1922. He was assistant to Julian HUXLEY on the Oxford University expedition to Spitzbergen (1921), where Elton carried out ecological studies of the region's animal life. Further Arctic expeditions were made in 1923, 1924 and 1930. Such experience prompted his appointment as biological consultant to the Hudson's Bay Company. In 1932 Elton helped establish the Bureau of Animal Population at Oxford—an institution that subsequently became an international center for information on and research into animal numbers and their ecology. In the same year he became editor of the new *Journal of Animal Ecology,* launched by the British Ecological Society, and in 1936 was appointed reader in animal ecology as well as a senior research fellow by Oxford University. Elton was one of the first biologists to study animals in relation to their environment and other animals and plants. At the outbreak of World War II Elton conducted intensive research into methods of controlling rats and mice, thus conserving food for the war effort.

Éluard, Paul (Eugène-Émile Paul Grindel) *(1895–1952)* French poet. Born in Saint-Denis and educated in PARIS, Éluard launched the surrealist movement in the 1920s with André BRETON and Louis ARAGON. He collaborated on experimental works with Breton as well as with Max ERNST and Pablo PICASSO. His most famous books are *Les Dessous d'une vie, ou la pyramide humaine* (The underside of life, or the human pyramid, 1926) and *Capitale de la douleur* (Capital of sorrow, 1926). His first wife, Gala, from whom he separated in 1930, became famous as the wife of Salvador DALÍ. Éluard supported the Republicans in the SPANISH CIVIL WAR, joined the RESISTANCE in 1942 and identified himself with the Communist Party. He is most important as an influence on an international younger generation of writers who were inspired by the avant-garde experiments of the surrealist group to break with traditional forms.

Elvehjem, Conrad Arnold *(1901–1962)* American biochemist. Elvehjem, the son of a farmer, graduated from and spent his whole career at the University of Wisconsin. He obtained his Ph.D. in 1927 and served as professor of biochemistry from 1936 until 1958, when he became president of the university—a position he held until his retirement in 1962. In 1937, following discoveries by Casimir Funk and Joseph Goldberger, Elvehjem succeeded in producing a new treatment for pellagra. He also worked on the role of trace elements in nutrition, showing the essential role played by such minerals as copper, zinc and cobalt. Elvehjem was a prolific author with more than 800 papers to his credit.

Ely, Paul *(1897–1975)* French commander in INDOCHINA after the fall of DIEN BIEN PHU. In 1954 General Ely announced in Saigon the partition agreement reached in Geneva ending France's eight-year war in Indochina. He was chief of the French general staff from 1953 to 1961, except for brief periods during that time.

Elytis, Odysseus (Odysseus Alepoudelis) *(1911–1996)* Greek poet. The son of a successful manufacturer in Crete, Elytis studied law at the University of Athens but did not complete a degree there. When he began writing, Elytis changed his name because of its commercial associations. Influenced by the poet Paul ÉLUARD and the surrealist movement, Elytis published his first poems in *Ta Nea Grammata* (New letters) in 1935. He rejected the despair he found in the work of the modernist poets; his early work is characterized by a bright and hopeful tone. After fighting in Albania during World War II, he served as a literary and art critic for the newspaper *Kathimerini* (Daily). In 1948 he went to PARIS, where he studied at the Sorbonne and became acquainted with Pablo PICASSO, Henri MATISSE and others of the Paris art world. Elytis's next major work, *To Axion Esti* (Worthy it is, 1959), was an autobiographical piece alternating between prose and verse in which he explored the use of conversational and literary Greek. Elytis moved to France in 1969 to protest the 1967 coup in GREECE. His works from this time include *O Ilios o iliatores* (The Sovereign Sun, 1971), *To fotodendro ke i dekati tetarti omorfia* (The Light Tree and the Fourteenth Beauty, 1971) and *Maria Nefeli* (1978), finished after he returned to Greece. Elytis was awarded the NOBEL PRIZE in literature in 1979. (See also MODERNISM; SURREALISM.)

Embden, Gustav George *(1874–1933)* German physiologist. Embden was educated at the Universities of Freiburg, Munich, Berlin and Strasbourg. From 1904 he was director of the chemical laboratory in the medical clinic of the Frankfurt hospital, becoming director (1907) of the Physiological Institute (which evolved from the medical clinic) and director (1914) of the Institute for Vegetative Physiology (which in its turn evolved from the Physiological Institute). In 1918 Otto

MEYERHOF threw considerable light on the process of cellular metabolism by showing that it involved the breakdown of glucose to lactic acid. Embden spent much time in working out the precise steps involved in such a breakdown, later known as the **Embden-Meyerhof pathway.** Embden's earlier work concentrated on the metabolic processes carried out by the liver.

Emeleus, Harry Julius *(1903–1993)* British inorganic chemist. Emeleus was educated at Imperial College, London, and at Karlsruhe and Princeton. He returned to Imperial College in 1931 and taught there until 1945, when he moved to Cambridge University—where he served as professor of inorganic chemistry until his retirement in 1970. In collaboration with John Anderson, he published (1938) the well-known work *Modern Aspects of Inorganic Chemistry.* He also worked on fluorine, publishing a monograph on the subject in 1969: *The Chemistry of Fluorine and its Compounds.*

Emerson, Peter Henry *(1856–1936)* British photographer; one of the world pioneers of nature photography. His works provide an invaluable pictorial record of the British countryside prior to the full-fledged industrial development of the 20th century. Major book collections by Emerson include *Life and Landscape of the Norfolk Broads* (1886) and *Pictures of East Anglia* (1888). Emerson was the first photographer to put forward a written theoretical justification of photography as an independent art.

Emiliani, Cesare *(1922–1995)* Italian-American geologist. Emiliani was educated at the University of Bologna. He moved to America in 1948, obtaining his Ph.D. from the University of Chicago in 1950. After teaching at Chicago (1950–56) he moved to the University of Miami, where he was appointed professor of geology in 1963 at the Institute of Marine Science. Emiliani specialized in using oxygen isotopic analysis of microfossils from ocean sediments. Eduard Bruckner had established (1909) the long-held orthodox view that four ice ages had occurred during the Pleistocene. In his fundamental paper *Pleistocene temperatures* (1955) Emiliani produced evidence that there had been more. Using the principle established by Harold UREY that the climate of past ages can be estimated by the ratio of oxygen 16 to oxygen 18 present in water (that is the less oxygen 18 present the colder the climate must have been), he examined the oxygen 18 content of fossils brought up from the mud of the Carribbean. By choosing fossils that he knew had lived near the surface, he could reconstruct the climatic history, and consequently identified seven complete glacial cycles.

Eminem (Marshal Bruce Mathers III) *(1973–)* American rap musician. Born in Kansas City, Kansas, Mathers moved to Detroit in 1985. By 1988 he had dropped out of high school before finishing his freshman year and began to pursue a career as a rapper (see HIP HOP). In 1997 Mathers gave himself the onstage nickname Eminem for the first letter in his first and last names and released his first album, *Infinite,* through FBT records, an independent company. It was not until later in 1997, when he won the *Wake Up Show's* Freestyle Performer of the Year Award and was the runner-up in the Los Angeles rap Olympics, that he began to receive positive national attention within the rap community. In 1998 Eminem released *The Slim Shady EP,* an album containing several rap hits that inspired Aftermath Records founder Dr. Dre to sign Eminem to a contract. In 1999 Dre and Eminem released *The Slim Shady LP,* which included popular singles such as "Guilty Conscience," which featured Dre as the voice of conscience and Eminem as the diabolic conscience of three individuals.

Eminem followed this with the release of *The Marshal Mathers LP* in May 2000, which immediately shot to number one on the pop charts. However, his lyrics in his *Slim Shady* and *Marshal Mathers* albums drew protests from women's groups, which objected to his indifferent references to spousal abuse, and from several groups within the gay community objecting to his use of the word *faggot.* In 2002 Eminem released *The Eminem Show,* which contained the popular singles "Without Me," followed by his acting debut in the largely autobiographical film *8 Mile;* for the film, Eminem composed the single "Lose Yourself," which won an Academy Award for best new song (2003).

Empire State Building New York City skyscraper of ART DECO design, for many years the tallest building in the world. This structure of 1929–31 was designed by the film of Shreve, Lamb & Harmon as an 85-floor office tower, but a plylon was added to the top, supposedly as a mooring mast for dirigibles, increasing the height to 102 stories (1,239 feet) and establishing a height record that lasted until 1972. The building has the setback form typical of tall buildings constructed in the 1920–50 era of zoning regulations and regarded as the "skyscraper style." Details are in the Art Deco mode, as are the interiors of the public spaces. The design was generally regarded as banal and commercial, but recent boredom with the INTERNATIONAL STYLE buildings of the post–World War II era has created a cult of reaction that now admires the 1930s skycrapers, of which this is the largest and most spectacular. Its status as a tourist attraction remains undiminished.

Empson, William *(1906–1984)* British poet and critic. Empson was educated at Winchester and Magdalene College, Oxford, where he studied physics and English with I. A. RICHARDS, under whose tutelage Empson wrote his dissertation. This work evolved into his first critical book, *Seven Types of Ambiguity* (1930), which made his reputation and became a seminal text in 20th-century literary criticism. Empson taught in China and Japan and then became a professor of English at Sheffield. His first volume of poems, *Poems* (1935), shows the influence of John Donne. In his second volume, *The Gathering Storm* (1940), which draws on his experiences in Asia, his voice is more his own. Empson's complex poetry incorporates ideas of modern physics and mathematics and strongly influenced the writers of The MOVEMENT. His critical works, which include *The Structure of Complex Words* (1951) and *Milton's God* (1961), are considered to be a springboard of the NEW CRITICISM, which, ironically, he attacked in a posthumously published collection of essays, *Using Biography* (1984).

END (European Nuclear Disarmament) British-based movement formed in 1980, originally seeking removal of all nuclear weapons from Europe. It became a pressure group for a reunited Europe free of Soviet or American domination.

Enders, John Franklin *(1897–1985)* U.S. virologist. In 1954, during his long association with Harvard University, he shared the NOBEL PRIZE in medicine or physiology with two of his former students for their development of a method for culturing the polio virus in large quantities. This procedure made possible the mass production of a safe polio vaccine. Enders conducted other research that led not only to the development of vaccines against measles, German measles and mumps but also to advances in growing tumor viruses.

Enesco, Georges *(1881–1955)* Romanian composer. A musical prodigy and violin virtuoso, he began his studies at the Vienna Conservatory at the age of seven. He later studied at the Paris Conservatory under Gabriele FAURÉ and Jules Massenet. He became an influential teacher, numbering Yehudi MENUHIN among his many students. Enesco toured extensively as a violin soloist and conductor, traveling throughout Europe and the U.S. As a composer, he was influenced by the folk music of his native Romania and evolved a highly personal style. His works include *Romanian Rhapsodies* (1901–02) and other orchestral works, chamber music, three symphonies and the opera *Oedipus* (1932).

Engel v. Vitale *(1962)* U.S. Supreme Court decision barring state-sponsored school prayer. For many years it was customary for public school children to recite mandatory prayers at the start of the school day. Critics (primarily atheists and Jehovah's Witnesses) charged that requiring the recitation of a state-designated nondenominational school prayer amounted to the establishment of religion. The Supreme Court held that such recitation was not mandatory and that children could either remain silent or be excused during the prayer. Later cases held that daily Bible readings were also unconstitutional.

Engler, Heinrich Gustav Adolf *(1844–1930)* German botanist. Engler studied botany at Breslau University, gaining his Ph.D. in 1866. After teaching natural history he became custodian of the Munich botanical collection and then professor of botany at Kiel University; in 1884 he returned to Breslau to succeed his former teacher in the chair of botany. At Breslau, Engler replanned the botanic garden, ordering the plants according to their geographical distribution. In 1887 he took up the important chair of botany at Berlin and successfully reestablished the garden in Dahlem. Between 1878 and his retirement from Berlin in 1921, Engler contributed greatly to the development of plant taxonomy with his classifications, presented in such books as *The Natural Plant Families* (1887–1911) and *The Plant Kingdom* (1900–37). Much of his work was drawn from firsthand observation gained during travels through Africa, Europe, India, China, Japan and America.

English Channel Tunnel (Chunnel) A 32.2-mile tunnel running 23.6 miles under the English Channel connecting Folkestone, England, and Calais, France. The long-debated Euro-tunnel was begun in 1986 when Prime Minister Margaret THATCHER and President François MITTERRAND signed the Channel Tunnel Treaty. Tunneling was begun from both ends; the two halves of the service tunnel met on December 1, 1990. The Chunnel actually consists of three tunnels. The outer two are for high-speed trains bearing automobiles and their passengers; in the center is a connected service tunnel, which can also be used for emergency evacuation. The trains carry freight in off-hours. The largest privately financed engineering project ever undertaken, the Chunnel became the world's longest undersea tunnel. The tunnel aroused controversy. Many Britons were reluctant to surrender their island status, and many worried about the environmental impact of the tunnel. The tunnel opened in 1994.

ENIAC Acronym for Electronic Numerical Integrator And Computer. Designed by J. Presper Eckert Jr. and John MAUCHLY and built at the University of Pennsylvania in 1946, the ENIAC was the first true electronic digital COMPUTER. ENIAC occupied an entire large room and used some 18,000 vacuum tubes. It could perform calculations with a rapidity previously unheard of, although by the standards of later computers it was slow and inefficient. Because of its size and complexity, it was never commercially available. In 1951 it was superseded by the more advanced UNIVAC

Enigma German cipher machine used to code and decode secret messages during WORLD WAR II. (See also ULTRA.)

Eniwetok Unpopulated atoll at the northwest end of the Ralik chain in the northwestern MARSHALL ISLANDS of the western Pacific Ocean. Mandated to JAPAN by the LEAGUE OF NATIONS in 1920, it was captured by U.S. forces in February 1944 during WORLD WAR II and became a naval base. In the 1940s and 1950s it was used as a site for atomic weapons testing. (See also BIKINI.)

Enniskillen bombing (*November 8, 1987*) The explosion of a bomb planted by the outlawed Provisional IRISH REPUBLICAN ARMY killed 11 persons and injured more than 60 others in Enniskillen, County Fermanagh, NORTHERN IRELAND. The explosion came as hundreds of people were gathering for the traditional wreath-laying ceremonies on Britain's Remembrance Day. The death toll was the highest from a single incident in the ongoing strife in Northern Ireland since 17 people were killed in a pub bombing in 1982. All of the 11 killed in the Enniskillen bombing were civilians; seven of them were retired persons over the age of 60. The following day the IRA claimed that the bomb had been intended for soldiers and police who would have been marching in the Remembrance Day parade and said that the bomb had gone off prematurely. Both British prime minister Margaret THATCHER and Irish TAOISEACH Charles Haughey, among other political leaders, condemned the bombing.

Enosis (*Greek:* "to unite") Greek Cypriot movement for the political union of CYPRUS and GREECE. It dates from the 19th century, having been revived in 1954 by Archbishop MAKARIOS III and opposed both by the Turkish minority on the island and by the Turkish government. TURKEY invaded and partitioned the island in 1974. (See also CYPRIOT WAR OF 1963–1964, CYPRIOT WAR OF 1974.)

Entebbe, raid on (*July 3, 1976*) Half-hour battle in which Israeli commandos rescued 106 predominantly Jewish aircraft passengers at Entebbe Airport, UGANDA. The plane had been hijacked by guerrillas of the **Popular Front for the Liberation of Palestine** demanding the release of 53 Arab terrorists. Twenty Ugandan soldiers, seven hijackers, three passengers and one Israeli soldier were killed. (See also Idi AMIN.)

Entente Cordiale (Anglo-French Entente) A bilateral agreement reached between the UNITED KINGDOM and FRANCE on April 8, 1904. Overcoming their traditional antagonisms, the two countries ended their colonial rivalry. The pact resolved various international disputes, principally in Egypt, which the British were to develop, and in Morocco, where the French were given free rein. Earlier, an 1890s agreement had sealed the rapprochment between France and Russia. Later, the ANGLO-RUSSIAN ENTENTE of 1907 was to cement

A mushroom cloud rises over Eniwetok after a hydrogen bomb test. (LIBRARY OF CONGRESS, PRINTS AND PHOTOGRAPHS DIVISION)

relations between England and Russia. These international relationships formed the basis of the TRIPLE ENTENTE that opposed the TRIPLE ALLIANCE in WORLD WAR I.

Enver Bey *(1881–1922)* Turkish army general. As one of the leaders of the reformist YOUNG TURKS group, Enver Bey led the rebellion in 1908. Later known as Enver Pasha, he served as military attaché in Berlin (1909–10) and sought German military support. By 1911 he was de facto ruler of TURKEY. He commanded Turkish forces in the Italo-Turkish War (1911) and the BALKAN WARS (1912). As the war minister in 1913, he commanded Turkish forces against RUSSIA in the Caucasus. After the RUSSIAN REVOLUTION, Enver Bey became involved in a "Pan-Turanian" attempt to unite Turkish people, mostly in Russia. After the Turkish defeat in WORLD WAR I (1918), Enver fled to Turkestan, where he was killed leading an anti-BOLSHEVIK revolt.

Environmental Protection Act The National Environmental Protection Act (NEPA), signed into law by President NIXON in 1970, declared it a federal policy to consider the environmental impact of government activities. By 1970 Americans had tired of the abuse of the environment and demanded the federal government assume a leadership role. The act established the Council on Environmental Quality, which sets the federal government's environmental policy, and also the better-known Environmental Protection Agency (EPA), which enforces federal environmental laws (its director was later elevated to cabinet rank). Yet even the EPA proved not to be immune from political manipulation and scandals (see EPA-SUPERFUND CONTROVERSY).

NEPA required the federal government to prepare environmental impact statements assessing the environmental effects of any major federal projects. The EPA was given enforcement power over the Clean Air Act and the Clean Water Act and other environmental legislation that also applied to private industry, and the EPA developed national clean air and water standards. Because of this legislation and increased awareness of environmental problems, the degradation of the environment was slowed in the final quarter of the 20th century. During the first presidential

term of George W. BUSH, environmental groups complained that the federal government was failing to enforce laws designed to protect the environment.

EOKA (Ethniki Organosis Kypriakou Agonos, National Organization of Cypriot Struggle) Anti-British Greek Cypriot guerrilla movement. EOKA members of the National Guard overthrew Archbishop MAKARIOS III, precipitating the Turkish invasion and the partition of CYPRUS. (See also CYPRIOT WAR OF 1974.)

EPA-Superfund controversy Controversy involving collusion between managers of the Environmental Protection Agency (EPA) and industry during the administration of President Ronald REAGAN. (The Superfund had been established by Congress to clean up the most polluted sites in the country.) When Reagan came into office he had a mandate to reduce government regulation, so lax enforcement of environmental regulations became the order of the day. During the 1980s Congress investigated allegations that Rita Lavelle, the EPA's assistant administrator, had given special favors to her former employer and to others. On orders from the president, EPA head Ann Burford refused to turn over subpoenaed documents to Congress; she was held in contempt of Congress. After months of stalemate Burford resigned, and Reagan fired Lavelle after she refused to resign. Lavelle later served a few months in prison for committing perjury during House hearings. The EPA eventually turned over the requested documents to congressional investigators.

Ephemeris Time See Gerald Maurice CLEMENCE.

Epstein, Sir Jacob *(1880–1959)* American-born British sculptor. Epstein, who was born in New York City and studied art as a young man in Paris, lived for most of his life in Britain. There he became renowned as one of the foremost creators of public works of art on the grand scale and was ultimately knighted. But his early career was not without controversy. A massive stone sculptural facade that Epstein produced for the headquarters of the British Medical Association (1907–08) was decried as an aesthetic horror. His memorial

sculpture of Oscar Wilde (1911) was similarly received. But Epstein gained ground with the artistic establishment through his famous busts of Joseph CONRAD, Albert EINSTEIN and Jawaharlal NEHRU, among other notables of the day.

Epstein brothers Julius J. Epstein (1909–2000) and his twin brother, **Philip G. Epstein** (1909–52), formed one of the most renowned screenplay-writing teams in the history of HOLLYWOOD. They were born on the Lower East Side of New York City, where their Jewish father ran a livery stable. After writing some comedies that were performed on Broadway, they went to work for WARNER BROS. in 1938. It was in Hollywood that the Epstein brothers made their true mark, coauthoring 20 films, including such classics as *Yankee Doodle Dandy* (1942), starring James CAGNEY, *Casablanca* (1943), featuring Ingrid BERGMAN and Humphrey BOGART, and *Arsenic and Old Lace* (1944), with Cary GRANT. After Philip's death in 1952, Julius went on to write numerous screenplays, notably *Pete 'n Tillie* (1972) and *Reuben Reuben* (1983).

equal employment opportunity Legally mandated nondiscrimination in employment. During the first half of the 20th century, employers typically discriminated against females and members of minority groups in hiring. In the last half of the century, Congress attempted to enforce the policy of equal employment opportunity by enacting a number of federal laws, including the Equal Pay Act (1963), the CIVIL RIGHTS ACT OF 1964, the Age Discrimination in Employment Act (1967) and the Vocational Rehabilitation Act of 1973. These laws, applying to public and private employers alike, prohibited discrimination in hiring or promotion on the basis of race, religion, national origin, sex, age or physical handicap. The federal government also established the Equal Employment Opportunity Commission (EEOC) to enforce the law by addressing workers' complaints.

Equal Rights Amendment (ERA) An amendment to the U.S. Constitution, first proposed in 1923, to guarantee the legal equality of men and women. The U.S. Congress passed the ERA in 1972, and it was passed on to the 50 state legislatures for their approval or rejection. However, after an intense lobbying campaign by supporters and opponents of the measure, only 35 states had ratified the measure by the 1982 deadline. This number was three short of the three-quarters majority of 38 required under the Constitution, and the amendment was defeated. The Equal Rights Amendment read: "Equality of rights under the law shall not be denied or abridged by the United States or any state on account of sex."

Equatorial Guinea (República de Guinea Ecuatorial) Equatorial Guinea consists of a mainland area (Río Muni) of 10,042 square miles on the coast of west-central Africa; and the islands of Bioko (formerly Acias Nguema, for-

---

EQUATORIAL GUINEA

1885	The mainland territory of Mbini (formerly Río Muni) comes under Spanish rule; the whole colony is known as Spanish Guinea, with the capital at Malabu on Bioko Island.
1959	The region becomes a Spanish overseas province; the African population is finally granted full citizenship.
1963	The region achieves internal autonomy.
1968	Equatorial Guinea formally proclaims its independence, with Macias Nguema Biyogo as president and Atanasio Ndong as foreign minister.
1969	Foreign Minister Ndong is accused of fomenting unrest and is arrested and reportedly killed; mass purge of Macias Nguema Biyogo's political enemies follows.
1970	PUNT is formed and declared the sole legal political party in the country.
1972	Macias Nguema Biyogo is proclaimed president for life.
1973	Under a program of Africanizing geographical names, Fernando Po is renamed Macias Nguema Biyogo, Santa Isabel is renamed Malabo, Annabon is renamed Pagalu, and Río Benito is renamed Mbini.
1974	Government launches a campaign of terror, causing nearly 100,000 citizens to seek asylum in neighboring countries. In a parallel campaign against the Catholic Church, Spanish bishops and nuns are expelled, Catholic schools and churches are closed, African nuns and priests are arrested, and Equatorial Guineans are compelled by decree to drop their Christian names.
1976	United States suspends diplomatic relations with Equatorial Guinea.
1979	President Macias is overthrown in a coup led by his nephew Teodoros Obiang Mguema Mbasogo, who sets up the Supreme Military Council with himself as president; Macias is arrested, tried on a number of charges, including treason, embezzlement, genocide, and other atrocities, found guilty, and shot by a firing squad. King Juan Carlos of Spain visits the country and receives a warm welcome, signifying the pro-Spanish and pro-Western tilt of the new regime. Relations with the United States are restored.
1982	Obiang Nguema Mbasogo is appointed president for a second term of seven years. New constitution is approved by 95% of the voters.
1983	Equatorial Guinea joins the Customs and Economic Union of Central Africa and the Central African Economic Community.
1989	Obiang is elected president in a contest in which he is the only candidate.
1990	Amnesty International accuses Equato-Guinean authorities of torturing political prisoners.
1992	A 1991 law allowing for a multiparty democracy goes into effect.
1996	President Nguema Mbasogo is reelected with 99% of the votes cast.
1999	Legislative elections dominated by the ruling Democratic Party of Equatorial Guinea are widely condemned as fraudulent.
2004	A coup plot by foreign mercenaries is foiled.

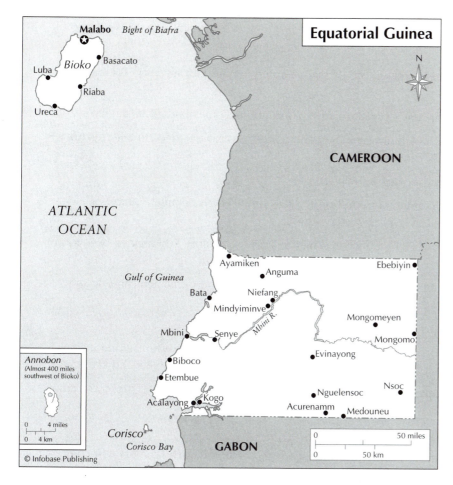

Malabo · Bight of Biafra
Equatorial Guinea
N

Bioko
Luba · Basacato
Ureca · Riaba

ATLANTIC
OCEAN

Gulf of Guinea

CAMEROON

Ayamiken · Ebebiyin
Anguma
Bata · Niefang
Mindyiminve
Mongomeyen
Mbini · Senye · Mongomo
Mbini R.
Biboco · Evinayong
Etembue
Nsoc
Nguelensoc
Acalayong · Kogo
Acurenamm · Medouneu

Annobon
(Almost 400 miles
southwest of Bioko)

0   4 miles
0   4 km

Corisco
Corisco Bay   **GABON**

© Infobase Publishing

0   50 miles
0   50 km

merly Fernando Poo), Annobon (Paualu), Corisco, Elobey Granoe and Elobey Chico in the Gulf of Guinea—for a total offshore area of 10,828 square miles. A Spanish colony since 1778, the area was systematically developed after 1939. Granted partial autonomy in 1963, Equatorial Guinea achieved full independence in 1968. Francisco Macías Nguema ruled the country until 1979, when he was overthrown by his nephew Teodoro Obiang Nguema Mbasogo. Multiparty elections scheduled for 1993 were supposed to alleviate the nation's several political and economic problems. However, the 1993, 1996, 1999 and 2002 national elections failed to end opposition unrest due to widespread reports of electoral fraud in favor of the ruling Democratic Party of Equatorial Africa. In 2004 a coup attempt by foreign mercenaries was foiled.

ER Television drama series created for NBC. Premiering in 1994, the series revolved around the professional and personal trials of the medical staff at County General Hospital in Chicago,

Illinois. Initially the show focused on the activities of Dr. Doug Ross (George Clooney), Dr. Mark Greene (Anthony Edwards), head nurse Carol Hathaway (Julianna Margulies), Dr. Benton (Eriq La Salle) and intern John Carter (Noah Wyle). However, with the exception of Wyle, the premier members of the ensemble cast had left by 2002, forcing *ER* executive producers Michael CRICHTON and John Wells to introduce several new characters, such as Dr. Elizabeth Corday (Alex Kingston), Dr. Luka Kovac (Goran Visnjic), Abby Lockhart (Maura Tierney) and Dr. Gregory Pratt (Mekhi Phifer). By the end of its ninth season (2002–03) *ER* had won 18 Emmy awards, including an award for outstanding drama series (1996) and a supporting actress award for Margulies.

ergonomics Systematic study of relationship between products and human users. The forms and layout of controls and instruments, the design of finger and hand grips, and the arrangement of seating surfaces and other furniture elements to promote efficiency, comfort and physiologically optimum

forms are special concerns of ergonomic study. The term has come into wide use in the promotion of chairs, such as the Herman Miller Ergon chair designed by Bill Stumpf, and other products that are claimed to be designed to maximize human convenience and comfort in use.

Erhard, Ludwig *(1897–1977)* Chancellor of West Germany (1963–66). Head of an economics research institute before World War II and professor of economics at Munich University from 1945 to 1949, Erhard was a Christian Democrat member of the Bundestag from 1949 to 1966. He became federal minister of economic affairs (1949–63) and presided over West Germany's "economic miracle," its transition from wartime devastation to prosperity. Deputy chancellor under Konrad ADENAUER (1957–63), he became chancellor on Adenauer's retirement in 1963. Erhard lacked Adenauer's skill in international affairs and, fearing an economic recession, proposed a series of tax increases that were defeated in the Bundestag (1966). He subsequently resigned from office.

Erikson, Erik Homburger *(1902–1994)* German-born American psychologist. As a young man, Erikson studied art before turning his attention primarily to psychology as a result of undergoing psychoanalytic therapy with Anna FREUD in Vienna in 1927. Erikson then proceeded to train in psychoanalysis, specializing in work with children. Exiling himself from Nazi Germany, he came to the U.S. in 1937. He taught at the University of California, Berkeley, but was forced to leave in 1950 due to his refusal to sign a McCARTHY-era loyalty oath. For the next three decades, Erikson taught primarily at Harvard University. His first major work, *Childhood and Society* (1950), posited eight major stages of formative personality development. Erikson applied these eight stages to biographical analysis in such renowned works as *Young Man Luther* (1958) and *Gandhi's Truth* (1969). *Insight and Responsibility* (1964) continued Erikson's theoretical researches into developmental issues.

Eritrea Italian colony (1898–1941), British trust territory (1941–52), province of ETHIOPIA (1952–93) and independent nation (1993–). In 1990

ERITREA

1889	The Italian colony of Eritrea is created out of areas formerly under Ottoman control and the coastal districts of Ethiopia.
1935–36	Eritrea is used as a base for Italy's conquest of Ethiopia and becomes part of Italian East Africa.
1941	Britain wrests Eritrea from Italy and rules over the country as an occupied enemy territory under a United Nations (UN) mandate.
1950	UN calls for Eritrean federation with Ethiopia.
1952	Eritrea federated with Ethiopia for a period of 10 years after which complete union or independence to be determined by Eritrean referendum.
1961	The Eritrean Liberation Front (ELF) launches armed resistance against Ethiopian subversion of the federal provisions.
1962	Emperor Haile Selassie of Ethiopia arbitrarily dissolves the Eritrean parliament and declares Eritrea an Ethiopian province.
1970	Eritrean nationals within the ELF split and form the EPLF.
1974	Emperor Haile Selassie overthrown in a military coup to be replaced by the Dergue military committee, whose hard stand on Eritrea escalates the war, precluding a mediated settlement.
1988	In the Battle of AfAbet, Ethiopian troops suffer a serious defeat in which EPLF fighters demolish a third of the Ethiopian army.
1991	EPLF liberates Eritrea on May 24.
1992	Eritrea conducts a national referendum for independence or union with Ethiopia. Outcome confirms overwhelming vote for independence.
1993	Eritrea declares its independence on April 24.
1998	War breaks out between Eritrea and Ethiopia.
2000	Eritrea and Ethiopia sign a peace agreement.
2001	Ethiopia and Eritrea complete their troop withdrawal from the border zone; the UN continues to monitor the peace process.

---

the Eritrean People's Liberation Front (EPLF), one of the factions rebelling against Ethiopian control, seized the provincial capital of Massawa. After brokering an agreement with the Ethiopian government that called for a provincial referendum on independence, the province's residents provided a near unanimous approval for making Eritrea an independent state in April 1993, and Eritrea entered the UN on May 28, 1993. In 1994 Eritrea ceased to have relations with SUDAN, which it claimed was harboring terrorists trying to overthrow Eritrea's government. A year later Eritrea invaded the Yemeni island of Hānīsh al Kabīr, but withdrew its troops when an arbitration committee ruled the island belonged to Yemen. In 1998 border clashes resulted in a civil war between Ethiopia and Eritrea that killed more than 10,000 soldiers before a cease-fire was declared in June 2000 and a peace accord was signed in December 2000. In 2003 Eritrea joined the U.S.-led coalition of the willing that entered Iraq in March 2003 and removed the regime of Iraqi dictator Saddam HUSSEIN.

Erlander, Tage (1901–1985) Premier of Sweden (1946–69). A Social Democrat, Erlandeer held office longer than any other premier in a modern Western democracy. In a period of industrial growth unprecedented in Sweden, he presided over the vast expansion of the nation's welfare system while maintaining Sweden's neutrality in foreign affairs. (See also WELFARE STATE.

Erlanger, Joseph (1874–1965) American neurophysiologist. Erlanger was educated at the University of California and Johns Hopkins University in Baltimore, where in 1899 he obtained his M.D. After working on the staff for a few years, Erlanger moved to the University of Wisconsin (1906) to accept the chair of physiology. In 1910 he moved to Washington University, St. Louis, where he held the chair of physiology in the medical school until his retirement in 1944. Between 1921 and 1931 Erlanger carried out some fundamental research on the functions of nerve fibers with his former pupil and colleague Herbert

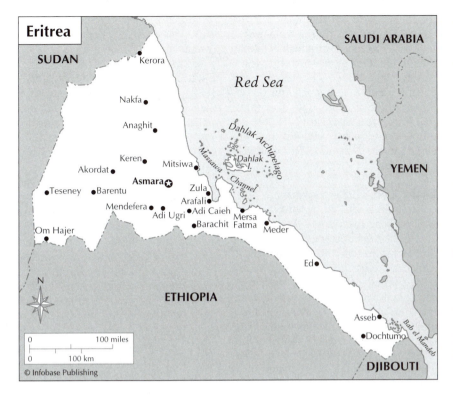

Eritrea

GASSER. They investigated the transmission of a nerve impulse along a frog nerve. Their innovation was to study the transmission with the cathode-ray oscillograph, which enabled them to picture the changes the impulse underwent as it traveled along the nerve. They found that when a nerve was stimulated, the resulting electrical activity indicating the passage of an impulse was composed of three waves, as observed on the oscillograph. They explained this by proposing that the one stimulus activated three different groups of nerve fibers, each of which had its own conduction rate. They went on to measure these rates. Erlanger and Gasser produced an account of their collaboration in *Electrical Signs of Nervous Activity* (1937), and they were awarded the 1944 NOBEL PRIZE in physiology or medicine for their work.

Ernst, Max (*1891–1976*) German painter and writer. Ernst, who began his artistic career as a follower of DADA, emerged in the 1920s as one of the leading painters of SURREALISM. He was a pioneer figure in the use of collage in surrealist art, gaining fame and notoriety from his exhibition (1920) of highly unusual collage assemblages such as *Phallustrade* and *The Wet Nurse of the Stars*. Ernst was also a major theoretician of the surrealist movement, who

was influenced by the credo of 19th-century French poet Arthur Rimbaud that the true artist should make a conscious effort to disorder all of his senses. Ernst wrote, "I have done everything to render my soul *monstrous*. Blind swimmer, I have made myself see. *I have seen*." During the Nazi era, Ernst immigrated to the U.S., where he exercised a considerable influence as teacher and exemplar over the postwar generation of American painters. In 2005 the Metropolitan Museum of Art in New York City mounted a major retrospective of his work.

Ershad, Hussain Mohammed (*1930– *) President of BANGLADESH (1986–90). Ershad was appointed to the 2nd East Bengal Regiment of the Pakistan army after finishing Officers' Training School in 1952. He was promoted to Bangladesh army chief of staff in 1978. General Ershad was instrumental in capturing the assassins of President ZIAUR RAHMAN in 1981. In 1982 he declared martial law and assumed full power. He was elected president in October 1986, in an election boycotted by the major opposition parties. Ershad was replaced by Shahabuddin Ahmed in 1990.

Erskine, John (*1879–1951*) American writer, musician and educator.

Erskine was one of the most versatile and influential figures in American academia in the first half of the 20th century. He served as a professor of English at Columbia University from 1909 to 1937, where he taught numerous future writers including Carl Van Doren and Mortimer ADLER. Erskine was also a gifted concert pianist and became the president (1928–37) of the renowned Juilliard School of Music. Remarkably, Erskine also wrote a number of humorous novels, most notably the best-selling *The Private Life of Helen of Troy* (1925), as well as volumes of poetry and literary criticism. His autobiography is in four volumes: *The Names of Certain Persons* (1947), *My Life as a Teacher* (1948), *My Life as a Musician* (1950) and *My Life as a Writer* (1951).

Erté (Romain de Tirtoff) (*1892–1990*) Russian-born ART DECO designer. De Tirtoff adopted the name Erté in 1913 and created hundreds of covers for *Harper's Bazaar* magazine between 1915 and 1937. As a theatrical designer, he created costumes for musicals, films, operas and ballets, as well as for the Folies-Bergère and the ZIEGFELD FOLLIES. His lithographs, most of which featured elegant women in Art Deco fashions, became extremely popular in the 1970s and 1980s.

Ertesezek, Olga (*?–1989*) Polish-born founder of the U.S. manufacturer Olga Co. She designed many of the firm's products and was credited with inventing the seamless brassiere and the nightgown with the built-in bra. She was featured in a widely published series of advertisements for the firm.

Ervin, Samuel James, Jr. (*1896–1985*) American politician; best known for his role as chairman of the Senate committee that investigated the WATERGATE affair. A North Carolina Democrat, in 1954 he was appointed to fill a vacant seat in the U.S. Senate, where he served for 20 years, winning election in his own right four times. A conservative known for his integrity and his respect for the Constitution, he cast his votes according to his strict constructionist principles. Ervin believed that an activist federal government interfered with STATES' RIGHTS and threatened individual liberties, and he opposed many liberal federal domestic programs and most civil rights legislation. In early 1973 Ervin was named chairman of the Senate Select Committee on Presidential Campaign Activities, known as the Watergate Committee. The Watergate hearings were broadcast on national television, and Ervin became an American folk hero as he directed the probe that played a key role in the resignation of President Nixon in August 1974. He often quoted from the Bible and the works of Shakespeare, but at one point described himself as simply "an old country lawyer." At one point during the Watergate hearings he sadly remarked, "I think that Watergate is the greatest tragedy this country has ever suffered. I used to think the Civil War was the greatest tragedy, but I do remember some redeeming features in the Civil War in that there was some spirit of sacrifice and heroism displayed on both sides. I see no redeeming features in Watergate."

Ervine, St. John Greer (*1883–1971*) Irish playwright and author. Born in Belfast, he was acquainted with AE, George Bernard SHAW and others associated with the ABBEY THEATRE, where Ervine's first play, *Mixed Marriage* (1911), was performed and where he served as manager in 1915. His early plays, which also include *Jane Clegg* (1913) and *John Ferguson* (1915), were realistic social dramas that examined the strife in NORTHERN IRELAND. Ervine later moved to London, where he was drama critic for *The Observer* and the *Morning Post* and continued to write plays, novels and biographies. He achieved success in the London theater with *The First Mrs. Fraser* (1929), which was followed by many other popular comedies. His biographical works include the lives of C. S. Parnell and General Booth, and the notable *Bernard Shaw: His Life, Work and Friends* (1956).

Erving, Julius Winfield "Dr. J" (*1950–   *) American basketball player. A standout player in college, Erving signed after his junior year with the Virginia Squires of the fledgling American Basketball Association. He gave the ABA credibility and drew crowds with his dazzling moves and hang time. After leading the New York Nets to three ABA titles, he was again traded,

this time to the Philadelphia 76ers of the NBA. With Erving the team was a four-time championship finalist, taking the title in 1983. A five-time first-team All-Star, at 6 feet 7 inches he was equally adept at both small and power forward. He became only the third player in league history to amass 30,000 points. In 1993 Erving was elected to the Naismith Memorial Basketball Hall of Fame.

Esaki, Leo (*1925–   *) Japanese physicist. Esaki graduated in physics at the University of Tokyo in 1947, where he later gained his doctorate in 1959. His doctoral work was on the physics of SEMICONDUCTORS, and in 1958 he reported an effect known as tunneling. The phenomenon of tunneling is a quantum-mechanical effect in which an electron can penetrate a potential barrier through a narrow region of solid, where classical theory predicted it could not pass. Esaki was quick to see the possibility of applying the tunnel effect, and in 1960 reported the construction of a device with diode-like properties—the tunnel (or Esaki) diode. Important characteristics of the tunnel diode are its very fast speed of operation, its small physical size and its low power consumption. It has found applications in many fields of electronics—principally computers, microwave devices and where low electronic noise is required. Esaki shared the NOBEL PRIZE in physics in 1973 with Brian JOSEPHSON and Ivar GAIEVER.

Eschenmoser, Albert (*1925–   *) Swiss chemist. Eschenmoser was educated at the Federal Institute of Technology, Zurich, where he has taught since 1956 and where, in 1960, he was appointed professor of organic chemistry. He is best known for his work in synthesizing a number of complex organic compounds. His first success came with an alkaloid that has important applications in genetic research. He also collaborated with Robert Woodward on the synthesis of vitamin B-12, which had first been isolated and crystallized by Karl Folkers in 1948. Its empirical formula was soon established, and in 1956 Dorothy Hodgkin established its structure. It took many years, with samples passing between Zurich and Harvard, before Eschenmoser and Woodward were finally able

to announce its synthesis in 1965. In 2000, he was awarded the Oparin Award.

Escher, Maurits Cornelis (*1898–1972*) Dutch artist. Escher was one of the modern masters of graphic art, specializing in woodcut, wood engraving and lithography. His visually striking and paradoxical works—in which surreal details and trompe l'oeil techniques abound—achieved great popularity in the 1960s and 1970s. Escher was born in Leeuwarden in northern Holland. He began his college studies in Haarlem, Holland, intending to become an architect, but soon switched to the graphic arts, to which he devoted the rest of his life. Escher lived in Italy from 1923 to 1935, and Italian settings predominate in his work of this period. He returned to Holland in 1941. His works of the last three decades of his life—such as *Reptiles* (1943), *Three Spheres I* (1945), and *Relativity* (1953)—tend toward introspective, abstract themes.

Escobar, Pablo (*1949–1993*) Colombian drug lord. During the 1980s Escobar created the MEDELLÍN CARTEL, named after the city that served as its center of operations. As head of the cartel, Escobar amassed billions in profits and controlled a sizable portion of Colombia's arable land, which he used to grow, refine and airlift cocaine to the U.S. In 1986 he attempted to use his resources to enter politics and offered, if he was elected, to pay off Colombia's national debt of $10 billion. When the Colombian government responded by barring him from public office, Escobar began a guerrilla campaign against the government, assassinating policemen, government officials and political candidates, including Luis Galán, the 1989 presidential nominee of the Liberal Party. In response the U.S. dispatched military advisers to train the Colombian Search Bloc, a military unit created to capture Escobar. In 1991 the Colombian government persuaded Escobar to turn himself in; however, he was allowed to build his own jail compound, which contained many of the trappings of a country estate. In 1992 Escobar escaped from his self-made compound but was cornered and killed by government troops in one of his Medellín hideouts on December 2, 1993.

Esenin, Sergei Alexandrovich *(1895–1925)* Russian poet. Founder of the Imagist school of Russian poets. Esenin presented himself as a "peasant poet" and recited in Moscow salons wearing a peasant smock. He welcomed the revolution, without really understanding it. He married Isadora DUNCAN, the American dancer, in 1922, but they separated after a year, and he returned to Russia with an international reputation as a drunken exhibitionist. He never succeeded in adapting either to the new, urban Soviet society or to the changed peasant world; he hanged himself in Leningrad in 1925. His *Confession of a Hooligan* was published in 1918.

Esnault-Pelterie, Robert *(1881–1957)* French aviation pioneer and aeronautical engineer. Esnault-Pelterie became interested in rocketry in middle age. In 1927 he and banker Andre Louis Hirsch established a 5,000-franc prize to be awarded annually for the best technical book on astronautics (the REP-Hirsch Award). The first award went to German rocket pioneer Hermann OBERTH in 1928. In 1930 Esnault-Pelterie published his own classic, *L'Astronautique,* still regarded as a major work in the history of astronautics. Elected to the French Academy of Sciences in 1936, he was working on the development of a gasoline- and liquid-oxygen-fueled rocket motor when the German occupation cut short his research and forced his retirement in 1940.

Espíritu Santo Island, also known as Marina, in an autonomous group of islands formerly known as the NEW HEBRIDES but now called VANUATU; in the southwestern Pacific Ocean. A large U.S. airbase was here during WORLD WAR II. Part of an Anglo-French condominium until 1980, independence saw separatist unrest that had to be put down in 1980.

Esposito, Anthony James "Tony" *(1943–   )* Canadian hockey player. Esposito began his career as backup goaltender for the Montreal Canadiens, then came into his own upon joining the Chicago Black Hawks. He won the

Calder Trophy as rookie of the year in 1970 and was an All-Star five times. That year, he faced his brother Phil in the Stanley Cup finals, but the Hawks lost in four straight games. Esposito was a Vezina Trophy winner three times for lowest goals-against average and finished his career with 76 shutouts and a 2.92 goals-against average. Active in the Players' Association throughout his career, he went on to a career in hockey administration.

Esposito, Philip Anthony *(1942–   )* Canadian hockey player. Esposito began his career in Chicago, but the Black Hawks lost patience with the lumbering, slow-developing center and traded him to the Boston Bruins in 1967, thus losing one of the game's greatest players. Although he never became a fluid skater, Esposito's extraordinary balance and puck sense allowed him to score at a virtual goal-a-game rate during the 1971 season. A five-time scoring champion and perennial All-Star, he was a leader in Team Canada's last-minute triumph over the Soviet Union in 1972. In 1975 he was traded along with Carol Vadnais to the archrival New York Rangers for Jean Ratelle and Brad Park in what is regarded as the biggest trade in hockey history. At first refusing to report, Es-

posito learned to love New York and went on to become general manager and coach of the team in the late 1980s. He was named to the Hall of Fame in 1984.

Estonia Situated on the Gulf of Finland, directly south of Finland itself, Estonia is the northernmost Baltic republic and covers an area of 17,370 square miles. The territory of present-day Estonia was annexed to Russia by Peter the Great in 1709. At the end of WORLD WAR I Estonia became an independent republic, governed by dictator Konstantin Paets (1934–39). The Soviet Union annexed the country in 1940. In 1968 Estonians staged the first mass protests against Soviet occupation since World War II. By 1988 the bid for independence had reached its zenith with the mass demonstrations known as the Singing Revolution. Following the collapse of the Soviet Union in December 1991, the Russian Federation recognized the independence of Estonia. Three years later Estonia joined the EUROPEAN UNION and NATO's PARTNERSHIP FOR PEACE. In 1992 the Republic of Estonia officially came into being, and elections were held that same year. Estonia joined the Council of Europe in 1993, and the last of the Russian occupying forces left

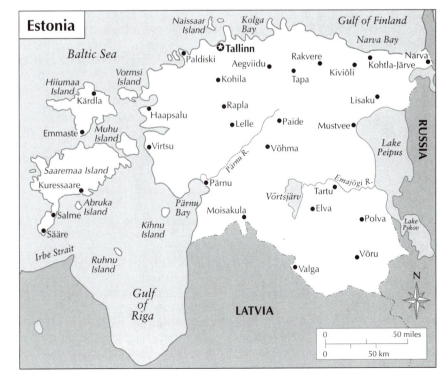

ESTONIA	
1918	Estonia declares independence from Russia and engages in an armed struggle against both German and Russian forces.
1940	Soviets invade Estonia.
1968	First open, mass protests against Soviet occupation since the end of World War II.
1988	"The Singing Revolution": mass demonstrations by 300,000 Estonians in Tallinn, marked by singing.
1991	Estonia declares its independence and is recognized by Moscow.
1992	The Republic of Estonia is reestablished and elections are held.
1993	Estonia becomes a member of the Council of Europe.
1994	The last Russian troops leave Estonia.
2004	Estonia joins the European Union and NATO.

Estonia in 1994. Estonia joined the European Union and NATO in 2004.

Estonian War of Independence *(1917–1920)* During WORLD WAR I Russian-controlled ESTONIA proclaimed independence on November 28, 1917, following the BOLSHEVIK REVOLUTION. Bolshevik troops advanced to retake the country, but the Germans occupied it. Estonia then declared independence again on February 24, 1918. Although the Treaty of BREST-LITOVSK granted independence to the Baltic states, Soviet forces invaded Estonia after Germany's defeat in renunciation of the treaty. The Estonians, with aid from a British flotilla, expelled the Soviets, and an anti-Bolshevik army from Estonia led by Nikolai Yudenich attempted to seize Petrograd (Leningrad) in October 1919. Leon TROTSKY hastily assembled a force and forced Yudenich's army to retreat to Estonia. Soviet recognition of Estonian independence came about in the Treaty of Dorpat (Tartu) on February 2, 1920. Soviet troops later occupied Estonia in 1940, when it became a Soviet republic.

Estrada, Joseph (Joseph Ejercito) *(1935–   )* Filipino film actor and director (1957–89), mayor of San Juan (1969–86), senator (1987–92), vice president (1992–98) and president (1998–2001). Born Joseph Ejercito in Manila, he changed his last name to Estrada when his family objected to his withdrawal from college to pursue an acting career. By 1961 he had established himself as a Filipino movie star with his role in *Asiong Salonga,* in which he played an underdog who overcame elitist opposition to triumph in the end. During a film career that included roles in 107 movies over 32 years, he generally played Robin Hood-esque characters who helped the poor at the expense of the rich.

In 1969 he used his status as a film star to win election as mayor of San Juan, a borough of the capital city of Manila. In 1987, after 17 years as mayor, Estrada was elected to the Philippine Senate. During his five years as a senator he became well known for his efforts to end the leases possessed by the U.S. for bases in the Philippines, such as Subic Bay. In 1992 Estrada was elected vice president because of his name recognition among the voters. Six years later he won election as Filipino president.

Despite some notable achievements as president, Estrada was impeached by the Filipino House of Representa-

tives in November 2000 on charges of corruption. Estrada's trial before the Senate was conducted amid massive street protests against him; the Supreme Court declared the office of president vacant on January 20, 2001, and swore in his vice president, Gloria ARROYO, as president.

ETA (Euzakadi Ta Askatasumar, "Basque Homeland of Liberty") A radical group split from the **Basque Nationalist Party** in 1959. It employs terrorist tactics. Between September 1998 and December 1999 a brief truce emerged between the ETA and the Spanish government. However, the truce ended when the Spanish government refused to negotiate with the ETA on its demand for Basque independence. In March 2006 the ETA declared a permanent cease-fire.

Ethiopia A country on the central plateau of East Africa; bordered by ERITREA and DJIBOUTI to the north, SUDAN to the west, KENYA to the south and SOMALIA to the east. Formerly known as Abyssinia, it is circled by mountains and has one navigable river, the Blue Nile. In 1882 ITALY, supported by Britain, took the Red Sea harbor of Aseb but was stopped from moving inland by the Ethiopian army, at Dogali in 1887. In 1889 Menelik II came to power and ended a treaty with Italy, which then claimed Abyssinia as a protectorate. Menelik II denounced the claim, and his army crushed an Italian invasion at Adwa (Adowa) in 1896. Global respect grew, but the new capital at Addis Ababa became a diplomatic hotbed in pitting the colonial powers against one another.

Italy never forgot its 1896 defeat and its interest in Ethiopia. In 1935 Benito MUSSOLINI's Fascist fist came down heavily on the medieval country, which nevertheless resisted the weapons of modern warfare for six months before succumbing. Emperor HAILE SELASSIE escaped to Britain but returned in 1941 after Allied forces defeated the Italians. Great Britain labored to upgrade the army and bureaucracy, and full sovereignty was regained after the war; in 1952 Ethiopia took control of the former Italian colony of Eritrea. Eritrea was to have been an autonomous province, but unrest grew as its status

ETHIOPIA

1928	Ras Tafari is crowned as Emperor Haile Selassie (Power of the Trinity) I.
1931–32	Haile Selassie gives Ethiopia its first written constitution and abolishes slavery.
1936	Ethiopia, never before colonized, is conquered and occupied by Italy under Mussolini.
1941	Italians are driven out by British troops during World War II.
1962	Ethiopia annexes Eritrea; secessionists intensify ongoing struggle for independence.
1974	Haile Selassie deposed; military Dergue (coordinating committee) led by Lieutenant Colonel Mengistu Haile Mariam declares Ethiopia a socialist state, institutes large-scale land reform and expands offensive against Eritrean People's Liberation Front (EPLF).
1977	Mengistu government trains peasant militia of 100,000 with Cuban assistance and airlifts them to Eritrea to fight EPLF secessionists and to Ogaden, where rebels seek union with Somalia.
1985	An estimated 1 million die of starvation; in the West Live Aid, an all-star rock telethon broadcast to 152 countries, raises $70 million for famine relief.
1991	Rebels make key advances against Ethiopian government troops; Mengistu flees the country; talks begin on forming new, democratic government.
1993	Eritrea obtains independence from Ethiopia after referendum.
1995	New constitution adopted; Meles Zenaive becomes prime minister.
1997	War breaks out between Ethiopia and Eritrea over disputed territory.
2002	A new border plan by an independent boundary commission is accepted by Ethiopia and Eritrea.
2005	Protests over possible fraud during the multiparty elections causes a re-vote for more than 30 seats. An international court in The Hague rules that Eritrea broke international law when it invaded Ethiopia in 1998.

was gradually eroded; Eritrean nationalist guerrillas battled the Ethiopian government throughout the 1960s and 1970s. After a cruel famine in September 1974, Haile Selassie was ousted by the military; in December 1974 Ethiopia was proclaimed a socialist state and began a closer relationship with the USSR under left-wing radical Colonel MENGISTU HAILE MARIAM. All-out war between Eritrean and Ethiopian factions started in 1975, while Somalia challenged Ethiopia's control of the Ogaden region. Intermittent famines persisted throughout the country. Rebel victories forced Mengistu to flee in 1991, ending the Marxist rule of Ethiopia. In 1993 an Eritrean referendum gave the province its independence. However, both Ethiopia and Eritrea remained embroiled in a dispute over the border town of Badme until signing a June 2000 cease-fire accord that arranged for a UN force to administer the withdrawal of Ethiopian

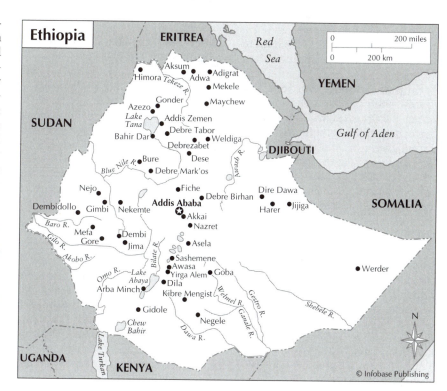

troops from Eritrea. In 2002 Ethiopia and Eritrea accepted a new common border provided by an independent commission. In 2005 multiparty elections were held, but protests over fraud led to re-runs for more than 30 seats. That same year an international court in The Hague ruled that Eritrea broke international law when it invaded Ethiopia in 1998.

Ethiopian-Eritrean Guerrilla War

(1961–1993) Under British control (1941–52), ERITREA became an autonomous province in a federal ETHIOPIA, giving the latter a frontier on the Red Sea. Ethiopian undermining of Eritrean autonomy led to armed resistance in 1961 by the Eritrean Liberation Front (ELF). Two additional guerrilla parties, the Eritrean Peoples Liberation Front, or EPLF (1970), and the ELF/PLF soon appeared. The rivals often fought among themselves, weakening the anti-Ethiopian effort; the war was characterized by small skirmishes. A massive military push by Ethiopia (1967) forced out thousands of Eritrean refugees. Martial law, established in 1971, famines in 1973 and 1975, the fall of Ethiopia's imperial government in 1974, reduction of Ethiopian control to Eritrean urban centers by 1977 and rebellions in Ethiopia itself—all complicated the war. Ethiopian-Soviet-Cuban fighters suffered a severe loss at Asmara in 1978. The guerrilla war ended in 1993 when an Eritrean referendum resulted in Eritrea's independence.

Ethiopian-Somali Border War

(1963–1988) SOMALIA, the union of Italian and British Somaliland in 1960, demanded additional territories on independence—in DJIBOUTI, KENYA and the Haud, partly in ETHIOPIA's OGADEN, where Somalis had grazed their herds. As early as 1963 Somalis and Ethiopians fought—Somalis rejecting Ethiopian control of the Ogaden. Discovery of oil (1973), the fall of Ethiopia's imperial government and a major revolt by Somalis in the Ogaden (1977) complicated the issue. In March 1978 Ethiopian troops, with Cuban and Soviet help, drove the Somalis from the Ogaden. The Somalis returned three months later as the Western Somali Liberation Front, and sporadic fighting along the Somali-Ethiopian border ensued. In 1988 the two countries signed

a peace treaty ending their border dispute.

ethnic cleansing An attempt by one or more ethnic groups to create ethnic homogeneity in a particular region by removing other ethnic groups from the region. Such exclusion could be the result of a peaceful transfer of peoples, as occurred between the Greeks and the Turks after the GRECO-TURKISH WAR OF 1920–1922, when GREECE agreed to accept the compulsory transfer of all Greeks living in TURKEY to Greece, while Turkey agreed to accept the Turks residing in Greece. However, the more common examples of ethnic cleansing in the 20th century were attempts to exterminate or expel by force certain ethnic minorities within states. Examples of the former include the HOLOCAUST, the genocide and forced evacuation conducted by the OTTOMAN EMPIRE against its Armenian minority during WORLD WAR I (see ARMENIA), and the attempts by CROATIA, SERBIA and the Bosnian Serbs to expel unwanted minorities from their respective areas of the former YUGOSLAVIA between 1991 and 1999.

E.T.: The Extra-Terrestrial *(1982)*

Movie directed by Steven SPIELBERG. It was, at the time, the most successful motion picture ever made, grossing more than $700 million worldwide.

Euler-Chelpin, Hans Karl August Simon von

(1873–1964) German-Swedish biochemist. Euler-Cheplin was educated at the Universities of Berlin, Strasbourg and Göttingen as well as the Pasteur Institute. In 1898 he moved to Sweden, being appointed to the staff of the University of Stockholm, where in 1906 he became professor of general and inorganic chemistry. He also became director of the Institute of Biochemistry (1929), where he remained until his retirement in 1941. Although he became a Swedish citizen in 1902, he served Germany in both world wars. In 1904 important work by Arthur Harden had shown that enzymes contained an easily removable nonprotein part—a coenzyme. In 1923 Euler-Chelpin worked out the structure of the yeast coenzyme, showing that the molecule was made up of a nucleotide similar to that found in nucleic acid. Euler-Chelpin shared the

1929 NOBEL PRIZE in chemistry with Harden for this work. His son, **Ulf von Euler,** won the NOBEL PRIZE in physiology or medicine in 1970 for his work on neurotransmitters and the nervous system. Von Euler had earlier (1935) discovered the substance prostaglandin, which he named. From 1966 to 1975 von Euler was president of the Nobel Foundation.

Euratom See EUROPEAN ATOMIC ENERGY COMMUNITY.

euro Unit of currency for most of the members of the EUROPEAN UNION (EU, 1999–) designated by the symbol €. The critical economic provision of the 1991 Treaty of MAASTRICHT, the euro was the final component of the EU's roadmap for Economic and Monetary Union (EMU). This union called for the creation of a single currency issued by a newly created European Central Bank that would function throughout the EU, facilitating intra-union investment and trade by eliminating the transactional costs of currency conversion. The greatest challenge to the establishment of the euro was the problem of how to prevent the steep devaluation of some member states' old currencies as a result of their integration with the weaker currencies of other states. To guard against such a development, the EU established tight restrictions on a nation's inflation rate, national budget deficit and the ability of a nation's currency to maintain a stable value prior to incorporation into the euro. Three EU members—Britain, Sweden and Denmark—considered the merging of their currencies with the euro too great a loss of sovereignty and refused to adopt the common currency.

To regulate the inflation rate, monetary supply and convertibility of the euro, the EU established the European Central Bank (ECB) in June 1998. On January 1, 1999, the ECB and the euro officially went into operation as the official central bank and currency of the EU, respectively. However, the consequences of the reform were not immediately evident, as euro coins and banknotes did not enter into circulation until 2002. Until then, the euro only functioned as a currency in bank transfers and credit card payments. On January 1, 2002, euro coins and notes entered circulation, superceding the national currencies of the participating states. After falling against the dollar during its first year in circulation, the euro rose sharply against the U.S. currency.

Although it became one of the most visible symbols of European integration, the euro also allows for a certain degree of national identity by the states that have adopted its use. The 1-, 2-, 5-, 10-, 20- and 50-cent euro coins (a full euro equals 100 cents) are decorated on one side by a design common to all coins and on the other side with a design specific to the country in which they were minted. (See also EUROPEAN MONETARY SYSTEM.)

Eurocorps A military organization of the EUROPEAN UNION numbering 35,000 troops. Created in 1992 under the auspices of the Western European Union, the fledgling security force of the EU, the Eurocorps represented an early concrete step toward European defense cooperation. Its original five members were Belgium, France, Germany, Luxembourg and Spain. Its headquarters are located in Strasbourg, France. It was initially thought by some observers that the Eurocorps might become a rival of the COLD WAR–era NATO alliance. However, to avoid complaints among European statesmen that the Eurocorps might undermine the American pledge to participate in the defense of the continent, the European members of the organization agreed to the creation of formal links between the Eurocorps and NATO's high command. In more recent years this fear has subsided; the Eurocorps has remained a very small military force, and became available as a Rapid Reaction Corps headquarters for both the EU and NATO.

European Atomic Energy Community (Euratom) Community formed in 1958, along with the EUROPEAN ECONOMIC COMMUNITY (EEC), under the terms of the 1957 Treaty of Rome. Its purpose is to achieve the common development and growth of the peaceful nuclear industries of its member states. Euratom is particularly active in the development of nuclear power. It accomplishes its aims by providing technical assistance, permitting the free movement of nuclear materials and equipment, concluding contracts,

setting standards for the protection of workers and the public, and establishing common procedures. Euratom became a part of the EUROPEAN COMMUNITY in 1967.

European Coal and Steel Community (ECSC) Proposed by French foreign minister Robert Schuman and formulated in the 1951 Treaty of Paris; officially founded in July 1952 by France, West Germany, Italy, Belgium, the Netherlands and Luxembourg, its goal was to unify the coal, iron and steel industries of the member countries. The organization established a single authority to encourage these industries, to eliminate tariffs and other bars to free trade and to favor a free labor market within member states. The community was extremely successful, and its achievements helped to foster other forms of European economic cooperation. The central institutions of the ECSC were merged with the EUROPEAN ECONOMIC COMMUNITY and the EUROPEAN ATOMIC ENERGY COMMUNITY in 1967, forming the EUROPEAN COMMUNITY. When Great Britain, Denmark and Ireland became members of the Common Market in 1973, they also became members of the ECSC.

European Community (EC) Collective term for three post–World War II organizations whose common aim is to create an economically integrated Europe. The EC emerged from the economic philosophy of Jean MONNET and was implemented by France's foreign minister, Robert Schuman. The member communities are the EUROPEAN ECONOMIC COMMUNITY (EEC), the EUROPEAN COAL AND STEEL COMMUNITY (ECSC) and the EUROPEAN ATOMIC ENERGY COMMUNITY (Euratom). Under the provisions of a 1965 treaty, the executive agencies of these organizations were merged in 1967, forming an integrated administrative system. The original member states were Belgium, France, Luxembourg, the Netherlands, Italy and West Germany. In 1973 Denmark, Ireland and Great Britain became members; Greece joined in 1981 and Portugal and Spain in 1986. The EC achieved, and continues to achieve as the refashioned EUROPEAN UNION (EU), its economic aims by creating a common customs tariff, attempting to

reduce economic differences between regions, abolishing restrictions on international trade, allowing the free flow of people and services among member states, aiding overseas development, promoting the movement of capital among members, establishing common agricultural goals and, through Euratom, working together to develop the nuclear power industry and other peaceful uses for nuclear energy. Indeed, there was no aspect of the economic life of Europe, including taxes, currency, transportation, antitrust regulations, health, food and much more, that was not governed to some degree by the EC. Implementing the concept of a truly economically unified Europe, the Single European Act, ratified by the community in 1987, set the close of 1992 as the deadline for the removal of all nontariff barriers among member states.

The community's main policymaking body is the Council of Ministers. With one representative from each member nation, it works closely with the Committee of Permanent Representatives. With a membership of 17 appointed by the council, the committee proposes legislation to the council and carries out the council's decisions in treaties. Both these administrative groups have their headquarters in Brussels; the European Parliament, headquartered in Strasbourg, is the community's advisory body, with a membership of over 500. Supervising its executive agencies, it has power over the budget and can dismiss the commission by the vote of a two-thirds majority. Located in Luxembourg, the European Court of Justice is the community's supreme court. With a judge from each member nation, it decides disputes among member countries that arise from community treaties or legislation. Made up of the heads of state of each member nation and formed in 1974, the European Council meets for general discussions three times a year.

In 1992 the signing of the MAASTRICHT TREATY by the EC's members led to the creation of the EU, a successor organization to the EC that increased political, economic and security cooperation among EC states. In 1999 the EU oversaw the implementation of the EURO as the sole currency among all EU nations except Britain, Sweden and Denmark.

European Defense Community

(EDC) Proposed European army, international in character but with common institutions. It was originally suggested by French prime minister René Pleven in 1950. The proposal was formalized in the 1952 Treaty of Paris, signed by the six nations that formed the EUROPEAN COAL AND STEEL COMMUNITY. In spite of the willingness expressed in the treaty, signatory nations, particularly France and Italy, were reluctant to establish this kind of supranational army. The EDC was nipped in the institutional bud when the French National Assembly, largely due to its fears of a loss of sovereignty refused to ratify the Paris treaty in 1954.

European Economic Community

(EEC) Also known as the Common Market, the EEC was created to integrate the economies of Western Europe through the formation of one economic market for their resources. It is the best known and most important of the three communities in the EUROPEAN UNION (EU). The EEC and the EUROPEAN ATOMIC ENERGY COMMUNITY (Euratom) were formed through the provisions of the 1957 Treaty of Rome, whose signatories were Belgium, France, Italy, Luxembourg, the Netherlands and West Germany. During the first decade of its operation, the EEC succeeded in abolishing trade restrictions, particularly tariffs, among member nations. It also formulated and put into operation a common tariff in dealing with other world nations. The EEC's success was reflected in the large increase its member states experienced in their production and in their domestic and international sales. The EEC was also responsible for developing a Common Agricultural Policy (CAP), established in 1962 to cover domestic prices paid to farmers and govern the import of all foreign foodstuffs. This community also adopted policies to permit the free flow of goods, people, services and capital among its members and to create uniform taxation. In addition, it worked to create standardized and improved social programs. Largely due to their early achievements, the EEC, Euratom and the EUROPEAN COAL AND STEEL COMMUNITY were formally merged under an umbrella administration in 1967, creating the EUROPEAN COMMU-

NITY. In 1973 the EEC admitted Great Britain (whose membership had previously been blocked by French president de GAULLE), Denmark and the Republic of Ireland as members. Norway, however, rejected a proposed membership by popular referendum in 1972. Greece joined the EEC in 1981, and Spain and Portugal became members in 1986. In addition, associate status has been granted to a number of nations. The Common Market set 1992 as the date for the abolition of trade and legal barriers among all nations of the EEC, and the deadline was met. The EEC's goal of full economic integration fell under the jurisdiction of the EU, the successor organization to the EC created by the MAASTRICHT TREATY.

European Free Trade Association

(EFTA) An organization formed in 1959 to promote economic expansion and free trade; headquarters are in Geneva, Switzerland. EFTA's original seven members were Austria, Denmark, Great Britain, Norway, Portugal, Sweden and Switzerland; Finland joined as an associate member in 1961, and Iceland became a full member in 1970. All members were for a variety of political reasons originally opposed to membership in the EUROPEAN ECONOMIC COMMUNITY (EEC), which was formed two years earlier. EFTA removed all nonagricultural tariffs among member states, in a gradual reduction over a period of seven years. Unlike the EEC, member states maintained preexisting national tariffs on other imports. EFTA was less effective than the EEC in promoting European trade and providing sweeping economic reform. Denmark and Great Britain left EFTA in 1972 to join the EEC in 1973. Thereafter, the remaining six members negotiated a new agreement with the EEC, providing for mutual tariff removal and free industrial trade among all of Western Europe's major nations. In 1995 Austria, Finland and Sweden left the EFTA to join the EUROPEAN UNION.

European Monetary System

(EMS) A system of financial exchange-rate controls among nations of the EUROPEAN ECONOMIC COMMUNITY; instituted in 1979. Members include Belgium, Denmark, France, Greece, Ireland, Italy,

Luxembourg, the Netherlands and Germany. After initial opposition, Britain joined, but it has been wary of full participation. The EMS sets international currency exchange rates among member states. By the late 1980s some European leaders had proposed a monetary union of all member states, in which individual national currencies would eventually be replaced by a common European currency, designated the ECU (for *European Currency Unit*). Supporters of this plan felt that it would improve trade among member nations; it would also be a step toward the political unification of Europe. British prime minister Margaret THATCHER strongly opposed this plan, feeling that Britain would lose its national sovereignty. Her open disagreement with leading members of her cabinet over endorsement of the plan led to her resignation in late 1990. In 1999 the EURO, the new EUROPEAN UNION (EU) currency, went into circulation as the sole currency in all EU member states except Britain, Sweden and Denmark.

European Union

(EU) A supranational organization created within Europe as a result of the 1991 Treaty of MAASTRICHT (formerly known as the Treaty on European Union). The purpose of the EU was to apply the principles of economic integration developed in the 1950s and 1960s in the EUROPEAN ECONOMIC COMMUNITY (later renamed the EUROPEAN COMMUNITY [EC]) and apply them to political and social issues while deepening the economic links of the member states.

Politically, the EU partially relies on the incorporation of the 1967 EC, with the principles of intergovernmental cooperation established through the Common Foreign and Security Policy (CFSP) and the Justice and Home Affairs (JHA); collectively, these three entities are referred to as the "pillars" of the EU. While each of these pillars has the right to deal with matters within its purview, no European state has ceded its final authority to these bodies. As a result, decisions concerning the CFSP and JHA require unanimity, and both structures depend on EU members for the enforcement of their resolutions.

The principal organs of the EU are the European Commission, the Council of the European Union, the European Parliament, and the European Court of Justice. Of these, the European Commission is the EU's highest administrative body. It possesses the power to establish and enforce policies throughout the EU. It is also responsible for managing the EU's finances and making certain that EU policies are implemented. Unlike the European Commission, the Council of the European Union is not concerned with administrative issues. Instead, this body serves as the EU's main decision-making agency, as its 15 members directly represent each of the EU governments. Unlike the commission, which has a fairly permanent roster, the delegates to the council from each state change according to the topic of any convened meetings; for instance, if the topic is foreign relations, each nation normally sends its foreign minister. After reaching a decision, the council's instructions are transmitted to the European Commission. One limitation of the council is the voting system applied during its meetings. Though some issues can be resolved by a simple majority vote, others require qualified majority voting (QMV), in which each state is allotted a certain number of votes in proportion to its population, with a two-thirds vote required for the passage of a proposal.

While the council's members represent the governments of the EU states, the European Parliament (EP) directly represents the citizenry of the EU. Directly elected by popular vote since 1979, the members of this legislative body wield authority on a variety of issues concerning the EU. The EP has the power to reject a proposed EU budget, to force the removal of the entire European Commission with a vote of no confidence and to prevent the admission of new states to the EU. Apart from these limited powers, the parliament acts only as a consultative body and will only increase its power if the governments of the member states agree.

The last key branch of the EU is the European Court of Justice. With a court composed of 25 judges, one selected by each member state, it has the authority to issue rulings on matters of EU law; the court has established the precedent that EU law supplants the laws of its various nations, although it has on occasion ruled in favor of national at the expense of EU law.

In economic matters the Maastricht treaty established an Economic and Monetary Union (EMU), which called for all participants to fully integrate their economies under the EU and adopt a single currency, the EURO; however, the United Kingdom, Sweden and Denmark, three signatories of the Maastricht treaty, declined to adopt the euro as their currency for fear that by doing so they would cede a vital component of their national sovereignty to the European Central Bank.

With these political and economic organs, the EU and its members have encountered difficulties on a number of issues. The requirement of unanimity, the minimal authority of the European Parliament and the restrictions placed on the Council of the European Union (on which the European Commission depends for its instructions) have all impeded the ability of the EU to act as a genuinely supranational body whose policies benefit the union as a whole. Also, the goal of greater economic integration, associated with the phenomenon of GLOBALIZATION, has provoked protests from European farmers, particularly those in France, who oppose all efforts by the EU to reform the Common Agricultural Policy (see José BOVÉ). Finally, foreign policy developments in the early 21st century revealed a sharp split within the EU. One faction, largely associated with France, Belgium, Luxembourg and, to a lesser extent, Germany, favors the adoption of policies increasingly designed to identify the EU and its members as a collection of states independent from the policies and actions of the U.S. However, other states, including the more recent inductees into the organization from eastern Europe such as Poland and the Czech Republic, as well as Britain and the Netherlands, have tended to align with American foreign and defense policies.

Since the creation of the EU, with the entry into force of the Maastricht treaty, the union has dramatically expanded its membership. Austria, Finland and Sweden joined in 1995. In 2004 the union admitted Cyprus, the Czech Republic, Estonia, Hungary, Latvia, Lithuania, Malta, Poland, Slovakia and Slovenia.

In 2005 a constitution for the EU was submitted to the 25 member states for ratification. After nine countries approved the constitution, the French and Dutch electorate decisively rejected the document, disrupting the EU's progress toward greater political integration.

Evans, Bill (*1929–1980*) Jazz pianist. Evans, along with BEBOP practitioner Bud Powell, helped redefine the course of postwar improvisation. After early engagements with guitarist Mundell Lowe, clarinetist Tony Scott and vanguard composer George Russell, Evans catapulted to jazz stardom in 1958 when hired by trumpeter Miles DAVIS; his collaboration with Davis for the seminal recording "Kind of Blue" (1959), which elevated MODAL JAZZ as a viable alternate to bebop, crystallized Evans's place as one of jazzdom's most significant innovators. While assimilating the bebop lexicon of Bud Powell, Evans evolved a highly lyrical and advanced harmonic approach. His greatest accomplishments were achieved in trio contexts with double bass and drums, where highly contrapuntal, interactive dialogues with bassists Scott La Faro, Chuck Israels, Eddie Gomez and Marc Johnson set new standards for the jazz piano format. Evans's rhythmic flair, consistent inventiveness and well-modulated touch also made him a superb accompanist, as his recordings with flutist Jeremy Steig, guitarist Jim Hall and singer Tony Bennett demonstrate. Evans's influence can be discerned in the work of such major contemporary pianists as Chick COREA, Herbie HANCOCK and Richard Beirach. Evans also left a body of provocative compositions, including such standards of the jazz repertory as "Waltz for Debbie," "Peace Piece," "Funkallero" and "Peri's Scope."

Evans, Robley Dunglison (*1907–1995*) American physicist. Evans was educated at the California Institute of Technology, where he obtained his Ph.D. in 1932. He went to the Massachusetts Institute of Technology in 1934 and was appointed professor of physics (1945). In 1940 Evans suggested that radioactive potassium 40 could be of use in geologic dating. It is widespread in the Earth's crust, has an exceptionally long half-life of more than a billion years and allows estimates of the age of potassium-bearing rocks ranging from 100,000 to about 10 million years. This method proved to be particularly valuable as it permitted accurate dating beyond the limits of Willard LIBBY's carbon-14 technique.

Evans, Walker (*1903–1975*) American photographer. Born in St. Louis, Missouri, Evans began his career as a photographer in 1928. As a documentary photographer for the Farm Security Administration from 1935 to 1937, he created superbly precise photographs of the depression-era South, sharp-focused images that ranged from beautifully composed, sign-dotted facades of rural buildings to the deeply lined faces of poor sharecroppers. In 1936 he accompanied writer James AGEE on a tour of Alabama, and his strikingly dignified portraits of tenant farmers and other working families are an integral part of their highly acclaimed book *Let Us Now Praise Famous Men* (1941). Walker's other projects included a series of portraits of New York City subway riders (1938–41). Walker was an editor, photographer and writer at *Fortune* magazine (1945–65) and a professor at Yale (1965–75). His books include *American Photographs* (1938), *Many Are Called* (1966), *Walker Evans: Photographs* (1971) and the posthumous *First and Last* (1978).

Everest, Mount Mountain in the central Himalayas, on the edge of NEPAL and TIBET. At 29,028 feet, Everest is the tallest mountain in the world. After eight unsuccessful attempts, it was finally scaled on May 28, 1953, by New Zealand explorer and mountain climber Edmund HILLARY and Tenzing Norkay of Nepal. It has since been ascended by numerous expeditions. Everest was named after Sir George Everest, British surveyor of the Himalayas.

Everglades Swampy area of about 5,000 square miles in southern Florida (U.S.); it spreads from Lake Okeechobee in the north to Florida Bay and is only seven feet above sea level at its highest point. The region is surrounded by water, saw grass, islands of vegetation, coastal mangrove forests and black slime. In the 20th century southern Florida's private and com-

mercial real estate boom drastically upset the area. Drainage and construction enterprises upset the water flow into the Everglades, and plant and animal life are continually menaced. Hunting, fishing and backwoods life continue to flourish in many sections. At the southwestern end is Everglades National Park (1.4 million acres).

Evergood, Philip (*1901–1973*) American painter. Born in New York City, Evergood studied at Eton, Cambridge, London's Slade School, New York's Art Students League and Paris's Académie Julien. He is best known for a mixture of figurative realism in his oils and etchings. Evergood gained particular recognition for his 1930s murals, which often explored themes of social deprivation and war. These large works include the narrative Richmond Hill Public Library mural (1936–37), *Cotton from Field to Mill* (1938) for the Post Office in Jackson, Georgia, and a commission for Kalamazoo College. His later works included more symbolism and often portrayed specifically American subjects, as in *My Forebears Were Pioneers* (1940, Georgia Museum of Art, Athens), or religious imagery, for instance, *The New Lazarus* (1954, Whitney Museum, New York City).

Evers, Medgar W. (*1926–1963*) American worker in CIVIL RIGHTS MOVEMENT. Evers was born in Decatur, Mississippi. A graduate of Alcorn A&M University, he served in World War II and received two Bronze Stars. For the nine years preceding his death, Evers was Mississippi field secretary for the NAACP. In 1963 civil rights protests in the state were at their height, and early on the morning of June 12, Evers was ambushed and shot to death in the driveway of his Jackson, Mississippi, home, as he was returning from an integration rally at a nearby church. Blacks in Jackson held mass demonstrations on June 12 to protest the murder, resulting in 158 arrests. Ten days after the killing, Bryon De la Beckwith, of Greenwood, Mississippi, was charged with the crime, but two mistrials were declared and no conviction was ever obtained in the case. Beckwith was rearrested in 1991. In 1994, following a third trial, De la Beckwith was convicted for assassinating Evers; he died in prison.

Evert, Christine Marie (*1954–   *) American tennis player. The daughter of a tennis instructor, she was the dominant woman player of the 1970s. She first reached the finals of the U.S. Open at the age of 16 in 1971 but lost to Billie Jean KING. She turned professional in 1972 and won more than $4 million during the remainder of the decade. She was the U.S. Open singles champion from 1975 to 1978 and came back to win it again in 1980 and 1982. A three-time Wimbledon winner, in 1974 she shared the Wimbledon spotlight with her then-fiancé Jimmy CONNORS, winner of the men's singles title that year. While married to tennis player John Lloyd, she was known as **Chris Evert Lloyd.** Following her fifth round loss to Zina Garrison at the U.S. Open in 1989, Evert retired from professional tennis.

Evian Agreements (*March 1962*) Overwhelmingly ratified by referenda in FRANCE (April 1962) and ALGERIA (July 1962), the Evian Agreements ended the ALGERIAN WAR OF INDEPENDENCE fought against France since 1954 with an immediate cease-fire and a guarantee of French withdrawal by the end of the year. The talks leading up to the agreements were held in Evian-les-Bains, France; the main participants were French prime minister Georges POMPIDOU and the Algerian nationalist leader Mohammed Ahmed BEN BELLA.

Evren, Kenan (*1917–   *) Turkish statesman and president. Evren rose through an orthodox military career and became chief of the general staff. Under his guidance, the Turkish armed forces' National Security Council (NSC) took over the government in a bloodless coup in 1980. Under the new constitution of 1982, Evren became president of TURKEY. His firm and straightforward personality has earned him respect and popularity. Known for his modesty, he denied a desire for permanent political power. Evren's term ended in 1989, and he was succeeded by TURGUT ÖZAL.

Ewing, Sir James Alfred (*1855–1935*) British physicist. Ewing was educated at the University of Edinburgh, where he studied engineering. In 1890 he was appointed professor of applied mechanics at Cambridge but in 1903 moved into higher levels of administration—first as director of naval education and from 1916 until his retirement in 1929 as principal and vice-chancellor of Edinburgh University. During WORLD WAR I Ewing was in charge of the cryptologists at the admiralty from 1914 to 1916. He described his work there in the posthumously published book *The Man in Room 40* (1939).

Ewing, William Maurice *(1906–1974)* American oceanographer. Ewing was educated at the Rice Institute, Houston, and earned his Ph.D. in 1931. He taught at Lehigh University, Pennsylvania, from 1934 until moving in 1944 to Columbia University, New York, where he organized the newly established Lamont Geological Observatory into one of the most important research institutions in the world. Ewing pioneered seismic techniques to obtain basic data on the ocean floors. He was able to establish that the Earth's crust below the oceans is only about 3–5 miles thick, while the corresponding continental crust averages 25 miles. In 1956 Ewing and his colleagues were able to show that the Mid-Atlantic Ridge constituted a mountain range extending throughout the oceans of the world and was some 40,000 miles long. In 1957, working with Marie Tharp and Bruce Heezen, he revealed that the ridge was divided by a central rift, which was in places twice as deep and wide as the Grand Canyon. Ewing also proposed, with William Donn, a mechanism to explain the periodic ice ages, but no hard evidence has yet been found to support that theory.

Ewins, Arthur James *(1882–1957)* British pharmaceutical chemist. Ewins went straight from school to join the brilliant team of researchers at the Welcome Physiological Research Laboratories at Beckenham. He worked on alkaloids with George Barger; in 1914, with Henry Dale, he isolated the important neurotransmitter acetylcholine from ergot. Following wartime experience in manufacturing arsenicals with the Medical Research Council, he became head of research with the pharmaceutical manufacturers May and Baker, where he remained until retirement in 1952. Under Ewins in 1939, the company produced sulfapyridine, one of the most important of the new sulfonamide drugs. An important later discovery was the antiprotozoal drug pentamidine (1948). He was elected a fellow of the Royal Society in 1943.

exclusionary rule A controversial rule of evidence that bars the introduction of evidence gathered in violation of a defendant's constitutional guarantees. Under the U.S. Constitution's Fourth Amendment, citizens are protected against unreasonable searches and seizures. In 1914 the U.S. Supreme Court, in the case *Weeks v. United States,* announced that citizens could bar the introduction of evidence gathered in violation of their Fourth Amendment rights. The rule was later termed the *exclusionary rule.*

Although the rule originally applied only to searches by federal officers, it was later applied to searches by state officers as well. The rule was attacked because it only indirectly deters unlawful searches; critics argue that the rule excludes potentially relevant evidence while failing to punish the police officers who unlawfully obtain the evidence. However, despite the criticism, the rule has withstood numerous proposals for its abolition.

executive privilege The discredited concept that a special legal privilege protects the U.S. president's confidential conversations. In 1973 Congress initiated an investigation of the circumstances surrounding a break-in at DEMOCRATIC PARTY headquarters during the 1972 presidential campaign. The ensuing scandal that rocked the administration of President Richard M. NIXON became known as the WATERGATE scandal, after the hotel in which the break-in occurred. When a special prosecutor subpoenaed taped transcripts of President Nixon's conversations, the president asserted that the tapes were protected by an executive privilege—similar to the attorney-client privilege—that covered the tapes' confidentiality.

In *UNITED STATES V. NIXON* (1974) the U.S. Supreme Court unanimously rejected the concept of executive privilege, ruling that the prosecutor had a legal right to the tapes. After the tapes were made public the House of Representatives voted to initiate impeachment proceedings, after which Nixon became the first U.S. president to resign from office.

existentialism Twentieth-century school of philosophy, perhaps the most influential school of philosophical thought to have emerged in the century. Important 19th-century precursors to existentialism include German philosophers Arthur Schopenhauer and Friedrich Nietzsche and Russian novelist Fyodor Dostoyevsky, all of whom wrote of a world in which ultimate meaning was lacking and humans were called upon to confront the absurdity of existence. Another key precursive influence was PHENOMENOLOGY, a philosophical viewpoint developed largely by German philosopher Edmund HUSSERL, which stressed the epistemological necessity of viewing the world without preconceived value judgments. Existentialism holds that life has no meaning beyond that which each individual accords to it. Atheistic existentialists, such as Martin HEIDEGGER and Jean-Paul SARTRE, denied the existence of the divine. Religious existentialists, such as Martin BUBER and Gabriel MARCEL, asserted that the absurdity of life could be transcended through faith achieved by way of an existential encounter with the divine.

Exner, Virgil *(1909–1973)* American automobile designer usually credited with having a major role in the design on the 1947 Studebaker. Exner worked on automotive styling in the 1930s under Harley EARL at GENERAL MOTORS. In 1939 he went to work for Raymond LOEWY, eventually developing the Studebaker body that has come to be regarded as a classic of postwar American design. In 1949 he returned to Detroit to work for Chrysler.

Explorer 1 The first American satellite, launched from CAPE CANAVERAL on January 31, 1958. After the Soviet Union launched the first artificial satellite (SPUTNIK 1, October 4, 1957), the U.S. was eager to send its own satellite into orbit and recoup some of its scientific and national prestige—especially after the launchpad explosion of a VANGUARD rocket in December 1957. *Explorer 1* was a pointed cylinder 80 inches long and some six inches in diameter, weighing just over 18 pounds (including 11 pounds of instruments). It achieved an elliptical orbit with an apogee (farthest point from the Earth) of 1,587 miles and a perigee (closest point) of 219 miles. *Explorer*'s instruments included a Geiger counter for measuring cosmic radiation, thermometers for measuring temperatures in space and inside the satellite gauges to detect the number and effect of micrometeorites striking the satellite, and two radio transmitters to relay all this information to Earth. The instruments and experiments were designed by physicist James VAN ALLEN. Among the findings relayed to Earth by *Explorer 1* was the existence of a belt of radiation above the equator, subsequently named the Van Allen Belt. The information received from *Explorer 1* was made available to the world scientific community as part of the INTERNATIONAL GEOPHYSICAL YEAR OF 1957–1958. Over the following months, a series of Explorer satellites was sent into orbit. In August 1959 *Explorer 6* became the first satellite to send back television pictures of the Earth from space.

expressionism Movement in art, literature and theater that developed in GERMANY from about 1910 to 1925. Influenced by the paintings of Vincent Van Gogh and Eduard MUNCH, expressionist artists aimed at intense depictions of inner reality. Expressionism's distorted forms and often grotesquely unnatural colors led to increasingly abstract works. Wassily KANDINSKY, Paul KLEE and Oskar KOKOSCHKA were among the movement's artists. Inspired by such authors as Dostoyevsky and STRINDBERG, expressionist writers—among them playwrights Georg KAISER and Ernst TOLLER—stressed a protagonist's psychological state. Expressionism's theme of individual alienation was echoed in the fiction of Franz KAFKA and the plays of both Eugene O'NEILL and Bertolt BRECHT. Brecht's dramatic technique also included such expressionist devices as highly stylized action, dialogue and setting.

Exxon Valdez On March 24, 1989, shortly after leaving the Alaskan port of Valdez with a full cargo (1,260,000 barrels) of crude oil, the tanker *Exxon Valdez* ran aground on a reef in Prince William Sound. Over the following days, some 11 million gallons of crude oil leaked into the sound, creating a slick more than 45 miles long—the worst oil spill in U.S. history. Much of the oil washed up on the numerous islands in the sound and on the mainland itself, causing extreme damage to local wildlife and threatening the region's fishing industry. Cleanup crews proved inadequate to cope with the magnitude of the spill, although hundreds of workers scoured the region during the next year. Meanwhile, a routine investigation had revealed that the *Exxon Valdez*'s captain had been drinking shortly before the accident and that the ship was being piloted by the third mate, who was not certified to operate the ship in those waters. The state of Alaska, the federal government and environmental groups claimed that the ship's owner, Exxon, had been criminally negligent. Exxon insisted that the disaster had been a simple accident and that no safety regulations had been violated. However, in 1991, Exxon pleaded guilty to four criminal misdemeanor charges and agreed to pay a $100 million fine—the largest fine ever assessed for an environmental crime. Moreover, the corporation agreed to pay $900 million over the next decade (until 2000) to settle civil suits brought by the state of Alaska and the U.S. government. In 1994 a federal court returned a verdict against Exxon, ordering the company to pay $5 billion in punitive damages. That verdict was overturned in 2001. The *Exxon Valdez* itself was towed to California, repaired and subsequently sailed under a new name.

Eyde, Samuel (*1866–1940*) Norwegian engineer and industrialist. Eyde was a civil engineer, trained in Berlin. Until 1900 he worked in Germany and on harbor and railroad station projects in Scandinavia. There he became interested in industrial electrochemical processes—a subject of some potential in Scandinavia because of the availability of cheap hydroelectric power. In 1901 Eyde met Kristian Birkeland, with whom he developed a process (1903) for the fixation of atmospheric nitrogen by reaction of oxygen in an electric arc. Because the **Birkeland-Eyde process** needed plentiful and cheap supplies of electricity, it led to an explosive growth in the production of hydroelectric power. In 1900 Norway had an output of little more than 100,000 kilowatts; by 1905, production had jumped to 850,000 kilowatts. In the same year Eyde started the company Norsk Hydro-Elektrisk Kvaelstof, with the help of French capital, to produce fertilizers by the Birkeland-Eyde process. As a result of this, Norway's export of chemicals was to treble before the start of World War I. Eyde retired from the firm in 1917. He was also a member of the Norwegian parliament.

Eyring, Henry (*1901–1981*) Mexican-American physical and theoretical chemist. Eyring was a grandson of American missionaries who had become Mexican citizens. He thus first came to America in 1912 as a Mexican citizen and did not take U.S. citizenship until 1935. He was educated at the University of Arizona and the University of California, where he obtained his Ph.D. in 1927. He then held a number of junior appointments before joining the Princeton faculty in 1931, becoming professor of chemistry there in 1938. Eyring moved to a similar chair at the University of Utah, holding the post until his retirement in 1966. He wrote nine books and over 600 papers and as a chemist was as creative as he was productive. His main work was in the field of chemical kinetics with his transition-state theory. Eyring also worked on the theory of the liquid state and made contributions in molecular biology.

Eyskens, Gaston (*1905–1988*) Belgian prime minister (1949–50, 1958–61, 1968–72). A professional economist and academic, he served in the Belgian parliament for the Christian Social Party from 1939 to 1973, leading five Belgian governments between 1949 and 1972. Eyskens's first term ended in the controversy surrounding the return to BELGIUM of King LEOPOLD III. During a later tenure in office, he oversaw the independence of the Belgian Congo (later known as ZAIRE, then as the Democratic Republic of the CONGO), but the onset of the Congolese Civil War (1960–68) forced his resignation. Eyskens also served as finance minister under several administrations.

F

Faber & Faber British publishing company. A leading publisher of modernist poetry and belles lettres in the 1920s and 1930s (see MODERNISM), Faber & Faber grew out of the Scientific Press, which had been inherited by Lady Gwyer. With the arrival of Geoffrey Faber in 1924, the company became Faber & Gwyer. In 1929 he bought out Lady Gwyer and established Faber & Faber, although Sir Geoffrey was the only Faber involved. Faber, a poet himself, encouraged his staff to foster innovative writers. T. S. ELIOT served as a director for many years, publishing such writers as W. H. AUDEN, Ezra POUND, and Stephen SPENDER. Faber died in 1961, but the company has maintained its reputation as a leading literary publisher. Other Faber & Faber authors have included James JOYCE, Edith SITWELL, Sylvia PLATH, Philip LARKIN, Samuel BECKETT, Ted HUGHES and Seamus HEANEY, to name but a few.

Fabian Society British socialist organization formed in 1884. The Fabian Society was begun by a group of middle-class intellectuals, including Beatrice and Sydney WEBB, who were committed to infusing the British system with socialistic principles of public welfare. They took their name from Quintus Fabius Maximus (d. 203 B.C.), a Roman general who avoided battles with the Carthaginians but drained them with a series of harassments instead. The Fabians rejected revolutionary tactics and felt that a long period of political evolution—encouraged by their well-intentioned needling—was necessary for democratic socialism to take hold. The society was instrumental in the formation of the Labour Representation Committee, which evolved into the LABOUR PARTY. The Fabian Society now acts largely as the party's research and support organization. Other prominent members of the society during its history have included George Bernard SHAW (who wrote many of the tracts they distributed), Rupert BROOKE and Shirley WILLIAMS.

Face the Nation Long-running CBS television public affairs program; premiered on Sunday, November 7, 1954, with newsman Ted Koop as moderator. Over the years hosts have included Stuart Novins, Howard K. Smith, Paul Niven, Martin Agronsky, George Herman, Leslie Stahl, and Bob Schieffer. The format has always been the same: Leading politicians and other public figures answer questions from a panel of journalists. One of the most famous guests was Nikita KHRUSHCHEV, soon-to-be Soviet premier, who became something of a television celebrity in 1957 when he consented to be a guest on *Face the Nation*. Filmed in Moscow, the program aired on June 2 and was subsequently acclaimed by *Time* magazine as "the season's most extraordinary hour of broadcasting." The media experience may have served Premier Khrushchev well in 1959, in his "Kitchen Debate" in Moscow with Vice President Richard NIXON.

Faeroe Islands Island group in the North Atlantic, between the Shetland Islands and ICELAND. Colonized by Norsemen in the eighth century A.D., the Faeroes have belonged to DENMARK since 1380. Mounting patriotism in the 19th century nurtured a longing for independence, which grew during WORLD WAR II when Denmark fell to GERMANY in 1940 and Great Britain was forced to set up a protectorate. After the war, the islands were awarded self-government under the authority of Denmark.

Fagerholm, Karl-August *(1901–1984)* Three-time prime minister of Finland and one of its best known post–World War II political figures, Fagerholm was premier during a major crisis with the USSR in 1958; his coalition government fell within four months because of silent Soviet pressure and internal squabbling. A Social Democrat, Fagerholm was a conciliatory politician who advocated Finnish cooperation with Scandinavian nations. He served as premier three times, as speaker of the chamber five times and as a member of parliament for 36 years. He retired from politics in 1966.

Fahd bin Abdul Aziz *(1923–2005)* Saudi government official and king of Saudi Arabia (1982–2005). The 11th son of IBN SAUD, the man who established the kingdom of SAUDI ARABIA in 1932, Fahd effectively ruled the state from 1982 until a stroke in 1995 substantially reduced his authority and ability as a statesman.

Educated at the Saudi royal court and in Britain, Fahd was appointed minister of education in 1953. Nine years later he was named to minister of the interior, a post he held for five years until designated second deputy prime minister. He helped Saudi Arabia negotiate an agreement with the U.S. in 1974 and three years later conferred with U.S. president Jimmy CARTER about the conflict between Israel and the Palestinians.

Upon the death of King Khalid in 1982, Fahd ascended to the throne of Saudi Arabia. He continued his predecessor's efforts to make the kingdom's economy less dependent on the production and sale of oil. When Iraqi president Saddam HUSSEIN invaded KUWAIT on August 2, 1990, and appeared to be threatening Saudi Arabia as well, Fahd agreed to allow the deployment of U.S. troops along the Saudi border with IRAQ and Kuwait as part of Operation Desert Shield to deter Hussein from invading the kingdom. When Kuwait was liberated under Operation Desert Storm in the winter of 1991, Fahd led the call for reparations from Iraq to pay for the damage Hussein caused in Kuwait and for economic sanctions against Hussein's regime. When, in 1992, appeals came within and outside Saudi Arabia for the introduction of democratic reform in the kingdom, Fahd agreed to create a 60-member "Majlis al-Shura," or Consultative Council, to advise the monarch in affairs of state. Fahd also made an effort to curb Islamic extremists within Saudi Arabia who opposed the royal government. These radicals criticized the continued presence of "infidel" troops near the holiest sites of Islam and its effect on the purity of the Saudi people. In November 1995 Fahd suffered a stroke that required him to hand power over to his half brother Abdullah for one month. Although he again resumed the title of king in December, his continuing health problems relegated him to the position of a purely symbolic ruler with no actual authority. He died in 2005, and his half brother Abdullah became king.

Faid Pass Pass in the Atlas Mountains of northern Tunisia. On February 14 and 20, 1943, during the North African phase of WORLD WAR II, Ger-

man forces led by ROMMEL targeted the Tunisian mountains to their west via the Faid and KASSERINE Passes. After initial setbacks, the invading Americans counterattacked and recaptured the Faid Pass in April, concluding the last Axis offensive in North Africa.

Fairbank, William Martin (*1917–1989*) American physicist. Working at Stanford University in California, Fairbank specialized in experiments in low-temperature superconductivity. He also worked on research into the existence of gravity waves and the subatomic particles known as quarks. Some of his work formed the basis for an ongoing multimillion-dollar satellite project intended to test a final unproven prediction from Albert EINSTEIN's general theory of relativity.

Fairbanks, Douglas (Julius Ullman) (*1883–1939*) American motion picture actor and producer whose swashbuckling style and physical agility dominated 43 films from 1915 to 1934. Born in Denver, Colorado, Fairbanks began acting in the Frederic Warde Shakespeare Company. After a succession of juvenile roles on Broadway, he came to HOLLYWOOD in 1914 under contract with the newly established Triangle Film Company. For the next five years he exploited talents for comedy and physical action in dozens of peppy, contemporary comedies breezily satirizing the fads and social pretensions of the day (for example, *His Picture in the Papers, Wild and Wooly,*

When the Clouds Roll By). But with the unexpected success of a period drama about old California, *The Mark of Zorro* (1920), Fairbanks settled into a notable, expensively produced series of costume dramas for which he is best remembered today: *The Three Musketeers* (1921), *Robin Hood* (1922), *The Thief of Bagdad* (1924), *The Black Pirate* (1926), *The Gaucho* (1927) and others. He married Mary PICKFORD in 1920, and the couple established residence in BEVERLY HILLS in a home they named "Pickfair," the prototype of subsequent celebrity homes in the area. He retired in 1934 after his last film, *The Private Life of Don Juan*, and devoted the rest of his life to traveling and planning film projects with his son, actor and producer **Douglas Fairbanks Jr.** Apart from his inimitable pantomimic style—a blend of balletic grace and rough-and-tumble acrobatics—Fairbanks was a powerful force in the film industry. With Pickford, Charles CHAPLIN and D. W. GRIFFITH, he formed UNITED ARTISTS in 1919. *The Black Pirate* introduced Technicolor to the commercial arena. He also served as the first president of the Academy of Motion Picture Arts and Sciences. He died of a heart attack in 1939.

Fair Deal President Harry TRUMAN's domestic program. Following President Franklin ROOSEVELT's death, Vice President Truman assumed the presidency in 1945. After the end of WORLD WAR II, Truman sought to continue and extend the programs initiated by

Douglas Fairbanks and Mary Pickford at their California estate. Pickfair (LIBRARY OF CONGRESS, PRINTS AND PHOTOGRAPHS DIVISION)

FDR's NEW DEAL reforms. Although Truman put forward his domestic program shortly after assuming office, he first used the term *fair deal* in his 1949 State of the Union address. The Fair Deal proposals centered on a full-employment law, a higher minimum wage, fair employment practices and extension of the Social Security program. Truman also called for a national housing program to eliminate slums, better price supports for farmers and increased aid to education. Although much of the program was enacted, the results were less dramatic than the New Deal reforms. Shortly after Truman's reelection in 1948 the KOREAN WAR diverted attention from the Fair Deal program.

Fair Labor Standards Act The Fair Labor Standards Act (1938), more commonly known as the Wage-Hour Law, prohibits oppressive child labor, establishes maximum working hours and fixes a federal minimum wage for many workers. Although Congress had made earlier attempts at regulating wages and hours in private employment, the Supreme Court had struck down all prior laws as beyond congressional power.

The act outlaws oppressive child labor, which includes any labor for a child under 16 years of age and labor that is hazardous to the health of a child under age 18. It establishes 40 hours as the maximum workweek, unless overtime pay is paid at one and one-half times the normal wage. The act also sets a minimum wage, which has been gradually increased over the years. The wage and hour rules do not apply to administrative or professional workers, outside sales representative and certain service and retail workers.

Faisal (*1906–1975*) King of Saudi Arabia (1964–75). Faisal served as prime minister from 1953 to 1964, before succeeding his brother, Saud as king. He used SAUDI ARABIA's oil wealth to transform the country into a modern nation. In the early 1970s, following the ARAB-ISRAELI WAR OF 1973, he directed the OPEC oil embargo against the U.S. to show his displeasure with America's support for ISRAEL. Faisal was assassinated by his nephew, Prince Faisal ibn Musad Abdel Aziz. He was succeeded

by his half brother, Crown Prince Khalid Abdel Aziz Al Saud.

Faisal I (*1885–1933*) King of Iraq (1921–33). Third son of Husein Ibn Ali of Mecca, he was educated in Constantinople. After serving with the Turkish forces in Syria during WORLD WAR I, he left the Turkish army and joined T. E. LAWRENCE in the Arab revolt and entered Damascus with Lawrence in 1918. Becoming king of SYRIA in 1920, within months he was forced to abdicate by the French. Faisal was elected king of IRAQ in 1921 under the British mandate, and he maintained a pro-British policy while obtaining Iraq's independence in 1932. He died a year later and was succeeded by his son, Ghazi.

Faisal II (*1935–1958*) King of Iraq (1939–58). Grandson of FAISAL I, he assumed the throne upon the death of his father, King Ghazi. Educated at Harrow, he ruled under the regency of his uncle, Emir Abdul Ilah, until his 18th birthday. During his reign he and his cousin, King HUSSEIN of Jordan, attempted to form a federation of their two nations. Faisal was killed on July 14, 1958, in a revolution led by Abdul Karim KASSEM, who overthrew the monarchy and proclaimed IRAQ a republic.

Falange Spanish extremist political group that favored nationalism and a fascist-type political and economic structure. It was founded in 1933 by José Antonio Primo de Rivera, son of the former Spanish dictator Miguel PRIMO DE RIVERA. After José Antonio's execution by Spanish Republicans in 1936 at the start of the SPANISH CIVIL WAR, the party moved closer toward a FASCISM inspired by MUSSOLINI. General Francisco FRANCO organized the party into the only legal political movement in Nationalist SPAIN. The Falange under Franco's leadership ruled Spain for many years, but in later years Franco moved away from its ideology. The Falange's influence declined considerably, and it was formally abolished on April 1, 1977.

Falkland Islands (*Spanish:* **Islas Malvinas**) Cluster of 200 islands in the South Atlantic, 300 miles east of the Strait of Magellan; now a depend-

ent territory of the UNITED KINGDOM. Discovered and claimed by John Davis in 1592, it was colonized from 1765 to 1774, and the islands have been continuously occupied since 1833. ARGENTINA also claims the islands, although it failed at colonizing them between 1829 and 1833. The remote islands were the site of a strategic naval battle during WORLD WAR I when on December 8, 1914, a British naval force shattered the German Pacific squadron, which had approached from the Straits of Magellan. In early April 1982 Argentina, asserting its claim to the islands, seized them by force. Great Britain quickly sent a large task force to recover the Falklands and set up a "total exclusion zone" around the islands. In late April the British recovered South Georgia, a chain of islands some 800 miles east of the Falklands, then moved on to attack the main islands. The Argentine cruiser *General Belgrano* and the British destroyer *Sheffield* were sunk, with much loss of life. In May the British established a beachhead on East Falkland. Darwin and then Stanley were secured, and by June 22 the British had triumphed. Although diplomatic relations have since been reestablished between Great Britain and Argentina, there has been no discussion of Britain's continued sovereignty in the islands.

Falkland Islands War (Islas Malvinas War) (*1982*) The dispute over control of the FALKLAND ISLANDS dates back to the 17th century. In 1833 the British reinforced their claim by deporting Argentine inhabitants, but Latin American nations supported the Argentine claims. Negotiations ended unresolved on February 27, 1982; Argentine forces invaded the Falklands on April 2, 1982, securing all points. Diplomatic efforts to defuse the crisis failed, British prime minister Margaret THATCHER dispatched a large naval task force under Rear Admiral John Woodward. The Argentine air force inflicted extensive damage on the British fleet. On May 21, 1982, British infantry landed at Port San Carlos led by Major General Jeremy Moore; after establishing a bridgehead they moved inland, forcing the surrender of the Argentines under General Mario Menéndez at Stanley on June 14, 1982. The British victory boosted Thatcher's government, while bringing down Argentine president Leopoldo Fortunato GALTIERI.

Fall, Albert (*1861–1944*) U.S. secretary of the interior involved in the TEAPOT DOME SCANDAL. A rancher, Fall was elected senator from New Mexico. When Warren Harding became president in 1921 he appointed his friend Fall to the Interior cabinet post. In 1922 Fall secretly leased the Navy oil reserve lands at Elk Hills, California, and Teapot Dome, Wyoming, to oil companies controlled by his crony Edward Doheny and Harry Sinclair. About the same time he received $100,000 from Doheny and a $260,000 "loan" from Sinclair. When the leases were revealed, Fall at first explained the $100,000 payment as a loan from an eccentric millionaire named Edward McLean, who promptly denied making any such loan. Fall eventually admitted the source of the funds. The press had a field day when Doheny termed the $100,000 payment "a mere bagatelle." Fall eventually went to prison for one year but emerged an invalid until his death in 1944.

Falla, Manuel de (*1876–1946*) Spanish composer. Born in Cádiz, he studied at the Royal Conservatory in Madrid and with composer Felipe Pedrell. Living in Paris from 1907 to 1914, he met DEBUSSY, DUKAS and RAVEL and was somewhat influenced by their impressionist style. He settled in Granada in 1921, living there until 1939 when he moved to Argentina, where he died. Falla's music is brilliantly Spanish in character. An expert on flamenco, he succeeded in capturing its driving rhythms while incorporating the brilliance and color of his homeland into the classic structure of his compositions. His most celebrated works include the opera *La vida breve* (1913); *Nights in the Gardens of Spain* (1911–15), which symphonically evokes Granada; and his most famous compositions, the ballets *El amor brujo* (1914–15) and *The Three-Cornered Hat* (1917). He also created many piano pieces, songs, orchestral works, the guitar solo *Homenajes* (1920–39) and *La atlántida,* a massive cantata unfinished at his death and completed by his ex-pupil Ernesto Halffter.

Fall Gelb (*German:* "yellow case" or "yellow plan") "Fall Gelb" was the code name for the German invasion of France, Luxembourg and the Low Countries (Belgium and the Netherlands) in May–June 1940. In broad terms, the plan of attack was similar to the German plan of World War I, the SCHLIEFFEN PLAN. However, it was much better executed. The Germans were well organized and were able to use their superiority in planes and tanks to overrun France in six weeks. However, they failed to destroy the British and French armies at DUNKIRK.

Fallingwater Famous house by Frank Lloyd WRIGHT at Bear Run, Pennsylvania, designed in 1936 for the Kaufmann family of Pittsburgh. Wright placed dramatic concrete cantilevers over a rocky waterfall in a wooded, rural site. The house is generally regarded as one of Wright's most striking masterpieces. Its dramatic form and the charm of its interiors are universally admired. It is again open to the public following a three-year restoration, begun in 2001, to strengthen the main cantilever.

Falun Gong A largely Chinese, but increasingly international, quasi-religious movement organized in the early 1990s by Hongzhi Li, a Chinese citizen. A union of traditional Chinese breathing exercises and physical regimens with Taoist and Buddhist philosophies, Falun Gong members describe their movement as nonhierarchical and consisting largely of informal groups of individuals who collectively seek to enhance and preserve their physical and psychological health through proper exercise and lifestyle habits. The movement continued to gain participants throughout the 1990s, and in April 1999 held a meeting of more than 10,000 of its members in Beijing, China. The increasing size of Falun Gong and the unregulated nature of the movement alarmed the Chinese government, which outlawed the movement in 1999 and arrested and imprisoned many of its practitioners.

Falwell, Jerry (*1933– *) American fundamentalist Christian preacher, televangelist and political activist. While a student at Lynchburg College, Virginia, Falwell became a "born-again" Christ-ian; after graduating from a Baptist Bible college, he started his own church in Lynchburg. He took to the television airwaves with a weekly program, *The Old Time Gospel Hour,* which was eventually broadcast over some 350 stations throughout the U.S., and gained a large following. In 1979 Falwell founded the **Moral Majority,** a grass-roots conservative lobbying group that was influential throughout the 1980s. The Moral Majority was formed to counter what Falwell and his followers saw as a rising tide of permissiveness, both in politics and in everyday life. Falwell stressed traditional values and scorned contemporary liberal movements; he was a strong supporter of Ronald REAGAN and other conservative candidates in 1980. Falwell disbanded the Moral Majority in 1989, saying that the organization had achieved its goal of getting conservative Christians involved in politics. He subsequently devoted himself to his Lynchburg ministry. Falwell came under criticism for his statement following the SEPTEMBER 11, 2001, terrorist attacks that implied that the attacks were a punishment from God for the actions of groups such as the ACLU, homosexuals and secularists.

Fangio, Juan Manuel (*1911–1995*) Argentine race car driver who dominated Grand Prix auto racing during the 1950s. Five-time world Grand Prix champion, Fangio won 16 Grand Prix races during the decade. After his racing career ended he became president of the Argentine branch of Mercedes-Benz.

Fang Lizhi (*1937– *) Chinese astrophysicist. Fang's name became internationally known in early 1987 when he was accused by the Communist Party of instigating student demonstrations for general democratic reforms. Fang was expelled from the party for promoting "bourgeois liberalization," but he retained his academic posts and in January 1988 was promoted from fourth- to second-grade academician of the Chinese Academy of Sciences. Dubbed by some the Chinese SAKHAROV, Fang does not want to be considered a dissident and believes that China will eventually become democratic. He and his wife took refuge in the U.S. embassy in Beijing following the army crackdown in June

1989; they later moved to the U.S. (See also TIANANMEN SQUARE MASSACRE.)

Fanon, Frantz Omar (1925–1961)

Martinique-born psychiatrist and social critic. Fanon, a black raised under French colonial rule, was seared as a youth by racism and the cultural prejudices of colonialism. He examined the psychological and political significance of these early experiences in his first major work, *Black Skin, White Masks* (1952), which argued that white colonialism imposed an existentially false and degrading existence upon its black victims to the extent that it demanded their conformity to its imperialistic social values. In 1953 Fanon began to practice in a psychiatric ward in Algeria and soon allied himself with the Algerian liberation movement that sought to throw off French rule. In his subsequent writings—*Studies in a Dying Colonialism* (1959), *The Wretched of the Earth* (1961) and *Toward the African Revolution* (1964)—Fanon argued for violent revolution as the only means of ending colonial repression and cultural trauma in the Third World.

Fantasia

Fantasia Classic Walt DISNEY motion picture. *Fantasia* combined the talents of conductor Leopold STOKOWSKI and Disney, excerpts from classical music and visual interpretations by the Disney animators. Although it lost money after its premiere on November 13, 1940, at the Broadway Theatre in New York (the location of the premiere of Disney's *Steamboat Willie* in 1928), it has since been frequently revived and was accorded cult status by audiences in the 1960s. Stokowski recorded the eight classical selections in the Disney Hyperion Studios and at the Philadelphia Academy of Music. The sequences and their visual interpretations were in the following order: 1) "Toccata and Fugue in D minor," by J. S. Bach—abstract shapes shift and change through a universe of freely mixing colors; 2) "The Nutcracker Suite," by Tchaikovsky—flowers and fairies twinkle in the muted twilight; 3) "The Sorcerer's Apprentice," by Paul DUKAS—MICKEY MOUSE brings to life a bunch of sinister brooms; 4) *Le Sacre du printemps* (*The RITE OF SPRING*), by Igor STRAVINSKY—dinosaurs galumph about a primeval landscape; 5) the Sixth Symphony ("Pastoral"), by Beethoven—cupids, nymphs and satyrs cavort about Mount Olympus; 6) "Dance of the Hours," by Ponchielli—hippos and alligators whirl in a mad ballet; 7) "Night on Bald Mountain," by Moussorgsky—an amphibian creature presides over an unholy bacchanale; 8) "Ave Maria," by Schubert—a pilgrim's procession greets the dawning light. Not merely a tour de force of state-of-the-art animation, it was a technical innovation in sound. Stokowski used a nine-track sound system that in some theaters was reproduced by a number of sound horns placed behind the screen and around the walls. This "Fantasound" anticipated stereophonic sound. Disney's attempt to popularize classical music has been both praised and damned by critics. "Gee," Disney allegedly said after viewing the "Pastoral" sequence, "this'll make Beethoven!" Which perhaps accounts for the extra twinkle in Mickey's eye—provided by animators Fred Moore and Les Clark, who placed pupils in his eyes for the first time.

Farabundo Martí National Liberation Front (FMLN)

Farabundo Martí National Liberation Front (FMLN) Leftist guerrilla movement in EL SALVADOR in opposition to the government (1972–89) and subsequently a political party (1992–   ). Formed in opposition to the ruling party in El Salvadoran politics, the Party of National Conciliation (PCN), the FMLN waged a guerrilla war against the government and its military forces in response to the PCN's nullification of the 1972 presidential election, which was won by a coalition candidate supported by the Christian Democratic Party (PDC) and the National Revolutionary Movement (MNR). The FMLN continued to wage covert warfare against right-wing death squads, some of which were supported by some Salvadoran governmental officials. Alfredo Cristiani, the leader of the Nationalist Republican Alliance (ARENA), negotiated a truce with the FMLN in 1991 that led all sides to cease fighting on February 1, 1992. The FMLN was drawn into the COLD WAR in its last years, as it received arms shipments from CUBA and the Soviet Union; this caused American president Ronald REAGAN to label the movement communist and provide the Salvadoran government with military aid a means of suppressing it.

When the conflict ended the FMLN transformed itself into a political party and led a leftist coalition intent on gaining power in El Salvador. Its main competition came from ARENA, a rightist umbrella political party formed in 1982 that gained control of El Salvador seven years later. In the 2000 national legislative elections FMLN cut into ARENA's lead, winning more seats than its competitor for the first time (31 to 29), although ARENA managed to hold on to political control through forming a coalition with the third-place PCN.

Far Eastern Republic (1920–1922)

The Far Eastern Republic served as a buffer state between Soviet Russia and Japan. One of the first "people's democracies," it was annexed by the USSR after the Japanese left Vladivostok.

Fargue, Léon-Paul (1876–1947)

Fargue was an enduring force in the various French poetic movements of the first half of the 20th century. In his earliest verse of the 1890s, he allied himself with the symbolist circle. *Tancrède* (1894) is his major work of this period. In the years prior to World War I, Fargue was influenced by cubist poetics, as is evident in *Poèmes* (1912) and *For Music* (1918) (see CUBISM). His later collections include *Espaces* and *Sous la lampe* (both 1929). A noted raconteur, Fargue was acquainted with most of the major French literary figures of the day. His memoirs, *Le Pieton de Paris* (1939), remain a key source work of the period.

Faris, Muhammed (1951–   )

Syrian cosmonaut-researcher. The first Syrian in space (July 22–30, 1987), Faris spent six days aboard the Soviet space station *MIR* after being launched and landed there by the SOYUZ TM-3 spacecraft. A pilot in the Syrian air force, Faris, with Munir Habib, was one of two Syrians to be trained for the mission in the Soviet Union's Star City complex.

Farkas, Bertalan (1949–   )

Hungarian cosmonaut-researcher. The first Hungarian citizen to make a spaceflight, Farkas, a skilled air force pilot, was aboard *Soyuz 36* (May 1980).

Farley, James A. (1888–1976)

American politician. A life-long Democrat,

Farley rose through the party ranks in his native New York, becoming state DEMOCRATIC PARTY chairman. In this position he managed Franklin D. ROOSEVELT's electoral races for governor and finally for president in 1932. After managing Roosevelt's landslide reelection in 1936, Farley was able to quip "As goes Maine, so goes Vermont." Roosevelt appointed Farley postmaster general. Farley, who also became chairman of the national Democratic committee, was responsible for building grassroots enthusiasm for Roosevelt's NEW DEAL reform program. In 1940, however, Farley and Roosevelt had a falling out—perhaps over Roosevelt's plan to run for a third term—and Farley quit his twin national posts. He became an executive with the Coca-Cola Corporation but remained active in politics until his death.

Farnsworth House Famous project of Ludwig MIES VAN DER ROHE, weekend house beside the Fox River near Plano, Illinois, built from 1945 to 1951 for Dr. Edith Farnsworth. The house is an ultimate example of the architect's effort to reduce building to minimal and universal terms. It consists of floor and roof planes supported by eight steel columns placed along their outer edges, with an all-glass rectangular enclosure that extends about two-thirds of the building's length. The interior is totally open except for a small rectangular block enclosing baths, utilities, and storage. Generally regarded as one of Mies's finest works, the house was unfortunately the cause of a bitter and notorious conflict between architect and client. The design seems to have been the inspiration for the equally famous Glass House of Philip JOHNSON at New Canaan, Connecticut.

Farouk *(1920–1965)* King of Egypt (1938–52). Farouk attained his majority in 1938 and ousted the WAFD government of Nahas Pasha, who had ruled following the death of Farouk's father in 1936. He tried to launch schemes of land reform and economic advancement, but corruption was rife, and his popularity rapidly dwindled. Strains in relations with Britain during and after WORLD WAR II and failure of the army in PALESTINE (1948) focused criticism against him, and he was

forced to abdicate as a result of a military coup in 1952.

Farr, Tommy *(1914–1986)* Welsh boxer. After winning the British heavyweight crown, Farr nearly took the world heavyweight title from Joe LOUIS in an August 1937 match at Yankee Stadium. In that title defense by Louis, Farr became the first of only three challengers to go the 15-round distance. Farr fought professionally from 1926 to 1953, winning 80 of 125 fights.

Farrand, Clair Loring *(1895–1981)* American electronics engineer and inventor. A pioneer in the radio industry, Farrand invented the radio loudspeaker. He worked with WARNER BROS., developing sound, color and cinematography technologies. He also founded and headed several companies, which together eventually held more than 1,000 patents on devices ranging from B-52 bombsights to simulator windows used in the U.S. space program.

Farrar, Geraldine *(1882–1967)* American opera singer. A great soprano of the early 20th century, Farrar made her debut with the Berlin Royal Opera in 1901 as Marguerite in *Faust*. After successful performances throughout Europe, she made her debut with the Metropolitan Opera in 1906 as Juliet. In 1907 she sang the title role in the American premiere of PUCCINI's *Madama Butterfly*, the role with which she became most identified. Other roles for which she was famous were Carmen and Tosca. She was a star of the Met until her retirement in 1922 and appeared in many world premieres, such as Paul DUKAS's *Ariane et Barbe-bleue* (1911). In addition, she acted in more than a dozen films, including Cecil B. DEMILLE's *Maria Rosa* (1915). She went on several concert tours before finally giving up public life to pursue philanthropic works.

Farrell, James Thomas *(1904–1979)* American novelist. Farrell was born in Chicago and worked at a variety of jobs to finance his education at the University of Chicago and later New York University. A naturalist writer, he is best known for his trilogy consisting of the novels *Young Lonigan*

(1932), *The Young Manhood of Studs Lonigan* (1934) and *Judgement Day* (1935). The novels portray Studs Lonigan, a poor Irish Catholic, from his childhood through his various attempts, some illegal, to get ahead and ultimately, his death from a heart condition aggravated by poverty. Farrell somberly depicts Chicago during the GREAT DEPRESSION and the deadening effects of poverty, both physical and spiritual. His writing has been compared to that of Theodore DREISER, whose work Farrell edited in *A Dreiser Reader* (1962). Other works include *The Collected Poems of James T. Farrell* (1965), *The Dunne Family* (1976) and *The Death of Nora Ryan* (1978).

Farrell, Suzanne *(1945–)* American dancer. One of the outstanding ballerinas of the 1960s–80s, she is most closely identified with the works of George BALANCHINE. Farrell joined the NEW YORK CITY BALLET in 1961 and quickly became Balanchine's muse, creating roles in many of his ballets, such as *Don Quixote* (1965) and *Jewels* (1967). From 1970 to 1974 she was the star ballerina with the Ballet of the 20th Century and created roles in such ballets as *Sonate* (1971) and *Nijinsky, Clown of God* (1971) by Maurice BÉJART. Returning to NYCB in 1975, she continued to create roles in Balanchine ballets, such as *Vienna Waltzes* (1977). She retired from dancing in 1989.

fascism Political ideology and form of government that emphasizes a strong one-party dictatorship (often embodied in a charismatic leader), extreme militarism and the glorification of the state. Fascist governments seek to instill uniformity and obedience in the populace, which is often manipulated by means of PROPAGANDA and coerced by secret police and informers. Unlike COMMUNISM, which professes to serve the people and to be an international movement, fascism makes little pretense about its dictatorial character or its nationalist and often racist aims. Fascism also allows privately owned industries, although there is some state regulation of the economy. In other respects, however, fascism and communism have generally proved to be merely two sides of the same totalitarian coin. Most 20th-century fascist governments have arisen during severe political and economic crises as people looked for simple, bold solutions to complex social problems. The two main manifestations of fascism in the 20th century occurred in ITALY under Benito MUSSOLINI from 1922 to 1945 and in GERMANY under Adolf HITLER from 1933 to 1945. (However, fascism and NAZISM are not technically equivalent.) Military regimes incorporating some aspects of fascism have also operated in SPAIN (under FRANCO and the FALANGE, 1939–75), HUNGARY (during WORLD WAR II), ROMANIA (again during WORLD WAR II, under ANTONESCU and the Iron Guard), CHILE (under General PINOCHET, 1973–89) and elsewhere. There have also been fascist-style political parties in FRANCE, the United Kingdom (led by Oswald MOSLEY) and other democratically governed countries, but these have had limited appeal. While fascism proved popular in certain places at certain times during the 20th century, it has not proved a durable ideology. At most times and in most places, *fascist* and *fascism* have been used as pejorative terms.

Fassbinder, Rainer Werner (*1946–1982*) German film director and actor. Fassbinder was one of the most prolific and controversial directors of the postwar era. He began his career in the theater, working with the avant-garde Anti-Theater in West Germany in the 1960s. Over a 13-year film career that began in 1969, Fassbinder completed an astonishing 41 films, for most of which he wrote the screenplays and appeared as an actor. Left-wing in his politics and a self-proclaimed homosexual, Fassbinder aroused strongly partisan or hostile feelings among cinema audiences. The political and social corruption of postwar Germany was a major theme in his films. Among Fassbinder's best-known films are *The Marriage of Maria Braun* (1979), *Lola* (1981) and *Veronika Voss* (1982). Fassbinder also directed a critically acclaimed 15.5-hour epic, *Berlin, Alexanderplatz* (1979).

Fast, Howard Melvin (*1914–2003*) American novelist, playwright and screenwriter. Fast is best known for his popular historical novels, which include *Two Valleys* (1933), written when he was 18; *Spartacus* (1951), which he first published privately and for which he later coauthored the screenplay with Dalton Trumbo (1960); and a trilogy with more modern themes—*The Immigrants* (1977, televised 1979), *The Second Generation* (1978) and *The Establishment* (1979). Fast was a member of the Joint Anti-Fascist Refugee Committee and as a result he was called before the HOUSE UN-AMERICAN ACTIVITIES COMMITTEE. Following his refusal to cooperate with the committee, he was jailed for a period in 1950. Many of Fast's novels have been adapted for film and television. Other works include the plays *The Hammer* (1950) and *The Crossing* (1962); the screenplays *The Hill* (1965) and *The Hessian* (1971), which were both based on his novels of the same titles; and the novels *The Dinner Party* (1987), *The Pledge* (1988), *The Confession of Joe Cullen* (1989), *An Independent Woman* (1997), *Redemption* (1999) and *Greenwich* (2000).

Fatah Revolutionary Council Palestinian terrorist organization founded in 1974 by ABU NIDAL. It was a radical breakaway group from Yasir ARAFAT's al-Fatah and the PALESTINE LIBERATION ORGANIZATION (PLO). The council received financial, military and intelligence aid from East Germany, Poland, North Korea, Iraq, Syria and Libya. Its targets included Israel, Westerners, Arab moderates and members of rival Palestinian organizations. At its peak during the late 1970s and early 1980s, the council had some 400 members operating in tightly-knit secret cells in the Mideast, Europe and Asia, plus more than 1,000 Palestinian recruits in training. It claimed more than 900 victims in at least 20 countries, including 56 people killed in the hijacking of an Egyptian airliner in 1985, 21 in the bombing of an Istanbul synagogue in 1986 and several dozen Arab diplomats and PLO officials assassinated in various operations. In 1988 the U.S. State Department characterized the group as "the most dangerous terrorist organization in existence." Since the end of the 1980s the Fatah Revolutionary Council has not orchestrated any attacks on Western targets. In August 2002 the leader of the council, Abu Nidal, was found shot dead in his Baghdad home.

Faubus, Orval Eugene (*1910–1980*) American politician. As governor of Arkansas (1956–67), Faubus summoned the state National Guard (1957) to block federally directed integration at LITTLE ROCK Central High School. His stand, which forced the use of federal troops to carry out integration, gained Faubus the popularity that won him many terms as governor. (See also BROWN V. BOARD OF EDUCATION.)

Faulk, John Henry (*1913–1990*) American humorist and radio host. In 1956, while serving as host of the popular radio show *Johnny's Front Porch,* Faulk was accused by an anticommunist watchdog group, Aware Inc., of having communist ties. The accusations were based, in part, on his having attended a UNITED NATIONS dinner for Soviet foreign minister Andrei GROMYKO. The chief sponsor of his show pulled out, CBS radio fired him later that year. He sued Aware Inc. and two of its founders and was awarded $3.5 million by a jury in 1962. His book about the case, *Fear on Trial,* was made into a television movie in 1975.

Faulkner, William (*1897–1962*) American novelist, widely considered one of the most original and important American literary figures of the 20th century. Born in Mississippi to a family with well-established roots there, Faulkner was an indifferent student and later held sundry menial positions before and after serving in the Royal Canadian Air Force in WORLD WAR I. Working as a journalist in New Orleans in 1924, he met Sherwood ANDERSON, who encouraged Faulkner to produce his first novel, *Soldier's Pay* (1926). Following a sojourn in Europe, Faulkner returned to Mississippi and began writing the notable series of novels that take place there—in the fictitiously renamed Jefferson in Yoknapatawpha County. *Sartoris* (1929) is the first of these, followed by *The Sound and the Fury* (1929), which depicts the degeneration of the South. *As I Lay Dying* (1930) is a darkly comic story of a poor family's attempt to fulfill a wish of their dying mother; *Sanctuary* (1931) is considered by some to be a sensationalized attempt to increase sales; and *Light in August* (1932) and *Absolom, Absolom* (1936) both firmly established Faulkner as a distinguished modern novelist. The publication of *The Portable William Faulkner* (1946), edited by Malcolm COWLEY, led to Faulkner's receiving the NOBEL PRIZE in literature in 1949. Faulkner also worked as a screenwriter in HOLLYWOOD; among his film credits is the *The Big Sleep* (1946). Faulkner's later works, less celebrated than his earlier novels, include *The Hamlet* (1940) and *Intruder in the Dust* (1948).

Faure, Edgar *(1908–1988)* French politician. Faure twice served as premier of FRANCE, for 40 days in 1952 and again in 1955–56. Faure held 11 cabinet posts during his 30-year political career and became minister of education after the 1968 Paris student riots.

Fauré, Gabriel Urbain *(1845–1924)* French composer. A student of Camille Saint-Saens, he was an outstanding organist and teacher. Fauré became a professor of composition at the Paris Conservatory and was its director from 1905 to 1920. His long list of students included Nadia BOULANGER, George ENESCO and Maurice RAVEL. Subtle and intimate, Fauré's compositions are remarkable for their melodic lyricism. He was extremely prolific, composing chamber music, orchestral works, nearly 100 songs, piano pieces and two operas. Among his best-known works are the *Pavane* and the *Requiem* (both 1887) and *Pelléas et Mélisande* (1898).

fauvism Name given to the work of a group of French painters who exhibited at the 1905 Parisian Salon d'Automne and who were called by outraged critics "fauves" (wild beasts), a name they happily embraced. Fauvism, perhaps the first truly modernist movement in 20th-century painting, is most strikingly marked by vivid, spontaneous and often violent color as well as by distorted forms, expressive brushwork and flat patterns—all characteristics that entered the canon of modern art. The movement lasted a brief time (1905–08), but its influence was felt throughout the world and the century. Among the fauves, not all of whom exhibited in the 1905 show, were such masters as Henri MATISSE, often considered their leader; Maurice de Vlaminck, Georges Rouault, Albert Marquet, André Derain, Georges BRAQUE, Raoul DUFY and Kees van Dongen, as well as a number of lesser-known artists.

Fawzi, Mahmoud *(1900–1981)* Egyptian diplomat and statesman. During his 50-year career the polylingual Fawzi served as EGYPT's ambassador to many nations. During the reign of King FAROUK he was Egypt's first ambassador to the UNITED NATIONS (1946–52). He was a leading figure in the administration of President NASSER, serving as foreign minister (1952–64) during the SUEZ CRISIS and ARAB-ISRAELI WAR OF 1956. He was subsequently Nasser's deputy prime minister (1964–67) and vice president (1967–68) and President SADAT's prime minister (1972–74) and co–vice president (1972–74).

Fay brothers Frank J. Fay (1970–1931) and William George Fay (1872–1947) were Irish theatrical actors and directors. They are best remembered for their active involvement in the Irish National Theater movement and in the creation, in 1904, of the Dublin-based ABBEY THEATRE company. As actors, they appeared in a number of Abbey Theatre productions. William played the lead role of Christy Mahon in the premiere of *THE PLAYBOY OF THE WESTERN WORLD* (1907), by John Millington SYNGE. In 1908 the brothers traveled to the U.S. to perform in a repertory of Irish plays. In the 1920s, after Frank had retired from the theater to work as a speech teacher, William remained active as an actor and director in England.

February Revolution *(1917)* Revolution during which the Russian monarchy fell and the provisional government and the Soviets of workers' and soldiers' deputies were established. Over 14 million peasants were engaged in military service, which in turn led to acute food shortages; this proved to be one of the factors that triggered the revolution. Having taken command of the army in 1915, Czar NICHOLAS II was at the front, and the czarina, with the help of RASPUTIN, was responsible for much of the decision making on domestic matters. In February 1917 (old calendar, March new calendar) there were widespread bread riots, strikes and demonstrations in Petrograd; the troops, summoned to restore order, mutinied. This led to the abdication of the czar, and a provisional government, led by KERENSKY, assumed power. The provisional government and the Soviets vied with one another for power, and the government proved to be incapable of dealing with the rising power of the BOLSHEVIKS.

Fedayeen *(Arabic:* "those who risk their lives for a cause"*)* Palestinian guerrillas who carried out raids in ISRAEL. They were eventually absorbed into the PALESTINE LIBERATION ORGANIZATION.

Federal Deposit Insurance Corporation (FDIC) The FDIC is a U.S. government corporation that insures customer deposits in U.S. banks. The 1929 STOCK MARKET CRASH was followed by a number of bank failures in which depositors lost their savings. In 1934 the federal government established the FDIC with the role of providing federal insurance for bank deposits. The current insured limit is $100,000 per account in each bank; however, banks are not required to carry the federal insurance. The depositor insurance is funded by premiums paid by member banks. No depositor has ever lost any money in an FDIC-insured account. After the failure of a number of savings and loan associations in the 1980s, the FDIC absorbed another government corporation, the Federal Savings and Loan Insurance Corporation (FSLIC), which was near insolvency.

Federal Reserve System The U.S. government's central bank, which controls both the money supply and credit within the economy. Although its board is appointed by the president, the "Fed" enjoys considerable independence and the chairman of the Fed is influential in setting monetary and exchange policy.

Created in 1913, the Federal Reserve System is comprised of 12 Federal Reserve banks and the Federal Reserve Board, consisting of seven members appointed by the president.

The Fed issues U.S. currency—federal reserve notes—and controls monetary policy, lending and interest rates through its reserve requirements and the discount rate for member banks. The Fed also operates in the foreign exchange markets. Each of the 12 Federal Reserve banks regulates private banks in its geographic area and provides them with services such as check clearing and fund transfers.

Federal Writers' Project Part of the Federal Artists' Project of the WPA, the Federal Writers' Project existed from 1935 to 1939 and was directed by Henry G. Alsberg. The project aimed to hire writers to produce works on American themes, and it was responsible for many groundbreaking studies of black culture, folklore and regional histories. A major accomplishment was the American Guide Series, which profiled each of the 48 states. Many notable writers worked for the project, among them Nelson ALGREN, Conrad AIKEN, Ralph ELLISON, John CHEEVER and Kenneth FEARING.

Fefer, Itsik (Isaak Solomonovich) *(1900–1952)* Yiddish poet. Having joined the Communist Party in 1919, Fefer volunteered for the Red Army and took part in the Civil War of 1917–20 and in the war of 1941–45. He first work was published in 1919. In 1943 he toured the U.S. and Great Britain in the capacity of the first official representative of Soviet Jews. He held a number of important government offices but was arrested in 1948 during the purge of Jewish writers. He was executed in 1952. The author of lyrical poems, Fefer drew upon his experiences in the civil war for the subject matter of much of his writing. He also wrote several plays.

Feiffer, Jules *(1929–   )* American cartoonist, playwright and screenwriter. Feiffer studied at the Art Students League in New York City, worked for various cartoon syndicates and served in a cartoon animation unit in the U.S. Army Signal Corps before the *Village Voice* began printing his political cartoons with their uniquely neurotic characters in 1956. His first venture as a playwright was the satirical review *The Explainers,* produced in 1961—the same year his animated film *Munro* won

an Oscar as the best short-subject cartoon. Feiffer wrote the screenplay for the film *Carnal Knowledge* (1971), which was banned in Georgia and subsequently at issue in the U.S. Supreme Court (1974). His other works include the cartoon collection *Jules Feiffer's America, from Eisenhower to Reagan* (1982) and the play *Eliot Loves* (1990). In 1997 Feiffer quit the *Village Voice* over a salary dispute. He went on to create the *New York Times's* first comic story, which ran until 2000.

Feld, Eliot *(1942–   )* American dancer, choreographer and dance company director. Feld began his career as a dancer in the Broadway and film productions of *West Side Story.* In 1963 he joined the AMERICAN BALLET THEATRE, receiving acclaim for his roles in many ballets, including *Fancy Free* and *Billy the Kid,* and for his first choreographed works, *Harbinger* and *At Midnight* (1967). He founded and directed the American Ballet Company as the resident company at the Brooklyn Academy of Music (1969–71), then formed the Eliot Feld Ballet in 1974. His early choreography was characterized by its athleticism and combination of classical, jazz and modern dance elements. Major works included *Intermezzo* (1970), *Seraphic Songs* (1974) and *Santa Fe Saga* (1978). As choreographer and director of Feld Ballets of New York, he produced such highly acclaimed works as *The Grand Canyon* (1985), *Yo Shakespeare* (1997) and *Mending* (1999). In 2004 he resurrected his Ballet Tech dance company for a memorable engagement at the Joyce Theater for the Mandance Project, a combination of ballet and modern dance.

Fellini, Federico *(1920–1993)* Italian film director and writer. An internationally acclaimed filmmaker, Fellini is noted for his use of personal symbolism and the surrealistic quality of his films, which often deal with the relationship between illusion and reality. He began his career as a cartoonist, journalist and radio scriptwriter (1936–43). Collaboration with actor Aldo Fabrizzi and director Roberto ROSSELLINI on *Open City* (1945) brought him widespread critical acclaim. Among the many subsequent films he directed (and collaborated on as screenwriter) are *Variety Lights*

(1950), *La Strada* (1955), *La Dolce Vita* (1959), *8½* (1963), *Juliet of the Spirits* (1965) and *Fellini Satyricon* (1969). In 1993 he received an Academy Award for lifetime achievement.

fellow traveler Term coined by Leon TROTSKY in 1925. It described intellectuals, especially writers, who were not communists but had sympathy with COMMUNISM or a modified Soviet regime. During the COLD WAR, and especially during the period of McCARTHYISM in the 1950s, the term was also used disparagingly by American conservatives to describe U.S. intellectuals with leftist political leanings.

Feltsman, Vladimir *(1952–   )* Russian pianist. Feltsman studied at the Moscow Conservatory and won first prize in the prestigious Marguerite Long Competition in Paris (1971). Hailed by the Soviets as a major pianist, during the 1970s he performed with orchestras throughout the Soviet Union and toured Europe and Japan. In 1979 he and his wife applied to immigrate to Israel. Their application was refused, and thereafter Feltsman was forbidden to perform in the USSR. During the 1980s the Feltsman case became an international cause célèbre. Various foreign governments and individuals pressured the Soviets until the Feltsmans were granted exit visas in 1987 under GORBACHEV's policy of GLASNOST. Feltsman's arrival and initial concerts in the U.S. were greeted with rapturous acclaim. Feltsman has since established a successful concert and teaching career in the West.

feminism Political, social and personal growth movement dedicated to bettering the lives and raising the status of women. The suffragists campaign to gain the vote for women in the U.S. was a vital precursor of modern feminism. As the term is presently used, it refers to a broad movement that came of age internationally in the 1960s and is directed at all aspects of the status of women—sexual, personal, social, economic and political. Key issues include the right to equal pay and to self-determination with regard to reproductive rights. Major theorists and writers in the feminist movement include Simone de BEAUVOIR, Betty FRIEDAN, Germaine GREER and Gloria STEINEM. Feminism has developed different emphases throughout its existence. In the 1980s "Second Wave" feminism emerged, which stressed women's liberation from feminine norms such as fashion. In the 1990s "Third Wave" feminism surfaced, which united traditional feminist desires for full equality with the acceptance of feminine social norms.

Fender, Percy George Henry *(1892–1985)* English cricketer. A legendary captain of Surrey, Fender won 13 England caps as an all-rounder in the 1920s. In 1920, in a match against Northamptonshire, he scored a 35-minute century, the fastest in first-class cricket history. He retired as the world's oldest Test cricketer.

Ferber, Edna *(1885–1968)* American author. Ferber began her career as a reporter in the Midwest. After the publication of her first novel, *Dawn O'Hara* (1911), she took up writing full time. She was a prolific writer of popular magazine stories, which were gathered together in several book collections. With the publication of *So Big* in 1924, she gained a place on the best seller lists and also won the PULITZER PRIZE. As a keen observer of American life and times, she was noted for her characterizations and choice of settings

Pulitzer Prizewinning author Edna Ferber, 1945 (LIBRARY OF CONGRESS, PRINTS AND PHOTOGRAPHS DIVISION)

for her novels. The highly popular *SHOW BOAT* (1926) formed the basis of musicals and motion pictures. Ferber was the author of many other famous novels, including *Saratoga Trunk* (1941, filmed 1945) and *Giant* (1952, filmed 1956). With George S. KAUFMAN she co-authored several plays, including the perennial *Dinner at Eight* (1932, filmed 1933). Although she was dismissed as a light romantic by many critics, others have praised Ferber's serious approach to her many themes. She wrote two autobiographical works, *A Peculiar Treasure* (1930) and *A Kind of Magic* (1963).

Ferdinand I *(1861–1948)* King of Bulgaria (1908–18); a prince of Saxe-Coburg, in 1887 he was elected prince of BULGARIA, then under Turkish sovereignty. The early part of his reign was made difficult by Russian opposition, but in 1896 he was finally recognized by the European powers. In 1908 Ferdinand declared Bulgaria independent and himself king. Forming an alliance with other Balkan countries, he was victorious in the first of the BALKAN WARS (1912–13) against the Turks but was overwhelmingly defeated in the second of these conflicts (1913). Hoping to win back territory he had lost, Ferdinand brought Bulgaria into WORLD WAR I on the CENTRAL POWERS' side (1915); when his fortunes in war went sour again, he was forced to abdicate (1918). His son, BORIS III, assumed the throne, and Ferdinand went into exile in Germany.

Ferencsik, János *(1907–1984)* Considered Hungary's foremost 20th-century orchestra and opera conductor, Ferencsik helped spread Hungarian music abroad. Educated at the conservatory in Budapest, he conducted at the Budapest State Opera in 1930. He later helped establish the Hungarian State Symphony Orchestra, which he directed from 1952 until his death. He was also music director of the Budapest State Opera (1957–74) and conducted frequently in Europe, the USSR, the U.S. and South America, as well as in Japan and Australia. Ferencsik was a leading interpreter of Hungary's two greatest 20th-century composers, Béla BARTÓK and Zoltán KODÁLY, whom he knew personally. He twice received Hungary's

highest award, the Kossuth Prize (1951, 1961).

Ferguson, James Edward *(1871–1944)* U.S. politician. A champion of the small farmer, Ferguson became governor of Texas in 1915. Accused of corruption, he was impeached during his second term in 1917 but resurfaced as "the man behind the governor" when his wife, Miriam A. Wallace FERGUSON, served as Texas governor in 1924 and again in 1932.

Ferguson, Maynard *(1928–2006)* Canadian-born jazz trumpet virtuoso; a child prodigy whose exceptional technique, range and brassy flair gained him initial prominence in the big bands of Boyd Raeburn and Charlie Barnet during the late 1940s. In 1950 Ferguson was hired by Stan KENTON, who showcased the trumpeter's stratospheric wizardry and helped make Ferguson a star. In the mid-1950s, after achieving acclaim with recordings for Kenton and under his own name, Ferguson formed his first important unit, the Birdland Dream Band, which debuted in New York City to rave reviews and wildly enthusiastic crowds. From that point on, Ferguson has helmed a string of successful bands; in addition to acclaim for his variously sized jazz outfits, Ferguson achieved popularity in the 1970s with the jazz-rock hits "MacArthur Park" (1970) and "Gonna Fly Now" (1978), the theme from the motion picture *Rocky*. Ferguson has secured a place in jazz history by virtue of his exceptional control over the trumpet's high register and BEBOP acrobatics. Like Kenton, Ferguson has been an active jazz educator through his many clinics and school concerts. He has also encouraged a host of players who went on to jazzdom's front ranks; in 1990, when Ferguson returned to a solid, swinging jazz approach with his Big Bop Nouveau band, he featured the gifted 17-year-old bassist, Nathan Berg. Ferguson can also be regarded as the last of the active big band leaders whose careers were built and sustained by being constantly on the road, playing one-nighters, club engagements and festivals.

Ferguson, Miriam A. *(1875–1961)* U.S. governor Texas. Ferguson was the wife of state governor James Edward FERGUSON. When he was not allowed to run for reelection in 1924, she ran in his place, winning the vote of small farmers. Although she held the office, it was generally known that her husband was the one who ran the state. She was reelected governor of Texas in 1932.

Ferlinghetti, Lawrence (1919–)

American poet and publisher. Ferlinghetti was one of the key poetic figures to emerge from the BEAT GENERATION. Two volumes of his poems from the 1950s, *Pictures from the Gone World* (1955) and *A Coney Island of the Mind* (1958), sold in the hundreds of thousands—extraordinarily well for poetry—and established Ferlinghetti as a bridge between literary and popular culture. Ferlinghetti, who earned a doctoral degree in literature from the Sorbonne in Paris, has also been highly influential as the founder of City Lights Press in San Francisco, an avant-garde publishing house that has published key works by Allen GINSBERG, William S. BURROUGHS and others. In 2003 Ferlinghetti received several honors, including the Authors' Guild Lifetime Achievement Award and the Poetry Society of America's Robert Frost Medal. He was elected to the American Academy of Arts and Letters in the same year.

Fermi, Enrico (1901–1954)

Italian-American physicist, without doubt the greatest Italian scientist since Galileo and in the period 1925–50 one of the most creative physicists in the world. In an age of ever-growing specialization he excelled as both an experimentalist and a theoretician. Fermi's intelligence and quickness of mind were apparent from an early age, and he gained admission in 1918 to the Scuola Normale in Pisa, a school for the intellectual elite of Italy. He completed his education at the University of Pisa, where he gained his Ph.D. in 1924. After spending time abroad, Fermi returned to Italy, where he was appointed to a professorship of physics at the University of Rome—a considerable achievement for one so young. This advancement was largely due to the reputation he had already established with the publication of some 30 substantial papers and the support of O. M. Corbino, the

Atomic research pioneer Enrico Fermi, 1942 (LIBRARY OF CONGRESS, PRINTS AND PHOTOGRAPHS DIVISION)

most distinguished Italian physicist at the time. Fermi published the first Italian text on modern physics, *Introduzione alla Fisica Atomica* (1928). His reputation attracted the brightest of the younger Italian physicists, but the growth of FASCISM in Italy led to the dispersal of its scientific talent. By 1938 Fermi, with a Jewish wife, was sufficiently alarmed by growing ANTI-SEMITISM to move to America.

However, his period in Rome turned out to be remarkably productive, with major advances in both the theoretical and the experimental field. His experimental work arose out of attempts to advance the efforts of Irène and Frédéric JOLIOT-CURIE, who had announced in 1934 the production of artificial radioactive isotopes. Fermi realized that the neutron, discovered by James CHADWICK in 1932, was perhaps an even better tool for creating new isotopes. Fermi stumbled on the phenomenon of slow neutrons, the production of which was later to have a profound impact in the field of nuclear energy. However, Fermi's immediate task was to use them to irradiate as many of the elements as possible and to produce and investigate the properties of a large number of newly created radioactive isotopes. It was for this work, for "the discovery of new radioactive substances . . . and for the discovery of the selective power of slow neutrons" that Fermi was awarded the 1938 NOBEL PRIZE in physics. In the course of their systematic irradiation of the elements, Fermi and his colleagues bombarded uranium with slow neutrons. Fermi thought that transuranic elements were being produced, but in

1938 Otto Frisch and Lise MEITNER first realized that nuclear fission was taking place in such reactions. On the theoretical level Fermi's major achievement while at Rome was his theory of beta decay—the process in unstable nuclei whereby a neutron is converted into a proton with the emission of an electron and an antineutrino. In 1933 Fermi gave a detailed analysis that introduced a new force into science, the so-called weak force.

In America Fermi soon became involved in the attempt to create a controlled nuclear chain reaction. In 1942 he built the first atomic pile in the stadium of the University of Chicago at Stagg Field. Using pure graphite as a moderator to slow the neutrons and enriched uranium as the fissile material, Fermi and his colleagues began the construction of the pile. It consisted of some 40,000 graphite blocks, in which some 22,000 holes were drilled to permit the insertion of several tons of uranium. At 2:20 P.M. on December 2, 1942, the atomic age began as Fermi's pile went critical, maintaining a self-supporting chain reaction for 28 minutes. In a historic telephone call afterward, Arthur COMPTON informed the managing committee that "the Italian navigator has just landed in the new world." Fermi continued to work on the project and was in fact present in July 1945 when the first atomic bomb was exploded in the New Mexico desert (see ATOMIC BOMB DEVELOPMENT). He is reported to have dropped scraps of paper as the blast reached him and, from their displacement, to have calculated the force as corresponding to 10,000 tons of TNT. After the war Fermi accepted an appointment as professor of physics at the University of Chicago, where he remained until his untimely death from cancer.

Fermi National Accelerator Laboratory (Fermilab)

A U.S. Department of Energy physics research laboratory, near Batavia, Illinois. It is named in honor of Enrico FERMI, the physicist who produced the first nuclear chain reaction. Fermilab contains one of the world's largest particle accelerators, also known as an atom smasher. Within a circular underground tunnel, one and one-third miles in diameter, protons are accelerated almost to the speed of light. The protons are directed at a target and the result of the collision is studied. Fermilab is managed by Universities Research Association, Inc., a consortium of 53 universities reporting to the U.S. Department of Energy.

Fernández, Emilio *(1904–1986)* Mexican actor, screenwriter and director. His socially aware films of the 1940s *(María Candelaria, Flor silvestre, The Pearl)* were the first to draw international attention to the Mexican cinema. Known as "El Indio" for his half-Indian ancestry, Fernández gained notoriety when he shot and wounded a film critic. He was imprisoned for several years in the 1970s for killing a farm laborer in a brawl. He acted in a number of Hollywood films, including *The Wild Bunch* and *Under the Volcano.*

Ferrari, Enzo *(1898–1988)* Italian entrepreneur; founder and chairman of the Italian car company that bears his name. Ferrari's factory near Modena produced about 1,000 cars a year, world renowned for their blood-red color, hair-raising power and acceleration, precise high-speed handling and exclusivity and expense. The Ferrari Formula 1 racing car, with its distinct prancing black stallion motif, became a symbol of national strength and weaknesses, winning nine world titles since 1952. A race car driver himself, he said that he "built racing cars with the same feverish pleasure with which drug addicts sniff cocaine."

Ferraro, Geraldine *(1935–   )* American politician. Ferraro earned her law degree at Fordham University's evening division while teaching during the day. In 1978 she was elected to the House of Representatives from Queens, New York, and served three terms (1979–85). A liberal Democrat, Ferraro became secretary of the Democratic Caucus in the House and a protégée of House Speaker Thomas P. O'Neill. In 1984 she became the first woman vice presidential candidate of a major party when presidential candidate Walter MONDALE named her as his running mate; they lost the election. Ferraro's career was later troubled by allegations of impropriety against her husband, John Zaccaro, in his real estate business, and by her son's arrest for selling cocaine. In 1992 and 1998 Ferraro was an unsuccessful Democratic candidate for a U.S. Senate seat from New York.

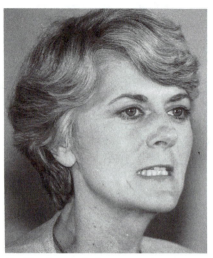

Geraldine Ferraro, the first woman chosen as a vice presidential candidate by a major political party (LIBRARY OF CONGRESS, PRINTS AND PHOTOGRAPHS DIVISION)

Ferraro was named U.S. ambassador to the UN Human Rights Commission in 1993.

Ferrier, Kathleen *(1912–1953)* British concert singer noted for her performances of the vocal music of Handel, Bach and MAHLER and the lieder of Schubert, Schumann and other masters. Ferrier's career was tragically brief; yet her vocal, musical and personal qualities made her one of the most beloved performers of her time. She possessed one of the purest and most distinctive contralto voices ever recorded. Born in Lancashire, she originally made her living as a piano accompanist and also worked as a telephone operator. After winning first prize in a voice competition she had casually entered in 1938, she devoted herself to the study of singing. She made her professional singing debut as a soloist in Bach's *Passion According to St. Matthew* in 1942 and quickly won the attention of other musicians, critics and the public. During WORLD WAR II she sang for soldiers and civilians throughout England—often in bomb shelters, hospitals or factories. At the GLYNDEBOURNE FESTIVAL in 1946 she sang the title role in the world premiere of Benjamin BRITTEN's opera *The Rape of Lucretia.* The next year at the festival she triumphed as Orfeo in Gluck's *Orfeo ed Euridice,* the only other operatic role she performed during her career. She first appeared at the EDINBURGH FESTIVAL in 1947 under the baton of Bruno WALTER, who became her friend and mentor. In 1948 she made her American debut in

Mahler's *Das Lied von der Erde* with the New York Philharmonic, again conducted by Walter. She toured the U.S. in concert (1948–49; 1950–51) and also appeared throughout Europe. Her career was cut short at its peak when she was stricken with cancer.

Fessenden, Reginald Aubrey *(1866–1932)* Canadian electrical engineer. After an education in Canada, Fessenden worked for the EDISON COMPANY as an engineer and later as head chemist (1886–90) and as an engineer (1890–91) for the Westinghouse Co., Edison's great rival. In 1900 he was appointed special agent for the U.S. Weather Bureau, adapting the technique of radio telegraphy, newly developed by Guglielmo MARCONI, to weather forecasting and storm warning. In 1902 he became general manager of the National Electric Signaling Co., which was formed by two financiers from Pittsburgh to exploit his ideas. From 1910 he was consultant engineer at the Submarine Signal Co. Fessenden's inventions were prolific and varied: At the time of his death he held over 500 patents. In 1900 he developed an electrolytic detector that was sufficiently sensitive to make radio telephony feasible. His most significant invention was the technique of amplitude modulation. This involved the use of carrier waves to transmit audio signals; he varied the amplitude of a steady high-frequency radio signal so that it corresponded to variations in the sound waves and thus carried the audio information. Using this principle he transmitted on Christmas Eve 1906 what was probably the first program of music and speech broadcast in America. The program was heard by ships' radio operators at distances of up to several hundred miles.

Festung Europa See FORTRESS EUROPE.

Fetchit, Stepin (Lincoln Theodore Monroe Andrew Perryl) *(1902–1985)* African-American actor. Stepin Fetchit was the first black actor to be prominently cast in American movies not aimed specifically at black audiences. His career peaked in the early and mid-1930s, when he starred in the all-black *Hearts in Dixie* and was given featured billing with such stars as Will ROGERS and Shirley TEMPLE. He generally portrayed a languorously lazy, simpleminded servant in roles that were later denounced as racist stereotypes. He countered this criticism by stating that he had paved the way for the success of such stars as Bill COSBY and Sidney POITIER. Once a millionaire, in the 1940s he declared bankruptcy and supported himself with nightclub appearances and occasional film roles.

Feuchtwanger, Lion (1884–1958)

German novelist and essayist. Born into an Orthodox Jewish family in Munich, Feuchtwanger rose to prominence in German letters with the publication of his novel *The Ugly Duchess* (1923). *Jus Süss* (1925, translated as *Jew Seuss* in 1926), his most famous novel, probed the tensions of life as a Jew in German society; in a bitter turnabout, the Nazis adopted this novel into an anti-Semitic propaganda film in 1940. Feuchtwanger fled Germany in 1932, going first to France and then, in 1941, to the U.S. His novels emphasized the molding forces of history and religion over and above the personality traits of the individuals. Major works by Feuchtwanger include a trilogy on Jewish life in Germany—*Success* (1930), *The Oppermanns* (1933) and *Paris Gazette* (1939)—and a second trilogy set in the biblical era—*Josephus* (1932), *The Jew of Rome* (1935) and *Josephus and the Emperor* (1936). *Jephta and His Daughter,* published in 1957, was Feuchtwanger's final novel.

Feydeau, Georges (1862–1921)

French playwright, actor and director; one of the most popular figures in French theater in the 1900s. Feydeau was especially renowned for his farces, such as *Hotel Paradiso* (1894) and *A Flea in Her Ear* (1907), which featured witty and stylized dialogue, quick plot twists, frantic action and imaginative use of stage decor and props. He frequently appeared in his own productions; English translations include *Four Farces* (1970) and *Feydeau, First to Last* (1982).

Feynman, Richard Phillips (1918–1988)

American physicist. Feynman received a B.S. in physics from the Massachusetts Institute of Technology (1939) and a Ph.D. from Princeton (1942) after publishing his dissertation on quantum mechanics. During WORLD WAR II, Feynman played a key role in ATOMIC BOMB DEVELOPMENT at Los Alamos, New Mexico. On the MANHATTAN PROJECT he came into contact with many of the century's greatest physicists, including Hans BETHE, Niels BOHR, Aage BOHR, Enrico FERMI and J. Robert OPPENHEIMER. After the war he taught for several years at Cornell University (and later at the California Institute of Technology), where he carried out the work on quantum electrodynamics that led to the 1965 NOBEL PRIZE in physics, which he shared with Julian S. Schwinger and Sin-itiro Tomonaga. The Feynman diagrams that he developed gave physicists a way of explaining the behavior of light and matter in terms of fundamental particles. His 1985 autobiography, *Surely You're Joking, Mr. Feynman,* became a surprise best seller. A turning point in the presidential probe of the space shuttle *CHALLENGER* DISASTER came when Feynman demonstrated the loss of resiliency in the critical O-ring seals at low temperatures. As well as being an important physicist, Feynman was also a brilliant teacher in the classroom and influenced many younger physicists by his unique approach to problem solving.

Fianna Fáil (Irish Gaelic: "soldiers of destiny")

Political party formed by Eamon DE VALERA in 1926 from moderate members of SINN FÉIN, reflecting a reversal of previous opposition to dominion status for IRELAND. One of the two major Irish political parties, it formed the government in 1951–54, 1957–73, 1977–81, 1982–83 and 1987–94 and 1997–. Fianna Fáil is considered the most nationalist of Ireland's political parties and generally follows conservative domestic policies. It seeks the reunification of Ireland through peaceful means. (See also FINE GAEL.)

Fiat

Largest Italian automobile manufacturer, with original factories near Turin. Founded in 1899 by Giovanni Agnelli, Fiat has often supported design excellence. The 1935 500 Topolino, the 1978 Ritmo, and the 1979 Strada—each small, functional and unpretentious—are good examples of Fiat's dedication to producing basic cars for a mass market. The 124 Spider sports car is an example of quality design, in the tradition of Italian coach building, aimed at a special luxury market.

Fibber McGee and Molly

American radio network show. This classic NBC radio show ran from 1935 to 1957 and starred Jim Jordan and his real-life wife, Marjorie. The McGees' home at Wistful Vista became a familiar place on the U.S. cultural landscape. As one critic commented in 1940, the characters "get their humor from simple things, like fixing the brakes or playing checkers." Molly's rejoinder to her husband, "Tain't funny, McGee," became a national catchphrase.

fiberglass

Generic version of the trade name Fiberglas used by the Owens-Corning Glass Company for the hybrid material made from polyester PLASTIC reinforced with glass fibers. Fiberglass makes it possible to give high strength to glass parts that may be molded, or "hand laid-up," that is, built up on a mold with layers of glass cloth soaked in plastic resin. Fiberglass is increasingly used for automobile body parts and the hulls of small boats. It is also used for various household products and is the material of the first successful plastic chairs designed by Charles EAMES and Eero SAARINEN.

fiber optics

A branch of optics dealing with the passage of light along optical fibers, usually slender strands of glass or plastic. Bundles of fiber optic cables are much thinner and lighter than wire cables, can carry much more information and are immune to electromagnetic interference. Fiber optical cables are widely used in communications equipment, where they can link computers, transmit television signals, carry thousands of telephone conversations or perform a number of other functions. They have also found wide application in medicine, where fiber optic tubes such as the endoscope are often employed to examine the interior of the body without the use of X-ray or exploratory surgery.

Fiedler, Leslie Aaron (1917–2003)

American literary critic and author. Educated at New York University, the University of Wisconsin and Harvard University, Fiedler served in a variety of academic posts in the U.S. and abroad. He is perhaps best known for the critical work *Love and Death in the American Novel* (1960), in which he compares American and European novels and contends that Americans are obsessed with death and unable to write about sex, portraying women as either sinners or saints. His many provocative works of criticism include *The Jew in the American Novel* (1959, second edition 1966), *The Inadvertent Epic: From Uncle Tom's Cabin to Roots* (1980) and *Olaf Stapeldon; A Man Divided* (1983). In *Being Busted* (1969) Fiedler describes his own false arrest and incarceration for marijuana use while he was a faculty adviser to a student group fighting for the legalization of marijuana. His fiction includes *The Messengers Will Come No More* (1974) and the short stories *Nude Croquet and Other Stories* (1969). In 1988 Fiedler was elected to the American Academy of Arts and Letters.

Field, Marshall, III *(1893–1956)* American businessman, publisher and philanthropist. The grandson of the wealthy department store owner Marshall Field I (1834–1906), Field was born in Chicago. After his father's apparent suicide in 1906, he was taken to England, where he attended Eton and Cambridge. He returned to the U.S. in 1914, and in 1936 he abandoned his many business activities to devote himself to liberal political and social causes. He was a cofounder (1940) of the liberal New York City newspaper *PM* and established the Field Foundation to aid in child welfare and race relations. The following year he founded the Chicago *Sun*, which through merger became the *Sun Times* in 1948. Consolidating his ventures into Field Enterprises Inc. in 1944, he also published *The World Book Encyclopedia* and the Sunday supplement *Parade*. He owned four radio stations and other communications enterprises. His social and political philosophy was expressed in his book *Freedom Is More Than a Word* (1945).

Fields, Dorothy *(1904–1974)* American lyricist and librettist. Fields first gained success with songwriter Jimmy McHugh by writing lyrics for songs in the Cotton Club revues in HARLEM. An early hit was "I Can't Give You Anything but Love, Baby" (1928). Other hits with McHugh included "On the Sunny Side of the Street" and "I'm in the Mood for Love." She also wrote lyrics for Broadway musicals—*Annie Get Your Gun* (1946), *A Tree Grows in Brooklyn* (1951), *Redhead* (1959) and *Sweet Charity* (1964). Fields collaborated on movie musicals with both Harold ARLEN and Jerome KERN. Several songs written with

KERN have become standards—"A Fine Romance," "The Way You Look Tonight" and "Lovely to Look At."

Fields, Gracie (Grace Stansfield) *(1898–1979)* British music-hall singer and comedian. Born in Rochdale, Lancashire, she first appeared in the town's Hippodrome in 1910. During the 1920s, 1930s and 1940s she performed frequently in London and toured throughout Great Britain. In her heyday she was believed to be the world's highest-paid star and is thought to have sold more records than any other British performer in the mid-1920s. Known for her sassy ditties, warm ballads and stouthearted warbling, she was especially popular during WORLD WAR II, entertaining the troops and civilians alike during Britain's darkest hours. Even after her popularity waned she remained a national institution.

Fields, William Claude (William Claude Dukenfield) *(1879–1946)* American comedic stage and film actor. Fields remains one of the best-loved comic figures in the history of the cinema. He began his career as a teenage juggler on the vaudeville circuit. By his early 20s, he was a top-billed star, and in the 1900s and 1910s he was featured with the renowned ZIEGFELD FOLLIES in New York. Fields's first film was a silent short, *Pool Sharks* (1915). In the 1920s Fields enjoyed success on Broadway with *Poppy* (1923) and also appeared in the D. W. GRIFFITH silent film *Sally of the Sawdust* (1925), which established Fields in HOLLYWOOD at the late age of 46. In the 1930s, with the arrival of the talkies, Fields became a star in his persona as the crafty con artist with a heart of gold. Between 1931 and 1941 Fields made his best films; these include *It's a Gift* (1934), *The Man on the Flying Trapeze* (1935), *You Can't Cheat an Honest Man* (1939), *My Little Chickadee* (1940, with Mae WEST) and *The Bank Dick* (1940).

fifth column Term used just prior to and during WORLD WAR II to denote Nazi sympathizers in Allied and neutral countries who collaborated with the Germans, disseminated pro-German propaganda or committed other treasonous acts. The term was coined during the SPANISH CIVIL WAR by the nationalist general Emilio Mola (1887–1937). Although the attack on Madrid was made by four columns of troops, Mola asserted that he also had a "fifth

column," a cadre of pro-FRANCO agents in the city. Fifth-column activities in WORLD WAR II were encouraged and financed by Germany, partially by the creation of German minority organizations under the Nazi Party's foreign relations section. Playing upon the themes of anticommunism and ANTI-SEMITISM, fifth-column propaganda was somewhat effective among European civilians. Countries in which fifth-column activities were particularly strong included Norway, Belgium, France and Yugoslavia. The term is also more generally used to denote enemy agents or sympathizers who attempt to undermine any nation's structure or institutions from within.

Figueres Ferrer, José *(1906–1990)* Costa Rican politician. Affectionately known as "Don Pepe," he helped establish democracy in COSTA RICA after years of political turmoil. In 1948 he led a brief civil war against a leftist government that had sought to annul the results of an election. He emerged from the struggle as president. In 1949 he dissolved the country's army, leaving only a civil defense force. He also undertook major social and economic reforms, including the adoption of a constitution and the nationalization of the country's banks. Elected to two more terms (1953–58 and 1970–74), Figueres was one of the first Costa Rican leaders to play a major international role in Latin America.

Fiji (Fiji Islands) Island nation in the southwest Pacific, 1,300 miles north of New Zealand. The archipelago of islands, strategically placed and agriculturally fertile, was seized by Great Britain in 1858. A prime Allied supply site in WORLD WAR II, Fiji was named an independent dominion of the COMMONWEALTH in 1970. Tensions between the Fijian majority (of Melanesian-Polynesian origin) and the Indian minority came to a head in April 1987, when an Indian-dominated coalition won the general election. Two coups were followed by the declaration of a Fijian republic (October 1987) and Fiji's decision to withdraw from the Commonwealth. The country returned to civilian rule of the beginning of 1990, but ethnic tensions lingered. To the outside world, however, Fiji remains an island paradise, and it is a popular stopover for travelers between the U.S. and Australia or New Zealand.

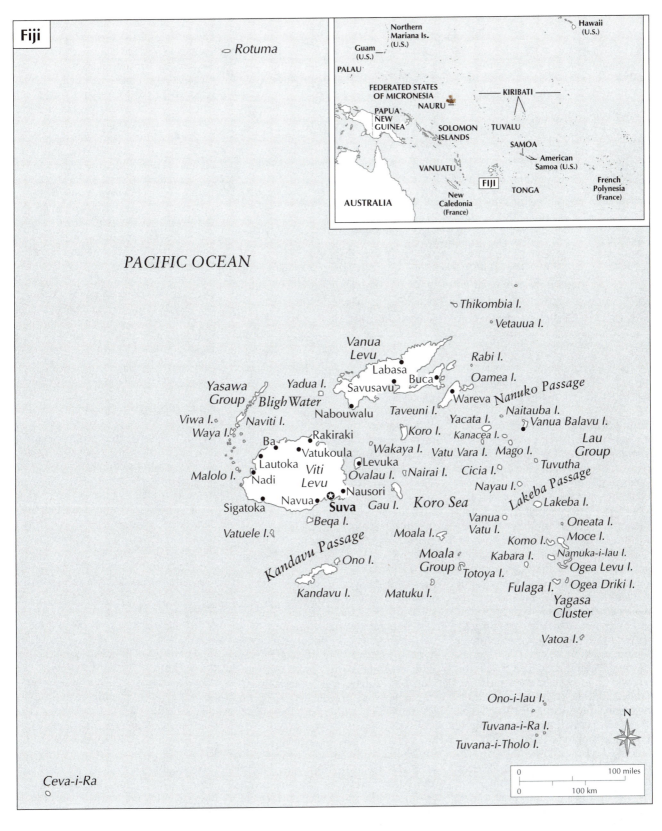

Fiji

Rotuma

PACIFIC OCEAN

Thikombia I.

Vetauua I.

Vanua
Levu

Rabi I.

Labasa

Buca

Oamea I.

Yasawa
Group

Yadua I.

Savusavu

Wareva

Nanuko Passage

Bligh Water

Nabouwalu

Taveuni I.

Naitauba I.

Viwa I.

Naviti I.

Yacata I.

Vanua Balavu I.

Waya I.

Koro I.

Kanacea I.

Lau
Group

Ba

Rakiraki

Wakaya I.

Vatu Vara I.

Mago I.

Lautoka

Vatukoula

Viti
Levu

Levuka

Tuvutha

Malolo I.

Nadi

Ovalau I.

Nairai I.

Cicia I.

Nayau I.

Lakeba Passage

Sigatoka

Navua

Nausori

Suva

Gau I.

Koro Sea

Lakeba I.

Beqa I.

Vanua
Vatu I.

Oneata I.

Vatuele I.

Moala I.

Komo I.

Moce I.

Kandavu Passage

Ono I.

Moala
Group

Kabara I.

Namuka-i-lau I.

Totoya I.

Ogea Levu I.

Kandavu I.

Matuku I.

Fulaga I.

Ogea Driki I.

Yagasa
Cluster

Vatoa I.

Ono-i-lau I.

Tuvana-i-Ra I.

N

Tuvana-i-Tholo I.

Ceva-i-Ra

| 0 | | 100 miles |
| 0 | | 100 km |

Following its adoption of a constitution that did not discriminate in favor of indigenous Fijians, Fiji was readmitted into the Commonwealth in 1997. However, Fiji was suspended from the Commonwealth in 2000 after Prime Minister Mahendra Chaudhry was taken hostage during a coup attempt in May of that year. The country was readmitted in December 2001 following the restoration of democratic rule that August.

Filene, Edward Albert (1860–1937) U.S. merchant. The president of William Filene's Sons in Boston, he was noted for his innovations in retail distribution, particularly his "bargain basement." He helped organize both

FIJI	
1943	Fiji is occupied by Allied forces waging the Solomon Islands campaign.
1970	Fiji becomes a sovereign and independent state
1987	Colonel Sitiveni Rabuka leads a military coup that overthrows the government; Rabuka revokes the constitution and declares Fiji a republic.
1990	Rabuka resigns from the cabinet; the new constitution is promulgated by decree of the president.
1997	Fiji rejoins the Commonwealth.
2000	Fijian ethnic nationalists take hostage the prime minister and 26 others in an attempt to roll back Fiji's efforts at creating a multiethnic society; the military storms the rebel stronghold and releases the hostages.

the Boston Chamber of Commerce and the U.S. Chamber of Commerce and was active in civic reform.

Filling Station, The Landmark modern American ballet. It was the joint collaboration in 1938 of composer Virgil THOMSON, choreographer Lew Christensen and impresario Lincoln KIRSTEIN for the newly formed Ballet Caravan of New York. With another Caravan production that same year, BILLY THE KID, it was one of the first ballets to draw primarily upon American national idioms and characters. The filling station itself was the intersection of a diverse group of travelers. Mack, the attendant, is visited by several characters—a golfer and his family, two truck drivers, a tipsy society couple and a gangster. After a holdup, a state trooper arrives to arrest the thief. "Using American music this way was quite avant-garde at the time," recalled Todd Bolender, who danced in the original production in 1938. "Audiences were startled to find anything so intrinsically American could be danced. And they loved the parodies of classical ballet, like the pas de deux danced by the drunken socialites and the use of a more modern jazz style. [Kirstein] wanted Americans to be aware that dance could be an integral part of our own culture and not so dependent upon the Europeans." The ballet is frequently revived, most recently by the State Ballet of Missouri and the San Francisco Ballet.

film noir A term applied by French film critics to certain American motion pictures from the WORLD WAR II and postwar era. It was not a specific genre; rather, the term denotes a particular mood and worldview found in a wide range of movies. From roughly the early 1940s to the late 1950s a sense of fatality, despair and nightmare appeared, born out of disillusionment with the recent war. Influential were the psychopathology of themes and characters and the dramatic lighting schemes of the German émigré filmmakers Fritz LANG, Robert Siodmak, and John Alton; the weakening censorship restrictions in HOLLYWOOD; and influences from the Italian neorealist films of the time. In short, after two decades of bright musicals and fairytale romances, suddenly the American screen was ripe for the ruthless hard-boiled detectives Sam Spade and Philip Marlow in, respectively, John HUSTON's *The Maltese Falcon* (1940) and Edward Dmytryk's *Murder, My Sweet* (1943). There were documentary-like police procedure thrillers, like Jules Dassin's *The Naked City* (1949) and Alfred Werker's *Dragnet* prototype, *He Walks by Night* (1949). *Double Indemnity* (1944) and *The Postman Always Rings Twice* made adultery, murder and sultry passion the cornerstones of romance and inspired a latter-day film noir, *Body Heat* (1981). Alfred HITCHCOCK attacked the smugness of American values in *Shadow of a Doubt*

(1943), and Nicholas Ray questioned the future of a new generation of teenagers in *They Live by Night* (1947). Robert Aldrich envisioned in *Kiss Me Deadly* (1957) nothing less than global holocaust. Not even the western and musical genres were left untouched: Raoul WALSH brought psychoanalysis to *Pursued* (1947) and Vincente MINNELLI inserted a Mike Hammer–like character into a sleazy ballet number in *The Band Wagon* (1953). Miraculously, in the face of such unremitting pessimism these movies displayed a dramatic, pictorial flair. Low-key lighting, the violent contrasts of rich chiaroscuro and crazy camera angles brought a breathtaking look even to conventional thrillers like *T-Men* (1947) and *The Big Combo* (1955). Through the 1990s film noir remained an important genre within the American film industry, with such critically and financially successful films as *The Last Seduction* (1994), *The Usual Suspects* (1995) and *L.A. Confidential* (1997).

final solution (German: *Endlosung*) Nazi euphemism for the secret German plan to exterminate systematically all European JEWS during WORLD WAR II, otherwise known as the HOLOCAUST. Adolf HITLER expressed his extreme ANTI-SEMITISM as early as 1923 in *MEIN KAMPF*, and anti-Semitism was fundamental in the rise of NAZISM and the Nazi Party during the 1930s. From the mid-1930s until the end of 1941, hundreds of thousands of Jews (at first in GERMANY, and later in the German-occupied countries) were deprived of their property and livelihood and confined to ghettos or sent to CONCENTRATION CAMPS. Hitler did not actually proclaim his deliberate extermination policy, however, until late 1941. The plan to destroy the European Jews—the so-called final solution to the Jewish problem—was formalized at the Wannsee Conference chaired by Reinhard HEYDRICH on January 20, 1942. Responsibility for implementing the final solution was given to Heinrich HIMMLER, who was assisted by Adolf EICHMANN and hundreds of lesser Nazi functionaries. The extermination policy was carried out at selected concentration camps, of which AUSCHWITZ was the most notorious.

Finch, George Ingle (1888–1970) Australian physical chemist. Finch was educated at Wolaroi College in Australia and the École de Médecine in Paris. Finding the study of medicine unappealing, he moved to Switzerland and studied physics and chemistry, first at the Federal Institute of Technology in Zurich and later at the University of Geneva. On moving to Britain in 1912 he worked briefly as a research chemist at the Royal Arsenal, Woolwich, joining the staff of Imperial College, London, in 1913. Finch remained there until his retirement in 1952, having been appointed professor of applied physical chemistry in 1936. After his retirement Finch traveled to India, where he was the director of the National Chemical Laboratory (1952–57).

Finch worked mainly on the properties of solid surfaces. In the 1930s he developed the technique of low-energy electron diffraction, using the wavelike properties of electrons, demonstrated by George Thomson and Clinton J. DAVISSON in 1927, to investigate the structure of surfaces. Finch was also widely known as a mountaineer. As one of the leading climbers of his generation he was a member of the 1922 Everest expedition, climbing to the then-unequaled height of 27,300 feet.

Fine Gael (*Irish Gaelic:* "Irish tribe") Moderate national party and one of two major Irish political parties. It won elections in 1973, 1982 and 1983. It generally avoids the nationalist rhetoric of the rival FIANNA FÁIL party and has shown willingness to compromise on the complex NORTHERN IRELAND issue. In 1994 the party formed a coalition with the Labour and Democratic Left Parties known as the "Rainbow Coalition," which governed Ireland until 1997.

Fini, Gianfranco (*1952–*) Political leader of the far right-wing Italian political party, the National Alliance. Fini is largely credited for the transformation of the Italian Social Movement, a quasi-fascist party, into the National Alliance. He succeeded in convincing its core members to cease performing stiff-armed salutes and expressing admiration and sympathy for the views of Jean-Marie LE PEN, a far-right French political leader.

In 1994, the year Fini and four other Alliance politicians entered the first government of Prime Minister Silvio BERLUSCONI, he provoked great controversy in ITALY and abroad. In an interview with the Turin daily newspaper *La Stampa* he was quoted as praising fascist dictator Benito MUSSOLINI as "the greatest statesman of the century." In 2002 Fini was designated by Berlusconi as the Italian representative to a European convention called to offer amendments to the 16 draft articles of the European constitution. During the proceedings Fini sided with British delegates who wished to avoid the adoption of a federal model, as called for in the original articles. He also opposed the admission of Turkey to the union and proposed an amendment specifying that all power possessed by the European Union and its organs be recognized as complementing rather than superseding its various members' national legislatures.

Fini, Leonor (*1908–1996*) Italian-Argentine painter. Raised in Buenos Aires, Fini received no formal artistic training as a youth, but after immigrating to Italy, she was influenced by painter Carlo CARRA while living in Milan and became one of his protégées. In 1933 Fini moved to Paris, where she became involved in the surrealist movement (see SURREALISM. Her fantastical paintings of the 1930s remain her best-known works. In the 1940s Fini won renown as a portraitist of famous personages of her era. She also did ballet stage designs and set designs for films.

Finland, Republic of (Finnish: Suomi) Nation of northeastern Europe; located between the Gulf of Bothnia and the Gulf of Finland and

FINLAND

1900	Finland enjoys limited autonomy within the Russian Empire, with its own legislature (the Diet) and a tradition of personal freedoms.
1905	Russian campaign to restrict freedoms and the power of the Diet is resisted in the "National Strike."
1906	Its power restored, the Diet guarantees freedom of press and assembly and universal suffrage; first film made.
1910	Russians reassert authority; freedoms erode.
1917	Diet declares independence during Russian Revolution.
1918	Brief civil war; "Whites" backed by Germany defeat and massacre "Reds" backed by Moscow.
1919	Republic declared; Staahlberg is first president.
1920	Treaty of Tartu with Soviet Union.
1925	Cultural renaissance in Helsinki, with composer Sibelius, architect Saarinen and others.
1930	Unsuccessful revolt by "Lapua," right-wing peasant movement.
1939	Soviet invasion meets tough resistance in Winter War.
1940	Finland cedes territory in Treaty of Moscow but retains independence.
1941	Embittered Finland joins Hitler's invasion of Soviet Union.
1944	Finland defeated by Soviet army.
1947	Treaty of Paris grants more territory and enormous reparation to Soviets.
1948	President Paasikivi seeks to placate Soviet neighbor through close cooperation, signs limited defense pact.
1952	Olympics held in Helsinki.
1955	Joins Nordic Council; this and other economic ties to the West, coupled with final stabilization of Soviet question, allows for long period of economic growth under center-left coalition governments.
1969	First Finnish auto factory opens as industry booms.
1975	Helsinki Conference and Accords—attempt by 35 nations to achieve East-West cooperation; accords set out basic human rights standards worldwide.
1987	Harri Holkeri becomes Finland's first post–World War II conservative prime minister.
1992	Finland nullifies 1948 defense pact with defunct USSR.
1995	Finland admitted to European Union.
2000	Social Democratic Party member Tarja Halonen becomes Finland's first female president.
2002	The euro replaces the local markka.

flanked by NORWAY and SWEDEN on the north and west and RUSSIA on the east and south. The north of Finland stretches above the Arctic Circle, in Lapland, and the south is flecked with lakes and waterways. Independent since 1917, Finland has been connected with either Russia or Sweden for much of its history; in fact, Swedish continues as one of the country's two official languages. The capital, Helsinki, is on the southern coast. After the RUSSIAN REVOLUTION in 1917, the Finns proclaimed their independence from the new USSR. Right-wing factions emerged triumphant after a five-month civil war in 1918; in 1920 the Soviet Union acknowledged the new republic in the Treaty of Tartu (see FINNISH WAR OF INDEPENDENCE). Finnish politics were unstable during the 1920s and 1930s, as reminders of the civil war were slow to fade. At the beginning of WORLD WAR II, in the winter of 1939–40, Finland was attacked by the USSR, in violation of a nonaggression pact. The Finns fought bravely but were defeated; quickly recuperating, they themselves attacked Russia when GERMANY invaded the USSR in 1941. The Finns were victorious at first but were routed in 1944, losing the Isthmus of Karelia, Vyborg, the Finnish shores of Lake Ladoga and the Pechenga region to the Soviet Union. After 1945 relations with the USSR were relatively harmonious. Finland's industries have grown considerably. In 1992 Finland nullified its friendship treaty with the Soviet Union, following the December 1991 disintegration of the latter country. Later that year Finland and Russia negotiated a new treaty that included no military accords. In 1995 Finland was admitted to the European Union, and in 2002 Finland adopted the euro as its currency.

Finley, David *(1890–1977)* Planner and first director (1938–56) of the National Gallery of Art in Washington, D.C. He was chairman of the U.S. Commission of Fine Arts (1950–63) and headed the National Trust for Historic Preservation during the same period.

Finney, Albert *(1936–   )* British stage and film actor and stage director. Finney remains most familiar to audiences worldwide for his tour de force performance in the title role of the film *Tom Jones* (1963), based on the picaresque 18th-century novel by Henry Fielding. Other films starring Finney include *Two for the Road* (1967) and *Shoot the Moon* (1982). But the bulk of his acting work took place on the London stage, where he earned critical acclaim for his lead roles in plays as diverse as *Billy Liar* (1960), *Luther* (1961), *Hamlet* (1975) and *Tamburlaine the Great* (1976). In 1983 he both directed and starred in *Armstrong's Last Goodnight,* by British playwright John Arden, in a production by the Old Vic Company. Finney has since appeared in several notable films, including *Erin Brockovich* (2000), in which he portrayed lawyer Ed Masry opposite Julia Roberts in the title role; *Traffic* (2000), in which he depicted the U.S. chief of staff, and *The Gathering Storm* (2002), a Home Box Office film in which he played Winston CHURCHILL and for which he received an Emmy nomination.

Finnish War of Independence *(1918–1920)* In 1917 the new Russian provisional government granted Finland a democratic government. After the BOLSHEVIK REVOLUTION, the Finns declared independence on December 6, 1917. The new Soviet government recognized it, but Finland's coalition government was ousted by Soviet-backed Finnish radicals (Reds) on January 28, 1918. This started a civil war between WHITES in the north, led by Baron Carl Gustaf MANNERHEIM, and Reds controlling the south. Mannerheim attacked the Reds but was halted until aid arrived from German troops under Count Rudiger von der Goltz, who seized Helsinki and drove the Reds from the country. At the **Battle of Vyborg,** April 29, 1918, the Whites forced the Reds to surrender and then launched a terror campaign, killing thousands of suspected communists. A republic was established on June 17, 1919, but desultory fighting continued with Russia over conflicting claims to western Karelia until the Treaty of Dorpat (Tartu), October 14, 1920, ended hostilities, reaffirming Finland's independence.

Finsen, Niels Ryberg *(1860–1904)* Danish physician and medical researcher. He was educated in Reykjavík, Iceland, and at the University of Copenhagen, where he earned his M.D. In the 1890s Finsen began to investigate previous suggestions that light could be used to kill bacteria. He experimented and found that ultraviolet rays had the greatest power to kill bacteria. In 1896 he founded the Institute of Phototherapy, directing it until his death. Here he used ultraviolet light to treat lupus vulgaris, a skin infection caused by the tubercle bacillus. Half of his 800 lupus vulgaris patients were completely cured, and nearly all the rest showed significant improvement. For this work he received the 1903 NOBEL PRIZE in physiology or medicine. Finsen was not only among the first to use light to treat medical conditions, but he was also among the first to note the effects of sunlight, and its absence, on mood.

fireside chats Informal radio talks begun by U.S. president Franklin Delano ROOSEVELT. The first fireside chat was broadcast on March 12, 1933; the format proved popular and was continued by Roosevelt's successors.

Firth of Clyde See CLYDE RIVER AND FIRTH OF CLYDE.

Fischer, Emil Hermann *(1852–1919)* German organic chemist, widely regarded as the father of biochemistry. During the 1870s he worked closely with Adolf von Bayer. Before the end of the 19th century he did important work in three fields: purines, sugars and peptides. This work helped lay the foundation for 20th-century biochemistry, and Fischer received the 1902 NOBEL PRIZE in chemistry. Later he was the first scientist to produce a polypeptide containing 18 amino acids (1907) and the first to synthesize a nucleotide (1914). He also studied enzymes and recognized the importance of proteins as building blocks of life.

Fischer, Ernst Otto *(1918–   )* German inorganic chemist. Fischer was educated at the Munich Institute of Technology, where he obtained his Ph.D. in 1952. He taught at the University of Munich, serving as professor of inorganic chemistry from 1957 to 1964, when he became the director of the Institute for Inorganic Chemistry at the Institute of Technology. Fischer is noted for his work on inorganic complexes. He shared the NOBEL PRIZE in chemistry with Geoffrey Wilkinson in 1973. Fischer went on to do further work on transition-metal complexes with organic compounds and is one of the leading workers in the field of organometallic chemistry.

Fischer, Hans *(1881–1945)* German organic chemist. Fischer gained his doctorate in chemistry at the University of Marburg in 1904. He also studied medicine at the University of Munich, earning his M.D. in 1908. He was assistant to Emil FISCHER before occupying chairs of medical chemistry at Innsbruck (1916) and Vienna (1918). In 1921 he succeeded Heinrich Wieland as professor at the Technical Institute in Munich. Fischer's life work was the study of the immensely important biological molecules hemoglobin, chlorophyll and the bile pigments, especially bilirubin. He synthesized hemin in 1929 and extensively investigated similar molecules—the porphyrins. He was awarded the NOBEL PRIZE in chemistry for this work in 1930. He then turned to the chlorophylls. Fischer took his own life at the end of WORLD WAR II, after his laboratories had been destroyed in the bombing of Munich.

Fischer, Joseph Martin "Joschka" (*1948– *) German Green Party politician, foreign minister of Germany (1998–). Born to ethnic Germans expelled from Hungary at the end of WORLD WAR II, Fischer spent the late 1960s and early 1970s demonstrating against the VIETNAM WAR and mingled with such activists as Daniel "Danny the Red" Cohn-Bendit (the French student leader who organized the 1968 Paris uprising against de GAULLE) and Hans-Joachim Klein (later charged with participating in a 1975 attack on OPEC oil ministers that killed three people). In 1976 he left the radical movement when it was revealed that two of its members had conspired with terrorists who later hijacked a plane in order to find and murder Israeli passengers.

In 1983 Fischer was elected to the Bundestag, the West German parliament, as a member of the pro-environment Green Party, and two years later joined the government of Helmut KOHL as minister of the environment. In 1998 he was selected as the political leader of the Green Party, which entered into a coalition government with Gerhard SCHRÖDER's Social Democratic Party, and Fischer became foreign minister.

Fischer differentiated himself from the majority of the Greens' constituents when in 1999 he supported the participation of German military forces in the NATO-led KOSOVO war, agreeing that the dangers of continued genocide and ETHNIC CLEANSING by Serbian forces in Kosovo justified the action. Fischer also promoted a German foreign policy that called for greater integration under the EUROPEAN UNION (EU). Also, although he supported the Schröder government's opposition to

the 2003 Anglo-American military operation against IRAQ, Fischer called for better relations with the U.S. after the conflict ended.

Fischer, Robert James "Bobby" (*1943– *) American chess champion. Considered among the greatest chess players of all time, Fischer was known for his aggressive style of play as well as for his demanding personality. He became a grandmaster in 1958, then went on to win the U.S. championship. In 1972 he beat the Soviet Union's Boris SPASSKY for the world championship, becoming the first American to hold that title; he then abruptly quit all competitive play. During his brilliant career Fischer helped to popularize chess throughout the world and helped to break the Soviet domination of the sport. In 1992 Fischer emerged from seclusion for a rematch against Spassky. Although Fischer won the rematch, held in Sarajevo, Yugoslavia, he quickly returned to anonymity. Following the terrorist attacks of SEPTEMBER 11, 2001, Fischer, living in Japan, gave a series of radio interviews in which he denounced the U.S. and made virulently anti-Semitic statements. Authorities in the U.S. later sought his extradition, claiming that by playing in Sarajevo in 1992 he had violated international sanctions then in force against the former Yugoslavia.

Fischer-Dieskau, Dietrich (*1925– *) German lieder (art song) and operatic baritone singer. His interpretations of the great German lieder cycles of Schubert, Schumann and Wolf are incomparable. He was born in Berlin and studied voice with G. A. Walter and Hermann Weissenborn. While serving in the German army during WORLD WAR II, he was captured by American forces near Pisa, Italy, and spent the remainder of the war singing lieder to his fellow prisoners. His subsequent concert and recording career with accompanists Joerg Demus, Gerald MOORE and Hartmut Hoell has encompassed an incredibly diverse roster of composers, from Purcell and Handel to Meyerbeer and Strauss to Pfitzner, Charles IVES, Hans-Werner HENZE and Benjamin BRITTEN (for whom he inspired the baritone part in the *War Requiem,* 1962). On the opera stage Fischer-Dieskau has

particularly excelled in the roles of Falstaff, Don Giovanni and Macbeth. In recent years he has established a conducting career, written several books (*Wagner and Nietzsche,* 1974; *Robert Schumann,* 1981; and a biographical study of Schubert's songs, 1976) and presented distinguished master classes. Arguably, his finest achievement was a 25-record project in the late 1960s for the Deutsche-Grammophone label of the approximately 600 Schubert songs. Many of these songs had never before been publicly performed and/or recorded. Although there are some detractors who criticize his tendency to "push" what is a rather lightweight vocal instrument, there is no denying his unparalleled dramatic insight and his complete command of any concert stage. Fischer-Dieskau made his final concert appearance in December 1992 at the Bavarian State Opera House in Munich, Germany, in the title role of Verdi's *Falstaff.*

Fisher, Dorothy Canfield (*1879–1958*) American author and humanitarian. Using the name Dorothy Canfield, she contributed many stories to magazines. After graduating from Ohio State University in 1899, she went to the Sorbonne in Paris and took a Ph.D. in 1904 from Columbia University. After marrying John R. Fisher, she lived on her ancestral farm near Arlington, Vermont, for the rest of her life. During WORLD WAR I she and her husband undertook relief work in France, resulting in her collection of short stories *Home Fires in France* (1918). She was selected as the only woman on the board of the Book-of-the-Month Club, continuing for 24 years. She introduced and popularized the Montessori method of early childhood education in *A Montessori Manual* (1913). Her work includes *The Bent Twig* (1915); *Understood Betsy* (1916), considered a children's classic; *Day of Glory* (1919) and *American Portraits* (1946).

Fisher, Geoffrey Francis (Lord Fisher of Lambeth) (*1887–1972*) English clergyman, archbishop of Canterbury. Fisher, who also served as primate of the Church of England, was one of the leading supporters of ecumenical unity in the modern Anglican Church. In 1960 he paid a visit to Pope

JOHN XXIII in the Vatican. That occasion marked the first formal meeting between the heads of the Anglican and the Roman Catholic Churches since the initial split between the two churches in 1534. In a 1961 speech, Fisher declared that the terms *Catholic* and *Protestant* were out of date and no longer held real meaning. Fisher's ultimate goal was what he termed a *commonwealth of churches*—with all denominations spiritually unified while each maintained organizational independence. Fisher served as Bishop of Chester (1932) and of London (1939) before becoming archbishop of Canterbury (1945–61).

Fisher, Sir John *(1892–1983)* British naval officer and government official. Fisher was one of those responsible for the "little ships" evacuation of Allied troops from DUNKIRK early in WORLD WAR II. Fisher was serving director of the coastal division of Britain's Ministry of War when he planned **Operation Dynamo,** in which an armada of small boats, most of them privately owned and sailed by civilians, ferried 338,226 Allied troops to England in May and June 1940.

Fisher, John Arbuthnot (first baron Fisher of Kilverstone, 1909) *(1841–1920)* British admiral. He joined the navy in 1854 and, while trained in sailing ships, became an advocate of technical advances and aided in the development of the torpedo. He developed ordnance (1886–90) and served as third sea lord (1892–97), commander in chief in the Mediterranean (1899–1902), second sea lord (1902–03) and first sea lord (1903–10). Largely responsible for revamping Britain's navy to face the emerging threat from Germany, the fiery admiral helped to build the *Dreadnought* and encouraged the construction of an expanded fleet and the development of the SUBMARINE. He retired in 1910 but returned as first sea lord at the outbreak of WORLD WAR I (1914). Opposed to CHURCHILL's Dardanelles expedition, he resigned in 1915.

Fisher, Mary Frances Kennedy *(1908–1992)* American author. After attending the University of California, Fisher spent three years in France studying at the University of Dijon. The author of numerous essays and books on food and cookery, Fisher is known for the clarity and elegance of her writing as well as her ability to intersperse personal reflection and reminiscence throughout her culinary books. Her prose has been praised by W. H. AUDEN, among others. Her works include *Serve It Forth* (1937), which she published as Mary Frances Parrish, using her second husband's name; *Here Let Us Feast: A Book of Banquets* (1946); *An Alphabet for Gourmets* (1949); *Not Now but Now: a Novel* (1982) and *Dubious Honors* (1988). Fisher also translated into English *The Physiology of Taste,* by Jean Anthelme Brillat-Savarin (1946).

Fisk, James B. *(1910–1981)* American physicist. Fisk headed a group that pioneered the development of RADAR during WORLD WAR II. He was appointed the first director of the U.S. Atomic Energy Commission (AEC) in 1947. In 1958 President EISENHOWER sent him to Geneva to head a team of scientists preparing the groundwork for negotiations on the NUCLEAR TEST BAN TREATY. From 1959 to 1973 Fisk was president of Bell Laboratories.

Fitch, Val Logsdon *(1923–)* American physicist. Fitch was educated at McGill and Columbia Universities and obtained his Ph.D. from Columbia in 1954. He then joined the staff of Princeton University, where he became professor of physics in 1960. Working with Leo James Rainwater, Fitch was the first to observe radiation from muonic atoms, that is, from species in which a muon is orbiting a nucleus rather than an electron. This work indicated that the sizes of atomic nuclei were smaller than had been supposed. He went on to study kaons and in 1964 collaborated with James CRONIN, James Christenson and Rene Turley in an experiment that disproved CP conservation. In 1980 Fitch and Cronin shared the 1980 NOBEL PRIZE in physics for this fundamental work.

Fitzgerald, Barry (William Joseph Shields) *(1888–1961)* Irish actor. Born in Dublin, Fitzgerald acted part-time at the ABBEY THEATRE from 1918 until 1929, after which he became a permanent member of the company. Fitzgerald established his reputation in the role of Captain Boyle, in Sean O'-Casey's *Juno and the Paycock* (1924). He appeared first in London in O'Casey's *The Silver Tassie* (1929). Following 1937, Fitzgerald appeared primarily in films, such as *Going My Way* (1944) and *The Quiet Man* (1952).

Fitzgerald, Ella *(1918–1996)* American jazz and popular singer known for her elegant song stylings. Born in Newport News, Virginia, Fitzgerald was raised by her aunt in New York. After winning the Harlem Amateur Hour contest, she became a vocalist with the Chick WEBB band in 1934. She first gained wide attention with her recording (with Webb) of "A-Tisket, A-Tasket"; although the song itself is mediocre, Fitzgerald's vocalization made it an instant hit. She displayed her characteristic traits—swing rhythm, improvisatory spirit, vocal range, control and clarity. After Webb's death (1939) she became the leader of the band. Fitzgerald's career was remarkable for its longevity and its sustained excellence. She worked with many of the notable jazz musicians of her time, toured extensively in the U.S. and Europe and made numerous concert, festival, nightclub and television appearances. Her repertoire, well represented in recordings, ranged from the lyrics of George and Ira GERSHWIN to BLUES and scat songs.

Fitzgerald, Francis Scott *(1896–1940)* American novelist and short story writer. F. Scott Fitzgerald captured in his writings the perceived moral emptiness of the wealthy American society of the "Roaring Twenties." Although not a member of the wealthy set, his elite education in private schools provided insight into the life of the privileged. Born in St. Paul, Minnesota, he attended Princeton University but resigned to join the army (1917) and served in France during WORLD WAR I. While in the army, he published his first book, *This Side of Paradise,* in 1920. In *Tales of the Jazz Age* (1922) he coined the term *Jazz Age* to describe his era. In 1924 Fitzgerald went to Europe, where he lived for six years. He published his best-known work, *The GREAT GATSBY* (1925), while living abroad. *Gatsby* is now widely acclaimed both for its formal perfection and for its insights into the American experience, but its initial reception was disappointing. The mental illness of his wife, Zelda Sayre Fitzgerald, and his

F. Scott and Zelda Fitzgerald (Library of Congress, Prints and Photographs Division)

bouts with alcohol hampered his literary progress and left Fitzgerald in a difficult financial position. *Tender Is the Night* (1934), perhaps his most ambitious book, was a financial failure. Fitzgerald turned to scriptwriting for Hollywood in 1936 and died of a heart attack before his novel *The Last Tycoon* was finished.

Fitzgerald, Robert Stuart (*1910–1985*) American scholar, critic and poet. Fitzgerald was a Harvard professor best known for his translation of the Greek classics. In 1961 his version of Homer's *Odyssey* won the first Bollingen award for translation of poetry. He also translated some major modern French literature.

Fitzmaurice, George (*1877–1963*) Irish playwright. Fitzmaurice's first play, *The Country Dressmaker* (1907), was performed at the Abbey Theatre and was an enormously popular realistic comedy. His later works, which include *The Pie-Dish* (1908), *The Dandy Dolls* (1908) and *The Magic Glasses* (1913), were more difficult, involving elements of the fantastic and grotesque; they were not popular during his lifetime. He remained a civil servant in Dublin. Following his death there was a revival of interest in his work, which has been compared to that of James Stephens.

Fitzsimmons, Frank Edward (*1908–1981*) American labor leader and head of the International Brotherhood of Teamsters (1971–81). Beginning as a truck driver, Fitzsimmons rose through the union ranks. He took temporary charge of the largest U.S. union when Jimmy Hoffa, his predecessor, was sent to prison (1967). After his election as head of the Teamsters, he expanded the union as a political force, improved relations with the AFL-CIO and maintained close ties with the White House. Nonetheless, charges of misuse of funds and other abuses continued to plague Fitzsimmons and the Teamsters.

five-year plan In communist and socialist countries, a plan during which the economic growth of the country is structured for the following five years. The first five-year plan was ordered in the Union of Soviet Socialist Republics by Joseph Stalin and lasted from 1928 to 1932. In 1958 Nikita Khrushchev hit on the idea of a seven-year plan. Although the USSR made immense industrial strides through its five-year plans during the Stalinist period, the cost in human suffering was also immense. Invariably, five-year plans have failed to meet their ambitious goals; they are often seen more as propaganda exercises than as realistic programs.

Flagstad, Kirsten (*1895–1962*) Norwegian opera singer, considered the greatest Wagnerian soprano of the 1930s and 1940s. Flagstad made her debut in *Tiefland* in Oslo (1913) and continued to sing in operettas until she joined the Storm Theater in Göteborg, Sweden (1930) and devoted herself to opera. Her performance as Sieglinde in *Die Walküre* in Bayreuth (1934) established her international reputation. Her 1935 debut in the same role at the Metropolitan Opera in New York was a triumph, and her subsequent soldout appearances over the next five years helped save the Met from financial ruin during the Great Depression. Her greatest roles were as Sieglinde, Isolde (*Tristan and Isolde*), Kundry (*Parsifal*) and the three Brünnhildes of Wagner's Ring Cycle. After retiring from live performance in 1954, she founded the Norwegian State Opera in 1959 and became its director.

Flaherty, Robert (*1884–1951*) American documentary filmmaker. Flaherty came to know the Canadian and Alaskan wildernesses as a child when he accompanied his father in travels throughout the Northwest Territory. These experiences came to fruition when Flaherty shot a silent documentary, *Nanook of the North* (1922), that documented Eskimo (Inuit) life and became a box-office success. He followed with *Moana* (1926), a documentary on the South Sea islands. *Man of Aran* (1934) is the work most acclaimed by film critics—a beautifully photographed study in black and white of the harsh conditions of village life on the Aran Islands of Ireland. *Elephant Boy* (1936) was a film on India. Flaherty's final documentary, sponsored by Standard Oil, was *Louisiana Story* (1948).

Flanagan, (Father) Edward Joseph (*1886–1948*) American priest and founder of Boys Town. A parish priest in Nebraska, Father Flanagan became interested in the treatment of homeless or lawbreaking boys and founded Boys Town near Omaha in 1917. The work began with five boys in a rented house. The next year he bought a small tract of land where he and the boys began to build the institution. Boys Town was incorporated as a municipality in 1922. His belief that "there is no such thing as a bad boy" was confirmed by his spectacular success in training young men, many of whom went on to successful careers. Father Flanagan's work was featured in the popular 1938 movie *Boys Town*. Following World War II, he became a special consultant on youth to the U.S. government and traveled to Asia and Europe to inspect youth work and facilities.

Flanders Ancient, strategically located area on the English Channel–North Sea coast of Europe, running from what is now the north of France through Belgium and into the Netherlands. Parts of it are in the French departments of Pas-de-Calais and Nord, the Belgian provinces of East and West Flanders and the Zeeland province of the Netherlands. It has had a turbulent history and was a perpetual battlefield during WORLD WAR I and a critical area during WORLD WAR II. The continuous battles in both French and West Flanders during World War I were depicted in John McCrae's poem "In Flanders' Fields." During World War II the battle of Flanders commenced with the Nazi attack on Belgium in 1940 and finished with the capitulation of the Belgian army and the British evacuation at DUNKIRK, from May 26 to June 4, 1940.

Flanner, Janet (*1892–1978*) American writer. Flanner was a correspondent for The NEW YORKER magazine for almost 50 years. Her regular "Letter from Paris" feature in the magazine gave insight into the French mind and way of life. She also wrote profiles of such diverse figures as Adolf HITLER, Henri MATISSE and Queen Mary.

Fleetwood Mac Anglo-American ROCK band. While the band Fleetwood Mac has experienced numerous changes in musical personnel since its founding in 1967, its most prominent members have been guitarist Lindsay Buckingham, drummer Mick Fleetwood, pianist and vocalist Christine McVie, bass player John McVie and vocalist Stevie Nicks. Fleetwood and John McVie, the two key founders of the band, met in the 1960s while playing together in a British group, John Mayall's Bluesbreakers. In 1969 Fleetwood Mac enjoyed a number-one hit in Britain with an instrumental single, "Albatross." In 1974 Americans Buckingham and Nicks joined the band and still greater commercial success ensued. A 1977 album, *Rumours*, became the first album by a rock-and-roll band to produce four singles that each reached the *Billboard* Top Ten pop chart—"Go Your Own Way," "Dreams," "Don't Stop" and "You Make Loving Fun." Fleetwood Mac disbanded for a time in the mid-1980s, but the group

later reunited and resumed actively performing and recording. Nicks also pursued a successful solo career.

Fleischer, Max (*1883–1972*) American cartoonist. Fleischer created the *Popeye* and *Out of the Inkwell* cartoon series (1917). He also invented more than 20 devices used in animation and motion picture production.

Fleming, Sir Alexander (*1881–1955*) British bacteriologist. After his early education at Kilmarnock Academy and the London Polytechnic Institute, Fleming began his career at the age of 16 as a shipping clerk in a London office. With encouragement from his brother, who was a doctor, he became a medical student at St. Mary's Hospital Medical School in 1902 and graduated from the University of London in 1908. He worked at St. Mary's all his life apart from his service in the Royal Army Medical Corps (1914–18). During his time with the medical corps he became interested in the control of wound infections and was a vigorous supporter of the physiological treatment of wounds rather than treatment using harsh chemicals, such as carbolic acid.

In 1928 Fleming was appointed professor of bacteriology, and in the same year he made his most important discovery. After accidentally leaving a dish of staphylococcus bacteria uncovered, Fleming noticed certain clear areas in the culture. He found these areas were due to contamination by a mold he identified as *Penicillium notatum*, which produced a substance that killed the bacteria. Fleming named this substance PENICILLIN and tested the bactericidal effect of the mold on various bacteria, observing that it killed some but not others. He appreciated the potentialities of his discovery but was unable to isolate and identify the compound. It was not until WORLD WAR II, with the urgent need for new antibacterial drugs, that penicillin—the first antibiotic—was finally isolated by Howard Florey and Ernst CHAIN. Fleming was awarded the 1945 NOBEL PRIZE in physiology or medicine jointly with Florey and Chain for his discovery, which initiated a whole new range of life-saving antibiotics. He received a knighthood in 1944 and many other honors.

Fleming, Lady Amalia (**Amalia Koutsouris**) (*1909–1986*) Greek political activist. She was the wife of Sir Alexander FLEMING, the discoverer of PENICILLIN. She became internationally known for her resistance to the military junta that ruled GREECE from 1967 to 1974. Expelled from Greece in 1971, she returned there after democracy was restored. In 1977 she was elected to Parliament as a Socialist Party member and later reelected in 1981 and 1985.

Fleming, Ian Lancaster (*1908–1964*) British novelist and journalist. The son of a Conservative M.P., Fleming was educated at Eton, Sandhurst and the Universities of Munich and Geneva. He served as Moscow correspondent for Reuters from 1929 to 1933 and later as a reporter for the *Times* of London. Fleming wrote the enormously popular series of espionage novels featuring JAMES BOND, agent 007, the embodiment of many a male adolescent fantasy. The Bond books, nearly all of which have been filmed, include *Casino Royale* (1953, filmed 1967), *Goldfinger* (1959, filmed 1964) and *The Spy Who Loved Me* (1962, filmed 1977). The series was given an additional boost in the U.S. by the praise of President John F. KENNEDY. Fleming also wrote the children's book *Chitty-Chitty-Bang-Bang* (1964, adapted as a musical film, 1968) and contributed to many periodicals under the pseudonym Atticus. The popular James Bond image of the spy as a glamorous superhero has been largely refuted by John LE CARRÉ.

Fleming, Peggy Gale (*1948– *) U.S. figure skater. One of the great balletic stylists, she won the first of her five straight U.S. women's championships at the age of 15. The world champion from 1966 through 1968, she was an Olympic gold medal winner in 1968. After the Olympics, she turned professional and performed with a number of ice shows and in professional competitions. Fleming has continued to receive awards and honors since her retirement, including the 1997 U.S. Olympic Committee Spirit Award and the 2003 Vince Lombardi Award of Excellence.

Fleming, Williamina Paton Stevens (*1857–1911*) U.S. astronomer.

She was a housekeeper in Boston when her employer, E. C. Pickering, hired her onto his Harvard College Observatory staff in 1881. Here she helped develop the "Pickering-Fleming" stellar classification system of photographic spectroscopy. She published her *Draper Catalogue of Stellar Spectra* of over 10,000 stars in 1890. She also established the first photographic system of measuring stellar magnitude, discovered half of the then known novae and over 200 variable-magnitude stars. In 1898 Harvard appointed her curator of astronomical photographs, and between 1892 and 1910 she cataloged over 200,000 plates. During her lifetime, Fleming was America's most famous woman astronomer.

Flerov, Georgi *(1913–1990)* Soviet nuclear physicist. Educated at the Leningrad Industrial Institute of Science, Flerov started his career at the Leningrad Institute of Physics and Technology in 1938. He later became chief of the laboratory of multicharged ions at the Kurchatov Institute of Atomic Energy, Moscow. Throughout his life Flerov was involved in the search for new elements and isotopes through synthesis and discovery. In many ways his work paralleled that of Glenn SEABORG in America. In 1960 Flerov became director of the nuclear radiation laboratories of the Joint Institute for Nuclear Research, Dubna, near Moscow.

Fletcher, Harvey *(1884–1981)* American physicist and expert on electronic acoustics. Fletcher joined Bell Telephone Laboratories in 1916. His acoustical research resulted in the development in 1934 of stereophonic sound. As head of physical research at Bell from 1933 to 1949, he helped develop the first electronic hearing aids and directed pioneering work on sound in motion pictures, television and transistors.

Fletcher, John Gould *(1886–1950)* American poet and critic. Born in Arkansas, Fletcher later lived for many years in England. His early poetry, such as *Irradiations: Sand and Spray* (1915) and *Goblins and Pagodas* (1916), was experimental and associated with that of the imagist poets. Fletcher later became concerned with issues of philosophy and spirituality, during which period he published *The Black Rock* (1928). This poetry, although mystical in nature, is more traditional in form. Late in life Fletcher returned to rural Arkansas, retreating from what he deemed the dehumanization of modern life. For *Selected Poems* (1938) he was awarded the PULITZER PRIZE in poetry. Other works include *The Epic of Arkansas* (1936) and *South Star* (1941). (See also IMAGISM.)

Flexner, Simon *(1863–1946)* American pathologist and authority on infectious diseases. In 1900, as professor of pathology at Johns Hopkins, Flexner discovered the bacillus that was causing a virulent form of dysentery among American troops in the Philippines; the organism was later named *Shingella flexneri*. In 1907, in response to an outbreak of meningitis in New York City, Flexner, then director of the laboratories at the Rockefeller Institute for Medical Research, developed a serum that remained a standard treatment of the disease for three decades. He headed the Rockefeller Institute from 1920 until 1935.

Florensky, Paul Alexandrovich *(1882–1943)* Russian Orthodox priest, philosopher and physicist. One of the founders of the Union of Christian Struggle as a student, he then lectured at the Moscow Theological Academy. Banished to Central Asia before the 1917 Bolshevik seizure of power, he returned afterward and studied advanced physics at the Academy of Sciences. He was deported to a CONCENTRATION CAMP in the 1920s, and nothing more is known about him. His *The Pillar and Foundation of Truth* (1914) has influenced philosophical and theological thought in the USSR.

Florida ballot controversy *(2000)* Crisis in the U.S.'s Electoral College brought about by the recounting of the popular vote in the state of Florida during the 2000 presidential election, amid allegations of ballot tampering. On November 7, 2000, in a tightly contested presidential race between Republican candidate George W. BUSH and Democrat Al GORE, original polling projections from the state of Florida made it appear that Bush had won the state's popular vote and therefore would receive all of Florida's 25 electoral votes, giving him a total of 271, enough to ensure his election. This prompted most news networks to call the presidential race in favor of Bush; Gore phoned the Bush camp to congratulate his opponent on the election's outcome. However, it was soon revealed that Bush's margin of victory only stood at a few thousand. Florida law required a recounting of all ballots to make certain that machine error did not result in illegitimate election results. Gore decided not to concede until the final tally was certified.

During the recount, and with the arrival of absentee and overseas voting forms, numerous reports surfaced of voting irregularities in several Florida counties. Democrats also claimed that defective voting machines had resulted in computer cards (used to tabulate individuals' votes) in which holes indicating how the person had voted were not completely punched out, which disqualified the ballot. This prompted calls from Democratic leaders for a hand recount in certain counties. While the controversy continued and the absentee ballot tally reduced Bush's lead to 950 votes, the Florida supreme court agreed to extend the recount deadline by 12 days.

On November 26, Katherine Harris, Florida's Republican secretary of state and the chairwoman of Bush's campaign in Florida, certified the recount as indicating that Bush won the popular vote by 537 votes. However, after the U.S. Supreme Court refused to permit a hand count of the ballots, Gore appealed his case to Florida's supreme court, which on December 6 agreed to order the counting of an estimated 40,000 ballots that computers had rejected for not including a vote on the presidential race. In response Bush filed a countersuit before the U.S. Supreme Court, which on December 12 voted 5-4 to overturn the decision reached by the Florida court, thus confirming Harris's original certification of Bush as the winner of the Florida vote and the recipient of all 25 electoral votes. The following day Gore conceded the election to Bush, who won 271 electoral votes to Gore's 266.

Floyd, Charles Arthur "Pretty Boy" *(1901–1934)* American gangster. Raised in Oklahoma's Cherokee Indian Territory, bank robber Floyd became a folk hero to depression-era sharecroppers in his home state. Unable to find work, he turned to robbery in the mid-1920s. He served (1925–26) one short term in jail, escaped (1930) a second, longer sentence, and was soon robbing banks throughout the Midwest with a succession of partners. Along the way, he made a considerable reputation as a Robin Hood, distributing money to the poor and ripping up bank mortgages. At the same time he became a confirmed killer, murdering an estimated 10 men. Labeled "public enemy number one" in the early 1930s, he was killed in an Ohio cornfield on October 22, 1934, by FBI agents under Melvin PURVIS.

Flying Tigers Popular term for the American Volunteer Group (AVG), an organization formed in 1941 by Colonel Claire Chennault and directed by him. Recruited from the U.S. Armed Forces, the men of the Flying tigers fought for CHIANG KAI-SHEK's China against the Japanese from 1941 to 1942. Based in Burma, the three squadrons that comprised the AVG flew American P-40 fighter planes, their wings marked with the Chinese Nationalist sun, their noses emblazoned with menacing red, white and blue shark's teeth. The Flying Tigers proved invaluable in protecting the BURMA ROAD supply line from Japanese incursions and were an important factor in delaying the Japanese capture of Rangoon until March 1942. Four months later, the AVG was transferred to American auspices and ceased to exist as a separate military entity.

Flynn, Errol (1909–1959) Australian-born film actor; achieved enduring success during the 1930s and 1940s as the archetypal HOLLYWOOD swashbuckler. Born on the island of Tasmania off the Australian coast, Flynn began his acting career with roles on the British stage before coming to Hollywood in 1934. After playing a few bit parts, he shot to stardom playing the romantic lead in the pirate film *Captain Blood* (1935), directed by Michael Curtiz and featuring Olivia de Havilland as Flynn's leading lady. Flynn then enjoyed a string of hits including *The Charge of the Light Brigade* (1936), *The Adventures of Robin Hood* (1938), *Dodge City* (1939) and *They Died with Their Boots On* (1941). In 1942 he was charged with statutory rape but ac-

quitted, prompting the popular saying "In like Flynn." In his last years Flynn returned to character roles in films including *The Sun Also Rises* (1957) and *The Roots of Heaven* (1958). *My Wicked, Wicked Ways* (1959) is his revelatory autobiography.

FNLA (National Front for the Liberation of Angola) An independence movement that fought alongside UNITA against the ultimately victorious MPLA in the ANGOLAN CIVIL WAR begun in 1975. It was funded by CHINA, and initially by the U.S. and ZAIRE. In the 1990s the FNLA emerged as a political party and participated in the political process organized by the 1991 BICESSE ACCORD and the 1994 LUSAKA ACCORDS.

Fo, Dario (1926–) Italian playwright, actor and theatrical producer. Fo has been a highly political figure in the postwar Italian theater and has avoided the twin extremes of COMMUNISM and FASCISM. He first attained success as a cabaret mime artist in the 1950s, performing satiric reviews with his wife, Franca Rama. Fo subsequently began to write plays that parodied the prevailing COLD WAR politics of the time. His work includes *Archangels Don't Play the Pin-Tables* (1959) and *Seventh: Thou Shalt Steal a Little Less* (1964). Fo achieved success throughout Europe with his play *Accidental Death of an Anarchist* (1970). His more recent plays include *We Won't Pay! We Won't Pay!* (1974) and *Trumpets and Raspberries* (1984). In 1997 Fo received the NOBEL PRIZE in literature in recognition of his contribution to the stage.

Foch, Ferdinand (1851–1929) French general. A veteran of the Franco-Prussian War of 1870–71 and commandant of the École de Guerre (1907–11), Foch was an official observer at Germany's army maneuvers in 1913. At the outbreak of WORLD WAR I he led the French Ninth Army at the MARNE. He also served in FLANDERS and commanded a French army group on the SOMME in 1916. After a brief retirement, he became General PÉTAIN's chief of staff in May 1917. His impressive performance led to his appointment as supreme commander of Allied forces on the Western Front in the spring of 1918 (see WORLD WAR I ON THE WEST-

ERN FRONT). He commanded the successful Marne counteroffensive (July 1918) and the subsequent offensive that led the Germans to sue for an armistice in November 1918. At the PARIS PEACE CONFERENCE (1919) he urged CLEMENCEAU to impose strong conditions on Germany. Foch was created a marshal of France in 1918; he was also made an honorary field marshal in the British army, the only Frenchman so honored.

Focke, Heinrich (1890–1979) German aircraft designer. Focke was an aviation pioneer whose FW-61 helicopter made the first free flight of a rotary-wing aircraft (1936). His VA-61 was the world's first helicopter to receive a certificate of airworthiness. One of his airplanes held the altitude record until 1954.

Fogel, Robert (1926–) American economist. Born in New York to Russian immigrants, Fogel attended Cornell University (B.A. 1948) and obtained an M.A. in economics from Columbia University (1960) and a Ph.D. in economics from Johns Hopkins University (1963). He was a professor at the University of Rochester (1960–75), the University of Chicago (1968–75) and Harvard University (1975–81). Fogel investigated the effects of technological innovations, government policy and changes in American structural institutions and environmental awareness on the development of American economic growth in the 19th and 20th centuries. He also helped develop cliometrics, a subdivision of the field of history that uses numerical data to quantify the importance of causal factors in producing a set of historical events. In 1993 Fogel was awarded the NOBEL PRIZE in economics on account of his research and efforts to refine the methods and formulae by which economists determine the reasons for fluctuations in a nation's monetary supply, economic health and foreign and domestic trade.

Fokine, Michel (1880–1942) Russian dancer and choreographer. He was one of the founders of modern ballet. Isadora DUNCAN inspired Fokine to free himself from the rigid classical discipline of the Imperial Ballet to create ballets in which dancing, music and scenery are combined in a related whole. *Le Cygne* (*The Dying Swan,* 1905), created as a solo for Anna PAVLOVA, and *Chopiniana* (later known as *Les Sylphides,* 1906) were early works. His great period was with DIAGHILEV in Paris (from 1909), when he created *Petrushka, Scheherazade, The Firebird* and *Le Spectre de la rose.* He left Russia for France at the outbreak of the revolution and moved to the U.S. during World War II.

Fokker, Anton Hermann Gerard (*1890–1939*) German-American aircraft designer and manufacturer. Born in Java of Dutch parents, Fokker moved to Germany, where he established a number of airplane factories. During WORLD WAR I he manufactured more than 40 kinds of airplanes for the German military, including the famous Fokker biplanes and triplanes. In addition, he developed a system for gear synchronization that allowed pilots to fire machine guns through spinning propellers. In 1922 he settled in the U.S., where he became a citizen and concentrated on the development of commercial aviation. His autobiography, *The Flying Dutchman,* was published in 1931.

Folsom, James Elisha "Big Jim" (*1908–1987*) American politician. Folsom served two terms as governor of Alabama (1947–51; 1955–59). Known as "the little man's big friend," he stood six feet eight inches tall. In an era when his state was regarded as a bastion of racism, he was regarded as a moderate or liberal on most issues.

Fonda, Henry (*1905–1983*) American actor. Widely acclaimed as one of America's greatest actors, Fonda starred in 80 films, 15 plays and numerous television dramas during a career that spanned nearly 50 years. Born in Nebraska, he joined the University Players in New England (1928), where he met Joshua LOGAN as well as James STEWART, who became a lifelong friend and later a frequent costar. In the early 1930s he appeared on Broadway, then moved to HOLLYWOOD to appear in films. In 1939 he began a long and successful collaboration with director John FORD, starring (as Abraham Lincoln) in *Young Mr. Lincoln* and in *Drums Along the Mohawk.* His role in Ford's adaptation of John STEINBECK's *The Grapes of Wrath* (1940) established his

quintessential screen persona as a soft-spoken but determined idealist. Among his notable later films are *The Ox-Bow Incident* (1943), *My Darling Clementine* (1946), *Mr. Roberts* (1955), *Twelve Angry Men* (1956), *Fail-Safe* (1964) and *On Golden Pond* (1981), his last movie. Fonda was equally adept in comedies, westerns and social dramas. He returned to the stage periodically and gave acclaimed performances in such plays as *Mr. Roberts* and *Clarence Darrow.* Many of his roles reflected his commitment to liberal social and political causes. His daughter, Jane FONDA, is also a noted actress and controversial social activist; his son **Peter Fonda** has been somewhat less successful as an actor, director and producer.

Fonda, Jane (*1937– *) American film actor; from a renowned HOLLYWOOD family that includes her father Henry FONDA, and her brother, Peter. At age 16, Fonda acted alongside her father in an Omaha stage production of *The Country Girl.* She made her film debut in *Tall Story* (1960). In 1965 Fonda married French film director Roger Vadim and starred in a number of his films, notably the futuristic sex fantasy *Barbarella* (1968), before their divorce. In the late 1960s she became a leading anti–VIETNAM WAR activist, visiting HANOI and making documentaries such as *Introduction to the Enemy* (1974); her widely publicized and highly controversial visit stirred charges that she was at best naive, at worst a traitor. During this period Fonda married political activist Tom Hayden. She enjoyed a major Hollywood success with the thriller *Klute* (1971), for which she won an ACADEMY AWARD as best actress. She has been a major star ever since, with films including *Julia* (1977), *Coming Home* (1978), for which she won a second best actress Oscar, *Nine to Five* (1981), *On Golden Pond* (1981), in which she costarred with her father, and *The Old Gringo* (1989). Fonda also became well known for her physical fitness books and videotapes. In 1991 Fonda married cable television entrepreneur Ted TURNER. The couple divorced in 2001. Fonda published a well-received autobiography, *My Life So Far,* in 2005.

Fontanne, Lynn See LUNT AND FONTANNE.

Fonteyn, Dame Margot (Margaret Hookham) (*1919–1991*) Legendary British ballerina considered one of the greatest dancers of the 20th century. Born in England to an English father and a Brazilian-Irish mother, Fonteyn spent much of her childhood with her parents in North America and China. She entered the Sadler's Wells Ballet School (now the Royal Ballet School) in 1934, making her dancing debut in a child's role in *The Nutcracker.* She soon come to the attention of Dame Ninette de VALOIS, who selected her (1935) to follow Alicia MARKOVA as the company's prima ballerina. At 17, Fonteyn danced the title role in *Giselle,* and for more than four decades thereafter she held center stage in British ballet. At the Royal Ballet she was known for her brilliant characterizations and flawless technique in such classics as *Swan Lake* and *The Sleeping Beauty,* as well as for the dances created for her by the choreographer Sir Frederick ASHTON, including *Ondine* (1958) and *La Fille mal gardée* (1960). In 1962 Fonteyn began a legendary partnership with Rudolf NUREYEV. Created a Dame of the British Empire in 1956, she retired from dancing at 60 and was awarded the rarely bestowed title *prima ballerina assoluta.* Her husband was the Panamanian politician Roberto Emilio ARIAS. Fonteyn devoted her later years to caring for her husband, who had been paralyzed by a would-be assassin.

Foot, Michael (*1913– *) British politician and journalist. After leaving Oxford, Foot became a journalist noted for his disputatious left-wing columns. He entered Parliament in 1945, served as editor of the LABOUR PARTY journal *Tribune* from 1948 to 1952 and from 1955 to 1960 and was secretary of state for employment from 1975 to 1979. In 1976 Foot became deputy prime minister and leader of the House of Commons. Following James CALLAGHAN's resignation in 1980, Foot served as leader of the Labour Party until 1983, attempting to maintain the party's traditional lines against resistance by the more conservative Social Democrats. A gifted orator, Foot is also the author of a two-volume biography of Aneurin BEVAN published in 1962 and 1973. In 1992 Foot retired from the House of

Commons. (See also SOCIAL DEMOCRATIC PARTY.)

Forbes, Esther *(1891–1967)* U.S. novelist and biographer. After studying writing at the University of Wisconsin (1916–18), she worked for publisher Houghton Mifflin in Boston (1919–26). She was awarded the O. Henry Prize for her story "BreakNeck Hill" in 1920. She published a steady stream of successful novels blending sexual passion and social repression in Puritan New England. Among the most famous are: *O, Genteel Lady* (1926), *A Mirror for Witches* (1928) and *Miss Marvel* (1935). She also wrote the PULITZER PRIZE–winning biography *Paul Revere and the World He Lived In* (1942) and the Newberry Prize–winning *Johnny Tremain* (1943).

Forbes, Malcolm Stevenson *(1919–1990)* American businessman. Forbes was chairman of Forbes Inc. and publisher of *Forbes* business magazine, which had been founded by his father in 1917. He was a flamboyant millionaire who was known for his love of yachting, motorcycling and hot-air ballooning. In his later years a frequent escort of actress Elizabeth TAYLOR, Forbes generated widespread publicity in 1989 with a $2 million 70th-birthday party he threw for himself in Morocco shortly before his death. His son **Steve Forbes** was a candidate for the Republican presidential nomination in 1996 and 2000.

Forbush, Scott E. *(1904–1984)* American geophysicist who pioneered research into cosmic rays. Forbush gave his name to the **Forbush effect**, a sharp lessening of the incidence of cosmic rays on Earth as the planet passes through a cloud of gas ejected by a solar flare.

Ford, Edsel Bryant *(1893–1943)* U.S. automotive executive and son of Henry FORD. In 1919 he succeeded his father as president and treasurer of the Ford Motor Company. However, industry opinion held that Ford authority was almost entirely nominal and that he merely carried out his father's wishes. Together the Fords established the FORD FOUNDATION. Henry Ford resumed the presidency when Edsel died in 1943. Edsel's name is perhaps best remembered for the ill-fated Edsel car of the 1950s, which proved to be well ahead of its time and now is in great demand as a classic car.

Ford, Ford Madox (Ford Hermann Hueffer) *(1873–1939)* British novelist. Ford changed his name in 1917 because of its German connotations. (His maternal grandfather was the noted pre-Raphaelite painter Ford Madox Brown.) Ford was the son of a music critic, and his childhood environment was an intellectual one. He was educated at University College School in London and converted to Catholicism at the age of 18. Ford published some fairy tales in the early 1890s and became acquainted with Joseph CONRAD, with whom he collaborated on the novels *The Inheritors* (1901) and *Romance* (1903). The two parted due to disagreements, the details of which Ford later obfuscated in his memoirs. On his own, Ford published *The Fifth Queen* (1906), the first of a trilogy about Catherine Howard, wife of Henry VIII; and in 1908 founded and edited the *English Review*. It was with the publication of *The Good Soldier* (1915), still considered Ford's most important novel, that he received some critical attention; however, he was never to realize great success in his lifetime. Also in 1915 he enlisted in the army, later to be invalided home in 1917, after having been gassed. His next major work, *Parade's End,* was published originally in four separate parts: *Some Do Not* (1924), *No More Parades* (1925), *A Man Could Stand Up* (1926) and *The Last Post* (1928). The books characterize the era prior to WORLD WAR I. In 1922 Ford moved to Paris, where he founded the seminal *Transatlantic Review,* which published work by James JOYCE and Ezra POUND, among others. Ford's interesting and idiosyncratic memoirs include *Return to Yesterday* (1931) and *It Was the Nightingale* (1933). His last publication was an original work of literary criticism, *The March of Literature* (1938). Although his work has never garnered popular acclaim, Ford's writing has received important critical recognition. As an editor, Ford had an enormous influence on subsequent 20th-century literature.

Ford, Gerald *(1913–)* American statesman and president of the UNITED STATES *(1974–77)*. Ford served in the navy during WORLD WAR II, then practiced law until he was elected to the

Gerald Ford, 38th president of the United States (LIBRARY OF CONGRESS, PRINTS AND PHOTOGRAPHS DIVISION)

U.S. House of Representatives from Michigan in 1948. A conservative Republican, Ford served as minority leader from 1965 to 1973, when President Richard M. NIXON named him to replace Spiro T. AGNEW as vice president. In 1974, after Nixon resigned, Ford became the 38th president. His pardon of Nixon and his program of limited amnesty for Vietnam-era deserters and draft dodgers stirred controversy. In foreign affairs Ford pursued a policy of DETENTE with the Soviet Union, signing the Vladivostok Arms Limitation Agreement in 1974. On the domestic scene he was plagued by an inflation-recession economy, incurring huge budget deficits. He survived two separate assassination attempts in 1975. Although he lost the 1976 presidential election to Jimmy CARTER, Ford remained politically active. In 1999 Ford received the Presidential Medal of Freedom from U.S. president Bill CLINTON.

Ford, Henry *(1863–1947)* American automobile manufacturer. Starting as a mechanic in Detroit, Ford began experimenting with engines about 1890 and completed his first gasoline engine in 1893. The first Ford automobile was completed in 1896. Encouraged by

A row of completed
Model Ts comes off the
Ford assembly line.
(HULTON ARCHIVE)

Thomas EDISON, Ford organized the Ford Motor Company in 1903. He started the development of the Model T car in 1908 and managed to reduce the price to within the reach of almost everyone. The car brought fame and fortune to the company, which in turn shared its profits with employees. To avoid stockholders' complaints about profit sharing, Ford bought them all out. From 1919 to 1956 the Ford family had sole control of the company. In 1932 Ford developed the V-8 engine.

Ford paid expenses for 150 people for a "peace trip" to Europe in 1915, but the trip ended in failure. While opposed to the entry of the U.S. into WORLD WAR I and WORLD WAR II, Ford quickly made his plants available for the manufacture of war materials. The Willow Run, Michigan, plant was the largest aircraft assembly plant in the world; during World War II it manufactured B-24 bombers until hostilities ceased.

Ford established Greenfield Village and the Ford Museum in Dearborn, Michigan. With his son Edsel FORD he established the FORD FOUNDATION. He passed on the presidency of the company to Edsel in 1919 and then resumed the office when Edsel died in 1943. In 1945 he once again relinquished the company presidency, to Edsel's son Henry FORD II.

Ford, Henry, II (*1917–1987*) Grandson of Henry FORD, the younger Ford was named president of Ford Motor Company in 1945 at the age of 28. Unlike his grandfather, who was an autocratic manager and foe of unionism,

Ford developed a flexible policy toward unions. He also initiated a sweeping reform of the administrative structure of the company to modernize the firm's inefficient managerial system and production techniques. In 1960 he became chairman and chief executive officer of the corporation. He resigned as chairman in 1979.

Ford, John (**Sean Aloysius O'Feeney**) (*1895–1973*) American film director best known for his westerns and Americana films. Ford was one of the screen's greatest lyric poets and a master of the offhand gesture and the fugitive moment. He was born in Cape Elizabeth, Maine. In 1913 he joined his older brother in HOLLYWOOD and was soon making films of his own. His first major project was a western, *Straight Shooting* (1917), whose central character and specific imagery anticipate his later, fully mature works, especially *The Searchers* (1956). During WORLD WAR II Ford headed a film unit for the OSS and made such classic documentaries as *The Battle of Midway* (1942). In 1947 he formed his own production company, Argosy Productions, for which he made some of his best-known westerns between 1947 and 1950.

Over the course of 60 years and 112 films, Ford remained remarkably consistent. Whether chronicling America's Manifest Destiny (*The Iron Horse* [1924], *Wagonmaster* [1950]) or his own Irish heritage (*The Informer* [1935] and *The Quiet Man* [1952]), Ford's big subject is the institution of the family. His wagon trains, coal miners, cavalry, "Okies," West Point cadets,

air mail pilots and homesteaders are all different kinds of family under threat of dissolution and change. Ford celebrates their tradition and laments their passing. Despite his brusque manner and frequent fights with studio heads and film crews, Ford earned several ACADEMY AWARDS (*The Informer; The Grapes of Wrath* [1939]; *How Green Was My Valley* [1941]; and *The Quiet Man*) along with the loyalty of friends like John WAYNE and Maureen O'Hara. In 1939–41 alone, he directed seven masterpieces: *Drums Along the Mohawk, Stagecoach, The Grapes of Wrath, Young Mr. Lincoln, The Long Voyage Home, Tobacco Road* and *How Green Was My Valley*—a feat unequaled by any other American filmmaker. Describing Ford's essential genius, Orson WELLES remarked "He knows what the earth is made of."

Ford Foundation World's wealthiest philanthropic organization, established by Henry FORD and his son Edsel FORD. The organization seeks to promote human welfare through grants for educational purposes. In its early years the foundation served only the state of Michigan, but in 1950 it became national. The foundation has awarded or pledged nearly $4.8 billion since its establishment in 1936. The money has gone to 95 countries outside the U.S. and to 7,100 organizations within the U.S. Foundation money supports programs in the fields of education and research, the arts, national and international affairs, communications, resources and environment. Foundation money helped establish the Public Broadcasting Service.

Ford Peace Ship Vessel used by Henry FORD on his peace mission to Europe. On December 4, 1915, Ford and 150 men and women left New York City on a ship privately chartered by the auto pioneer. Ford's object was to organize a conference of peace advocates who would then attempt to influence WORLD WAR I's warring governments to come to terms early. Ford returned home after reaching Christiania (Oslo), Norway, but the rest of the mission continued on through Sweden, Denmark, Germany and the Netherlands. This peace mission was not sponsored by the U.S. government, and despite the best intentions, no peace was achieved.

Ford Trimotor Airplane developed under the auspices of Henry FORD. Generally remembered for his role in the development of the automobile, Ford also did a great deal to promote the aircraft industry. With W. B. Stout he developed the famous Trimotor plane based on Stout's all-metal airplane, which Ford bought in 1925. He developed the single-engine plane into a plane of three engines, still all-metal. The Trimotor had a great influence on the development of the commercial air travel industry.

Foreman, Carl (1914–1984) American film producer and screenwriter. In 1951 Foreman appeared before the HOUSE UN-AMERICAN ACTIVITIES COMMITTEE (HUAC) investigating alleged communist influence in HOLLYWOOD. He was labeled an "uncooperative witness" and later blacklisted. Unable to find work, Foreman moved to London, where he continued to write film scripts under a pseudonym. His script for *High Noon* (1952) was nominated for an ACADEMY AWARD, as were his scripts for *Champion* (1949), *The Men* (1950), *The Guns of Navarone* (1961) and *Young Winston* (1972). Foreman also coauthored the Academy Award–winning screenplay for David LEAN's *The Bridge on the River Kwai* (1958), but as a blacklisted writer working under a pseudonym he was unable to claim the award.

Foreman, George (1949–) American boxer. Foreman came to world attention as the flag-waving Olympic heavyweight champion during the politically fraught 1968 OLYMPIC GAMES. His professional career included 40 consecutive victories, culminating in an upset victory over Joe FRAZIER for the heavyweight crown in 1973. Foreman lost the title the following year to Muhammad ALI in the "rumble in the jungle" at Kinshasha, Zaire. Foreman retired in 1977 with a 46-2 record and became a preacher but, amazingly, hit the comeback trail in 1990. Initially, he fought unknowns before small crowds, but he earned his way back to the top and fought Evander Holyfield for the heavyweight championship 18 years after he first won the crown. Foreman's late-blooming wit and self-deprecating humor, unusual in the world of boxing, made him a popular favorite, but he was defeated by Holyfield in a unanimous

decision. Many considered the 42-year-old Foreman's going the distance with Holyfield a victory in itself. In 1994 Foreman regained the IBF and WBA heavyweight titles when he knocked out Michael Moorer in the 10th round. Foreman retired from the ring in 1997 after a controversial loss. After his retirement from boxing, Foreman reinvented himself by marketing a line of barbecue grills that earned him much more money than he had ever made in boxing.

Foreman, Percy (1902–1988) American trial attorney who compiled a remarkable record in defending accused murderers. Foreman was known for his ability to save convicted murderers from the gallows. He is perhaps best remembered for his unsuccessful defense of James Earl Ray, the man who allegedly shot CIVIL RIGHTS MOVEMENT leader Martin Luther KING Jr. Following Foreman's advice, Ray pleaded guilty but later appealed, arguing unsuccessfully that he had been misled about the plea.

Forester, Cecil Scott (1899–1966) American novelist and screenwriter. Forester was born in Cairo, Egypt, and studied medicine. He began his literary career writing the biographies *Napoleon and His Court* (1924) and *Josephine, Napoleon's Empress* (1925). He brought his knowledge to bear on his popular series of historical novels about Horatio Hornblower, a fictional British sailor in the Napoleonic Wars. These books include *Beat to Quarters* (1937), *Lieutenant Hornblower* (1952) and *Hornblower and the Atropos* (1953). Forester worked intermittently as a screenwriter, often adapting his own fiction for the screen, notably in *The African Queen* (1935, filmed 1951) and *Captain Horatio Hornblower,* an adaptation of the first three Hornblower novels filmed in 1951.

Formalists Name given to Soviet literary critics belonging to the Opoyaz group (Society for the Study of Poetic Language). Leading Formalist critics include V. Shklovskiy, B. Eykhenbaum and R. Jakobson. The Formalists issued their manifesto, a collection of essays entitled *Poetika*, in 1919. For the Formalists, art was mainly a collection of devices and techniques; attention was paid to style rather than to ideas

expressed or the "message" conveyed. A typical work of Formalist criticism is Shklovskiy's essay "The Plot as a Phenomenon of Style." The extremists amongst the Formalists identified the study of literature with that of linguistics and were interested primarily in the phonetic qualities of poetry; Osip Brik, for instance, produced a study of the phonetic structure of Pushkin's verse. The more moderate Formalists, the "Petersburg Group," shared a keen interest in the way in which historical processes have affected literature. The school as a whole was suppressed in 1930.

Forman, Miloš (1932–) Czech-born film director. Forman, who was left an orphan by the Nazis during WORLD WAR II, went on to become the most prominent Czech director of his generation. He studied at the Prague film school. His first feature, *Talent Show* (1963), was a fictional story constructed out of various documentary film clips. *Loves of a Blonde* (1965) and *The Fireman's Ball* (1967), which were widely shown in the West during the loosened political atmosphere of the PRAGUE SPRING, established Forman's international reputation. Following increased Soviet artistic repression, Forman immigrated to America in the 1970s. His highly successful Hollywood-based films include *One Flew Over The Cuckoo's Nest* (1975), *Hair* (1979), *Ragtime* (1980) and *Amadeus* (1985), which won the ACADEMY AWARD for best picture. Forman continued to direct dramatic films throughout the 1990s, such as *The People vs. Larry Flint* (1996) and *Man on the Moon* (1999).

Forrestal, James Vincent (1892–1949) American government official. Born in Beacon, New York, he attended Princeton, was an aviator in WORLD WAR I and became an investment banker during the 1920s. A supporter of President Franklin D. ROOSEVELT's program to regulate the stock market, he helped to draft the Securities and Exchange Act (1933) and entered government service as an administrative assistant to the president. He served as undersecretary of the navy (1940–44) and secretary of the navy (1944–47). With the merger of the War and Navy Departments into the Department of Defense in 1947, he was named the nation's first secretary of defense by President Harry S TRUMAN. Adamantly opposed to COMMUNISM, Forrestal was highly suspicious of post–World War II expansionism by the USSR and repeatedly warned both Roosevelt and Truman. He later attempted to end interservice squabbling by members of the military and to raise Defense Department appropriations in order to resist any possible Soviet aggression. Forrestal resigned in 1949 after policy disputes with Truman and the deterioration of his own health. Suffering from paranoia and severe depression, he was hospitalized and committed suicide two months later.

Forrester, Maureen *(1930–)* Canadian contralto. Born in Montreal, Forrester studied voice and made her debut there in 1953. Debuts in Europe (1955) and the U.S. (1956) followed. the *New York Times* called her voice "darkly resonant . . . a superb voice of generous compass and volume." Her international career has included recitals at the EDINBURGH FESTIVAL and the Casals Festival in Puerto Rico, solo engagements with symphony orchestras, such as the New York Philharmonic, and opera roles with major companies. She is especially known for her interpretations of the works of MAHLER and Handel and has performed extensively in her native Canada. In 2000 Forrester received the Ruby Mercer Opera Award, the highest honor in Canadian opera.

Forssmann, Werner Theodor Otto *(1904–1979)* German surgeon and urologist. Forssmann was educated at the University of Berlin, where he qualified as a physician in 1929. He then worked in the 1930s as a surgeon in various German hospitals. After the war he practiced as a urologist at Bad Kreuznach from 1950 until 1958, when he moved to Düsseldorf as head of surgery at the Evangelical Hospital. In 1929 Forssmann introduced the procedure of cardiac catheterization into medicine. He was struck by the danger inherent in the direct injection of drugs into the heart (frequently demanded in an emergency). He proposed introducing a catheter through the venous system from a vein in the elbow directly into the right atrium of the heart. Drugs could then be introduced through this.

After practice on cadavers and an unsuccessful attempt on himself made with the aid of a nervous colleague, Forssmann decided to do the whole thing himself. He consequently introduced a 26.5-inch catheter for its entire length, walked up several flights of stairs to the X-ray department and calmly confirmed that the tip of the catheter had in fact reached his heart. There had been no pain or discomfort. Further development was inhibited by criticism from the medical profession, which assumed that the method must be dangerous. Consequently it was left to André COURNAND and Dickinson Richards to develop the technique into a routine clinical tool in the 1940s; for this work they shared the NOBEL PRIZE in physiology or medicine with Forssmann in 1956.

Forster, Edward Morgan *(1879–1970)* British novelist and critic. Born in London, E. M. Forster was named for his father, an architect, who died a year after Forster's birth. Forster was educated at Tonbridge school, which he detested, and at King's College, Cambridge, where he thrived under the influence of G. E. MOORE and Goldsworthy Lowes Dickinson, whose biography Forster wrote in 1934. In 1901 Forster was elected to the Apostles, the Cambridge intellectual society, and through his associations there later came in contact with the BLOOMSBURY GROUP. After Cambridge, he traveled in Italy and Greece and drew on these experiences in his early short stories and novels. In 1903 he began writing for the *Independent Review*, where he published his first short story in 1904. His first novel, *Where Angels Fear to Tread* (1905), satirized English tourists and established one of Forster's major themes—the inhibition of the English as contrasted with the sensuality and openness of other cultures. *The Longest Journey* (1907), *A Room with a View* (1908, filmed 1986) and *Howards End* (1910, filmed 1992) followed, establishing him as an important modern novelist (see MODERNISM).

In 1912 and 1913 Forster traveled in India, and in 1913 he visited E. Carpenter in England. Carpenter's influence was brought to bear in *Maurice*—a novel portraying homosexuality—which Forster circulated pri-

vately at the time. It was published posthumously in 1971 and later filmed (1987). Forster spent WORLD WAR I working for the Red Cross in Alexandria, Egypt. His last and most important novel, *A Passage to India* (1924, filmed 1984), begun during the war, was highly critical of British colonialism; it also examined the ambiguous relationship between perception and reality. Some critics consider *A Passage to India* to be the most perfectly constructed English novel of the 20th century. Throughout his life, Forster, an outspoken liberal and humanist, fought censorship. He opposed the suppression of *The Well of Loneliness*, a novel about lesbianism by Marguerite Radclyffe Hall, and testified at the trial of the publishers of D. H. LAWRENCE's *Lady Chatterley's Lover*. He also gained some notoriety for saying that if he had to choose between his friends and his country, he would choose his friends.

Forsyte Saga, The Three novels and two "interludes" by John GALSWORTHY published in 1922. The novels are *A Man of Property* (1906), *In Chancery* (1920) and *To Let* (1921). The interludes consist of the two short stories "The Indian Summer of a Forsyte," which was originally published in the collection *Five Tales* (1918), and "The Awakening" (1920). The *Saga* follows five generations of the Forsytes, a quintessential upper-middle-class Edwardian family. The *Saga* satirizes the rigid conventionality of the Forsytes' class and remains immensely popular as a portrait of Edwardian England. It has also been deemed by some as middlebrow soap opera. Two more Forsyte trilogies followed; in 1967 BBC television dramatized the first six novels. Another television adaptation was produced in the early 2000s.

Fortas, Abe *(1910–1982)* Associate justice, U.S. Supreme Court (1965–69). Fortas is best remembered as President Lyndon B. JOHNSON's unsuccessful choice for chief justice and also for his later forced resignation from the Court. Fortas, a graduate of Southwestern College and Yale Law School, was a brilliant lawyer who, after a brief stint as a law professor at Yale, rose in federal posts at an early age. In 1946 Fortas started a Washington, D.C., law firm, later known as Arnold & Porter, and became wealthy representing large corporations. During this time he became a close associate of Senator Lyndon Johnson, who as president later appointed Fortas to the Supreme Court. In 1968, as Johnson was about to leave office, Earl WARREN, the presiding chief justice, retired. Johnson nominated Fortas as chief justice, but the nomination was attacked in the Senate because of Fortas's close ties to Johnson. Subsequently Fortas was forced to resign from the Court after it was disclosed that he had a financial relationship with a former client who was under federal investigation. He returned to private law practice.

Fortress Europe (German: Festung Europa) Term used by the Germans in WORLD WAR II to describe the alleged invulnerable status of Europe provided by a defensive "wall." After 1942, as German defeats on all fronts escalated, the Nazi PROPAGANDA machine maintained that Allied attempts could never shatter the impenetrable walls of Fortress Europe provided by German defensive fortifications. The walls proved to be largely a fantasy. Only a few strategic sites had truly effective defenses. Most important, Fortress Europe had no roof, allowing Allied air forces to batter key German targets from the air.

47 Workshop See George Pierce BAKER.

Fosse, Bob (Robert Louis Fosse) **(1927–1987)** American dancer, choreographer and director. Fosse became a major figure in Broadway musicals in the 1950s. He won a Tony award for the first Broadway show he choreographed, *Pajama Game* (1954). He won additional Tonys for, among other shows, *Damn Yankees* (1955), *Sweet Charity* (1966) and *Big Deal* (1986). In 1973 he won two Tony awards for *Pippin,* as well as an Oscar for *Cabaret* and an Emmy for a TV special with Liza Minnelli. In 1975 he had a massive heart attack, an experience on which he based the film *All That Jazz* (1979). He was working on a revival of *Sweet Charity* when he died of another heart attack.

Fossey, Dian **(1932–1985)** American naturalist. Fossey went to Africa in the 1960s to study the rare mountain gorilla in its central African habitat. She

established a research institute in Rwanda and campaigned to prevent the gorillas' extinction. Fossey was murdered in her cabin on December 26, 1985, possibly by poachers. Her life was dramatized in the film *Gorillas in the Mist* (1989), starring Sigourney Weaver.

Foster, Norman *(1935–)* British architect. Born in Manchester, England, Foster developed an early interest in architecture when he began to study the works of the American architect Frank Lloyd WRIGHT and the French design theoretician LE CORBUSIER. Although greatly interested in the forms of Wright and the spatial theories of Le Corbusier, Foster left school in 1951 to work at the Manchester City Treasury. After military service in the Royal Air Force, he returned to his study of architecture by enrolling in the Manchester University School of Architecture and City Planning.

Graduating in 1961, Foster won a fellowship that allowed him to receive his master's degree in architecture at Yale University. While studying in the U.S. he encountered fellow Briton Richard Rogers, who shared Foster's passion for Wright's architectural style. They often traveled together to see first-hand many of Wright's buildings. When Fosters and Rogers returned to the United Kingdom in 1965 they formed Team 4, a design firm. The first building they designed, the Reliance Controls electronics factory in Swindon, England, demonstrated their willingness to develop a more modern style and use of space. Two years after his return to Britain Foster left Team 4 and created his own architectural firm, Foster and Partners. Building on his earlier work, Foster cultivated a style that maximized the entry of natural light through glass supported along a steel skeleton and minimized the use of concrete. In 1974 Foster incorporated these elements into his design of the Willis Faber and Dumas Building in Ipswich, England. Its ubiquitous use of glass, employment of escalators (rather than the more cloistered elevators) and roof-level gardens won him much acclaim. These achievements resulted in the offer of multiple commissions to construct the Sainsbury Centre for the Visual Arts in Norwich, the Hong Kong and Shanghai Bank in Hong Kong, the Stansted Airport in

Essex and the new Reichstag headquarters in Berlin. The last of these buildings also expressed Foster's appreciation for the environment, as its electrical needs were completely provided through the use of vegetable oil. For his innovative designs Foster received the Pritzker Prize in Architecture in 1999, the highest honor available in the architectural world. His commercial office tower for the Swiss Re Company, known as "The Gherkin," won the 2004 RIBA Stirling Prize for the best new building.

Foucault, Michel *(1926–1984)* French philosopher, psychologist and social critic. He was one of the most learned and versatile French thinkers of the postwar era. He studied at the Sorbonne, earning degrees in philosophy and psychology, and went on to further graduate work in psychopathology at the University of Paris. During his subsequent teaching career, Foucault lectured at universities throughout Europe. Strongly influenced both by Marxism and by STRUCTURALISM (the theory that comparative cultural analyses should focus on the overall structures of information and belief), Foucault devoted many of his works to probing the psychological and economic assumptions that prevailed in France and other nations throughout history. His major works include *Madness and Civilization* (1961), *The Order of Things: An Archaeology of the Human Sciences* (1966) and the three-volume *The History of Sex* (1976–84).

Fouche, Jacobus Johannes "Jim" *(1898–1980)* President of South Africa (1968–75). Fouche was first elected to the South African Parliament in 1941 as a member of the National Party. He served as defense minister from 1959 to 1966, during which time the country cut its ties to Britain and became an independent republic (1961). He was the republic's second president.

Fournier, Pierre *(1906–1986)* French cellist. Fournier's elegant and subdued manner of playing typified French musical style. His repertoire ranged from the unaccompanied sonatas of Bach to music written for him by such 20th-century composers as Bohuslav MARTINU and Francis POULENC. As much concerned with chamber music as with solo performance, he succeeded

Pablo CASALS in the famous trio whose other members were violinists Jacques THIBAUD and pianist Alfred CORTOT.

Four Quartets Four interrelated poems by T. S. ELIOT, published as a complete book in 1944. The four poems are "Burnt Norton" (1941), "East Coker" (1940), "The Dry Salvages" (1941) and "Little Gidding" (1942). Regarded by many critics as the crowning masterpiece of Eliot's poetic career, these symmetrical meditations on philosophical and religious subjects reflect Eliot's view of history, time and the nature of human experience. Originally conceived as a long poem loosely based on a scheme of the four seasons and four elements, it also contains autobiographical elements. It combines lyric, dramatic and narrative styles, successfully weaving its themes into an intricate formal pattern akin to that of the musical string quartet. *Four Quartets* is at once public, abstract, elegiac and optimistic.

Fourteen Points Peace program formulated by U.S. president Woodrow WILSON and presented by him to a joint session of Congress on January 8, 1918. Through this idealistic yet practical plan, Wilson established himself as moral leader of the WORLD WAR I Allies and hoped to appeal to a wide variety of those involved. These included the more liberal forces in the Central Powers, the Allies, the people of the U.S. and the newly emerged Bolshevik government in Russia. The first five points were general and included the following: (1) rejection of secret diplomacy (the famous "open covenants openly arrived at"), (2) freedom of the seas, (3) removal of economic barriers to international trade to the greatest degree possible, (4) arms reduction as low as demands for domestic safety would permit and (5) fair adjustment of colonial claims taking into consideration self-determination and other factors. The next eight points concerned specific territorial issues. Point 14 called for the formation of an association of nations to provide for the political independence of each. Although many of these points were abrogated or compromised at the PARIS PEACE CONFERENCE (1919–20), the spirit of the Fourteen Points was, to some degree, maintained in the final settlement.

Moreover, point 14 formed the basis for the establishment of the LEAGUE OF NATIONS.

Fowler, Alfred *(1868–1940)* British astrophysicist. Born in Bradford, Fowler attended the Normal School of Science (later the Royal College of Science). He joined the Solar Physics Observatory, London, becoming a professor of astrophysics in 1915. A cofounder of the International Astronomical Union (1919), he was its general secretary until 1925. Fowler was a research professor at the Royal Society from 1923 to 1934. His particular field of study was solar and stellar spectroscopy, and he was especially interested in spectrographic analysis, duplicating the light emissions of the Sun and other stars in the laboratory. Among his discoveries were the presence of magnesium hydride in sunspots and carbon monoxide in comets' tails. Fowler was also active in the spectrographic analysis of atomic structure.

Fowler, William Alfred *(1911–1995)* American astrophysicist. Born in Pittsburgh, Pennsylvania, Fowler attended Ohio State University and the California Institute of Technology, where he served as a professor of physics since 1946. Fowler's work mainly involved nuclear spectroscopy and nuclear physics, concentrating on the nature of energy-producing nuclear reactions in the immensely hot core of stars and the chemical elements synthesized thereby. His investigations in this area are outlined in a work cowritten by Fowler and Fred HOYLE entitled *Nucleosynthesis in Massive Stars and Supernovae* (1965). After the mid-1960s, Fowler's inquiries centered on fundamental questions that bear on the age and future of the universe, such as the amount of the elements of helium and deuterium present in the universe.

Fowles, John Robert *(1926–2005)* British novelist. Fowles was educated at Bedford School and New College, Oxford. He achieved recognition with his first novel, *The Collector* (1963, filmed 1965), a psychological thriller about a man who begins to collect human "specimens." Fowles experimented in his writing with varied styles and themes. *The Magus* (1966, revised 1977) bears traces of MAGIC REALISM; *Daniel Martin* (1977), of an ex-

perimental naturalism. His other works include *The French Lieutenant's Woman* (1969, filmed 1981 with screenplay by Harold PINTER), *Mantissa* (1982), the nonfiction books *The Tree* (1979) and *The Enigma of Stonehenge* (1980), and *Wormholes,* a book of essays and reviews (1998).

Fox, Harold Munro *(1889–1967)* British zoologist. Born in London, Fox was educated at Cambridge University, where he was a fellow from 1920 to 1928. He served as professor of zoology at Birmingham University from 1928 to 1941 and at Bedford College from 1941 until his retirement in 1954. Fox's earlier experiments concerned siphon growth in the sea squirt (*Ciona intestinalis*). His best-known work involved investigations of invertebrate blood pigments, with emphasis on research into the relationship of water-borne oxygen and the synthesis of hemoglobin in the water flea (*Daphnia*) as it bears on the relative red or clear coloration of that tiny crustacean.

Fox, John *(1907–1984)* American newspaper publisher. Fox was best known as a leading crusader against COMMUNISM during the 1950s. With a fortune he amassed as a securities broker, he purchased the *Boston Post* (1952), which became a forum for his views. The paper failed in 1956. In 1958, testifying before a congressional committee, Fox accused President EISENHOWER's chief aide Sherman ADAMS of financial misconduct. Fox's testimony was not substantiated, but other testimony eventually led to Adams's resignation. In the 1960s, after losing his fortune, Fox became a JAZZ pianist in Boston's waterfront bars.

Fox, Sidney Walter *(1912–1998)* American biochemist. Born in Los Angeles, Fox attended the University of California and the California Institute of Technology. He held brief teaching posts at Berkeley and the University of Michigan but spent most of his early career as professor of biochemistry at Iowa State University (1947–54) and professor of chemistry at Florida State University (1954–64). In 1964 he became director of the Institute of Molecular and Cellular Evolution at the University of Miami. Fox's researches led him to posit answers to questions involving the origin of life. From experiments (1958) that produced proteinlike amino acid polymers from the application of heat and the production of tiny spheres resembling bacteria from the cooling of these so-called protenoids, he concluded that proteins were the first elements of life on Earth.

Fox, Terry *(1958–1981)* Canadian popular hero. In 1977 Fox lost a leg to cancer. In 1980, fitted with an artificial limb, he attempted to run across Canada from coast to coast to raise money for cancer research and to show that people with cancer could still live active lives. His well-publicized run gained him the admiration of millions of people throughout Canada and the U.S. and raised more than $20 million. Fox's marathon was cut short at the halfway point when he was struck with lung cancer, and he died soon thereafter at the age of 22. His run was the subject of a TV movie.

Fox, Uffa *(1898–1972)* British designer of sailing yachts, better known (at least in England) as a sailor and frequent member of the crew of Prince Philip when he sailed in races. Fox was the designer of exceptionally fast racing dinghies and keelboats such as *Avenger* of 1928 and the racing class known as Flying Fifteen. It was *Coweslip* of this class, owned by Prince Philip, that brought special fame to Fox, leading to his reputation as a writer, lecturer and broadcaster and making him something of a celebrity.

Fox Quesada, Vicente *(1942–)* President of Mexico (2000–06). Born in Mexico City into a family with Mexican (his father), Spanish (his mother) and Irish-American roots (his paternal grandfather), Fox obtained a position in the Coca-Cola Company after graduating from college and began working on improving the soft-drink company's performance in Mexico. His success in this endeavor led to a series of promotions until he became president of Coca-Cola's Mexican and Latin American division. In the 1980s Fox left Coca-Cola and formed his own company, Grupo Fox, which produced shoes and agricultural products.

In 1988 Fox joined the National Action Party (PAN) and was elected to the

Mexican president Vicente Fox (EMBASSY OF MEXICO)

Chamber of Deputies, Mexico's lower legislative house. In 1995 Fox was elected governor of the state of Guanajuato by a sizable margin. As governor he encouraged foreign investment in his state, particularly American firms eager to set up shop in MEXICO with its low labor costs under the newly instituted NORTH AMERICAN FREE TRADE AGREEMENT (NAFTA). In 1999 Fox resigned as governor of Guanajuato and began to mount a presidential campaign under the PAN banner. Partly as a result of allegations that former president Carlos SALINAS DE GORTARI of the ruling Institutional Revolutionary Party (PRI) and his family had embezzled millions from the government and partly because of Fox's impressive record as governor, he defeated the PRI candidate, Francisco Labastida Ochoa, to become the first non-PRI president of Mexico since the 1920s.

The Fox presidency was marked by several problems, including deteriorating relations with the U.S. caused by disagreements over immigration and the U.S.-led military intervention in Iraq in 2003. However, President Fox won a significant victory in January 2004 when President Bush proposed a major overhaul of the U.S. immigration system to grant legal status to millions of undocumented workers in the U.S., most of whom are Mexican citizens.

Foxx, Jimmie (James Emory Foxx) *(1907–1967)* American baseball player. Foxx was one of baseball's greatest hit-

ters, driving in over 100 runs for 13 seasons. Known for his power at the plate, he led major league batters in all three categories—average, home runs and runs batted in—in his best year, 1932. As a fielder, he was known for his skill at first base, although he also played both sides of the battery as pitcher and catcher. Foxx began his career with Connie MACK's Athletics and later played for the Red Sox and the Cubs. He made a comeback during the war years and pitched nine games in 1945. His lifetime batting average was .325, and at the end of his career was only second to Babe Ruth on the all-time home run list with 534. Known for his affability and generosity, Foxx was named to the Baseball Hall of Fame in 1951.

Foyt, A. J. *(1935–)* American race car driver. Foyt is considered one of the outstanding race car drivers of the 20th century; he is the only driver to win all three crown jewels of motorsports: the Indianapolis 500, the Daytona 500 and the 24 Hours of Le Mans. In his career he has driven in more Indianapolis 500 races than any other driver (35 consecutive years, beginning in 1959) and shares the record of four Indianapolis 500 victories (1961, 1964, 1967 and 1977) with Rick Mears and Al Unser Sr. In 2000 Foyt formed his own full-time NASCAR Winston Cup team in Mooresville, North Carolina.

Fracci, Carla *(1936–)* Italian ballerina. Especially noted for such roles as Giselle and Juliet in the romantic ballets, Fracci is the first Italian ballerina of the 20th century to garner an international reputation. She joined the La Scala Ballet Company in Milan in 1954, becoming prima ballerina in 1958, and appeared as a guest artist with numerous other companies, most notably AMERICAN BALLET THEATRE. In 1969 she danced opposite Erik BRUHN in the film version of *Giselle,* and her television film, *Serata Con C.F.,* won the Golden Rose of Montreux Award in 1973. In addition, she appeared in several ballets, such as *The Seagull* (1968) and *The Stone Flower* (1973), produced by her husband—theater director Beppe Menegatti—and choreographed by Loris Gai. Fracci has overseen the ballet theaters of Naples (1990–91) and Verona (1995–97) and the Balletto dell'Opera in Rome (1997–).

Fraenkel-Conrat, Heinz L. *(1910–1999)* German-American biochemist. Trained as a physician at the University of Breslau, he left Germany in 1934 to study at the University of Edinburgh, where he obtained a Ph.D. in 1936. He immigrated to the U.S., became a citizen in 1941 and joined the University of California, Berkeley in 1951 as professor of virology and of molecular biology. His extensive work on the tobacco mosaic virus (TMV) proved that viral RNA, like DNA, can be the transmitter of genetic information. Working with Wendell Stanley, he also outlined the complete 158 amino acid–long chain of the TMV protein. He also did significant research on snake neurotoxins and wrote several virology texts.

Frame, Janet (Janet Paterson Frame Clutha) *(1924–2004)* New Zealand novelist and poet. Frame was born in Dunedin, New Zealand. Her first novel was *Owls Do Cry* (1957), followed by the more acclaimed *Faces in the Water* (1961), which, with its pessimistic and morbid tone, is characteristic of Frame's work. She draws on her own experiences with mental illness and hospitalization in that and subsequent works, such as *A State of Siege* (1966), *Intensive Care* (1970) and *The Carpathians* (1988). Frame's work is also noted for its intelligent portrayal of New Zealand geography. Her poetic works include *The Pocket Mirror* (1967), and she also wrote the autobiographies *An Angel at My Table* (1984, filmed in 1991) and *The Envoy from Mirror City* (1985).

France Western European country, officially called the French Republic, bordered by the English Channel to the north; GERMANY, SWITZERLAND and ITALY to the east; the Mediterranean Sea and SPAIN to the south, and the Atlantic Ocean to the west. At the turn of the century, France was strong and prosperous, with many colonies in Africa and Asia, although engaged in territorial disputes with Germany. At the outbreak of WORLD WAR I Germany invaded France, which suffered huge losses of life and wealth during the war. In 1919 France and Germany signed the Treaty of VERSAILLES, restoring to France the provinces of Alsace and Lorraine, which had been seized by Germany in 1871. Following the

war, the Third Republic government was beset by economic strife and instability, and it directed its foreign policy toward weakening Germany and exacting postwar reparations from it. Adolf HITLER's Nazi Party rose to power, however, and France declared war on Germany after the Nazis invaded POLAND in 1939. In 1940 Germany, later joined by Italy, invaded and defeated France. The country was subsequently divided temporarily, with the northern part occupied by Germany and the south governed by Marshal Henri Philippe PÉTAIN, a French war hero, in VICHY. General Charles de GAULLE formed the FREE FRENCH RESISTANCE movement to continue to fight the Germans. In 1944 Allied forces launched the Invasion of NORMANDY on June 6, arriving in Paris

on August 25 and effectively liberating France from German rule. A provisional government was established in Paris led by de Gaulle. In 1946 the constitution was revised to create the Fourth Republic, which changed the French colonial empire to the French Union and strengthened the National Assembly. De Gaulle resigned because it did not provide enough executive power. In a 1947 election—the first in which French women voted—Vincent AURIOL was elected president.

In 1946 revolution had begun in French INDOCHINA, which was later divided into CAMBODIA, LAOS and North and South VIETNAM. After much loss of life, the French withdrew from Indochina in 1954. That same year the colony of ALGERIA began struggling for

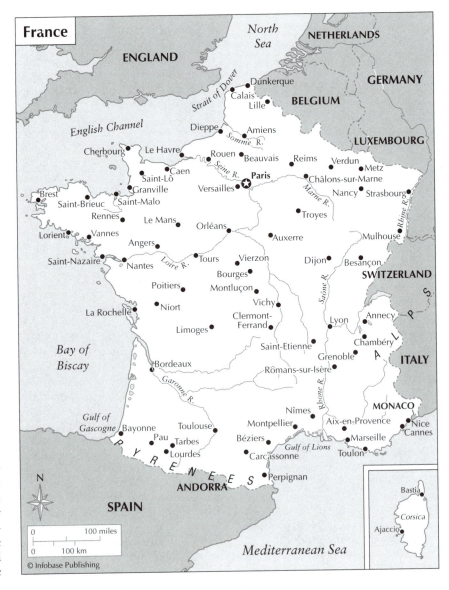

FRANCE

1914–18 France suffers nearly 1.4 million dead and 4.25 million wounded in World War I.

1919 Alsace-Lorraine returned to France under Treaty of Versailles.

1939 France declares war on Germany after German invasion of Poland; start of World War II.

1940 Marshal Henri Philippe Pétain signs armistice with Germany; Germans occupy 60% of France; collaborationist Vichy government established in unoccupied France; General Charles de Gaulle forms alternative "Free French" government in London.

1942 Germany occupies the rest of France.

1944 Allies liberate Paris on August 25.

1946 (Oct. 13) Constitution of France's Fourth Republic approved, allowing French colonies varying degrees of autonomy; de Gaulle serves as provisional president.

1949 France becomes founding member of NATO.

1951 France leads in formation of European Coal and Steel Community, forerunner of European Economic Community (EEC).

1954 France suffers defeat at Dien Bien Phu and is forced to withdraw from Indochina.

1957 France signs Treaty of Rome establishing the European Economic Community.

1958 Fifth Republic established, with de Gaulle as first president.

1960 France tests its first atomic bomb.

1962 Algerian independence granted despite terrorist campaign by right-wing French soldiers.

1963 De Gaulle vetoes Britain's request to enter the Common Market.

1965 France signs the Treaty of Brussels, setting up the European Community (later the European Nation).

1966 France withdraws from NATO; its headquarters are moved to Brussels.

1969 Georges Pompidou, a Gaullist, is elected president.

1974 Pompidou dies and Finance Minister Valéry Giscard d'Estaing is elected president.

1979 Giscard's administration is rocked by scandal when it is discovered that as finance minister in 1973 he received $250,000 in diamonds from Emperor Bokassa of the Central African Republic.

1981 François Mitterrand is elected the first socialist president of the Fifth Republic; later introduces economic austerity program.

1985 Greenpeace ship *Rainbow Warrior* sunk by French Frogmen on orders of the defense ministry; defense minister resigns and head of secret service is sacked.

1988 Mitterrand is reelected.

1989 Bicentennial celebration of the French Revolution commences on January 1 with balloonists taking to the air and actors reading the Declaration of the Rights of Man in major towns.

1991 French forces participate in Operation Desert Storm to oust Iraq from Kuwait during Persian Gulf War.

1995 Jacques Chirac succeeds Mitterrand as president.

2002 The euro replaces the franc as the national currency. Chirac is reelected president in a landslide victory against right-wing National Front leader Jean-Marie Le Pen.

2004 French voters reject the constitution for a European Union in a nationwide referendum.

2005 Immigrants riot in the northwest suburbs of Paris sparking violent protests nationwide.

2006 A new labor law leads to protest and mass demonstrations, forcing lawmakers to scrap the legislation.

independence. Hoping to retain Algeria and prevent revolutions in the colonies of MOROCCO and TUNISIA, France granted the latter two independence. The continuing war in Algeria, however, was a divisive issue that led many French military personnel and Algerian settlers to threaten rebellion if the war ceased and independence was granted. In 1958 de Gaulle returned as prime minister, and his government drafted the new constitution of the Fifth Republic, of which he became first president. This constitution granted extensive executive power. In spite of opposition from rebellious French soldiers, France granted Algeria its independence in 1962 (see O.A.S.).

Although allied with the Western nations during the COLD WAR, de Gaulle strove to maintain a policy independent from the U.S. and NATO. Many people, however, were becoming disillusioned by de Gaulle's government. In 1968 Parisian students began a violent protest (see PARIS STUDENT DEMONSTRATIONS), which was joined by workers across the country and threatened to turn into civil war. De Gaulle managed to avert a crisis but was compelled to resign in 1969. His nationalist policies were largely maintained by his successors: George POMPIDOU and Valéry GISCARD D'ESTAING.

In 1981 Socialist François MITTERRAND won a landslide victory over Giscard. Mitterrand's government nationalized some major industries and private banks. Mitterrand was reelected in 1986 and 1988. In 1985 *Rainbow Warrior,* a vessel of the Greenpeace environmental organization that was monitoring nuclear tests, was mined in Auckland Harbor, New Zealand, by the French secret service. Mitterrand later accepted responsibility for the event. France was a member of the UNITED NATIONS coalition and took part in the fighting against IRAQ during the PERSIAN GULF WAR (1990–91). In 1995 Jacques CHIRAC succeeded Mitterrand. He proved able to work with Socialists after appointing PSF leader Lionel Jospin prime minister in 1997. Chirac defeated Jospin and far-right politician Jean-Marie LE PEN in the 2002 presidential election. In the winter of 2002–03 Chirac antagonized the administration of U.S. president George W. BUSH by openly opposing the president's

plan to overthrow the Iraqi government of Saddam HUSSEIN without the approval of the UN Security Council. In 2004 French voters dealt the cause of European political unity a major setback by rejecting the proposed constitution of the EUROPEAN UNION in a referendum. In 2005 the suburbs of Paris were rocked by riots led by alienated North African and other immigrants that spread across France. In 2006 new demonstrations occurred over a new youth employment law, which was subsequently abandoned.

France, Anatole (Jacques Anatole François Thibault) (1844–1922)
French novelist and critic. The son of a book dealer, France was educated at the College Stanislas in Paris. France began his literary career writing a column, "La Vie Litteraire" (The literary life), for the newspaper *Le Temps.* His first work of fiction—two short novels, *Jocaste* (Jocasta) and *Le Chat maigre* (The famished cat)— was published in 1879. But it was *Le Crime de Sylvestre Bonnard* (1881) that brought him success, which he maintained with *La Rotisserie de la Reine* (1893) and *Les opinions de M. Jerome Coignard* (1893). These social satires introduce variations on a prototypical France character (the bemused, scholarly professor), and they captured the mood of the country at the time. France's reputation gained him entrée into the literary and social salon of Leontine Arman de Caillavet, for whom he later left his wife. France's work evidences his erudition and keen observation of French politics and society. Other important works include *Histoire contemporaire* (1897–1900), which consists of four novels, *L'Île de pingouine* (1908) and *Les Dieux ont soif* (1912). France was awarded the NOBEL PRIZE in literature in 1921.

France, Battle of (1940) France's
heavily fortified MAGINOT LINE afforded little security from GERMANY when, in June 1940, Nazi armies broke through north of the line as well as from Belgium into Brittany. A third force broke through at Champagne and attacked the line from the rear. Italy, having declared war on France (June 10, 1940), advanced from the south. The Allies had to retreat from eastern and central France, and on June 14 Paris fell without a fight, the French government

fleeing to Tours, then Bordeaux. On June 22, 1940, France accepted German terms for armistice; aged general Henri Philippe PÉTAIN became premier, assisted by Pierre LAVAL—a Nazi collaborator—and set up a French government at VICHY, while Germans occupied northern and eastern France. Thousands of French troops escaped to continue fighting, while others joined the RESISTANCE to continue the covert struggle within France.

Francis, David Rowland (1850–1927) U.S. statesman. Starting as a grain merchant, Francis was mayor of St. Louis, Missouri (1885–89), before becoming Democratic governor of the state (1889–93). Secretary of the interior (1896–97) under President Grover Cleveland, he gained a presidential proclamation that set aside millions of acres of forest reserves. In 1916 he was appointed ambassador to RUSSIA and remained at his post throughout the RUSSIAN REVOLUTION, trying to keep Russia in the war against Germany.

Francis, Thomas, Jr. (1900–1969)
American virologist. Born in Gas City, Indiana, he attended Allegheny College and Yale University, receiving an M.D. in 1925. He was a researcher at the Rockefeller Institute (1925–38) and professor of bacteriology at the New York University College of Medicine (1938–41) before becoming professor of epidemiology at the University of Michigan (1941–69). From the mid-1930s to the mid-1950s Francis worked on the epidemiology of the influenza virus, detecting a strain of the first-discovered type (1934) and an entirely new type (1940). He was also active in developing flu vaccines. Francis gained wide public attention in 1954, when he evaluated the newly developed SALK polio vaccine trial.

Franck, James (1882–1964) German-American physicist. Born in Hamburg, he studied at Heidelberg and Berlin, receiving his doctorate in 1906. In 1913 he began a collaboration with **Gustav Hertz,** examining the interaction of electrons and atoms. Their discovery of quantized energy transfer in these interactions led to their being awarded the 1925 NOBEL PRIZE in physics. After distinguished service in WORLD WAR I, Franck accepted the chair in experi-

mental physics at Göttingen but fled Germany after the rise of HITLER. After a year in Copenhagen, he immigrated to the U.S. (1935), where he became a professor of physics at Johns Hopkins University (1935–38) and professor of physical chemistry at the University of Chicago (1938–49). In the U.S. Franck primarily investigated the physical chemistry of photosynthesis. He worked on the MANHATTAN PROJECT during WORLD WAR II and was responsible for the *Franck Report,* in which he and several other outstanding scientists argued against the use of the newly developed atomic bomb without first demonstrating its devastating effect on an unpopulated island.

Franco (L'Okanga La Ndju Pene Luambo Makiadi) *(1939–1989)* Zairean jazz guitarist and band leader. During his lifetime he was one of Africa's most popular and influential musicians. He was noted for creating the soukous style, a fusion of Afro-Cuban rhumba music with JAZZ, gospel and African rhythms, and for lyrics that sometimes ridiculed Africa's ruling classes and offended the Zairean government. Following his death, however, Zairean president MOBUTU SESE SEKO declared an official four-day mourning period.

Franco, Francisco *(1892–1975)* Spanish general and head of the government of Spain. Born in El Ferrol in Galicia, Franco was a career army officer who became a brigadier general in 1926 at age 33. In 1934 he successfully suppressed a communist-led miner's revolt. The same year he was appointed chief of the Spanish army. In 1936, as governor of the Canary Islands, he led the antisocialist revolt that started the SPANISH CIVIL WAR. The Nationalists proclaimed him head of state, and by 1939 his regime, having won the civil war, received British and French diplomatic recognition. During World War II he led Spain on a fascist Italian model, under a single political party—the FALANGE. However, he maintained Spain's neutrality. After the war his regime received U.S. patronage but was opposed bitterly by intellectuals. In 1969 he nominated Prince JUAN CARLOS, grandson of ex-king ALFONSO XIII, to succeed him after his death. Franco resigned from the position of premier in 1973 but retained his functions as head of state until his death.

Frank, Anne *(1929–1945)* Jewish diarist of the HOLOCAUST. Her book, *The Diary of Anne Frank* (1947), which poignantly recounts the thoughts and experiences of a young Jewish girl living in hiding from the Nazis during WORLD WAR II, has been widely acknowledged as one of the spiritual classics of the 20th century. A best seller that has been published around the world, the *Diary* has also been successfully adapted to the Broadway stage (1956) and as a Hollywood film (1959). Frank, who fled with her family from Germany to Holland, went into hiding—along with her family and a few others—in a Dutch warehouse office from 1942 to 1944. In 1944 they were discovered by the Nazis. Frank died in the BERGEN-BELSEN CONCENTRATION CAMP. Her diary, which is most noteworthy for Frank's remarkably enduring faith in human nature, was discovered by her father after the war.

Frank, Leo See LYNCHING OF LEO FRANK.

Frankenheimer, John *(1930–2002)* American motion picture and television director. Frankenheimer was born in New York, served in the air force in the early 1950s and after his discharge joined other young men like Sidney LUMET at CBS to pursue a career in television. Quick, versatile and technically adept in the new medium, he directed a religious series, *Lamp unto My Feet;* an interview series with Edward R. MURROW, PERSON TO PERSON; and a variety show, *The Garry Moore Show.* His subsequent movies carry oh this eclecticism and virtuoso technique. His best-known works include *The Manchurian Candidate* (1962), a surreal tale of brainwashing and assassination; *Seven Days in May* (1963), a political thriller; and *Grand Prix* (1966), a Cinerama racing epic. Less familiar, but no less full of quirky surprises, are *The Train* (1965), a WORLD WAR II thriller about protecting art masterpieces from invading Nazis; *French Connection II* (1975), a sequel to the original; and *The Fourth War* (1990), an offbeat war movie that reflected the thaw in the COLD WAR tensions between East and West. *Seconds* (1966), arguably his finest, if most neglected film, nicely sums up his restless camera technique and nightmarish sense of mood and image. A man's search for lost youth and a new identity becomes an exercise in Kafkaesque horror—quite one of the scariest movies of the 1960s. Frankenheimer continued to direct films until his death, receiving an Emmy award for his direction of the television film *George Wallace* (1997). He also directed the motion picture *Reindeer Games* (2000).

Frankenstein *(1931)* Prototype of the American horror film. Mary Shelley's 1818 novel had been filmed as early as 1910 by Edison, in a silent version that ran a scant 10 minutes. In 1931 UNIVERSAL Studios, cashing in on its recent success with *Dracula,* brought in writer/director Robert Florey and its new star, Bela LUGOSI, to make the first TALKING PICTURE version. Unhappy with the project, the studio transferred them to another film (*Murders in the Rue Morgue* [1932]) and brought in another team: director James WHALE and newcomer Boris KARLOFF. The results were superior to the rather static *Dracula,* as for the first time we see the archetypal horror formula assuming shape: the "creation" sequence ("It's alive!"); the Old World atmosphere (via sets borrowed from Universal's ALL QUIET ON THE WESTERN FRONT); and the restless, torch-carrying locals storming the castle. Set designer

Spanish general and premier Francisco Franco. 1954
(LIBRARY OF CONGRESS, PRINTS AND PHOTOGRAPHS DIVISION)

Charles Hall twisted his interiors into the distorted shapes of German EXPRESSIONISM, Kenneth Strickfaden stitched the air with dazzling electrical effects and makeup ace Jack Pierce devised the effective Monster makeup (reportedly after consulting with surgeons and pathologists). Above all, director James Whale infused the proceedings with a certain diabolical humor that has worn well over the years. Not even the numerous sequels, including *Abbott and Costello Meet Frankenstein* (1948) and Mel BROOKS's satiric *Young Frankenstein* (1974), can take the dark bloom off this eldritch rose.

Frankenthaler, Helen (*1928– *) American painter. Born in New York City, she studied with a number of artists, notably Hans Hofmann and Jackson POLLOCK. Influenced by art critic Clement GREENBERG and such painters as Pollock, Willem DE KOONING and Arshile Gorky, Frankenthaler developed a lyrical color-field technique that involves staining and saturating the canvas with color. Lyrical in mood, her works include *Mountains and Sea* (1952, Metropolitan Museum of Art, New York City) and *Arden* (1961, Whitney Museum of American Art, New York City).

Frankfurter, Felix (*1882–1965*) Associate justice, U.S. Supreme Court (1939–62). Born in Austria, Frankfurter was raised in poverty in New York City's Lower East Side. He attended City University and Harvard Law School. After brief stints in pri-

Supreme Court associate justice Felix Frankfurter (LIBRARY OF CONGRESS, PRINTS AND PHOTOGRAPHS DIVISION)

vate practice, the U.S. Attorney's Office and the War Department, he returned to Harvard Law School as a professor for 25 years, interrupted by three years in various posts in Washington. Frankfurter was an active Zionist and also became involved in many controversial legal battles of the era, including the defense of SACCO AND VANZETTI. He was a founder of the AMERICAN CIVIL LIBERTIES UNION. He was also a close adviser of President Franklin D. ROOSEVELT, who appointed him to the Supreme Court in 1939 to replace Justice CARDOZO. Frankfurter generally supported NEW DEAL legislation. In later years he generally favored the doctrine of judicial restraint, which holds that the courts should not substitute their views for those of the elected legislatures.

Franklin, John Hope (*1915– *) U.S. educator and historian. With a Ph.D. from Harvard (1941), he taught on several college faculties before joining the Howard University staff in 1947. He was a Fulbright Scholar (1954) and a William Pitt Scholar (1962), both at Cambridge University. He became chairman of the history department at the University of Chicago in 1969. He was a trustee of the Chicago Symphony from 1976 to 1980. Considered one of the foremost historians of his time, he emphasized social, political and cultural history and biography in his writings and teachings. His writings include *From Slavery to Freedom: A History of Negro Americans* (1947), *The Militant South* (1956) and *The Emancipation Proclamation* (1963). He was named to the Oklahoma Hall of Fame in 1978. Franklin received a series of awards throughout the 1990s, including the Charles Frankel Prize for Contributions to the Humanities (1993), the Presidential Medal of Freedom (1995) and the NAACP's Spingarn Medal (1995). In 1995 the John Hope Franklin Research Center for African and African-American Documentation was established at Duke University (1995). In 1997 Franklin served as chairman of President Bill CLINTON's Initiative on Race, a presidential council established to examine race relations in the U.S.

Franklin, (Stella Maria Sarah) Miles (*1879–1954*) Australian nov-

elist. Franklin first realized success with *My Brilliant Career* (1901). Written when she was 16, the novel depicts pioneer life in the Australian bush through the eyes of the young heroine who longs to escape it. In her lifetime, she was best known for *All That Swagger* (1936), also about the desolation of life in the bush. *Some Everyday Folk and Dawn* (1909) deals with women's suffrage (see WOMEN'S MOVEMENT.) The filming of *My Brilliant Career* in 1980 led to a renewed interest in Franklin's work.

Franklin, Rosalind (*1920–1958*) British crystallographer and biophysicist. A graduate of Cambridge, Franklin worked for the British Coal Utilisation Research Associates from 1942 to 1947 and the Paris Laboratoire Centrale des Services Chimique from 1947 to 1950, when she returned to England. There she was a researcher at King's College (1951–53) and Birbeck College (1954–58). Franklin had an important part in the epoch-making discovery of the structure of DNA by James WATSON and Francis CRICK. Using X-ray diffraction photography, she showed that the DNA molecule's phosphates lay on its outside and provided information that indicated that DNA had a helical chain structure. Franklin's work and her alleged lack of cooperation with fellow-researcher Maurice Wilkins were described in Watson's book *The Double Helix* (1968). She also did important research on the structure of carbon and the tobacco mosaic virus.

Franz Ferdinand (*1863–1914*) Austrian archduke, after 1889 heir apparent to his uncle, Emperor Franz Joseph II. He was married to Sophie Chotek, a Czech countess. Because of her relatively low rank, their two sons were not granted the right of succession. On a trip to Sarajevo in 1914, he and his wife were assassinated by the Serbian nationalist Gavrilo Princip—provoking Austria's declaration of war against SERBIA. This event was the spark that erupted into the conflagration of WORLD WAR I.

Franz Joseph II (*1906–1989*) Prince of Liechtenstein. Becoming head of state of the small European principality in 1938, he oversaw LIECHTENSTEIN's development from a poor, rural country to a wealthy tax and banking haven with one of the world's highest per capita incomes. A keen sportsman, he served on the International Olympic Committee for more than 35 years. In 1984 he handed his executive powers over to his son, Crown Prince Hans Adam.

Franz Joseph Land (Russian: Zemlya Frantsa Josifa) Archipelago north of Novaya Zemlya in Russia, constituting the northern boundary of the Barents Sea. Found and named in 1873 by an Austrian expedition, Franz Joseph Land was scouted by several other polar expeditions including NANSEN's and has also been known as Fridtjof Nansen Land. Claimed by Russia in 1914, the archipelago was formally annexed in 1926 by the Soviet Union. The world's northernmost weather station is located here.

Fraser, James Earle *(1876–1953)* American sculptor. After studying art at the Art Institute of Chicago in 1894, Fraser moved to Paris to study at the École des Beaux-Arts. His most famous work, *The End of the Trail,* depicting an exhausted Indian on horseback, was completed in 1896. In 1898 he became the student-assistant of famed sculptor Augustus St. Gaudens. As an artist Fraser was the recipient of hundreds of awards from national and international organizations. Principal works of Fraser include a bust of Theodore ROOSEVELT on display in the U.S. Senate chamber; two heroic figures, *Justice* and *Law,* in front of the Supreme Court building; statues of Albert Gallatin and Alexander Hamilton for the Treasury Building (all in Washington, D.C.); the Buffalo nickel; and monuments to Thomas Edison for the Edison Institute in Dearborn, Michigan.

Fraser, Malcolm *(1930–   )* Prime minister of Australia (1975–83). A member of the Australian LIBERAL PARTY, Fraser was educated at Oxford University. Returning to Australia, he entered politics and was elected to the Australian House of Representatives in 1955. He held various cabinet posts from 1966 to 1971. Fraser succeeded Gough WHITLAM as prime minister in 1975, following a budget crisis that brought down Whitlam's LABOUR PARTY government, and formed a ruling coalition with the National Party. He gener-

ally followed conservative economic and foreign policies. He was defeated by the Labour Party, led by Robert HAWKE, in 1983. Throughout the 1990s Fraser served as an Australian goodwill ambassador, observing the Pakistan national elections of 1997 and obtaining the release of Australian humanitarian workers held in the former Yugoslavia in 1999.

Frasier American comedy television series (1993–2004). Originally conceived as a spin-off series from NBC's popular comedy, CHEERS, *Frasier* became a comic force in its own right. Starring Cheers alumnus Kelsey Grammer, the series focused on the arrival of Dr. Frasier Crane as he relocated from Boston to Seattle to escape his ex-wife, Lillith, and begin a new life. Frasier finds work as a radio psychiatrist and interacts with his brother and fellow psychiatrist Niles (David Hyde Pierce), their father, retired police detective Martin Crane (John Mahoney), his father's caretaker, Daphne Moon (Jane Leeves) and Roz Doyle (Peri Gilpin), a coworker of Frasier's at the radio station. The series won numerous Emmys.

Frazier, Joe *(1944–   )* American boxer, known as "Smokin' Joe." The world heavyweight champion from 1971 to 1973, Frazier was one of the most devastating fighters of his or any other time. He was discovered in Philadelphia by trainer Yank Durham, then worked his way up through the boxing ranks, taking on such opponents as Buster Mathis and Jerry Quarry, before defeating the champion Muhammad ALI in a 15-round unanimous decision at Madison Square Garden, New York, in 1971. Frazier lost his title to George FOREMAN two years later. In 1975 he again met Ali in one of the most vaunted fights of all time, the "thriller in Manila." Despite Frazier's superior power, Ali rallied to defeat him with a 15th-round TKO.

Frederick, Pauline *(1918–1990)* American radio and television news commentator. Frederick had her own news programs on three networks— ABC, NBC and National Public Radio—and served as NBC's UNITED NATIONS correspondent for 21 years. In 1976 she became the first woman to

moderate a presidential debate—the one between Gerald R. FORD and Jimmy CARTER.

Frederika *(1917–1981)* Queen of Greece (1947–64). Born in Germany, she was a member of an ancient German princely family. The strong-willed wife of King Paul, she intervened in Greek politics after her son King CONSTANTINE came to the throne in 1964; her activities helped pave the way for the overthrow of the monarchy in 1967. After GREECE was officially proclaimed a republic in 1973, she went into self-imposed exile.

Freedom of Information Act During the administration of President Richard NIXON, it was revealed that the federal government had systematically maintained files on American citizens suspected of being disloyal. Both the FBI and the CIA were involved in domestic surveillance of citizens. After the WATERGATE scandal and the end of the VIETNAM WAR, public opinion demanded access to these files. The 1976 Freedom of Information Act allows citizens and businesses to request copies of government records. Certain records are exempted, including those that touch on trade secrets of businesses and national security. Citizens can not only learn if federal agencies maintain any files pertaining to them but also receive copies of such files. This law has also been used successfully by scholars and researchers. The U.S. government and a number of states have "sunshine" or "open meeting" laws that require all governmental meetings to be announced in advance and open to the public. A "sunset law" is a provision— in any act that empowers a government body—requiring a government body to automatically go out of existence unless the legislature specifically votes to reinstate it. The act is intended to promote more efficient government by eliminating nonessential bodies and agencies. In 1996 President William Jefferson CLINTON signed an updated Freedom of Information Act to account for the recording of government information on computers, CDs and diskettes.

Freedom Party Conservative political party in Austria, headed by Jörg HAIDER, the governor of the Austrian state of Kärnten. The Freedom Party rose to international and national attention during Austria's 1999 elections for the legislature, the Nationalrat, when Haider and his party capitalized on concerns and anger among the Austrian working class by arguing that Austria's continued high immigration rate (primarily from Turkey) and its obligations to the EUROPEAN UNION (EU) would siphon off jobs from natural-born Austrian citizens. Haider also made public preelection comments praising aspects of the Nazi regime of Adolf HITLER but later retracted these statements and apologized for them. In October 1999 the Freedom Party tied the People's Party, a moderate-conservative political organization, with 52 seats in the Nationalrat. The two parties formed a coalition government in February 2000, in which Freedom Party members obtained ministerial posts. Haider, however, was not included in this coalition government. International pressure on Austria from several foreign governments and the EU prompted demands in Vienna for a change in the Freedom Party's leadership, forcing Haider's resignation as head of the party.

Free French Movement headed by General Charles de GAULLE during WORLD WAR II as an alternative to the collaborationist VICHY regime. After the fall of France in 1940 to the Nazis, de Gaulle headed RESISTANCE activities from exile in London, calling on his countrymen to resist the German occupation and organizing an army of French and colonial volunteers. By 1942 Free French troops numbered about 70,000 men, who participated in battles in Africa and in various naval engagements. After the Allied invasion of North Africa in 1942, a provisional Free French government was established in Algiers in 1943 (see NORTH AFRICAN CAMPAIGN). When Paris was liberated by Free French and other Allied forces in August 1944, the French government was moved to the capital. De Gaulle headed a provisional French government until the establishment of the Fourth Republic in 1946.

free jazz A term initially applied to the relatively open-ended improvisations of alto saxophonist Ornette COLEMAN and pianist Cecil Taylor. The term derived from Coleman's seminal recording, *Free Jazz* (1960), a sprawling, open-ended improvisation for two pianoless quartets that set the tone for the free jazz movement of the 1960s. Free jazz generally involves collective improvisation; also, although soloists often step forward, as in mainstream jazz, there is much more initiative and interaction among the others in the group. The abandonment of traditional song forms and harmonic structures associated with the mainstream is significant; in place of traditional sound ideals generally thought of as "beautiful" or "sonorous," avant-garde players, especially in the early years, incorporated wails, honks, shrieks and other "voice-like" sounds connoting anger and frustration. These emotive qualities were especially important to black American musicians who saw free jazz as a part of the larger CIVIL RIGHTS MOVEMENT and BLACK POWER movements of the 1960s. In Europe, free jazz provoked controversy among both musicians and critics, who attacked its "free" aspect as license for an essentially undisciplined, musically illiterate, "anything goes" approach. Nonetheless, free jazz remains, especially in Europe, an important alternative to more mainstream styles; it has also provided a significant repertoire of gestures and even attitudes that have been incorporated into the music of such contemporary jazz artists as guitarists John SCOFIELD, Pat Metheny and John Abercrombie.

Free Officers Army officers in EGYPT who overthrew King FAROUK in 1952.

free speech movement (*1964–1965*) The free speech movement refers to a series of student-led demonstrations conducted on the campus of the University of California at Berkeley (1964–65). The central issue giving rise to the demonstrations was the ban placed by the university administration, headed by President Clark Kerr, on speech related to off-campus political issues being conducted on-campus at Bancroft Strip. The free speech movement, which was led by student Mario Savio, became a cause celebre that received support from such luminaries as Norman MAILER and Bertrand RUSSELL. The free speech movement ultimately prevailed by virtue of an overwhelming majority vote by the Academic Senate. More important, it became a paradigm of student protest in the 1960s.

Frei Montalva, Eduardo (*1911–1982*) President of Chile (1964–70). A self-proclaimed radical reformer, Frei was the first Christian Democrat ever to lead a nation of the Western Hemisphere. During his presidency he began an ambitious land distribution program but failed in his stated goal to give land to 100,000 poor farmers. He also started the nationalization of CHILE's copper industry that was completed under his successor, Salvador ALLENDE GOSSENS. The hero of the democratic moderates, Frei was a leading opposition figure during the military government of General Augusto PINOCHET.

FRELIMO (Frente de Libertação de Moçambique) Marxist liberation movement that waged a guerrilla war against the Portuguese in MOZAMBIQUE from 1964 to 1974. The dominant political force in the country after independence.

Frenay, Henri (*1905–1988*) French politician. Frenay was one of the top leaders of the French RESISTANCE during WORLD WAR II. For a time he sought to challenge Charles de GAULLE. Frenay created a national liberation movement, Combat, which he intended to be independent of the Anglo-Saxon powers and the communists as well as de Gaulle. After the war he supported European federation.

French, Sir John Denton (first earl of Ypres) (*1852–1925*) British field marshal. A longtime army officer, French served in the Sudan (1884–85) and the SOUTH AFRICAN WAR (1899–1902) before becoming chief of the imperial general staff (1912–14). He was promoted to the rank of field marshal in 1913. During the first year of WORLD WAR I French commanded the British Expeditionary Force in France and Belgium (1914–15) but was unable to coordinate with French forces and incurred heavy casualties in both the first and second battles of YPRES and the battle of Loos. Replaced by General Douglas HAIG in December, 1915, he returned to England, where he organized civil defenses. Later he was appointed lord lieutenant of Ireland (1918–21) and was made an earl upon his retirement in 1922.

French Community (Communauté française)

Established in 1958 to succeed the FRENCH UNION, the French Community included FRANCE, its overseas departments and territories, and 12 African colonies given autonomy at the time (in 1958 GUINEA had voted for instant independence). In 1960 these countries were given independence and the option of leaving the community; SENEGAL, GABON, CHAD, CONGO, the CENTRAL AFRICAN REPUBLIC and MADAGASCAR stayed; MALI, MAURITANIA, Upper Volta (now BURKINA FASO), Dahomey (now BENIN,), NIGER and the Ivory Coast (CÔTE D'IVOIRE) relinquished formal membership but continued a connection through special accords. The community's management was aimed at drafting common foreign, economic and military policies for its members, but the operation dwindled during the 1960s, eventually to be succeeded by bilateral agreements, fostered by powerful economic and cultural bonds, between France and the other community participants.

French Equatorial Africa (French Congo)

A former confederation of French colonies in West Africa that now make up the states of GABON, CONGO, CHAD and the CENTRAL AFRICAN REPUBLIC. The grouping was formed in 1910 and was a consolidated colony between 1934 and 1946. The capital, Brazzaville, became the nucleus of African operations for the FREE FRENCH in WORLD WAR II. In 1958 French Equatorial Africa disappeared when its constituent regions became autonomous members of the FRENCH COMMUNITY.

French Guiana (French: Guyane française)

On the Atlantic coast of northeastern South America, it is an overseas region of FRANCE. During WORLD WAR II French Guiana supported the VICHY government after the Nazi defeat of France, but in 1943 the FREE FRENCH assumed control. In 1958 French Guiana approved the constitution of France's Fifth Republic and chose to remain an overseas department, with its own representatives in the French parliament. It became a region in 1974. Beginning in the 1990s French Guiana served as the base for the rocket launches of the European Space Agency (ESA) and its ARIANE 5 rockets. (See also GUYANA.)

French Indochina War of 1946–1954

After the Japanese invaders withdrew from French INDOCHINA at the end of WORLD WAR II, the French were not in a strong position to reassert immediately their authority. In the north the VIET MINH, a political party led by HO CHI MINH, proclaimed the independent Democratic Republic of VIETNAM. France agreed to recognize Vietnam as a free state within the French Union, but negotiations dragged on. In 1946 French forces attacked Viet Minh forces and Vietnamese civilians. During the ensuing years guerrilla activity increased in the countryside. In 1949 a Vietnamese provisional government headed by Emperor BAO DAI was established and recognized by France, and in 1950 by the U.S. The communist-dominated Viet Minh rejected any remnant of French authority and consequently attacked French outposts along Vietnam's border with China, from whom they received substantial military aid.

In 1951 the Viet Minh created a common front with communist groups in Laos and Cambodia (Kampuchea) and became more and more aggressive. They were led by General VO NGUYEN GIAP, who launched an attack on March 18, 1954, against the strategic French stronghold at DIEN BIEN PHU in northwestern Vietnam. Giap's siege lasted 56 days; his Viet Minh troops continually attacked with artillery and mortar fire until the French defenders, short of ammunition, surrendered on May 7, 1954. Meanwhile, an international conference in Geneva was working out an agreement whereby the fighting would cease and the French would withdraw. The Viet Minh set up a government north of the 17th parallel, while Vietnamese noncommunists set up a government south of the demarcation line. The war was unpopular in France, most of whose citizens were relieved when it was over, in spite of their defeat and loss of influence in Southeast Asia. In July 1954 Vietnam was divided into the Democratic Republic of Vietnam (North Vietnam) and the Republic of Vietnam (South Vietnam). (See also VIETNAMESE CIVIL WAR OF 1955–1965; VIETNAM WAR.)

French Polynesia

Overseas area of France, formerly known as French Oceania, consisting of nearly 105 islands in the South Pacific Ocean. The five main groups are the Gambier Islands and the Marquesas, Society, Tuamotu and Tubuai, or Austral, Islands. Unpopulated Clipperton Island, 670 miles southwest of Mexico, is managerially a part of the region. Tahiti is the primary island, and the capital of the territory is Papeete on Tahiti. Some islands are volcanic; others are coral atolls; the citizens are mainly Polynesian. France claimed and annexed the island groups from 1842 to 1881. In 1903 the groups were united under a single administration as French Oceania (or Etablissements françaises de l'Océanie); in 1946 they were reconsolidated as an overseas territory and renamed French Polynesia. The inhabitants voted in 1957 to remain connected to the FRENCH COMMUNITY, with representation in the French parliament. From time to time France conducted nuclear tests in the islands. In 1995 France resumed nuclear testing on the Mururoa atoll of French Polynesia.

French Southern and Antarctic Territories

These islands lie in the southern Indian Ocean and cover a total area of 3,003 square miles. They include the extinct volcanoes Île Amsterdam and Île Saint-Paul, and Îles Kerguelen and Crozet. France also claims an area known as Terra Adelie in Antarctica as part of its territories, a claim not recognized by the U.S. Administered as dependencies of the former French colony of Madagascar from 1924 to 1955, the islands became a separate overseas territory in 1955. Scientific stations form the only permanent settlements.

French Union

Formed by the French Constitution of 1946, this was a federation of FRANCE, its overseas departments and territories, and the associated states of INDOCHINA, MOROCCO and TUNISIA. With the French Union allowing more autonomy to territories and protectorates, a number of them became ready for independence. The union paved the way for a transition of France's colonial empire into the FRENCH COMMUNITY, which succeeded the union in 1958.

French West Africa A former federation of French colonies in West Africa that are now the states of BENIN, BURKINA FASO, GUINEA, CÔTE D'IVOIRE, MALI, MAURITANIA, NIGER and SENEGAL. Organized in 1895, the federation ended in 1958 when Guinea voted for immediate independence. The remaining constituent regions of French West Africa became autonomous constituents of the FRENCH COMMUNITY, achieving independence in 1960. (See also FRANCE.)

Freud, Anna *(1895–1982)* Austrian psychologist. Freud was the daughter of Sigmund FREUD, the founder of psychoanalysis, and she devoted much of her career to applying and defending the theoretical principles first articulated by her father. As a result of Nazi threats, Freud left Austria for Britain with her dying father in 1938. Over the next four decades, Freud became a major force in British psychology. Her highest achievement was the founding, in 1947, of the Hampstead Child Therapy Clinic in London. Freud specialized in the application of psychoanalysis to children. She also argued for the value of psychoanalytical insights in the interpretation of normal, as opposed to neurotic, behavior patterns. *The Ego and the Mechanisms of Defense* (1936) was her major work.

Freud, Sigmund *(1856–1939)* Austrian psychiatrist and founder of psychoanalysis. Freud is, beyond question, the most influential psychological theorist of the 20th century, although his insights have been frequently misstated and oversimplified. Born of Jewish parentage in Moravia, Freud studied medicine in Vienna and Paris. In 1884 he studied under Josef Breuer, a Viennese physician who introduced Freud to the cathartic method of treating hysteria. This method, which focused on allowing patients to confront the root element of their abiding fears, became the essential starting point of psychoanalysis. In 1895 Freud and Breuer coauthored *Studies in Hysteria.* In 1900 Freud published a landmark work, *The INTERPRETATION OF DREAMS,* which established the importance of the psychoanalytic movement. In *Three Essays on the Theory of Sexuality* (1905) Freud spelled out his insistence on the primal importance for personality development of unconscious sexual drives that emerge during infancy. In his later works Freud analyzed cultural and religious issues and concluded that both artistic creation and religious belief were the result of sublimated sexual energy held in check by societal taboos. In 1938 Freud, who had been condemned by the Nazis, fled to London, where he died of throat cancer weeks after the outbreak of WORLD WAR II. Freud's ideas have had an enormous influence on 20th-century art, literature and social thought.

Freyssinet, Eugène *(1879–1962)* French structural engineer best known for his extraordinary constructions of reinforced concrete. Freyssinet designed vast twin airship hangars, built in 1916–21 at Orly Airport near Paris, using a continuous parabolic concrete arch with a span of 195 feet. The hangars were destroyed in 1944. Freyssinet was also the designer of various concrete bridges, including an arch bridge with a span of 430 feet over the Seine at Pierre du Vauvray, built in 1922 and reconstructed in 1946, and of some buildings of the Gare d'Austerlitz in Paris of 1929.

Frick, Ford C. *(1894–1978)* Commissioner of baseball from 1951 to 1965. Frick was originally a newspaperman and then a radio announcer. He also served as president of baseball's National League for 17 years. He was elected to the Baseball Hall of Fame in 1970.

Fried, Alfred *(1864–1921)* Austrian journalist and pacifist. Fried ran a publishing company in Berlin and created the German Peace Society in 1892. Inspired by the first Hague peace conference in 1899, he devoted himself to promoting it and the cause of internationalism. He began publishing the *Annuaire de la vie internationale* (Annual of international life) in 1905 and authored several books, notably, *Handbuch der Friedensbewegung* (Handbook of the peace movement, 1911). Fried was a joint recipient of the 1911 NOBEL PRIZE for peace along with Tobias ASSER.

Friedan, Betty *(1921–2006)* American feminist leader and author; one of the most prominent figures in the feminist movement since the publication of her landmark work, *The Feminine Mystique* (1963). In that work Friedan captured wide public attention for her central thesis that women are culturally stereotyped in America as suited only to economically dependent and intellectually vacant lives as housewives and mothers. Friedan, who had for a time given up her own professional aspirations to live as a housewife in the sub-

Feminist activist and author Betty Friedan. 1967 (LIBRARY OF CONGRESS, PRINTS AND PHOTOGRAPHS DIVISION)

urbs, drew on her own surveys of a wide range of American women to support her then-controversial findings. In 1966 she founded the National Organization of Women (NOW) to serve as a lobbying and public opinion force on behalf of feminist political issues. In 1970 Friedan headed a nationwide Women's Strike for Equality. Her other books include *It Changed My Life* (1977) and *The Second Stage* (1981). In 1993 Friedan published *The Fountain of Age,* a work that examined the changing perceptions of old age in American society. Seven years later she published her memoir, *Life So Far.*

Friedman, Elizabeth S. *(1894–1980)* American pioneer cryptographer. Friedman helped decipher codes used by enemies of the U.S. during WORLD WAR I and WORLD WAR II. She also aided in the solving of international drug and liquor smuggling cases. Working with her husband, Colonel **William Friedman,** she broke the top-secret Japanese **purple code,** which was used by Japanese diplomats before and during World War II.

Friedman, Herbert *(1916–2001)* U.S. rocket astronomy pioneer. After studying physics at Brooklyn College, Friedman did his graduate work at Johns Hopkins University in 1940. Joining the U.S. Naval Research Laboratory, he became involved in rocket astronomy during World War II and after the war was primarily concerned with RADAR detection devices and solar physics. In 1949 he directed a team that sent a V-2 rocket carrying scientific instruments into space, proving that X-rays emanated from the Sun. During this same period Friedman did pioneering work in ultraviolet mapping. Beginning in 1956 he began working with the Vanguard satellite development program, in an effort to continue his studies of X-rays and ultraviolet radiation from the Sun. In 1960 he made the first X-ray photographs of the Sun and made observations proving that neutral hydrogen is present throughout the solar system. Friedman was elected to the National Academy of Sciences in 1960 and was awarded more than 40 patents in the field of rocket and satellite astronomy. He was recipient of the 1987 Wolf Prize in Physics.

Friedman, Milton *(1912–   )* American economist; leader of the monetarist, or "Chicago" school of economics. Friedman was born in New York City, the son of immigrants from eastern Europe. He graduated from Rutgers University in 1932 and received his doctorate from Columbia University in 1946. After World War II he taught for two years at the University of Minnesota before joining the economics department of the University of Chicago, where he labored for the next three decades. In his 1957 book *A Theory of the Consumption Function,* Friedman introduced the extremely influential "permanent income hypothesis," which suggested, in contradiction to John Maynard KEYNES, that individuals base spending decisions on expected long-term income rather than on current income.

In 1963 Friedman, with his collaborator David Meiselman, continued his attack on Keynesian economics by arguing that money supply rather than government spending is the chief determiner of economic health. An economic adviser to Presidents NIXON and REAGAN, Friedman argued for a laissez-faire policy toward business and trade and played an important role in the creation of an all-volunteer army and on other questions of public policy. He won the 1976 NOBEL PRIZE in economics. In 1977 Friedman retired from the University of Chicago and became a senior research associate at the Hoover Institution. In 1980 he published his best-selling book *Free to Choose,* which also became the basis of a television series. He was awarded the Medal of Freedom in 1988. (See also MONETARISM.)

Friedmann, Alexander Alexandrovich *(1888–1925)* Soviet astronomer. The son of a composer, Friedmann was educated at the University of St. Petersburg. He began his scientific career in 1913 at the Pavlovsk Observatory in St. Petersburg and, after war service, was appointed professor of theoretical mechanics at Perm University in 1918. In 1920 he returned to the St. Petersburg Observatory, where he became director shortly before his early death from typhoid at the age of 37. Friedmann established an early reputation for his work on atmospheric and meteorological physics. However, he is better known for his 1922 paper on the

expanding universe. This arose from work of EINSTEIN in 1917 in which he attempted to apply his equations of general relativity to cosmology. Friedmann developed a theoretical model of the universe using Einstein's theory, in which the average mass density is constant and space has a constant curvature. Different cosmological models are possible depending on whether the curvature is zero, negative or positive. Such models are called Friedmann universes. (See also BIG BANG THEORY.)

Friel, Brian *(1929–   )* Northern Irish playwright. Friel has become an influential playwright in the British Isles by virtue of plays that probe the deep and persistent social, political and religious divisions between England and Ireland. In particular, Friel's plays have explored the violence and unrest that have persisted in his native NORTHERN IRELAND under British rule. His first play was *This Doubtful Paradise* (1959). Subsequent theatrical successes included *Philadelphia, Here I Come!* (1964), *Lovers* (1967), *The Freedom of the City* (1973), *Faith Healer* (1979), *Translations* (1980) and *Aristocrats* (1988). Friel also translated (1981) the classic play *Three Sisters* by Anton CHEKHOV.

Friend, Charlotte *(1921–1987)* American medical microbiologist. She was known for her important cancer research. In 1956 she discovered a virus that caused leukemia in mice; the **Friend virus,** as it came to be known, emerged as a major tool for study of the links between viruses and cancer.

Friends Service Council (FSC) Organization established by the Quakers in London in 1927. It was formed by merging the Friends Foreign Mission Association, which had been founded in 1868 to organize and operate schools, hospitals and Quaker societies abroad, and the Council for International Service, which was formed in 1919 to establish peace centers throughout the world. Headed from 1932 by Carl Heath, the FSC initially sponsored conferences that discussed problems brought on by the Treaty of VERSAILLES, and interceded with governments to relieve persecuted minorities. After World War II the FSC took over various relief activities that had been conducted by another Quaker organization during the war. Along with its U.S. counterpart, the AMERICAN FRIENDS SERVICE COMMITTEE, the FSC received the 1947 NOBEL PRIZE for peace. The FSC has continued its humanitarian work throughout the world, operating relief camps for Palestinian refugees, aiding riot victims in INDIA, helping civilian victims of war in KOREA and VIETNAM, feeding people in famine-stricken Africa and conducting other relief and peace-related programs.

fringe theater A general term for British experimental theater groups; first became a prominent usage in British theatrical circles in the 1950s, when the annual Edinburgh Drama Festival—which featured the best in accepted professional stage productions—became a stimulus for a number of alternative theatrical groups to perform their own experimental plays at the same time as the official festival productions. This informal competition between the "fringe" and the mainstream has continued to serve as an effective stimulus to British theater. A major playwright who emerged from the early "fringe" movement is Tom STOPPARD; subsequent "fringe" playwrights have included Howard Brenton and David HARE.

Frisch, Max (1911–1991) Swiss novelist and playwright. Frisch, who began his career as an architect, achieved his first literary success with his play *When the War Was Over* (1949), which showed the strong influence of Frisch's close friend, the German playwright Bertolt BRECHT. In the 1950s Frisch turned his attention to fiction; his novel *I'm Not Stiller* (1954) earned international acclaim and enabled Frisch to devote himself full time to writing. Frisch's most prominent themes are the pervasive nature of Nazi postwar guilt and the necessarily continuous struggle for political and personal freedom. His other novels include *Homo Faber* (1957), *Montauk* (1975) and *Man in the Holocene* (1979). Other plays by Frisch include *Andora* (1961) and *Biography: A Game* (1967). Frisch also produced several volumes of memoirs, most notably *Sketchbook 1946–49* (1977) and *Sketchbook 1966–71* (1974).

Friuli (German: Friaul) In the ancient world, Forum Julii, a region on the Adriatic Sea south of Austria; now split between SLOVENIA and the Friuli-Venezia Giulia area of northeastern ITALY. During WORLD WAR I the area was a battlefield; afterward, the victorious Italy took all of old Friuli but had to cede the eastern section to YUGOSLAVIA after WORLD WAR II. The balance was united with Venezia Giulia as a region in 1947. Trieste was made its capital in 1954.

Fromm, Erich (1900–1980) German-born psychoanalyst, social philosopher and humanist. Fromm obtained his Ph.D. from the University of Munich (1922) and also studied at Berlin's Psychoanalytic Institute. He started his own practice in 1925, and four years later began his lifelong teaching career. He emigrated from Nazi Germany to the U.S. in 1934 and subsequently lectured at Columbia, Yale and other universities. Schooled in traditional Freudian analysis, he developed his own eclectic theories to explain human behavior. These theories stressed social and economic factors as well as unconscious drives. Fromm wrote some 20 books, including influential works on the theories of Karl Marx and Sigmund FREUD, the religious precepts of Judaism and Christianity, and the COLD WAR and the alienation of the individual.

Front National (National Front) Far-right political party in France headed by Jean-Marie LE PEN. Formed in the early 1980s by Le Pen, a former French paratrooper in the Algerian War, the Front National (FN) derived its support largely from its stance against continued immigration into France. Until the 2002 presidential election, the party remained on the fringe of French politics, as it never gained more than 12% of the popular vote in parliamentary or presidential contests. However, its continued appeal among some constituencies forced governments under President François MITTERRAND and the government of his successor, Jacques CHIRAC, to compromise on issues such as social programs and immigration policy.

The front blamed immigrants to France, primarily those coming from North Africa, for the high French unemployment rate and the increase in urban crime. In the first round of the 2002 French presidential elections Le Pen's party rose even further to national prominence. Riding a wave of popular discontent, Le Pen edged out the Socialist candidate for president, Prime Minister Lionel Jospin, to receive the second-highest number of votes in the election behind Chirac. In the second round Chirac handily defeated Le Pen with support from leftist voters. Yet Le Pen's strong showing demonstrated the willingness of French voters, particularly native-born working-class citizens, to support his party's anti-immigration positions.

Frost, Robert Lee (1874–1963) American poet. Frost dropped out of Dartmouth in 1892 to work as a mill laborer and teacher in Lawrence, Massachusetts. He attended Harvard, 1897–99; then moved to New Hampshire to farm and teach English. He lived in England briefly (1912–15) before returning to farm near Franconia, New Hampshire. Though his first poem appeared in 1894, his first success was in England with the publication of *A Boy's Will* (1913) and *North of Boston* (1914), written under the influence of his friend Edward THOMAS. Frost received the PULITZER PRIZE four times (1924, 1931, 1937, 1943) and was poetry consultant to the Library of Congress in 1958. Additional accolades included the Congressional Gold Medal awarded on his 88th birthday and more than 40 honorary degrees; he won a new, wide audience when he read at the inaugura-

Poet Robert Frost (LIBRARY OF CONGRESS, PRINTS AND PHOTOGRAPHS DIVISION)

tion of President John F. KENNEDY in 1961. Throughout his lifetime Frost cultivated the persona of a gentle, folksy, white-haired country farmer who wrote popular poems such as "Stopping by Woods on a Snowy Evening," "The Death of the Hired Man" and "Mending Wall," staples in every high school English class in the middle of the 20th century. However, his work and thought have more complex undercurrents than are at first apparent. While scholars and biographers have revealed a dark side to Frost's life and personality, he is universally acknowledged as a master craftsman and a major poet.

Fry, Christopher *(1907–2005)* British playwright; achieved his greatest theatrical successes in the 1930s and 1940s. Fry was noted for his highly poetic and elevated style that dealt with romantic and mystical themes. His first play to gain attention was *The Boy with a Cart* (1937). In 1940 he was appointed director of the Oxford Playhouse, where his work was performed regularly throughout the decade. A number of leading British actors appeared in Fry's plays, including John GIELGUD in *The Lady's Not for Burning* (1948), Lawrence OLIVIER in *Venus Observed* (1950) and Edith EVANS in *The Dark Is Light Enough* (1954). Other plays by Fry include *A Phoenix Too Frequent* (1946), *The First-born* (1948) and *A Yard of Sun* (1970).

Fry, (Edwin) Maxwell *(1899–1987)* British architect. As a pioneer of modern architecture in Great Britain, his work included a housing project at Kensal Green in London that set new standards for its time. He was also involved in major architectural projects in British colonial West Africa, notably the design of the University of Ibadan in Nigeria. From 1951 to 1954 he was a member of the team of architects that worked with LE CORBUSIER on the design and initial construction of Chandigar, the new capital of the Punjab region of India.

Fry, Roger Eliot *(1866–1934)* British art critic, painter and author. Fry was educated at King's College, Cambridge, where as a member of the Apostles he became acquainted with members of the BLOOMSBURY GROUP, with which he would later be associated. Fry was a friend of and strong influence on Clive

BELL. Fry wrote art criticism for the *Athenaeum* beginning in 1901 and helped found the *Burlington Magazine*. He worked at the Metropolitan Museum of Art in New York City from 1905 to 1910. Fry coined the term POST-IMPRESSIONISM and presented a landmark exhibition of the style to a doubtful British public in 1910. Fry was named Slade Professor of Fine Art at Cambridge in 1933. His books include *Vision and Design* (1920), *Transformations: Critical and Speculative Essays on Art* (1926) and *The Arts of Painting and Sculpture* (1932). Virginia WOOLF wrote a biography of Fry which was published in 1940.

Frye, (Herman) Northrop *(1912–1991)* Canadian literary critic. Frye, who was educated at Oxford and taught for several decades at the University of Toronto, was one of the most influential literary critics of the post–World War II era. He is best known for his insistence on the underlying importance of myth and symbol as influences upon both creativity and formal literary structure. His major works include *Fearful Symmetry* (1947), a study of the British mystical poet William Blake, *Anatomy of Criticism* (1957), *Fables of Identity* (1963) and *The Well-Tempered Critic* (1967). In *The Great Code: The Bible and Literature* (1981), Frye argued for a pervasive shared symbolism between the Bible and the great works of Western literature.

Fuad I *(1868–1936)* First king of modern Egypt (1922–36). The second son of Ismail Pasha, he was educated in Europe and succeeded his brother Hussein Kamil as sultan in 1917. He was proclaimed king in 1922, a year before Britain's recognition of his country's independence. In conflict with the WAFD party, he abrogated the existing constitution and introduced a new constitution in 1928 but was forced to restore the earlier document in 1935. Fuad was succeeded by his son FAROUK.

Fuchs, (Emil) Klaus Julius *(1911–1988)* German physicist and Soviet agent. Fuchs was active in the anti-Nazi underground movement before fleeing to France and later to England. He worked on ATOMIC BOMB DEVELOPMENT in Britain and in the U.S. during WORLD WAR II. After the war he helped

direct nuclear research in Britain but also passed crucial nuclear secrets to the Soviet Union and was arrested for espionage in February 1950. Fuchs's case led to the exposure of a nuclear espionage ring that included Julius and Ethel ROSENBERG. Upon his release from prison in 1953 he flew to East GERMANY, where he became deputy director of the national nuclear research institute and a member of the central committee of the East German Communist Party.

Fuchs, Sir Vivien Ernest *(1908–1999)* British explorer and geologist. The son of a farmer of German origin, Fuchs was educated at Cambridge University, where he obtained his M.A. in geology in 1929 and his Ph.D. (1935). From 1929 he traveled on a series of expeditions as geologist, the first being the Cambridge East Greenland Expedition (1929). In 1947 he became a member of the Falkland Islands Dependencies Survey and in 1950 its director. As a result of his involvement with the survey, Fuchs led an expedition to Graham Land in ANTARCTICA (1948) to reassert the British claim to the territory, which was being challenged by Argentina. He was stranded on Storing Ton Island by bad weather until 1950. Fuchs is best known for the Commonwealth Trans-Antarctic Expedition he jointly led with Edmund HILLARY in the Weddell INTERNATIONAL GEOPHYSICAL YEAR (1957–58). Leaving Shackleton Base on the Weddell Sea on November 24, 1957, he reached the South Pole and met Hillary on January 19, 1958, then continued on to reach Scott Base, Victoria Land, on March 2. Fuchs was knighted in 1958.

Fuentes, Carlos *(1928–)* Mexican writer and diplomat. A liberal lawyer and political activist, Fuentes is one of Mexico's leading novelists and short story writers. His experimental novels are usually set in postrevolutionary Mexico and explore the mythology of his country's past and the social conditions of its present. His first work was a collection of surrealist stories, published in 1954. His first novel, *Where the Air Is Clear* (1958, translated in 1960), examined the lives of various inhabitants of Mexico City since the revolution of 1910. Fuentes achieved international acclaim with his novel

The Death of Artemio Cruz (1962, translated in 1964). Fuentes's other fiction includes the novels *A Change of Skin* (1967, translated in 1968), *Terra Nostra* (1975, translated in 1976), *Distant Relations* (1980), *The Old Gringo* (1985) and *Instinto de Inez* (2001). He is also a playwright and essayist.

Fuerzas Armadas Revolucionarias de Colombia (FARC)

A guerrilla band in COLOMBIA formed in 1966 by Manuel "Sureshot" Marulanda; the name in English is Revolutionary Armed Forces of Colombia. Originally an obscure leftist force fighting the conservative government and parties of Colombia in the hopes of establishing a communist state, FARC remained one of many such organizations with an appeal and influence confined mainly to peasants who had turned isolated jungles in Colombia into agriculturally productive land. In the 1980s the power of FARC increased dramatically when it began to encourage the cultivation of coca and opium poppies on the territory it controlled, which it refined into cocaine and heroin and exported throughout the world, mainly to the U.S. Its increasing cultivation of narcotics led the group to adopt the trappings of a government. It taxes all aspects of drug production, including the processing of chemicals and the air transportation of processed drugs. It also has regularly engaged in kidnapping and extortion of government and business officials in Colombia.

In the 1980s FARC attempted to establish a political party to provide a platform for the expression of its views in Colombian elections, the Patriotic Union (UP). But severe government repression of the UP convinced FARC to abandon the political route and to concentrate on its continued guerrilla operations. These efforts intensified between 1996 and 1999, when its bands captured more than 500 members of the security forces in Colombia, prompting the government to initiate negotiations with FARC in an effort to end the constant raids, assassinations and kidnappings. In 1998 FARC obtained a "safe haven" of 42,000 square kilometers as a result of a negotiated settlement with the government of President Andrés Pastrana. However, in 2002 the Pastrana administration ended the ongoing negotiations after FARC forces hijacked and kidnapped a Colombian senator. In response FARC launched a mortar attack on the presidential palace in Bogotá during the inauguration of Pastrana's successor, Álvaro Uribe, resulting in the death of 21 nearby residents. But the ability of FARC's estimated 12,000 military personnel to intimidate the Colombian government declined in the first few years of the 21st century, in part because of intensive training by U.S. military advisers of Colombian security forces as part of the ongoing U.S. war on drugs.

Fugard, Athol (1932–)

South African playwright, actor and director; achieved worldwide fame for his searing plays depicting the physical and psychological horrors of APARTHEID. Fugard began his career as an actor in Cape Town in the 1950s. His first play was *No Good Friday* (1959), in which he also acted. His first major theatrical success was *The Blood Knot* (1961). In 1963 he founded his own theatrical troupe, the Serpent Players, which became a dominant force in South African theater. *Sizwe Bansi Is Dead* (1972) represented a shift for Fugard into a more experimental, improvisational mode of playwriting. More recent works include *Statements after an Arrest under the Immorality Act* (1972), *Dimetos* (1975), *A Lesson from Aloes* (1978) and the acclaimed *Master Harold and the Boys* (1982), which featured American actor James Earl JONES.

Fugitives and Agrarians (1920s– 1930s)

Literary movement by American writers of the South. The Fugitive literary movement—which was renamed the Agrarian movement in the 1930s—began in the years following World War I. John Crowe RANSOM, an eminent poet and literary critic, was teaching at Vanderbilt University. Among the students drawn to his classes were poet, critic and biographer Allen TATE and poet Robert Penn WARREN. Ransom inspired these writers and others to view the agrarian heritage of the South, along with its Confederate STATES' RIGHTS political background, as a vital cultural base for literary works. The Fugitives and Agrarians opposed industrialism and the policies of the NEW DEAL while promoting a new clas-sicism for literature. *The Fugitive*, edited by Tate, was a major literary journal of the 1920s. Ransom went on to edit the influential *Kenyon Review* from 1938 to 1959.

Fujimori, Alberto (1938–)

President of Peru (1990–2001). Born in Lima, PERU, to Japanese immigrants, Fujimori studied agriculture at the Agricultural National University in La Molina, Peru, and the University of Wisconsin. He later served as an agricultural engineer, a dean of the science faculty at La Molina and the host of a TV show. After defeating the novelist Mario VARGAS LLOSA in the presidential election of 1990, Fujimori tackled the twin problems facing Peru: continued terrorist attacks from leftist rebel organizations such as the SHINING PATH and an economy on the verge of complete collapse. In an effort to stimulate economic growth Fujimori privatized state-owned enterprises, ended government subsidies to domestic companies and industries and removed many of the regulatory controls on the private sector. In April 1992, with the support of the Peruvian military, he dissolved Peru's national legislature and court system on the grounds that these bodies hindered the campaign against the rebels. Fujimori's authoritarian crackdown seemed vindicated five months later when Peruvian forces captured Abimael Guzmán, the head of the Shining Path. Fujimori was reelected in 1995 based on his successes in curbing hyperinflation and suppressing left-wing insurgents. Critics of Fujimori argued that his victories stemmed largely from his use of the Peruvian intelligence service to bully his opponents and from his control of governmental organizations and manipulation of the media. In 1999 Fujimori provoked an additional outcry from his opponents when he announced he again would run for reelection, seemingly in violation of the 1993 constitution, which restricted presidents to two terms. When Peru's constitutional court challenged his right to run, Fujimori removed several of those judges from their positions. His election victory over Alejandro Toledo in May 2000 provoked a series of demonstrations that prompted him to announce he would resign by July 2001. The surfacing of a videotape indicating that his intelligence chief, Vladimiro Montesinos, had bribed a congressman caused Fujimori to flee the country in November 2000 and seek asylum in Japan, which refused to extradite him to Peru. After announcing his intention to run in Peru's 2006 presidential election, he traveled to Chile and was detained by Chilean authorities.

Fukada, Takeo *(1905–1995)* Japanese politician, a member of the Liberal Democratic Party (LDP, a conservative party), representative in the Japanese House of Representatives and prime minister of Japan (1976–78). In the years after WORLD WAR II he served as deputy finance minister, director of the National Banking Bureau and director of the Budget Bureau.

In 1952, after 21 years in the Ministry of Finance, Fukada was elected to the House of Representatives as a candidate for the LDP (then the dominant party in Japanese politics). In 1965 he was appointed minister of finance. In 1966 he was elected president of the LDP and for two years helped shape the party's campaign strategy and national policy. After stepping down from the party post in 1968, Fukada served as minister of finance, minister of foreign affairs, director general of the Administrative Management Agency and deputy prime minister. On December 24, 1976, Fukada was elected prime minister. He promptly enunciated the Fukada Doctrine in 1977, which pledged that Japan would use its business investments and foreign aid in Asia to allay concerns that an economically resurgent Japan would threaten the other nations of Asia. Fukada's government lasted only 714 days, and he was forced to leave office on December 7, 1978, although he remained in the House of Representatives until his death on July 5, 1995.

Fulbright, James William *(1905–1995)* U.S. senator. Raised in Fayetteville, Arkansas, Fulbright graduated from the University of Arkansas in 1925, then studied at Oxford as a Rhodes scholar before earning a law degree at George Washington University. After serving as president of the University of Arkansas from 1939 to 1941, he was elected in 1942 to the U.S. House of Representatives and in 1944 to the U.S. Senate. In 1946 Fulbright sponsored the legislation establishing the foreign exchange program that bears his name. In 1959 he became chairman of the Senate Foreign Relations Committee. During the 1960s Fulbright urged the U.S. to reduce its expenditures supporting the COLD WAR with the Soviet Union and to concentrate its resources instead on domestic problems. In the early days of the VIETNAM WAR he was a supporter of President Lyndon JOHNSON's policies, and it was Fulbright who introduced the TONKIN GULF RESOLUTION in the Senate on August 6, 1964, supporting the administration's use of force. However, beginning in 1966, he publicly questioned the wisdom of U.S. involvement in VIETNAM, and in 1967 his book *The Arrogance of Power* became a best seller. In 1968 Fulbright denounced the Gulf of Tonkin Resolution. By 1970, when the resolution was repealed by Congress, Fulbright had emerged as a leading critic of the war. In 1974, after five full terms in the Senate, he was defeated by Arkansas governor Dale Bumpers in the Democratic Senate primary. In 1993 Fulbright received the Presidential Medal of Freedom from President Bill CLINTON.

Fuller, Loie (Mary Louise Fuller) *(1862–1928)* American dancer and choreographer. A self-taught dancer, Fuller created her first dance, *Serpentine Dance,* in 1891 after working as an actress, playwright and producer in the American theater for several years. Her 1892 solo dance debut at the Folies-Bergère in Paris was acclaimed. Hailed by the Impressionists and the ART NOUVEAU movement as an innovator for her experimentation with light, color and stage devices, Fuller's choreographic style was characterized by improvised movement for the body clothed in masses of silk, which created a sculpted effect. She created 130 dances, including *Fire* (1895) and *Ballet of Light* (1908); founded a school in 1908; invented and patented costume designs, stage devices and lighting machines; was honored by French scientists for her contributions to lighting theories and inspired such artists as Toulouse-Lautrec and Auguste Rodin and the poet W. B. YEATS.

Fuller, R(ichard) Buckminster *(1895–1983)* Self-described "engineer, inventor, mathematician, architect, cartographer, philosopher, poet, cosmogonist, comprehensive designer and choreographer." He was best known for his 1947 invention of the **geodesic dome**, a sphere composed of triangles that provided maximum strength with great economy of materials. He designed many other innovative structures, including a futuristic three-wheeled automobile (1932) that was never built and the DYMAXION House, a prefabricated glass-walled building that had rooms suspended from a pole. (Conceived in 1927, the first Dymaxion House was constructed in 1944.) Fuller, who attended Harvard but never graduated, wrote 25 books, held scores of patents and received 39 honorary doctorates in fields ranging from the fine arts to engineering. In his later years he dedicated himself to encouraging efficient use of resources; in the 1960s he had a cultlike following among those who saw his "alternative lifestyle" as a solution to modern ecological problems. He received the Presidential Medal of Freedom from President Ronald Reagan in 1983.

Fuller, Roy Broadbent *(1912–1991)* British poet and novelist. Fuller was a solicitor who in the 1930s began contributing poetry to *New Verse* and other left-wing literary journals. His first volume of poetry, *Poems,* was published in 1939. His early work shows the influence of W. H. AUDEN and Stephen SPENDER. His experiences in the Royal Navy during WORLD WAR II provided inspiration for the collections *The Middle of a War* (1942) and *A Lost Season* (1944). His later poetry, including *From the Joke Shop* (1975) and *The Reign of Sparrows* (1980), is more sarcastic and bitter in tone. Of his novels, which range from thrillers to children's books, perhaps most notable is *Image of a Society* (1956). Fuller was a professor of poetry at Oxford from 1968 until 1973. He published the memoirs *Souvenirs* (1980), *Vamp Til Ready* (1982) and *Home and Dry* (1984). Fuller's son **John Fuller** *(1937–)* is also a noted poet and novelist. His works include the poetry collections *Cannibals and Missionaries* (1972) and *Lies and Secrets* (1979) and the novel *Flying to Nowhere* (1983).

Funston, Frederick *(1865–1917)* U.S. Army officer. Educated at the University of Kansas, he received a Medal of Honor for his leadership of U.S.

troops in the Philippines in 1899. Returning to the U.S., Funston commanded the army departments of the Colorado, the Columbia, the Lake and California. His handling of the disaster of the 1906 SAN FRANCISCO EARTHQUAKE and fire further enhanced his national reputation. He served as the commander of U.S. forces along the Mexican border in 1916.

Furmanov, Dimitri Andreyevich
(1891–1926) Russian writer. Originally a journalist, he wrote several "Sketches from the Front" after joining the Russian army in 1914 (see WORLD WAR I ON THE EASTERN FRONT). They were published in *Russkoye Slovo* in 1916. He joined the Communist Party in 1918 and served as a political commissar in CHAPAYEV's guerrilla forces. In 1923 he wrote the novel *Chapayev* about his experiences (filmed 1934). Other works include *Red Sortie* (1922), *Riot* (1923–25) and an unfinished novel, *Writers.*

Furman v. Georgia *(1972)* U.S.
Supreme Court decision that temporarily overruled all state death penalties. By the 1970s some states had outlawed the death penalty as too cruel and unusual a punishment. However, other state courts sentenced prisoners to death for a variety of offenses. Petitioners challenged the Georgia death penalty statute by showing that the death penalty was inconsistently applied and fell most heavily on members of minority groups.

The Court did not hold that the death penalty was per se unconstitutional for being cruel and unusual but reasoned that the states must have a formal procedure to ensure that the death sentence would be applied consistently, with ample opportunity for appeal. (See also CAPITAL PUNISHMENT.)

Furtwängler, Wilhelm *(1886–1954)*
German conductor, widely revered (with Arturo TOSCANINI) as one of the two greatest conductors of the 20th century. Furtwängler, the son of a distinguished archaeologist, was born in Berlin. After studying with Josef von Rheinberger, he was music director in Lubeck, Mannheim and Frankfurt before succeeding Richard STRAUSS as music director of the Berlin State Opera in 1920. Two years later he became music director of the Berlin Philharmonic. During the 1920s through the 1940s his mastery of the standard Austro-German repertoire—Beethoven, Brahms, Bruckner and Wagner—became increasingly evident. He toured widely and conducted in the U.S., including a year as director of the New York Philharmonic (1937–38). He remained in Germany during WORLD WAR II; however, unlike his chief musical rival in Germany, Herbert von KARAJAN, Furtwängler was never a Nazi. Rather, he believed that he could serve the values of civilization by remaining in Germany and making the best of a bad situation. He defended Jewish musicians in the Berlin Philharmonic and also championed Paul HINDEMITH, whom the Nazis denounced. However, he was forbidden to conduct until 1948, when the Allies cleared him of Nazi sympathies. In later years, despite increasing deafness, he continued to conduct in Germany, Austria and Switzerland. Initially indifferent and occasionally hostile to recording technology, Furtwängler nonetheless left a rich legacy of records, including an incomparable *Tristan und Isolde* (1953) and a legendary radio recording of the *Ring* cycle (1953).

fusion jazz Also known as jazz-rock, fusion jazz encompasses such amalgams as jazz-and-rock, jazz-and-blues and jazz-and-pop. First introduced in the 1960s, fusion was adopted by younger musicians (and audiences) who had grown up with both ROCK and roll and jazz. It also reflected evolving technologies in the manufacture of musical instruments and recordings. For example, in fusion the electric bass guitar replaces the acoustic upright bass, various electronic keyboards substitute for the acoustic piano and acoustic instruments such as the saxophone and trumpet are electronically amplified and modulated. Rhythmically, the fluid swing feel of jazz is discarded; instead of constant alterations between oscillating pulses of tension and release, the beat becomes metronomic, indeed, mechanistic, especially in groups of the 1980s using drum machines. Instead of supple walking bass lines, fusion tends to employ repeated ostinato figures. Harmonically, the traditionally sophisticated chordal changes associated with Tin Pan Alley and Broadway give way to simpler harmonic schemes, often borrowed from the MODAL JAZZ approach of saxophonist John COLTRANE.

The most important of the early fusion artists arose from the groups of trumpeter Miles DAVIS in the late 1960s and early 1970s. Keyboardists Herbie HANCOCK and Chick COREA, guitarist John McLaughlin and drummer Tony Williams all went on to establish notable solo careers as fusion group leaders. While much of fusion can be dismissed as commercially motivated, formulaic pap, the jazz-rock of such contemporary guitarists as John SCOFIELD, John Abercrombie and Pat Metheny embodies a genuine artistic quest for new sounds and new forms.

Futurama Name of the GENERAL MOTORS exhibit at the NEW YORK WORLD'S FAIR of 1939–40. Norman BEL GEDDES conceived and designed this famous exhibition pavilion to house a conveyer belt ride above an imagined world of the future (1960) created in model form, in which dramatic superhighways connected futuristic cities. The most popular exhibit at the fair, Futurama has often been credited as the key influence in the development of the superhighway network constructed after World War II.

futurism Futurism was a theoretical movement that influenced literature, painting, theater and the arts in general in the early decades of the 20th century. The term *futurism* was coined by the Italian poet F. T. MARINETTI in a 1909 manifesto. Marinetti urged that artists should turn their backs on past eras of artistic creation and instead embrace the "dynamism" of the industrial era with its hectic urban pace of life and its machine-influenced aesthetics. While Marinetti concentrated on the applications of futurism to poetic language, Italian painters such as Umberto Boccioni, Carlo CARRA and Luigi Russolo produced canvases filled with mechanical forms and the pulsing energy of the city. Russia was another country in which the influence of futurism showed itself strong, particularly in the work of poet Vladimir MAYAKOVSKY. In the 1920s Marinetti continued to write on futurism and allied the movement with Italian FASCISM.